BRAZIL

A TRAVEL SURVIVAL KIT

Andrew Draffen
Robert Strauss
Deanna Swaney

D0972916

Brazil – a travel survival kit

2nd edition

Published by
> **Lonely Planet Publications**
> Head Office: PO Box 617, Hawthorn, Vic 3122, Australia
> Branches: PO Box 2001A, Berkeley, CA 94702, USA and London, UK

Printed by
> Singapore National Printers Ltd, Singapore

Photographs by
> Kim Bartholemew (KB)
> Greg Caire (GC)
> Andrew Draffen (AD)
> William Herzberg (WH)
> John Maier (JM)
> Scott Plous (SP)
> Mitchell Schoen (MS)
> Vivian Stirling (VS)
> Robert Strauss (RS)
> Deanna Swaney (DS)
> Front cover: Boats moored at São João da Barra, Ilha de Santa Catarina (AD)
> Back cover: Morning light on araucaria pines, near Canela, Rio Grande do Sul (GC)

First Published
> August 1989

This Edition
> August 1992

Although the authors and publisher have tried to make the information as accurate as possible, they accept no responsibility for any loss, injury or inconvenience sustained by any person using this book.

National Library of Australia Cataloguing in Publication Data

Draffen, Andrew.
Brazil: a travel survival kit.

2nd ed.
Includes index.
ISBN 0 86442 141 9.

1. Brazil – Description and travel – 1981 – – Guidebooks. I.
Swaney, Deanna. II. Strauss, Robert. III. Schoen, Mitchell. Brazil: a
travel survival kit. IV. Title.

918.10463

Andrew Draffen

Australian-born Andrew has travelled and worked his way around Australia, Asia, North America and the Caribbean, settling just long enough in Melbourne to complete an Arts degree, majoring in history. During his first trip to South America in 1984, Andrew fell in love both with Brazil and his future wife, Stella. They have since toured extensively in Brazil, Europe and Asia, and today travel with their young daughter, Gabriela, whose great-great-grandfather introduced football to Brazil.

Deanna Swaney

After completing her university studies, Deanna made the standard European tour and has been addicted to travel ever since. Despite an erstwhile career in computer programming, she made a break for South America, where she wrote Lonely Planet's *Bolivia – a travel survival kit*. Subsequent travels resulted in four more travel survival kits: *Tonga*; *Samoa*; *Iceland, Greenland & the Faroe Islands*; and *Zimbabwe, Botswana and Namibia*.

Robert Strauss

In the early '70s Robert took the overland route to Nepal and then studied, taught and edited in England, Germany, Portugal and Hong Kong. For Lonely Planet he has worked on travel survival kits to *China*, *Tibet*, and *Japan*. For Bradt Publications he wrote the *Trans-Siberian Rail Guide*. He has contributed photos and articles to other books, magazines and newspapers in the USA, Australia and Asia.

Mitchell Schoen

Mitchell's initial interest in Latin America was sparked by an exiled Chilean friend. He studied political and economic development at the University of California at Berkeley, wtih an emphasis on Latin America, where he has travelled extensively.

William Herzberg

William studied biochemisty at Harvard and spent his college summers writing for the *Let's Go* travel guide series. He is now a physician in San Francisco.

From the Authors

From Andrew Special thanks to my Brazilian family in São Paulo, especially Vera Miller – my favourite mother-in-law; Iara Costa da Pinto (São Paulo) for her hospitality on many Brazil trips; Arnaldo Alves da

Motta (São Paulo) for his input – especially in the music section; Mari from Regina Turismo (São Paulo) for her *paulistana* efficiency; Áhmad Schabib Hany (Corumbá); TURIMAT (Cuiabá); the Secretaria de Turismo de Canela; Dona Lillian Argentina Braga Marques (Instituto Gaúcho de Tradição e Folclore, Porto Alegre); Alan Pires (USA) for his intimate knowledge of pharmaceuticals and cachaça brands; Simon Rooney (Australia); Greg Caire (Australia); Monica Costa (Rio); Sophia Rondon (Aquidauana); Frank & Helen Draffen (Australia) for their support over the years; and Stella & Gabriela Draffen, who make it all worthwhile.

I would like to dedicate my chapters to Vera Motta, my sister-in-law and Gabriela's beloved *madrinha*, who lost her life in a tragic car crash on the way to Ilhabela in January 1992. We all miss her very much. *Agora, ela esta em paz.*

From Deanna & Robert Special thanks to the following persons in Brazil and further afield: Eugênia Silva de Medeiros (IBAMA, Piauí); Ana Elisa Carvalho Teles (PIEMTUR, Piauí); Giacomo Maistroianni (and furry friend, Amanda) (Fortaleza); Rosângela Lima (Fortaleza); Paulo Sadao (São Paulo); Phil Schwartz (Porto Alegre); Luís Krug and the Luísmobile (Lençóis); Edivaldo da Silva (IBAMA, Belém); Seth Dechtman (USA); Rose Bratsiotis (São Paulo); Salatiel Silva Reis (São Paulo); Verena Henman (São Paulo & UK); Leif Örnestrand & Suzanne Gabrielsson (João Pessoa & Sweden); Oliveira Reis Turismo (Olinda); The Ghostbusters (Olinda); Dr Marc & Betsy van Roosmalen (Manaus); Laura Silvani Hurtado (Spain); Dave Dault (Alaska); Mark Dunlop & Heather Weidenhamer (Canada), Douglas Trent (Focus Tours: Belo Horizonte & USA) and Commander M K Barritt (Royal Navy, UK) for his information on Bahia and other states.

Robert would like to dedicate his slice of this book to Claudio Ohnstein, a spirited Paulista who shared travels in Tibet and Christmas in Macau. In 1989, whilst returning from the beach (his favourite pleasure), Claudio was killed in a road accident.

This Book

The first edition of *Brazil – a travel survival kit* was written by Mitchell Schoen and William Herzberg. This edition was tackled by a fresh set of authors: Andrew covered the Southeast, South, and Central West; Robert and Deanna covered the Northeast and North. All three writers covered overlapping sections of these regions.

From the Publisher

This edition of *Brazil – a travel survival kit* was edited by Michelle de Kretser and Michelle Coxall. Trudi Canavan was responsible for design, drawing new maps and updating maps drawn by Todd Pierce for the 1st edition of this book. Illustrations were drawn by the aforementioned Trudle, Ann Jeffree and Greg Herriman. Thanks to Krzysztof Dydynski for permission to use material from *Colombia – a travel survival kit* for the Leticia section.

Warning & Request

Things change – prices go up, schedules change, good places go bad and bad places go bankrupt nothing stays the same. So if you find things better or worse, recently opened or long since closed, please write and tell us and help make the next edition better!

Your letters will be used to help update future editions and, where possible, important changes will also be included as a Stop Press section in reprints. All information is greatly appreciated and the best letters will receive a free copy of the next edition, or any other Lonely Planet book of your choice.

To all those readers who wrote to us about the first edition of this guide – thank you! Your names are recorded for prosperity on page 626.

Contents

INTRODUCTION...9

FACTS ABOUT THE COUNTRY.. 11

History 11
Geography 26
Flora & Fauna........................29
Ecology & Environment 33
National Parks 39

Climate 43
Government 44
Economy 45
Population & People.................48
Education 53

Arts.......................................53
Culture..................................58
Religion.................................59
Language...............................62

FACTS FOR THE VISITOR 66

Visas......................................66
Documents.............................67
Customs.................................68
Money....................................68
When to Go 71
What to Bring 71
Tourist Offices 72
Useful Organisations 72
Business Hours & Holidays 73

Festivals & Cultural Events 73
Post & Telecommunications 74
Time.......................................76
Electricity...............................77
Weights & Measures.................77
Books & Maps 77
Film & Photography 83
Health....................................84
Women Travellers....................96

Dangers & Annoyances 97
Work.....................................103
Activities..............................103
Highlights.............................105
Accommodation.....................106
Food 109
Drinks...................................113
Entertainment.......................115
Things to Buy.......................116

GETTING THERE & AWAY 119

Air...119

Land.......................................125

Tours.....................................127

GETTING AROUND...129

Air...129
Bus...131
Train......................................133

Taxi..133
Car & Motorbike 134
Bicycle...................................135

Hitching.................................135
Boat 135
Local Transport.......................135

THE SOUTHEAST - 137

RIO DE JANEIRO CITY...139

Orientation.............................142
Information.............................144
Walking Tour 147
Beaches..................................151

Museums................................155
Popular Hikes & Climbs.........159
Carnival.................................161
Places to Stay........................163

Places to Eat..........................169
Entertainment........................173
Getting There & Away 177
Getting Around 178

RIO DE JANEIRO STATE...181

West of Rio de Janeiro 183
Ilha Grande 183
Angra dos Reis 184
Parati.....................................185
Around Parati 190
The Mountains 191
Petrópolis...............................191
Vassouras...............................192
Teresópolis.............................193

Nova Friburgo........................196
The Itatiaia Region............198
Resende.................................198
Penedo...................................198
Visconde de Mauá 199
Parque Nacional do Itatiaia 200
East of Rio de Janeiro 202
Saquarema 202
Arraial do Cabo 204

Cabo Frio 205
Búzios....................................206
Barra de São João 208
Rio das Ostras 208
Macaé....................................208
Reserva Biológica do Poço
das Antas 208
Macaé to Campos 208
Barra da Itabapoana 209

ESPÍRITO SANTO 210

Vitória....................................210
Guarapari 214
Anchieta.................................214

Piúma 215
Marataízes 215
Domingos Martins 216

Santa Teresa 216
Conceição da Barra.................217

MINAS GERAIS 218

Belo Horizonte 220
Historical Towns **224**
Sabará 224
Congonhas 226
Ouro Prêto 227

Mariana 235
São João del Rei 235
Tiradentes 240
Prados 242
Diamantina 242

Mineral Spa Towns **245**
Caxambu 245
São Lourenço 248
São Tomé das Letras 250
National Parks **251**

SÃO PAULO STATE 253

São Paulo City **253**
The Paulista Coast **269**
Ubatuba 269
Caraguatatuba 270

São Sebastião 270
Ilhabela 271
Boiçucanga 272
Guarujá 273

Santos 273
Iguape 273
Cananéia 274
Campos do Jordão 274

THE SOUTH - 277

PARANÁ 279

Curitiba 279
Morretes 285
Antonina 286

Paranaguá 286
Paraná Beaches 289
Ilha do Mel 289

Other Baía de Paranaguá
Islands 291
Foz do Iguaçu 293

SANTA CATARINA 299

Joinville 300
Joinville to Florianópolis 303

Blumenau 304
Florianópolis 306

Ilha de Santa Catarina 309
São Joaquim 313

RIO GRANDE DO SUL 314

Porto Alegre 314
Litoral Gaúcho 317
Pelotas 319

Rio Grande 320
Serra Gaúcha 321

Parque Nacional de Aparados
da Serra 323
Jesuit Missions 324

CENTRAL WEST - 327

Distrito Federal **329**
Brasília 329
Around Brasília 336
Goiás **336**
Goiânia 336
Goiás Velho 339
Pirenópolis 341
Caldas Novas 342

Parque Nacional das Emas 343
Rio Araguaia 343
Mato Grosso **343**
Cuiabá 344
Chapada dos Guimarães 349
Cáceres 350
Barão de Melgaço 350
Poconé 351

The Pantanal **351**
Mato Grosso do Sul **359**
Corumbá 359
Aquidauana 364
Campo Grande 364
Coxim 367
Bonito 367
Ponta Porã 368

THE NORTHEAST - 371

BAHIA 374

Salvador **377**
Around Salvador **396**
Itaparica 396
Other Baía de Todos os Santos
Islands 398
The Recôncavo Region ...**398**
Cachoeira 398
Candeias 403
Santo Amaro 403
Nazaré 404
North of Salvador **405**

Arembepe 405
Praia do Forte 405
South of Salvador **408**
Valença 408
Ilhéus 411
Porto Seguro 416
North of Porto Seguro 421
Santa Cruz Cabrália 421
South of Porto Seguro 421
Arraial d'Ajuda 422
Trancoso 423

Caraíva 424
Parque Nacional de Monte
Pascoal 424
Prado & Alcobaça 424
Caravelas 425
West of Salvador **426**
Feira de Santana 426
Lençóis 426
Parque Nacional da Chapada
Diamantina 430
Rio São Francisco 434

SERGIPE & ALAGOAS 436

Sergipe **436**

Estância 436

São Cristóvão 437

Laranjeiras 437	**Alagoas**.......................... **442**	North of Maceió.....................451
Aracaju 438	Maceió 442	
Propriá 441	South of Maceió 448	

PERNAMBUCO 453

Recife...........................453	Pontas de Pedra..................472	Garanhuns 474
Beaches South of Recife 464	Caruaru 472	Triunfo 474
Olinda 465	Tracunhaém 474	**Fernando de Noronha 475**
Beaches North of Olinda.........470	Fazenda Nova & Nova	
Igarassu 470	Jerusalém 474	

PARAÍBA & RIO GRANDE DO NORTE 479

Paraíba........................ **479**	Barra do Cunhaú 486	Ponta Negra.......................486
João Pessoa 479	Tibau do Sul 486	Natal 487
South of João Pessoa 484	Senador Georgino Alvino to	North of Natal 491
Baía da Traição 484	Búzios 486	Areia Branca 492
Sousa 485	Pirangi do Sul & Pirangi do	Tibaú 493
Rio Grande do Norte...... 485	Norte 486	
Baía Formosa 485	Barreira do Inferno 486	

CEARÁ, PIAUÍ & MARANHÃO 494

Ceará........................... **494**	Pacatuba 509	Pedro Segundo 517
Fortaleza 494	Parque Nacional de Ubajara ... 510	**Maranhão** **518**
Beaches South-East of	Serra da Ibiapaba 511	São Luís 518
Fortaleza 503	Juazeiro do Norte 511	Ilha de São Luís 527
South to Rio Grande do Norte.506	**Piauí** **512**	Alcântara 528
Beaches North-West of	Teresina 512	Parque Nacional Lençóis
Fortaleza 506	Litoral Piauiense 515	Maranhenses 530
Sobral 508	Parque Nacional de Sete	The North Coast 531
Maranguape 508	Cidades 516	Reserva Biológica do Gurupi . 531

THE NORTH - 533

PARÁ, AMAPÁ & TOCANTINS 538

Pará.............................. **538**	Serra Pelada 555	Serra do Navio 562
Belém............................538	Santarém 555	National Parks, Reserves &
Ilha do Mosqueiro 550	Parque Nacional da Amazônia 559	Research Stations in Amapá ... 562
Praia do Algodoal & Marudá ..551	**Amapá**.......................... **560**	**Tocantins**...................... **563**
Salinópolis 551	Macapá.............................560	Rio Araguaia 563
Ilha de Marajó 551	Rio Araguari & The Pororoca 562	Ilha do Bananal 563

AMAZONAS & RORAIMA 565

Amazonas..................... **565**	Tabatinga & Benjamin	Boa Vista 588
Manaus 565	Constant 583	Around Boa Vista...............591
Manacapuru 582	Leticia (Colombia) 585	Santa Elena (Venezuela) 591
Maués 583	Islandia (Peru) 587	Mt Roraima & The Gran
Tefé 583	**Roraima** **588**	Sábana 592

RONDÔNIA & ACRE 594

Rondônia...................... **594**	Guajará-Mirim 601	Brasiléia 609
Porto Velho 595	Guayaramerín (Bolivia)....... 603	Cobija (Bolivia) 610
Vilhena..........................601	**Acre** **605**	Assis Brasil & Iñapari (Peru).. 612
Forte Príncipe da Beira &	Rio Branco 606	Cruzeiro do Sul 613
Costa Marques 601	Xapuri 608	

INDEX ....

Maps 619	Text 620

Map Legend

BOUNDARIES

—‥—‥—‥—	.... International Boundary
—‥—‥—‥—	.... Internal Boundary
‥‥‥‥‥‥‥‥‥	.... National Park or Reserve
– – – – – – –	.... The Equator
‥‥‥‥‥‥‥‥‥	.... The Tropics

SYMBOLS

◉ NEW DELHI	.... National Capital
● BOMBAY	.... Provincial or State Capital
● Pune	.... Major Town
• Barsi	.... Minor Town
■	.... Places to Stay
▼	.... Places to Eat
☎	.... Post Office
✈	.... Airport, Airstrip
i	.... Tourist Information
⊖	.... Bus Station or Terminal
66	.... Highway Route Number
☧ ☩ ☩	...... Mosque, Church, Cathedral
∴	.... Temple or Ruin
✚	.... Hospital
※	.... Lookout
▲	.... Camping Area
⌐	.... Picnic Area
⌂	.... Hut or Chalet
▲	.... Mountain or Hill
	.... Railway Station
	.... Road Bridge
	.... Railway Bridge
	.... Road Tunnel
	.... Railway Tunnel
	.... Escarpment or Cliff
	.... Pass
	.... Ancient or Historic Wall

ROUTES

————————	.... Major Road or Highway
– – – – – – –	.... Unsealed Major Road
————————	.... Sealed Road
– – – – – – –	..... Unsealed Road or Track
════════	.... City Street
+++++++	.... Railway
◉═══◉	.... Subway
‥‥‥‥‥‥‥	.... Walking Track
– – – – – – –	.... Ferry Route
+н+н+н+	.... Cable Car or Chair Lift

HYDROGRAPHIC FEATURES

	.... River or Creek
	.... Intermittent Stream
	.... Lake, Intermittent Lake
	.... Coast Line
	.... Spring
	.... Waterfall
	.... Swamp
	.... Salt Lake or Reef
	.... Glacier

OTHER FEATURES

	Park, Garden or National Park
	.... Built Up Area
	... Market or Pedestrian Mall
	.... Plaza or Town Square
	.... Cemetery

Note: not all symbols displayed above appear in this book

Introduction

For hundreds of years Brazil has symbolised the great escape into a primordial, tropical paradise. No country ignites the Western imagination as Brazil does. From the mad passion of Carnival to the enormity of the dark Amazon, Brazil is a country of mythical proportions.

Roughly the size of the continental USA, Brazil is a vast country encompassing nearly half of South America, and bordering each of the continent's lesser nations with the exceptions of Ecuador and Chile. After 40 years of internal migration and population growth, Brazil is also an urban country: more than two out of every three Brazilians live in a city. São Paulo, with its 17 million inhabitants, is one of the most populous megalopolises in the world. Nevertheless, Brazil's population is clustered along the Atlantic coast and much of the country – including the massive Amazon Basin – remains scarcely populated and inaccessible.

For most, the Brazilian journey begins in Rio de Janeiro. For some it goes no further. One of the world's great tourist cities, Rio has developed a highly advanced culture of pleasure. It revolves around the planet's most famous beaches – Copacabana and Ipanema – and is fuelled by the music and dance of samba, the beauty of Corcovado and Pão de Açúcar (Sugar Loaf Mountain), the athleticism of football, the happiness to be found in an ice-cold *cerveja* (beer), the camaraderie of *papo* (chitchat) and the cult of the body-beautiful. This hedonism reaches its climax in the big bang of ecstasy that is Carnival – four days of revelry and debauchery, unrivalled by any other party on the globe.

The state of Rio de Janeiro is blessed with some of the country's best beaches: from the world renowned Búzios to the unknown and undeveloped Ilha Grande. Inland, the coastal mountains rise rapidly from under their blanket of lush green tropical forest, culminating in spectacular peaks. The mountains are punctuated by colonial cities and national parks that are home to Brazil's best hiking and climbing.

The Amazon is the world's largest tropical rainforest, fed by the world's largest river, and home to the richest and most diverse ecosystem on the earth. It is the ultimate naturalist's fantasy! Though it is threatened by rapid and senseless deforestation, the Brazilian Amazon still offers years of exploration for the adventurous traveller.

South of the Amazon, in the centre of the continent, is Brazil's best kept secret – the Pantanal. The world's largest wetlands, the Pantanal is home to the greatest concentration of fauna in South America. When the floodwaters recede in March, the Pantanal becomes an ornithologist's playground, with over 200 bird species displaying their stuff:

macaws, parrots, toucans, rheas and jaburú storks are just a few of the more exotic species to be seen. Caimans (alligators), deer, capybara, anteater, anaconda, river otter, and the rare jaguar also thrive in the Pantanal, although several of these species are severely threatened by poaching.

The Iguaçu Falls, at the border of Argentina, Paraguay and Brazil, may be Brazil's most dazzling spectacle. The mighty waterfalls are one of the natural wonders of the world, and are superior, in size and grandeur, to both Niagara and Victoria.

Wherever the traveller goes in Brazil, from the standing-room only crowds of Copacabana to the quieter white-sand beaches along the banks of the Amazon, Brazilians are at their beaches playing. In Brazil, the beach is the national passion – everything and everyone goes there. Fortunately, with over 8000 km of coastline, there are loads of superb beaches, and if you want to find your own tropical hideaway, there's no problem.

The mixing of races in Brazil – Indian, Black and White – is most pronounced in the historic Northeast. Miscegenation and the tenacity of the traditional way of life have created a unique and wonderful civilisation, with much of Brazil's most beautiful music, dance and art, and a series of fascinating 16th and 17th-century cities like Recife, Olinda, Fortaleza, São Luís and, of course, Salvador.

Once the capital of Brazil, and one of the richest cities of the New World, Salvador is today the centre of Afro-Brazilian culture. Against a backdrop of 17th-century colonial houses, gilded churches and lively beaches, Salvador de Bahia breathes Africa: the rhythms of *afoxé*; the dance of *capoeira*; the spirituality of Candomblé, the Afro-Brazilian religion; and the many colourful pageants and festivals, particularly from December to Carnival.

Perhaps Brazil is not the paradise on earth that many travellers once imagined, but it is a land of often unimaginable beauty. There are stretches of unexplored rainforest, islands with pristine tropical beaches, and endless rivers. And there are the people themselves, who delight the visitor with their energy, fantasy and joy.

Facts about the Country

HISTORY
Indians
Anthropologists believe that at least 20,000 years ago, American Indians migrated across the Bering Strait from north-eastern Asia. They were hunter-gatherers who followed the animals across the land bridge connecting Asia and North America. The tribes were highly mobile and once they crossed into Alaska they moved south to warmer climates. Eventually, they reached the Amazon Basin in Brazil and spread out from there. It's also likely that a separate, later migration took place across the oceans, jumping from island to island.

The Brazilian Indians never developed an advanced, centralised civilisation like the Inca or Maya. They left little for archaeologists to discover: only some pottery, shell mounds and skeletons. The shell mounds *(sambaquis)* are curious. They are found on the island of Marajó, the home of Brazil's most advanced pre-Columbian civilisation, and along the coast in the south. Typically as tall as a human and about 50 metres long, the mounds are naturally formed by the sea and were used as burial sites and sometimes as dwellings.

The Indian population was quite diverse. At the time of the Portuguese conquest the Tupi were most prevalent on the coast and best known to the White conquerors. Today, most of the animals in Brazil, nearly all the rivers and mountains, and many of the towns have Tupi names.

There were an estimated two to five million Indians living in the territory that is now Brazil when the Portuguese first arrived. Today there are fewer than 200,000. Most of them live in the hidden jungles of the Brazilian interior.

The Indians of Brazil, as the Portuguese were to learn, were divided into many groups and were primarily hunter-gatherers. The women did most of the work while the men, who were magnificent archers and fishers, went to war. They lived in long communal huts. Music, dance and games played a very important role in their culture. Little surplus was produced and they had very few possessions. Every couple of years the village packed up and moved on to richer hunting grounds.

This natural life, which became the ideal of the noble savage in European minds and inspired many social thinkers such as Rousseau and Defoe, was punctuated by frequent tribal warfare and ritual cannibalism. After battles, captured enemies were ceremonially killed and eaten.

Early Colonisation
In 1500, Pedro Cabral sailed from Lisbon, bound for India, with 13 ships and 1200 men. Following Indies trailblazer Vasco da Gama's directions, his fleet sailed on a south-westerly course in order to exploit the favourable westerly trade winds in the southern hemisphere. In his slow sailing ships he was vulnerable to the strong equatorial current, which took him further west than intended. Some historians say it was his secret destination all along, and his official 'discovery' was reported to the king in such matter-of-fact terms that it seems that the existence of Brazil was already well known to mariners. In fact Portuguese records dating from 1530 suggest that the country had been colonised for more than 40 years.

Cabral landed at present-day Porto Seguro on 22 April. He and his crew were immediately greeted by some of the many Indians living along the Brazilian shore. Staying only nine days, the Portuguese built a cross and held the first Christian service in the land they dubbed Terra de Vera Cruz (Land of the True Cross). The Indians watched with apparent amazement and then, complying with the exhortations of their guests, knelt before the cross. But it wasn't Catholicism that grabbed their attention. It was the building of the cross. The Indians, living in a stone age culture, had never seen iron tools.

Cabral sailed on, leaving behind two convicts to learn the Indian's ways and taking some logs of the *pau brasil* – brazil wood tree, which produced a red dye. Subsequent Portuguese expeditions were disappointed by what they found in Brazil. They had little interest in colonisation; instead they sought the riches of India and Africa where they established trading stations to obtain spices and ivory. Brazil offered the merchants little: the Indians' stone age culture produced nothing for the European market, and the land was heavily forested, barely passable and very wild.

However, the red dye from brazil wood provoked the interest of a few Portuguese merchants and the king granted them the rights to the brazil wood trade. They soon began sending a few ships a year to harvest the trees, depending entirely on Indian labour which they procured in exchange for metal axes and knives – objects that are used to this day by Brazilians contacting unknown Indians.

Brazil wood remained the only exportable commodity for the first half of the 16th century – long enough for the colony to change its name from Terra de Vera Cruz to Brazil, an act that was later interpreted, as reports of Brazilian godlessness reached superstition-ridden Portugal, as the work of the devil. But the brazil wood trade was already in jeopardy. It was never terribly profitable and the most accessible trees were rapidly depleted. French competition for the trees intensified and fighting broke out. The Indians stopped volunteering their labour.

In 1531, King João III of Portugal sent the first settlers to Brazil. Martin Afonso de Sousa was placed at the head of five ships and a crew of 400; after exploring the coastline he chose São Vicente, near the modern port of Santos in São Paulo, to set up shop. In 1534, fearing the ambitions of other European countries, the king divided the coast into 12 parallel captaincies. These hereditary estates were given to friends of the crown *(donatários)*, who became lords of their

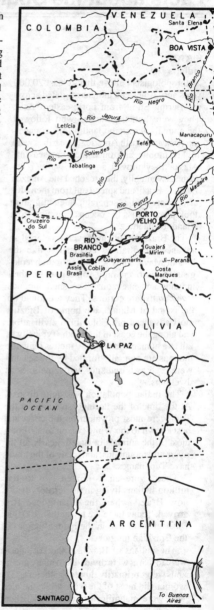

Brazil

0   250   500 km

land. Each captaincy comprised 50 leagues (about 300 km) of coastline and unlimited territory inland.

This was one of the earliest European attempts to set up a colony in the tropics. The king's scheme was designed to minimise the cost to the crown while securing the vast coastline through settlement. He wanted to give the captaincies to Portuguese nobility, but the wealthy nobles were interested in the riches of Asia. So instead the captaincies were given to common *fidalgos* (gentry), who lacked the means to overcome the obstacles of settlement in Brazil. They were hampered by the climate, hostility from the Indians and competition from the Dutch and French. One of the donatários, Duarte Coelho, wrote to the king: 'We are obliged to conquer by inches, the land that your Majesty has granted us by leagues.' Four captaincies were never settled and four were destroyed by Indians. Only Pernambuco and São Vicente were profitable.

In 1549 the king sent Tomé de Sousa to be the first governor of Brazil, to centralise authority and to save the few remaining captaincies. Despite the fact that the Indians had recently driven the Portuguese from the area, the king chose Bahia for Sousa to rule from; the Baía de Todos os Santos (Bay of All Saints) was one of Brazil's best, as was the land surrounding it.

Ten ships and 1000 settlers arrived safely. On board were Portuguese officials, soldiers, exiled prisoners, New Christians (converted Jews) and the first six Jesuit priests. The great Caramuru, a Portuguese living among the Indians and married to a chief's daughter, selected a spot on high ground for Salvador de Bahia, the new capital of Portuguese Brazil, a position it held until the colonial capital was transferred to Rio in 1763.

The colonists soon discovered that the land and climate were ideal for growing sugar cane. Sugar was coveted by a hungry European market that used it initially for medicinal purposes and as a condiment for almost all foods and even wine. To produce the sugar cane, all the colonists needed were workers. Growing and processing the cane was hard work. The Portuguese didn't want to do the work themselves so they attempted to enslave the Indians.

Up and down the coast, the Indians' response to the Portuguese was similar. First, they welcomed and offered the strangers food, labour and women in exchange for iron tools and liquor. They then became wary of the Whites, who abused their customs and beliefs, and took the best lands. Finally, when voluntary labour became slavery and land abuse became wholesale displacement, the Indians fought back and won many victories.

The capture and sale of Indian slaves became Brazil's second commerce. Organised expeditions from São Paulo hunted the Indians into the Brazilian interior, exploring and claiming vast lands for the Portuguese and making fortunes supplying the sugar estates with Indian slaves. These expeditions were called *bandeiras* (flags) after the flags they followed. Each group had its own flag, and the men who followed them came to be known as *bandeirantes* (flag-bearers). Their bravery was eclipsed only by their brutality.

The Jesuit priests went to great lengths to save the Indians from the slaughter. They inveighed against the evils of Indian slavery in their sermons, though they said little about Black slaves. They pleaded with the king of Portugal. They set up *aldeias* (missions) to settle, protect and Christianise the Indians.

Fear of God failed to deter the colonists. The monarchy was ambivalent about Indian slavery and too weak to do anything about it. Most of the Indians not killed by the guns of the bandeirantes or the work on the sugar plantations died from introduced European diseases and the alien life in the missions. The Jesuits may have delayed the destruction of the Brazilian Indians, but they certainly didn't prevent it. Nonetheless, the Jesuits battled heroically to save the Indians. One Brazilian statesman wrote: 'Without the Jesuits, our colonial history would be little more than a chain of nameless atrocities.'

By the end of the 16th century about 30,000 Portuguese settlers and 20,000 Black slaves lived in isolated coastal towns surrounded by often hostile Indians. There were about 200 prosperous sugar mills; most were in Pernambuco and Bahia. In an often quoted passage, a historian lamented in 1620 that the Brazilian settlers were satisfied with 'sidling like crabs along the coastline from one sugar plantation to another'.

But there were good reasons for this. The export economy looked only to Europe, not inland where the forests were dense, the rivers were wild and hostile Indians prevailed. Sugar was extremely lucrative, whereas the gold of El Dorado was elusive. The sugar trade needed the rich coastal soil and access to European markets. Thus the Portuguese settled almost exclusively at the mouths of rivers on navigable bays. Where sugar grew – mainly Bahia, Pernambuco and Rio – so did the fledgling colony.

The captaincy system failed, but sugar succeeded. The sparsely settled land – that would eventually encompass half a continent – already had the elements that were to define it even into the 19th century: sugar and slavery.

Sugar & Slaves

The sugar plantations were self-sufficient economic enclaves. They were geared to large-scale production that required vast tracts of land and specialised equipment to process the sugar cane. In Brazil this meant the sugar baron needed land, a fair amount of capital and many workers, typically 100 to 150 slaves, both skilled and unskilled.

By the 1550s the wealthier sugar barons began to buy African slaves instead of Indians. The Africans were better workers and more immune to the European diseases that were slaughtering the Indians faster than the Portuguese guns. Soon tremendous profits were being made by merchants in the slave trade. The infamous triangular trade brought slaves and elephant tusks from Africa; sugar, sugar cane liquor and tobacco from Brazil; and guns and luxury goods from Europe.

19th century engraving of the selling of African slaves

Throughout the 17th century Blacks replaced Indians on the plantations. In the early 1600s about 1500 slaves were arriving each year. From 1550 to 1850, when the slave trade was abolished, about 3½ million African slaves were shipped to Brazil – 38% of the total that came to the New World.

Those Africans who didn't die on the slave ships generally had short and brutal lives. The work on the plantations was hard and tedious. During the busy season slaves worked 15 to 17 hours a day. But working and living conditions, not the amount of work itself, were largely responsible for the high mortality rate of Brazil's slaves. Disease was rampant in Brazil: many succumbed to dysentery, typhus, yellow fever, malaria, syphilis, tuberculosis and scurvy.

The plantation owners ruled colonial Brazil. Their control over free Whites who worked as share-croppers was almost total, and over slaves it was absolute. Slave were dependent on their masters. Some were kind, most were cruel and often sadistic.

Slave families were routinely broken up. Masters mixed slaves from different tribes to prevent collective rebellion. The slaves from Islamic Africa, culturally superior to most Portuguese, were particularly feared by the White masters.

Resistance to slavery took many forms. Some slaves responded to their misery with *banzo*, the longing for Africa, which culminated in a slow suicide. Many documents of the period refer to slaves who would stop eating and just fade away. Many slaves fled. Mothers killed their babies. Sabotage and theft were frequent, as were work slow-downs, stoppages and revolts.

Those that survived life on the plantations found solace in their African religion and culture, in their dance and song. The slaves were given perfunctory indoctrination into Catholicism. Except for the Islamic element, a syncretic religion rapidly emerged. Spiritual elements from many of the African tribes such as the Yoruba, Bantu and Fon were preserved and made palatable to the slave masters with a facade of Catholic saints and ritual objects. These are the roots of modern Macumba and Candomblé, prohibited by law until very recently.

Portugal was not an overpopulated country. There was no capitalist revolution and no enclosures, as in England, forcing the peasantry off the land. Consequently, the typical Brazilian settler emigrated by choice with the hope of untold riches. These settlers were notoriously indisposed to work. They came to Brazil to make others work for them, not to toil in the dangerous tropics. Even poor Whites had a slave or two. There was a popular saying that 'the slaves are the hands and the feet of the Whites'.

The sugar barons lived on the plantation part time and escaped to their second houses in the cities, where they often kept *mulatto* (mixed race) mistresses. The White women led barren, cloistered lives inside the walls of the *casa grande* (big house). Secluded from all but their family and servants, the women married young – usually at 14 to 15 years of age – and often died early.

Sexual relations between masters and slaves were so common that a large mulatto population soon emerged. Off the plantation, with the shortage of White women, many poorer settlers lived with Black and Indian women. Prostitution was prevalent. Many of the free mixed-race women could only survive by working as concubines or prostitutes. Brazil was famous for its sexual permissiveness. By the beginning of the 18th century it was known as the land of syphilis. The disease had reportedly wrought devastation even in the monasteries.

The church was tolerant of any coupling that helped populate the colony. Many priests had mistresses and illegitimate children. As Gilberto Freyre, Brazil's most famous social scientist, said of the priests, 'a good part if not the majority of them assisted in the work of procreation, and their cooperation was so gratefully accepted that the courts did not arrest or issue warrants for any cleric or friar on the charge of keeping a concubine'.

In the poorer regions of Pará, Maranhão, Ceará and São Paulo, the settlers couldn't afford Black slaves. Indian slaves were more common. Here, miscegenation was more prevalent between Whites and Indians and just as tolerated (this is evident in the racial mix of the people's faces in those states today). As in the rest of the colony, sexual relations were rather licentious. As the Bishop of Pará summed it up: 'the wretched state of manners in this country puts me in mind of the end that befell the five cities, and makes me think that I am living in the suburbs of Gomorrah, very close indeed, and in the vicinity of Sodom'.

17th Century

Sugar plantations were the first attempt at large-scale agricultural production, not just extraction, in the New World. Thanks to a virtual monopoly and increasing European demand, they were highly profitable. The sugar trade made the Portuguese colonisation of Brazil possible. In later years, as Portugal's Asian empire declined, the tax revenues from the sugar trade kept the Portuguese ship of state afloat.

Although Spain and Portugal had divided the New World exclusively between themselves with the Treaty of Tordesillas, competing European powers – principally France and Holland – were not deterred from South America. France had successfully operated trading stations in Brazil for many years and had friendly relations with many Indians, who saw the French as a lesser evil than the hated Portuguese.

In 1555 three boatloads of French settlers led by Admiral Nicolas Durand de Villegagnon landed on a small island in Baía de Guanabara. They intended to add a large part of southern Brazil to their empire, which was to be called Antarctic France. After some bloody battles they were finally expelled by the governor-general of Brazil, Mem de Sá, in 1567. In a second attempt in 1612 the French took São Luis but were driven out by the Portuguese a few years later.

The Dutch posed a more serious threat to Portuguese Brazil. Dutch merchants had profited from the Brazilian sugar trade for many years, but when Portugal was unified with Spain, the traditional enemies of the Dutch, peaceful trade quickly collapsed. The Dutch set up the Dutch West India Company to gain control of part of Brazil. A large expedition took Bahia in 1624. A year later, after bloody and confused fighting, the Portuguese retook the city; they repulsed two more attacks in 1627.

The Dutch next conquered Pernambuco in 1630 and from there took control of a major chunk of the Northeast from Sergipe to Maranhão and founded what they called 'New Holland'. With their superior sea power the Dutch sailed to Africa and captured part of Portuguese-held Angola to supply slaves for their new colony. In 1637, the Dutch prince, Maurice of Nassau, took over as its governor. An enlightened administrator, he was successful in increasing the number of sugar plantations, creating large cattle farms and re-establishing the discipline of his troops and civil administrators. Hospitals and orphanages were founded and freedom of worship guaranteed in an attempt to win over the local population.

But Nassau was undermined and frustrated by a lack of support from Holland. When he returned home in 1644, the rot set in. The Pernambucan merchants, resenting the Protestant invaders, funded Black and Indian soldiers who fought the Dutch on land. The Portuguese governor of Rio de Janeiro and Angola, Salvador de Sá, sailed from Rio and expelled the Dutch from Angola. Finally, when provisions failed to arrive, the Dutch troops mutinied and returned to Europe. A peace treaty was signed in 1654.

Bandeirantes

Throughout the 17th and 18th centuries, bandeirantes from São Paulo continued to march off into the interior to capture Indians. Most bandeirantes, born of Indian mother and Portuguese father, spoke both Tupi-Guaraní and Portuguese. They also learned the survival skills of the Indians and the use of European weaponry, and wore heavily padded cotton jackets that deflected Indian arrows. Travelling light in bands that ranged from a dozen to a couple of hundred, they would go off for months and years at a time, living off the land and plundering Indian villages. By the mid-1600s they had traversed the interior as far as the peaks of the Peruvian Andes and the lowlands of the Amazon forest. These super-human exploits, more than any treaty, secured the huge interior of South America for Portuguese Brazil.

The bandeirantes were ruthlessly effective Indian hunters. The Jesuits, who sought desperately to protect their flock of Indians – who had come to the missions to escape bandeirante attacks – built missions in the remote interior, near the present-day borders with Paraguay and Argentina. Far from São Paulo, the Jesuits hoped that they were beyond the grasp of the bandeirantes. They were wrong, and this was to be their last stand. The Jesuits armed the Indians and desperate battles took place. The bandeirantes were slowed down but they were never stopped. Finally, with the collusion of the Portuguese and Spanish crowns, the missions fell and the Jesuits were expelled from Brazil in 1759.

Gold

El Dorado and other South American legends of vast deposits of gold and precious stones clouded European minds and spurred roving bandeirantes to excess. Despite incessant searching, riches failed to materialise until the 1690s, when bandeirantes discovered a magical lustre in the rivers of the Serra do Espinhaço, Brazil's oldest geological formation, an inaccessible and unsettled region inland from Rio de Janeiro.

Soon, the gold rush was on. People dropped everything to go to what is now the south central part of Minas Gerais. Unaware of the hazardous journey, many died on the way. In the orgy to pan no one bothered to plant, and in the early years terrible famines swept through the gold towns. The price of basic provisions was always outrageous and the majority suffered. But the gold was there – more than seemed possible.

When gold was first discovered, there were no White settlers in the territory of Minas Gerais. By 1710 the population was 30,000 and by the end of the 18th century it was half a million.

For 50 years, until the mines began to decline, Brazilian gold caused major demographic shifts in three continents. Paulistas came from São Paulo, followed by other Brazilians, who had failed to strike it rich in commercial agriculture. Some 400,000 Portuguese arrived in Brazil in the 18th century, many headed for the gold fields. Countless slaves were stolen away from Africa, to dig and die in Minas.

Fuelled by competition over scarce mining rights, a Brazilian species of nativism arose. Old-time Brazilians, particularly the combative Paulistas, resented the flood of recent Portuguese immigrants who were cashing in on their gold discoveries. The recent arrivals, numerically superior, loathed the favourable treatment they saw the Paulistas receiving. Gold stakes were more often than not settled by guns, not judges, and armed confrontations broke out in 1708. The colonial government was faced with a virtual civil war which lasted over a year, with miners carrying pans in one hand and guns in the other, before government intervention slowed the hostilities.

Most of the gold mining was done by Black slaves. An estimated third of the two million slaves who reached Brazil in the 18th century went to the gold fields, where their lives were worse than in the sugar fields. Most slave owners put their slaves on an incentive system, allowing the slaves to keep a small percentage of the gold they found. A few slaves who found great quantities of gold were able to buy their own freedom, but for the majority disease and death came quickly.

Wild boom towns arose in the mountain valleys: Sabará, Mariana, São João del Rei, and the greatest, Vila Rica de Ouro Prêto (Rich Town of Black Gold). Rich merchants built opulent mansions and churches. Crime, gambling, drinking and prostitution ruled the streets. A class of educated artisans created some stunning baroque church architecture. Portuguese officials provided a sense of European civilisation. The absence of White women led to a large number of mulatto offspring.

Most of Brazil's gold wealth was squandered. A few merchants and miners became incredibly rich and lived on imported European luxury goods. But the gold did little to develop Brazil's economy, create a middle class or better the common worker. Most of the wealth went to Portuguese merchants and the king, where it paused before being traded for English goods.

By 1750, after a half-century boom, the mining regions were in decline, the migration to the interior was over and coastal Brazil was returning to centre stage. Apart from some public works and many beautiful churches, the only important legacy of Brazil's gold rush was the shift in population from the Northeast to the Southeast. Some stayed in Minas Gerais and raised cattle on its rich lands. Many ended up in Rio, whose population and economy grew rapidly as gold and supplies passed through its ports.

19th Century

In 1807 Napoleon's army marched on Lisbon. Two days before the invasion, 40 ships carrying the Portuguese prince regent (later known as Dom João VI) and his entire court of 15,000 had set sail for Brazil under the protection of British warships. When the prince regent arrived in Rio his Brazilian subjects celebrated wildly, dancing in the streets. He immediately took over rule of Brazil from his viceroy.

As foreigners have been doing ever since, Dom João fell in love with Brazil. A great lover of nature, he founded Rio's botanical gardens and introduced the habit of sea bathing to the water-wary inhabitants of Rio. Expected to return to Portugal after Napoleon's Waterloo in 1815, he stayed in Brazil. The following year his mother, mad queen Dona Maria I, died and Dom João VI became king. Despite demands to return to Portugal and rule, he refused and declared Rio the capital of the United Kingdom of Portugal, Brazil and the Algarves. Brazil became the only New World colony to ever have a European monarch ruling on its soil.

Five years later he finally relented to political pressures and returned to Portugal, leaving his son Pedro in Brazil as prince regent.

According to legend, in 1822, Pedro pulled out his sword and yelled 'Independendência ou morte!' (Independence or Death), putting himself at the country's head as Emperor Dom Pedro I. Portugal was too weak to fight its favourite son, not to mention the British, who had the most to gain from Brazilian independence and would have come to the aid of the Brazilians. The Brazilian Empire was born. Without spilling blood, Brazil had attained its independence and Dom Pedro I became the first emperor of Brazil.

Dom Pedro I only ruled for nine years. From all accounts he was a bumbling incompetent who scandalised even the permissive Brazilians by siring several soccer teams of illegitimate children. He was forced to abdicate, paving the way for his five-year-old son to become emperor.

Until Dom Pedro II reached adolescence, Brazil suffered through a period of civil war under the rule of a weak triple regency. In 1840, the nation rallied behind the emperor, and his 50-year reign is regarded as the most prosperous period in Brazilian history. He nurtured an increasingly powerful parliamentary system, went to war with Paraguay, meddled in Argentine, Paraguayan and Uruguayan affairs, encouraged mass immigration, abolished slavery, and became the first man in Brazil to have his photograph taken and to speak on the telephone (though not at the same time). Ultimately, he forged a nation that would do away with the monarchy forever.

In 1889 a military coup supported by the coffee aristocracy and a popular wave of republican sentiment toppled the antiquated Brazilian Empire. The emperor went into exile and died in Paris a couple of years later. A military clique ruled for four years until elections were held, but because of land and literacy requirements, ignorance and threats, only about 2% of the adult population voted. Little changed, except that power to the military and the coffee growers increased, while the sugar barons lost power.

A New Empire

At the beginning of the 19th century Brazil was a country of masters and slaves. There were about three million people, not including the Indians, and roughly one million of them were African slaves. In the poorer areas there were fewer Black slaves, more poor Whites and more Indians. The central west region – Minas, Goiás, the Mato Grosso –

was settled only in isolated pockets where precious metals had been found. The North-eastern interior, the *sertão*, was the most settled inland section of the country. The arid *sertão* was unable to sustain much agriculture, but cattle could graze and survive. It was a poor business, constantly threatened by drought, but the hardy *sertanejo* (inhabitant of the sertão) – often of mixed Portuguese and Indian extraction – was able to eke out a living.

The south was another story. Settled by

19th century engraving of South America

farmers from the Portuguese Azores who brought their wives with them, the area was economically backward. Few could afford slaves. The Indians had been clustered in the Jesuit missions far to the west to save them from the bandeirantes. The south was, and remains, Brazil's most European region.

Slave Revolts & Abolition

Slavery in Brazil was not abolished until 1888, 25 years after abolition in the USA and 80 years behind Britain. Resistance to slavery grew throughout the 19th century and the spectre of Haiti – the site of the first successful slave revolt – haunted the Brazilian planters who, as a result, became more brutal towards their slaves.

In Bahia there were several urban insurrections between 1807 and 1835. Most were led by Muslim Blacks – those who were free and those in slavery. The uprising of 1807 in Bahia was carefully planned so that slaves from the sugar plantations would meet the city slaves at the entrance to the city and together attack the Whites, seize ships and flee to Africa. However, the plot was betrayed and the leaders killed. The following year, a similar plan was carried out and the Blacks were defeated in battle. In Minas Gerais, 15,000 slaves congregated in Ouro Prêto and 6000 in São João do Morro, demanding a constitution and freedom. The last big slave revolt in Bahia was in 1835, and was almost successful.

Slaves fought their oppressors in many ways, and many managed to escape from their masters. *Quilombos*, communities of runaway slaves, scattered throughout the countryside, were common throughout the colonial period. The quilombos ranged from small groups hidden in the forests, called *mocambos*, to the most famous, the great republic of Palmares, which survived much of the 17th century.

Palmares covered a broad tract of lush tropical forest near the coast of northern Alagoas and southern Pernambuco states. At its height, 20,000 people lived under its protection. Most were Black, but there were also Indians, mulattos, mestiços and bandits.

They lived off the land, growing mostly corn. Agriculture was collective and productivity was higher than on the slave plantations.

Palmares was really a collection of semi-independent quilombos united under the rule of one king to fight off the Portuguese forces. Led by the African king Zumbí, the citizens of Palmares became pioneers of guerrilla warfare and defeated many Portuguese attacks. Fearing Palmares' example, the government desperately tried to crush it. Between 1670 and 1695 Palmares was attacked on an average of every 15 months, until it finally fell to a force led by Paulista bandeirantes.

Palmares is now the stuff of movies and myths, but there were many quilombos in every state. As abolitionist sentiment grew in the 19th century, the quilombos received more support and ever greater numbers of slaves fled. Only abolition itself in 1888 stopped the quilombos.

Insurrections

With populated settlements separated by enormous distances, few transportation or communication links, and an economy oriented toward European markets rather than local ones, the Brazilian nation was weak and there was little sense of national identity. Throughout the 19th century the Brazilian Empire was plagued by the revolts of local ruling elites demanding greater autonomy from the central government, or even fighting to secede. Rio Grande do Sul was torn by a civil war, called the Farrapos rebellion. There were insurrections in São Paulo and Minas Gerais, and insurrections swept through the North and Northeast in the 1830s and '40s.

The bloodiest and most radical was the Cabanagem in the state of Pará. The rebels laid siege to the capital of Belém, appropriating and distributing supplies. They held the city for a year before their defeat at the hands of a large government force. The peasants fled to the jungle with the army in pursuit and eventually 40,000 of the state's 100,000 people were killed.

The most serious revolts, like the Cabanagem, were the ones that spread to the oppressed peasants and urban poor. But the empire always struck back and the revolts all failed, in part because the upper and middle classes, who led the revolts, feared the mobilised poor as much as they feared the government.

The 19th century was also a period of messianic popular movements amongst Brazil's poor. Most of the movements took place in the economically depressed backlands of the Northeast. Canudos is the most famous of these movements. From 1877 to 1887, Antônio Conselheiro wandered through the backlands preaching and prophesising the appearance of the Antichrist and the coming end of the world. He railed against the new republican government, and eventually gathered his followers (who called him the Counsellor) in Canudos, a settlement in the interior of Bahia.

In Canudos, the government sensed dissenting plots to return Brazil to the Portuguese monarchy. They set out to subdue the rebels, but miraculously, a force of state police and then two attacks by the federal army were defeated.

Hysterical demonstrations in the cities demanded that the republic be saved from the revolutionary-monarchist followers of the Counsellor. Canudos was again besieged. A federal force of 4000 well-supplied soldiers and cannon took the settlement after ferocious house-to-house and hand-to-hand fighting. The military was disgraced and suffered heavy casualties and the federal government was embarrassed, but Canudos was wiped out. The military killed every man, woman and child, and then burned the town to the ground to erase it from the nation's memory.

The epic struggle has been memorialised in what is considered the masterpiece of Brazilian literature, *Os Sertões* (Rebellion in the Backlands) by Euclides da Cunha (more recently Mario Vargas Llosa's wrote of Canudos in a lesser work, *The War of the End of the World*).

Coffee & Rubber

Popular legend has it that the coffee bean was

Lampião

Every country has famous bad guys somewhere in its history. The USA has its Western outlaws, the UK has its highwaymen, Australia has its bushrangers and Brazil has its *cangaçeiros* (bandits).

At the end of the 19th century, the harsh poverty and social injustice in the drought-plagued sertão of the Northeast caused the formation of gangs of outlaws known as *cangaços*, who attacked towns, *fazendas* (ranches) and army outposts. The most famous cangaçeiro was Lampião, who terrorised the sertão for more than 20 years.

Lampião was a cowboy until his parents were killed by a cruel landowner. He and his brothers swore revenge and headed for the sertão to join the roaming outlaw bands.

Around 1920, two years after he had become a cangaçeiro, Lampião became head of his own gang. He gained his nickname, The Lamp, because of the bright flashes given off by his rifle when he fought the police. Unlike other cangaço leaders, who were known for their generosity to the suffering people of the sertão, Lampião was renowned for his cruelty.

With his band, whose numbers varied between 15 and 50 men, he roamed the backlands of Pernambuco, Paraíba, Alagoas and Ceará. His fame grew as stories and songs of his deeds spread throughout the Northeast.

In 1929 he met Maria Bonita, who became his lover and the first woman to join the cangaço. For another nine years the cangaço continued to be a thorn in the side of the state and federal governments, who tried many times to bring Lampião to justice. Protected by the frightened general population and scared landowners, the cangaço became careless. One night in July 1938, they were surrounded by a group of polícia militar from Sergipe. Lampião and Maria Bonita were both killed, along with nine other gang members. Their heads were cut off and for almost 30 years remained on display in the Salvador Medical Institute. They were finally buried in 1969.

The last cangaçeiro and surviving member of Lampião's band, Corisco, was killed in 1940, and the era of the cangaços came to an end. ■

introduced to Brazil in the early 18th century by Francisco de Mello Palheta, an officer from Maranhão, who went to Cayenne in French Guiana in order to settle a border dispute. He reputedly won the heart of the governor's wife, who put some coffee beans into his cup as a parting gift. On his return to Brazil, he planted them. It was to be another 100 years, however, until coffee rose to become Brazil's new monoculture.

The international sugar market began a rapid decline in the 1820s. The sugar planters had depleted much of their best soil. They had failed to modernise and were unable to compete with the newly mechanised sugar mills in the West Indies. As rapidly as sugar exports fell, coffee production rose.

The coffee tree did poorly in the harsh northern climate, but flourished on the low mountain slopes of the Paraíba valley from north-east of São Paulo city up to Rio de Janeiro state and along the border with Minas Gerais. As these lands were snatched up, the coffee plantations moved westward into Minas Gerais and western São Paulo.

Coffee production was labour intensive. Because of the large investment needed to employ so many workers, production excluded the small farmer and favoured large enterprises using slave labour. The master-slave sugar plantation system, complete with the big house and slave quarters, was reproduced on the coffee fazendas of São Paulo and Minas Gerais.

Coffee exports increased rapidly throughout the 19th century and profits soared with the introduction of machinery and Brazil's first railroads. In 1889 it totalled two-thirds of the country's exports. The modernisation of coffee production also eased the coffee plantations' transition to a free labour force with the end of slavery in 1888. During the next decade 800,000 European immigrants, mostly Italians, came to work on the coffee fazendas. Millions more immigrants – Japanese, German, Spanish and Portuguese – flooded into the cities from 1890 to 1916.

Brazil was still a rural society – only 10% of the population lived in cities in 1890 – but cities were growing rapidly. São Paulo and Rio in particular were the main beneficiaries of the coffee boom.

In the last decades of the 19th century and the first of the 20th, the Amazon region was the scene of another incredible economic boom. Its protagonist was *Hevea brasiliensis* – the rubber tree – a native of the American tropics. Things started to inflate in 1842, with the discovery of the vulcanisation process, which turned rubber into an important industrial material. Demand started to increase, but really pumped up in 1890, with the invention of the pneumatic tyre and the expansion of the fledgling automobile industry in the USA. The price of rubber sky-rocketed, and brought huge wealth and a rapid surge of progress to the main Amazonian cities of Belém, Manaus and Iquitos, as well as a large population increase to the region.

In 1912, Manaus boasted electric lights, trams and a magnificent opera house. Rubber production that year reached its peak, when 42,000 tonnes of latex were exported, accounting for almost 40% of Brazilian export revenue. It was second only to coffee on the list of most valuable export commodities.

Then the puncture occurred. Unfortunately for Brazil, in 1876, seeds from the rubber tree had been smuggled out of the Amazon and sent to Kew Gardens in England. The seedlings quickly found their way to the British colonies in South-East Asia, where large rubber plantations were created. These plantations started to produce in 1910 and proved to be extremely efficient. The price of latex on the world market plummeted. The Brazilian rubber boom became a blowout.

Brazil's place in the world economy remained that of an exporter of agricultural commodities and importer of manufactured goods. Some seeds of modernisation had been planted, but there was no economic take-off, no qualitative leap forward. In 1917, after repeated sinkings of Brazilian ships by Germans, Brazil entered WW I on the Allied side. The production of foodstuffs during the war years restored a brief period

Henry Wickham – Executioner of Amazonas

Henry Alexander Wickham was the man who punctured the Brazilian rubber boom. A classic Victorian character, it's surprising that no movie has ever been made about his famous 'seed snatch' from the Amazon.

The idea of setting up rubber plantations in the British colonies in Ceylon, Malaya and the Dutch East Indies was one which had not escaped the crafty British botanists, but the seedlings or seeds of the *Hevea brasiliensis* would not survive the trip to England.

In 1876, Wickham, who had been drifting through South America for some time, made a deal with Sir Joseph Hooker at Kew Gardens, who assured him he'd get £10 for every 1000 rubber seeds he could provide.

As luck would have it, on March 1, a 1000-tonne liner, the SS *Amazonas*, had its entire cargo stolen from the docks in Manaus. Wickham chartered the ship and instructed the captain to sail at once and meet him in Santarém. Wickham himself went up river by canoe, to a spot already chosen for the large numbers of rubber trees that grew there. For the next week he and his Indian helpers collected seeds by listening for the sharp crack of the exploding seed capsules that scatter seeds up to 50 metres from the tree. He then packed the precious cargo between dried banana leaves and stored them in cane baskets. When he boarded the *Amazonas* in Santarém he had with him 70,000 seeds.

As they reached the Brazilian Customs House in Belém, the captain held the ship in the harbour under a full head of steam while Wickham visited the customs officials, declaring: 'All we have here are exceedingly delicate botanical specimens specially designated for delivery to Her Majesty's own Royal Gardens of Kew'.

Immediately on arrival in Le Havre, en route to Liverpool, Wickham jumped ashore and caught a fast boat across the Channel. He finally arrived at Kew Gardens at 3 am, and woke up a surprised Sir Joseph Hooker, who sent a goods train to Liverpool to meet the *Amazonas* and ordered workers to clear the hothouse of its other tropical plants in anticipation.

The speed of the whole operation succeeded in bringing live rubber seeds to England, and in August of the same year, the first seedlings were shipped to Ceylon – thus ensuring the collapse of the Brazilian rubber industry.

Wickham was nicknamed the 'Executioner of Amazonas' by the Brazilian rubber barons. He went off to spend his £700 trying to grow tobacco and coffee in North Queensland, Australia. In 1920 he was knighted by King George V for services to the plantation industry. ■

---

of prosperity, but after the war there were continuing economic crises and local political revolts.

Vargas Era

Coffee was king until the global economic crisis of 1929 put a big hole in the bottom of the coffee market and badly damaged the Brazilian economy. The coffee planters of São Paulo, who controlled the government, were badly weakened. In opposition to the pro-coffee policies of the government, a liberal alliance formed around the elites of Minas Gerais and Rio Grande do Sul and nationalist military officers. When their presidential candidate, Getúlio Vargas, lost the 1930 elections, the military took power by force, handing over the reins to Vargas.

Vargas proved to be a gifted political manoeuverer and was to dominate the political scene for the next 20 years. He skillfully played off one sector of the ruling elite against another, but was careful not to alienate the military. His popular support came from the odd bit of social reform combined with large slabs of demagoguery and nationalism.

In 1937, on the eve of a new election, Vargas sent in the military to shut down congress and took complete control of the country. His regime was inspired by Mussolini's and Salazar's fascist states. Vargas banned political parties, imprisoned political opponents and censored the press. When WW II struck, Vargas sided with the Allies and when the war ended, the contradiction between fighting for democracy in Europe while operating a quasi-fascist state at home was too glaring. Vargas was forced to step down by the military authorities but he remained popular.

In 1951 he was legally elected to the presidency and, with the economic opportunities afforded by the war in Europe, Brazil began its fitful march towards industrialisation and urbanisation. A large network of state corporations, including national petroleum and steel companies, was established, the first minimum wage was set and peasants flocked to the cities for a better life. But Vargas' administration was plagued by corruption. The press, especially a young journalist named Carlos Lacerda, attacked him viciously and the military withdrew their support. In August of the same year, Vargas' bodyguards made an attempt to murder Lacerda, but killed an air force major who was with him. In the resulting scandal, the military demanded Vargas' resignation. He responded melodramatically by shooting himself in the heart. Popular reaction proved extremely sympathetic to the dead president. Antigovernment newspapers were burned and the US Embassy was attacked. Lacerda was forced into exile, but later returned to become a dynamic governor of Rio.

Late 20th Century

Juscelino Kubitschek, popularly known as JK, was elected president in 1956. His motto was '50 years' progress in five'. His critics responded with '40 years' inflation in four'. The critics were closer to the mark, although industrial production did increase by 80% during Kubitschek's five years.

The dynamic Kubitschek was the first of Brazil's big spenders. Deficit spending and large loans funded roads and hydroelectric projects. Foreign capital was encouraged to invest and Brazil's auto industry was started. Kubitschek built Brasília, a new capital which was supposed to be the catalyst for development of Brazil's vast interior.

In the 1961 elections, former São Paulo governor Janio Quadros took over the presidency on a wave of public euphoria. He gained 48% of the vote, the highest majority ever. Quadros had huge plans for political reform, but a moralistic streak saw him

trying to prohibit the wearing of bathing costumes at beauty contests, bikinis on the beaches and the use of amyl nitrate at Carnival. An uphill battle indeed. He then decorated Che Guevara in a public ceremony in Brasília, a move which upset the right-wing military, who started to plot. A few days later Quadros resigned after only six months in office, claiming that 'occult forces' were at work.

João 'Jango' Goulart, his vice-president and the labour minister under Vargas, took over the presidency. Opposition to Goulart's leftist policies and the fact that he hadn't been elected led to his overthrow by the military in 1964. Within hours of the coup, President Johnson cabled his warmest good wishes. The USA immediately extended diplomatic relations to the military regime and suspicions ran deep that the USA had masterminded the coup.

Much of the middle class welcomed the military and the Revolution of 1964, as it was called at first. Brazil's military regime was not as brutal as those of Chile or Argentina; the repression tended to come and go in cycles. But at its worst, around 1968 and 1969, the use of torture and the murder of political opponents was widespread. For almost 20 years political parties were outlawed and freedom of speech was curtailed.

Borrowing heavily from the international banks, the generals benefited from the Brazilian economic miracle; year after year in the late '60s and early '70s Brazil's economy grew by over 10%. The transformation to an urban and semi-industrialised country accelerated.

Spurred on by the lack of any effective rural land reform, millions came to the cities, and *favelas* (shanty towns) filled the open spaces. The middle class grew, as did the bureaucracy and military.

More mega-projects were undertaken to exploit Brazil's natural resources, to provide quick fixes to underdevelopment and to divert attention from much needed social reforms. The greatest of these was the opening of the Amazon, which has brou~ great wealth to the few and little to

Brazilians, while helping to turn attention away from the issue of land reform.

The military's honeymoon didn't last. Opposition grew in 1968 as students, and then many in the church – which had been generally supportive of the coup – began to protest against the regime. Inspired by liberation theology, the church had begun to examine Brazilian misery. Church leaders established base communities among the poor to fight for social justice. They were appalled by the military's flagrant abuse of human rights, which broke all religious and moral tenets.

In 1980 a militant working-class movement, centred around the São Paulo auto industry, exploded onto the scene with a series of strikes under the charismatic leadership of Lula, the Lech Walesa of Brazil.

With the economic miracle petering out and popular opposition picking up steam, the military announced the so-called *abertura* (opening): a slow and cautious process of returning the government to civilian rule.

A presidential election was held in 1985, under an electoral college system designed to ensure the victory of the military's candidate. Surprisingly, the opposition candidate, Tancredo Neves, was elected. Millions of Brazilians took to the streets in a spontaneous outburst of joy at the end of military rule. Tragically, Tancredo died the day before assuming the presidency and was succeeded by the vice-president, José Sarney, a relative unknown who had supported the military until 1984.

During Sarney's term of office the economy was hampered by severe inflation, and by 1990 Brazil had run up a US$25 billion domestic deficit and a US$115 billion foreign debt. However, the congress did, during this period, manage to hammer out a new, more liberal constitution that guaranteed human rights.

The first democratic presidential election since the military takeover was held in 1989. In a hard-fought campaign, Fernando Collor de Mello, ex-Brazilian karate champion and former governor of the small state of Alagoas, narrowly gained victory over the Workers Party candidate, Lula. Lula's campaign was not helped by the fact that a few days before the election his ex-lover revealed on national TV that Lula had offered her money for an abortion 16 years before.

Collor made all kinds of promises, the two main ones being to give the chop to inflation and attack corruption in government. When he assumed control in March 1990, he took some drastic measures: reducing his ministries from 23 to 12, authorising the sale of much government property, cutting subsidies to industry and, in an attempt to reduce inflation caused by excess liquidity in the market, confiscating 80% of every bank account worth more than US$1200, promising to release it 18 months later with interest. He also announced moves to privatise many state-owned companies and open Brazilian markets to foreign competition and capital. Collor professed to be a committed 'green' president, who has vowed to prevent the destruction of the Amazon forest. He recently announced that Brazil would trade up to US$100 million a year of its US$118 billion foreign debt to finance Amazon protection projects – a dramatic turnaround for the Brazilian government, which has long been touchy about 'Gringo greenmail' threatening its sovereignty in the Amazon.

By early 1992, however, few of Collor's promises had been fulfilled. He had already used up much of the goodwill from his election. The government was being shaken yet again by scandal and corruption linked directly with his family, and inflation was heading yet again into astronomical figures.

As Brazil approaches the 21st century, many lingering problems remain – corruption, violence, urban overcrowding, lack of essential health and education facilities, environmental abuse and dramatic extremes of wealth and poverty. It has long been known as a land of the future. But the future never seems to arrive.

GEOGRAPHY

Brazil is the world's fifth largest country – after Russia, Canada, China and the USA. It

The States of Brazil

NUMBERED STATES
1 RIO GRANDE DO NORTE
2 PARAÍBA
3 PERNAMBUCO
4 ALAGOAS
5 SERGIPE

borders every country in South America, except Chile and Ecuador, and its 8½ million sq km occupies almost half the continent. Gigantic Brazil is larger than the continental USA, 2½ times the size of India, and larger than Europe excluding Russia. It spans three time zones and is closer to Africa than it is to Europe or the USA.

As amazing as the size of this enormous expanse, is its inaccessibility and inhospitality to humans. Much of Brazil is scarcely populated: 36% of the nation's territory is in the Amazon Basin which, along with the enormous Mato Grosso to its south, has large

regions with population densities of less than one person per sq km. Most of this land was not thoroughly explored by Europeans until this century. New mountains, new rivers and new Indian tribes are still being discovered. The Amazon is being rapidly settled, lumbered and depleted.

Brazil's geography can be reduced to four primary regions. The long, narrow, Atlantic coastal band that stretches from the Uruguayan border to the state of Maranhaõ; the large highlands – called the Planalto Brasileiro or central plateau – which extend over most of Brazil's interior south of the

Amazon Basin; and two great depressions – the Amazon Basin and the Paraguay Basin in the south-east.

The coastal band, stretching for 7408 km, is bordered by the Atlantic and the coastal mountain ranges that lie between it and the central plateau. From Rio Grande do Sul all the way up to Bahia the mountains are right on the coast. Sheer mountainsides, called the Great Escarpment, make rivers impossible to navigate. Especially in Rio and Espírito Santo, the littoral is rocky and irregular, with many islands, bays and sudden granite peaks, like Pão de Açucar in Rio.

North of Bahia, the coastal lands are flatter and the transition to the highlands more gradual. Rounded hills signal the beginning of the central plateau. There are navigable rivers and the coast is smooth and calm, well protected by offshore reefs.

The Planalto Brasileiro is an enormous plateau that covers a part of almost every Brazilian state. It is punctuated by several small mountain ranges that reach no more than 3000 metres – the highest of these are centred in Minas Gerais – and is sliced by several large rivers. The average elevation of the Planalto is only 500 metres.

From Minas Gerais the Planalto descends slowly to the north. The great Rio São Francisco, called the river of national unity or more informally *velho chico*, which begins in the mountains of Minas, follows this northerly descent. There are several other rivers slicing through the Planalto. The large tablelands or plains between these river basins are called *chapadões*.

From the Brazilian Planalto to the south, the Andes to the west and the Guyana shield to the north, the waters descend to the great depression of the Amazon Basin. In the far west the basin is 1300 km wide, to the east, between the Guyana massif and the Brazilian Planalto, it narrows to less than 100 km wide.

There are an estimated 1100 tributaries flowing into the Amazon River, 10 of which carry more water than the Mississippi River. The 6275-km-long Amazon is the world's largest river. With its tributaries it carries an estimated 20% of the world's freshwater.

The Amazon forest contains 30% of the remaining forest in the world.

In the south, there's the Paraná-Paranagua basin. This depression, which is not as low-lying as the Amazon, includes the Pantanal and runs into the neighbouring countries of Paraguay and Argentina. It is characterised by open forest, low woods and scrubland. Its two principal rivers, the Paraguay and the Paraná, run south through Paraguay and Argentina.

For political and administrative purposes, Brazil is generally divided into five regions: the North, the Northeast, the Central West, the Southeast and the South.

The North is the Amazon forest. It encompasses 42% of Brazil's land and includes the states of Amazonas, Pará, Rondônia, Acre, Tocantins and the territories of Amapá and Roraima. This is Brazil's least populated region and contains most of the country's Indian population. The two major cities are Manaus and Belém, the former on the Rio Negro, and the latter on the Amazon River.

The Northeast, Brazil's poorest region, has retained much of Brazil's colonial past. It's also the region where the African influence is most evident. It contains 18% of Brazil's area and includes, moving up the coast, the states of Bahia, Sergipe, Alagoas, Pernambuco, Paraíba, Rio Grande do Norte, Ceará, Piauí and Maranhão. These states are divided into a littoral, the *zona da mata*, and the sertão (the dry interior).

In the old days the Central West was called the *mato grosso* (thick forest). It includes the states of Goiás, Mato Grosso, Mato Grosso do Sul and the federal district of Brasília: 22% of the national territory. Only recently opened to road transport, this is Brazil's fastest growing region.

The Southeast is developed, urban Brazil. The states of Rio de Janeiro, São Paulo, Minas Gerais and Espírito Santo make up 10% of the national territory but have 43% of the population and 63% of industrial production.

In the South, Brazil is more European, and comprises the prosperous states of Paraná (the location of the magnificent Iguaçu Falls)

Santa Catarina, with its very visible German presence, and Rio Grande do Sul.

FLORA & FAUNA

The richness and diversity of Brazilian fauna and flora is astounding, and the country ranks first in the world for numbers of species of primates, amphibians, and plants; third for bird species; and fourth for species of butterflies and reptiles.

The following is a rough overview of this extraordinary diversity which, for ease of reference, is divided into general vegetation zones with a few examples of the fauna and flora.

For details about related topics (National Parks; Ecology & Environment) refer to the respective sections in this chapter.

The Pantanal

A vast wetlands area in the centre of South America, the Pantanal is about half the size of France – some 230,000 sq km spread across Brazil, Bolivia and Paraguay. Something less than 100,000 sq km is in Bolivia and Paraguay, the rest is in Brazil, split between the states of Mato Grosso and Mato Grosso do Sul.

The Pantanal – 2000 km from the Atlantic Ocean yet only 100 to 200 metres above sea level – is bounded by higher lands: the mountains of the Serra de Maracaju to the east; the Serra da Bodoquena to the south; the Paraguayan and Bolivian Chaco to the west; and the Serra dos Parecis and the Serra do Roncador to the north. From these highlands the rains flow into the Pantanal to form the Rio Paraguai and its tributaries, which flow south and then east, draining into the Atlantic Ocean between Argentina and Uruguay.

During the rainy season, from October to March, the rivers flood their banks – inundating much of the low-lying Pantanal for half the year and creating *cordilheiras*, patches of dry land where the animals cluster together. The waters reach their high mark, as much as three metres, in January or February, then start to recede in March, and don't stop until the rainy season returns some six months later.

This seasonal flooding has made systematic farming impossible and severely limited human incursions into the area. It has also provided an enormously rich feeding ground for wildlife.

The flood waters replenish the soil's nutrients, which would otherwise be very poor due to the excessive drainage. The waters teem with fish, and the ponds provide excellent ecological niches for many animals and plants. Enormous flocks of wading birds gather in rookeries several sq km in area.

Later in the dry season, the water recedes, the lagoons and marshes dry out, and fresh grasses emerge on the savannah (Pantanal vegetation includes savannah, forest and meadows which blend together, often with no clear divisions). The hawks and jacaré compete for fish in the remaining ponds. The ponds shrink and dry up and the jacarés (caimans) crawl around for water, sweating it out until the rains return.

The food economy of the extremely diverse and abundant marshland birdlife is based on snails, insects and fish. All three abound in the Pantanal and may account for the presence of over 600 bird species: kites and hawks, limpkins, cardinals, herons and egrets, woodpeckers, ibises and storks, woodrails, kingfishers, cuckoos, hummingbirds, parakeets, thornbirds, shrikes, wrens, jays, blackbirds, finches, toucans and macaws.

A mere list doesn't do justice to the colour of a flock of parakeets in flight or the clumsiness of the *tuiuiú* (jaburú stork), the metre-high, black-hooded, scarlet-collared symbol of the Pantanal, nor can it suggest the beauty of *ninha* birds settling like snow in the trees or the speed of a sprinting herd of *emas* (rheas). Keep an ear unclogged for the call of the *quero-quero* (I want, I want) bird, which is named for its sound to Brazilian ears.

Birds are the most frequently seen wildlife, but the Pantanal is also a sanctuary for giant river otter, anacondas and iguanas, jaguars, ocelets, cougars, thousands upon thousands of jacaré, pampas and swamp deer, giant and lesser anteaters, black howler monkeys, zebu bulls and capybaras, the world's largest rodents.

Capybaras

The capybara is the most visible mammal in the Pantanal. These rodents have guinea pig faces and bear-like coats. They grow up to 63 kg and can be seen waddling in the swampy half of the Transpantaneira, where they feed on aquatic plants. They are equally at home on land or in water and are often seen in family groups of two adults and four or five young, or in large herds.

The two species of anteater in the Pantanal are endangered and not readily seen. The hairy giant anteater roams the dry savannah ground in search of the hard termite mounds which it'll excavate for 10 to 15 minutes at a time. The lesser anteater, smaller and

Giant Anteater

lighter coloured than the giant, spends most of its time in trees eating ants, termites and larvae. Both are slow footed, with poor vision, but an excellent sense of smell.

The anteater's strong arms and claws, which keep even the jaguars at bay, offer no protection from the local Pantaneiros, who prize their meat. The killing of anteaters has led to an increase in ants and termites in the last decade, and many Pantaneiros now use deadly pesticides to try to destroy the mounds, ignoring the fact that the pesticides are absorbed by cattle and wildlife feeding in the area.

With thousands of jacaré sunning themselves on the edge of each and every body of water, it's hard to believe that they are endangered by poachers, who slaughter an estimated one to two million each year.

The jacaré feed mainly on fish, and are the primary check on the growth of the piranha population, which has been growing rapidly due to the jacaré slaughter. The size of an adult jacaré is determined by the abundance of food, and varies noticeably: jacaré on the river's edge are often considerably larger than those that feed in small ponds. Although they eat young or injured animals, jacaré rarely attack people or capybara, and many birds mingle amongst the jacaré in complete peace and harmony.

Visitors to the Pantanal are always fascinated by the passivity of the jacaré. I've seen Pantaneiros swimming in rivers lined with jacaré, but there are times to be on guard. It's not safe to enter the water where there is only one jacaré. It could be a female guarding her eggs or her young. She can attack and, for short distances, run faster than a horse.

During the rainy season you must be careful walking in the water. The jacarés are not aggressive and will usually swim away before you get close. But if stepped on the jacaré will grab a leg and roll. This has probably never happened to a tourist, and only once in a blue moon does a Pantaneiro suffer this end, but the rare jacaré attack is used nonetheless to justify their slaughter.

The jacaré, not known for its voice, makes one of the strangest sounds in the Pantanal.

Every now and then a jacaré will curl its body, with head and tail stretching to the sky, open its mouth and let out a weird, deep rattle-roar. Then, suddenly, thin lines of water shoot up from the jacaré's back, and soon after it returns to its state of inactivity.

The cattle that live side by side with all this wildlife graze during the dry season and gather on the little islets that form during the wet season. Amazingly, the cattle live in harmony with the wildlife, as have humans until recently.

Jaguar

Jaguars attack only sick or injured cattle, and some eat only their natural prey, capybara and tapir. Nevertheless, many cattle ranchers kill jaguars to protect their cattle. Jaguars are also killed for their skins. They are a highly endangered species and are threatened with extinction, as are the swamp deer and the giant river otter (the 'jaguar of the waters').

The Pantaneiros believe that eating jaguar meat boosts masculine qualities like strength and virility, qualities the traditional hunter of the jaguar, the *zagaeiro*, has in abundance. Using only a *zagara*, a wooden spear with a metal tip, the zagaeiro chases the jaguar up a tree and then taunts the cat until it is ready to leap and attack. At the last moment the zagaeiro plants the spear in the ground and when the jaguar jumps on the man it impales itself, dying instantly.

See the Pantanal section in the Mato Grosso chapter for more details on the region.

The Amazon

This is the largest equatorial forest in the world and occupies approximately 42% of Brazil's area.

The rainforest ecosystem is stratified into four layers of plant and animal life. Most of the activity takes place in the canopy layer, 20 to 40 metres above ground, where plants compete for sunshine and the majority of the birds and monkeys live. The dense foliage of the canopy layer blots out the sunlight at lower levels, while a few tall trees poke above the canopy and dominate the forest skyline. A poorly defined middle layer or understorey merges with the canopy from below, and epiphytes hang at this level.

Bushes and saplings up to five metres in height constitute the shrub layer, while the ground layer is composed of ferns, seedlings and herbs – plants adapted to very little light. Ants and termites, the so-called social insects, live here. The *saubas* (leaf-cutter ants) are farmers and use leaves to build underground nests for raising fungus gardens, while army ants swarm through the jungle in huge masses, eating everything in their path. Fungi and bacteria, the decomposers, keep the forest floor clear. It's tidy in comparison to temperate forests.

The forest is not homogeneous; plant species vary with the land and its exposure to water. Plants of the *igapó* and flooded lowlands are mostly palms and trees with elevated roots. The valuable hardwoods and the brazil nut tree prefer land that is high and dry. The rubber trees and other plants of the *várzea*, land by the river's edge, have adapted to spending half of the year below water and half the year dry. Then there are

Saubas (leaf-cutter ants)

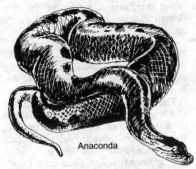
Anaconda

the aquatic plants of the river itself like the giant vitória regia water lilies (named after Queen Victoria), *mureru, camarans* and *manbeca*. There are floating marshes with grasses adapted to an amphibious lifestyle. These plants have both earth and aquatic roots, depending on the season and local conditions.

The forest still keeps many of its secrets: to this day major tributaries of the Amazon are unexplored. Of the estimated 15,000 species of Amazon creatures, thousands of birds and fish and hundreds of mammals have not been classified, and after each foray into the jungle botanists still manage to bring back dozens of unclassified plants.

A cursory sampling of known species of animals found in the forest – some common, some rare, some virtually extinct – would include jaguar, tapir, peccary, capybara, spider monkey, howler monkey, sloth, armadillo, caiman, alligator, river dolphin, manatee and turtle; and various species of snakes such as the boa constrictor and anaconda. Typical species of birds for the forest include toucans, parrots, macaws, hummingbirds, woodpeckers, and hawks. Insect life is well represented with over 1800 species of butterflies and more than 200 species of mosquitoes. Well-known species of fish include piranha, tucunaré, pirarucu, surubim, pintado and electric eel. The enormous diversity of fish in the Amazon means that biologists are unable to catalogue or identify 30% of the catch they come across in the markets of Belém.

Unfortunately, deforestation is taking place on such a vast scale that countless unknown species of animals and plants will be destroyed. We will lose a genetic library that has already given us so much: rubber, manioc, cocoa, anti-malarial drugs, cancer drugs and thousands more medicinal plants.

For more details about the problems facing the Amazon rainforest, see the Ecology & Environment section in this chapter.

Mata Atlântica

Reduced by sugar-cane farming, logging, coffee plantations and acid rain to less than 1% of its original size, the surviving coastal rainforest, known in Brazil as the Mata Atlântica, now only occurs in isolated pockets. The largest, the Estação Ecológica da Jureia, on the southern coastal escarpment in São Paulo state, owes its survival to the shelving of plans to build a nuclear power plant.

Separated from the Amazon by non-rainforest terrain, the Mata Atlântica evolved independently, with only a limited overlap of species. It contains many unique and endangered animals, such as the spider monkey (the largest primate in the Americas), howler monkey, puma, giant anteater, otter and golden-lion tamarin. Its distinctive flora includes many large trees: brazil wood, iron wood, Bahian jacaranda and cedar, as well as a number of rare tree ferns. The Mata Atlântica is also home to 115 bird species, 94 of which are unique. These include: harpy and black-hawk eagles, tinamous and the extremely rare Spix macaw.

See the Ecology & the Environment section in this chapter for more details.

Mata da Araucaria

The mountainous regions of south-west and southern Brazil were once covered by coniferous forests which were dominated by the prehistoric-looking araucaria, or parana pine tree. It grows to a height of 30 to 40 metres, has clear trunks and candelabra-like heads of upturned branches that form flattened crowns. Its seeds, *pinhões*, are edible.

Faces of Brazil (JM)

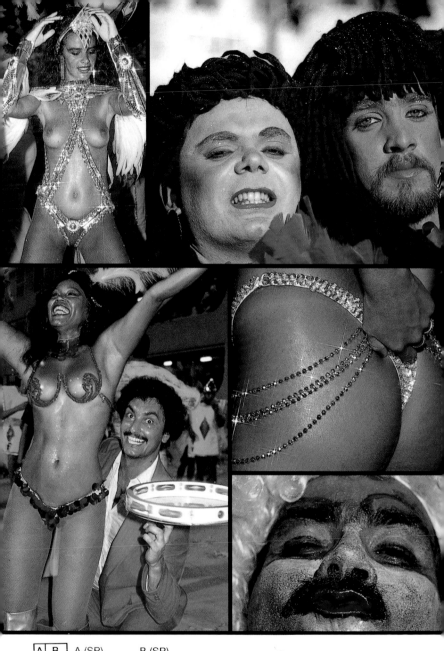

A (SP)   B (SP)
C (JM)   D (SP)
E (SP)

Decimated by timber cutters, the araucaria forests are now more scattered, but are much in evidence in the south, where their animal inhabitants include foxes, tree squirrels, skunks, spotted cats and monkeys.

Caatingas

These are dry areas, such as those of the sertão in the Northeast, where vegetation consists mainly of cacti and thorny shrubs which have adapted to lack of water and extreme heat. Much of the wildlife in these areas – anteaters and armadillos for example – has been severely depleted by hunting and habitat destruction. The list of endangered species for the caatingas includes the Spix and Lear's macaws, and the three-banded armadillo.

Cerrados

These open lands, which also occur in the form of savannah, are usually grassy plains dotted with small trees such as the mangaba and carobeira. This landscape extends from the borders of Maranhão in the Northeast down through Minas Gerais and as far as the south-west. Armadillos, foxes and rheas are some of the well-known species in these areas. The use of this land for agricultural purposes has also reduced available habitat for wildlife, such as the maned wolf, which is native to this region but is now an endangered species.

Further Reading

See the Books & Maps section in the Facts for the Visitor chapter.

ECOLOGY & ENVIRONMENT

The early '90s have seen a dramatic surge in international and domestic interest in Brazil's ecological progress and environmental attitudes. This is clearly demonstrated by the choice of Brazil as the venue for ECO-92, a mega environmental and ecological bash organised by the United Nations to thrash out appropriate priorities for the environment and economic development.

In the '70s, the military government attempted to tame the Amazon with an ambitious plan entitled Plano de Integração National (PIN). Long roads, like the 3000-km Transamazônica, were cleared from the jungle and settlers from the Northeast soon followed in the tracks of the bulldozers. The roads were said to be safety valves to ease the social tensions and overpopulation of the drought-stricken Northeast. Thousands left the Northeast to build homesteads in the newly cleared forest. The majority of these hopeful settlers failed to establish a foothold and either perished or abandoned the land for the favelas of Manaus and Belém.

During the '80s, the Brazilian government acted as if the forest were an impediment to progress, an asset to be used to pay back the debt incurred during the 20 years of military dictatorship. Encouraged by the IMF and the World Bank, the Brazilian government provided large incentives to coax multinational timber and mining firms to exploit the Amazon. These gigantic projects were designed to yield short-term profits and pay off the foreign debt regardless of environmental and social consequences. The economic plan was launched with purely extractive goals, which perceived the forests and precious metals as resources to be exploited at top speed until they were gone.

Ironically, many of the loans for these gigantic projects have simply worsened Brazil's foreign debt, which now stands at US$118 billion as opposed to US$100 billion in 1984, and created even more pressure to meet these payments without considering the cost to the environment. Despite increasing criticism at home and abroad, the general shape of this plan is still being maintained and will eventually achieve the end result of totally exhausting Brazil's resources.

Although the international media generally centres its attention on destruction of the Amazon rainforest, there are a number of other environmental issues in Brazil which are very serious.

The Mata Atlântica, a region of forest which covered 1.5 million sq km during the 16th century and stretched from the states now known as Rio Grande do Norte and Rio

Grande do Sul, has been reduced to a mere 10,000 sq km. Some Brazilian sources, such as Fundação SOS Mata Atlântica, believe that even these remnants will be finished in 15 years, along with more than 300 species of wildlife that are already on the brink of extinction.

The Pantanal is threatened by pollution and poaching – described in more detail at the end of this section. The Northeast region, already experiencing extreme poverty and social breakdown, is literally losing ground to desertification; and beaches throughout Brazil (particularly those near industrial areas) are threatened by indiscriminate dumping of major pollutants or malfunctioning sanitation systems. Further problems involve huge burns of land in parks and reserves; widespread and unchecked use of dangerous pesticides; and the concomitant reduction or extinction of hundreds of plant and wildlife species – an irretrievable genetic loss.

The Pantanal – Under Threat from Poaching & Pollution

According to Dr Maria Padua, a Pantanal biologist and conservationist, poachers are doing more damage to the Pantanal than the Amazon. The Brazilian government has not done much to stem the slaughter of the animals.

Fifteen Polícia Florestal (Forest Police) with only 12 jeeps patrol an area of land that's one-tenth the size of the Amazon. They are up against a well-organised and well-funded army of poachers, who have aircraft and hidden jungle airstrips, and corrupt national and state officials on their side. Lately, though, the police have been shooting first and asking questions later.

Anywhere from 500,000 to two million animals are killed each year in the Pantanal, smuggled over the Bolivian border (where poaching is also illegal, but requisite laws are not even tokenly enforced) and exchanged for cocaine, guns and cash.

The slow and fearless jacarés are easily shot at short range. A jacaré skin commands a price of US$200, but only a fraction of it is used – the supple, small-scaled skin of the jacaré's flanks is sought after to make fashionable wallets, belts, purses and shoes. The rest of the carcass is useless to poachers and is discarded.

A park ranger told me of the hundreds of jacaré carcasses, their skulls in neat piles, crates of handguns and rifles, bags of cocaine, and the many jaguar and ocelot pelts which were found in a recent raid on some poachers, who worked two hours by boat from Porto Jofre.

Just as poachers supply the fashion industry with skins, they supply American pet shops with rare tropical fish and birds. A hyacinth macaw will sell for US$5000 in the USA; compare that to the minimum monthly wage of a Brazilian and it's easy to see the great temptation for farmers, truckers, government officials, in fact anyone in the area, to get involved in poaching. The depletion in the numbers of jacaré is causing unchecked growth in the piranha population, which in turn will affect the numbers of different fish and bird populations.

As well as the threat posed by poachers, the delicate environment is also threatened by mercury in gold slurries and ever-expanding farm and ranch lands. Sugar mills and factories that produce álcool (sugar cane fuel) in São Paulo and Mato Grosso dump poisonous waste into rivers that drain into the Pantanal. Scientists have also detected use of the defoliant Thordon, a component of Agent Orange.

A popular TV soap opera, filmed in the Pantanal (and also, funnily enough, named *Pantanal*), has brought the area to the attention of many Brazilians. The hope is that wildlife tourism in the Pantanal will make conservation a profitable enterprise. Club Med certainly thinks so – it recently purchased a large chunk of land in the region.

The Fate of the Amazon

The Amazon, a very large, complex and fragile ecosystem – comprising one-tenth of the planet's entire plant and animal species, producing one-fifth of the world's oxygen and containing one-fifth of the world's freshwater – is endangered. Unless things change, the rainforests will be cleared for more ranches and industries, the land will be stripped for mines and the rivers will be dammed for electricity. Already jaguars, caimans, dolphins, monkeys and a host of other wildlife and plant species are threatened with extinction. As in the past, the Indians will die with their forests, and the invaluable, irreplaceable Amazon may be lost forever.

The construction of roads is a prerequisite for exploiting the Amazon. This process was initiated with the construction of the Transamazônica highway in 1970. The ensuing decades saw over US$10 billion thrown into gargantuan projects and schemes offering financial incentives to exploit resources regardless of the effects on the environment. Those involved included the World Bank, the IMF, US and other international banks, and a variety of Brazilian corporations, politicians, and military figures. According to calculations made using Landsat photos, the damming of rivers, burning, and clearing of the forests between 1970 and 1989 destroyed about 400,000 sq km or around 10% of the Amazon forest.

At the end of 1988, Chico Mendes, a rubber tapper and opponent of rainforest destruction, was assassinated in the town of Xapurí (Acre state) by a local landowner. This sparked an international reaction which eventually pressured the World Bank and the IMF to declare that they would no longer fund destruction of the rainforest. For more on Chico Mendes, see the Rondônia & Acre chapter.

Despite this commitment, it seems there will be no appreciable slackening in the destruction. The Perimetral Norte, a highway which is projected to stretch in a huge loop from Macapá (Amapá state) via Boa Vista (Roraima state) all the way to Cruzeiro do Sul (Acre state), is still being touted as a viable project. In the state of Acre, the extension of BR-364 from Rio Branco to Cruzeiro do Sul is being supported by Japanese finance. The inevitable conclusion is that new highway projects such as these will follow the old pattern of development and open up the Brazilian Amazon to even more destruction.

President Collor has promised to tackle Brazil's environmental problems, but he cannot count on unified support. The military have long had an interest in securing a slice of the country's resources and recently claimed in all seriousness that the environmental issues surrounding the Amazon had been exaggerated by foreigners intent on invading the region! Collor is also unlikely to receive much encouragement from Gilberto Mestrinho, governor of Amazonas state, whose absurd comments on the environment would be amusing oddities if it were not for the chilling fact that he is responsible for governing over 1½ million sq km of the Brazilian Amazon. The following are samples of his pearls of ecological wisdom:

I like trees and plants, but they are not indispensable. After all, men have managed to live in space for almost a year without trees...

Man is the centre of the environment and I will be the governor of men, not of animals and the forest...

There are hardly any healthy trees in Amazônia and they should be used before woodworm gets to them.

Much of what is being promised overseas and in Brazil appears to be 'Greenspeak', a type of lip service whereby the speaker certifies green intentions for a hazy point in the future without putting these into deeds. Whatever results are obtained from ECO-92, there will hopefully be more deeds and a lot less 'Greenspeak'.

Economic Development of the Amazon

Most biologists doubt that the Amazon can support large-scale agriculture; the lushness of the jungle is deceptive. Apart from volcanic lands and flood plains which can support continuous growth, the jungle topsoil is thin and infertile; most of it is acidic and contains insufficient calcium, phosphorus and potassium for crops.

Small-scale slash and burn, a traditional agricultural technique adopted by nomadic

Indians, seemed to work best at supporting small populations on such fragile lands without ecological compromises. Indians would fell a five or 10-acre plot of land and burn off remaining material. The resulting ash would support a few years of crops: squash, corn, manioc, plantains and beans. After a few seasons, however, the nutrients would be spent and the Indians would move on. The clearings were small in size and number and the land was left fallow long enough for the jungle to recover.

In contrast, modern agricultural techniques are enormous in scale, directed to the production of animal protein rather than vegetable protein, and fail to give the jungle an opportunity to recover. Nowadays ranchers clear huge areas of land – some cattle ranches are larger than European nations. These lands are never left fallow, so that nutrients contained at one point in the biomass of the forest and a thin topsoil are permanently squandered.

Farming and ranching is almost incidental to the deforestation process. Vast tracts of land are bought so that the buyers can speculate for the treasures buried beneath the earth, not those growing on it. Since Brazilian law requires that one third of the land be put to use, the owners set fire to the land (killing wildlife indiscriminately), plant some grasses and raise cattle. The government then approves the land rights and the important mineral rights are secured.

Effects of Development The Indian tribes in the Brazilian Amazon have borne the brunt of the destruction which has systematically wiped out their lands and the forest, their sole livelihood. New roads have attracted settlers and *garimpeiros* (miners) into the last refuges of these tribes, which have been virtually wiped out by new diseases, violent disputes over land, pollution from mining or the construction of huge dams which simply flood them out of the area. For more details about the Indians see the History and Population & People sections in this chapter.

Giant hydroelectric schemes, such as Balbina (Amazonas state) and Tucuruí (Pará state), are also a source of controversy. In the case of Balbina, a US$750 million project funded by the World Bank, there are doubts as to the usefulness of flooding over 2000 sq km. Apart from the loss of wildlife and wastage of valuable lumber, the possible chemical effects of such large quantities of submerged, decomposing, vegetal matter on the water quality and the surrounding region have not been sufficiently researched. Over 70 major hydroelectric schemes are planned in the Brazilian Amazon by the year 2010.

Thousands of garimpeiros have swarmed into the region to mine the streams and rivers. Unfortunately, their principal mining technique involves the use of mercury separation to extract gold from ore. Large quantities of mercury, a highly poisonous substance, are washed into the water, where they become a major health hazard for local Indians, wildlife, and the garimpeiros.

One of the most dramatic and disturbing sights in the forest is the burning of immense tracts to clear the area for agriculture or cattle ranching. Whilst travelling in the region we noticed that many airports – Porto Velho, Cuiabá, Imperatriz, and Açailândia are just a few examples – were regularly closed to air traffic because of the smoke. During broad daylight, we found ourselves sitting outside in semi-gloom (induced by huge clouds of smoke obscuring the sun) at a restaurant in Porto Velho, whilst a light rain of vegetal ash descended on the tables.

It is quite obvious that no attention whatsoever is being paid to legislation which restricts the number of fires on any one day; and it would be a Herculean task to try and enforce such a law. During 1991, it was reliably reported that on one day alone, over 60,000 fires were blazing in the Brazilian Amazon.

According to meteorologists, the smoke cloud has already reached Africa and Antarctica. Scientists generally agree that the torching of the forest on such a massive scale contributes to the greenhouse effect, but opinions differ as to the scale involved. Although scientists no longer consider the

Amazon forests to be a prime source of the world's oxygen, they are becoming increasingly concerned by the regional and global climatic changes caused by massive deforestation. The water cycle, which depends on transpiration from the forest canopy, has been interrupted and neighbouring lands, such as eastern Pará, are receiving less rainwater than usual, while the spent soils of the surrounding areas and deforested zones are being baked by the sun into desertified wastelands.

Perhaps the most devastating long-term effect is the annual loss of thousands of forest species which disappear into extinction and thereby reduce the genetic pool which is vital (as a source of foods, medicines and chemicals) for sustaining life on earth.

The Search for Solutions

It is only fair to point out that many of the countries outside Brazil which have criticised Brazil's development of the Amazon were once actively encouraging such development, and have only recently been reminded that their own treatment of the environment was hardly exemplary. The general consensus for the '90s, however, is that a series of different approaches must be tried to halt and remedy the destruction. The following are a few samples of what's being attempted.

Debt-for-nature swaps are international agreements whereby a portion of a country's external debt is cancelled in exchange for local funding of conservation initiatives. Negotiation of such swaps requires that the sovereignty of recipient countries is kept intact, and that inflationary effects on their economies are avoided. Brazil is saddled with an enormous external debt and has shown interest in such a swap, but the sovereignty issue is controversial, especially with the military, and the inflationary track record of the economy is well known.

Extractive reserves gained worldwide attention when Chico Mendes, an enthusiastic advocate of these reserves, was assassinated in Acre state. The aim of this concept is to set aside reserves for the sustainable harvesting of brazil nuts, rubber, and other non-timber products. The idea is to use the forest as a renewable resource, without destroying it.

Alternatives are also being researched to stop wasteful clear-cutting of timber. In many cases, huge tracts of forest are wiped out in order to extract only a few commercially valuable tree species, whilst the rest is considered waste. Different methods are being tried to control the type of timber cut, the size of the area that is logged, and the manner in which forests are harvested – preferably as part of an overall management scheme to retain forests as a sustainable resource.

If any success is to be achieved, these schemes will have to be underpinned with finance and enforcement. A number of foreign organisations are eyeing the idea of providing finance for Brazil's environmental needs, but experience has shown that any funds provided should be watched carefully. Much of what is currently promised in Brazil exists only on paper, and funds have a strange habit of missing their destination or drifting into private accounts. Many of the country's environmental protection units suffer from lack of funds, staff and equipment, and a consequent inability to act. Depredation of parks and reserves will have to be stringently protected by reliable, well-informed and committed 'green rangers'. Otherwise, there will be no change in the sort of situation where, for example, the Parque Nacional da Amazônia in the state of Pará has only four park guards responsible for physically protecting nearly one million hectares.

Environmental Movements

Brazil's environmental movement is about 20 years behind those in Europe, Japan and the USA. Rallying behind the slogan 'Vamos a preservar a Natureza' (let's preserve nature), the nascent conservation movement is beginning to make inroads. The environmentalists have demonstrated the benefits to industry of not polluting, and industry is beginning to respond. Nowadays environmental impact studies accompany all major industrial projects, but this does not mean that the companies concerned will feel compelled to act on recommendations made in such studies.

If Brazil's environment is to be preserved it will be through the efforts of groups like these within Brazil and abroad – groups that can educate the public and enlist its support to control consumption of tropical forest products; to pressure domestic and international banks and institutions to stop financing destructive development projects; and to persuade the Brazilian government to adopt more rational uses for the Amazon.

Ecotourism is also being considered as a powerful tool to encourage countries such as Brazil to earn more from preserving the environment than from destroying it. It is important that the organisations which proclaim an interest in ecotourism prove they are not just jumping onto the 'green' bandwagon, but also actively preserving the environment. An example of active involvement is the growing pressure exerted by consumers, who can change economic trends on a global scale by simply changing purchasing patterns. Contact the environmental and ecological organisations in the following list for more information about environment and ecology in Brazil. For more details about tour operators, see under Tours in the Facts for the Visitor chapter.

Australia

Friends of the Earth/Aust, 222 Brunswick St, Fitzroy, 3065 (☎ (03) 419-8700)

Greenpeace Australia Ltd, 3/389 Lonsdale St, Melbourne, 3000 (☎ (03) 670-1633)

Brazil

Fundação SOS Mata Atlântica, Rua Manoel da Nóbrega, 456, São Paulo (SP), CEP 04001

União dos Defensores da Terra Oikos, Avenida Brig Luís Antônio, 4442, São Paulo (SP), CEP 01402

Centro de Estudos e Atividades de Conservação da Natureza (Ceacon), Rua Augusta, 2690, cj. 217, São Paulo (SP), CEP 01412

Associação de Defesa da Juréia, Rua Cardoso de Almeida, 1479, Casa 2, São Paulo (SP), CEP 05013

União Protetora do Ambiente Natural (Upan), Rua Lindolfo Collor, 560, Caixa postal 189, São Leopoldo (RS), CEP 93001

Associação Capixaba de Proteção ao Meio Ambiente (Acapema), Caixa Postal 2304, Vitória (ES), CEP 29000

Associação Gaúcha de Proteção ao Ambiente Natural (Agapan), Rua João Telles, 524, Porto Alegre (RS), CEP 90020

Associação Paraíbana de Amigos da Natureza, Rua Empresário João Rogrigues Alves, 103, conj. UPFB, João Pessoa (PB), CEP 58000

Associação Pernambucana de Defesa da Natureza (Aspan), Rua Conselheiro Aguiar, 3686/206, Recife (PE), CEP 51020

Grupo Ambientalista da Bahia (Gamba), Rua Itabuna, 217, Salvador (BA), CEP 41910

Fundação Bio Diversitas, Avenida Otacílio Negrão de Lima, 8210, Belo Horizonte (MG), CEP 31390

Associação Mineira de Defesa Ambiental (AMDA), Rua Campos Gerais, 23, Belo Horizonte (MG), CEP 30710

Fundação Chico Mendes, Rua Dr Batista de Moraes, 180, Xapuri (AC), CEP 69920

Fundação Brasileira para a Conservação da Natureza (FBCN), Rua Miranda Valverde, 103, Rio de Janeiro (RJ), CEP 22281

Fundação Pró-Natura (Funatura), SCLN 107, Ed Gemini Center II, Bloco B, salas 201/13, Brasília (DF), CEP 70743

Instituto de Estudos Amazônicos (IEA), Rua Monte Castelo, 380, Curitiba (PR), CEP 82500

Grupo de Estudos e Defesa dos Ecosistemas do Baixo e Médio Amazonas (Gedebam), Avenida Almeida Barroso, 71, s/28, Belém (PA), CEP 66050

UK

Friends of the Earth/UK, 26/28 Underwood St, London N17JU

Survival International, 310 Edgeware Road, London W2 1DY (☎ (071) 723-5535)

USA

The Rainforest Action Network (RAN), 301 Broadway, Suite A, San Francisco CA 94133 (☎(415) 398-4404)

Conservation International, 1015 18th St, NW, Suite 1000, Washington, DC 20036 (☎ (202) 429- 5660)

Cultural Survival, 11 Divinity Avenue, Cambridge, MA 03128

The Nature Conservancy, 1815 Lynn Street, Arlington, VA 22209 (☎ (703) 841-5300)

Survival International USA, 2121 Decatur Place, NW, Washington, DC 20006

Friends of the Earth/USA, 218 D St, SE, Washington, DC 20003 (☎ (202) 544-2600)
Greenpeace, 1436 U St, NW, Washington, DC 20009 (☎ (202) 462-8817)
Earthwatch, 680 Mt Auburn St (PO Box 403), Watertown, MA 02272 (☎ (617) 926-8200)
The Chico Mendes Fund, Environmental Defense Fund, 257 Park Ave South, New York, NY 10010
Rainforest Alliance, 270 Lafayette St, Suite 512, New York, NY 10012
The Rainforest Foundation, Inc, 1776 Broadway 14th floor, New York, NY 10019

Further Reading
Refer to Books and Maps in the Facts for the Visitor chapter.

NATIONAL PARKS
On a federal and state level, there are 350 parks and ecological stations, ensuring the protection of over 300,000 sq km – roughly 5% of the national territory. Unfortunately, about 70% of them exist only on paper. Only 33% of Brazilian natural reserves have a minimum infrastructure (warden offices and fences) and only 19.5% have vehicles, supporting equipment, weapons and personnel on an appropriate level. Of all national parks, the government has managed to regulate only 22% of them. To pay out the owners of the land would cost US$1 billion. The Brazilian Environment & Natural Resources Institute (IBAMA) still hasn't expropriated any land, so ranchers continue to use it.

IBAMA makes the distinction between Parques Nacionais (National Parks), Reservas Biológicas (Biological Reserves) and Estações Ecológicas (Ecological Stations). Only Parques Nacionais are open to the public for recreational use. Reservas Biológicas and Estações Ecológicas are only open to researchers. To visit them you need permission from IBAMA.

Despite all this, there are some fantastic parks to visit. IBAMA has a minuscule budget which only allows it to publish a small amount of literature in Portuguese and even less in English. We have tried to locate and make available in this book as much information as possible. Any feedback from

readers regarding visits to these parks would be much appreciated.

If you're prepared to rough it a bit and do some camping, you'll experience some spectacular places. The following is a quick overview of Brazil's main national parks, divided for ease of reference into regions. See the regional chapters for more detailed information.

Southeast
In Rio, the Parque Nacional da Tijuca, surrounded by the city, is a popular day trip and offers magnificent panoramic views. The Parque Nacional do Itatiaia, 155 km to the south-east of the city, is a favourite with trekkers and climbers, its big attraction being the Agulhas Negras mountain with a 2787-metre peak. Another climbing mecca is the Parque Nacional da Serra dos ÓrgãosParque Nacional da Serra dos Órgãos, 86 km from Rio. As well as its spectacular peaks it offers some great walks. These last two parks both possess a well-developed tourist infrastructure.

On the border of Rio and São Paulo states, close to Parati, the Parque Nacional da Serra da Bocaina is where the coastal escarpment meets the sea, and the Atlantic rainforest quickly changes to high-altitude araucaria forest as you move up from the coast. There doesn't, as yet, exist any infrastructure for tourists.

In Minas Gerais, there are some great parks to visit. The Parque Nacional de Caparaó in the east of the state, on the border with Espírito Santo, contains the third highest peak in the country: O Pico do Bandeira, at 2890 metres, and you don't have to be a climber to get up there. The tourist infrastructure is well developed, especially for campers. In the south-west of the state, 350 km from Belo Horizonte, the Parque Nacional da Serra da Canastra is where the Rio São Francisco, the river of national unity, begins. The area is very beautiful and contains the spectacular Cascada D'Anta waterfall. The park is also home to many endangered species, such as the maned wolf, giant anteater, pampas deer, giant armadillo

National Parks, Biological Reserves & Ecological Stations

and thin-spined porcupine. Camping is permitted.

The Parque Nacional da Serra do Cipó, 100 km from Belo Horizonte, is an area full of mountains, waterfalls and open country-side. Its highlands are an arm of the Serra do Espinhaço. The 70-metre waterfall, Cachoeira da Farofa, and the Canyon das Bandeirinhas are its two principal attractions. Unfortunately, it contains no tourist infrastructure.

Also in Minas, near its borders with Bahia and Goias, the Parque Nacional Grande Sertão Veredas is made up of cerrado, caatinga, *veredas* (swampy plains between hills and rivers), and a few stands of wine-palms. Inhabitants of the park include the maned-wolf, giant armadillo, banded ant-eater and rhea. Once again, this is another park with no tourist infrastructure and access is difficult.

South

In the southern region, the most famous national park is Iguaçu, which contains the falls. Also in Paraná, but near the coast, is the Parque Nacional do Superagui, which con-

● NATIONAL PARKS

1 Parque Nacional de Cabo Orange
6 Parque Nacional da Amazônia
8 Parque Nacional do Jaú
12 Parque Nacional de Monte Roraima
13 Parque Nacional do Pico da Neblina
16 Parque Nacional da Serra do Divisor
19 Parque Nacional de Pacaás Novos
23 Parque Nacional da Chapada dos Guimarães
25 Parque Nacional do Pantanal Matogrossense
26 Parque Nacional das Emas
27 Parque Nacional de Brasília
28 Parque Nacional da Chapada dos Veadeiros
29 Parque Nacional do Araguaia
32 Parque Nacional dos Lençóis Maranhenses
33 Parque Nacional de Sete Cidades
34 Parque Nacional de Ubajara
38 Parque Nacional da Serra da Capivara
41 Parque Nacional da Chapada Diamantina
42 Parque Nacional de Grande Sertão Veredas
44 Parque Nacional de Monte Pascoal
45 Parque Nacional Marinho dos Abrolhos
51 Parque Nacional de Caparaó
52 Parque Nacional da Serra do Cipó
53 Parque Nacional da Serra da Canastra
55 Parque Nacional do Itatiaia
57 Parque Nacional da Serra dos Órgãos
59 Parque Nacional da Tijuca
60 Parque Nacional da Serra da Bocaina
63 Parque Nacional do Superagui
65 Parque Nacional de Iguaçu
67 Parque Nacional de São Joaquim
69 Parque Nacional de Aparados da Serra
70 Parque Nacional da Lagoa do Peixe

■ BIOLOGICAL RESERVES

3 Reserva Biológica do Lago Piratuba
5 Reserva Biológica do Rio Trombetas
15 Reserva Biológica do Abufari
18 Reserva Biológica do Jarú
20 Reserva Biológica do Guaporé
30 Reserva Biológica de Tapirapé
31 Reserva Biológica do Gurupi
36 Reserva Biológica de Saltinho
37 Reserva Biológica de Serra Negra
40 Reserva Biológica de Santa Isabel
43 Reserva Biológica de Una
46 Reserva Biológica do Córrego Grande
47 Reserva Biológica do Córrego do Veado
48 Reserva Biológica de Sooretama
49 Reserva Biológica Nova Lombardia
50 Reserva Biológica de Comboios
56 Reserva Biológica de Tinguá
58 Reserva Biológica do Poço das Antas

▼ ECOLOGICAL STATIONS

2 Estaçõe Ecológica de Maracá-Jipioca
4 Estaçõe Ecológica do Jari
7 Estaçõe Ecológica de Anavilhanas
9 Estaçõe Ecológica de Niquiã
10 Estaçõe Ecológica de Caracaraí
11 Estaçõe Ecológica da Ilha de Maracá
14 Estaçõe Ecológica de Juami-Japurá
17 Estaçõe Ecológica do Rio Acre
21 Estaçõe Ecológica de Iqué
22 Estaçõe Ecológica da Serra das Araras
24 Estaçõe Ecológica de Taiamã
35 Estaçõe Ecológica de Seridó
39 Estaçõe Ecológica de Uruçui-Una
54 Estaçõe Ecológica de Parapitinga
61 Estaçõe Ecológica de Tupinambás
62 Estaçõe Ecológica dos Tupiniquins
64 Estaçõe Ecológica de Guaraqueçaba
66 Estaçõe Ecológica de Carijós
68 Estaçõe Ecológica de Aracuri/Esmeralda
71 Estaçõe Ecológica do Taim

sists of the Peças and Superagui islands. Notable attractions of the park are the huge number of wild orchids and the abundant marine life. Created in 1989, it contains no infrastructure for tourists.

Santa Catarina boasts the Parque Nacional de São Joaquim, in the highlands of the Serra do Mar, where it even snows sometimes. As yet, it contains no tourist infrastructure.

Rio Grande do Sul contains one of the most unforgettable parks in Brazil, the Parque Nacional de Aparados da Serra, with its famous Itaimbézinho canyon. Camping is possible and there's a small hotel inside the park. Close to the town of Rio Grande, in the south of the state, the Parque Nacional da Lagoa do Peixe is an important stopover for many species of migratory birds. It also contains the largest saltwater lagoon in the state. A visitors' centre is still on the drawing board.

Central West

This region has its share of parks too. Just 10 km from the national capital, Brasília, is the Parque Nacional de Brasília, a favourite weekend spot with the city's inhabitants. It contains a visitors' centre, and a leisure area with natural swimming pools. Parque Nacional da Chapada dos Veadeiros, 200 km north of Brasília, in the state of Goiás, contains some rare fauna and flora, as well as some spectacular waterfalls and canyons. Camping is the only option here. In the extreme south-west of the state is the Parque Nacional das Emas. Its main attraction is its great abundance of wildlife and the ease with which you can spot it in the open country, especially in the dry season. Accommodation is available inside the park, and camping is permitted.

Close to the city of Cuiabá is another popular park, the Parque Nacional da Chapada dos Guimarães, with its waterfalls, huge valleys and strange rock formations. Accommodation inside the park is limited to camping, but there are hotels in the nearby town of the same name.

Halfway between Cuiabá and Corumbá, near the fork of the Paraguai and Cuiabá rivers, the Parque Nacional do Pantanal Matogrossense is deep in the Pantanal and can only be reached by river or by air. Porto Jofre, 100 km upriver, is the closest you'll get by land. Permission from IBAMA in Cuiabá is required to visit this park. Camping is the only option here.

Northeast

In Bahia, the Parque Nacional da Chapada Diamantina has a network of trails, and great hiking to peaks, waterfalls and rivers. See the Bahia chapter for full details about this easily accessible park and the attractive old mining town of Lençóis which functions as its hub.

On the southern border of the state is the Parque Nacional de Monte Pascoal, which contains a variety of ecosystems ranging from Atlantic rainforest to mangroves, beaches and reefs, and rare fauna and flora. A visitors' centre has been in the planning stage for several years.

Approximately 80 km offshore in the extreme south of the state is Parque Nacional Marinho dos Abrolhos, which was designated in 1983 as Brazil's first marine park. The attractions are the coral reefs which are visited on organised scuba diving tours, and the birdlife on the numerous reefs and islets.

The state of Pernambuco recently incorporated the archipelago of Fernando de Noronha, which lies approximately 525 km east of Recife. A section of this archipelago has been designated as the Parque Nacional Marinho de Fernando de Noronha. The attractions here are the exceptionally varied and abundant marine life and birdlife. Organised tours, almost always in the form of package tours which include transport from the mainland to the archipelago and back, are readily available and the tourist infrastructure is rapidly being developed.

The state of Ceará contains the Parque Nacional de Ubajara, which is renowned for its limestone caves. Tourist infrastructure is available, and access to the caves has been re-established with a new cable car which has replaced the system destroyed by landslides in 1987.

In the northern region of the state of Piauí is the Parque Nacional de Sete Cidades. The park's interesting set of rock formations resembling 'seven cities' *(sete cidades)* are accessible via a hiking trail. Tourist infrastructure, including transport and accommodation, is available.

In the southern region of the state, the Parque Nacional da Serra da Capivara contains prehistoric sites and rock paintings which are still being researched. Over 300 sites have been discovered so far, and this park is already being considered one of the top prehistoric monuments in South

America. Tourism infrastructure is still very limited, since it is difficult to combine ongoing research with public access, but a museum and guided tours are planned.

In the state of Maranhão, the Parque Nacional dos Lençóis Maranhenses has a spectacular collection of beaches, mangroves, dunes and fauna. Infrastructure is limited, but transport and basic accommodation are available.

North

The national parks in the northern region of Brazil are best known for their diverse types of forests harbouring an astounding variety of fauna and flora. Most of these parks require that visitors obtain permits before arrival. They provide little infrastructure, and access normally entails lengthy and difficult travel by plane and/or boat.

The Parque Nacional de Cabo Orange extends along the coastline at the northern tip of Amapá state. This park has retained a diverse variety of wildlife, including rare or endangered species such as the manatee, sea turtle, jaguar, anteater, armadillo and flamingo. At present there is no tourist infrastructure available for transport or accommodation in the park.

In the state of Pará, the vast forests enclosed by the Parque Nacional da Amazônia are being rapidly eroded by illegal encroachment and destruction. The wildlife includes a wide variety of rainforest species, but poaching is making rapid inroads into their numbers. And it's difficult to see any change in this situation when only four park guards are responsible for nearly one million hectares. Limited infrastructure for accommodation and transport of visitors is provided.

The Parque Nacional de Monte Roraima lies on the northern boundary of Roraima state. Established in 1989, this park contains Monte Roraima (2875 metres), one of Brazil's highest peaks.

In the state of Amazonas, the Parque Nacional do Pico da Neblina adjoins the Venezuelan border and contains Brazil's highest peaks: Pico da Neblina (3014 metres) and Pico 31 de Março (2992 metres). Visitors normally require a permit from the IBAMA office in Brasília. No standard tourist infrastructure is available, but visitors can arrange access by using a combination of air and river transport.

Brazil's largest national park, Parque Nacional do Jaú, lies close to the centre of Amazonas state. Visitors normally require a permit from the IBAMA office in Brasília. No standard tourist infrastructure is available, but visitors can arrange access by using a combination of air and river transport.

The Parque Nacional de Pacaás Novos lies close to the town of Ji-Parana in the state of Rondônia. The principal rivers of the state, the Madeira and the Guaporé, originate within the park, where small communities of indigenous Indians have sought refuge from the massive deforestation and destruction still raging through the state. See the chapter on Rondônia for details about visiting the biological reserves of Guaporé and Jaru.

The Parque Nacional da Serra do Divisor lies in the extreme western part of the state of Acre and adjoins the border with Peru. Established in 1989, it does not yet possess any tourist infrastructure.

The Parque Nacional do Araguaia now lies in the recently created state of Tocantins. The park area covers the northern end of the Ilha do Bananal, the world's largest river island, formed by the splitting of the Rio Araguaia. The park has no standard tourist infrastructure, but visitors may be able to make arrangements in Santa Teresinha.

CLIMATE

Many travel guides suggest a certain sameness to the weather in Brazil. This is misleading. It's true that only the south has extreme seasonal changes like Europe and the USA, but most of the country does have noticeable seasonal variations in rain, temperature and humidity. In general, as you go from north to south, the seasonal changes are more defined.

The Brazilian winter is from June to August. It doesn't get cold in Brazil – except in the southern states of Rio Grande do Sul,

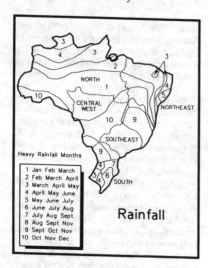

Heavy Rainfall Months
1 Jan Feb March
2 Feb March April
3 March April May
4 April May June
5 May June July
6 June July Aug
7 July Aug Sept
8 Aug Sept Nov
9 Sept Oct Nov
10 Oct Nov Dec

Rainfall

tinue for days nonstop), or you want more heat, head to the Northeast.

The Northeast coast gets about as hot as Rio during the summer, but due to a wonderful tropical breeze and less humidity, it's rarely stifling. Generally, from Bahia to Maranhão, temperatures are a bit warmer year-round than in Rio, rarely far from 28°C. All in all, it's hard to imagine a better climate.

In general the highlands or planalto, such as Minas Gerais and Brasília, are a few degrees cooler than the coast and not as humid. Here, summer rains are frequent, while along the coast the rains tend to come intermittently.

Although there are variations in rainfall (see map), throughout Brazil rain is a year-round affair. The general pattern is for short, tropical rains that come at all times. These rains rarely alter or interfere with travel plans. The sertão is a notable exception – here the rains fall heavily within a few months and periodic droughts devastate the region.

The Amazon Basin receives the most rain in Brazil, and Belém is one of the most rained on cities in the world, but the refreshing showers are usually seen as a godsend. Actually, the Amazon is not nearly as hot as most people presume – the average temperature is 27°C – but it is humid. The hottest part of the basin is between the Rio Solimões and Rio Negro. From June to August the heat tends to decrease a bit.

Whenever you decide to travel in Brazil, there are few regions that can't be comfortably visited all year around.

GOVERNMENT

Brazil slowly returned to democracy in the '80s. In 1988 a new constitution guaranteed freedom of speech and the right to strike, and outlawed the use of torture. It also gave 16 year olds and illiterates the right to vote.

In 1989, Fernando Collor de Mello became the first president elected by popular vote in 28 years to take office. (Tancredo Neves was the first elected president, but he never took office.) The 1988 constitution

Santa Catarina, Paraná and São Paulo, where the average temperature during the winter months of June, July and August is between 13°C and 18°C. There are even a few towns that can get snow, which is very strange to most Brazilians, who have never touched the white flakes. The rest of the country boasts moderate temperatures all year long.

The summer season is from December to February. With many Brazilians on vacation, travel is difficult and expensive while from Rio south the humidity can be oppressive. It's also the most festive time of year, as Brazilians escape their small, hot apartments and take to the beaches and streets. School vacation, corresponding with the hot season, begins sometime in mid-December and goes through to Carnival, usually in late February.

In summer, Rio is hot and humid; temperatures in the high 30°Cs are common and sometimes reach the low 40s. Frequent, short rains cool things off a bit, but the summer humidity makes things uncomfortable for people from cooler climes. The rest of the year Rio is cooler with temperatures generally in the mid 20°Cs, sometimes reaching the low 30s. If you are in Rio in the winter and the weather's lousy (the rain can con-

allows him to choose ministers of state, initiate pieces of legislation and maintain foreign relations. It also names him as commander-in-chief of the armed forces and gives him the power of total veto. These presidential powers are balanced by a bicamaral legislature, which consists of a 72-seat senate and a 487-seat chamber of deputies. Presidential elections are slated to be held every five years, with congressional elections every four. State government elections are also held every four years, and municipal elections every three years.

Elections are colourful affairs, regarded by the democracy-starved Brazilians as yet another excuse for a party. Posters cover every available wall space and convoys of cars cruise through the cities creating as much noise as possible in support of their chosen candidate.

Politics itself remains largely the preserve of the wealthy. In the 1990 elections for state governors and senators, several candidates were forced to drop out because of costs. Inducements to voters are common.

In October 1993, the existing system may change. There is to be a rederendum to decide the form of government – republic or constitutional monarchy (unlikely) – and the system of government – a presidency or a parliamentary system.

A parliamentary system, which divides the functions of chief of state and chief of government, would considerably reduce the power of the president. Strong arguments in favour of a parliamentary system in Brazil include the flexibility of the mandate, which would allow for change if the existing government proved inefficient and the possibility of a more efficient and rational government. Opponents of the parliamentary system argue that in a country like Brazil, strong presidential power is needed to bring about significant social and economic changes.

ECONOMY

The only certainty in the economy is its uncertainty. Wild boom and bust cycles have decimated the economy in recent years. Record-breaking industrial growth fuelled by foreign capital was followed by negative growth and explosive hyperinflation. This stagnation led Brazilian economists to call the '80s the Lost Decade.

Since WW II Brazil has seen tremendous growth and modernisation, albeit in fits and starts. Today, Brazil's economy is the world's 10th largest. It's called a developing country. The military dictators even had visions of Brazil joining the ranks of the advanced, industrialised nations by the year 2000. No one believes that is possible now, but no one denies that tremendous development has occurred.

Brazil is a land of fantastic economic contrasts. Travelling through the country, you will witness incredibly uneven development. Production techniques barely changed from the colonial epoch dominate many parts of the Northeast and Amazonia, while São Paulo's massive, high-tech auto, steel, arms and chemical industries successfully compete on the world market.

Brazil's rulers, at least since President Kubitschek invented Brasília, have had a penchant for building things big and they have, of course, been encouraged by the IMF and the World Bank. The government borrowed heavily to finance Brasília's construction. The country's external debt began to take off exponentially and a couple of years later inflation followed.

Economic development is slow, but there always seem to be some highly visible megaprojects under way. Many of these are economically ill advised and some never get completed. The funding dries up, is pocketed by corrupt bureaucrats, or the politician who started it leaves office and the political enemy who takes over decides to abandon the project. Whatever the reason, huge amounts of money are wasted. The megaprojects which do get finished may produce wealth, but they don't create many jobs, at least once they are built. Utilising the latest technology, much of Brazil's new development is capital intensive. Few jobs are created – not nearly enough to employ the millions of urban poor who have fled the countryside.

Brazil now has an estimated 64 million working people: one third are women; 17% work in agriculture, most as small or landless peasants; 12% work in industry. A majority of the rest cannot find decent work and are forced to sell their labour dirt cheap in jobs that are economically unproductive for society and a dead end for the individual.

Cheap labour and underemployment abound in Brazil. Middle-class families commonly hire two or more live-in maids. This contrasts with five-year-old kids, who will never go to school, selling chewing gum or shining shoes. People are hired just to walk dogs, to watch cars, to deliver groceries. Large crews of street cleaners work with home-made brooms. Hawkers on the beaches sell everything and earn almost nothing. Restaurants seem to have more waiters than customers.

Unlike Mexico or Turkey, the poor in Brazil have no rich neighbours where they can go for jobs. With the exception of some minor agrarian reforms, there is no relief in sight. The *fazendeiros* (estate owners), with their massive land holdings, are very influential with the government. Apart from the occasional token gesture they are unlikely to be interested in parting with their land.

Instead of land reform, the government built roads into the Amazon: the Belém to Brasília road in 1960 and the Transamazônica and the Cuiabá to Porto Velho roads in the '70s. The idea was to open up the Amazon to mineral and agricultural development, and also encourage settlement by the rural poor.

The mineral-poor Amazonian soil proved hard for the peasants to farm. After cutting down forest and opening up the land the peasants were forced off by the hired guns of big cattle ranchers. The settlement of the Amazon continues today, particularly along the Cuiabá-Porto Velho-Rio Branco strip, where violent boom towns, deforestation and malaria follow in the wake of the settlers.

Brazil is a capitalist country constrained by state intervention and state ownership. In the last six years prices and wages have been frozen by the government five times. There are restrictions on foreign capital and the government has set up protectionist barriers to help local industry.

All this government tampering politicises economic decision-making. Investments are made in a climate of inflation and interest-rate uncertainty and government favours, like special subsidies, special licences, special exemptions from regulations. This leads to many unhappy capitalists and incredible waste. Petrobras, the national oil company, claims to be the largest company in the southern hemisphere. It handles 40% of the country's imports and 20% of its exports. They are now sitting on one of the world's largest untapped oil deposits off the coast of Rio. Although one of 600 state-owned companies in Brazil, the question with Petrobas is who owns whom. General Geisel was the head of Petrobras before he became president of Brazil in 1974. Called a government within a government, Petrobras seems to resist pressure – mostly from the IMF – to streamline its operations. Like many government jobs, working for Petrobras is considered a plum. Salaries are among Brazil's best. Housing for most of its white-collar workers is provided at a Rio building called the hanging gardens of Petrobras.

Over 50% of Brazil's industry is clustered in and around São Paulo city. Most important is the car industry. Labour relations with the workers at Volkswagen, General Motors and Ford were managed by a system modelled on fascist Italy: government-approved unions backed by the power of the military state. From 1968 to 1978 the workers were silent and passive, until the day 100 workers at a bus factory went to work and sat down in front of their machines. Within two weeks 78,000 metalworkers were on strike in the São Paulo industrial belt.

Rapidly, the strikes spread to other industries. The government-sponsored unions were replaced; decisions were made by mass assemblies of workers in soccer stadiums. At the invitation of the Catholic Church, union offices were moved to the cathedral of São Bernardo. Caught by surprise the corporations and military gave in to substantial wage increases. Both sides prepared for the next time.

In 1980 there was a new wave of strikes. They were better organised, with greater rank-and-file control. Demands were made to democratise the workplace, with shop floor union representation and factory and safety committees. Many improvements were won, many have since been lost, but the industrial working class had flexed its muscles and no one has forgotten.

Skyrocketing inflation and the world recession have battered the Brazilian economy in the last few years. When Collor took office he pledged to reduce inflation, then running at 72% a month, to 3% per month in 18 months. He also promised to: cut back government spending, responsible for the majority of the country's US$118 billion foreign debt; privatise inefficient state-owned companies; and open Brazil's markets to foreign competition and capital.

His first 'draconian' measure was to freeze 80% of all bank accounts with a balance of over US$1200 for a period of 18 months. This certainly stopped inflation for a while, but the economy ground to a halt. The following recession hit hardest in the manufacturing industry, putting hundreds of thousands out of work in São Paulo. In São Bernardo do Campo, 2000 workers stormed the Ford plant, fighting with security guards and wrecking equipment, in protest at a perceived unfair wage rise.

By late 1991, the economy had plunged back into inflation on a grand scale. Brazilians were able to temporarily staunch their disappointment by reading Zélia: A Passion, the best-selling biography of former economy minister, Zélia Cardoso de Mello, who used the book to reveal some bizarre facts about the economy and her love life – at the same time. According to her: the wrong man was given the plum job of central bank chief because a secretary misunderstood the name; the target figure of US$115 billion set during controversial freezing of bank accounts was simply chosen at random; and she regularly exchanged love notes with a former justice minister during crucial cabinet meetings.

There's no doubting that the Brazilian economy has great potential. All the ingredients for progress are there: a large labour force, the means of production, transport systems and markets for the products. The challenge is whether or not they can be co-ordinated efficiently. The harsh reality is that seven out of 10 Brazilians still live in poverty.

Social Conditions

The richest 10% of Brazilians control a whopping 54% of the nation's wealth; the poorest 10% have just 0.6% – and the gap is widening. Sixty million live in squalor without proper sanitation, clean water or decent housing. Over 60% of the people who work make less than twice the minimum wage. Unemployment is rampant.

Wealthy Brazilians live 'closed', First-World existences in luxurious houses behind high walls protected by armed guards and guard dogs.

These inequities occur in a country with the world's 10th largest economy, a country with nuclear power plants (that don't work), a country that has the capacity to process uranium, a country with the world's largest hydroelectric dam and a country that exports automobiles and arms.

In this developing country of 148 million people, 40 million people are malnourished; 25 million live in favelas; 12 million children are abandoned and more than seven million between the ages of seven and 14 don't attend school. Brazil, with its military dreams of greatness, has misery that compares with the poorest countries in Africa and Asia.

As always, these ills hit some groups much harder than others. If you are a woman, a Black, an Indian or from the North or Northeast the odds against escaping poverty are great. One third of the women employed in Brazil work as maids and nannies, and most earn less than the minimum wage. Of

A favela in Rio with Cristo Redentor (Christ the Redeemer) behind

Brazil's 21 million illiterates, 13 million are Black. Life expectancy in the Northeast is 51 years, compared to 61 for the whole country.

The Indians are fighting for survival; less than 200,000 remain from an estimated five million when the Portuguese arrived. They still suffer violent attacks from ranchers and gold prospectors laying claim to their land.

The killing of peasant leaders, trade unionists and church workers involved in land disputes and strikes continues.

Even though torture has been outlawed by the constitution, reports of death in custody after its use as a means of obtaining a confession continue, although there are very few eye-witnesses. The killing of criminal suspects by uniformed and off-duty police in 'death-squad' operations, especially in Baixada Fluminense, on the outskirts of Rio de Janeiro, is widely reported.

The federal government is aware of the scale of human rights violations and the chronic failure to administer justice at state and local levels, but will not accept responsibility for matters it deems beyond its jurisdiction.

All these facts illustrate the obvious: for the majority, Brazil is, as it has always been, a country of poverty and inequality, where reforms are as elusive as the wind.

POPULATION & PEOPLE

According to the 1991 census, Brazil's population is just over 148 million, making it the world's sixth most populous country. The population has been rising rapidly over the last 45 years, although in the last 10 years it seems to have slowed a little. There were only 14 million Brazilians in 1890, 33 million in 1930, 46 million in 1945, and 71 million in 1960. The population has doubled in the last 30 years.

Still, Brazil is one of the least densely populated nations in the world, averaging only 15 people per sq km. The USA, by comparison, averages 25 people per sq km. The population in Brazil is concentrated along the coastal strip and in the cities. There are around 10 million in the enormous expanses of the North and less than 10 million in the Central West, while there are over 65 million in the Southeast and over 42 million in the Northeast. Brazil also has a young population: half its people are less than 20 years old, 27% under 10.

There are 12 million *abandonados*, children without parents or home. Many are hunted by the so-called 'death squads' made up of vigilantes who take it upon themselves to torture and murder the children under the pretence that 'they grow up to become criminals anyway so why not get rid of them now?' The fate of these children is one of the most pressing social problems facing Brazil today.

Brazil is now an urban country whereas 40 years ago it was still a predominantly rural society. Due to internal migration, two-thirds of Brazilians now live in nine large urban areas: São Paulo, Rio de Janeiro, Belo Horizonte, Porto Alegre, Salvador, Recife, Fortaleza, Brasília and Belém. Greater São

Paulo has over 17 million residents, greater Rio over 10 million.

Some 500 years ago Cabral landed in Brazil. When he departed, only nine days later, he left behind two convicts who subsequently married natives. Thus, colonisation through miscegenation was how the Portuguese managed to control Brazil. This strategy was pursued, often consciously and semi-officially, for hundreds of years. First with native Indians, then with the Black slaves and finally between Indians and Blacks, miscegenation thoroughly mixed the three races. Brazilians use literally dozens of terms to describe people's various racial compositions and shades of skin tones. Most Brazilians have some combination of European, African, Amerindian, Asian and Middle Eastern ancestry.

Accurate statistics on racial composition are difficult to obtain in Brazil. Many people are no doubt counted as White who have some Black or Indian blood, but the 1980 census showed about 55% technically White, 6% Black and 38% mulatto. Anyone who has travelled in Brazil knows these figures are ridiculous. They reflect what people want to think rather than reality. Whiteness in Brazil, they often say, is as much a reflection of one's social standing as the colour of one's skin.

Brazil has had several waves of voluntary immigration. After the end of slavery in 1887, millions of Europeans were recruited to work in the coffee fields. The largest contingent were from Italy, but there were also many Portuguese and Spaniards, with smaller groups of Germans and Russians. Japanese immigration began in 1908 and today São Paulo has the largest Japanese community outside of Japan.

Some 50,000 Portuguese came to Brazil from 1974 to 1975 with the liberation of Portugal's African colonies. During the '70s many Latin Americans fleeing military dictatorships in Argentina, Chile, Uruguay and Paraguay settled in Brazil.

Indians

FUNAI, the government Indian agency, has documented 174 different Indian languages and dialects. Customs and belief systems vary equally widely.

Growing international concern over the destruction of the Amazon rainforest has also highlighted the plight of the region's Brazilian Indians, who are facing extinction early next century – if not sooner. At present the number of Indians in Brazil is estimated at less than 200,000. Of the several hundred tribes already identified, most are concentrated in the Amazon region and virtually all Brazilian Indians face a host of problems which threaten to destroy their environment and way of life. An estimated 40 tribes have never been in contact with outsiders. For more details about Indians and their status in Brazil refer to the following separate sections in this chapter: History; Ecology & Environment; Indian Art; and Culture.

Indian Policy During the 20th century, the general thrust of official Brazilian policy towards the Indians and their lands has concentrated on pacification, integration, and dispossession.

In 1910, Marechal Cândido Rondon (1865-1958), who favoured a humane and dignified Indian policy, founded the Serviço de Proteção ao Indio (SPI) as an attempt to protect the Indians against massacres and land dispossession. Unfortunately, Rondon's good intentions were quickly swept aside and SPI became notorious as a tool for corrupt and greedy officialdom to physically eliminate Indians or force them off their lands. By the late '60s, SPI had become the target of fierce national and international criticism.

In 1967, SPI was replaced by the Fundação Nacional do Indio (FUNAI) which was intended to redress the SPI wrongs. FUNAI was set the ambitious and controversial tasks of protecting Indian reserves, administering to the medical and educational needs of the Indians, and contacting and pacifying hitherto unknown tribes.

FUNAI has been criticised for adopting a patronising attitude toward Indians, and for manipulating against Indian interest in favour of other claims to Indian lands. It's difficult to see how this grossly underfunded and understaffed organisation can escape contradictions when it represents the will of the Indians and simultaneously acts in the interests of the government and military, which have both been expropriating Indian lands for industry and settlement. In early 1991, FUNAI was lacking 97% of its allotted annual budget, and of the 4000 officials working for FUNAI, only 1000 were actually employed in the field.

Religious organisations, such as Conselho Indígenista Missionário (CIM) and Centro Ecumênico de Documentação e Informação (CEDI) have attempted to right the imbalance, but there appears to be little interest in reducing patronising attitudes or giving the Indians a chance to represent their rights as decreed by Brazilian law. The Brazilian constitution recognises Indian rights to their traditional lands, which cover approximately 87 million hectares (about 10% of Brazil's territory). Current laws require full demarcation and protection for all these Indian lands by October 1993. In 1991, only half of these lands had been demarcated.

FUNAI recently started using a computer network and satellite photographs to secure the borders of large and remote tracts of land from invading lumber workers and prospectors. The system is composed of many reservations and posts plus five major parks: Xingu and Aripuanâ parks in Mato Grosso, Araguaia Park on Ilha do Bananal island in Tocantins, Tumucumaque Park on the Guyanese border of Pará and the Yanomami Park in Roraima.

Recent Developments During the '80s, Indian tribes which had seen their people and lands destroyed by development projects (particularly highway construction) in the '70s were stung to take independent action to protect themselves.

In 1980, nearly 1000 Xavante Indians, who had tired of FUNAI inactivity, started marking the boundaries of their reserve in Mato Grosso state. When a fierce conflict arose with encroaching ranchers, 31 Xavante leaders paid a surprise visit to the president of FUNAI in Brasília and demanded immediate boundary demarcation. Further pressure was exerted on FUNAI when Txucarramãe Indians killed 11 agricultural workers whom they had caught trespassing on their Xingu reserve and clearing the forest. In 1982, over 200 Indian leaders assembled in Brasília to debate land ownership at the First National Assembly of Indigenous Nations.

Subsequent years saw a spate of hostage takings and confiscations by Indians, who were thereby able to force rapid decisions from the government. As an attempt to deflect criticism and placate public opinion, the government hired and fired FUNAI officials in quick succession: a convenient scapegoat technique which continues to be employed in the '90s, changing names and little else. In 1989, the First Meeting of the Indigenous Nations of Xingu included a huge cast of Brazilian Indians, foreign environmentalists, and even the rock star Sting. Two Kayapo chiefs, Raoni and Megaron, then accompanied Sting on a world tour to raise funds for the preservation of the Amazon rainforest.

During the '90s, international attention has focused on the plight of the Yanomami (see the next section). Environmentalists and ecologists attending ECO-92 will be pressing for practical changes to benefit the Indians and their environment – nobody wants to be fobbed off any more with speeches and papers which are simply a public relations exercise to be forgotten and filed.

The Yanomami The Yanomami are one of the newly discovered Indian peoples of the Amazon. Until some Yanomami were given metal tools by visitors, all their implements were made of stone, ceramic, animal hides and plants. They are literally a stone-age people rapidly confronting the 20th century. The plight of the Yanomami has aroused considerable foreign interest, since the problems experienced by the Yanomami are considered typical of those encountered by other Indians in Brazil.

In 1973 the Yanomami had their first contact with Westerners: Brazilian Air Force pilots and religious missionaries. In 1974 and 1975 as BR-210 (Perimetral Norte) and BR-174 cut through the Catramani and Ajarani tributaries of the Rio Negro, people from several Yanomami villages mixed with the construction workers and contracted and died from measles, influenza and VD. Over a dozen villages were wiped out.

In 1988, the government instituted an absurd plan to create 19 separate pockets of land for the Yanomami, thereby depriving the Indians of 70% of their territory. Thousands of garimpeiros swarmed into the area and ignored all boundaries. Two years later, growing international and national criticism of the genocide being perpetrated on the Yanomami forced the authorities to backtrack and declare only a handful of designated zones open for mining. The garimpeiros continued to prospect at random and resisted all efforts, even force, to dislodge them.

In 1991, the Venezuelan government officially recognised the Yanomami territory on the Venezuelan side of the Brazilian border as a special Indian reserve; a few months later President Collor defied opposition and followed suit on the Brazilian side. The Brazilian military continues to oppose the decision and prefers instead to encourage development and settlement of the border areas as a buffer against possible foreign intrusions. Although Collor's decision has now been made on paper, it will only be worthwhile if it can be effectively enforced against powerful opponents such as the military, and if the Yanomami are finally allowed to live as they choose on their own territory.

The Yanomami are slight people, with Oriental features. Their estimated 18,000 seminomadic tribespeople are scattered over 320 villages on either side of the Brazilian-Venezuelan border. They speak one of four related languages: Yanomam, Yanam, Yanomamo and Sanumá.

The centre of each community is the Yano, a large circular structure where each family has its own section facing directly onto an open central area used for communal dance and ceremony. The Yano is built with palm-leaf thatch and timber posts. Each family arranges its own section by slinging hammocks around a fire which burns constantly and forms the centre of family life.

Inter-tribal visits are an opportunity to eat well: if the hunt is successful everyone gets to eat monkey, which is a delicacy. Otherwise tapir, wild pig and a variety of insects make up the protein component of the meal, which is balanced with garden fruits, yams, plantains and manioc. The Yanomami also grow cotton and tobacco. Once their garden soils and hunting grounds are exhausted, the village moves on to a new site.

The Yanomami hold elaborate ceremonies and rituals and place great emphasis on inter-tribal alliances. The latter are intended to minimise any feuds or violence which, as has often happened in the past, can escalate into full wars. The importance attached to inter-tribal hostility is demonstrated in the widespread belief that disease comes from evil spirits sent by the shamans of enemy tribes. Disease is cured with various herbs, shaman dances and healing hands. Sometimes the village shaman will enlist the good spirits to fight the evil spirits by using *yakoana*, a hallucinogenic herbal powder.

The Yanomami have some curious practices. When a tribal person dies, the body is hung from a tree until dry, then burned to ashes. The ashes are mixed with bananas, which are then eaten by friends and family of the deceased to incorporate and preserve the spirit. The mourning ritual is elaborate: one member of the tribe is assigned to cry for a month (as determined by the phases of the moon, since the Yanomami have no calendar and the only number they have greater than two is 'many'). Friends or allies from other communities will travel three to four days to join the mourning tribe.

These days even such remote tribes are exposed to encroaching civilisation in the shape of clearance roads for the Perimetral

Norte, illegal airstrips built by garimpeiros, and FUNAI posts. Despite the latest positive moves from the Brazilian government, the Yanomami lands are not adequately protected against encroachment and dispossession by brute force. More details about providing support for the Yanomami can be obtained from Survival International – for the address refer to the Ecology & Environment section in this chapter.

Information & Further Reading There are several governmental and religious organisations which publish information on Brazilian Indians. *Poratim* is a newsletter published by the Conselho Indígenista Missionário (CIM) (☎ (061) 225-9457), Edifício Venâncio III, Sala 310, Caixa Postal 11.1159, CEP 70084, Brasília, DF . In the past, FUNAI's own publication, *Jornal da Funai*, was produced at the same address as CIM, but future publishing plans for it are unclear. *Aconteceu* is a bi-weekly journal (with strong ecological emphasis) published by the Centro Ecumênico de Documentação e Informação (CEDI) (☎ (021) 224-6713), Rua Santo Amaro, 129, Rio de Janeiro, CEP 22211, RJ.

There are also various individuals or small groups working on alternative projects for tribes such as the Ticuna and Wapichana. In the state of Amazonas, there's Alírio Mendes Moraes (Ticuna), Coordenação das Organizações Indígenas da Amazônia Brasileira (COIAB) (☎ (092) 624-2511), Avenida Leopoldo Peres, 373, Caixa Postal 3264, Manaus, CEP 69000, AM. In the same state, education is the main emphasis of the Organização Geral dos Professores Ticuna Bilingüe (☎ (092) 415-5494), Avenida Castelo Branco, 594, Projeto Alto Solimões, Benjamin Constant, CEP 69630, AM. In the state of Roraima, another group has been set up by Clovis Ambrósio (Wapichana), Conselho Indígena de Roraima (CIR) (☎ (095) 224-5761), Avenida Sebastião Diniz, 1672 W, Bairro São Vicente, Boa Vista, CEP 69300, RR.

If you contact any of these organisations, groups or individuals, remember that they operate on minimal budgets, so you should at least pay return postage and material costs in advance. It is also worth pointing out that truth and facts about the Indians are hard to pinpoint, and official information is often presented in a flexible manner to suit the political, financial, or cultural agenda of those involved.

Outside Brazil, one of the most active and reputable organisations providing information on Indian affairs in Brazil is Survival International, which has campaigned especially hard for the Yanomami Indians and has members and offices worldwide (for address details see the Ecology & Environment section in this chapter). Survival International members receive a regular newsletter, Urgent Action Bulletins, campaign documents, and an annual review.

For suggested reading, see the Books & Maps section in the Facts for the Visitor chapter.

Visiting a Reservation If you are a physician, anthropologist or sociologist with an authentic scholarly interest, you can apply to FUNAI for authorisation to visit a reservation.

If you are not a Brazilian citizen you must first submit a research proposal together with your curriculum vitae, a letter of introduction from your research institute, a letter from the Brazilian researcher or research institute taking responsibility for you and your work and who agrees to accompany you into the field, a declaration that you speak Portuguese and know Brazilian law, vaccination certificates for yellow fever, typhoid and tetanus and an X-ray to show that you are free from tuberculosis.

All documentation must be in Portuguese and must first be presented to the embassy or consulate of your home country. They must send it to the Ministry of Foreign Relations in Brasília, which will in turn forward it to CNPQ (National Centre for Research). CNPQ will take a minimum of 90 days to consider your proposal. If they agree to authorise your project, the file is passed to the FUNAI office in Rio at the Museu do

Índio (Indian Museum) where Professor Neyland further processes it and Dra Cláudia scribbles the final signature.

The procedure is intentionally difficult. It is intended to protect the Indians from the inadvertent spread of diseases to which they have no natural immunity as well as from overexposure to alien cultural ideals. Nevertheless, many applicants make it through all the obstacles, and as many as 60 projects have been approved in one three-month period.

EDUCATION

The government claims a literacy rate of 80% but according to EDUCAR, the government department for adult education, only 40% of Brazilians old enough to be in the workforce are capable of reading a newspaper with comprehension. The government considers literate those who can write their names, know the alphabet and sound out a few words. In the workplace it has become obvious that these people are functionally illiterate. According to the government, half of the nation's pupils do not pass the first school year and many do not attempt to repeat it. Only two out of every 10 students make it through elementary school. The remainder drop out to support themselves and their family.

Education in Brazil is based on class. Public schools are so bad that anyone with the means sends their children to private school. Almost all university students are from the private schools, so very few poor children reach university and the poverty cycle is renewed. Many poor children must work to eat and never attend school. Even for those who are able to go, there aren't enough schools, teachers or desks to go around.

The Brizola government of Rio de Janeiro was one of the first to understand and act upon the connections between poverty, hunger and illiteracy, and has set up food programmes in schools. The kids come to school for the food and stay for the lessons. Some schools have classes at night for those children who work during the day. Brizola recently presented Collor with a plan to build 5000 special schools all over Brazil that would also contain health services for the surrounding community and be used as homes for street children at night. The plan has been approved, but like any project in Brazil, believe it when you see it.

Mass media has also been used in Brazil with some success. Since 1972, TV and radio educational programmes have been on the air. They concentrate on primary (*primeiro grau*) and secondary (*segunda grau*) students, but not exclusively. One course consists of 235 radio and TV programmes, with the objective of qualifying primary teachers. In 1989 Universidade Aberta (Open University), a tertiary education programme, was introduced. You'll often see the workbooks on newsstands.

While these measures are not enough – many primary school students still have only three hours of classes per day – they show that some programmes are successful.

ARTS
Music

Brazilians are the most musical people on the planet. Wherever you go, you'll find people playing, singing and dancing. Perhaps because of its African roots, Brazilian music is a collective act, a celebration, a festa.

Brazilian popular music has always been characterised by great diversity. Shaped by the mixing of a variety of musical influences from three different continents, the music of the people is still creating new and original forms.

Thus the *samba canção*, for example, is a mixture of Spanish bolero with the cadences and rhythms of African music. *Bossa nova* was influenced by North American music, particularly jazz, and samba. And the music called *tropicalismo* is a mix of musical influences that arrived in Brazil in the '60s, including Italian ballads and bossa nova.

Samba *Tudo dá samba*: everything makes for a samba. The most popular Brazilian rhythm, samba was first performed at the Rio Carnival in 1917, though its origins go back much further.

It is intimately linked with African rhythms; notably the Angolan tam-tam, which provided the basis for its music and distinctive dance steps. It caught on quickly after the advent of radio and records and has since become a national symbol. It is the music of the masses.

The 1930s is known as the Golden Age of Samba. By then, samba canção had also evolved, as had *choro*, a romantic, intimate music with a ukulele or guitar as its main instrument, playing off against a recorder or flute.

The most famous Brazilian singer of this period, perhaps of all time, is Carmen Miranda. A star of many Hollywood musicals of the period, she was known for her fiery, Latin temperament and her 'fruity' costumes. She has since become a cult figure among Rio's gay community, and Carnival in Rio sees many of them impersonating her.

Bossa Nova In the '50s came bossa nova, and the democratic nature of Brazilian music was altered. Bossa nova was new, modern and intellectual. It also became an international hit. The middle class stopped listening to the old interpretations of samba and other regional music like the *forró* of the Northeast.

Bossa nova was more than a musical style or movement. It initiated a new style of playing instruments and singing. The more operatic, florid style of singing was replaced by a quieter, more relaxed sound; remember the soft sound of 'The Girl from Ipanema'. João Gilberto is the founding father of bossa nova, and many leading figures, like Antônio Carlos (Tom) Jobim (composer of 'The Girl from Ipanema'), Baden Powell and Nara Leão, are still playing in Rio. Another bossa nova voice, who became Brazil's most beloved singer, was Elis Regina.

Bossa nova was associated with the rising middle class of urban, university-educated Brazil. It was a musical response to other modernist movements of the '50s and '60s such as the Cinema Novo, the Brazilian Modern Architecture of Oscar Niemeyer et al, and other aspects of the cultural life of the

Musician from Salvador playing a *berimbau*, an instrument used in capoeira

nation during the optimistic presidency of Juscelino Kubitschek from 1956 to 1960.

Tropicalismo At the end of the '60s the movement known as tropicalismo burst onto the scene. Tropicalismo provoked a kind of general amnesty for all the forgotten musical traditions of the past. The leading figures – Gilberto Gil, Caetano Veloso, Rita Lee, Macalé, Maria Betânia, Gal Costa – said that all musical styles were important and relevant. All the styles and traditions in Brazilian music could be freely mixed. This kind of open thinking led to innovations like the introduction of the electric guitar and the sound of electric samba.

Música Popular Brasileira Paralleling these musical movements are several incredibly popular musicians who are hard to categorise: they are simply known as exponents of MPB – Música Popular Brasileira (Popular Brazilian Music).

Chico Buarque de Holanda, who mixes traditional samba with a modern, universal flavour, is immensely popular, as is Paulinho da Viola, a master *sambista* who also bridges the gap between traditional samba and pop music. Jorge Bem comes from a particular Black musical tradition of the Rio suburbs, but plays an original pop samba without losing its characteristic Black rhythms. Another example is Luis Melodia, who combines the samba rhythms of the Rio hills with more modern forms from the '70s and '80s, always with beautiful melody. Then there are people like Egberto Gismonti from Minas who is a wizard with experimental, instrumental music.

Milton Nascimento, also from Minas, was recently elected by readers of *DownBeat* magazine as the number one exponent of World music. He has long been famous in Brazil for his fine voice, stirring anthems and ballads which reflect the spirituality of the Mineiro (someone from Minas).

Brazilian Rock Derived more from English than American rock, this is the least Brazilian of all the Brazilian music. It's all the rage with the youngsters. Groups like Titãs, Kid Abelha, Legião Urbana, Capital Inicial and Plebe Rude are all worth a listen if you like rock music. Heavy metal bands like Sepultura and Ratos do Porão have huge followings.

Regional Music Samba, tropicalismo and bossa nova are all national musical forms. But wherever you go in Brazil you'll hear regional specialities.

The Northeast has perhaps the most regional musical styles and accompanying dances. The most important is the forró, a mix of Northeastern music with Mexican music – maybe introduced via Paraguay – with nuances of the music of the Brazilian frontier region. The forró incorporates the European accordion, the harmonica, and the *zabumba* (an African drum).

Another distinctive type of music is the wonderful *bumba meu boi* festival sound from São Luís in Maranhão. *Frevo* is a music specific to Recife. The *trio elétrico*, also called *frevo baiano*, began much more recently and is more of a change in technology than music. It began as a family joke when, during Carnival in Salvador, Dodô and Osmar got up on top of a truck and played frevo with electric guitars. The trio elétrico is not necessarily a trio, but it is still the backbone of Salvador's Carnival, when trucks piled high with speakers, with musicians perched on top, drive through the city surrounded by dancing mobs. But it wasn't popularised until Caetano Veloso, during the period of tropicalismo, began writing songs about the trio elétrico.

Afoxé is another important type of Black music of Brazil. Religious in origin, it is closely tied to Candomblé, and primarily found in Bahia. Afoxê is the most African-sounding music in Brazil. It has been rejuvenated by the strong influence of reggae and the growth of a Black consciousness movement in Bahia.

The influence of the music of the Indians was absorbed and diluted, as was so much of the various Indian cultures in Brazil. In musical terms, several Whites have idealised what they thought those influences were. The *carimbó*, the music of the Amazon region – where the majority of Indians live today – is influenced primarily by the Blacks of the littoral. Maybe the forró is the Brazilian music that was most influenced by the Indians, via Nordestinos (people from the Northeast) who have occupied a good part of the Amazon region since the end of the past century.

Recent Trends *Pagode*, a type of samba that has existed for some time, was recently picked up and promoted by the record producers. For some of the best of pagode, listen to Bezerra da Silva, who was popular in the favelas before ever recording. Pagode, samba, frevo and forró all have corresponding dances – perhaps a reflection of the

African influence on Brazilian music and the Brazilian use of music as a celebration of communication.

Lambada is a rhythm with a sensual dance that has become another international success story. Originating in Belém, and influenced by various Caribbean rhythms like rumba, merengue and salsa, lambada became really popular in Porto Seguro, which today is considered its home. From there it spread to the cities of Brazil and eventually to Europe and the USA. It even inspired a couple of terrible Hollywood movies.

The most successful lambada artist is Beto Barbosa and her group Kaoma, made up of Brazilian, Argentine and French musicians. Other Brazilian musicians who have recorded some lambada tracks include Lulu Santos, Pepeu Gomes and Moraes Moreira, and even Caetano Veloso.

The latest rage is *sertanejo*, a kind of Brazilian country and western music that has long been a favourite with truckdrivers and cowboys, but has only recently entered the mainstream of popular Brazilian music. Usually sung by male duets wearing cowboy hats, fringe jackets and large belt-buckles, sertanejo is characterised by its soaring harmonies and, of course, its lyrics about broken hearts, life on the road, etc. Popular exponents are: José Rico and Millionario, Chitãozinho and Xororó, and Leandro e Leonardo.

If you want to have a listen to some Brazilian music before you arrive, the 'Brazil Classics' series, compiled by David Byrne and distributed by Warner Brothers, is a good starting point. The records are readily available, and cover samba and forró, and some individuals like Bahian Tom Zé. Bossa nova records are reasonably plentiful, especially the Grammy-winning collaborations between Brazilian and American artists, like João Gilberto and Stan Getz. *The Rhythm of the Saints*, a recent album by Paul Simon, is heavily influenced by Brazilian music. It includes backing by Milton Nascimento and the increasingly popular Grupo Cultural Olodum from Bahia.

Purchasing Records & Tapes On arrival in Brazil, the widest selection of records can be found in the large cities, like São Paulo and Rio. Folk music enthusiasts should check out the selection available at the Museu Folclorico Edson Carneiro in Rio.

Records and tapes cost around US$7. Compact discs are now available in Brazil, but there are doubts as to their quality compared to 'imported' CDs. They cost around US$12 to US$15.

Art

The first painters of the colonial period were the Jesuit and Benedictine missionaries, who painted their churches and sacred objects in a European baroque style. The Dutch invasion in the north brought with it some important Flemish artists, such as Frans Post, who painted the flora and fauna in its tropical surroundings.

Brazilian baroque art peaked in the 18th century, when the wealth provided by the gold rush allowed talented artists to reach their full potential and create many beautiful works. The acknowledged genius of this period is the sculptor and architect Antônio Francisco Lisboa, better known as Aleijadinho (see the Minas Gerais chapter for details of his life and works).

In the 19th and 20th centuries Brazilian artists have followed the international trends of neo-classicism, romanticism, impressionism, academicism and modernism.

The internationally best known Brazilian painter is Candido Portinari. Early in his career he made the decision to paint only Brazil and its people. Strongly influenced by the Mexican muralists like Diego Rivera, he managed to fuse native, expressionist influences into a powerful, socially conscious and sophisticated style.

Indian Art In its original form, Indian art was created for religious or utilitarian purposes and was considered part of the Indian way of life.

After first contacts had been made, Indians were soon visited by traders who perceived their art as a valuable item to be acquired by bartering and then sold as a curiosity or collectible in Brazil and abroad. Today many Indians produce art items for sale as tourist curios – the income pays their keep on the margin of a society which has destroyed their environment, their way of life, and left no other purpose for their art.

The Indians are renowned for a wide range of artistic handicrafts. The plumage of forest birds is used to create necklaces, bracelets, earrings, headdresses, capes and blankets. Some tribes pluck the original feathers from a bird such as a macaw, and smear the plucked area of the bird's skin with a vegetable dye which changes the colour of the new plumage. Members of some tribes use dyes and tattoos to decorate their bodies with intricate designs of great beauty.

Ceramic arts were a speciality of the Marajó Indians, who flourished long before the arrival of the Portuguese, and today the Carajás tribe in the state of Tocantins is famed for its skillfully painted figurines. Grasses, leaves and bark from the forests are used in highly developed Indian handicrafts such as weaving and basketry. The Kaxinawá tribe in the state of Acre is especially skilled at producing woven bags and baskets to transport or store forest foods. For more details about the Indians of Brazil, refer to the Population & People section in this chapter.

Architecture

Many Brazilian examples of outstanding architecture have been proclaimed by UNESCO as part of the world's cultural heritage.

Representing the colonial period are Olinda, in Pernambuco, and the historic centre of Salvador, which is considered to be the finest example of Portuguese colonial architecture in the world.

In Minas Gerais, the town of Ouro Prêto and Aleijadinho's masterpiece, the church of Bom Jesus de Matzinhos in Congonhas, represent the golden age of Brazilian baroque architecture.

The remains of the 17th-century Jesuit missions in Rio Grande do Sul, on the border between Brazil, Argentina and Paraguay, are notable for the fine woodcarving and masonry of the Guaraní Indians, who achieved their own distinct style.

The central urban plan of the capital, Brasília, also earns a UNESCO rating as a striking example of modern architecture.

Literature

There are a few dozen excellent Brazilian works of fiction translated into English but, sadly, many of today's best writers have not been translated.

Machado de Assis is simply world class. The son of a freed slave, Assis worked as a typesetter and journalist in late 19th-century Rio. A tremendous stylist, with a great sense of humour, Assis had an understanding of human relations which was both subtle and deeply cynical, as the terse titles of books like *Epitaph of a Small Winner* (Avon Bard, 1977) and *Philosopher or Dog* (Avon Bard, 1982) might suggest. He wrote five major novels; my favourite is *Dom Casmurro* (Avon Bard, 1980).

The most famous writer in Brazil is the regionalist Jorge Amado. Born near Ilhéus, Bahia, in 1912, and a long-time resident of Salvador, Amado has written colourful romances of Bahia's people and places. Strongly influenced by Communism during his early work, Amado's later books are better, although the subjects are lighter. His books are widely translated and easy to obtain. The best are *Gabriela, Clove and Cinnamon* (Avon Bard, 1974), which is set in Ilhéus, and *Dona Flor and her Two Husbands* (Avon Bard, 1977), whose antics occur in Salvador. Amado's *Tent of Miracles* (Avon Bard, 1978) explores racial relations in Brazil and *Pen, Sword and Camisole* (Avon Bard, 1986) laughs its way through the petty worlds of military and academic politics. *The Violent Land* (Avon Bard, 1979) is another of Amado's classics. The three short stories about a group of Bahian characters that make up *Shepherds of the Night* (Avon Bard, 1980) inspired my first visit to Brazil.

Without a word to waste, Graciliano Ramos tells of peasant life in the sertão in his best book, *Barren Lives* (University of Texas Press, 1965). The stories are powerful portraits. Strong stuff. Autran Dourado's *The Voices of the Dead* (Taplinger, 1981) goes into the inner world of a small town in Minas Gerais. He has also penned a couple of books about Minas Gerais, his home state. Read anything you can find by Mário de Andrade, one of Brazil's pre-eminent authors. His *Macunaíma* is comic and could only take place in Brazil.

Clarice Lispector has several collections of short stories, all of which are excellent. Lídia Fagundes Telles' books contain psychologically rich portraits of women in today's Brazil. Dinah Silveira de Queiroz's *The Women of Brazil* is about a Portuguese girl who goes to 17th-century Brazil to meet her betrothed.

Márcio Souza is a modern satirist based in Manaus. His biting humour captures the horror of the Amazon and his imaginative parodies of Brazilian history reveal the stupidity of personal and governmental endeavours to conquer the rainforest. Both the *Emperor of the Amazon* (Avon Bard, 1980), his first book, and *Mad Maria* (Avon Bard, 1985) shouldn't be missed if you're going to the Amazon, but his latest farce, *The Order of the Day* (Avon Bard, 1986), is disappointing. *The Impostors* (Avon Bard, 1987) by Pablo Vierci is a humorous novel about Amazon mayhem.

The bizarre and brutal *Zero* (Avon Bard, 1983), by Ignácio de Loyola Brandão, had the honour of being banned by the military government until a national protest helped lift the ban. *The Tower of Glass* (Avon Bard, 1982), by Ivan Ângelo, is all São Paulo: an absurdist look at big-city life where nothing that matters, matters. It's a revealing and important view of modern Brazil, 'where all that's solid melts into air'. João Ubaldo Ribeiro's *Sergeant Getúlio* (Avon Bard, 1980) is a story of a military man in Brazil's Northeast. No book tells better of the sadism, brutality and patriarchy which run through Brazil's history.

CULTURE

Brazilian culture has been shaped not only by the Portuguese, who gave the country its language and religion, but also by native Indians, Black Africans, and other settlers from Europe, the Middle East, and Asia.

Although often ignored, denigrated or feared by urban Brazilians, Indian culture has helped shape modern Brazil and its legends, dance and music. Many native foods and beverages, such as tapioca, manioc, potatoes, maté, and guaraná, have become Brazilian staples. The Indians also gave the colonisers numerous objects and skills which are now in daily use in Brazil, such as hammocks, dugout canoes, thatched roofing, and weaving techniques. For more details about the Indians refer to the sections on Indian Art and Population & People in this chapter.

The influence of African culture is also very powerful in Brazil, especially the Northeast. The slaves imported by the Portuguese brought with them their religion, music and cuisine, all of which have profoundly influenced Brazilian identity.

All these elements have combined to produce a nation of people well known for their spontaneity, friendliness and lust for life. As you would expect from such a diverse population mix, there are many regional differences and accents. One of the funniest aspects of this regional diversity is the rivalry between the citizens of Rio and São Paulo. Talk to Paulistas (inhabitants of São Paulo state) and they will tell you that Cariocas (inhabitants of Rio) are hedonistic, frivolous and irresponsible. Cariocas think of Paulistas as materialistic, neurotic workaholics. Both Paulista and Carioca agree that the Nordestinos, from the Northeast, do things more slowly and simply, and are the worst drivers! Mineiros, from the state of Minas Gerais, are considered the thriftiest and most religious of Brazilians – Cariocas claim they're saving up for their tombs!

In Brazil, time is warped. The cities and their 20th-century urban inhabitants exist only a short distance from fisherfolk, cowboys and forest dwellers whose lifestyles have varied little in 300 years. In the forests, the ancient traditions of the native Brazilians remain untouched by TV soap operas – for the time being.

Brazilians have an excellent sense of humour. They adore telling jokes about the Portuguese, in the same way that Americans tell Polish jokes and Australians and Brits tell Irish jokes.

If you manage to get a grasp of the language, listen to Brazilians when a group of them get together on the beach or in a corner bar. If you can get past the fact that they all talk at once, you'll discover that the conversation almost always turns to football, criticism of the government, family matters or the latest twist in the current soap opera.

So what unifies the Brazilians? The Portuguese language, love of football, Carnival and the sound of samba. Listen and watch their expressive way of communicating; go to a football game and watch the intensity and variety of emotions, both on the field and in the stands; experience the bacchanal of Carnival and attempt to dance the samba and you may begin to understand what it is to be Brazilian.

RELIGION

Officially, Brazil is a Catholic country which claims the largest Catholic population of any country in the world. However, Brazil is also noted for the diversity and syncretism of its many sects and religions, which offer great flexibility to their followers. For example, without much difficulty you can find people from Catholic backgrounds who frequent the church and have no conflict appealing for help at a *terreiro de umbanda*, the house of one of the Afro-Brazilian cults.

Historically, the principal religious influences have been Indian animism, Catholicism and African cults brought by the Blacks during the period of slavery. The slaves were prohibited from practising their religions by the colonists in the same way that they were kept from other elements of their culture, such as music and dance, for fear that it would reinforce their group identity. Religious persecution led to religious syncretism. To avoid persecution the slaves gave Catholic names and figures to all their African gods. This was generally done by finding the similarities between the Catholic images and the *orixás* (gods) of Candomblé (described later in this section). Thus, the slaves worshipped their own gods behind the representations of the Catholic saints.

Under the influence of liberalism in the 19th century, Brazilians wrote into their constitution the freedom to worship all religions. But the African cults continued to suffer persecution for many years. Candomblé was seen by the White elites as charlatanism that showed the ignorance of the poorest classes. The spectrum of Brazilian religious life was gradually broadened by the addition of Indian animism to Afro-Catholic syncretism, and by the increasing fascination of Whites with the spiritualism of Kardecism (described later in this section).

Today Catholicism retains its status as the official religion, but it is declining in popularity. Throughout Brazil, churches are closing or falling into disrepair for lack of funds or priests, and attendance at services is dwindling to attendance at the basics: baptism, marriage, and burial. The largest numbers of converts are being attracted to Afro-Brazilian cults, and spiritist or mystic sects. Nowadays, the intense religious fervour of Brazilians extends across gradations and subdivisions of numerous sects: from purist cults to groups that worship Catholic saints, African deities and the Cabóclos of the Indian cults simultaneously.

Note that in this book, we use the abbreviation NS for 'Nossa Senhora' (Our Lady) or 'Nosso Senhor' (Our Lord): eg, NS do Pilar.

Afro-Brazilian Cults

These cults do not follow the ideas of major European or Asian religions; neither do they use doctrines to define good and evil. One of the things that was most shocking to Europeans in their first contact with the African images and rituals was the cult of Exú. This entity was generally represented by combined human and animal images, complete with a horn and an erect penis. Seeking parallels between their own beliefs and African religions, European Catholics and Puritans identified Exú as the devil. For Africans, however, Exú represents the transition between the material and the spiritual worlds. In the ritual of Candomblé, Exú acts as a messenger between the gods and human beings. For example, everything related to money, love, and protection against thieves comes under the watchful eye of Exú. Ultimately, Exú's responsibility is the temporal world.

Candomblé This is the most orthodox of the cults brought from Africa by the Nago, Yoruba, and Jeje peoples. Candomblé, which is an African word denoting a dance in honour of the gods, is a general term for the cult in Bahia. Elsewhere in Brazil the cult is known by different names: in Rio it's known as Macumba; in Amazonas and Pará, Babassuê; in Pernambuco and Alagoas, Xangô; in Rio Grande do Sul, either Pará or Batuque; and the term Tambor is used in Maranhão. For suggested reading on Candomblé, see the Books & Maps section in the Facts for the Visitor chapter.

The Afro-Brazilian rituals are practised in a *casa-de-santo* or *terreiro* directed by a *pai* or *mãe de santo* (literally father or mother of the saint – the Candomblé priest or priestess). This is where the initiation of novices takes place as well as consultations and rituals. The ceremonies are conducted in the Yoruba tongue. The religious hierarchy and structure is clearly established and consistent from one terreiro to the next. Not all ceremonies are open to the public.

If you attend a Candomblé ceremony, it's best to go as the invited guest of a knowledgeable friend or commercial guide. If your request to visit is declined, you should accept the decision. Some ceremonies are only open to certain members of a terreiro, and there is genuine concern that visitors may not know the customs involved and thereby interrupt the rituals.

Although the rules for Candomblé ceremonies are not rigidly fixed, there are some general points which apply to most of these ceremonies. If in doubt, ask the person who has taken you to the ceremony. Dress for men and women can be casual, but shorts should not be worn. White is the preferred colour; black, purple, and brown should be avoided. Hats should not be worn inside the terreiro; and if you wish to smoke, you should only do so outside. On arrival at the terreiro, make sure you do not stand blocking the doorway. There's usually someone inside who is responsible for directing people to their seats – men are often seated on the right, women on the left. The seating pattern is important, so make sure you only sit where indicated. Watch respectfully and follow the advice of your friend or guide as to what form of participation is being expected of you. Sometimes drinks and food are distributed. Depending on the ritual involved, these may be intended only as offerings, or else for your consumption. In the case of the latter, there's no offence taken if you don't eat or drink what's offered. For a description of An

Candomblé rite participant

Evening of Candomblé see the Bahia chapter.

According to Candomblé, each person has an orixá which attends from birth and provides protection throughout life. The orixá for each person is identified after a pai or mãe de santo makes successive throws with a handful of *búzios* (shells). In a divination ritual known as Jogo dos Búzios (Casting of Shells) the position of the shells is used to interpret your luck, your future, and your past relation with the gods.

The Jogo dos Búzios can be traced back to numerology and cabalism. It is a simple version of the Ifa ceremony in which the orixá Ifa is invoked to transmit the words of the deities to the people. The mãe de santo casts 16 seashells on a white towel. She interprets the number and arrangement of face-up and face-down shells to predict the future.

The Jogo dos Búzios is a serious, respected force in Bahia. In 1985 it was used by many politicians to forecast the election returns. In Salvador, visitors can consult a mãe-de-santo for Candomblé-style fortune telling any day of the week, except for Fridays and Mondays, but Thursdays are best.

Like the gods in Greek mythology, each orixá has a personality and particular history. Power struggles and rulership conflicts amongst the many orixá are part of the history of Candomblé.

Although orixá are divided into male and female types, there are some which can switch from one sex to the other. One example is Logunedé, son of two male gods, Ogun and Oxoss. Another example is Oxumaré who is male during six months of the year and female during the other months. Oxumaré is represented by the river that runs from the mainland to the sea or by the rainbow. These bisexual gods are generally, but not necessarily, the gods of homosexuals. Candomblé is very accepting of homosexuality and this may explain the foundation of these practices and why they are legitimised by the cult's mythology.

To keep themselves strong and healthy, followers of Candomblé always give food to their respective orixá. In the ritual, Exú is the first to be given food because he is the messenger for the individual to make contact with the orixá. Exú likes *cachaça* and other alcoholic drinks, cigarettes and cigars, strong perfumes and meats. The offering to the orixá depends on their particular preferences. For example, to please Iemanjá, the goddess/queen of the sea, one should give perfumes, white and blue flowers, rice and fried fish. Oxalá, the greatest god, the god and owner of the sun, eats cooked white corn. Oxúm, god of fresh waters and waterfalls, is famous for his vanity. He should be honoured with earrings, necklaces, mirrors, perfumes, champagne and honey.

Each orixá is worshipped at a particular time and place. For example, Oxósse, who is god of the forests, should be revered in a forest or park, but Xangô, god of stone and justice, receives his offering in rocky places.

In Bahia and Rio, followers of Afro-Brazilian cults turn out in huge numbers to attend a series of festivals at the year's end – especially those held during the night of 31 December and on New Year's Day. Millions of Brazilians go to the beach to pay homage to Iemanjá, the queen of the sea. Flowers, perfumes, fruits and even jewellery are tossed into the sea for the mother of the waters, to please or gain protection, and for good luck in the new year.

Umbanda Umbanda, or white magic, is a mixture of Candomblé and spiritism. It traces its origins from various sources, but in its present form it is a religion native to Brazil. The African influence is more Angolan/Bantu. The ceremony, conducted in Portuguese, incorporates figures from all of the Brazilian races: *preto velho*, the old Black slave, *o caboclo* and other Amerindian deities, *o guerreiro*, the White warrior, etc. In comparison to Candomblé, Umbanda is less organised and each pai or mãe de santo modifies the religion.

Quimbanda is the evil counterpart to Umbanda. It involves lots of blood, animal sacrifice and nasty deeds. The practice of Quimbanda is illegal.

Kardecism

During the 19th century, Allan Kardec, the French spiritual master, introduced spiritism to Brazilian Whites in a palatable form. Kardec's teachings, which incorporated some Eastern religious ideas into a European framework, are now followed by large numbers of Brazilians. Kardecism emphasises spiritism associated with parlour seances, multiple reincarnations and speaking to the dead. Kardec wrote about his teachings in *The Book of Spirits* and *The Book of Mediums*.

Other Cults

Brasília has become the capital of the new cults. In the Planaltina neighbourhood, visit Tia Neiva and the Vale do Amanhecer, and Eclética de Mestro Yocanan (see the Brasília chapter).

A few of the Indian rites have been popularised among Brazilians without becoming part of Afro-Brazilian cults. Two such cults are União da Vegetal in São Paulo and the South; and Santo Daime in Rondônia and Acre. A hallucinogenic drink called *ayahuasca*, made from the root and vine of two plants, *cipó jagube* and *folha chacrona*, has been used for centuries by the indigenous peoples of South America. This drink is central to the practices of these cults, which are otherwise very straight – hierarchy, moral behaviour, and dress follow a strict code. The government tolerates the use of ayahuasca in the religious ceremonies of these cults, which also tightly control the production and supply.

The cult of Santo Daime was founded in 1930 in Rio Branco, Acre, by Raimundo Irineu Serra. Today it claims around 10,000 members, including notable Brazilian figures such as the flamboyant singer Ney Matogrosso, the cartoonist Glauco, and the anthropologist Edward Macrae. The cult has 10 churches and communities in Brazil. The two major communities are Ceú da Mapiá in Amazonas, and Colônia Cinco Mil in Rio Branco, Acre.

LANGUAGE

Quem tem boca vai á Roma.
(If you can speak you can get to Rome.)

When they settled Brazil in the 16th century, the Portuguese encountered the diverse languages of the Indians. These, together with the various idioms and dialects spoken by the Africans brought in as slaves, extensively changed the Portuguese spoken by the early settlers. Along with Portuguese, Tupi-Guaraní, written down and simplified by the Jesuits, became a common language, understood by the majority of the population. It even became the main language spoken by the general public until the middle of the 18th century, but its usage diminished with the great number of Portuguese gold-rush immigrants and a royal proclamation in 1757 prohibiting its use. With the expulsion of the Jesuits in 1759, Portuguese was well and truly established as the national language.

Still, many words remain from the Indian and African languages. From Tupi-Guaraní come lots of place names (eg Guanabara, Carioca, Tijuca and Niterói), animal names (eg piranha, capivara and urubu) and plant names (eg mandioca, abacaxí, caju and jacarandá). Words from the African dialects, mainly those from Nigeria and Angola, are used in Afro-Brazilian religious ceremonies (eg Orixá, Exú and Iansã), cooking (eg vatapá, acarajé and abará) and general conversation (eg samba, moleque and mocambo).

Within Brazil, accents, dialects and slang (*gíria*) vary regionally. The Carioca inserts the 'sh' sound in place of 's'. The gaúcho speaks a Spanish-sounding Portuguese, the Baiano (from Bahía) speaks slowly and the accents of the Cearense are often incomprehensible to outsiders.

Portuguese is similar to Spanish on paper, but sounds completely different. You will do quite well if you speak Spanish in Brazil, although in general, Brazilians will understand what you say, but you won't get much of what they say. So don't think studying Portuguese is a waste of time. Listen to language tapes. Develop an ear for Portuguese – it's a beautiful-sounding language.

Brazilians are easy to befriend, but unfortunately the vast majority speak little or no English. This is changing, as practically all Brazilians in school are learning English. All the same, don't count on finding an English speaker, especially out of the cities. The more Portuguese you speak, the more you will derive from your trip. Take the time and learn some of the language.

Most phrasebooks are not very helpful; their vocabulary is often dated and contains the Portuguese spoken in Portugal, not Brazil. Notable exceptions are Lonely Planet's *Brazilian Phrasebook*, and a Berlitz phrasebook for travel in Brazil. Make sure any English-Portuguese dictionary is a Brazilian Portuguese one.

If you're more intent on learning the language, try the US Foreign Service Institute (FSI) tape series. It comes in two volumes. Volume 1, which includes 23 cassettes and accompanying text, costs US$130 and covers pronunciation, verb tenses and essential nouns and adjectives. Volume 2 includes 22 tapes with text and sells for US$115. It includes useful phrases and travel vocabulary. For fluent Spanish speakers, FSI also has: 'Portuguese – From Spanish to Portuguese', which consists of two tapes and a text explaining similarities and differences between these languages. This one costs US$20. To get hold of these, write to or call the National Audiovisual Centre (☎ (301) 763-1896), Information Services PF, 8700 Edgeworth Drive, Capitol Heights, Maryland, USA, 20743-3701.

In Australia, a condensed version of the FSI tapes is available from Learn Australia Pty Ltd (☎ (008) 338-183), 726 High St, East Kew, Victoria, 3102. Twelve 90-minute tapes cost A$195.

Combine these with a few Brazilian samba tapes and some Jorge Amado novels and you're ready to begin the next level of instruction on the streets of Brazil. If that doesn't suffice, it's easy to arrange tutorial instruction through any of the Brazilian-American institutes where Brazilians go to learn English, or at the IBEU (Instituto Brazil Estados Unidos) in Rio.

Useful Words & Phrases

yes	*sim*
no	*não*
perhaps	*talvez*
please, thank you	*por favor*
thank you	*obrigado* (males)
	obrigada (females)
that's alright	*nada*
good morning	*bom dia*
good afternoon	*boa tarde*
good evening	*boa noite*
goodbye	*tchau*
see you soon	*até logo*
How are you?	*Como vai?* or
	Tudo bem?
good	*bom*
a pleasure	*muito prazer*
(meeting you)	
speak more slowly	*fale mais devagar*
I don't speak	*Não falo português.*
Portuguese.	
Do you speak	*Você fala inglês?*
English?	
excuse me	*com licença*
pardon me	*desculpe*
sorry	*perdão*
the bill please	*a conta por favor*
how much?	*quanto?*
How much time does	*Quanto tempo*
it take?	*demora?*
where	*onde*
Where is...located?	*Onde fica...?*
left/right	*esquerda/direita*
when	*quando*
how	*como*
who	*quem*
what	*que*
why	*porque*
I want to buy...	*Eu quero comprar...*
expensive	*caro*
cheap	*barato*
more	*mais*
less	*menos*
yesterday	*ontem*
today	*hoje*

tomorrow	*amanhã*
morning	*a manhã*
afternoon	*a tarde*
night	*a noite*
What time is it?	*Que horas são?*

Numbers

0	*zero*
1	*um, uma*
2	*dois, duas*
3	*três*
4	*quatro*
5	*cinco*
6	*seis* (when quoting telephone or house numbers, Brazilians will often say *meia* instead of *seis*)
7	*sete*
8	*oito*
9	*nove*
10	*dez*
11	*onze*
12	*doze*
13	*treze*
14	*catorze*
15	*quinze*
16	*dezesseis*
17	*dezessete*
18	*dezoito*
19	*dezenove*
20	*vinte*
30	*trinta*
40	*quarenta*
50	*cinqüenta*
60	*sessenta*
70	*setenta*
80	*oitenta*
90	*noventa*
100	*cem*

first	*primeiro*
last	*último*

Days of the Week

Sunday	*domingo*
Monday	*segunda-feira*
Tuesday	*terça-feira*
Wednesday	*quarta-feira*
Thursday	*quinta-feira*
Friday	*sexta-feira*
Saturday	*sábado*

Slang

Brazilians pepper their language with strange oaths and odd expressions (literal translation in parentheses):

curse word	*palavrão*
shooting the breeze	*batendo um papo*
gosh!	*nossa!* (Our Lady!)
great, cool, OK	*'ta lógico, 'ta ótimo, 'ta legal*
I'm mad at...	*eu fiquei chatiado com...*
money	*grana*
whoops!	*opa!*
wow!	*oba!*
hello	*oi*
you said it!	*falou!*
bum	*bum-bum/bunda*
bald	*careca*
a mess	*cambalacho*
the famous Brazilian bikini	*fio dental* (dental floss)
marijuana	*fumo* (smoke)
guy	*cara*
girl	*garota*
my god	*meu deus*
it's crazy, you're crazy	*'ta louco*
everything OK?	*tudo bem?*
everything's OK	*tudo bom*
that's great, cool	*chocante*
that's bad, shit	*merda*
a fix, a troublesome problem	*abacaxí*
Is there a way?	*Tem jeito?*
There's always a way	*Sempre tem jeito*

Body Language

Brazilians accompany their oral communication with a rich body language, a sort of parallel dialogue. The thumbs up of *tudo bem* is used as a greeting, or to signify OK or thank you. The authoritative *não, não* finger-wagging is most intimidating when done right under a victim's nose, but it's not a threat. The sign of the *figa*, a thumb inserted between the first and second fingers of a

A B
C D
  E

A (SP)

B

C (JM)

D (JM)

E (JM)

A Armadillo (tatu) (DS) B Monkey, Pantanal (DS)
C Tapir (RS) D Piranha (GC)
E Capybaras (RS) F Hyacinth Macaw (RS)
G Jacaré (AD)

clenched fist, is a symbol of good luck derived from an African sexual charm. It's more commonly used as jewellery than in body language.

To indicate *rápido!* (speed and haste), thumb and middle finger touch loosely while rapidly shaking the wrist. If you don't want something *(não quero)*, slap the back of your hands as if ridding yourself of the entire affair.

Touching a finger to the lateral corner of the eye means I'm wise to you.

Facts for the Visitor

VISAS

At the time of writing, Brazilian visas were necessary for visitors who were citizens of countries which required visas for visitors from Brazil. American, Canadian, Australian and NZ citizens required visas, but UK citizens did not. Tourist visas are issued by Brazilian diplomatic offices and are valid for arrival in Brazil within 90 days of issue and then for a 90-day stay in Brazil. They are renewable in Brazil for an additional 90 days.

It should only take about three hours to issue a visa, but you need a passport valid for at least six months, a single passport photograph (either B&W or colour) and either a round-trip ticket or a statement from a travel agent, addressed to the Brazilian diplomatic office, stating that you have the required ticketing. If you only have a one-way ticket they may accept a document from a bank or similar organisation proving that you have sufficient funds to stay and buy a return ticket, but it's probably easier to get a letter from a travel agent stating that you have a round-trip ticket.

Visitors under 18 years of age must submit a notarised letter of authorisation from their parents or legal guardian.

Tourist Card

When you enter Brazil, you will be asked to fill out a tourist card, which has two parts. Immigration officials will keep one part, and the other one will be attached to your passport. When you leave Brazil, this will be detached from your passport by immigration officials. Make sure you don't lose your part of the card whilst travelling around Brazil. If you do lose your portion, your departure could be delayed until officials have checked your story. For added security, make a photocopy of your section of the tourist card and keep this in a safe place, separate from your passport.

Whilst researching this edition, we crossed the Brazilian borders many times. At one stage, whilst travelling from Brazil to Uruguay, we missed the fact that the requisite part of our tourist card had not been collected on departure. Several weeks later, when we arrived at Ponta Porã on the Paraguay-Brazil border, the immigration authorities explained that we had not technically left Brazil! After considerable cogitation and friendly banter, the officials asked us to make a certified deposition concerning the details of our 'disappearance'. Then the old cards were doctored, and we were issued with new cards.

Renewing Visas

The Polícia Federal handles visa extensions and they have offices in major Brazilian cities. You must go to them before your visa lapses, or suffer the consequences. Don't leave it until the last minute either. Go for an extension about 15 days before your current visa expires. The tourist office can tell you where they are. In most cases a visa extension seems to be pretty automatic, but sometimes they'll only give you 60 days. The police may require a ticket out of the country and proof of sufficient funds, but this seems to be entirely at the discretion of the police officer.

When applying for an extension, you will be told to go to a *papelaria* (stationery shop) and buy a DARF form. After filling it out, you must then go to a Banco do Brasil (or another bank nearby) and pay a fee of about US$5. You then return to the Polícia Federal with the DARF form stamped by the bank. The extension should then be routinely issued.

If you opt for the maximum 90-day extension and then leave the country before the end of that period, you cannot return until the full 90 days have elapsed. So if you plan to leave and re-enter Brazil you must plan your dates carefully.

Brazilian Embassies & Consulates

Brazilian embassies and consulates are maintained in the following countries:

Australia
19 Forster Crescent, Yarralumla, ACT 2600 (☎ (062) 732-372)
Canada
255 Albert St, Suite 900, Ottawa, Ontario K1P-6A9
France
34 Cours Albert, 1er, 75008 Paris (☎ (1) 259-9250)
Germany
Kurfürstendamm 11, 1 Stock, 1 Berlin 15 (☎ (30) 883-1208)
New Zealand
New Zealanders must apply to the Brazilian Embassy in Australia for their visas; this can be done easily through a travel agent.
UK
32 Green St, London W1Y 4AT (☎ (071) 499-0877)
USA
630 Fifth Ave, Suite 2720, New York, NY 10111 (☎ (212) 687-0530); there are also consulates in Atlanta (☎ (404) 659-0660), Chicago (☎ (312) 372-2179), Houston (☎ (713) 961-3063), Los Angeles (☎ (213) 382-3133), Miami (☎ (305) 374-2263), and San Francisco (☎ (212) 981-8170)

Visas for Adjoining Countries

The following information is intended as a rough guide only. Visa regulations are notoriously quick to change, so check them before you travel. For details of the relevant embassies and consulates, refer to individual cities mentioned.

Argentina
Australians and New Zealanders require visas. Citizens of most West European countries, Canada, and the USA do not. There are Argentine consulates in Porto Alegre, Foz do Iguaçu, Rio, São Paulo, and Brasília.
Bolivia
Australians, New Zealanders, Dutch, French, and Canadians require visas. Citizens of the UK, and the USA do not require visas. There are Bolivian consulates in Brasília, Rio, São Paulo, Corumbá, Campo Grande, Manaus, and Guajará-Mirim.

Colombia
Australians, New Zealanders, Canadians, and citizens of the USA require visas. Citizens of most West European countries do not require visas. There are consulates in Brasília, Manaus, Rio, São Paulo, and Tabatinga.
Guyana
Most visitors require visas. Guyana has consulates in Brasília and São Paulo.
French Guiana
Citizens of the USA, Canada, and the European Community do not require visas. Australians and New Zealanders require visas, which can be obtained at French consulates in Brasília, Belém, Recife, Rio, São Paulo, and Salvador.
Paraguay
Australians and New Zealanders require visas. There are Paraguayan consulates in Brasília, Campo Grande, Corumbá, Curitiba, Foz do Iguaçu, Porto Alegre, Ponta Porã, Rio, and São Paulo.
Peru
Australians and New Zealanders require visas. There are Peruvian consulates in Brasília, Manaus, Rio Branco, Belém, Rio, and São Paulo.
Surinam
Visas are not required by UK or Canadian citizens. There is an embassy for Surinam in Brasília.
Uruguay
Australians and New Zealanders require visas. There are Uruguayan consulates in Brasília, Chuí, Jaguarão, Porto Alegre, Rio, and São Paulo.
Venezuela
All overland travellers require visas. There are Venezuelan consulates in Brasília, Manaus, Belém, Boa Vista, Porto Alegre, Rio, and São Paulo.

DOCUMENTS

The only papers you really need are your passport and visa, an airline ticket, a yellow WHO health certificate and money.

By law you must carry a passport with you at all times, but many travellers opt to carry a photocopy (preferably certified). A credit card is quite handy, as is an International Youth Hostel card if you plan to use the *albergues de juventude* (youth hostels). The International Student Identity Card is practically useless. To rent a car you must be at least 25 years old, and have a credit card and a valid driver's licence. You should also carry an International Driver's Permit or Inter-Americas licence.

It's convenient to have several extra passport photographs for any documents or visas you might acquire in Brazil. As a backup for emergencies, it's handy to have photocopies of the following: your passport (including relevant visas), tourist card (provided when entering Brazil), travellers' cheque numbers, and airline tickets. For more hints on safety, see the Security section under Dangers & Annoyances in this chapter.

CUSTOMS
Travellers entering Brazil are allowed to bring in one radio, tape player, typewriter, video and still camera. Personal computers are allowed.

At airport customs, they use the random check system. After collecting your luggage you pass a post with two buttons; if you have nothing to declare, you push the appropriate button. A green light means walk straight out; a red light means you've been selected for a baggage search.

Customs searches at land borders are more thorough, especially if you're coming from Bolivia.

MONEY
Currency
Anyone who's ever been famous in Brazil has a good chance of getting their picture on a banknote – the currency changes so often. Since 1986 the name of the currency has changed four times, from cruzeiro to cruzado to cruzado novo and back to cruzeiro.

At the moment, the monetary unit of Brazil is the cruzeiro. It's made up of 100 centavos, but in reality the only time anyone sees a 50 centavo coin is when the supermarket checkout operator wants to give exact change. You may come across one lying in the street. It's so worthless that nobody can be bothered to pick it up. Other coins are almost as worthless. These are the 1, 5 and 10 cruzeiro coins.

Old 50, 100, 200 and 500 cruzado novo notes are worth their face value in cruzeiros. Also in circulation are the 1000, 5000, 10,000 and 50,000 cruzeiro notes. By the time you read this, 100,000 cruzeiro notes should be around too.

Exchange Rates
There are currently three types of exchange rate operating in Brazil: official (also known as *comercial* or *câmbio livre*), *turismo* and *paralelo*.

Until recently, the official rate has always been much lower than the other two rates. A few years ago, all dollars exchanged at banks were changed at the official rate as were all credit card transactions, making it an extremely unfavourable transaction. But thanks to a certain amount of deregulation in an attempt to wipe out black market trading it's now possible to change cash dollars and travellers' cheques at banks using the turismo rate, which is only slightly less than the parallel 'black market' rate.

Full parallel rates are usually available only at borders and in the larger cities like Rio and São Paulo anyway.

Exchange rates are written up every day on the top, right-hand corner of the front page of *O Globo* and in the *Dinheiro* section of the *Folha de São Paulo*. They are always announced on the evening TV news.

Approximate bank rates as at March 1992 were as follows:

US$1 = Cz$1752.95
UK£1 = Cz$3053.70
A$1 = Cz$1337.50
NZ$1 = Cz$961.54
C$1 = Cz$1477.90
DM1 = Cz$1068.47
FFr1 = Cz$315.50
SwFr1 = Cz$1175.51
Y100 = Cz$1310.85

Cash & Travellers' Cheques

US cash dollars are easier to trade and are worth a bit more on the parallel market, but travellers' cheques are an insurance against loss, and now that they can be exchanged at the turismo rate it's good value and good sense to use them.

American Express is the most recognised brand, but they charge 1% of the face value of the cheque (on top of the interest that your money makes while sitting in their banks), and sometimes, with all the non-accidental losses of cheques, they're a little squirrely about giving your money back on the spot. They have offices in Rio de Janeiro, Salvador, Recife, Brasília, Belo Horizonte and São Paulo. Thomas Cook, Barclays and First National City Bank are also good. Get travellers' cheques in US dollars and carry some small denominations for convenience. Have some emergency US cash to use when the banks are closed.

Learn in advance how to get refunds from your travellers' cheque company. Keep a close, accurate and current record of your travellers' cheque expenditures. This speeds up the refund process. Guard your travellers' cheques: they are valuable to thieves even without your counter signature.

Changing Money

Changing money in Brazil is easy in the large cities. Almost anyone can direct you to a *casa de câmbio* (money exchange house). Many new casas de câmbio have sprung up in response to the recent deregulation of foreign currency by the federal government.

Most large banks now have a foreign section where you can change money at the slightly lower turismo rate, but sometimes this may involve a bit of time-wasting bureaucracy. At present, the two banks officially allowed to change travellers' cheques are Banco do Brasil and Banco Econômico, but you can also exchange travellers' cheques at most casas de câmbio. Make sure you ask them before you sign the cheque.

In small towns without a bank, you'll have to ask around. Someone will usually be able to direct you to someone who buys cash dollars.

Changing money at weekends, even in the big cities, can be extremely difficult, so make sure you have enough to last until Monday. If you do get stuck, the best places to try are the large hotels, expensive restaurants, travel agents, jewellery stores or souvenir shops. Be prepared to lose a few dollars on the transaction.

Incidentally, if the banks are told to stop using the turismo rate and go back to a lower, regulated official rate, the above-mentioned places are the best bets for changing at parallel rates, except on weekends! Don't change money on the streets, follow exchangers into unfamiliar areas, or give money or unsigned cheques up front.

Small Change

There is a chronic shortage of change in Brazil. When you change money, for example at the Banco do Brasil, ask for lots of small bills – and take very few notes in denominations larger than the equivalent of US$10. Change, variously referred to as *troco* or *miúdo*, is often unobtainable at newsagents, restaurants, street stalls, in taxis, on buses, etc. Although the shortage clearly exists, it is also commonly used as an excuse to simply retain a fat tip. If you encounter this problem, insist that the seller finds change and hang around until it is procured. If you want to find out if the seller has change – preferably *before* you purchase – ask *tem troco?* (do you have change?). If you want to convey that you don't have change, say *não tem troco* (there is no change) which makes it clear that you neither have change nor have been able to find any in the vicinity – thus heading off the seller's inevitable request that you hunt around the vicinity! Sometimes sweets are used instead of small change.

Credit Cards

International credit cards like Visa and American Express are accepted by the more expensive hotels, restaurants and shops. At present, you get billed at the turismo rate in cruzeiros. Sometimes, the hotel/restaurant/store will try to add an extra charge for using the card. It's illegal to do this, and you can make a complaint to the relevant credit card company, which may decide to terminate its contract with the offending establishment. There have been reports that Varig is charging the official rate of exchange for purchases of domestic flights on international credit cards, whereas other Brazilian airlines, such as VASP, follow official policy and charge the turismo rate. Vote for fair play with your credit card!

New-style credit card coupons do not have carbon paper inserts and offer more protection against misuse. If you sign an old-style coupon, be sure to ask for the carbon inserts and destroy them after use: a worthwhile precaution against unwanted duplication of your credit card!

American Express card-holders can purchase US dollar travellers' cheques from Amex offices in the large cities.

Buying Foreign Cash

Rules and regulations regarding the purchase of foreign currency by foreigners at banks seem to change with monotonous regularity. In recent years, even Brazilians wanting to travel have had to show their plane ticket in order to buy dollars at banks. One of the reasons for this reluctance to sell dollars was that the official exchange rate has always been much lower than the parallel, black-market rate. It simply wasn't realistic to sell a dollar to someone for 50 cruzeiros when that same person could walk around the corner and exchange that dollar on the black-market for 80 cruzeiros.

By early 1992, after the dollar had been 'floated' by the government, the difference between the official and black-market rates had become very small, so the advantage of being able to buy dollars at a drastically lower, official rate had disappeared.

Both Brazilians and foreigners can now buy foreign cash at the many casas de câmbio that have appeared in the large cities, with no restrictions. The problem is that no one can say for sure just how long this situation will last.

Costs

Because of wild fluctuations in the economy, it's difficult to make any solid predictions about how much you'll spend. During my first couple of trips to Brazil in 1984 and '85, prices were frozen in an attempt to halt inflation and budget travel was ridiculously cheap, as the value of the dollar kept rising on the black market. Then on another trip in early 1990, just after Collor froze everyone's bank account, prices skyrocketed, and budget travellers headed for the borders as fast as they could. During this research trip, there was a price freeze which caused the cheap hotels (which don't take much notice of price freezes anyway) to become relatively expensive and the more expensive hotels to be relatively cheap.

If you're travelling on buses every couple of days, staying in hotels for US$10 a night, and eating in restaurants and/or drinking in bars every night, US$30 a day would be a rough estimate. It's possible to do it for less of course. If you plan to lie on a beach for a month, eating rice, beans and fish every day, US$10 to US$15 would be enough.

Tipping

Most services get tipped 10%, and as the people in these services make the minimum wage – which is not enough to live on – you can be sure they need the money. In restaurants the service charge will often be included in the bill and is mandatory. If a waiter is friendly and helpful you can give more. Even when it is not included, it's still customary to leave a 10% tip; unless the service is atrocious, the waiter shouldn't be punished for giving you the option. There are many places where tipping is not customary but is a welcome gesture. The local juice stands, bars, coffee corners, street and beach vendors are all tipped on occasion.

Because of the massive amount of unemployment in Brazil, some services that may seem superfluous are customarily tipped anyway. Parking assistants are the most notable, as they receive no wages, and are dependent on tips, usually the equivalent of 25c to 50c. Gas station attendants, shoe shiners and barbers are also frequently tipped.

Taxis are not usually tipped. Most people round the price up, but tipping is not expected.

Bargaining

Bargaining for hotel rooms should become second nature. Before you agree to take a room, ask for a better price. *Tem desconto?* (Is there a discount?) and *Pode fazer um melhor preço?* (Can you make a better price?) are phrases to use. There's often a discount for paying *á vista* (cash) or for staying during the *época baixa* (low season) when hotels need guests to cover running costs. It's also possible to reduce the price if you state that you don't want a TV, private bath, or air-con. If you're staying longer than a couple of days, ask for a discount. Once a discount has been quoted, make sure it is noted on your bill at the same time – this avoids 'misunderstandings' at a later date. Bargain also in markets and unmetered taxis.

WHEN TO GO

See the Climate section in Facts about the Country for details of seasonal factors that may influence your decision on when to visit the country. There are few regions that can't be comfortably visited all year round.

WHAT TO BRING

The happiest travellers are those who can slip all their luggage under their plane seats. Pack light. Backpacks with detachable daypacks make a versatile combination. Travel packs are backpacks which can be converted into more civilised-looking suitcases. They are cleverly compartmentalised, and have internal frames and special padding.

Use small padlocks to secure your pack, particularly if you have to leave it unattended in one of the more down-market hotels that you are bound to encounter. For more details about security, refer to the section on Dangers & Annoyances in this chapter.

What you bring will be determined by what you do. If you're planning a river or jungle trip read the Amazon chapter in advance. If you're travelling cheap, a cotton sheet sleeping-sack will come in handy.

With its warm climate and informal dress standards, you don't need to bring many clothes to Brazil. Except for the South and Minas Gerais, where it gets cold in the winter, the only weather you need to contend with is heat and rain, and whatever you're lacking you can purchase while travelling. Buying clothes in Brazil is easy and has the added advantage of helping you appear less like a tourist – if you like to stand out in a crowd try wearing Birkenstock sandals and an American-style bathing suit on Brazil's beaches. The only exception is if you wear big sizes, which can be difficult to find, particularly for shoes.

However, you should be aware that unlike other basic necessities, clothing is not particularly cheap in Brazil. Shoes are the notable exception. You can get some good deals on leather shoes. Tennis shoes are the norm in Brazil, as are light jeans. Bring a pair of comfortable shorts and a light rain jacket. Bring your smallest bathing suit – men and women – which will certainly be much too modest for Brazil's beaches. So plan on buying a Brazilian suit *(maiô)* anyway. There are many funny T-shirts that are practical garments to buy along the way, and are also good souvenirs.

You don't need more than a pair of shorts, trousers, a couple of T-shirts, a long-sleeved shirt, bathing suit, towel, underwear, walking shoes, thongs and some raingear. Quick-drying, light cotton clothes are most convenient. Bring suntan lotion from home. Most other toiletries (even the same brand names) are available in Brazil.

Usually, one set of clothes to wear and one to wash is adequate. It's probably a good idea if one set of clothes is somewhat presentable or could pass as dress-up for a good restaurant or club (or to renew your visa at the federal police station). While dress is informal, many Brazilians are very fashion-conscious and pay close attention to both their own appearance and yours.

For information regarding compiling a basic medical kit, see the Health section in this chapter.

TOURIST OFFICES
Local Tourist Offices
Embratur, the Brazilian Tourist Board, recently moved its headquarters to Brasília, but still maintains an office in Rio de Janeiro at Rua Mariz e Barros 13 on the 14th floor. In Brasília, their new address is: Embratur, Setor Comercial Norte, Quadra 2, Bloco G, Brasília, DF, CEP 70710.

Tourist offices elsewhere in Brazil are generally sponsored by individual states and municipalities. In many places, these offices rely on shoestring budgets which are chopped or maintained according to the whims (or feuds!) of regional and local politicians. Some tourist offices clearly function only as a sinecure for the family and relatives of politicians; others have dedicated and knowledgeable staff who are interested in providing information. Some offices are conveniently placed in the centre of town; others are so far out of range that you'll need to launch an expedition and spend an entire

RESPEITE O TURISTA.

Respect the tourist.

day getting there. Keep your sense of humour, prepare for pot luck, and don't expect too much!

Overseas Reps
Brazilian tourism is represented outside Brazil exclusively by Funtur, the National Tourism Foundation. To date, Funtur has only two offices outside Brazil:

Germany
    Klein Hochstrasse 9, 6000 Frankfurt am Main 1
    (☎ (69) 289-683, fax (69) 29-5974)
USA
    551 5th Ave, Room 519, New York, NY 10176
    (☎ (212) 286-9600, fax (212) 490-9294)

Brazilian consulates and embassies are able to provide more limited tourist information.

USEFUL ORGANISATIONS
One of the most useful sources for visitors to South America is the South American Explorers Club, 126 Indian Creek Road, Ithaca, New York, USA 14850. This club provides services, information, and support

to travellers, scientific researchers, mountaineers, and explorers. It also sells a wide range of books, guides, and maps for South America, and publishes a quarterly journal and a mail order catalogue. If you're travelling elsewhere in South America, the club maintains clubhouses in Ecuador and Peru. Considering the massive package of benefits offered, membership is quite a bargain.

The Brazilian American Cultural Center (BACC; (☎ (212) 7301010; or toll-free (1-800) 222-2746), 16 West 46th St, New York, NY 10036, is a tourism organisation which offers its members discounted flights and tours. Members also receive a monthly newspaper about Brazil and the Brazilian community in the USA, and can send money to South America using BACC's remittance service. The organisation can also secure tourist visas for members through the Brazilian Consulate in New York.

For information about the growing network of Brazilian youth hostels, contact the Federação Brasileira dos Albergues de Juventude (FBAJ; (☎ (021) 252-4829), Rua da Assembléia 10, sala 1211 Centro, Rio de Janeiro, CEP 20011, RJ. Include an envelope and postage.

Disabled travellers in the USA might like to contact the Society for the Advancement of Travel for the Handicapped (☎ (718) 858-5483), 26 Court St, Brooklyn, New York, NY 11242. In the UK, a useful contact is the Royal Association for Disability & Rehabilitation (☎ (071) 242-3882), 25 Mortimer St, London W1N 8AB.

BUSINESS HOURS & HOLIDAYS
Business Hours
Most shops and government services (eg post office) are open Monday to Friday from 9 am to 6 pm and Saturday from 9 am to 1 pm. Because many Brazilians have little free time during the week, Saturday mornings are usually spent shopping. Some shops stay open later than 6 pm in the cities and the huge shopping malls often stay open until 10 pm. Banks, always in their own little world, are generally open from 10 am to 4.30 pm. Business hours vary by region and are taken less seriously in remote locations.

Holidays
National holidays fall on the following dates:

1 January
    New Year's Day
6 January
    Epiphany
February or March (four days before Ash Wednesday)
    Carnival
March or April
    Easter & Good Friday
21 April
    Tiradentes Day
1 May
    May Day
June
    Corpus Christi
7 September
    Independence Day
12 October
    Our Lady of Aparecida Day
2 November
    All Souls' Day
15 November
    Proclamation Day
25 December
    Christmas Day

Most states have several additional local holidays when everyone goes fishing.

FESTIVALS & CULTURAL EVENTS
Major festivals include:

January
    Torneio de Repentistas (Olinda, Pernambuco)
    Festa de São Lázaro (Salvador, Bahia)
1 January
    New Year & Festa de Iemanjá (Rio de Janeiro)
    Procissão do Senhor Bom Jesus dos Navegantes (Salvador, Bahia)
1 to 20 January
    Folia de Reis (Parati, Rio de Janeiro)
3 to 6 January
    Festa do Reis (Carpina, Pernambuco)
6 to 15 January
    Festa de Santo Amaro (Santo Amaro, Bahia)
2nd Sunday in January
    Bom Jesus dos Navegantes (Penedo, Alagoas)
2nd Thursday in January
    Lavagem do Bonfim (Salvador, Bahia)
24 January to 2 February
    NS de Nazaré (Nazaré, Bahia)

February
   Grande Vaquejada do Nordeste (Natal, Rio Grande do Norte)
2 February
   Festa de Iemanjá (Salvador, Bahia)
1st Saturday in February
   Buscada de Itamaracá (Itamaracá, Pernambuco)
February or March
   Lavagem da Igreja de Itapoã (Itapoã, Bahia)
   Shrove Tuesday (and the preceding three days to two weeks, depending on the place)
March
   Procissão do Encontro (Salvador, Bahia)
After Easter Week (usually April)
   Feiras dos Caxixis (Nazaré, Bahia)
Mid-April
   Drama da Paixão de Cristo (Brejo da Madre de Deus, Pernambuco)
15 days after Easter (April or May)
   Cavalhadas (Pirenópolis, Goiás)
45 days after Easter (between 6 May and 9 June)
   Micareta (Feira de Santana, Bahia)
Late May or early June
   Festa do Divino Espírito Santo (Parati, Rio de Janeiro)
June
   Festas Juninas & Bumba meu boi (celebrated throughout June in much of the country, particularly São Luis, Belém and throughout Pernambuco and Rio states)
   Festival Folclórico do Amazonas (Manaus, Amazonas)
22 to 24 June
   São João (Cachoeira, Bahia & Campina Grande, Paraíba)
July
   Festa do Divino (Diamantina, Minas Gerais)
   Regata de Jangadas Dragão do Mar (Fortaleza, Ceará)
17 to 19 July
   Missa do Vaqueiro (Serrita, Pernambuco)
Mid-August
   Festa da NS de Boa Morte (Cachoeira, Bahia)
15 August
   Festa de Iemanjá (Fortaleza, Ceará)
September
   Festival de Cirandas (Itamaracá, Pernambuco)
   Cavalhada (Caeté, Minas Gerais)
12 & 13 September
   Vaquejada de Surubim (Surubim, Pernambuco)
October (2nd half)
   NS do Rosário (Cachoeira, Bahia)
12 October
   Festa de Nossa Senhora Aparecida (Aparecida, São Paulo)
Starting 2nd Sunday in October
   Círio de Nazaré (Belém, Pará)
November
   NS da Ajuda (Cachoeira, Bahia)

1 & 2 November
   Festa do Padre Cícero (Juazeiro do Norte, Ceará)
4 to 6 December
   Festa de Santa Barbara (Salvador, Bahia)
8 December
   Festa de Nossa Senhora da Conceição (Salvador, Bahia)
   Festa de Iemanjá (Belém, Pará & João Pessoa, Paraíba)
31 December
   Celebração de Fim de Ano & Festa do Iemanjá (Rio de Janeiro)

POST & TELECOMMUNICATIONS
Postal Rates
Postal services are pretty good in Brazil. Most mail seems to get through, and airmail letters to the USA and Europe usually arrive in a week or so. For Australia, allow two weeks. The cost, however, is ridiculously high for mail leaving Brazil, almost US$1 for an international letter or postcard. Rates are raised very frequently, and are now amongst the highest in the world.

There are mail boxes on the street but it's a better idea to go to a post office. Most post offices *(correios)* are open 9 am to 6 pm Monday to Friday, and Saturday morning.

Receiving Mail
The *posta restante* system seems to function reasonably well and they will hold mail for 30 days. A reliable alternative for American Express customers is to have mail sent to one of its offices.

Telephone
International Calls Phoning abroad from Brazil is very expensive, and charges continue to be revised upwards at frequent intervals. To the USA and Canada, figure approximately US$3 a minute. Prices are 25% lower from 8 pm to 6 am daily and all day Sundays. To the UK the charge is US$3.50 a minute, and to Australia and New Zealand, US$5 a minute. There are no cheaper times to these last two countries.

Every town has a *posto telefônico* (phone company office) for long-distance calls, which require a large deposit. If you're

calling direct from a private phone dial 00, then the country code number, then the area code, then the phone number. So to call New York, you dial 001-212-(phone number). For information on international calls dial 000333. Some of the country code numbers are: UK 44, USA 1, Australia 61, New Zealand 64, Canada 1, Argentina 54, Chile 56, Peru 51, Paraguay 595.

International collect calls *(a cobrar)* can be made from any phone. To get the international operator dial 000111 or 107 and ask for the *telefonista internacional*. If they don't speak English you could experiment with some of the following phrases:

I would like to make an international call to...
Quero fazer uma ligação internacional para...
I would like to reverse the charges.
Quero fazê-la a cobrar.

I am calling from a public (private) telephone in Rio de Janeiro.
Estou falando dum telefone público (particular) no Rio de Janeiro.
My name is...
Meu nôme é...
The area code is...
O código é...
The number is...
O número é...

If you're having trouble, reception desks at the larger hotels can be helpful. Also, the phone books explain all this, but in Portuguese (although some have English translations).

National Calls National long-distance calls can also be made at the local phone company office, unless you're calling collect. All you need is the area code and phone number, and a few dollars. For calling collect within Brazil dial 107.

Area codes for the major cities are as follows:

Aracaju – 079
Belém – 091
Belo Horizonte – 031
Boa Vista – 095
Brasília – 061
Campo Grande – 067
Cuiabá – 065
Curitiba – 041
Florianópolis – 0482
Fortaleza – 085
Goiânia – 062
Macapá – 096
Maceío – 082
Manaus – 092
Natal – 084
Porto Alegre – 0512
Porto Velho – 069
Recife – 081
Rio Branco – 068
Rio de Janeiro – 021
Salvador – 071
São Luis – 098
São Paulo – 011
Teresina – 086
Vitória – 027

Local Calls Brazilian public phones are nicknamed *orelhões* (big ears). They use *fichas*, coin-like tokens, which can be bought at many newsstands, pharmacies, etc. They cost less than 5c, but it's a good idea to buy a few extra fichas as phones often consume them liberally.

On almost all phones in Brazil you wait for a dial tone and then deposit the ficha and dial your number. Each ficha is generally good for a couple of minutes, but the time can vary considerably. When your time is up, you will be disconnected without warning, so it's a good idea to deposit an extra ficha. To call the operator dial 100; for information call 102.

Phone Books There are several kinds of *lista telefônica* (telephone book) available. In larger cities there are two types of lista: *assinantes*, which lists names in alphabetical order; and *endereço*, which lists street names

in alphabetical order followed by house numbers, and the householder's name and phone number. The Brazilian equivalent of yellow pages is called Páginas Amarelas. Phone books for other parts of the country can be found at the larger telephone offices. Recently, telephone companies have been including excellent maps in phone books – see the Books & Maps section later in this chapter.

Fax, Telex & Telegraph
Post offices send and receive telegrams and the larger branches also have fax services. Fax costs US$13 per page to the USA and Canada, US$20 to Australia and New Zealand, and US$16 to the UK.

TIME
'Delay in Brazil is a climate. You live in it. You can't get away from it. There is nothing to be done about it...a man in a hurry will be miserable in Brazil.'

(*Brazilian Adventure* by Peter Fleming)

Brazil has four official time zones, generally depicted on maps as a neat series of lines. However, in the real world, these lines are subject to administrative convenience. This means that travellers are subject to the vagaries (and inconvenience) of geodesic demarcation, state boundaries, and the euphemistic term that saves the bacon of all officials – *acidentes geográficos* (geographical accidents). The Brazilian time system rewards unhurried travellers moving short distances – most other travellers have a few tales to tell about connections missed due to temporal ignorance.

The standard time zone for Brazil covers the eastern, north-eastern, southern, and south-eastern parts of Brazil, including Brasília, Amapá, Goiás, Tocantins, and a portion of Pará. This zone is three hours behind GMT. So when it is noon in Brazil it is 3 pm in London; 10 am in New York; 7 am in San Francisco; 1 am the next day in Sydney or Melbourne; and 11 pm in New Zealand.

Moving westwards, the next time zone

Time Zones

Hours Behind GMT

- 3 hours
- 4 hours
- 5 hours

Allow for daylight savings during summer (clocks move forward 1 hour).

ELECTRICITY

Electrical current is not standardised in Brazil, so it's a good idea to carry an adaptor if you can't travel without your hairdryer. In Rio de Janeiro and São Paulo, the current is almost exclusively 110 or 120 volts, 60 cycles, AC. Salvador and Manaus have 127 volt service. Recife, Brasília and various other cities have 220 volt service. Check before you plug in.

Speaking of plugs, the most common power points have two round sockets.

LAUNDRY

If you own the kind of clothes we do, it's cheaper to buy new ones than to have them cleaned at many city laundromats. While all other services are cheap in Brazil, oddly washing clothes isn't, at least if you send out. Most Brazilians wash their own clothes or have domestics do it. If you don't wish to wash your own, enquire at your hotel, as often the housekeepers will wash clothes at home to make a few extra cruzeiros.

WEIGHTS & MEASURES

Brazil uses the metric system. There is a metric conversion table at the back of this book.

BOOKS & MAPS
History

Brazil has a fascinating and fantastic history, but for some reason none of the good surveys of Brazilian history have been translated into English. So the best way to go, if you want to understand the flow of Brazilian history in English, is via several excellent narratives.

John Hemming's *Red Gold: The Conquest of the Brazilian Indians* follows the colonists and Indians from 1500 to 1760, when the great majority of Indians were effectively either eliminated or pacified. Hemming, a founder of Survival International and eloquent campaigner for Indian rights, has extended his analysis of Indian history in *Amazon Frontier: The Defeat of the Brazilian Indians* (Harvard University Press, 1987).

Caio Prado Junior, Brazil's leading economic historian, presents a descriptive

covers part of Pará; Roraima, Rondônia, Mato Grosso, Mato Grosso do Sul; and all but the far western fringe of Amazonas. This zone is one hour behind Brazilian standard time, and four hours behind GMT.

The time zone for the far west covers Acre and the western fringe of Amazonas, which are two hours behind Brazilian standard time, and five hours behind GMT.

The island of Fernando de Noronha, far to the east of the Brazilian mainland, has its own time zone, which is one hour ahead of standard Brazilian time, and two hours behind GMT.

Finally, connoisseurs of Brazilian timekeeping will be thrilled to hear that all these time zones may vary if Brazil continues to adopt daylight savings time, which requires clocks to be set one hour ahead in October, and one hour back in March or April.

Brazilians, by the way, are not noted for their punctuality! Don't be surprised, or angry, if they arrive a couple of hours later than expected. To them it is acceptable, and they always have the most inventive reasons for not arriving on time. If you find yourself arriving late, you might like to blame it on an accident – geographical perhaps?

analysis of the legacy of Brazil's colonial past in *The Colonial Background of Modern Brazil*. It's probably the single best interpretation of the colonial period in English: Prado presents a sweeping view of Brazil's lack of development, which he blames on the export-based economy and the social relations of slavery.

Celso Furtado, a leading economist and the current Minister of Culture in Brazil, has written a good introductory economic history of the country titled *The Economic Growth of Brazil* (Greenwood, 1984).

Charles R Boxer is from the good old school of British economic history, which took writing seriously. All his books are fine reading and illuminating history. His *Golden Age of Brazil, 1695-1750* (University of California Press, 1962) has an excellent introductory chapter summarising life in 17th-century Brazil, and then focuses on the gold rush in Minas Gerais and its consequences in the rest of the colony. Boxer has also written *Salvador de Sá & the Struggle for Brazil & Angola, 1602-1686* and *The Dutch in Brazil, 1624-1654*.

The most famous book on Brazil's colonial period is Gilberto Freyre's *The Masters & the Slaves: A Study in the Development of Brazilian Civilization* (University of California Press, 1986). There's a new paperback edition from the University of California Press, which is also publishing Freyre's other works: *The Mansions & the Shanties: The Making of Modern Brazil* (University of California Press, 1986) and *Order & Progress: Brazil from Monarchy to Republic* (University of California Press, 1986).

Freyre's argument that Brazilian slavery was less harsh than in the USA and that through miscegenation Brazil has avoided the racial problems of the USA is deeply flawed. It contributed to the myth of racial democracy in Brazil and has been severely rebuked by academics over the last 20 years. Still, Freyre's books can be read on many levels, including social history, and there are fascinating comments (read the footnotes) on folklore, myths and superstition, religion, sexuality, etc.

Emília Viotti da Costa has a collection of well-written essays in English which is one of the best treatments of 19th-century Brazil. *The Brazilian Empire: Myths & Histories* (University of Chicago Press, 1986) interweaves the ideological and economic components of Brazilian history, and the results are illuminating and suggestive. Her essays, particularly on slavery and the landless poor, explode many of the harmony myths that hide the realities of oppression and poverty.

The English narratives on 20th-century Brazilian history are less satisfying. Peter Flynn's *Brazil: A Political Analysis* presents a political history from 1889 to 1977. Thomas Skidmore's *Politics in Brazil, 1930-1964* is good. And Irving L Horowitz covers the Goulart era in *Revolution in Brazil*.

Alfred Stepan has edited a collection of essays called *Authoritarian Brazil: Origins, Policies & Future* (Yale University Press, 1973). These are often theoretically heavy, but quite interesting, particularly the essays by Fishlow, Cardoso and Schmitter.

Finally, the not-to-be-believed rebellion in Canudos by the followers of the mystic Antônio Conselheiro has been immortalised in *Rebellion in the Backlands* (University of Chicago Press, 1985), by Euclides da Cunha. Mixing history, geography and philosophy, *Os Sertões* (in Portuguese) is considered the masterpiece of Brazilian literature. It's an incredible story about the outcasts of the Northeast, and is a sort of meditation on Brazilian civilisation. The story of the author and the rebellion is told by Mário Vargas Llosa in his novel *The War of the End of the World* (Avon Bard, 1985); entertaining, light reading for the traveller.

Fiction

For a description of Brazilian literature and suggested reading, refer to the Arts section (Literature) in the Facts about the Country chapter.

Travel

Peter Fleming's *Brazilian Adventure* (Penguin, 1978) is about the young journalist's expedition into Mato Grosso in search of Colonel Fawcett, who had disappeared. At the time this area was the world's last, vast unexplored region. What Fleming found is less important than the telling: written with the humour of the disenchanted Briton, travel adventures don't get any funnier than this. Highly recommended.

While it's not all about Brazil, Peter Mattheissen's *The Cloud Forest* (Collins Harrill, 1960), an account of his 30,000-km journey across the South American wilderness from the Amazon to Tierra del Fuego, is well worth a read. Mattheissen is a master at describing the environment that surrounds him. Moritz Thomsen's *The Saddest Pleasure: A Journey on Two Rivers* (1990, Graywolf Press) is a highly recommended book – skip the sickly introduction – about the author's experiences in South America, including journeys through Brazil and along the Amazon.

Although currently out of print, *Valley of the Latin Bear* by Alexander Lenard merits reading if you're interested in village life in the interior of southern Brazil. The Hungarian author is best known for his *Winnie ille Pu*, a Latin translation of the famous Edward Bear book.

For readers who like their history with a dose of fiction, *Brazil* (Simon & Schuster, 1986) by Errol Lincoln Uys, is an interesting novel that traces the history of two Brazilian families from pre-Cabral times to the foundation of Brasília.

In the 19th century, practically every Westerner who visited Brazil seems to have written a travelogue, and some, with their keen powers of observation, are quite good. Maria Graham's *Journal of a Voyage to Brazil & Residence there During Part of the Years 1821, 1822, 1823* is as precise as the title suggests. Henry Koster wrote *Travels in Brazil* in 1816; Herbert H Smith wrote *Brazil, the Amazon & the Coast* in 1880.

The Amazon & Indians

The first and last word on the history of the Portuguese colonisation, the warring and the enslavement of the Indian is *Red Gold* (Harvard University Press, 1978) by John Hemming. Hemming has brought Indian history up to date in *Amazon Frontier: The Defeat of the Brazilian Indians* (Harvard University Press, 1987).

Other interesting titles are *The Last Indians: South America's Cultural Heritage* by Fritz Tupp, *Aromeri Brazilian Indian Feather Art* by Norberto Nícola and Sónia Ferraro and *Aborigines of the Amazon Rain Forest: The Yanomami* (Time Life Books, 1982) by Robin Hanbury-Tenison. *Amazonia* (1991), by Loren McIntyre, the renowned explorer and photographer, records in magnificent photographs the gradual demise of the region and its original inhabitants. To learn more about McIntyre's many journeys in search of the source of the Amazon and his extraordinary psychic experiences with indigenous tribes, pick up a copy of *Amazon Beaming* (1991) by Petru Popescu.

The works of Márcio Souza (see Literature in the Facts about the Country chapter), a skillful Brazilian satirist, are set in the Amazon. Anthropologist Darcy Ribeiro's interesting novel *Maíra* (Random House 1983) is about the clash between Indian animism and Catholicism.

Alex Shoumatoff has written three excellent Amazon books, all of them entertaining combinations of history, myth and travelogue. His latest work, *The World is Burning* (Little Brown, 1990), recounts the Chico Mendes story.

Armchair adventurers will enjoy Spix & Martius' *Travels Brazil*, a three-volume chronology of the pair's 3½-year journey from 1817 to 1820. Illustrated with wonderful etchings, it is a biologist's record of customs, social life, ethnology and a description of flora and fauna. You may still be able to find secondhand copies of George Woodcock's *Henry Walter Bates, Naturalist of the Amazons* (Faber & Faber, 1969), a fascinating account of Bates' many years spent in pursuit of plantlife during the mid-19th century .

Those interested in *yagé*, the hallucinogenic drug used by certain tribes of the upper

Amazon, will find *Wizard of the Upper Amazon – the Story of Manuel Córdova-Rios* (Houghton Mifflin, 1975) and the sequel *Rio Tigre and Beyond* by F Bruce Lamb interesting reading.

The Fate of the Forest: Developers, Destroyers, and Defenders of the Amazon (Verso, 1989) by Susanna Hecht & Alexander Cockburn is one of the best analyses of the complex web of destruction, and provides ideas on ways to mend the damage. Arnold Newman's *Tropical Rainforest: A World Survey of Our Most Valuable and Endangered Habitat with a Blueprint for its Survival* is a massive analysis of rainforest destruction and possible alternatives for sound forest management. *People of the Tropical Rainforest* (University of California Press & Smithsonian Institute, 1988) is a compilation of writings about the rainforest by experts on the subject. Augusta Dwyer delivers a fierce indictment of corruption and mismanagement in the Amazon in *Into the Amazon: The Struggle for the Amazon.*

The Rainforest Book (Living Planet, 1990) by Scott Lewis is a concise analysis of rainforest problems and remedies. It's packed with examples which link consumer behaviour with rainforest development; listings of organisations to contact; and advice on individual involvement. A similar publication compiled by the Seattle Audubon Society and the Puget Consumers Co-operative is the booklet entitled *Rainforests Forever: Consumer Choices to Help Preserve Tropical Rainforests* (1990).

Flora & Fauna Guides

Rainforests – A Guide to Tourist and Research Facilities at Selected Tropical Forest Sites in Central and South America by James L Castner is full of information and well worth getting hold of if you want to do some research or even just visit the rainforest.

Margaret Mee's *In Search of the Flowers of the Amazon Forest* is beautifully illustrated, and highly recommended for anyone (not just botanists) interested in the Amazon.

Neotropical Rainforest Mammals: A Field Guide by Louise Emmons & François Feer provides colour illustrations to identify mammals of the rainforest. For a reference work, rather than a field guide, you could consult the *World of Wildlife: Animals of South America* (Orbis Publishing, 1975) by F R de la Fuente.

Birders in the Amazon region of Brazil often use field guides for adjacent countries – many species overlap. Amateur interests should be satisfied with titles such as *South American Birds: A Photographic Aid to Identification* (1987) by John S Dunning; or *A Guide to the Birds of Venezuela* by Rodolphe de Schauensee & William Phelps. For a definitive tome, rather than a lightweight guide, you could start with *A Guide to the Birds of South America* (Academy of Natural Science, Philadelphia).

Last, but not least, for some fascinating oddities you should dip into *Ecology of Tropical Rainforests: An introduction for Eco-tourists* (Free University Amsterdam, 1990) by Piet van Ipenburg & Rob Boschhuizen. This mini-booklet is packed with intriguing and bizarre scientific minutiae about sloths, bats, the strangling fig, etc; and more extraordinary details of rainforest ecology. Available in the UK from J Forrest, 64 Belsize Park, London NW3 4EH; or in the USA from M Doolittle, 32 Amy Rd, Falls Village, CT 06031. All proceeds from sales of this booklet go to the Tambopata Reserve Society, which is funding research in the Tambopata Reserve in the rainforests of south-eastern Peru.

Travel Guides

A Brazilian travel guide is published annually by Quatro Rodas. Called *Quatro Rodas: Guia Brasil*, it's readily available at most newsagents and contains a wealth of information about accommodation, restaurants, transport, sights, etc. If you buy it in Brazil it also comes with an excellent fold-out map of the country. It doesn't cover budget options, and you need a reasonable knowledge of Portuguese to make the most of it. For details of additional mapping published by Quatro Rodas, see the section on maps later in this chapter.

The *South American Handbook* (Trade & Travel Publications) contains a huge volume of information. It is useful for travel in Brazil, but haphazard updating has resulted in contradiction and a confusing layout. Travellers planning river trips on their own will find practical advice in *South American River Trips* (Bradt Publications, 1982) and *Up the Creek* (Bradt Publications, 1986). *Backcountry Brazil* (Bradt Publications, 1990) provides useful supplementary information if you want to skip the cities.

Religion

The strength and cultural richness of Candomblé has attracted and inspired a number of perceptive Western authors, several of whom were converted. *Orixás* by Pierre Fatumbi Verger is a photo book comparing the Brazilian and African religions. *The African Religions of Brazil* (John Hopkins, 1978), by the well-known French anthropologist Roger Bastide, is a scholarly look at social forces which shaped Candomblé. Ruth Landes' *The City of Women* is about Candomblé in Bahia. For a quick overview in Portuguese, dip into *ABC do Candomblé* by Vasconcelos Maia. Edison Carneiro, a famous student of Candomblé, has written about the subject in *Candomblé da Bahia*. For light reading, try Jorge Amado's novel *Dona Flor and Her Two Husbands*, which is available in English translation.

Other Subjects

Florestan Fernandes' *The Negro in Brazilian Society* was one of the first books to challenge the myth of racial democracy. Thomas Skidmore's *Black into White: Race & Nationality in Brazilian Thought* is an intellectual history of the racial issue.

Carolina Maria de Jesus lived and wrote in the slums of São Paulo. Her book *Child of the Dark* (NAL, 1965) is strong and compelling. It was published in the UK and Australia under the title *Beyond All Pity*. In *The Myth of Marginality: Urban Politics &*

Poverty in Rio de Janeiro (University of California Press, 1976) Janice Perlman debunks some of the myths of life in the favelas.

Maps

Given the size of Brazil, it's essential to be armed with decent mapping which gives a clear idea of scale. It's very easy to underestimate distances and the time required for travel, particularly if you plan to visit several regions using the roads rather than the airports.

In the USA, Maplink (☎ (805) 965-4402), 25 E Mason St, Dept G, Santa Barbara, CA 93101, is an excellent and exhaustive source for maps of Brazil and just about anywhere else in the world. A similarly extensive selection of mapping is available in the UK from Stanfords (☎ (071) 836-1321), 12-14 Long Acre, London WC2E 9LP.

For general mapping of South America with excellent topographical detail, it's hard to beat the sectional maps published by International Travel Map Productions (Canada). Coverage of Brazil is provided in *South America – South* (1987); *South America – North East* (1989); *South America – North West* (1987); and *Amazon Basin* (1991).

Within Brazil, the mapping used by most Brazilian and foreign travellers is produced by Quatro Rodas, which also publishes the essential *Quatro Rodas: Guia Brasil*, an annually updated travel guide in Portuguese. This guide is complemented by *Guia Rodoviário*, a compact book of maps in a handy plastic case, which covers individual states and provides useful distance charts.

The city maps provided in *Quatro Rodas: Guia Brasil* help with orientation. It's very much a question of pot luck if you hunt for maps from tourist offices. If you're after detailed street layout, take a look at the phone books. The telephone companies in many states include excellent city maps either in the Lista Telefônica (White Pages) or in the Páginas Amarelas (Yellow Pages); and the same companies are also starting to distribute 'Shopping maps' which are equally useful.

MEDIA

Brazil's media industry is concentrated in the hands of a few organisations. The companies that own the two major TV stations, O Globo and Manchete, also control several of the nation's leading newspapers and magazines.

Newspapers & Magazines

English In major Brazilian cities you will find three daily newspapers in English. The best by far is the Latin American edition of the *Miami Herald*. This paper isn't cheap, but it's current and fairly comprehensive. Its strong points are Latin America and the American sports scene.

The *Brazil Post* is published Tuesday to Saturday in Brazil. It has advertisements in English for both São Paulo and Rio, including apartment rentals, and general news. The *International Herald Tribune* has articles from the *New York Times* and the *Washington Post*, but it's a pretty thin paper, and more expensive than the other two newspapers.

Time and *Newsweek* magazines are available throughout Brazil. What can one say about these icons? Their coverage is weakest where the *Miami Herald* is strongest: Latin America and sports. The *Economist* is sold in Rio and São Paulo, but it costs about US$4. In the big cities you can find all sorts of imported newspapers and magazines at some newsstands, but they are very expensive.

Portuguese The *Folha de São Paulo* is Brazil's finest newspaper. It has excellent coverage of national and international events and is a good source for entertainment in São Paulo. The Turismo section in the Thursday edition always has a table showing costs of internal flights, and another giving bus times and costs (from São Paulo). It's available in Rio and other major cities. The *Jornal do Brasil* and *O Globo* are Rio's main daily papers. Both have entertainment listings. *Balcão* is a Rio weekly with only classified advertisements, a good source for buying anything. *O Nacional* is a weekly paper that has some excellent critical columnists. *O Povo* is a popular daily with lots of gory photographs.

Among weekly magazines, *Veja*, the Brazilian *Time* clone, is the country's best-selling magazine. It's easy reading if you want to practise your Portuguese. *Isto É Senhor* has the best political and economic analysis, and reproduces international articles from the British *Economist*, but it's not light reading. It also provides good coverage of current events.

The latest environmental and ecological issues (both national and international) are covered in the monthly magazine, *Ecología e Desenvolvimento*, which was launched in 1991 by Editora Terceiro Mundo (☎ 252-7440), Rua da Glória, 122, Salas 105-6, CEP 20241, Rio de Janeiro, RJ.

Sources of information and literature about Brazilian Indians are given in the Population & People section of the Facts about the Country chapter, and in the Books & Maps section of this chapter.

TV

English If you are having second thoughts about visiting Brazil because you don't want to miss the Superbowl, Wimbledon or, perhaps, The Miss Teen America Pageant, relax and go ahead and make those reservations. Thanks to the parabolic antenna, cable TV and the hospitality of the Sheraton, the Inter Continental or any of several other big hotels, all the major American TV events are shown in Rio and São Paulo.

Portuguese Many of the worst American movies and TV shows are dubbed into Portuguese and shown on Brazilian TV. Brazil's most famous TV hosts, who have to be seen to be believed, are Xuxa, the queen of kiddy titillation, and Faustão. Both are strong statements on the evil of TV. Both are on the tube for countless hours, Xuxa on weekdays, Faustão on Sundays.

Xuxa has coquettishly danced and sang her way into the hearts of tiny Brazilians everywhere. She is living proof that Freud had it right about children's sexuality. Faustão hosts *Domingão de Faustão*, a seemingly endless bump'n'grind variety show.

What is worth watching? On Sunday nights, starting at 9 or 10 pm, you can see the highlights of soccer matches played that day. And there's a good comedy show that starts daily at 5.30 pm called *Escolinha do Professore Raimundo*.

The most popular programmes on Brazilian TV are the *novelas* (soap operas), which are followed religiously by many Brazilians. These are actually quite good, and easy to understand if you speak some Portuguese. They often feature some of Brazil's best actors, and pioneer new techniques in the genre; several have had successful runs on European TV. The novelas go on the air at various times from 7 to 9 pm.

The news is on several times a night, but broadcast times vary from place to place. O Globo and Manchete, the two principal national networks, both have rather pedestrian national news shows. *Aqui Agora* (Here Now) is a sensational news show on SBT that is worth a look, even if you don't understand Portuguese. Among other things, it has a nightly economic comment from the Brazilian heavyweight boxing champion wearing a tuxedo and boxing gloves.

Cable TV is a recent addition to the airwaves, with ESPN (the sports network), CNN (Cable News Network), RAI (Radio Televisione Italia), and, of course, MTV (music television) available to those few who can afford them.

FILM & PHOTOGRAPHY

Cameras are expensive and cumbersome objects. They will certainly be abused on the road and they may get broken, lost or stolen. But there are so many good shots out there that you'll kick yourself if you don't bring one along.

Your choice of camera will depend on your photographic requirements. Automatic 35-mm rangefinders will suffice for standard portraits and landscapes . But if you want to take general wildlife shots, a 200-mm or 300-mm zoom lens is essential. A 400-mm or 500-mm telephoto (fixed focal length) lens is preferred by photographers who are after close-up shots of wildlife.

If you want to get the right exposure, photography in the rainforest will require careful consideration of the lack of light. You'll have to experiment with a combination of fast film (400 ASA and upwards), tripod, flash unit, and cable release. When exposed to the humid conditions of the forest for an extended period of time, your cameras and lenses may have their functioning impaired by fungus growth. The standard preventative is to keep your photographic gear sealed in bags together with silica-gel packs. Unseal only for use and reseal everything immediately after each photo session.

If you're shooting on beaches, remember to adjust for the glare from water or sand; and keep sand and salt water away from your equipment.

Useful accessories would include a small flash, a cable release, a polarising filter, a lens cleaning kit (fluid, tissue, aerosol), plenty of silica-gel packs, and a bean bag (or clamp ormonopod). Don't carry a flashy camera bag – use something less likely to attract the attention of thieves; and make sure your equipment is insured.

Photographic equipment and accessories are expensive in Brazil and you'd be well advised to buy your film and equipment before arrival. However, Kodak and Fuji print film is sold and processed almost everywhere. You can only get Ektachrome or Kodachrome slide film developed in the big cities and it's expensive to buy. If you're shooting slides it's best to bring film with you and have it processed back home. Heat and humidity can ruin film, so remember to keep it in the coolest, driest place available. Use a lead film bag to protect film from airport X-ray machines. This is especially important for the sensitive high-ASA films.

If you must get your film processed in Brazil, have it done either at a large lab in São Paulo or in Rio at Kronokroma Foto (☎ 285-1993) at Rua Russel 344, Loja E, near Praia do Flamengo's Hotel Glória. Bring in exposed film in the morning, when the chemical baths are fresh. In Rio the

Fomar Photo Store (☎ 221-2332) at Rua São Jose 90 off Avenida Rio Branco sells some camera accessories. Their friendly staff do quick camera cleaning. If your Nikon is on the blink, speak to Louis (☎ 220-1127) at Franklin Roosevelt 39 on the 6th floor near the US Consulate.

It's foolish to bring a camera to a beach unless it will be closely guarded – for more advice on camera security see the Dangers & Annoyances section in this chapter. Some Candomblé temples do not permit photography. Respect the wishes of the locals and ask permission before taking a photo of them.

HEALTH

Travel health depends on predeparture preparations, day-to-day attention to health-related matters, and the manner of handling medical emergencies if they do arise. The following health section may seem like a who's who of dreadfully unpleasant diseases, but your chances of contracting a serious illness in Brazil are slight. You will, however, be exposed to environmental factors, foods and sanitation standards that are probably quite different from what you're used to; but if you take the recommended jabs, faithfully pop your antimalarials and use common sense, there shouldn't be any problems.

While there's no worry of any strange tropical diseases in Rio and points further south, Amazonas, Pará, Mato Grosso, Amapá, Rondônia, Goiás, Espírito Santo and the Northeast have some combination of the following: malaria, yellow fever, dengue fever, leprosy, and leishmaniasis. Health officials periodically announce high rates of tuberculosis, polio, sexually transmitted diseases, hepatitis and other endemic diseases.

The following rundown of health risks includes some preventative measures, symptom descriptions and suggestions about what to do if there is a problem. It isn't meant to replace professional diagnosis or prescription, and visitors to the developing world should discuss with their physician the most up-to-date methods used to prevent and treat

the threats to health which may be encountered.

Predeparture Preparations
Health Insurance A travel insurance policy to cover theft, loss and medical problems is a wise idea. Before heading abroad, travellers should get up-to-date information. There is a wide variety of policies; contact either your travel agent or one of the organisations mentioned under Travel Health Information.

When buying a policy, it's important to check the small print. Some policies specifically exclude 'dangerous activities' which can include scuba diving, motorcycling or even trekking. If these activities are on your agenda, such a policy would be of limited value.

You may prefer a policy which pays doctors or hospitals directly rather than requiring you to pay first and claim later. If you must claim after the fact, however, be sure you keep all documentation. Some policies ask you to phone (reverse charges) a centre in your home country where an immediate assessment of the problem will be made.

Check on the policy's coverage of emergency transport or evacuation back to your home country. If you have to stretch out across several airline seats, someone has to pay for it!

Travel Health Information In the USA you can contact the Overseas Citizens Emergency Center and request a health and safety information bulletin on Brazil by writing to the Bureau of Consular Affairs Office, State Department, Washington, DC 20520. This office also has a special telephone number for emergencies while abroad: (202) 632-5525.

Read the Center for Disease Control's *Health Information for International Travel* supplement of *Morbidity & Mortality Weekly Report* or the World Health Organisation's *Vaccination Certificate Requirements for International Travel & Health Advice to Travellers*. Both of these sources (CDC and WHO) are superior to the Travel Information

Manual published by the International Air Transport Association.

The International Association for Medical Assistance to Travelers (IAMAT) at 417 Center St, Lewiston, New York, NY 14092 can provide you with a list of English-speaking physicians in Brazil.

In the UK, contact Medical Advisory Services for Travellers Abroad (MASTA; (☎ (071) 631-4408), Keppel St, London WC1E 7HT). MASTA provides a wide range of services, including a choice of concise or comprehensive 'Health Briefs' and a range of medical supplies. Another source of medical information and supplies is the British Airways Travel Clinic (☎ (071) 831-5333).

In Australia you could contact the Traveller's Medical & Vaccination Centre in Sydney (☎ (02) 221-7133) or Melbourne (☎ (03) 650-7600) for general health information pertaining to Brazil.

In Brazil, the Rio Health Collective (☎ 325-9300 extension 44) can put you in touch with an English-speaking doctor. They have a 24-hour answering service.

Public Health in Brazil

Life expectancy, like infant mortality, is a gross index of health care and development. In the southern states of Santa Catarina and Rio Grande do Sul the figures approach those of the USA and Western Europe; cancer and circulatory diseases are the biggest threats. In the North and Northeast, where infectious and parasitic diseases exact a very high toll, the life expectancy is less than 50 years. Pockets of poverty in the Northeast, like the border region between Pernambuco and Paraíba, have life expectancies as low as 39 – rivalling the worst of war-torn Third World nations in Africa and Asia.

The infant mortality rate is about 90 per 1000 in Northeastern Brazil, but poor health is not confined to the North and the Northeast. The urban slums of the large southern cities are just as miserable. In Nova Iguaçu, a poor and dangerous suburb of Rio de Janeiro, 150 out of every 1000 babies die before the end of their first year. These figures are shocking in comparison to wealthier Brazilian community rates of 10 per 1000.

These statistics are attributable to diarrhoea and other infectious diseases caused by lack of sanitation, inadequate access to medical care and poor nutrition. According to government statistics, nearly one-third of Brazil's population is undernourished. The huge discrepancy in longevity and the quality of health is an indicator of the vast difference between the wealthy and poor in Brazil.

According to transmissible disease reports, there are 160,000 new cases of malaria per year. In 1986 there were 430,000 cases of malaria and 600,000 by 1991. In 1986 there were said to be some six million sufferers of Chagas' disease, between six and eight million people with schistosomiasis, 220,000 with leprosy (there are even some cases in the South), 72,000 with measles, 56,000 with tuberculosis, 4200 with typhoid fever, 300 with bubonic plague (there was an outbreak in Paraíba) and 156 victims of polio.

Hospitals & Pharmacies It's not necessary to take with you every remedy for every illness you might conceivably contract during your trip. Pharmacies stock all kinds of drugs and sell them much more cheaply than in the West. There are few restricted medications, so practically everything is sold over the counter. In the past, foreign pharmaceutical industries sold drugs which had exceeded their shelf life to South American firms, but fortunately this practice is not as widespread as it was previously. Nearly all drugs are manufactured by firms in São Paulo under foreign licence. However, when buying drugs anywhere in South America, be sure to check expiry dates and storage conditions. Some drugs available there may no longer be recommended, or may even be banned, in other countries.

In addition, travellers should be aware of any drug allergies they may have and avoid using such drugs or their derivatives while travelling in Brazil. Since common names of prescription medicines in South America are likely to be different from the ones you're used to, ask a pharmacist before taking anything you're not sure about.

Pharmacies in Brazil are known as *farmácias* and medicines are called *remédios*. The word for doctor is *doutor* or *médico*; and medicine tablets are known as *comprimidos*.

Some pharmacists will give injections (with or without prescriptions). This is true of the Drogaleve pharmacy chain. Sometimes hygiene is questionable, so always purchase fresh needles, and make sure other health professionals take similar precautions.

Some private medical facilities in Rio de Janeiro and São Paulo are on a par with US hospitals, but be wary of public hospitals in the interior. They are notorious for re-using syringes after quick dips in alcohol baths, for lack of soap, and other unsanitary practices. University hospitals are likely to have English-speaking physicians. UK and US consulates have lists of English-speaking physicians.

Brazilian blood banks don't always screen carefully. Hepatitis B is rampant, so if you should require a blood transfusion, do as the Brazilians do: have your friends blood-typed and choose your blood donor in advance.

Medical Kit It's a good idea to carry a small, straightforward medical kit, which may include:

- Aspirin or paracetamol (acetominophen in North America) – for pain or fever
- Antihistamine (such as Benadryl) – useful as a decongestant for colds and allergies, to ease itching from insect bites, or to prevent motion sickness
- Antibiotics – useful if you're travelling off the beaten track. Most antibiotics are prescription medicines
- Kaolin and pectin preparation such as Pepto – Bismol for stomach upsets and Imodium or Lomotil to bung things up in case of emergencies during long-distance travel
- Rehydration mixture – for treatment of severe

diarrhoea. This is particularly important when travelling with children.
- Antiseptic liquid or cream and antibiotic powder for minor injuries
- Calamine lotion – to ease irritation from bites and stings
- Bandages and band-aids
- Scissors, tweezers, and a thermometer – but remember that you cannot transport mercury thermometers on airlines
- Insect repellent, sunblock (15+), suntan lotion, chap stick and water purification tablets (or iodine)
- Sterile syringes are recommended for travel in Amazônia, particularly Brazil, due to the AIDS risk. Be sure you have at least one large enough for a blood test – those normally used for injections are too small. For sources of requisite medical supplies, refer to the Travel Health Information section.

Ideally, antibiotics should be administered only under medical supervision and should never be taken indiscriminately. Overuse of antibiotics can weaken your immune system and can reduce the drug's efficacy in the future. Take only the recommended dosage at the prescribed intervals and continue using the antibiotic for the prescribed period, even if you're feeling better sooner. Antibiotics are quite specific to the infections they will react with so if you're in doubt about a drug's effects or suffer any unexpected reactions, discontinue use immediately.

Health Preparations Make sure you're healthy before embarking on a long journey, have your teeth checked and if you wear glasses or contacts, bring a spare pair and a copy of your optical prescription. Losing your glasses may be a real problem in remoter areas, but in larger Brazilian cities you can have a new pair made with little fuss.

At least one pair of good-quality sunglasses is essential, as the glare is terrific and dust and blown sand can get into the corners of your eyes. A hat, sunscreen lotion and lip protection are also essential.

Particular medications may not be available locally. Take the prescription with the generic rather than brand name so it will be universally recognisable. It's also wise to carry a copy of the prescription to prove you're using the medication legally.

Customs and immigration officers may get excited at the sight of syringes or mysterious powdery preparations. The organisations listed in the Travel Health Information section can provide medical supplies such as syringes, together with multilingual customs documentation.

Immunisations Vaccinations provide protection against diseases you may encounter along the way. A yellow fever vaccination and related documentation is strongly recommended for every traveller in Brazil. In addition, Brazilian authorities will not grant entrance, especially in Amazônia, without it. The vaccination certificate remains effective for 10 years. Other commonly recommended jabs for travel to South America are typhoid, tetanus DPT, polio, and meningitis vaccines as well as gamma globulin as protection against hepatitis. Some physicians will also recommend a cholera vaccine but its effectiveness is minimal.

Cholera Although many countries require this vaccine, it lasts only six months and is not recommended for pregnant women.

Tetanus DPT Boosters are necessary at least every 10 years and are highly recommended as a matter of course.

Polio Polio is endemic in Brazil; recent outbreaks have been reported in the southern states of Paraná, Santa Catarina and Rio Grande do Sul. A complete immunisation series should be boosted if more than 10 years have elapsed since the last course.

Typhoid Protection lasts for three years and is useful if you are travelling for longer periods in rural tropical areas. The most common side effects from this vaccine are pain at the injection site, fever, headache, and a general unwell feeling.

Gamma Globulin Gamma globulin is not a vaccination but a ready-made antibody which has proven successful in reducing the chances of contracting infectious hepatitis (hepatitis A). Because it may interfere with the development of immunity, it should not be given until at least 10 days after administration of the last vaccine needed, and as near as possible to departure due to its relatively short-lived effectiveness – normally about six months.

Yellow Fever Protection lasts for 10 years and is recommended for all travel to South America. You usually need to visit a special yellow fever vaccination centre. Vaccination isn't recommended during pregnancy, but if you must travel to a high-risk area, it is still probably better to take the vaccine. Once you've taken the jabs, keep the yellow WHO certificate in your passport to avoid problems when passing through Acre, Amapá, Amazonas, Maranhão, Mato Grosso and Mato Grosso do Sul, Tocantins, Pará, Rondônia and Roraima.

Basic Rules

Food & Water Care in what you eat and drink is the most important health rule; stomach upsets are the most common travel health problem but the majority of these upsets will be minor. Don't be paranoid about sampling local foods – it's all part of the travel experience and shouldn't be missed.

As a general rule, Brazilian tap water isn't potable. The simplest way to purify suspect water is to boil it for eight to 10 minutes. Simple filtering won't remove all dangerous organisms, so if you can't boil suspect water, it should be treated chemically. Chlorine tablets (Puritabs, Steritabs and other brand names) will kill many but not all pathogens. Iodine is very effective and is available in tablet form (such as Potable Aqua) but follow the directions carefully and remember that too much iodine will be harmful.

If you can't find tablets, tincture of iodine (2%) or iodine crystals may be used. Add two drops of tincture of iodine per litre or quart of water and let stand for 30 minutes. Iodine crystals can also be used to purify water, but this is a more complicated and dangerous process since you first must prepare a saturated iodine solution. Iodine loses its effectiveness if exposed to air or damp so keep it in a tightly sealed container. Flavoured powder will disguise the normally foul taste of iodine-treated water and is an especially good idea for those travelling with children.

When it's hot, be sure to drink lots of liquids. Excessive sweating can lead to loss of salt and cause muscle cramping. Failure to urinate or dark yellow urine is a sign of dehydration. Always carry a bottle of water on long trips.

Reputable brands of bottled water or soft drinks are normally fine, although sometimes water bottles are refilled and resold – check the seals before buying. In rural areas, take care with fruit juices since water may have been added. Milk should be treated with suspicion as it is often unpasteurised. Boiled milk is fine if it is kept hygienically and yoghurt is always good. Tea or coffee should also be OK, since the water used was probably boiled.

Salads and fruit should be washed with purified water or peeled where possible. Ice cream is usually OK but beware of ice cream that has melted and been refrozen. Thoroughly cooked food is safest but not if it has been left to cool or if it has been reheated. Take great care with shellfish or fish and avoid undercooked meat. If a place looks clean and well run and the vendor also looks clean and healthy, then the food is probably all right. In general, look for places that are packed with locals.

Diseases of Insanitation

Diarrhoea Few travellers escape the inevitable misery of Montezuma's Revenge and there is very little you can do to prevent the onslaught. Also called *turista* and a dozen other descriptive nicknames, there is no escaping the fact that plain old travellers' diarrhoea can happen to you anywhere.

This problem is not caused by lack of sanitation or 'bad' food but primarily by a change in diet and a lack of resistance to local strains of bacteria. The first thing to remember is that every case of diarrhoea is not dysentery, so don't panic and start stuffing yourself with pills. If you've spent all your life living out of sterilised, cellophane-wrapped packets and tins from the supermarket, you'll have a hard time until you adjust.

Flies live on various wastes produced by humans and other animals. In many places, local people shit fairly indiscriminately whenever the urge takes them. Rural facilities are rare or unspeakable and sewage treatment isn't always top rate. Most gut infections stem from the connection of food and shit via flies. There are very few public lavatories in rural areas and facilities at bus stops and roadside restaurants are rarely sanitary. If you need to make use of the bush ensure that no paper or sanitary products are left behind.

If and when you get a gut infection, avoid rushing off to the chemist and loading up on antibiotics. In this case, taking antibiotics can do more harm than good. If the bacteria in your body are able to build up immunity to them, the antibiotics may not work when you really need them. Try to starve out the bugs first. If possible, eat nothing, rest and avoid travelling (or pop an Imodium or Lomotil to plug the drain). Drink lots of liquids – diarrhoea will cause dehydration and may result in stomach cramps due to a salt imbalance in the blood. Chewing a small pellet of paregoric, a stronger version of Milk of Magnesia, will relieve the pain of the cramps.

If you can't hack starvation, keep to a light diet of dry toast, biscuits and black tea. To keep up your liquids, drink bottled water or lemonade. Once you're headed towards recovery, try some yoghurt but stay away from sweets, fruit, and dairy products. If you don't recover after a couple of days, it may be necessary to visit a doctor to be tested for other problems, which could include giardia, dysentery, cholera and so on.

It's interesting that, in addition to the initial 'shakedown', most people experience upon arriving in South America, they experience it again upon arriving home. One therefore suspects that South Americans may have similar discomforts when they visit other countries (the Yankee Quickstep or the Wallaby Hops?) thanks to unfamiliar diet and bacteria.

Giardia This is prevalent in South America and is first characterised by a swelling of the stomach, pale-coloured faeces, diarrhoea, frequent gas, headache and later by nausea and depression. Many doctors recommend Flagyl (metronidazole) tablets (250 mg) twice daily for three days. Flagyl, however, can cause side effects and some doctors prefer to treat giardiasis with two grams of Tiniba (tinadozole), taken in one fell swoop to knock the bug out hard and fast. If it doesn't work the first time, the treatment can be repeated for up to three days.

Dysentery This serious illness is caused by contaminated food or water and is characterised by severe diarrhoea, often with blood or mucus in the stool, and painful gut cramps. There are two types: bacillary dysentery, which is uncomfortable but not enduring; and amoebic dysentery which, as its name suggests, is caused by amoebas. This variety is much more difficult to treat and is more persistent.

Bacillary dysentery hits quickly, and because it's caused by bacteria it responds well to antibiotics and is usually treated symptomatically with a kaolin and pectin or a bismuth compound. On the other hand, since the symptoms themselves are actually the best treatment – diarrhoea and fever are both trying to rid the body of the infection – it may be best to just hole up for a few days and let it run its course. If activity or travel is absolutely necessary during the infection, you can take either Imodium or Lomotil to plug the drain, so to speak, until reaching a more convenient location to R&R (rest and run).

Amoebic dysentery, or amoebiasis, is a much more serious variety. It is caused by protozoans, or amoebic parasites, called *Endamoeba histolytica*, which are also transmitted through contaminated food or water. Once they've invaded, they live in the lower intestinal tract and cause heavy and often bloody diarrhoea, fever, tenderness in the liver area and intense abdominal pain.

If left untreated, ulceration and inflammation of the colon and rectum can become very serious. If you see blood in your faeces over two or three days, seek medical attention. If that's not possible, try the antiparasitic Flagyl (metronidazole). You'll need three tablets three or four times daily for 10 days to rid yourself of the condition. Flagyl should not be taken by pregnant women. The best method of preventing dysentery is, of course, to avoid eating or drinking contaminated items.

Cholera The cholera vaccine is between 20 to 50% effective according to most authorities, and can have some side effects. Vaccination is not usually recommended, nor is it legally required by Brazilian authorities. If you are travelling further afield, and want to avoid unplanned-for jabs, it may be worth getting a shot before you leave.

During 1991, a major epidemic of the disease was reported in South America, particularly in Peru and the upper reaches of the Brazilian Amazon; be particularly wary of shellfish or other seafood. Keep up to date with information about this and other diseases by contacting travellers' clinics or vaccination centres, and avoid areas where there are outbreaks.

Cholera is characterised by a sudden onset of acute diarrhoea with 'rice water' stools, vomiting, muscular cramps and extreme weakness. You need medical attention, but your first concern should be rehydration. Drink as much water as you can – if it refuses to stay down, keep drinking anyway. If there is likely to be an appreciable delay in reaching medical treatment, begin a course of tetracycline – which, incidentally, should not be administered to children or pregnant women. Be sure to check the expiry date since old tetracycline can become toxic.

Viral Gastroenteritis This is not caused by bacteria but, as the name implies, a virus. It is characterised by stomach cramps, diarrhoea, vomiting and slight fever. All you can do is rest and keep drinking as much water as possible.

Hepatitis This incapacitating disease is caused by a virus which attacks the liver. Hepatitis A is contracted through contact with contaminated food, water, toilets, or individuals. The victim's eyes and skin turn a sickly yellow and urine orange or brown. An infected person will also experience tenderness in the right side of the abdomen and a loss of appetite.

If you contract infectious hepatitis (hepatitis A) during a short trip to South America, you probably should make arrangements to go home. If you can afford the time, however, and have a reliable travelling companion who can bring food and water, the best cure is to stay where you are, find a few good books and only leave bed to go to the toilet. After a month of so, you should feel like living again. Drink lots of fluids and keep to a diet high in proteins and vitamins. Avoid alcohol and cigarettes absolutely.

Type A can be caught by eating food (especially shellfish), drinking water or using cutlery or crockery contaminated by an infected person. Avoid urban beaches after rainy days, when there's a higher probability of contracting infectious hepatitis from sewage-contaminated run-off. Like the daily smog report in Los Angeles, newspapers in Rio do daily beach reports on the *E coli* counts.

The best preventative measure available is a gamma globulin jab before departure from home and booster shots every three or four months thereafter while you're away (beware of unsanitary needles!). A jab is also in order if you come in contact with any infected person; and if *you* come down with hepatitis, anyone who has been in recent contact with you should take the shot too. Hepatitis B, formerly known as serum hepatitis, can only be caught by having sex with an infected person, or by skin penetration – eg tattooing with a contaminated needle or using the same syringe as an infected person. If type B is diagnosed, fatal liver failure is a real possibility and the victim should be sent home and/or hospitalised immediately. Gamma globulin is not effective against hepatitis B.

A vaccine does exist for hepatitis B, but it is not readily available and is extremely expensive. It consists of a course of three shots over a period of six months.

A variant of the B strain, called hepatitis C, now also exists. Transmission and symptoms are similar to hepatitis B; however, there is presently no vaccine against hepatitis C. It is not a very common strain, though, and should not be of too much concern to travellers.

Typhoid Contaminated food and water are responsible for typhoid fever, another gut infection that travels the faecal-oral route. Vaccination against typhoid isn't 100% effective. Since it can be very serious, medical attention is necessary.

Early symptoms are like those of many other travellers' illnesses – you may feel as though you have a bad cold or the flu combined with a headache, sore throat and a fever. The fever rises slowly until it exceeds 40°C while the pulse slowly drops. These symptoms may be accompanied by nausea, diarrhoea or constipation.

In the second week, the fever and slow pulse continue and a few pink spots may appear on the body. Trembling, delirium, weakness, weight loss and dehydration set in. If there are no further complications, the fever and symptoms will slowly fade during the third week. Medical attention is essential, however, since typhoid is extremely infectious and possible complications include pneumonia or peritonitis (burst appendix).

When feverish, the victim should be kept cool. Watch for dehydration. The recommended antibiotic is chloramphenicol but ampicillin causes fewer side effects.

Insect-Borne Diseases

Malaria Malaria, endemic in many parts of Brazil, is caused by the blood parasite *plasmodium* which is transmitted by the nocturnal *anopheles* mosquito. Only the females spread the disease but you can contract it through a single bite from an insect carrying the parasite. Malaria sporozites enter the bloodstream and travel to the liver, where they mature, infect the red blood cells and begin to multiply. This process takes between one and five weeks. Only when the infected cells re-enter the bloodstream and burst do the dramatic symptoms begin. For this reason, malaria can be extremely dangerous because the victim by this time has often left the malarial area, so the disease is not suspected and therefore is improperly treated.

There are four types of malaria: *Plasmodium falciparum*, the deadliest, *P malarie*, which is still universally sensitive to chloroquine, and finally *P vivax* and *P ovale*, which are harboured outside the blood and can relapse. The drug-resistant status of different malarial strains in different parts of the world is constantly in flux.

Diagnosis is confirmed by a blood test in which the plasmodium and its strain can be identified. Some strains, particularly *Plasmodium falciparum*, can be fatal if not immediately and properly treated. Malarial symptoms include (in this order) gradual loss of appetite, malaise, weakness, alternating shivering and hot flashes, diarrhoea, periodic high fever, severe headache, vomiting and hallucinations.

The most effective form of malaria prevention, of course, is to avoid being bitten. Mosquitoes bite at dusk, so you can avoid bites by covering bare skin at this time and using an insect repellent. Sleep under a mosquito net or at least light a mosquito coil. Next best – but hardly 100% effective – is a course of antimalarials, which are normally taken two weeks before, during and several weeks after travelling in malarial areas.

The malaria parasite mutates rapidly and although pharmacology manages to keep one step ahead of it, advice on which antimalarials you'll need to take goes out of date very quickly. Your doctor or travellers' health clinic will have access to the latest information.

Currently, the recommended prophylactic is chloroquine. If you develop malarial symptoms, seek medical advice immediately. If you have *Plasmodium falciparum* and reach the headache stage, you may be in serious danger. If you are not within reach of medical attention, the treatment for all strains (until you can reach a doctor) is one single dose of four tablets (600 mg) of chloroquine followed by two tablets (300 mg) six hours later and two tablets on each subsequent day. As an alternative (requisite for chloroquine-resistant strains) take a single dose of three tablets of Fansidar. *Never* use Fansidar as a prophylactic.

Chagas' Disease There is a very small possibility of contracting this disease. It is caused by a parasite which lives in the faeces of the *Reduvid* beetle which, in turn, lives in the thatching of dirty huts in the lowland, Northeast and Chaco regions of Bolivia, Argentina, Paraguay and Brazil.

The disease, transmitted through the bite of this beetle (more colourfully called the assassin bug), causes progressive constriction and hardening of blood vessels, which places increasing strain on the heart. At present there is no cure and Chagas' is always fatal over a period of years. Researchers in developed countries seem to be largely unaware of this serious disease. The best prevention is to use a mosquito net if you'll be sleeping in thatched buildings. If you are bitten, wash the affected area well and don't scratch the bite, or the faeces and consequently the parasite may be rubbed into the wound.

Haemorrhagic Fever Incidences of this illness have been reported in low-lying rainforest areas, especially in the Amazon Basin. It is transmitted by mosquitoes and can be prevented by using the same mosquito protection recommended against malaria.

The most salient symptom is an odd pinprick-type rash which is caused by capillary haemorrhaging. Accompanying symptoms include chills, fever, fatigue, congestion and other influenza-like symptoms. It can be very dangerous and professional attention, preferably in a hospital, should be immediately sought.

Worms The majority of people living in rural Brazil have worms. If you adopt the diet and lifestyle of the interior, you are also likely to acquire a worm load. The most common form you're likely to contract are hookworms. They are usually caught by walking barefoot on infected soil. They bore through the skin, attach themselves to the inner wall of the intestine and proceed to suck the blood. Abdominal pain and sometimes anaemia are the result.

Threadworms, or *strongyloidiasis*, are also found in low-lying areas and operate very much like hookworms, but symptoms are more visible and can include diarrhoea and vomiting. If you stay long and travel rough you can become home for a tribe of cattle and pig tapeworms, Ascaris, hookworm or trichura. Schistosomiasis is endemic to Brazil and thus freshwater bathing (rivers, streams, ponds, irrigations ditches, etc) can be dangerous.

Prevent exposure to parasitic worms (and other faecal-oral diseases) by drinking and brushing teeth with boiled, bottled or filtered water only. Wash produce in the same clean water and make sure all foods, particularly meat, fish, molluscs and pork, are well cooked – they harbour flukes and tapeworms. Don't walk around barefoot, always wash your hands before preparing meals and after using the toilet, and keep your nails short and clean.

A stool test when you return home isn't a bad idea if you think you may have contracted worms. Infestations may not be obvious for some time and although they are generally not serious, they can cause further health problems if left untreated. Worms may be treated with thiabendazole or mabendazole taken orally twice daily for three or four days. As usual, however, medical advice is best because the symptoms of worms so closely resemble those of other, more serious conditions.

Myiasis This very unpleasant affliction is caused by the larvae of some tropical flies which lay their eggs on damp or sweaty clothing. The eggs hatch and the larvae burrow into the skin, producing an ugly boil as the parasite develops. To kill the invader, place drops of hydrogen peroxide, alcohol or oil over the boil to cut off its air supply, and then squeeze the boil to remove the bug. However revolting the process, at this stage the problem is solved.

Yellow Fever Yellow fever is endemic in much of South America, including the Amazon Basin. This viral disease, which is transmitted to humans by mosquitoes, first manifests itself as fever, headache, abdominal pain and vomiting. There may appear to be a brief recovery before it progresses into its more severe stages, when liver failure becomes a possibility. There is no treatment apart from keeping the fever as low as possible and avoiding dehydration. The yellow fever vaccination, which is highly recommended for every traveller in South America, offers good protection for 10 years.

Typhus Typhus is spread by ticks, mites or lice and begins as a severe cold followed by a fever, chills, headache, muscle pains, and rash. There is often a large and painful sore at the site of the bite and nearby lymph nodes become swollen and painful.

Trekkers may be at risk from cattle or wild game ticks. Seek local advice on areas where ticks are present and check yourself carefully after walking in those areas. A strong insect repellent can help and regular bushwalkers should consider treating boots and trousers with repellent.

Cuts, Bites, & Stings

Cuts & Scratches The warm, moist conditions of the tropical lowlands invite and promote the growth of 'wee beasties' that would be thwarted in more temperate climates. Because of this, even a small cut or scratch can become painfully infected and lead to more serious problems.

Since bacterial immunity to certain antibiotics can build up, it's not wise to take these medicines indiscriminately or as a preventative measure. The best treatment for cuts is to cleanse the affected area frequently with soap and water and apply Mercurachrome or an antiseptic cream. Where possible, avoid using bandages, which keep wounds moist and encourage the growth of bacteria. If, despite this, the wound becomes tender and inflamed, then use of a mild, broad-spectrum antibiotic may be warranted.

Bichos de Pé These small parasites live on

Bahian beaches and sandy soil. They burrow into the thick skin of the foot at the heel, toes and under the toenails and appear as dark boils. They must be incised and removed completely. Do it yourself with a sterilised needle and blade. To avoid *bichos de pé* wear footwear on beaches and dirt trails, especially where animals are present.

Snakebite Although threat of snakebite is minimal in Brazil, those walking around the forested northern areas may wish to take precautions. The most dangerous snakes native to Brazil are the bushmaster and the fer-de-lance *(jararacussu* or *jararaca)* – the latter is responsible for the highest number of reported snakebites in Brazil. To minimise chances of being bitten, wear boots, socks and long trousers when walking through undergrowth. A good pair of canvas gaiters will further protect your legs. Don't put your hands into holes and crevices, and be careful when collecting firewood. Check shoes, clothing and sleeping bags before use.

Snakebites do not cause instantaneous death and antivenenes are usually available, but it is vital that you make a positive identification of the snake in question or, at very least, have a detailed description of it.

If someone is bitten by a snake, keep the victim calm and still, wrap the bitten limb as you would for a sprain and then attach a splint to immobilise it. Tourniquets and suction on the wound are now comprehensively discredited. Seek medical help immediately and, if possible, bring the dead snake along for identification (but don't attempt to catch it if there is a chance of being bitten again). Bushwalkers who are (wisely) concerned about snakebite should carry a field guide with photos and detailed descriptions of the possible perpetrators.

Insects Ants, gnats, mosquitoes, bees and flies will be just as annoying in Brazil as they are at home. Brazilian mosquitoes are not like their North American brethren: they are smaller, quicker, and are less detectable during the big drill. Their bites are vicious, their appetites insatiable and they're harder

to smack. Cover yourself well with clothing and use insect repellent on exposed skin. Burning incense and sleeping under mosquito nets in air-conditioned rooms or under fans also lowers the risk of being bitten. Protect yourself especially from dusk to dawn, when mosquitoes, including the malaria-transmitting *Anopheles*, like to feed. Also nasty are the bites of the pium flies.

If you're going walking in humid or densely foliated areas, wear light cotton trousers and shoes, not shorts and sandals or thongs. Regardless of temperature, never wear shorts or thongs in the forest and remember to carry an effective insect repellent. Bee and wasp stings are usually more painful than dangerous. Calamine lotion offers some relief and ice packs will reduce pain and swelling.

Body lice and scabies mites are also common in South America, so a number of shampoos and creams are available to eliminate them. In addition to hair and skin, clothing and bedding should be washed thoroughly to prevent further infestation.

Diseases Spread by People & Animals
Tetanus This potentially fatal disease is found in underdeveloped tropical areas and is difficult to treat, but is easily prevented by vaccination. Tetanus occurs when a wound becomes infected by a bacterium which lives in human or animal faeces. Clean all cuts, punctures, and bites. Tetanus is also known as lockjaw and the first symptom may be difficulty in swallowing, followed by a stiffening of the jaw and neck, and then by painful convulsions of the jaw and whole body.

Rabies Throughout Brazil, but especially in low-lying humid areas, rodents and bats carry the rabies virus and pass it on to larger animals and humans. Avoid any animal that appears to be foaming at the mouth or acting strangely. Bats, especially vampire bats, are common in the Amazon Basin and are notorious carriers of rabies. Be sure to cover all parts of your body at night, especially your feet and scalp. Dogs are also particularly notable carriers. Any bite, scratch or even lick from a mammal should be cleaned immediately and thoroughly. Scrub with soap and running water and then clean with an alcohol solution. If there is any possibility that the animal is infected, help should be sought. Even if the animal isn't rabid, all bites should be treated seriously as they can become infected or result in tetanus. A rabies vaccination is now available and should be considered if you spend a lot of time around animals.

If you do get bitten, try to capture or kill the offending animal so that it may be tested. If that's impossible, then you must assume the animal is rabid. The rabies virus incubates slowly in its victim, so while medical attention isn't urgent, it shouldn't be delayed.

Meningococcal Meningitis The disease is spread by close contact with people who carry it in their throats and noses. They probably aren't aware they are carriers and pass it around through coughs and sneezes. This very serious disease attacks the brain and can be fatal. A scattered blotchy rash, fever, severe headache, sensitivity to light and stiffness in the neck preventing nodding of the head are the first symptoms. Death can occur within a few hours, so immediate treatment with large doses of penicillin is vital. If intravenous administration is impossible, it should be given intramuscularly. Vaccination offers reasonable protection for over a year but you should check for reports of recent outbreaks and try to avoid affected areas.

Diptheria Diptheria can appear as a skin infection or a more serious throat infection. It is spread by contaminated dust coming in contact with the skin or being inhaled. About the only way to prevent the skin infection is to keep clean and dry – not always easy in South America. The throat infection is prevented by vaccination.

Gonorrhoea & Syphilis Sexual contact with an infected partner spreads a number of unpleasant diseases. While abstinence is 100% effective, use of a condom will lessen your risk considerably. The most common of these diseases are gonorrhoea and syphilis which in men first appear as sores, blisters or rashes around the genitals and pain or discharge when urinating. Symptoms may be less marked or not evident at all in women. The symptoms of syphilis eventually disappear completely but the disease continues and may cause severe problems in later years. Antibiotics are used to treat both syphilis and gonorrhoea.

AIDS AIDS is another issue. It is a very serious problem in Brazil to a degree unfamiliar to most Western travellers and should be a major concern to all visitors. At present, AIDS is a death sentence and will continue to be until a cure is found – and that may not be for a while. Although in the West it is most commonly spread through intravenous drug abuse and male homosexual activity, in South America it is transmitted primarily through heterosexual activity.

Most people affected by the AIDS virus are not aware they have it, and hospitals are likely to diagnose their symptoms as something more mundane. The obvious way to best avoid the disease is to remain celibate. Not everyone can – or is inclined to be. If you do have sex in South America, cut the risk by using a condom. Even then, you are still far from being 100% safe. Condoms are available in Brazil and are generally known as *preservativos*; however, they are not particularly reliable. If you are anticipating amorous encounters whilst in Brazil, bring a sufficient supply of condoms with you.

You can also pick up AIDS through blood transfusions. Don't take any chances. It is also possible to pick up the virus through injection with an unsterilised needle. If you must have an injection, either provide your own sterilised syringe or make absolutely sure it is either new or properly sterilised.

Sun, Heat & Exertion
Sunburn Most of Brazil lies in the humid tropics, where the sun's rays are more direct

and concentrated than in temperate zones. Even in cooler highland areas, everyone – particularly fair-skinned people – will be susceptible to hazardous UV rays. The use of a strong sunscreen is essential because serious burns can occur after even brief exposure. Don't neglect to apply it to any area of exposed skin, especially if you're near water.

To be safe, choose the highest rated sunscreen available. In addition, a hat will serve to shade your face and protect your scalp. Sunglasses will prevent eye irritation (especially if you wear contact lenses).

Prickly Heat Prickly heat is an itchy rash caused by excessive perspiration trapped under the skin. It usually strikes those newly arrived in a hot climate whose pores have not opened enough to accommodate profuse sweating. Frequent baths and application of talcum powder will help relieve the itch.

Heat Exhaustion In the humid lowlands of Brazil and on the beach, heat combined with humidity and exposure to the sun can be oppressive and leave you feeling lethargic, irritable and dazed. A cool swim or lazy afternoon in the shade will do wonders to improve your mood. You'll also need to drink lots of liquids and eat salty foods in order to replenish your supply of these products lost during sweating.

Serious dehydration or salt deficiency can lead to heat exhaustion. Take time to acclimatise to high temperature and, again, be sure to drink sufficient liquids. Salt deficiency, which can be brought on by diarrhoea or nausea, is characterised by fatigue, lethargy, headaches, giddiness and muscle cramps. Salt tablets will probably solve the problem. Anhidrotic heat exhaustion, caused by inability to sweat, is quite rare but can strike even those who have spent some time in hot climates.

Heatstroke This serious, sometimes fatal, condition can occur if the body's thermostat breaks down and body temperature rises to dangerous levels. Continuous exposure to high temperatures can leave you vulnerable to heatstroke. Alcohol intake and strenuous activity can increase chances of heatstroke, especially in those who've recently arrived in a hot climate.

Symptoms include minimal sweating, a high body temperature (39 to 40°C), and a general feeling of unwellness. The skin may become flushed and red. Severe throbbing headaches, decreased coordination, and aggressive or confused behaviour may be signs of heatstroke. Eventually, the victim will become delirious and go into convulsions. Get the victim out of the sun, if possible, remove clothing, cover with a wet towel and fan continually. Seek medical help as soon as possible.

Motion Sickness If you're susceptible to motion sickness, then come prepared because the roads in Brazil aren't always straight and smooth.

If Dramamine works for you, take some along. Eating very lightly before and during a trip will reduce the chances of motion sickness. Try to find a place that minimises disturbance: near the wing on aircraft or near the centre on buses. Fresh air almost always helps, but reading or cigarette smoking (or even being around someone else's smoke) normally makes matters worse.

Commercial motion sickness preparations, which can cause drowsiness, have to be taken before the trip; after you've begun feeling ill, it's too late. Dramamine tablets should be taken three hours before departure and scopolamine patches (which are available only by prescription in most places) should be applied 10 to 12 hours before departure. Scopolamine will dilate the pupils if it accidentally comes in contact with the eyes and has been known to cause drowsiness, so caution should be exercised. Ginger can be used as a natural preventative and is available in capsule form.

Women's Health
Gynaecological Problems Poor diet, lowered resistance due to use of antibiotics, and even contraceptive pills can lead to

vaginal infections when travelling in hot climates. To prevent the worst of it, keep the genital area clean, wear cotton underwear, and skirts or loose-fitting trousers.

Yeast infections, characterised by a rash, itch and discharge, can be treated with a vinegar or lemon juice douche or with yoghurt. Nystatin suppositories are the usual medical prescription. Trichomonas is a more serious infection which causes a discharge and a burning sensation when urinating. Male sexual partners must also be treated, and if a vinegar and water douche is not effective, medical attention should be sought. Flagyl is the most frequently prescribed drug.

Pregnancy Most miscarriages occur during the first trimester of pregnancy, so this is the most risky time to be travelling. The last three months should also be spent within reasonable reach of good medical care, since serious problems can develop at this stage as well. Pregnant women should avoid all unnecessary medication but vaccinations and malarial prophylactics should still be taken where possible. Additional care should be taken to prevent illness, and the chances of complications will certainly decrease with particular attention to proper nutrition and diet.

Back Home

Be aware of illness after you return; take note of odd or persistent symptoms of any kind, get a check-up and remember to give your physician a complete travel history. Most doctors in temperate climes will not suspect unusual tropical diseases. If you have been travelling in malarial areas, have yourself tested for the disease.

WOMEN TRAVELLERS

Depending on where they travel in Brazil, lone women will be greeted with a range of responses. In São Paulo, for example, where there are many people of European ancestry, foreign women without travelling companions will scarcely be given a sideways glance. In the more traditional rural areas of the Northeast, where a large percentage of the population is of mixed European, African and Indian origin, blonde-haired and light-skinned women – especially those without male escorts – will certainly arouse curiosity.

Although *machismo* is an undeniable element in the Brazilian social structure, it is manifested less overtly than in Spanish-speaking Latin America. Perhaps because attitudes toward sex and pornography are quite liberal in Brazil, males feel little need to assert their masculinity or prove their prowess in the eyes of peers. Flirtation – often exaggerated – is a prominent element in Brazilian male/female relations. It goes both ways and is nearly always regarded as amusingly innocent banter; no sense of insult, exploitation – or intent to carry things further – should be derived from it. If unwelcome attention is forthcoming, you should be able to stop it by merely expressing disgust or displeasure.

Once you've spent an hour in Copacabana or Ipanema, where some women run their errands wearing *fio dental*, the famous Brazilian skimpy bikini, you'll be aware that dress restrictions – at least in some parts of Brazil – aren't as strict as they could be. It seems largely a matter of personal taste, but it's still best to synchronise your dress to local standards. What works in Rio will not necessarily be appropriate in a Northeastern city or a Piauí backwater.

Although most of the country is nearly as safe for women as for men, there are a few caveats which are also likely to apply at home. It's a good idea to keep a low profile in the cities at night and avoid going alone to bars and nightclubs if you'd rather not chance being misconstrued. Similarly, women should not hitch either alone or in groups; and even men or couples should exercise discretion when hitching. Most important, some of the more rough-and-ready areas of the north and west, where there are lots of men but few local women, should be considered off limits to lone female travellers.

DANGERS & ANNOYANCES
Security

Hard facts presented in a recent Gallup survey show that Brazil is the world's second most violent nation, surpassed only by Colombia. Robberies on buses, city beaches and heavily touristed areas are extremely common. Thieves tend to work in gangs, are armed with knives and guns, and are capable of killing those who resist them. Much of the petty street crime in Rio, São Paulo, Salvador, and Manaus is directed against tourists – Rio's thieves refer to them as *filet mignon*. Foreign tourists have got lots of money and expensive cameras. They are easy to pick out in a crowd, are unfamiliar with the turf and language, and are very vulnerable.

Not surprisingly, a recent official survey of foreign visitors to Brazil reported that concern about safety and security was one of the major reasons for feeling apprehensive about travelling to Brazil. Since many readers may not have previously experienced the type and extent of crime evident in Brazil, this section has been written in detail to heighten awareness. However, it is neither necessary nor helpful to become paranoid; our intention is to demonstrate that there are many things travellers can do to reduce the risks.

Predeparture Precautions

If you work on the elements of vulnerability, you can significantly reduce the risks. For starters, you should take with you only those items which you are prepared to lose or replace. Travel insurance is essential for replacement of valuables and the cost of a good policy is a worthwhile price to pay for minimum disturbance or even abrupt termination of your travel plans. Loss through petty theft or violence is an emotional and stressful experience which can be reduced if you think ahead. The less you have, the less you can lose.

Don't bring any jewellery, chains, or expensive watches, and if you have to wear a watch, then use a cheapie worth a few dollars. Even better, buy your cheapie watch in Brazil and keep it in your pocket, not on

your wrist. In the words of a local in Salvador, 'It is considered an insensitive affront to the less fortunate if tourists stroll around wearing expensive jewellery, watches, and cameras'.

Be prepared for the worst – make copies of your important records: a photostat of your passport (page with passport number, name, photograph, location where issued and expiration date; all visas); tourist card (issued on entry to Brazil); travellers' cheque numbers; credit card numbers; airline tickets; essential contact addresses, etc. Keep one copy on your person, one copy with your belongings and exchange one with a travelling companion.

By law you must carry a passport with you at all times, but many travellers opt to carry a photocopy (preferably certified) whilst they amble about town, and leave the passport locked up somewhere safe. A passport is worth several thousand dollars to some people, so keep a close eye on it. If you do lose it, photostats of the lost passport and a copy of your birth certificate can usually speed up the issuing of a new passport at embassies and consulates.

Credit cards are useful in emergencies and for regular purchases. Make sure you know the number to call if you lose your credit card and be quick to cancel it if lost or stolen. New-style credit card coupons do not have carbon paper inserts and offer more protection against misuse. If you sign an old-style coupon, be sure to ask for the carbon inserts and destroy them after use. Similarly, destroy any coupons which have been filled out incorrectly. These are worthwhile precautions against unwanted duplication of your credit card!

Cabling money is difficult, time-consuming and expensive. You must know the name and address of both the bank sending (record this and keep this with your documents) and the bank receiving your money. In Rio, Casa Piano on Avenida Rio Branco is the most experienced with overseas transactions. The Brazilian American Cultural Center (BACC), which has offices in the USA and Brazil, provides a special remittance service for members – for details and main address of BACC, refer to the Useful Organisations section in this chapter.

Security Accessories Make sure that your backpack is fitted with double zippers which can be locked using small combination locks. Padlocks are also good, but are easier to pick. A thick backpack cover or modified canvas sack improves protection against pilfering, 'planting' of drugs, and general wear and tear. Double zippers on your daypack can be secured with safety pins, which reduce the ease of access favoured by petty thieves. A bicycle combination lock or padlock (steel or chain) is highly recommended for many purposes, such as chaining luggage to racks in buses, trains, and to hotel fixtures. A medium-size combination lock or padlock is useful to replace the padlock on your hotel door. Rubber wedges are handy to prevent access to doors or windows. To deter thieves operating with razors, you can line the inside of your daypack (and even your backpack) with lightweight wire mesh.

Don't keep all your valuables together: distribute them about your person and baggage to avoid the risk of losing everything in one fell swoop. Various types of money belt are available to be worn around the waist, neck or shoulder; and leather or cotton material is more comfortable than synthetics. Such belts are only useful if worn *under* clothing – pouches worn outside clothing are easy prey and attract attention. Determined thieves are wise to conventional money belts, and some travellers now also use cloth pouches sewn into trousers or attached inside with safety pins. Other methods include belts with concealed zipper compartment; and bandages or pouches worn around the leg.

If you wear glasses, secure them with an elastic strap to deter petty theft. Better still, wear contact lenses.

Finally, the extra pair of eyes provided by a travelling companion are an obvious asset!

Security Precautions in Brazil

There are certain key things you can do to reduce attention from criminals. Your style of dress should be casual and preferably something that blends in – inexpensive clothes bought in Brazil would be an obvious choice.

If you carry a daypack, *always* wear it local fashion: strapped to the chest like a kangaroo pouch! Whether you're in a bus station, restaurant, shop, or elsewhere, whenever you have to put your daypack down, *always* put your foot through the strap. Both these ploys make things more difficult for furtive fingers or bag-slashers.

If you have a camera with you, never wander around with it dangling over your shoulder or around your neck – keep it out of sight as much as possible. It's also unwise to keep it in a swanky camera bag, which is an obvious target. We sometimes carried a camera in a sturdy plastic bag from a local supermarket.

Get used to keeping small change and a few banknotes in a shirt pocket so that you can pay bus tickets and small expenses without extracting large amounts of money which could quickly attract attention. This easily accessible money is also useful to rapidly appease a mugger. If you carry a wallet, make sure it's small and kept in a zippered or buttoned inside pocket, and don't use it on public transport or in crowded places where it might attract unwelcome attention.

Before arriving in a new place, make sure you have a map or at least a rough idea about orientation. Try to plan your schedule so you don't arrive at night, and do use a taxi if this seems the appropriate way to avoid walking through high-risk areas. A travelling companion is useful, since solo travellers are more easily distracted. Be observant and learn to look like a street-smart local.

Favourite Scams Distraction is a common tactic employed by street thieves. The 'cream technique' is now very common throughout South America, and Brazil is no exception. The trick commences when you're walking down the street or standing in a public place, and someone surreptitiously sprays a substance on your shoulder, your daypack or anything else connected with you. The substance can be anything from mustard to chocolate or even dog muck. An assistant (young or old; male or female) then taps you on the shoulder and amicably offers to clean off the mess...if you'll just put down your bag for a second. The moment you do this, someone makes off with it like a flash. The golden rule is to ignore any such attempt or offer and simply endure your mucky state until you can find a safe place, such as your hotel, where you can wash. Just a couple of hours after arrival in Rio, we experienced an unsuccessful attempt of this kind.

Another distraction technique involves one or more people working to divert you or literally throw you off balance. This trick usually happens when you're standing in the street or somewhere busy like a bus station. One or more characters suddenly ask you a question, 'bump' into you or stage an angry discussion or fight around you, and whilst you are off balance or diverted, there'll be an attempt to pick your pockets or whip your gear.

Never change money on the street; always ignore itinerant moneychangers who whisper favourable rates into your ear as you pass; and never follow any of these types into a sidestreet for such a transaction. No exceptions: never means never.

Druggings have also been reported. Exercise caution when you are offered cigarettes, beer, sweets, etc. If the circumstances make you suspicious or uneasy, the offer can be tactfully refused by claiming stomach or other medical problems.

These scams are continuously being developed, and imported or exported across borders. Keep abreast of new scams by talking to other travellers. In our experience, theft and security are sources of endless fascination and stories: some are true, some are incredible, and some are taller than Corcovado! If you think this section is useful and would like to forewarn other travellers about new developments, we'd appreciate your feedback. You might even derive consolation from letting off steam, and satisfaction from steering other travellers out of the clutches of criminals.

On the Beach Don't bring anything to city beaches apart from just enough money for lunch and drinks. No camera, no bag and no jewellery. Wear your bathing suit and bring a towel. That's it. If you want to photograph the beach go with a friend, then return the camera to your room before staying on the beach. Don't hang out on city beaches at night.

In the Northeast, male travellers have reported that 'good-time' ladies at beach bars make friendly advances over drinks which are then drugged. The semi-comatose traveller is then accompanied back to his hotel, where the woman explains that she needs the key to help her 'drunken friend' to his room – where she cleans out all his valuables and then makes a quick exit.

Here's a typical beach mugging as experienced by one of the authors in Rio:

I didn't look like a tourist; I wasn't carrying a camera or wearing flashy jewellery, just a cheap digital watch. I had the equivalent of US$50 in Brazilian currency, plus another US$100 in travellers' cheques. I knew better than to go to Copacabana beach with a lot of money, but then I thought nothing bad could happen to me.

Lulled by the beauty of Copacabana and the sound of the surf, I felt safe. I stripped down to my bathing suit, held my jeans, T-shirt and sandals in my hands like weights, and started running along the shoreline. There were no bathers or people lying on the sand, but there were plenty of joggers running in pairs and lots of soccer games going on. A man jogging alone on the hard-packed sand called for the time; a minute later he turned back, pointed to his bare wrist and shouted hoarsely. He said something about the watch which I couldn't understand, but I shouted back the time anyway: 'It's 4.30'. The sun wouldn't set for an hour and a half.

Ducking my head under the lines of some surfcasters, I slowed down to wade in the water and cool off, holding my things above the water. I turned around in the foot-deep surf and a crazed man with an eight-inch blade raised over his head was yelling at me in Portuguese, 'Give me everything you have. Give me your money'. I pulled the wallet out of my jeans and handed it to him.

'And the clothes!', he said. His head and neck were

cocked to the side, trembling. Two surfcasters were only 20 feet away and they didn't do a damn thing. I could see people in the distance, but the incline of beach at the water's edge seemed like a wall of sand. I didn't shout, so as not to alarm the thief.

'The watch too!'

I fumbled with the watch band.

'Come on hurry up! The watch.'

He came towards me. I circled backwards in the water, afraid to trip, afraid he would lose his patience and kill me for the watch. I gave it to him.

The thief sprinted 100 yards down the beach and dropped to the ground with the bundle. He left my clothes and my travellers' cheques on the sand.

A soccer player left his game and approached me. 'It's a good thing you gave him the money because that guy was working with a group. They were standing right there, five men, two with pistols. The bandits, they don't bother us. We have an understanding with them.'

Maybe he was telling the truth or just covering up for not helping me. But I felt a lot better about just handing over my money. You hear stories about how dangerous Copacabana is, yet it's so beautiful, so wide-open that it puts you off guard. The beach doesn't fit your conception of what a dangerous place should look like. And yet it may well be the most likely place to get robbed in Brazil.

Streets, Buses & Taxis Thieves watch for people leaving hotels, car-rental agencies, American Express offices, tourist sights – places with lots of foreigners. Then they follow their targets. If you notice you are being followed or closely observed, it helps to pause and look straight at the person(s) involved or, if you're not alone, simply point out the person(s) to your companion. This makes it clear that the element of surprise favoured by petty criminals has been lost.

Don't advertise the fact that you're a foreigner by flashing big bills or wearing jewellery. Keep your watch out of sight in your pocket. Don't carry much money in the streets and even less on the municipal buses. Carry just enough money on your person for the evening's entertainment and transport, and keep it discreetly stashed away in a money belt, money sock, secret pockets or shoe.

Always have enough money on hand to appease a mugger (about US$2 to US$5). We've heard of Israeli tourists (fresh from military training) foiling attempted muggers, disarming them, and breaking all their fingers, but we do not recommend resistance. There have been other reports of tourists shot dead whilst pursuing muggers – an absurd price to pay for the loss of valuables. Don't carry weapons: in many cases this could make matters much worse. In any case, if you've prepared for your trip along the lines mentioned earlier in this section, you'll probably feel happier just letting the unpleasant event pass.

If you ride the buses, have your change ready before boarding. You're less of a target once you have passed the turnstile. Avoid the super-crowded buses. If you talk out loud, it's easier for thieves to identify you as a target. If you have valuables, take taxis rather than buses.

Long-distance bus travel is usually well organised. If you hand over luggage to be placed in the baggage compartment, make sure you receive and keep your receipt. Two or more items can be padlocked together. If you place luggage on the overhead racks inside the bus, padlock it to the rack. If you have to place baggage on the roof, secure it with a padlock. These last two points are especially important during night trips.

Although taxi drivers and their tricks with taxi fares can be irritating (see the Getting Around chapter for more details), taxis currently pose minimal problems with outright theft.

When entering or leaving a taxi, it's advisable (particularly for solo travellers) to keep a passenger door open during the loading or unloading of luggage – particularly if this is being done by someone other than the driver. This reduces the ease with which a taxi can drive off with your luggage, leaving you behind! A neater solution for those who travel light is to fit luggage inside the taxi rather than in the boot.

Also, when entering or leaving a taxi, always remember to watch your luggage (slip your foot or your arm through the appropriate strap). Opportunistic thieves are quick to make off with items whilst you are distracted by price-haggling or baggage arrangement. If you're travelling as a pair (or larger group), it's a good general precaution to always have at least one person remain close to the open passenger door or inside the taxi whenever luggage is still in the taxi.

Before starting, immediately question the presence of any 'shady' characters accompanying the driver, and don't hesitate to take another taxi if you feel uneasy. If there are mechanical or orientation problems en route, do not allow yourself to be separated from your luggage. When you arrive at your destination, *never* hand over your luggage to a person who tries to help you out of the car and offers to carry something, unless you are quite positive about their identity. Otherwise, you may see your luggage disappearing down the street. We noted an unsuccessful attempt of this particular kind when we arrived outside the Hotel Pelourinho in Salvador.

Hotels If you consider your hotel to be reliable, place valuables in its safe and get a receipt. Make sure you package your valuables in a small, double-zippered bag which can be padlocked, or use a large envelope with a signed seal which will easily show any tampering. Count money and travellers' cheques before and after retrieving them from the safe – this should quickly identify any attempts to extract single bills or cheques which might otherwise go unnoticed.

Check the door, doorframe, and windows of your room for signs of forced entry or unsecured access. If your hotel provides a padlock, it's recommended to use your own combination lock (or padlock) instead. A hotel padlock obviously increases the number of people with access to your room; and there have been reports of criminals holding up hotel receptionists at gunpoint whilst an accomplice takes the keys and cleans out the rooms. Although it's not recommended to leave valuables in your room, some travellers padlock baggage to room fixtures or tape items in concealed places. If you tape things, don't leave them behind as a windfall for the cleaner!

Boats Passengers on local boats, particularly in northern Brazil, are the target of thieves who take advantage of crowded conditions, long journeys, and unsecured baggage – particularly at night. Before boarding, beware of entrusting your baggage to someone wearing an official uniform who requests to see your ticket and even issues a receipt. We met a German traveller who had done this in Belém, only to return several hours later to find that the official had been bogus, the padlock for the boat's 'storage room' had belonged to the impostor, and the German's backpack had disappeared.

On board, make sure you keep all valuables on your person, never flash your money around, and keep your camera out of sight as much as possible. Double zippers on your baggage should be padlocked and a bicycle padlock or chain is useful to secure your baggage to a fixture on the boat. Some travellers use a large eyelet hook and a rope to suspend baggage from the ceiling next to their hammock. Do not assume cabins have secure access.

It is important that any baggage you are not carrying on your person is secured to the boat. Thieves prefer to rifle through unsecured and unobserved baggage, extract valuables and then simply dump large evidence (the baggage) overboard. This happened to one of the authors when a daypack was stolen and dumped overboard during a long Amazon trip. The loss of money was sustainable (and replaceable), but the biggest blow was the loss of dozens of rolls of film (for another book) and personal effects.

The Police

If something is stolen from you, you can report it to the police. No big investigation is going to occur but you will get a police form to give to your insurance company. The police aren't to be trusted, however. Brazilian police are known to plant drugs and sting gringos for bribes. The bribes are like pyramids: the more people are involved, the bigger the bribe becomes.

Drugs

Marijuana and cocaine are plentiful in Brazil, and very illegal. The military regime had a rather pathological aversion to drugs and enacted stiff penalties. Nevertheless, marijuana and cocaine are widely used, and, like many things in Brazil, everyone except the military and the police has a rather tolerant attitude towards them. Bahia seems to have the most open climate. But because of the laws against possession, you won't bump into much unless you know someone or go to an 'in' vacation spot with the young and hip like Arraial d'Ajuda, Morro de São Paulo, Canoa Quebrada, etc.

There are some wild hallucinogenic substances in the Amazon. The best known is *Banisteriopsis caapi*, better known as yagé or ayahuasca, which comes from a jungle vine and has ritual uses amongst certain tribes and cults. For more details about the cults refer to the Other Cults section under Religion in the Facts about the Country chapter. For further reading on the topic of drugs, refer to the Amazon & Indians section under Books & Maps in this chapter.

Drugs provide a perfect excuse for the police to get a fair amount of money from you, and Brazilian prisons are brutal places. Police checkpoints along the highways stop cars and buses at random. Police along the coastal drive from Rio to São Paulo are notorious for hassling young people and foreigners. Border areas are also very dangerous. A large amount of cocaine is smuggled out of Bolivia and Peru through Brazil. Be very careful with drugs. Don't buy from strangers and don't carry anything around with you.

If you're coming from one of the Andean countries and have been chewing coca leaves, be especially careful to clean out your pack before arriving in Brazil. Here's what happened to a traveller who didn't:

I got out of jail after four days with the help of the consul, and was supposed to stay in Rio for 14 days waiting for trial, but my lawyer found out that the judge wanted to send me to jail so he suggested I leave immediately. The consul gave me a passport and I flew south to Porto Alegre and crossed the border into Uruguay without difficulty before flying home.

My parents were very happy of course, but it cost them a lot of money to get me out. A lady from the consulate in Rio wrote and told me that I'd been sentenced to four years in jail, and it was only 17.7 grams of coca leaves!

I'm glad to be home, safe and in one piece, and I don't have to fight with those disgusting cockroaches! Just think of it – four years in a Brazilian jail! I can't even imagine it but it was so close.

Name witheld for obvious reasons

This woman was one of the lucky ones. Don't forget to clean out that pack!

Beggars

A disconcerting aspect of travel in Brazil, particularly in the cities of the Northeast, is the constant presence of beggars. With no social welfare system to sustain them, the elderly, blind, crippled, mentally ill and jobless take to the streets and try to arouse sympathy in any way they can.

Since giving even a pittance to every beggar encountered will be financially impossible for most visitors, everyone has to formulate their own idea about what constitutes an appropriately humanitarian response. Some travellers choose to give to only the most pathetic cases or to those enterprising individuals who provide some value for the money, such as by singing or playing a musical instrument. Others simply feel that contributions only serve to fuel the machine that creates beggars and ignore them.

All we can offer on this issue is a couple of guidelines: the rest must be left to your conscience. The physically impaired are always underemployed, and frequently have to fall back on selling lottery tickets and telephone tokens, but they do manage to earn something. The mentally indigent or the elderly, who would appear to have no other possible means of support, may be especially good candidates. Keep in mind, however, that many families simply set their older members on the pavement with a tin bowl hoping to generate a little extra income. For those who go begging for bones, scraps and leftovers, or others who are truly trying to change their situations, a bowl of soup or a nutritious hot meal will go a long way.

Regarding the numerous children who beg, it's probably best not to give money since it will lead to their exploitation by unscrupulous adults and will give the impression that something can be had for nothing. For a child who appears truly hungry, a piece of fruit or other healthy snack will be greatly appreciated; if such gifts are refused and money is demanded, it should be fairly obvious what's really going on.

Plumbing
Much of the plumbing in Brazil is jerry-built or poorly installed and can pose 'shocking' problems to the uninitiated. Therefore, some explanation and instruction for use may be helpful.

First of all, bathtubs are rare outside of expensive tourist hotels, as are hot and cold running water. It is possible however, to have hot, or tepid, showers thanks to a frightening and deadly-looking device that attaches to the shower head and electrically heats the water as it passes through. Bare wires dangle from the ceiling or run into the shower head.

The dangling variety indicates that you're not going to get a hot shower because the device is broken, as many are. Don't bother getting undressed until you've verified that it's working.

On the wall, you will find a lever that looks suspiciously like an old-time electrocutioner's switch. You have to flip the switch after the water is running (yes, really), so it's best to leave your shoes or flip-flops on and not get wet until this is done.

When the heater is activated, it will begin to emit an electrical humming sound and the lights in the room will dim or go out altogether. This is because the heater requires a great deal of electricity to operate effectively.

The temperature of the water can then be adjusted by increasing or decreasing the flow. A larger volume of water cannot be adequately heated in the time it takes to pass through the shower head, so a shower of a bearable temperature often becomes nothing but a pressureless drip.

When it's time to turn the water off, don't touch the controls until you've dried off and have your footwear on. This may be tricky, especially if the shower stall is small. Before turning the water off, flip the switch on the wall and then turn off the water.

WORK
Travellers on tourist visas aren't supposed to work in Brazil. The only viable paid work is teaching English in one of the big cities, but you need to speak a bit of Portuguese and allow enough time to get some pupils. I taught English in São Paulo for five months a few years ago and found that I was able to earn between US$5 and US$10 per hour. Teaching company executives during their lunch hour and taking private pupils at home were my most lucrative classes, but both these take some time to set up.

To find work, look in the classifieds under 'Professor de Ingles', or ask around at the English schools.

Volunteer work with welfare organisations is quite easy to find if you're prepared to do some door-knocking. One traveller I met walked up to the front door of a Catholic home for abandoned children in Recife and asked if there was anything he could do. The priests in charge gave him a place to sleep and he spent the next two months helping to cook, getting the children out of jail, telling them stories and breaking up knife fights. He said it was the highlight of his trip.

ACTIVITIES
Windsurfing
Windsurfing is catching on. In Rio you can rent equipment down at Barra da Tijuca. I saw lots of windsurfing at Ilhabela in São Paulo, Porto Seguro and Belém, among other places.

Hang-Gliding
It's easy to fly *duplo* in Rio. Go to Pepino beach, where you'll see the gliders landing, and for US$60 someone will take you up (straight up) Pedra Bonita and fly down with you on a glider-built-for-two (see the Rio de Janeiro chapter for more information).

Surfing

Today surfing is popular all along the coast and there are some excellent waves to be had, especially in the south. Santa Catarina has the best surfing beaches and holds the Brazilian championships at Joaquina beach near Florianópolis. In Rio state, Saquarema has the best surf. Búzios and Itacoatiara beach in Niterói are also popular breaks. There's also plenty of surf close to the city of Rio – see the Rio de Janeiro chapter for details. Waves are best in the Brazilian winter (from June to August).

Surfing Vocabulary Despite their reputation for aggressiveness in the water, once on land Brazilian surfers become very interested in foreign surfers and their travels. They also are reasonably willing to lend their boards if you ask politely.

surfer	*surfista*
wave	*onda*
surfboard	*prancha*
to break	*quebrar*
wind	*vento*
Are there any waves?	*Tem ondas?*
Could I borrow your board please?	*Pode me emprestar sua prancha por favor?*
Let's go surfing	*Vamos pegar ondas*

Other Water Sports

As you would expect in a place with such a long coastline and so many beach lovers, all

the different water sports are popular. And as you would expect in a place with such a large gap between rich and poor, they're restricted to those who can afford them. What this means to the traveller is that in order to rent the equipment needed to practise any of the above activities you need to go to established resorts.

Sailing is big in Búzios in Rio state and the larger resorts along the coast. Diving doesn't match the Caribbean, but it is worthwhile if you're keen. Angra dos Reis is the best place in Rio state, and Porto Seguro in Bahia and Brasma in Recife have been recommended.

Fishing in the interior of Brazil is fantastic. The Rio Araguaia in Goiâs and Tocantins is known as a fishing paradise, with a large variety of fish including the pintado, dourado and tucunaré. In the Pantanal, licenced fishing is allowed on the Taquari, Coxim, Aquidauana, Cuiabá and Paraguay rivers. Fishing for piranha is not undertaken by serious fishers, though it's good fun.

Hiking & Climbing

Hiking and climbing in Brazil are best during the cooler months of the year – April to October. During the summer, the tropical sun heats the rock up to oven temperatures and turns the jungles into steamy saunas. Climbing during the summer is still pursued, although only primarily in the early morning or late afternoon when the sun's rays are not so harsh.

The best thing about rock climbing in Brazil is that one hour you can be on the beach, and the next on a world-class rock climb 300 metres above a city. Brazil has lots of fantastic rock climbs, ranging from the beginner level to still unconquered routes. In Rio de Janeiro, the centre of rock climbing in Brazil, there are 350 documented climbs that can all be reached within 40 minutes from the city centre.

There are lots of great places to hike in Brazil, both in the national and state parks and along the coastline. Lots of good hikes are mentioned in the appropriate chapters. It's also a good idea to contact some of the climbing clubs (see the Rio city chapter for addresses), who have details of trekking options.

Climbing Vocabulary Although most Brazilians in the clubs know a little English, not everyone does. It helps to know a little Portuguese to smooth the way.

equipment	equipamento
bolt	grampo
rope	corda
carabiner	mosquetão
harness	baudrie
backpack	mochila
webbing	fita
chalk powder	pó de magnésio
rock	rocha
summit	topo/cume
crack	fenda
route	via/rota
a fall	queda
to be secured	estar preso
a hold	uma agarra
to belay	dar segurança
to make a stupid mistake and fall	tomar uma vaca

HIGHLIGHTS

Brazil offers much more than Carnival and Amazon river trips. The following are suggestions for you to explore and enjoy the country.

Historical Cities & Architecture

Salvador and Pelourinho; Olinda; Alcântara and São Luís; Lençóis; Cachoeira; Goiás Velho; Ouro Preto and other historical cities in Minas Gerais; Parati.

Museums

Museu Emílio Goeldi (Belém); Museu Histórico (Alcântara); Museu do Homem do Nordeste (Recife); Museu da Borracha (Rio Branco); Museu Dom Bosco (Campo Grande); Museu Folclorico Edson Carneiro and Museu da República (Rio de Janeiro); Museu Biológico de Professor Melo Leitão (Santa Teresa).

Beaches

Prainha (Natal, Rio Grande do Norte); Tambaba (Paraíba); Prejuiças (Lençóis Maranhenses, Maranhão); Morro de São Paulo (Bahia); Jericoacoara (Ceará); Pepino and Barra (Rio de Janeiro); Parati (Rio state); Joaquina (Florianópolis); Ilha do Mel (Paraná).

Festivals

Boa Morte (Cachoeira); Bumba Meu Boi (São Luís); Carnival (Olinda); Círio de Nazaré (Belém); Cavalhadas (Pirenópolis); Semana Santa (Goiás Velho); New Year's Eve on Copacabana beach (Rio de Janeiro).

Food & Drinks

Baiana cuisine; exotic forest fruits & juices; mineiro cuisine; fresh fruit batidas; a well-made caipirinha. (See the Food section for details.)

Restaurants

Miako (Japanese, Belém); Casa do Benin (African, Salvador); Pousalegre (baiana and Chinese, Lençóis); Raizes (Northeastern specialities, Natal); Cervantes (meat and pineapple sandwiches, Rio de Janeiro); Tio Flor (gaúcho cuisine, Porto Alegre); Colombo (coffee, cakes and atmosphere, Rio de Janeiro).

Accommodation

Canto das Águas (Lençóis); Pousada dos Quatro Cantos (Olinda); Hotel Rio Branco (Rio Branco); Pousada do Mordomo Régio (Alcântara); Nhundiaquara (Morretes); Pouso Chico Rei (Ouro Preto).

Music & Dance

Sunday night in Pelourinho (Salvador); forro on Ilha do Mel (Paraná); forró at the Estudantina club (Rio de Janeiro); Samba do Enredo at the Rio Carnival.

Wildlife Viewing

Pantanal Matogrossense; Tefé (Amazonas).

National Parks & Natural Attractions

Parque Nacional de Aparados da Serra

Doing it Yourself
One of our readers offers his comments on climbing in Brazil:

If you're a climber travelling to Brazil, don't hesitate to bring a bit of gear and do some routes. You don't need much – a pair of boots, a chalk bag, harness, 10-mm rope, 10 quick-draws and a couple of long slings are enough. You can sell used gear very quickly and easily in Rio – just contact the clubs for interested members. Practically all routes are bolted; most bolts are really solid, though those around the sea-cliff areas can be rusty and a bit dubious.

Hanging belays are very common – they usually consist of a single bolt. It can be very unnerving: you're 200 metres off the ground, leading off a single anchor 20 metres to the next piece of protection.

The routes are usually long and interesting, (if a little run-out). Cracks aren't very abundant and when they exist they usually peter out fairly quickly. The rock is old and weathered, and generally very solid. Friction is excellent – but the small, sharp edges (especially on the crags around Rio) can be pretty severe on boots. You tend to lose quite a bit of rubber. It's easy and cheap to get boots resoled in Rio, however: I had an old pair of Rocksters resoled for US$15. It was a very neat and professional job. Just call Eduardo Cabral (☎ 239-2773), or contact Club Excursionista Carioca. You can also stay at the club for US$3 a night. It has a fridge, bathroom and toilet and is only a block from Copacabana beach.

Most of the climbing in Brazil is centred around the southern states as far north as Rio. Some interesting areas include:

Pedra do Bau This is a 300-metre rock pinnacle near Campos do Jordão in the Serra da Mantiquéira. The valley itself is popular for hang-gliding and para-gliding. Two peaks provide various free and artificial routes: Pedra do Bauzinho, the smaller of the two, has some easy climbs but is mainly used as a descent route (via two abseils) to a knife-edge ridge which provides access to Pedra do Baú – a striking, isolated pinnacle of rock. Several climbs of moderate grades ascend the pinnacle, and all are provided with bolts.

(Itaimbezinho canyon); Iguaçu Falls; Parque Nacional da Chapada dos Guimarães; Parque Nacional de Caparaó; Parque Nacional da Chapada Diamantina; Parque Nacional dos Lençóis Maranhenses; Parque Nacional Marinho de Fernando de Noronha; Parque Nacional da Serra da Capivara.

Religious Experience
Candomblé (Bahia); Colônia Cinco Mil (Rio Branco); Vale de Amanhecer (Brasília).

Sports
Capoeira (Bahia); football (Rio).

Offbeat Attractions & Activities
Olaria de Brennand (Recife); train ride from Cuiabá to Paranaguá (Paraná); dune buggy rides (Natal); Ribeirão do Meio water slides (Lençóis); catamaran excursions from São Luís to Alcântara; nudist beach at Tambaba

(João Pessoa); pororoca tidal bore (Amapá); Salão Internacional de Humor do Piauí (International Humour Festival of Piauí, Teresina); steam train from São João del Rei to Tiradentes (Minas Gerais); hot spa at the Parque das Águas (Caxambu); double hang-gliding (Rio); tubing down the Rio Nhundiaquara (Morretes); piranha fishing (Pantanal); Butantan snake farm (São Paulo).

ACCOMMODATION
We have managed to tackle the problem of inflation reasonably well by quoting all prices in US dollars, but it is impossible to counteract the weird price changes caused when the government freezes prices, unfreezes them, then freezes them again. Most of the prices listed will be reasonably accurate, but once in a while there is bound to be a shocker. For advice about security and

Três Picos This is an amazing place near Nova Friburgo in Rio state. From Nova Friburgo, ask for directions to the bus stop for the No 620 bus to São Lourenço. The 1½-hour trip to Três Picos traverses mostly dirt roads – ask to be let off at the Três Picos turnoff. Walk up this dirt road for about six km (all uphill) and head for the three granite domes which dominate the valley. If unsure of the way, ask for directions to Renaldo's fazenda – his farm is the last in the valley, at the base of the cliffs. Renaldo has two huts which he allows climbers to use; one has electric light. It's customary to give him 50c per person per night for the use of the huts, though he won't ask for it. The last bus leaves Nova Friburgo for São Lourenço at 6.50 pm.

This is one of the best climbing areas in Brazil. The rock is small-crystal granite, with great friction. Routes vary in size from 400 to 700 metres, on three separate granite domes: Capacete (400 metres), Pico Maior (700 metres) and Pico Médio (500–600 metres). The grades vary from 5.9 to 5.12 and above (Australian grade 18 and beyond). From the summit, views are spectacular – to the south lies the Serra dos Órgãos (Dedo de Deus, etc); to the east lies Rio (visible on a clear day); and north and west lie rolling, mountainous valleys. The potential for new routes is enormous – you could spend a long time here. It's wise to take up a few days' food, as the round trip to the nearest shop, on foot, is about 14 km. Drinkable spring water is provided at the huts.

Rio Pão de Açúcar (Sugar Loaf) is the stereotypical, 'must-do' climbing area close to the city. The easy solo route described in the Rio chapter of this book is worthwhile. It's more bushwalking than climbing, though one exposed section requires caution. I've clambered up this route dozens of times and have yet to tire of it. If you start the walk at about 3 pm you'll get to the top in time to see the sun set over Rio – a worthwhile experience. It's not necessary to pay the cost of the cable-car ride back down – just hop on.

On Saturdays, the Carioca Climbing Club opens up the artificial climbing wall built into the side of the topmost cable-car station. Anybody's welcome to join in – just bring boots, harness and chalk-bag. The wall has several routes, all bolted, with a tendon-grinding roof and overhung section.

The more serious routes on Pão de Açúcar start from the base of the cliff under the cable car. Routes include: 'Cavallo Louco' (a classic), 'Italiano', 'Cisco Kid', 'Babylonia' and 'Acid Wall'.

It's possible to climb some routes at night, under the floodlights set up for the tourist lookout. ■

Greg Caire

---

accommodation, refer to the Dangers & Annoyances section in this chapter.

Camping

Camping is becoming increasingly popular in Brazil and is a viable alternative for travellers on limited budgets or those who want to explore some of the country's national or state parks. For detailed information on camping grounds it's a good idea to buy the *Guia Quatro Rodas Camping Guide* from any newsstand. You may also want to contact the Camping Club of Brazil, Rua Senador Dantas 75, 25th floor, Rio de Janeiro. The club has 52 sites in 14 states.

Minimum Impact Camping The following guidelines are recommended for those camping in wilderness or other fragile areas of Brazil:

- Select a well-drained campsite and, especially if it's raining, use a plastic or other type of waterproof groundsheet to prevent having to dig trenches.
- Along popular routes, set up camp in established sites.
- Biodegradable items may be buried but anything with food residue should be carried out – including cigarette butts – lest it be dug up and scattered by animals.
- Use established toilet facilities if they are available. Otherwise, select a site at least 50 metres from water sources and bury wastes in a cat-hole at least several inches deep. If possible, burn the used toilet paper or bury it well.
- Use only biodegradable soap products (you'll probably have to carry them from home) and to avoid thermal pollution, use natural temperature water where possible. When washing up dishes with hot water, either let it cool to outdoor temperature before pouring it out or dump it in a gravelly, non-vegetated place away from natural water sources.
- Wash dishes and brush your teeth well away from watercourses.

When building a fire, try to select an established site and keep fires as small as possible. Use only down dead wood and when you're finished, make sure ashes are cool and buried before leaving. Again, carry out cigarette butts.

Youth Hostels

Youth hostels in Brazil are called *albergues de juventude*, and in the last few years the Brazilian organisers have been getting their act together. There are now more than 90 hostels and more are planned. Most state capitals and popular tourist areas have at least one. Although quality varies widely, the cost is very reasonable and is regulated by the federation in Brazil. A night in a hostel will cost between US$5 to US$7 per person, depending on inflation. It's not always necessary to be a member to stay in one, but it'll cost you more if you're not. International Youth Hostel cards are accepted, but if you arrive in Brazil without one you can buy guest membership cards for about US$10 from the head office in each state. Booklets listing the hostels and describing how to get there (in Portuguese) are available at these offices and most travel agents.

The head office of the Federação Brasileira dos Albergues de Juventude (FBAJ; (☎ (021) 2524829) is at Rua da Assembléia 10, sala 1211, Centro, Rio de Janeiro, CEP 20011, RJ. The FBAJ publishes a useful directory of Brazilian hostels.

Dormitórios

A *dormitório* is dorm-style sleeping with several beds to a room. These are usually the cheapest places in town, often costing as little as US$2 or US$3 a head per night.

Pensões

Most budget travellers stay at a *pensão* (small guesthouse) where a room without a bathroom can go for as little as US$4 or US$5 per person. These rooms with communal bathrooms down the hall are called *quartos*. With a private bathroom, similar rooms are called *apartamentos*, and cost a couple of dollars more.

Hotels

If you want to travel in style, Brazil has modern luxury hotels all over the place. The best hotels can cost as little as US$30 a double per night and, at the other end of the scale, as much as US$100 to US$150 per night in Rio and São Paulo. Often a 10% tax is added to the bill.

Aparthotels, available in the larger cities, provide the comforts of a good hotel without some of the glitter. They are also a bit cheaper. A good, medium-priced aparthotel should cost somewhere from US$40 per night for a double room.

Most hotels in Brazil are regulated by Embratur, the federal tourism authority. They also rate the quality of hotels from one to five stars. Regulated hotels must have a price list with an Embratur label which is usually posted on the wall in every room and behind the reception desk. Even so, it still pays to bargain.

It's a good idea to look at a room before deciding to take it. Check the shower for hot water, check the bed, check the lock on the door. Two big sleep killers in Brazil are mosquitoes and heat. Fans do wonders for stopping both. Many medium-priced and expensive hotels have safes which are 'safe' to use so long as you get a receipt.

In the off season many hotels have promotional rates. Ask about them. Sometimes good hotels have a few quartos or cheaper rooms which are not advertised. It pays to enquire about these, as they allow you to use all the facilities of the hotel while paying considerably less than the other guests. For more details about bargaining, refer to Bargaining under the Money section in this chapter.

There are a few games played by hotel clerks to get you into a more expensive room. If you want a single room there are only doubles; if you want a quarto, there are only apartamentos. Don't say yes too quickly – if you feign a desire to look for alternative lodging, they will often remember that there is a cheaper room after all. In reality, some hotels don't have singles. It is generally much cheaper to travel with someone, as rooms for two are nowhere near twice as expensive as rooms for one.

Reservations If you're staying in middle to high-class hotels, reservations are a good idea in touristed centres (especially in Rio) during vacations (July, and December to February) and in any vacation Mecca (eg Búzios) during weekends. We try to list hotel phone numbers for this purpose, but you can also get them from travel agents and tourist information offices. Be wary of taxi drivers, particularly in Rio, who know just the hotel for you. You may find yourself being taken to an expensive hotel which pays the cabby a commission.

To avoid summer crowds, it is not a bad idea to travel during the week and stay put, usually in a city, during the weekends, when the locals are making their pilgrimages away from the cities. This minimises your contact with crowded buses and hotels and gets you into the city for the weekend music and festivities.

Motels

Motels are a Brazilian institution and should never be confused with hotels. They have names like Alibi, Ilha do Capri, L'Amour and Wet Dreams. Rented by the hour, for short stays only, the motel is the Brazilian solution to the lack of privacy caused by overcrowded living conditions. Used by adults who still live with their parents, kids who want to get away from their parents, and couples who want to get away from their kids, they are an integral part of the nation's social fabric, a bedrock of Brazilian morality, and are treated by Brazilians with what most outsiders consider to be incredible nonchalance.

The quality of motels varies, reflecting their popularity with all social classes. Most are out of the city centre, with walled-in garages for anonymity. A personal favourite is the Swing in São Paulo. In a three-storey apartment, it has a hot tub on the top floor with skylights that open. On the 2nd floor is a sauna and bathroom. The suites have circular vibra-beds with mirrors overhead, a video recorder with adult movies piped over loudspeakers, and room service with a menu full of foods and sex toys (with instructions).

Most travellers don't spend much time in motels, but they can be quite useful, and a lot of fun if you're travelling as a couple. If you're having trouble finding accommodation, they're not too expensive. I for one wouldn't hesitate to head straight for a motel in that situation.

Accommodation in Remote Areas

If you're travelling where there are no hotels – the Amazon or the Northeast – a hammock and a mosquito net are essential. With these basics, and friendly locals, you can get a good night's rest anywhere. Most fishing villages along the coast have seen an outsider or two and will put you up for the night. If they've seen a few more outsiders, they'll probably charge you a couple of dollars.

FOOD

Vou matar quem 'tá me matando.
I'm going to kill the person who's killing me.
(A popular saying when sitting down to eat)

The hub of the Brazilian diet revolves around *arroz* (white rice), *feijão* (black beans) and *farofel* (manioc flour). It's possible to eat these every day in Brazil and in some regions it's hard not to. The tasty black beans are typically cooked in bacon. The white rice is often very starchy. Farofel, the staple of the Indians, slaves and Portuguese for hundreds of years, is a hardy root that grows everywhere. It seems to be an acquired taste for foreign palates.

From the rice-bean-farofel group, meals go in one of three directions: *carne* (steak), *galinha* (chicken) and *peixe* (fish). This makes up the typical Brazilian meal and is called *prato feito* (set meal) or *prato do dia* (plate of day) in lanchonetes from Xique Xique to Bananal. They are typically enormous meals and incredibly cheap, but after a while they can become a trifle monotonous. If quantity is your thing, you can live like a king.

What is done with the meat, chicken or fish? It's cooked, and that's about it. Don't

Food vendor

get me wrong, it's generally very good meat, but Brazilians don't do much with it. Steak is the national passion. They like it big and rare. The best cuts are *filet* and *churrasco*. Chicken is usually grilled, sometimes fried. Fish is generally fried.

But that's not the end of the story. In the cities you can get many of the dishes that you like back home. There's also fine dining. For US$5 to US$10 you can have a superb Italian, Japanese or Indian dinner in Rio or São Paulo. *Churrascarias* and *rodízios* bring you all the meat you can eat and a variety of other goodies for a fixed price (around US$5 in Rio). They must be tried – vegetarians have no problem filling up either if they don't mind seeing all that meat. Rodízios are especially good in the South.

Lanchonetes are stand-up fast-food bars where you can order sandwiches and *pasteis* (crumbed hors d'oeuvres). *Restaurantes* have more proper sit-down meals. Never order *um almoço* (a lunch) unless you have a big appetite or care to share with a friend. Portions are immense.

Regional Cuisine

Despite much sameness there are regional differences. The cooking in the Northern interior *(comida do sertão)* has a heavy Indian influence, using many unique, traditional tubers and fruits. On the Northeastern coast the cuisine *(comida baiana)* has a distinct African flavour: it uses peppers, spices and the delicious oil of the *dendê* palm tree. The slaves also introduced greater variety in the preparation of meat and fish, and dishes like *vatapá* and *caruru*.

Minas Gerais is the home of *comida mineiro*, a heavy but tasty cuisine based on pork, vegetables like *couve* (spinach-like leaf) and *quiabo* (bean-like vegetable); and *tutú*, a kind of refried bean-paste. In the South, *comida gaúcha* from Rio Grande do Sul revolves around meat, meat and more meat. This cuisine has the most extensive vocabulary for different cuts of meat that you're ever likely to hear.

Breakfast

Breakfast is called *café da manhã*; it's often

shortened to *café*, which is also the word for coffee. Served at most hotels (with the possible exception of the very cheapest places), for no extra charge, café includes coffee, steamed milk, fruit, biscuits or bread, maybe cheese and meat, and rarely eggs. If you tire of this, or don't like it in the first place go into any *padaria* (bakery) or market and buy a good *iogurte* (yoghurt), then get some fruit, always abundant and delicious.

Lunch

Lunch is the main meal for Brazilians. Lanchonetes, as mentioned earlier, are everywhere. Portions are almost always big enough for two. Most cities now have vegetarian restaurants with salads, casseroles, brown rice, etc. With any luck the food might be healthy, but it's rarely tasty. A better choice may be a *suco* (juice) bar for a natural fruit juice and sandwich.

Dinner

Dinner doesn't vary much from lunch, unless you go to a better restaurant. Most dishes can be easily divided between two people (if you can't eat it all ask for a doggie bag *(embalagem)* and give it to someone on the street).

In the cities, Brazilians dine late. Restaurants don't get busy in Rio and São Paulo until 10 pm on weekends. A 10% tip is generally included in the bill. If not it's customary to leave at least 10%. Most places in Rio will bring you a *couvert*, whether you ask or not. This is optional, so you are perfectly within your rights to send it back. The typical couvert is a ridiculously overpriced and tedious basket of bread, crackers, pheasant eggs and a couple of carrot and celery sticks. Most restaurants will still bring bread with your soup at no extra charge.

Standard operating procedure in most Rio restaurants is to overcharge the customer. Some places don't even itemise their bills. Don't hesitate to look at the bill and ask the waiter: *pode discriminar?* (can you itemise?). Also, take your time and count your change – short-changing is very common in Brazil. It's all part of the game. They good-naturedly overcharge and you can good-naturedly hassle them until the bill is fixed. They are used to it.

Brazilian Dishes

Acarajé – this is what the Baianas, Bahian women in flowing white dresses, traditionally sell on street corners throughout Bahia. The Baianas are an unforgettable sight but you're likely to smell their cooking before you see it. It's the wonderful-smelling dendê oil. Acarajé is made from peeled brown beans, mashed in salt and onions, and then fried in dendê oil. Inside these delicious fried balls is *vatapá* (see this list), dried shrimp, pepper and tomato sauce. Dendê oil is strong stuff. Many stomachs can't handle it.

Angú – a cake made with very thin corn flour, called *fubá*, and mixed with water and salt.

Bobó de camarão – manioc paste cooked and flavoured with dry shrimp, coconut milk and cashew nut.

Camarão á paulista – unshelled fresh shrimp fried in olive oil with lots of garlic and salt.

Canja – a big soup with chicken broth. More often than not a meal in itself.

Caranguejada – a kind of crab cooked whole and seasoned with water.

Carne de sol – a tasty, salted meat, grilled and served with beans, rice and vegetables.

Caruru – one of the most popular Brazilian dishes brought from Africa, this is made with okra or other vegetables cooked in water. The water is then drained, and onions, salt, shrimps and malagueta peppers are added, mixed and grated together with the okra paste and dendê oil. Traditionally, a sea fish such as garoupa is then added.

Casquinha de carangueijo or *Siri* – stuffed crab. The meat is prepared with manioc flour.

Cozido – any kind of stew, usually with more vegetables than other stew-like Brazilian dishes (eg potatoes, sweet potatoes, carrots and manioc).

Dourado – found in freshwater throughout Brazil; a scrumptious fish.

Feijoada – the national dish of Brazil, feijoada is a meat stew served with rice and a bowl of beans. It's served throughout the country and there are many different variations, depending on what animal happens to be walking through the kitchen while the chefs are at work. All kinds of meats go into feijoada. Orange peels, peppers and farinha accompany the stew.

Frango ao molho pardo – chicken pieces stewed with vegetables and then covered with a seasoned sauce made from the blood of the bird.

Moqueca – a kind of sauce or stew and a style of cooking from Bahia. There are many kinds of moqueca: fish, shrimp, oyster, crab or a combination. The moqueca sauce is defined by its heavy use of dendê oil and coconut milk, often with peppers and onions. A moqueca must be cooked in a covered claypot.

Moqueca capixaba – a moqueca from Espírito Santo uses lighter *urucum* oil from the Indians instead of dendê oil.

Pato no tucupi – roast duck flavoured with garlic and cooked in the *tucupi* sauce made from the juice of the manioc plant and *jambu*, a local vegetable. A very popular dish in Pará.

Peixada – fish cooked in broth with vegetables and eggs.

Peixe a delícia – broiled or grilled fish usually made with bananas and coconut milk. Delicious in Fortaleza.

Prato de verão – this dish, which translates literally as summer plate, is served at many suco stands in Rio. Basically, it's a fruit salad.

Pirarucu ao forno – pirarucu is the most famous fish from the rivers of Amazônia. It's oven-cooked with lemon and other seasonings.

Tacacá – an Indian dish of dried shrimp cooked with pepper, jambu, manioc and much more.

Tutu á mineira – a bean paste with toasted bacon and manioc flour, often served with cooked cabbage. Typical of Minas Gerais.

Vatapá – a seafood dish with a thick sauce made from manioc paste, coconut and dendê oil. Perhaps the most famous Brazilian dish of African origin.

Xinxim de galinha – pieces of chicken flavoured with garlic, salt and lemon. Shrimp and dendê oil are often added.

Fruit

Expand your experience of fruit juices and ice creams beyond pineapple and orange to play blind man's buff in Brazil with your taste buds. From the savoury nirvana of *graviola* to the confusingly clinical taste of *cupuaçú*, fruits and juices are a major Brazilian highlight. For more details about styles of juices, refer to Fruit Juices under Drinks in the following section.

To get you started, we have included here a partial list of Brazilian fruits, particularly those found in Rio. Many of the fruits of the Northeast and Amazon have no English equivalent, so there's no sense in attempting to translate their names: you'll just have to try the exotic tastes of *ingá, abiu, mari-mari, pitanga, taperebá, sorva, pitamba, uxí, pupunha, seriguela, bacuri* and *jambo*. The following taste descriptions are unashamedly subjective: be bold with your choices and enjoy!

abacate – avocado

abacaxí – pineapple

açaí – gritty, forest berry taste and deep purple colour. This fruit of the açaí palm tree is also used in wines and syrups.

acerola – wonderful cherry flavour. Megasource of vitamin C.

ameixa – plum, prune

bacaba – Amazonian fruit used in wines and syrups.

betarraba – beetroot

biribá – Amazonian fruit eaten plain.

buriti – a palm-tree fruit with a mealy flavour and a hint of peach followed by an odd aftertaste. Also used in ice cream and for wine.

cacau – pulp from cocoa pod; tastes wonderfully sweet and creamy. Nothing like cocoa, which is extracted from the bean.

caja – pear-like taste

cajú – fruit of cashew (the nut is enclosed in

an appendage of the fruit). Tart taste like a cross between lemon and pear.

carambola – starfruit. Tangy, citrus flavour.

cenoura – carrot

cupuaçú – cool taste, strangely clinical. Best with milk and sugar.

fruto-do-conde green, sugar-apple fruit, very popular.

gengibre – ginger. Commonly drunk as *atchim* (a mixture of lemon and ginger).

genipapo – what could be imagined as curdled cow piss – not everyone's favourite! Better as a liqueur.

goiaba – guava

graviola – custard apple. Aromatic and exquisite taste.

jaca – large fruit of the jackfruit tree.

laranja – orange

limão – lemon

mamão – papaya (pawpaw)

manga – mango

mangaba – tart flavour, similar to pear.

maracujá – passion fruit

melancia – watermelon

melão – honeydew melon

morango – strawberry

murici – mealy fruit with vague caramel taste.

pera – pear

pêssego – peach

pupunha – a fatty, vitamin-rich Amazonian fruit taken with coffee.

sapotí – gritty, semi-sweet Worcestershire sauce. Brits may even recognise a hint of Marmite. Rather confusing for a fruit!

tamarindo – pleasantly acidic, plum-like.

tangerina – mandarin orange, tangerine

tapereba – gritty texture, flavour resembles cross between acerola and sweet potato.

uva – grape

DRINKS
Fruit Juice

Sucos in Brazil are divine. They vary by region and season (the Amazon has fruits you won't believe). Request them *sem açúcar e gelo* or *natural* if you don't want sugar and ice. Often you'll get some water mixed into a suco; if you're worried about getting sick ask for a *vitamina*, which is juice with milk. Banana and avocado are great with milk.

Another way to avoid water is to drink orange juice, which is rarely adulterated and it mixes well with papaya, carrot, and several other fruits. An orange juice, beet and carrot combo is popular in Rio. There are an incredible variety of fruits and good combinations. Spend some time experimenting.

Caldo de cana is a tasty juice extracted directly from lengths of sugar cane, usually while you wait. The machine that does the crushing is a noisy, multi-cogged affair that has to be cranked up every time someone wants a drink. Caldo and pasteis are a favourite combination amongst Brazilians.

Coffee

Brazilians take their coffee as strong as the devil, as hot as hell, and as sweet as love. They call it *cafezinho* and drink it as an espresso-sized coffee without milk and cut with plenty of sugar. The cafezinho is taken often and at all times. It's sold in stand-up bars and dispensed in offices to keep the workers perky. I've known Brazilians to take one to bed with them to go to sleep. If you don't like the sugar, hunt around for a coffee stand that has espresso. They're easy to find in cities and large towns. *Café com leite* is coffee with hot milk, usually drunk for breakfast.

Chá or tea is not nearly as important a drink as coffee, except in the state of Rio Grande do Sul, where the gaúchos drink *maté*, a strong tea drunk through a silver straw from a hollow gourd.

Soft Drinks

Soft drinks *(refrigerantes)* are found everywhere and are cheaper than bottled water. Coke is number one, Guaraná is number two. Made from the berry of an Amazonian plant, Guaraná has a delicious, distinctive taste.

Alcohol

Para que nossas mulheres não fiquem viúva.
May our wives never be widows (a drinking toast).

Cachaça is found everywhere – even in the

most miserable frontier shantytowns. Bottled beer usually follows the introduction of electricity to a region. At the pinnacle of Brazilian civilisation is *chopp* (see below), which is only found in large and prosperous economic centres with paved roads and electricity.

Beer Brazilians, like most civilised people, enjoy their beer served icy cold *(bem gelada)*. A *cerveja* is a 600-ml bottled beer. Of the common brands, Antártica is the best followed by Brahma (although some Brazilians argue that Brahma is better in Rio), Skol, Kaiser and Malt 90. The best beers are the regional ones, like Bohemia and Cerpa from Pará and Cerma from Maranhão. Bavaria is a tasty beer which only comes in 300-ml bottles and is found in the more up-market bars. Caracu is a stout-like beer, also only available in 300-ml bottles.

Brazilians gesture for a tall one by horizontally placing the Boy Scout sign (three fingers together) a foot above their drinking tables. A *cervejinha* is 300-ml of bottled or canned beer. Cans are more expensive than bottles. Some experts argue that it tastes better from the can – this is a debatable subject and one on which you'll have to form your own opinion after researching the matter. If you're buying beer to take away, you'll be charged a hefty deposit for the bottles unless you trade in empties.

Chopp (pronounced 'shoppee') is a pale blond pilsner draft, lighter and far superior to canned or bottled beer. In big cities you may even find *chopp escuro* a kind of light stout. Usage: *Moço, mais um chopp!* (waiter, one more 'shoppee'!).

Wine Jorge Amado wrote a satire about nationalist generals running Brazil who drink Brazilian wine in public and avoid the stuff like the plague in private. Well, Brazilian wine is improving but it's not great. Forrestier is at the top of a very low heap of vintages. The whites are better than the reds and the Argentine wines are much better than both.

Cachaça *Cachaça, pinga* or *aguardente* is a high-proof, dirt cheap, sugar-cane alcohol produced and drunk throughout the country. Cachaça literally means booze. Pinga (which literally means drop) is considered more polite, but by any name it's cheaper than spit and far more toxic. The production of cachaça is as old as slavery in Brazil. The distilleries grew up with the sugar plantations, first to supply local consumption and then to export to Africa to exchange for slaves.

There are well over 100 brands of cachaça, with differences in taste and quality. A cheap cachaça can cut a hole in the strongest stomach lining. Velho Barreiro, Ypioca, Pitú, Carangueijo, and São Francisco are some of the better labels. Many distilleries will allow

Beer Labels

you to take a tour and watch the process from raw sugar to rot gut and then sample some of the goodies. The smaller distilleries usually make a much smoother cachaça than the commercial brands.

Other Alcoholic Drinks *Caipirinha* is the Brazilian national drink. The ingredients are simple: cachaça, lime, sugar and crushed ice, but a well-made caipirinha is a work of art. *Caipirosca* is a caipirinha with vodka replacing cachaça. *Caipirissima* is still another variation, with Bacardi rum instead of cachaça. *Batidas* are wonderful mixes of cachaça, sugar and fruit juice.

ENTERTAINMENT
Movies
English Most movies in the cinemas are screened in their original language with Portuguese subtitles; consequently there are plenty of films in English. Brazil gets most of the hits from the USA, including many of the violent Rambo-type films. Brazilians also adore comedians like Woody Allen and the Marx Brothers. I must admit I don't completely understand why. When I saw *Hannah & Her Sisters* in Rio I was the only person in the theatre laughing; in the scene where Woody becomes a Catholic and tries to explain his existential crisis to his father, a New York Jew, I realised that the Brazilians didn't have a clue as to why it was so funny.

The Marx Brothers films are dubbed, which raises the pun problem. When Groucho tells Chico that the loot is out near the viaduct and Chico responds, in his thick accent, 'Vi-a-duck, Vi not a chicken', there is no way this exchange can be duplicated in Portuguese.

Portuguese From the romanticism of *Black Orpheus* to the realism of *Cinema Novo* and Glauber Rocha, Brazil has produced a number of excellent films. Since the end of the dictatorship there has been a film renaissance. *Pixote*, Hector Babenco's compelling film about young street urchins, won the best film award at Cannes. Many recent Brazilian films are historical, providing special insight into the country.

Rio has many film aficionados and special events. The Cineclub Botafogo is always a good venue. There are special events like the annual film festival in September, and cinema on the beach at Copacabana in the summer.

Spectator Sports
Football Soccer was introduced to Brazil after a young student from São Paulo, Charles Miller, returned from his studies in England with two footballs and a rule book and began to organise the first league. It quickly became the national passion, and Brazil has since won three World Cups. Brazilians are crazy about the game.

The government is prepared to spend whatever it takes to win the World Cup, but becomes worried because of the financial drain when no one goes to work on game days. When the team lost to arch-rivals Argentina in the 1990 World Cup, millions cried on the streets and a mass depression gripped the country for weeks.

Fans worship their heroes. Matches are played on Sundays and Wednesdays. Announcers have the ability to stretch the word 'goal' for at least 20 seconds (GOOOOOOOOOOOOOOOOOOOOOL!). Brazilians play the world's most creative and artistic style of football. You'll see tiny kids playing skilled, rough matches in the streets, on the beaches, just about anywhere.

Go to a game. It's an intense spectacle, and one of the most colourful pageants I've ever seen. The fans are insane but they know their football. Each good play is rewarded with superlatives. A fancy dribble past an opponent receives a Spanish bullfight *olé*; a goal results in delirium.

Volleyball Surprisingly volleyball is Brazil's second sport. A natural on the beach, it's also a popular spectator sport on TV. A local variation you'll see on Rio's beaches is volleyball played without the hands (*footvoley*). It's quite fun to watch but it's bloody hard to play.

Pelé – King of Brazil

On 23 October 1940, Édson Arantes do Nascimento was born in Três Corações, Minas Gerais. He became the greatest soccer player in the world, known to everyone as Pelé. Although he has long retired, Pelé's presence is everywhere in Brazil – on TV advertising a department store, in the newspapers receiving an award for community service, on billboards promoting shoes, and in the hearts and minds of every Brazilian. If he ran for president he'd be a sure thing. But Pelé is above politics – he is king of Brazil.

His public image is impeccable. He's never smoked, never been photographed with a drink in hand and NEVER been involved with drugs. Even when an illegitimate daughter surfaced after 25 years, his name remained untarnished. Of course he did the right thing by including her in his will.

In his 22-year career, the teams in which he played gained 53 titles; three World Cup titles (Sweden in 1958, Chile in 1962 and Mexico in 1970), dual world club championships (with Santos in 1962 and 1963), two South American championships, 11 paulista state championships and four Rio-São Paulo tournaments.

In 1971, Pelé retired from the Brazilian team and in 1974 from Santos. In 1975 the New York Cosmos coaxed him north to the USA. He played there until 1977, when they won the American championship. He finally retired at the end of that year, after a game between the Cosmos and Santos, in which he played the first half for the Cosmos and the second half with Santos.

In 1363 games (112 for the Brazilian team), he scored 1282 goals. When he scored his 1000th goal in 1969 he dedicated it 'To the Children of Brazil'. Pelé called getting the goal: 'One of the greatest blessings a man could ever expect to receive from God'.

In 1981 he received the title Athlete of the Century from the French magazine *L'Equipe*. In Brazil he is known simply as O Rei (The King). ∎

Motor Racing Brazilians love speed. Taxi drivers may give you a hint of it, and since the early '70s Brazilians have won more Formula One Grand Prix world championships than any other nationality. Emerson Fittipaldi was world champion twice in the '70s, Nelson Piquet won his third world championship in 1987, and Ayrton Senna took it out for the first time in 1988. The Brazilian Grand Prix traditionally kicks off the Formula One season in Rio around March each year.

THINGS TO BUY

A smart souvenir hunter can do well in Brazil, provided they know a little about Brazilian culture. Most people find the best souvenirs to be music, local crafts and artwork.

Brazilian music (discussed in the Facts about the Country chapter) is sure to evoke your most precious travel memories. The best record stores in the country are in the big shopping malls of São Paulo.

Although nearly everything can be found

in Rio and São Paulo, there is a premium for moving craft and art pieces from the hinterland to the fancy stores of the big cities. The inexpensive exceptions include the weekly hippie fair at Ipanema (see the Rio de Janeiro city chapter), the ubiquitous FUNAI stores and museum gift shops.

Most of the Indian crafts sold in FUNAI stores are inexpensive, but the quality generally matches the price. Museum gift shops, on the other hand, stock some very worthwhile souvenirs. They are particularly good for prints of local art. The Carmen Miranda museum in Rio de Janeiro sells great T-shirts of the great lady herself complete with her fruit headdress.

Outside the big cities, your best bet for craftwork are artisan fairs, cooperative stores and government-run shops. The Northeast has a rich assortment of artistic items from which to choose. Salvador and nearby Cachoeira are notable for their rough-hewn wood sculpture. Artisans in Fortaleza and the southern coast of Ceará specialise in fine lace cloths. The interior of Pernambuco, in particular Caruaru, are famous for the wildly imaginative ceramic figurines and the traditional leather hats worn by the sertanejos. Functional and decorative hammocks are available in cities throughout the Amazon. These string, mesh or cloth slings are fixtures in most Brazilian homes. They are indispensable for travellers and make fine, portable gifts.

The state of Minas Gerais is most famous for its gemstones. However, if you're in the market for fine jewellery and precious stones, wait until you return to the big cities to make your purchases. Buy from a large and reputable dealer like Amsterdam-Sauer, Roditi or H Stern. Stern is an international dealer based in Ipanema whose reputation for quality and honesty is beyond reproach. It isn't a discount store, but their jewellery is less expensive in Brazil than in their outlets in other parts of the world.

Brazilian leather goods are moderately priced, but the leather isn't particularly supple. The better Brazilian shoes, belts, wallets, purses and luggage are sold in the up-market shops of Ipanema and Copacabana. Brazilian shoes are extremely good value, but much of the best is reserved for export and larger sizes are difficult to find. High-quality, cheap, durable, leather soccer balls with hand-stitched panels are sold all over Brazil in sporting goods stores. Inflated soccer balls should not be put in the cargo hold of a plane.

In an effort to draw industry to the Amazon, the Brazilian government lifted many tax and tariff restrictions in Manaus. The advantage to tourists in this free trade zone is minimal unless you are particularly interested in picking up electrical equipment which has been assembled in Brazil.

Finally, here are a few more ideas for the avid souvenir hunter. Coffee-table picture books on Brazil, videotapes of Carnival and videotapes of highlights of the Brazilian national team and Pelé in various World Cup matches are hawked in the streets of Copacabana. Guaraná powder, a stimulant (said to be an aphrodisiac), is sold in health

Sticker advertising Bum Bum bikinis

food stores and chemists around the country. Mounted reprints of old Rio lithographs are sold in Rio's Cinelândia district on the steps of the opera house. The smallest of Brazil's bikinis are sold at Bum-Bum or Kanga shops. Candomblé stores are a good source of curios, ranging from magical incense guaranteed to bring good fortune and increase sexual allure, wisdom and health, to amulets and ceramic figurines of Afro-Brazilian gods. If you are travelling in Brazil during Carnival make sure you pick up a copy of the Carnival edition of *Manchete* magazine.

Neotropic Cormorants

Getting There & Away

INTRODUCTION

Most travellers start their Brazilian odyssey by flying down to Rio, but this is only one of many ways to arrive. Other gateway airports include: Recife, popular with German package tourists on their way to one of the many beach resorts catering to their needs, and Manaus, capital of the state of Amazonas, which is halfway between Rio and Miami.

Brazil also has land borders with every other country in South America, with the exception of Chile and Ecuador, so while some travellers may be bussing in from Uruguay in the south, others may be arriving via the *trem da morte* (death train) from Bolivia. By river, many travellers take a slow boat down the Amazon from Iquitos in Peru or into the Pantanal via the Rio Paraguay from Asunçion.

However you're travelling, it's worth taking out travel insurance. Work out what you need – you may not want to insure that grotty old army surplus backpack, but everyone should be covered for the worst possible case: an accident, for example, that will require hospital treatment and a flight home. It's a good idea to make a copy of your policy, in case the original is lost. If you are planning to travel for a long time, the insurance may seem very expensive – but if you can't afford it, you certainly won't be able to afford to deal with a medical emergency overseas.

AIR

Cheap deals on air travel are volatile. With some legwork you can usually save a couple of hundred dollars. Check newspapers and discount or Latin American specialist travel agents for good deals.

Varig, Brazil's international airline, flies to many major cities in the world. From the USA the basic carriers which serve Brazil are Varig, American Airlines, and Japan Airlines (JAL) (from the west coast); from England, British Airways and Varig; and from Australia, Qantas, Aerolineas Argentinas and Lan Chile.

Discount tickets have restrictions. The most pernicious is the limit on the amount of time you can spend in Brazil. Charter flights often restrict a stay to as little as three weeks. Most other tickets have a 90-day limit. There's usually a premium for tickets valid over 180 days. Although the Brazil Air Pass is no longer the bargain it once was, it's worth mentioning here that you *must* purchase it outside Brazil. (See the Getting Around chapter for more information.)

If you are planning to stay in Brazil for more than 90 days, cheap airline tickets are a big problem. You are required to buy a return ticket before you will be issued with a visa in the USA, but it's not hard to get around this (see the Visa section in the Facts for the Visitor chapter). Unfortunately, the cost of a one-way ticket is more than twice the price of a return economy fare. For example: from Los Angeles to Rio return costs about US$900 if you buy from the airlines, but you may be able to obtain a discount ticket for as little as US$700 from a specialist travel agent. The fare for a one-way ticket is US$850, and for a round trip valid for over three years the fare is doubled. Absurd! This means it may be cheaper to buy a discounted return ticket with a 90-day limit, bury the return portion ticket and then buy a ticket in Brazil when you are ready to go home.

If you plan to stay more than six months in Brazil you also have to consider leaving the country to get a new visa. Ask about package deals. We were able to get a round-trip Aerolineas Argentinas ticket from New York to Buenos Aires with an unlimited stopover in Rio. This gave us a free ride to Buenos Aires to get new visas after several months in Brazil – but check if this is still available.

To/From the USA

The *New York Times*, the *LA Times*, the *Chicago Tribune* and the *San Francisco Examiner* all produce weekly travel sections in which you'll find any number of travel agents' ads. Council Travel and STA Travel have offices in major cities nationwide. The Brazilian American Cultural Center (BACC; ☎ (1-800) 222-2746) offers its members low-priced flights to Brazil (for more details about BACC, see the section on Useful Organisations in the Facts for the Visitor chapter).

Also highly recommended is the newsletter *Travel Unlimited* (PO Box 1058, Allston, MA 02134) which publishes details of the cheapest airfares and courier possibilities for destinations all over the world from the USA. Courier flight prices from Miami recently quoted in this magazine included US$450 (return flight, stay up to 21 days) for Rio; US$250 (return flight, stay up to 21 days) for Quito (Ecuador); and US$250 (return flight, stay up to 14 days) for Caracas (Venezuela).

From the USA the gateway cities for major carriers are New York, Los Angeles and Miami. All have basically the same fare structure. Economy fares often have to be purchased two weeks in advance and restrictions commonly require a minimum stay of two weeks and a maximum of three months. For this type of return ticket to Rio, a rough starting point for prices would be around US$600 (ex Miami); US$700 (ex New York); and US$800 (ex Los Angeles). A popular choice for budget travellers is the cheap Miami-Asunción-Rio de Janeiro flight operated by Lineas Aereas Paraguayas (LAP).

Some of the cheapest flights from Brazil to the USA are charters from Manaus to Miami (the Disneyworld express!). Manaus, which lies halfway between Rio and Miami, is a useful gateway city if you plan to make a long circuit around Brazil.

To/From Canada

Travel CUTS has offices in all major cities. The *Toronto Globe & Mail* carries travel agents' ads, and the magazine *Great Expeditions* (PO Box 8000-411, Abbotsford BC V2S 6H1) is useful. Travellers interested in booking flights with Canadian courier companies should obtain a copy of the newsletter published by Travel Unlimited (see the USA section for details).

To/From the UK

Look for travel agents' ads in the Sunday papers, the travel magazine *Complete Traveller*, and listings magazines such as *Time Out* and *City Limits*. Also look out for the free magazines widely available in London – start by looking outside the main train stations.

To initiate your price comparisons, you could contact travel agents such as: Journey Latin America (JLA; ☎ (081) 747-3108) which publishes a very useful *Flights Bulletin*; Travel Bug (☎ (061) 721-4000); Trailfinders (☎ (071) 938-3444); STA (☎ (071) 937-9962); and South American Experience (☎ (071) 379-0344). For courier flight details, contact Polo Express (☎ (081) 759-5383) or Courier Travel Service (☎ (071) 351-0300).

The Globetrotters Club (BCM Roving, London WC1N 3XX) publishes *Globe*, a newsletter for members which covers obscure destinations and can help find travelling companions.

Prices for discounted flights between London and Rio start around £300 one way or £550 return – bargain hunters should have little trouble finding even lower prices.

To/From Europe

The newsletter *Farang* (La Rue 8 á 4261, Braives, Belgium) deals with exotic destinations, as does the magazine *Aventure au Bout du Monde* (116 Rue de Javel, 75015 Paris).

To/From Australia & New Zealand

Aerolineas Argentinas flies over the south pole once a week (twice during peak periods) via Sydney-Auckland-Buenos Aires-Rio de Janeiro for A$3207. This ticket is valid for six months. Aerolineas has some other interesting fares: a Circle Americas fare to South and North America for A$2969; Circle Pacific fares via South America for A$3455; a Two-Continents fare that includes Africa and South America for A$3500; and a Round-the-World fare via South America for A$3199 that's valid for one year. Lan Chile and Qantas fly once a week via Sydney-Papeete-Easter Island-Santiago-Rio de Janeiro for A$3340.

Qantas flies Sydney-Rio de Janeiro via Los Angeles for A$4200. The LA-Rio leg is on Varig; a maximum of two stopovers are allowed in the Pacific in places like Honolulu and Tahiti. A Qantas/Varig Round-the-World fare costs A$3700.

To/From Asia

Hong Kong is the discount plane ticket capital of the region. Its bucket shops, however, are at least as unreliable as those of other cities. Ask the advice of other travellers before buying a ticket.

STA, which is reliable, has branches in Hong Kong, Tokyo, Singapore, Bangkok and Kuala Lumpur.

From the Orient, the hot tickets are JAL and Singapore Airlines. JAL flies Tokyo-Los Angeles-Rio de Janeiro-São Paulo, and they often have the best fares to Rio from the west coast of the USA.

Round-the-World Tickets & Circle Pacific Fares

Round-the-World (RTW) tickets which include a South American leg have become very popular in the last few years. These tickets are often real bargains, and can work out no more expensive or even cheaper than an ordinary return ticket. From the UK, a RTW ticket including Rio starts at around UK£1300. From the USA, a RTW ticket including Rio starts at around US$2500.

Official airline RTW tickets are usually made available by cooperation between two airlines which permit you to fly anywhere you want on their route systems, as long as you don't backtrack. Other restrictions are that you (usually) must book the first sector in advance and cancellation penalties then apply. There may be restrictions on how many stops you are permitted and usually the tickets are valid from 90 days up to a year. An alternative type of RTW ticket is one put together by a travel agent using a combination of discounted tickets.

Circle Pacific tickets use a combination of airlines to circle the Pacific – combining Australia, New Zealand, South America, North America and Asia. As with RTW tickets there are advance purchase restrictions and limits to how many stopovers you can take.

Arriving in Brazil by Air

Information regarding arriving in Brazil by air can be found in the Getting Around sections for individual cities.

Leaving Brazil by Air

To buy a ticket out of Brazil, non-resident foreigners have to change at a bank the equivalent in US$ of the price of the ticket. After presenting the receipt given by the bank to the travel agent or airline company, the ticket can be issued. Another option is to use an international credit card, which is then debited by calculating the cruzeiro at the turismo rate.

In the past, the official dollar rate was much less than the parallel rate. This meant that travellers, who required a bank receipt to purchase tickets out, effectively had to pay more for flights than locals, who could change dollars at the parallel rate.

At the time of writing, the official dollar rates and the parallel rates were very close and it appeared that these discrepancies would end. Unfortunately that hasn't happened. Here's why.

Travel agents now offer a number of discounted tickets, but to buy one a foreigner has to go to the bank and change the US$ equivalent of a full-price ticket. With the receipt, the ticket can be issued at the discount price, but it leaves the buyer with a couple of hundred dollars worth of cruzeiros. The alternatives are to spend them quickly before inflation eats away their value, or to

Air Travel Glossary

Apex Apex, or 'advance purchase excursion', is a discounted ticket which must be paid for in advance. There are penalties if you wish to change it.

Baggage Allowance This will be written on your ticket: usually one 20-kg item to go in the hold, plus one item of hand luggage.

Bucket Shop An unbonded travel agency specialising in discounted airline tickets.

Bumped Just because you have a confirmed seat doesn't mean you're going to get on the plane — see Overbooking.

Cancellation Penalties If you have to cancel or change an Apex ticket there are often heavy penalties involved: insurance can sometimes be taken out against these penalties. Some airlines impose penalties on regular tickets as well, particularly against 'no show' passengers.

Check In Airlines ask you to check in a certain time ahead of the flight departure (usually 90 minutes on international flights). If you fail to check in on time and the flight is overbooked, the airline can cancel your booking and give your seat to somebody else.

Confirmation Having a ticket written out with the flight and date you want doesn't mean you have a seat until the agent has checked with the airline that your status is 'OK' or confirmed. Meanwhile you could just be 'on request'.

Discounted Tickets There are two types of discounted fares — officially discounted (see Promotional Fares) and unofficially discounted. The lowest prices often entail drawbacks like flying with unpopular airlines, inconvenient schedules, or unpleasant routes and connections. A discounted ticket can save you other things than money — you may be able to pay Apex prices without the associated Apex advance booking and other requirements. Discounted tickets only exist where there is fierce competition.

Full Fares Airlines traditionally offer 1st class (coded F), business class (coded J) and economy class (coded Y) tickets. These days there are so many promotional and discounted fares available from the regular economy class that few passengers pay full economy fare.

Lost Tickets If you lose your airline ticket an airline will usually treat it like a travellers' cheque and, after enquiries, issue you with another one. Legally, however, an airline is entitled to treat it like cash and if you lose it then it's gone forever. Take good care of your tickets.

No Shows No shows are passengers who fail to show up for their flight, sometimes due to unexpected delays or disasters, sometimes due to simply forgetting, sometimes because they made more than one booking and didn't bother to cancel the one they didn't want. Full-fare passengers who fail to turn up are sometimes entitled to travel on a later flight. The rest of us are penalised (see Cancellation Penalties).

---

buy US$ from a casa de câmbio at the parallel rate of exchange.

It should be stressed that this situation could change at any time, so find out about any restrictions well before you plan on buying a ticket.

To Europe, the cheapest tickets are Recife-Madrid or Recife-Lisbon. The cost is US$1300 one way. From Rio it costs about US$100 more.

To the USA, Manaus-Miami costs US$750 one way. Recife-Miami is around US$950 one way. From Rio add another US$100.

To Australia the cheapest flights are the trans-polar Acrolineas Argentina flights, which cost around US$2000 one way. Note that all these are full-price fares. Discounts are available and worth hunting around for, even if you do have to go through the paper-shuffling described above.

At the time of writing, the airport tax for

On Request An unconfirmed booking for a flight (see Confirmation).

Open Jaw A return ticket where you fly out to one place but return from another. If available this can save you backtracking to your arrival point.

Overbooking Airlines hate to fly empty seats, and since every flight has some passengers who fail to show up (see No Shows) airlines often book more passengers than they have seats. Usually the excess passengers balance those who fail to show up but occasionally somebody gets bumped. If this happens guess who it is most likely to be? The passengers who check in late.

Promotional Fares Officially discounted fares like Apex fares which are available from travel agents or direct from the airline.

Reconfirmation At least 72 hours prior to departure time of an onward or return flight you must contact the airline and 'reconfirm' that you intend to be on the flight. If you don't do this the airline can delete your name from the passenger list and you could lose your seat. You may not have to reconfirm the first flight on your itinerary or if your stopover is less than 72 hours – check this with the airline. It doesn't hurt to reconfirm more than once.

Restrictions Discounted tickets often have various restrictions on them – advance purchase is the most usual one (see Apex). Others are restrictions on the minimum and maximum period you must be away, such as a minimum of 14 days or a maximum of one year (see Cancellation Penalties).

Standby A discounted ticket where you only fly if there is a seat free at the last moment. Standby fares are usually only available on domestic routes.

Tickets Out An entry requirement for many countries is that you have an onward or return ticket – in other words, a ticket out of the country. If you're not sure what you intend to do next, the easiest solution is to buy the cheapest onward ticket to a neighbouring country or a ticket from a reliable airline which can later be refunded if you do not use it.

Transferred Tickets Airline tickets cannot be transferred from one person to another. Travellers sometimes try to sell the return half of their ticket, but officials can ask you to prove that you are the person named on the ticket. This is unlikely to happen on domestic flights, but on an international flight, tickets may be compared with passports.

Travel Agencies Travel agencies vary widely and you should ensure you use one that suits your needs. Some simply handle tours, while full-service agencies handle everything from tours and tickets to car rental and hotel bookings. A good one will do all these things and can save you a lot of money, but if all you want is a ticket at the lowest possible price, then you really need an agency specialising in discounted tickets. A discounted ticket agency, however, may not be useful for other things, like hotel bookings.

Travel Periods Some officially discounted fares, Apex fares in particular, vary with the time of year. There is often a low (off-peak) season and a high (peak) season. Sometimes there's an intermediate or shoulder season as well. At peak times, when everyone wants to fly, not only will the officially discounted fares be higher but so will unofficially discounted fares, or there may simply be no discounted tickets available. Usually the fare depends on your outward flight – if you depart in the high season and return in the low season, you pay the high-season fare. ∎

domestic flights was about US$3, and for international flights, around US$16. The appropriate tax is usually added to the price of your ticket.

Buying a Plane Ticket

Your plane ticket will probably be the single most expensive item in your budget, and buying it can be an intimidating business. There is likely to be a multitude of airlines and travel agents hoping to separate you from your money, and it is always worth putting aside a few hours to research the current state of the market. Start early: some of the cheapest tickets have to be bought months in advance, and some popular flights sell out early. Talk to other recent travellers – they may be able to stop you making some of the same old mistakes. Look at the ads in newspapers and magazines (not forgetting the South American press if you have access to it). Consult reference books and watch for special offers, and then phone round travel agents for bargains. (Airlines can supply information on routes and timetables; however, except at times of inter-airline war they do not supply the cheapest tickets.) Find out the fare, the route, the duration of the journey and any restrictions on the ticket. (See restrictions in the Air Travel Glossary.) Then sit back and decide which is best for you.

You may discover that those impossibly cheap flights are 'fully booked, but we have another one that costs a bit more...' Or the flight is on an airline notorious for its poor safety standards and leaves you in the world's least favourite airport mid-journey for 14 hours. Or they claim only to have the last two seats available for Brazil for the whole of July, which they will hold for you for a maximum of two hours. Don't panic – keep ringing around.

Use the fares quoted in this book as a guide only. They are approximate and based on the rates advertised by travel agents at the time of going to press. Quoted airfares do not necessarily constitute a recommendation for the carrier.

If you are travelling from the UK or the USA, you will probably find that the cheapest flights are being advertised by obscure bucket shops whose names haven't yet reached the telephone directory. Many such firms are honest and solvent, but there are a few rogues who will take your money and disappear, to reopen elsewhere a month or two later under a new name. If you feel suspicious about a firm, don't give them all the money at once – leave a deposit of 20% or so and pay the balance when you get the ticket. If they insist on cash in advance, go somewhere else. And once you have the ticket, ring the airline to confirm that you are actually booked on the flight.

You may decide to pay more than the rock-bottom fare by opting for the safety of a better known travel agent. Firms such as STA, who have offices worldwide, Council Travel in the USA or Travel CUTS in Canada are not going to disappear overnight, leaving you clutching a receipt for a non-existent ticket, but they do offer good prices to most destinations.

Once you have your ticket, write its number down, together with the flight number and other details, and keep the information somewhere separate. If the ticket is lost or stolen, this will help you get a replacement.

It's sensible to buy travel insurance as early as possible. If you buy it the week before you fly, you may find, for example, that you're not covered for delays to your flight caused by industrial action.

Air Travellers with Special Needs

If you have special needs of any sort – you've broken a leg, you're vegetarian, travelling in a wheelchair, taking the baby, terrified of flying – you should let the airline know as soon as possible so that they can make arrangements accordingly. You should remind them when you reconfirm your booking (at least 72 hours before departure) and again when you check in at the airport. It may also be worth ringing round the airlines before you make your booking to find out how they can handle your particular needs.

Airports and airlines can be surprisingly helpful, but they do need advance warning. Most international airports will provide escorts from check-in desk to plane where needed, and there should be ramps, lifts, accessible toilets and reachable phones. Aircraft toilets, on the other hand, are likely to present a problem; travellers should discuss this with the airline at an early stage and, if necessary, with their doctor.

Guide dogs for the blind will often have to travel in a specially pressurised baggage compartment with other animals, away from their owner, though smaller guide dogs may be admitted to the cabin. All guide dogs will be subject to the same quarantine laws (six months in isolation, etc) as any other animal when entering or returning to countries currently free of rabies such as the UK or Australia.

Deaf travellers can ask for airport and

in-flight announcements to be written down for them.

Children under two travel for 10% of the standard fare (or free, on some airlines), as long as they don't occupy a seat. They don't get a baggage allowance either. 'Skycots' should be provided by the airline if requested in advance; these will take a child weighing up to about 10 kg. Children between two and 12 can usually occupy a seat for half to two-thirds of the full fare, and do get a baggage allowance. Push chairs can often be taken as hand luggage.

LAND

To/From Argentina

Coming from or going to Argentina, most travellers pass through Foz do Iguaçu (see the Foz do Iguaçu section in the Paraná chapter for more information).

To/From Bolivia

Corumbá Corumbá, opposite the Bolivian border town of Quijarro, is the busiest port of entry along the Bolivia/Brazil border. It has both rail and bus connections from São Paulo, Rio de Janeiro, Cuiabá and southern Brazil.

Between Quijarro and Santa Cruz, there's a daily train during the dry season, but during the wet, there may be waits of several days. Taxis are available between the railhead at Quijarro and the frontier. For further information, see under Corumbá in the Central West chapter.

Cáceres From Cáceres, north of Cuiabá, you can cross to San Matías in Bolivia. There are daily buses which do the 4½-hour trip for US$10. Bolivia's Transportes Aereos Militares (TAM) operates flights each way between San Matías and Santa Cruz, Bolivia (via Roboré), on Saturdays. During the dry season, there's also a daily bus between the border town of San Matías and San Ignacio de Velasco (in Bolivia's Jesuit Missions), where you'll find flights and bus connections to Santa Cruz.

Coming from Bolivia, there are daily micros (again, only during the dry season)

from San Ignacio de Velasco to the border at San Matías, from where you'll find onward transport to Cáceres and Cuiabá.

Guajará-Mirim Another popular crossing is between Guajará-Mirim in Brazil and Guayaramerín, Bolivia, via motorboat ferry across the Rio Mamoré. Guayaramerín is connected with Riberalta by a road which should be extended to Cobija/Brasiléia in the near future – and another long dusty route strikes southward toward Rurrenabaque and La Paz with a spur to Trinidad, the capital of the Bolivian Amazon. The Madeira to Mamoré railway from Guajará-Mirim to Porto Velho has long since been abandoned, but there are bus connections twice daily (during the dry season) between Porto Velho and Guajará-Mirim – a minimum 12-hour bus ride.

It's possible to take a six-day river trip up the Mamoré to Trinidad, and from there on to Puerto Villarroel near Cochabamba. When the water is high enough to accommodate cargo transport, it's also possible to travel up the Rio Beni from Riberalta at least as far as Rurrenabaque, which is 15 hours by bus from La Paz. Conditions are basic, so be prepared. Alternatively, Lloyd Aero Boliviano (LAB) has three flights per week from both Guayaramerín and Riberalta. For further information see under Guajará-Mirim and Guayaramerín in the Rondônia & Acre chapter.

Brasiléia In Acre state, in the far west of Brazil, there's a border crossing between Brasiléia and Cobija, Bolivia. You can either take a rowboat ferry across the Rio Acre or a taxi across the international bridge over the Rio Abunã. For more details, see under Brasiléia and Cobija in the Amazonas & Roraima chapter.

To/From Colombia

Leticia The Colombian border crossing is at Leticia/Tabatinga. For further information on the Triple Frontier region, refer to Benjamin Constant, Tabatinga and Leticia in the Amazonas & Roraima chapter.

To/From French Guiana

Both Brazilians and foreigners may enter French Guiana from Oiapoque by motorised dugout, but it is reportedly not possible for non-Brazilian passport holders to enter Brazil overland from French Guiana. The obvious corollary is that you shouldn't enter French Guiana at St Georges (the French Guianese town opposite Oiapoque) unless you intend to fly from Cayenne or to re-enter Brazil elsewhere. This route will be feasible during the dry season only. Those who require a French visa should pick it up in Belém. For further information see under Macapá in the Amapá chapter.

To/From Guyana

The border crossing is at Bonfim in Roraima state and is reached via Boa Vista. You may want to save yourself the trouble of a difficult overland passage by flying directly to Georgetown on one of the two weekly Varig/Cruzeiro flights from Boa Vista. See under Boa Vista for more details.

To/From Paraguay

Foz do Iguaçu/Ciudad del Este and Ponta Porã/Pedro Juan Caballero are the two major border crossings. See the Foz do Iguaçu section in the Paraná chapter and the Ponta Porã section in the Mato Grosso chapter for details.

To/From Peru

Islandia & Ramón Castilla The main route between Brazil and Peru is along the Amazon between Iquitos and Islandia (the Peruvian port village on an island at the junction of the Rio Yauari and the Amazon, opposite Benjamin Constant. Some boats leave from Ramón Castilla a few km further upstream in Peru. For further information on the Triple Frontier region, refer to Benjamin Constant, Tabatinga and Leticia in the Amazonas and Roraima chapter.

Iñapari There is another border crossing into Peru at Assis Brasil. From Brasiléia, take a bus 110 km west to Assis Brasil where you'll get an exit stamp. Across the Rio Acre from

Assis Brasil is the muddy little Peruvian settlement of Iñapari where you must officially check into Peru with the police. For more details, see sections on Brasiléia and Assis Brasil.

To/From Surinam

It isn't possible to enter Surinam overland from Brazil without first passing through either French Guiana or Guyana.

To/From Uruguay

Coming from Uruguay, travellers usually pass through the border town of Chuy/Chuí: Chuy is the Uruguayan town on one side of the main street and Chuí is the Brazilian town on the other side. See the Rio Grande do Sul chapter for details.

There are four other border crossings: at Aceguá; from Rivera to Santana do Livramento; from Artigas to Quaraí; and at Barra do Quaraí near the border with Argentina.

If you're driving from Brazil, you'll need to stop at the Brazilian checkpoint to get an exit stamp and the Uruguayan checkpoint for the Uruguayans to check that you have a Brazilian exit stamp and a Uruguayan visa (if you need one). Buses will stop at the checkpoints.

To/From Venezuela

Santa Elena From Boa Vista (Roraima state) you can cross into Venezuela via the border town of Santa Elena. There's a Venezuelan Consulate in Boa Vista, open Monday to Friday, 8 am to noon. Everyone requires a visa to enter Venezuela overland. You'll need a photo, an onward ticket, sufficient funds, and probably a letter from your embassy, bank and/or employer guaranteeing that you're gainfully employed or financially sound. Further information is included under Boa Vista and Santa Elena in the Amazonas and Roraima chapter.

Road

Drivers of cars and riders of motorbikes entering Brazil will need the vehicle's registration papers, and an international driver's permit in addition to their domestic licence. You should also carry liability insurance. You may also need a *carnet de passage en douane*, which is effectively a passport for the vehicle, and acts as a temporary waiver of import duty. The carnet may need to have listed any more expensive spares that you're planning to carry with you, such as a gearbox. This is necessary when travelling in many countries, including South America, and is designed to prevent car import rackets.

Another document used in South America is the *libreta de pasos por aduana*, a booklet of customs passes. It supposedly takes the place of the carnet, but since the refundable bond for the libreta is only US$100, it doesn't seem much of a deterrent to selling a vehicle.

Some travellers recently reported that the only documents they required were the title of the vehicle and a customs form issued on arrival which must be presented upon departure. Contact your local automobile association for details about all documentation. Remember that it's always better to carry as much as you can.

Anyone planning to take their own vehicle with them needs to check in advance what spares and petrol are likely to be available. Lead-free is not on sale worldwide, and neither is every little part for your car. Brazil has plenty of Volkswagen spares.

You don't see many long-distance cyclists in Brazil. Crazy drivers who only respect vehicles larger than themselves, lots of trucks on the main roads spewing out unfiltered exhaust fumes, roads without shoulder room and the constant threat of theft are just some of the reasons. I wouldn't recommend cycling in Brazil. It seems a downright dangerous thing to do.

If you're still determined to tackle Brazil by bike, before you leave home, go over your bike with a fine-toothed comb and fill your repair kit with every imaginable spare. As with cars and motorbikes, you won't necessarily be able to buy that crucial gizmo for your machine when it breaks down somewhere in the back of beyond as the sun sets.

Bicycles can travel by air. You *can* take them to pieces and put them in a bike bag or box, but it's much easier simply to wheel your bike to the check-in desk, where it should be treated as a piece of baggage. You may have to remove the pedals and turn the handlebars sideways so that it takes up less space in the aircraft's hold; check all this with the airline well in advance, preferably before you pay for your ticket.

RIVER

One novel way to enter Brazil from Paraguay is to sail up the Rio Paraguay on either the *Presidente Carlos Antonio López* or the *Bahía Negra*, from Asunción to Corumbá, in the Brazilian state of Mato Grosso do Sul.

These boat services are supposed to leave twice monthly, but sailings depend on favourable river conditions. The journey is via Concepción (310 km and 26 hours from Asunción) continuing to Corumbá, a further 830 km (72 hours). Boats depart on Fridays at 8 am from Asunción, and the fare is US$35 tourist class, or US$25 for deck space only. For further information, contact the Flota Mercantil del Estado (☎ 448-544) at Estrella 672, Asunción.

TOURS

The following listing of organisations and tour agencies provides a sample of the tour options available for independent travellers with special interests.

Brazil

Tatu Tours (☎ (071) 237-3161), Rua Afonso Celso 447, sala 105, Barra, Salvador, CEP 40160, BA, specialises in natural and cultural history tours around Bahia. See also details for Traveller's Tree, which represents Tatu Tours in the UK. Focus Tours (☎ (031) 223-0358), Rua Alagoas 1460/s503, 30130, Belo Horizonte, MG, runs a variety of tours with a strong emphasis on the environment and ecology; see also the section on the USA for their American office.

UK

The boom in ecotourism worldwide has prompted the creation of groups and organisations in the UK and elsewhere to monitor the effects of tourism and provide assessments and recommendations for those involved. For more information on ecotours, try contacting: the Centre for the Advancement of Responsible Travel (☎ (0732) 35-2757); Tourism Concern (☎ (081) 878-9053); and Green Flag International (☎ (0223) 89-3587). The Brazilian tour agency, Tatu Tours, is represented in the UK by Traveller's Tree (☎ (071) 935-2291), 116 Crawford St, London W1H 1AG .

USA

Assessments and information about ecological and other types of tours can be obtained from: the North American Coordinating Center for Responsible Tourism, 2 Kensington Rd, San Anselmo, CA 94960; One World Family Travel Network, PO Box 4317, Berkeley, CA 94703; and Travel Links, Co-op America, 2100 M St NW, Suite 310, Washington DC 20036.

Focus Tours (☎ (612) 892-7830), 14821 Hillside Lane, Burnsville, MN 55337, is rated highly for its dedication to conservation and use of naturalists as guides. Tour members are given the use of telescopes and bird identification books; and guides also use professional recording equipment to call out otherwise shy animals. Tour destinations include the Pantanal (and Chapada das Guimarães); Minas Gerais; Amazon; Parque Nacional do Itatiaia; and Serra da Canastra.

Brazilian Views (☎ (212) 472-9539), 201 E 66th St, Suite 21G, New York, NY 10021, is a small agency offering a wide range of special-interest tours based on topics such as horticulture, weaving, birdwatching, arts and crafts, gems and minerals, etc. Victor Emanuel Nature Tours (☎ (1-800) 328-8368), Box 33008, Austin, TX 78764, specialises in birdwatching trips. Earthwatch (☎ (617) 926-8200), 680 Mt Auburn St (PO Box 403), Watertown MA 02272, organises trips for volunteers to work overseas on scientific and cultural projects with a strong emphasis on protection and preservation of ecology and environment. Other organisations which provide tours with a similar emphasis include Conservation International (☎ (202) 429-5660), 1015 18th St, NW, Suite 1000, Washington DC 20036 and The Nature Conservancy (☎ 703-8415300), 1815 N Lynn St, Arlington VA 22209.

For more addresses, see the Environment & Ecology section in the Facts about the Country chapter.

Getting Around

AIR

Flying in Brazil is not cheap, but with the seemingly endless expanses of sertão, Amazon and Pantanal between many destinations, the occasional flight can be an absolute necessity. And even if you don't use it, having extra money to fly can add flexibility to your travel plans.

Brazil has three major national carriers and several smaller regional airlines. The biggies are Varig/Cruzeiro, VASP, and Transbrasil. Together, they cover an extensive network of cities; they don't all go to the same places, but at least one of them goes to every major city. As this edition was being researched, there was a price war between these three airlines. Among the offers to attract customers were a 30% discount on flights booked seven days in advance, 30% discount on night flights and even a 50% discount given to couples going on their honeymoon! If you plan on doing a bit of flying, check whatever special discounts are available.

If you use a credit card to purchase domestic flights with Varig, make sure you check which rate of exchange is used. Unlike other Brazilian airlines, Varig has been known to charge for domestic flights in dollars at the official rate of exchange – most unfavourable for the credit-card holder.

Strange routes, bizarre connections, long lay-overs and frequent stops are always a danger on domestic flights. Planes flying along the coast often stop at every city, so if you're going from Rio to Fortaleza it's possible that the plane will stop at Salvador, Maceió, Recife and João Pessoa on the way. Sometimes these outrageously indirect flights are unavoidable, but not always.

The smaller domestic airlines include Nordeste, Rio Sul, TABA, Votec and Tam. They mostly use the Bandeirante, a small Brazilian-built prop-plane (which some claim is not too safe) and fly to smaller cities where the major carriers don't go. We used Nordeste to fly to Ilhéus once when we couldn't get a seat on a plane directly to Salvador.

There are also many air-taxi companies, which mostly fly in the Amazon region. These flights are expensive, although the price usually drops if there are more passengers – and sometimes you can bargain.

FAB (Força Aerea Brasileira) has been known to give free flights when they have extra space. Go to the desk marked CAN in the airport and ask about the next military flight, then show up again two days before scheduled departure time and sign up. It helps to have a letter of introduction from a consulate. Some air bases restrict flights to Brazilian nationals (eg, Santarém), but it's not as rigid as it often appears. The whole process is hit and miss but it's worth a try, particularly in the North in cities like Boa Vista, Macapá, Porto Velho, Manaus, Santarém, Rio Branco, Belém, and São Luís.

Air Pass

The Brazil air pass is no longer the great deal that it once was. It now costs US$440 and buys you five flight coupons for five flights. It's possible to pay US$100 each for an additional four flight coupons, adding up to US$840 for nine flights. All travel must be completed within 21 days.

Before buying an air pass, you should sit down and work out whether it is really a good investment for your purposes. There are often delays flying in Brazil and it's rare that you don't waste a day in transit. Unless you're intent on a whistle-stop tour of the country, there are only so many flights that you will want to take in two or three weeks.

The pass must be purchased outside Brazil, where you'll get an MCO in your name with Brazil Air Pass stamped on it, which you exchange for an air pass from one of the three airlines in Brazil. All three airlines offer the same deal, and all three fly to most major cities, although Varig/Cruzeiro

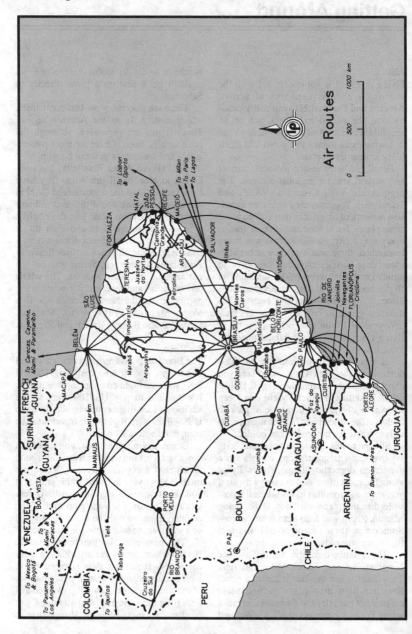

flies to more cities than the other two. If you are buying an air pass and have specific plans to go to a smaller city, you may want to check with a travel agent to see which airline goes there (for example, only VASP flies to Corumbá, the port of entry to the southern Pantanal).

Air-pass holders who get bumped from a flight for any reason should reconfirm all their other flight reservations. I was bumped from a Manaus-Foz do Iguaçu flight once and then found that because I wasn't on that particular flight, all my other air-pass reservations had been scrubbed from the computer. This experience has also been reported by other travellers.

The air pass cannot be used to fly on the Rio to São Paulo shuttle, which lands at the downtown airports of both cities, but it can be used to fly between the international airports of both cities. The MCO is refundable if you don't use it in Brazil.

Airport Tax
At the time of writing, the airport tax for domestic flights was about US$3. The exact figure for the appropriate tax can vary slightly, but is usually added to the price of your ticket.

Reservations
Air reservations can appear and disappear mysteriously. If you have a reservation it's often necessary to both confirm it and reconfirm it, even if you've already bought the ticket. If you have been told a flight is full, keep trying to make the reservation and perhaps alter your tactics by going directly to the airline's central ticket office or the airport.

Because flying is expensive, it's rarely difficult getting on a flight, with the exception of the vacation periods from December up to Carnival and July. Make reservations as early as possible for Carnival time! However, if you get caught short, don't assume all is lost. Several times travel agents were unable to get us reservations, assuring us that there wasn't a ticket to Salvador within two months of Carnival, and we got

the reservation simply by going to the airline counter at the airport.

BUS
Onde fica essa cidade? Lá onde o vento faz a volta.
Where is that city? There where the wind turns around.
(Popular saying about distances in Brazil.)

Except in the Amazon Basin, buses are the primary form of long-distance transportation for the vast majority of Brazilians. Bus services are generally excellent. Departure times are usually strictly adhered to, and the buses are clean, comfortable, and well serviced Mercedes, Volvos and Scanias. The drivers are generally good, and a governor limits their wilder urges to 80 km per hour.

Bus travel throughout Brazil is very cheap (fares work out to less than US$2 per hour): for example, the six-hour trip from Rio to São Paulo costs US$11; the 22-hour trip from Rio to Foz do Iguaçu is US$37.

All major cities are linked by frequent buses – one leaves every 15 minutes from Rio to São Paulo during peak hours – and there is a surprising number of scheduled long-distance buses. It's rare that you will have to change buses between two major cities, no matter what the distance. For tips on security and bus travel, see the Dangers & Annoyances section in the Facts for the Visitor chapter.

'Progress is roads' goes the saying in Brazil. And wherever there is a road in Brazil, no matter what condition it's in, there is a bus that travels it. We will never forget the bus that rescued us on an almost deserted peninsula out near Ponta do Mutá – a place where no one goes, and no one ever seems to have heard of. How we got there is hard to explain, how the bus got there is impossible to explain. The 'road' was more like a wide trail, impassable by normal car and apparently unknown to Brazilian cartographers. But the bus came and eventually delivered us to a humble fishing village of no more than a hundred people.

Like everything in Brazil, bus service varies by region. The South has the most and the best roads. The coastal highways are usually good, at least until São Luís. The Amazon and the sertão are another story. It's no surprise that roads in the sertão are bad. It's the way in which they are bad that's so strange. In several areas the road alternates every few hundred metres between dirt (which is better) and pot-hole infested paved road (which is much worse). This pattern is without logic, it conforms to no obvious geographical or human design, and it forces a constant speeding-up or slowing-down.

There has been a tremendous increase in road construction in previously unsettled regions in Brazil. This applies particularly to the Transamazônica highway and the Amazon region where roads have become the cornerstone of government strategies for economic development and military schemes to defend Brazilian borders. But many of these roads are precarious at best. Most are unpaved and are constantly being washed out during the rainy season when buses get stuck and are always being delayed. In the dry season buses are usually scorching hot, dusty and stuffed with people. As countless books have documented, bus transportation in the Amazon is always an adventure, teaching a healthy respect for the power and the size of the forest.

Bus Types

There are two types, or classes, of long-distance buses. The ordinary or *comum* is the most common. It's quite comfortable, usually with air-conditioning and a toilet. The *leito* or *executivo* is Brazil's version of the couchette. Although they usually take as long to reach their destination as a comum and cost twice as much, leitos, which often depart late at night, are exceptionally comfortable. They have spacious, fully reclining seats, blankets and pillows, and more often than not a steward serving coffee, soda and água mineral. If you don't mind missing the scenery, a leito bus can get you there in comfort and save you the cost of a hotel room.

With or without bathrooms, buses generally make pit-stops every three or four hours.

These stops are great places to meet other bus passengers, buy bizarre memorabilia and wish you were back home eating a healthy vegetarian quiche.

Bus Terminal (Rodoviária) Information

In every big city, and most small ones, there is a central bus terminal *(rodoviária)*. The rodoviárias are most frequently on the outskirts of the city. Some are modern, comfortable stations. All have restaurants, newsstands, toilets, etc, and some even have post offices and long-distance telephone facilities. Most importantly, all the long-distance bus companies operate out of the same place, making it easy to find your bus.

Inside the rodoviária you'll find ticket offices for the various bus companies. They usually post bus destinations and schedules in their windows; occasionally they are printed on leaflets; sometimes you just have to get in line and ask the teller for information. This can be difficult if you don't speak much Portuguese and the teller is in a highly agitated state after his 23rd cafezinho or speaks with an accent from the interior of Ceará. The best strategy is probably to have a pen and paper handy and ask him to write down what you need to know.

When you find a bus company that goes to your destination, don't assume it's the only one; there are often two or more and the quality may vary.

Ticket Purchase & Reservation

Usually you can go down to the rodoviária and buy a ticket for the next bus out. Where this is difficult, for example in Ouro Preto, we try to let you know. In general though it's a good idea to buy a ticket at least a few hours in advance, or if it's convenient, the day before departure. On weekends, holidays and from December to February this is always a good idea.

Aside from getting you on the bus, buying a ticket early has a few other advantages. First, it gets you an assigned seat – many common buses fill the aisles with standing passengers. Second, you can ask for a front row seat, with extra leg space, or a window seat with a view (ask for a *janela* or an odd-numbered seat).

You don't always have to go to the rodoviária to buy your bus ticket. Selected travel agents in major cities sell long-distance bus tickets. This is a great service which can save you a long trip out to an often chaotic rodoviária. The price is the same and the travel agents are more likely to speak some English and are usually less rushed.

TRAIN

There are very few railway passenger services in Brazil, despite the fact that there is over 30,000 km of track. Most trains only carry cargo. Of the passenger services that do exist, many have been scaled down or even discontinued in the last few years, as the national railway company becomes more and more debt-ridden. The most recent service to go off the rails was the night train between São Paulo and Rio.

Enthusiasts should not despair, however, as there are still some great train rides. The Curitiba-Paranaguá train that descends the coastal mountain range offers some unforgettable views, as does the steam train that runs from São Paulo to Santos every weekend. Speaking of steam trains, affectionately known in Brazil as *Maria Fumaças* (Smoking Marys): the 13 km run from São João del Rei to Tiradentes in Minas Gerais, is great fun. Other pleasant short trips are those from Joinville to the island of São Francisco do Sul, in Santa Catarina, and the ride through the mountains from Campos do Jordão to Santo Antônio do Pinhal, in São Paulo, the highest stretch of track in the country. It's still possible to go from São Paulo to Brasília by rail, but the service has been cut to once a week.

Probably the train of most interest to travellers is the route from São Paulo to Corumbá, on the Bolivian border. It still runs regularly. (See the São Paulo chapter for details.)

TAXI

Taxi rides are reasonably priced, if not cheap, but you should be aware of various tricks

used by some drivers to increase the charges. We encountered some superb, friendly, honest, and knowledgeable taxi drivers; however, we also met plenty of rogue cabbies with unsavoury characteristics.

Taxis in the large cities usually have meters with prices which are subject to frequent updates using a *tabela* (price sheet) to convert the price on the meter to a new price. This is OK as long as the meter works and the tabela is legal and current (don't accept photocopies). Unless you are certain about a standard price for a standard trip (and have verified this with the driver) or you have purchased a ticket from a taxi ticket office (described later in this section), you must *insist* that drivers turn on their meters (no excuses) at the beginning of the ride and show you a valid tabela at the end.

What you see is what you pay – no extras if you've only loaded a couple of pieces of baggage per person or the driver thinks the trip to the town centre has required 'extra' fuel. If the meter doesn't work or the driver won't engage it for whatever reason, then negotiate a fare before getting on board or find another cab. If you want to get a rough idea about the 'going rate' prior to taking a taxi ride into town, ask a newsagent or an official at the rodoviária, train station, airport, etc.

As a general rule, Tarifa I (standard tariff) applies from approximately 6 am to 10 pm (Monday to Saturday); Tarifa II (higher tariff) applies outside these hours, on holidays, and outside city limits. Sometimes there is a standard charge, typically for the trip between the airport and the city centre. Many airports and rodoviárias now have a system for you to purchase a taxi ticket from a *bilheteria* (taxi ticket office).

The same general advice applies to taxis without meters. You *must* agree on the price beforehand, and make sure there is no doubt about it. Learn the numbers in Portuguese. If the driver hesitates for a long time or starts using fingers instead of talking to you about numbers, you may find the price has been grasped from imagination rather than being the normal rate. You don't want to have an argument at the end of the ride; it's not worth it, even if you win.

If the driver claims to have 'no change', hold firm and see if this is just a ploy to extract more from you. We often found that change mysteriously appeared out of the driver's pocket when we said we'd be happy to wait in the taxi until change could be found. You can avoid this scenario by carrying change. (More tips can be found under the heading called Small Change in the Money section of the Facts for the Visitor chapter.)

If possible, orient yourself before taking a taxi, and keep a map handy in case you find yourself being taken for a blatant detour. Never use taxi touts – an almost certain ripoff. Deal directly with the taxi driver at the taxi rank, or with the taxi company. The worst place to get a cab is wherever the tourists are. Don't get a cab near one of the expensive hotels. In Rio, for example, walk a block away from the beach at Copacabana to flag down a cab. Many airports have special airport taxis which are about 50% more expensive than a regular taxi which is probably waiting just around the corner. If you are carrying valuables, however, the special airport taxi, or a radio-taxi can be a worthwhile investment. These are probably the safest taxis on the road.

For more tips on security and taxi travel see the Dangers & Annoyances section in the Facts for the Visitor chapter.

CAR & MOTORBIKE

The number of fatalities caused by motor vehicles in Brazil is estimated at 80,000 per year. The roads can be very dangerous, especially busy highways like the Rio to São Paulo corridor. Most of the problems stem from the Brazilian driver. If you thought the Italians were wild drivers, just wait. This isn't true everywhere, but in general the car owner is king of the road and shows it. Other motorists are treated as unwelcome guests at a private party. Pedestrians are shown no mercy, and certainly no courtesy.

Especially in Rio, the anarchic side of the Brazilian personality emerges from behind the driver's wheel as lane dividers, one-way streets and even sidewalks are disregarded and violated. Driving is unpoliced, traffic violations unheard of. Despite all appearances to the contrary, Brazil does hold to the convention that a red light means 'stop'. In practice, this old-fashioned, but often useful, concept has been modified to mean 'maybe we'll stop, maybe we'll slow down – but if it's night we'll probably do neither'.

Drivers use their horns incessantly, and buses, which have no horns, rev their engines instead. One of the craziest habits is driving at night without headlights. This is done, as far as we can tell, so that the headlights can be flashed to warn approaching vehicles.

Many drivers are Formula I racing fans and tend to drive under the influence, pretending they are Ayrton Senna. The worst are the Rio bus drivers, or maybe the São Paulo commuter, or maybe the Amazonian truck driver, or maybe...we could go on and on. This cult of speed, a close cousin to the cult of machismo, is insatiable; it's only positive aspect is that, unlike grandma driving to church on Sunday, these drivers tend to be very alert and rarely fall asleep at the wheel.

Driving at night is hazardous, at least in the Northeast and the interior, where roads are often poor and unreliable. Like malaria, pot holes are endemic and poorly banked turns are the norm. It's always a good idea to slow down when you enter a town, since many have speed bumps, variously known as *quebra-molas*, *lombadas*, *ondulações* or *sonorizadores*, which you never see until it's too late. Another big danger are the farm trucks with inexperienced drivers carrying workers and cargo to town.

On the bright side, many trucks and buses in the Northeast help you pass at night with their indicators. A flashing right indicator means it's clear to go, a flashing left means that a vehicle is approaching from the opposite direction. Everything happens more slowly in the Northeast, and this holds true for driving too.

Car Rental

Renting a car is expensive, with prices

similar to those in the US and Europe. But if you can share the expense with friends it's a great way to explore some of the many remote beaches, fishing villages and back roads of Brazil. Several familiar multinationals dominate the car-rental business in Brazil and getting a car is safe and easy if you have a driver's licence, a credit card and a passport. You should also carry an international driver's licence.

There is little competition between the major rental companies. Prices are usually about the same, although there are occasional promotional deals (the only ones we encountered were during off-season weekends in non-tourist towns). Fiat Unos are the cheapest cars to rent, followed by the Volkswagen Golf and Chevette (which has a good reputation). Sometimes the rental companies will claim to be out of these cheaper models; if this is the case, don't hesitate to shop around. Also, when you get prices quoted on the phone, make sure they include insurance, which is required. When looking at the contract, pay close attention to any theft clause which appears to load a large percentage of any loss onto the hirer.

The big companies have offices in most cities; they are always out at the airport and often in the centre of town as well. In the phone book, look under *autolocadoras* or *locadoras de automóveis*. There are usually small discounts for weekly and monthly rentals, and no drop-off charges.

Motorcycles

Mar e Moto (☎ 274-4398) in Rio rents motorcycles, but it's quite expensive. If you want to buy a bike, Brazil manufactures its own, but they are also expensive.

Motorcycles are popular in Brazil, especially in and around the cities. Theft is a big problem; you can't even insure a bike because theft is so common. Most people who ride keep their bike in a guarded place, at least overnight. For the traveller this can be difficult to organise, but if you can manoeuvre around the practical problems, Brazil is a great place to have a motorcycle.

BICYCLE

You don't see many long-distance cyclists in Brazil. I wouldn't recommend cycling there, as conditions are very dangerous. See the Road section in the Getting There & Away chapter for more details.

HITCHING

Hitching in Brazil, with the possible exception of the Amazon and Pantanal, is difficult. The word for hitching in Portuguese is *carona*, so *pode dar carona* is 'can you give (me/us) a lift'. The best way to hitch – practically the only way if you want a ride – is to wait at a petrol station or a truck stop and talk to the drivers. But even this can be difficult. A few years back there were several assaults by hitchhikers and the government began to discourage giving rides in public service announcements.

BOAT

Although river travel in Brazil has decreased rapidly due to the construction of a comprehensive road network, it is still possible to travel by boat between some of the river cities of the Rio São Francisco. See the River Travel section in the Bahia chapter, and the São Francisco River Trip heading under Belo Horizonte in the Minas Gerais chapters for more details.

For information on river travel in the Amazon region, see the North chapters.

LOCAL TRANSPORT
Local Bus

Local bus services tend to be pretty good in Brazil. Since most Brazilians take the bus to work every day, municipal buses are usually frequent and their network of routes is comprehensive. They are always cheap and crowded.

In most city buses, you get on at the back and exit from the front. Usually there's a money collector sitting at a turnstile at the rear of the bus, with the bus price displayed nearby. If you're unsure if it's the right bus, it's easy to hop on the back and ask the money collector if the bus is going to your

Coupons given as change on buses in some cities.

destination – *você vai para...?* If it's the wrong bus no one will mind if you hop off, even if the bus has gone a stop or two.

Crime can be a problem on buses. Rather than remain at the rear of the bus, it's safer to pay the fare and go through the turnstile. Try to avoid carrying valuables if you can. If you must take valuables with you then keep them well hidden. For more tips about security and travel on local buses, see the Dangers & Annoyances section in the Facts for the Visitor chapter.

Jumping on a local bus is one of the best ways to get to know a city. With a map and a few dollars you can tour the town and maybe meet some of the locals.

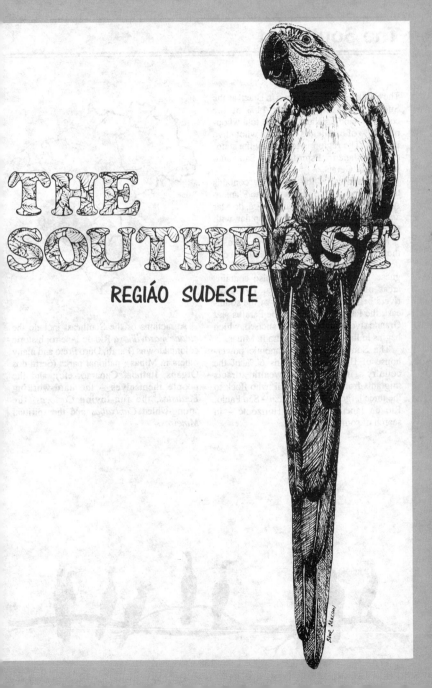

THE SOUTHEAST

REGIÁO SUDESTE

The Southeast

The Southeast region, known in Brazil as the Sudeste, comprises almost 11% of the country's land area and is home to a whopping 44% of brasileiros – 90% of whom live in cities. The region is formed by the states of Rio de Janeiro, Espirito Santo, São Paulo and Minas Gerais.

Geographically, the Southeast contains the most mountainous areas of the Planalto Atlântico: the serras da Mantiqueira, do Mar and do Espinaço, making it popular with hikers and climbers.

Most of the region was once covered by the lush Mata Atlântica, but this has been devastated since the arrival of the Portuguese. Inland, Minas Gerais also contains areas of cerrado and caatinga. Two great rivers begin in the mountains of the southeast; the Paraná, formed by the Paraíba and Grande rivers; and the São Francisco, which begins in the Serra da Canastra in Minas.

The Southeast is the economic powerhouse of Brazil and contains 60% of the country's industry. This wealth attracts migrants from all over Brazil, who flock to the three largest cities of Brazil – São Paulo, Rio de Janeiro and Belo Horizonte – in search of something better.

Attractions of the Southeast include the *cidade maravilhosa* Rio de Janeiro; historic colonial towns (Parati, Ouro Preto and many others in Minas); national parks (Serra dos Órgãos, Itatiaia, Caparaó, etc); and the people themselves – the hard-working *Paulistas*, the fun-loving *Cariocas*, the strong-willed *Capixabas* and the spiritual *Mineiros*.

Rio de Janeiro City

Rio is the cidade maravilhosa (marvellous city). Jammed into the world's most beautiful city setting – between ocean and escarpment – are seven million Cariocas, as the inhabitants are called. This makes Rio the world's biggest tropical city and one of the most densely populated places on earth. This thick brew of Cariocas pursues pleasure like no other people: beaches and the body beautiful; samba and cerveja; football and cachaça.

Rio has its problems, and they are enormous. A third of the people live in the favelas that blanket many of the hillsides. The poor have no schools, no doctors, no jobs. Drug abuse and violence are endemic. Police corruption and brutality are commonplace. There is no law or order. Rio's reputation as a violent city has even caused a sharp reduction in tourism in the last few years. Between 1988 and 1990 the number of foreign tourists disembarking at Galeão, the international airport, fell by 30%, from 760,000 to 540,000.

Nevertheless, in Rio everything ends with samba – football games, weddings, work, political demonstrations and, of course, a day at the beach. There's a lust for life, and a love of romance, music, dance and talk that seem to distinguish the Carioca from everyone else. For anyone coming from the efficiency and rationality of the developed capitalist world this is potent stuff. The sensuality of Carnival is the best known expression of this Dionysian spirit, but there are plenty more.

Rio has its glitzy side, its international tourism crowd, its lives of the rich and famous. But happily it's also a good city for the budget traveller. There are plenty of cheap restaurants and hotels. The beaches are free and democratic. There's lots to explore in the city centre and in several other neighbourhoods with their parks and museums. Mass transportation is fast and easy. And if you can meet some locals – not nearly so hard as in New York, London or Sydney – well, then you're on easy street.

History

Gaspar de Lemos set sail from Portugal for Brazil in May 1501 and entered a huge bay in January 1502. Mistaking the bay for a river, he named it Rio de Janeiro. It was the French, however, who first settled along the great bay. Like the Portuguese, the French had been harvesting brazil wood along the Brazilian coast, but unlike the Portuguese they hadn't attempted any permanent settlements until Rio de Janeiro.

As the Portuguese colonisation of Brazil began to take hold, the French became concerned that they'd be pushed out of the colony. Three ships of French settlers reached the Baía de Guanabara in 1555. They settled on a small island in the bay and called it 'Antarctic France'. Almost from the start, the town seemed doomed to failure. It was torn by religious divisions, isolated by harsh treatment of the Indians and demoralised by the puritanical rule of the French leader, Nicolas de Villegagnon. Antarctic France was weak and disheartened when the Portuguese attacked and drove the French from their fortress in 1560.

A greater threat to the Portuguese were the powerful Tamoio Indians, who had allied with the French. A series of battles occurred, but the Portuguese were better armed and better supplied than the French, whom they finally expelled. They drove the Tamoio from the region in a series of bloody battles.

The Portuguese set up a fortified town on the Morro Castelo in 1567 to maximise protection from European invasion by sea and Indian attack by land. They named it São Sebastião do Rio de Janeiro, after King Sebastião of Portugal. The founding 500 Cariocas built a typical Brazilian town: poorly planned, with irregular streets in the medieval Portuguese style. By the end of the century the small settlement was, if not

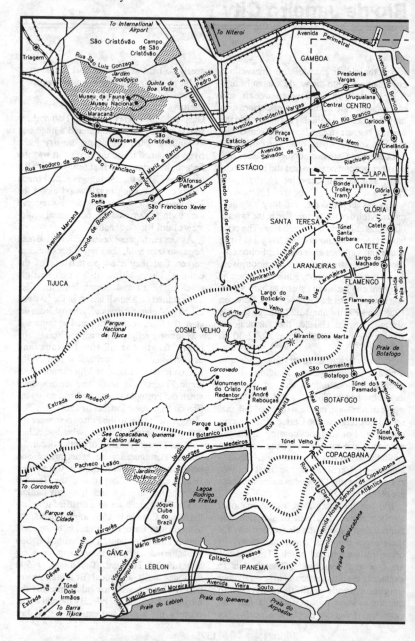

See Central Rio Map

Ilha das Cobras

Aeroporto Santos Dumont

Parque do Flamengo

ATLANTIC OCEAN

See Glória, Catete & Flamengo Map

Fortaleza de São João

Praia de Fora

URCA

Pão de Açúcar

Avenida Portugal

Pasteur

Praia Vermelha

Avenida Princesa Isabel

Forte Duque de Caxias

Ponta do Leme

Praia do Leme

Rio de Janeiro

0   1   2 km

exactly prosperous, surviving on the export of brazil wood and sugar cane, and from fishing in the Baía de Guanabara.

In 1660 the city had a population made up of 3000 Indians, 750 Portuguese and 100 Blacks. It grew along the waterfront and what is now Praça 15 de Novembro (often referred to as Praça Quinze). Religious orders came – the Jesuits, the Franciscans and the Benedictines – and built austere, closed-in churches.

With its excellent harbour and good lands for sugar cane, Rio became Brazil's third most important settlement (after Salvador de Bahia and Recife-Olinda) in the 17th century. Slaves were imported and the sugar plantations thrived. The owners of the sugar estates lived in the protection and comfort of the fortified city.

The gold rush in Minas Gerais at the beginning of the 18th century changed Rio forever. In 1704 the Caminho Novo, a new road to the Minas gold fields, was opened. Until the gold began to run out, half a century later, a golden road went through the ports of Rio. Much of the gold that didn't end up in England, along with many of the Portuguese immigrants who didn't end up in Minas, stayed in Rio.

Rio was now the prize of Brazil. In 1710 the French, who were at war with Portugal and raiding its colonies, attacked the city. The French were defeated, but a second expedition succeeded and the entire population abandoned the city in the dark of night. The occupying French threatened to level the city unless a sizeable ransom in gold, sugar and cattle was paid. The Portuguese obliged. During the return voyage to an expected heroes' welcome in France, the victors lost two ships and most of the gold.

Rio quickly recovered from the setback. Its fortifications were improved, many richly decorated churches were built and by 1763 its population had reached 50,000. With international sugar prices slumping and the sugar economy in the doldrums, Rio replaced Salvador de Bahia as the colonial capital in 1763.

In 1808 the entire Portuguese monarchy

and court – fleeing an imminent invasion by Napoleon's armies – arrived in Rio. The city thus came to house the court of the Portuguese Empire – or at least what was left of it. With the court came an influx of money and talent that helped build some of the city's lasting monuments, like the palace at the Quinta da Boa Vista and the Jardim Botânico (a pet project of the king). The Portuguese court was followed by talented French exiles, such as the architect Jean de Montigny and the painters Jean Baptiste Debret and Nicolas Antoine Taunay.

The coffee boom in the mountains of São Paulo and Rio revitalised Brazil's economy. Rio took on a new importance as a port and commercial centre, and coffee commerce modernised the city. A telegraph system and gas street lights were installed in 1854. Regular passenger ships began sailing to London (1845) and Paris (1851). A ferry service to Niterói began in 1862.

At the end of the 19th century the city population exploded because of European immigration and internal migration (mostly ex-slaves from the declining coffee and sugar regions). In 1872 Rio had 275,000 inhabitants; by 1890 there were about 522,000, a quarter of them foreign born. By 1900 the population had reached 800,000. The city spread rapidly between the steep hills, bay and ocean. The rich started to move further out, in a pattern that continues today.

Climate

Expect some rain in Rio. In the summer, from December to March, it gets hot and humid. Temperatures in the high 30°Cs are common. There's more rain than at other times but it rarely lasts for too long. In the winter, temperatures range from the 20°Cs to low 30°Cs, with plenty of good days for the beach.

Orientation

Rio is divided into a *zona norte* (north zone) and a *zona sul* (south zone) by the Serra da Carioca, steep mountains that are part of the Parque Nacional da Tijuca. These mountains descend to the edge of the city centre, where the zonas norte and sul meet. Corcovado, one of these mountain peaks, offers the best way to become geographically familiar with the city, as from it you have views of both zones.

Rio is a tale of two cities. The upper and middle classes reside in the zona sul, the lower class, except for the favela dwellers, in the zona norte. Favelas cover steep hillsides on both sides of town – Rocinha, Brazil's largest favela with somewhere between 150,000 and 300,000 residents, is in Gávea, one of Rio's richest neighbourhoods. Most industry is in the zona norte, as is most of the pollution. The ocean beaches are in the zona sul.

Unless they work in the zona norte, residents of the zona sul rarely go to the other side of the city. The same holds true for travellers, unless they head north to the Maracanã football stadium or the Quinta da Boa Vista, with the national museum, or the international airport, which is on the Ilha do Governador.

Centro Rio's centre is all business and bustle during the day and absolutely deserted at night. It's a working city – the centre of finance and commerce. The numerous high-rise office buildings are filled with workers who pour onto the daytime streets to eat at the many restaurants and shop at the small stores. Lots of essential services for the traveller are in the centre. The main airline offices are here, as are foreign consulates, Brazilian government agencies, money exchange houses, banks and travel agencies.

The centre is the site of the original settlement of Rio. Most of the city's important museums and colonial buildings are here. Small enough to explore on foot, the city centre is lively and interesting, and occasionally beautiful (despite the many modern, Bauhaus-inspired buildings).

Two wide avenues cross the centre: Avenida Rio Branco, where buses leave for the zona sul, and Avenida Presidente Vargas, which heads out to the sambódromo and the zona norte. Rio's modern subway follows these two avenues as it burrows under the city. Most banks and airline offices have their headquarters on Avenida Rio Branco.

Cinelândia At the southern edge of the business district, Cinelândia's shops, bars, restaurants and movie theatres are popular day and night. There are also several decent hotels that are reasonably priced. The bars and restaurants get crowded at lunch and after work, when there's often samba in the streets. There's a greater mix of Cariocas here than in any other section of the city. Several gay and mixed bars stay open until late.

Lapa By the old aqueduct that connects the Santa Teresa trolley and the city centre is Lapa, the scene of many a Brazilian novel. This is where boys used to become men and men became infected. Prostitution still exists here but there are also several music clubs, like the Circo Voador and Asa Branca, and some very cheap hotels. Lapa goes to sleep very late on Fridays and Saturdays.

Santa Teresa This is one of Rio's most unusual and charming neighbourhoods. Situated along the ridge of the hill that rises from the city centre, Santa Teresa has many of Rio's finest colonial homes. In the 1800s Rio's upper crust lived here and rode the *bonde* (tram) to work in the city. The bonde is still there but the rich moved on and out long ago.

During the '60s and '70s many artists and hippies moved into Santa Teresa's mansions. Just a few metres below them the favelas grew on the hillsides. Santa Teresa was considered very dangerous for many years and is now heavily policed. It's still necessary to be cautious here, especially at night.

Catete & Flamengo Moving south along the bay, you'll come to Catete and Flamengo, two areas which have the bulk of inexpensive hotels in Rio. Flamengo was once Rio's finest residential district and the Palácio do Catete housed Brazil's president until 1954, but with the new tunnel to Copacabana the upper classes began moving out in the 1940s.

Flamengo is still mostly residential. The apartments are often big and graceful, although a few high-rise offices have recently been built amongst them. With the exception of the classy waterfront buildings, Flamengo is mostly a middle-class area.

There is less nightlife and fewer restaurants here than in nearby Botafogo or Cinelândia, which are five minutes' away by subway.

Parque do Flamengo Stretching along the bay from Flamengo all the way to the city centre, the Parque do Flamengo was created in the 1950s by an enormous landfill project. Under-utilised during the week, with the exception of the round-the-clock football games (joining a few hundred spectators at a 3 am game is one of Rio's stranger experiences), the park comes to life on weekends.

The museum of modern art is at the northern end of the park; at the south end is Rio's, a big outdoor restaurant that's ideal for people and bay watching. The park is not considered safe at night.

Botafogo Botafogo's early development was spurred by the construction of a tram that ran up to the botanical garden linking the bay and the lake. This artery still plays a vital role in Rio's traffic flow and Botafogo's streets are extremely congested. There are several palatial mansions here that housed foreign consulates when Rio was the capital of Brazil. This area has fewer high-rise buildings than much of the rest of Rio.

There are not many hotels in Botafogo but there are lots of good bars and restaurants where the locals go to avoid the tourist glitz and high cost of Copacabana.

Copacabana The famous curved beach you know about. What's surprising about Copacabana is all the people who live there. Fronted by beach and backed by steep hills, Copacabana is for the greater part no more than four blocks wide. Crammed into this narrow strip of land are 25,000 people per sq km, one of the highest population densities in the world. Any understanding of the Rio way of life and leisure has to start with the fact that so many people live so close together and so near to the beach.

Only three parallel streets traverse the length of Copacabana. Avenida Atlântica runs along the ocean. Avenida NS de Copacabana, two blocks inland, is one way, running in the direction of the business district. One block further inland, Rua Barata Ribeiro is also one way, in the direction of Ipanema and Leblon. These streets change their names when they reach Ipanema.

Copacabana is the capital of Brazilian tourism. It's possible to spend an entire Brazilian vacation without leaving it, and some people do just that. The majority of Rio's medium and expensive hotels are here and they are accompanied by plenty of restaurants, shops and bars. For pure city excitement, Copacabana is Rio's liveliest theatre. It is also the heart of Rio's recreational sex industry. There are many *boîtes* (bars with strip shows) and prostitutes; anything and everyone is for sale.

From Christmas to Carnival there are so many foreign tourists in Copacabana that Brazilians who can't afford to travel abroad have been known to go down to Avenida Atlântica along the beach and pretend they are in Paris, Buenos Aires or New York. As always when there are lots of tourists, there are problems. Prices are exorbitant, hotels are full and restaurants get overcrowded. The streets are noisy and hot, and Copacabana is the place where you are most likely to get robbed in Brazil.

Ipanema & Leblon These are two of Rio's most desirable districts. They face the same stretch of beach and are separated by the Jardim de Alah, a canal and adjacent park. They are residential, mostly upper class and becoming more so as rents continue to rise. Most of Rio's better restaurants, bars and nightclubs are in Ipanema and Leblon; there are only a few hotels, although there are a couple of good aparthotels.

Barra da Tijuca Barra is the 'in' suburb with Rio's rich and famous. The beach is beautiful, and apartments in the closed condominiums are expensive. Like fungi in a rainforest, hundreds of buildings have sprung up wherever there happens to be an open space. Whether condo, restaurant, shopping centre or discotheque, these big, modern structures are, without exception, monstrosities.

Information

Tourist Offices Riotur (☎ 242-8000) has a tourist information hotline. Call them from 9 am to 5 pm, Monday through Friday, with any questions. The receptionists speak English and more often than not they'll be able to help you.

Riotur (☎ 297-7177) is the Rio city tourism agency. The main office is at Rua da Assembléia 10, 8th floor, Centro, but the special 'tourist room' is on the 9th floor in *sala* (room) 924. There, you'll find free brochures (in Portuguese and English), which include maps, and some excellent, cheap posters for sale. It's open weekdays from 9 am to 6 pm; the metro stop is Carioca.

You can also get the brochures at their information booths at: the main rodoviária (open daily from 6 am to 11 pm); the Cinelândia subway station (Monday to Saturday, from 8 am to 8 pm); Pão de Açúcar (daily, from 8 am to 7 pm); the international airport at Galeão (daily, from 5 am to 11 pm); Cosme Velho at the Corcovado railway station (daily, from 7 am to 7 pm); Avenida Rio Branco 44 (daily, from 10 am to 5 pm); and sometimes in your hotel. When arriving in Rio by bus, the Riotur booth at the rodoviária can save you a lot of time by calling around town to find a vacant hotel and making a reservation. The staff only have lists of the mid-range to top-end hotels, but if you give them the phone number of a cheaper one they're happy to call it. Riotur is also in charge of Carnival and puts out a special programme during this time.

TurisRio (☎ 211-8422) is the Rio state tourism agency. Its office is in the same building as Riotur's (metro stop Carioca), on the 7th floor. Embratur (☎ 273-2212) is Brazil's national tourism agency. The main office is in Brasília, but there's a branch at Rua Mariz e Barros 13 near Praça da Bandeira on the north side of town. For the average traveller, neither of these agencies is worth a special trip.

Money Changing money in Rio at the parallel rate is easy, especially if you have cash. Have a look at the *dólar paralelo (comprar)* exchange rates posted on the front page of *O Globo* or *Jornal do Brasil*. The exchange houses should give you the listed rate for cash and a few points less for travellers' cheques.

In the centre of the city, there are several travel agencies/casas de câmbio on Avenida Rio Branco, a couple of blocks before and after the intersection with Avenida Presidente Vargas (be cautious carrying money in the city centre). The Casa Piano office at Avenida Rio Branco 88 is one of the best places to change. There's also an office in Ipanema at Visconde de Pirajá 365. Cambitur has several offices: Rua Visconde de Pirajá 414, Ipanema; Avenida NS de Copacabana 1093, Copacabana;and Avenida Rio Branco 31, Centro. Another is Exprinter at Avenida NS de Copacabana 371, Copacabana, and Avenida Rio Branco 128 and 57, Centro.

Most of the banks in the city also have currency exchange facilities, but they change at the turismo rate, which is a bit less than the parallel.

At the international airport, there are three exchange houses: Imperial, which only changes cash and is open daily from 6 am to midnight, Cambitur, which changes travellers' cheques but closes at 2 pm on the weekend and Escobar, which also changes travellers' cheques and is open daily from 6 am to 10 pm. All change at the turismo rate. Porters and cleaners at the airport will also offer to change money. They don't change travellers' cheques, but change cash at the 'gringo rip-off' rate.

If there is a crackdown and the government shuts down the exchange houses you may have to get a bit more creative. Hotels, travel agents and jewellers are good places to make enquiries. Perseverance is the key.

Post & Telecommunications Any mail addressed to Posta Restante, Rio de Janeiro, Brazil, ends up at the post office at Rua Primeiro de Março 64, in the city. They hold mail for 30 days and are reasonably efficient. This same post office is also the place to go if you want to send a fax or a telex.

Telephone International phone calls can be made from the following locations in Rio:

Aeroporto Santos Dumont – 6 am to 11 pm
Centro – Praça Tiradentes 41, open 24 hours
Copacabana – Avenida NS de Copacabana 462, open 24 hours
Ipanema – Rua Visconde de Pirajá 111, 6 am to 11 pm
Rodoviária Novo Rio – open 24 hours
Méier – Dias da Cruz 182, 6.30 am to 11 pm

There are certain emergency phone numbers for which you don't need fichas to call from public phones: police 190, ambulance 192, fire 193. There is a special police department for tourists called Poltur (☎ 259-7048), open 24 hours a day at Avenida Humberto de Campos 315, Leblon, across the street from Scala.

American Express The American Express agent in Rio is Kontik-Franstur SA (☎ 235-1396). The address is Avenida Atlântica 2316-A, Copacabana CEP 20040, Copacabana, Rio de Janeiro, Brazil. They do a pretty good job of getting and holding onto mail. Beware of robbers when leaving their office.

Foreign Consulates The following countries have consulates in Rio:

Argentina
    Praia de Botafogo 228, 2nd floor, Botafogo (☎ 551-5498); open Monday to Friday, noon to 5 pm
Australia
    Rua Voluntários da Pátria 45, 5th floor, Botafogo (☎ 286-7922); open Monday to Friday, 9 am to noon. Note that this is only an office; for the Australian Embassy call Brasília (☎ 061) 248-5569.

Bolivia
Avenida Rui Barbosa 664, No 101, Botafogo
(☎551-1795); open Monday to Friday, 8.30 am
to 1 pm
Canada
Rua Dom Gerardo 35, 3rd floor, Centro (☎ 233-
9286); open Monday to Friday, 9 am to 1 pm
Chile
Praia do Flamengo 344, 7th floor, Flamengo
(☎ 552-5349); open Monday to Friday, 8.30 am
to 12.30 pm
Colombia
Praia do Flamengo 82, No 202, Flamengo
(☎ 225-7582); open Monday to Friday, 9 am to 1
pm
Ecuador
Praia do Botafogo 528, No 1601, Botafogo
(☎ 552-4949); open Monday to Friday, 8.30 am
to 1 pm
Paraguay
Avenida NS de Copacabana 427, No 301,
Copacabana (☎ 255-7572); open Monday to
Friday, 9 am to 1 pm
Peru
Avenida Rui Barbosa 314, 2nd floor, Botafogo
(☎ 551-6296); open 9 am to 1 pm
Uruguay
Rua Arthur Bernardes 30, Catete (☎ 225-0089);
open 8 am to 1 pm
UK
Praia do Flamengo 284, 2nd floor, Flamengo
(☎ 552-1422); open Monday to Friday, 8.30 am
to 12.30 pm and 1.30 to 5 pm
USA
Avenida Presidente Wilson 147, Centro (☎ 292-
7117); open Monday to Friday, 8 am to 5 pm

Visa Extension If you need to renew your
visa for another three months, go to the
Polícia Marítima building (☎ 203-2142,
ramal (extension) 37) at Avenida Venezuela
2, Centro (near the far end of Avenida Rio
Branco). It's open from 8 am to 4 pm for visa
extensions. Bring a passport and money (the
fee is around US$5).

Travel Agencies Rio has no shortage of
tourist agents eager to give advice, book bus
and plane tickets and organise tours. They
can also save you unnecessary trips to the
rodoviária by selling bus tickets in advance.
Many agents are brusque and unhelpful but
some are quite the opposite, so it's usually
worth walking out on type one to find type
two.

In Copacabana, try Extra Brazil Touren
(☎ 267-3741) at Rua Julio de Castilho
63/402. Le Monde Passagems, Viagems e
Turismo (☎ 287-4042) in the shopping
centre at Rua Visconde de Pirajá 260,
Ipanema, is useful (speak to Mark or Carlos).
Just around the corner at Vinícius de Moraes
120 is Brazilclub Tours (☎ 267-5093), which
doesn't sell bus tickets but, unlike Le Monde,
is open on Saturday mornings. Talk to Victor,
who speaks English and French. Dantur
Passagems e Turismo (☎ 205-1144) at Largo
do Machado 29, shop 41, is useful if you're
staying in the Catete/Botafogo/Flamengo
area.

Guidebooks There are several guidebooks
to Rio. *Guia Rio* by Quatro Rodas has the
most comprehensive list of restaurants,
hotels, bars and activities. It's well worth
buying if you understand Portuguese and are
going to be in Rio a long time; it's sold at
newsstands. However, it covers only the
upper end of the price spectrum. The
Insider's Guide to Rio by Christopher
Pickard covers a lot of ground, has excellent
descriptions of Rio's fine restaurants and is
in English, but it too is not oriented to the
budget traveller (you can find it in hotel
souvenir shops).

If you're a student of colonial architecture
and plan on seeing the remains of old Rio,
the Riotur office at Assembléia sells a book
in Portuguese entitled *Guia do Patrimônio
Cultural Carioca Bens Tomados*, filled with
detailed maps and descriptions of the city's
historic buildings.

Bookshops Finding good English books is
difficult outside Rio and São Paulo, so stock
up before heading into the interior. Nova
Livraria Leonardo da Vinci is Rio's best
bookshop; it's at Avenida Rio Branco, 185
(it's one floor down on the *sobreloja* level).
Edifício Marques do Herval (☎ 224-1329) is
a serious bookstore, with Rio's largest collection of foreign books and a knowledgeable staff who, for a tidy sum, will order just
about any book you want. It's open 9 am to

7 pm Monday to Friday and 9 am until noon on Saturday.

Livraria Dazibão at Rua Visconde de Pirajá 571-B in Ipanema stocks many Penguin paperbacks. Livraria Kosmos, next to the Copacabana Palace Hotel, has many foreign-language books. Each of the Livraria Siciliana chain has a collection of paperbacks in English. They are at Visconde de Pirajá 511, Ipanema, and Avenida NS de Copacabana 830, Copacabana.

Stúdio Livros at Rua Visconde de Pirajá 462 has current magazines and paperbacks in English. At the Leblon end of Ipanema, at Rua Visconde de Pirajá 640, there's a small used-book store that has old, funky and cheap books in English.

Libraries Instituto Brasil-Estados Unidos (IBEU; ☎ 255-8939) has an English library with a large fiction collection, many books about Brazil in English and a good selection of current magazines from the USA. To check out books you have to take classes there or buy a membership, but it's cheap. The library is at Avenida NS de Copacabana 690, 3rd floor.

With an American passport you can get into the American Consulate, which has a fantastic periodical room. It's on the corner of Avenida Presidente Wilson and Rua México; open 8 am to 4 pm, Monday to Friday.

Language Classes IBEU (☎ 255-8939) has a variety of Portuguese language classes that start every month or two. The cost for a four-week course that meets three times a week is about US$120. For information stop by Avenida NS de Copacabana 690, 5th floor. There are several companies that offer group and private lessons, but they are expensive; for information check the English-language newspaper the *Brazil Post*.

Next door to IBEU is a Casa Matos store which sells the language books for the IBEU courses. It's a good place to pick up a book or dictionaries to study Portuguese on your own.

Health The Rio Health Collective (☎ 325-9300 extension 44) offers a free telephone referral service. The staff speak English and can hook you up with an English-speaking doctor or specialist, in any part of the city.

24-Hour Pharmacies These include Farmácia Piauí at: Avenida Ataulfo de Paiva 1283, Leblon (☎ 274-8448); Rua Barata Ribeiro 646, Copacabana (☎ 255-6249); Rua Ministro Viveiros de Castro 32, Leme (☎ 275-3847); and Praia do Flamengo 224, Flamengo (☎ 284-1548).

Laundry There are laundromats in Copacabana at Rua Miguel Lemos 56 and Avenida NS de Copacabana 1226. In Flamengo, there's one at Rua Marquês de Abrantes 82. All are open Monday to Saturday from 8 am to 10 pm.

Art Supplies Casa Matos is the big chain. There's a store in Copacabana at Avenida NS de Copacabana 690. The small Arte Técnica shop is in Flamengo, at Rua do Catete 228, *loja* (shop) 119. It has better quality supplies and also sells poster tubes which can carry home some of Rio's best gifts – art prints, giant photos, posters, etc.

Walking Tour
There's more to Rio than beaches. Don't miss exploring some of the city's museums, colonial buildings, churches (of course) and traditional meeting places – restaurants, bars, shops and street corners. The centre of Rio, now a pot pourri of the new and old, still has character and life. Here's our suggested walking tour. Many of the places mentioned are described in more detail in the appropriate sections.

Take a bus or the metro to **Cinelândia** and find the main square along Avenida Rio Branco; called **Praça Floriano**, it's the heart of Rio today. Towards the bay is the Praça Mahatma Gandhi. The monument was a gift from India in 1964. Behind the praça and across the road, the large aeroplane hangar is the **Museu de Arte Moderna**.

Praça Floriano comes to life at lunch time

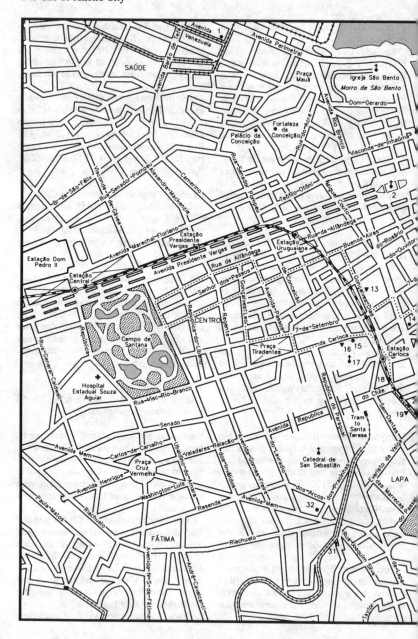

Ilha das Cobras

Baía de Guanabara

Ferry to
Niterói
& Paqueta

▼ PLACES TO EAT

6 English Bar
9 Restaurante Alba Mar
13 Confeitaria Colombo
16 Bar Luis
19 Suco (Juice) Bars
23 Outdoor Cafés &
    Political Debating
26 Café Bohemia
27 Hotel Ambassador
31 Arco da Velha Bar e Restaurante

OTHER

1 Polícia Federal (Visa Extensions)
2 Igreja NS da Candelaria
3 Post Office
4 Igreja e Museu da Santa
   Cruz dos Militares
5 Igreja da Lapa
7 Praça Quinze de Novembro
8 Igreja e Museu do Carmo
10 Museu Naval e Oceanográfico
11 Igreja de São José
12 TurisRio & Riotur (State &
    City) Tourist Offices
14 Riotur Booth
15 Casa Oliveira
17 Convento de Santo Antonio
18 Crafts Market
20 Teatro Municipal
21 Museu Nacional de Belas Artes
22 Praça Ana Amelía
24 Buses to Southern Suburbs:
    Flamengo, Copacabana etc
25 Praça Floriano
28 US Consulate
29 Varig Airlines Main Office
30 Praça Mahatma Gandhi
32 Circo Voador

CASTELO

Aeroporto
Santos Dumont

Central Rio

0   250   500 m

Museu de
Arte Moderna

Monumento
aos Mortos
da II Guerra

··············· Walking Tour

and after work when the outdoor cafes are filled with beer drinkers, samba musicians and political debate. The square is Rio's political marketplace. There's daily speech-making, literature sales and street theatre. Most city marches and rallies culminate here on the steps of the old **Câmara Municipal**.

Across Avenida Rio Branco is the **Biblioteca Nacional**. Built in 1910 in the neoclassic style, it's open to visitors and usually has an exhibition. The most impressive building on the square is the **Teatro Municipal**, home of Rio's opera, orchestra and gargoyles. The theatre was built in 1905 and revised in 1934 under the influence of the Paris Opéra. The front doors are rarely open, but you can visit the ostentatious Assyrian Room Restaurant & Bar downstairs (entrance on Avenida Rio Branco). Built in the '30s, it's completely covered in tiles, with beautiful mosaics. In Avenida Rio Branco you'll also find the **Museu Nacional de Belas Artes**, housing some of Brazil's best paintings.

Now do an about-face and head back to the other side of the Teatro Municipal and walk down the pedestrian-only Avenida 13 de Maio (on your left are some of Rio's best suco bars). Cross a street and you're in the Largo da Carioca. Up on the hill is the recently restored **Convento de Santo Antônio**. The original church here was started in 1608, making it Rio's oldest. The church's Santo Antônio is an object of great devotion to many Cariocas in search of husbands. The church's sacristy, which dates from 1745, has some beautiful jacaranda-wood carving and Portuguese blue tiles.

Gazing at the skyline from the convent, you'll notice the Rubix-cube-like **Petrobras building**. Behind it is the ultra-modern **Catedral Metropolitana** (the inside is cavernous with huge, stained-glass windows). If you have time for a side trip, consider heading over to the nearby bonde (tram) that goes up to **Santa Teresa**.

Next find the shops along 19th-century Rua da Carioca. The old wine and cheese shop has some of Brazil's best cheese from the Canastra mountains in Minas Gerais.

They also have bargains in Portuguese and Spanish wines. Two shops sell fine Brazilian-made instruments, including all the Carnival rhythm-makers, which make great gifts. There are several good jewellery stores off Rua da Carioca, on Rua Ramalho Ortigão.

Whenever I'm near Rua da Carioca 39 I stop at the **Bar Luis** for a draft beer and lunch or snack. Rio's longest running restaurant, it was opened in 1887 and named Bar Adolf until WW II. For decades, many of Rio's intellectuals have chewed the fat while eating Rio's best German food here.

At the end of the block you'll pass the **Cinema Iris**, which used to be Rio's most elegant theatre, and emerge into the hustle of Praça Tiradentes. It's easy to see that this was once a fabulous part of the city. On opposite sides of the square are the **Teatro João Caetano** and the **Teatro Carlos Gomez**, which show plays and dance performances. The narrow streets in this part of town house many old, mostly dilapidated, small buildings. It's worth exploring along Rua Buenos Aires as far as **Campo de Santana** and then returning along Rua da Alfândega. Campo de Santana is a pleasant park, once the scene – re-enacted in every Brazilian classroom – of Emperor Dom Pedro I, King of Portugal, proclaiming Brazil's independence from Portugal.

Back near Avenida Rio Branco, at Rua Gonçalves Dias 30, hit the **Confeitaria Colombo** for coffee and turn-of-the-century Vienna. Offering succour to shopping-weary matrons since 1894, the Colombo is best for coffee (very strong) and desserts.

From here, cross Avenida Rio Branco, go down Rua da Assembléia, stop at Riotur and TurisRio if you want tourist information, then continue on to **Praça 15 de Novembro**. In the square is the **Pyramid Fountain**, built in 1789, and a **crafts market**. Facing the bay, on your right is the **Palácio Imperial**, which was the royal palace and the seat of government. With independence it was ingloriously relegated to the Department of Telegraphs but has recently been restored.

On the opposite side of the square is the

historic **Arco de Teles**, running between two buildings. Walking through the arch you'll see, immediately on your left, the elegant and very British **English Bar** – a good place for a quiet, expensive lunch or drink. The stores along the stone streets here have a waterfront character. There are several seafood restaurants, fishing supply stores and a couple of simple colonial churches. It's a colourful area.

Back at Praça 15 de Novembro, take the overpass to the **waterfront**, where ferries leave to **Niterói** and **Ilha da Paquetá**. The ferry to Niterói takes only 15 minutes and you never have to wait long. Consider crossing the bay and walking around central Niterói if you have some time (the feel is different from Rio – much more like the rest of Brazil). Even if you return immediately the trip is worth it just for the view.

When you're facing the bay, the **Alba Mar** restaurant is a few hundred metres to your right. It's in a green gazebo overlooking the bay. The food is good and the atmosphere just right. On Saturdays the building is surrounded by the tents of the **Feira de Antiguidades**, a strange and fun hodgepodge of antiques, clothes, foods and other odds-and-ends.

Beaches

The beach, a ritual and way of life for the Carioca, is Rio's common denominator. People of all walks of life, in all shapes and sizes congregate on the sand. To the casual observer one stretch of sand is the same as any other. Not so. The beach is complex. Different times bring different people. Different places attract different crowds. Before and after work, exercise is the name of the game. Tanning is heaviest before 2 pm. On prime beach days, the fashionable pass the morning out at Pepino or Barra beaches and the afternoon back at their spot in Ipanema.

Every 20 metres of coastline is populated by a different group of regulars. For example, Arpoador has more surfers and people from the zona norte. In front of the luxury hotels you'll always find tourists and

a security force watching over them. Wherever you do go, don't take valuables.

Swimming isn't recommended at any of the bay beaches because of the sewage and industrial waste that pollutes the water.

Flamengo This popular beach is a thin strip of sand on the bay, with a great view. The park and beach were a landfill project. Within an easy walk of most of the budget hotels in Catete/Flamengo, there's a different class of Carioca here than on the luxurious beaches to the south, and it's fun to watch them play.

Botafogo This small beach is on a calm bay inlet looking out at Pão de Açúcar. The Rio Yacht Club and Bâteau Mouche are next door.

Copacabana/Leme The world's most famous beach runs 4½ km in front of one of the world's most densely populated residential areas. From the scalloped beach you can see the granite slabs that surround the entrance to the bay – a magnificent meeting of land and sea. The last km to the east, from Avenida Princesa Isabel to the Leme hill, is called Praia do Leme. When you go to Copacabana, which you must, do as the locals do: take only the essentials with you. This is the best place in Brazil to get robbed. It's also not a good idea to walk down by the water at night.

There's always something happening on the beach during the day and on the sidewalks at night: drinking, singing, eating and all kinds of people checking out the scene; tourists watching Brazilians, Brazilians watching tourists; the poor, from nearby favelas, eyeing the rich, the rich avoiding the poor; prostitutes looking for tricks, johns looking for treats.

Arpoador This small beach is wedged between Copacabana and Ipanema. There's good surfing here, even at night when the beach is lit, and a giant rock that juts out into the ocean with a great view.

Ipanema/Leblon These two beaches are really one, although the beach narrows on the Leblon side, separated by the canal at Jardim de Alah. Ipanema, like the suburb, is Rio's richest and most chic beach. There isn't quite the frenzy of Copacabana, and the beach is a bit safer and cleaner. There are only two sidewalk cafes facing the ocean in Ipanema – Barril 1800 and Albericos – and one in Leblon – Canecão.

Ipanema is an Indian word for Dangerous, Bad Waters. The waves can get big and the undertow is often strong. Be careful, and swim only where the locals are swimming.

Different parts of the beach attract different crowds. Posto nine is Garota de Ipanema beach, right off Rua Vinícius de Morais. Today it's also known as the Cemetério dos Elefantes because of the old leftists, hippies and artists who hang out there. The Farme de Armoedo at Rua de Armoedo, also called Land of Marlboro, is the gay beach. In front of the Caesar Park Hotel there's a very young crowd.

Vidigal Under the Sheraton Hotel and the Morro Dois Irmãos, this beach is a mix of the hotel and favela dwellers who were pushed further up the hill to make way for the Sheraton.

Pepino/São Conrado After the Sheraton there is no beach along the coast for a few km until Pepino beach in São Conrado. You can also take Avenida Niemeyer to the tunnel leading to Barra da Tijuca.

Pepino is a beautiful beach, less crowded than Ipanema. Currently Rio's most 'in' beach, it's popular with the surfing set and many in their 20s. Along the beach are two big resort hotels, the Hotel Inter-Continental and Hotel Nacional. Behind them, nestled into the hillside, is Brazil's biggest favela, Rocinha.

Bus No 546, 547 or 557 goes to Pepino. Don't take valuables, as these buses are frequent targets of robbers. There is also an executive bus (No 2016 'São Conrado') that goes along Copacabana and Ipanema beaches to Pepino.

Praia Barra da Tijuca The next beach out is Barra. It's 12 km long, with clean, green water. The first few km are filled with bars and seafood restaurants (Peixe Frito is recommended). Further out there are only barracas on the beach. It's calm on weekdays, and crazy on hot summer weekends.

Barra's population has doubled in the last 10 years and it's currently the most fashionable place to live in Rio. There are more than a hundred closed condominiums, and the area is now known as the 'California Carioca'.

Further Out The beaches further south – Prainha, Grumari, Marambaia – are very beautiful and worth exploring but not easily accessible by public transport. They only get busy on weekends, when bus lines swell. All have barracas. Prainha, the next beach past Barra, is one of the best surfing beaches in Rio. Grumari is arguably the prettiest beach near the city. There is a restaurant on the beach where the crabs are good.

To reach these beaches by car you can turn off the Rio to Santos road, BR-101, at Barra and follow the beach road. If it's a busy weekend, wait a few km and turn left at Estrada Bemvindo Novais, at Recreio dos Bandeirantes or Estrada Vereador.

Maracanã

This stadium, Brazil's temple of soccer and a colossus among coliseums, easily accommodates over 100,000 people and on occasion – the World Cup Game of 1950 or Pelé's last game – has squeezed in close to 200,000 crazed fans (although it's difficult to see how). If you like sports, if you want to understand Brazil, or if you just want an intense, quasi-psychedelic experience, then by all means go see a game of *futebol*, preferably a championship game or one between rivals Flamengo (Fla) and Fluminense (Flu).

Brazilian soccer is the most imaginative and exciting in the world. Complementing the action on the field, the stands are filled with fanatical fans who cheer their team on in all sorts of ways: chanting, singing and shouting; waving banners and streamers with team colours; pounding huge samba drums; exploding firecrackers, Roman candles and smoke bombs (in the team colours); launching incendiary balloons; throwing toilet paper, beer and even dead chickens – possibly Macumba inspired. The scene, in short, is sheer lunacy.

Obviously, you have to be very careful if you go to Maracanã. Don't wear a watch or jewellery. Don't bring more money than you need for tickets, transport and refreshments. The big question is how to get to and from the game safely.

The big games are held on Sundays at 5 pm year-round. Tourist buses leave from major hotels at 2.30 pm (they often run a bit late) for 5 pm Sunday games. They cost about US$22, which is a rip-off, but it's the safest and easiest way to get to the game. They drop you off and pick you up right in front of the gate and escort you to lower-level seats. Unfortunately this is not the best perspective for watching the game, but it is the safest because of the overhead covering which protects you from descending objects.

However you get to the stadium, it's a good idea to buy these lower-level seats, called *cadeira*, instead of the upper-level bleachers, called *arquibancada*. The price is US$8, unless it's a championship game, when it's more.

The metro is closed on Sundays, and taking a bus or cab can be a hassle. Getting to the stadium isn't too difficult: catch a bus marked 'Maracanã' (from the zona sul, No 433, 432, 464 or 455; from Centro, No 260, 238 or 239) and leave a couple of hours before game-time. Returning to your hotel by bus is often a drag. The buses are flooded with passengers and thieves set to work on the trapped passengers. Taking a cab is a possible alternative, but they can be hard to flag down; the best strategy is to walk away from the stadium a bit.

Surprisingly, driving a car to the stadium is pretty easy. You should leave a couple of hours before kick-off and, for easy departure, park away from the stadium. The traffic isn't all that bad and if you arrive early you can watch the preliminary games.

Pão de Açúcar (Sugar Loaf)

Sugar Loaf, God's gift to the picture postcard industry, is dazzling. Two cable cars lift you 1300 metres above Rio and the Baía de Guanabara. From here, Rio is undoubtedly the most beautiful city in the world. There are many good times to make the ascent, but sunset on a clear day is the most spectacular. As day becomes night and the city lights start to sparkle down below, the sensation is delightful.

Everyone must go to Sugar Loaf, but if you can, avoid going from about 10 to 11 am and 2 to 3 pm when most tourist buses are arriving.

The two-stage cable cars (☎ 295-8244) leave about every 30 minutes from Praça General Tibúrcio at Praia Vermelha in Urca. They operate daily from 8 am to 10 pm and cost US$6. On top of the lower hill there's a restaurant/theatre. The Beija Flor samba school puts on a show on Monday from 9 pm to 1 am. Less touristy shows are the Friday and Saturday Carioca Nights. They have some excellent musicians; check the local papers for listings.

To get to Sugar Loaf take a bus marked 'Urca' from Centro and Flamengo (No 107); from the zona sul, take No 500, 511 or 512. The open-air bus that runs along the Ipanema and Copacabana beaches also goes to Sugar Loaf.

Corcovado & Cristo Redentor

Corcovado (Hunchback) is the mountain and Cristo Redentor (Christ the Redeemer) is the statue. The mountain rises straight up from the city to 709 metres. The statue, with its welcoming outstretched arms, stands another 30 metres high and weighs over 1000 tonnes (a popular song talks about how the Cristo should have its arms closed against its chest because for most who come to Rio the city is harsh and unwelcoming).

The statue was originally conceived as a national monument to celebrate Brazil's 100 years of independence from Portugal. The 100 years came and went in 1922 without the money to start construction, but in 1931 the statue was completed by French sculptor

Paul Landowski, thanks to some financial assistance from the Vatican.

Corcovado lies within the Parque Nacional da Tijuca. You can get there by car or by taxi, but the best way is to go up in the cog train – sit on the right-hand side going up for the view. The round trip costs US$8 and leaves from Rua Cosme Velho 513 (Cosme Velho). You can get a taxi there or a bus marked 'Rua Cosme Velho' – a No 422, 498 or 108 bus from Centro, a No 583 from Largo Machado, Copacabana and Ipanema, or a No 584 from Leblon.

During the high season, the trains, which only leave every 30 minutes, can be slow going. Corcovado, and the train, are open from 8 am to 6.30 pm. Needless to say, the view from up top is spectacular.

Santa Teresa Bondinho

The *bondinho* (little tram) goes over the old aqueduct to Santa Teresa from Avenida República do Chile and Senador Dantas in Centro. Santa Teresa is a beautiful neighbourhood of cobbled streets, hills and old homes. Favelas down the hillsides have made this a high-crime area. Young thieves jump on and off the tram very quickly. Go, but don't take valuables. Public transport stops at midnight, so you'll need a car if you are going anywhere after that time.

There's a small Museu do Bonde at the central tram station with a history of Rio's tramways since 1865 for bonde buffs. You may wonder why people choose to hang onto the side of the tram even when there are spare seats. It's because they don't have to pay.

The Museu Chácara do Céu (☎ 224-8991), Rua Murtinho Nobre, 345 Santa Teresa, has a good collection of art and antiques.

Parks & Gardens

Parque Nacional da Tijuca Tijuca is all that's left of the tropical jungle that once surrounded Rio de Janeiro. In 15 minutes you can go from the concrete jungle of Copacabana to the 120-sq-km tropical jungle of Parque Nacional da Tijuca. A more rapid and drastic contrast is hard to imagine. The

The bondinho

forest is exuberant green, with beautiful trees, creeks and waterfalls, mountainous terrain and high peaks. Candomblistas leave offerings by the roadside, families have picnics, and serious hikers climb the summit of Pico da Tijuca (1012 metres).

The heart of the forest is the Alto da Boa Vista with several waterfalls (including the 35-metre Cascatinha Taunay), peaks and restaurants. It's a beautiful spot. You can get maps at the entrance.

The entire park closes at sunset and is rather heavily policed. Kids have been known to wander off and get lost in the forest – it's that big. It's best to go by car, but if you can't catch a No 221, 233 or 234 bus.

The best route by car is to take Rua Jardim Botânico two blocks past the botanical garden (heading away from Gávea). Turn left on Rua Lopes Quintas and then follow the Tijuca or Corcovado signs for two quick left turns until you reach the back of the botanical garden, where you go right. Then follow the signs for a quick ascent into the forest and past the Vista Chinesa (get out for a view) and the Mesa do Imperador. Go right when you seem to come out of the forest on the main road and you'll see the stone columns to the entrance of Alto da Boa Vista on your left in a couple of km.

You can also drive up to Alto da Boa Vista by heading out to São Conrado and turning right up the hill at the Parque Nacional da Tijuca signs.

Jardim Botânico Open daily from 8.30 am to 5.30 pm, the garden was first planted by order of the prince-regent Dom João in 1808. There are over 5000 varieties of plants on 141 hectares. Quiet and serene on weekdays, the botanical garden blossoms with families and music on weekends. The row of palms, planted when the garden first opened, and the Amazonas section with the lake containing the huge Vitória Regia water lilies, are some of the highlights. It's not a bad idea to take insect repellent.

The garden is on Rua Jardim Botânico 920. To get there take a 'Jardim Botânico' bus: from Centro, No 172, 409 or 438; from the zona sul, No 558 or 571; from Leblon, No 574. Note that these buses don't coincide with Rio tourist booklet info.

After the garden walk, go a few blocks down Rua Jardim Botânico, away from the beach, to Alfaces at Rua Visconde da Graça 51 for an excellent light lunch with an assortment of salads, good desserts and outdoor tables.

Parque Lage Just a few blocks down from the Jardim Botânico at Rua Jardim Botânico 414, this is a beautiful park at the base of Parque Nacional da Tijuca. There are gardens, little lakes and a mansion which now houses the Instituto de Belas Artes – there are often art shows and sometimes performances there. It's a tranquil place, with no sports allowed and a favourite of families with small children. It's open from 8 am to 5.30 pm. Take a 'Jardim Botânico' bus.

Parque do Flamengo Flamengo is a park with loads of fields and a bay for activities and sports. There are three museums – Museu Carmen Miranda, Museu dos Mortos da Segunda Guerra Mundial, and Museu de Arte Moderna. Inside the park, along the bay, the Barracuda Rio restaurant (☎ 265-4641) is a great spot for bay and people watching. There's a deck and tables outside where you

can drink or eat, and inside you can get a more substantial meal; it's also open for dinner.

To get there take buses marked 'Via Parque do Flamengo': from Centro No 125 or 132, and from the zona sul No 413 or 455.

Parque da Catacumba With high-rise buildings on both sides, Catacumba is on the Morro dos Cabritos, which rises from the Lagoa Rodrigo de Freitas. It was the site of a favela which was destroyed to make the park. A shaded park for walkers only, it's a good place to escape the heat and see some excellent outdoor sculptures. At the top of the hill there is a great view. Catacumba also has free Sunday afternoon concerts during the summer in its outdoor amphitheatre, featuring some of Rio's best musicians. Check the Sunday newspaper for details.

Parque da Cidade Up in the hills of Gávea, this park is also calm and cool, and popular with families. Open daily from 8 am to 5.30 pm, the Museu da Cidade is on the park grounds.

Parque do Catete The grounds of the old presidential palace are now the Parque do Catete, a quiet refuge from the city; the park has monkeys hanging from the giant trees.

Quinta da Boa Vista Rio's main park and museum of natural history makes a great Sunday outing, and if you want to make a day out of it the nordeste fair (see Things to Buy) and Maracanã soccer stadium are both nearby. The park is open daily from 8 am to 7 pm.

Museums
Museu Nacional This museum and its grand imperial entrance are still stately and imposing, and the view from the balcony to the royal palms is majestic. However, the graffitied buildings and unkempt grounds have suffered since the fall of the monarchy. The park is large and busy, and because it's on the north side of the city you'll see a good cross-section of Cariocas.

The museum is open Tuesday to Sunday from 10 am to 5 pm, and admission is about US$1 (free on Thursdays). There are many interesting exhibits: dinosaur fossils, sabre tooth tiger skeletons, beautiful pieces of pre-Columbian ceramics from the littoral and planalto of Peru, a huge meteorite, hundreds of stuffed birds, mammals and fish, gory displays of tropical diseases and exhibits on the peoples of Brazil.

The latter are most interesting. Rubber-gatherers and Indians of the Amazon, lace workers and *jangadeiro* fishers of the Northeast, candomblistas of Bahia, gaúchos of Rio Grande do Sul and *vaqueiros* (cowboys) of the sertão are all given their due. What's interesting about these exhibits is that with a little bit of effort and a lot of travelling you can see all of these peoples in the flesh. The Indian exhibit is particularly good – better than that of the FUNAI Museu do Índio.

The museum is at the Quinta da Boa Vista. To get there from Centro take the metro to São Cristóvão or bus No 284; from the zona sul take bus No 460, 461, 462 or 463.

Museu Nacional de Belas Artes At Avenida Rio Branco 199 is Rio's premier fine art museum (☎ 240-0160). There are over 800 original paintings and sculptures in the collection. The most important gallery is the Galeria de Arte Brasileira, with 20th-century classics such as Cândido Portinari's *Café*. There are also galleries with foreign art (not terribly good) and contemporary exhibits.

The museum is open Tuesday to Friday from 10 am to 5.30 pm; and Saturday, Sunday and holidays from 3 to 6 pm. Photography is prohibited. Take any of the city-bound buses and get off near Avenida Rio Branco, or take the metro to Carioca station.

Museu Histórico Nacional Restored in 1985, this former colonial arsenal (☎ 220-5829) is filled with historic relics and interesting displays, one of the best being the re-creation of a colonial pharmacy. The building is near the bay at Praça Marechal Âncora.

Museu Folclorico Edson Carneiro The small Edson Carneiro museum should not be missed – especially if you're staying nearby in the Catete/Flamengo area. It has excellent displays of folk art – probably Brazil's richest artistic tradition – a folklore library, and a small crafts store with some wonderful crafts, books and folk records at very cheap prices.

The museum is next to the grounds of the Palácio do Catete. The address is Rua do Catete 181, Catete, and it's open Tuesday to Friday from 11 am to 6 pm, and Saturday, Sunday and holidays from 3 to 6 pm.

Museu da República & Palácio do Catete The Museu da República and the Palácio do Catete have been wonderfully restored. Built between 1858 and 1866 and easily distinguished by the bronze eagles on the eaves, the palace was occupied by the president of Brazil from 1896 until 1954, when Getúlio Vargas killed himself here. His bedroom, where it took place, is on display. The museum, which occupies the palace, has a good collection of art and artefacts from the republican period. It's open Tuesday to Friday from noon to 5 pm. Admission costs 30c.

Museu do Índio At Rua das Palmeiras 55, Botafogo, the Museu do Índio (☎ 286-8799) has a good library with over 25,000 titles, a map and photo collection and a quiet garden. The Indian exhibits in the Museu Nacional at the Quinta da Boa Vista are better.

Museu H Stern The headquarters of the famous jeweller H Stern, at Rua Visconde de Pirajá 490, contains a museum. You may find the 12-minute guided jewellery tour interesting if you're in the neighbourhood. With a coupon you can get a free cab ride to and from the store and anywhere in the zona sul.

Museu Carmen Miranda The small Carmen Miranda Museum in Parque do Flamengo is across the street from Avenida Rui Barbosa 560 and is open Tuesday to Friday from 11 am to 5 pm, and Saturday and Sunday from

1 to 5 pm. Carmen, of course, was Hollywood's Brazilian bombshell, although she was actually born in Portugal. She made it to Hollywood in the 1940s and has become a cult figure in Rio. During Carnival hundreds of men dress up as Carmen Miranda look-a-likes. The museum is filled with Carmen memorabilia and paraphernalia, including costumes, posters, postcards, T-shirts, records and a small exhibit.

Museu Villa-Lobos This museum is in a century-old building and is dedicated to the memory of Heitor Villa-Lobos. This great Brazilian composer, regarded as the father of modern Brazilian music, was the first to combine folkloric themes with classic forms. As well as personal items, there's also an extensive sound archive. At Rua Sorocaba 200 in Botafogo, it's open from Monday to Friday from 10 am to 5.30 pm.

Museu de Arte Moderna At the northern end of Parque do Flamengo, looking a bit like an airport hangar, is the Modern Art Museum. Construction began in 1954, but for much of the past few years all that one has been able to see of the museum are its grounds, done by Brazil's most famous landscape architect, Burle Marx (who landscaped Brasília).

The museum was devastated by a fire in 1978 which consumed much of its collection. It is still being renovated and therefore is often closed, so call 210-2188 before going there.

Museu Naval e Oceanográfico This museum chronicles the history of the Brazilian navy from the 16th century to the present. It's close to Praça 15 de Novembro and is open every day from noon to 4.45 pm.

Museu Naval In Bauru, behind the Modern Art Museum, the Naval Museum is open Tuesday to Friday from 11.30 am to 5.30 pm, Saturday and Sunday from 9 am to 5.30 pm. It documents the Brazilian navy's role in WW II and has ship models.

Ilha da Paquetá

This island in the Baía de Guanabara was once a very popular tourist spot and is now frequented mostly by families from the zona norte. There are no cars on the island. Transport is by foot, bicycle (there are literally hundreds for rent) and horse-drawn carts. There's a certain dirty decadent charm to the colonial buildings, unassuming beaches and businesses catering to local tourism. Sadly, the bay is too polluted to safely swim in and the place gets very crowded.

Go to Paquetá for the boat ride through the bay and to see Cariocas at play – especially during the Festa de São Roque, which is celebrated over five days in August. Boats leave from near the Praça 15 de Novembro in Centro. The regular ferry takes one hour and costs 50c. The hydrofoil is worth taking, at least one way. It gets to the island in 25 minutes and costs US$5. The ferry service (☎ 231-0396) goes from 5.30 am to 10.30 pm, leaving every two to three hours. The hydrofoil leaves every hour on the hour from Rio (8 am to 5 pm) and returns every hour from Paquetá (8 am to 5.30 pm).

Jóquei Clube

There's lots to see at the race track. The stadium, which seats 35,000, is on the Gávea side of the Lagoa Rodrigo de Freitas at Praça Santos Dumont 31 (take any of the buses that go to Jardim Botânico). It's a beautiful horse-racing track with a great view of the mountains and Corcovado; it costs only a few cents to enter. It's rarely crowded and the fans are great to watch – it's a different slice of Rio life. Racing usually takes place every Saturday and Sunday afternoon, and Monday and Thursday night.

City Sunset

Sunset is a nice time to be around the central plaza in the city. The sky can be beautiful and floodlights illuminate the big buildings like the municipal theatre and national library.

Surfing

In Rio city, surfing is very popular, with the locals ripping the fast, hollow beach breaks.

When the surf is good, it gets crowded. Arpoador, between Copacabana and Ipanema, is where most surfers congregate, though there are some fun beach breaks further out in Barra, Grumari, Joá and Prainha. Boards can be rented in Rio, but they're so cheap that you'd be crazy not to buy one, especially if you've planned a surfing expedition down the coast. A brand-new board is a steal at US$150 to US$200, and I saw some decent second-hand ones for as little as US$40. Galeria River (pronounced heever), at Rua Francisco Otaviano 67 in Arpoador, is an arcade full of surf shops. Loja three of Ocean has a reasonable selection.

Hang-Gliding

If you weigh less than 80 kg (about 180 lb) and have US$60 you can do the fantastic – hang-glide off Pedra Bonita on to Pepino beach in São Conrado. This is one of the giant granite slabs that towers above Rio. No experience is necessary. To arrange a double flight *(voo duplo)* go out to Pepino and the pilots will be waiting on the beach. We're told that the winds are very safe here and the pilots know what they are doing. Guest riders get their bodies put in a kind of pouch that is secured to the kite.

Our pilot, Assad, picked us up in his beat-up Volkswagen with the *asa delta* (hang-glider) rack. The climb up to the take-off point was awesome. Pedra Bonita looms over São Conrado's Pepino beach like Fantasia's Bald Mountain. The road winds up through the lush green Tijuca forest. Assad's driving was not soothing – in fact if his driving was any indication of how he was going to pilot the hang-glider, I didn't want to have anything to do with him. We were waved on through the private entrance to the hang-gliding area and the engine whined as we climbed the extremely steep hill.

When we reached the top Assad assembled the glider, untangled the cables, tightened the wing nuts and slipped elastic bands over the wing struts. Up close the glider looked flimsy. We put on our flight suits and practised a few take-off sprints near the platform, literally a five-metre-long runway of wooden boards inclined 15° downhill. We were 550 metres above sea level and a few km inland from the beach. If I were a rock and Rio were a vacuum, it would take me over 10 seconds to kiss the dirt.

I wore old sneakers for traction and two good luck charms to amuse the ambulance crew I anticipated would be piecing through the tangled ball of crumpled metal, torn nylon and mangled flesh down below.

With the glider resting at the top of the runway, we clipped ourselves onto it and checked the balance of the craft as we hung side by side. Assad adjusted his weight belt, all the straps, the velcro leg cuffs and helmet and gave me very brief instructions: hold on to the cuff of his shorts, keep my hands to myself, resist the temptation to hold the control bar or cables (this can throw the glider, so don't touch), and when he gave the count 'um, dois, tres, ja!', go very fast.

Assad checked the windsocks on either side of the platform, the surface of the sea and the rippling of the leaves to ascertain the direction, speed and flow of the wind. He wanted a smooth wind coming inland from a flat sea. 'Um, dois, tres, ja!' Four bounding steps and we were flying. It's not the free-fall sinking feeling you get from elevators, but a perfect calm. I closed my eyes and felt as if I was still – the only movement, a soft wind caressing my face. Miraculously, it seemed I was suspended between earth and sky. To our left was Rocinha, the most famous of the zona sul's favelas, to the right Pedra Bonita, and below us the fabulous homes of Rio's rich and famous. We floated over skyscrapers and Pepino beach, made a few lazy circles over the water and before I knew it, it was time for the descent. Upon landing we stood upright, Assad pointed the nose up, the glider stalled and we touched down on the sand gentle as a feather.

It wasn't until after the flight that Assad told me that he is not without recourse. In an emergency, like a sudden change in weather, a hang-glider pilot can fly down to the beach in less than 90 seconds. Assad also carries a never-used parachute which is designed to support the weight of two passengers and the glider itself, which is supposed to fall first and cushion the blow.

Flight Information Assad can mount a camera with flash, wide-angle lens, motor drive and a long cable release on a wing tip to take pictures of you in flight. Other flyers too provide this service. If you want to take pictures yourself you must realise that take-off and landing pictures are impossible since you can't be encumbered with equipment. Your camera must fit into the velcro pouch in the front of your flight suit. It's a good idea to have the camera strap around your neck and a lens cover strapped to the lens or you will risk beaning a Carioca on the head and losing equipment. Flights are usually extremely smooth so it's possible to take stable shots. Hang-gliders themselves are dramatic shots, especially when taken from above.

Know your exact weight in kg in advance. Ideally your pilot should be heavier than you. If you're heavier than the pilot, he will have to use a weight belt and switch to a larger glider. If you're over 80 kg, you're out of luck. You don't need any experience or special training – anyone from seven to 70 years can do it.

Cautious flights depend on atmospheric conditions. Assad reckons he can fly on all but three or four days per month, and conditions during winter are even better. For the experience of a lifetime, it's not that expensive: US$60 for anywhere from 10 to 25 minutes of extreme pleasure. For US$80 Assad will supply film and camera gear. These prices include being picked up and dropped off at your hotel. Arrive early and allow for plenty of time to get things assembled, move things around, etc. If you fly early in the day, you have more flexibility with delays.

The best way to arrange a flight is to go right to the far end of Pepino beach on Avenida Prefeito Mendes de Morais, where the fly-boys hang out (and Niemeyer is building the headquarters of the Voo Livre club). Assad can be reached on 322-5417. Ruy Marra is another excellent tandem glider pilot. For more information call the Associação Brasileiro de Voo Livre (☎ 220-4704), which also offers classes.

Popular Hikes & Climbs

Excellent hiking is possible surprisingly close to the city. There are three national parks with trail systems in Rio state: Parque Nacional da Tijuca (see entry later this chapter), Parque Nacional da Serra dos Órgãos and Parque Nacional do Itatiaia (see the Rio de Janeiro State chapter for information on these latter two parks).

Clubs

For anyone interested in climbing and hiking, Rio's clubs are the single best source of information as well as the best meeting place for like-minded people. The clubs meet regularly and welcome visitors. All of the following clubs are well organised and have bulletin boards listing excursions on the weekends.

Centro Excursionista Brasileiro
Avenida Almirante Barroso 2-8 Andar, Centro, Rio de Janeiro, RJ CEP 20031. CEB has a membership of 900, meets on Wednesday and Friday evenings and is geared toward trekking and day hikes. CEB also runs a small restaurant which is open from 6 pm, Monday to Friday, where people meet informally to plan excursions.

Centro Excursionista Rio de Janeiro
Avenida Rio Branco 277/805, Centro, Rio de Janeiro, RJ CEP 20040. CERJ, with an active membership of 50, meets on Tuesday and Thursday evenings. CERJ offers the greatest diversity of activities ranging from hikes to technical climbing.

Clube Excursionista Carioca
Rua Hilário de Gouveia 71/206, Copacabana, Rio de Janeiro, RJ CEP 22040.(☎ Marcelo Ramos (021)227-8398) Meeting on Wednesday and Friday evenings at 10.30 pm, this club specialises in difficult technical climbing.

Tijuca The Parque Nacional da Tijuca is a 120-sq km park with an excellent trail system. It is also home to different species of birds and animals including iguanas and monkeys. The Alto da Boa Vista section of Tijuca forest, which is part of the national park, has several good day hikes. Maps of the forest are obtained at the small artisan shop just inside the park entrance, which is open from 7 am to 9 pm daily. To get there take bus 221 from Praça 15 in the centre to Praça Afonso Viseu in Alto da Boa Vista.

Pão de Açúcar On Pão de Açúcar (396 metres), Rio's Sugar Loaf, there are 32 established climbing routes. Climbers are often seen scaling the western face below the cable cars. One of the best hikes is up the back side of Pão de Açúcar. Besides the breathtaking view of the ocean below, one is also compensated by not having to pay for the cable-car ride. The hike takes 1½ hours and doesn't require equipment or a lot of climbing experience, but does have two 10 to 15-metre exposed parts that require agility and commonsense.

The hike begins on the left-hand side of Praça General Tibúrcio (the same praça where the cable cars are boarded), where a paved jogging track runs for 1200 metres along the base of Morro de Tijuca and Pão de Açúcar. At the end of the track pick up the trail on the other side of the cement tank in the tall grass. Follow this trail (always taking the uphill forks) for 100 metres. At the old foundations, some 30 metres above the water, the trail ascends steeply for 60 metres until levelling off on the narrow ridge. From the ridge, the broad eastern flank of Pão de Açúcar is seen. The trail to follow is up the far left-hand side ridge.

At the base of the rock the trail deviates slightly to the right for the next 40 metres until coming to two iron bolts on the smooth exposed rock. This is the first exposed area, which,while crossed easily without ropes, requires agility and alertness. There is nothing to break a fall except the rocks in the ocean, 120 metres below.

From the second bolt stay next to the rock slab for the following six metres. In the gap between the first rock slab and the next slab it is safer to step up on to the second rock slab rather than continuing along the exposed face. Twenty metres higher up there is a third iron bolt, which is a good place to take in the view before tackling the crux of the climb – above the clearly defined path. At the fourth bolt, the hike becomes a climb for the next 10 metres. This section is best climbed by finding the holds behind the rock slabs and pulling yourself up. After the sixth and final bolt, the climbing is over. Follow the well-defined path up 200 metres to the small children's park at the top.

Corcovado Corcovado (710 metres) offers technically difficult climbs with fantastic views of Pão de Açúcar and Lagoa Rodrigo. Private guides and the clubs are the best means for unravelling its many diverse routes. Well-equipped and experienced climbers can easily climb its eastern face on the route K-2 (rated 5.9).

The climb begins 200 metres below the summit. To get to the base of the climb, take the train to the top and instead of ascending the stairs to the left, follow the road out of the parking lot for 15 minutes. After the first rocky outcrop, on the northern side, descend two more turns in the road. At the second turn there is a cement railing, behind which is a poorly maintained trail.

Follow this trail as it hugs the base of the rock for 200 metres around to the eastern face of the mountain. Don't get discouraged by the tall grass which obstructs the trail; just keep to the base of the rock. On the eastern face the start of the climb is at the 20-metre crack in the whitened rock. From there the climb is clearly marked with well-placed bolts to the top, just underneath the statue of Christ.

Bâteau Mouche

On New Year's Eve 1988, 55 people out of the 59 on board drowned when an over-loaded Bâteau Mouche bay cruise capsized in Baía de Guanabara. This private company still runs cruises, and they're much more careful with the number of passengers they let on board. Their modern boats cruise the bay and go out into the Atlantic. They usually have a morning and afternoon cruise that costs from US$20 to US$30. The scene is too slick-touristy for my taste but the voyage out into the ocean is undeniably beautiful. Don't take their bay cruise, because for a 50th of the price you can take a ferry or hydrofoil to Paquetá island and cover much of the same ground while travelling with the locals.

Ferry to Niterói

This is the poor person's Bâteau Mouche. It costs about 15c and the views are great, particularly returning to Rio around sunset. Over at Niterói you can walk around a bit to see Rio's poor relation or catch a local bus to Niterói's beaches. Leaving from Praça 15 de Novembro (in Centro), the ferry goes every 20 minutes and is always full of commuters. Buses to Praça 15 de Novembro include: from Flamengo, No 119; from Copacabana, No 119, 413, 415, 154, 455 or 474; and from Ipanema, No 474 or 154.

Carnival

Carnival is a pagan holiday originating perhaps in the Roman bacchanalia celebrating Saturn or in the ancient Egyptian festival of Isis. Carnival was a wild party during the Middle Ages until tamed in Europe by Christianity, but the sober church of the Inquisition could not squelch Carnival in the Portuguese colony, where it came to acquire African rhythms and Indian costumes.

People speculate that the word Carnival derives from *caro-vale*, meaning 'goodbye meat'. The reasoning goes something like this: for the 40 days of Lent, nominally Catholic Brazilians give up liver or flank steaks. To compensate for the big sacrifices ahead, they rack up sins in a delirious carnal blowout in honour of King Momo, the king of Carnival.

Carnival is celebrated everywhere in Brazil and each region has a particular way of celebrating. In Bahia, Carnival is celebrated in the streets under the blasting loudspeakers of the trio elétrico trucks; in Recife and Olinda merry-makers dance the frevo. These are more authentic Carnivals than Rio's glitzy celebration, which has become the big draw for the tourism industry. More than anywhere else in Brazil, Carnival in Rio is a spectator event, but it's a fantastic spectacle nonetheless.

Every year wealthy and spaced-out foreigners descend on Rio en masse, get drunk, get high, bag some sunrays and exchange exotic diseases. Everyone gets a bit unglued at this time of year and there are lots of car accidents and murders. Some of the leaner and meaner Cariocas can get a little ugly with all the sex, booze and flash of money. Apartment rates and taxi fares triple and quadruple and some thieves keep to the spirit of the season by robbing in costume.

The excitement of Carnival builds all year and the pre-Lenten revelry begins well before the official dates of Carnival. A month before Carnival starts, rehearsals at the *escolas de samba* (samba clubs) are open to visitors on Saturdays. The rehearsals are usually in the favelas. They're fun to watch, but for your safety go with a Carioca. Tourist

Carnival shows are held all year round at Scala, Plataforma 1 and up top at Pão de Açúcar.

The escolas de samba are actually predated by *bandas* (nonprofessional equivalents of the escolas de samba), which are now returning to the Carnival scene as part of the movement to return Rio's Carnival to the streets. Last year there was a Banda da Ipanema, a Banda do Leblon, a Banda da Boca Maldita and a Banda Carmen Miranda, among others. The bandas are great fun, a good place to loosen up your hip-joints for samba, and excellent photo opportunities; transvestites always keep the festivities entertaining.

Riotur has information on the scheduled bandas, or you could just show up in Ipanema (most of them are in Ipanema), at Praça General Osório or Praça Paz around 5 pm or so, a couple of weekends before official Carnival. Other street festivities are held in Centro on Avenida Rio Branco. Riotur has all the information in a special Carnival guide.

Carnival Balls Carnival balls are surreal and erotic events. In one ball at Scala I saw a woman (transsexual?) bare her breasts and offer passers-by a suck while rickety old ladies were bopping away in skimpy lingerie. A young and geeky rich guy was dancing on tables with whores past their prime, young models and lithe young nymphets, all in various stages of undress. Breasts were painted, stickered with adhesive tattoos, covered with fish-net brassieres or left bare. Bottoms were spandexed, G-stringed or mini-skirted.

In Monte Líbano, all the action took place on the stages. One stage had a samba band, the other was crushed with young women. They didn't dance, but ground their hips and licked their lips to the incessant, hypnotic music and the epileptic flashing of the floor lights. Throngs of sweaty photographers and video crews mashed up to the stage. Everyone played up for the camera, vying for space and the attention of the photographers. The Vegas headdresses, the pasty-faced bouncers and the rich men in private boxes overlooking the dance floor lent a Mafiosi feel to the place.

Carnival is the holiday of the poor. Not that you could tell from the price of the tickets to the balls. Some of them cost more than the monthly minimum wage. There are snooty affairs like the Pão de Açúcar ball (☎ 541-3737, tickets about US$75) and the Hawaiian ball at the yacht club, and raunchier parties in Leblon at Scala (☎ 239-4448, US$40) and Monte Líbano (☎ 239-0032, US$20). Tickets go on sale about two weeks before Carnival starts and the balls are held nightly for the week preceding Carnival and through Carnival.

In 1991 Scala held the Flamengo soccer club's Baile Vermelho e Preto (Red and Black Ball) and the inimitable Gala Gay Ball. Monte Líbano, the wildest place safe enough for tourists, hosted many hot events: Panther Night, the World Ball and the Grand Gala among others. There are three rules of thumb: beautiful, flirtatious and apparently unescorted women are either escorted by huge, jealous cachaça-crazed men wielding machetes, or else they are really men dressed up as women; everything costs several times more within the club than outside; and, finally, don't bring more money than you're willing to lose – the club bouncers are big, but not that effective.

The Sambódromo Parades

In the *sambódromo*, a tiered street designed for samba parades, the Brazilians harness sweat, noise and confusion and turn it into art. The 16 top-level samba schools prepare all year for an hour of glory in the sambódromo. The best escola is chosen by a hand-picked set of judges on the basis of many components including percussion, the *samba do enredo* (theme song), harmony between percussion, song and dance, choreography, costume, storyline, floats and decorations and others. The championship is hotly contested; the winner becomes the pride of Rio and Brazil.

The parades begin with moderate mayhem, then work themselves up to a higher plane of frenzy. The announcers introduce the escola, the group's colours and the number of wings. Far away the lone voice of the *puxador* starts the samba. Thousands more voices join him, and then the drummers kick in, 600 to 800 per school. The booming drums drive the parade. This samba do enredo is the loudest music you're ever likely to hear in your life. The samba tapes flood the air waves for weeks prior to the beginning of Carnival. From afar the parade looks alive. It's a throbbing beast – and slowly it comes closer, a pulsing, Liberace-glittered, Japanese-movie-monster slime-mould threatening to engulf all of Rio in samba and vibrant, vibrating mulattas.

The parades begin with a special opening wing or *abre-alas*, which always displays the name of the school and the theme of the escola. The whole shebang has some unifying message, some social commentary, economic criticism or political message, but it's usually lost in the glitter. The abre-alas is then followed by the *commissão de frente*, who greet the crowds. The escola thus honours its elderly men for work done over the years.

Next follow the main wings of the escola, the big allegorical floats, the children's wing, the drummers, the celebrities and the bell-shaped Baianas twirling in their elegant hoop skirts. The Baianas honour the history of the parade itself, which was brought to Rio from Salvador de Bahia in 1877. The *mestre-sala* (dance master) and *porta-bandeira* (standard bearer) waltz and whirl. Celebrities, dancers and tambourine players strut their stuff. The costumes are fabulously lavish: 1½-metre-tall feathered headdresses, flowing sequin capes, rhinestone-studded G-strings.

The floats gush neo-baroque silver foil and gold tinsel. Sparkling models sway to the samba, dancing in their private Carnivals. All the while the puxador leads in song, repeating the samba do enredo for the duration of the parade. Over an hour after it began, the escola makes it past the arch and the judges' stand. There is a few minutes' pause. Globo and Manchete TV cranes stop bobbing up and down over the Pepsi caps and bibs of the foreign press corps. Now garbage trucks parade down the runway clearing the way for the next escola. Sanitation workers in orange jump suits shimmy, dance and sweep, gracefully catch trash thrown from the stands and take their bows. It's their Carnival, too. The parade continues on through the night and into the morning, eight more samba schools parade the following day, and the week after, the top eight schools parade once more in the parade of champions.

Getting tickets at the legitimate prices can be tough. Many tickets are sold 10 days in advance of the event; check with Riotur on where you can get them, as the outlet varies from year to year. People queue up for hours and travel agents and scalpers snap up the best seats. Seats in private boxes have been sold for US$200. If you do happen to buy a ticket from a scalper (don't worry about finding them – they'll find you), make sure you get both the plastic ticket with the magnetic strip and the ticket showing the seat number. Different days have different coloured tickets, so check the date as well.

But don't fret if you don't get a ticket. It's possible to see the show without paying an arm and a leg. The parades last eight to 10 hours each and no one can or wants to sit through them that long. Unless you're an aficionado of an escola that starts early, don't show up at the sambódromo until midnight, three or four hours into the show. Then you can get tickets at the grandstand for about US$16. And if you can't make it during Carnival, there's always the cheaper (but less exciting) parade of champions the following week.

If you can avoid it, don't take the bus to or from the sambódromo; it's safer to take a taxi.

Dates Starting dates for Carnival in coming years are:

1993	21 February
1994	13 February
1995	26 February
1996	18 February
1997	9 February

Places to Stay

Rio has a star system. Hotels are ranked from one star for the cheapest to five for the most luxurious. Rio has 12 five-star hotels to choose from, 17 four-star hotels, 27 three-star hotels, 29 two-star hotels, three one-star hotels and 47 hotels unclassified by Embratur (our speciality), but still regulated. Hotels which are not regulated by Embratur sometimes slip in additional charges and other assorted petty crimes against the tourist. Threaten to call Sunab price regulation if this happens, discuss a price before accepting a room, and also ask if a 10% service charge is included.

Unless otherwise indicated, breakfast is included in the cost of the following hotels.

At Carnival time hotel prices go up and everyone gives dire warnings of no place to stay. For the past couple of years, however, there have been enough rooms, as many people go to other cities for Carnival.

Also, when there is a big discrepancy between the official and parallel exchange rates, the big hotels will try to hold their rooms for overseas bookings, which are paid at the official rate. This means that sometimes these hotels claim to be booked up far in advance and then will have rooms available at the 11th hour.

Places to Stay – bottom end

The best area for budget hotels is Glória/Catete/Flamengo. This used to be a desirable part of the city and is still quite nice. Many of the places used to be better hotels, so you can get some pleasant rooms at very reasonable prices. These hotels are often full from December to February, so reservations are not a bad idea.

From Glória to Lapa, near the aqueduct, on the edge of the business district, there are several more budget hotels. Generally, these are hardly any cheaper than the hotels further from the city in Catete, yet they are run-down and the area is less safe at night. If, however, everything else is booked up you'll see several hotels if you walk along Rua Joaquim Silva (near the Passeio Público), then over to Avenida Mem de Sá, turn up

Avenida Gomes Freire and then turn right to Praça Tiradentes. The *Hotel Marajó* at Avenida Joaquim Silva 99 is recommended.

Glória The *Hotel Turístico* (☎ 225-9388), Ladeira da Glória 30, is one of Rio's most popular budget hotels and there are always plenty of gringos staying here. It's across from the Glória metro station, 30 metres up the street that emerges between two sidewalk restaurants. The rooms are clean and safe, with small balconies. The hotel is often full but they do take reservations. Singles/doubles start at US$10/12 for quartos and US$13/15 for apartamentos.

Right near the Glória metro station, the *Hotel Benjamin Constant*, Rua Benjamin Constant 10, is one of the cheapest places around. The rooms are small and dingy, but the cost is only US$2.50 per person. There's a youth hostel, *Hostel Bello* (☎ 222-8576), at Rua Santo Amaro 162. It's a reasonable place to stay but a bit of a hike from the metro.

Catete & Flamengo The *Hotel Ferreira Viana* (☎ 205-7396) at Rua Ferreira Viana 58 has cramped, but cheap, rooms at US$7/10 for singles/doubles (US$13 with air-con) and an electric shower down the hall.

On busy Rua do Catete are three budget hotels worthy of note. The *Hotel Monte Blanco* (☎ 225-0121) at Rua do Catete 160, a few steps from the Catete metro stop, is very clean, has air-con, and singles/doubles for US$9/11. Ask for a quiet room in the back; they have round beds and sparkling wall paint.

The *Hotel Imperial* (☎ 205-0212) at Rua do Catete 186 is a tacky hotel with parking. The quality and prices of the rooms vary from US$16/20 for doubles without/with bathrooms. Some of the rooms have air-con. The *Hotel Rio Claro* (☎ 225-5180), a few blocks down at Rua do Catete 233, has musty singles for US$10 and doubles with air-con, TVs and hot showers for US$15.

The *Hotel Hispánico Brasileiro* (☎ 225-7537) at Rua Silveira Martins 135 has big, clean apartamentos. Singles are US$12 and doubles US$14.

Turn down the quiet Rua Arturo Bernardes for a couple more budget hotels: the *Monterrey* (☎ 265-9899) and *Hotel Rio Lisboa* (☎ 265-9599) are at Nos 39 and 29 respectively. The first is cheaper and friendlier. Single/double quartos go for US$3/6 and apartamentos cost US$10. At the Rio Lisboa, single quartos cost US$5 and apartamentos are US$8/10 for singles/doubles. These two are the cheapest places in Catete.

Copacabana The best place for budget travellers to stay in Copacabana is the *Copacabana Praia* youth hostel (☎ 236-6472) at Rua Tenente Marones de Gusmão 85. Although it's a few blocks from the beach it's still excellent value. A relaxed and friendly place, they charge US$7 for members, US$9 for non-members and US$20 for double apartments with a stove and a refrigerator. They will also rent you sheets if you don't have any.

Places to Stay – middle

If you want to be near the beach, there are several reasonably priced hotels in Copacabana, a couple in Ipanema and even some in Leblon. They all get busy in the high season, so it might pay to book ahead. For the same price you can get a cheerier room in Flamengo or in the centre near Cinelândia (the Cinelândia hotels are also convenient if you're heading to the airport or rodoviária soon). But if you want to stay where the sun always shines and the lights never go out, you can probably find a Copacabana hotel room for US$15 to US$20.

Another relatively inexpensive option in Copacabana, Ipanema and Leblon is to rent an apartment by the week or the month. There are loads of agencies. You could try Brasleme Imóveis (☎ 542-1347), Rua Barata Ribeiro 92-A, Copacabana. They rent apartments for a minimum of three days starting from US$75. Apartur Imóveis (☎ 287-5757), Rua Visconde de Pirajá 371 S/204, Ipanema, offers similar deals. If you are

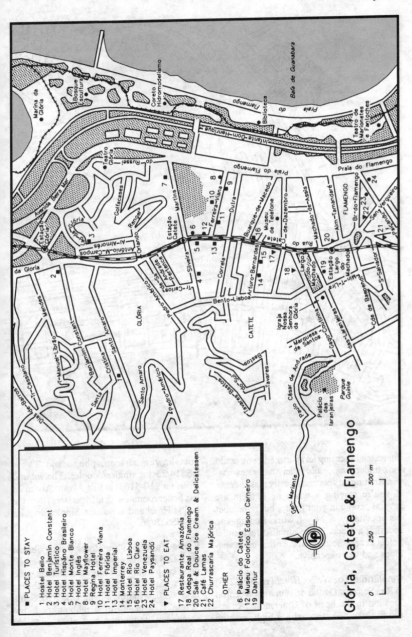

Glória, Catete & Flamengo

PLACES TO STAY
■ 1 Hostel Bello
2 Hotel Benjamin Constant
3 Hotel Turístico
4 Hotel Hispâno Brasileiro
5 Hotel Monte Blanco
7 Hotel Inglês
8 Hotel Mayflower
9 Regina Hotel
10 Hotel Ferreira Viana
11 Hotel Flórida
13 Hotel Imperial
14 Monterrey
15 Hotel Rio Lisboa
16 Hotel Rio Claro
23 Hotel Venezuela
24 Hotel Paysandú

▼ PLACES TO EAT
17 Restaurante Amazônia
18 Adega Real do Flamengo
20 Salé & Douce Ice Cream & Delicatessen
21 Café Lamas
22 Churrascaria Majórica

OTHER
6 Palácio do Catete
12 Museu Folclórico Edson Carneiro
19 Dantur

0   250   500 m

interested in renting an apartment, you could look under *temporada* in any daily newspaper. Renting an apartment really makes sense if you're staying a while or if there are several people in your group, but remember it's inevitably a bit of work finding and securing a place. There are also residential hotels or aparthotels that are often more spacious and less expensive.

Cinelândia The *Nelba Hotel* (☎ 210-3235) at Rua Senador Dantas 46 is in a good central location in the heart of Cinelândia. A two-room, three-bed suite with a high-pressure

hot shower, air-con, phone and TV is US$14/25 for singles/doubles. The *Itajuba Hotel* (☎ 210-3163) at Rua Álvaro Alvim 23 has better rooms (with refrigerators) than the Nelba Hotel and is quieter. Singles/doubles are US$18/26.

Santa Teresa The *Hotel Santa Teresa* (☎ 222-4355) is attractive and has a small pool, car parking and rates that include three meals. Singles/doubles with a bath are US$16/20; without a bath, US$9/16. Santa Teresa is a beautiful neighbourhood, but somewhat dangerous and after midnight

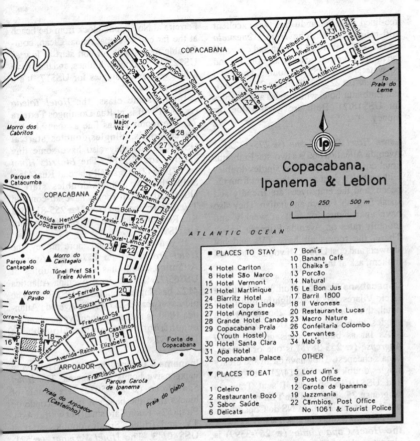

Copacabana,
Ipanema & Leblon

0   250   500 m

ATLANTIC OCEAN

■ PLACES TO STAY

4   Hotel Carlton
8   Hotel São Marco
15 Hotel Vermont
21 Hotel Martinique
24 Biarritz Hotel
25 Hotel Copa Linda
27 Hotel Angrense
28 Grande Hotel Canada
29 Copacabana Praia
    (Youth Hostel)
30 Hotel Santa Clara
31 Apa Hotel
32 Copacabana Palace

▼ PLACES TO EAT

1   Celeiro
2   Restaurante Bozó
3   Sabor Saúde
6   Delicats

7   Boni's
10 Banana Café
11 Chaika's
13 Porcão
14 Natural
16 Le Bon Jus
17 Barril 1800
18 Il Veronese
20 Restaurante Lucas
23 Macro Nature
26 Confeitaria Colombo
33 Cervantes
34 Mab's

OTHER

5   Lord Jim's
9   Post Office
12 Garota da Ipanema
19 Jazzmania
22 Câmbios, Post Office
    No 1061 & Tourist Police

there is no public transport. The hotel is at Rua Almirante Alexandrino 660. To get there take the bondinho to Vista Alegre and then follow the tracks downhill to the old mission-style building.

Catete & Flamengo The *Hotel Flórida* (☎ 245-8160), one of Rio's best budget hotels, is at Rua Ferreira Viana 81, near the Catete metro station. The Flórida has only two faults: it's not in Ipanema and it always seems to be booked up. Rooms have private baths with good, hot showers and polished parquet wood floors. Singles/doubles cost

US$20/23 (air-con is available). There's a cheap little restaurant and a safe deposit for valuables. Make your reservations well in advance for stays during the high season.

Down the block at Rua Ferreira Viana 29, the *Regina Hotel* (☎ 225-7280) is a respectable mid-range hotel with a snazzy lobby, clean rooms and hot showers; singles/doubles start at US$20/25.

At Rua Silveira Martins 20 is the *Hotel Inglês* (☎ 265-9052), a good two-star hotel where singles/doubles cost US$17/20.

Further into Flamengo, near the Largo do Machado metro station, the elegant palm-tree-lined Rua Paiçandú has two excellent mid-range hotels. The *Hotel Venezuela* (☎ 205-2098) at No 34 is clean and cosy. All the rooms have double beds, air-con, TV and hot water; it costs US$16 a double. The *Hotel Paysandú* (☎ 225-7270) at No 23 is a two-star Embratur hotel with singles and doubles for US$18/21. Both are good value for money.

Leme *Hotel Praia Leme* (☎ 275-3322) at Avenida Atlântica 866 is a two-star Embratur hotel costing US$26/29 for singles/doubles with bath. It's right across the street from the beach, and the employees are friendly and speak English, French and Italian. They also have apartments for rent at weekly and monthly rates on Avenida Princesa Isabel. There, the rooms all have TVs and hot showers and cost US$22. If you're interested in them, ask at the hotel.

Copacabana Near the youth hostel, at Rua Décio Vilares 316, is a delightful mid-range hotel, the *Santa Clara* (☎ 256- 2650) with singles/doubles starting at US$22/25.

As far as budget hotels go, the *Hotel Angrense* (☎ 255-3875) is one of Copacabana's cheapest. They have clean and dreary singles/doubles for US$14/21 with a bath and US$10/15 without. It's at Travessa Angrense 25. The road isn't on most maps but it intersects Avenida NS de Copacabana just past Rua Santa Clara. A few blocks away, the *Hotel Copa Linda* (☎ 267-3399) is almost as cheap. The small and basic rooms cost US$16 a single and US$20 a double. It's at Avenida NS de Copacabana 956 on the 2nd floor.

There are several hotels that offer more for the money than the two just mentioned. Right nearby, the *Grande Hotel Canada* (☎ 257-1864), Avenida NS de Copacabana 687, has singles for US$20 and doubles for US$25 (there is no elevator for the cheapest rooms). The rooms are modern, with air-con and TV.

The *Hotel Martinique* (☎ 521-4552) combines a perfect location with good rooms at a moderate cost. It's on the quiet Rua Sá Ferreira at No 30, one block from the beach at the far end of Copacabana. Clean, comfortable rooms with air-con start as low as US$22/32 for singles/doubles, and they have a few very small singles for US$17. It's a friendly place.

In the same class, the *Hotel Toledo* (☎ 257-1990) is at Rua Domingos Ferreira 71. The rooms are as fine as many higher priced hotels. Singles/doubles start at US$28/32 and they also have some tiny singles for US$17. The *Biarritz Hotel* (☎ 521-6542) is a small place at Rua Aires Saldanha 54. Singles/doubles start at US$16/30 and all rooms have air-con and TV. Also try the *Apa Hotel* (☎ 255-8112) at Rua República do Peru 305. Singles/doubles are US$28/38.

If you want to spend more money, the *Hotel Trocadero* (☎ 257-1834), Avenida Atlântica 2064, has singles/doubles at US$65/72. The *Riviera*, Avenida Atlântica 4122, has singles/doubles for US$56/60. The old *Excelsior* (☎ 257-1950), Avenida Atlântica 1800, is the least expensive hotel on the beachfront, with singles/doubles at US$44/52.

Ipanema & Leblon There are two relatively inexpensive hotels in Ipanema. The *Hotel San Marco* (☎ 239-5032) is a couple of blocks from the beach at Rua Visconde de Pirajá 524. Rooms are small but with air-con, TV, and fridge. Singles/doubles start at US$40/43. The *Hotel Vermont* (☎ 521-0057), Rua Visconde de Pirajá 254, also has very simple rooms at US$31/35. Call for reservations at both these hotels.

You can get an oceanside apartment at the *Arpoador Inn* (☎ 247-6090), Rua Francisco Otaviano. This six-floor hotel is the only hotel in Ipanema or Copacabana that doesn't have a busy street between your room and the beach. The beachfront rooms are more expensive than those facing the street but the view and the roar of the surf makes it all worthwhile. Singles cost from US$30 to US$60 and doubles from US$32 to US$63. The *Hotel Carlton* (☎ 259-1932), Rua João Lira 68, is on a very quiet street in Leblon.

It's a small, friendly hotel, away from the tourist scene. There is an excellent hotel bar. Singles/doubles are US$34/38.

Places to Stay – top end

The *Rio Flat Service* (☎ 274-7222) has three residential hotels that are more like apartments. All apartments have a living room and a kitchen. Without the frills of fancy hotels, they still have a swimming pool, breakfast and room service. Apartments start at US$50. The *Apart Hotel* (☎ 256-2633), Rua Barata Ribeiro 370, Copacabana, and the *Copacabana Hotel Residência* (☎ 256-2610), Rua Barata Riveiro 222, are both very similar to Rio Flat Service.

Of the many top hotels in Rio, the old-style *Copacabana Palace* (☎ 255-7070), at Avenida Atlântica 1702, is the one favoured by royalty and rock stars. Standard apartments cost US$110/125 a single/double, or you might like to try the Presidential suite for only US$1250 a night. In Ipanema, the *Caesar Park* (☎ 287-3122) at Avenida Vieira Souto 460 is favoured by ex-dictators, and business people with large expense accounts. Singles/doubles begin at US$230/255. The Imperial suite is a steal at US$2500 a night.

Places to Eat

As in most of Brazil, restaurants in Rio are abundant and cheap. The plates at the many lanchonetes are big enough to feed two and the price is only US$1 to US$2. For something lighter, and probably healthier, you can eat at a suco bar. Most have sandwiches and fruit salads. Make a habit of asking for an *embalagem* (doggie bag) when you don't finish your food. Wrap it and hand it to a street person.

Centro *Bar Luis*, Rua da Carioca 39, is a Rio institution that opened in 1887. The city's oldest cervejaria, on Rio's oldest street, is a bar-less old dining room serving good German food and dark draft beer at moderate prices. It's open Monday to Saturday for lunch and dinner, until midnight.

Hotel Ambassador, at Rua Santa Luzia 651 off Avenida Graça Aranha, has a business lunch buffet which is a good way to fill your belly. For US$4 it's all you can eat, with plenty of fruits and desserts included.

Café do Teatro (☎ 262-6164) at Avenida Epitácio Pessoa 1244 under the Teatro Municipal is a place to recall the good old days. Entering the dark, dramatic Assyrian Room, with its elaborate tilework and ornate columns, is like walking into a Cecil B De Mille film. The 70-year-old restaurant is where Rio's upper crust used to dine and drink after the theatre; it must be seen to be believed. They serve lunch only and close on Saturdays and Sundays. It's somewhat expensive and semi-formal, but don't be deterred – you can have a drink and light snack by the bar, listen to piano music, and breathe in the Assyrian atmosphere.

Confeiteria Colombo is at Rua Gonçalves Dias 34, one block from and parallel to Rio Branco. It's a big Viennese coffee house/restaurant where you can sit down for a meal, or stand if you're having just a dessert or cake. The Colombo is best for coffee and cake or a snack. Another old-style coffee house is *Casa Cavé* on the corner of Rua 7 de Setembro and Uruguiana. They have good ice cream.

The *English Bar* (☎ 224-2539) at Travessa do Comércio 11, Arco do Teles, is open 11.30 am to 4 pm Monday to Friday. It's a quiet and classy English pub that serves a good lunch. Steaks go for US$6 to US$7, fish for a bit less. It's off the Praça 15 de Novembro, right through the Arco do Teles.

The green gazebo structure near the Niterói ferry is *Alba Mar* (☎ 240-8378) at Praça Marechal Âncora 184. It looks out on the Baía de Guanabara and Niterói. Go for the view and the seafood. It stays open from 11.30 am to 10 pm Monday to Saturday. Dishes start at US$5 and the peixe brasileira is recommended.

Cheio de Vida is a reasonably priced place in the centre at Avenida 13 de Maio 33, 403. It's not the easiest place to find, but it's worth it. Their food has a 'natural' touch. Try the zucchini pizza. *Simples Delírio do Nectar* at Avenida General Justo 365A has top salad plates for US$2 and main course dishes like pork and potatoes, or shrimp with mandioca, for around US$3.

Cinelândia *Macrobiótica* (☎ 220-7585) is one floor up at Rua Embaixador Regis de Oliveira 7. Macrobiotics is pretty popular in Brazil's cities and the food here is inexpensive and simple. Try the soup and rice dishes. They are open Monday to Friday from 11 am to 5.45 pm.

Lanchonete Bariloche is at Rua Alcindo Guanabara 24-D, across from Rua Senador Dantas. This cheap little counter joint has wood-grilled steaks for US$3 and is open until 2 am. *Churrascolândia Restaurante* (☎ 220-9534) at Rua Senador Dantas 31 is a steakhouse which also has tasty steaks cooked on a wood grill for US$4.

Lapa & Santa Teresa *Arco da Velha Bar e Restaurante* at Praça Cardeal Câmara 132, Lapa, is literally under the arch of the viaduct that the trolley crosses to head up to Santa Teresa. The Arco da Velha has great Bahian food and there is live music upstairs. It's a good place to eat if you're going to a show in the city. In Santa Teresa at Rua Almirante Alexandrino 316-B, *Bar do Arnaudo* has excellent carne do sol. It's closed Mondays.

Catete & Largo do Machado Area *Salé & Douce Ice Cream & Delicatessen* (☎ 285-7347) is at Rua do Catete 311, next to the São Luis cinema and across from the Largo do Machado subway entrance. In addition to Babushka's ice cream they have healthy sandwiches for about US$2. *Leg Leg Lanches*, Rua da Catete 228, loja 111, is behind a shopping plaza. This little lunch and pastry place has some excellent, light and healthy lunches for less than US$2

Restaurant Amazónia (☎ 225-4622) at Rua do Catete 234 has good steak and a tasty broiled chicken with creamed corn sauce, both for about US$3.

Adega Real do Flamengo (☎ 265-7549) at Largo do Machado 30-A is an Iberian-style bar and restaurant, with garlic and meat hanging from the ceiling and wine bulging off the shelves. It serves various fish and

meat dishes that vary from the usual Rio fare. Try the *bolinhos de bacalhau* (cod fish balls) for 50c each with a Portuguese wine. For a feast try the roast *cabrito* (kid – the four-legged kind with little horns growing out of its head) for US$5.

For an early morning (or late afternoon) juice in Catete, you can't go past *O Rei dos Sucos* (The King of Juices) on the corner of Rua Catete and Rua Silveira Martins. They have a top range of fruits which they juice, including a lot of Amazonian ones with hard-to-pronounce names.

Botafogo & Flamengo David, the owner of *Rajmahal* (☎ 541-6999) at General Polidoro 29, Botafogo, is British, but the food is all Indian and quite good. Meals cost about US$7 and the place is a bit off the beaten path. The restaurant is spacious and refreshingly calm for Rio. It's open in the evenings from Tuesday to Sunday.

Sol e Mar (☎ 295-1896), Avenida Repórter Nestor Moreira 11, is somewhat pricey and stuffy, and comes complete with serenading violinists. It's one of the few places in the city that's right on the bay and the outdoor tables provide a spectacular view. Seafood dominates the menu. The restaurant is next to the Bâteau Mouche at Botafogo beach and is open daily from 11 am to 3 am. A favourite with wealthy tourists.

The popular *Churrascaria Majórica* (☎ 245-8947), Rua Senador Vergueiro 11/15, Flamengo, has good meat, reasonable prices and an interior done in gaúcho kitsch. It's open for lunch and dinner.

Cafe Lamas (☎ 205-0198) at Rua Marques de Abrantes 18-A, Flamengo, has been operating since 1874 and is one of Rio's most renowned eateries. It has a lively and loyal clientele and is open for lunch and dinner with a typical meaty menu and standard prices; try the grilled linguiça, or filet mignon.

Leme *Mário's* (☎ 542-2393), at Avenida Atlântica 290, Leme, has an all-you-can-eat deal for US$6. Many people think this is Rio's best churrascaria and they may be right. Be prepared to wait during prime time as they get a big tourist crowd. It's open from 11.30 to 1.30 am.

Restaurante Shirley at Rua Gustavo Sampaio 610-A has delicious seafood plates from US$5 to US$10. Try the mussel vinaigrette appetiser or the octopus and squid in ink for US$8.

Copacabana *Lope's Confeiteria* at Avenida NS de Copacabana 1334, off Júlio de Castilhos, is an excellent lanchonete with big portions and little prices for typical Brazilian food.

The *Americana Restaurant*, on Avenida Rainha Elizabete off Avenida NS de Copacabana, has lunches and dinners which are hearty and reasonably priced. The steak with potatoes or vegies is excellent for US$4.50.

Restaurante Lucas at Avenida Atlântica 3744 is across from Rua Lima and has reasonably priced German dishes starting at US$4.

Confeitaria Colombo, at the intersection of Avenida NS de Copacabana and Barão de Ipanema, is a smaller version of the Colombo in the centre, but with the same colonial charm. For coffee, desserts and snacks stay downstairs, but take a look upstairs at the elegant dining room. Their café Viennese is excellent. They now serve a great breakfast too.

Arataca at Rua Domingues Ferreira 41 (near the American Express office) is one of several Arataca restaurants in Rio which feature the exotic cuisine of the Amazon. This place is actually a counter lunch stand and deli, around the corner from one of their regular restaurants, with the same food as at the restaurants but for only half the price. In addition to the regional dishes such as vatapá for US$4 and *pato* (duck) for US$5, they serve real guaraná juice (try it) and delicious sorbets made from Amazonas fruits.

Mab's, on Avenida Atlântica (the Copacabana side of Princesa Isabel, across from the Meridien), has excellent seafood soup in a crock, chock full of piping hot creepy-crawlies for US$4.

Cervantes, on Avenida Prado Junior, is Rio's best sandwich joint and is also a late night hangout for a strange and colourful crew. It's on the infamous Avenida Prado Junior, where everyone and everything goes at night. Meat sandwiches come with pineapple (US$2). The steaks and fries are excellent too.

Macro Nature, down the Travessa Cristiano Lacorte, is the best vegetarian restaurant/health food store in Copacabana. The menu is brief and very organic; the soups excellent. They have sucos, sandwiches, yoghurt and health foods to go and everything is cheap. The *ponto de encontro de pessoas saudáveis* (the meeting point for healthy people) as they call themselves is open Monday to Friday from 9 am to 10.30 pm, Saturday and Sunday from 9 am to 6 pm.

Ipanema If you can't afford to stay at the *Caesar Park* hotel, go down there one Wednesday or Saturday from noon to 4 pm and sample their famous Brazilian feijoada. President Collor considers it the best around, and for US$15 it's excellent value for money.

Via Farme (☎ 227-0743) at Rua Farme de Amoedo 47 offers a good plate of pasta at a reasonable price, something which is usually hard to find. The four-cheese pasta and the seafood pasta dishes are excellent and portions are large enough for two to share. Most dishes are less than US$5. They are open from noon to 2 am.

Barril, at both 1800 Avenida Vieira Souto and Avenida Rainha Elizabete at the beach, is open late into the night. This trendy beach cafe, below Jazzmania (see Entertainment), is for people meeting and watching. After a day at Ipanema beach, you can stroll over to the *Shell Station* across the street from Barril 1800 for Babushka's terrific ice cream.

Boni's, Rua Visconde de Pirajá 595, is a favourite for fast food. Excellent pastries and fresh coffee with enough force to turn Bambi into Godzilla. *Chaika's*, Rua Visconde de Pirajá 321, is open from 8 am to 2 pm; this is where the girl from Ipanema really eats. There's a stand-up fast-food bar, and a restaurant in the back with delicious hamburgers, the sweetest pastries and good cappuccino (a rarity in Rio). Chaika's stays busy late into the night.

Il Veronese, Rua Visconde de Pirajá 29A, is off Gomes Carneiro. For an inexpensive meal, Veronese has takeaway Italian pastas (the best in Rio according to local sources), pizzas and pastries.

Porcão (☎ 521-0999), Rua Barão da Torre 218, has steadily been moving up in the churrasco ratings game. Again, it's all you can eat for about US$6 a person. They open at 11 am and close at 2 am.

Bar Lagoa, on the lake, is Rio's oldest bar/restaurant. It doesn't open till 7 pm but only closes at 3 am. There's always a good crowd and you can just drink beer, or you can eat a full meal for US$5 to US$6. The food is excellent, the menu typical, and the atmosphere great.

Natural (☎ 267-7799) at Rua Barão da Torre 171 is a very natural health food restaurant which has an inexpensive lunch special with soup, rice, vegies and beans, for less than US$3. Other good dishes are pancakes with chicken or vegetables.

Delicats, at Avenida Henrique Dumont near Rua Visconde de Pirajá, is Rio's only deli and has lots of homemade food. They make the best potato knish (dumplings) south of New York. They also have pastrami, herring, rye bread and other treasures from the old country, but sadly no bagels.

Le Bon Jus at the corner of Teixeira de Meio and Visconde de Pirajá is one of the best juice and sandwich stands in the city.

Banana Café, at Rua Barão da Torre 368, is a trendy bar/restaurant. They have 19 different types of pizza and eight types of sandwich. If you're drinking, try a 'Black Velvet' (dark chopp with champagne). They're open till 6 am.

Chez Michou, Rua Paul Redfern 44, is a popular creperie with a young crowd. They open till 4 am, but are closed on Tuesday.

Fans of Japanese food should hit the *Kabuki Japanese Buffet*, Rua Visconde de Pirajá 365. It's reasonably priced and open Monday to Saturday from 10 am to 7 pm.

Leblon *Sabor Saúde*, Avenida Ataulfo de Paiva 630, is Rio's best health food emporium and is open daily from 8.30 am to 10.30 pm. They have two natural food restaurants: downstairs has good meals for US$3 while upstairs is more expensive (they have great buffet feasts for US$6). There's also a small grocery store and takeaway food counter.

Celeiro, at Rua Dias Ferreira 199, has a fantastic salad bar. It's open from 11.30 am to 5 pm every day except Sunday. Don't let the silly name put you off at *Restaurante Bozó* (☎ 274-0147), Rua Dias Ferreira 50 – these people are very serious about their food. Try the scrumptious and filling medallions of filet mignon wrapped in bacon and smothered in pepper sauce.

Most Cariocas have a favourite churrascaria. The serious carnivores have a current favourite because last month's favourite has slipped a bit. Prices don't vary much between churrascarias: it's usually all you can eat for about US$8. *Plataforma* (☎ 274-4052) at Rua Adalberto Ferreira 32 is one of the best. It's always busy late at night and is a big hangout for actors and musicians. Tom Jobim is a big fan of its chopp. The restaurant is open from 11 am to 2 am daily.

Café Leblon specialises in sandwiches. The turkey with plum chutney for US$2 is great. The decor is interesting too, with marble tables and photos of old Rio. It's at Avenida Bartolomeu Mitre 297 and stays open late.

Gávea *Guimas* (☎ 259-7996), Jose Roberto Macedo Soares 5, is my favourite restaurant. The food is terrific, although the prices are just a bit more than you'll pay for a typical filet at any one of 100 Rio restaurants. That's because the portions are not enormous.

Guimas offers what most restaurants in Rio lack: creative cooking. Try the pernil de carneiro (lamb with onions) for US$6 or the Oriental shrimp curry (US$10) and a Rio salad. The small, but comfortable open-air restaurant opens at 8 pm and gets crowded later in the evening.

Parque Nacional da Tijuca *Os Erquilos* is

a beautiful colonial restaurant in Alto da Boa Vista. It has a typical menu which is not expensive. It is open Tuesday to Sunday from noon to 7 pm.

Ice Cream *Babushka's* and *Alex* are the two best ice-cream chains in town.

Fine Dining Rio is loaded with fancy restaurants which are not that expensive for the visitor. In most you can spend less than US$15 – especially if you decline the couvert, which is always a rip-off – and the most expensive are often less than US$30. Here's a list of some of the best:

Chinese
> *Mr Zee*, Rua General San Martin 1219, Leblon (☎ 294-0591)

French
> *Laurent*, Rua D Mariana 209, Botafogo (☎ 266-3131)
> *Club Gourmet*, Rua General Polidoro 186, Botafogo (☎ 295-1097)
> *Ouro Verde*, Avenida Atlântica 1456, Copacabana (☎ 542-1887)

Italian
> *Quadrifoglio*, Rua Maria Angélica 43, Jardim Botânico (☎ 226-1799)

Polish
> *A Polonese*, Rua Hilário de Gouveia 116, Copacabana (☎ 237-7378)

Portuguese
> *Antiquarius*, Rua Aristides Espinola 19, Leblon (☎ 294-1049)

Swiss
> *Casa da Suiça*, Rua Cândido Mendes 157, Glória (☎ 252-2406)

Entertainment

To find out what's going on at night, pick up the *Jornal do Brasil* at any newsstand and turn to the entertainment section. On Fridays they insert an entertainment magazine called *Programa* which lists the week's events. If you can't deal with another word of Portuguese, the big shows and fancier clubs will have announcements in the *Brazil Post*.

Nightlife varies widely by the neighbourhood. Leblon and Ipanema have up-market, trendy clubs with excellent jazz. Botafogo has cheaper, popular clubs with more dancing and samba. Cinelândia and Lapa in the centre have a lot of samba and pagode and are also the heart of gay Rio. Try some of the bars around Sala Cecília Mendez. Copacabana is a mixed bag, with some good local hangouts but also a strong tourist influence with a lot of sex for sale.

Entertainment is less organised and more spontaneous in Rio than you'd expect. Much of Rio's nightlife happens on the streets, in front of bars, in restaurants, anywhere outside with room to drink and sing. Most bars stay open until 4 am on busy weekend nights and to around 2 am other nights.

Centro & Lapa Getting a taxi late at night in Lapa or Cinelândia isn't a problem; there is also limited bus service all night long. You can catch buses to the zona sul along the Praça Mahatma Gandhi on Avenida Luis de Vasconcelos.

Suburban Dreams at Pedro Lessa 41, Centro, behind the Biblioteca Nacional, is a bar, open until late very late, and right in the centre. It's the only thing open on the block. The suburbs referred to here are the poorer areas on the outskirts of the city. The bar is frequented by many gays, Blacks and zona norte people. It's a good change from the zona sul club scene but don't bring too much money to this part of town late at night. There's no cover charge.

Café Bohemia is a vegetarian restaurant by day and has wild transvestite shows on Friday, Saturday and Sunday nights. For a couple of dollars you get dancing and a very funny show if you can get by in Portuguese. It's on Avenida Santa Luzia; turn right off Avenida Rio Branco. The show starts about 1 or 2 am.

Bar Brasil in Lapa is an old bohemian hangout and is always lively. Some Cariocas who live in the zona sul only come into the centre to go to Bar Brasil. Lapa is generally an interesting area to explore at night.

Botafogo O Viro da Ipiranga (☎ 225-4762) at Rua Ipiranga 54 is a warm bar with a relaxed scene, great local musicians and it costs only a couple of dollars to get in. The music varies but they have a couple of nights a week of *chorinho*, a bittersweet instrumental music from Rio.

Manga Rosa (☎ 266-4996) at Rua Dezenove de Fevereiro 94 is off Rua Voluntários da Pátria. There are tables inside and out, in a pleasant courtyard, and they have samba and karaoke music from Thursday to Sunday with a minimal cover charge.

Beco Da Pimenta, Rua Real Grandeza 176, is a great little joint for samba, pagode and traditional Rio music and it's very cheap. There's a lively, mixed crowd that knows how to dance and drink.

Cochrane, off Rua Voluntários da Pátria, is one of Rio's more popular gay bars. Vaticano, Rua da Matriz 62, is a hip bar, popular with the artsy Rio set.

Copacabana Galeria Alaska on Avenida NS de Copacabana has a transvestite show and dancing and is a centre of gay Rio.

If you are homesick for punk culture, try Kitschnet at Barata Ribeiro 543. It's frequented by 'darks' – Brazilian punks who wear black clothing and listen to Brazilian rock – they've come a long way from 'The Girl from Ipanema' days.

Ipanema & Leblon Jazzmania (☎ 287-0085), Rua Rainha Elizabete, is Rio's most serious jazz venue. They have more international stars than any other club, but also the best of Brazilian jazz. The club is expensive at around US$10 cover on weekends and a little less on weekdays. The music starts about 11 pm and goes late.

People's (☎ 294-0547), at Avenida Bartolomeu Mitre 370 in Leblon, is a posh club with some of the best names in jazz. To hear the great music you have to endure a US$8 cover charge and incessant smoking and talking from a snobby crowd. When it gets crowded the Yves St Laurent crowd seems to get in and seated, while the Lonely Planet crowd gets left at the door.

There are several other expensive restaurants/clubs in Ipanema and Leblon which have good jazz but look like a scene right out of Los Angeles or New York. Chiko's Bar, Avenida Epitácio Pessoa 560 on the lake,

goes late and has no cover charge. Mistura Up at Rua Garcia D'Avila 15 and Un Deux Trois (☎ 239-0198) at Rua Bartolomeu Mitre 123 are also popular.

If you want to speak English, Lord Jim's British pub is the place. It's at Rua Paul Redfern 63 in Ipanema. The Garota de Ipanema is at Rua Vinícius de Morais 49 and has open-air dining. There are always a few foreigners checking out the place where Tom Jobim was sitting when he wrote 'The Girl from Ipanema'.

My favourite bar is also Rio's oldest. In a town that's losing its traditions rapidly to modern Western schlock, Bar Lagoa is a comforting breeze. They tried to close it down to build a high-rise, high-tech, condo complex, but opposition was too strong. It's open from about 9 pm to 3 or 4 am with food, drink and a loud Carioca crowd.

Botanic (☎ 294-7448) is a bar frequented almost exclusively by women. It is in Jardim Botânico at Rua Pacheco Leão 70.

Brazilian Dancing The following clubs have popular Brazilian music like samba and forró and Rio's popular dance classes. You're unlikely to find any tourists, or middle-class Brazilians there. If you want to learn about Brazil and dance, or just watch Brazilians dancing, these are the places.

Pagode da Passarela has samba and pagode on Friday and Saturday nights. It's very crowded because it's affordable to almost everyone: 50c for women and US$1 for men. It's in the centre near Praça 11. Bola Preta (☎ 240-8049) is a big dance house with different types of popular music each night. They have serestas, roda de samba and pagode. The club's right in the centre, on Avenida 13 de Maio. Another good place to samba, but out in the suburbs, is Pagode Domingo Maior (☎ 288-7297) at Rua Gonzaga Bastos 268, Vila Isabel. It's probably a good idea to go with a Brazilian if you don't speak Portuguese.

If you'd rather not go into town, Clube do Samba (☎ 399-0892) is out in Barra at Estrada da Barra 65. They have samba and pagode Friday and Saturday nights. On

Sunday you can get a feijoada there. This is a middle-class club, with admission costing about US$3.

Forró is the popular dance music of Brazil's Northeast and there are plenty of Northeasterners in Rio going out dancing every weekend. I actually like the accordion-laced forró more than most of the current samba, and the dancing is a blast. Forró Forrado (☎ 248-0524) is close to the budget hotels in Catete at Rua do Catete 235. From Thursday to Sunday nights they do the forró, starting up at 10 pm and going late. Admission is US$2.50 for men and US$1 for women. Another club for forró is Estudantina (☎ 232-1149) at Praça Tiradentes 79, Centro. They go Thursday, Friday and Saturday nights until about 4 am. The cover charge is US$2.

Samba Schools As early as October or November the samba schools begin holding rehearsals and dances, typically on Saturday nights. These are generally open to the public for watching and joining in the samba. Almost all the escolas da samba are on the north side of town and, of course, things get going late, so you need a car or a taxi. Check with Riotur or the newspaper to get the schedules and locations. Each school has a club/arena but they also hold rehearsals around town. The school addresses are:

Portela
Rua Clara Nunes 81, Madureira
Mocidade Independente de Padre Miguel
Rua Coronel Tamarindo 38
São Clemente
Rua Assunção 63, Botafogo
Império Serrano
Avenida Ministro Edgard Romero 114, Largo de Madureira
Mangueira
Rua Visconde de Niterói 1072, Mangueira
Beija Flor
Rua Praçinha Wallace Paes Leme 1562, Nilópolis
Império da Tijuca
Rua Conde de Bonfim 1226, Usina da Tijuca

Big Shows Circo Voador under the Arcos da Lapa is a big tent with reggae, samba and trio elétrico music. The crowd is mostly from the north side. It's one of my favourites and is very reasonably priced. They get many of the best bands from Bahia and São Paulo. Their Sunday night dance gets really crowded. It starts at 11 pm and goes till late. Cover charge is US$3.

Down the block is Asa Branca (☎ 252-0966). They have samba and pagode shows that aren't for tourists, though they are staged shows. Scala, Plataforma I and Oba Oba have expensive Vegas-style shows with naked samba. Scala II has many top musicians like Gilberto Gil playing there these days. It's a show house, flashy and artificial, but I'd go anywhere to see a Gil show.

Pão de Açúcar has a regular performance of the samba school Beija Flor on Mondays from 9 pm to 1 am. It's expensive and touristy, but it's samba. Carioca Nights are held Fridays and Saturdays from 10 pm to 4 am. Mostly rock, but not always, the shows are not terribly expensive and are under the small pavilion on Morro da Urca – the first stop to Sugar Loaf. It's a spectacular view.

Canecão also gets the big stars of music. It's right next to the giant Rio Sul shopping mall at the entrance to the Copacabana tunnel.

Maracanãzinho is the smaller stadium next to Maracanã in São Cristóvão. The biggest shows, like Milton Nascimento, play there.

Parque Catacumba, along the lake, often has free outdoor concerts on Sundays at 5 pm. Check the newspaper.

Discos There are many discos with bright lights and loud music in the big city, but I can't help you much here if you're interested – pick up a tourist brochure. Interestingly, many of the discos have stiff dress codes and admission charges, designed in part to deter the many prostitutes who come to meet tourists. Some are even called private clubs and require you to pay US$20 through a concierge at your five-star hotel in order to enter.

Help calls itself the biggest disco in Latin America and no one seems to doubt it. It's at Avenida Atlântica 3432 in Copacabana. Lots of drunken gringos seem to get robbed just outside. Calígola in Ipanema is where the rich and famous hang out. The current favourite is Resumo da Ópera; it's in Lagoa at Avenida Borges de Medeiros 1426.

Things to Buy

Most stores are open Monday to Friday from 9 am to 7 pm (some stay open even later). Saturday is a half-day of shopping, from 9 am to 1 pm. The malls usually open from 10 am to 10 pm, Monday to Friday, and 10 am to 8 pm on Saturdays. It's illegal for stores to open on Sundays.

Pé de Boi This store sells the traditional artisan handicrafts of Brazil's Northeast and Minas Gerais, and it's all fine work. There's lots of wood, lace, pottery and prints. It's not an inexpensive store; you have to buy closer to the source to get a better price, but if you have some extra dollars – US$10 to US$20 at a minimum – these pieces are the best gifts to bring home from Brazil: imaginative and very Brazilian.

The small store is worth a visit just to look around. Ana Maria Chindler, the owner, knows what she's selling and is happy to tell you about it. Pé de Boi (Bull's Foot; ☎ 285-4395) is in Botafogo on Rua Ipiranga 53. It is open Monday to Friday until 7 pm and on Saturdays from 10 am to 1 pm.

FUNAI Brazil's Indian agency has a tiny craft shop at Avenida Presidente Wilson 16-A (it's actually around the corner from the main entrance). Open Monday to Friday from 9 am to noon and 1 to 6 pm, the store has woven papoose slings for US$5, jewellery from 50c to US$5 and musical instruments.

Casa Oliveira This beautiful music store (☎ 222-3539) is at Rua da Carioca 70 in Centro – Rio's oldest street. It sells a wide variety of instruments, including all the noise makers that fuel the Carnival *baterias* (rhythm sections), a variety of small mandolin-like string instruments, accordions and electric guitars. These make great presents

and it's a fun place to play even if you don't buy.

Rio Sul Brazilians, like Americans, seem to measure progress by shopping malls. They love to shop at these monsters. Rio Sul was the first mall to maul Rio. There are all kinds of stores. The C&A department store has a good range of clothes and is inexpensive. Rio Sul is right before you enter the Copacabana tunnel in Botafogo. There are free buses from Copacabana.

Bum Bum Since your bathing suit has too much fabric attached to the seams, resign yourself to buying a new one. Bum Bum is the trendsetter of the bikini world, and it knows it. It's not cheap, but you're paying for style not fabric. It's in Ipanema at Rua Visconde de Pirajá 437. If you're on a budget, there are plenty of other boutiques that sell bikinis for less money but with just as little fabric. Ki-Tanga is a good example.

Hippie Fair This is an arts and crafts fair, with many booths selling jewellery, leather goods, paintings, samba instruments, clothes, etc. There is some awful stuff here and some OK stuff. Prices go way up during the peak tourist season and the air rings with the sounds of New Yorkers hunting down good buys.

The fair takes place every Sunday at the Praça General Osório in Ipanema. But you can find the same items at Praça 15 de Novembro in Centro or at the northern end of Copacabana beach. If you're just beginning to travel in Brazil, skip it.

Nordeste or São Cristóvão Fair The nordeste fair is held at the Pavilhão de São Cristóvão on the north side of town every Sunday, starting early and going until about 3 pm. The fair is very Northeastern in character. There are lots of *barracas* (stalls) selling meat, beer and cachaça; bands of accordions, guitars and tambourines playing the forró; comedy, capoeira battles and people selling magic potions. It's a great scene.

Of course there's plenty to buy. Besides food, they have lots of cheap clothes, some good deals on hammocks and a few good nordeste gifts like leather vaqueiro (cowboy) hats. If you're ready for adventure and have a car, it's best to arrive the night before the market. This is set-up time and also party time. At about 9 or 10 pm the barracas open for dinner and beer. Some vendors are busy setting up, others are already finished. Music and dance starts, and doesn't stop until sunrise. It's great fun so long as you're careful.

Getting There & Away

Air From Rio, flights go to all of Brazil and Latin America. Shuttle flights to São Paulo leave from the conveniently located Aeroporto Santos Dumont, in the city centre along the bay. Almost all other flights – domestic and national – leave from Aeroporto Galeão.

Incoming visitors at Galeão pass through customs and then continue into a large lobby where there's a tourist information counter run by a private company called RDE which can arrange hotel and taxi reservations. The staff also try to palm off a 'travellers passport' for the outrageous sum of US$25,and attempt to pressure befuddled travellers with the argument that government regulations require purchase of this junk package. This is a load of nonsense and a blatant rip-off attempt.

All three major Brazilian airlines have their main offices in the centre (metro stop Cinelândia). You can also walk over to Aeroporto Santos Dumont where they have ticket counters and make reservations from there.

Varig/Cruzeiro (☎ 292-6600 for reservations or 282-1319 for information) has its main office in Centro at Avenida Rio Branco 277. There are also offices at Rua Rodolfo Dantas 16 in Copacabana (☎ 541-6343), and Rua Visconde de Pirajá 351, Ipanema (☎ 287-9440). The city office is much more reliable and knowledgeable than the other Varig offices.

VASP (☎ 292-2080) has a city office at Rua Santa Luzia 735. They also have offices at Aeroporto Santos Dumont (☎ 292-2112), at Avenida NS de Copacabana 262 (☎ 292-2112) in Copacabana, and at Rua Visconde de Pirajá 444 (☎ 292-2112) in Ipanema.

Transbrasil (☎ 297-4422) is in the centre at Avenida Calógeras 30. The other office is at Avenida Atlântica 1998 (☎ 236-7475) in Copacabana.

Nordeste Linhas Aéreas (☎ 220-4366) is at Aeroporto Santos Dumont. It goes to Porto Seguro, Ilhéus and other smaller cities in the Northeast. Rio Sul (☎ 262-6911) does the same for the south and is also at Aeroporto Santos Dumont.

International airlines include:

Aerolineas Argentinas
Rua São José 40, Centro (☎ 224-9242);
Avenida NS de Copacabana, Copacabana 312 (☎ 255-7144)

Aero Peru
Praça Mahatma Gandhi 2, Centro (☎ 210-3124)

Air France
Rua Lauro Muller 116, No 3801, Rio Sul Tower, Botafogo (☎ 542-5442.

Alitalia
Presidente Antônio Carlos 40, Centro (☎ 210-2192)

Avianca
Avenida Presidente Wilson 165, No 807 (☎ 240-4413)

British Airways
Avenida Rio Branco 108, 21st floor, Centro (☎ 221-0922)

Ecuatoriana
Avenida Almirante Barroso 63, No 1908, Centro (☎ 240-1075)

Iberia
Avenida Presidente Antônio Carlos 51, 8th floor, Centro (☎ 282-1336)

Japan Air Lines
Avenida Rio Branco 156, No 2818, Centro (☎ 220-6414)

KLM
Avenida Rio Branco 311, Centro (☎ 210-1342)

Lan Chile
Rua São José 70, 8th floor, Centro (☎ 242-1423)

LAP-Lineas Aereas Paraguayas
Avenida Rio Branco 245, 7th floor, Centro (☎ 220-4148)

Lloyd Aero Boliviano
Avenida Calógeras 30, Centro (☎ 220-9548)

Lufthansa
Avenida Rio Branco 156, Centro (☎ 262-0273)

Pan American
    Avenida Presidente Wilson 165, Centro (☎ 210-3214)
SAS
    Avenida Presidente Wilson 231, 21st floor, Centro (☎ 210-1222)
Viasa
    Rua do Carmo 7, 4th floor, Centro (☎ 224-5345)

Bus From Rio , there are buses to everywhere. They all leave from the loud Novo Rio Rodoviária (☎ 291-5151 for information), Avenida Francisco Bicalho in São Cristóvão, about 20 minutes north of the centre. At the rodoviária you can get information on transport and lodging if you ask at the Riotur desk on the ground floor.

Excellent buses leave every 15 minutes or so for São Paulo (six hours). Most major destinations have *leito* (executive) buses leaving late at night. These are very comfortable. Many travel agents in the city sell bus tickets. It's a good idea to buy a ticket a couple days in advance if you can.

National Bus Schedules

Angra dos Reis	2¾ hours
Belém	60 hours
Belo Horizonte	7 hours
Brasília	18 hours
Cabo Frio	3 hours
Curitiba	11 hours
Florianópolis	20 hours
Foz do Iguaçu	22 hours
Goiânia	18 hours
Ouro Preto	7 hours
Parati	4 hours
Petrópolis	1½ hours
Porto Alegre	27 hours
Recife	38 hours
Salvador	28 hours
São João del Rei	5½ hours
Vitória	8 hours

International Bus Schedules

Asunción, Paraguay	25 hours
Buenos Aires, Argentina	46 hours
Montevideo, Uruguay	39 hours
Santiago, Chile	74 hours

Getting Around

To/From the Airport All international and nearly all domestic flights use Galeão international airport, 15 km north of the city centre on Ilha do Governador.

Aeroporto Santos Dumont is in the heart of the city on the bay. It's used for the São Paulo shuttle and some flights to a variety of other destinations like Porto Seguro or Belo Horizonte. You can take the same bus as for Galeão airport or get to the city and take a taxi, or simply walk to the airport from Centro.

Bus – air-conditioned There are two air-con airport bus routes operating from 5.20 to 12.10 am, every 40 minutes to one hour (about US$3). One route goes to the centre and to Santos Dumont airport, the other route goes to the city centre and along the beaches of Copacabana, Ipanema, Leblon, Vidigal, and São Conrado. The driver will stop wherever you ask along the route. On both routes, you can stop at the rodoviária if you want to catch a bus out of Rio immediately. If you want to catch the metro, ask the driver to let you off right outside the entrance to Carioca metro station.

You can catch the bus on the 2nd floor (arrivals) of the main terminal, at the Galeão sign. The tourist desk inside the airport has schedule and price information. If you're heading to the airport you can get the bus in front of the major hotels along the beach, but you have to look alive and flag them down. The bus company is Empresa Real. Galeão should be written on the direction sign.

It is safer to catch one of these buses or take a taxi rather than a local bus if you have many valuables.

Bus – local On the far corner, to your right as you leave the main terminal at Galeão, there is a small terminal for local buses on Rua Ecuador. There are bus numbers and routes posted, so it's pretty easy to get oriented.

For Copacabana, the best is bus No 126, 127 or 128. The best bus to Ipanema and Leblon is No 128, but you can also take No 126 or 127 to Copacabana and then catch another bus to Ipanema and Leblon.

For the budget hotels in Catete and Glória, take bus No 170 ('Gávea – via Jóquei'), which goes down Rua do Catete and then turns up Rua Pedro Americo and along Rua Bento Lisboa. If you want the Catete budget hotels, get off at the stop near the corner of Bento Lisboa and Rua Silveira Martins and walk a block down to Rua Catete.

An alternative is to take any bus that goes to the centre on Avenida Rio Branco. Get off near the end of Avenida Rio Branco and hop on the metro. Get off the metro at Catete station, which is in the heart of the budget hotel area.

Taxi Many taxis from the airport will try to rip you off. The safe course is to take a radio-taxi, where you pay a set fare at the airport. This is also the most expensive way to go. A yellow-and-blue comum (common) taxi is about 20% cheaper if the meter is working and if you pay what is on the fare schedule. A sample fare from the airport to Copacabana is US$18 in a yellow-and-blue taxi versus US$24 in a radio-dispatched taxi. If you're entering Brazil for the first time, on a budget, a good compromise is to take a bus to somewhere near your destination and then take a short taxi ride to your hotel.

Sharing a taxi from the airport is a good idea. Taxis will take up to four people. To ensure a little bit of security, before entering the taxi at the airport you can usually get a receipt with the licence plate of your taxi and a phone number to register losses or complaints. If you're headed to Leblon or Ipanema, the Tunnel Reboucas is more direct than the beach route.

Bus The buses are a real mixture of the good, the bad and the ugly. The good: Rio's buses are fast, frequent, cheap and, because Rio is long and narrow, it's easy to get the right bus and usually no big deal if you're on the wrong one. The bad: Rio's buses are often crowded, slowed down by traffic and driven by raving maniacs who drive the buses as if they were motorbikes. The ugly: Rio's buses are the scene of many of the city's robberies.

Don't carry any valuables on the buses. Don't advertise being a foreigner, and do have your money ready when you enter the bus. Be particularly cautious if you're boarding a bus in a tourist area. If you feel paranoid about something on the bus, get off and catch another.

In addition to their number, buses have their destinations, including the areas they go through, written on the side. Nine out of 10 buses going south from the centre will go to Copacabana and vice versa. All buses have the price displayed above the head of the money collector. The buses you need to catch for specific destinations are listed under individual sights.

There are also special air-conditioned buses (see To/From the Airport). The Castelo-Hotel Nacional and Castelo-São Conrado buses are good to take for Pepino beach. From the Castelo station there are buses to Petrópolis and Terosópolis, which saves a trip out to the rodoviária. There is an open-air tourist bus that goes along the beaches and then over to Pão de Açúcar.

If you're staying in the Catete/Flamengo area and want to get to the beaches by bus, you can either walk to the main roadway along Parque do Flamengo and take any bus marked 'Copacabana' or you can walk to Largo do Machado and take the No 570 bus.

Train The train station, Estação Dom Pedro II, is at Praça Cristiano Ottoni on Avenida Presidente Vargas. To get there take the metro to Central station.

Metro Rio's excellent subway system is limited to points north of Botafogo and is open from 6 am to 11 pm daily, except Sundays. The two air-conditioned lines are cleaner, faster and cheaper than buses (discounts are offered with multiple tickets). The main line from Botafogo to Saens Pena has 15 stops, of which the first 12 are: Botafogo, Flamengo, Largo do Machado, Catete, Glória, Cinelândia, Carioca, Uruguiana, Presidente Vargas, Central, Cidade Nova and Estácio, which is common to both lines. At Estácio the lines split: the main line continues west towards the neighbourhood of Andarai, making stops at Afonso Pena, Engenho Velho and Tijuca, and the secondary line goes north towards Maracanã stadium and beyond. The main stops for Centro are Cinelândia and Carioca.

Taxi Rio taxis are quite reasonably priced, if you're dividing the fare with a friend or two. Taxis are particularly useful late at night and when carrying valuables, but they are not a completely safe and hassle-free ride. First, there are a few rare cases of people being assaulted and robbed by taxi drivers. Second, and much more common, the drivers have a marked tendency to exaggerate fares.

Here's how the taxi is supposed to operate: there should be a meter and it should work; there should be a current tabela to determine the fare; upon reaching your destination, check the meter and look that up on the tabela, usually posted on the passenger window, which is used to determine the fare.

Now, what to watch out for: most importantly, make sure the meter works. If it doesn't, ask to be let out of the cab. The meters have a flag that switches the meter rate; this should be in the number one position (20% less expensive), except on Sundays, holidays, between 10 pm and 6 am and when driving outside the zona sul (some taxis will switch to the high rate near the airport, which is legal). Make sure meters are cleared before you start (find out the current starting number). Make sure the tabela is original, not a photocopy. The taxi drivers that hang out near the hotels are sharks. It's worth walking a block to avoid them. Most people don't tip taxi drivers, although it's common to round off the fare to the higher number.

The meters are weighted towards distance not time. This gives the drivers an incentive to drive quickly (for a head rush tell your driver that you are in a bit of a hurry) and travel by roundabout routes. Taxis don't always run during thunderstorms because alcohol-powered cars stall easily in the wet, but buses usually plough on ahead. It's illegal for cabs to take more than four passengers. This is, of course, irrelevant except for the fact that most cabs won't do it because of conventions of the trade.

The white radio-taxis (☎ 260-2022) are 30% more expensive than the comums, but they will come to you and they are safer.

Car Car rental agencies can be found at the airport or clustered together on Avenida Princesa Isabel in Copacabana. There doesn't seem to be much price competition between the companies. Prices are not cheap, at about US$40 a day, but they go down a bit in the off season. When they give prices on the phone the agencies usually leave out the cost of insurance, which is mandatory. Most agencies will let you drop off their cars in another city without an extra charge.

Motorcycle Mar e Moto (☎ 274- 4398) rents motorcycles but it is cheaper to rent a car. It's in Leblon at Avenida Bartolomeu Mitre 1008.

Walking For God's sake be careful! Drivers run red lights, run up on sidewalks and stop for no one and nothing.

Rio de Janeiro State

The small state of Rio de Janeiro offers the traveller much more than just the cidade maravilhosa. Within four hours of travel from any point in the state, and often much less, are beaches, mountains and forests that equal any in Brazil. Many of these places offer more intimate settings in which to meet Cariocas who have known about the natural wonders surrounding the city for years. You won't find virgin sites, undeveloped for tourism, as you'll find in the Northeast. Tourism here is fairly developed and prices are higher than in most of Brazil. But if you have only a couple of weeks in Brazil and think that you'll be returning some day, an itinerary that covers the entire state of Rio would be one of the best possible. And if you have all the time in the world, it's easy to pass a month or two here.

Rio de Janeiro state, which lies just above the Tropic of Capricorn, has an area of 44,268 sq km – about the size of Switzerland – and a population of more than 14 million. The littoral is backed by steep mountains which descend into the sea around the border with São Paulo and gradually rise slightly further inland in the north. This forms a thin strip of land nestled between the lush green mountains and the emerald sea, with beaches that are the most visually spectacular in Brazil.

Divided by the city of Rio and the giant Baía de Guanabara, which has 131 km of coast and 113 islands, there are two coastal regions, each with somewhat different natural characteristics: the Costa Verde to the west and the Costa do Sol to the east.

Along the Costa Verde, where the mountains kiss the sea, there are hundreds of islands, including Ilha Grande and the Restinga de Marambaia, which make for easy swimming and boating. The calm waters, coupled with the natural ports and coves, allowed safe passage to the Portuguese ships that came to Parati to transport sugar cane, and later gold, to Europe. They also pro-

tected pirates, who found a safe haven on Ilha Grande.

There are beaches waiting to be explored, particularly further away from Rio city, where the coastal road stays close to the ocean and the views are spectacular. The most famous spots are Angra dos Reis, Parati and Ilha Grande.

To the east, the mountains begin to rise further inland. The littoral is filled with lagoons and swamp land. Stretching ever further from the coast are *campos* (plains) which extend about 30 km to the mountains. Búzios and Cabo Frio, famous for their beauty and luxury, are only two hours from Rio by car. Saquarema, one of Brazil's best surfing beaches, is even closer.

Driving due north from Rio city, after passing through the city's industrial and motel sections, you soon reach a wall of jungled mountains. After the climb, you're in the cool Serra dos Órgãos. The resort cities of Petrópolis and Teresópolis are nearby, as well as many smaller villages where Cariocas go to escape the tropical summer heat. Hiking and climbing among the fantastic peaks of the Parque Nacional da Serra dos Órgãos, outside Teresópolis, are superb.

The other mountain region where Cariocas play is the Itatiaia area, in the corner of the state that borders São Paulo and Minas Gerais. Getting there is a longer trip, although it still takes only four hours. The route passes near the steel city of Volta Redonda.

Indian Names
Many place names in Rio state are derived from Indian words. Among them are:

Araruama – place where the macaw eats
Baré – in the middle of many fish
Cunhambebe – women who speak too much
Grataú – ghost's den
Grumari – a kind of tree
Guanabara – arm of the sea

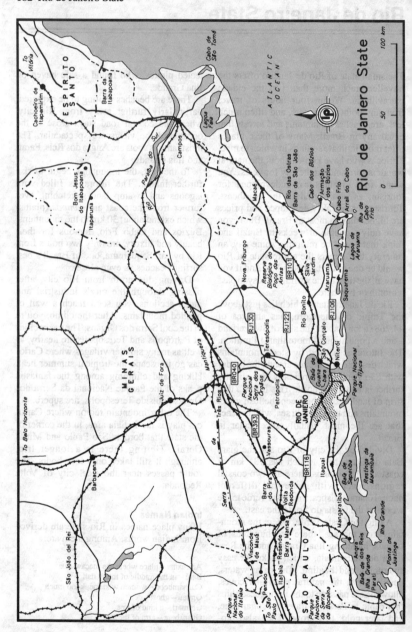

Guaratiba – place with much sun or place with many holes

Ipanema – place that gives bad luck or place of dangerous sea

Itacuruçá – stone's cross

Itaipu – stone that the sea hits

Itaipuaçu – little Itaipu

Jabaquara – crack in the earth

Jeribá – a kind of coconut palm

Mangaratiba – banana orchard

Maricá – belly

Parati – a kind of fish

Paratininga – dry fish

Sapeca – burned

Saquarema – lagoon without shells

Tijuca – putrid-smelling swamp

West of Rio de Janeiro

ILHA GRANDE

Ilha Grande is what Hawaii must have been before the arrival of the British. It's all tropical beach and jungle, and because of a maximum security prison and a limitation on new hotels it is likely to remain this way. There are only three towns on the island. Freguesia de Santana is a small hamlet with no regular accommodation. Parnaioca has a few homes by a lovely strip of beach near the prison. Abraão has plenty of pousadas, camping grounds and ferry connections to Mangaratiba and Angra dos Reis.

If you really want to get away from it all, Ilha Grande may well be the place to go. The options are pretty attractive. You can rent a boat in Abraão for US$6 per hour, and buzz around to Freguesia or Parnaioca. There are trails through the lush steamy jungle to various beaches around the island. For instance, it is a 2½-hour trek to Praia Lopes Mendes, claimed by some to be the most beautiful beach in all Brazil. Praia de Parnaioca also ranks up there. And these are only two of the island's 102 beaches!

Ilha Grande has been declared a park and there is a Forest Office where you can find maps and information regarding trekking in the jungle, beaches and campsites. In case the office is closed, anybody around can show you the ranger's house where you can directly go and ask. Getting a special permit at the

military police station it's possible to organise a nice daily trip to Dos Rios (the location of the prison), using a military bus, and from there a trek to the largest and wildest beaches on the island: Praia de L'este and Praia do Sul. Don't forget to bring water for the treks and watch for snakes that are likely to be found in the jungle

Paolo Vacchina (USA)

Abraão

Abraão could be a movie set for *Papillon*. It has a gorgeous, palm-tree studded beachfront of pale, faded homes and a tidy white church. Guards and military police compete for beer and curb space. It's OK to rouse the dogs sleeping on the dirt and cobblestone streets. They're friendly and seem to enjoy tramping around the island to the abandoned old prison, to the beaches, to the forest, to the hills and the waterfalls.

Orientation & Information

In Abraão, to the left of the dock (when you're facing the ocean), are the ferry ticket office, a guest house for military police, the road to the commandant's house and the trail to the ruined old prison. To the right of the dock is the cobblestoned Rua da Igreja, and at the far end of the beach a clockwise trail leads around the island to Praia Lopes Mendes and the other beaches of Ilha Grande.

The tourist office in Angra dos Reis has information on accommodation available on Ilha Grande.

Money

There is an informal money exchange for cash dollars at the Hotel Mar da Tranquilidade or at Bar la Vento on the main beach.

Places to Stay & Eat

Cheap lodging on Ilha Grande can be difficult to find. There are expensive hotels and mid-range pousadas on the island, and a few campgrounds in Abraão. It may be possible to arrange a stay in a private home in Freguesia. Offsite camping is forbidden and not advised.

Cheaper accommodation possibilities in Abraão include *Pousada Teté*, which has singles/doubles for US$15/25. The *Tropicana*, Rua da Praia 28, is run by a French/Brazilian couple and is similarly priced, with singles/doubles for US$13/24. The cheapest option is to camp. *Camping Renato*, up a small path beside Dona Pena's, has well-drained, secure sites and basic facilities, as well as a café/bar onsite. They charge US$4 per person. Other campgrounds include *Holandes*, which also has rooms, *Gilson* and *César*.

At right angles to the beachfront, Rua da Igreja is the second most important street on the island. It features a white church, a few bars and the *Hotel Mar da Tranquilidade* (☎ 789-1614 or for reservations from Rio (021) 392-8475). The hotel has charming but expensive doubles with hot showers and includes breakfast and lunch for US$60. Singles are US$30. The hotel restaurant is open to everyone – just give the cook several hours' advance notice.

Right around the corner is *Restaurante Janethe's*, which serves prato feitos with abundant portions of fresh fish (US$3). Rua da Igreja becomes a dirt road and continues over a little footbridge to the house of Dona Pena. Look for the yellow gate on the right hand side. Dona Pena has gone up-market in the last few years, though she does have one room for US$16 a double. Ilha Grande's most expensive hotel, *Paraiso do Sol*, is minutes away by boat or two hours away on foot from Abraão at Praia das Palmas, on the trail to Praia Lopes Mendes. Doubles with full board are US$200. For information and reservations call (021) 263-6126.

Getting There & Away

Catch a Conerj ferry from either Mangaratiba or Angra dos Reis. If you take the 5.30 am bus from Rio to Mangaratiba, you can catch the daily 8.30 am ferry from Mangaratiba to Abraão. There are five buses a day from Rio to Mangaratiba: at 6 and 9 am, and 12.30, 3 and 7 pm. Outgoing bus schedules are similarly staggered, but begin half an hour earlier.

The boat returns from Abraão to Mangaratiba on Mondays, Wednesdays and

Fridays at 4.30 pm, on Tuesdays and Thursdays at 11 am and on Saturdays and Sundays at 4 pm. Mangaratiba is nothing more than a poor little fishing town. If you're stuck there, you can stay at the *Hotel Rio Branco*, a small and dumpy place on the main square with US$7 doubles (US$12 with private bath).

The ferry schedule from Angra dos Reis to Abraão is Mondays, Wednesdays and Fridays at 3 pm, returning from Abraão at 10.15 am on the same days. It's a 90-minute, US$5 ride. If you miss the ferry you can hire a fishing boat to the island for about US$24 from either Mangaratiba or Angra.

Life on Ilha Grande

We were on our way out the door to Praia Lopes Mendes when Dona Pena suggested we go to the police station and enquire about the fugitive situation. The convicts – some of Brazil's most dangerous and hardened criminals – make regular breaks from the prison and hide on the island until they can find a boat and take off. We didn't think much of Dona Pena's cautionary advice, but nevertheless we stopped by the DPO. Half a dozen armed military police were milling about the chief's desk.

'Have any fugitives escaped?' we asked.

'Yes, seven,' replied an MP.

'Is it dangerous?' we queried.

'Where do you want to go?'

'Praia Lopes Mendes.'

'On foot?'

Without waiting for our answer, the chief raised an eyebrow and continued, 'Are you going to camp there?'

'No. Is it dangerous?'

There was no answer or comforting looks from the other men. We persisted, 'Would you go?'

'You can go. I am not going to stop you. But they are desperate men. They have nothing to lose.'

We joined up with three fishermen and two prison guards who were drinking chopp and snacking on olives. Their conversation turned toward the prison break. 'The fugitives? They escaped 10 days ago and they're certainly off the island by now. You have nothing to worry about.'

We walked a km so down the beach, where a Carioca sporting speedos, a tan and a martini led us to the trailhead to Praia Lopes Mendes.

ANGRA DOS REIS

Angra dos Reis is a base for nearby islands and beaches, not a tourist attraction in itself. The savage beauty of the tropical, fjord-like coastline along this stretch of BR-101 has been badly blemished by industrialisation. Super-tankers dock in Angra's port, a rail line connects Angra to the steel town of Volta Redonda, there's a Petrobras oil refinery and – thanks to the military government and the IMF – a controversial nuclear power plant has been built nearby.

The closest beaches are at Praia Grande and Vila Velha. Take the 'Vila Velha' municipal bus.

Information

Tourist Office The Centro de Informaçoes Turisticas is in Largo da Lapa, right across from the bus station. Staff have information about places to stay on Ilha Grande.

Post & Telephone The post office is just behind the tourist office in Praça Lopes Trovão and long-distance phone calls can be made from Avenida Raul Pompéia 97, right next to the Hotel Londres.

Places to Stay

No real cheapies here. The *Cherry Hotel* at Rua Peroia Peixoto 64 is in the heart of Angra off Rua Coronel Carvalho and they charge US$10 per person without breakfast. The *Hotel Sol da Praia* (☎ 65-0605), Estrada do Contorno 1890, Praia Grande, Angra dos Reis, is on the right-hand side, 200 metres before the Angra Inn. Take the 'Vila Velha' bus from the rodoviária. The hotel has a nice courtyard and classy doubles for US$17.

The *Palace Hotel* (☎ 65-0032) at Rua Coronel Carvalho 275 is a clean three-star Embratur hotel with TV, air-con, telephone, hot water and US$40 doubles. There's also the *Grande Hotel Acrópolis* (☎ 65-0226) at Rua da Conceição 231 with singles/doubles for US$25/30.

Places to Eat

A couple of good seafood places are *Taberna 33* and *Costa Verde*, almost next door to one another near the corner of Rua Coronel Carvalho and Rua Raul Pompéia. If your budget doesn't run to seafood, there's *Pastelaria Verolme* on the corner of Travessa Santa Luzia near the waterfront. Their fresh pasteis

washed down with caldo da cana (sugar cane juice) are excellent.

Getting There & Away

Angra dos Reis is almost three hours (150 km) from Rio de Janeiro's Novo Rio bus station. To Rio, buses leave every hour from 4.30 am to 9 pm and cost US$7. To Parati, six buses a day make the two-hour trip for US$5. The first leaves at 6 am.

PARATI

Oh! Deus, se na terra houvesse um paraíso, não seria muito longe daqui!
(Oh! God, if there were a paradise on earth, it wouldn't be very far from here!)

Américo Vespúcio

Américo was referring to steep, jungled mountains that seem to leap into the sea, a scrambled shoreline with hundreds of islands and jutting peninsulas, and the clear, warm waters of the Baía da Ilha Grande, as calm as an empty aquarium. All this still exists, if no longer in a pristine state, along with one of Brazil's most enchanting towns – the colonial village of Parati, which Américo did not get to enjoy.

Parati is both a great colonial relic, well preserved and architecturally unique, and a launching pad for a dazzling section of the Brazilian coastline. The buildings are marked by simple lines that draw the eye to the general rather than the specific, and earthy colours and textures that magnify, through contrast, the natural beauty that envelops the town. So while the individual buildings in Parati may well be beautiful, the town when viewed as a whole is truly a work of art.

Dozens of secluded beaches are within a couple of hours' boat or bus ride from Parati. There are good swimming beaches close to town, but the best are along the coast toward São Paulo and out on the bay islands.

One of the most popular spots between Rio and São Paulo, Parati is crowded and lively during the summer holidays, brimming with Brazilian and Argentine holiday-makers, and good music. That the town is all tourism there is no doubt; there are too many boutiques and too few cheap places to eat and sleep for it to be anything else. If you get around these obstacles Parati is a delight, and there are plenty of beaches to accommodate all visitors.

History
Parati was inhabited by the Guianas Indians, when Portuguese from the capitania of São Vicente settled here in the early part of the 16th century. With the discovery of gold in Minas Gerais at the end of the 17th century, Parati became an obligatory stopover point for those coming from Rio de Janeiro, as it was the only point where the escarpment of the Serra do Mar could be scaled. The precarious road was an old Guianas Indian trail that cut past the Serra do Facão (nowadays Cunha, São Paulo) to the valley of Paraíba and from there to Pindamonhangaba, Guaratinguetá and then the mines.

Parati became a busy, important port as miners and supplies disembarked for the gold mines and gold was shipped to Europe. The small town prospered and, as always, the wealthy built churches to prove it. There was so much wealth in Parati that in 1711 Captain Francisco do Amaral Gurgel sailed from Parati to save Rio de Janeiro from a threatened French siege by handing over a ransom of 1000 crates of sugar, 200 head of cattle and 610,000 gold cruzados.

The town's glory days didn't last long. After the 1720s a new road from Rio to Minas Gerais via the Serra dos Órgãos cut 15 days off the route from Parati and it started to decline. In the 19th century the local economy revived with the coffee boom, and now, with the recent construction of the road from Rio, the town's coffers are once again being filled.

Parati is easy to look around: just walk on the *pes-de-moleque* (street urchins' feet), the local name for the irregular cobblestone streets washed clean by the rains and high tides. The town is a couple of km off the Rio to Santos highway, at the south-west corner of Rio de Janeiro state. Until 1954 the only access to Parati was by sea. In that year a road

was built through the steep Serra do Mar, passing the town of Cunha, 47 km inland. In 1960 the coastal road from Rio, 253 km away, was extended to Parati, and beyond to São Paulo 330 km away.

Climate
Like Rio, Parati gets hot and muggy in the Brazilian summer. The rains are most frequent in November, January, and May. Be ready for plenty of nasty mosquitoes.

Orientation
Parati is small and it's easy to find your way around, but one thing that becomes confusing is street names and house numbers. Many streets have more than one name, which has the locals, as well as the tourists, thoroughly perplexed. The house-numbering system seems totally random.

Information

Tourist Office The Centro de Informações Turísticas (☎ 71-1266 extension 20) on Avenida Roberto Silveira is open daily from 7 am to 7 pm. The Secretaria de Turismo e Cultura (☎ 71-1256), in the Antigo Quartel do Forte near the port, is open daily from 8 am to 6 pm.

Money The Banco do Brasil is on Avenida Roberto Silveira and changes cash and travellers' cheques between the hours of 11 am and 2.30 pm. Don't get in line, go straight to the manager's desk.

Post & Telephone The post office is on the corner of Rua da Cadeia and Beco do Proposito. The Telerj stations are in front of the Centro de Informações Turísticas and at Rua Dr Samuel Costa 29. Hotel Pousada Pardeiro and the Restaurante Mare Alta, among others, have *fale facil* (easy-speaking) phones.

Churches
Parati's 18th-century prosperity is reflected in its beautiful old homes and churches. Three main churches were used to separate the races – NS do Rosário (1725) for slaves,

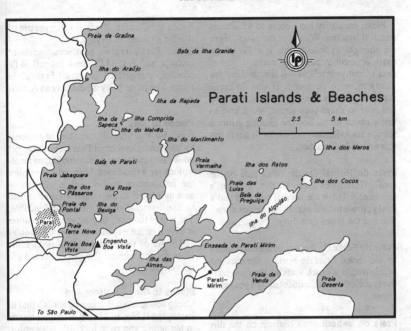

Santa Rita for freed mulattos and NS das Dores for the White elite.

The Igreja NS do Rosário e São Benedito dos Homens Pretos (1725), Rua Samuel Costa, was built by and for slaves. Renovated in 1857, the church has gilded wood altars dedicated to Our Lady of the Rosary, St Benedict and St John. The pineapple crystals are for prosperity and good luck.

Igreja Santa Rita dos Pardos Libertos (1722), Praça Santa Rita, has a tiny museum of sacred art and some fine woodwork on the doorways and altars. Igreja de NS das Dores (1800), Rua Dr Pereira, was renovated in 1901. The cemetery is fashioned after the catacombs.

Matriz NS dos Remédios (1787), Praça Mons Hélio Pires, was built on the site of two 17th-century churches. Inside there is art from past and contemporary local artists. The construction of the church, according to legend, was financed by a pirate treasure hidden on Praia da Trindade.

Forte Defensor Perpétuo

The Forte Defensor Perpétuo was built in 1703 to defend the gold being exported from Minas Gerais from pirate attacks. The fort was rebuilt in 1822, the year of Brazilian independence, and was named after Emperor Dom Pedro I. It's on the Morro da Vila Velha, the hill just past Praia do Pontal, a 20-minute walk north from town. The fort houses the Casa de Artista e Centro de Artes e Tradições Populares de Parati.

Beaches & Islands

The closest fine beaches on the coast – Vermelha, Lulas and Saco – are about an hour away by boat (camping is allowed on the beaches). The best island beaches nearby are probably Araújo and Sapeca, but many of the islands have rocky shores and are private. The mainland beaches tend to be better. These beaches are all small and idyllic; most have a barraca serving beer and fish and, at most, a handful of beachgoers.

Parati reputedly has access to 65 islands and 300 beaches. Whatever the count, there are enough. Following this is a list of the most accessible beaches, north of town. Don't limit yourself to this list, as there are plenty more to be found. If you do come across any really special beaches, and you can bear to share your secret, we'd love to know about them. See the Getting Around section for information on how to get to the less accessible beaches.

Praia do Pontal On the other side of the canal, 10 minutes away on foot, is Parati's city beach. There are several barracas and a lively crowd but the beach itself is not attractive and the water gets dirty.

Praia do Forte On the side of the hill, hidden by the rocks, Praia do Forte is the cleanest beach within a quick walk of the city, relatively secluded and frequented by a youngish crowd.

Praia do Jabaquara Continue on the dirt road north past Praia do Pontal, over the hill, for two km to Praia do Jabaquara, a big, spacious beach with great views in all directions. There is a small restaurant and a campground that's better than those in town. The sea is very shallow and it's possible to wade way out into the bay.

Festivals
Parati is known for its colourful and distinctive festivals. The two most important are the Festa do Divino Espírito Santo, which begins nine days before Pentecostal Sunday, and the NS dos Remédios on 8 September. The former is planned throughout the year and features all sorts of merrymaking revolving around the *fólios*, musical groups that go from door to door singing and joking.

The Festas Juninas during the month of June are filled with dances, including the *xiba*, a circle clog dance, and the *ciranda*, a xiba with guitar accompaniment. The festivals culminate on 29 June with a maritime procession to Ilha do Araújo. Parati is a good

option for Carnival if you want to get out of Rio for a couple of days.

The Parati region produces excellent cachaça, and in 1984 the town council, in its wisdom, inaugurated an annual Festival da Pinga. The pinga party is held over an August weekend.

Places to Stay
Parati has two very different tourist seasons. From about October to February hotels get booked up and room prices double, so reservations are a good idea. Many places require the full amount to be paid in advance – usually placed in their bank account in Rio or São Paulo. This is often nonrefundable. The rest of the year, finding accommodation is easy and not expensive, the town is quiet and some of the boutiques and restaurants close for the winter. The prices quoted are off-season rates.

Places to Stay – bottom end
Cheap accommodation can be hard to find in Parati, but if Noemi Maciel is renting rooms in her house you're in luck. It's a beautiful, big, 300-year-old house at Rua da Praia 41. Noemi is friendly and relaxed about sharing her place. She charges US$7 a person for a bed in a room with anywhere from two to seven beds. The showers are incredibly good and you can use her living room and kitchen. It's a terrific place. If Noemi isn't there when you arrive, she's probably at Café Paraty.

The *Pousada Familiar* (☎ 71-1475), at Rua José Vieira Ramos 262, is close to the bus station and charges US$8 per person, including a good breakfast. It's a friendly place, run by Lúcia, a Brazilian, and her Belgian husband, Joseph. Joseph speaks English, French, German, Spanish and, of course, Flemish and is very helpful. The pousada also has clothes-washing facilities.

Another recommended place is the *Pousada Marendaz* (☎ 71-1369) at Rua Dr Derly Ellena 9. Run by Rachel and her four sisters, it's more of a family home than a hotel. They charge US$9 per person.

The *Hotel Estalagem* (☎ 71-1626), Rua da Matriz, charges US$10 a person. Try and get the room upstairs – it has a great view. They also have kayaks for rent. The *Pousada da Matriz* (☎ 71-1610), Rua Mal Deodoro 334, is well located and has rooms for as little as US$10 per person.

Camping There are several campgrounds on the edge of town, just over the bridge.

Places to Stay – middle

The *Hotel Solar dos Geránios* (☎ 71-1550) on Praça da Matriz (also known as Praça Monsenhor Hélio Pires) is a beautiful old hotel with wood and ceramic sculptures, flat brick and stone, rustic heavy furniture and *azulejos* (Portuguese tiles). Rooms have hot showers. Singles/doubles start as low as US$15/25.

The *Bela Vista* (☎ 71-1429), Rua do Comércio 46, is a good choice with doubles from US$35 to US$40.

Places to Stay – top end

There are three splendid, four-star, colonial pousadas in Parati. Owned by a famous Brazilian actor, the *Pousada Pardeiro* (☎ 71-1370), Rua do Comercio 74, has a tranquil garden setting, refined service and impeccable decor. This is one of Brazil's best hotels, with singles/doubles for US$80/100.

The *Hotel Coxixo* (☎ 71-1568), Rua do Comercio 362, is just a notch below the Pousada Pardeiro, but they have some standard rooms that are a good deal at US$35. The pousada is cosy and colonial, with beautiful gardens and a pool, the rooms are simple but comfortable and pretty. To get the US$35 doubles make reservations early. Most doubles go for US$60.

Pousada do Ouro (☎ 71-1311), Rua da Praia 145, is the kind of place where you can imagine bumping into Mick Jagger, Sonia Braga, Tom Cruise or Marcello Mastroianni, especially when you enter the hotel lobby and see photos of them posing in front of the pousada. The hotel has everything – bar, pool and a good restaurant. Doubles cost US$65 to US$75.

Places to Eat

Parati has many pretty restaurants that all seem to charge too much. To beat the inflated prices in the old part of town, try the sandwiches at the lanchonete on Praça da Matriz.

The best restaurants in the old town include the *Galeria do Engenho*, Rua da Lapa, which serves large and juicy steaks for US$6 and *Vagalume*, Rua da Ferraria. *Hiltinho*, Rua da Cadeia, at the edge of the Praça da Matriz, is more expensive, but there's a good menu and ample portions. Another recommended restaurant is *Mare Alta*, Praça da Bandeira. They have tasty pizzas.

Entertainment

Café Paraty is a popular hangout on the corner of Rua do Comercio and Rua da Lapa. Bar da Terra over the bridge gets pretty lively and the Taberna Pub, near the Hiltinho restaurant, is the place to hear some jazz. Or just wander the streets and you'll hear some music outside at the restaurants by the canal or inside one of the bars.

Getting There & Away

The rodoviária (☎ 71-1186) is on the main road into town, Rua Roberto Silveira, a half-km up from the old town.

There are six daily buses from Parati to Rio; it's a four-hour trip, with the first bus leaving at 4.30 am and the last at 7.30 pm. Buses leave Rio for Parati at 6 and 9 am, 12.30, 3, 6.20 and 8 pm. It's a US$10 trip.

Six daily buses go from Parati to Angra dos Reis, taking two hours. The first leaves at 5.40 am, the last at 6.45 pm. It costs US$5. There are two daily (11 am and 11.30 pm) buses for São Paulo which take six hours. Three daily buses go to Ubatuba (7 am, noon and 7 pm) and three more go to Cunha.

Getting Around

To visit the beaches that aren't easily accessible, many tourists take the big schooner that leaves from the docks at noon and returns at 5 pm (on Sunday it leaves at 9 am and returns at 3 pm). It costs US$15 per person. Lunch is served on board for an additional US$7. The boat makes three beach stops for about 45 minutes each. Because it's the least expensive cruise in the bay, the schooner is usually crowded and stifling.

A much better alternative is to rent one of the many small motorboats at the port. For US$10 per hour (somewhat more in the summer) the skipper will take you where you want to go. Bargaining is difficult but you can lower the cost by finding travelling companions and renting bigger boats – they hold from six to 12 passengers.

At a minimum, if you figure on a one-hour boat ride and an hour at the beach, you need to rent a boat for three hours. Of course, there are even more beautiful beaches further away.

The strategy of the boat drivers, since they usually can't return to port for another boatload, is to keep you out as long as possible. So don't be surprised if the first beach you go to is out of beer, or the next beach would be much more pleasant because of its cleaner water. These can be very compelling reasons not to return as scheduled, but paradise has a price.

AROUND PARATI
Praia Barra Grande
About 20 km up the Rio to Santos highway, Barra Grande is an easy-to-reach alternative to the beaches in Baía de Parati. There are 11 municipal buses a day leaving from Parati, the first at 7.10 am.

Praia de Parati-Mirim
For accessibility, cost and beauty, this beach is hard to beat. Parati-Mirim is a small town, 27 km from Parati. The beach has barracas and houses to rent. From Parati, it's a couple of hours by boat; if you're on a budget, catch a municipal bus that makes the 40-minute trip for only 50c. Get the 'Parati Mirim' bus from the rodoviária at 6.50 am, or 1 or 4.40 pm.

Praia do Sono
They don't get much prettier than this beach. Past Ponta Negra on the coast going south,

about 40 km from Parati, Praia Sono can have rough water and is sometimes difficult to land on. It's a four to five-hour boat ride. The much cheaper alternative is to take the Laranjeiras bus from Parati and get directions in Laranjeiras for the 1½-hour walk to Sono. Buses leave Parati at 5.15 am, and 12.30 and 6.40 pm. There's food but no formal lodging at the beach.

Praia da Trindade
About five km before Sono, this is another beautiful beach. It has a simple pousada so you can stay here for a night or two. The beach is accessible by boat, as well as by the same bus as for Praia do Sono. Ask the driver to let you off at the entrance to Trindade.

Inland
The old gold route, now the road to Cunha (6 km), is a magnificent jungle ride up the escarpment. The steep dirt part of the road gets treacherous in the rain. Catch the 'Cunha' bus.

Take the 'Ponte Branca' bus from Parati to the Igrejinha da Penha, a small, triple-turreted hillside church. You'll find a 750-metre jungle trail to a beautiful waterfall and water slide. Buses charge 25c for the round trip, and leave at 5.45, 9 and 11.30 am and 2 and 6 pm.

Fazenda Bananal-Engenho de Murycana is four km off the Parati to Cunha road, 10 km from town. It's a touristy spot with an old sugar mill, a restaurant, a zoo, and free samples of cachaça and batidas.

Parque Nacional da Serra da Bocaina
On the border between Rio and São Paulo, where the mountains of the Serra do Mar meet the sea, is the Parque Nacional da Serra da Bocaina. Rising from sea level to the 2132 metre Pico da Boa Vista, the park contains a mixture of vegetation; from mata atlântica in the lower altitudes to mata araucária and windswept grassy plateaus in the higher altitudes.

Wildlife is plentiful and includes a large population of the rare spider monkey, as well as other monkeys like the howler and ring-

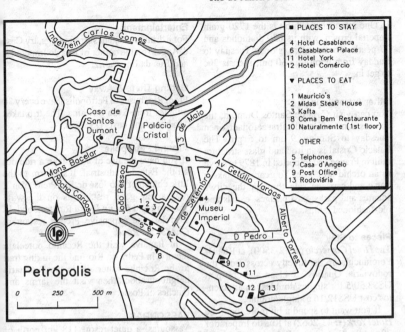

PLACES TO STAY

4 Hotel Casablanca
6 Casablanca Palace
11 Hotel York
12 Hotel Comércio

PLACES TO EAT

1 Mauricio's
2 Midas Steak House
3 Kafta
8 Coma Bem Restaurante
10 Naturalmente (1st floor)

OTHER

5 Telphones
7 Casa d'Angelo
9 Post Office
13 Rodoviária

Petrópolis

0   250   500 m

tailed. Other animal species include the tree-porcupine, sloth, deer, tapir, giant-anteater and otter. Birds found in the park include the harpy and black-hawk eagles and the black-beaked toucan.

Places to Stay

Unfortunately the park possesses no tourist infrastructure. There is an expensive hotel near the park: *Pousada Vale dos Veados* (☎ (0125) 77-1192) which charges US$80 a double. Advance reservations are necessary.

Getting There & Away

Travellers going from Parati to Cunha actually pass through the southern end of the park. If you have a car and are driving in from the coast, take the Cunha-Campos Novo road to the park. If you're coming from the Rio-São Paulo Dutra (multi-lane highway), turn off at Queluz and drive for 37 km, passing through the town of Areias and con-tinuing on to São José dos Barros, the closest town to the park.

The Mountains

PETRÓPOLIS

Petrópolis is a lovely mountain retreat with a decidedly European flavour. It's only 60 km from Rio de Janeiro, making it an ideal day trip. This is where the imperial court spent its summer when Rio got too muggy. Petrópolis is still the home of the heir to the throne, Princess Isabel's grandson, 78-year-old Dom Pedro de Orleans e Bragança. He runs a real estate business and can often be seen riding his horse around town.

Museu Imperial

Petrópolis' main attraction is the Museu Imperial, the perfectly preserved and impeccably appointed palace of Dom Pedro

II. One interesting exhibit is the 1720-gram imperial crown, with its 639 diamonds and 77 pearls. The museum is open Tuesday to Sunday from noon to 5.30 pm; it costs 30c to get in.

Other Attractions

You can visit Casa de Santos Dumont, the curious home of Brazil's first aeronaut; open Tuesday to Sunday, 9 am to 5 pm. The Palácio Cristal is an iron and glass structure built in France and imported in 1879 to serve as an orchid hothouse. You can also take a horse-and-carriage ride through the city's squares and parks, past bridges, canals and old-fashioned lamps.

Places to Stay

The *Hotel Comércio* (☎ 42-3500), at Rua Dr Porciúncula 56, is directly across from the rodoviária. Quartos are clean and cheap at US$3.50/5 for singles/doubles. Apartamentos cost US$12/16 a single/double.

If you want to spend a bit more, both the *Hotel York* (☎ 43-2662) at Rua do Imperador 78 and the *Casablanca Palace* (☎ 42-0162), Rua 16 de Março 123, have singles/doubles for US$25/28. The York is closer to the rodoviária.

The *Hotel Casablanca* (☎ 42-6662) is almost right next to the Museu Imperial, at Avenida 7 de Setembro 286, and has singles/doubles for US$30/35. Yes, the two Casablanca hotels are run by the same people.

Places to Eat

Naturalmente is a good place to go for a healthy vegetarian buffet lunch. It's upstairs in the shopping centre at Rua do Imperador 288. You get all you can eat for US$5. Another all-you-can-eat deal for lunch (US$2) is offered by *Coma Bem Restaurante*, upstairs at Rua do Imperador 563. They also have à la carte dishes in the evening.

Rua 16 de Março has lots of places, like *Kafta*, the Arab restaurant at No 52, *Maurício's* seafood place at No 154 and the *Midas Steak House* at No 170.

Entertainment

For a drink in elegant surroundings, try Casa d'Angelo on the corner of Rua do Imperador and Rua da Imperatriz.

Getting There & Away

From Rio, buses to Petrópolis leave every 30 minutes from 5 am onwards. The trip takes 1½ hours and costs US$2.50.

Around Petrópolis

If you have the use of a car, take a ride out on the Estrada Industrial. It's 70 km to the little church of São José de Rio Preto. You'll pass a few good restaurants on the way: *Tarrafa's* and *Boi na Brasa* for steak and, in Correias, the expensive French restaurant *One for the Road*.

In Itapaiva visit the Recanto porcelain factory. In Pedra do Rio find the hiking trail to the Rocinha waterfalls in the Secretaria neighbourhood, then visit the farms and ranches of Posse.

VASSOURAS

Vassouras, a quiet resort 118 km north of Rio, was the most important city in the Paraíba valley in the first half of the 19th century. Surrounded by the huge fazendas of the 19th-century coffee barons, the town still wears the money they poured into it. They were literally barons, for 18 of them were given titles of nobility by the Portuguese crown. With the abolition of slavery in 1888 and the resulting decline in coffee production, Vassouras' importance diminished and this preserved the town.

Museu Chácara da Hera

Vassouras' favourite grande dame is the noble heiress Eufrásia, a woman who claimed devotion to Vassouras despite palaces in London, Brussels and Paris. Her home, the Museu Chácara da Hera, is located on Rua Fernandes Junior and is open from Wednesday to Sunday from 11 am to 5 pm.

Fazendas

There are a few old churches in the centre as well as old buildings of the schools of med-

Top: Ipanema, Rio de Janiero (SP)
Bottom: Hang-gliding at the beach, Rio de Janiero (JM)

Climbing Pão de Açucar (the Sugarloaf) (Who needs a cable car?), Rio de Janiero (GC)

icine, philosophy and engineering, but the real attractions of Vassouras are the coffee fazendas. Unfortunately, if you don't have a car you're in for some long hikes. Although the fazendas are protected by the historical preservation institutes, permission must be requested from the owners before touring the grounds. For more information, ask at the Casa de Cultura, next to the cinema on Praça Barão do Campo Belo.

Nine km from town is the Fazenda Santa Eufrásia, one of the oldest in the area, dating from the end of the 18th century. If you have a car, take the road to the small town of Barão de Vassouras, five km away. Pass through the town and after 3 km you'll see the most impressive Fazenda Santa Mônica situated on the banks of the Rio Paraiba. The Fazenda Paraiso and the Fazenda Oriente are further out on the same road.

Places to Stay & Eat

Pensão Tia Maria, just up from the bus station at Rua Domingos de Almeida 134, charges US$10 per person. They don't have any double beds. Other accommodation is expensive. The *Mara Palace* (☎ 71-1993), at Rua Chanceler Dr Raul Fernandes 121, charges between US$32 and US$45 for a deluxe double. The *Hotel Parque Santa Amália* (☎ 71-1346), at Avenida Rui Barbosa 526, charges US$40 for doubles.

Pensão Tia Maria and a few other places nearby have reasonable *comida caseira* (home cooking), but as for top restaurants, you're 100 years too late.

Getting There & Away

The bus station is on Praça Juiz Machado Jr. Frequent buses make the 2½-hour trip to Rio for US$5. The first leaves at 6.45 am and others leave every 1½ hours after that.

TERESÓPOLIS

Do as Empress Teresina did and escape the steamy summer heat of Rio in the cool mountain retreat of Teresópolis (910 metres), the highest city in the state, nestled in the strange, organ-pipe mountains of the Serra dos Órgãos. The road to Teresópolis first passes the sinuous curves of a padded green jungle, then winds and climbs past bald peaks which have poked through the jungle cover to touch the clouds.

The city itself is modern, prosperous and dull. The principal attraction is the landscape and its natural treasures – in particular the strangely shaped peaks of Pedra do Sino (2263 metres), Pedra do Açu (2230 metres), Agulha do Diabo (2020 metres), Nariz do Frade (1919 metres), Dedo de Deus (1651 metres), Pedra da Ermitage (1485 metres) and Dedo de Nossa Senhora (1320 metres). With so many peaks, it's no wonder that Teresópolis is the mountain climbing, rock climbing and trekking centre of Brazil.

There are extensive hiking trails in the region and it's possible to trek over the mountains and through the jungle to Petrópolis. Unfortunately the trails are unmarked and off the maps, but it's easy and inexpensive to hire a guide at the Parque Nacional.

Teresópolis is not simply for alpinists: it's a centre for sports lovers of all kinds. The city has facilities for motorcross, volleyball and equestrianism – many of Brazil's finest thoroughbreds are raised here – not to mention soccer. The city bears the distinction of hosting Brazil's World Cup soccer team; the national team is selected and trained here.

Orientation

Teresópolis is built up along one main street which changes names every few blocks. Starting from the highway to Rio in the Soberbo part of town and continuing north along the Avenida Rotariana (with access to the national park), the road is renamed Avenida Oliveira Botelho, Avenida Alberto Torres, Feliciano Sodré and then Avenida Lúcio Meira. Most of the sites are west of the main drag and up in the hills. The cheap hotels are found in the neighbourhood of the Igreja Matriz de Santa Tereza, Praça Baltazar da Silveira.

Information

Tourist Office The Terminal Turistico tourist office is in Soberbo at the intersection

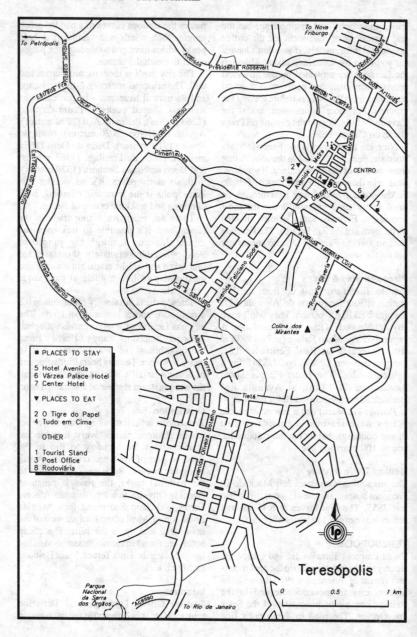

PLACES TO STAY
5 Hotel Avenida
6 Várzea Palace Hotel
7 Center Hotel

PLACES TO EAT
2 O Tigre do Papel
4 Tudo em Cima

OTHER
1 Tourist Stand
3 Post Office
8 Rodoviária

Teresópolis

0   0.5   1 km

with the road to Rio. It's open daily from 8 am to 11 pm and the view of Rio from the office is great. If you're travelling by bus, however, it's a hassle to get to, and you can pick up the same maps at the tourist stand on Avenida Lúcio Meira, which is open from Monday to Friday from 8 am to 5 pm.

Post & Telephone The post office is on Avenida Lúcio Meira. The rodoviária has a Telerj station for long-distance calls.

Parque Nacional Serra dos Órgãos

The main entrance to the national park is open daily from 8 am to 5 pm (admission 25c). There's a 3½-km walking trail, waterfalls, swimming pools, tended lawns and gardens. It's a very pretty park for a picnic. There are some chalets for rent at the park substation, 12 km towards Rio. There are also camping sites.

Other Attractions

The Mulher de Pedra (Rock Woman) rock formation, 12 km out towards Nova Friburgo, does indeed look like a reclining woman.

Colina dos Mirantes is a good place to view the Serra dos Órgãos range and the city. On clear days you can see as far as the Baía de Guanabara. To get there, take Rua Feliciano Sodré. The Quebra Frascos, the royal family of the Second Empire, lived in this neighbourhood. The best spot for viewing the Dedo de Deus peak is from Soberbo.

Places to Stay – bottom end

The *Várzea Palace Hotel* (☎ 742- 0878) at Rua Prefeito Sebastião Teixeira 41/55, behind the Igreja Matriz, is a grand old white building with red trim which has been a Teresópolis institution since 1916. Can this be a budget hotel? Cheap and classy singles/ doubles without a bath are US$12/15. With a bath they cost US$15/18.

Other relatively cheap hotels are nearby, including the *Center Hotel* (☎ 742-5890) at Sebastião Teixeira 245 which has singles/ doubles for US$17/23. The *Hotel Avenida*

(☎ 742-2751) is in front of the Igreja Matriz, at Rua Delfim Moreira 439. Singles/doubles here cost US$20/28.

Places to Stay – top end

The more expensive hotels are out of town. *Hotel Alpina* (☎ 742-5252) is three km on the road to Petrópolis and has singles/ doubles for US$34/40. *Hotel Rosa dos Ventos* (☎ 742-8833) is at Km 23 on the Nova Friburgo highway and has rooms for honeymooners and couples. No one under 16 is permitted to stay here. Rooms are US$72/82 for singles/doubles with breakfast and lunch included. The similarly priced *São Moritz* (☎ 741-1135) is further along at Km 36.

Places to Eat

Restaurante Irene (☎ 742-2901) at Rua Seada 730 (parallel to Rua Sebastião Teixeira) basks in its reputation for Teresópolis' best *haute cuisine*. Reservations are required.

Bar Gota da Água at Praça Baltazar da Silveira 16 is also known as *Bar do Ivam* and is a comfy little place which serves trout with a choice of sauces for US$7. Try it with alcaparra, a bitter pea-like vegetable, or almond sauce. For dessert have some apple strudel and Viennese coffee a few doors down at *Lanches Mickey*. *Tudo em Cima*, Avenida Delfim Moreira 409, serves an admirable soufflé of bacalhau for US$4. *O Tigre de Papel* is a good Chinese restaurant in the centre at the end of Rua Francisco Sá.

Getting There & Away

The rodoviária is on Rua 1 do Maio, off Avenida Tenente Luiz, and has buses to Rio every 30 minutes from 5 am to 10 pm (US$3.80, 1½ hours, 95 km). There are seven buses to Petrópolis (from 6 am to 9 pm) and plenty to Novo Friburgo.

Getting Around

To get to the park from the centre, take the 'Albequerque Soberbo' bus for 50c. It runs every hour and its last stop is the Terminal Turistico in Soberbo.

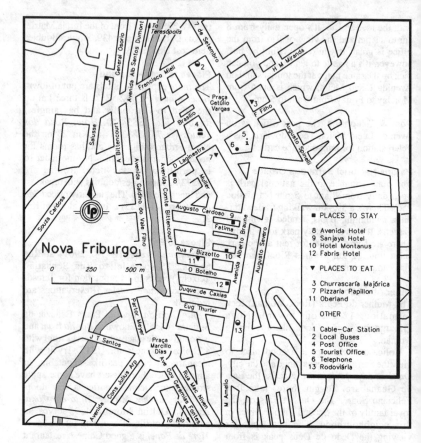

Nova Friburgo

0   250   500 m

PLACES TO STAY

8 Avenida Hotel
9 Sanjaya Hotel
10 Hotel Montanus
12 Fabris Hotel

▼ PLACES TO EAT

3 Churrascaría Majórica
7 Pizzaria Papillon
11 Oberland

OTHER

1 Cable–Car Station
2 Local Buses
4 Post Office
5 Tourist Office
6 Telephone
13 Rodoviária

NOVA FRIBURGO

During the Napoleonic wars, Dom João II encouraged immigration to Brazil. At the time people were starving in Switzerland, so 300 families in the Swiss canton of Friburg packed up and took off for Brazil in 1818. The passage to Brazil was horrible; many died, but enough families survived to settle in the mountains and establish a small village in the New World.

Like Teresópolis and Petrópolis, Nova Friburgo has good hotels and restaurants as well as many lovely natural attractions, waterfalls, woods, trails, sunny mountain mornings and cool evenings. (It's chilly and rainy during the winter months from June through August.) The Cónego neighbourhood is interesting for its Germanic architecture and its apparently perpetually blooming flowers.

Information

Tourist Office The tourist office on Praça Dr Demervel B Moreira is open daily from 8 am to 8 pm and is most efficient. The staff speak some English. As well as maps they have a complete list of hotels, including the cheapest, with updated prices.

Post & Telephone Both the post office and telephone office are on Praça Getúlio Vargas. There's also a branch of the post office at the bus station.

Things to See & Do

Most of the nice sights are a few km out of town. Scout out the surrounding area from Morro da Cruz (1800 metres). The cable-car station is in the centre at Praça do Suspiro. Cable cars to Morro da Cruz run from 9 am to 5.30 pm. Pico da Caledônia (2310 metres) offers fantastic views and jump-off sites for hang-gliders.

You can hike to Pedra do Cão Sentado or explore the Furnas do Catete rock formations, visit the mountain towns of Bom Jardim (23 km north on BR-492), or Lumiar (25 km from Mury and a little bit before the entrance to Friburgo). Hippies, cheap pensions, waterfalls, walking trails and white-water canoe trips abound in Lumiar.

Places to Stay – bottom end

Fabris Hotel (☎ 22-2852) at Avenida Alberto Braune 148 asks US$12/14 for clean singles/doubles. *Hotel Montanus* (☎ 22-1235) at Rua Fernando Bizzotto 26 has simple singles/doubles for the same price but you can bargain them down. The *Avenida Hotel* (☎ 22-1664), at Rua Dante Laginestra 89, is a bit cheaper, with quartos for US$9/10 a single/double.

Places to Stay – middle & top end

A good mid-range place in the centre is the *Sanjaya Hotel* (☎ 22-6052) at Avenida Alberto Braune 58. They charge US$28 a single and US$32 a double.

Rates at the top hotels are all for double occupancy and include full board. *Sans Souci* (☎ 22-7752), in town at Rua Itajai, charges US$40/50 for doubles/singles. *Hotel Olifas* (☎ 22-7840), in Lagoinha at Parque Olifas, charges US$60/90 for singles/doubles. *Hotel Garlipp* (☎ 42-1330) is in Mury, 10 km out on the road to Niterói, and charges US$40/50 for singles and US$50/60 for doubles.

Places to Eat

If you want to eat very well, try one of the two Swiss/German delicatessens on Rua Fernando Bizzotto for a hefty cold-cut sandwich on black bread with dark mustard. One of the two delis, *Oberland* (☎ 22-9838) at No 12, doubles as a restaurant. It's a very cosy wood-panelled room where the menu is short and the food is great. Try the weisswurst (veal sausage) with sauerkraut for US$2 and the chocolate cakes for desert.

The *Churrascaría Majórica*, in the centre at Praça Getúlio Vargas 74, serves a decent cut of filet mignon for US$6. *Pizzaria Papillon*, on the other side of Praça Getúlio Vargas, makes excellent pizzas.

Entertainment

There's dancing at both the White Streams club in Cónego and at Catina Camping, eight km away.

Things to Buy

Cinderela Artesanato works with semiprecious stones and sells heraldic family shields. Praça Getúlio Vargas has shops where home-made liqueurs and jams are sold.

Getting There & Away

Nova Friburgo is a little over two hours (US$5) by bus from Rio via Niterói on 1001 Lines. The ride is along a picturesque, winding, misty, jungle road. From Novo Friburgo, buses to Rio leave every 30 minutes to one hour. To Teresópolis there are four daily buses, at 7 and 11 am and 3 and 6 pm. The two-hour trip costs US$3. If you're heading to the coast, an adventurous trip is to catch a bus to Lumiar and from there catch another to Macaé.

Getting Around

The local bus terminal is behind Praça Getúlio Vargas. Local buses go to just about all the tourist attractions. Ask for details at the tourist office.

The Itatiaia Region

The Itatiaia region, a curious mix of Old World charm and New World jungle, is comprised of Itatiaia, Penedo and Visconde de Mauá. This idyllic corner of Rio de Janeiro state was settled by Europeans – Penedo by Finns, Itatiaia and Visconde de Mauá by Germans and Swiss – but is now very popular among Brazilians of all ethnic groups. Resende is the main centre for the area.

The climate is alpine temperate and the chalets are Swiss, but the vegetation is tropical and the warm smiles are purely Brazilian. There are neatly tended little farms with horses and goats, and small homes with clipped lawns and flower boxes side by side with large tracts of dense jungle untouched by the machete. This is a wonderful place to tramp around green hills, ride ponies up purple mountains, splash in waterfalls and blaze jungle trails without straying too far from the comforts of civilisation: a sauna, a fireplace, a soft bed, a little wine and a well-grilled trout! Budget travellers beware: the region is frequented by wealthy Cariocas and Paulistas, so food and lodging tend to be expensive.

The region lies in the Serra da Mantiqueira's Itatiaia massif in the north-west corner of Rio de Janeiro, and borders the states of São Paulo and Minas Gerais. The Parque Nacional do Itatiaia is due north of the Serra de Bocaina. Itatiaia Turismo (☎ 511-1147) at Rua Visconde de Pirajá 540 in Rio arranges weekend bus tours from Rio to Penedo, Mauá and Itatiaia.

RESENDE

Resende, the largest city in the area, is the transport hub for Itatiaia, Penedo and Visconde de Mauá. Resende has no tourist attractions, but it is the home of Brazil's military academy (Academia Militar das Agulhas Negras) and a university.

Places to Stay

The military presence and the university may account for the presence of very cheap hotels in the Campos Elízio part of the city. The best is the *Hotel Presidente* (☎ 54-5464) at Rua Luis Pistarni 43, with simple but clean single and double quartos for US$3/6. Double apartamentos are US$10. Lodging doesn't come much cheaper in this part of Brazil. Unless you are camping you are likely to pay at least twice as much in Penedo, Mauá or the national park, but I think it's worth the extra to stay in those places rather than commute from Resende.

Getting There & Away

Buses from Rio de Janeiro and São Paulo go to and from Resende several times a day. From Resende it's reasonably easy to hitch, taxi, or bus to your final destination. Cidade de Aço lines runs 11 buses a day to Resende from Rio. The first bus leaves at 7 am, the last at 9 pm for the 2½-hour, US$5 ride.

PENEDO

Finnish immigrants, led by Toivo Uuskallio, settled Penedo in 1929. If the beautiful Scandinavian woodwork doesn't convince you of this, the number of saunas will. The Finns planted citrus groves along the banks of the Rio das Pedras, but when this enterprise failed they turned to preparing Finnish jams and jellies, home-made liqueurs and sauces.

Apart from jungle and waterfalls, there are not many attractions. The Museu Kahvila at Travessa da Fazenda 45 is a lanchonete which also displays Finnish clothing, books and photographs. You can have the locals point out the hotels of two near-celebrities: Captain Asa (Captain Asa entertained children years ago on radio and TV) and Baby Consuelo's stepmother (Baby Consuelo and husband Pepeu Gomes are strange and popular Baiano singers), whose hotel/restaurant has been closed by the Department of Public Health.

Activities

There are three waterfalls worth visiting. They are Tres Cachoeiras near Tião,

Cachoeira do Roman, which is very pretty but on private grounds and 10 minutes uphill from the Pousada Challenge, and Cachoeira do Diabo right near the Pousada Challenge.

About 40 minutes of uphill hiking from Hans Camping takes you into very dense jungle, although there are trails inside. Hopefully you will run into the large bands of big monkeys and steer clear of the wildcats. At the point where Penedo's main asphalt road turns to dirt you can hire horses for US$2.50 per hour, or a horse and carriage for US$5 per hour.

Dances Among an assortment of Brazilian people there is now only a sprinkling of Finns, but they get together for polkas, mazurkas, *letkiss* and *jenkiss* dances every Saturday night at the Clube Finlandia. The second Saturday of each month is particularly interesting. The Finnish dancers put on their Old World togs and do traditional dances (admission US$3, starts at 9 pm and by 1 am it's over).

Saunas Next door and across the street from the Clube Finlandia are the Sauna Bar and Sauna Finlandesa. The sweat shops are open to the public from early afternoon until 10 pm and later if there are enough people interested (US$2 admission).

Places to Stay & Eat

Penedo is expensive, due to the number of weekend tourists who come up from Rio, but the accommodation is well above average, the food is good and daily rates usually include breakfast and lunch. *Hans Camping*, several km up from the last bus stop, charges US$6 per person for campsites and has a sauna, swimming pool, bar and a waterfall nearby.

The *Pousada Challenge* (☎ 51-1389), about a km up from Tião on the Estrada da Fazendinha, has very clean pre-fab chalets which sleep three. It costs US$35 for doubles and includes breakfast, lunch and use of the pool and sauna.

The *Hotel Baianinha* (☎ 51-1204), next to Tião on the Cachoeiras, asks US$20/25 for singles/doubles. The Baianinha kitchen specialises in fish and Bahian dishes which range in price from US$5 to US$12. The food is good and portions are huge. *Restaurante Mariska*, Rua Esporte Clube near the Telerj station, serves tasty but expensive Hungarian food.

Things to Buy

Paulo of Mato Grosso builds and sculpts wonderful things from hard eucalyptus woods. He's ecologically minded and uses felled wood he finds in the forest. Penedo's small craft shops specialise in jellies, honey, chutneys and preserves, chocolates, cakes and candles.

Getting There & Away

From Resende it's much easier to get to Penedo and Itatiaia than to Mauá. There are 22 Penedo-bound buses daily from 6 am to 11 pm. The bus services the three-km main street (which is considered to be the centre of town) and continues past the end of the paved road to Tião, which is the final stop. The Hotel Baianinha is the second-last stop. Pousada Challenge is a brisk 30-minute walk from Tião and Hans Camping is 20 minutes further up.

VISCONDE DE MAUÁ

Mauá is prettier and a little more tranquil than Penedo, and harder to reach. It's a lovely place, with streams, tinkling goat bells, cosy chalets and country lanes graced with wildflowers. There are horses for hire by the footbridge for US$2.50 per hour, but some of them are pretty small.

Orientation & Information

Mauá is actually made up of three small villages a few km apart. The bus stops first at Vila Mauá, the largest village. Vila Maringá, on the other side of the Rio Preto, is actually in Minas Gerais, and has lots of restaurants and places to stay. At the end of the bus route is Vila Maromba, which has restaurants and pousadas, but not as many as Maringá. Most travellers stay in Maringá or

Maromba. Hitching around here is fairly easy.

Things to Do

The Santa Clara Cachoeira, the nicest waterfall in the area, is a 40-minute walk from Vila Maromba in Maringá. For a mini jungle experience, climb up on either side of the falls through the bamboo groves.

The young and the restless can follow the trail from Maromba to the Cachoeira Veu de Noiva in the Parque Nacional do Itatiaia. It's a full day's hike each way. It's possible to kayak the rapids of the Rio Preto if you are so inclined. The Rio Preto, which divides Minas Gerais from Rio, also has small river beaches and natural pools to explore.

Places to Stay

Most pousadas offer full board with lodging. It's easy to find them because at each intersection there are lots of small signposts.

In Maringá, the cheapest place to stay is *Tia Sophia's*. She charges US$7 per person without full board. *Hotel Casa Alpininha* has US$30 doubles with full board and fireplace. For reservations call Rio (021) 217-3506, or São Paulo (011) 259-5226. There are many other hotels of this calibre in this price range, but the cheapest places to stay are the campgrounds. Try *Camping do Torto* or *Camping do Casarão*.

In Maromba, *Pousada Aguas Claras*, right next to the bus stop, is the cheapest place to stay; it charges US$18 a single and US$35 a double with full board. Three km from Maromba is *Pousada Tiatiaim*, which is in a great location and charges US$35 a double.

Places to Eat

Natural/vegetarian food is served at *Pureza* in Maringa. People here like brown rice, granola with tropical fruits and yoghurt mixed in, and caipirinhas with natural honey. The food is good, but expensive.

Restaurante Maina, also in Maringá, serves abundant portions of standard fare at low prices. Big meals cost US$4, prato feito costs US$2.

Things to Buy

The Companhia Visconde de Mauá is a hippie store selling embroidered blouses, T-shirts, natural perfumes and soaps.

Getting There & Away

The one daily bus from Resende to Visconde de Mauá (about 2½ hours on a winding dirt road, US$2) leaves Monday to Saturday at 4 pm, so you must catch the 1 pm bus from Rio to make it, or else hitch or pay for a taxi which costs US$35. The bus leaves for Resende at 8.30 am every day, except for Sundays when it leaves at 5 pm.

PARQUE NACIONAL DO ITATIAIA

This is a national park established in 1937 to protect 120 sq km of ruggedly beautiful land. It contains over 400 species of native birds, jaguars, monkeys, sloths, lakes, rivers, waterfalls, alpine meadows and primary and secondary Atlantic rainforests. Don't let the tropical house plants fool you: it gets below freezing point in June! Itatiaia even has a few snowy days some years!

Museum

The park headquarters, museum and Lago Azul (Blue Lake) are 10 km in from the Via Dutra highway. The museum, open Tuesday to Sunday from 8 am to 4 pm, has glass cases full of stuffed and mounted animals, pinned moths and snakes in jars.

Activites

Mountain climbing, rock climbing and trekking enthusiasts will want to pit themselves against the local peaks, cliffs and trails.

Every two weeks a group guided by Senhor Hans Bauermeister from Penedo scales the Agulhas Negras peak, which at 2787 metres is the highest in the area. For more information call the Grupo Excursionista de Agulhas Negras (☎ 54-2587) and refer to the section on Hiking & Climbing in the Facts for the Visitor chapter.

A walk to the Abroucas refuge at the base of Agulhas Negras is a 26-km, eight-hour jungle trek from the park entrance. The mountain refuge can sleep 24 people and is

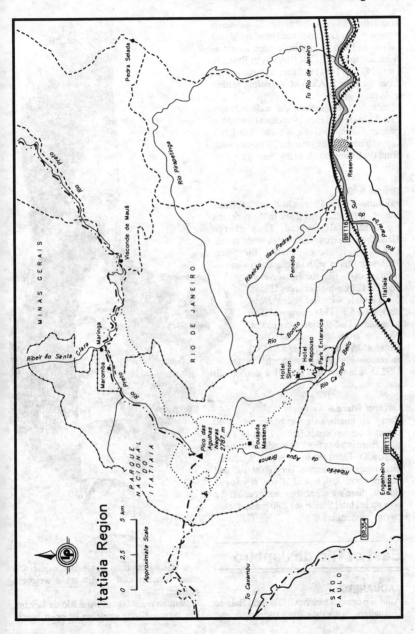

Itatiaia Region

0   2.5   5 km

Approximate Scale

accessible by car from the Engenheiro
Passos to São Lourenço road near the Minas
Gerais and Rio de Janeiro border. Reservations are required. Call IBAMA in Resende
(☎ (0243) 52-1461) and get maps and advice
from the park IBAMA office before setting
off.

Simpler hikes include the walk between
Hotel Simon and Hotel Repouso (where the
painter Guignard lived, worked and left a
few of his paintings), and the 20-minute walk
from the Sítio Jangada to the Poronga waterfalls.

Places to Stay
Pousada do Elefante, close to the Hotel
Simon, is the cheapest place in the park. It's
basic but well located. They charge
US$20/40 for singles/doubles with board.
Other hotels are expensive, three-star
Embratur affairs with saunas and swimming pools – like the *Hotel Simon*
(☎ 52-1122), which charges US$90
for a double with full board. *Hotel
do Ypê* (☎ 52-1453) charges US$60
a double or US$80 to stay in a chalet.
Not far from the park entrance,
Hotel Aldéia da Serra (☎ 52-1152)
is reasonably priced, with chalets for
US$35 a single and US$50 a double, all
inclusive.

Getting There & Away
Every 20 minutes on weekdays, every 40
minutes on weekends (from 7 am to 11.20
pm), there is a bus from Resende to the town
of Itatiaia. From the town take a 'Circular'
bus to the park entrance. They go at 6.45 and
10 am, noon, 2, 4, 6, and 10 pm. If you can
time it, there's a schoolbus that goes all the
way up to Hotel Simon at 12.30 pm and takes
paying passengers.

East of Rio de Janeiro

SAQUAREMA
After the famous beaches of Rio and Baía de
Guanabara, with their high-rise hotels and

Sloth

bars spilling out onto the sands, the quiet and
clean beaches east of Rio are a welcome
change.

Saquarema, 100 km from Rio de Janeiro,
sits between long stretches of open beach,

lagoons and jungled mountains. The town takes unusual pride in the natural beauty of its setting. Polluting industries are forbidden in the municipality, so it's still possible to find sloths and bands of monkeys in the jungles. Motorboats aren't allowed to muck up the lakes and lagoons, which means the water is still pure, and the fish and shrimp are abundant. The long shoreline of fine, white sand and clean water attracts surfers, sports fishers and sun worshippers.

Saquarema is a horse-breeding and fruit-growing centre. You can visit the orchards and pick fruit, or hire horses and take to the hills. Adventurers who tramp the jungle trails in search of the elusive micro-leão monkey are sure to discover beautiful waterfalls, if not primates. All in all, there are plenty of things to do away from the beach.

Ah, but the beaches...Bambui, Ponta Negra and Jaconé, south of town, are long and empty save for a couple of fishing villages. The waves are big, particularly in Ponta Negra and three km north of Saquarema in Praia Itaúna, where an annual surfing contest is held during the last two weeks of May.

History

On 17 March 1531, Martim Afonso de Sousa founded a Portuguese settlement here and met with the Tamoio Indian chief Sapuguaçu. Nonplussed by de Sousa's five ships and 400 sailors, Sapuguaçu chose to ally the Tamoios with the French. In 1575 Antônio Salema, then Governor of Rio de Janeiro, decided to break the Tamoio-French alliance, and with an army of over 1000 men massacred the Indians and their French military advisors.

The next big event in Saquarema's history was the slave revolt of Ipitangas, in which 400 slaves took over the plantation mansion and kicked out their master. For a few days, the slaves held the town and fought against the cavalry which rode out from Niterói. The town pillory, Bandeque's Post, named after the leader of the slave revolt, was in use as recently as the end of last century.

Information

Tourist Office The Secretaria de Turismo at the Prefeitura is quite useless. The best place to go for information, especially about places to stay, is Toulouse Lagos Turismo (☎ 51-2161) at Rua Coronel João Bravo 28, shop G, a stone's throw from the bus stop. The manager, Conceição, has a complete listing of hotels and she is happy to call around to see if there are any vacancies.

Money There's a Banco do Brasil in town. If they aren't changing money, ask Conceição at her travel agency.

Post & Telephone The post office is close to the bus stop in Praça Oscar de Macedo Soares. The posto telefônico is right next to the Shell petrol station after crossing the bridge.

Festival

Saquarema hosts the NS de Nazaré mass on 7 and 8 September. It attracts 150,000 pilgrims, which is second only to the Nazaré celebrations of Belém.

Places to Stay

A great place to stay is *Pousada da Mansão* at Avenida Oceanica 353. Rooms in the old mansion go for US$10 a single and US$20 a double, and there's camping there too. Sonia, who runs the place, speaks English and French. For reservations phone (021) 259-2100 in Rio. The *Hotel Saquarema* (☎ 51-2275) is right at the bus stop. They charge US$10 per person, but stay there only as a last resort. It's OK, but there are better places for the same price.

Pousada da Titia (☎ 51-2508), at Avenida Salgado Filho 774, is a good alternative, with quartos for US$14 a double and apartamentos for US$20. *Pousada dos Socos*, at Rua dos Socos 592, charges US$25 a double.

There are stacks of places charging around US$40 a double. A couple of popular ones are the *Maasai Hotel Club* (☎ 51-1092) near Itaúna beach and *Espuma da Praia* (☎ 51-2118) at Rua das Pintangas 143.

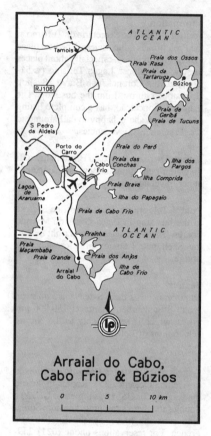

Arraial do Cabo,
Cabo Frio & Búzios

0   5   10 km

ARRAIAL DO CABO

Arraial do Cabo sits on a square corner of land, with Cabo Frio due north 10 km and Praia Grande stretching due west 40 km (continuous with Praia Maçambaba). The village of Arraial do Cabo spreads out from the edges of four bays and has beaches that compare with the finest in Búzios, but unlike Búzios, Arraial is a place where people live and work. The saltworks of the Companhia Nacional de Alcalis, north of town, extract table salt and *barrília*, a type of phosphate tied to the salt.

Information

There's no tourist office in Arraial, but you don't really need one as the layout is fairly straightforward and the attractions are the beaches. The post office is in Praça Castelo Branco and the Telerj office is next to Hotel Praia Grande.

Beaches

'Discovered' years ago by Américo Vespúcio, Praia dos Anjos has beautiful turquoise water and a little too much boat traffic for comfortable swimming. The favourite beaches in town are Praia do Forno, Praia Brava and Praia Grande. Stretching along a pretty piece of road to Cabo Frio, Praia do Forte has bleached white sand and a backdrop of low scrub, cacti and grasses. The Museu Oceanográfico on Praia dos Anjos is open Tuesday to Sunday from 9 am to 4.30 pm.

To get to the Gruta Azul (Blue Cavern) on the far side of Ilha de Cabo Frio, ask fisherfolk at Praia dos Anjos for a tour – it should cost about US$15 – or enquire at the Pousada Restaurante dos Navegantes. Be alert to the tides: the entrance to the underwater cavern isn't always open.

To see the wild orchids between Cabo Frio and Arraial do Cabo, ask the bus driver to let you off at the access road and then hike inland.

Places to Stay

In the centre of town, the *Hotel Praia Grande* (☎ 22-1369) at Rua Dom Pedro 41

Places to Eat

For prato feito, *Pensão Tia Tiana* is a favourite with locals. *Giovani Pizzaria* is recommended. There are lots of lanchonetes at Itaúna.

Getting There & Away

From Rio to Saquarema there are seven buses a day from 6.30 am to 6.30 pm. The same number go the other way from 5.50 am to 7.50 pm. The two-hour trip costs US$4. To get to Cabo Frio, take a local bus to Bacaxá. From there, buses to Cabo leave every 30 minutes.

is a good cheapie, with US$10 singles and US$14 doubles. On the same street at number 16, the *Dom Viega* has doubles for US$17. Singles here are the same price. *Hotel Churrascaria Gaucha* (☎ 22-1533), Praça Lions Clube 35, has large, beat-up rooms with hot showers and plenty of mosquitoes for US$10 per person. It's not worth it.

The *Pousada Restaurante dos Navegantes* (☎ 22-1611) on Praia Grande is a very pretty resort hotel with a courtyard pool and singles for US$20, doubles for US$27. *Camping Praia Grande* is a walled-in grassy area reasonably close to the beach.

Places to Eat

Garrafa de Nansen Restaurante is a classy seafood place where you can eat very well for about US$8 per person. Cheaper eats are available at the *Hotel Churrascaria Gaucha*, where US$3 buys you a prato feito with chicken, beef, sausage, salad, manioc, rice and beans. At Praia Grande, the *Canoa Quebrada* restaurant is a good choice, especially if you're in the mood for seafood moqueca. It's at Rua Epitácio Pessoa 26.

Getting There & Away

Take the municipal bus from Cabo Frio (30c), which loops around Arraial and returns to Cabo Frio every 20 minutes.

CABO FRIO

The Cabo Frio district formerly comprised Cabo Frio, the most populous town, Búzios, the wealthy and sophisticated resort, and Arraial do Cabo, which has since become independent politically and economically because of its salt industry.

History

According to local historian Márcio Verneck, Cabo Frio was inhabited at least 5500 years ago. Before the Portuguese arrived, the warring Tamoio and Goitacazes tribes lived here. In 1503 the Portuguese armada, under the command of Américo Vespúcio, landed at Praia dos Anjos in Arraial do Cabo. Twenty-four men were left behind to start a settlement, one of the first in the Americas. Fantastic reports about this community were the model for Thomas More's *Utopia*.

The economy of the Portuguese settlement was based on the coastal brazil wood, which was felled and shipped back to Europe. Portuguese vessels were at the mercy of Dutch and French corsairs until 1615, when the Portuguese defeated their European foes, founded Santa Helena de Cabo Frio and took the French-built fort of São Mateus to protect their trade. In time the Franciscans joined the settlement and built the NS dos Anjos convent. They were followed by the Jesuits at Fazenda Campo Novo. By the 1800s the brazil wood stands were completely destroyed and the economy was geared toward fishing and, more recently, tourism, saltworks and chemical industries.

Orientation

Canal do Itajuru links the Lagoa de Araruma to the ocean. Cabo Frio lies to one side of this canal. The town is a two-km hike from the bus station along Avenida Júlia Kubitschek. There's a map of Cabo Frio on the wall there.

Information

Tourist Office There is a tourist office (English spoken) in Praça Porto Rocha. Staff sell guides for US$1.50 which include a detailed map of the city. They also have information on hotels and will call to make reservations for you.

Money There's a Banco do Brasil at Praça Porto Rocha 44.

Post & Telephone The post office is at Largo de Santo Antônio 55, in the centre and the Telerj office is in Praça Porto Rocha near the tourist office.

Forte São Mateus

The Forte São Mateus, a stone fortress stronghold against pirates, was built in 1616 and is open from 10 am to 4 pm Tuesday to Sunday. It's at the end of Praia do Forte.

Dunes

There are three spots in and about Cabo Frio with sand dunes. The dunes of Praia do Peró, a super beach for surfing and surfcasting, are six km north in the direction of Búzios, near Ogivas, and after Praia Brava and Praia das Conchas. The Dama Branca (White Lady) sand dunes are on the road to Arraial do Cabo. The Pontal dunes of Praia do Forte town beach stretch from the fort to Miranda hill. The dunes can be dangerous because of robberies, so get the low-down from the locals before heading out to the beaches and dunes.

Place to Stay

Cabo Frio is a bit too built up for my tastes and it's hard to understand why anyone would want to stay here instead of at Arraial do Cabo or Búzios. If you do enjoy staying in crummy beach cities, there are a couple of youth hostels very close to the bus station, both of which charge the maximum of US$7 a night. *Pousada Suzy* (☎ 43-1742) is about 100 metres to the right as you leave the bus station, at Avenida Júlia Kubitschek 22. The owners are very friendly. Much nicer though is the *Albergue Muxarabi*, directly behind Pousada Suzy in Rua R.

The cheapest hotels are located on Rua José Bonifácio and Rua Jorge Lossio, close to the tourist office.

Getting There & Away

The old coastal road takes longer than BR-101 but it's a beautiful level route winding around foggy green mounds. There are regular buses from Rio de Janeiro and Niterói (3 hours, US$6).

Getting Around

To get to Arraial do Cabo from Cabo Frio, catch a local bus from the bus stop just up to the right as you leave the bus station. To get to Búzios, cross the road and get a bus from the stop on your left. Local buses cost 40c.

BÚZIOS

Búzios, a lovely beach resort, is a peninsula (scalloped by 17 beaches) which juts into the Atlantic. It was a simple fishing village until 'discovered' by Brigitte Bardot and her Brazilian boyfriend. The village is now littered with boutiques, fine restaurants, fancy villas, bars and posh pousadas. It's twice the price of the rest of Brazil but affordable for foreigners.

Búzios is not a single town but three settlements on the peninsula – Ossos, Manguinhos, and Armação – and one further north on the mainland called Rasa. Ossos (Bones) at the northernmost tip of the peninsula is the oldest and most attractive. It has a pretty harbour with a yacht club, a few hotels, bars and a tourist stand. Manguinhos at the isthmus is the most commercial and even has a 24-hour medical clinic. Armação, in between, has the best restaurants, along with city necessities like international phones, a bank, petrol station, post office and pharmacy. North-west along the coast is Rasa and the island of Rasa, where Brazil's political dignitaries and rich relax.

Information

The Ekoda Tourist Agency (☎ 23-1490) in Armação at Avenida José Bento Ribeiro Dantas 222 is open seven days a week from 10 am to 8 pm. Staff sell maps of Búzios, change money, represent American Express, speak English, French, German and Spanish, and arrange accommodation and tours.

Boat Trips

The schooner *Queen Lory* makes daily trips out to Ilha Feia, Tartaruga and João Fernandinho. There is a 2½-hour trip which costs US$12 and a four-hour trip for US$20. These trips are excellent value, especially since caipirinhas, soft drinks, fruit salad and snorkelling gear are included in the price. To make a reservation, ask at your pousada or visit Queen Lory Tours, Rua Angela Diniz 35.

Beaches

In general the southern beaches are trickier to get to, but they're prettier and have better surf. The northern beaches are more sheltered and closer to the towns.

Working anticlockwise from south of Maguinhos, the first beaches are Geribá and Ferradurinha (Little Horseshoe). These are beautiful beaches with good surf but the Búzios Beach Club has built condos here.

Next on the coast is Ferradura, which is large enough for windsurfing, and Lagoinha, a rocky beach with rough water. Praia da Foca and Praia do Forno have colder water than the other beaches. Praia Olho de Boi (Bull's Eye) was named after Brazil's first postage stamp. It's a pocket-size beach reached from the long clean beach of Praia Brava by a little trail.

João Fernandinho and João Fernandes are both good for snorkelling, as are the topless beaches of Azedinha and Azeda. Praia dos Ossos, Praia da Armação, Praia do Caboclo and Praia dos Amores are pretty to look at, but not for lounging around. Praia da Tartaruga is quiet and pretty. Praia do Gaucho and Manguinhos are town beaches further along.

Places to Stay

Lodging is somewhat on the expensive side, especially in the summer, so consider staying in Saquarema or Cabo Frio or renting a house and staying for a while. In the off season, however, you should be able to find a place for the same price as you'd pay in Cabo Frio or Arraial. Most places charge the same price for singles as they do for doubles. Búzios is a romantic place and solo travellers are unusual. In general, rooms to let are cheaper than pousadas. All accommodation listed has showers and includes a light breakfast. Prices range from US$15 to US$70 for doubles in the low season. The high season is December to March and again in July.

In Ossos, *Pousada dos Sete Pecados Capitais* (☎ 23-1408, reservations 399-1431) on Praça Eugênio Harold (also known as Praça dos Ossos) charges US$15 off-season and US$30 in the high season for a small double. The place is clean, attractive and among Búzios' cheapest. *Casa Márcia Vanicoru* (☎ 23-1542), Rua João Fernandes 60, is a private home with rooms to let. Márcia runs a progressive household and has

doubles for US$28 off-season, US$40 in the high season. Márcia speaks English, is an excellent cook and will rent you bikes to get to the beaches.

Vila Mediterrânea (☎ 23-1322) at Rua João Fernandes 58 is a white-washed and tiled little hotel. Off-season doubles with a lovely inland view are US$30. *Pousada la Chimere* (☎ 23-1460), Praça Eugênio Harold 36, is an excellent splurge: it has a lovely courtyard and large well-appointed rooms with a view over the square. Low-season doubles are US$45, high season US$60. Ten minutes' walk from the bus station, *Don Quijote* (☎ 23-1165), Estrada da Usina Velha 300, is good value, charging US$30 a double off-season.

In Armação, try *Pousada do Arco Iris* (☎ 23-1256) at Rua Manoel Turibe de Farias 182, with US$15 doubles off-season, US$30 high season.

Camping
If you want to camp, *Fênix Camping* at Praia de Manguinhos is a good spot.

Places to Eat
For good cheap food, have grilled fish right on the beaches. Brava, Ferradura and João Fernandes beaches have little thatched-roof fish and beer restaurants. Most of the better restaurants are in or about Armação. *Restaurante David* in Armação, on Rua Manoel Turibe de Farias, has good cheap food. An ample US$4.50 prato feito usually includes shark fillet (cassão) with rice, beans and salad. *Gostinho Natural*, also in Armação, is very popular and their servings are huge.

Búzios is also a good place to indulge in some fancy food. *Le Streghe* (The Witch) in Armação, on Rua das Pedras, has great pasta and northern Italian dishes, and obsequious service. *Au Cheval Blanc*, a few doors down, has a reputation for fine French food. Both have main courses starting at US$10 and up.

Chez Michou Crêperie, also on Rua das Pedras, is a popular hangout because of their incredible crepes. They'll make any kind of crepe you want and the outdoor bar has delicious pinha coladas for US$2. On Avenida Beira Mar, between Ossos and Armação, are *Satíricon*, with overpriced Italian seafood, and *La Nuance*, a fun, outdoor French restaurant and bar.

Getting There & Away

From Cabo Frio to Búzios (Ossos) take the municipal bus for a 50-minute, 20-km bone-crunching cobblestone run. There are four direct buses daily to Rio from the bus stop on Rua Turibe de Faria in Armação. The three-hour trip costs US$7.

BARRA DE SÃO JOÃO

Barra de São João, not to be confused with São João da Barra further north up the coast, is an easygoing place set on a narrow spit of land between a small river and the Atlantic. Old, well-preserved colonial homes with azulejos give it a warm Portuguese feel. The village architecture is protected by law. The long, quiet beach is good for surfcasting.

Places to Stay

Don't get the idea that accommodation will be any cheaper here than in Búzios. All the 'simple' pousadas in town charge at least US$30 a double. They include *Pousada Lua Azul* (☎ 64-1356) at Rua Octavio Moreira 100, *Pousada Bouganville* (☎ 64-1154), Rua Dr Sá Pinto 279, and the *Hotel Brasil* on the highway.

Getting There & Away

Thirty-five km from Macaé and 57 km from Cabo Frio, Barra de São João is serviced by 10 daily buses.

RIO DAS OSTRAS

Rio das Ostras is 10 km north of Barra de São João and is full of hotels and restaurants, but isn't nearly as charming as Barra de São João. The best beaches are Costa Azul and Praia da Joanna, near the yacht club across the wooden bridge.

Places to Stay & Eat

The *Hotel Restaurante Ostrão* (☎ 64-1379), Avenida Beira Mar, has clean but overpriced doubles (US$40 but bargain) with fridge-bar, TV and ocean views. There are several cheaper hotels back on the highway. Try *Sandy's* for light snack food, drinks and breakfast.

MACAÉ

Macaé was once a calm fishing village but now it's a fast-growing petroleum refinery city with Petrobras oil rigs 100 km offshore. A few years ago the place was swarming with American technicians, resulting in the gas pipeline which is now being built to Rio. Due to helicopter traffic to and from the oil rigs, Macaé is perhaps the third busiest airport in Brazil after Rio and São Paulo. The best beach in town, Praia Cavalheras, is not polluted...yet.

Places to Stay & Eat

The *Pousada Del Rey* (☎ 62-2896) at Rua Vereador Manuel Braga 192, only a block from the bus station, is clean and a good deal, with US$8 singles and US$12 doubles. The owner, Daniel, a Spaniard from Salamanca, recommends the *Cantinho do Bobo* for family-style food.

RESERVA BIOLÓGICA DO POÇO DAS ANTAS

A few km off BR-101, between Casmiro de Abreu and Silva Jardim, the Poço das Antas reserve was created to protect the endangered mico-leão (Golden-Lion Tamarin monkey) and its natural habitat, coastal jungle. Fifty mico-leãoes were sent from a breeding programme in the USA. The small monkeys with their golden, lion-like manes are hard to spot. More monkey business is conducted in nearby Cachoeiras de Macaco in the Instituto de Estúdos de Simiologia (Simian Studies Institute).

MACAÉ TO CAMPOS

From Macaé to Campos is rolling ranch land. Here and there are remnants of tropical forest, palms and scraggly undergrowth in uncleared ravines and hill clefts. A dark mountain range runs along the coast 50 km inland. Most of the land between the Atlantic and the mountains is planted with sugar cane.

BARRA DA ITABAPOANA

At the extreme north-east corner of Rio de Janeiro state is Barra da Itabapoana, which borders the Atlantic Ocean and Espírito Santo on the far side of the Rio Itabapoana. There's not much to the town: a beat-up church, a few riverboats, two or three street lights, a Telerj station, a fish market and a menagerie of pigs, chickens, horses and dogs. The beach is two km from the church (turn left at the cemetery).

Places to Stay & Eat

Dona Sede runs a pension near the church and charges US$6 per person. She can fix you meals, but your best bet is *Restaurante São Remo* by the fish market. It is possible to get good food in the middle of nowhere: their pasteis de camarão are superb, and US$3 buys a plate of fried fish with shrimp sauce plus rice, beans and salad.

Getting There & Away

There is one daily bus at 6 am that crosses into Cachoeiro do Itapemirim, Espírito Santo. From here the choice is either to head directly to Vitória or take the slower, more picturesque coastal route.

Two buses go the three hours and 76 km of dirt road from Barra da Itabapoana to Campos. One bus leaves at 3 pm, the other at 6 pm.

Espírito Santo

If Brazil were to have a contest for the least appealing state, Sergipe would be a contender, but Espírito Santo would win the prize. Perhaps Espírito Santo suffers most due to the glory of its neighbouring states, Minas Gerais, Rio de Janeiro and Bahia. In any case it's a small state with little to interest the traveller.

Colonised in the 16th century, Espírito Santo grew as an armed region to prevent gold from being smuggled out of Minas. In the 1800s, Germans and Italians came to the state and settled in the hills of the interior. Until the 1960s, coffee plantations were the prime source of income but that has been superseded by heavy industry.

The coastline away from Vitória is clean but not particularly pretty. The turbulent surf kicks up sand which gives the water a muddy brown hue rather than the aquamarine found in Bahia or Rio.

In all fairness, Espírito Santo does have some attractions, humble as they may be. Some of the fishing villages and beaches on the southern coast are attractive; however, they have no provisions for tourists. To the north, Conceição da Barra and the nearby sand dunes at Itaúnas are worth a visit. Excellent seafood is available in Espírito Santo; especially noteworthy is the moqueca capixaba which is made without dendê oil.

Espírito Santo

0   50   100 km

VITÓRIA

Being 521 km from Rio de Janeiro and 602 km from Porto Seguro, Vitória, capital of the state of Espírito Santo, is a convenient place to break the journey between Rio and the state of Bahia. Founded in 1551, Vitória has remarkably little to show of its colonial past. It's a port city, connected by rail with Minas Gerais. Large amounts of export coffee and timber pass through here, and the port at nearby Tubarão is the outlet for millions of tonnes of iron ore.

Orientation

The main bus station is a km from the centre of town. There are two strips of beach: Praia de Camburí, a 10-minute bus ride away to the north-east of the city, and Praia da Costa, 12 km away to the south at Vila Velha.

Information

Tourist Office Emcatur, the state tourism authority, has the tough job of promoting tourism in Espírito Santo. It maintains

210

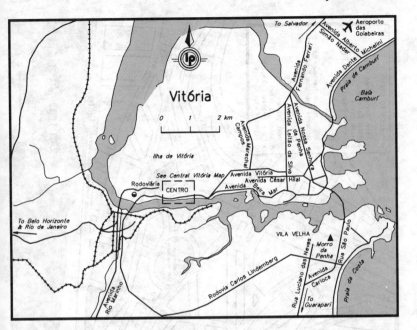

Map of Vitória

booths at the airport and the main bus station. They're supposed to be open daily from 8 am to 7 pm, but don't bet on this. They have lots of coloured brochures of the various points of interest in the state, but no decent maps of the city.

The Emcatur advisors also have hotel information (but not prices) in the mid to top-end range, but they can't make reservations because they don't have a phone.

The best map of the city and its surrounds can be found in the middle pages of the local telephone directory, unless you happen to look in the copy I got mine from.

Money The quickest and easiest way to change cash is to go to the Escal souvenir shop just off Avenida Marechal Mascarenhas and round the corner from the Banco do Brasil in Avenida Governador Bley. You'll have to go there or the BEMGE (State Bank of Minas Gerais) nearby to change travellers' cheques.

Post & Telephone The main post office is in the centre on Avenida Jerônimo Monteiro and there's a branch at the rodoviária. There are three posto telefônicos: at the rodoviária, the airport and in the centre on Rua do Rosário. They all open at 6.30 am and close between 10.30 and 11 pm.

Praia de Camburí
This five-km stretch of beach is where you'll find lots of restaurants, mid-range hotels and nightspots. It's not good for swimming, as its proximity to the port at Tubarão means there's usually some oil or chemicals in the water.

Vila Velha
This was first place colonised in Espírito Santo. The most interesting thing to do here is climb up to the Convento da Penha. On top of a 154-metre granite outcrop, this is a major pilgrimage centre where, in the week after Easter, thousands of devotees come to

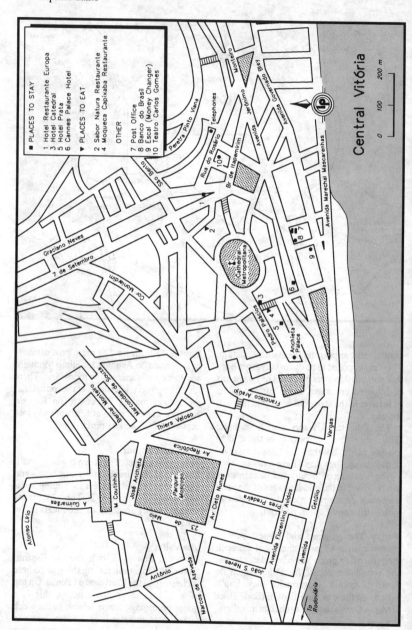

PLACES TO STAY
1 Hotel Restaurante Europa
3 Hotel Catedral
5 Hotel Prata
6 Cannes Palace Hotel

▼ PLACES TO EAT
2 Sabor Natura Restaurante
4 Moqueca Capixaba Restaurante

OTHER
7 Post Office
8 Banco do Brasil
9 Escol (Money Changer)
10 Teatro Carlos Gomes

Central Vitória

0   100   200 m

pay homage to the image of NS de Penha, some even making the climb on their knees. The convent is presently undergoing restoration, but the panoramic view of Vitória makes the trip up worth it.

Praia da Costa is close to the convent. It's the main Vila Velha beach and has fewer hotels and restaurants than Camburí, but it's better for swimming.

Around Town

The pink Anchieta Palace, on Praça João Climaco, is a 16th-century former Jesuit college and church. It's now the seat of state government, and the only part you can enter is the tomb of Padre Anchieta, co-founder of São Paulo. Close by is the Catedral Metropolitana, with it's neo-gothic exterior and interesting stained-glass windows.

Teatro Carlos Gomes on Praça Costa Pereira is a replica of La Scala in Milan. The Parque Moscoso is where the Capixabas, as natives of the state are called, go for a break.

Places to Stay

There is a row of 'crash-pad' hotels across from the bus station, the best of which is the *Spala*, at US$5 per person. The centre is easy to get to, however, and it's worth making the effort to get away from the bus station and its uninspiring surroundings.

In the centre are lots of cheap hotels. *Hotel Restaurante Europa*, at the start of Rua 7 de Setembro next to Praça Costa Pereira, is a good deal with clean quartos for US$2 a head and big apartamentos for US$4 a head. The food in their restaurant is cheap, with large servings. *Hotel Catedral* (☎ 223-4173) is, you guessed it, near the cathedral at Rua Pedro Palácios 213. The receptionist here reads the Bible in his spare moments – it's that kind of place. Quartos cost US$4/6 a single/double and apartamentos US$6/8; it's cheap, clean and honest.

Hotel Prata (☎ 222-4311) is right next to the Anchieta Palace at Rua Nestor Gomes 201. They charge US$12/14 for musty singles/doubles and you have to be out by 10 am. The breakfast is good, though. The *Cannes Palace Hotel* (☎ 222-1522), Ave-

nida Jerônimo Monteiro 111, is a more expensive option at US$25/35 for singles/doubles – but if you're going to spend that sort of money you may as well be on the beach.

Out at Camburí, the cheapest place on the beachfront is the *Hotel Praia* (☎ 227-3197), Avenida Dante Michelini 207, with singles for US$20 and doubles for US$25. The *Camburi Praia* (☎ 227-1322), Dante Michelini 1007, costs a few dollars more.

If you want to stay at Praia da Costa in Vila Velha, the *Hostess* (☎ 329-2111), Avenida Antonio Gil Velloso 442, is a three-star hotel with singles/doubles for US$25/37. *Hotel Senac* (☎ 325-0111), Ilha do Boi, is the five-star hotel in Vitória. Rooms start at US$60 a double.

Places to Eat

Restaurante Piratas at Avenida Dante Michelini 747, Praia de Camburí, has a good squid vinaigrette for US$7. Ask for the couvert. *Churrascaria Minuano* at Avenida Dante Michelini 337 has a US$6 rodízio.

In the centre, the *Sabor Natura Restaurante* for vegetarians is near Praça Costa Pereira, at Rua 13 de Maio 90. They're open from 8 am to 6.30 pm daily, but their US$2 set lunch only goes from 11 am to 3 pm. Another good lunch buffet in the centre is the US$4, all-you-can-eat session at the *Cannes Palace Hotel*, Avenida Jerônimo Monteiro 111. The *Moqueca Capixaba Restaurante* is a good place to eat the dish of the same name. It's on the steps leading down from the park in front of the cathedral; closed on Sunday.

Getting There & Away

It's all too easy to get here – the trick is to get away. The bus station on Ilha do Príncipe has connections to all major cities. To Belo Horizonte, nine buses a day make the eight-hour trip for US$12. Direct to Ouro Preto, there's a bus at 10.45 pm. To Porto Seguro, there's one daily bus at 9 am. The 11-hour trip costs US$14. To Rio de Janeiro, 11 buses make the eight-hour journey for US$9.

Getting Around

To/From the Airport The airport is 10 km from the city centre. There's a local bus that goes there from the bus station for 50c. Funnily enough, it's marked 'Aeroporto'.

Bus All local buses run from the various stops outside the main rodoviária. As in Rio de Janeiro, the route is written on the side of the bus. To get into the centre, catch any bus that goes along Avenida Vitória. When you pass the pink palace on the left-hand side, get out at the next stop. It's only a three-minute ride.

For Camburí, catch any bus that goes along Avenida Dante Michelini. To Vila Velha, catch an all yellow or all blue bus. To get to Praia da Costa, you'll have to catch another bus from the Vila Velha terminal.

GUARAPARI

Guarapari is the most prominent resort town of Espírito Santo. It's too big a city to be a proper beach town but there are 23 beaches in the municipality, each with a lovely mountain backdrop. The best beach is Praia do Morro; unlike the others it doesn't have too many stones, and it does have the healing monazitic radioactive sands touted in Espírito's brochures.

Guarapari was an excellent base for a family holiday. We enjoyed being off the beaten tourist track in a genuine Brazilian holiday resort – albeit out of season. From Praia do Morro there is an excellent walk around the headland through brushland where birds abound, to lovely unspoiled coves. There are superb views back towards Guarapari and Muquicaba with the backdrop of the dramatic coastal range of mountains. To the south of Guarapari, at the tiny resort of Meaípe, there is a magnificent beach. At lunchtime, stroll off the sand into the Cantina de Curuca for excellent lobster and prawns.

Commander M K Barritt Royal Navy (UK)

Places to Stay

From the bus station it's a 10-minute walk to the centre. There are two budget places on Rua Dr Silva Melo, in the centre of town only a block from Praia do Meio and Praia da Areia Branca. At No 98, *Hotel Maryland*

(☎ 261-0553) has single/double apartamentos for US$11/18. Almost next door is the *Areia Preta* (☎ 261-2717), which as well as running a reasonable Chinese restaurant, charges US$10 for singles and US$17 for doubles. A bit more upmarket in the same vicinity are the *Solar da Ruth* (☎ 261-1836), Silva Melo 215, a very friendly one-star hotel close to the beach with singles/doubles for US$16/25, and the *Coronado* (☎ 261-1709), a three-star job right on the beach with singles/doubles for US$25/32.

The best place close to the bus station is the *Star* (☎ 261-2439). It's popular with travellers who only want to stay for the night and don't want to carry their bags into town. It's a couple of blocks from Prainha beach at Rua Santo Antonio 287. It costs US$10 a single and US$16 a double. The youth hostel and campground, *Guaracamping*, isn't far from the bus station and it's well signposted. *Hotel Porto do Sol* (☎ 261-0011) at Avenida Beira Mar 1, by Muquiçaba beach, is Guarapari's four-star hotel with singles/doubles for US$80/87.

Places to Eat

Pizzaria do Angelo, on the corner of Silva Melo and Joaquim Silva Lima, is a good, cheap place in a pleasant, green setting. *Cabana Ali Babá e os 40 Quibes* is an interestingly named restaurant at Avenida Beira Mar 382. They serve good Arab food. For seafood, *Peixada do Irmão*, at Rua Jacinto de Almeida 72, is highly recommended.

Getting There & Away

From Vitória, buses make the 75-minute run every hour from 6 am to 9 pm. The cost is US$1.20. To Vitória, buses run hourly from 6 am to 9.30 pm. Frequent buses make the 28-km trip to Anchieta.

ANCHIETA

Anchieta is 88 km south of Vitória. Its attractions are the 16th-century church of NS de Assunção and, alongside, the Museu Padre Anchieta. The church walls are original; they were built by Padre Anchieta and the local Indians. The museum is no big deal, although it contains the chair of Padre Anchieta and some relics (closed Monday).

Places to Stay

There aren't any real cheapies here. *Hotel Porto Velho* (☎ 536-1181) is right above the bus stop. Their rooms with TV, refrigerator, etc go for US$20/28 a single/double. A bit cheaper and 100 metres further down the road is the *Anchieta* (☎ 536-1258), which combines a pleasant, colonial style with some wild floral wallpaper and curtains. Singles cost US$17 and doubles US$20.

Places to Eat

Ressacas Bar at Rua Costa Pereira 204 serves good seafood dishes. One of their US$6 plates will serve two people easily. The *Restaurante Peixada do Garcia* on Praia Ubu, 10 km north towards Guarapari, is reputedly excellent.

Getting There & Away

To Guarapari, buses run every 20 to 30 minutes from 6 am to 6.50 pm. To Piúma, 12 km away, they run every 30 to 40 minutes from 6 am to 7.20 pm.

PIÚMA

Known as the 'City of Shells', Piúma is a small village 100 km south of Vitória. The rarest shell in the world, Oliva Zelindea, is occasionally found here. There are some nice beaches around here and some offshore islands very close by which are worth a look.

The coastline here is dominated by the 300-metre-high, cone-shaped Monte Aghá, which is good for hang-gliding and climbing.

Islands

Ilha do Gamba is connected to the mainland by a thin isthmus, and is home to lots of seabirds. Ilha dos Cabritos, 15 minutes away by boat, has a good seafood restaurant. Ilha do Meio preserves wild orchids and native trees, and a large variety of lobsters, sea horses and starfish are found in the surrounding waters. To get a boat to the islands, ask the fishers along the beach.

Beaches

Praia Boca da Barra and Praia Maria Nenen are surf beaches, while Praia Acaiaca has calm water.

Places to Stay

The best deal in town is the *Solar de Brasilia* (☎ 520-1620), 50 metres from the beach at Avenida Eduardo Rodrigues 15. Singles/doubles are US$7/14. The breakfast is excellent and they have a swimming pool. Similarly priced, but nowhere near as good, is *Pousada Barbara* at Rua Mimoso do Sul. The cheapest place in town is a dormitorio close to the bus station on the corner of the town square. You can sleep here for US$3. The three-star *Monte Aghá* (☎ 534-1190), Avenida Minas Gerais 20, is the priciest hotel in Piúma, with singles/doubles for US$35/42.

Places to Eat

Most of the restaurants are located along the beachfront on Avenida Beira Mar. *Belabatok* has great seafood and carne do sol. *D'Angelus*, right alongside Belabatok, is also very popular.

Getting There & Away

Frequent buses go to Anchieta and Marataizes. Only four buses a day go to Vitória.

MARATAÍZES

The town of Marataízes caters to the working-class, Mineiro holiday crowd during high summer season, but lives off its small fishing industry the rest of the year. Every morning the town beach throbs with fishers, who pull lines in teams, haul in and sort the catch, fix nets and push tiny boats into the foamy sea. It is possible to hire a boat from Marataízes or Itapaiva beach to the islands of Francês, Ovos or Itaputera.

Places to Stay

There are lots of cheap places and a few more expensive ones. The cheapest (and furthest from the bus station) is *Pousada Cantinha do Valdir* (☎ 532-2604) at Avenida Costa e

Silva 132. Valdir himself is quite a character and he loves the sound of his own voice. He charges US$3 per person and US$5 for two-person apartments with a kitchen, so you can cook the local fish any way you want. It's pretty basic, but then it's very cheap. *Pensão Santa Izabel* (☎ 532-1439), at Rua Soares 80, is cheap and clean at US$5 a head or US$10 if you want meals as well. *Hotel Atlântico* (☎ 532-1427) has apartamentos for US$7 per person. Close to the Praia Hotel, at Rua Alegre 83, it's only a block from the beach.

Across the road from the bus station, the *Hotel Marataízes* (☎ 532-1383) charges US$5 per person. From here it's a three-minute walk to the main beach.

Of the expensive hotels, the *Praia Hotel* (☎ 532-2144) is the pick of the bunch; it faces the beach at Avenida Atlântica 99. Singles are US$28 and doubles are US$40, but they give a 20% discount in the off season.

Places to Eat

The strip along Avenida Atlântica is full of bars and restaurants. *Gaivota* at No 712 has all the seafood dishes, as does the popular *Mar Azul* at No 630. The restaurant in the *Praia Hotel* is a bit more expensive, but highly recommended. Near the bus station is *Bar Restaurante Pic Tot*: a friendly place and the serves are huge.

Getting There & Away

Three buses a day go to Vitória, at 6 and 6.15 am, and 3.10 pm. There's also a bus to Rio de Janeiro which leaves at 10.30 pm.

Around Marataízes

Praia Marape is a lovely beach adjacent to a poor little fishing village about 30 km south of Marataízes. There is no formal accommodation here, but hardy travellers can make do. Praia das Neves, Praia Moroba and Praia Lagoa Boa Vista are reasonable beaches further to the north.

DOMINGOS MARTINS

Domingos Martins, also known as Campinho, is a small village settled by Germans in 1847. The pride of the town is the musical water clock decorated with figures of the 12 apostles; it's in the Restaurante Vista Linda, seven km before the town proper.

Recanto dos Colibris, which is in town at the far end of Avenida Presidente Vargas, is a pretty gathering spot. The town is a good base for exploring the streams and forests of the mountains. Fifty km further into the mountains at Aracê are some fancier resort hotels with horses for hire.

Places to Stay

The cheapest hotel is the *Campinho*, which is close to the bus stop. Singles/doubles here are US$7/12. *Hotel e Restaurante Imperador* (☎ 268-1115) at Rua Duque de Caxias 275 has a sauna and charges US$25 for doubles.

Places to Eat

Try the restaurant in the *Imperador*, or the *Vista Linda* out of town. There's a great view of the valley and, of course, of the musical clock.

Getting There & Away

Nine buses a day make the 41-km, hour-long trip from Vitória. It costs US$1.50.

SANTA TERESA

Santa Teresa is a small town settled by Italian immigrants. The town has a pretty, flowered plaza and a cool, mountain climate suitable for vineyards. Nearby trips include the valley of Canaã and the Reserva Biológica Nova Lombardia.

Museu Biológico de Professor Melo Leitão

This museum is the town's main attraction. It represents the life's work of Augusto Ruschi, a staunch envionmentalist and world-renowned hummingbird expert, who died in 1986 after being poisoned by a frog. The museum also has a small zoo, a butterfly garden, a snake farm and a large number of orchids and other flora. It's open only on weekends, from noon to 5 pm. Time your visit here accordingly, as it's very interesting.

Places to Stay

Hotel Pierazzo (☎ 259-1233) at Avenida Getúlio Vargas 115 has very nice singles/doubles for US$15/20. The cheaper alternative is the *Globo* at Rua Jerônimo Vervloet 190, which charges US$4 per person.

Places to Eat

A few doors down from the Pierazzo is the *Restaurante Zitus*, which does good pasta. Go upstairs from the lanchonete.

Getting There & Away

Santa Teresa is two hours and 76 km from Vitória. Seven buses a day make the journey. It costs US$2.

CONCEIÇÃO DA BARRA

Situated in the north of the state, 254 km from Vitória, Conceição da Barra is a small town that lies between the mouths of the Itaúnas and Cricaré rivers.

There are some quiet beaches in the area, like Praia da Barra, Bugia and Guaxindiba, but the main attractions are the Dunas de Itaúnas: 20 to 30-metre-high dunes of fine sand that engulfed the small village of Vila de Itaunas. Only the church tower is still visible. From the top of the dunes it's possible to see the sea, the Rio Itaúnas and the surrounding Atlantic rainforest. The dunes are 23 km from Conceição da Barra.

Places to Stay & Eat

There are plenty of places to stay in town. The *Dunas de Itaúnas* (☎ 762-1302) has single/double apartamentos for US$9/14. It's in the centre on Rua Mendes de Oliveira. Another place in the centre is *Rustico's Hotel* (☎ 762-1193) at Rua Muniz Freire 299. Single/double apartamentos cost US$12/20.

The top-end place to stay is the *Barramar Praia Hotel* (☎ 762-1311 at Praia de Guaxindiba. It's a three-star job that charges US$27/34 a single/double.

Budget travellers should think seriously about trying to sling a hammock in a fisher hut at Bugia or camping out near the dunes.

The best places to eat are the barracas on the beaches, which serve the local speciality: *puã de caranguejo*, a tasty crab stew. These shacks also serve coconut milk, fried fish and, of course, killer batidas.

Getting There & Away

There is only one daily direct bus from Vitória. It leaves at 10 am and arrives in Conceição at 2 pm. The trip costs US$9. Alternatively, you could catch a bus to São Mateus and then catch one of the frequent buses that make the 35-km trip from there to Conceição; or catch any bus going to Bahia along BR-101, get off at the turnoff to Conceição, and hitch or walk the 15 km to town.

Minas Gerais

The state of Minas Gerais, which is as large as France, is part of a vast plateau that crosses Brazil's interior. Rising along the state's southern border with Rio and São Paulo is the Serra da Mantiqueira, which has some of Brazil's highest peaks. These mountains stalled the development of Minas Gerais until the gold boom at the beginning of the 18th century. Running south to north, from São João del Rei through Ouro Prêto and past Diamantina, is the Serra do Espinhaço, Brazil's oldest geological formation. This range separates Minas' two principal river systems: the great São Francisco to the west and the Rio Doce to the east.

Minas has good roads, but travel is usually a sinuous affair. Much of the terrain is characterised by hills, deep valleys, and plateaus running off the larger mountains. Because of the plentiful rains, the south, east and much of the centre were once thickly forested, but the land has been cleared for mining and agriculture and today there is little forest left. In the rainy season the land is still green, but forests are pretty much limited to Minas' several large parks and reserves. The northern extension of the state is sertão and less populated than the rest of Minas. It's an arid land, with shrub-like trees that look dead during the dry season but quickly regain their foliage when it rains. The most common tree is the pepper tree (aroeira).

For the traveller, Minas presents a welcome contrast to the rest of Brazil. Nestled in the Serra do Espinhaço are the cidades históricas – historic colonial cities which grew up with the great gold boom. The foothills and streams of these mountains were scoured for gold throughout the 18th century. Minas' exquisite colonial towns are seemingly frozen in another epoch. Their baroque churches and sacred art – most of these are sculptures from one of the world's great artists, Aleijadinho – represent over half of Brazil's national monuments.

Minas also has several hydro-mineral spas in the mountainous south-west corner and a number of prehistoric caves close to the capital, Belo Horizonte. Founded as recently as 1897, Belo Horizonte is Brazil's third largest city. While residents often speak well of this sprawling place, there is little beauty, natural or otherwise, to stimulate the visitor.

The major historical cities are clustered in three main spots along the Serra do Espinhaço range. São João del Rei, with Tiradentes and Prados nearby, is 200 km south of Belo Horizonte. Ouro Prêto and Mariana are 100 km south-east of Belo Horizonte. Diamantina, with Serro further down the road, is 290 km north of Belo Horizonte.

Ouro Prêto, declared a World Cultural Heritage Site by UNESCO, has more of everything than any city in Brazil – more homogeneous baroque architecture, more churches, more Aleijadinho, more museums and more fame. It also has more tourists, more traffic, more boutiques, more locals hawking things to visitors and more expensive hotels and restaurants. If you go to Ouro Prêto and don't have time to visit the other clusters of historic cities, be sure to visit nearby Mariana, which remains less affected by tourism.

It's hard to tell anyone to bypass Ouro Prêto, and if you really like colonial or baroque art and architecture, or the sculpture of Aleijadinho and churches, then you should definitely go there. But if your time is limited and your visit is during the peak tourist season, it's worth considering spending more time at some of the other historic cities and less time at Ouro Prêto.

Diamantina has the fewest tourists and is the most tranquil of the historic cities. Its many buildings form a beautiful display of colonial architecture. São João and Tiradentes are a good combination to visit: the former has several churches and works of Aleijadinho in a small lively city with little

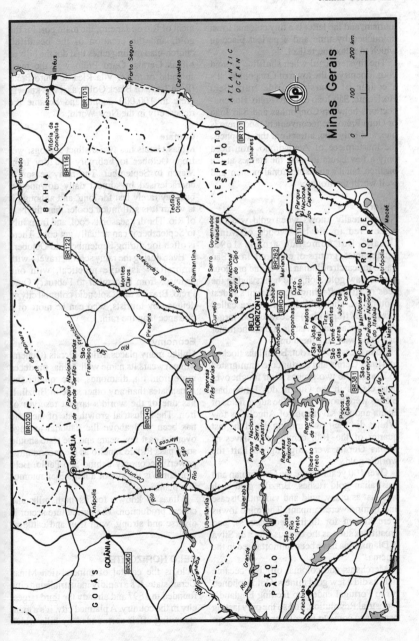

Minas Gerais

0   100   200 km

tourism, and the latter is a tiny colonial town untouched by time and a perfect place in which to relax and reflect.

The mystery card when shuffling around your itinerary is the town of Congonhas. It's a couple of hours' bus ride from Belo Horizonte, São João or Ouro Prêto. Bus connections between Congonhas and São João or Ouro Prêto are inconvenient, and there is one, and only one, attraction: the Prophets, the masterpiece of Aleijadinho. You need only a few hours to view the statues at the basílica, but it's an inspirational moment and well worth the trouble.

History

No one really knows when gold was first discovered in the backwoods of Minas Gerais. But sometime around 1695, bandeirantes, groups of explorers from São Paulo in search of Indian slaves and precious metals, saw gold along the banks and in the beds of rivers flowing from Brazil's oldest mountains. The gold deposits were called *faisqueiras* (sparkles) because the larger pieces were actually visible and all the miner had to do was pick them up.

Soon the word was out. Brazilians flocked to Minas Gerais and Portuguese immigrated to Brazil. The two groups soon fought over land claims in the Guerra dos Emboabas. Slaves were brought from the sugar fields of Bahia and the savannahs of Angola, as few Whites did their own mining. Until the last quarter of the 18th century the slaves of Minas Gerais were digging up half the world's gold.

Over 100 years before the Californian and Australian gold rushes, Brazil's gold rush was just as crazy, wild and violent. Disease and famine were rampant. The mine towns were known for their licentiousness, and prostitutes such as the famous Chica da Silva in Diamantina have been immortalised in the cinema.

Merchants and colonial officials became rich, as did a few gold miners. Gold siphoned off to Portugal ended up feeding England's Industrial Revolution, and so the only lasting benefits to come to Brazil were the develop-

ment of Rio de Janeiro, the main port for the gold, and the creation of the beautiful, church-clad mining cities that dot the hills of Minas Gerais. Ouro Prêto was the most splendid of these. Vila Rica de Ouro Prêto (Rich Town of Black Gold), as it was known, grew to 100,000 people and became the richest city in the New World.

Climate

Minas Gerais has two distinct seasons: wet from October to February and dry from March to September. The rainy season is characterised by almost daily downpours, but they rarely last for long, and although it is warm it is still much cooler than the heat of Rio. The dry season is cool, and from July to September it can actually get cold. There is often fog during September and October.

Even during the rainy season, travel – with umbrella – is quite practical, with one proviso: from December to February Ouro Prêto, Brazil's most splendid colonial city, is deluged by tourists, who can be more of a nuisance than the rain.

Economy

Unlike many places, Minas Gerais (General Mines) wears its name well. Minas produces more iron, tin, diamonds, zinc, quartz and phosphates than any other state in Brazil. It has one of the world's largest reserves of iron. The industrial growth rate of the state has been well above the national average over the past few years and the state should soon pass Rio de Janeiro as the second most powerful economy behind São Paulo. Belo Horizonte is the site of a large Fiat automobile plant.

Minas is known for its high milk and cheese production. The agriculture sector is diverse and strong, with fruit and cattle as well.

BELO HORIZONTE

Belo is the capital of mineral-rich Minas Gerais state. It's a rapidly industrialising city, founded in 1897 and already the third largest city in the country. A planned city, it's a giant sprawling affair surrounded by hills which

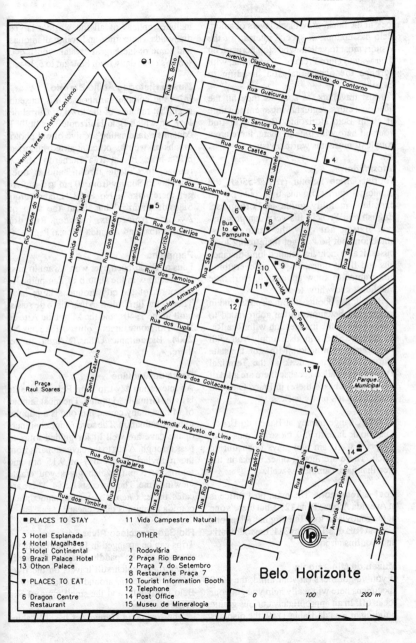

Belo Horizonte

■ PLACES TO STAY
3 Hotel Esplanada
4 Hotel Magalhães
5 Hotel Continental
9 Brazil Palace Hotel
13 Othon Palace

▼ PLACES TO EAT
6 Dragon Centre Restaurant

11 Vida Campestre Natural

OTHER
1 Rodoviäria
2 Praça Rio Branco
7 Praça 7 do Setembro
8 Restaurante Praça 7
10 Tourist Information Booth
12 Telephone
14 Post Office
15 Museu de Mineralogia

0   100   200 m

lock in the thick, grey-black layers of smog. Belo has nothing of special interest for the visitor; most travellers who stop here are on their way to Ouro Prêto or Diamantina, with perhaps the occasional soul heading to Brasília.

Most travellers, as soon as they hit the historical cities, regret having spent any time at all in Belo Horizonte. But if you find yourself here with time to spare, there are a couple of museums worth a visit.

Information

Tourist Office Belotur (☎ 222-5500), the municipal tourist organisation, puts out an excellent monthly guide in Portuguese, English and French. It's very comprehensive, listing not only the main tourist attractions but how to get there using local buses. It also includes detailed long-distance bus and flight times, as well as everything you wanted to know about Belo Horizonte but didn't know how to ask.

Belotur has booths at both airports, and in Praça 7 do Setembro (often abbreviated to Praça Sete) at the intersection with Rua Rio de Janeiro. Staff can also supply you with state tourist information. Minastur, the state tourist body, has a desk at the Terminal Turístico (so called because there are a lot of travel agents based there) in Praça Olegário Maciel, but it's pretty useless.

Money Change money at Banco do Brasil, Rua Rio de Janeiro 750, close to Praça Sete. It opens at 10 am and stays open during lunch. There are lots of other banks in the area that have câmbios as well.

Post & Telephone The main post office is at Avenida Afonso Pena 1270, but there's one at the rodoviária too. Telemig has telephone posts at Rua dos Tamoios 311, the rodoviária and Confins airport.

Museu de Mineralogía

If you've got rocks on your mind, the 5000 specimens here will really help you get your rocks off. In an appropriately curious gothic building at Rua da Bahia 1149, the displays include replicas of all the world's largest diamonds, meteorites and rough diamonds, and some of the largest crystals you'll ever see. It's open daily from 8.30 am to 5.30 pm.

Museu Historico Abílio Barreto

In an old colonial farmhouse, this museum is all that remains of the town of Curral del Rey, on which Belo Horizonte was built. It contains a fascinating archive of old photographs as well as other assorted historical bric-a-brac. It's at Rua Bernardo Mascarenhas, in Cidade Jardim, and is open Tuesday to Sunday from 10 am to 5 pm. To get there, take a No 8902 'Luxemburgo/Sagrada Familia' bus from the stop on Avenida Amazonas, between Rua dos Tupinambas and Avenida Afonso Pena.

Pampulha

Fans of Oscar Niemeyer won't want to miss his creations in the suburb of Pampulha, in the north of the city around a large lake. There's the Igreja de São Francisco de Assis, built in the 1940s, and the Museu de Arte de Belo Horizonte, among others. Take bus No 2004 'Bandeirantes/Olhos/D'Agua' to get there.

Gruta de Maquiné

An interesting day trip from Belo Horizonte is to the Gruta de Maquiné. The most famous of Minas' many caves, this one is a popular tourist destination. The seven huge chambers of the cave are well lit for guided tours to pass through. A bus to the caves departs from the rodoviária every day at 9.15 am and returns at 3 pm, which gives you ample viewing time. The trip costs US$4. There are cafés there: *Chero's* is recommended;their comida mineira is quite cheap.

Rio São Francisco River Trip

Trips can be arranged in Belo Horizonte for passage on the paddle-steamer *Benjamin Guimaraes*, which still travels on the river between Pirapora, around 320 km north of Belo Horizonte, and the small town of São Francisco.

The *Benjamin Guimaraes* has 12 cabins

and a bar/restaurant on board. The five-day tourist trip begins every Sunday and costs US$300 per person, which includes the bus from Belo Horizonte to Pirapora. Ring (031) 201-7144 in Belo Horizonte for more details and to confirm that the schedule hasn't changed. For more information regarding the history of the 'River of National Unity', see the Rio São Francisco section in the Bahia chapter.

Places to Stay

You'll see lots of hotels right next to the rodoviária but they're pretty dingy and the area is sleazy and red light after dark. However, there are lots of hotels that are centrally located and not too far from the rodoviária. Prices are generally inexpensive, and there are many cheap places. From the front of the rodoviária there are several hotels within 10 blocks along the following routes: walk down Avenida Santos Dumont and then turn right and go up Rua Espírito Santo; or walk down Avenida Afonso Pena, the major diagonal street.

Places to Stay – bottom end

Hotel Magalhães (☎ 222-9233) at Rua Espírito Santo 237 has singles/doubles for US$4/7 without bath, and doubles with bath for US$10. It is clean and comfortable.

Next door, *Hotel São Salvador* (☎ 222-7731) at Rua Espírito Santo 235 has singles/doubles for US$6/10 without bath and US$14 doubles with bath.

Youth Hostels There are two youth hostels in town: *Pousada Beagá* (☎ 275-3592) at Rua Timbiras 2330 and *Pousadinha Mineira* (☎ 446-2911), Rua Januária 206. Both charge US$6 per head.

Places to Stay – middle & top end

At Rua Espírito Santo 284, the *BH Centro* (☎ 222-3390) has singles/doubles without bath for US$10/14 and doubles with bath for US$25. The *Hotel Continental* (☎ 201-7944) at Avenida Paraná 241, in the centre, is a couple of blocks from the west side of Avenida Afonso Pena. It's clean, friendly,

not too noisy and some rooms have little balconies. Fifties-style apartamentos are a good deal at US$13/22.

The *Hotel Esplanada* (☎ 222-7411), a two-star Embratur hotel at Avenida Santos Dumont 304, charges US$13/17 for singles/doubles without bath or US$19/26 with bath. The *Brazil Palace Hotel* (☎ 273-3811) at Rua dos Carijos 269 has singles/doubles for US$20/26.

The *Hotel Amazonas* (☎ 201-4644) at Avenida Amazonas 120 is a classy three-star Embratur place. They charge US$52 for doubles with TV, air-con and balcony. In the centre, across from the park, the *Othon Palace* (☎ 273-3844) is Belo Horizonte's five-star hotel. It has singles/doubles for US$100/115.

Places to Eat

There are lots of lanchonetes and fast-food places clustered around Praça Sete – like *Bang Bang Burguer* (try saying that in Portuguese), where the waiters all wear cowboy hats, at Rua São Paulo 679. Wander around and see what you feel like.

For lunch, *Vida Campestre Natural* at Rua Afonso Pena 774 has good, cheap natural food. The *Dragon Centre* is a reasonable Chinese restaurant close to Praça Sete at Afonso Pena 549.

Most of the really flash restaurants are in the suburb of Savassí, and the Belotur monthly guide has a good listing.

Entertainment

Olimpia is a good dance spot at Avenida Olegário Maciel 1206, Lourdes. Danceterias in the centre include Champagne and Cassino, at Rua Rio de Janeiro 1245 and 1299 respectively. Right near the central hotels on Praça Sete is the Restaurante Praça 7, which has a beer-hall atmosphere with good local music from 10 pm to 3 am. If you can stand the horrible sound system, it's fun.

Cantina do Adnan is a somewhat sleazy place, but has some terrific, very unusual local music. It's a few blocks up from the Hotel Magalhães, on Rua Espírito Santo.

Things to Buy

The Centro de Artessanato Mineiro (☎ 222-2765) on Avenida Afonso Pena 1537, Palácio das Artes (at the edge of the Parque Municipal), has a varied assortment of mineiro crafts: ceramics, jewellery, tapestries, rugs, quilts and soapstone sculptures. It's open Saturday from 9 am to 8.45 pm and Sunday from 9 am to 1.45 pm. It's a government store.

The Gem Centre is not far from the municipal park, at Avenida Alvares Cabral 45. There are around 20 reputable gem dealers with small shops in the building.

There's a huge Feira de Arte e Artesano on Sundays from 9 am to 1 pm on Avenida Afonso Pena between Rua da Bahia and Rua Guajajaras, with good food and local crafts. If you're around check it out.

Getting There & Away

Air Belo Horizonte is connected to Rio and São Paulo by frequent one-hour VASP/Cruzeiro/Transbrasil *ponte aerea* (air bridge) flights. There are daily flights to just about anywhere in Brazil.

Transbrasil is at Rua dos Tamoios 86 (☎ 226-3433) and Confins airport (☎ 689-2475). Varig/Cruzeiro is at Rua Espírito Santo 643 (☎ 273-6566) and Confins airport (☎ 689-2244). The VASP office is at Rua dos Carijos 279 (☎ 335-9888) and the airport (☎ 689-2400).

Bus Buses take seven hours to Rio (US$7), 9½ to São Paulo (US$15), 12 hours to Brasília (US$20) and around 22 to Salvador (US$35). There are buses leaving every hour for Ouro Prêto. The first leaves at 6 am and the last at 8.15 pm. The trip takes 1¾ hours and costs US$4.

There are eight daily buses to Mariana, from 6 am to 11 pm. The two-hour trip costs US$4.50. Six daily make the 5½-hour run to Diamantina (US$10), the first at 5.30 am and the last at midnight. Seven daily go to São João del Rei, the first at 6.15 am and the last at 7 pm. From 1 am to midnight buses run to Sabará every 15 minutes. Catch this one

downstairs at the local bus section of the rodoviária.

If you're heading to the mineral spring resorts, there are four daily buses to Poços das Caldas (US$24), two to Caxambu (US$7), at 7.30 am and 11 pm, and three to São Lourenço (US$8), at 12.30 am, and 3 and 9.30 pm.

Getting Around

To/From the Airport There are two airports. Most planes use the new international Aeroporto Confins (also known as Aeroporto Tancredo Neves), which is 40 km from the city. The closer, sleepy Aeroporto da Pampulha has some of the Rio and São Paulo shuttle flights.

The best way to get to the airport is by bus from the rodoviária. There's a conventional bus that leaves every 30 minutes to one hour depending on the time, between 4.45 am and 10.30 pm; the trip costs US$1.50. Even though it's not advertised, this bus will stop at Aeroporto da Pampulha on the way to Aeroporto Confins – but make sure the driver knows your destination.

There is also an executivo bus that costs US$4 and is air-conditioned. It leaves from the executivo terminal every 45 minutes to one hour, between 5.15 am and 9.45 pm.

Historical Towns

SABARÁ

Sabará stands on the muddy banks of the Rio das Velhas (Old Ladies' River). It was the first major gold-mining centre in the state, and during its peak was one of the world's wealthiest towns. This is reflected in its houses, mansions, churches, statues, waterfountains and sacred art. It's now a poor town dominated by a Belgian metal works. In the boom years of the early 1700s, when the Rio das Velhas was 15 times wider, slave boats would sail all the way down the Rio São Francisco from Bahia. Sabará produced more gold in one week than the rest of Brazil produced in one year. You can still pan

Top: Igreja de Bom Jesus de Matinhos, Cogonhas, Minas Gerais (AD)
Left: Fountain in Ouro Prêto, Minas Gerais (WH)
Right: Street in Tiradentes, Minas Gerais (MS)

Top: CEAGESP Market, São Paulo (AD)
Bottom: São Paulo cityscape, viewed from Edifício Itália (AD)

the river bed for gold flakes, but the nuggets are long since gone.

Orientation & Information

There aren't any hotels or pensôes in Sabará, but since it's only 25 km and 30 minutes by bus from Belo Horizonte, it's an easy and interesting day trip. There's an information booth at the entrance to town, but it's useless. The major sights are signposted from Praça Santa Rita anyway.

Matriz de NS de Conceição

The Portuguese Jesuits, cultural ambassadors of the far-flung Portuguese Empire, were among the first Westerners to make contact with the Orient. As a result, the Matriz de NS de Conceição (1720) is a fascinating blend of Oriental arts and Portuguese baroque – overwhelming with its gold leaf and red Chinese scrolls.

Restationed in Brazil, the Jesuits brought the Oriental arts to Sabará, as is evident in the pagodas on some of the church door panels by the sanctuary. There are several other interesting little details in the church. Floorboards cover the graves of early church members. Gold and silver nuggets nailed on these tablets indicate whether the deceased was rich or poor.

On the ceiling of the church is the patron saint of confessors, John Nepomuceno of 14th-century Czechoslovakia, who is shown holding his tongue. King Wenceslau ordered St Nepumeco's tongue cut out because the saint refused to reveal whether or not the Moldavian queen was faithful. Nepumeco died of his wound but became very popular posthumously in Czechoslovakian cult circles and, inexplicably, in Minas Gerais during the gold era. Note the little angel at his side shushing churchgoers with a finger to his lips. The church is open from 8 am to noon and 2 to 6 pm daily. It's on Praça Getúlio Vargas.

Igreja de NS do Ó

Captain Lucas Ribeiro de Almeida survived an attack by his own troops in 1720 and built a chapel in thanks to the Virgin Mary. Like NS de Conceição, the chapel has Oriental details, and is just as popular with pregnant women (and those praying for fertility). Plain on the outside, gilded on the inside, the chapel gives no clues as to the meaning of its name, Our Lady of O. It's open from 8 am to noon and 2 to 6 pm.

Igreja de NS do Rosário

Only half built, this church on Praça Melo Viana was started and financed by slaves but never got finished. It now stands as a memorial to the abolition of slavery in 1888. Open daily from 8 am to noon and 2 to 6 pm.

Igreja NS do Carmo

Aleijadinho had a lot to do with the decoration of this church. His touch is everywhere, especially in the faces of the statues of São Simão and São João da Cruz. It's on Rua de Carmo.

O Teatro Imperial

Sabará has an elegant old opera house, O Teatro Imperial (1770). The crystal lamps and three tiers of seats in carved wood and bamboo cane are testimony to the wealth of days gone by. On Rua Dom Pedro 11, it's open Tuesday to Sunday from 8 am to 5 pm.

Gold Museum

Housed in an old gold foundry (1730), the Gold Museum, on Rua da Intendência, contains art and artefacts of Sabará's glory years, mostly related to the gold-mining industry. The museum is open Tuesday to Sunday from 8 am to 5 pm.

Places to Eat

This is a good opportunity to try a feijão mineiro with couve at *Restaurante 314* on Rua Commandante Viana 314. *Quinto do Ouro* at Rua Borba Gato 45 does a good frango com quiabo.

Getting There & Away

Viação Cisne buses shuttle the 25 km to Belo Horizonte. They leave every 15 minutes from the bus stop on Avenida Victor Fantini;

you can also catch one on the road out of town.

CONGONHAS

Little is left of Congonhas' colonial past except the extraordinary Prophets of Aleijadinho at the Basílica do Bom Jesus de Matosinhos. While the town is commonplace, these dramatic statues are exceptional. They are Aleijadinho's masterpiece and Brazil's most famed work of art. It's worth taking the trouble to get to Congonhas just to see them. Congonhas is 72 km south of Belo Horizonte, three km off BR-040. The city grew up with the search for gold in the nearby Rio Maranhão and is set in a broad valley. The economy today is dominated by iron mining in the surrounding countryside.

The 12 Prophets

Already an old man, sick and crippled, Aleijadinho sculpted the Prophets from 1800 to 1805. Symmetrically placed in front of the Basílica of Bom Jesus do Matosinhos, each of the prophets from the Old Testament was carved out of one or two blocks of soapstone. Each carries a message: six of them are good, six bad, and all are in Latin.

Much has been written about these sculptures: their dynamic quality, the sense of movement (many talk of the appearance they give of a Hindu dance or a ballet), how they complement each other and how their arrangement in front of the church prevents them from being seen in isolation. The poet Carlos Drummond de Andrade wrote that the dramatic faces and gestures are 'magnificent, terrible, grave and tender' and commented on 'the way the statues, of human size, appear to be larger than life as they look down upon the viewer with the sky behind them'.

Before working on the Prophets, Aleijadinho carved or supervised his assistants in carving the wooden statues which were placed in the six little chapels that represent the Passion of Christ: The Last Supper, Calvary, Imprisonment, Flagellation and Coronation, Carrying of the Cross and The Crucifixion.

Some of the figures, like the Roman soldiers, are very crude and clearly done by assistants, while others are finely chiselled. The statues were restored in 1957 by the painter Edson Mota and the gardens were designed by Burle Marx.

Festivals

From 7 to 14 September the Jubileu do Senhor Bom Jesus do Matosinhos is one of the great religious festivals in Minas Gerais. Each year, approximately 600,000 pilgrims arrive at the church to make promises and do penitence, receive blessings and give and receive alms. The Holy Week processions in Congonhas are also famous, especially the dramatisations on Good Friday.

Places to Stay & Eat

The *Colonial Hotel* (☎ (031) 731-1834) is antique and basic, but it has a pool and it's right across the street from the Prophets. Single rooms cost US$8/12 without/with bath, and doubles are US$16/24. There is a good restaurant, the *Cova do Daniel*, downstairs.

Do yourself a favour and don't stay in this town – there's nothing to keep you here after you've seen the Prophets.

Getting There & Away

If you get an early start, you can avoid spending a night in Congonhas. We've included detailed bus schedules to enable you to make quick connections.

There are six daily buses from Belo Horizonte to Congonhas (one hour and 40 minutes, US$4). The last return bus to Belo Horizonte leaves Congonhas at 8 pm. Buses leave every 30 minutes for Conselheiro Lafaiete, where you can get a midnight bus to Rio.

To get from Congonhas to Ouro Prêto you can go to Belo Horizonte or make a connection in Conselheiro Lafaiete. The latter route can be faster if you make a good connection. The drive from Lafaiete to Ouro Prêto is almost all dirt road; it's very slow and often crowded, but quite scenic, with a view of several large mining projects. Try to get to

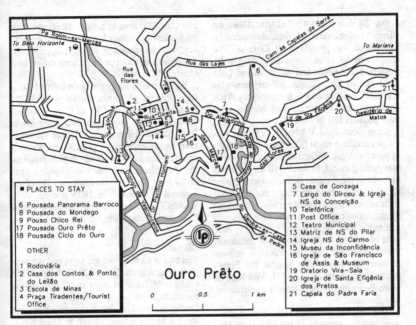

PLACES TO STAY

6 Pousada Panorama Barroco
8 Pousada do Mondego
9 Pouso Chico Rei
17 Pousada Ouro Prêto
18 Pousada Ciclo do Ouro

OTHER

1 Rodoviária
2 Casa dos Contos & Ponto do Leilão
3 Escola de Minas
4 Praça Tiradentes/Tourist Office

5 Casa de Gonzaga
7 Largo do Dirceu & Igreja NS da Conceição
10 Telefônica
11 Post Office
12 Teatro Municipal
13 Matriz de NS do Pilar
14 Igreja NS do Carmo
15 Museu da Inconfidência
16 Igreja de São Francisco de Assis & Museum
19 Oratorio Vira–Saia
20 Igreja de Santa Efigênia dos Pretos
21 Capela do Padre Faria

Ouro Prêto

0   0.5   1 km

Lafaiete a bit early to make sure you get a bus, although if you miss the last bus there are a couple of hotels across from the rodoviária.

From Lafaiete to Ouro Prêto is US$4 and 2½ hours. Buses run: Monday to Friday, at 7.15 and 9.40 am, noon, 3 and 6.45 pm; Saturday, at 7.15 am, noon, 3 and 6 pm; Sunday, at 6 am, 3 and 6 pm.

From Ouro Prêto to Lafaiete, buses leave Monday to Saturday at 5 (except Saturday) and 9 am, noon, 2.40 and 6 pm; on Sunday they leave at 6 am, noon, 2.40 and 6 pm.

There are no direct buses from Congonhas to São João del Rei, so catch a local or a Conselheiro Lafaiete bus to the turnoff at Murtinho. There's a Petrobras station there called Posto Queluz. Stand on the side of the road, where there are probably people already waiting, and catch a bus to São João – or to Lagoa Dourada, from where there are frequent buses to São João.

Getting Around

From the Congonhas rodoviária the 'Basílica' bus leaves every 30 minutes and costs 20c. It's a 15-minute ride up the hill to the basilica and the Prophets. Try to get off the bus just after passing the church, as it begins to go downhill, for the best approach and first view of the statues. The same bus returns you to the rodoviária.

OURO PRÊTO

History

According to the Jesuit Antonil, a mulatto servant in the Antonio Rodrigues Arzão expedition went to the rivulet Tripui to quench his thirst and pocketed a few grains of an odd black metal he found in the stream bed. The little nuggets were reported to the governor of Rio and turned out to be gold. The exact location of the river was forgotten during the long expedition and only the strange shape of the peaks of Itacolomy were remembered.

On 24 June 1698, Antônio Dias de Oliveira rediscovered the area, convinced he had found the promised El Dorado. The mines were the largest deposits of gold in the western hemisphere and the news and gold fever spread fast. Stories tell of men who acquired fabulous wealth from one day to the next, and others who died of hunger with their pockets full of gold.

King Dom João V back in Portugal was quick to claim a royal fifth in tax, and a chain of posts was established to ensure the crown was getting its cut. In theory, all the gold was brought to these *casas de intendencias* to be weighed and turned into bars, and the royal fifth set aside. Tax shirkers were cast into dungeons or exiled to Africa. One common technique used to avoid the tax was to hide gold powder in hollow images of the saints. Bitter over the tax, the Paulista miners rebelled unsuccessfully against the Portuguese. Two years later in 1711, Vila Rica de Ouro Prêto, the present town's predecessor, was founded.

The finest goods from India and England were made available to the simple mining town. The gold bought the services of baroque artisans, who turned the city into an architectural gem. At the height of the gold boom in the mid-18th century there were 110,000 people in Ouro Prêto (the vast majority of whom were slaves) versus 50,000 in New York and about 20,000 in Rio de Janeiro. The royal fifth, estimated at 100 tonnes of gold in the 18th century, quickly passed through the hands of the Portuguese court, built up Lisbon and then financed the British Industrial Revolution.

The greed of the Portuguese led to sedition on the part of the inhabitants of Vila Rica (1720). As the boom tapered off, the miners found it increasingly difficult to pay ever-larger gold taxes. In 1789, poets Claudio da Costa and Tomas Gonzaga, the dentist Tiradentes and others whose heads were full of the French revolutionary philosophies hatched the Inconfidência Mineira. This attempt to overthrow the Portuguese was crushed by agents of the crown in the early stages. Gonzaga was exiled to Mozambique,

and Costa did time in prison. Tiradentes, the only man not to deny his role in the conspiracy, was abandoned by his friends, jailed for three years without defence, then drawn and quartered.

By decree of Emperor Dom Pedro I, Vila Rica, capital of Minas Gerais since 1721, became the Imperial City of Ouro Prêto. In 1897 the state capital shifted from Ouro Prêto to Belo Horizonte. This was the decisive move that preserved Ouro Prêto's colonial flavour. The former capital assumes the symbolic role of state capital once a year on 24 June. The city was declared a Brazilian national monument in 1933 and in 1981 UNESCO proclaimed Ouro Prêto a World Cultural Heritage Site.

Climate

The city is a km above sea level and temperatures vary from 2°C to 28°C. Winters are pretty cold. It can be rainy and foggy all year round, but you can expect daily showers in December and January. Perhaps the best time to visit Minas is from March to August.

Orientation

The odd-shaped peak of Itacolomy (1752 metres), 18 km out of town, is the first clue that you're approaching Ouro Prêto. The first bandeirantes to penetrate the region used it as a reference point. Ouro Prêto is in the remote Serra do Espinhaço range.

Praça Tiradentes, a few blocks down from the rodoviária on the main road, is the town centre. Ouro Prêto is divided into two parishes. If you stand in Praça Tiradentes, facing the Museu da Inconfidência, the parish of Pilar is to the right, the parish of Antônio Dias to the left.

All of Ouro Prêto's streets have at least two names: the official one and the one used by the locals because the other one is too much of a mouthful. Rua Conde Bobadella, the street leading off to the right from Praça Tiradentes as you're facing the Museu da Inconfidência, is commonly known as Rua Direita. Similarly, Rua Conselheiro Quintiliano is Rua das Lajes and Rua Senador

Rocha Lagoa is Rua das Flores. To add to the confusion, the names are rarely posted.

The town is very hilly and the rain-slicked, cobblestone streets are extremely steep. Bring comfortable walking shoes with good tread.

If you plan to spend only one day in Ouro Prêto, make sure it's not a Monday, as almost all the museums and churches are closed then.

Information

Tourist Office The tourist office at Praça Tiradentes 41 is open from 8 am to 6 pm during the week and 8 am to 5 pm on weekends. English is spoken, and staff give out a leaflet which indicates the opening times of the museums and churches; they also sell good maps for US$2 and copies of the *Guia de Ouro Prêto* by Manuel Bandeira in Portuguese. It costs US$4. *Passeio a Ouro Prêto* by Lucia Machado de Almeida has sections in English, French and Portuguese and costs US$5. Also by the same author is the *Minas Gerais Roteiro Turistico-Cultural das Cidades Historicas* (Embratur-AGGS). I'd like to thank Embratur for permission to use this material when discussing the myths and legends of Ouro Prêto.

If you want to pack in a lot of sightseeing with little effort, hire an official guide (US$25 for a full-day tour) at the tourist office. Cássio is one who speaks excellent English and really knows his baroque. Beware of unofficial guides: there are some nasty characters hanging around.

Money The Banco do Brasil câmbio is at Rua São José 195, and most of the jewellery stores in town will change close to the parallel rate.

Post & Telephone The post office is in Rua Direita, on the right-hand side at the bottom of the hill as you walk down from Praça Tiradentes. The telefônica for long-distance calls is on the steep Rua das Flores, on the left as you walk down from the praça.

Things to See

Apart from Niemeyer's Grande Hotel Ouro Prêto and two other modern monstrosities, no 20th-century buildings defile this stunningly beautiful colonial city. Spend a day walking on the cobblestone roads around the dark rock walls of the village admiring its carved fountains, statues and crumbling orange-tiled roofs. Gaze through the mist at a skyline of bare green hills, church steeples and grey skies.

The following itinerary of sights was made keeping the quirky schedule of visiting hours in mind. The itinerary is crowded for one day of sightseeing, but if you hustle it's possible to see most of the sights in the Antônio Dias parish in the morning, lunch in or about Praça Tiradentes and spend the afternoon visiting the Pilar parish, and the Mineral and Inconfidência museums. Bear in mind that you need at least two days to see the town properly, and more if you intend to visit some of the other nearby historical towns.

Start at about 7.30 am from Praça Tiradentes and walk along Rua das Lajes, the road to Mariana, for a panoramic view of town.

Capela do Padre Faria

Work your way downhill off the road to this chapel. Padre Faria was one of the original bandeirantes, and the chapel (built between 1701 and 1704) is Ouro Prêto's oldest house of worship. The chapel is set behind a triple-branched papal cross (1756), the three branches representing the temporal, spiritual and material powers of the pope. It's the richest chapel in terms of gold and artwork, but unfortunately due to poor documentation the artists are anonymous. In 1750 the church bell rang for Tiradentes (when his body was brought to Rio); later, it rang once again for the inauguration of Brasília. Note that the angel on the right-hand side of the high altar has butterfly wings. The church is open from 8 am to noon.

Igreja de Santa Efigênia dos Prêtos

Descending the Ladeira do Padre Faria back

Chico-Rei

The first abolitionist in Brazil was Chico-Rei, an African tribal king. Amidst the frenzy of the gold rush an entire tribe, king and all, was captured in Africa, placed in chains, sent to Brazil and sold to a mine owner in Ouro Prêto. Chico-Rei worked as the foreman of the slave-miners. Working Sundays and holidays, he finally bought his freedom from the slave master, then freed his son Osmar. Together father and son liberated the entire tribe. The collective bought the fabulously wealthy Encardadeira gold mine and Chico-Rei assumed his royal functions, once again holding court in Vila Rica and celebrating African holidays in traditional costume. News of this reached the Portuguese king, who immediately prohibited slaves from purchasing their own freedom. Chico-Rei is a folk hero among Brazilian Blacks. ■

towards town, you'll come to the Igreja de Santa Efigênia dos Prêtos. The church was built between 1742 and 1749 by and for the Black slave community. Santa Efigênia, patron saint of the church, was the Queen of Nubia, and the featured saints, Santo Antônio do Nolo and São Benedito, are Black. The slaves prayed to these images that they wouldn't be crushed in the mines.

The church is Ouro Prêto's poorest in terms of gold and richest in artwork. The altar is by Aleijadinho's master, Francisco Javier do Briton. Many of the interior panels are by Manuel Rabelo de Souza (see if you can find the painting of Robinson Crusoe), and the exterior image of NS do Rosário is by Aleijadinho himself. The church was financed by gold extracted from Chico-Rei's gold mine, Encardadeira. Slaves contributed to the church coffer by washing their gold-flaked hair in baptismal fonts. Others managed to smuggle gold powder under fingernails and inside tooth cavities. The church is open from 8 am until noon.

Oratorio Vira-Saia

At the beginning of the 18th century there was a rash of ghost incidents in the city. Phantoms would spring from the walls near Santa Efigênia church and wing through town spooking the townspeople. The simple village folk would faint and drop their bags of gold powder, which the bandit-like ghosts would snatch. The terrorised people asked the bishop for permission to build oratories and the bishop complied. Designed to keep evil spirits at bay, the oratories (glass-encased niches containing images of saints)

were built on many street corners. Not many oratories remain, but there's one on Rua dos Paulistas (also called Bernardo Vasconcelos) and another on Antônio Dias; the most famous one of all is the Oratorio Vira-Saia. Nowadays these few remaining oratories are used to scare off evil spirits during Holy Week.

The small oratory of Vira-Saia is at the bottom of the Ladeira de Santa Efigênia (also known as Vira-Saia), on the corner with Rua Barão do Ouro Branco. *Vira-saia* has two possible meanings: it either originates from the Portuguese *virar* (turn) and *sair* (depart) or is the direct translation of vira-saia, which means turncoat or traitor.

In the latter part of the 18th century, gold caravans destined for the Portuguese crown were robbed on a regular basis, despite measures to cloak shipments by altering dates and routes. It didn't take long to surmise that it was an inside job. Someone working in the Casa de Fundição was leaking information.

Who would suspect that Antônio Francisco Alves, pillar of the community, upstanding citizen, mild-mannered businessman and gentle father, was in reality the head and brains behind the Vira-Saia bandits – the very same outfit which looted the government's gold caravans? After a caravan's route was planned, Alves would steal out to the oratory and turn the image of NS das Almas within the sanctuary to face the direction of the gold traffic.

The plot thickened. A reward was posted for revealing the secret identity of the criminal. Finally a member of Alves' own band, Luis Gibut, turned him in. Gibut was a

French Jesuit who fell in love with a beautiful woman, abandoned the order, became a highway bandit and the turncoat's turncoat. This same Luis Gibut was responsible for teaching Aleijadinho misspelled Latin phrases which the artist incorporated into many of his works.

Alves, his wife and his daughters were dragged off into the jungle to meet their fate. Sra Duruta, a good neighbour, came to the rescue and saved Alves, but it was too late for his wife and kids. Alves was one step ahead of the long arm of the law, but he didn't get off scot free. Shortly afterwards, he was plugged by another unnamed Vira-Saia. The criminal gang continued to do successful robberies without its first chief. Luis Gibut, ex-Jesuit, traitor and poor speller, is probably still doing time in purgatory.

Largo do Dirceu

Largo do Dirceu is next, just before you get to the Igreja Matriz NS da Conceição de Antônio Dias. This used to be a popular hangout of the poet Tomás Antônio Gonzaga and his girlfriend and muse, Marília. It figures prominently in *Marília de Dirceu*, the most celebrated poem in the Portuguese language.

Matriz NS da Conceição de Antônio Dias & Around

The cathedral of the Antônio Dias parish, Matriz NS da Conceição de Antônio Dias, was designed by Aleijadinho's father, Manuel Francisco Lisboa, and built between the years 1727 and 1770. Note the painting of the eagle: its head points downwards, symbolising the domination of the Moors by the Christians. Aleijadinho is buried by the altar of Boa Morte. The cathedral is open from 8 to 11.30 am and 1 to 5 pm.

The Museu do Aleijadinho adjoins the church and has the same hours. Nearby is Encardideira, the abandoned mine of Chico-Rei. Ask around for directions. It's rumoured to be haunted, dangerous, full of crumbling secret passageways and ripe for an Indiana Jones adventure.

Casa de Tomás Antônio Gonzaga

Rua do Ouvidor 9 is the address of Tomás Antônio Gonzaga's house, now the seat of the municipal government. Back in 1789, the gold tax and antimonarchist sentiment in Minas were rising concurrently. This is where Gonzaga, his poet-friend Claudio da Costa (author of *Vila Rica*), Tiradentes the dentist and others conspired unsuccessfully to overthrow the Portuguese monarchy. The sad little event came to be known as the Inconfidência Mineira.

Igreja de São Francisco de Assis

Across the street from Gonzaga's house is the Igreja de São Francisco de Assis. After the Prophets in Congonhas, Aleijadinho's masterwork, it is the single most important piece of Brazilian colonial art. The entire exterior, a radical departure from the military baroque style, was carved by Aleijadinho alone, from the soapstone medallion to the cannon waterspouts and the military (two-bar) cross. The interior was painted by Aleijadinho's long-term partner, Manuel da Costa Ataíde.

The sacristy is haunted by the spirit of an 18th-century woman. In the dead of night her head dissolves into a skull and she screams, 'I'm dying, call Father Carlos!'. The church and adjoining Aleijadinho museum is open from 8 to 11.30 am and 1 to 5 pm.

Praça Tiradentes

Praça Tiradentes is the centre of town and a good place to have lunch, catch your breath by the statue of Tiradentes or take in some museums before the churches of the Pilar parish open in the afternoon.

The Museu da Inconfidência, formerly the old municipal building and jail, is an attractive civic building built between 1784 and 1854. Used as a prison from 1907 until 1937, the museum contains the Tiradentes tomb, documents of the Inconfidência Mineira, torture instruments and important works by Ataíde and Aleijadinho. The museum is open noon to 5.30 pm.

Aleijadinho

The church of São Francisco de Assis, the Carmo church facade, the Prophets of Congonhas do Campos and innumerable relics in Mariana, Sabará, Tiradentes and São João del Rei were all carved by Aleijadinho (Antonio Francisco Lisboa). Brazil's Michelangelo lost the use of his hands and legs at the age of 30 but, with hammer and chisel strapped to his arms, advanced art in Brazil from the excesses of the baroque to a finer, more graceful rococo. The Mineiros have reason to be proud of Aleijadinho – he is a figure of international prominence in the history of art. Aleijadinho angels have his stylistic signature: wavy hair, wide-open eyes and big, round cheeks.

The son of a Portuguese architect and a Black slave, Aleijadinho lived from 1730 to 1814 and was buried in the Matriz NS da Conceição, within 50 paces of his birth site. By federal decree he was declared patron of Brazilian arts in 1973. For many years Manuel da Costa Ataíde, from nearby Mariana, successfully collaborated with Aleijadinho on many churches: Aleijadinho would sculpt the exterior and a few interior pieces, and Ataíde would paint interior panels. With his secretly concocted vegetable dyes, Costa the colour man fleshed out much of Aleijadinho's work. ■

Igreja NS do Carmo

The Igreja NS do Carmo was a group effort by the most important artists of the area. Begun in 1766 and completed in 1772, the church features a facade by Aleijadinho. It's open 8 to 11.30 am and 1 to 5.30 pm.

Casa de Tiradentes

The home of Joaquim Jose da Silva Xavier (better known as Tiradentes – Toothpuller) is nearby. After his failed rebellion against the Portuguese and execution in Rio, his head was paraded around town, his house was demolished and the grounds were salted so that nothing would grow there.

Escola de Minas

The Escola de Minas in the old governor's palace in Praça Tiradentes has a very fine museum of mineralogy. It's open noon to 5 pm, Monday to Friday.

Casa dos Contos

The Casa dos Contos (Counting House) is now a public library and art gallery. Claudio da Costa was imprisoned here after participating in the Inconfidência Mineira. It is open 12.30 to 5 pm. Next door is the old Ponto do Leilão, where slaves were taken to be tortured.

Matriz de NS do Pilar

The Matriz de NS do Pilar is the second most opulent church in Brazil (after Salvador's São Francisco) in terms of gold, with 434 kg of gold and silver and one of Brazil's finest showcases of artwork. Note the wild bird chandelier holders, the laminated beaten gold, the scrolled church doors, 15 panels of Old and New Testament scenes by Pedro Gomes Chaes, and the hair on Jesus (the real stuff, donated by a penitent worshipper).

Legend has it that both the Pilar and Antônio Dias parishes vied for the image of

NS dos Passos. In order to settle the argument, the image was loaded on a horse standing in Praça Tiradentes and rockets were fired to scare the horse; the idea was that the image would belong to the parish to which the horse bolted. Since the horse only knew one path it galloped straight to the Matriz do Pilar. The church is open from noon to 5 pm.

Teatro Municipal

Built in 1769 by João de Souza Lisboa, the Teatro Municipal is the oldest theatre in Minas Gerais and perhaps in all of Brazil. The theatre is open to visitors from 1 to 5 pm.

Other Attractions

This is only a partial list of places to see in Ouro Prêto. If you're still enthusiastic for more, the tourist office can sell you some fine guidebooks. If you're after something more strenuous, hike to the peak of Itacolomy; it takes three hours to walk the 18 km from Praça Tiradentes.

Parque Itacolomy (easiest approach from Mariana) is a pleasant excursion – the park has good walking trails, waterfalls and orchids, and the colonial town of Mariana is only 12 km away. Buses leave every half-hour.

Festivals

The Semana Santa (Holy Week) procession held on the Thursday before Palm Sunday and sporadically until Easter Sunday is quite a spectacle. The Congado is to Minas what Candomblé is to Bahia and Umbanda is to Rio: the local expression of African-Christian syncretism. The major Congado celebrations are for NS do Rosário on 23 to 25 October (at the Capela do Padre Faria), for the New Year and for 13 May, the anniversary of abolition.

The Cavalhada held in Amarantina (near Ouro Prêto) during the Festa de São Gonçalo from 17 to 23 September isn't as grand as the one in Pirenópolis, but is impressive nonetheless. The Cavalhada is a re-enactment of the battles between Christians and Moors in Iberia.

Places to Stay – bottom end

Ouro Prêto is a university town with schools of pharmacy and biochemistry, mineralogy, geology and engineering. No less than 20% of the homes in Ouro Prêto are devoted to student lodging known as repúblicas. Although they are the cheapest places to stay in town, most of the repúblicas are closed from Christmas to Carnival. Another problem with repúblicas is their lack of security, as they put strangers together in the same room. From a security point of view, I wouldn't recommend staying in one. For an extra couple of dollars you're better off in a pousada. The tourist office has a complete list of places to stay, including the cheapest, and they'll ring around to find a vacancy for you. On weekends, holidays and during exam periods, the town gets crowded, but finding a room shouldn't be a problem.

A selection of good pousadas includes the *Pousada Panorama Barroco* (☎ 551-3366), only a 15-minute walk from the bus station or 10 minutes from Praça Tiradentes, at Rua das Lajes 722. It's run by David, an Arizonian, and his Brazilian wife Lucia. Apart from having the best view in town, their charming place is set up with the traveller in mind: video player, washing machine and dryer, book exchange and even a telescope for baroque voyeurs. They also sell Indian crafts and mineral specimens for the collector and do trips into the countryside. They charge US$7 per person, which includes a good breakfast.

Another pousada worth checking out is *Pousada Ouro Prêto* (☎ 551-3081), Largo Musicista José das Anjos Costa (also called das Mercês) 72, right in front of Igreja NS das Mercês. It's another friendly place, and Gerson, who runs it, speaks English. He charges US$7 per person as well.

Youth Hostel The youth hostel, *Pousada Ciclo do Ouro* (☎ 551-3201) at Rua Felipe dos Santos 241, is a small, friendly, family-run place that charges US$6 for members and US$8 for others. They also have a lanchonete with good snacks.

Places to Stay – middle

There are a number of mid-range hotels closer to the centre of town. *Hotel Pilão* (☎ 551-3066), Praça Tiradentes 57, has quartos for US$10/12 a single/double and apartamentos for US$13/15. *Hotel Colonial* (☎ 551-3133) at Travessa Camilo Veloso 26 has apartamentos for US$16/23 a single/double.

Places to Stay – top end

Pouso Chico Rei (☎ 551-1274), Rua Brigideiro Mosqueira 90, has wonderful doubles completely furnished in antiques for US$30 without bath and US$44 with bath. If you're lucky, there's one single room for US$13. Reserve way in advance. *Pousada do Mondego* (☎ 551-2040), Largo do Coimbra 38, is close to Igreja São Francisco; it's in an 18th-century colonial mansion. Singles are US$70 and doubles are US$80, a bit more if you want the view. This is an excellent top-end choice.

Places to Eat

Most of the restaurants are clustered in two areas: along Rua Direita and Rua São José. It's really just a matter of deciding what you want to eat. Ouro Prêto is a good place to try some regional cooking. One typical Minas dish is tutu a mineira, a black bean feijoada with couve, a type of kale. *Restaurante Casa Do Ouvidor* on Rua Direita is the place to try it. If the mineiro food is a bit heavy for you, *Cheiro Verde* is the natural food restaurant in town. It's at Rua Getúlio Vargas 248, close to the Rosário church, and is closed on Mondays.

Entertainment

The kids hang out in Praça Tiradentes before thronging to Club Ouro Prêto for some slow and steamy dancing. It's open Saturday and Sunday nights from 8 to 11 pm.

Things to Buy

A soapstone quarry 28 km away in Santa Rita de Ouro Prêto provides endless supplies for attractive Henry Moore-style carvings, and imitations of Aleijadinho. Unglazed ceramics, woodcarvings and basketwork are sold in the souvenir shops of Praça Tiradentes. Wilson Prolin, a fine local painter, has a studio in town.

Although imperial topaz is found only in this area of Brazil, don't buy any here unless you are knowledgeable about gem stones. The larger firms in Rio and São Paulo, like Stern, Roditi and Amsterdam Sauer, are more trustworthy.

Getting There & Away

There are 11 buses a day from Belo Horizonte to Ouro Prêto. The first bus leaves at 6.45 am and the last bus at 10.15 pm (98 km, 1¾-hour trip). During the peak tourist period, buy bus tickets at least a day in advance, or you may find yourself without a ride. Nine buses a day make the seven-hour trip to Rio for US$13.

Around Ouro Prêto

Minas de Passagem I got a kick out of Minas de Passagem. It is probably the best gold mine to visit in the Ouro Prêto region. The immense system of tunnels goes way down deep, then spreads horizontally. Only a fraction of the mine is open to the public, but for most terrestrials it's enough. The descent into the mine is made in an antique, steam-powered cable car (though the guide is quick to assure you that the cable itself is new) that gives you a very good idea of just how dangerous and claustrophobic mining can be.

The mine was opened in 1719. Until the abolition of slavery it was worked by Black slaves, many of whom died (not from the cable car ride as you might think after taking it, but from the job of dynamiting into the rock). My guide, who had been working in the mine as recently as 1985, and was then earning the minimum wage of US$35 a month, told us that the life of the 'free' miner was little better than that of the slave.

The mandatory guided tour, led by former miners, is short and quite informative, especially if someone in the group asks the right questions. The mine is open from 9 am to 6 pm daily and the entry fee is US$7.

The mine is between Ouro Prêto and Mariana. Take any local bus that runs between the two and ask the driver to let you off at Minas de Passagem.

MARIANA

Mariana is a beautiful old mining town with a character unlike its busy neighbour, Ouro Prêto. Only 12 km by paved road from Ouro Prêto, Mariana is touristed but not overrun. Founded in 1696, it retains the high-altitude tranquillity of many of the mining towns and is a great place in which to unwind. It's also a good place in which to stay if you want to avoid Ouro Prêto by night.

Information

The tourist terminal, where the bus from Ouro Prêto will stop, contains an information office which sells maps (US$2) and guide books in Portuguese. This is the place to arrange a guide if you want one.

Things to See

There are plenty of interesting sights. The 18th-century churches of São Pedro dos Clérigos, NS da Assunção, São Francisco, and the Catedral Basílica da Sé, with its fantastic German organ dating from 1701, are all worth while. The museum at Casa Capitular is also worth a look. While walking through the old part of town, you'll come across painters and wood sculptors at work in their studios.

Places to Stay

Hotel Providência (☎ 557-1444), Rua Dom Silveiro 233, is an interesting cheapie. Originally the living quarters for nuns, who still run a school next door, there is a chapel if you're feeling pious and an excellent swimming pool with individual changing boxes. You have to go through the school to get to it, so don't walk around in your swimming gear or the nuns might have heart attacks. Quartos are US$7 per person and apartamentos US$9.

Hotel Central (☎ 557-1630), Rua Frei Durão 8, is a real budget hotel with quartos for US$5/8 a single/double. *Hotel Faisca*

(☎ 557-1206), Rua Antônio Olinto 48, is similarly priced. *Hotel Muller* (☎ 557-1188), Avenida Getúlio Vargas 34, is US$11 for a single room.

The best hotel in town is the *Pouso da Typographia* (☎ 557-1577) at Praça Gomes Freire 220. It's worth going in just to look at the two antique printing presses in the foyer. Singles/doubles cost US$36/52, but you can get the price down during the week.

Places to Eat

Portão da Praça, on Praça Gomes Freire at No 108, serves excellent regional food and tasty Sirio/Lebanese sandwiches if you want something lighter. *Papinna Della Nonna* at Rua Dom Viçoso 27 is Mariana's Italian restaurant and a good one at that; it's very close to Praça Gomes Freire. *Restaurante Tambaú*, near the town square, also has good regional cooking at reasonable prices.

Getting There & Away

A bus leaves Ouro Prêto for Mariana every 30 minutes from the far side of the Escola de Minas. The trip takes 35 to 40 minutes. There are direct buses from Mariana to Belo Horizonte, 113 km away.

SÃO JOÃO DEL REI

One of Minas Gerais' original gold towns, São João del Rei is a thriving small city with an old central section with several of Brazil's finest churches. With hotels and sights all within walking range in the old city centre, there's little cause to see the more modern part of town; nevertheless, it's evident that the city hasn't been frozen in time, unlike most of the other historic cities of Minas Gerais.

The old section is protected by Brazil's Landmarks Commission and police guard the churches at night. The city is cut in half by Rio Lenheiro, which is traversed by two 18th-century stone bridges. In addition to the Aleijadinho-inspired churches, there are several fine colonial mansions – one of which belonged to the late and still popular Tancredo Neves – a good museum, and a

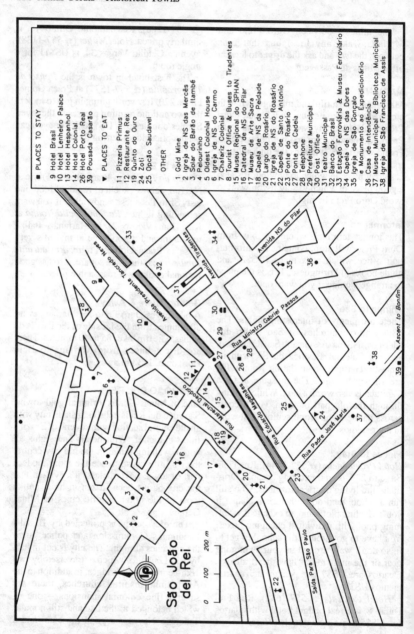

São João del Rei

0   100   200 m

■ PLACES TO STAY
9 Hotel Brasil
10 Hotel Lenheiro Palace
13 Hotel Hespanhol
14 Hotel Colonial
26 Hotel Porto Real
39 Pousada Casarão

▼ PLACES TO EAT
11 Pizzeria Primus
12 Restaurante Rex
19 Quinto do Ouro
24 Zoti
25 Opção Saudavel

OTHER
1 Gold Mine
2 Igreja de NS das Mercês
3 Solar do Barão de Itambé
4 Pelourinho
5 Oldest Colonial House
6 Igreja de NS do Carmo
7 Chafariz Colonial
8 Tourist Office & Buses to Tiradentes
15 Museu Regional do SPHAN
16 Catedral de NS do Pilar
17 Museu de Arte Sacra
18 Capela de NS da Peidade
20 Largo do Rosário
21 Igreja de NS do Roasário
22 Capela de Santo Antonio
23 Ponte do Rosário
27 Ponte da Cadeia
28 Telephone
29 Prefeitura Municipal
30 Post Office
31 Teatro Municipal
32 Banco do Brasil
33 Estação Ferroviária & Museu Ferroviário
34 Capela de NS das Dores
35 Igreja de São Gonçalo
36 Casa de Intendência
   e Monumento ao Expedicionário
37 Museu Municipal & Biblioteca Municipal
38 Igreja de São Francisco de Assis

surprising variety of other sites and activities.

The city sits between the Serra de São José and Serra do Lenheiro, near the southern end of the Serra do Espinhaço. It's hilly country near the Rio das Mortes (River of the Dead), where many prospectors were killed during the gold rush days. The most famous incident took place in 1708, when a band of Emboadas, recent Portuguese immigrants, surrounded about 50 Paulistas or bandeirantes, natives of São Paulo of mixed Portuguese and Indian blood. The Paulistas were massacred after laying down their arms in surrender. This was the bloodiest atrocity in the near civil war that these two groups fought over control of the mines; the place where it happened is called the Capão da Traição (Copse of Treason).

Orientation

The city is sandwiched between two hills, both of which provide excellent views, particularly at sunset. The Cristo Redentor monument, overlooking the city, stands on one hill and the Capelinha do Senhor do Bonfim on the other. Both hilltops are the last stop for the local city bus 'Sr dos Montes', which leaves from in front of the train station.

Information

Tourist Office The tourist information office is in the Terminal Turistico in Praça Antonio Vargas, a block from Avenida Presidente Tancredo Neves. It's open from 6 am until 6 pm. Bosco Tavares, who works there, speaks English and is very helpful. This is also where you catch the bus to Tiradentes.

Money There's a Banco do Brasil on Avenida Ermilia Alves and the BEMGE state bank has a câmbio close to the Hotel Lenheiro Palace.

Post & Telephone The post office is on Avenida Tiradentes. There are telephone posts on Rua Gabriel Passos and at the rodoviária for long-distance calls.

Churches

Floodlights illuminate the churches at night and give them a fantastic appearance. Be sure to take a walk at night.

Igreja de São Francisco de Assis This exquisite baroque church, full of curves and carvings, looks out on a palm-tree-lined plaza shaped like a lyre. Begun in 1774, the church was Aleijadinho's first complete project, but much of his plan was not realised. Still, the exterior, with an Aleijadinho sculpture of the Immaculate Virgin and several angels, is one of the finest in Minas. There is some uncertainty about what work Aleijadinho did and did not do on the interior. He probably did the main altar, but his work was completely altered. In the second altar to the left there is an image of São João Evangelista which is the work of Aleijadinho, as is the Santo Antonio. Notice the fine woodwork, particularly in the rear of the church.

Tancredo Neves, the man who led Brazil from military rule, is buried in the graveyard out the back.

The church is open from 8.30 am to noon and 1.30 to 6 pm. On Sundays the local Coalhada (all-White) orchestra and choir perform at the 9.15 am mass.

Igreja de NS do Carmo Begun in 1732, this church was designed by Aleijadinho. He also did the frontispiece and sculpture around the door. In the second sacristy is a famous unfinished Christ. The church is open from 4 to 7 pm.

Catedral de NS do Pilar Begun in 1721, this church has exuberant gold altars. There are also fine Portuguese tiles. The mulatta Rapadura orchestra and choir accompany the 7 pm mass here on Wednesday. On Thursday and Friday the Coalhada takes their place. The church is open from 7 to 11 am and 2 to 4 pm.

Catedral de NS do Rosário This simple church was built in 1719 to honour the protector of the slaves. It's open from 9 to 11 am.

Museums

Museu Regional do SPHAN One of the best museums in Minas Gerais, this well-restored, 1859 colonial mansion has good sacred art on the first two floors and an industrial section on the 3rd floor with tools and instruments. It's open from noon to 5.30 pm daily except Mondays.

Museu Ferroviário Train freaks take heart: you are one with the Mineiros, who also love their trains. Expertly renovated, the railway museum has a wealth of artefacts and information about the old train days in the late 19th century. It's in the train station. Don't forget to walk down the track to the large rotunda that looks like a coliseum: it houses the trains and is the best part of the museum. The museum costs 50c and is open Tuesday to Sunday from 8 am to 5 pm, though it's sometimes closed for lunch.

Museu do Estanho John Somers This is a pewter factory with a display and store for visitors. It's owned by an Englishman (there is a small English community in São João). The museum is down the river towards the rodoviária at Avenida Leite de Castro 1150. It is open daily from 8 am to 6 pm.

Museu de Arte Sacra Open daily except Monday from 8 am to 5 pm, the museum has a small but impressive collection of art from the city's churches. Look closely at the figure of Christ mourned by Mary Magdalene and you'll see that the drops of blood are rubies.

Mina de Ouro-Tancredo Neves

This former gold mine is a thin wedge that descends 53 metres through solid rock. Apart from the adrenalin rush you get from going into the mine, it's an interesting demonstration of the regional mining techniques. Very impressive, and free.

Wear decent walking shoes and follow the signs from town till you reach a steep hill. Walk up the hill into the favela and turn left along the footpath. The mine is right there behind the 'Exportak' sign.

Maria Fumaça Train

Chugging along at 25 km/h on the steam-powered Maria Fumaça along a picturesque stretch of track from São João to Tiradentes makes a great 30-minute train ride. The line has operated nonstop since 1881 with the same Baldwin locomotives and is in perfect condition after being restored. The 76-cm gauge track stretches 13 km between the two towns.

The train runs only on Fridays, Saturdays, Sundays and holidays, leaving São João at 10 am and 2.15 pm and returning from Tiradentes at 1 and 5 pm. This schedule often changes, so it's best to double-check. The train is often crowded, so get there early. It costs US$2.50. Going to Tiradentes, sit on the left side for a better view. Don't forget that if you're only going to Tiradentes for the day and need more time than the return train allows, you can easily take a later bus back to São João.

Festivals

São João has a very lively Carnival – the locals claim it's the best in Minas Gerais. With all the music in town – there's a school of music and several bands and orchestras – it's a credible boast. The Semana da Inconfidência from 15 to 21 April celebrates Brazil's first independence movement and the hometown boys who led it (it's also held in Tiradentes).

Another important festival is the Inverno Cultural, during July, when there is lots of theatre, concerts, dances, etc. The list of festivals just goes on and on – 15 religious and 10 secular on one calendar – so stop by the tourist office to get a calendar of events; there's a good chance someone is celebrating something in São João.

Places to Stay – bottom end

There is a good stock of inexpensive hotels in the old section of the city, right where you want to be. The *Hotel Brasil* (☎ 371-2804), just around the corner from the Terminal

Turistico at Avenida Presidente Tancredo Neves 395 facing the river, is a former grand hotel and is a real bargain at US$3 a single.

The historic *Hotel Colonial* (☎ 371-1792) is clean, if a bit funky, and very colonial. Rooms without bath go for US$5 a person and most have a view of the river. The *Aparecida Hotel* (☎ 371-1548), right next to the Terminal Turistico, has singles for US$4; it's not bad if the other hotels are full. The *Hotel Hespanhol* (☎ 371-4677) at Rua Marechal Deodoro 131 has quartos for US$7/14 a single/double and apartamentos for US$10/20. All rooms are clean and relatively spacious.

Places to Stay – top end

The *Hotel Lenheiro Palace* (☎ 371-3914), facing the river at Avenida Presidente Tancredo Neves 257, has charm and style for US$32 a single and US$42 a double. Up the hill behind the Igreja de São Francisco is the *Pousada Casarão* (☎ 371-1224), at Rua Ribeiro Bastos 94. Like many of Minas' elegant mansions turned pousada, this place is exquisite. There is a small swimming pool and the cost is US$20/28 for singles/doubles.

The *Hotel Porto Real* (☎ 371-1201) is São João's modern hotel – it's also the biggest eyesore on the riverfront. They have singles/doubles for US$32/35.

Places to Eat

Pizzeria Primus has good pizza – try the primus special. It's open late at Rua Arthur Bernardes 97. The *Cantina do Italo* on Rua Ministro Gabriel Passos has a good reputation for pasta. For regional cooking try *Restaurante Rex* at Rua Arthur Bernardes 137, *Quinto do Ouro* at Praça Severiano de Resende 4 or *Gruta Mineira* on Marechal Deodoro.

For a vegetarian lunch and a good juice, *Opção Saudavel*, Avenida Tiradentes 792, has a set menu, but you need to drop in at least an hour before to tell them you're coming, because they bring the food from home. On the same street, *Zoti* is a lively late-night place for beer and light meals.

Entertainment

The music of Minas is extremely good and different from anything else you've ever heard. Try the Teatro Municipal for weekend concerts. The restaurant Cabana da Espanhola has live music Thursday to Sunday. It's at Avenida 31 de Março. Another central place to try is Feitiç O Mineiro, near the Catedral do Pilar; it's open from Wednesday to Friday.

Getting There & Away

Bus The long and winding road from Rio to São João traverses the Serra da Mantiqueira. The roads and scenery are good on this 5½-hour bus ride. São João is 190 km south of Belo Horizonte, 3½ hours away by bus.

Buses leave Rio direct for São João daily at 9 am, and 4 and 11 pm. The return bus from São João to Rio leaves at 8 am, 4 and 11.30 pm Monday to Saturday, and at 4, 10 and 11.30 pm Sunday. The fare is US$9. There are also frequent buses to Juiz de Fora, where you can then transfer to a São João or Rio bus.

From São João to Belo Horizonte – via Lagoa Dourada – there are seven buses a day. From Monday to Friday, the first bus leaves at 6 am and the last at 6.30 pm. There are extra buses on Sunday night until 10 pm. The trip takes 3½ hours and costs US$6. This is also the bus to Congonhas, two hours and US$4 down the road. You won't be able to buy a ticket directly to Congonhas, but ask for a ticket there anyway. Let the driver know you are going to Congonhas and you'll be dropped off at the Congonhas turnoff. From there you can either wait for a local bus, or cross the road where you see a statue and walk 500 metres down to the rodoviária on the right-hand side to catch a 'Basilica' local bus.

For the quickest route to Ouro Prêto, catch a bus to Conselheiro Lafaiete and from there take the bus to Ouro Prêto (for schedules see the Congonhas section).

Train For details of the picturesque train ride to Tiradentes, see the earlier section on the Maria Fumaça Train.

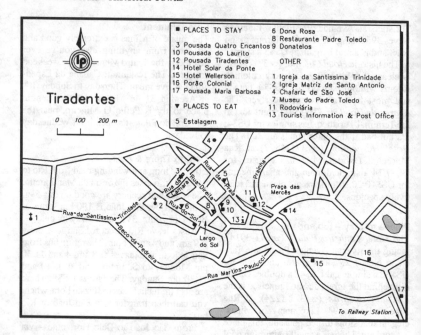

Tiradentes

0   100   200 m

■ PLACES TO STAY

3 Pousada Quatro Encantos
10 Pousada do Laurito
12 Pousada Tiradentes
14 Hotel Solar da Ponte
15 Hotel Wellerson
16 Porão Colonial
17 Pousada Maria Barbosa

▼ PLACES TO EAT

5 Estalagem

6 Dona Rosa
8 Restaurante Padre Toledo
9 Donatelos

OTHER

1 Igreja da Santissima Trinidade
2 Igreja Matriz de Santo Antonio
4 Chafariz de São José
7 Museu do Padre Toledo
11 Rodoviária
13 Tourist Information & Post Office

Getting Around

The yellow local buses will get you to the rodoviária in 10 minutes. They leave from the small bus stop in front of the train station. You can also take a taxi for US$4. To get to the Terminal Turistico from the rodoviária, catch any yellow bus from the bus stop to your left as you walk out, not from the more obvious one directly in front. All of them stop at the Terminal Turistico.

TIRADENTES

They don't make 'em any prettier than Tiradentes. Ten km down the valley from São João del Rei, its gold-era rival, colonial Tiradentes sits on a hill below a mountain. With few signs of change over the last two centuries, the town has that magic quality of another age – and for some odd reason that's a very good feeling.

Originally called Arrail da Ponta do Morro (Hamlet on a Hilltop), Tiradentes was renamed to honour the martyred hero of the Inconfidência, who was born at a nearby farm. The town's colonial buildings run up a hillside, where they culminate in the beautiful Igreja Matriz de Santo Antonio. If you stand between the church's Aleijadinho-carved frontispiece and famous sundial, there is a colourful view of the terracotta-tiled colonial houses, the green valley and the towering wall of stone formed by the Serra São Jose.

Information

Tourist Office The Secretaria de Turismo is at Rua Resende Costa 71. You can't miss it as it's the only three-storey building in town. The staff have maps and other useful information. Luiz Cruz speaks good English and is very helpful. Ask about guides and walks into the surrounding mountains. The post office is in the same building.

Igreja Matriz de Santo Antônio

In 1710 construction began on this church,

which is named after the town's patron saint; it is built on the site of a former church. Restored in 1983, this is one of Brazil's most beautiful churches. There are two bell towers and a frontispiece by Aleijadinho, one of the last that he completed. Leandro Gonçalves Chaves made the sundial in front of the church in 1785.

The inside is all gold, and rich in symbols from the Old Testament. There is a painting by João Batista showing the miracle of Santo Antonio making a donkey kneel before the pope. There is also a polychrome organ built in Portugal and brought to Tiradentes by donkey in 1798. Ask about performances. The church is open from 8 am to 5 pm but usually closes from noon till 1 pm for lunch.

Museu do Padre Toledo

This museum is dedicated to another hero of the Inconfidência, Padre Toledo, who lived in this 18-room house where the Inconfidêntes first met. The museum features regional antiques and documents from the 18th century.

Igreja da Santissima Trindade

After a short walk on Rua da Santissima Trindade, you arrive at this simple pilgrimage church. Dating from 1810, it was built on the site of a small chapel where Tiradentes chose the triangle, symbolising the holy trinity, as the flag for the new nation.

Solar da Ponte

This colonial mansion, now an expensive hotel, is impeccably restored and decorated and is well worth walking through. It's the first building on the other side of the little stone bridge and it's marked by a small sign.

Chafariz de São José

Constructed by the town council in 1749, this beautiful fountain has three sections, one for drinking, one for washing clothes and one for watering horses. The water comes from Mãe d'Agua via an old stone pipeline.

Serra de São Jose

This area is one of the remaining untouched segments of Atlantic rainforest in Minas. Mãe d'Agua is at the base of these mountains. Lush with moss and plants, the waters are clear and fresh. A 25-minute walk from Tiradentes, Mãe d'Agua can also be reached by car. Other walks include: A Calçada, a stretch of the old road that linked Ouro Prêto with Rio de Janeiro; Cachoeiras do Mangue, the falls where you can see an old gold mine on the road made by slaves; and Cachoeira do Bom Despacho, a waterfall on the Tiradentes-Santa Cruz road. All of these take about four or five hours. A seven-hour walk will allow you to cross the range. For guides and information about walks into the mountains, ask at the tourist office.

Places to Stay

Tiradentes has lots of good but expensive pousadas and only a few cheap places. If you can't find anything within your budget ask around for homes to stay in, or commute from São João del Rei. Try to avoid staying here on the weekend, as it gets crowded and the prices quoted below double.

Pousada do Laurito is the best cheapie in town, with a good central location and singles/doubles for US$6/12. Next to the bus station, *Pousada Tiradentes* (☎ 355-1232) has charm and costs US$8 a single and US$13 a double. *Hotel Wellerson* (☎ 355-1226) has singles/doubles for US$10/20. Similarly priced, with a great little garden, is *Pousada Quatro Encantos*, near the Santo Antônio church.

If you want to stay in a nice place a bit further out of town with a bit of space, try *Pousada da Terra*. It's 800 metres from the train station along a dirt road. They charge US$8 per person.

Near the train station are both the *Porão Colonial* (☎ 355-1251) and the *Pousada Maria Barbosa* (☎ 355-1227). Both have pools and cost around US$14/28 for singles/doubles.

Hotel Solar do Ponte (☎ 355-1255) is an old colonial mansion. The rooms are simple, small and beautifully decorated. There's a salon and sauna, and afternoon tea is included in the US$88 a double price.

Places to Eat

Restaurante Padre Toledo has excellent *bife acebolada* (beef with onions). *Estalagem* does a mean *feijão com lombo* (beans with pork). Try *Dona Rosa* for some regional specialities. *Donatelos* is the pasta place in town, and *Quinto do Ouro* is the most up-market restaurant, with both regional and international dishes.

Things to Buy

Tiradentes has surprisingly good antiques, woodwork and silver jewellery for sale. There is furniture, clocks, china and even chandeliers in the antique stores.

Getting There & Away

Tiradentes is about 20 minutes from São João del Rei. The best approach is the wonderful railroad trip from São João del Rei (see that city for details).

Buses come and go between São João and Tiradentes every 40 minutes (slightly less frequently on weekend afternoons). From São João, the first and last buses leave for Tiradentes Monday to Friday at 5.50 am and 5.45 pm, Saturday at 7 am and 5.45 pm, Sunday at 8.15 am and 10 pm. From Tiradentes, the last bus back to São João del Rei leaves at 6.20 pm from Monday to Saturday and at 8.40 pm on Sunday. There is no direct bus service to other places from Tiradentes.

PRADOS

Prados is a small colonial town with virtually no tourism. The town has good colonial buildings and the Igreja da NS da Conceição, built in 1711. It's a quiet place with a certain charm, but few important sights.

Places to Stay

The town hotel, the *São Sebastião*, is simple and cheap, with singles/doubles for US$7/12.

Getting There & Away

The journey, an hour by bus from São João, costs US$2. Buses leave São João: Monday to Friday at 7.30 and 10.30 am, 12.15, 3.30, 5.30 and 6.30 pm; Saturday at 7.30 am, 12.15, 3.30 and 6 pm; and Sunday at 12.15 and 10 pm.

DIAMANTINA

Diamantina is a 5½-hour drive north from Belo Horizonte. After passing the town of Curvelo (the geographical centre of Minas), the stark landscape of northern Minas, with its rocky outcrops and barren highlands, is a sharp contrast to the lush hills in the south of the state.

One of Brazil's prettiest and less touristed colonial gems, the city boomed when diamonds were discovered in the 1720s after the gold finds in Minas. The diamonds have petered out, but fine colonial mansions and excellent hiking in the surrounding mountains still draw visitors. Diamantina also happens to be the birthplace of Juscelino Kubitschek, former president and founder of Brasília.

Because of its isolation, Diamantina is a well-preserved colonial city. The centre, apart from the relatively new cathedral and a couple of incongruous traffic lights, hasn't changed for hundreds of years. Most of the churches and historical houses remain closed, but it doesn't matter much because the exteriors are more interesting anyway.

Information

Tourist Office At Praça Antonio Eulálio 57, a short walk from the cathedral, is the tourist office, where you'll find a *roteiro turístico* (tourist guide) in Portuguese which includes a map. The staff also have access to the keys to most of the tourist attractions, many of which are undergoing restoration indefinitely.

Money The Banco do Brasil is in a beautiful colonial building in the main praça.

Post & Telephone There are two post offices: at Rua Quintanda 31 and Praça Dr Prado 71. Long-distance calls can be made from the telephone post opposite the Hotel Dália.

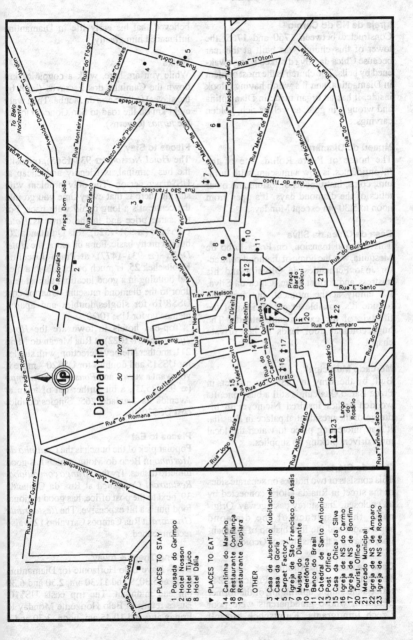

Diamantina

PLACES TO STAY

- 1 Pousada do Garimpo
- 2 Hotel Nosson
- 3 Hotel Tijuco
- 8 Hotel Dália

▼ **PLACES TO EAT**

- 14 Cantina do Marinho
- 18 Restaurante Confiança
- 19 Restaurante Grupiara

OTHER

- 3 Casa de Juscelino Kubitschek
- 4 Casa da Gloria
- 7 Carpet Factory
- 9 Igreja de São Francisco de Assis
- 10 Museu do Diamante
- 11 Telefónica
- 12 Banco do Brasil
- 13 Catedral de Santo Antonio
- 15 Casa da Chica da Silva
- 16 Igreja de NS do Carmo
- 17 Igreja de NS de Bonfim
- 20 Tourist Office
- 21 Mercado Municipal
- 22 Igreja de NS de Amparo
- 23 Igreja de NS de Rosario

Igreja de NS do Carmo

Constructed between 1760 and 1765, the tower of this church was built at the rear because Chica da Silva disliked being awakened by bells. The church is the most opulent in Diamantina, and it's worth having a look inside. It has an organ made in Diamantina and wrought in gold, as well as rich, golden carvings.

Museu do Diamante

The house of Padre Rolim, one of the Inconfidêntes, is now a museum, with furniture, coins, instruments of torture and other relics of the diamond days. It's open from noon to 5.30 pm except Mondays.

Casa da Chica da Silva

This colonial mansion, on Praça Lobo de Mesquita, was the home of diamond contractor João Fernandes de Oliveira and his mistress and former slave, Chica da Silva. It's empty at the moment, but from the outside it's possible to get an idea of the lifestyle of the extravagant mulatta. The huge colonial door leads to her private chapel.

Mercado Municipal

Built by the army in 1835, the market, in Praça Barão Guaicuí, is still a busy one. Its wooden arches inspired Niemeyer in his design of the presidential palace in Brasília. It's an interesting place to watch the local mule drivers picking up supplies.

Casa da Glória

This consists of two houses on separate sides of the street in Rua da Glória connected by an enclosed, 2nd-storey passageway. Originally the residence of the diamond supervisors and the first bishop of Diamantina, today it's the Institute of Geology.

Casa de Juscelino Kubitschek

This small house at Rua São Francisco 241 reflects the simple upbringing of the former president, whose grandparents were poor Czech immigrants. Kubitschek himself believed that his early life in Diamantina influenced him greatly.

Walks

While you are here, walk a couple of km down the Caminho dos Escravos (built by the slaves) to the Serra da Jacuba. Then walk eight km on the road to São Goncalo to see the *furnas* (caverns).

Places to Stay

The *Hotel Nosson* (☎ 931-1565), opposite the bus terminal, is friendly and cheap at US$4 per person. The only problem with staying there is that every time you go into the centre it's a long uphill walk back. For the same price and in the centre is *Hotel Carvalho* (☎ 931-1526), Rua Quintanda 20, but it's pretty basic. For a bit extra, the *Hotel Dália* (☎ 931-1477), at Praça Juscelino Kubitschek 25, is much better. It's in a nice old building in a good location, almost next door to the diamond museum. Quartos cost US$8/16 for singles/doubles and apartamentos go for US$10/20.

Top-end hotels in town are the *Hotel Tijuco* (☎ 981-1022) at Rua Macau do Meio 211, another Niemeyer erection, with singles for US$15 and doubles for US$20 – more if you want a view – and *Pousada do Garimpo* (☎ 931-2523), a bit further out of town at Avenida da Saudade 265. Singles/doubles cost US$30/40.

Places to Eat

Popular pick of the bunch is the *Cantina do Marinho* in Beco do Motta, which has good mineiro dishes. Try their *frango com quiabo*. *Restaurant Confiança* at Rua da Quitanda 39, next to the post office, has good regional food but is a bit expensive. The *Restaurante Grupiara* at Rua Campos Carvalho 12 is also recommended.

Getting There & Away

Buses leave Belo Horizonte for Diamantina daily at 5.30, 9 and 11.30 am, 2.30 and 6.30 pm and midnight. The trip costs US$10. Buses return to Belo Horizonte Monday to Friday at 6 and 10.45 am, noon, 3.30 and 6 pm; Saturday at 6 and 10.45 am, noon, 3.30 and 6 pm; and Sunday at 6 am, noon, 3.30 and 6 pm.

SERRO

Dominated by the Igreja de Santa Rita, Serro is a tranquil cidade histôrica, 90 km from Diamantina. It's a cold, windy place surrounded by granite hills, which in the past provided refuge for runaway slaves. It's a city rich in folkloric traditions and is the home of the famous *queijo serrano* – one of Brazil's finest cheeses.

Colonial Buildings

As well as the Igreja Santa Rita, Serro contains other historic churches, like the Igreja NS do Carmo, dating from 1781, in Praça João Pinheiro, and the Igreja Senhor Bom Jesus de Matosinhos in Praça Cristiano Otoni.

Other colonial buildings worth a look are the Casa do Barão de Diamantina – now used as the town hall – with 40 rooms which were to have held Dom Pedro II and his entourage during a visit that never happened, and the Chácara do Barão do Serro, across the valley, which has a small museum.

Festival

The Festa do Rosário, which takes place on the first Sunday in July, features folkloric characters – *catopês*, *caboclinhos* and *marujos* – who dance and stage mock fights in the streets.

Places to Stay & Eat

Pousada Vila do Principe (☎ 941-1485) at Rua Antônio Honório Pires 38 has apartamentos for US$9/13 a single/double.

The *Itacolomi* in Praça João Pinheiro is a hotel/restaurant that's a good place to stay and eat mineiro cooking. Single/double apartamentos cost US$8/11.

Another popular place to stay and camp is the small town of Milho Verde, about halfway between Diamantina and Serro.

Getting There & Away

From Diamantina there is only one daily bus to Serro. It leaves at 4 pm and takes two hours.

Mineral Spa Towns

The southern mineral spa towns of Minas are well-developed health resorts possessing excellent mineral springs with various therapeutic applications. Of the 13 spa towns, Caxambu, with its century-old Parque das Aguas, and São Lourenço, surrounded by the green hills of the Serra da Mantiqueira, are of most interest to the traveller. Been travelling hard and fast? Recovering from a tropical disease? Sick of seemingly idyllic beaches? Overdosing from too much baroque? If the answer is yes to one or all of these questions, the spa towns await you.

CAXAMBU

Caxambu is a combination of two African words: *cacha* (drum) and *mambu* (music). A *cacha-mambu* or *caxambu* is a conically shaped drum from the Congo which the founders of the city likened to the knolls of the area. In 1748, with the construction of a chapel dedicated to Our Lady of Cures in the parish of Baependi, the settlement of Cachambum, later called Caxambu, was put on the map.

In 1814, according to tradition, the first mineral fountains were discovered by an illustrious European traveller whose name was not recorded, but it wasn't until 1870 that the springs were first tapped. Realising the curative properties of the waters, medical practitioners flocked to the town. In 1886 Dr Policarpo Viotti founded the Caxambu water company (nationalised in 1905).

The water of Caxambu was celebrated on the international water circuit, winning gold medals long before Perrier hit Manhattan singles bars. Caxambu took the gold medal in Rome's Victor Emmanuel III Exposition of 1903, and another gold medal in the St Louis International Fair of 1904, then the Diploma of Honour in the University of Brussels Exposition of 1910.

These water Olympics were discontinued during WW I, and Caxambu's history was uneventful until 1981, when Supergasbras and Superagua, private firms, took over the government concession. Caxambu is sold throughout Brazil, and in Miami, Florida, where the US Food & Drug Administration has approved it. Caxambu is the only Brazilian mineral water thus honoured.

Caxambu is a tranquil resort for the elderly and middle class – people come here to escape the heat of Rio and the madness of Carnival. The town has not changed for 50 years and some couples have been coming here every summer for 30 years and more.

Information

Tourist Office In Praça 16 de Setembro, the tourist office is open from 8 to 11 am and noon to 6 pm. The staff have maps and other information.

Money For some unknown reason the Banco do Brasil won't change money here. Try the larger hotels.

Post & Telephone The post office is on Avenida Camilo Soares, right next to the Hotel Gloria. Phone calls can be made from Rua Major Penha 265.

Parque das Aguas

The Parque das Aguas is like a Disneyland for the rheumatic. Given the proper temperament and surroundings, nursing your ailments can be fun. People come to take the mineral waters, smell the sulphur, compare liver spots, watch the geyser spout every two or 2½ hours, rest in the shade by the canal or walk in the lovely gardens.

The park is not only good, it's good for you. Liver problems? Go to the Dona Leopoldina magnesium fountain. Skin disorders? Take the sulphur baths of Tereza Cristina. Anaemic? The Conde d'Eu e Dona Isabel fountains are rich in iron. VD? The Duque de Saxe fountain helps calm the bacteria that cause syphilis. For stomach troubles, drink the naturally carbonated waters of Dom Pedro (there's a water-bot-

tling plant on the premises). The alkaline waters of the Venancio and Viotti fountains are good for dissolving kidney stones, while the Beleza waters soothe the intestines. The multipurpose water of the Mayrink fountains 1, 2 and 3 is good for gargling, eye irritations and table water (without the bubbles).

The park is open daily from 7 am to 6 pm, and admission to the grounds is 50c. Separate fees are required for paddleboats, the rifle range, hydrotherapeutic massages at the bathhouse, the jacuzzi, sauna, clay tennis courts, swimming pool, skating rink and chairlift to the top of Morro Cristo.

Other Attractions

Morro Cristo hill has an eight-metre-high image of Jesus. On Rua Princesa Isabela is the Igreja Santa Isabel da Hungria, built by the princess once she conceived due to the miraculous waters of Caxambu.

Take a horse-and-buggy tour into the countryside; a 1½-hour ride from the park entrance will only set you back US$12. The standard tour includes a mini-zoo, the Fabrica de Doce and the Chacarra Rosallan. The mini-zoo at the Hotel Campestre has caged monkeys, a wilting peacock, and a sariema bird which looks like an eccentric European aristocrat, disgraced and in exile. The Fabrica de Doce has locally produced honey (US$3), liqueurs (50c) and preserves (US$2). The last stop is Chacara Rosallan's, an old farm with a flower orchard and fruit grove. Rosallan is famous for two of her fruit liqueurs: jaboticaba and bottled tangerine. Empty bottles are passed over the tiny tangerines and strapped to the tree; the tangerine grows within the bottle and weeks later is made into a liqueur.

Places to Stay

Unlike São Lourenço, Caxambu lacks really cheap places to stay. The *Lider Hotel* (☎ 341-1398) at Rua Major Penha 225 is a broken-down one-star Embratur hotel with humble charm. Singles/doubles with full board are US$20/28. With breakfast only, the cost is US$12/16.

Hotel São José (☎ 341-1094) at Rua

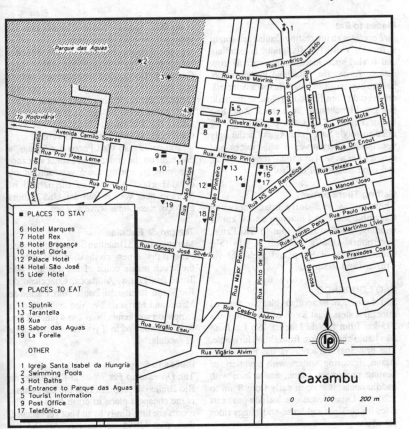

Parque das Aguas

To Rodoviária

Rua Américo Machado

Rua Cons Mavrink

Rua Oliveira Mafra

Avenida Camilo Soares

Rua Prof Paes Leme

Rua Dr Viotti

Rua Alfredo Pinto

Rua João Carlos

Rua João Pinheiro

Rua NS dos Remedios

Rua Costa Guedes

Rua Dr Mario Milward

Rua Plinio Mota

Rua Dr Enout

Rua Teixeira Leal

Rua Manoel João

Rua Paulo Alves

Rua Martinho Livio

Rua Praxedes Costa

Rua Afonso Pena

Rua Pinto de Moura

Rua Barbosa

Rua Cônego José Silvério

Rua Major Penha

Rua Cesário Alvim

Rua Virgílio Esaú

Rua Vigário Alvim

Ave Olímpio de Almeida

Caxambu

0   100   200 m

PLACES TO STAY

6 Hotel Marques
7 Hotel Rex
8 Hotel Bragança
10 Hotel Gloria
12 Palace Hotel
14 Hotel São José
15 Lider Hotel

PLACES TO EAT

11 Sputnik
13 Tarantella
16 Xua
18 Sabor das Aguas
19 La Forelle

OTHER

1 Igreja Santa Isabel da Hungria
2 Swimming Pools
3 Hot Baths
4 Entrance to Parque das Aguas
5 Tourist Information
9 Post Office
17 Telefônica

Major Penha 264 is an apartment-hotel with TVs, big double beds, and hot showers. Singles/doubles are US$14/26 with breakfast. The *Hotel Marques* (☎ 341-1013) at Rua Oliveira Mafra 223 has singles/doubles for US$14/28, or US$23/40 with full board. Next door, the *Hotel Rex* (☎ 341-1331) is similarly priced.

The four-star *Hotel Gloria* (☎ 341-1233) at Avenida Camilo Soares 590 is a very posh resort complex with a range of activities for the leisure set. Doubles with TV, bath, bar, telephone and three meals a day are US$110 for two. Facilities include a big gym with indoor basketball court, tennis (clay courts in the park), physical rehabilitation centre and sauna.

The *Hotel Bragança* (☎ 341-1117), directly in front of the Parque das Aguas entrance, is not quite as fancy but more than adequate. Singles/doubles are US$40/60 and the rates include full board. An excellent top-end deal can be had at the impressive *Palace Hotel* (☎ 341-1044). Although with full board the prices are US$60/80 for singles/doubles, with breakfast only the cost drops to US$20/28. Their food must be pretty good!

Places to Eat

La Forelle is an interesting Danish restaurant at Rua Dr Viotti 190. Its fondue is excellent and it also specialises in salmon and trout dishes. *Tarantella*, Rua João Pinheiro 326, has the best pasta and pizza in town. *Sputinik*, on Avenida Camilio Soares close to the park, is a good lanchonete for a snack. *Xua*, Rua Major Penha 225, is the place to go for mineiro food. *Sabor das Aguas* is the only vegetarian alternative; it sells juices and sandwiches as well as natural food products, and is on Rua João Pinheiro.

Getting There & Away

There are seven daily buses between Caxambu and São Lourenço on 49 km of winding, wooded road; four to São Paulo, (6½ hours, US$9); and two to Rio (5½ hours, US$8), at 8 am and midnight via Cruzeiro and Resende.

SÃO LOURENÇO

São Lourenço is another pleasant city of mineral waters. Just south of Caxambu, it's 275 km from Rio de Janeiro, 296 km from São Paulo and 401 km from Belo Horizonte. The principal attraction is the Parque das Aguas, featuring waters with a variety of healing properties, sauna, and a lake with paddle boats. It is open daily from 8 am to 5.20 pm. Other diversions include goat cart rides for children and horse-and-buggy rides for adults.

Information

Tourist Office In front of the Parque das Aguas, the tourist office is open every day from 8 to 11 am and 1 to 6 pm. Staff have a list of hotels and a map of the attractions.

Money The Banco do Brasil is at Avenida Dom Pedro II 266.

Post & Telephone The post office is on Rua Dr Olavo Gomes Pinto. The telefônica is at Rua Celso José Justino 647.

Circuito das Aguas

VW Kombi van half-day tours of the Circuito das Aguas (Water Circuit) can be arranged for US$12 per person. If possible organise it the day before. The vans will take up to eight people and normally visit Caxambu, Baependi, Cambuquira, Lambari and Passo Quatro, but you can also talk (bribe?) the driver into taking you to the mysterious stone village of São Tomé das Letras (80 km away). Taxis and VW vans congregate at Avenida Getúlio Vargas.

You could also visit Poços das Caldas, a city built on the crater of an extinct volcano; this mineral spring town was settled by crystal glass blowers of the island of Murano, near Venice. Full-day US$25 tours to Poços das Caldas leave at 7 am.

Templo da Euboise

Members of the Brazilian Society of Euboise believe that a new civilisation will arise in the seven magic cities of the region – São Tomé das Letras, Aiuruoca, Conceição do Rio Verde, Itanhandu, Pouso Alto, Carmo de Minas and Maria da Fe. You can visit their temple on weekends from 2 to 4 pm, but you won't be allowed in if you're wearing shorts or sandals.

Places to Stay

The *Dormitorio Per Noite* at Rua Barão do Rio Branco 45, right next to the bus station, is the cheapest place to crash in town. The rooms are tiny, dimly lit and not very secure; they cost US$4 per person. Around the corner at Avenida Dom Pedro II 611 is the *Hotel Colombo* (☎ 331-1577), which is several notches above the dormitory in quality, with clean, carpeted rooms. Apartamentos are US$10/16 a single/double. If you can be bothered walking a bit further, the *Hotel Estância* (☎ 331-3369), Rua Dr Olavo Gomes Pinto 195, is cheaper and nicer, with singles/doubles for US$8/15.

The *Hotel Metropole* (☎ 331-1290), Rua Wenceslau Braz 70, has quartos ranging from US$12 to US$20 with breakfast and US$24 to US$40 with full board. Apartamentos cost US$4 more than quartos. They also have a pool. The *Hotel Miranda* (☎ 331-1033), Rua Dom Pedro II 545, is not

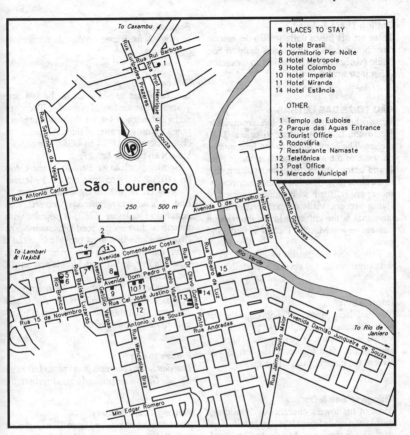

■ PLACES TO STAY

4 Hotel Brasil
6 Dormitorio Per Noite
8 Hotel Metropole
9 Hotel Colombo
10 Hotel Imperial
11 Hotel Miranda
14 Hotel Estância

OTHER

1 Templo da Euboise
2 Parque das Aguas Entrance
3 Tourist Office
5 Rodoviária
7 Restaurante Namaste
12 Telefônica
13 Post Office
15 Mercado Municipal

São Lourenço

0   250   500 m

a bad deal, with quartos at US$20/24 a single/double with full board. On the same street at No 587, the *Hotel Imperial* (☎ 331-1762) has apartamentos at US$28/40 with full board.

Hotel Brasil (☎ 331-1422) at Rua João Loage 87, across from the park, is the top-of-the-line four-star hotel in São Lourenço. Doubles with full board start at US$120 – less 30% out of season.

Places to Eat

The restaurants in town can't compete with the food served in the hotels. *Restaurante Namaste*, just across from the park entrance, is a good place for lunch. It's open from 9.30 am to 4 pm every day except Tuesday. There's also a good health food restaurant in the park itself.

Entertainment

The nightlife is pretty tame. In the evenings teenagers and young adults dress up and hang out on the fence and entrance of the Hotel Metropole. The club there has dances with a large-screen music video and bar. If that's not your scene, there's a cinema on Avenida Dom Pedro II.

Getting There & Away

There are six buses daily to Rio de Janeiro (five hours, US$7), five buses daily to São Paulo (six hours, US$8) and 11 to Caxambu (45 minutes, 75c).

SÃO TOMÉ DAS LETRAS

In southern Minas, 310 km from Belo Horizonte, Letras is a stone village at 1450 metres. The name refers to the inscriptions on some of the many caverns in the region. If you're into mysticism or superstition, this is the place to go. Fuelled by the inscriptions, the town is filled with strange stories of flying saucers, visits of extraterrestrials, a cave that is the entrance to a subterranean passageway to Macchu Picchu in Peru, and more.

This is also a beautiful mountain region, with great walks and several waterfalls.

Information

The Prefeitura Municipal is opposite the bus stop in the main square, but can provide only verbal information in Portuguese. There's a shop in the main square, to the left as you look at the church, that sells maps.

Things to See & Do

Most of the town's churches and buildings are old and made from slabs of quartzite. One that isn't is the Igreja Matriz de São Tomé, dating from 1785, in the main square. It contains some excellent frescoes by the artist Joaquim José da Natividade. Right next to the church is the Gruta de São Tomé, a small cave which, as well as its shrine to São Tomé, has some of the strange inscriptions. The Igreja de Pedra is made of stone and worth a photograph. The lookout only 500 metres up from town provides great views and is a good place to watch the sunset or sunrise.

The caves Carimbado (3 km) and Chico Taquara (3½ km) both contain the puzzling inscriptions. Popular waterfalls to walk to are Euboise (3 km), Prefeitura (7 km) and Véu de Noiva (12 km).

Festivals

In August, the Festas de Agosto attract lots of pilgrims.

Places to Stay

São Tomé has grown a lot in the last few years so there are lots of pousadas. There are no five-star hotels yet, but the way things are going it's only a matter of time. All pousadas charge between US$4 to US$8 per person, but not all provide breakfast.

Spotlessly clean is *Pensão Dona Célia* (☎ (101) 244), Rua Joaquim José Mendes Peixoto 11. There's no sign, but it's easy to find. Ask anybody. *Pousada Arco Iris*, Rua Armando Duplessis Vilela, is popular with travellers. Just up the road, *Pousada Serra Branca* is one that does provide breakfast. Near the bus stop in the main square is *Pousada Por do Sul*, very simple and one of the cheapest.

There's a youth hostel 20 metres up behind the stone church to the right, and camping at Gruta do Leão, which supposedly has enchanted water.

Places to Eat

Bar das Letras serves a good prato feito and *Bar do Gê* is a surprisingly good restaurant.

Getting There & Away

The town is best reached from Três Corações (which happens to be Pelé's birthplace and has a statue of him), 38 km to the west. Buses leave Monday to Saturday at 3.30 pm. The dirt road up the mountains is precarious and buses are cancelled during hard rains.

Hitching is possible, but not easy. To try hitching from Três Corações, cross the river next to the bus station and turn into the first street on the right, the one with the train track down the middle. About 50 metres down on the left-hand side there's a bus stop. Take the 'B Ventura' bus to its final destination. It'll save you a long uphill walk through town.

São Tomé das Letras can also be reached from Caxambu, 60 km to the south, but not by local bus.

National Parks

Parque Nacional de Caparaó

This park is popular with climbers and hikers from all over Brazil. The panoramic views are superb, taking in the Caparaó valley that divides Minas Gerais and Espírito Santo. Caparaó contains the highest mountains in southern Brazil, including the third highest peak in the country: the Pico da Bandeira, at 2890 metres. Other peaks include Cristal (2798 metres) and Calçado (2766 metres). All three can be reached via a good network of trails that exist within the park. Climbing gear isn't necessary.

Despite being ravaged by fire in 1988 and by human interference for the last 300 years, the park has a few lush remnants of mata atlântica, mostly in Vale Verde, a small valley split by the Rio Caparaó.

Wildlife in the park is not exactly plentiful, but there are still some opossums, agoutis and spider monkeys to be seen. Birdlife includes various species of eagles, parrots and hummingbirds.

Between November and January there's lots of rain and it's too cloudy for good views. The best time to visit the park is from June to August. Although these are the coldest months, the days are clear. Bring warm clothes!

The park is open daily from 7 am to 5 pm and costs 50c to enter. Make sure you pick up a map.

Places to Stay

It's possible to camp inside the park. There are two official campsites: Tronqueira, eight km from the park entrance, and Terreirão, a further 4½ km and halfway to the summit of Pico da Bandeira.

Camping costs US$2 a night, but it's a good idea to reserve a site about a week before you arrive by ringing IBAMA in Belo Horizonte on (☎ (031) 275-4266).

If you don't have a tent, the nearest place to stay is the *Caparaó Park Hotel* (☎ 741-2559), a short walk from the park entrance.

It's a pleasant, friendly place, but a bit on the expensive side, with singles/doubles for US$30/35. If that's too steep, ask around for a room to rent in Alto do Caparaó, the village closest to the park.

Getting There & Away

Caparaó can be reached via Belo Horizonte or Vitória, in Espírito Santo. You'll need to catch a bus to the town of Manhumirim and then another local bus to Alto do Caparaó, a further 25 km away.

Unfortunately the bus timetables work against the budget traveller. There are two buses a day to Manhumirim from both Belo Horizonte and Vitória. From Belo, they leave at 10 am and 5 pm; from Vitória at 9.30 am and 3.30 pm. The trip from either takes around five hours. The problem is that there are only two local buses a day to Alto do Caparaó: at 8 am and noon. To avoid staying in Manhumirim, catch one of the many buses going to Presidente Soares and ask to be dropped off at the Caparaó turnoff, and hitch the rest of the way. Alternatively, if you can afford it, take a taxi from Manhumirim to Alto do Caparaó. It costs between US$10-20, depending on the mood of the driver and your own bargaining ability.

Parque Nacional da Serra do Cipó

Formed by mountains, rivers, waterfalls and open grasslands, the Parque Nacional Serra do Cipó is one of Minas' most beautiful. Its highlands, together with an arm of the Serra do Espinaço, divide the water-basins of the São Francisco and Doce rivers.

Most of the park's vegetation is cerrado and grassy highlands, but the small river valleys are lush and ferny, and contain a number of unique orchids. Animal species include the maned-wolf, tamarin monkeys, banded anteaters, tree hedgehogs, otters, jaguars and large numbers of bats. Birdlife includes woodpeckers, blackbirds and hummingbirds. The park is also home to a small, brightly coloured frog which secretes deadly toxins from its skin. Brazilians call it Sapo-de-Pijama – the Pyjama-Frog.

Other attractions of the park include the

70-metre waterfall, Cachoeira da Farofa, and the Canyon das Bandeirantes, named after the early adventurers from São Paulo who used the area as a natural road to the North in their search for riches.

Unfortunately, the park contains no infrastructure for tourism.

Getting There & Away

Located about 100 km to the north-east of Belo Horizonte, the park is reached by catching a bus to Lagoa Santa, and then another one to Conceição do Mato Dentro. The road passes next to the park and Cardeal Mota, the nearest town.

Parque Nacional da Serra da Canastra

In the south-east of Minas Gerais, the Parque Nacional da Serra da Canastra is the birthplace of the Rio São Francisco – the river of national unity. With altitudes varying between 900 to 1500 metres, the vegetation is cerrado with grassy tablelands. Although the fauna has been devastated by hunting and bushfires over the years, the park is a reasonable place to see animals, especially early in the morning. Maned-wolves, deer, armadillos, banded anteaters and jaguars may be spotted, as well as eagles, vultures and owls. Another big attraction is the 200 metre high Casca D'anta waterfall. The best time to visit the park is between April and October.

Places to Stay

The park contains a campsite, but no hotels. The closest town, São Roque de Minas, has basic hotels.

Getting There & Away

From Belo Horizonte to São Roque de Minas is a distance of about 350 km. From São Roque, it's a further 40 km to Casca D'anta.

São Paulo State

São Paulo is another world. It is South America's richest state – the industrial engine that motors Brazil's economy: 30 of Brazil's 50 largest companies are in São Paulo, as is 50% of the nation's industry. The state contains South America's largest city – a megalopolis with 17 million inhabitants in the metropolitan area. One in every nine Brazilians lives here.

São Paulo City

The city of São Paulo is Brazil's most cosmopolitan and modern. It is a city of immigrants and ethnic neighbourhoods. Millions of Italians came here at the end of the 19th century. Millions of Japanese have come in this century. Millions of Brazilians from the countryside and from the Northeast are still pouring in. From this diversity and industrial development has sprung Brazil's largest, most cultured and educated middle class. These Paulistanos (inhabitants of the city; inhabitants of the state are called Paulistas) are lively and make well-informed companions. They call their city Sampa and, despite constantly complaining about street violence, traffic problems and pollution, they wouldn't dream of living anywhere else.

São Paulo is on a high plateau and it gets cold in the Brazilian winter and smoggy-hot in the summer. It can be an intimidating place, but if you know someone who can show you around or if you just like big cities, it's worth a visit. At its best it offers the excitement and nightlife of one of the world's great cities.

History
Founded in 1554 when a group of Jesuit priests led by Manoel de Nóbrega and José de Anchieta arrived at the Piratinanga plateau, São Paulo remained an unimportant backwater for many years. By the beginning of the 17th century it had a few churches and a small village. The growing slave trade in Indians saw the town become a headquarters for the bandeirantes, the slave-trading pioneers who, in their treks into the Brazilian interior, explored much unknown territory. For them, the Treaty of Tordesillas, which divided South America between Spain and Portugal, was nothing more than a line on a map and they were largely responsible for expanding the boundaries of Portuguese territory.

By the 18th century, the bandeirantes had turned their attention to mineral exploration and had discovered gold mines in Minas Gerais, Goiás and Matto Grosso. São Paulo was used as a stopover by the increasing number of pioneers, explorers and fortune-hunters heading for the interior, as well as by sugar dealers on their way to the port of Santos with their shipments.

During the early part of the 19th century, two events significantly changed São Paulo. The first was the declaration of Brazilian independence, which led to the city becoming a provincial capital. The second occurred a few years later with the founding of the Law Faculty, which attracted a new, transient population of students and intellectuals. As a political and intellectual centre, São Paulo became a leader in both the campaign to abolish slavery and the founding of the republic.

The last decades of the 19th century brought dramatic change. The rapid expansion of coffee cultivation in the state, the construction of railroads and the influx of millions of European immigrants caused the city to grow rapidly. São Paulo's industrial base began to form, and the import restrictions caused by WW I meant rapid industrial expansion and population growth, which continued after the war. The population reached 580,000 by 1920, 1.2 million by 1940, two million by 1950, 3.1 million by

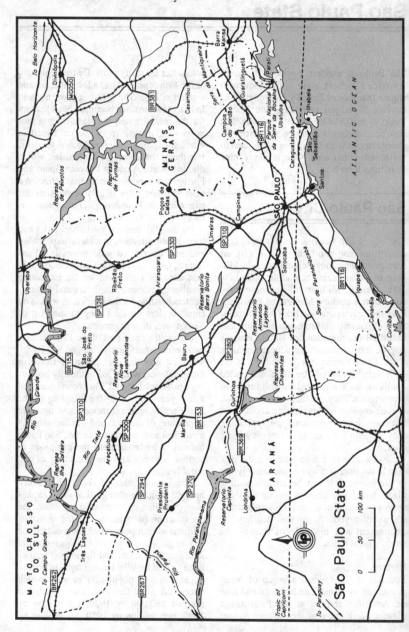

1960, and 5.2 million by 1970. By the year 2005 the population is expected to top 25 million.

Orientation

Getting around São Paulo can be difficult even if you speak Portuguese, have a car, time and money, and know the streets and traffic patterns. For the traveller it takes much longer to get a feel for the layout of São Paulo than just about any city in the world. Why? First, it's a big, sprawling city. Second, there is no plan or pattern to the arteries. Third, there are few natural or artificial landmarks by which to orient oneself. There is no ocean or river (of importance), and either few dominating boulevards or so many, depending on how you look at it, that they are of little use to the visitor. Visibility is limited by buildings everywhere. Even maps reflect the difficulty of bringing the city down to comprehensible dimensions. At first glance, they are of practically no use. The solution is to go underground. The Metrô, São Paulo's subway system, is one of the best in the world. And it's cheap too.

Parks, museums, art galleries, zoos, you name it are spread throughout the metropolitan area. It's best to pick up *Veja* at a newsstand or go to a tourism booth for a good list.

As a city of immigrants, certain suburbs of São Paulo are associated with the nationalities that settled there. Liberdade, just south of Praça da Sé, is the Oriental area. Bela Vista and nearby Bixiga are Italian. Bom Retiro, near Estação da Luz train station (the metro runs through here too), is the old Jewish quarter. The large Arab community is based around Rua 25 de Março, to the north of Praça da Sé. In all these areas, you'll find restaurants to match the tastes of their inhabitants.

Avenida Paulista, to the south-west of the centre, is an avenue of skyscrapers, and the adjoining suburb of Cerqueira César contains the city's highest concentration of good restaurants, cafés and nightclubs. When people refer to São Paulo as the 'New York of the Tropics', this is the area they have in mind. Adjoining Cerqueira César is the stylish Jardins district, home to many of the city's middle and upper-class residents.

Information

Tourist Office The city's many tourist information booths have excellent city and state maps, as well as *São Paulo this Month* – a monthly entertainment guide with an English section. They are also good for bus and metro information. English is spoken.

The information booth on Praça da República (along Avenida Ipiranga) is very helpful. Balthazar, who works there, is a Paulistano who loves his city and enjoys meeting travellers. It's open daily from 6 am to 6 pm. There's a post office attached to this booth.

Other tourist offices are found at: Praça da Sé (in front of the Sé metro station entrance; 6 am to 6 pm); Praça da Liberdade (in front of Liberdade metro station entrance; 6 am to 6 pm); Teatro Municipal (open weekends from 9 am to 4 pm); Avenida São Luis (on the corner of Praça Dom José Gaspar; 10 am to 4 pm daily); and Aeroporto de Congonhas (open 24 hours a day). The shopping centres Ibirapuera and Iguatemi also have information booths. The phone number for the main tourism office is 267-2122, extension 627 or 581 (on weekends).

The state tourist office is located in the beautiful, deco Banco de São Paulo building at Praça Antonio Prado 9, and is worth a visit if you plan on staying for a while.

Paulistanos would not dream of driving in the city without one of several large city street directories. If you are staying in the city for a while, the *Guia São Paulo* by Quatro Rodas has street maps and hotel and restaurant listings. *O Guia* has the clearest presentation of any street guide and it lists tourist points as well. Probably the best street guide to check out is the *Guia Caroplan*, as it has an extensive English section.

Money Changing money is easy in São Paulo and you'll get top rates. The only time you're likely to have a problem is on weekends. There are several travel agencies and

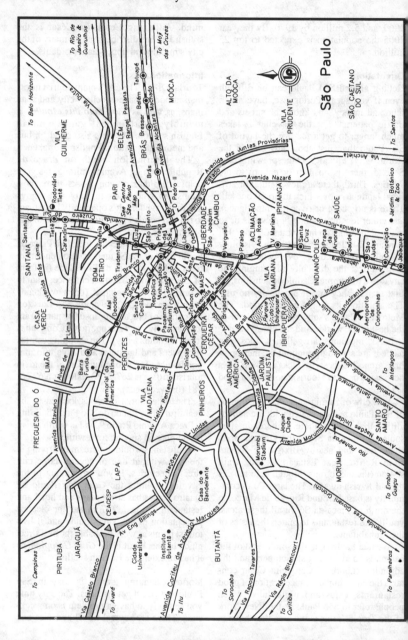

casas de câmbio across from the airline offices on Avenida São Luis, close to Praça da República, which are a good bet. Most banks in this area have foreign exchange counters too.

Post & Telecommunications The main post office is in the Praça do Correio, right where Avenida São João meets Anhangabaú. The Posta Restante is downstairs. They hold mail for 30 days. Fax services are available in the same building.

The Telesp long-distance phone call office is close to Praça da República on the Ipiranga side. It's 200 metres down Rua 7 de Abril, on the right as you walk away from the praça.

American Express American Express/Kontik-Franstur (☎ 259-4211) is at Rua Marconi (1st floor). From the Praça da República, on the Avenida Ipiranga side, go down Barão de Itapetininga and turn left after two blocks. They close for mail pick-up from noon to 2 pm. You also come here if you need to purchase travellers' cheques with your Amex card.

Foreign Consulates
The following countries have consulates in São Paulo:

Argentina
    Rua Araújo 216, 8th floor (☎ 256-8555); open 9 am to 1 pm
Bolivia
    Rua Quirino de Andrade 219, 3rd floor (☎ 255-3555); open 9 am to 1 pm
Canada
    Avenida Paulista 106, 1st floor (☎ 287-2122); open 9 am to 3 pm
Chile
    Avenida Paulista 1009, 10th floor (☎ 284-2044); open 8.30 am to 1.30 pm
Paraguay
    Avenida São Luis 112, 10th floor (☎ 259-3579); open 9 am to 1 pm.
Peru
    Rua Suécia 114 (☎ 853-9375); open 8 am to 4 pm
UK
    Avenida Paulista 1938, 17th floor (☎ 287-7722); open 8.30 am to 12.30 pm and 1.30 to 5 pm

USA
    Rua Padre João Manoel 933 (☎ 881- 6511); open 8.30 am to 3 pm

Visa Extension For visa extensions, the Polícia Federal office is at Avenida Prestes Maia 700. It's open from 10 am to 4 pm. Go up to the 1st floor.

Bookshops There's a good selection of English books at the Book Centre at Rua Gabus Mendes 29, near the Praça da República.

Livraria Cultura at Avenida Paulista 2073 has a wide variety of titles as well.

Health For serious health problems, Einstein Hospital (☎ 845-1233) is one of the best in Latin America.

Tourist Police Deatur is the English-speaking tourist police service. It has two offices in the city: Avenida São Luis 115 (☎ 256-4856) and Rua 15 de Novembro (☎ 37-8332). They're not open on weekends.

The Historic Centre
The triangle formed by Praça da Sé, Estação da Luz train station and Praça da República contains the old centre of São Paulo, and it's certainly worth having a look round this area. A good place to start is the **Mercado Municipal** at Rua da Cantareira 306. Dating from 1933, this lively market used to be the city's wholesale market until the CEAGESP (a huge new market) was built. Check out the German-made, stained-glass windows with their agricultural themes.

Not far from the market is the geographical centre of the city, Praça da Sé and the **Catedral**, completed in 1954. There's a lot of busking here, but don't bring any valuables as there are lots of pickpockets and bagsnatchers. Close by is the **Patío do Colégio**, where the city was founded in 1554 by the Jesuits José de Anchieta and Manoel da Nóbrega. The church and college have been reconstructed in colonial style.

A couple of blocks from Praça da Sé, in the Largo São Francisco, is the traditional

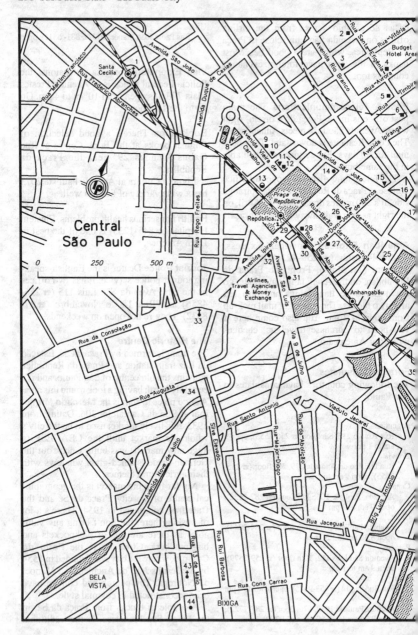

Central
São Paulo

0   250   500 m

■ PLACES TO STAY

2	Galeão Hotel
4	Luanda Hotel
5	Pauliciéa Hotel
6	San Remo Hotel
9	Hotel Itamarati
12	Hotel Amazonas
17	Municipal Hotel
19	Britannia Hotel
20	Hotel Central
26	Hotel Joamar
27	Hotel Rivoli
28	Hotel São Sebastião
41	Isei Hotel
42	Ikeda Hotel

▼ PLACES TO EAT

3	Lanches Aliados
8	Dinho's Place
10	Baby-Beef Rubaiyat
11	Casa Ricardo
15	Ponto Chic
18	Bar e Restaurante Leão
34	Ca'd'Oro

OTHER

1	Igreja Santa Cecília
7	Mercado de Flores
13	Bus to Airports
14	Bar Brahma
16	Largo de Paissandu
21	Post Office
22	Mosteiro São Bento
23	Mercado Municipal
24	State Tourist Information
25	Teatro Municipal
29	Tourist Information Booth
30	Telesp (Telephone)
31	Deatur Tourist Police
32	Edifício Italia
33	Igreja NS de Consolação
35	Igreja São Francisco de Assis & Law Faculty
36	Igreja de Santo Antonio
37	Patio do Colégio
38	Catedral
39	Igreja São Gonçalo
40	Igreja das Almas
43	Igreja NS Achiropita
44	Museu Memórias do Bixiga

Law Faculty of the University of São Paulo. The surrounding bars are local student hangouts, especially **Bar & Restaurante Itamaraty**.

Up Rua Libero Badaró and across the **Viaduto do Chá**, the bridge that crosses the Vale do Anhangabaú, is the **Teatro Municipal** – pride of the city; it's built in baroque style with art nouveau elements. The area between here and Avenida Ipiranga is for pedestrians only, and gets really busy during the day. There are plenty of clothing stores, shoe shops, bookshops, travel agents, record stores, one-hour photo places and lunch counters.

Up on Avenida Ipiranga, on the corner with Avenida São Luis, is the tallest building in town, the 41-storey **Edifício Itália**. There's a restaurant and piano bar at the top, as well as a viewing terrace. Strictly speaking, you're supposed to be a customer to go there, so if you're not – act like one. The best time to go up is right on sunset. This is the only time you'll ever get to see the horizon, and as the sun goes down over the nearby hills and the city lights start to sparkle, you could almost convince yourself that São Paulo is beautiful.

Next to the Itália is another one of the city's landmarks, **Edifício Copan**, with its famous curve – yet another Niemeyer project. Along Avenida Ipiranga, just past Praça da República, is the intersection with Avenida São João. When people get nostalgic about the city (yes – some do) this is the place they write songs about. **Bar Brahma** on the corner is a classic bar where you may want to go and try to compose yourself.

The area between here and the Estação da Luz gradually deteriorates. Rua Santa Efigênia is where Paulistanos go for cheap electronic goods, and the area between here and the station is known as *boca do lixo* (mouth of trash) – it's a red-light area with strip-tease shows and desperate characters hang out here after dark.

Museu de Arte de São Paulo (MASP)

This museum has Latin America's best collection of Western art, including many French impressionists. There are also a few great Brazilian paintings: the Candido Portinaris alone are worth the trip. There are also temporary exhibits and a pleasant cafeteria in the basement, and outside on Sundays, from 9 am to 5 pm, there is the Feira de Antiquidades do MASP. The fair is full of old odds and ends, big and small – including furniture, books and toys.

The museum is open 1 to 5 pm from Tuesday to Friday and 2 to 6 pm on weekends. Go early, as the light can be very bad late in the day. The MASP is at Avenida Paulista 1578. To get there take the metro to Paraiso station, and then change for Trianon.

For a bit of R&R after the museum, visit the small park – a tropical oasis in the midst of the mountains of concrete – across Avenida Paulista.

Parque do Ibirapuera

There's lots to do in this park and many people doing it on weekends. The best way to get here is to take the metro to Ana Rosa station and then catch 'Monções' bus No 675-C. The large edifice across the street from the park is the São Paulo state legislature. Just outside the park, at the end of Avenida Brasil, is Victor Brecheret's huge monument 'Bandeiras', built in memory of the pioneers of the city.

Inside the park is a planetarium, lake, monuments, a Japanese pavilion and several museums.

Museu de Arte Contemporânea

This museum has many of the big names in modern art and a good collection of modern Brazilian artists. It's housed, at least part of it, in the Bienal building, which also has a couple of enormous exhibition halls. The rest of the collection is at the Cidade Universitária, which is open Tuesday to Sunday from 1 to 6 pm.

The Bienal is worth a mention too. It's the largest art exhibition in Brazil and if you happen to be in town when it's on, don't miss it. It takes place every odd year.

Museu de Arte Moderna

This is the oldest modern art museum in the country. It's open Tuesday to Friday from 1 to 7 pm, Saturday and Sunday from 11 am to 7 pm.

Museu de Folclore & Museu Aeronautica

These two museums are in the dome-shaped building. The former includes an Afro-Brazilian cult altar and folkloric costumes from all over Brazil. The latter includes the flying machines of Santos Dumont, considered the father of Brazilian aviation. Both museums are open Tuesday to Sunday from 2 to 5 pm.

Museu de Arte Sacra & Jardim da Luz

This is the best of many sacred art museums in Brazil. It's at Avenida Tiradentes 676. Take the metro to Tiradentes. The museum is open Tuesday to Sunday from 1 to 5 pm. After your visit you can walk two blocks down Avenida Tiradentes to the park, Jardim da Luz, and the old British-built train station, Estação da Luz.

Museu Lasar Segall

Lasar Segall was a great Lithuanian expressionist artist who made Brazil his home and became leader of the modernistic movement in the country in the 1920s. In addition to his work, the museum gets some very good exhibitions. Unfortunately, it's a long way from town at Afonso Celso 362, Vila Mariana (☎ 572-8211). It's open Tuesday to Sunday from 2.30 to 6.30 pm.

Fundação Maria Luisa e Oscar Americano

Another sight that's a long way from the centre, in the posh suburb of Morumbi, is this modern Brazilian home in beautifully landscaped surroundings. It contains lots of imperial antiques and eight oils by the Dutch artist Frans Post, painted in Olinda. This is a great place to come for afternoon tea. It's at Avenida Morumbi 3700 and is open Tuesday to Sunday from 10 am to 5 pm.

The Butantã Snake Farm & Museum

The most popular tourist sight in town, the Instituto Butantã is also an important research centre. It has many snakes that are milked for their poison to make serum, and it's quite a sight for both the serpentologist and lay person. Open Tuesday to Sunday from 9 am to 4.45 pm, the farm and museum are at Avenida Vital Brasil 1500 at the edge of the Cidade Universitária. Take the No 702-U bus marked 'Butantã-USP' from in front of the tourist booth at Praça da República.

Casa do Bandeirante

Not far from the snake farm is this typical pioneer's abode, with a sugar mill, ox cart and farm implements. It's in Praça Monteiro Lobato and is open Tuesday to Sunday from 9 am to 5 pm. Interesting if you're in the area.

Memorial America Latina

Close to Barra Funda metro station at Rua Mario de Andrade 664, this group of buildings is another Niemeyer creation. Outside is a seven-metre cement hand. Inside are the Centre of Latin American studies, an auditorium with free concerts, and various handicraft exhibits. Portinari's painting *Tiradentes* hangs in the Salão de Atos, and huge panels by Carybé and Poty represent the people of South America.

Organised Tours

One of the best ways to see the city, saving time and money, is to take an organised tour. Government-sponsored, multilingual bus tours take place on Sundays and cost US$2. There are eight different itineraries and they include some of those hard-to-get-to spots. Tickets are available from the tourist booth in Praça da República from Tuesday to Sunday. If you have time, buy your ticket a couple of days before, and that'll give you a chance to choose your itinerary. The three-hour tours begin from the praça.

Places to Stay

São Paulo has plenty of hotels and they come in groups, which makes it easy to go to a street and find one that suits your style. Prices tend to be reasonable. Most hotels have a 10% surcharge, but many give weekend discounts of 20%. Rooms are hardest to find midweek, and for the middle to top-end hotels it's a good idea to make reservations a week or so in advance.

Places to Stay – bottom end

Down and out in São Paulo is done in an area between the Estação da Luz and the Praça da República. There are dozens of budget and below-budget hotels on Rua dos Andradas and Rua Santa Efigênia and the streets that intersect them from Avenida Ipiranga to Duque de Caxias. The area is pretty safe during the day but is seedy at night. There's much prostitution, and many of the hotels cater to this high-turnover clientele. These are often the cheapest hotels and the management will usually indicate that you're not welcome.

There are several cheap places on Santa Efigênia. The *Pauliceía Hotel* (☎ 220-9733), Rua Timbiras 216 (at the corner of Santa Efigênia), is a very good deal, and is clean and safe. A single quarto goes for US$8 and a double for US$12. Apartments cost US$12/15 a single/double. At Santa Efigênia 348, the *Luanda Hotel* (☎ 222-3666) has singles for US$9/12 without/with bath. Doubles cost US$13/16. At Santa Efigênia 163, the *San Remo Hotel* (☎ 229-6845) is similar in quality and price to the Luanda. The *Galeão Hotel* (☎ 220-8211) at Rua dos Gusmões 394 is excellent. It's really a mid-range hotel (apartments start at US$13), bus has cheap quartos which cost US$10 per person. They also do laundry.

In the pedestrian part of Avenida São João, between the post office and Largo de Paissandu, are three relatively cheap places – the *Municipal Hotel* (☎ 228-7833) at 354, the *Britannia Hotel* (☎ 222-9244) at 300 and the *Hotel Central* (☎ 222-3044) at 288. The first has quartos from US$12 and apartamentos from US$15 a single. The second has single/double quartos for US$8/10 and apartamentos for US$12/15. The Central is around the same price. I'd stay around here instead of in a similar place on Rua Santa Efigênia, unless of course you enjoy being surrounded by electronics stores.

Places to Stay – middle

Centre There are loads of middle-priced hotels on the streets around Praça da República. They tend to come in clusters, by price, along certain streets.

In the pedestrian streets close to Praça da República, are a few places worth a mention. A stone's throw from the tourist booth, at Rua 7 de Abril 364, is the *Hotel São Sebastião* (☎ 257-4988) with single/double apartamentos for US$14/16. Around the corner at Rua Dom José de Barros 28, the *Hotel Rivoli* (☎ 231-5633) has apartamentos for the same price and quartos a couple of dollars cheaper. A nice little place a bit further down the same street at No 187 is *Hotel Joamar* (☎ 221-3611), with apartamentos for US$15/19 a single/double.

On the other side of Praça da República, in Avenida Vieira de Carvalho, are a couple of favourites. It's a dignified, quiet street with some very expensive hotels as well. The *Hotel Itamarati* (☎ 222-4133) is at No 150. It's a well-kept old place, the rooms are clean and the management helpful. Single/double quartos are US$12/14 and apartamentos are only a dollar more. The *Hotel Amazonas* (☎ 220-4111) is in a great spot, at the corner where Avenida Vieira de Carvalho meets the Praça da República. With lots of wood panelling, this one is a fine mid-range choice. Singles/doubles start at US$22/26. Both these hotels are very close to the airport bus stop.

Across from the Estação da Luz, the *Hotel Florida* (☎ 220-2811) has singles/doubles for US$22/28. Good place – crummy location.

There are three big hotels to choose from on the 700 block of Avenida Ipiranga with rooms starting in the same price range: *Plaza Maraba Hotel* (☎ 220-7811) with singles/doubles for US$26/35, the *Terminus* (☎ 222-2266) with singles/doubles for US$34/43 and the *Excelsior* (☎ 222-7377), the best and

the most expensive of the three, with singles/doubles for US$45/54.

Liberdade An alternative to staying in a hotel in the central district is to head over to Liberdade, the Japanese, Chinese and Korean district. The subway stops very close to the hotels, and it's quieter, safer and more interesting at night. You can also pig out on cheap Japanese food. There are several less expensive hotels as you walk downhill from the metro station at Praça da Liberdade (there's an information booth here that can give directions). The *Ikeda Hotel* (☎ 278-5853) at Rua dos Estudantes 134 has singles starting at US$10. The *Hotel Isei* (☎ 278-6677) at Rua de Glória 290 has singles/doubles for US$16/26.

More expensive places in Liberdade include the *Banri* (☎ 270-8877) at Rua Galvão Bueno 209. They have singles/doubles starting at US$30/40. The *Osaka Palace* (☎ 270-1311) is right across the street from the metro. It has all the modern amenities and doubles starting at US$60. Reservations are often needed about a week in advance for these two hotels.

Around Avenida Paulista Close to Avenida Paulista, there are no real bargains, but the two-star *Pamplona Palace* (☎ 285-5301), Rua Pamplona 851, is the closest you'll get, with singles/doubles for US$27/40.

Places to Stay – top end

As in Rio, the residential hotels are an excellent deal. The *Trianon Residence* (☎ 283-0066) – near Avenida Paulista at Alameda Casa Branca 363, Cerqueira César – features an excellent location, close to the centre but not in it. It has comfortable doubles for US$70. The *Augusta Park Residence* (☎ 255-5722), Rua Augusta 922, Consolação, is similar value.

The *Nikkey Palace* (☎ 270-8511) in Liberdade at Rua Galvão Bueno 425 has a sauna and restaurant. Singles/doubles cost US$75/100.

In the centre there is the *Othon Palace*

(☎ 239-3277) at Rua Libero Badaró 190 with singles/doubles starting at US$75/83.

Over on Avenida Casper Libero, a quiet street for the centre of town, there are three hotels. The *Marian Palace* (☎ 228-8433) has singles/doubles starting at US$65/75. Down the block, the *Planalto* (☎ 227-7311) has all the amenities too. It's a bargain with singles/doubles starting at US$30/40. The same applies to the *Delphos* (☎ 228-6411) next door, with singles/doubles for US$35/44. The *São Paulo Centre* (☎ 228-6033) at Largo Santa Efigênia 40 is an old, elegant beauty. Singles/doubles cost US$70/86 and up.

São Paulo's luxury hotels include the *Maksoud Plaza* (☎ 251-2233) with singles/doubles for US$150/185, the *Grand Hotel Ca'd'Oro* (☎ 256-8011), the *São Paulo Hilton* (☎ 256-0033) with singles/doubles for US$130/160, and the *Sheraton* (☎ 284-5544), Alameda Santos 1437, the priciest place in town, with singles/doubles for US$180/200.

Places to Eat

The best reason to visit São Paulo is to eat. Because of the city's ethnic diversity you can find every kind of cuisine and, if you can spend a few dollars, it's easy to find great food at reasonable prices. There are also a million cheap lanchonetes, great pizzerias and churrascarias, and some of the best Italian and Japanese food that you'll find outside those countries.

Paulistanos love to go out to dinner and they go out late. Although they open earlier, most restaurants don't fill up until 9 or 10 pm on weekdays and later on weekends. Many stay open on weekends until 2 or 3 am.

The places mentioned in this section are the more traditional ones. That they've been around for a long time is a recommendation in itself, as Paulistanos are very particular diners. The selection given is limited to areas easily reached by public transport. If you have a car or don't mind grabbing a taxi, there are hundreds more places to choose from. The best place to get a listing of good restaurants is in the São Paulo lift-out section of the weekly *Veja* magazine. The bilingual *São Paulo this Month* also has a decent listing with prices included. If you're really keen, Guia Quatro Rodas publishes a small guide to the best restaurants in São Paulo and Rio. It's available from any newsstand.

Central District If you're staying here, there are a few inexpensive places that are close by and several notches above the rest. *Ponto Chic* is a friendly, informal restaurant, but the best reason to go is the famous Brazilian sandwich, the *bauru*, which Ponto Chic invented many moons ago. The bauru consists of beef, tomato, pickle and a mix of melted cheeses served on French bread. The price is US$2. Not only is it popular in urban and backland Brazil, it is also served in Paris. Ponto Chic is only a few blocks from the Praça da República at Largo Paissandu 27, and is open until 4 am.

Another winner is the *Lanches Aliados* at the corner of Avenida Rio Branco and Rua Vitória. It's a cheap lunch spot with excellent food. The *Casa Ricardo* features 20 different sandwiches and is reasonable. Open until 7 pm, it's at Avenida Vieira de Carvalho 48.

For vegetarians *Superbom* is pretty fair. It's open Monday to Friday for lunches only

(closes at 3 pm). There are branches at the Praça da República 128 (4th floor), 9 de Julho 180 and Praça da Sé 62. The *Mel* has some excellent natural and vegetarian lunches. The curried mushroom and tofu pancake is particularly tasty. It's open from 11 am to 4 pm Monday to Friday at Rua Araújo 75.

If it's lean meat you seek, *Baby-Beef Rubaiyat* has three churrascarias: the one in the centre (☎ 222-8333) is at Avenida Vieira de Carvalho 116. A bit less expensive, *Dinho's Place* (☎ 221-2322) at Largo do Arouche 246 has a feijoada every Wednesday and Saturday.

Also in Avenida Vieira de Carvalho, *Carlino* (☎ 223-1603), at No 154, is a reasonably cheap Italian restaurant that's been there for over a century. The *Bar e Restaurante Leão* at Avenida São João 320 has all-you-can-eat Italian meals and a salad bar, at reasonable prices.

Ca'd'Oro (☎ 256-8011), in the hotel of the same name at Rua Augusta 129, is considered one of the best. It's very expensive; sports jacket and reservations are recommended.

Bela Vista & Bixiga These districts are loaded with Italian restaurants and bars; they're one of the best places in the city at night. In Bela Vista, there are two very good and very Italian restaurants on Rua Avanhandava. *Gigetto* and *Famiglia Mancini* have large selections of pastas and wines, stay crowded until very late with the after-theatre crowd and are moderately priced – US$4 buys a large plate of pasta. Gigetto is supposed to be an actors' hangout.

In Bixiga, *Cantina e Pizzeria Lazzarella* (☎ 288-1995), Rua 13 de Maio 589, is full of Brazil kitsch. The live, if dated, music features a multilingual sing-along. It's festive, the food is good and large plates of pasta are only US$4. *Speranza* (☎ 288-8502), at Rua 13 de Maio 1004, is one of the best pizzerias in town.

Cerqueira César There are lots of restaurants and bars in the area bounded by Avenida Paulista, Rua da Consolação, Rua Estados Unidas and Alameda Ministro Rocha Azevedo. Most are fairly expensive but there are quite a few reasonable ones. A good sandwich place is the very traditional *Frevo*, Rua Oscar Freire 603. If you want to be really Paulistano, order one of their *beirute á modas* and a chopp. Waiters calling for a chopp yell for a *rabo de peixe* (fish tail). *Baguette*, another sandwich and beer place at Rua da Consolação 2426, in front of the cinema, is open 24 hours a day and is packed at 3 am.

Almanara (☎ 853-6916) at Rua Oscar Freire 523 serves good Arab food. The churrascarias *Wessel Grill* (☎ 280-9107), Rua Bela Cintra 1855, *Rodeio* (☎ 883-2322), Rua Haddock Lobo 1498, and *Esplanada Grill* (☎ 881-3199), Rua Haddock Lobo 1682, are all excellent but expensive.

An interesting place with a great view is *Jinro* (☎ 283-2543), a Korean restaurant on the 25th floor at Avenida Paulista 807. The food is good and the prices reasonable.

There are a few French restaurants in the area, but nothing cheap. If bucks aren't a worry, try *Marcel* (☎ 881-7557) at Alameda Lorena 1852. The soufflés are famous.

There are several fine and reasonably priced Italian restaurants. *L'Osteria do Piero* (☎ 853-1082) at Alameda Franca 1509 features roast kid with broccoli and agnollotti. It is closed on Monday. *Babbo Giovanni* (☎ 853-2678), Rua Bela Cintra 2305, has good inexpensive pizza.

For a big splurge, many think *Massimo* (☎ 248-0311) at Alameda Santos 1826 is the city's best Italian restaurant. *Z Deli* at Alameda Santos 1518 is a Jewish deli that's a popular lunch spot with Paulistanos. Vegetarians won't feel left out in this area. *Associação Macrobiótica*, Rua Bela Cintra 1235, has a healthy fixed menu and *Sattva* at Rua da Consolação 3140 has some imaginative vegetarian dishes.

Liberdade Liberdade has lots of inexpensive Oriental restaurants and good food at the Sunday street fair. There are several good Japanese restaurants to choose from on Rua

Tomás Gonzaga. *Gombe* at No 22 is always full. They have great sushis and sashimis and excellent kushi-yaki. Other favourites include *Takão* at Rua Barão de Iguapé 324 which has a delightful karaoke, the *Diego* at Praça Almeda Jr 25 with its strong, Okinawan dishes and the *Sushi-Yassu* – the most famous and most expensive at about US$10 a meal. It's at Rua Tomás Gonzaga 110-A and is closed Mondays.

Entertainment

This city swings at night. Everyone is out playing until the wee hours and you feel it – where else can you get stuck in a traffic snarl at 3 am. São Paulo's nightlife approaches the excitement, diversity and intensity of New York's. To enjoy it, all you need is money and transportation.

The best list of events is probably found in the weekly *Veja* magazine, which has a special São Paulo edition. It also lists restaurants, bars, museums, fairs, etc. Another good source is the *illustrada* section of the *Folha de São Paulo*.

Rua 13 de Maio in Bixiga hums at night. There are several clubs, restaurants and even a revival movie theatre. It attracts a young crowd so prices are reasonable. You can go there, look around and plan out a full evening in one neighbourhood. The biggest club is the Café Piu-Piu at No 134. They have music every night but Monday: jazz, rock and a sequin-shirted, 20-gallon-hatted band that plays American country music. Café do Bixigaat No 76 is a traditional bar that stays open late. Try their pinga com mel.

Bela Vista is another good area for nightlife. There's lots happening and it's central, although the clubs are not as close together as in Bixiga. Spazio Pirandello at Rua Augusta 311 is always lively – the crowd includes both gay and straight clientele. There's art on the walls and a bookstore downstairs.

For the best jazz in town try Café Teatro Opus 2004 (☎ 256-9591), Rua da Consolação 2004. At the Luar do Sertão (Sertão Moonlight) you'll find the music of the sertão, and many Nordestinos swaying to the

forrós, the *xotes* and various other wild dances. This music is one of the great cultural treasures of Brazil, and with the mass migration from the Northeast to São Paulo there's plenty of authentic talent from which to draw.

The Bar Brahma is the city's oldest drinking establishment. It's at the corner of Rua São João and Avenida Ipiranga, in the heart of the central hotel district. From 7 pm to midnight the antique surroundings are accompanied by equally dated live music. The best tables are upstairs. The bar is friendly and relaxing, and is a popular after-work hangout for many Paulistano professionals.

Another time-capsule bar is the Riviera Restaurant & Bar at the corner of Rua Consolacão and Avenida Paulista. This bar takes you back to the seedy '40s. It's inexpensive and unassuming; a good place to go with a friend to talk and unwind. Finnegan's Pub at Alameda Itú 1541 in Cerqueira César is where to go if you want to speak some English. Paulistanos know it as a 'gringo' bar and it gets lively. The Paris Cafe is the famous café hangout by the university.

Vou Vivendo is a medium-size music club/restaurant. It's informal and prices are reasonable. Upstairs there's excellent samba, jazz, etc. It's at Avenida Pedroso de Moraes 1017, Pinheiros. Across the street the Avenida Club features orchestra dancing – for couples – on Sundays from 10 pm to 4 am. The 18-piece orchestra plays old tunes and the dance hall is a fantastic recreation of the '30s scene. The cover charge is US$5 for men and US$4 for women.

Popular discos include Colúmbia on the corner of Rua Augusta and Rua Estados Unidas, US Beef Rock at Rua Estados Unidas 1626, and Woodstock, Rua Consolação 3247.

The gay scene is lively in São Paulo. A popular club is Corintho, Alameda dos Imarés 64, with live shows from Wednesday to Sunday starting at 11 pm. Homo Sapiens at Rua Marques de Itú and Nostro Mondo at Rua da Consolação 2556 are a couple of others.

Things to Buy

Shopping is almost as important to Paulistanos as eating out. Those who can afford it like to do it in one of the many large shopping malls that dot the city. For the traveller, these malls don't hold much interest – prices tend to be higher than those you'd find in the centre of town. However, if you're a big fan of malls you'll find a list of addresses in the *São Paulo this Month* guide.

More interesting are the many markets and fairs that take place around town, especially on weekends. One of the most popular is held in the Praça da República on Sundays from 8 am to 2 pm. It's a great place for people watching. Things for sale include Brazilian precious stones, leather gear, woodcarvings, handmade laces and paintings. Some of the painters, especially the naive artists, are excellent. My favourite is Tavares, from the interior of the state. His themes include football games and trips to the dentist.

Liberdade, the Oriental district, has a big street fair all day Sundays and is only five minutes from the centre by metro. The fair surrounds the metro station.

A couple of markets worth a look are the Mercado Municipal (see The Historic Centre) and the huge CEAGESP market on Avenida Doutor Gastão Vidigal in the suburb of Jaguaré. This huge market is the centre of food distribution for the whole city, and is quite a sight. The best time to go is Tuesday to Friday from 7 am to noon, when there's a flower market as well. On other days you just have lots and lots of produce.

Another excellent market to check out takes place every weekend in Embu, 28 km from São Paulo. It's renowned for its rustic furniture, ceramics, paintings and leather items. You'll find things here from all over Brazil. If you can't make it to the fair on the weekend, it's still worth coming during the week, as most of the artists have permanent shops and there are stacks of handicraft stores. While you're in Embu, have a look at the old Jesuit church in the main square; it contains a small sacred art museum and the first organ made in Brazil.

Getting There & Away

Air From São Paulo there are flights to everywhere in Brazil and many of the world's major cities. Before buying your ticket be sure to check which airport the flight departs from and how many stops it makes (flights to coastal cities often make several stops along the way).

The São Paulo to Rio shuttle flies every 30 minutes or less from Congonhas airport into Santos Dumont, in central Rio. The flight is less than an hour and you can usually go to the airport, buy a ticket and be on a plane within the hour. They still use the old Lockheed Elektra planes, but they're slowly being phased out, much to the dismay of many Elektra fans.

Most of the major airlines have offices on Avenida São Luis, near the Praça da República. Varig/Cruzeiro (☎ 231-9244) is at Rua da Consolação 362, Transbrasil (☎ 259-7066) is at Avenida São Luis 250 and VASP (☎ 220-3622) is at Rua Libero Badaró 106.

Bus The Terminal Tietê rodoviária is easy to reach – just get off at the Tietê metro station, which is adjacent to and connected with it. It's an enormous building but easily navigated. The information desk in the middle of the main concourse on the 1st floor is of limited value. Only Portuguese is spoken.

Bus tickets are sold on the 1st floor, except for the Rio shuttle, which has its ticket offices on the ground floor at the rear of the building. Buses leave for destinations throughout Brazil, and there are also buses to major cities in Argentina, Paraguay, Chile and Uruguay.

All the following buses leave from the Terminal Tietê. Frequent buses traverse the 429 km of the Via Dutra highway to Rio in six hours. The cost is US$11 for the regular bus, US$18 for the leito. There are also buses to: Brasília (14 hours, US$28); Belo Horizonte (9½ hours, US$15); Foz do Iguaçu (15 hours, US$26); Cuiabá (24 hours, US$35); Campo Grande (14 hours, US$21); Salvador (33½ hours, US$45); Curitiba (6 hours, US$10); and Florianópolis (12 hours, US$20).

Buses to Santos, Guarujá and São Vicente leave every five minutes from a separate bus station at the end of the southern metro line (Jabaquara station). It's a one-hour trip.

If you're staying outside the city centre, find out if there is a local bus station nearby where the buses make a stop on their way out of town. For example, there's Itapemirim Turismo (☎ 212-5402) at Avenida Valdemira Feirrara 130, near the Cidade Universitária. Several southbound buses stop here on their way to Florianópolis, Curitiba, etc. If you catch the bus here, it will save an hour's drive into the city and an hour's drive back.

Train Estação da Luz train station services the long-distance routes to Brasília and Bauru (from where you can get to Campo Grande and Corumbá – see below). To get there take the metro to Luz station. Long-distance routes have been severely cut back in recent times, so it'll pay to check the following information. The information booth (☎ 227-3299, 991-3062) at Luz station has all the details.

The 22-hour trip to Brasília offers daylight and interesting terrain. It leaves on Sundays at 8.25 pm with stops at the bigger cities along the way.

You can't get a direct train to Campo Grande or Corumbá from São Paulo – you have to take the train or bus from São Paulo to Bauru. The 11 pm train that leaves São Paulo for Bauru every Tuesday, Thursday and Sunday connects with the 11 am train from Bauru to Campo Grande. For connections from Campo Grande to Corumbá and Bolivia, see the Campo Grande section. The trip from São Paulo to Corumbá, which crosses the southern edge of the Pantanal, takes close to 40 hours.

Steam-train enthusiasts, or anybody for that matter, will enjoy the spectacular rail trip to Santos, which descends the Piritinanga plateau to the port city. It leaves from Barra Funda station on Saturday, Sunday and holidays at 8.15 am, arriving in Santos at noon,

and departs Santos at 5.30 pm. Fares are US$4 one way and US$7 return.

Getting Around

To/From the Airport São Paulo has three airports. Congonhas serves Rio and other local destinations. It is the closest airport – 14 km south of the city centre. Avoid the radio-taxis at the front of the terminal and ask for the comums (regular taxis); there's a small sign marking the place. The ride into town is about US$8.

To catch a bus into the city, walk out of the terminal and to your right, where you'll see a busy street with a pedestrian overpass. Head to the overpass, but don't cross: you should see a crowd of people waiting for the buses along the street, or ask for the bus marked 'Banderas'. The trip takes about an hour, and the last bus leaves around 1 am.

The Aeroporto Viracopos is 97 km from the city, near Campinas. Avoid this airport if possible. A taxi from here into town will cost about US$60.

Aeroporto Internacional de São Paulo/Guarulhos is 30 km east of the city. There's a bus that goes to Praça da República, Terminal Tietê rodoviária and Congonhas airport. It costs US$8. There's another bus for the same price that does a circuit of 11 four and five-star hotels in the Jardims area and the centre. A comum taxi will cost US$20 to the centre and a radio-taxi US$30.

Metro If you're on a limited budget, a combination of metro and foot is the best way to see the city. The metro is new, cheap, safe and fast. It's open from 5 am to midnight. You can buy all sorts of tickets, but the most useful if you're going to be around for a few days is the *multiplo* 10, which gives you 10 rides for US$3. A single ride costs 40c.

There are currently three lines. Two intersect at Praça da Sé, and the other, newer line gives access to Avenida Paulista. It begins at Paraiso station. Liberdade is one stop away from Praça da Sé, the budget hotel area is served by the Luz and República stations, and the rodoviária, Terminal Tietê, is four stops north of Luz. Get off at Tietê.

Bus Buses are slow, crowded during rush hours and not too safe. Unlike Rio, you can wait quite a while for the one you want, and trying to figure out which that is can be difficult. The tourist information booths are excellent sources of information about buses.

Taxi Both the comum and radio-taxi services are metered. Radio-taxi (☎ 251-1733) costs 50% more than the comum and will pick you up anywhere in the city.

The Paulista Coast

UBATUBA

The Ubatuba littoral is a stunning stretch of beach along the northern São Paulo coast. It's the pre-eminent beach resort for the well-to-do of São Paulo and there are many elegant beach homes and hotels, especially to the south of the town of Ubatuba. To the north of town, all the way to Parati, the beaches are wilder, cleaner and often deserted. There are few hotels, but plenty of campsites.

Most travellers don't go to Ubatuba, unless they are spending some time in São Paulo and want to escape for the weekend, or are driving the Rio-Santos coastal road. It's not that the beaches aren't top-notch – they are, but they get crowded in the summer, are rather expensive and there is little that remains of the old fishing culture that animates so many coastal towns in Brazil.

Information

Tourist Office There's a tourist office shack in Ubatuba where Rua Profesor Thomaz Galhardo hits the bay. It's open from 8 am to 6 pm; staff are somewhat helpful, but don't have any maps. By some strange coincidence, the newsstand next door sells an Ubatuba guidebook with a good map for US$2.

Money The Banco do Brasil is on the corner of Rua Dona Maria Alves and Rua Carvalho.

Post & Telephone The post office is on Rua Dona Maria Alves and the posto telefônico is at Rua Professor Thomaz Galhardo 81.

Beaches

Beaches, beaches and more beaches. Within the district of Ubatuba there are some 74 beaches and 15 islands. If you're staying in the city and don't have wheels, there's a fine beach a couple of km south of town with barracas and some surfing. Other recommended beaches south of Ubatuba include Toninhas and Enseada (eight km away), Flamengo (12 km), Lazaro and Domingas Dias (14 km).

To the north of town the beaches are hidden away down the steep hillside. They are harder to find, but well worth the effort. The best beaches are Vermelha (nine km away), Itamambuca (11 km), Promirim (22 km), and Ubatumirim (32 km).

Port

The port is at Praia de Saco de Rebeiro, 12 km south of Ubatuba. Mykonos Turismo (☎ 41-1388) has offices at the port and offers daily cruises into the Baía da Enseada and out to the Ilha Anchieta. The four-hour cruise costs US$15.

Festival

On 29 June, Ubatuba celebrates the Festa de São Pedro Pescador with a big maritime procession.

Places to Stay

Staying in Ubatuba is the most convenient place if you don't have a car, because you can catch local buses to some of the beaches. Hotel deals within a couple blocks of the bus station include the *Hotel Xareu* (☎ 32-1525) at Rua Jordão Homem da Costa 413, the *Hotel São Nicolau* (☎ 32-1267) at Rua Conceição 213, and, next door, the *Parque Atlântico* (☎ 32-1336) at Rua Conceição 185. None of these hotels are cheap and all of them charge around US$30 a single and US$40 a double.

For cheaper accommodation, your best bet is to go over to Praia do Perequê, a 10-minute walk away, and check in at the *Jangadeiro Hotel* (☎ 32-1365), Avenida Abreu Sodré 111. It's a very friendly place and singles/doubles cost US$8/12. There's a campground nearby at Avenida Leovegildo dias Viera 1854, Itaguá.

Ubatuba Palace (☎ 32-1500) is the city's finest hotel, with singles/doubles for US$60/70.

Places to Eat

A good fish restaurant is *Ladis*, on the waterfront at Avenida Leovegildo dias Viera 196. Also on the waterfront but a bit closer to the centre is *Cantina Perequim*, an Italian restaurant that's popular with the locals. It's at Rua Guarani 385. *Gauchão* is the best churrascaria in town, at Rua Guarani 378.

Getting There & Away

Bus There are two bus stations in Ubatuba, less than two blocks apart. The main rodoviária is on Rua Profesor Thomaz Galhardo between Rua Hans Staden and Rua Cunhambebe. The Reunidas bus company, which also runs buses to Rio and São Paulo, has a ticket office in a lanchonete on the corner of Rua Profesor Thomaz Galhardo and Rua Coronel Domiciano.

To São Paulo, there are eight daily buses, the first leaving at 12.30 pm and the last at 6.30 pm. The four-hour trip costs US$7. Buses to Parati leave at 9.30 am, 5 and 9.30 pm. For Rio, buses leave at 12.45 pm and 9.45 am. The five-hour trip costs US$9.

Car Ubatuba is 72 km south-west of Parati on the paved coastal road: a 1½-hour drive at a reasonable speed. Rio is 310 km away: a five-hour drive. Heading south on the coast, you reach Caraguatatuba, 54 km away, São Sebastião and Ilhabela, 75 km away, and Santos, 205 km away. After Caraguatatuba the road begins to deteriorate and an unending procession of speed bumps rear their ugly heads.

São Paulo is 240 km from Ubatuba. The fastest route, by a long shot, is to turn off the coastal road at Caraguatatuba on SP-099 and climb the escarpment until you meet the Rio-São Paulo highway, BR-116, at São José dos Campos. This is a beautiful, rapid ascent, and the road is in good condition.

CARAGUATATUBA

The coastal town of Caraguatatuba is 55 km from Ubatuba and 25 km from São Sebastião. This is not a very attractive town, and the beaches around the city are below the regional standard and not worth visiting.

Places to Stay & Eat

If you do get stuck here there are a few cheap hotels – ask around for *Hotel Central*, *Hotel Atlântico* or *Hotel Binoca* – and plenty of restaurants. There are also several hotels at Praia Massaguaçu, 10 km north of town.

Getting There & Away

The rodoviária is at Avenida Brasília 50 and buses leave for points north and south along the coast, and for São Paulo and Rio.

SÃO SEBASTIÃO

The coastal town of São Sebastião faces the Ilha de São Sebastião, popularly known as Ilhabela, which is only a 15-minute ferry trip across the channel. Huge oil tankers anchor in the calm canal formed by the island and mainland, waiting to unload at São Sebastião. The town itself is unassuming. There's not much here, but at least it has avoided the tourist industry blight, thanks to the poor beaches. Most visitors stay in São Sebastião either because they can't find lodging at Ilhabela or to enjoy the canal's excellent windsurfing conditions.

Information

There's a very helpful tourist office where English is spoken, on the waterfront at Avenida Dr Altino Arantes 174. It doesn't have information on Ilhabela, just the coastal towns towards Guarujá. It's open 8 am to 6 pm from Monday to Friday and 6 to 10 pm on weekends.

Places to Stay

The *Porto Grande* (☎ 52-1101), on the coast road just north of town, is the best hotel around and the owner changes dollars at close to parallel market rates. Basic singles/doubles are US$56/70, while more luxurious singles/doubles are US$80/95. They also have a good dinner and a maritime museum, and the hotel is right on the beach.

For something cheaper, and right in the centre of town, try the *Hotel Roma* (☎ 52-1016) at the Praça Major João Fernandes 174. Doubles start at US$15. Also good value is the *Pousada da Sesmaria* (☎ 52-2437) at Rua São Gonçalo 190, close to the centre. Singles/doubles start at US$12/20.

Places to Eat

Along the waterfront you'll find several good fish restaurants, including *Superflipper*. Eat the fish, not the shrimp.

Getting There & Away

The rodoviária, at Praça da Amizade 10, has a regular service to São Paulo, Rio, Santos and Caraguatatuba.

The Rio-Santos highway is slow going between São Sebastião and Santos. A much quicker route to São Paulo (200 km) is through Caraguatatuba, despite a zillion speed bumps along the coastal road.

ILHABELA

With an area of 340 sq km, Ilhabela is the biggest island along the Brazilian coast. The island's volcanic origin is evident in its steeply rising peaks, which are covered by dense, tropical jungle. There are 360 waterfalls and the flatlands are filled with sugar cane plantations. The island is known for it's excellent jungle hiking and fine cachaça.

Although it's a beautiful place, visiting Ilhabela can be a bit of a drag. During the summer the island is besieged by multitudes of Paulistas, and the normal population of 13,000 swells to over 100,000. Besides the threat this poses to the environment, the crowds create all sorts of logistical difficulties: many hotels fill up, waits of two to three hours for the car ferry are common and prices

soar. To add to all that, the bugs are murder, especially the little bloodsuckers known as *borrachudos*. Use plenty of repellent at all times.

The time to go to Ilhabela is weekdays in the off season. Once you arrive, the name of the game is to get away from the west coast, which faces the mainland, and where almost all human activity is concentrated. To get to the other side of the island requires either a car, catching a boat, or a strong pair of hiking legs.

Information

The Secretaria de Turismo de Ilhabela is in Vila Ilhabela, the main settlement, at Rua Dr Carvalho 234. Staff sell maps for US$1 and have a complete list of hotels, pousadas, chalés and camping grounds. The post office and ticket office for buses to São Paulo are in the same street.

There's a tourist information post at the roundabout 200 metres from the ferry dock in Barra Velha. It's open every day from 9 am to noon and 2 to 6 pm. Staff have information about hotels (including prices) and sightseeing trips, and a serviceable map of the island.

Colonial Buildings

Vila Ilhabela has quite a few well-preserved colonial buildings, including the slave-built Igreja NS da Ajuda, dating from 1532, the Fazenda Engenho d'Agua in Itaquanduba, constructed in 1582 and the Fazenda Santa Carmen at Feiticeira beach.

Beaches

There are more than 50 beaches on the island, but most of them are hard to get to and can only be reached by boat or by walking.

Of the sheltered beaches on the island's north side, Praia Pedra do Sino and Praia Jabaquara are recommended. On the east side, where the surf is stronger, try Praia dos Castelhanos (good camping and surf), Praia do Gato or Praia da Figueira.

Waterfalls

Cachoeira das Tocas, two km inland from Perequê beach, is made up of various small waterfalls with accompanying deep pools and water slides. It costs US$1 to get in, which includes all the insect repellent you want. It's a great place to go if you're sick of the beach. Cachoeira de Água Branca, in the middle of the jungle, is another waterfall to check out. Access is from Veloso beach.

São Sebastião

If you're feeling energetic, the 1379-metre-high peak of São Sebastião, in the suburb of Barra Velha, provides a great view.

Activities

Paulistas on vacation like their toys, so consequently you can rent almost anything: power boats, yachts, kayaks, jet skis, windsurfers, motorbikes, dune buggies, bicycles, tennis courts, diving gear and helicopters are just some of the alternatives.

Places to Stay

There's a lack of cheap lodging on Ilhabela, which is why many people choose to stay in São Sebastião where the hotels are cheaper.

On Rua Dr Carvalho try the *Hotel São Paulo* (☎ 72-1158) for relatively inexpensive lodging at US$25/30 a single/double. The *Pousada dos Hibiscos* (☎ 72-1375), Avenida Pedro Paula de Morais 714, is a bit cheaper, with doubles for US$25. It's 800 metres from town and is near the beach. Still close to town, the *Costa Azul* (☎ 72-1365), Rua Francisco Gomes da Silva Prado 71, is similarly priced.

If you plan on staying a few days, self-contained chalés àre reasonably priced. *Chalé Praia Grande* (☎ 72-1017), in the southern part of the island, is the cheapest at US$12 per day. There are lots of campgrounds near Barra Velha, where the ferry stops, and just a bit further south at Praia do Curral.

There is certainly no lack of top-end hotels on the island. The five-star *Itapemar* (☎ 72-1329), close to town in Saco da Capela, costs US$85 a double. Other top-end recommen-

dations from people 'in-the-know' include: *Porto Pousada Saco da Capela* (☎ 72-2255) and *Ilhabela Turismo Ltda* (☎ 72-1083), both in Saco da Capela; and *Petit Village* (☎ 72-1393) on Rua Morro da Cruz in Itaguassú. Reservations are a good idea here, especially on weekends.

Places to Eat

There are new restaurants opening up all the time on Ilhabela. In Vila Ilhabela itself there are a few good, cheap lanchonetes, two in the pedestrian mall and a couple on Rua Dr Carvalho. Right on the pier is *Pier Pizza* where you can have a tasty chopp and watch the fishers pull in a few swordfish. Other places a bit further from Vila are *Deck* at Avenida Almirante Tamandaré 805, a popular seafood restaurant, and *Stefan's* at Perequê, which specialises in German dishes. *Recanto da Samba*, on the waterfront, is a great place to have a beer, stare at the mainland and listen to some samba.

Getting There & Away

The ferry takes 15 minutes and runs frequently. The service starts at 5.30 am and goes until midnight, although during the summer it often goes much later. Pedestrians travel free.

BOIÇUCANGA

A popular weekend spot for Paulistas, Boiçucanga is well serviced by simple hotels and decent restaurants. While the beach here is not as good as the nearby ones at Maresias and Camburi, there are some good walks into the Mata Atlântica, the Atlantic rainforest.

Information

A good source of information here is José Mauro B Pinto y Silva, who runs a tourist information service/câmbio/video rental place called Amart (☎ 65-1276) at Avenida Walkir Vergani 319. An experienced budget traveller who speaks good English, José is a friendly guy who can help you out with just about anything, including cheap places to stay. He's a good person to see about treks into the forest.

Beaches

There are some great beaches along this stretch of coastline and if you have a car you'll be able to explore them easily. If you're relying on buses it's a bit harder, but still possible.

Maresias and Camburi are both good surf beaches. Barra do Sahy is a beach with calmer water and some nearby offshore islands which you can visit. Kayaks can be rented on the beach for US$5 an hour.

Places to Stay & Eat

There are campgrounds at all the beaches and they are a good, cheap option. Cheaper hotels in Boiçucanga include the *Dani* (☎ 65-1299) at Avenida Walkir Vergani 455, with singles/doubles for US$15/20, and *Pousada Boiçucanga* at No 522, with rooms for US$15. The *Big Pão* padaria on the corner nearby has good snacks and *Le Moussier* at Rua Luziana 226 has an excellent chicken pie as well as coffee and cakes.

At Camburi, an enjoyable top-end place to stay is *Pousada das Praias*, just off the main road on the old SP-55 road (Antiga SP-55) at No 22. During the week their doubles go for US$40 but on weekends the price goes up to US$60.

Getting There & Away

There are regular buses running along the coast. José has a timetable posted in his shop window.

GUARUJÁ

The closest beach to the city of São Paulo, 87 km away, Guarujá is the biggest and most important beach resort in the state. If you enjoy beach cities, it has plenty of hotels, restaurants, boutiques, etc.

Places to Stay & Eat

If you do end up here, *Hotel Rio* (☎ 86-6081), a block from Praia das Pitangueiras at Rua Rio de Janeiro 131, is the best budget deal, with singles/doubles for US$12/24. It's small and popular. There are many other, more expensive places.

There are stacks of restaurants and bars along the waterfront.

Getting There & Away

The rodoviária is just outside town at Santos Dumont 840. From there catch a local bus into the city. Buses to São Paulo leave every 30 minutes. The US$2 trip takes just over an hour. On the way you'll pass through Cubatão, one of the most polluted places in the world.

SANTOS

Santos is the largest and busiest port in Latin America. Founded in 1535 by Brás Cubas, the city has seen better days. As a destination for travellers, Santos holds little interest. Only the facades remain of many of the grand 19th-century houses built by wealthy coffee merchants, and the water at the beaches is definitely suspect.

Information

There are tourist information booths at Praça das Bandeiras, Praia do Gonzaga and at the rodoviária. If you need to change money, try Casa Branco in the centre at Praça da República 29.

Places to Stay & Eat

On the waterfront at Avenida Presidente Wilson 36, the *Hotel Gonzaga* (☎ 4-411) is quite a decent cheapie, with single/double quartos for US$11/13. There are lots of other hotels along the seafront, and this is also where most of the restaurants are located.

Getting There & Away

The bus station is right in the centre at Praça dos Andradas 45. There are frequent buses to São Paulo, 72 km away.

IGUAPE

One of the oldest towns in Brazil, Iguape was founded in 1538.

Information

Tourist information is available from the pre-ifeitura at Rua 15 de Novembro 272. It's open on weekdays from 8 to 11 am and 1 to 5 pm.

Things to See

The attractions of the town are the Museu de Arte Sacra in the limestone Igreja do Rosário, and the Mirante do Morro do Espia, a lookout with a good view of the port and surrounding area. The most popular beaches in the area are Varela, Prelado, Rio Verde, Una and Juréia. Five minutes by ferry from Iguape is Ilha Comprida, with a 74-km stretch of beach.

Places to Stay

The *Solar Colonial* (☎ 41-1591) in the centre of town has good doubles for US$12. *Rio Verde* (☎ 41-1493) at Rua Antônio José de Morais 86 is a bit cheaper, with singles/doubles for US$6/10. On Ilha Comprida, the *Alpha* (☎ 42-1270), Rua São Lourenço 14, and *Vila das Palmeiras* (☎ 42-1349), Rua Júlio de Almeida, charge US$15 a double. At Juréia beach, the *De Ville* (☎ 42-1238) charges US$15 a double.

Places to Eat

Seafood and more seafood. Try *Gaivota* and *Arrastão*, both on the seafront at Ilha Comprida.

Getting There & Away

Four buses a day, the first at 6 am and last at 8 pm, make the trip to São Paulo. To get to Cananéia, take a bus to Pariquero and switch from there. An alternative route is to hitch along the beach on Ilha Comprida.

CANANÉIA

Considered the oldest city in Brazil, Cananéia was the first port of call of Martim Afonso de Sousa's squadron, and was founded in 1531.

Beaches

The town doesn't have its own beach, but Ilha Comprida is only 10 minutes away by boat. To the south, popular beaches are Prainha, Ipanema with its waterfall, and Ilha do Cardoso, an ecological reserve with some nice, deserted places; it's a two-hour boat ride away.

Other Attractions

In the town itself, there's not a lot to do. The colonial buildings are in really poor shape. There's a marine museum at Rua Profesor Besnard 133 if you're hard up, or you could walk up Morro de São João for a good view of the surrounding islands.

Places to Stay

The *Recanto do Sol* (☎ 51-1162) on Rua Pedro Lobo has reasonable rooms. Singles/doubles cost US$8/12. The *Beira-Mar* (☎ 51-1115) is a cheaper alternative, at Avenida Beira-Mar 219. *Hotel Coqueiro* (☎ 51-1255) on Avenida Independência has doubles for US$20 and a swimming pool.

Places to Eat

There are a couple of excellent Japanese restaurants in Cananéia; the *Naguissa* at Rua 33, No 25, is open for lunch and dinner from Tuesday to Sunday; it's closed Mondays. The *Bom Abrigo*, on Avenida Luís Wilson Barbosa, is only open for dinner and is closed on Tuesdays. Cananéia is renowned for its oysters.

Getting There & Away

To São Paulo, there's a direct bus at 4.30 pm.

CAMPOS DO JORDÃO

Three hours by bus from São Paulo, Campos do Jordão is a popular weekend mountain getaway for Paulistas, who like to feel cold and eat *pinhão* (large pine nuts). At 1700 metres in the Serra da Mantiqueira, Campos is a good place from which to check out some of the last remaining virgin *araucária* (Parana pine) forests, and to hike to the top of some high peaks, with their spectacular views of the Paraíba valley and the coastal mountain range, the Serra do Mar. The train line which connects Campos with Santo Antônio do Pinhal is the highest in Brazil.

Orientation

Campos is made up of three main suburbs:

Abernéssia, the oldest, Jaguaribe, where the rodoviária is located, and Capivari, the tourist centre with a large concentration of restaurants, chocolate shops and three-star hotels. Capivari is the best base for visitors. The three suburbs are connected by a tram line.

Information

Tourist Office If you're driving, there's a tourist information office at the gateway to the valley, just before Abernéssia. There's another office in Capivari, close to the tram stop in the old railway station. Normally, they're open from 8 to 11.30 am and 1.30 to 6 pm weekdays, but during the peak period in July they open from 8 am to 6 pm every day. They have handouts with average maps and a list of all the hotels. Nobody in the office speaks English, but they are reasonably helpful.

Money There's a Banco do Brasil in Abernéssia, but you should be able to get close to parallel rates from some of the boutiques in Capivari.

Post & Telephone Telesp has a posto telefônico in Abernéssia in front of the tram stop. The post office is also in Abernéssia on Avenida Dr Januário Miraglia.

Things to See & Do

The state park, better known as Horto Florestal, 14 km from Capivari, contains the largest araucária reserve in the state, and there are some fine walks. The reception desk near the trout farm hands out maps.

The Gruta dos Crioulos (Creoles' Cave) was used as a hiding place by slaves escaping from the surrounding fazendas. The cave is seven km from Jaguaribé on the road to Pedra do Baú, which is a huge, rectangular granite block, 1950 metres high. To get to the top you have to walk 2 km and climb up 600 steps carved in the rock. It's 25 km from Campos.

Another spot that deserves a visit is the Pico do Itapeva (Itapeva Peak), 15 km away. With an altitude of 2030 metres, it's possible to see almost all of the Paraíba valley, with its industrial cities and the Rio Paraíba.

Close to Capivari is a chairlift to the top of the 1800-metre-high Morro do Elefante, which has a good view of the town. The Palácio Boa Vista is the state governor's summer residence, and contains many antiques. It's open Wednesdays, weekends and holidays from 10 am to noon and 2 to 5 pm. It's 3½ km from Abernéssia.

The train ride from Campos to Santo Antônio do Pinhal is a three-hour round trip, including the 40 minutes spent in Santo Antônio. The train makes the journey twice a day from Campos, at 10.20 am and 3.25 pm. For the best views, sit on the right-hand side when leaving Campos.

Places to Stay

July is peak tourist period in Campos and hotel prices double or even triple. *Pousada Emilio Ribas* (☎ 63-2711), close to the tourist office, on Avenida Emilio Ribas, is worth a try. They charge US$9 a head without breakfast. You won't find any cheaper in the centre.

There's a youth hostel a few km out of town at Recanto Feliz. To get there, take the 'Recanto Feliz' local bus to its final destination. The hostel itself is OK but the surroundings are crummy.

Hotel Saint Moritz (☎ 63-1450), Rua Marcondes Machado 119, is close to the centre and costs US$20 a head with breakfast. The *Nevada Hotel* (☎ 63-1422) includes all meals in their price of US$60 a double. The oldest and most stylish place to stay is the *Toriba* (☎ 62-1566) on Avenida Ernesto Diedericksen, four km from Abernéssia. Singles go for US$100 and doubles for US$150.

Places to Eat

There are lots of restaurants in Capivari. *Esquina do Pastel* at Avenida Macedo Soares 203 has excellent pastels. *Baden-Baden*, Rua Djalma Forjaz 93, is a German food place. *Matterhorn* in the mock-Tudor Blvd Geneve is a fashionable delicatessen.

Don't forget to eat the tasty pine nuts. Try some fried in butter or mixed with rice.

Getting There & Away

From São Paulo there are seven daily buses to Campos, from 6 am to 6.15 pm. From Campos to São Paulo, there are also seven daily buses, from 6 am to 6.20 pm. The trip costs US$6.

See the Things to See & Do section for details of the train ride to Santo Antônio do Pinhal.

Getting Around

The tram that connects the suburbs of Campos is itself a tourist attraction. It runs every half-hour between 6.30 am and 8 pm, and gets very crowded. Local buses also run out to the state park. Take the 'Horto Florestal' to its final stop.

Bicycles, including mountain bikes, can be rented in Capivari from Verde Vital in Cadij shopping centre if you feel like a bit of a pedal. If you want to horse around, rent one near the chairlift or 10 km out on the road to the park, where the trails are better.

THE SOUTH

REGIÁO SUL

The South

The Southern region, known in Brazil as Região Sul, includes the states of Paraná, Santa Catarina and Rio Grande do Sul. It covers almost 7% of the country's land area and contains 23 million inhabitants – just over 15% of Brazil's population. Most of these people are descendants of the German, Italian, Swiss and Eastern European immigrants who settled the region in the latter half of the 19th century. They have kept alive their customs, language and architecture, so you'll see painted wooden houses with steep roofs and onion-spire churches, and find small towns where Portuguese is still the second language.

Some of the natural attractions of the region include the Iguaçu Falls and Ilha do Mel in Paraná, the beautiful beaches of Florianopolis in Santa Catarina and the mountain areas of Rio Grande do Sul.

Geographically, Paraná, Santa Catarina and the northern part of Rio Grande do Sul are dominated by *planaltos* (tablelands): near the coast, the Planalto Atlântico, is formed of granite; and in the interior, the Planalto Meridional is formed by volcanic basalt, with rich, red soil known as *terra roxa*. In the southern interior of Rio Grande do Sul are the *pampas* – the grassy plains, while on the coast there are three large saltwater lagoons: Patos, Mirim and Mangueira.

With the exception of the north of Paraná, the climate is subtropical and the vegetation varies from Mata Atlântica remnants on the Paraná and Santa Catarina coast to the almost extinct Mata Araucária and pine forests of the Planalto Meridional. Snow is not uncommon on the Planalto Meridional during winter.

The economy of the region has changed dramatically in the last 30 years. The pampas, where once roamed huge herds of cattle driven by *gaúcho* cowboys, is now dominated by endless fields of soya beans – much of which goes to feed European cattle. Heavy industry, encouraged by cheap electricity from the Itaipu Dam, has transformed the south into Brazil's second most developed region.

Proud of their differences to other Brazilians, *Sulistas* (Southerners) – especially the gaúchos from Rio Grande do Sul – are growing increasingly dissatisfied with the inefficient and corrupt central government in Brasília. Talk of separatism is rife. A recent poll in the three southern states showed 40% in favour of independence.

Paraná

CURITIBA

Curitiba, the capital of Paraná, is one of Brazil's urban success stories. As in many of Brazil's cities, thousands began to flood into Curitiba in the 1940s. With only 140,000 residents in 1940 the city has grown tenfold to more than 1½ million people today. Yet, with the assistance of a vibrant local and state economy, Curitiba has managed to modernise in a sane manner – historic buildings have been preserved, a handful of streets have been closed to cars and there are many parks, gardens and wide boulevards.

Surprisingly, a progressive mayor instituted several incentives, including lower bus prices, to get people out of their cars – and the strategy worked. Traffic congestion was reduced and today there's an ease to getting around in Curitiba. Drivers go slowly and stop at red lights, few horns honk, pedestrians cross streets without blood-type identification bracelets, and although I haven't researched it, I bet Curitiba's divorce, heart attack, murder and dog abandonment rates are all down.

The local Curitibanos are mostly descended from Italian, German and Polish immigrants. There is also a large university population, which gives the city a young feel, and a good music scene as well.

At 900 metres above sea level, Curitiba is atop the great escarpment along the route from Rio Grande do Sul to São Paulo. Due to this location, it flourished briefly as a pit-stop for gaúchos and their cattle until a better road was built on an alternative route.

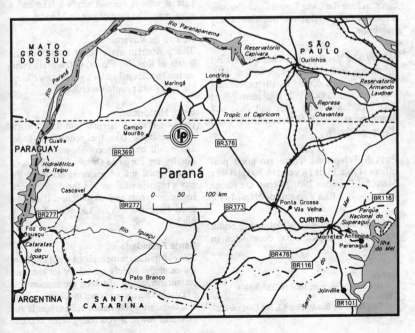

Curitiba quickly went back to sleep. It wasn't until the tremendous growth of the coffee plantations in northern Paraná at the beginning of the 20th century that the modern city of Curitiba began to take shape.

Like the gaúchos of old, most visitors are just passing through Curitiba. The highway from São Paulo (400 km away) to Florianópolis (300 km) and Porto Alegre (710 km) intersects Curitiba, and it's the turnoff for the train ride to Paranaguá and the bus to the Iguaçu Falls.

There's not much here for the out-of-towner, but it's still possible to pass a pleasant day in a park, museum and older neighbourhood waiting for your bus or train to leave. It's an easy city to walk around and if you have errands to do or clothes to buy, this is a good place for it.

Information

Tourist Office The tourist information booths at the rodoferroviária are useless. You can purchase the *Guia Turístico do Curitiba e Paraná* from bookstores, but it's not very helpful.

Money The travel agencies are the best bet for money exchange and information. ABC is at Rua Buenos Aires 178, Brementur is at Rua Candido Lopes 352, Diplomatur is at Rua Presidente Faria 143, and Jade and Esatur are at Rua 15 de Novembro 477 and 384 respectively.

Post & Telephone There are good post offices at Rua 15 de Novembro 700 and Rua Marechal Deodoro 298. Telepar, the phone company, is at Rua Visconde de Nácar 1415.

Foreign Consulates The following South American countries have consulates in Curitiba:

Bolivia
    Rua Bruno Filgueira 1662 (☎ 232-5698)
Chile
    Rua Barão do Rio Branco 63, No 1301 (☎ 225-1369)
Paraguay
    Rua Voluntários da Pátria 400, 5th floor (☎ 222-9226)
Peru
    Rua Alameda Dr Murici 926, 2nd floor (☎ 233-4711)
Uruguay
    Rua Saldanha Marinho 961 (☎ 232-0436)

Many European countries also have consulates in Curitiba.

Bookshops English books are available at Livraria-Curitiba, Rua Vol da Pátria 205 (Praça Santos Andrade), Rua Marechal Deodoro 275 and Rua 15 de Novembro; and at the Livraria Ghignone, Rua 15 de Novembro 409.

Passeio Público

Take a stroll in the Passeio Público, where Curitibanos have relaxed since 1886. Because it's right in the centre of town on Avenida Presidente Carlos Cavalcanti the park is always busy. There's a lake and a small zoo. The park closes on Mondays.

Rua 15 de Novembro

This pedestrian mall, better known by the locals as Rua das Flores, is the main commercial boulevard and it's good for walking, shopping and people watching.

Setor Histórico

Over by Praça Tiradentes and the Catedral Metropolitana, take the pedestrian tunnel and you'll be in the cobblestoned historic quarter, the Largo da Ordem. They've done a very good job of restoring some of the city's historic edifices and there are several restaurants, bars and art galleries. It's also a good place for a drink and some music at night.

Santa Felicidade

The old Italian quarter, about eight km from the centre, is widely touted for its bars and restaurants, many of which are monuments of kitsch. There's really not much to see here, and there are good Italian restaurants in the centre of town. If you really want to come

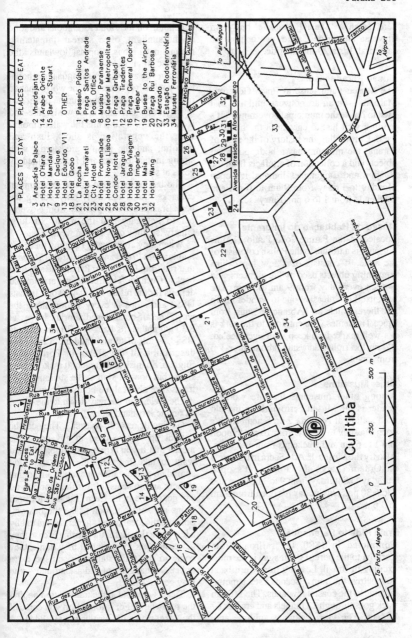

■ PLACES TO STAY   ▼ PLACES TO EAT

3   Araucária Palace
5   Hotel O'Hara
7   Hotel Mandarin
9   Hotel Cacique
13 Hotel Eduardo V11
18 Hotel Globo
21 La Rocha
22 Hotel Itamarati
23 City Hotel
24 Hotel Promenade
25 Hotel Nova Lisboa
26 Condor Hotel
28 Hotel Jaragua
29 Hotel Boa Viagem
30 Hotel Imperio
31 Hotel Maia
32 Hotel Wang

2   Vherdejante
14 Arabe Oriente
15 Bar do Stuart

OTHER

1   Passeio Público
4   Praça Santos Andrade
6   Post Office
8   Museu Paranaense
10 Catedral Metropolitana
11 Praça Garibaldi
12 Praça Tiradentes
16 Praça General Osorio
17 Telepar
19 Buses to the Airport
20 Praça Rui Barbosa
27 Mercado
33 Estação Rodoferroviária
34 Museu Ferroviária

Curitiba

here, catch a 'Santa Felicidade' bus from Travessa Nestor de Castro, just behind the cathedral. It's a 20-minute ride.

Museu Paranaense

The Museu Paranaense at Praça Generoso Marques is in an art nouveau building that used to house the municipal government. It's worth a visit just to check out the building itself. Chronicling the history of the state of Paraná, the museum has a hodgepodge of objects and a collection of artefacts from the Guarani and Caigangues Indians. It's open Monday to Friday from 9 am to 6 pm and weekends from 1 to 6 pm. Entry is free.

Museu da Habitação do Imigrante

Located in the Parque João Paulo 11, this museum is a tribute to the Polish colonists of the state. It consists of a few log cabins containing objects used by the pioneers, and is open every day from 9 am to 5 pm. The park itself is a pleasant one to wander in. To get there, catch an 'Abranches' bus from Praça Tiradentes. The entrance to the park is not well marked, so keep your eyes peeled. It's on the right-hand side, about three km from town.

Other Museums

Among other museums that are worth a gander is the Museu Ferroviária in the old train station at Avenida 7 de Setembro. It's open Tuesday to Friday from 10 am to noon and 1 to 6 pm and weekends from 1 to 6 pm. Also try the Museu de Arte Sacra in the Igreja da Ordem (Largo da Ordem). It's open Tuesday to Saturday from 9 to 11.50 am and 2 to 6.30 pm. On Sunday it's open from 9 am to 3 pm.

Train Ride to Paranaguá

Completed in 1880, the railroad from Curitiba to the port of Paranaguá is the most exciting in Brazil. Leaving from Curitiba at 900 metres, the train descends a steep mountainside to the coastal lowlands. The 110-km track goes through 13 tunnels and crosses 67 bridges. The view below is sublime and,

depending on the cloud formations and tone of the sunlight, often surreal: threatening mountain canyons, tropical lowlands, the vast blue Atlantic.

When you arrive in Paranaguá three hours later you've just witnessed the world change rapidly and radically: the climate is hot and muggy, and often rainy in the winter; the land is flat and low until it hits the wall of mountain; the vegetation is short, lush and uniform; and the people are sturdy, with strong Indian features and faces defined by years at sea.

The bad news is that due to government cutbacks, trains run daily only during the peak Brazilian tourist periods: from November to February and the month of July. Otherwise, they only run on weekends.

When they are actually running, there is a regular train *(trem)* and tourist train *(litorina)* that run from Curitiba to Paranaguá and then back to Curitiba. The trem leaves at 7 am and departs for the return trip at 4.30 pm. It costs US$2 and stops at every station along the way. The air-conditioned litorina leaves at 8.30 am and starts back at 3.30 pm. It costs US$8, is full of tourists and has a recorded description of the sights in Portuguese, English, Spanish and French. It makes photo stops, but doesn't stop at the stations. Both trains take about three hours each way. For the best view on the way down to the coast, sit on the left-hand side.

Getting tickets can be tricky. They can be bought up to two days in advance. This means that if you arrive in Curitiba late and want to take the train the next day, you should go to the station at about 6 am so that if there are no seats left for the litorina you can get on the trem. Even if tickets for both trains are sold out, don't take the bus yet. Some of the local travel agencies seem to buy a few extra tickets for the litorina in case they get customers for a tour; if they don't, they come to the train station to sell the extra tickets, so hang about and ask around – you may get lucky.

Tickets are sold at the train station behind the rodoviária. For information you can call the ticket office in Curitiba on 234-8441.

Places to Stay – bottom end

Across from the rodoferroviária, there are lots of inexpensive hotels. The *City Hotel* (☎ 264-3366), at Rua Francisco Torres 806, is good value at US$4.50/6 a single/double. Lots of Brazilians use this one so it fills up quickly. At Avenida Presidente Afonso Camargo 549 is the *Hotel Wang*, which has deteriorated a bit in the last few years, but is still cheap at US$3.50 a single and US$5.50 a double.

On the same street as the Wang there are three hotels in a row. The *Hotel Maia* (☎ 264-1684) has singles/doubles with bathroom for US$10/16. Next door at No 367 is the *Hotel Imperio* (☎ 264-3373). It's very clean and friendly, and charges US$8/14 for singles/doubles. Right alongside is the *Hotel Boa Viagem*, the cheapest of the bunch with singles for US$2.50 and doubles for US$4. They have a sense of humour there: when I asked the manager whether they had apartamentos, he just laughed and said they only had *apartamentos* (*apertar* is Portuguese for pinch or squeeze!).

Another good one to head for is the *Hotel Itamarati* (☎ 222-9063) at Rua Tibagi 950. In a quieter street, it's excellent value, with singles/doubles for US$8/12. Across from the market, on Avenida 7 de Setembro, is the *Hotel Nova Lisboa* (☎ 264-1944), with singles for US$9 and doubles for US$16.

If you want something closer to the centre, take Avenida Presidente Afonso Camargo to Avenida 7 de Setembro and then turn right on Rua João Negrão. About halfway between the rodoferroviária and the centre of town is *La Rocha* (☎ 233-6479), at Rua João Negrão 532. Singles and doubles cost US$3/6 but their pride and joy are the apartamentos with colour TV. They cost US$6/8.

In the centre itself, a couple of decent places are the *Mandarin* (☎ 233-6915) at Travessa Tobias de Macedo 120, close to the Museu Paranaense, which has apartamentos for US$14 a single and US$18 a double, and the *Hotel Cacique* (☎ 233-8122) at No 26, right on Praça Tiradentes. It's quite a bit cheaper, at US$7 a single and US$9 a double.

There is a *Casa dos Estudantes* (☎ 222-4911) on the Passeio Público, but phone before you go there, as at the time of research the visitors' quarters were being renovated and no one had any idea as to how long this would take.

Youth Hostel There is a youth hostel at Rua Padre Agostinho 645, in the suburb of Mercês. Catch the 'Campina do Siqueira – Capão do Imbui' bus, which heads to Campina do Siqueira from outside the bus station. Get out at Praça 29 de Março and walk two blocks along Rua Desembargador Molta to the crossroads with Rua Padre Agostinho.

Places to Stay – middle

A bit more expensive, but popular with travellers is the *Condor Hotel* (☎ 262-0322), a few doors up from the Nova Lisboa on Avenida 7 de Setembro. Singles/doubles with bathroom cost US$20/25.

An excellent mid-range alternative in the centre is the *Hotel O'Hara* (☎ 232-6044) in a colonial building at Rua 15 de Novembro 770, opposite Praça Santos Andrade. At US$19/27 for singles/doubles, it's good value for this price range. Also centrally located is *Hotel Globo* (☎ 234-7013). It's at Rua Senador Alencar Guimarães 72, very close to Praça General Osorio. Singles and doubles are US$21 and US$26.

Places to Stay – top end

Top-end hotels across from the rodoferroviária are the *Hotel Jaragua* (☎ 264-4322) at Avenida Presidente Afonso Camargo 279, which charges US$36 for singles and US$47 for doubles, and the *Hotel Promenade* (☎ 224-3022) at Rua Mariano Torres 976, with singles/doubles for US$50/62.

In the centre, the *Hotel Eduardo VII* (☎ 232-0433), close to Praça Tiradentes at Rua Cândido de Leão 15, has singles/doubles for US$30/43. The *Araucária Palace* (☎ 224-2822) is opposite the performing arts centre, at Rua Amintas de Barros 73. Singles/doubles cost US$70/83.

Places to Eat

The *Bologna* (☎ 223-7102) has the city's best Italian food. Moderately priced, it's at Rua Carlos de Carvalho 150 and is open for lunch and dinner daily except Tuesdays. Their tortellini has a city-wide reputation. Also in the city centre is the *Arabe Oriente* at Rua Ebano Pereira 26 on the 1st floor. Open daily for lunch and dinner, they have big portions and good food. The *Yuasu* has inexpensive Japanese meals at Avenida 7 de Setembro 1927. They are open for lunch and dinner daily, except Mondays.

There are several very pleasant, medium-priced restaurants in the Largo da Ordem area. It's a good place to walk around, look at menus and see what looks best. The *Vherdejante* vegetarian restaurant has excellent self-serve, fixed-price lunches, and is open daily except Sundays at Rua Presidente Faria 481, in front of the Passeio Público. They also serve chicken and fish dishes.

The *Bar do Stuart* has great small meals and a classy ambience. It's open daily until midnight (except Sundays when they close at 2 pm) at Praça General Osorio 427. For coffee and cake, try *Confeitaria Schaffer* at Rua 15 de Novembro 424 or the *Petit Café* at Rua Cruz Machado 258.

Entertainment

Up in Largo da Ordem there are several bars with rock. There's also the Casa Nilo Samba at Rua Mateus Leme 65 which has samba and choro. Up the hill, John Edwards Bar is at Rua Jaime Reis 212. It's a bit pricey but they have good jazz, blues and bossa nova from Wednesday to Sunday nights. John Edwards, the owner, is an American from San Francisco.

Another good place is the Cristal Bar, right next to the Araucária Palace Hotel. It's a small place with great local jazz, informal and cheap and always crowded with a mix of mostly artsy and university types. The music starts late and goes late.

Things to Buy

The Feira de Arte e Artisano is held in Praça Garibaldi on Sundays from 10 am to 2 pm. They have a good variety of arts and crafts.

Getting There & Away

Air There are flights to all major cities in Brazil.

Bus The rodoferroviária (☎ 234-8441) is clean and well organised. The entrance is on Avenida Presidente Afonso Camargo. Bus schedules are posted and easy to understand, and some companies even have printed schedules that they hand out.

There are many daily buses to São Paulo (six hours) and Rio (11 hours) and all major cities to the south. There are 13 buses a day to Foz do Iguaçu: the first leaves at 6.45 am and the last two at 9.15 and 10 pm (these last two are leitos). The price is US$12 for a regular bus and US$23 for a leito.

From Curitiba you can also get direct buses to Asunción (US$21), Buenos Aires (US$57) and Santiago (US$87).

If you miss the train, or there just isn't one, there are plenty of buses to Morretes, Antonina and Paranaguá. Try to get a bus that goes along the Estrada da Graciosa, the old pioneer road completed around 1873. The trip isn't as stunning as by train but it's still pretty. It takes just over 1½ hours to get to Paranaguá.

Train See the Train Ride to Paranaguá earlier in this section for details of this scenic train trip.

Getting Around

To/From the Airport Alfonso Pena airport is a 20 to 30-minute drive from the city. A taxi costs about US$13 and there are cheap public buses marked 'Aeroporto' that leave every hour or so from opposite the Hotel Presidente on Rua Westfalen. For other information call the airport on 282-1143.

Bus You can walk to most places of interest, as the city is fairly compact, but if you're footsore there's an excellent local bus network. Destinations are well marked and fares are 20c. The main bus terminals are on

Praça Tiradentes, Praça General Osorio and Praça Rui Barbosa.

Particularly useful is the white 'Circular Centro' minibus. It does regular circuits of the city and stops at the Passeio Público, Praça Tiradentes, Praça Santos Andrade near the university and outside the rodoviária. Look for the bus stop with the white acrylic top.

Around Curitiba

Vila Velha An interesting day trip is a visit to the 'stone city' of Vila Velha, 93 km from Curitiba on the road to Foz do Iguaçu. Here you'll find an interesting collection of sandstone pillars created by millions of years of erosion. There's also a place to swim and an elevator ride into a crater lake.

To get there, catch a semi-direito bus to Ponta Grossa from the rodoferroviária and ask to be let out at the entrance to the state park. Unless you camp, there's nowhere to stay in the park, but there are always plenty of buses back to Curitiba. If you're going on to Foz, catch a bus or hitch into Ponta Grossa, 22 km away.

MORRETES

Founded in 1721 along the banks of the Rio Nhundiaquara, there's nothing here but a tranquil little colonial town in the midst of the lush coastal vegetation zone. That's its attraction and it's a good place in which to relax, swim in the river and take some walks in the nearby state park.

Several buses and the train stop at Morretes on the way to Antonina and Paranaguá. If you like the feel of the place just hop off. The spectacular part of the train ride is over anyway. The town itself is very small and it's easy to find your way around.

Marumbi State Park

The park offers some great hikes. It's very popular with Curitibanos, who get off the train at one of its many stops and hike down the old pioneer trails that were the only connections between the coast and the Paranaense highland in the 17th and 18th centuries. The best two to walk on are the

Graciosa trail, which passes close to the Estrada da Graciosa, and the Itupava trail. Views from both are fantastic.

To get to the park from Morretes, catch a bus to São João de Graciosa. It's a couple of km from there to the park entrance, where you can pick up a trail map. Don't forget to take some insect repellent!

Rio Nhundiaquara

This river served as the first connection between the coast and the highlands. Now one of the best things to do on it is hire a truck inner tube from the guy who runs the service station and go 'tubing'. The same guy who rents the tubes will also take you up river and drop you off. It takes about four hours to float back down. See Dona Gloria at the Hotel Nhundiaquara for more details.

Cascatinha

Five km from Morretes on the Rio Marumbi is Cascatinha, a large lake which is good for swimming. It's a fine place to camp. There's a cachaça factory nearby.

Places to Stay

There are three hotels in Morretes. The *Hotel Nhundiaquara* (☎ 462-1228) is the best place to stay. It's on the river at Rua General Carreiro 13. The owner, Dona Gloria, is really helpful. She charges US$7/14 for singles/doubles with bathroom, and US$5/8 without. Being next to a fast-flowing river, it's also free from mosquitoes!

The *Hotel Bom Jesus* (☎ 462-1282) on Rua 15 de Novembro is cheaper with rooms for as little as US$4. The most expensive hotel in town is the *Porto Real Palace* (☎ 462-1344). It has singles for US$16 and doubles for US$26 and is just up from the railway station on Rua Visconde de Branco.

Places to Eat

The speciality of the region is a filling dish called *barreado*, a mixture of meats and spices cooked in a sealed clay pot for 24 hours. Originally it was cooked during Carnival, to give the revellers a huge protein fix, but today it's considered the state dish. There are a few places around town that serve it, but the best place to try it is in the restaurant of the *Hotel Nhundiaquara*.

ANTONINA

Antonina is 14 km east of Morretes and 75 km east of Curitiba on the Baía de Paranaguá. There are direct buses linking Antonina, Curitiba and Paranaguá. Similar to Morretes, Antonina is old and peaceful. Its first settlers panned for gold in the river. There's a fine church in the centre, the Igreja de NS do Pilar, that was begun in 1715 and rebuilt in 1927. Its festival is held on 15 August.

The beaches along the bay are not very good, but Antonina is an easy place in which to kick back and take in the great view of the Baía de Paranaguá.

Places to Stay

Of the five hotels in town, none could be considered a real bargain. The *Christina Hotel* (☎ 432-1533) on Rua 15 de Novembro and the *Monte Castelo* (☎ 432-1163) on Travessa Ildefonso both have medium-priced rooms for around US$15 a single and US$20 a double.

The cheapest place is the *Tokio*, close to the railway station at Rua Consuelo Alves de Araújo 287, but it's a long way from the waterfront. Singles/doubles cost US$3/6. The *Hotel Luz* (☎ 432-1625) on Rua Comendador Araújo 189 is good value at US$6/12 for singles/doubles, but again it's a bit of a walk to the water.

The most expensive hotel in Antonina is the *Regency Capela Antonina* (☎ 432-1357) at US$24 a single and US$40 a double – more if you want a view of the bay. It's at Praça Coronel Macedo 208.

Places to Eat

The *Vista Mar* on Travessa 7 de Setembro serves seafood and other dishes, as well as making some of the tastiest fruit batidas around. There's a great view of the bay. The restaurant is closed on Mondays. Along the waterfront, *Tia Rosinha* at Rua Antonio Prado 54, serves good seafood and barreado.

PARANAGUÁ

The train ride from Curitiba isn't the only reason to go to Paranaguá. It's a colourful city, with an old section near the waterfront that has a feeling of tropical decadence. There are several churches, a very good museum, and other colonial buildings that are worth a look. Although there has been some renovation, you still feel surrounded by decay. Fortunately, there aren't enough tourists around to destroy this air of authenticity. Paranaguá is also the place from which you leave for Ilha do Mel and the mediocre beaches of Paraná.

One of Brazil's major ports, Paranaguá is 30 km from the sea in the Baía de Paraná. Goods from a vast inland area, encompassing the state of Paraná, and parts of São Paulo, Santa Catarina, Mato Grosso do Sul and Rio Grande do Sul, are shipped from here.

The primary exports have been gold, mate, madeira and coffee, and are now corn, soy, cotton and vegetable oils.

Paranaguá's old section is small enough for wandering without a set itinerary. Without much effort you can see most of Paranaguá's colonial buildings and churches, waterfront bars and various markets.

Information

There's a tourist information office in front of the train station. Staff are helpful, friendly and often have maps as well as a list of hotels with prices. A few metres away there is a small telephone office for long-distance calls. It's open from 8 am to 10 pm. If you need to change money, try Diplomata Turismo at Faria Sobrinho 559. For travellers' cheques, the Banco do Brasil is at Largo Conselheiro Alcindino 103.

Museu de Arquelogia e Artes Popular

Don't miss the Museu de Arquelogia e Artes Popular. Many Brazilian museums are disappointing; this one is not. Housed in a beautifully restored Jesuit school that was built from 1736 to 1755 (the Jesuits didn't get to use the school for long, as they were expelled from Brazil in 1759), the museum has many Indian artefacts, primitive and folk art, and some fascinating old tools and wooden machines – an enormous basket-weaver, for instance.

At the front desk are notebooks with descriptions of the exhibits in English. The museum is at Rua 15 de Novembro 567 (near the waterfront). It's open Tuesday to Sunday from noon to 5 pm.

Churches

The city's churches are simple, unlike baroque churches. The Igreja de NS do Rosário is the city's oldest. Also worth visiting are the Igreja São Francisco das Chagas (1741) Igreja de São Benedito (1784) and the Igreja de NS do Rocio (1813).

Waterfront

Down by the waterfront you'll find the new and old municipal markets, and depending on the time and day, both can be quite lively. Nearby, there is a bridge that leads to the Ilha dos Valadares. There are 8000 people on the island, mostly fisherfolk, mostly poor. They

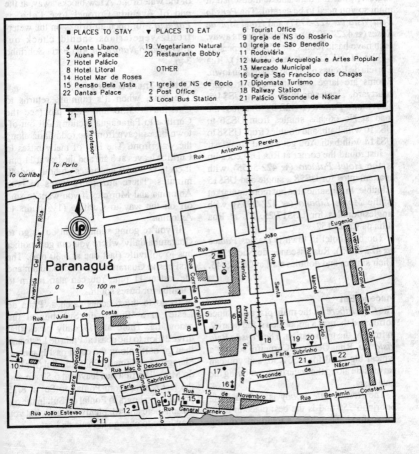

■ PLACES TO STAY	▼ PLACES TO EAT	6 Tourist Office
4 Monte Libano	19 Vegetariano Natural	9 Igreja de NS do Rosário
5 Auana Palace	20 Restaurante Bobby	10 Igreja de São Benedito
7 Hotel Palácio		11 Rodoviária
8 Hotel Litoral	OTHER	12 Museu de Arqueologia e Artes Popular
14 Hotel Mar de Roses		13 Mercado Municipal
15 Pensão Bela Vista	1 Igreja de NS de Rocio	16 Igreja São Francisco das Chagas
22 Dantas Palace	2 Post Office	17 Diplomata Turismo
	3 Local Bus Station	18 Railway Station
		21 Palácio Visconde de Nácar

Paranaguá

dance the Paraná fandango: a hybrid dance that combines the Spanish fandango and the dances of the Carijó Indians.

There are no regular boat trips to Ilha do Mel except during the summer, but there is a tourist boat that explores the river. The boats leave daily at 10.30 am, noon, 2 and 4 pm from the end of Avenida Arthur de Abreu, and the trip lasts 1½ hours.

Places to Stay – bottom end

The cheapest places are along the waterfront on Rua General Carneiro. The street has character, but it's dark and semideserted at night so you need to be careful. The *Pensão Bela Vista* (☎ 422-5737) and *Hotel Mar de Roses* (☎ 422-7397), a couple of doors away, both have basic rooms for US$3 per person.

The *Hotel Litoral* (☎ 422-0491), Rua Correia de Freitas 65, is the best deal in town. Rooms are large and open onto a sunny courtyard; singles/doubles go for US$4/6. The *Auana Palace* (☎ 422-0948) across the road at No 66 has singles from US$6 to US$10 with bath, and doubles from US$8 to US$14 with bath. You get a good breakfast.

Just round the corner at Rua Dr Leocádio is the *Hotel Palácio* (☎ 422-5655), with apartamentos for US$8 a single and US$15 a double. In the same area but more upmarket is the *Monte Libano* (☎ 422-2933), with singles/doubles for US$17/25. It's at Rua Julia da Costa 152.

The best hotel in town is *Dantas Palace* (☎ 422-1555), Rua Visconde de Nácar 740. Their singles and doubles start at US$35/45.

Place to Eat

The *Cafe Itibere* on the main praça has super coffee and there is a good suco stand nearby, in front of the train station. The *Pensão Bela Vista* on Rua General Carneiro serves a typical big meal for US$2.50, and you can eat outside along the waterfront, enjoying the bela vista.

The *Restaurante Bobby* is at Rua Faria Sobrinho 750 and is the best place in town for seafood. They have a traditional dining room and serve good size portions of fish, shrimp and meat that come with the best American-style condiments in Brazil. Most meals are US$4 to US$7, but you can easily spend less by ordering one meal for two people. The seafood moqueca is excellent. The restaurant is open daily for lunch and dinner, except for lunch on Mondays.

The *Restaurante Danúbio Azul Panorâmico* has seafood upstairs, beer and pizza downstairs. Meals are US$3 to US$6, and this place is open daily for lunch and dinner, except Sunday dinner. It's down at Rua 15 de Novembro 95 and has an excellent view of the waterfront. A few blocks away, at the end of Avenida Coronel José Lobo, is *Palhano's* for open-air drinks on the waterfront. Vegetarians should check out *Vegetariano Natural* at Rua Faria Sobrinho 346.

Getting There & Away

The train, when it's running, returns to Curitiba at 3.30 and 4.30 pm (see the Curitiba to Paranaguá section). All out-of-town buses leave from the rodoviária along the waterfront. The first of many buses to Curitiba leaves at 6 am and the last at 11 pm. It costs US$2.50 and takes an hour and 40 minutes. There are many buses to both Antonina and Morretes if you want to stop off on the way to Curitiba (1½ hours to Antonina).

If you're going south, eight buses go to Guaratuba daily, where you can get another bus to Joinville (last one at 5.30 pm). The first bus to Guaratuba leaves at 6.30 am and the last at 11 pm. You can also return to Curitiba for buses south.

To go to the beaches catch a 'Praia de Leste' or a 'Pontal do Sul' bus at the rodoviária. There are 17 daily buses that drive 30 km to the coast at Praia de Leste and then go north along the coast past Ipanema, Shangri-lá and finally Pontal do Sul (for Ilha do Mel). The first bus leaves at 5.50 am and the last returns from Pontal do Sul at 8.15 pm. It's 1½ hours to Pontal do Sul. In the off season there are still plenty of buses, but you may have to change at Praia de Leste.

Parque Nacional do Superagui

Comprising the Superagui and Peças islands in the Baia de Paranaguá, this marine park was created in 1989. It is reknowned for its mangroves and salt-marshes and also contains a great variety of orchids, dolphins, jaguars and parrots that are threatened with extinction as the mata atlântica shrinks.

The park doesn't possess any tourist facilities. It does, however, contain a small fishing community, Vila Superagui, where you may be able to sling a hammock. The closest town to the park is Guaraqueçaba. It can be reached by bus from Curitiba or Paranaguá. An alternative means of getting there would be to ask around the docks in Paranaguá about direct boats to the Superagui or Peças islands.

PARANÁ BEACHES

Descending the Serra do Mar from Curitiba you get a good view of the Paraná coast. The broad beach runs uninterrupted from Pontal do Sul to Caiobá. With the notable exception of Ilha do Mel, these are unspectacular beaches, hot and humid in the summer and too cold in the winter. There's plenty of camping and seafood barracas, and each town has a few hotels. Unfortunately, condominium blight is on the rise.

Praia de Leste

This is a small, unattractive town with a couple of hotels and the closest beach to Paranaguá, a bit more than 30 minutes away. The beach is open and windy, and there are some beach breaks for surfing.

You can check your luggage in at the rodoviária (50c) if you want to go for a swim. This is where you get buses south to Guaratuba. These get very crowded on summer weekends, so get there early.

Pontal do Sul

This is the end of the line and where you get off for Ilha do Mel. The bus stops three km from the canal where boats leave for Ilha do Mel. In between are summer homes and lots of open, unused beach.

ILHA DO MEL

The Ilha do Mel is an oddly shaped island at the mouth of the Baía de Paranaguá that wasn't discovered by the Portuguese until the 18th century. To secure the bay and its safe harbours from French and Spanish incursions, King Dom José I ordered a fort built in 1767. Since then not too much has happened. The few people on the island were ordered out during WW II in the name of national defence. Most significantly, the island is now part of the Patrimônio Nacional, which has prevented it from being turned into more cheesecake for the rich.

The island is popular in the summer because of its excellent beaches, scenic walks and relative isolation. Its undoing might be that it is becoming too popular. However, it is administered by the Instituto de Terras e Cartografia Florestal (ITCF), which intends to preserve the island more or less as it is.

From January to Carnival, and during Easter, the island is very popular with a young crowd, but there is still a lot of beach and there always seems to be room for an extra hammock. If you're travelling up or down the coast, it's crazy not to visit the island at least for a day. Many people end up staying much longer.

Orientation

The island has two parts, connected by the beach at Nova Brasília, where most of the locals live. The bigger part is an ecological station, thick with vegetation and little visited, except for Praia da Fortaleza. On the ocean side are the best beaches – Praia de Fora, Praia do Miguel and Praia Grande. All are reached by a trail that traverses the beaches, coves and steep hills that divide them. The bay side is muddy and covered with vegetation.

Your best bet is to catch a boat from Ponto do Sul direct to Nova Brasília. It'll set you down close to the main attractions of the island, as well as most of the pousadas. If you want the surf beaches and more nightlife, go to the right as you get off the boat. If you want something more mellow, cross over to

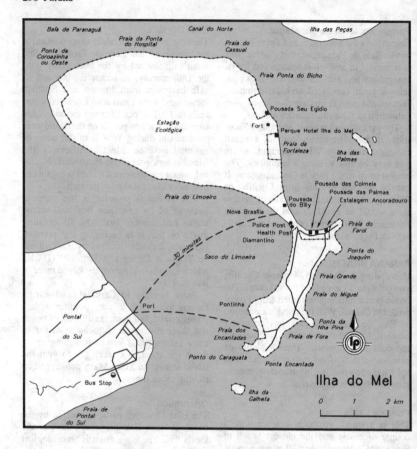

Bafá de Paranaguá
Canal do Norte
Ilha das Peças
Ponta da Coroazinha ou Oeste
Praia da Ponta do Hospital
Praia do Cassual
Praia Ponta do Bicho
Pousada Seu Egídio
Estação Ecológica
Fort
Parque Hotel Ilha do Mel
Praia da Fortaleza
Ilha das Palmas
Praia do Limoeiro
Pousada das Colmeia
Pousada das Palmas
Estalagem Ancoradouro
Pousada do Billy
Nova Brasília
Police Post
Health Post
Diamantino
Praia do Farol
30 minutes
Saco do Limoeira
Ponta do Joaquim
Praia Grande
Praia do Miguel
Port
Pontinha
Pontal do Sul
Ponta da Nha Pina
Praia dos Encantadas
Praia de Fora
Ponto do Caraguata
Ponta Encantada
Bus Stop
Ilha da Galheta
Praia de Pontal do Sul

Ilha do Mel

0   1   2 km

the ocean side and go left. It's a 30-minute walk to the fort. If there are a few of you or if you've got lots of luggage, it might be worth hiring a small cart to transport your stuff to a pousada. Look for them when you get off the boat. To Praia do Farol they cost US$6, US$8 to the fort and US$12 to Praia Grande.

The entire island can be walked in eight hours, but the best walking by far is along the ocean side (east) from the southern tip of the island up to Praia da Fortaleza. Bichos de pé are prevalent on the island, so keep something on your feet when you're off the beach.

Beaches

The best beaches face the ocean toward the east. Praia Grande is a 20-minute walk from Nova Brasília and a two-hour walk from Praia dos Encantadas. According to the local surfers, it has the best waves in Paraná, and during winter boatloads of surfers come across on the weekends. The walking is excellent along this stretch too.

Other Attractions

Points of interest include the Grutas das Encantadas, small caves at the southern tip (Ponta Encantada) where, legend has it, beautiful mermaids enchant all who come near them. The fort, Fortaleza de NS dos Prazeres, was built in 1769 to guard the bay at Praia de Fortaleza. From inside the fort, a trail leads up to the WW II gun emplacements and a magnificent view of the whole area. The Farol das Conchas lighthouse, built in 1872 on the orders of Dom Pedro II, stands at the island's easterly point at Praia do Farol. The fishers on the island regularly catch hammerhead sharks which they call 'Formula Ones'.

Festival

Ilha do Mel goes crazy at Carnival. Estimates for last year's attendance were 20,000.

Places to Stay

There are about 10 pousadas on the island, all charging between US$8 and US$10 per night. The best one is *Estalagem Ancoradouro*, run by Arnaldo, out towards the lighthouse. It's about a 10-minute walk from the police post at the far right of Brasília, as you face the island, but it's worth the walk. Other pousadas in the area are *Pousada das Colmeia* and *Pousada das Palmas*. About halfway between the lighthouse and the fort is *Pousada do Billy*. You can't miss it because it looks like a prison camp. Despite this it's a good place to stay; they charge US$8 per person, which includes breakfast.

At Praia da Fortaleza, 200 metres past the fort, there are a couple of places. Try *Pousada Seu Egidio*. Just before you get to the fort is the island's only hotel, the aptly named *Parque Hotel Ilha do Mel* (☎ (041) 223-2585), with rooms for US$40 a night. They have a boat that'll pick you up and take you directly to the hotel.

If you happen to arrive on the island on a holiday weekend or at another peak time, there's a chance there won't be any rooms, but it's easy to rent some space to sling a hammock. There's also plenty of room to camp. Watch out for the tides if you decide to sleep on the beach.

Places to Eat

There are barracas with food and drink at Brasília, Encantadas and Fortaleza. On Friday and Saturday nights there is music, and forró, and when the beer is gone it's time for pinga, the local cachaça. At Brasília, the *Davi* restaurant, just past the health post, has a good prato feito for US$2. Nearby, *Mierelles* serves an excellent pizza for US$3.

At Encantadas, Lucia is the most popular cook and speaks the best German on the island. Her *Bar Delirio* doesn't open for coffee until about 10.30 am because she stays open late.

Getting There & Away

Take the 'Ponto do Sul' bus from Paranaguá, or if you are coming from Guaratuba transfer at Praia de Leste for the same bus. The bus stops three km from the canal where the boats leave for Ilha do Mel. There's usually a taxi, which charges monopoly prices: US$3 for the five-minute ride. Look for someone else to split the cost with, or you can walk or hitch.

If you decide to walk when you get off the bus, return 20 metres to the paved main road and turn right. Follow this road for a little more than a km until it veers right and approaches the sea. Then turn left on a sandy but well-travelled road for about two km until the end, where you'll find several barracas and a few boats. That's it.

The boats cost US$1 and from December to March they make the 30-minute voyage to the island every hour or so, usually from 8 am to 5 pm. The rest of the year, they aren't as frequent, but you should have no problems finding one.

OTHER BAÍA DE PARANAGUÁ ISLANDS

There are several other islands in the Baía de Paranaguá that can be visited, but you'll have to do some scraping around to get there as there is no regular boat service.

The Ilha dos Currais is known for its birdlife ánd the Ilha da Cotinga for its mysterious inscriptions and ruins. The Ilha das

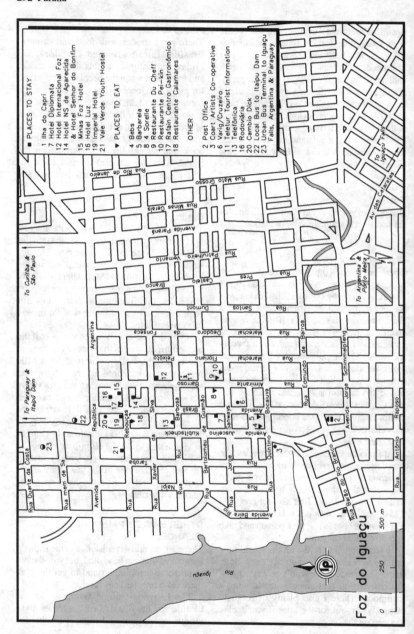

Foz do Iguaçu

PLACES TO STAY
1 Ilha do Capri
7 Hotel Diplomata
12 Hotel Internacional Foz
14 Hotel NS de Aparecida
   & Hotel Senhor do Bonfim
15 Minas Foz Hotel
16 Hotel Luz
19 Imperial Hotel
21 Vale Verde Youth Hostel

PLACES TO EAT
4 Bebs
5 Barbarela
8 4 Sorelle
9 Restaurante Du Cheff
10 Restaurante Pei-kin
17 Rafain Centro Gastronômico
18 Restaurante Calamares

OTHER
2 Post Office
3 Coart Artists Co-operative
6 Varig/Cruzeiro
11 Teletur Tourist Information
13 Telefônica
16 Rodoviária
20 Cambio Dick
22 Local Bus to Itaipu Dam
23 Urban Bus Terminal to Iguaçu
   Falls, Argentina & Paraguay

Peças and the Ilha do Superagui make up the Parque Nacional do Superagui.

FOZ DO IGUAÇU

The Rio Iguaçu arises in the coastal mountains of Paraná and Santa Catarina, the Serra do Mar, at the modest elevation of 1300 metres. The river snakes west for 600 km, pausing behind the Foz do Areia Cruz Machado and Salto Santiago dams and picking up a few dozen tributaries along the way. It widens majestically and sweeps around a magnificent jungle stage before plunging and crashing in tiered falls. The 275 falls are over three km wide and 80 metres high, which makes them wider than Victoria, higher than Niagara and more beautiful than either. Neither words nor photographs do them justice: they must be seen and heard. They're what the Romantic poets had in mind when they spoke of the awesome and sublime.

The falls were a holy burial place for the Tupi-Guaraní and Paraguas tribes thousands of years before they were 'discovered' by Whites. Spaniard Don Alvar Nuñes, also known as Cabeza de Vaca (Cow's Head), happened upon the falls in 1541 in the course of his journey from Santa Catarina on the coast to Asunción. He named the falls the Saltos de Santa Maria, but this name fell into disuse and the Indian name of Iguaçu, meaning Great Waters in Tupi-Guaraní, was readopted. No agreement has been made with spelling – in Brazil it's Iguaçu, in Argentina Iguazú and in Paraguay Iguassu. In 1986 the international commission of UNESCO declared the region (along with the Pantanal) a World Heritage site.

With a population increase from 35,000 to 150,000 as a result of the construction of the Itaipu dam, the Brazilian border town of Foz do Iguaçu is a frenzied place which can be dangerous, particularly at night. Ciudad del Este in Paraguay is a real pit, while Puerto Iguazú in Argentina is much more mellow.

Orientation

The falls are roughly 20 km east of the junction of the Paraná and Iguaçu rivers, which form the tripartite Paraguayan, Brazilian and Argentine border (marked by obelisks).

The Ponte Presidente Tancredo Neves bridges the Rio Iguaçu and connects Brazil to Argentina. The Rio Paraná, which forms the Brazilian-Paraguayan border, is spanned by the Ponte da Amizade; 15 km upstream is Itaipu, the world's largest hydroelectric project.

The falls are unequally divided between Brazil and Argentina, with Argentina taking the larger portion. To see them properly you must visit both sides – the Brazilian park for the grand overview and the Argentine park for a closer look. Travellers must allow at least two full days to see the falls. Even more time is required if you want to do it at a leisurely pace or visit Ciudad del Este or Itaipu dam.

The best time of the year to see them is from August to November. If you come during the May to July flood season you may not be able to approach the swollen waters on the catwalks. It's always wet at the falls. The area gets over two metres of rain per year, and the falls create a lot of moisture. Lighting for photography is best in the morning on the Brazilian side and in the late afternoon on the Argentine side.

Information

Tourist Office Teletur (☎ 139) maintains information booths at the airport and the Brazilian side of Ponte Presidente Tancredo Neves, but the best place to go is the main tourist office at Rua Almirante Barroso 485, next to the San Diego Hotel. Staff speak English and are very helpful. The office is open weekdays from 8 am to 6 pm. The telephone information service is attended from 8 am to 8 pm.

Money Recently the parallel market has been giving more favourable rates in Foz do Iguaçu. Go to Cambio Dick in Foz, near the bus station at Avenida Brasil 40, or Frontur at Avenida Brasil 75. There are plenty of others, but these two change both cash and travellers' cheques.

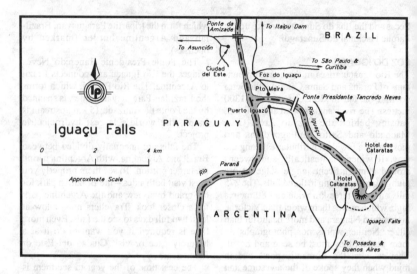

Post & Telephones The post office is on Praça Getúlio Vargas. International phone calls can be made from Rua Rui Barbosa 475, or Rua Marechal Floriano Peixoto 1222.

Visas Visitors who spend the day outside Brazil will not require visas, but those who intend to stay longer must go through all the formalities. In Foz do Iguaçu, the Argentine Consulate (☎ (0455) 74-2877) is at Rua Dom Pedro II 26 and the Paraguayan Consulate (☎ (0455) 73-1499) is at Rua Bartolomeu de Gusmão 777.

The Falls – Brazilian side

Although the Brazilian side has a smaller chunk of the falls, the Brazilians have The Grand View across the churning lower Rio Iguaçu to the raging falls. The Brazilian park is larger, with 1550 sq km of rainforest, but the Argentine forest is in better shape.

Walk to the observation tower by the Floriano falls, then over to Santa Maria falls, and then treat yourself to an outrageously beautiful helicopter ride over the waterfalls. US$40 will buy you seven minutes of intense pleasure in the air. The choppers will take up

to three passengers, but it's best to sit by the edge of the bubble. You can extend the ride to see Itaipu dam too. Helisul Taxi Aereo (☎ (0455) 74-2414) operates from Hotel das Cataratas, right at the waterfalls on the Brazilian side, from April to October between 9 am and 5 pm, and from November to March between 9 am and 7 pm. Travellers flying into Foz or Puerto Iguazú with accommodating weather and pilots can see the falls from the air.

You can catch a boat to the Garganta do Diablo (Devil's Throat) from near the observation tower. Sometimes the boat operators have an odd sense of humour and they'll cut the engine and float to the edge of the falls.

The Falls – Argentine side

The Argentine side is noted for its close-up views of the falls and the jungle. The entrance to the Argentine park is 18 km from Puerto Iguazú. There are three separate walks on the Argentine side: the Passeios Inferiores, the Passeios Superiores and the Garganta del Diablo, which should be saved until last for dramatic effect.

The Passeios Inferiores is a view of the falls from below on a 1½-km circuit. Take the boat to San Martin island (boat service 8 am to 5.30 pm, US$1.25) and enjoy spectacular close-up views of the falls.

The Passeios Superiores' concrete catwalks behind the waterfalls used to go as far as Garganta del Diablo until floods a few years back swept them over the edge. The path goes only as far as the Salto Adán y Eva.

There's a dirt road running a few km from the park entrance to Puerto Canoas. From here you can either walk along the catwalks or take a hair-raising boat ride out to Garganta del Diablo, where 13,000 cubic metres of water per second plunge 90 metres in 14 falls, arranged around a tight little pocket.

The view at the precipice is hypnotising. Visitors will be treated to a multisensory experience: roaring falls, huge rainbow arcs, drenching mist and, in the distance, parrots and hawks cruising over deep green jungle. Watch for the swifts, which drop like rocks into the misty abyss, catch insects in mid-air, shoot back up and dart behind the falls to perch on the cliffs.

The Itaipu Dam

How did Brazil ever manage to run up a huge foreign debt? Part of the answer is by engaging in mammoth projects like Itaipu, the world's largest hydroelectric works. The US$18 billion joint Brazilian-Paraguayan venture has the capacity to generate 12.6 million kilowatts – enough electricity to supply the energy needs of Paraguay and southern Brazil. Enough concrete was used in this dam to pave a two-lane highway from Moscow to Lisbon.

Fortunately the dam will not affect the flow of water in Iguaçu, as the Paraná and the Iguaçu rivers meet downstream of the falls. The Itaipu dam has, however, destroyed Sete Quedas – the world's largest waterfall with 30 times the water spilled by Iguaçu – and created a 1400 sq km lake. Local weather, and plant and animal populations have been altered, and the complete repercussions of the environmental changes will not be felt for decades. Guided tours of the Itaipu dam are given six times a day: at 8, 9 and 10 am, and 2, 3 and 4 pm. The

hour-long tours are free of charge. The Itaipu dam is 19 km from Foz.

Ciudad del Este (Paraguay)

Across the Ponte da Amizade is Ciudad del Este, where you can play roulette or baccarat at the Casino de Leste, purchase up to US$150 of duty-free imported goods (no great deals) or some nifty Paraguayan lacework and leather goods.

Jungle Tour (Argentina)

There's more to the 550 sq km Argentine park than just waterfalls. If you intend to do a jungle tour, do it on the Argentine side; they do a better job of protecting their park lands than the Brazilians. For an exceptional tour (in Spanish) ask for Juan Manuel Correa of Guembe Tours, Avenida Victoria Aguirre 481, Puerto Iguazú. Arrange the tour the evening before, and pick up a wildlife list and study it. Try to arrive in the park before 7 am (when the entrance fee of about US$1 is waived) or in the late afternoon, the best time to spot birds and wildlife.

Juan – biologist/park ranger/actor – is very friendly and extremely enthusiastic about his work. Go in a small, nature-loving group and bring binoculars and a tape recorder (to record the sounds of the jungle). You'll see fantastic butterflies (they congregate about pools of urine and on sweaty handrails to sip salts), parrots, antshrikes, parakeets, woodpeckers, hummingbirds, lizards, three-cm-long ants, beautifully coloured spiders and all sorts of orchids, lianas and vines.

I saw two species of toucan, but there are four species in the park. Juan explained that their long beaks are deceptive, being actually so light and spongy that the birds are backheavy and therefore clumsy flyers. The toucans eat fruit, eggs, chicks and leaves of the amba *(Cecropia adenopus)* tree. According to Juan, amba leaves are used to make a medicinal tea which is good for coughs.

There are other creatures in the park, including monkeys, deer, sloth, anteaters, racoons, jaguar, tapir, caiman and armadillo, but as is true of other tropical rainforests,

Green Toucan

large animals are not very abundant and they tend to be nocturnal. You can see them on display at the natural history museum at the Argentine park headquarters.

The foliage is lush and lovely. There are 2000 species of plants stacked in six different layers, from forest-floor grasses, ferns and bushes to low, middle and high tree canopies. The jungle cover, in addition to harbouring a wide variety of animals and insects, protects the soil from erosion, maintains humidity and moderates temperatures. Tarzan vines, lianas and epiphytes connect and blur the distinction between the forest levels.

Festival

The Pesca ao Dourado (Dorado Fishing Contest) takes place in the last week of October.

Places to Stay

Teletur keeps a complete list of rated (one-star and up) hotels at its main office, including current prices, so if you're not after a real cheapie, this should be your first stop when you hit town.

Places to Stay – bottom end

Around the bus station there are lots of cheap hotels. Two decent ones are the *Hotel NS de Aparecida* (☎ 74-5139) and *Hotel Senhor do Bonfim* (☎ 74-4540), next to each other in a small dead-end street just off Rua Almirante Barroso. They charge US$5 per person, and have fans in every room – something absolutely necessary when it's hot in Foz.

The *Minas Foz Hotel* (☎ 74-5208) at Rua Rebouças 641 is popular; it has apartamentos for US$8 per person and quartos for US$6 per person, without breakfast.

Youth Hostel At Rua Rebouças 335 is *Vale Verde* (☎ 74-2925) youth hostel; you don't have to be a member to stay there. They charge US$5 per person without breakfast, but for an extra US$1 you can eat it in the café out the front.

Camping There are three campgrounds on the Brazilian side. *Camping Club do Brasil* (☎ (0455) 74-1013) is the closest to the falls at Rodovia das Cataratas (eight km from Foz).

Places to Stay – middle

Moving up in price, right inside the rodoviária is the *Luz Hotel* (☎ 74-4311), which charges US$18/23 for singles/doubles. This place is only for sound sleepers. The *Imperial Hotel* (☎ 74-2422) at Avenida Brasil 168 is reasonable, with apartamentos for US$13/19 a single/double. The cheapest hotel in town with a pool is the *Ilha de Capri* (☎ 74-1300) at Rua Barão Rio Branco 409. Singles go for US$20 and doubles for US$24. The *Hotel Diplomata* (☎ 74-3155) at Avenida Brasil 678 also has a pool. They charge US$30/40 for singles /doubles, but if you ask them nicely they might let you use the pool anyway.

Places to Stay – top end

At the top end, the classiest place to stay is in the *Hotel das Cataratas* (☎ 74-2666), right at the waterfalls. Singles/doubles cost US$86/96, but Brazil airpass holders can get a 15% discount. Back in the city itself, the five-star *Hotel Internacional Foz* (☎ 74-4855), at Rua Almirante Barroso 345, charges US$100 a single and US$112 a double.

Places to Eat

The best buffet deal in town is *Restaurante Calamares* at Rua Rebouças 476. At US$3 for all you can eat, it's a good energy boost after a hard day at the falls. Along Rua Almirante Barroso between Rua Jorge Sanways and Rua Xavier da Silva are lots of good places. For Italian food, *4 Sorelle* is at No 650. For seafood, *Restaurante Du Cheff* is at No 683. It's expensive, but excellent.

A good churrascaria is *Búfalo Branco* at Rua Rebouças 530. *Restaurante Pei-kin*, Rua Jorge Samways 765, serves fair Chinese food. For a healthy sandwich and a really good juice, *Barbarela*, Travessa Julio Passa 77, is the place to go. For fast food, the *Rafain Centro Gastronômico* on the corner of Avenida Brasil and Rua Rebouças fits the bill. For a beer and a snack later on, *Bebs* at Avenida Juscelino Kubitschek 198 is a popular student hangout that gets pretty lively.

Getting There & Away

Air There are frequent flights from Foz do Iguaçu to Asunción, Buenos Aires, Rio and São Paulo. VASP (☎ (0455) 74-2999) is at Avenida Brasil 845; Transbrasil (☎ (0455) 74-3671) is at Avenida Brasil 1225; and Varig/Cruzeiro (☎ (0455) 74-3344) is at Avenida Brasil 821.

Aerolineas Argentinas and Austral have daily flights to Buenos Aires for US$160.

Bus From Foz do Iguaçu to Curitiba is 635 km and 12 hours. There are seven daily buses on BR-277, and it costs US$16. To São Paulo, eight buses make the 15-hour trip for US$26. To Rio there are six buses per day. It takes 22 hours and the fare is US$36.

There are several buses a day from Ciudad del Este to Asunción (320 km, seven hours, US$8).

There are three buses a day from Puerto Iguazú to Buenos Aires (20 hours, US$55). An alternative is to take one of 17 daily buses down Ruta 12 to Posadas (316 km, six hours, US$15), and then catch the train to Buenos Aires (1060 km, 20 hours) from Posadas.

Getting Around

To/From the Airport Catch a 'P Nacional' bus. They run from 5.30 am every 35 minutes until 7 pm, and then every hour until 11.15 pm. To get to the airport takes 30 minutes. A taxi there costs US$15; the bus costs 40c.

Bus All local buses leave from the urban bus terminal on Avenida Juscelino Kubitschek.

Brazilian Falls Catch a 'Cataratas' bus to get to the Brazilian side of the falls. On weekdays, the first bus leaves the terminal at 8 am and runs every two hours until 6 pm. The last bus leaves the falls at 7 pm. The fare is 40c. At the entrance to the park you'll have to get out and pay the US$1.20 entry fee. The bus will wait while you do this. On weekends and public holidays, the first bus leaves the terminal at 8 am, the second at 10 am; thereafter buses leave every hour until 6 pm. The last bus leaves the falls at 7 pm.

Argentine Falls In Foz, catch a bus to 'Puerto Iguazú' to get to the Argentine side of the falls. They start running at 7 am and run every hour until 9 pm. The fare is US$1.20. In Puerto Iguazú, transfer to a 'Trans Cataratas' bus.

At the bus station in Puerto Iguazú you can pay for everything in one go: the bus fares to and from the park, the bus to and from Puerto Canoas, entry to the park and the boat ride to Isla San Martin. The entrance fee for the park must be paid in Argentine australes. If you only have cruzeiros, the ticket seller at the bus station will exchange the appropriate amount of cruzeiros required for the park entrance to the equivalent in australes; this can then be paid on arrival at the park. This is the only time you'll need Argentine currency; everything else can be paid for with cruzeiros.

The 'Trans Cataratas' bus leaves every hour from 8 am to 6 pm – but not at 1 pm, which is siesta time.

Itaipu From the local bus stop opposite the urban terminal in Foz, take a 'Canteiro de Obras' bus heading east to get to Itaipu. There's one every 35 minutes. They run from 5.30 am until 7 pm.

Ciudad del Este From the urban terminal in Foz, buses for Ciudad del Este begin running at 7 am and leave every five minutes.

Neotropic Cormorants

Santa Catarina

The Germans and Italians who settled in Santa Catarina in the 19th century, unlike most immigrants in the rest of Brazil, owned their small family-run farms. This European model of land use has produced a far more egalitarian distribution of wealth than in most of Brazil – 83% of the farmland is owned by farmers with less than 1000 hectares.

Many of the state's four million people still own their rich farmland, which combined with some healthy small-scale industry has created one of Brazil's most prosperous states. This relative affluence, the very visible German presence and the efficient services give the state the feel of Europe rather than Brazil – at least in the highlands, which are green and pastoral. If Santa Catarina reminds one of Switzerland, it's less because of geography and more because of the sedate middle-class consumerism. Most travellers don't come to Santa Catarina to visit a foreign culture – they come for the beaches.

There's no doubt that the beaches are beautiful: they're wide and open, with Caribbean-like coves and bays, clear and clean emerald-blue water and views of offshore islands. The water is very warm during the summer months and there are plenty of calm, protected beaches for swimming. Santa Catarina also has some of Brazil's better surfing spots. The current can be very dangerous in places, so be careful.

While there are still fishing villages along the coast, you don't really find the kind of primitive fishing villages that predominate in the Northeast. The setting is less exotic and less tropical, the villagers less secluded and less friendly, and the escape from Western civilisation less complete.

Many of Santa Catarina's beaches have become 'in' vacation spots for well-to-do Paulistas, Curitibanos and Argentines, so during the holiday season between January and February, the beaches and hotels are jammed. Several little Copacabanas have sprouted up in beach towns like Camboriú,

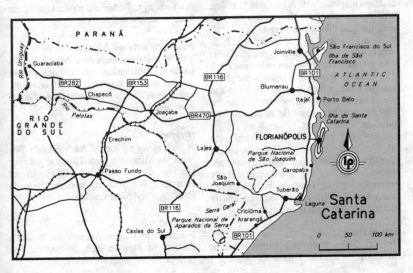

and this growth is changing the coastline at an unbelievable pace.

Santa Catarina's climate is nice and hot during the Brazilian summer. In the winter the wind along the coast picks up considerably, although it never gets too cold. The best months to go, unless you like the crowds, are March-April and November-December.

Compared with other parts of Brazil, this is a polite and proper place, where children are subdued and well mannered. You may be excluded from a restaurant because your jeans are worn, you probably will be excluded from a bar if you're not wearing a shirt and you must wear either bermuda-length shorts or long trousers on inter-city buses – no swim suits. What's so unusual about this Brazilian state is not that it has these rules, but that they are respected and enforced.

JOINVILLE

Imagine a city where blonds stroll through town on clean, well-lit, heavily policed streets, perusing Bavarian-facaded, neon-named shops full of modern Western appliances, with well-manicured lawns, flower festivals and a central park in which children play at night. A city that is polite, efficient and pleasant. Now here's the hard part: imagine this city in Brazil.

Santa Catarina's second largest city, Joinville (pronounced joyvilee) is described in its own tourist brochure as 'an industrial city'. The industry, however, is outside the pleasant inner city, which is quite habitable and seems like the kind of place to raise a family. For the traveller, Joinville is relaxed and pleasant, if unexciting.

Joinville is on the BR-101, 180 km north of Florianópolis and 123 km south of Curitiba. The road is good and the views are beautiful around the town, particularly where the highway traverses the lush coastal mountains. The drive down to Guaratuba on the coast to the north is stunning.

Information
Tourist Office There is a tourist office in front of the Colón Palace Hotel, open Monday to Sunday from 8 am to 6 pm. It offers mediocre maps and silly brochures, and the staff speak German and a little English. There is a travel agency behind the office.

The city centre is small. Most stores and services are concentrated on and around Rua 15 de Novembro and Rua Princesa Isabel.

Post & Telephone The telephone company and post office are both on Rua Princesa Isabel.

Museu Nacional da Imigração

At Rua Rio Branco 229, facing an impressive, palm-lined walkway, is the Museu Nacional da Imigração. Housed in the old palace, built in 1870, it's full of objects used by the pioneers of the state. From Tuesday to Friday it's open from 9 am to 6 pm, and on weekends from 9 am to noon and 2 to 6 pm.

Museu Arqueológico do Sambaqui

At Rua Dona Francisca 600 is the Museu Arqueológico do Sambaqui, an exposition of the Sambaqui Indian lifestyle. It's worth a visit on a rainy day. It's open from 9 am to 6 pm Tuesday to Friday and on weekends from 9 am to noon and 2 to 6 pm.

Museu de Arte de Joinville

This is quite an interesting one. It houses works by local artists, and contains a small restaurant. It's at Rua 15 de Novembro 1400, and is open Tuesday to Sunday from 9 am to noon and 2 to 8 pm.

Mirante

A high tower on top of the Morro da Boa Vista, the Mirante is a good place to get your bearings. It also provides a 360° view of Joinville, and you can see the Baía da Babitonga and São Francisco do Sul.

Festival

For the last 53 years, Joinville has hosted a Festival of Flowers each November. The orchids are the main attraction.

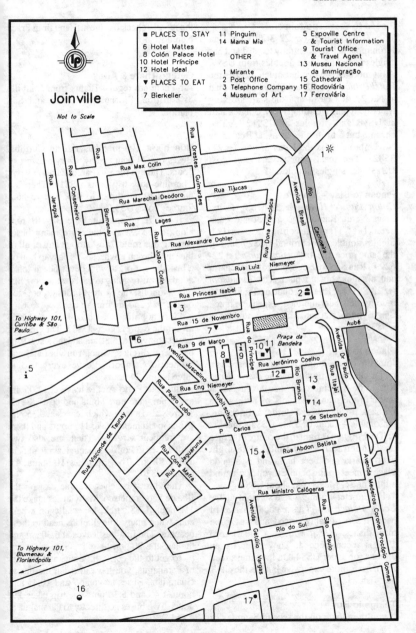

Joinville

Not to Scale

PLACES TO STAY

6 Hotel Mattes
8 Colón Palace Hotel
10 Hotel Príncipe
12 Hotel Ideal

PLACES TO EAT

7 Bierkeller
11 Pinguim
14 Mama Mia

OTHER

1 Mirante
2 Post Office
3 Telephone Company
4 Museum of Art
5 Expoville Centre
  & Tourist Information
9 Tourist Office
  & Travel Agent
13 Museu Nacional
   da Immigração
15 Cathedral
16 Rodoviária
17 Ferroviária

Places to Stay – bottom end

The *Hotel Ideal* (☎ 22-3660) on Rua Jerônimo Coelho is centrally located and has singles from US$4 and doubles from US$7. A bit more expensive but much nicer is the *Hotel Príncipe* (☎ 22-8555) just up the road at No 27. It's clean and the staff are very friendly. It tends to fill up early. Singles start at US$8 and doubles at US$12. A real cheapie but a bit further away, at Rua 15 de Novembro 811, is the *Hotel Mattes* (☎ 22-3582). The least expensive rooms cost US$3/6 for singles/doubles.

Places to Stay – top end

Colón Palace Hotel (☎ 22-6188), facing Praça Nereu Ramos, has a pool and great breakfast (try the chocolate milk). Singles/doubles cost around US$25/30. For the same price, the *Anthurium Palace* (☎ 22-6299), Rua São José 226, has colonial charm and a sauna, but no pool. The *Tannenhof* (☎ 22-8011) at Rua Visconde de Taunay 340 is Joinville's best and most expensive hotel. Single rooms start at US$30 and doubles at US$35.

Places to Eat

Joinville boasts good German food and is a major chocolate producer. The *Bierkeller* at Rua 15 de Novembro 497 has the city's best value in German food, lots of pork and a feijoada for lunch on Saturdays. Prices are reasonable – about US$3 to US$5 a meal.

The *Pinguim* is right in the centre off Praça da Bandeira. It's a popular, late-night churrascaria and beer hall, and is a good place to meet young people if you don't mind a little noise. Meals cost about US$4.

For quieter dining, the restaurant at the *Colón Palace Hotel* is a good change of pace; it's reasonably priced and has good meat dishes. *Mama Mia*, Rua Rio Branco 193, is recommended. They offer Italian dinners for under US$4. On the same street, *Pinheiro* is more expensive but has the city's best fish.

Things to Buy

If you're in town on the second Saturday of the month, check out the artisan fair in Praça Nereu Ramos.

Getting There & Away

Air There are regular flights from Joinville to Curitiba, Florianópolis, Rio and São Paulo.

Bus It's a 2½-hour bus ride to Curitiba. Buses run 24 hours a day, every one to two hours. The bus for São Paulo leaves at 9 pm. The nine-hour trip costs US$14. There's a bus at 8.20 pm direct to Rio. The 15-hour journey costs US$26.

If you're going south, the BR-101 runs along the coast and there are many buses serving this route. Most stop at any or all of the small beach towns, so it's easy to hop on a bus and get off at whichever beach looks good. If you're going to a set destination, like Florianópolis, the express buses do not stop on the way and are much faster.

Florianópolis is a three-hour bus ride away; the express costs US$7. The first bus leaves Joinville at 6.30 am and the last at 9.10 pm. Semi-direitos, which run via Itajaí and Balneário Camboriú, leave every two to three hours, 24 hours a day.

Buses to Porto Alegre leave at 11.05 am and 9 pm, take nine hours and cost US$12. There's also a leito which leaves at 9.35 pm. Buses to Blumenau take 1½ hours and there are frequent services. There are also two daily buses to Foz do Iguaçu, leaving at 5.10 and 9.30 pm. The trip takes 10 hours and costs US$20.

The closest beaches are due east on the Ilha de São Francisco. Many buses make the 1¼-hour, US$2 trek, especially on weekends when many Joinvilleians head to these beaches. The first bus leaves at 6.30 am and the last at 8.20 pm.

To get to the coast of Paraná and the city of Paranaguá, you have to catch the bus to Guaratuba. Buses leave at 7 and 10.45 am, noon, 1.45 and 5.30 pm. The trip takes 1½ hours. Two buses go directly to Paranaguá at 4 and 7.30 pm.

Train

There is a daily 8 am train to São Francisco do Sul. It returns at noon.

Getting Around

The airport is 12 km from the city and the rodoviária is two km out. There is a bus stop at the side of the airport terminal from where city buses leave every 20 minutes or so for the Praça da Bandeira in the centre.

JOINVILLE TO FLORIANÓPOLIS

There are many beautiful beaches along this coast, but it's being developed rapidly and without controls. In general, the more famous a beach, the more developed and ugly it is. Balneário Camboriú, the area's best known beach town, is the best example.

São Francisco do Sul

This historic city's island setting was 'discovered' way back in 1504 by the Frenchman Binot Paulmier de Goneville, but the city itself wasn't settled until the middle of the next century. It became the port of entry for the German immigrants settling the land around Joinville.

Beaches The beaches on the Ilha de São Francisco are good, but they are some of the most crowded because of their proximity to Joinville and even Curitiba. There is also a lot of surfing. On the positive side, there are several cheap hotels in the city and a variety of beaches accessible by local buses.

Both Prainha and Praia Grande to the south have big waves and are popular surfing beaches. Swimming is not safe. Closer to the city, Praia de Ubatuba and Praia de Enseada are pretty and safe for swimming, but they're developed and often crowded. For another option, ask in town about boats leaving from Capitania dos Portos to the Ilha da Paz.

Places to Stay Praia de Enseada has several hotels and you can catch a bus directly to Joinville. The *Enseada* (☎ 42-2122), Avenida Atlântica 1074, is on the beach and is reasonably priced. The *Turismar* (☎ 42-2060), Avenida Atlântica 1923, is similar

with singles/doubles for US$8.50/12. In town the *Kontiki* (☎ 44-0232), at Rua Camacho 33, across from the waterfront, is reasonable, charging US$8 per person.

Barra Velha

If driving south from Joinville on BR-101, this is the first point where the road meets the sea. Four km to the south of town, Praia do Grant is popular with the younger set. The surf beaches are Praia do Tabuleiro, two km from town, and Itajuba, five km away.

Places to Stay & Eat There are a few hotels and restaurants in town. The *Mirante* (☎ 46-0343), at Rua Governador Celso Ramos 106, has decent quartos for US$9/15 a single/double. *Camping Simone* (☎ 46-0226) is at Rua Lauro Ramos 69. For a fine fish dinner, try *Agua Viva* at Avenida Santa Catarina 248.

Piçarras

Piçarras, 14 km to the south of Barra Velha, has a good big beach and several small islands which can be visited. The town is lively in the summer but the campgrounds are often full then.

Places to Stay & Eat Apart from the three campgrounds, there are barracas and several hotels, including the cheaper *Real* (☎ 45-0706) at Avenida Nereu Ramos 607 and the *July* (☎ 45-0644) at Avenida Getúlio Vargas 44. Ask about houses to rent. There are lots of seafood restaurants. Try *Maneco* at Avenida Nereu Ramos 299.

Penha

Penha is a big fishing town, so it's not completely overrun by tourism. Only six km from Piçarras, the ocean is calm at the city beaches, Armação and Prainha. There are simple hotels at these beaches. The beaches south of these two are less crowded. From Praia da Armação, boats leave every half-hour or so to the nearby islands of Itacolomi and Feia.

Places to Stay & Eat A cheap hotel on the beach at Praia da Armação is *Itapocorot*

(☎ 45-0015), which has apartamentos for US$8/14 a single/double.

There are lots of campgrounds near the main beaches. There are several very good beachside seafood restaurants as well.

Itajaí

At the turnoff to Blumenau is Itajaí, an important port for the Itajaí valley. However, there's not much of interest to the tourist and the best beaches are out of town. There are a couple of hotels across from the rodoviária and several more on the main road going out of town to Camboriú. There are plenty of buses coming and going from Itajaí.

Balneário Camboriú

This little Copacabana, with sharp hills dropping into the sea, nightclubs with 'professional mulattos' and an ocean boulevard named Avenida Atlântica, is clearly out of control. In summer the population increases tenfold.

This is Santa Catarina's most expensive town, and here you can meet well-heeled Argentines, Paraguayans and Paulistas who spend their summers in the ugliest beach-hugging high-rise buildings you can imagine. The spoiling of this beachfront is surely a crime against nature.

Outside the city, there is a Museu Arqueológico e Oceanográfico that's worth visiting (six km south on BR-101, open daily from 9 am to 6 pm), and a nude beach (a rarity in Brazil) at Praia do Pinho, 13 km south of the city.

Porto Belo

The beaches around Porto Belo are the last good continental beaches before Ilha de Santa Catarina. Praia Bombas, three km away, and Praia Bombinhas, seven km from town by dirt road, are the prettiest beaches around. For a great walk, head out to Ponta do Lobo, 12 km from Praia Bombinhas. From Rua Manoel Felipe da Silva in Porto Belo you can catch a boat to the islands of Arvorerdo and João da Cunha. Both have fine beaches.

Places to Stay Both Praia Bombas and Praia Bombinhas have barracas and campgrounds and are relatively uncrowded. The *Hotel Bomar* (☎ 69-4136), which has singles/doubles for US$9/15, is at Praia de Bombas. There are many campgrounds along the beaches.

Places to Eat On Avenida Governador Celso Ramos in Porto Belo, *La Ponte* at No 1988 and *Petiscão* at No 2170 both have tasty seafood.

BLUMENAU

Blumenau is 60 km inland from Itajaí, 139 km from Florianópolis and 130 km from Joinville. Nestled in the Vale do Itajaí on the Rio Itajaí, Blumenau and its environs were settled largely by German immigrants in the second half of the 19th century. The area is serene, but the city itself wears its German culture way too loud. Everything is Germanicised with the commercial, but not creative, flair of Walt Disney. The city attracts tourists (mostly from not too far away) but isn't particularly recommended.

Information

There is an information post at the bus station which is pretty useless. Your best bet for information and money changing are the travel agencies. The telephone company is on Rua Uruguai near the bridge. The post office is on Rua Pe Jacobs.

Festival

Blumenau hosts an increasingly popular Oktoberfest, beginning on the first Friday in October.

Places to Stay

Hotels in Blumenau are very clean and efficiently run compared with those in the rest of Brazil, or in any other country for that matter. The *Hotel Herman* (☎ 22-4370), Rua Floriano Peixoto 213, has cheap singles/doubles from US$5/8. The manager is very friendly and loves to practise his German. Close by is the *City Hotel* (☎ 22-2205) at

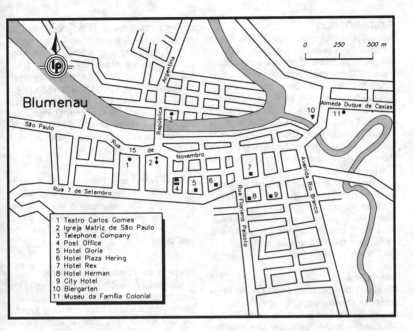

1 Teatro Carlos Gomes
2 Igreja Matriz de São Paulo
3 Telephone Company
4 Post Office
5 Hotel Gloria
6 Hotel Plaza Hering
7 Hotel Rex
8 Hotel Herman
9 City Hotel
10 Biergarten
11 Museu da Família Colonial

Rua Angelo Dias 263. They have singles starting at US$8 and doubles from US$12.

Moving up the price scale, the *Hotel Gloria* (☎ 22-1988) at Rua 7 de Setembro 954 is well located; it has singles from US$14 and doubles from US$27. On the same street, at No 640, the *Hotel Rex* (☎ 22-5877) has all the amenities and singles/doubles for US$38/45. Nearby, the *Hotel Plaza Hering* (☎ 22-1277) is Blumenau's fanciest sleepery with singles/doubles for US$64/76. For reservations from São Paulo call toll-free on (011) 800-8618.

Places to Eat

Unfortunately, the cheaper hotels in town don't provide any breakfast, so the best place to head is the *Cafehaus Gloria* in the Hotel Gloria. Their US$3.50 *café colonial* is excellent. It starts at 7 am. You could do a lot worse than go there for lunch or dinner, too.

For average German food and a good view, try *Frohsinn*, up the hill on Rua Itajaí.

They're open for lunch and dinner every day except Sunday. The *Gruta Azul* at Rua Rudolfo Freygang 8 has also been recommended. You could also try snacking at one of the chopperias near the República Argentina bridge. They're good places to go for a beer in the evening, as is the *Biergarten* in Praça Hercílio Luz.

Getting There & Away

There are plenty of buses to Florianópolis from Blumenau. The direct buses take 2½ hours and leave at 8 am, noon, 3 and 5 pm. Semi-direitos stop at Itajaí and Camboriú, and arrive in Florianópolis three hours after leaving Blumenau.

Getting Around

The rodoviária is at Rua 2 de Setembro 1222. Take the 'Rodoviária' or 'Fortaleza' bus from the city, or a taxi for US$5.

FLORIANÓPOLIS

Florianópolis, the state capital, fans out in both directions from the spot where the coast and the large Ilha de Santa Catarina almost connect. The central section is on the island facing the Baía Sul. Over the hill, on the north shore, there is a long row of luxury high-rises, none of which looks more than a couple of years old, and modern restaurants to feed their occupants. The mainland part of the city has the industry. Much of the city's shoreline appears barren due to undeveloped landfill.

The city is modern, with some large structures like the new rodoviária and many works in progress. The island side of the city, where you'll probably spend all your time, has a small-city feel. It's easy to get around by foot and there are regular public buses to the island's beautiful beaches.

Information

Tourist Office Setur (☎ 44-5822), the Florianópolis tourist bureau, is on the mainland side of the city just before the bridge at Rua Max de Sousa 236. Santur (☎ 24-6300), the state tourist office, is at Rua Felipe Schmidt 21 on the 9th floor. Neither is worth going out of your way to get to. There are information desks at the bus station and airport, which may be good for maps if they're actually open. The small building at the top of Praça 15 de Novembro is a more substantial tourist office, but isn't always open either.

Protur (☎ 22-4904), a private foundation promoting tourism on the island, is of more use. Their excellent brochure contains detailed maps of the walks you can do around Lagoa de Conceição, as well as lots of pretty pictures. They're at Rua Jerônimo Coelho 33, sala 403.

There are lots of touts at the bus station waiting for tourists, mostly Argentine or Uruguayan, to arrive. They have lots of information about places to stay (they get their commission of course) and can be useful. Adão is one who is quite helpful and speaks Spanish.

Money There's a very active street black market for cash dollars in the pedestrian mall on Rua Felipe Schmidt. These guys, mostly Spanish-speaking and armed with calculators and bulging money belts, change at the top rate, and the Argentine and Uruguayan tourists have no qualms about changing right there on the street. It's all done very openly. If the situation has changed, change your money at a travel agency. For travellers' cheques, go to the Banco do Brasil at Praça 15 de Novembro, No 20.

Post & Telephone The phone company is two blocks up the hill from Praça 15 de Novembro. It's open from 8 am to 11 pm Monday to Friday and closes an hour earlier on Saturdays, Sundays and holidays. The post office faces the praça.

Praça 15 de Novembro & Around

While you'll probably want to get out to the beaches as soon as possible, it's definitely worth your while to have a wander around the city and have a look at some of the colonial buildings.

From Praça 15 de Novembro and its 100-year-old fig tree, you can cross the road and go into the pink Palácio Cruz e Souza. It's the state museum, but the most interesting things to see are the ornate parquetry floors and the outrageous 19th-century ceilings. Entry is 20c and it's open on weekdays from 10 am to 8 pm and weekends from 10 am to 6 pm.

On the high point of the praça is the Catedral Metropolitana; it was remodelled this century, so not much from the colonial era remains. The least remodelled colonial church is the Igreja de NS do Rosário, further up from the cathedral.

Waterfront

Back down on the old waterfront are the Alfândega (Customs House) and the Mercado Municipal, both colonial buildings that have been well preserved. The market is a good place to have a chopp and watch the passers-by in the late afternoon.

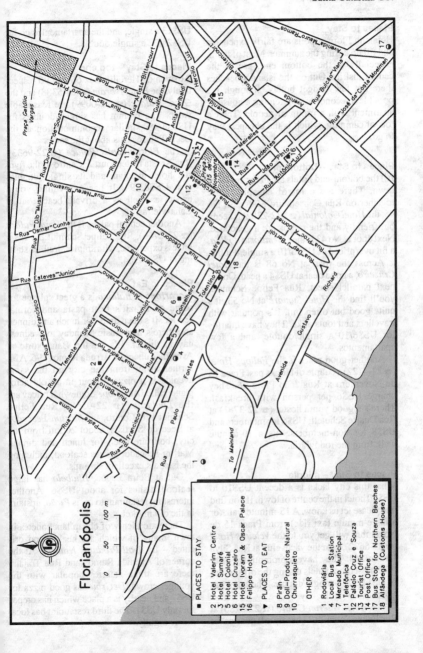

Florianópolis

0   50   100 m

PLACES TO STAY
2 Hotel Valerim Centre
3 Hotel Sumaré
5 Hotel Colonial
6 Hotel Cruzeiro
15 Hotel Ivoram & Oscar Palace
16 Felippe Hotel

PLACES TO EAT
8 Pirão
9 Doll – Produtos Natural
10 Churrasquieto

OTHER
1 Rodoviária
4 Local Bus Station
7 Mercado Municipal
11 Telefônica
12 Palácio Cruz e Souza
13 Tourist Office
14 Post Office
17 Bus Stop for Northern Beaches
18 Alfândega (Customs House)

Places to Stay

Hotels in Florianópolis are fairly expensive and fill up during the summer. Most of them, especially at the bottom end, are in the central district. Out on the island's beaches there are few budget hotels, although it's possible to economise by renting a house or apartment with a group of people. There's lots of camping, which is the cheapest way to go.

Places to Stay – bottom end

All the bottom-end hotels are in the centre of town. There are a lot of cheapies close together on Rua Conselheiro Mafra. At No 45, the *Hotel Colonial* (☎ 232-2302) is seedy but friendly and the rooms are a good size. Next door at No 43 is the *Dormitorio do Ilha*, a bit overpriced at US$6/10 a single/double.

Across the road at No 68 is the *Hotel Cruzeiro*, a good deal at US$4 a head. On the next parallel street, Rua Felipe Schmidt, you'll find the *Hotel Sumaré* at No 53; it's quite good but often full. It's popular with travellers and touts alike. They have quartos for US$6/10 a single/double, and a few apartamentos.

Another good place is the *Felippe Hotel* (☎ 22-4122) a couple of blocks past Praça 15 de Novembro at Rua João Pinto 26. They charge US$6 per person with breakfast. There's a good youth hostel (☎ 22-3781) at Rua Duarte Schutell; US$6 for members and US$8 for non-members. It's a 10-minute walk from the rodoviária.

Places to Stay – middle

What this city lacks is a decent US$10 to US$20 hotel in the centre of town. If you find one please let us know. A 15-minute walk (or a three-minute taxi ride) from Praça 15 de Novembro will get you to the *Veleiros Hotel* (☎ 23-6622), near the yacht club at Rua Silva Jardim 254. They have a promotional offer (like most other hotels during the off season) of US$12/22 a single/double. The hotel has a great view of the bay.

The *Hotel Valerim Centre* (☎ 22-3280) at Rua Felipe Schmidt 74 has rip-off quartos for US$13 a single, and the apartamentos go for US$24/32 a single/double.

Places to Stay – top end

At Avenida Hercilio Luz 66 and 90 respectively, the *Hotel Ivoram* (☎ 24-5388) and the *Oscar Palace* (☎ 22-0099) are reasonable value. The Ivoram has singles/doubles for US$34/38; similar accommodation at the Oscar Palace costs about the same.

The *Florianópolis Palace* (☎ 22-9633), Rua Artista Bittencourt 2, Centro, is the five-star hotel in town, and its singles/doubles cost US$83/94. It has everything you'd expect as well as a private beach out at Canasvieiras.

Another central palace is the *Faial Palace* (☎ 23-2766), Rua Felipe Schmidt 87. It's a bit less expensive, with singles/doubles starting at US$52/64.

Places to Eat

Macarronada Italiana is a great splurge for some of Brazil's best pasta and formal service. It's open daily for lunch and dinner, and there's live music Monday to Wednesday at dinner. It's on the Baía Norte at Avenida Rubens de Arruda Ramos 196. A bit further away from the city on the same avenida is a pizza parlour in an old aeroplane, called *Aeroflop*. Somewhat pricey are the *Lindacap* (☎ 22-0558), Rua Felipe Schmidt 178, Centro, and *Martim-Pescador* at Beco do Surfista, about 20 km from the city; both are open for lunch and dinner. Martim-Pescador serves seafood, including the island's excellent shrimps.

Out at Beira Lagoa, *Ilhabela* has large seafood dishes for about US$6. Another interesting restaurant to try is *Pirão*, upstairs in the old market.

There are plenty of cheap lanchonetes in town, many of which are health-food oriented – try *Doll-Produtos Natural*. At the corner of Avenida Ramos and Rua Trajano there are three eateries popular with the younger crowd. *DeGrau* has good pizza for US$2 and nearby is a place which has crepes for only US$1. The third restaurant has local music nightly.

Getting There & Away

Air There are daily direct flights to São Paulo and Porto Alegre, as well as connections to most other cities. Flights to Rio make at least one stop. Watch out for multiple-stop flights, with multiple plane changes.

The airlines all have offices in the centre: Varig/Cruzeiro (☎ 24-2811) at Rua Felipe Schmidt 34, Transbrasil (☎ 23-7177) at Praça Pereira Oliveira 16 and VASP (☎ 22-1122) at Rua Osmar Cunha 15.

Bus Costs and times for long-distance buses are: Porto Alegre US$10 and 7½ hours, Curitiba US$8 and five hours, São Paulo US$20 and 12 hours, Rio US$30 and 20 hours, Foz do Iguaçu US$24 and 16 hours, Buenos Aires US$50 and 27 hours, Montevideo US$35 and 21 hours.

There are frequent buses up and down the coast as well as inland to Blumenau, Brusque and Lajes. Travel along BR-101, the coastal highway, is considerably quicker by direct bus. Local indirect buses can be easily flagged down along the highway.

Getting Around

The airport is 12 km south of the city. A cab costs US$8. Buses marked 'Aeroporto' go regularly to the airport until 10 pm and leave from the first platform at the central rodoviária. It's a 30-minute ride by bus.

ILHA DE SANTA CATARINA

The island's east-coast beaches are the most beautiful, with the biggest waves and the greatest expanses of empty beach. They are also the most popular for day trips and most do not have hotels. The north coast beaches have calm, bay-like water and resorts with many apartment-hotels and restaurants. The west coast, facing the mainland, has great views and a quiet, Mediterranean feel. The beaches here are small and unspectacular.

East Coast

The following beaches are listed from north to south. Praia dos Ingleses, 34 km from Florianópolis, is becoming quite developed, and although the beach is a good one, the surroundings aren't very attractive. There are lots of hotels and restaurants catering to the Brazilian, Argentine and Uruguayan tourists but nothing's cheap. *Sol & Mar* (☎ 69-1271) has doubles for US$25.

Praia do Santinho has a few beach houses and barracas and one of the island's most beautiful beaches. The island's longest beach, Praia do Moçambique or Praia Grande, is 14 km long and undeveloped. It's hidden by a pine forest from the dirt road that runs a couple of km inland from it. The camping here is good.

Barra da Lagoa, a big curved beach at the end of Praia do Moçambique, is a short bus trip (No 403 'Barra da Lagoa') from Florianópolis. It still has many indigenous fisherfolk, descended from the original Azorean colonists. There are more hotels and restaurants here than anywhere else on the east coast, except Praia dos Ingleses, but there still aren't many of them and they are not modern eye-sores. The barracas are excellent, and it seems like every second house is for rent.

A good place to stay is the *Gaivota* (☎ (0482) 32-0177), run by a very friendly family. Try and get a front room for the great view. Singles/doubles cost US$8/US$12. This is the best beach to head to if you want to stay a few days. Praia Mole is a beautiful stretch of beach, with one hotel, the four-star *Cabanas da Praia Mole* (☎ 32-0231).

Praia da Joaquina hosts the Brazilian surfing championship in January and the Hang Loose championship in September. It has a couple of hotels. The *Joaquina Beach* (☎ 32-0059) is simple and on the beach. Singles cost US$16 and doubles US$24, but in season it's more expensive. *Hotel Cris* (☎ 32-0380) charges US$25 a single and US$50 a double, but midweek out of season you can get the prices down by half if you bargain. A bit cheaper is the *Estalagem das Açores*, on the approach road to Joaquina. There are also restaurants, and this is the busiest beach on the island. The crowd is young and hip and the surf pumps. Surfboards can be hired if the surf shop is open. They can also be hired at Barra da Lagoa.

Ilha de Santa Catarina

The three main beaches to the south are the most remote and quite spectacular. Praia do Campeche has a few barracas and the beach is long enough for everyone to find a private patch of sand. Praia da Armação is similar. As at Campeche, the current is often heavy. *Sol de Costa* (☎ 22-5071) has doubles for US$30. Pântano do Sul at the end of the paved road is a small fishing village with a couple of restaurants. The mountains here close in on the sea, which is calm and protected.

North Coast

The north coast is the most developed coast on the island and the beaches are narrow; however, the sea here is warm and calm, incredibly clean and perfect for swimming.

Canasvieiras, in particular, has many apartments, families with holiday homes, and nightlife (during the summer). In many ways it is the least attractive beach town on the island and there's plenty more construction on-line.

Of its many apartment-hotels, most are pricey, but a few are affordable if you have at least three or four people. There are no real budget hotels, so if you're alone it's expensive. The least expensive place is the *Ivoram Praia* (☎ 66-0041), a five-minute walk from the beach on the 'Camping Canasvieiras' road. They have one-bedroom apartments with big kitchens, and will add another bed so as to accommodate up to four people. It's tight, but for US$25 its a good deal for the area. Another possibility is the *Canasvieiras Praia* (☎ 66-0310) with doubles for US$30.

A few km west, Jurerê is similar to Canasvieiras but a bit quieter. Out at Praia do Forte are the ruins of the Fortaleza de São José da Ponta Grossa, built in 1750. Jurerê has two top-end hotels, the *Jurerê Praia Hotel* (☎ 66-0108) and the *Clube Atlântico Jurerê* (☎ 66-0783).

West Coast

If you want to explore the west coast, the town of Sambaqui is charming and peaceful. There are a handful of barracas and some beach-goers on weekends. After the town

and the barracas, keep walking on the dirt road a few hundred metres for a more private beach or keep going another km to reach an even more secluded area. Both of these beaches are tiny and cosy, with good views. The road is blockaded soon after this second beach.

On the south-west coast, Ribeirão da Ilha is an old colonial town. It has an impressive little church, the Igreja NS da Lapa.

The Interior

It's not just the beaches: the entire island is beautiful. Lagoa da Conceição is the most famous region in the interior. The views of the lagoon, surrounding peaks and sand dunes make for great walks or boat rides. Lots of boats are for hire right next to the bridge. Typical costs are US$16 for two hours, but the boats can take up to 10 people, so try to get a group together. There are several seafood restaurants in the town of Lagoa – *Ilha Bela* is very good. This town also has some simple hotels which are overpriced, but so is everything outside Florianópolis. The *Andrinus* (☎ 32-0153) has quartos for two at US$20 and apartamentos for two at US$28.

If you're down south, the turnoff to Lagoa do Peri is at Morro das Pedras. The lake is fun to explore.

Getting Around

Local buses serve all of the island's beach towns, but the schedule changes with the season so it's best to get the times at the tourist office or the central rodoviária in Florianópolis. Also there are additional microbuses during the tourist season that leave from the centre and go directly to the beaches.

The buses for the south of the island leave from the central rodoviária, platform one (closest to the bay). Buses for the north leave from the corner of Rua José da Costa Moelmann and Avenida Mauro Ramos. To get there, find Rua Antonio Luz at the bottom of Praça 15 de Novembro and walk away from the centre for about seven blocks, heading towards the hillside.

The buses, marked with their destinations, include services for Sambaqui, Lagoa da Conceição, Campeche, Barra da Lagoa, Canasvieiras (Jurerê) Ponta Grossa, Barra do Sul, Ribeirão da Ilha, Pantano do Sul, Ingleses-Aranhas and Ponta das Canas.

The island is one of those places where a one-day car rental is a good idea, although fairly expensive. With a car, or on one of the bus tours offered by the travel agencies (Ponto Sul (☎ 23-0399) is a good one: US$12 for an eight-hour tour), you can see most of the island and pick a beach to settle on.

Another excursion is with Scuna-Sul (☎ 24-1806). They have a big sailboat that cruises Baía Norte for three hours for a reasonable US$10. They leave from near the steel suspension bridge – Brazil's longest.

SOUTH OF FLORIANÓPOLIS
Garopaba

Garopaba is the first beach town south of Florianópolis. It's 95 km from Florianópolis, including a 15-km drive from the main BR-101 highway. The little town has not been overrun by tourism, the beaches are good and you can still see the fishers and view their way of life. Praia do Garopaba is a km from the town. Praia do Silveira, three km away, is good for surf, and Siriú, 11 km away, has some large sand dunes. Avoid the next town, Imbituba: it's polluted from a chemical plant.

Places to Stay There are half a dozen hotels. The *Pousada Casa Grande e Senzala* (☎ 5-4177) at Rua Dr Elmo Kiseski 444 is a good bet, with apartments for US$10 in the off season.

Ask about rooms in houses for a cheap sleep. There are plenty for rent. There are lots of campgrounds on Garopaba beach.

Places to Eat Try the *Unter Deck* on top of the hill at Rua Nereu Ramos – good food with a nice view. It's open every day for lunch and dinner. Also recommended is the *Rancho da Vovó* at Rua João Orestes Araújo 510.

Laguna

Laguna has an active fishing industry and is the centre of tourism for the southern coast. On the southern point of the line that divided the Americas between Spain and Portugal in the Treaty of Tordesillas in 1494, it's a historic city, settled by Paulistas in the 1670s. It was occupied by the farrapos soldiers and declared a republic in 1839 in the Guerra dos Farrapos, which was fought between republicans and monarchists.

Museums If it's a rainy day, have a look at Museu Anita Garibaldi, on Praça República Juliana, which honours the Brazilian wife of the leader of Italian unification. The museum is open from 8 am to 6 pm. The Casa de Anita Garibaldi on Praça Vidal Ramos contains some of her personal possessions. It's open daily from 8 am to 6 pm.

Beaches The best beaches in the area are out on the Cabo de Santa Marta, 16 km from the city plus a 10-minute ferry ride. The ferry operates from 6.30 am to 6.30 pm. There are beautiful dunes here, and it is possible to camp or to stay in barracas. Rooms can be also be rented in houses.

For something closer to town, try the Praia do Gi, five km north of town. There are hotels and restaurants along the beach.

From Mar Grosso, the city beach, you can get a boat to the Ilha dos Lobos, which is an ecological reserve and rather unspoilt. The trip lasts an hour each way.

Places to Stay Laguna is not cheap. There are several expensive hotels and restaurants. On the waterfront, opposite the market, the *Farol Palace* (☎ 44-0596) is your best bet. Singles/doubles here are US$8/12. The *Ondão* (☎ 44-0940) on Avenida Rio Grande do Sul is the cheapest place at Mar Grosso and has singles/doubles for US$10/15.

Places to Eat Seafood is the order of the day in Laguna. Try *Arrastão* at Avenida Senador Galotti 629 at Mar Grosso or *Baleia Branca* next to the beach at Mar Grosso on Avenida Rio Grande do Sul.

Further South

Further south are the coal mining towns of Tubarão and Criciúma. There's no reason to stay in either unless you want to go to the mineral baths. Both have a handful of hotels and are serviced by regular buses along the coastal route. From Tubarão you can get to several mineral baths, including Termas do Gravatal (20 km), Termas da Gurada (12 km) and baths on the Rio do Pouso (19 km).

The Termas do Gravatal are very popular and have many facilities. The radioactive waters are said to heal rheumatism, ulcers and a variety of other ailments. Unfortunately, none of the four-star hotels in the park grounds are inexpensive. There is camping, however, and you can easily come up for the day from Tubarão.

SÃO JOAQUIM

Not many overseas travellers come to Brazil to see snow, but if they did, this is where they'd come. The mountains are scenic in the winter. São Joaquim is Brazil's highest city, at 1355 metres.

Bom Jardim da Serra

Bom Jardim da Serra, in the middle of the Serra do Rio do Rastro, is a hair-raising but beautiful 45-km drive from São Joaquim. There you'll find access to the Parque Nacional de São Joaquim. The park is completely undeveloped, so ask the locals about a guide if you want to explore.

Places to Stay

There aren't many places to stay in town. The cheapest is the *Maristela* (☎ 33-0007) at Rua Manoel Joaquim 220. They have singles/doubles for US$7/10. Close by at No 213 is the *Nevada* (☎ 33-0259), with singles for US$9 and doubles for US$15. The *Minuano* (☎ 33-0656) has chalets for US$16. It's on Rua Uribici at No 230.

Places to Eat

Try the restaurant at the *Minuano* hotel for a good churrasco lunch. *Água na Boca* at Rua Marcos Batista 907 serves a decent pizza.

Getting There & Away

Buses run between São Joaquim and Florianópolis. There aren't too many of them, so check the schedules before heading out.

Rio Grande do Sul

PORTO ALEGRE

Porto Alegre, gaúcho capital and Brazil's sixth biggest city, lies on the eastern bank of the Rio Guaíba at the point where it empties into the huge Lagoa dos Patos. It's a modern city which makes a living predominantly from its freshwater port and commerce. Originally settled by the Portuguese in 1755 to keep the Spanish out, Porto Alegre was never a centre of colonial Brazil and is mainly a product of the 20th century, which is when many German and Italian immigrants arrived here.

Although most travellers just pass through Porto Alegre, it's an easy place in which to spend a few days. There are some interesting museums, some impressive neo-classical buildings and the friendly gaúchos and their barbecued meat – the city abounds in churrascarias.

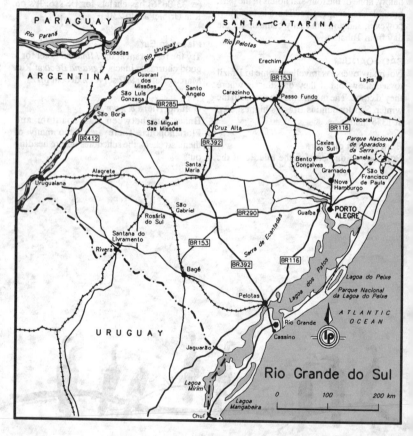

Rio Grande do Sul

314

Information
Don't forget that Porto Alegre has distinct seasonal weather changes: it gets very hot in summer (above 40°C) and you need a good jacket in the winter. City beaches are too polluted for swimming.

Tourist Office CRTur (☎ 28-7377), at Rua dos Andradas 1137 on the 6th floor of an arcade, is the state tourist office. It maintains branches at the airport and the bus station. Staff are efficient and hand out maps and a monthly guide.

Money There are lots of casas de câmbio in Porto Alegre. Try Exprinter (☎ 21-8266), Avenida Salgado Filho 247, or Aerotur (☎ 28-8144), on the ground floor in the same building as the tourist office on Rua dos Andradas.

Post & Telephone The post office is at Rua Siqueira Campos 1100. Make phone calls from CRT at Avenida Borges de Medeiros 512, on the corner of Avenida Salgado Filho.

Foreign Consulates The following South American countries are represented by consulates in Port Alegre:

Argentina
    Rua Prof Annes Dias 112, 1st floor (☎ 24-6799)
Paraguay
    Quintino Bocaiuva 655, sala 301 (☎ 46-1314)
Uruguay
    Rua Siqueira Campos 1171, 6th floor (☎ 24-3499)

Museu Histórico Júlio de Castilhos
Near the cathedral at Rua Duque de Caixas 1231, this interesting museum contains diverse objects concerning the history of the state: things like special moustache cups, a pair of giant's shoes and a very intricate wooden chair. It's open from 9 am to 5 pm, Tuesday to Sunday.

Museu de Arte do Rio Grande do Sul
In the Praça da Alfândega, this one has a good collection of works by gaúcho artists. Hours are 10 am to 5 pm, Tuesday to Sunday.

Mercado Público
Constructed in 1869, the market is a lively one and lots of stalls sell the unique tea-drinking equipment of the gaúchos: the *cuia* (gourd) and *bomba* (silver straw). These are good, portable souvenirs.

Parque Farroupilha
This big, central park is a good place to see gaúchos at play. If you're due for some exercise they have bikes to rent. On Sunday mornings, the Brique da Redenção, a market/fair, fills up a corner of the park with antiques, leather goods and music.

Instituto Gaúcho de Tradição e Folclore
If you're really interested in the traditions of the gaúcho, Dona Lilian, the chief archivist at this institution, can show you some excellent photographs. They also sell books (in Portuguese) relating to every aspect of gaúcho life. It's at Rua Siqueira Campos 1184, on the 5th floor.

Morro Santa Teresa
Porto Alegre is renowned for its stunning sunsets. The best place to watch one is Morro Santa Teresa, six km from the city centre. This 131-metre-high hill provides good views of the city and the Rio Guaíba.

Places to Stay
The *Hotel Uruguai* (☎ 28-7864), Rua Dr Flores 371, is a clean, secure and cheap place to stay. They have single quartos for US$3 and doubles for US$6. Apartamentos cost US$4/8. Nearby at Avenida Vigario José Inácio 644 is the *Hotel Palácio* (☎ 25-3467), popular with travellers and very friendly. Quartos cost US$7/13 a single/double and apartamentos go for US$10/15.

Over on Rua Andrade Neves, there are a few hotels and some good spots to eat. The *Hotel Marechal* (☎ 28-3076) is one of the cheapest with apartamentos for US$9/12 a single/double. For the same price, the *Hotel Gloria* (☎ 24-6433) across the road is good, but often full.

More expensive but in the same street, the *Metrópole* (☎ 26-1800), at Rua Andrade

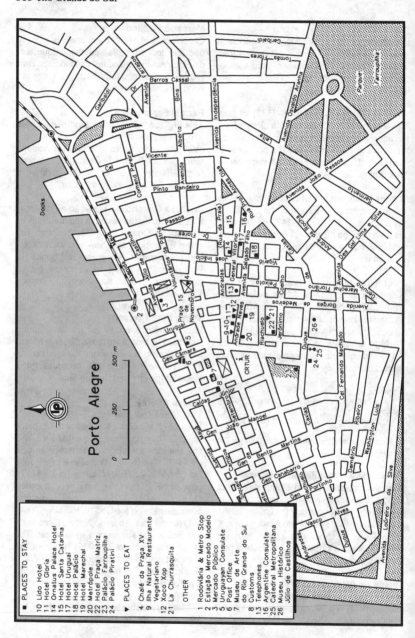

Porto Alegre

0   250   500 m

PLACES TO STAY

10 Lido Hotel
11 Hotel Gloria
14 Ornatus Palace Hotel
15 Hotel Santa Catarina
17 Hotel Uruguai
18 Hotel Palácio
19 Hotel Marechal
20 Metrópole
23 Hotel Praça Matriz
23 Palácio Farroupilha
24 Palácio Piratini

PLACES TO EAT

4   Chalé da Praça XV
9   Ilha Natural Restaurante
    Vegetariano
12 Xoco Xop
21 La Churrasquita

OTHER

1   Rodoviária & Metro Stop
2   Estação Mercado Modelo
3   Mercado Público
5   Uruguayan Consulate
6   Post Office
7   Museu de Arte
    do Rio Grande do Sul
8   Customs
13 Telephones
16 Argentine Consulate
25 Catedral Metropolitana
26 Museu Histórico
26 Júlio de Castilhos

Neves 59, has apartamentos for US$15/20 for singles/doubles. An interesting place to stay is the *Hotel Praça Matriz* (☎ 25-5772) at Largo João Amorim de Albequerque 72. In an ornate old building, it costs US$12 a single and US$20 a double with TV.

Hotel Santa Catarina (☎ 24-9044) is a good mid-range alternative with apartamentos for US$22. Forget it if you're alone though because you only get a 10% reduction on the room. It's at Rua General Vitorino 240. On the same street at No 146 is the *Ornatus Palace Hotel* (☎ 21-4555). Their apartamentos are US$33/42 for singles/doubles.

Back on Rua Andrade Neves, the *Lido* (☎ 26-8233) at No 150 is a top-end alternative with singles/doubles for US$40/50.

Across from the rodoviária try the *Terminaltur* (☎ 27-1656)which has doubles for US$22 and singles for US$18, with air-con and TV. Next door, the *Hotel Ritter* (☎ 21-8155) has three-star singles/doubles for US$45/51.

Places to Eat

Most of the good restaurants are in the suburbs and are a hassle to get to. Meat is the order of the day in the city and wherever you are a juicy steak will be nearby. At Rua Riachuelo 1331, *La Churrasquita* is one vegetarian's nightmare.

One place to try for sucos and sandwiches in the city is *Caseiro Natural*, in the subterraneo Malcom. Also try the Banca 40 at the Mercado Público. With an excellent US$3 buffet lunch, *Ilha Natural Restaurante Vegetariano*, Rua Andrade Neves 42, packs the locals in. Close by, at No 98, *Xoco Xop* has good cakes and juices.

Locals brag about the traditional gaúcho cooking at the *Pulperia*, Trevessa do Carmo 76 at the Cidade Baixa. Meals cost US$5 to US$8 but it's a good splurge. For traditional gaúcho cooking and a folkloric floorshow, try *Tio Flor*, Avenida Getúlio Vargas 1700. It's not too expensive and the show is well done. It's at the bottom of Morro Santa Teresa, so you could go there after watching the sunset.

One real Porto Alegre tradition is to have a late afternoon chopp at the *Chalé da Praça XV* on Praça 15 in front of the market. Constructed in 1885, it's the most traditional bar-restaurant in the city, and a great place to people watch.

Getting There & Away

There are international buses to Montevideo (13 hours, US$26), Buenos Aires (24 hours, US$40) and Asunción (16 hours, US$36). Foz do Iguaçu is 18 hours away and costs $25, Florianópolis 7½ hours and US$10, Curitiba 11 hours and US$17, São Paulo 18 hours and US$30 and Rio de Janeiro 27 hours and US$40. Road conditions in the state are generally excellent.

Getting Around

Porto Alegre has a one-line metro that the locals call Trensurb. It has 15 stations, but the only ones of any use to the visitor are the central station by the port called Estação Mercado Modelo, the rodoviária, which is the next stop, and the airport, which is three stops further. The metro runs from 5 am to 11 pm. A ride costs 10c.

LITORAL GAÚCHO

The Litoral Gaúcho makes up a 500-km strip along the state of Rio Grande do Sul – from Torres in the north until Chuí at the Uruguayan border. Of all Brazil's coast, this is the least distinguished, the least varied. The beaches are really one long beach uninterrupted by geographical variations, wide open, with little vegetation and occasional dunes. The sea here is choppier than in Santa Catarina, the water less translucent.

In winter, currents from the Antarctic bring cold, hard winds to the coast. Bathing suits disappear, as well as most people. Most hotels shut down in March and the summer beach season doesn't return until November at the earliest, with the arrival of the northern winds.

The three big resort towns on the north coast are Torres, Capão da Canoa and Tramandaí. Torres, the furthest from Porto Alegre, is only three hours away by car. All three have medium-size airports, luxury hotels and upscale nightlife, and they all fill up in the summer with Porto Alegrenses, Uruguayans and Argentinians. This is not where you go to get away from it all. There are many campgrounds and cheaper hotels in the towns, but the flavour is much more that of well-to-do weekend resorts than of fishing villages.

Torres

Torres is 205 km from Porto Alegre. It is well known for its fine beaches and the beautiful, basaltic rock formations along the coast. This is good country in which to walk and explore, and if you can get here early or late in the season, when the crowds have thinned out, it's especially worthwhile. There is also an ecological reserve on the Ilha dos Lobos.

Information There's a really good tourist office on the corner of Avenida Barão do Rio Branco and Rua General Osório. It publishes a list of hotels, including the cheapest ones. There are a few câmbios in town. Try Brasiltur, Rua Corte Real 950. For travellers' cheques, there is a Banco do Brasil.

Festival A big drawcard over the last few years has been the ballooning festival, held near the end of March.

Places to Stay Torres is full of hotels, and has a surprising number of simple places that are reasonably priced. If you're there in the off season, make sure you get an off-season rate, which should be considerably less than the summer price. Campgrounds are plentiful.

The cheapest hotel in town is *Hotel Medusa* (☎ 664-2378), Rua Benjamin Constant 828. Singles/doubles are US\$4/8. A good place at Avenida Barão do Rio Branco 148 is *Hotel Mar del Plata* (☎ 664-1665), with doubles for US\$17. The best hotel is the four-star *Continental Torres* (☎ 664-1811), at Rua Plínio Kroeff 405, next to the Rio Mampituba.

Places to Eat At last count there were more

than 35 restaurants in Torres. For seafood, *Mariscão*, Avenida Beira Mar 145, is recommended. For churrasco, *Bom Gosto* at Barão do Rio Branco 242 is excellent. A tasty pizza is served by *Ravena* at No 117.

Capão da Canoa

This is a smaller resort, 140 km from Porto Alegre, without the glamour and glitz of Torres. The best known beach is Praia de Atlântida, three km from the town. The beach is big and broad, and there's an active windsurfing scene on the lagoons.

Places to Stay As in Torres, there are several campgrounds here. For less expensive lodging, try the *Acapulco* (☎ 665-3121) at Rua Venâncio Aires 363, with singles/doubles for US\$9/15. At Atlântida beach threee km away, the *Johsil* at Rua 24, No 310 has rooms for around the same price.

Places to Eat Lots of the restaurants here close down over the winter. In summer, try the *Taberna Don Ciccilo* at Rua Guaracy 1826. They have a varied menu.

Tramandaí

Only 120 km from Porto Alegre, Tramandaí's permanent population of some 15,000 swells to half a million in January. On summer weekends the beaches are the busiest in the state; they're good, though not as nice as in Torres.

Festival There is a good festival here in late June, the Festa de São Pedro, with a procession of boats on the sea.

Places to Stay There's a lot of camping and several less-expensive hotels in Tramandaí, but reservations are still in order during January and February. In the centre, the *Junges* (☎ 661-1022), Avenida Fernando Amarel 522, is reasonable value. Singles/doubles cost US\$8/14. A bit better is the *Paulinho* (☎ 661-1209), Avenida Rio Grande 1060. Singles/doubles are US\$12/21. There's a good youth hostel (☎ 25-0599) on Rua Belém.

Places to Eat Most of the restaurants are on Avenida Emancipação. At No 265, *Palato* is good for seafood, as is *Taverna do Willy* at No 315. *Yellows*, at No 323, has a more varied menu.

Chuí

The small border town of Chuí is about 225 km south of Rio Grande on a good paved road. One side of the main street, Avenida Brasil, is Brazilian and the other side is the Uruguayan town of Chuy. The Brazilian side is full of Uruguayans doing their monthly grocery shopping, buying auto-parts and taking care of their clothing needs for the next six months. The Uruguayan side is a good place to change some money, buy cheap, duty-free Scotch whisky and post letters.

Visas It's much better to get your Uruguayan visa in Porto Alegre than at the border at Chuí, but it can be done here. You won't need a medical examination, but you'll have to wait overnight. The Uruguayan Consulate (☎ 65-1151) is at Rua Venezuela 311 and is open from 9 am to 3 pm. If you need one, visas cost US$20.

Places to Stay & Eat Hopefully, you've had the good sense to organise your visas well before arriving in Chuí and are on a direct bus to your destination. If you haven't, you're in travellers' purgatory: a dusty, dirty border town waiting overnight for your visa.

There are a few simple hotels. Try the *Hotel e Restaurante São Francisco* (☎ 65-1096) at Rua Columbia 741. It charges US$5 per person. Across the road, *Hospedagem Bianca* and *Hospedagem Roberto* are a bit cheaper. In Uruguay, the *Plaza Hotel*, Rua General Artigas 553, has singles/doubles for US$20/30.

The restaurant in the São Francisco is as good as any around town. There is lots of fast food in both countries.

Getting There & Away The rodoviária is at Rua Venezuela 247 and buses leave constantly for most cities in southern Brazil.

You can buy tickets to Montevideo on the Uruguayan side of Avenida Brasil. Seven buses leave daily for Punta del Este and Montevideo. The first leaves at 4 am and the last at midnight.

Crossing the Border All buses to Uruguay stop at the Polícia Federal on Avenida Argentina, a couple of km from town. You must get out to get your Brazilian exit stamp. In Uruguay, the bus will stop again for the Uruguayan officials to check if you have a Brazilian exit stamp.

PELOTAS

If they gave out awards for the most outrageous-looking bus station in Brazil, Pelotas would be a major contender in the 'Imaginative Uses of Concrete' category.

Pelotas, 251 km south of Porto Alegre, was a major port in the 19th century for the export of dried beef and was home to a sizeable British community. The wealth generated is still reflected in the grand, neo-classical mansions around the main square, Praça General Osório. Today the town is an important industrial centre, and much of its canned vegetables, fruits and sweets are exported.

There's really no reason to stay in Pelotas, but if you're waiting at the rodoviária for a bus connection, and you have some time to spare, it's worth going into the centre for a look.

Places to Stay

If you do get stuck here, *The Rex* (☎ 22-1163) at Praça Coronel Osório 205 has quartos for US$6/10 and apartamentos for US$8/12. The *Palace* (☎ 22-2223), at Rua 7 de Setembro 354, is a bit cheaper.

Places to Eat

The *Shanghai* at Rua 7 de Setembro 301 has reasonable Chinese food. On the same street at No 306, the *Bavaria* serves German food.

Pelotas is renowned for its sweets, which can be sampled from the many stalls on Rua 7 de Setembro, or at *Otto Especialidades*, next to the Bavaria.

RIO GRANDE

Once an important cattle centre, Rio Grande lies near the mouth of the Lagoa dos Patos, Brazil's biggest lagoon. To the north, the coast along the lagoa is lightly inhabited. There's a poor dirt road along this stretch, which is connected with Rio Grande by a small ferry boat. It's an active port city, and while not a great drawcard, it's more interesting than Pelotas if you want to break your journey in this area.

Information

There's a tourist office at Rua Riachuelo 355, but it's rarely open in the off season. The only tourist brochure in town is available from any travel agent or big hotel, like the Charrua. A good place to change money is at the Turisbel, a bar and gemstone shop at Rua Luíz Loreá 407. Its English-speaking Greek owner will even change Australian dollars. For travellers' cheques, there is a Banco do Brasil. The post office is at Rua General Netto 115.

Catedral de São Pedro

This cathedral is the oldest church in the state, and was erected by the Portuguese colonists. In baroque style, it's classified as part of the Patrimônio Histórico. Even if you don't usually look at churches, this is an interesting one.

Museu Oceanográphico

This museum is the most complete of its type in Latin America. Two km from the centre, it has a large shell collection and skeletons of whales and dolphins. It's interesting, and open daily from 9 to 11 am and 2 to 5 pm. It's on Avenida Perimetra.

Other Museums

The Museu da Cidade is in the old customs house, which Dom Pedro II ordered built on Rua Richuelo. It's open weekdays from 9.30 to 11.30 am and 2.30 to 5 pm and on Sundays from 2.30 to 5 pm. Across the road is the Museu do Departamento Estadual de Portos, Rios e Canais (DEPREC), which houses the machinery used during the construction of

the large breakwater. It's open weekdays from 8 to 11.30 am and 1.30 to 5.30 pm.

São José do Norte

Boats leave from the terminal at the waterfront every 40 minutes and make the trip across the mouth of the Lagoa dos Patos to the fishing village of São José do Norte. This is a nice trip to do around sunset. The last boat back to Rio Grande leaves at 7 pm. It costs US$1.50 for the round trip.

Places to Stay

There are a few cheap hotels in Rio Grande, but the one to head for is the *Paris* (☎ 32-8944). In a 19th-century building, this one's seen better days but is still impressive, and its courtyard is an excellent place in which to sit and contemplate the glory days of the city. It's at Rua Marechal Floriano 112; quartos cost US$5/9 and apartamentos US$8/12 for singles/doubles. Don't miss this one, even though it's a bit of a hike to get there.

Moving up in price but not character, there is the *Europa* (☎ 32-8133), opposite Praça Tamandaré at Rua General Netto 165. Singles/doubles cost US$18/25. The top hotel in town is the *Charrua Hotel* (☎ 32-8033), on Rua Duque de Caixas, opposite Praça Xavier Ferreira. They usually charge US$30 a double, but off season they'll cut this to US$20.

Places to Eat

For seafood, try the *Pescal* at Rua Marechal Andrea 269. They're closed on Sundays. *Marcos*, Avenida Silva Paes 400, has a varied menu and a nice ambience. For coffee and a sandwich, *Reastaurante Nova Gruta Baiana* on Rua Marechal Floriano, opposite Prac Xavier Ferreira, is good. For a buffet lunch, the *Charrua Hotel* puts on a good spread.

Getting There & Away

The rodoviária, at Rua Vice Admiral Abreu 737, is about six blocks from the centre. Buses connect with Uruguay and all major cities in southern Brazil.

Top: Flower of Iguaçu, Paraná (SP)
Bottom: Iguaçu Falls, Paraná (AD)

Top: Ruins of São Miguel Jesuit Mission, Rio Grande do Sul (AD)
Bottom: Fortaleza Canyon, Cambará do Sul, Rio Grande do Sul (AD)

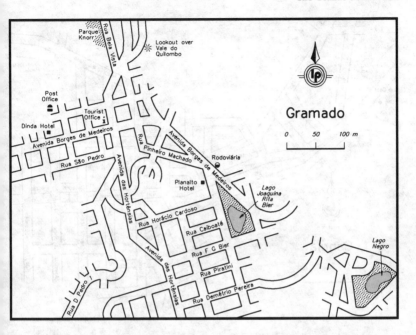

Gramado

0   50   100 m

Around Rio Grande

Cassino Twenty-five km south of Rio Grande, reached by local bus from Praça Tamandaré, Cassino is a D-grade beach resort popular in summer with Uruguayans and Argentinians. If you like littered, wind-swept beaches, brown sea water and cars zipping up and down the beach, this is the place for you.

SERRA GAÚCHA

North of Porto Alegre, you quickly begin to climb into the Serra Gaúcha. The ride is beautiful, as are the mountain towns of Gramado and Canela, 140 km from Porto Alegre. First settled by Germans in 1824 and later by Italians in the 1870s, the region is as close to the Alps as Brazil gets. It's known as the Região das Hortênsias (Geranium Region). Both towns are popular resorts and are crowded with Porto Alegrenses in all seasons, but particularly when it's hottest in the big city. There are many hotels and res-

taurants, particularly in Gramado, and many with a German influence. Prices are high for Brazil.

Hikers abound in the mountains here. In the winter there are occasional snowfalls and in the spring the hills are blanketed with flowers. The best spot is the Parque Estadual do Caracol, which is reached by local bus from Canela, eight km away.

Gramado

This touristy mountain resort is a favourite with well-to-do Argentinians, Uruguayans, Paulistas and gaúchos. It has lots of cosy restaurants, expensive, Swiss-style chalet/hotels and well-manicured gardens.

Information There's a useful Centro de Informações in the centre of town on Praça Major Nicoletti. It has maps and information on most hotels and restaurants.

Parks Well-kept parks close to town include

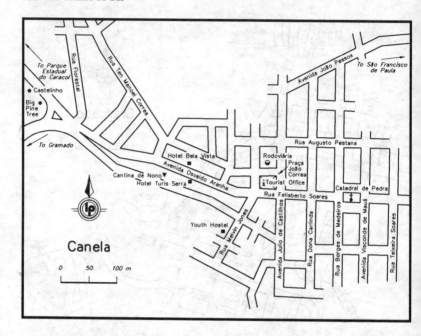

Canela

0   50   100 m

the Lago Negro at Rua 25 de Julho 175, which has lots of pine trees and a small lake, and the Parque Knorr at the end of Rua Bela Vista. The latter has lots of flowers and a good view of the spectacular Vale do Quilombo. There's also the Lago Joaquina Rita Bier, a lake surrounded by geraniums, at Rua Leopoldo Rosenfeldt.

Festival Each June Gramado hosts the Brazilian Film Festival.

Places to Stay There are no really cheap places in Gramado. The *Dinda Hotel* (☎ 286-1588), Rua Augusto Zatti 160, has apartamentos for US$15/20 a single/double and is in the middle of town. Another recommended hotel is the *Planalto* (☎ 286-1210), across from the rodoviária at Avenida Borges de Medeiros 554. It's pleasant and clean, with plenty of hot water and a balcony for each room. It's better than some more expen-

sive places, with single/double apartamentos for US$18/23.

There's no shortage of top-end places. The best ones are out on the road between Gramado and Canela, especially the *Villa Bella Gramado* (☎ 286-2688) has doubles from US$50.

Places to Eat Every second place in Gramado seems to be a restaurant, especially along Avenida das Hortênsias. Try *A Carreta* at No 3845 for some regional dishes. They also have live music. A good churrascaria is *4 Rodas* at No 5532. They have a rodízio and live music. Fondue lovers should try *Le Chalet de la Fondue* at No 1297.

Getting There & Away The rodoviária is close to the centre at Avenida Borges de Mendeiros 2100. Frequent buses make the two-hour, US$4 trip to Porto Alegre. To Canela, take a local bus from the rodoviária. The trip takes 15 minutes.

Canela

While not as up-market as Gramado, Canela is the best jumping-off point for some great hikes and bike rides in the area. There are cheaper hotels here than in Gramado, so budget travellers should make this their base.

Information The tourist office (☎ 282-1287) in Praça João Correa is helpful and hands out a brochure with some entertaining English translations.

Parque Estadual do Caracol Eight km from Canela, the major attraction of this park is a spectacular waterfall 130 metres high. You don't have to do any hiking to see it as it's very close to the park entrance. The park is open daily from 7.30 am to 6 pm. Entry is 40c. On the road to the park, two km from the centre of Canela, is a 700-year-old, 42-metre-tall araucária pine.

A public bus to the park, marked 'Caracol Circular', leaves the rodoviária at 8.15 am, noon and 5.30 pm.

Ferradura A seven-km hike from the park entrance brings you to Ferradura, a stunning 400-metre-deep horseshoe canyon formed by the Rio Santa Cruz.

You can camp in here, but you have to bring everything with you.

Castelinho One of the oldest houses in the area, on the road to the park, Castelinho is a pioneer museum, a German restaurant and chocolate shop.

Festival From 26 to 28 May, 80,000 pilgrims arrive to celebrate the Festa de NS de Caravaggio. There is a six-km procession from the Igreja Matrix to the Parque do Saiqui.

Places to Stay The *Hotel Turis Serra* (☎ 282-2136) is the best cheapie in Canela. At Avenida Osvaldo Aranha 223, it's clean and friendly, and is excellent value at US$5 per person with breakfast. The *Hotel Bela Vista* (☎ 282-1327), at Rua Osvaldo Aranha 160, has rooms and separate cabanas for US$16 a single and US$22 a double.

Close to the Turis Serra, at Rua Melvin Jones 151 behind the Centro Educational Cidade das Hortênsias building, is a youth hostel. It costs US$5 but you need to be a member.

Camping is available at *Camping Club do Brasil*, eight km from town on the park road.

Places to Eat Highly recommended is *Cantina de Nono*, Avenida Osvaldo Aranha 161. They have excellent pizza and reasonable Italian food. Big meat eaters will enjoy *Bifão & Cia* at Avenida Osvaldo Aranha 456.

Getting There & Away The rodoviária is in the centre of town. There are frequent buses to Porto Alegre, all travelling via Gramado.

Getting Around Canela is a good place to do some scenic bike rides. Bikes can be hired in the park just outside the tourist office.

PARQUE NACIONAL DE APARADOS DA SERRA

This national park is Rio Grande do Sul's most magnificent area and one of Brazil's great natural wonders. It is 70 km north of São Francisco de Paula, and 18 km from the town of Cambará do Sul.

Things to See

The park preserves one of the country's last araucária forests (pine-like trees that stand up to 50 metres tall), but the main attraction is the Canyon do Itaimbézinho, a fantastic narrow canyon with sheer 600 to 720-metre parallel escarpments. Two waterfalls drop into this deep incision in the earth, which was formed by the Rio Perdiz's rush to the sea.

Another of the park's attractions is the Canyon da Fortaleza, a 30-km stretch of escarpment with 900-metre drops. You can see the coast from here. Nearby on one of the walls of the canyon is the Pedra do Segredo, a five-metre monolith with a very small base. It's 23 km from Cambará, but unfortunately in a different direction from Itaimbézinho.

Places to Stay

In Cambará do Sul there are two places to

stay: the *Pousada Fortaleza*, 300 metres to the left if you face the city square from the bus station, and the *Hotel São Jorge*, 50 metres to the right. Go to the Pousada Fortaleza first. Both are pretty basic and charge US$3 per person.

In the park itself is the *Paradouro do Itaimbezinho* (☎ 178, 191 in Cambará do Sul). This is easily the place you should stay. They charge US$7 per person and it's a good idea to ring before you go to see if they're open. Don't do any sleepwalking.

Camping is a good alternative here and there are good spots near the Paradouro hotel and near Fortaleza.

Getting There & Away

If you can't afford to take a US$45, four-hour taxi ride from Cambará do Sul, or to hire a car (or plane) for a day, put on your walking shoes if you expect to see both Itaimbézinho and Fortaleza. No public buses go to either and the hitching is lousy. The closest you can get is three km from Itaimbézinho, by taking the bus to Praia Grande and asking to be dropped at the park entrance. From the other entrance, on the road between Cambará and

Statue at the ruins of São Miguel Jesuit Mission

Tainhas, it's a 15-km walk to the canyon. To get to Fortaleza, you'll either have to walk 23 km or make a deal with Borges, the taxi driver, to take you out there. There and back would cost around US$25, but it's worth it.

There are various ways to get to the park itself. One is to come up from the coast via Praia Grande and get off the 'Cambará do Sul' bus at the park entrance. You could also come up from Torres and get off at Tainhas, but you'd have to change buses there, and if you miss the connection there's nowhere to stay. Both these roads from the coast are spectacular. Another route is to come up from São Francisco de Paula and get off at the other entrance to the park.

There's also the possibility of hiking 20 km from Praia Grande into the canyon itself, but it's dangerous without a guide. People have been trapped in the canyon by flash flooding.

JESUIT MISSIONS

Soon after the discovery of the New World, the Portuguese and Spanish kings authorised Catholic orders to create missions to convert the natives into Catholic subjects of the crown and the state. The most successful of these orders were the Jesuits, who created a series of missions in a region which spanned parts of Paraguay, Brazil and Argentina. In effect it was a nation within the colonies, a nation which at its height in the 1720s claimed 30 mission villages inhabited by over 150,000 Guarani Indians. Buenos Aires was merely a village at this time.

Unlike those established elsewhere, these missions succeeded in introducing Western culture without destroying the Indian people, their culture and their Tupi-Guaraní language.

In 1608 Hernandarias, Governor of the Spanish province of Paraguay, ordered the local leader of the Jesuits, Fray Diego de Torres, to send missionaries to convert the infidels, and so in 1609 the first mission was founded. Preferring indoctrination by the Jesuits to serfdom on Spanish estates or slavery at the hands of the Portuguese, the Indians were rapidly recruited into a chain of missions. The missions covered a vast region of land encompassing much of the present-day Brazilian states of Paraná, Santa Catarina and Rio Grande do Sul as well as portions of Paraguay and northern Argentina.

The Jesuit territory was too large to defend and the Portuguese bandeirantes found the missionary settlements easy pickings for slave raids. Thousands of Indians were captured, reducing the 13 missions of Guayra (Brazilian territory) to two. Fear of the bandeirante slavers caused these two missions to be abandoned, and the Indians and Jesuits marched westward and founded San Ignacio Miní (1632), having lost many people in the rapids of the Paraná. The missions north of Iguaçu were decimated by attacks from hostile Indian tribes and were forced to relocate south.

Between 1631 and 1638, activity was concentrated in 30 missions which the mission Indians were able to defend. In one of the bloodiest fights, the battle of Mbororé, the Indians beat back the slavers and secured their lands north of San Javier.

The missions, under administration based in Candelaria, grew crops, raised cattle and prospered. They were miniature cities built around a central church and included libraries, baptisteries, cemeteries and dormitories for the Indian converts and the priests. The missions became centres of culture and intellect as well as religion. An odd mix of European baroque and native Guarani arts, music and painting developed. Indian scholars created a written form of Tupi-Guaraní and from 1704 published several works in Tupi-Guaraní in one of the earliest printing presses of South America.

As the missions grew, the Jesuit nation became more independent of Rome and relations with the Vatican became strained. The nation within a nation became an embarrassment to the Iberian kings and finally in 1777 the Portuguese minister Marques de Pombal convinced Carlos III to expel the Jesuit priests from Spanish lands. Thus ended, in the opinion of many historians, a grand 160-year experiment in socialism, where wealth was equally divided, and religion, intellect and the arts flourished – a utopian island of progress in an age of monarchies and institutionalised slavery. Administration of the mission villages passed into the hands of the colonial government and the communities continued until the early 1800s, when they were destroyed by revolutionary wars of independence and then abandoned.

Today, there are 30 ruined Jesuit missions: seven lie in Brazil, in the western part of Rio Grande do Sul, eight are in the southern region of Itapuá, Paraguay, and the remaining 15 are in Argentina. Of these 15 Argentine missions, 11 lie in the province of Missiones, which hooks like a thumb between Paraguay and the Rio Paraná, and Brazil and the Uruguay and Iguaçu rivers.

Brazilian Missions

São Miguel das Missoes This mission, 58 km from Santo Angelo, is the most interesting of the Brazilian ones. Every evening at 8 pm there's a sound and light show. Also nearby are the missions of São João Batista (on the way to São Miguel) and São Lourenço das Missoes (10 km from São João Batista by dirt road).

Paraguayan Missions

The missions of Paraguay, long since abandoned, are only now being restored. The most important mission to see is Trinidad, 25 km from Encarnación. The red stone ruins are fascinating. If you have the time, see the missions of Santa Rosa, Santiago and Jesus.

Argentine Missions

In Argentina, the most important mission to see is San Ignacio Miní, 60 km from Posadas on Ruta Nacional 12. Of lesser stature is mission Santa Maria la Mayor, 111 km away from Posadas on Ruta 110, and mission Candelaria, 25 km from Posadas on Ruta 12 (now a national penitentiary). It's possible to cut across the province of Missiones to San Javier (Ruta 4) and cross by ferry to Brazil at Puerto Xavier, or further south at Santo Tome, and ferry across the Rio Uruguay to São Borja, Brazil.

The border at Uruguaiana, 180 km south of São Borja, is more commonly used. Uruguaiana is 180 km from São Borja or 635 km from Porto Alegre. Buses operate to Buenos Aires, Santiago do Chile and Montevideo. The Argentine Consulate (☎ (055) 412-1925) is at Rua Santana 2496, 2nd floor, while the Uruguayan Consulate (☎ (055) 412- 1514) is at Rua Domingos de Almeida, 1709.

Places to Stay & Eat

In Brazil, Santo Angelo has several modest but proper hotels, but it's great to stay out at São Miguel to see the sound and light show and the sunrise. The missions were always placed on high points in the countryside, so there's a great view. The *Hotel Barichello* is the only place to stay. It's very clean and run by a friendly family. Singles cost US$4 and doubles with a shower, US$9. It's a good place to eat, too.

In Paraguay, Encarnacion has a couple of cheap and modest hotels and Chinese restaurants.

Across the Rio Paraná from Encarnacion is the capital of the Argentine province of Posadas. A ferry operates from 8 am to noon, and from 2 pm until sundown. Everything is more expensive, but the food is better and the lodging (10 hotels to choose from) is fancier.

Getting There & Away

Use Encarnacion as a base for the missions of Paraguay. Riza buses leave daily from Ciudad del Este for Encarnacion, 320 km south; from Asuncion they depart daily for the 370 km journey to Encarnacion on Ruta 1. Either way, it's a pleasant ride through fertile rolling hills, a region where the locals (mostly of German descent) drink a variation of maté called *tererê*.

Getting Around

This is the sort of travelling that's best done by car, but unfortunately car rental fees are expensive and driving a rental car over borders is difficult. It's possible to hire a taxi from any of the three base cities, Posadas, Encarnacion and Santo Angelo.

leaf-cutter ants

THE CENTRAL WEST

REGIÃO CENTRO OESTE

The Central West

Known to Brazilians as the Centro-Oeste, this region includes almost 19% of the country's land area. It's the most sparsely populated region in Brazil, containing only 6% of the total population.

Made up of the states of Mato Grosso, Mato Grosso do Sul, Goiás and the Distrito Federal of Brasília, this massive terrain was until the 1940s the last great unexplored area on earth.

Here, the Planalto Brasileiro has been greatly eroded to form the Guimarães, Parecis and Veadeiros *chapadões* (tablelands) between the river basins. In the south-west of Mato Grosso and the west of Matto Grosso do Sul is the wildlife paradise called the Pantanal Matogrossense. It's a unique geographical depression formed by a huge inland sea which dried up millions of years ago. Large portions become covered by water during the rainy season.

As well as the Pantanal, which is the drawcard of the region, the Central West contains many other natural attractions: national parks in two of the abovementioned

tablelands (Chapada dos Guimarães and Chapada dos Veadeiros); the Parque Nacional das Emas; and the Rio Araguaia which extends into the northern state of Tocantins.

There are also interesting colonial towns (Goiás Velho and Pirenopolis) and large, planned cities (Goiânia and Brasília) that are worth a look.

Central West

Distrito Federal

BRASÍLIA

I sought the curved and sensual line. The curve that I see in the Brazilian hills, in the body of a loved one, in the clouds in the sky and in the ocean waves.

Brasília architect Oscar Niemeyer

Brasília is a utopian horror. It should be a symbol of power, but instead it's a museum of architectural ideas.

Art critic Robert Hughes

The impression I have is that I'm arriving on a different planet.

Cosmonaut Yuri Gagarin

Brasília must have looked good on paper and still looks good in photos. In 1987 it was added to the UNESCO list of World Heritage Sites, being considered one of the major examples of this century's modern movement in architecture and urban planning. But in the flesh, forget it. The world's great planned city of the 20th century is built for automobiles and air-conditioners, not people. Distances are enormous and no one walks. The sun blazes, but there are no trees for shelter.

It's a lousy place to visit and no one wanted to live there. Bureaucrats and politicians, who live in the model 'pilot plan' part of the city, were lured to Brasília by 100% salary hikes and big apartments. Still, as soon as the weekend comes they get out of the city as fast as possible to Rio, to São Paulo, to their private clubs in the country – anywhere that's less sterile, less organised, less vapid. Brasília is also one of the most expensive cities in Brazil.

The poor have to get out – they have no choice. Mostly from the Northeast, these *candangos* (pioneers) work in the construction and service industries. They live in favelas, which they call 'anti-Brasílias', as far as 30 km from the centre. This physical gulf between haves and have-nots is reminiscent of South Africa's township system.

All this is the doing of three famous Brazilians: an urban planner (Lucio Costa), an architect (Oscar Niemeyer) and a landscape architect (Burle Marx), all three the leading figures in their field. They were commissioned by President Juscelino Kubitschek to plan a new inland capital, a city that would catalyse the economic development of Brazil's vast interior. With millions of dirt-poor peasants from the Northeast working around the clock, Brasília was built in an incredible three years – it wasn't exactly finished but it was ready to be the capital (Niemeyer admits today that it was all done too quickly). On 21 April 1960, the capital was moved from Rio to Brasília and thousands of public servants fell into a deep depression.

An inland capital was an old Brazilian dream that had always been dismissed as expensive folly. What possessed Kubitschek

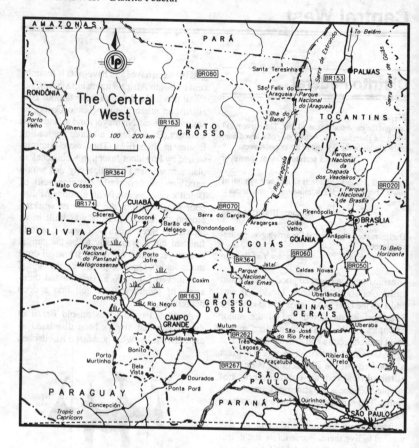

to actually do it? Politics. He made the building of Brasília a symbol of the country's determination and ability to become a great economic power. He successfully appealed to all Brazilians to put aside their differences and rally to the cause. In doing so he distracted attention from the country's social and economic problems, gained enormous personal popularity and borrowed heavily from the international banks. His legacy to the country was rampant inflation.

Orientation

Seen from above, Brasília looks like an aeroplane (symbolising the fastest way out of town) or a bow and arrow (signifying the penetration of the interior and the destruction of the indigenous people). The planned city, the *plano piloto*, faces the giant artificial Lago do Paranoá. In the plane's fuselage (or the arrow) are all the government buildings and monuments. The plaza of three powers – the president's Palácio do Planalto, the Palácio do Congresso and the Palácio da Justiça – is in the cockpit. Out on the wings (*asas*) are block after block of apartment buildings (known as Superquadras or Quadras) and little else.

You can rent a car, take a tourist tour or combine a city bus (circular buses leave from the city rodoviária) with some long walks to see the bulk of Brasília's edifices. Remember that many buildings are closed on weekends and at night.

Information

Tourist Office Detur is the government tourist information service. Its office is inconveniently located on the 3rd floor of the Centro de Convenções and is open Monday to Friday from 1 to 6 pm. It also operates a tourist desk at the airport, which is open Monday to Friday from 8 am to 1 pm and 2 to 7 pm. On weekends it's open from 10 am to 1 pm and 4.30 to 7.30 pm. If you're only after a map or a list of attractions, pick up a brochure in any one of the big hotels or travel agencies. The best map I found was in the phone book *Achei! (Found it!) O Guia de Brasília*. It also has lots of tourist information in Portuguese.

Money There are plenty of banks with moneychanging facilities in the Setor Bancário Sul (SBS – Banking Sector South) and Setor Bancário Norte (SBN – Banking Sector North). Both are close to the rodoviária.

Travel agencies will also change cash dollars.

Post & Telephone The post office is in the Setor Hoteleiro Sul (SHS – Hotel Sector South). There's a long-distance telephone office in the rodoviária.

Foreign Embassies Well, this is the capital, so they're all here. In the following addresses, SES stands for Setor de Embaixadas Sul.

Australia
    SHIS, Q I-9, cj 16, casa 1 (☎ 248-5569)
Canada
    SES, Avenida das Nações Q 803 lote 16 sl 130 (☎ 223-7517)
UK
    SES, Avenida das Nações, Q 801, cj K lote 8 (☎ 225-2710)
USA
    SES, Avenida das Nações, Q 801, lote 3 (☎ 321-7272)

Things to See

Start at the **Memorial JK**, open from 8 am to 6 pm. Along with the tomb of JK (President Kubitschek) there are several exhibits relating to the construction of the city.

Head to the 75-metre observation deck of the **TV tower**. It's open from 9 am to 8 pm. At the base of the tower on weekends there's a handicraft fair.

The **Catedral Metropolitana**, with its 16 curved columns and stained-glass interior, is worth seeing too. At the entrance are the haunting statues of the *Four Evangelists* carved by Ceschiatti, who also made the aluminium angels hanging inside. The cathedral is open from 8.30 to 11.30 am and 2 to 6 pm.

Down by the tip of the arrow you'll find the most interesting government buildings: the **Palácio do Itamaraty** (open Monday to Friday until 4 pm) is one of the best – a series of arches surrounded by a reflecting pool and landscaped by Burle Marx; there's also the **Palácio da Justiça**, the Supreme Court (open Monday to Friday from noon to 6 pm), with water cascading between its arches; and the **Palácio do Congresso** (open Monday to Friday from 10 to noon and 2 to 5 pm), with the 'dishes' and twin towers. The presidential **Palácio da Alvorada** is not open to visitors. If you're in town on a weekend, the big city park can be fun.

As impressive as the cathedral, or perhaps even more so, is the **Santuário Dom Bosco** (Dom Bosco's Shrine). Made of concrete columns and blue stained-glass windows, it's definitely worth a look. Located at Quadra 702 Sul, it's open daily from 8 am to 6.30 pm.

The **Parque Nacional de Brasília** is an ecological reserve, and is a good place in which to relax if you're stuck in the city. This park is open daily from 9 am to 5 pm, and is very popular on weekends. Apart from the attraction of its natural swimming pools, it is also home to a number of endangered

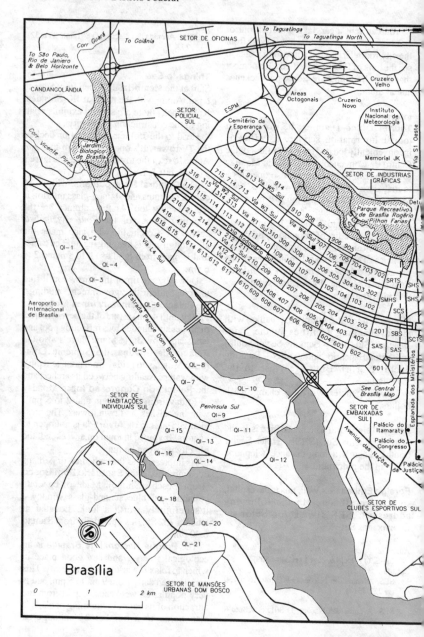

Brasília

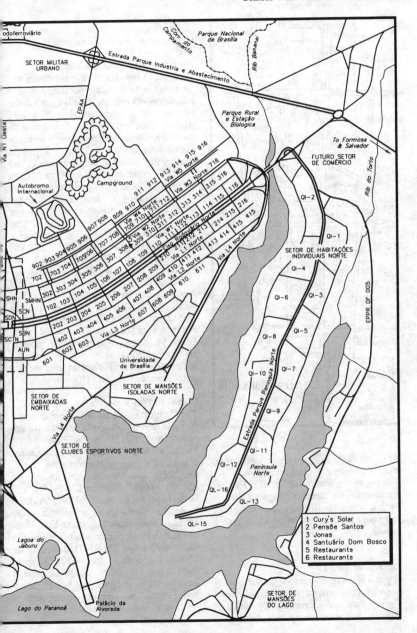

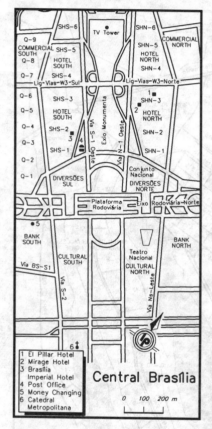

1 El Pillar Hotel
2 Mirage Hotel
3 Brasília Imperial Hotel
4 Post Office
5 Money Changing
6 Catedral Metropolitana

Central Brasília

0   100   200 m

animals, such as the maned-wolf, deer, banded anteater and giant armadillo.

Another good park is the **Parque Recreativo de Brasília Rogerio Pithon Farias**, where you'll find a swimming pool and small lunch places at which to grab a snack.

Organised Tours

If you want to save your feet, guided tours of the city cost around US$15. The Hotel Garvey-Park is the travel agency capital of Brasília and most companies there have sightseeing tours. You can also book bus tours at the airport or the rodoviária.

Places to Stay – bottom end

There aren't any cheap hotels in Brasília, but there are a few cheap pensions, mostly located on W3 Sul. The best is *Cury's Solar* (☎ 243-6252). Neusa Batista runs a very friendly place and it's a real favourite with travellers. Guests are encouraged to make themselves at home. There's a fridge, laundry facilities, TV, telephone and a good breakfast. Prices vary with room size: singles go from US$8 to US$12 and doubles from US$12 to US$24. Try this place first. To get there from the rodoviária, catch any bus going along W3 Sul and get off at the stop between Quadras 707 and 708. The house is in the second row from the street in 707. The address is Quadra 707 south, Block I, casa 15. There's no sign but it's easy to find.

A couple of other places close by are *Pensõe Santos* (☎ 244-6672) in Quadra 705 south, Block M, casa 43, which charges US$12 per person, and *Jonas* (☎ 224-6775), run by Jamira Batista, at Quadra 704 south, Block M, casa 9. She has clean shoebox singles for US$12.

Camping is possible not far from the city in the Setor de Garagens Oficiais.

Places to Stay – middle

The cheapest hotels fall into the mid-range, two-star category. A good one is the *Mirage Hotel* (☎ 225-7150) in the Hotel Sector North (SHN Q 02 Bloco N). They charge US$22/27 for singles/doubles. The restaurant there is good and the service very friendly. *El Pillar Hotel* (☎ 224-5915) is also in the Hotel Sector North (SHN Q 03 Bloco F) and has rooms for the same price as the Mirage. On the other side of the Eixo Monumental in Hotel Sector South, the *Brasília Imperial Hotel* (☎ 321-8747) has singles for US$21 and doubles for US$23. Keep in mind that any time there's a special event in Brasília, all these hotels will be full. Many hotels in the hotel sectors give discounts of up to 40% on the weekends.

There are cheaper hotels out of town

Brasília – Capital of the Third Millenium.

In 1883 an Italian priest, João Bosco, prophesied that a new civilisation would arise between parallels 15 and 20 and that its capital would be built between parallels 15 and 16, on the edge of an artificial lake. Brasília is considered by many people to be that city, and a number of cults have sprung up in the area.

About 45 km from Brasília you'll find the Vale do Amanhecer (Valley of the Dawn), founded in 1959 by a clairvoyant, Tia Neiva. The valley is actually a small town where you can check out Egyptian, Greek, Aztec, Indian, Gypsy, Inca, Trojan and Afro-Brazilian rituals. You can take part if you want. They take place daily at 12.30, 2.30 and 6.30 pm.

The 2000 mediums who live there follow the 'Doctrine of the Dawn'. They believe that a new civilisation will come with the third millenium. The main temple was inspired by the spiritual advice received by Tia Neiva. In the centre is an enormous star of David which forms a lake, pierced by an arrow.

About 80 km from the valley, near Santo Antônio do Descoberto, is the Cidade Ecléctica (Eclectic City), founded in 1956 by Yokanam, an ex-airline pilot. The main aim of its 3000 believers is the unification of all religions on the planet, and the values of fraternity and equality are expounded. Their ceremonies take place on Wednesdays and Fridays at 8 pm and on Sundays at 3 pm. There are strict dress regulations, but if you're not dressed suitably they will give you a special tunic to wear.

In Brasília itself, the Granja do Ipê (Ipê Estate) on the southern exit from the city is the site of the City of Peace & Holistic University. It aims to form a new generation with a mentality suited to the needs of the third millenium. The Templo da Boa Vontade (Temple of Goodwill) is at 915 Sul. It incorporates seven pyramids joined to form a cone that is topped with the biggest raw crystal you'll ever see.

Some people also believe that, in certain regions around Brasília, extraterrestrial contacts are more favorable – on Km 69 of the BR-351 highway, for instance, or on the plateau that exists in the satellite city of Brasilândia. Believe it or not. ■

---

towards Taguatinga in a sector called the SIA, but you'll only be saving a few dollars and spending a lot of time sitting on buses. Since you only need to stay in Brasília for one or two days to see everything, do yourself a favour and spend the extra money.

Places to Stay – top end

The *Hotel Nacional Brasília* (☎ 321-7575) and *Hotel Carlton* (☎ 224-8819) are two popular five-star lodgings. The former has an adjoining shopping mall and the latter is often the home for delegations from the USA. Both have doubles starting at US$100. There are lots of three and four, as well as a few more five-star hotels in the hotel sectors. The Detur desk at the airport has a complete list with prices.

Places to Eat

Both the shopping complexes near the rodoviária have lots of places to eat and many of them have lunchtime specials. The one on the north side (Conjunto Nacional) has the best selection.

Restaurants are located along the main avenues or else in between the quadras. A couple of places with a good selection of restaurants and bars are the space between Quadras 405 and 404 South and between Quadras 308 and 309 North.

In the following addresses, SCL means Setor Comércio Local, which is the space provided in the quadras for shops, restaurants, etc. N or S is North or South, followed by the quadra number, the block and the store number.

There are good restaurants scattered around too. The *Bom de Mais* has plenty of salads, other natural foods and live music, it's at SCLN 706 Bloco A, loja 60. It's open every day from 6 pm. *Bar Academia* is a popular place at SCLN 308, Bloco D, loja 11/19.

For nordestino cuisine the *Xique-Xique* has carne de sol and feijão verde with manteiga da terra. It's at SCLS 107 Bloco A, loja 1. *Tiragostas* is one of the city's oldest bar/restaurants. It's a famous meeting point for artists and musicians, and has outdoor tables under trees. The prices are reasonable and it's at SCLS 109 Bloco A, loja 2/4.

Vegetarians needn't feel left out. For some good natural food there's *Cheiro Verde*, SCLN 313, Bloco C, loja 20. It's open from Monday to Friday from 8 am to 8 pm. *Coisas da Terra* at SCLN 703, Bloco D, loja 41. On weekdays they're open from 11.30 am to 2.30 pm and 5.30 to 8 pm; weekend hours are from noon to 6 pm.

Getting There & Away
Air With so many domestic flights making a stopover in Brasília it's easy to catch a plane out of the city at almost any time. Almost all Brazilian cities are served and there are also Varig flights to Miami. Flying time to Rio is 1½ hours. To São Paulo it's one hour and 20 minutes.

Phone numbers for the airlines are: Transbrasil 243-6133, TAM 223-5168, Varig/Cruzeiro 226-2186 and VASP 321-3636.

Bus The giant rodoferroviária (☎ 233-7200) is due west of the centre. There are buses to places you've never heard of. It's three hours to Goiânia (US$6), 20 hours to Cuiabá (US$32 – buses from there to Porto Velho and Manaus), 2½ hours to Anápolis (US$5), 36 hours to Belém (US$56), 12 hours to Belo Horizonte (US$20), 18 hours to Rio (US$32), 14 hours to São Paulo (US$28) and 25 hours to Salvador (US$37).

Getting Around
To/From the Airport The international airport (☎ 248-5588) is 12 km south of the centre. There are two buses marked 'Aeroporto' that go from the city rodoviária to the airport every 15 minutes. The fare is 60c and it takes 35 minutes. A taxi will cost US$15.

Bus To get from the city rodoviária to the rodoferroviária (for long-distance buses), take the No 131 (you can also flag it down along the main drag).

Car There are car rental agencies at the airport and the Hotel Nacional Brasília and Hotel Garvey-Park.

AROUND BRASÍLIA
Estância de Agua de Itiquira
Itiquira is the Tupi-Guaraní Indian word for Water that Falls. From the viewpoint at this 170-metre free-fall waterfall, you can see the valley of the Paranãs to the south. There's forest, several crystal-clear streams with natural pools for a swim, and the requisite restaurants and bars.

Itiquira is 110 km from Brasília; you need a car. Leave through the satellite cities of Sobradinho and Planaltina and the town of Formosa. The road is dirt for the next 35 km.

Cachoeira Saia Velha
This is a pleasant swimming hangout, not too far from the city. Take the road to Belo Horizonte for about 20 km. When you reach the Monumento do Candango, a ridiculous statue made by a Frenchman for the people who built Brasília, there's a sign for the waterfall. The road is to the left of the monument.

For US$5 per car you can sample the live music on Saturdays, including food and beer. There are also several natural swimming pools. There is no hotel but there are camping areas.

Cachoeira Topázio
This is a pretty fazenda with a waterfall, camping facilities, food and drink. To get there, take the road to Belo Horizonte to the Km 93 marker. Turn to the right, taking the other road out to the cachoeira. Entry cost is US$5 a car.

Goiás

GOIÂNIA
The capital of the state of Goiás, Goiânia is 200 km south-west of Brasília and 900 km from both Cuiabá and São Paulo. Planned by urbanist Armando de Godói and founded in

1 Hotel Paissandú
2 Cabiúna Palace
3 Principe Hotel
4 Hotel Bandeirantes
5 Vila Rica
6 Goiânia Palace
7 Hotel Del Rey
8 Hotel Karajas
9 Telephone Centre

1933, it's a fairly pleasant place with lots of open spaces laid out around circular streets in the centre. There are three main zones – housing is in the south, administration is in the centre, and industry and commerce are in the north. The core of Goiânia's economy is based on the commercialisation of the region's cattle.

Information

Tourist Office Goiastur, the state tourist body, is located on the 3rd floor of the Serra Dourada stadium in the suburb of Jardim Goiás. It's an effort to get there and not worth it. Everything you ever wanted to know about Goiânia, and lots of things you didn't, can be found in the *Nova Guia Turístico de Goiânia*, a book available for US$2 at most newsstands. It includes a map of the city and details local bus routes.

Turisplan Turismo (☎ 224-1941) at Rua 8, 388 is a central travel agency that sells plane and bus tickets.

Money The Banco do Brasil is at Avenida Goiás 980. The Banco do Estado de Goiás (BEG!) is in Praça do Bandeirante 546, on the corner of Avenida Goiás and Avenida Anhanguera.

If you're going to Goiás Velho or Pirenópolis, change here.

Post & Telephone The post office is right in the centre of town at Praça Civica 11. Long-distance telephone calls can be made from the Setor Norte Rodoviária, the airport and the corner of Rua 3 and Rua 7.

Things to See & Do

There's not much for the visitor in Goiânia. If you have some time to kill, try the Parque Educativo on Avenida Anhanguera in Setor Oeste. It has a zoo, a zoological museum and an anthropology museum. It's open from 8 am to 6 pm. If you're so inclined you can also go water skiing at the Jaó Club (☎ 261-2122) on a reservoir.

Excursions from Goiânia include the Caldas Novas hot springs, Lake Pirapitinga, Pousada do Rio Quente and the rock formations of Parauna. All are within a 200-km radius of Goiânia.

Places to Stay

There are a couple of cheap places near the rodoviária. The *Star Hotel* at Rua 68, 537 gets a mention because the family who run it are friendly. Some strange characters live there but it's OK for a night. Very basic quartos go for US$5 per person. The centre of town is so close, however, that it's worth staying there instead.

The *Hotel Del Rey* (☎ 225-6306) is centrally located in the Rua 8 pedestrian mall at No 321. Apartamentos cost US$9/15 a single/double. Another cheapie is the *Hotel Paissandú* (☎ 224-4925) at Avenida Goiás 1290. All rooms have fans. Quartos are US$6/9 a single/double and apartamentos are US$10/14. The *Goiânia Palace* (☎ 225-0671) is the same price as the Paissandú, but it doesn't have fans. The *Principe Hotel* (☎ 224-0085) is a couple of dollars more but is better value. It's at Avenida Anhanguera 2936.

In the mid-range, the *Vila Rica Hotel* (☎ 223-2733) at Avenida Anhanguera 3456

and the *Cabiúna Palace* (☎ 224-4355) at Avenida Paranaiba 698 each charge US$24/30 a single/double. Both are two-star Embratur hotels.

At the top end there are plenty of alternatives. A couple of centrally located ones at the *Hotel Karajás* (☎ 224-9666) at Rua 3, 860 which charges US$35/40 a single/double and the *Hotel Bandeirantes* (☎ 224-0066), near the corner of Avenida Anhanguera and Avenida Goiás, which charges US$50/60 for singles/doubles.

Places to Eat

Since they are surrounded by cattle, the locals eat lots of meat. They also like to munch on *pamonha*, a green corn concoction that is very tasty. You'll see *pamonharia* stands all over town. Try it.

If you want to taste some typical Goiânian dishes like *arroz com pequi, arroz com guariroba* or *peixe na telha*, head for the *Centro de Tradições Goiánas*, Rua 4, 515, above the Parthenon Centre, or *Dona Beija* on Avenida Tocantins between Rua 4 and Avenida Anhanguera. My favourite dish is the *empadão de Goiás*, a tasty meat pie.

Praça Tamandare, a short bus ride or a long walk from the centre, has quite a few restaurants and bars surrounding it; try *Churrascaria e Chouparia do Gaúcho* for meat, beer and live music or *Modiglianni* for a good pizza. Wander around and see what takes your fancy.

The *Restaurante Macrobiótica Arroz Integral* at Rua 93, 326 in Setor Sul is Goiânia's anti-churrascaria. They're open from 11 am to 2 pm and 6 to 9 pm. Other natural food is available, naturally, at *Restaurante Naturalmente Natural* in the centre at Rua 15, 238.

Getting There & Away

Air In addition to the regular domestic carriers there are several air taxi companies which go any and everywhere in the Mato Grosso and Amazon, but they are expensive. One company quoted me US$1500 for a return trip to Parque Nacional das Emas, in a plane that would hold four people.

For major airlines call Varig/Cruzeiro (☎ 224-5049) or VASP (☎ 223-4266).

If you're interested in an air taxi call Sete Taxi Aereo (☎ 207-1200) or União (☎ 261-2333).

Bus The rodoviária (☎ 224-8466) is at Rua 44, 399. It's a huge, relatively new one, and it wins the award for the most TV sets on poles (22) in a rodoviária. The bus to Brasília takes three hours (US$6), to Goiás Velho 2½ hours (US$6, every hour from 5 am to 8 pm), to Cuiabá 16 hours (US$26), to Pirenópolis two hours (US$6, 7 am and 5 pm) and Caldas Novas three hours (US$7).

Distances from Goiânia to major cities are immense: Belém 2000 km, Belo Horizonte 900 km, Fortaleza 2620 km, Manaus 3289 km, Recife 2414 km, Rio 1340 km, Salvador 1730 km and São Paulo 900 km.

Getting Around

Aeroporto Santo Genoveva (☎ 207-1288) is six km from the city. A taxi there will cost US$10.

To get from the rodoviária to the corner of Avenida Anhanguera and Avenida Goiás is a 15-minute walk. Local buses can be caught from the bus stop 50 metres from the main terminal as you walk towards town. A couple to look for are the No 163 'Vila União – Centro' and the No 404 'Rodoviária-Centro'. Both go down Avenida Goiás. To get to Praça Tamandare, catch the 'Vila União'.

GOIÁS VELHO

The historic colonial city of Goiás Velho was formerly known as Vila Boa. Once the state capital, it is 144 km from Goiânia and is linked to Cuiabá by dirt road. The city and its baroque churches shine during the Semana Santa (Holy Week).

History

On the heels of the gold discoveries in Minas Gerais, bandeirantes pushed further into the interior in search of more precious stones and, as always, Indian slaves. In 1682, a bandeira headed by the old Paulista Bartolo-meu Bueno da Silva, visited the area. The Goyaz Indians gave him the nickname *anhanguera* (old devil) when after burning some cachaça (which the Indians believed to be water) on a plate he threatened to set fire to all the rivers if they didn't show him where their gold mines were. Three years later, having been given up for dead, the old devil and a few survivors returned to São Paulo with gold and Indian slaves from Goiás.

In 1722 his son, who had been on the first trip, organised another bandeira and the gold rush was on. It followed a pattern similar to that in Minas Gerais. First came the Paulistas, then the Portuguese Emboadas and soon the Black slaves. With everything imported from so far away, prices were even higher than in Minas Gerais and many suffered and died, particularly the slaves. The boom ended quickly.

Things to See

Walking through Goiás Velho, the former state capital, you quickly notice the main legacies of the gold rush: 18th-century colonial architecture and a large mulatto and mestizo population. The streets are narrow with low houses and there are seven churches. The most impressive is the oldest, the Igreja de Paula (1761) at Praça Zaqueu Alves de Castro.

The Museu das Bandeiras is also well worth a visit. It's in the old town council building (1766) at Praça Brasil Caiado. Other museums worth a look are the Museu de Arte Sacra in the old Igreja da Boa Morte (1779) on Praça Castelo Branco, with lots of 19th-century works by local Goiânian Viega Vale, and the Palácio Conde dos Arcos, the old governor's residence. All museums are open Tuesday to Saturday from 8 am to 5 pm and on Sundays from 8 am to noon.

Festival

The big occasion here is Semana Santa (Holy Week). The main streets of town are lit by hundreds of torches, carried by the towns-folk and dozens of hooded figures in a procession which re-enacts the removal of Christ from the cross and his burial.

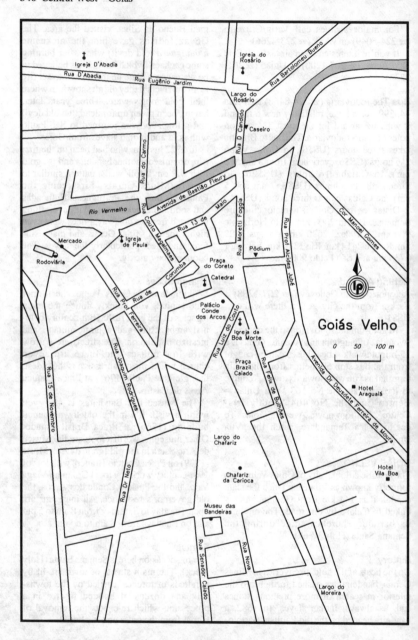

Goiás Velho

0   50   100 m

Places to Stay

The best low-budget place is the *Hotel Araguaiá* (☎ 371-1462), Avenida Dr Deusdete Ferreira de Moura. It's a bit of a hike from the bus station – about 15 minutes – but has very comfortable apartamentos for US$6 a single and US$10 a double. Another budget place in Praça Brasil Caiado should be open now too, run by the same people who used to run the Hotel Minas Goiás. Ask around at the praça.

The *Hotel Vila Boa* (☎ 371-1000) is up on a hill, and has a view and swimming pool. It was being renovated when I was there but should be open by now. Prices will be in the mid to top-end range. You can camp in town at the *Chafariz da Carioca*.

Places to Eat

Caseiro at Rua D Candido 31 is the place to go for some regional food. It's open from 11 am to 3 pm and 6.30 to 10.30 pm. Near the Praça do Coreto, *Pôdium* is a good place for a beer and a snack. The run-down place upstairs at the corner of the praça and Rua Moretti Foggia serves great empadãos for US$2.50.

Getting There & Away

There are frequent buses to Goiânia, 144 km away.

PIRENÓPOLIS

Another historic colonial gold city, Pirenópolis is 70 km from Anápolis and 128 km from Goiânia on the Rio das Almas. There are some unusual rock formations in the Serra dos Pirineus but you need a car to see them.

Pirenópolis was founded in 1727 by a bandeira of Paulistas in search of gold and was originally called Minas da NS do Rosário da Meia Ponte. In 1989 it was placed on the Patrimonio Nacional (National Heritage) register. The city's colonial buildings sit on striking red earth under big skies.

Churches

The Igreja Matriz (1732) is the oldest sacred monument in the state. The Igreja NS de Bonfim (1750) with its beautiful altars contains an image of the Senhor de Bonfim brought here from Portugal in 1755. The Igreja NS de Carmo (1750) was built by the Portuguese and is used today as the Museu das Artes Sacras.

Fazenda Babilônia

Twenty-six km from town, this fazenda has been placed on the Patrimonio Nacional list because it's considered one of the best examples of an 18th-century farmhouse and sugar mill. It's worth a visit if you can get out there.

Festival

The city is famous for the acting out of the story Festa do Divino Espírito Santo, 45 days after Easter. It's a tradition begun in 1819 and if you're in the neighbourhood make a point of seeing this stunning and curious spectacle, one of the most fascinating in Brazil.

For three days the town looks like a scene from the middle ages. *Cavalhadas, congadas, mascardos, tapirios* and *pastorinhos* perform a series of medieval tournaments, dances and festivities which includes a mock battle between Moors and Christians in distant Iberia. Riding richly decorated horses, the combatants wear bright costumes and bull-headed masks. In the end, proving that heresy doesn't pay, the Moors are defeated on the battlefield and convert to Christianity.

The festival is happy, and more folkloric than religious. The town's population swells several-fold during the festival.

Places to Stay

There are a few simple pousadas in town. *Pensão Central* at Praça Emanuel Jayme and *Dormitório da Geny* at Rua dos Pirineus 29 both charge around US$5 a head. The *Rex Hotel* (☎ 331-1121) is a step up but still pretty basic, with quartos for US$8/10 a single/double. The *Pousada das Cavalhadas* (☎ 331-1304) at Praça da Matriz 1 has apartamentos for US$20 a double.

A couple of expensive places have sprung up in the last few years: the *Hotel Fazenda Quinta da Santa Barbara* (☎ 331-1304) at

Rua do Bonfim 1 and *Pousada dos Pirineus* (☎ 331-1345) at Alto de Carmo.

All these places fill up during the festival, so most visitors camp out near the Rio das Almas or rent a room from a local.

Places to Eat

The *Restaurante As Flor*, in Avenida São Jayme, serves up good regional cuisine. Don't fill up on your main course, as they have an assortment of 18 different desserts, each one sweeter than the next. *Restaurante Arquinda* in Rua do Rosário is also recommended.

Things to Buy

Pirenópolis is considered the national silver capital. For silver jewellery check out Terra Nostra in Rua Mestre Propício, P-2 in Praça Benjamin Constant, and Baratos Afins at Alto de Carmo; the last also has leather, ceramics, woodwork and soapstone crafts.

Getting There & Away

There are bus services from Anápolis and Goiânia as well from as Brasília.

CALDAS NOVAS

Caldas Novas, 167 km from Goiânia and 393 km from Brasília, has more than 30 hot springs with average temperatures of 42°C (107°F). Now a very popular resort, the region has dozens of hotels at all levels of price and luxury. Studies have shown that the healing waters work particularly well with people suffering from high-blood pressure, poor digestion, weak endocrine glands or impotency.

Information

Tourist Office There's a tourist information booth in Praça Mestre Orlando that's open from 8 am to noon and 1 to 6 pm. It has lots of information about the various springs you can dip into, most of which are out of town.

Places to Stay

A couple of relatively cheap places in the centre are *Rio das Pedras* (☎ 453-1145) at Rua Orozimbo Correia Neto 200, and *Santa Clara* (☎ 453-1764) at Rua America 109. Both charge US$13/20 a single/double, but the Rio das Pedras has a pool.

The best place to stay is the *Pousada do Rio Quente* (☎ 421-2255), which is 28 km from town on the banks of the Rio Quente. They charge US$80 a double including lunch.

Places to Eat

A Caminho do Natural at Rua José Borges 550 is a self-serve, health-food place open from noon to 3 pm and 6 to 9 pm. It's closed Wednesdays. Meat eaters will prefer the rodízio at *Choupana* on the corner of Rua Rui Barbosa and Avenida Orcalino Santos. They're open from 11.30 am to 4 pm and 7 to 10.30 pm.

Getting There & Away

The rodoviária is at the end of Rua Antônio Coelho de Godoy. Frequent buses go to Brasília (US$15, 6 hours), Goiânia (US$7, 3 hours) as well as Rio de Janeiro and São Paulo.

PARQUE NACIONAL DA CHAPADA DOS VEADEIROS

Just over 200 km north of Brasília, this scenic park is located in the highest area of the Central West. With high waterfalls, natural swimming pools and oasis-like stands of wine-palms, it has become a popular destination amongst Brazilian ecotourists.

Animal life includes the maned-wolf, banded anteater, giant armadillo, capivara and tapir. Birds include rheas, toucans and vultures. The best time to visit the park is between May and October. The entry fee is US$.50c.

Places to Stay

Camping is the best option here. It costs about US$1 a night. Basic accommodation can be found in the small nearby town of São Jorge.

Getting There & Away

From Brasília, take a bus to Alto Paraiso de

Goias, from where you can either catch a local bus to São Jorge, or walk to the park, a couple of hours away.

If you have a car, take the road to Alto Paraiso and turn left 50 metres before entering the town. Follow the dirt road to Colinas for 30 km. Then follow the sign to the park entrance, five km away. São Jorge is a bit further on.

PARQUE NACIONAL DAS EMAS

Emas is a relatively small 1300 sq km park in the corner of the state of Goiás, where it meets the states of Mato Grosso and Mato Grosso do Sul. The park lies along the Brazilian great divide between the Amazon and Paraná river basins, at the head waters of the Araguaia, the Formoso and the Taquari rivers.

The three rivers take divergent paths to the Atlantic. The Araguaia courses north to the equator via the Tocantins and the mighty Amazon. The Rio Taquari travels westward to flood the Pantanal; it then flows south via the Paraguai. The Rio Formoso changes name midstream to Corrientes and flows into the Parnaiba and then the Paraná. The Paraguai and the Paraná flow on either side of Paraguay, meet at Argentina and enter the Atlantic a few hundred km east of Buenos Aires and some 35° latitude south of the mouth of the Amazon.

Surrounded by rapidly encroaching farmlands, Emas park is on a high plateau covered by grassy plains and open woodlands. There is little foliage to obstruct the sighting of wildlife, which includes anteaters, deer, capybara, foxes, tapir, peccaries, armadillos, and blue and yellow macaws. It is the home of endangered wolves, and is the exclusive sanctuary of the jacamari and other rare species. Another interesting spectacle in the park is the large number of termite mounds which, at certain times of the year 'glow' in the dark from a fluorescence produced by the termite larvae.

The dry season is from July to October. Be careful: the area is then dry enough for spontaneous brush fires. In 1988 a fire raged for five days and burned up 65% of the park area.

Places to Stay

There is basic accommodation inside the park which costs about US$4 per person per night. You'll need to take your own food, but there is a kitchen and a cook available. It's also possible to camp in the park, and this costs around US$2 a night per person.

Getting There & Away

Access to the park is tough. Even though it's surrounded by farmland there are no paved roads or regular bus routes. Visitors must arrange with private companies for 4WD or air taxis from as far away as Cuiabá, Goiânia and Campo Grande.

Adventurous types may consider taking BR-364 to Alto do Araguaia/Santa Rita do Araguaia (531 km from Goiânia, 423 km from Cuiabá), then hitching 63 km to Plaça dos Mineiros on a road that's being paved, and then 40 to 60 km further on dirt roads to the park.

RIO ARAGUAIA

Refer to the section on the Rio Araguaia in the Pará, Amapá & Tocantins chapter for information.

Mato Grosso

There's a rather well-known story about a naturalist in the Mato Grosso. Disoriented by the sameness of the forest, the naturalist asked his Indian guide – who had killed a bird, put it in a tree and, incredibly, knew where to return for it at the end of the day – how he knew where the tree was. 'It was in the same place,' the Indian replied.

To begin to appreciate the Mato Grosso's inaccessibility and vastness, read the classic *Brazilian Adventure* by Peter Fleming. It also happens to be one of the funniest travel books ever written. Fleming tells the story of his quest to find the famous British explorer Colonel Fawcett, who disappeared in the Mato Grosso in 1925 while searching for the hidden city of gold. For a more scientific report on the region see *Mato Grosso: Last Virgin Land* by Anthony Smith.

Mato Grosso means bundu, bush, savannah, outback; an undeveloped thick scrub. Part of the highland plain that runs through Brazil's interior, the Mato Grosso is a dusty land of rolling hills and some of the best fishing rivers in the world, such as the Araguaia.

This is also the land where many of Brazil's remaining Indians live. They are being threatened by rapid agricultural development, which is bringing in poor peasants from the south and Northeast who are desperate for land, and by a government which is less than fully committed to guaranteeing them their rights. In 1967, an entire government agency, the Indian Protective Service, was dissolved. No less than 134 of its 700 employees were charged with crimes and 200 were fired. In two years the director had committed 42 separate crimes against Indians including collusion in murder, torture and illegal sale of land.

There's a saying in Brazil that 'progress is roads'. Key routes such as the Belém to Brasília and the Cuiabá to Santarém roads have catalysed the opening of vast stretches of the Mato Grosso to cattle, rice, cotton, soybean, corn and manioc, as well as mining. Goiás, where wealthy ranchers fly from one end of their huge tracts of land to the other in private planes, is one of the fastest growing agricultural belts in the country.

This is Brazil's frontier, the wild west where an often desperate struggle for land between peasants, Indians, miners, rich landowners and their hired guns leads to frequent killings and illegal land expropriation.

CUIABÁ

Founded by gold and slave-seeking bandeirantes in 1719, Cuiabá has little historic or cultural heritage to interest travellers. However, it's a lively place and a good base for excursions into the Pantanal and Chapada dos Guimarães, as well as a rest stop on the way to the Amazon and expeditions to

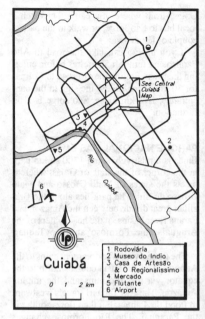

Parque Nacional das Emas and the Rio Araguaia.

The city is actually two sister-cities separated by the Rio Cuiabá: old Cuiabá and Várzea Grande (where the airport is located by the Rio Cuiabá). We found the people here incredibly friendly and gracious.

History

Imagine how hard it was to get here in the 18th century. A Paulista, Pascoal Moreira Cabral, was hunting Indians along the Rio Cuiabá when he found gold in 1719. A gold rush followed, but many gold-seekers never reached Cuiabá. Travelling by river over 3000 km from São Paulo took five months; along the way there was little food, many mosquitoes, rapids, portages, disease and incredible heat.

There was usually one flotilla of canoes each year, bringing supplies, slaves and miners and returning with gold. There were several hundred people in a flotilla, including many soldiers to protect the canoes against Indian attacks, but nevertheless the expeditions often failed. With the end of the gold boom and the decay of the mines Cuiabá would have disappeared, except that the gold was never completely exhausted (garimpeiros still seek their fortunes today); also, the soil along the Rio Cuiabá allowed subsistence agriculture while the river itself provided fish.

As in many mining towns, there was tension between Paulistas and recent Portuguese immigrants. In 1834, the small town was torn apart by the Rusga (Brawl), in which a nativist movement of Paulistas, inspired by wild rumours following Brazilian independence, slaughtered many Portuguese under the pretext that the victims wanted to return Brazil to Portuguese rule.

Today Cuiabá is a frontier boom town. New roads have opened the lands of the Mato Grosso and southern Amazon, bringing peasants desperate for land to the area and increasing export of agricultural products. Since the 1950s, Cuiabá's population has been growing at 14% annually, a national record. It is *the* boom town in the country of boom towns. In 1969 Cuiabá got its first TV channel, the litmus test of progress in Brazil. It was named the *boca de sertão* – the mouth of the backlands.

Indians

To reach Cuiabá the Portuguese had to cross the lands of several groups of Indians, many of whom were formidable warriors. They included the Caiapó, who even attacked the settlement at Goiás, the Bororo of the Pantanal, the Parecis, who were enslaved to mine the gold, the Paiaguá, who defeated several large Portuguese flotillas and caused periodic panic in Cuiabá itself, and the Guaicuru, skilled riders and warriors with many years' experience in fighting the Europeans.

As a result of being nomadic people in a region without abundant food, the Guaicuru women performed self-abortions, refusing to have children until they were near menopause. On the longer journeys, when the women stayed behind, the Guaicuru men took male transvestites with them as sexual partners. Both women and men could divorce easily and often did, several times a year.

Despite important victories, many Indians had been killed or enslaved by the time the gold boom began to fade in the mid-1700s. However, today there are several tribes still left in northern Mato Grosso, living as they have for centuries. The Erikbatsa, noted for their fine featherwork, live near Fontanilles and Juima; the Nhambikuraa are near Padroal; and the Cayabi near Juara. There are also the Indians of Aripuana park, and of course the tribes under the care of FUNAI at Xingu park. The only tribe left in the Pantanal which still subsists by hunting and fishing is the Bororo.

You probably won't be able to overcome FUNAI's obstacles to visiting the Indians, but if you want to visit FUNAI the office (☎ 321-2325) is at Rua São Joaquim 1047 and is open from 8 am to 5.30 pm. The condition of the building speaks volumes about the government's lack of concern with Indian affairs.

Information

Tourist Office Turimat (☎ 322-5363), the Mato Grosso tourist authority, is in the city centre in Praça da República. The staff are very helpful, speak English and have information on hotels in the Pantanal and a list of reasonably priced guides (live ones that is) for the Pantanal. The office is open Monday to Friday from 8 am to 6 pm.

Money Bemat, the state bank, has an exchange on the corner of Joaquim Murtinho and Avenida Getúlio Vargas. They change cash and travellers' cheques at the turismo rate and are open Monday to Friday from 10 am to 3.30 pm. The Banco do Brasil, a bit further up Avenida Getúlio Vargas, also exchanges money.

Post & Telephone The post office is in Praça da República, next to Turimat. The posto telefônico is on Rua Barão de Melgaço near the corner of Avenida Isaac Póvoas.

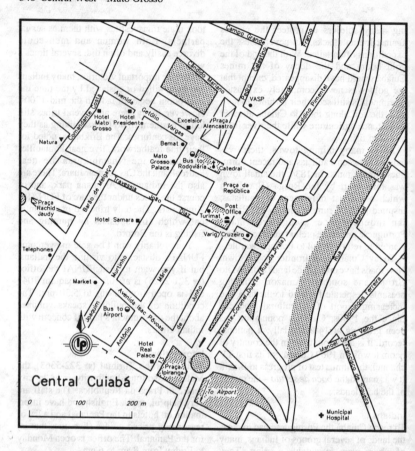

Central Cuiabá

0   100   200 m

Travel Agencies If you want help with an excursion use one of the travel agencies in town. They arrange reservations, guides and transport for photo-safaris into the Pantanal, weekend trips to Chapada dos Guimarães, and can help with the logistics of more ambitious trips to Emas. Ametur (☎ 321-4948), Rua Joaquim Murtinho 242, close to Turimat, has been recommended. Their tours are expensive (around US$75 a day) but well organised. Tuiutur (☎ 322-9330) at Avenida Isaac Póvoas 927 has lots of different packages and they're a bit cheaper. Confiança Turismo (☎ 321-4142) at Rua Cândido

Mariano 434 and JM Turismo in the same street at No 1280 are others you can try.

An alternative and relatively cheap excursion is with Joel Souza, a very enthusiastic guide who speaks fluent English and German. He can be reached at the airport (☎ 381-4827) or the Hotel Real Palace. His two-day trips into the Pantanal cost around US$100 including food, accommodation, transport and boat ride. You won't find anything cheaper than this in Cuiabá or Poconé.

Health Remember to start your antimalarials prior to visiting the Pantanal. Cuiabá's municipal hospital (☎ 321-7418) is on Avenida General Valle. Hospital Modelo (☎ 322-5599), a private clinic at Rua Comandante Costa 1262, is within walking distance of the Hotel Mato Grosso. Hospital Universidade (Jaime Muller) on Avenida CPA is only open business hours.

Museu do Indio
Cuiabá's tourist brochures make much noise about satellite tracking antennas, but they're no big deal. The Museu do Indio (Rondon) is, however, played down. The museum has exhibits of the Xavantes, Bororos and Karajas tribes and is worth a visit. It is at the university on Avenida Fernando Correia da Costa and is open Monday to Friday from 8 to 11.30 am and 1.30 to 5.30 pm. The university also contains a small zoo. To get there catch a No 133 bus, or any other 'Universidade' bus, on Avenida Tenente Coronel Duarte.

Market
The market by the bridge that crosses the Rio Cuiabá is a good one, at least before and after the heat of the day. It's interesting not so much for buying as for looking at the people and their products. They're a very friendly crowd. Try the waterfront bars for a drink afterwards.

Santo Antonio de Leverger
Santo Antonio de Leverger, Mato Grosso's Cidade Morena, is where Cuiabanos go for river beaching from June to October. It's on the Rio Cuiabá, 28 km south of Cuiabá in the direction of Barão de Melgaço.

Festival
The Festa de São Benedito takes place during the first week in July at Igreja NS do Rosário and the Capella de São Benedito. The holiday has a more Umbanda than Catholic flavour; it's celebrated with traditional foods like bola de queijo and bola de arroz, and regional dances like O Cururu, O Siriri, Danças do Congo, dos Mascarados, and others.

Places to Stay
There are some cheap hotels across from the rodoviária, but with the centre only a short bus ride away, there's little point in staying there. In town, one of the popular cheapies is the *Hotel Samara* (☎ 322-6001) at Rua Joaquim Murtinho 270. Their single quartos go for US$5 and double apartamentos cost US$9. The *Hotel Presidente* (☎ 321-6162) at Getúlio Vargas 345 has quartos for US$7/9 a single/double and apartamentos for US$9/11. It's a bit noisy, but very close to the Praça da República and the bus stop to/from the rodoviária. If you like the action around the waterfront market, you could stay in the *Hotel Rio* (☎ 321-4554) right on the Praça do Porto. Basic apartamentos cost US$9 a head.

For my money, the best value in town is the *Hotel Real Palace* (☎ 321-7703) at Praça Ipiranga 102, a couple of blocks from the airport bus' first/last stop. Their air-conditioned apartamentos are huge and the breakfast is excellent. It's a friendly place that's becoming very popular with travellers. Singles/doubles cost US$10/16.

Another travellers' favourite is the *Hotel Mato Grosso* (☎ 321-9121) at Rua Comandante Costa 2522. It has US$12/16 apartamentos and a good breakfast as well.

At the top end, the *Mato Grosso Palace* (☎ 322-9304) on Rua Joaquim Murtinho is a four-star job offering singles from US$50 and doubles from US$60. The *Hotel Excelsior* (☎ 322-6322) at Getúlio Vargas 264 is a bit cheaper, with singles/doubles for US$30/42.

Places to Eat
There are some great fish dishes to try, like *pacu assado com farofa de couve*, *piraputanga assado* and *pirão de Bagre*. A good place to splurge on one is the floating restaurant *Flutuante*, next to Ponte Nova bridge. It's six km from the centre and complicated to get to by public bus. From the waterfront market though, it's a 20-minute walk. It's open daily from 11 am to 11 pm.

O Regionalissimo serves excellent regional food. The cost is US$3.50 for buffet-style meals – lots of fish and the sweetest of sweets. It's open for lunch and dinner, closed Mondays, and is next to the Casa do Artesão, Rua 13 de Junho.

For a vegetarian lunch try *Natura* on Rua Comandante Costa near the Hotel Mato Grosso. For some beef, *Biehaus* at Avenida Isaac Póvoas 1200 is popular with the well-heeled locals. *Tucanos Restaurante e Chopparia*, Avenida CPA 674, has a good pizza and gets pretty lively on weekends.

Entertainment

I liked the Cuiabanos and I liked their nightlife. When the sun sets and it cools off a bit, the city comes to life. For some frontier-town fun head down near the bridge over the Rio Cuiabá. The outdoor bars have music and plenty of drinkers until the wee hours, but the centre of activity is on Avenida CPA, which has plenty of bars with good music and dancing.

Things to Buy

Casa do Artesão on Rua 13 de Junho has lots of local handicrafts, like ceramics, wood-carvings, straw baskets, paintings and hammocks. The FUNAI store at Avenida Barão do Melgaço 3944 is open from 7.30 to 11.30 am and 1.30 to 5.30 pm on weekdays and has Indian baskets, bows and arrows, jewellery and headdresses for sale. Guarana Maués at Avenida Isaac Póvoas 611 has lots of guaraná products.

Getting There & Away

Air There are flights between Cuiabá and the rest of Brazil with Transbrasil (☎ 381-3347), VASP (☎ 381-3737) and Varig/Cruzeiro (☎ 381-2051). Make reservations well in advance if you're travelling in July, when many Brazilians are on vacation.

Bus Cuiabá's rodoviária (☎ 321-4803) is on Avenida Marechal Rondon on the highway towards Chapada dos Guimarães. It's serviced by municipal bus from the city near the Praça da República. Six buses a day make the two-hour trip to Poconé for US$5; the first leaves at 6 am. To Barão de Melgaço

there are two daily buses, at 7.30 am and 3 pm. The three-hour trip costs US$11. For Chapada dos Guimarães, take the 8 am bus if you've only got a day to spend there. Five other buses make the 1½-hour journey for US$3.50.

Cáceres is a three-hour ride away, with three buses making the trip daily, at 7 and 10.15 am and 3 pm. The cost is US$11. To Porto Velho, it's a hard-core 24-hour ride for US$35. There are two buses daily, at 7 am and midnight. To Goiânia, the 16-hour ride costs US$25. Five buses make the trip daily. To Rondonópolis, Coxim and Campo Grande you take the one bus, of which there are six daily; they take three hours to get to Rondonópolis, seven to Coxim and 10 to Campo Grande.

Getting Around

To/From the Airport Marechal Rondon airport (☎ 381-2211) is in Varzea Grande. As you leave the airport, the city is seven km to your right. To catch the local bus to town, cross the road and walk to the left until you reach the Las Velas hotel. The bus stop is opposite the hotel entrance. Catch a 'Jardim Primavera', 'Cohabcanela' or 'Costa Verde' to the centre.

Bus In Cuiabá, you enter local buses through the front door. From the rodoviária, take the No 202 'Rodoviária' bus to its final stop in the city. You'll be on the corner of Joaquim Murtinho and Getúlio Vargas. Other buses go via the rodoviária, and it'll be written on the side, but if you're about to catch one, make sure it's going to the centre, as all local buses enter the rodoviária facing the same direction.

Car The car rental places all have branches in the centre and in or near the airport. There are often promotional rates, so shop around. The best car for the Pantanal is a Volkswagen Golf or Fiat Uno. Note that the Porto Jofre station only has gas and diesel; Poconé and Pousada Pixaim (55 km from Poconé, 85 km from Porto Jofre) have álcool.

On average, a rental car will cost around US$40 a day.

CHAPADA DOS GUIMARÃES

After the Pantanal, Chapada dos Guimarães is the region's leading attraction. This rocky plateau is 800 metres higher than and 64 km north-east of Cuiabá, in a beautiful region reminiscent of the American Southwest. Surprisingly different from the typical Mato Grosso terrain, this place is not to be missed. I spent two days here but would have loved to spend a week.

Information

If you don't have a car, your best bet is to to take an excursion with Jorge Mattos, who runs Ecoturismo (☎ 791-1393) on Praça Dom Wunibaldo in the town of Chapada. Jorge is an excellent guide, who really knows his way around Chapada. He speaks English and meets the 8 am bus from Cuiabá every day, when it arrives at 9.30 am. He runs three excursions: to the national park, which contains the most spectacular waterfalls; to the Blue Lake and Aroe Jari cavern; and to the stone city. To the park and the stone city it costs around US$15, and to the lake and cavern US$30 (much cheaper than if you organised something similar in Cuiabá).

Unfortunately, if Jorge doesn't find at least four people, the price goes up. All tours take between four and six hours, depending on the enthusiasm of the group. If you only want to spend a day there, he can have you on the last bus back to Cuiabá at 4 pm.

An alternative is to hire a car and explore the area on your own, stopping at different rock formations, waterfalls and bathing pools at leisure. If you do have the use of a car, drop by the Secretaria de Turismo, on the left-hand side as you drive into town, just before the square. It's open on weekdays from 8 to 11 am and 1 to 4 pm, and a useful map is available. You'll need it.

Véu de Noiva & the Mirante Lookout

The two exceptional sights in the Chapadas are the 60-metre Véu de Noiva (Bridal Veil) falls and the Mirante lookout, the geographic centre of South America. Both are quite easy to find. Six km after Salgadeira, you'll see the turnoff for Véu de Noiva on the right. It's well signposted.

Alta Mira is eight km from the town of Chapada. Take the last road in Chapada on your right, go eight km and look carefully for a 'capão de Boi' sign on your left. A hundred metres after the sign on your right is a dirt road with a sign saying 'Centro Geodésico'. Turn right and drive a couple of hundred metres to the rim of the canyon. The view is stupendous; off to your right you can see the Cuiabá skyline.

At about 2 pm, start walking downhill over the bluff, slightly to your right. There's a small trail that leads to a magical lookout perched on top of rocks with the canyon below. This is Chapada's most dazzling place.

Other Attractions

Driving to Chapada, you'll pass Rio dos Peixes, Rio Mutaca and Rio Claro, all popular weekend bathing spots for Cuiabanos. The sheer, 80-metre drop called Portão do Inferno (Hell's Gate) is also unforgettable.

Take a waterfall shower at Cachoeirinha and peek into the chapel of NS de Santãna, a strange mixture of Portuguese and French baroque. A hike to the top of Chapada's highest point, Morro do São Jerônimo, is well worthwhile.

A bit further out of town are the 1100-metre-long Aroe Jari cavern and, in another cave, the Lagoa Azul (Blue Lake).

Places to Stay

Lodging in the area ranges from the very basic but friendly *Hotel São José* (☎ 791-1152), Rua Vereador José de Souza 50, which charges US$2.50 per person, to the *Hotel Pousada da Chapada* (☎ 791-1330), a couple of km from town on the road to Cuiabá. They charge US$35 a double and can be booked in Cuiabá at Selva Turismo.

In between are a couple of good alternatives. The very popular *Turismo Hotel* (☎ 791-1176) at Rua Fernando Correo Costa

1065 is run by a German family and apartamentos here cost US$10 per person. *Rio's Hotel* (☎ 791-1126) at Rua Tiradentes 333 has rooms which start at US$10 a head.

All of these places, with the exception of the Pousada da Chapada, are close to the rodoviária. There is good camping at Salgadeira, just before the climb into Chapada, but if you wanted to rough it you could basically camp anywhere.

Places to Eat
On the main praça, *Nivios* has excellent regional food – all you can eat for US$5. The *Turismo Hotel* also has a restaurant.

Getting There & Away
Buses leave from Cuiabá's rodoviária every 1½ hours for Chapada dos Guimarães from 8 am to 6 pm. The other way, the first bus leaves at 6 am and the last at 4 pm. The cost is US$3.50.

CÁCERES
The city of Cáceres, founded in 1778 on the left bank of the Rio Paraguai, is an access point for a number of Pantanal lodges and San Mathias in Bolivia. Cáceres is 215 km from Cuiabá on BR-070 and close to the Ilha de Taiamã ecological reserve.

Lots of travellers arrive with the misunderstanding that they'll be able to get a cement barge to Corumbá. You'd have to be very lucky, and unless you have unlimited time to hang around, forget it. Even the port captain has no idea when the boats are likely to arrive.

If you're going to Bolivia, get a Brazilian exit stamp from the Polícia Federal office at Rua Antonio João 160.

Places to Stay
Cáceres has a number of modest hotels and restaurants for visitors. The best cheapie near the bus station is *Hotel Avenida* (☎ 221-1553), just around the corner in Avenida 7 de Setembro. It's a friendly place, and charges US$4 a head. Closer to the river, the *Rio Hotel* (☎ 221-1387), on Praça Major João Carlos, is a good option. Their apartamentos

with fans cost US$7/11 a single/double. You could also try the *Hotel Comodoro* (☎ 221-1525) on Praça Duque de Caixas, with apartamentos for US$12/20 a single/double.

The *Hotel Barranquinho* (☎ 221-2641 extension 3 or in São Paulo (011) 285-3022), at the confluence of the Jauru and Paraguai rivers and 18 km from the Pirapitanga waterfalls, is 72 km and 2½ hours from Cáceres by boat. *Frontier Fishing Safari* is 115 km by boat from Cáceres; for information and reservations call (011) 227-0920 in São Paulo.

Places to Eat
Corimba near the river at the corner of Rua 6 de Outubro and Rua 15 de Novembro is a good fish restaurant. *Pilão* in Praça Barão do Rio Branco is a decent churrascaria.

Getting There & Away
It's a three-hour trip from Cuiabá to Cáceres; the cost is US$11. Buses make the journey both ways regularly. To San Matías in Bolivia, there is a daily bus at 4 pm. The 4½-hour trip costs US$10. For more details, see the To/From Bolivia section under Land in the Getting There & Away chapter.

BARÃO DE MELGAÇO
Barão de Melgaço, 35 km south-east of Cuiabá, is, along with Cáceres and Poconé, a northern entrance into the Pantanal. Nearby there are ruined fortresses from the Paraguayan wars, and Sia Mariana and Chacororé, two huge bays full of fish.

Places to Stay
NS de Carmo Hotel (☎ 713-1141), Avenida A Leverger 33, 600 metres from the bus station, has double apartamentos for US$15. The top-end place is the *Barão Tur Hotel* (☎ 713-1166 or 322-1568 in Cuiabá) which charges US$50 a double.

Getting There & Away
Two buses a day make the three-hour, US$11 trip from Cuiabá. They leave at 7.30 am and 3 pm.

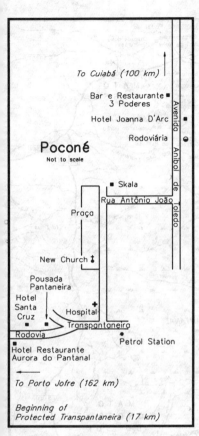

To Cuiabá (100 km)

Bar e Restaurante 3 Poderes ■

Hotel Joanna D'Arc

Rodoviária

Avenida Anibol de Toledo

Poconé
Not to scale

■ Skala

Rua Antônio João

Praça

New Church ↕

Pousada Pantaneira

Hotel Santa Cruz

✚ Hospital

Transpantaneira

Rodovia

● Petrol Station

Hotel Restaurante Aurora do Pantanal

← To Porto Jofre (162 km)

Beginning of Protected Transpantaneira (17 km)

POCONÉ

Poconé is the northern entry point to the Pantanal from Cuiabá and the beginning of the Transpantaneira 'highway'. In May the pink city of Poconé celebrates the week-long Semana do Fazendeiro e do Cavalo Panteiro with a cattle fair and rodeos. Most of the locals are descendants of Indians and Blacks. Many have hunted the *onça* (jaguar) and have amazing stories to tell. They wear some excellent straw hats.

Places to Stay & Eat

The *Hotel Joanna D'Arc* on Avenida Anibol de Toledo, near the rodoviária, has basic, beat-up rooms with fans for US$2 without breakfast. The nearby *Bar e Restaurante 3 Poderes* is better, with good, cheap rooms with fan for US$4 including breakfast. They also serve cheap and hearty food. It's all you can eat of over a dozen dishes. In the middle of town is the *Skala* (☎ 721-1407), Rua Bem Rondon 64. Singles start at US$11 with fan and doubles at US$19 with fan. Some rooms have baths as well for the same prices.

The best places to stay, especially if you intend to hitch the Transpantaneira, are out of town near the beginning of that road. The *Pousada Pantaneira* (☎ 721-1220) is the first one you'll pass. It's on the right-hand side and charges US$9 per person, though they will bargain. Their rooms are a bit on the dingy side, but it's a friendly place. They also serve an excellent prato feito. A further 500 metres up, on the left-hand side, is the *Hotel Restaurante Aurora do Pantanal* (☎ 721-1339). Their spacious apartamentos with fans cost US$9/13 a single/double. They also serve prato feito.

Getting There & Away

There are six buses a day from Cuiabá to Poconé from 6 am to 7 pm and six in the opposite direction from 6 am to 7.30 pm. The 100-km, two-hour, US$5 ride is often packed; get a seat early, or you are not likely to be able to appreciate the vegetation typical of the Pantanal's outskirts, *pequís, piúvas, babaçus, ipês* and *buritis*. The bus passes directly by the airport at Varzea Grande.

From Poconé to Porto Cercado there are two buses a week, on Tuesdays and Saturdays at 9 am. The return trip is on the same days at 11.30 am.

The Pantanal

The Amazon may have all the fame and glory, but the Pantanal is a far better place to see wildlife. In the Amazon, the animals hide in the dense foliage, but in the open spaces of the Pantanal, wildlife is visible to the most

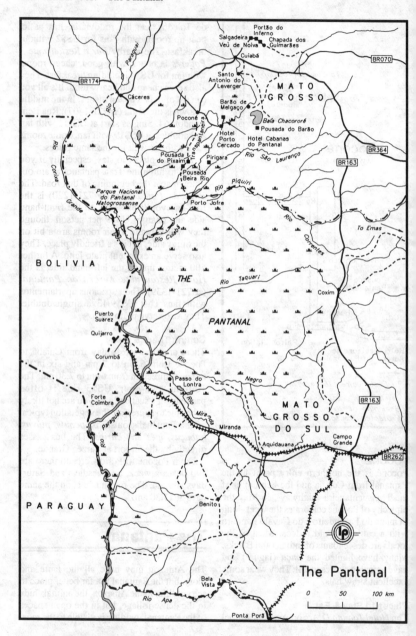

The Pantanal

0   50   100 km

Brasília (AD)

A Ministry Buildings from Congresso Nacional
B Disciples, by Ceshiati, with the Cathedral behind
C Disciple

D Congresso Nacional
E Interior of the Cathedral
F Disciple

Top: Morro do São Jerônimo, Chapada dos Guimarães, Mato Grosso (AD)
Bottom: Fishing for Piranha, Pantanal, Mato Grosso do Sul (GC)

Jaburú storks

casual observer. It's not easy to get to and almost impossible to do on the cheap, but if you like to see animals in their natural state, the Pantanal – with the greatest concentration of fauna in the New World – should not be missed.

A vast wetlands in the centre of South America, the Pantanal is about half the size of France – some 230,000 sq km spread across Brazil, Bolivia and Paraguay. Something less than 100,000 sq km is in Bolivia and Paraguay, and the rest is in Brazil, split between the states of Mato Grosso and Mato Grosso do Sul.

The Pantanal – Terra de Ninguem (Nobody's Land) – has few people and no towns. Distances are so large and ground transport so poor that people get around in small aeroplanes or motorboats; 4WD travel is restricted by the seasons. The only road that plunges deep into the Pantanal is the Transpantaneira, a raised dirt road sectioned by 89 small, wooden bridges, which ends 145 km from Poconé at Porto Jofre. Only a third of the intended route from Poconé to Corumbá has been completed because of lack of funds and ecological concerns.

The road and a strip of land on either side of it comprise the Transpantanal national park. Although IBAMA is trying to expand its jurisdiction to protect the entire Pantanal region, it only administers one other park in the Mato Grosso portion of the Pantanal, the Parque Nacional do Pantanal Matogrossense which encompasses the old Cará-Cará biological reserve.

Geography & Climate

Although *pantano* means swamp in both Spanish and Portuguese, the Pantanal is not a swamp, but rather a vast alluvial plain. In geological terms it is a sedimentary basin of quaternary origin, the drying remains of an ancient inland sea called the Xaraés which began to dry out along with the Amazon Sea 65 million years ago.

First sea, then immense lake, and now a periodically flooded plain, the Pantanal – 2000 km from the Atlantic Ocean yet only 100 to 200 metres above sea level – is bounded by higher lands: the mountains of the Serra de Maracaju to the east; the Serra da Bodoquena to the south; the Paraguayan and Bolivian Chaco to the west; and the Serra dos Parecis and the Serra do Roncador to the north. From these highlands, the rains flow into the Pantanal, forming the Rio Paraguai and its tributaries (which flow south and then east, draining into the Atlantic Ocean between Argentina and Uruguay).

During the rainy season, from October to March, the rivers flood their banks – inundating much of the low-lying Pantanal for half the year and creating cordilheiras, patches of dry land where the animals cluster together. The waters reach their high mark – as much as three metres – in January or February, then start to recede in March, and don't stop until the rainy season returns some six months later.

This seasonal flooding has made systematic farming impossible and severely limited human incursions into the area. It has also provided an enormously rich feeding ground for wildlife.

The flood waters replenish the soil's nutrients, which would otherwise be very poor due to the excessive drainage. The waters teem with fish, and the ponds provide excellent ecological niches for many animals and plants. Enormous flocks of wading birds gather in rookeries several sq km in area.

Later in the dry season, the water recedes, the lagoons and marshes dry out, and fresh grasses emerge on the savannah (Pantanal vegetation includes savannah, forest and meadows which blend together, often with no clear divisions). The hawks and jacaré compete for fish in the remaining ponds. The ponds shrink and dry up and the jacarés crawl around for water, sweating it out until the rains return.

When to Go

If possible, go during the dry season from April to September/October. The best time to go birding is during the latter part of the dry season, from July to September, when the birds are at their rookeries in great numbers, the waters have receded and the bright green grasses pop up from the muck. Temperatures are comfortable in the dry season, being hot by day and cool by night, with plenty of rain.

Flooding, incessant rains and deep heat make travel difficult during the rainy season from November to March, though not without some special rewards (this is when the cattle and exotic wildlife of the Pantanal clump together on the small islands). The heat peaks in November and December, when temperatures over 40°C are common. Roads turn to breakfast cereal. The mosqui-

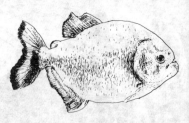

Piranha

toes are fierce and they're out in force. Many hotels close at this time.

The heaviest rains fall in February and March. Every decade or so the flooding is disastrous, destroying both humans and animals. In 1988, the southern Pantanal was devastated: fazendas were destroyed, cattle and wild animals drowned and starved, and the city of Corumbá was submerged for weeks.

Fishing is best during the first part of the dry season, from April to May, when the flooded rivers settle back into their channels, but Pantanal cowboys have been known to lasso 80-kg fish throughout the dry season and well into December. This is some of the best fishing in the world. There are about 20 species of piranha; many are vegetarians, and all are good eating. There's the tasty dourado, a feisty 10 to 20 pounder; and there are many other excellent catches, such as pacu, suribim, bagre, giripoca, piraputanga, piapara, cachara, pintado, pirancajuva and pintado to name a few.

Hunting is not permitted, but fishing – with required permits – is encouraged. Fishing permits are available from IBAMA in Cuiabá and Campo Grande. Enthusiasts can study their quarry at Cuiabá's fish market, located in the market near the bridge.

Guides

If you want to enhance your Pantanal experience and money isn't a problem, a good guide can identify animal and bird species, explain the diverse Pantanal ecology, and take care of any hassles along the way. But you don't need a guide. There's only one road to follow and the wildlife is hard to miss.

The tourist office (☎ (065) 322-5363) in Cuiabá has a list of local guides. The office is in the centre, at Praça da República. The cost, of a guide, without a car, is very little (US$20 a day) but you have to pay for their bread and board.

If language or time is a problem and money isn't, you can write to Douglas Trent of Focus Tours (☎ (612) 892-7830), 14821 Hillside Lane, Burnsville, MN 55337, USA; in Brazil, contact Focus (☎ (031) 223-0358) at Rua Alagoas 1460/s503, Belo Horizonte, MG. Focus specialises in nature tours and Doug is active in trying to preserve the Pantanal. For about US$1000, a guide'll take you to the Hotel Santa Rosa for a week and show you the ropes. They have all the bird calls on tape, and play them over a loud-speaker to attract the real thing. For more about Focus, see the Tours section in the Getting There & Away chapter.

Flora & Fauna
For details refer to the Flora & Fauna section in the Facts about the Country chapter.

Ecology & Environment
The fragile equilibrium of the Pantanal is under threat from poaching and pollution. For details refer to the Ecology & Environment section in the Facts about the Country chapter.

What to Bring
You can't buy anything in the Pantanal, so come prepared. The dry season is also the cooler season. Bring attire for days that are hot, though not brutal, cool nights, rain and mosquitoes. You'll need sunscreen, sunglasses, a hat and cool clothes, sneakers or boots, light raingear, and something for the cool evenings. Mosquito relief means long pants and long-sleeved shirts, vitamin B 12 and repellent. Autan is the Brazilian brand recommended by eight out of 10 Pantaneiros, but some travellers claim that the mosquitoes have become used to it and even started to like it.

Binoculars are your best friend in the Pantanal. Bring an alarm clock to get up before sunrise and a strong flashlight to go hunting for owls and anacondas after sunset. Don't forget plenty of film, a camera, tripod and a long lens – 300 mm is about right for the wildlife.

Places to Stay
Pantanal accommodation is divided into three general categories – *fazendas*, *pesqueiros* and *botels*. Fazendas are ranch-style hotels which usually have horses for hire and often boats. Pesqueiros are hangouts for fishers, and boats and fishing gear can usually be rented from them. A botel, a contraction of boat and hotel, is a floating lodge. Reservations are needed for all accommodation, especially in July, when lots of Brazilian tourists spend their holidays there.

Unfortunately, nearly all accommodation is expensive. It usually includes transport by plane, boat or 4WD from Corumbá or Cuiabá, good food and modest lodging. More often than not, reservations are handled through a travel agent and you must pay in advance. It's also a good idea to call ahead for weather conditions. The rainy and dry seasons are never exact and proper conditions can make or break a trip.

Transpantaneira Accommodation on the Transpantaneira, the elevated dirt road that begins just outside Poconé and extends 145 km to Porto Jofre, is limited to three places: there's the Pousada Pixaim and the Fazenda-Hotel Beira Rio, both at Km 65, and in Porto Jofre there's the Hotel Santa Rosa Pantanal.

The *Pousada Pixaim* (☎ (065) 322-8961) has a friendly manager, clean rooms with electric showers, tasty meals (included in the accommodation price) and the last álcool and gas pump until you return to Poconé – so fill up! This is the budget travellers' favourite at US$20 per person. Across the bridge, the *Fazenda-Hotel Beira Rio* (☎ (065) 321-9445) is more expensive, charging US$45 a single and US$60 a double. They rent boats for US$20 an hour and horses for US$12 an hour. Boats can also be rented at Pousada Pixaim for about the same price.

Porto Jofre is where the Transpantaneira meets its end at the Rio Cuiabá. It's a one-hotel town – in fact it's not even a town. Campers can stay at Sr Nicolino's near the river for US$2 per person. He provides clean bathrooms and cooking facilities, and also rents boats. Alternatively, take the turnoff (it's the only one) a couple of km to the *Hotel Santa Rosa Pantanal* (☎ 322-0948). For US$70/80 a single/double, the Santa Rosa will put you up in a bungalow that sleeps four and feed you three fish meals a day.

It's nothing fancy, but you get hot showers plus decent food (a choice of fried fish, grilled fish, stewed fish or salted fish). They have a swimming pool and foosball (table-top soccer) table; boats (very expensive), horses (expensive) and beer cost extra. Reservations are a good idea – the next hotel is probably in Bolivia. Estur in Cuiabá organises packages (US$220 for two days, US$330 for three days).

Lots of budget travellers get a shock when they get here and find out the price. Those that already know stay at the Pousada Pixaim. Perhaps you could persuade the manager to let you hang your hammock in the workers' apartments at the edge of the hotel grounds, but don't count on it.

Mato Grosso There are several fazendas in the northern Pantanal that are off the Trans-pantaneira. The *Hotel Porto Cercado* (☎ (065) 322-0178 in Cuiabá) is easily reached by car; it costs US$50 a day per person with meals included. It's along the Rio Cuiabá about 50 km from Poconé. The expensive *Hotel Cabanas do Pantanal* (☎ (065) 322-4142 in Cuiabá) is 42 km from Poconé. A three-day package costs US$300.

Camping Pirigara and *Pirigara Pantanal Hotel* (☎ (065) 322-8961 in Cuiabá) are on the banks of the Rio São Lourenço and Rio Cuiabá, 45 minutes by plane from Poconé and about six hours by boat from Porto Cercado. To stay in the hotel is only US$30 per person all inclusive, but the plane ride

costs US$200. The boat is cheaper but oper-ates only during the dry season.

Mato Grosso do Sul One of the cheapest places to stay in the Pantanal is the *Pesqueiro Clube do Pantanal* (☎ (067) 242-1464 in Miranda). It's 168 km from Corumbá in the direction of Campo Grande. They charge about US$25 per person with full board, and fishing trips by boats can be arranged. Also in the vicinity of Miranda is the *Miranda Pesca Clube* (☎ (067) 242-1323 in Miranda) five km from town, and the *Hotel Beira Rio* (☎ (067) 242-1262 in Miranda) eight km from town. The latter has air-con and hot showers and is rigged out like a pesqueiro. It is US$30 per person for full board.

There are a few places located down-stream of the Rio Miranda and a bit deeper into the Pantanal at Passo do Lontra, 120 km and two hours (dry season) from Corumbá; to get there, take the dirt road leading off the road to Campo Grande. Alternatively you can take the train to Campo Grande and have the lodge pick you up at the Carandazal station. The *Cabana/Pesqueiro do Lontra* (☎ (067) 383-4532) in Campo Grande and (011) 283-5843 in São Paulo) is pricier than many, charging US$60 per person including full board. Boat and fishing gear rental is expensive.

Sixteen km from Passo da Lontra is *Fazenda Santa Clara* (☎ (067) 231-5797). This one is popular with travellers for a couple of reasons. The first is that you can do it on your own and don't have to wait around for a group to form up. The second is that they're well organised, with an office in Corumbá (Rua Frei Mariano 502), and take people out to the fazenda every day. They charge US$76 for two days, US$91 for three days and US$115 for four days, full board included. They have boats, horses and fishing gear.

Around Aquidauana, there are a number of medium-priced to expensive hotel-fazen-das. *Aguapé Pousada* is 57 km away and charges US$80 a day, but you can camp there for US$5 a day and buy meals at the restau-rant. *Hotel-Fazenda Salobra* is 90 km away and costs US$50 a day. *Pousada Mimosa*, 170 km away, is for those who like a bit of adventure. They charge US$40 a day. *Pousada Rio Negro* is the old Rondon homestead where the soap opera *Pantanal* was filmed. It's around US$100 a day. For more information about these places, see Panbratour in Aquidauana.

Serious fishing enthusiasts should consider the *Pesqueiro Taruma* (☎ (067) 231-4197 in Corumbá), 70 km from Corumbá on the Rio Paraguai, which is small but well equipped, with air-con, hot shower, fridge and boats. They charge US$60 a day including meals. *Paraiso dos Dourados* (☎ (067) 231-5223 in Corumbá) at Fazenda Morrinhos, 72 km from Corumbá, offers its guests hot water, air-con, fridge, boats and good fishing.

Botels defy any permanent address. *Botel Flory* (☎ (067) 231-1968 is a 10-person boat that cruises the Rio Paraguai from Corumbá. *Corumbi*, *Trans-Tur* and *Amazonas* (all (☎ (067) 231-3016) have air-con, hot water and accommodations for eight. Phone (067) 231-4683 for the eight-person *Barco Cabexi*. It costs US$225 a day with a five-day minimum. All meals are included.

The *Cidade Barão de Melgaço* or *CBM* makes long, bi-monthly trips through the Pantanal on the Cuiabá, São Lourenço and Paraguai rivers. A US$700 fee includes ground transport to the boat from the airport and the cabins have bath and air-con. For reservations call 231-1460 in Corumbá.

Getting There & Away

There are two main approach routes to the Pantanal: via Cuiabá in the north and Corumbá in the south. From Cuiabá, the capital of Mato Grosso, there are three 'gateways' to the Pantanal – Cáceres, Barão de Melgaço and Poconé – all of which lead to Porto Jofre on the Transpantaneira. Corumbá is best accessed by bus from Campo Grande, capital of Mato Grosso do Sul; the route runs via Aquidauana and Miranda.

Coxim, a small town on BR-163, east of the Pantanal and accessible by bus or air-taxi

from either Campo Grande or Cuiabá, is a third point of entry to the Pantanal. However, it has a very limited tourist infrastructure.

Humming bird

Getting Around

Since the lodges are the only places to sleep, drink and eat, and public transportation doesn't exist, independent travel is difficult in the Pantanal. The cement boat that makes the run from Corumbá to Cáceres is very infrequent. You can always try to hitch a ride on a plane with one of the local fazendeiros. Driving is less expensive, but not easy. Only a few roads reach into the periphery of the Pantanal; they are frequently closed by rains and reconstructed yearly. Only the Transpantaneira highway goes deep into the region.

Transpantaneira It is of course impossible to know everything about travel in the Pantanal, but based on several trips and conversations with literally dozens of Pantanal experts we think the best way to visit the Pantanal, if you're in it for the wildlife and your budget is limited, is driving down the Transpantaneira, preferably all the way to Porto Jofre.

Why the Transpantaneira? First, it's the best place to see wildlife – especially in the meadows near the end of the road at Porto Jofre. Second, renting a car in Cuiabá and driving down the Transpantaneira is less expensive than most Pantanal excursions, which require flying, boating or hiring a guide with a 4WD. And third, if you're on a very tight budget, you can take a bus to Poconé and hitch from there (it's pretty easy) and if you have to, return to Poconé for cheap accommodation.

The Transpantaneira is the best place that I've seen in South America for observing wildlife, which is drawn to the roadway at all times of the year. During the wet season the roadway is an island, and during the dry season the ditches on either side of the road serve as artificial ponds drawing birds and game towards the tourist.

Thousands of birds appear to rush out from all sides, ocelots and capybara seem frozen by the headlights, and roadside pools are filled with hundreds of dark silhouettes and gleaming red jacaré eyes. It's very easy to approach the wildlife; you can walk within spitting range of the jacaré, and if you are so crazy as to go cheek to cheek with one you can spot the fleas which live off the lacrimal fluid of their eyeballs.

If you are driving from Cuiabá, get going early. Leave at 4 am and you'll reach the Transpantaneira by sunrise when the animals come to life, and have a full day's light in which to drive to Porto Jofre.

The approach road to the Transpantaneira begins in Poconé (two hours from Cuiabá) by the Texaco station. Follow the road in the direction of Hotel Aurora. The official Transpantaneira Highway Park starts 17 km south of Poconé. There's a sign and guard station (where you pay a small entry fee) at the entrance, but I've seen herds of ema, many birds and jacaré well before the park entrance. Thirty km down the road, stop off at Bar Figeira and meet Zico, the 'pet' jacaré.

Stopping to see wildlife and slowing down for 89 rickety little wooden bridges, it's easy to pass the whole day driving the Transpantaneira – arriving at the expensive Hotel Santa Rosa in time for dinner soon after sunset. Weekdays are best if you're driving, as there's less traffic kicking up dust.

Hitching down the Transpantaneira is easy enough – it's hitching back that's difficult. There aren't a lot of cars or trucks, but many stop to give rides. The best time to hitch is on weekends, when the locals drive down the Transpantaneira for a day's fishing. Make sure you get on the road early. I've done the entire route from Porto Jofre to Poconé several times with all sorts of folk: a rancher and his family, two American birders, an IBAMA park ranger, a photosafari guide, some Italian tourists, an ex-poacher and a photojournalist working on an article on jacaré poaching.

Macaw

Wildlife is abundant along the length of the Transpantaneira, but reaches a climax in the meadows about 10 to 20 km before Porto Jofre. The flora here is less arid, less scrubby. The birds, jacaré and families of capybara scurry into the ponds along the road. I've seen several toucans, flocks of luminescent green parrots and six blue hyacinth macaws in the big trees that divide the great meadows. There are enormous flocks of birds and individual representatives of seemingly every species. For details, see the Flora & Fauna section in the Facts about the Country chapter.

Car Rental In Cuiabá, there are several car rental agencies just outside the airport grounds to your right which are often cheaper than the agencies inside the airport. There is some competition, so shop around, and ask about promotional rates. No matter what anyone tells you, you don't need a 4WD to drive the Transpantaneira. The best car is a Volkswagon Golf or Fiat Uno. The Brazilian Gurgel looks like a 4WD but doesn't act like one. Stick with the Golf in the Pantanal. Flat tires can be a problem, so make sure you have a spare.

If you do plan to drive the Transpantaneira, protect yourself by reserving a Golf a few weeks in advance (there's no cost). You can always shop around for a better deal when you arrive. Don't forget to fill up your tank at Poconé and the Pousada Pixaim.

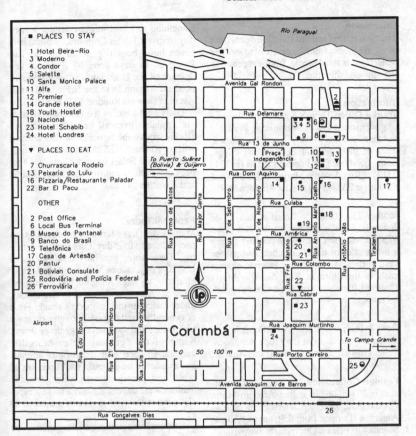

PLACES TO STAY

1 Hotel Beira–Rio
3 Moderno
4 Condor
5 Salette
10 Santa Monica Palace
11 Alfa
12 Premier
14 Grande Hotel
Youth Hostel
19 Nacional
23 Hotel Schabib
24 Hotel Londres

PLACES TO EAT

7 Churrascaria Rodeio
13 Peixaria do Lulu
16 Pizzaria/Restaurante Paladar
22 Bar El Pacu

OTHER

2 Post Office
6 Local Bus Terminal
8 Museu do Pantanal
9 Banco do Brasil
15 Telefônica
17 Casa de Artesão
20 Pantur
21 Bolivian Consulate
25 Rodoviária and Polícia Federal
26 Ferroviária

Mato Grosso do Sul

CORUMBÁ

Corumbá, a port city on the Rio Paraguai and the Bolivian border, is the southern gateway to the Pantanal. Corumbá, or Cidade Branca (White City), was founded and named in 1776 by Captain Luis de Albuquerque.

By 1840 it was the biggest river port in the world and boasted a dozen foreign consulates. Ships would enter the Rio de la Plata in the South Atlantic, sail up the Rio Paraná to

its confluence with the Rio Paraguai and then up to Corumbá. The crumbling but impressive buildings along the waterfront reflect the wealth that passed through during the 19th century. With the coming of the railway, Corumbá lost its importance as a port and went into decline.

The city is 403 km north-west of Campo Grande by road or rail. Due to its strategic location near the Paraguayan and Bolivian border (Puerto Suarez is only 19 km away), Corumbá has a reputation for drug traffic, gun running and poaching. Be cautious if you come here.

Orientation

The train station and bus station are near each other, six blocks from the centre of town. The waterfront is three blocks from the centre in the opposite direction.

Information

Tourist Office There's not much in the way of government tourist information available but there are lots of travel agencies in town, most of them promoting the same things. Some good ones are Pantanal Safari (☎ 231-2112) at Rua Antônio Maria Coelho 330 and Pantur (☎ 231-4343) at Rua América 969.

Money The Banco do Brasil at Rua 13 de Junho 914 has a câmbio on the 2nd floor. When I was there they were actually giving a better rate for travellers' cheques than for cash dollars. An alternative place to change cash is the store at Rua Antônio Maria Coelho 140, where you'll get close to parallel rates.

Post & Telephone The post office is in Rua Delamere across from the Praça República. Telems has a telefônica on Rua Dom Aquino.

Foreign Consulates The Bolivian Consulate (☎ 231-5606) is at Rua Antônio Maria Coelho 852, near the intersection of Rua América. It's open from 8.30 am to 1.30 pm Monday to Friday. Oddly, intending visitors to Bolivia may have to check out of Brazil before applying for a visa here.

The Paraguayan Consulate (☎ 231-2030) can be found on Rua Cuiabá. On the Bolivian side, the nearest Brazilian Consulate is in Santa Cruz.

Polícia Federal For a Brazilian entry/exit stamp, go to the Polícia Federal at the rodoviária.

Things to See & Do

Corumbá's star attraction is the Pantanal and you can get a preview of it from Morro Urucum (1100 metres). Tourists looking for something different might consider a two-day trip to Forte Coimbra, which is a seven-hour boat trip south on the Rio Paraguai. In days gone by it was a key defence of the Brazilian west, and you still need permission from the Brigada Mista at Avenida General Rondon 1735 to visit it.

Daily boat tours of the Corumbá vicinity are available from all travel agencies. An all-day trip on the boat *Pérola do Pantanal* will set you back US$25 and includes lunch. See Pantanal Safari for more details. Other packages include sightseeing trips to Bolivia and day trips by road.

Pantanal Tours

Many budget travellers are choosing to go on cheap three to four-day tours into the Pantanal. These trips, generally costing around US$20 a day, can be very rough-and-ready affairs – try and imagine boy scouts on cachaça. Accommodation is in hammocks, under thatch or in somebody's shack. Food is generally pretty good, though you must take water, and the trucks may break down. Some of the 'guides' are ex-crocodile hunters, so their attitude towards animals leaves a lot to be desired. You'll see lots of birds and plenty of crocodiles, but the mammals are understandably a bit shy, especially when they get chased by a truck at 80 km/h.

If you want something well organised, and riding around in the back of a pick-up truck doesn't grab you, pay a bit more and stay at a hotel-fazenda for a few days. If you're prepared to take it as it comes, you might have a good time.

Before signing on with one of these trips, and certainly before parting with any cash, there are a few things you should check out. Firstly, find out how far into the Pantanal you go – it should be at least 200 km, preferably more. Then ask about the itinerary and get it in writing if possible. Is the programme flexible enough to account for sudden weather changes? Check out the truck. Does it look OK? Does it have a radio or carry a first-aid kit in case of emergency? A bite from the *boca da sapo* snake will kill in 30 minutes if left untreated.

You should expect to spend at least one day simply travelling deep into the Pantanal, and one day to return. Then allow at least two days for seeing wildlife at close quarters. Definitely insist on doing this on foot – vehicles should be used for access only, *not* for pursuit. Your chances of enjoying the Pantanal and its wildlife are greatly increased if you go with a reputable guide who: forsakes the 'mechanical chase' approach; accompanies small groups (preferably less than five persons) on an extensive walking trip through the area for several days; camps out at night (away from drinking dens!); and takes you on walks at the optimum times to observe wildlife – before sunrise, at dusk, and during the night. A trip along these lines will need at least four days (preferably five).

Insist on meeting your guide (or make it clear in writing that you will only go with a designated guide) and avoid signing on through an intermediary. How many years has your guide been in the Pantanal? Remember that speaking English is less important than local knowledge. Someone who has spent their life in the Pantanal won't speak much English. Prior to departure, be sure to read the Pantanal section (especially the What to Bring part) earlier in this chapter.

There are a lot of shonky guides around. In Corumbá they're known as *guias piratas* (pirate guides). They're not registered with the Associação das Guias (Guides' Association), so if you have some complaint or want your money back, you have no course of action. On these shonky tours there is a lot of cachaça drinking, the theory being that since cachaça is cheaper than gasoline, it costs less to convince drunk tourists that they're having a good time. Then there's no need to drive as far as promised. Tales of woe with pirate guides include: abandonment in the marshes; assorted drunken mayhem; and even attempted rape.

The following guides are recommended: Clovis Carneiro (☎ 231-4473), an elderly guy with excellent local knowledge;

Rodrigues (☎ 231-6746); Ico (☎ 231-2629), president of the Associação das Guias; and Johnny Indiano (☎ 231-6835), who has spent his life in the Pantanal and is especially skilled at finding nests and newborn animals. Several travellers have complained about Necolândia Tours and in particular about two associated guides called Murilo and Nolasco.

Places to Stay

Close to the bus and train stations, the budget travellers favourite is the *Hotel Schabib* (☎ 231-1404) at Rua Frei Mariano 1153. About a five-minute walk from the stations, it's a friendly place, with English and French spoken. Well worth the US$3 a night they ask. If they're full, close by at Rua Joaquim Murtinho 1021 is *Hotel Londres* (☎ 231-6717), with quartos for US$4 a head and singles/doubles with fans for US$5/9.

In the centre, there are a number of cheapies located on Rua Delamere between Rua Antônio Maria Coelho and Rua Frei Mariano. *Salette* (☎ 231-3678) has rooms starting at US$5/9 a single/double. Next door at the *Condor* quartos with fan go for US$3 per and this is good value because the place is clean and friendly. A couple of doors along at No 911 the *Moderno* is also good value, with quartos for US$3.50 a head. There's a youth hostel (☎ 231-2305) at Rua Antônio Maria Coelho 677.

Moving up in price a bit, the *Grande Hotel* (☎ 231-1012) at Rua Frei Mariano 468 has good big quartos for US$9/12 and apartamentos for a bit more, but they don't include breakfast.

An interesting place to stay, though it's a bit out of the way, is on the waterfront at the *Hotel Beira-Rio* (☎ 231-2554), Rua Manoel Cavassa 109. Popular with fishers, they charge US$12 per person in air-con rooms.

Three hotels in a row along Rua Antônio Maria Coelho are the *Premier* (☎ 231-4937) at 389, with US$12 singles and US$15 doubles with air-con and TV. The rooms are on the small side.

Almost next door at 367 is the *Alfa* (☎ 231-6699), which is a bit cheaper because it doesn't have TVs. Hard to miss is the two-star *Santa Monica Palace* (☎ 231-3001) at No 345. They charge US$23/33 for singles/doubles with the lot.

The *Nacional* (☎ 231-6868) at Rua América 936 is the most expensive hotel in town. Singles/doubles go for US$40/50.

Places to Eat

Bar El Pacu on Rua Cabral is a good, cheap restaurant. Their fish is excellent. Try a delicious local speciality, *peixe urucum* (fish with cheese melted on top in a condensed milk sauce) for US$4. It's run by Herman the German, an interesting character who has spent a long time in the Pantanal.

Peixaria do Lulu in Rua Antônio João is another good fish restaurant. *Churrascaria Rodeio* at 13 de Junho 760 has live music as well as their tasty meat dishes. *Pizzeria/Restaurante Paladar* on Rua Antônio Maria Coelho has expensive but good pizza.

Things to Buy

The Casa de Artesão in the old prison at Rua Dom Aquino 405 has a good selection of Indian art, as well as the best Pantanal T-shirts in Corumbá.

Getting There & Away

Like Campo Grande, Corumbá is a transit point for travel to/from Bolivia and Paraguay. The Crossing the Border discussion at the end of this section gives details on crossing the border between Corumbá and Quijarro, Bolivia.

Air The airport (☎ 231-5842) is three km from the town centre. VASP is the only big company flying into Corumbá. Their office is at Rua 15 de Novembro 392 (☎ 231-4441) and at the airport (☎ 231-4308). They have connections with Brazilian capitals, while air taxis fly into remote points in the Pantanal.

For Bolivian air connections, contact Pantur (see the Information section under The Pantanal heading earlier in this chapter). Pantur is the agent for LAB (Lloyd Aereo Boliviano) and TAM (Transportes Aereos Militares).

There are LAB flights between Puerto Suarez and Santa Cruz on Monday, Wednesday and Saturday. The Pantur price for a one-way ticket is US$98, which includes transport between Corumbá and Puerto Suarez. If you arrange your own transport between the two places, the price drops to US$78.

TAM flights between Puerto Suarez and Santa Cruz operate on Tuesday and Saturday. The Pantur flight for a one-way ticket is US$85, including transport between Corumbá and Puerto Suarez, or US$69 if you arrange your own transport.

Bus From the rodoviária, buses run to Campo Grande eight times a day from 8.30 am to midnight. The seven-hour trip costs US$12 and is much quicker than the train.

Train To Campo Grande, there are trains every Tuesday, Thursday and Sunday leaving at 9 pm (Pullman class, US$8; sleeping berth US$20 double); and Monday, Wednesday and Friday at 8 am (2nd class, US$3; 1st class, US$5). Pullman seats *(poltronas leitos)* can only be reserved on the day of travel and there are no ticket sales on Saturday. To make a quick connection to Bauru, you need to take the morning train.

From Campo Grande to Corumbá, the day train operates on Tuesday, Saturday and Sunday and departs at 6.45 am. The night train departs on Monday, Wednesday and Friday at 9 pm.

Once across the Bolivian border, most people will be heading towards Santa Cruz. The rail line between Santa Cruz and Quijarro, the Bolivian border town opposite Corumbá, is known as the Death Train.

However, the journey is a beautiful one, passing through lush jungle, Chaco scrub, and oddly shaped mountains to the steamy, sticky Pantanal area near the frontier. The many cattle ranches, agricultural projects, logging operations and Mennonite colonies along the railway are all indicators of the current thrust into development of the long-neglected Bolivian Oriente (East). Despite all the economic changes and growth in the area, there is still a diverse and abundant supply of wildlife and vegetation. Colourful flowers, birds, and butterflies thrive in the warm, moist conditions, and larger species, though rarely seen, still exist in limited numbers.

Be sure to have plenty of mosquito repellent on hand, since there are often long and unexplained stops in low-lying, swampy areas and the zillions of skeeters get voraciously hungry in those parts.

Those taking the train should anticipate delays. Three classes of service are available – Pullman, 1st, and 2nd – but it's difficult to distinguish between them. There's a distinctly bovine feeling that comes over anyone riding this train. The boxcars have their drawbacks but they're still more comfortable than the overcrowded coaches!

From Quijarro to Santa Cruz, Pullman service runs on Tuesday and Saturday, the Rápido on Wednesday and Sunday. In the opposite direction, both the Pullman and the Rápido run on Monday and Friday. The trip takes anywhere from 20 to 25 hours. In either direction, Pullman fare is B$59, 1st class is B$39 and 2nd class, B$27. You'll have the same problems getting tickets in Quijarro as in Santa Cruz, although Quijarro taxi drivers will sell tickets at inflated prices – B$45/35 for 1st/2nd class. Make sure they're not already punched and that they're for the correct day and train.

Ferrobus The ferrobus, a bus on bogeys which is considerably faster than the train, goes from Quijarro to Santa Cruz on Wednesday and Sunday. It costs B$85 for a 1st-class ticket and B$68 for 2nd. From Santa Cruz to Quijarro, it leaves on Tuesday, Thursday and Saturday. Securing a ticket can be extremely difficult, but again, the taxi drivers in Quijarro may be able to help.

For real Bolivian-style luxury there's the Expreso Especial Bracha, a rapidly deteriorating rail car offering air-con, videos and minimal food service. Westbound, it runs on Tuesday and Saturday, and eastbound on Monday and Friday. In Corumbá, tickets should be reserved three or four days in advance through Receptivo Pantanal at Rua Frei Mariano, 502. They cost US$40 per person.

Boat The Paraguayan company Flota Mercantil del Estado runs boat services between Asunción and Corumbá. Boats leave every two weeks on Friday. The trip takes five days and costs US$40 for a cabin or US$30 for a hammock. It's much cooler if you take the cheap class and sling your hammock on deck. Meals are not included in the ticket price, but acceptable food is available in the restaurant on board. Some boats go as far south on the Paraguai as Buenos Aires. Boat transport up through the Pantanal is difficult and infrequent. Enquire at the Porto Geral.

Crossing the Border Today, the Bolivian border town of Quijarro is not much more than a muddy little collection of shacks. Taxis operate between Quijarro station and the border, a distance of about two km. You may have to bargain with the drivers over their unrealistic initial rates. They're banking on foreigners not knowing the distance to be travelled, who may agree to pay whatever they ask. The going rate is currently US$1 per person.

Moneychangers at the frontier will only accept cash and are more interested in dollars than cruzeiros. Have your requisite amount readily and discreetly available for a smooth transaction unless you relish the attention of onlookers. Since it appears the new cruzeiro is following in the footsteps of its hyperinflationary predecessors, it's impossible to quote a reliable exchange rate here; your best bet is to ask travellers going in the opposite direction what a fair rate will be.

Some people report being charged 50c for a Bolivian exit stamp. Others have paid US$2.50 to leave Bolivia at Quijarro but some pay nothing. It just depends on the officer on duty at the time.

Just over the bridge on the Brazilian side you may be subjected to a customs search, but Brazilian immigration is at the federal police post at the Corumbá rodoviária.

Anyone entering or exiting Brazil must check in here and complete immigration formalities. For about 15c a city bus will take you into Corumbá, five km from the border. Everyone entering Brazil from Bolivia is required to have a yellow fever vaccination certificate or they won't be admitted to the country. There is a vaccination clinic in Corumbá but it is only open one hour per day, Monday to Saturday, and not at all on Sunday.

Getting Around

A taxi from either the bus or the train station to the centre of Corumbá costs US$1.50. For a taxi from the centre to the Bolivian border, expect to pay US$3.50. The city bus between the centre and the Brazilian border runs about twice an hour and the ticket costs 60c. The Brazilian border post is open daily from 8 to 11 am, and from 2 to 5 pm.

AQUIDAUANA

Aquidauana and Anastácio are twin towns situated on the Rio Aquidauana, 138 km from Campo Grande. They represent the beginning of the Pantanal and there are a number of excellent hotel-fazendas in the area. In Aquidauana there's not much to interest the traveller, though it's a pleasant place in which to spend a night.

Information

Panbratour (☎ 241-2986), Rua 7 de Setembro 459, is an Aquidauana-based travel agency that specialises in the Pantanal. It also sells excellent photos of the area. Staff can give you the latest information on the hotel-fazendas available. Buriti Viagens e Turismo (☎ 241-2718) at Rua Manoel Antonio Paes de Barros 720 is another helpful agency. If you need to change money, try these places.

Places to Stay

A couple of popular cheapies close to the railway station are the *Hotel Fluminense* (☎ 241-2038), Rua Teodoro Rondon 365, and the *Hotel Londres* a couple of blocks

away. Both charge US$5/9 for single/double quartos and US$9/12 for apartamentos.

The *Portal Pantaneiro Hotel* (tel 241-4328) at Rua Pandía Calógeras 1067 is a very reasonably priced mid to top-end place, with singles starting at US$12 and doubles for US$20. Excellent value, this one.

Places to Eat

Churrascaria Princesa do Sul at Rua Marechal Mallet 1047 is popular. They're closed on Sundays. *Lanchonete Asa Branca* on Rua Manoel da Costa has a good prato feito.

Getting There & Away

Aquidauana is four hours by train or 2½ hours by bus from Campo Grande. Buses are frequent. The railway station is right in town but the bus station is a 15-minute walk from the centre.

CAMPO GRANDE

Founded around 1875 as the village of Santo Antonio de Campo Grande, Campo Grande really began to grow when the railway came through in 1914. The city became the capital of Mato Grosso do Sul in 1977 by decree of military president Ernesto Giesel, when the new state splintered off from Mato Grosso. It is known as the Cidade Morena because of its red earth. Manganese, rice, soy and cattle are the sources of its wealth. Campo Grande lies 716 km south of Cuiabá and 403 km south-east of Corumbá.

There are no tourist attractions in Campo Grande, but because it's a transport hub, most travellers end up staying overnight before heading out. Like all big cities, Campo Grande has plenty of hotels and restaurants, and gets lively on weekends when the cowboys come to town.

Information

Tourist Office Semcetur runs a small information booth in the pedestrian mall on Rua Barão do Rio Branco between Rua 14 de Julho and Rua 13 de Maio. It's open Monday to Saturday from 7.30 am to 7.30 pm.

Campo Grande

0   0.5   1 km

■ PLACES TO STAY   15 Hotel Jandaia
                    18 Novo Hotel

 1 Hotel Esperança
 2 Hotel Copacabana   OTHER
 3 Hotel Estação
 4 Hotel Gaspar   9 Restaurante Hong Kong
 5 Hotel União   12 Post Office
 6 Hotel Priape   13 Telefônica
 7 Hotel Tupi   14 Museu Dom Bosco
 8 Hotel Continental 16 Semcetur
10 Hotel Americano   17 Rodoviária
11 Palace Hotel

Money The Banco do Brasil has a câmbio at Avenida Afonso Pena 2202. If you're stuck, try the Hotel Jandaia.

Post & Telephone The post office is on the corner of Rua Dom Aquino and Avenida Calógeras. The telefônica is near the corner of Rua Rui Barbosa and Rua Dom Aquino.

Museu Dom Bosco
The Museu Dom Bosco, Rua Barão do Rio Branco 1843, is the only museum worth a look in town. It has an excellent collection of over 10,000 insects, including 7000 butter-flies. There are also lots of stuffed animals, and interesting exhibits about the Bororo, Moro, Carajá and Xavante Indians. It's open from 7 to 11 am and 1 to 5 pm.

Places to Stay – bottom end
If you're a light sleeper, bear in mind that hotels near the rail yards are pretty noisy. *Hotel Copacabana*, a stone's throw from the railway station at Rua Dr Temistocles 83, and the *Hotel Esperança* next door are two flop-houses where the cowboys and outlaws crash out. They're only for those on the tightest of tight budgets. Both charge US$3 a head. Of

Indian girl in Campo Grande

the two, the Esperança is the friendlier. The *Hotel Gaspar* (☎ 381-5121) is across from the railway station and has singles/doubles starting at US$9/14. Just down the road at Avenida Calógeras 2828, the *Hotel União* (☎ 382-4213) is a bit cheaper with singles/doubles for US$7/11.

Pick of the budget places, though, is the *Hotel Continental* (☎ 382-3072) at Rua Maracajú 229. It's very clean, and Carlos, the manager, is very hospitable. There's a washing machine for getting that red dust out too. Quartos with fan are US$5/10 and apartamentos go for US$9/14. If they're full, try the *Hotel Americano* (☎ 721-1454) at Rua 14 de Julho 2311. They have quartos for US$7/9 a single/double and apartamentos for US$13/16. Near the bus station, the *Novo Hotel* (☎ 721-0505), Rua Joaquim Nabuco 185, is very clean and charges US$9 per person.

Places to Stay – middle & top end

More expensive places include the *Palace Hotel* (☎ 384-4741) at Rua Dom Aquino 1501, an excellent place right in the centre and not too noisy either. Singles cost US$13 and doubles US$18. They're often full. At the top end, the *Hotel Jandaia* (☎ 382-4081), Rua Barão do Rio Branco 1271, is a four-star job that charges US$40 a single and US$50 a double.

Places to Eat

Restaurante Hong Kong is an excellent Chinese restaurant close to the cheap hotels. I can highly recommend their curry and tofu dishes. For a self-serve vegetarian lunch, *Natural Viva a Vida* at Rua Dom Aquino 1354 is open from 11 am to 2.30 pm every day except Saturday. The bars along the pedestrian mall on Rua Barão do Rio Branco also have standard menus. This mall is also a good place to come for a chopp or three.

Getting There & Away

Air There are daily connections to all major cities. For the major airlines call Varig (☎ 383-4070; 763-1213 at the airport and VASP (☎ 382-4091; 763-2389 at the airport.

Antonio João airport (☎ 763-2444) is seven km from town. Take the 'Vila Popular' bus from near the rodoviária to get there. There are several air taxis for trips into remote areas of the Pantanal.

Bus The rodoviária, at Rua Joaquim Nabuco 200, is a huge one, with lots of bars, barbers and a porno movie theatre. The visiting cowboys need never leave the bus station. An interesting aspect of this place is the touts. A number of bus companies run competing routes, so when you go to buy a ticket, touts come up and ask you where you want to go. Don't worry about this – the price of the ticket won't go up because of it. The touts get their commission from the company, so let them show you where to buy your ticket.

To Corumbá, there are seven buses a day; the first leaves at 6.30 am and the last at midnight. The trip takes seven hours (four hours less than the train) and costs US$12. To Cuiabá there are eight buses a day and the trip takes 10 hours. To Ponta Porã there are 10 buses a day. The 8 am bus will get you there by 1 pm. This is the fastest – the others are milk runs that stop for everyone. The cost is US$9. There are also daily buses to Brasília (23 hours, US$30), Belo Horizonte (23 hours, US$30), São Paulo (14 hours, US$21) and Foz de Iguaçu (13 hours, US$20).

Train The railway station is on Avenida Calógeras, close to the centre of town. Trains are cheaper than buses, except when you travel in cabins. Take mosquito repellent if you go by rail.

To Corumbá there is a train every day except Sunday. On Monday, Wednesday and Friday it leaves at 9 pm. On Tuesday, Thursday and Saturday it leaves at 7.03 am.

For the night train, cabins cost US$14/20 a single/double and are only sold from 1 to 5 pm and 6 to 8.50 pm on the day of the trip. Leito seats cost US$8, 1st class is US$5 and 2nd class is US$3.

To Bauru (and connections with São Paulo), trains leave every Monday, Wednesday and Friday at 8 pm. It's a 22-hour trip.

To Ponta Porã there is a daily train at 4.20 pm. It takes nine hours to get there. If you want to check rail information, call (0142) 22-4000 in Bauru or (067) 383-2762 in Campo Grande.

COXIM

Coxim is a small town about halfway between Cuiabá and Campo Grande on the eastern border of the Pantanal. Its drawcard is the Piracema, when fish migrate up the Taquari and Coxim rivers, leaping through rapids to spawn. The Piracema usually takes place from September to December; if you're travelling this road during that period, it's worth stopping off to have a look at it. The fishing (pacú, pintado, curimbatá, piracema and dourado) is good from August to December. A fishing licence is required. There are also some pretty waterfalls in the area, notably the Palmeiras falls on the Rio Coxim.

Places to Stay & Eat

There are a number of cheap hotels in town. If you arrive late at night, the *Hotel Neves* (☎ 291-1273) is close to the bus station. Clean quartos cost US$5 per person, a bit more if you want a fan or air-con. The town is three km away, on the banks of the river.

A couple of reasonable hotels with river frontage are the *Rio* (☎ 291-1295) at Rua Filinto Muller 651 and *Preto 27* (☎ 291-

1117) at No 238. Both have singles/doubles with fan for US$9/13. The Rio also has single quartos for US$5.

The *Piracema* (☎ 291-1219) is a good place right next to the river but it's three km out of town. Instead of going into town from the bus station, head down the highway for another half a km. It's next to the bridge. Their apartamentos with air-con and frigobar cost US$10. They also have a good fish restaurant open daily from 11 am to 3 pm and 6 to 11 pm. The *Grande Hotel* (☎ 291-1133) is the most expensive place, with singles/doubles for US$20/25.

Getting There & Away

All the buses going between Campo Grande and Cuiabá stop at Coxim.

Getting Around

All the hotels can arrange boats, the going rate for a day being around US$70. To get to the Palmeiras falls, 27 km away, a taxi will cost anywhere between US$15 to US$30 for a return trip. You need to ask a few different taxi drivers.

BONITO

Apart from the Pantanal, the small town of Bonito is one of the major tourist destinations in the state of Mato Grosso do Sul. The town itself has no attractions, but the natural resources of the area are impressive. There are many caves in the region, the main ones being Lago Azul, an underground lake that's 156 metres deep, and NS Aparecida. To visit the caves you need to take along a guide, because they are locked up and the guides have the keys.

Another attraction of the area is the incredibly clear rivers, where it's possible to go diving and see the fish eyeball to eyeball.

Information

Hapakany Tur (☎ 255-1315), Rua Pilad Rebuá 626, is a well-organised outfit. Sergio da Gruta, who runs it, knows the area very well and he's a good guy. He has a lot of different excursions, including a rubber-rafting day trip. Prices vary, but they're mostly around the US$30 mark.

Places to Stay

Camping five km out of town on the banks of the Rio Formoso at the *Balneário Municipal* would be the best place. In town, there are a few cheap hotels, notably the *Bonanza* (☎ 255-1162) at Pilad Rebuá 623, which charges US$8 a single and US$14 a double. There are a couple of cheaper places around the square where the bus stops.

Places to Eat

On the main square, *Lanchonete Rincão* has a good prato feito for US$2. The *Tapera*, just around the corner at Pilad Rebuá 480, has a reasonable pizza.

Getting There & Away

Bonito is 248 km from Campo Grande. There is one bus a day that leaves at 3 pm and runs via Aquidauana. The trip takes 6½ hours, because the roads are rough after Aquidauana.

There is a bus to Ponta Porã at 12.30 pm every day.

Getting Around

Unfortunately, most of the attractions are some distance from town and there's no public transport.

PONTA PORÃ

Ponta Porã is a border town divided from the Paraguayan town of Pedro Juan Caballero by Avenida Internacional. It was a centre for the yerba maté trade in the late 1800s, long before it started attracting Brazilians who like to play in the Paraguayan casinos, shop for perfumes, electronics and musical condoms, and hang out in ritzy hotels.

Information

Getting exit/entry stamps involves a bit of legwork, so if you're in a hurry, grab a cab. For Brazilian entry/exit stamps, go to the Polícia Federal on Avenida Brasil, near the corner of Rua Duque de Caxias. It's on the

2nd floor and is open weekdays from 7.30 to 11.30 am and 2 to 5 pm. The Paraguayan immigration office (☎ 2962), where you need to go for entry/exit stamps, is seven blocks away in Pedro Juan Caballero. It's inside Inmobiliaria Ycua Bolaños, a real estate office 5½ blocks from the border on Calle Curupayty. It's open from 7.30 to 11.30 am and 1 to 5 pm Monday to Saturday.

The Paraguayan Consulate is on Avenida Internacional, next to the Hotel Internacional in Ponta Porã. It's open from Monday to Friday from 8 am to noon. The Brazilian Consulate is almost directly opposite, on Avenida Dr Francia in Pedro Juan Caballero.

Places to Stay – bottom end & middle

There are plenty of cheap places in both countries. The ones on the Paraguayan side don't include breakfast. In Brazil, the *Hotel Alvorada* (☎ 431-5866) at Avenida Brasil 2977 is such good value that it's almost always full. Quartos go for US$6/12 a single/double and apartamentos for US$8/14.

A few blocks away at Rua Guia Lopes 57, the *Barcelona Hotel* (☎ 431-3061) is a reasonable alternative with apartamentos for US$10/15 a single/double, though their plumbing is a bit rough. Opposite, the *Hotel Guarujá* (☎ 431-1619) is more expensive but better, with singles for US$15 and doubles for US$28.

Next to the Paraguayan Consulate, at Avenida Internacional 2604, the *Hotel Internacional* (☎ 431-1243) has single quartos for US$8 and apartamentos for US$12/20 a single/double. It's in a good location.

Over in Paraguay there are a few hotels close to each other on Calle Mariscal López. A couple of good ones are the *Hotel Guavirá* (☎ 2743) at No 1327 and the *Hotel Peralta* (☎ 2346) at No 1257. Both charge around US$8 a single and US$14 a double.

Places to Stay – top end

At the top end, the best place in Brazil is the *Pousada do Bosque* (☎ 431-1181), Avenida Presidente Vargas 1151, with US$40/50 single/double rooms. In Paraguay, the *Hotel*

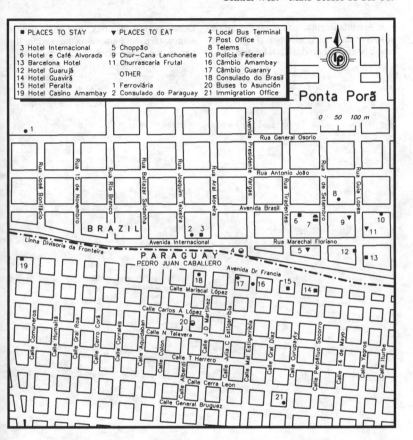

PLACES TO STAY
3 Hotel Internacional
6 Hotel e Café Alvorada
13 Barcelona Hotel
12 Hotel Guarujá
14 Hotel Guavirá
15 Hotel Peralta
19 Hotel Casino Amambay

▼ PLACES TO EAT
5 Choppão
9 Chur–Cana Lanchonete
11 Churrascaria Frutal

OTHER

1 Ferroviária
2 Consulado do Paraguay

4 Local Bus Terminal
7 Post Office
8 Telems
10 Polícia Federal
16 Câmbio Amambay
17 Câmbio Guarany
18 Consulado do Brasil
20 Buses to Asunción
21 Immigration Office

Casino Amambay (☎ 2573) is the dictators' choice.

Places to Eat

Choppão at Rua Marechal Floriano 1877 is a good place to go for a beer and a snack, as is the *Chur-Cana* lanchonete on the corner of Avenida Brasil and Rua Guia Lopes. *Churrascaria Frutal* at Rua Guia Lopes 288 is a huge, flashy place that's just right for a splurge.

Getting There & Away

To Campo Grande, 335 km away, there are nine buses a day; the first leaves at 1 am and the last at 9.30 pm. The 5½-hour trip costs US$9. To Asunción, there are constant buses leaving from the bus station on Calle Alberdi, three blocks from the border.

The train to Campo Grande leaves at 4.20 pm daily. It's a nine-hour trip that costs US$3.50 in 1st class and US$2 in 2nd.

There are also daily flights to São Paulo.

Getting Around

Public transport on the Brazilian side is excellent and simple. The local bus terminal is on Avenida Internacional, near the corner with Avenida Presidente Vargas. To get to the long-distance rodoviária, take the 'São Domingos (Rod)' bus. For the railway station, take the 'Ferroviária' bus and for the airport, the 'Aeroporto'.

THE NORTHEAST

Anaconda

REGIÃO NORDESTE

The Northeast

The Northeast region, known in Brazil as the Nordeste, covers more than 18% of the country's land area and contains 43 million inhabitants – nearly 30% of Brazil's population. The region is divided into nine states: Bahia, Sergipe, Alagoas, Pernambuco, Paraíba, Rio Grande do Norte, Ceará, Piauí, and Maranhão. The archipelago of Fernando de Noronha lies over 500 km east of Recife and was placed under the political administration of Pernambuco state in 1988.

The many attractions of the Northeast include: historical cities (São Luís, Olinda, and Salvador); colonial villages (Alcântara, Lençóis, etc); national parks (Lençóis Maranhenses, Chapada da Diamantina, Sete Cidades, etc); and the region's fascinating African heritage (music, dance, religion, cuisine, and festivals).

The geography of the Northeast is characterised by four divisions. The *zona da mata* (forest zone) covers the coastal area and extends up to 200 km inland. The forest, known as the *mata Atlântica*, now only exists in tiny pockets – the rest was destroyed to make way for sugar-cane cultivation during the colonial period. With the exception of Teresina in Piauí state, all the major cities of the Northeast were established in this zone.

Further west, the *agreste* forms a transitional strip of semifertile lands which merges into the *sertão*.

The sertão (backlands) is characterised by a dry and temperate climate. Droughts, sometimes lasting for many years, have been the bane of this area for many centuries. The land is commonly referred to as caatingas because the landscape is dominated by vast tracts of caatinga (a scrubby shrub plant). The largest towns of the sertão are dotted along the Rio São Francisco, which provides irrigation. The bleak and brutal life of the Sertanejo (inhabitant of the sertão) has received literary coverage in *Os Sertões* (published in English as *Rebellion in the Backlands*) by Euclides da Cunha, and the novel *Vidas Secas* (Dry Lives) by Graciliano Ramos. The Cinema Novo films of Glauber Rocha portray violence, religious fanaticism, official corruption and hunger in the sertão.

The state of Maranhão and the western margin of Piauí state form the *meio norte*, a transitional zone between the arid sertão and the humid Amazon region.

The social problems of the Northeast include crippling poverty, underemployment, housing shortages, a decaying educational system, and absence of basic sanitation. For example, in the state of Bahia, only 18 out of 415 cities have basic sanitation; out of every 1000 infants, over 43 do not survive their first year; 40% of Bahia's schools are inoperative due to lack of funds, and recent figures indicate that half the population is illiterate; and the number of unemployed in the state has been conservatively estimated at 1.5 million (around 30% of the workforce).

SUDENE (Superintendência do Desenvolvimento do Nordeste), the official government agency for development in the Northeast, has attempted to attract industry and boost the economy of the region, but these efforts have been hampered by the lack of energy sources, transport infrastructure, skilled labour, and raw materials. Many Nordestinos (inhabitants of the Northeast) have emigrated to the Southeast and Central West in search of a living wage or new land for cultivation.

The economy of the zona da mata depends on the cultivation of crops such as sugar and cacao, and the petroleum industry which is based on the coast. The inhabitants of the agreste make their living from subsistence farming, small-scale agriculture (vegetables, fruits, cotton, coffee) and cattle ranching (beef and dairy). In the sertão, the economy is based on cattle ranching, cotton cultivation, and subsistence farming, which puts the *carnaubeira*, a type of palm, to a multitude of uses. The meio norte is economically reliant on *babaçu*, another type of palm, which provides nuts and oil. The latter is converted into lubricating oil, soap, margarine, and cosmetics. São Luís has become a major centre for the production of aluminium.

Bahia

Bahia is Brazil's most historic state, and has retained strong links with its African heritage. Its capital, Salvador da Bahia, was also the capital of colonial Brazil from 1549 to 1763 and the centre of the sugar economy which sustained the country's prosperity until the 18th-century decline in international sugar prices.

The state of Bahia divides into three quite distinct regions: the *recôncavo*, the *sertão* and the *litoral* (littoral).

The recôncavo is a band of hot and humid lands which surrounds the Baía de Todos os Santos. The principal cities are Cachoeira, Santo Amaro, Maragojipe and Nazaré, which were once sugar and tobacco centres and the source of wealth for Salvador.

The sertão is a vast and parched land on

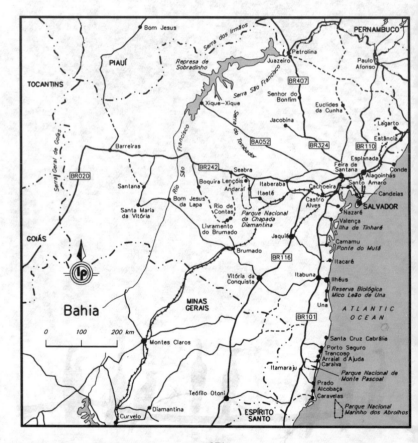

which a suffering people eke out a meagre existence raising cattle and scraping the earth. Periodically, tremendous droughts, such as the great drought of 1877 to 1879, sweep the land. Thousands of Sertanejos pile their belongings on their backs and migrate south or anywhere they can find jobs. But with the first hint of rain in the sertão, the Sertanejos return to renew their strong bond with this land.

The litoral, south of Salvador, with beautiful, endless beaches, is a cacao producing region and there are important cities like Valença, Ilhéus and Itabuna. North of Salvador the coast is only sparsely populated with a few fishing villages. The southern beaches are calm, while the northern beaches are often windy with rough surf.

Salvador is a fascinating city loaded with colonial relics – including many richly decorated churches, one for every day of the year according to popular belief. You should also take the time to explore outside Salvador and visit the smaller cities, towns and fishing villages in Bahia, where life is unaffected by tourism and even less affected by the 20th century.

If beaches are what you want, the only difficulty is choosing. You can go to Porto Seguro for beaches with fancy hotels and restaurants or cross the river to Arraial d'Ajuda for a hipper, less developed beach scene. To really escape civilisation you can go to the beaches up north around Conde.

The inland regions of Bahia are less well known, but are well worth a visit if you want a change from beaches. Cachoeira and Lençóis are both interesting colonial towns. Lençóis provides a handy base for hiking trips inside the Parque Nacional da Chapada Diamantina. Travellers might also like to explore the bizarre moonscapes of the sertão, where the Sertanejos have maintained a rich culture despite the poor environment.

Culture

Capoeira Capoeira is an African martial art developed by slaves to fight their oppressors. Prohibited by the slave-masters, capoeira was banished from the *senzalas* (slave barracks) and practised clandestinely in the forest. Later, in an attempt to disguise capoeira from the authorities, it was developed into a kind of acrobatic dance. The clapping of hands and plucking of the *berimbau*, a fishing rod-like instrument, originally served to alert fighters to the approach of the boss and subsequently became incorporated into the dance to maintain the rhythm.

As recently as the 1920s, capoeira was still prohibited and Salvador's police chief organised a police cavalry squad to ban capoeira from the streets. In the 1930s, Mestre Bimba established his academy and changed the emphasis of capoeira, from its original function as a tool of insurrection, to a form of artistic expression which has become an institution in Bahia.

Today, there are two schools of capoeira: the Capoeira de Angola led by Mestre Pastinha and the more aggressive Capoeira Regional of Mestre Bimba. The former school holds that capoeira came from Angola, the latter believes that it was born in the plantations of Cachoeira and other cities of the recôncavo region.

Capoeira is a fight, a game and a dance. The movements are always fluid and circular, the fighters always playful and respectful. It has become very popular in recent years and throughout Bahia and Brazil you will see *roda de capoeiras*, semicircles of spectator-musicians who sing the initial *chula* before the fight and provide the percussion during the fight. In addition to musical accompaniment with the berimbau, blows are exchanged to the beat of other instruments, such as *caxixi, pandeiro, recoreco, agogô* and *atabaque*.

Folk Art

Bahia has some of Brazil's best artisans, who usually have small shops or sell in the local market. You can buy their folk art in Salvador, but the best place to see or purchase the real stuff is in the town of origin because so much of the production is regional and specialised.

The main materials used in Bahian folk art

Capeoira

are leather, wood, earth, metal and fibre. Feira de Santana is known for its leather-work: the best examples are in the city's Casa do Sertão folklore museum. Maragojipinho, Rio Real and Cachoeira produce earth-enware. Caldas do Jorro, Caldas de Cipo and Itaparica specialise in straw crafts. Rio de Contas and Muritiba have metalwork. Ilha de Maré is famous for lacework. Jequié, Valença, and Feira de Santana are wood-working centres. Santo Antônio de Jesus, Rio de Contas and Monte Santo manufacture goods made of leather and silver.

Religion

Much of Bahian life revolves around the Afro-Brazilian religious cults known as Candomblé. To the Christian observer, Candomblé provides a radically different view of the world. It is also a medium for cultivating African traditions – music, dance, and language – into a system that aims to worship and enjoy life in peace and harmony.

Much of Candomblé is secret – it was prohibited in Bahia until 1970 – but the public ceremony, conducted in the original Yoruba tongue, takes place in a *terreiro*. In Salvador, Casa Branca on Avenida Vasco da Gama 463, in the Engenho Velho neighbour-hood is the centre for Candomblé.

See the Religion section of the Facts about the Country chapter for more detail about Candomblé and the Jogo dos Búzios (Casting of Shells). For suggested reading on religion, see the Books & Maps section of the Facts about the Country chapter.

An Evening of Candomblé

The mãe de santo or pai de santo runs the service. The *mãe pequena* is entrusted with the training of priestesses: two *filhas de santo*, one a girl over seven years of age, the other a girl under seven. The initiates are called *abian*.

On the morning of a day dedicated to a specific orixá, celebration commences with an animal sacrifice. Only initiates may attend this service. Later in the afternoon the *padê* ceremony is held to attract the attention of Exú; and this is followed by chanting for the orixás, which is accompanied by *alabés* (atabaque drummers).

The long evening of Candomblé in Casa Branca, Salvador's oldest terreiro, is quite an experience. The men drum complex and powerful African rhythms. The women dress in lace and hooped skirts, dance slowly, and chant in the Yoruba language. The terreiro is female dominated. Only the women dance, and only they enter a state of trance, the principal goal of the ceremony. The men play supporting roles. The dance is very African, with slow, graceful hand motions, swaying hips and light steps. When the trance strikes one dancer she shakes and writhes while assistants embrace and support her. Other dancers also fall into a trance while dancing. Sometimes, spectators even go into trances, which is discouraged.

The festival I witnessed was for Omolú, the feared and respected orixá of plague and disease. He is worshipped only on Mondays and his Christian syncretic counterpart is either St Lazarus or St Roque. His costume consists of straw belt encrusted with seashells, straw mask, cape and dress to cover his face and body which have been disfigured by smallpox.

When dancers have received the spirit of Omolú in their trance, some leave the floor. They return shortly with someone who represents Omolú: a figure covered from head to toe in long straw-like strands. The dancing resumes.

Although the congregants of Casa Branca are friendly and hospitable, they don't orient their practice to outsiders. Several Westerners attend, and many White Brazilians are members. After the ceremony the guests are invited to the far end of the house for sweets and giant cakes – one is decorated like the Brazilian flag. ■

Salvador

Population: Two million

Salvador da Bahia, often abbreviated to Bahia by Brazilians, is the capital of Bahia state and one of Brazil's cultural highlights. This city has managed to retain its African soul and develop its unique, vibrant culture – the best of its colonial legacy. Ornate churches still stand on cobblestone streets. Festivals are spontaneous, wild, popular and frequent. Candomblé services illuminate the hillsides. Capoeira and afoxé dance through the streets. It is also appropriate to mention that Salvador suffers from social and economic problems, with a great number of jobless, homeless, hungry, abandoned and sick citizens.

History

According to tradition, on 1 November 1501, All Saints' Day, the Italian navigator Amerigo Vespucci sailed into the bay, which was accordingly named Baía de Todos os Santos. In 1549 Tomé de Souza came from Portugal bringing city plans, a statue, 400 soldiers and 400 settlers including priests and prostitutes. He founded the city in a defensive location: on a clifftop facing the sea. After the first year, a city of mud and straw had been erected, and by 1550 the surrounding walls were in place to protect against attacks from hostile Indians. Salvador da Bahia became the capital of the new lands and remained Brazil's most important city for the next three centuries.

During its first century of existence the city depended upon the export of sugar cane, but tobacco cultivation was later introduced and cattle ranching proved profitable in the sertão. The export of gold and diamonds mined in the interior of Bahia (Chapada Diamantina) provided Salvador with immense wealth. The opulent baroque architecture in

PLACES TO STAY

12 Hotel Anglo–Americano
16 Hotel Caramuru
19 Hotel Porto da Barra

OTHER

1 Forte de Santo Antônio Além
  do Carmo
2 Forte do Barbalho
3 Igreja do Carmo
4 Igreja de Nazaré
5 Tomb of Ruy Barbosa
6 Museu de Arte Sacra da Bahia
7 Solar do Unhão Restaurant &
  Historical Senzala (Slave Quarters)
8 Museu de Arte Popular
9 Post Office
10 Museu de Instituto Feminino
11 Forte da Gamboa
13 Goethe Institut
14 Terminal do Campo Grande
   (City Bus Terminus)
15 Universidade Federal
17 Museu de Arte da Bahia
18 Forte São Diogo
20 Forte Santa Maria
21 Shopping Barra
22 Morro do Cristo
23 Forte de Santo Antônio
   da Barra
24 Farol do Barra

Salvador

0   250   500 m

the city is a testament to the prosperity of this period.

Salvador remained the seat of government until 1763 when, with the decline of the sugar-cane industry, the capital was moved to Rio. Overlooking the mouth of Baía de Todos os Santos, which is surrounded by the recôncavo, Brazil's richest sugar and tobacco lands, Bahia was colonial Brazil's economic heartland. Sugar, tobacco, sugar-cane brandy and, later, gold were shipped out, whilst slaves and European luxury goods were shipped in.

After Lisbon, Salvador was the second city in the Portuguese Empire: the glory of colonial Brazil, famed for its many gold-filled churches, beautiful colonial mansions, and numerous festivals. It was also renowned, as early as the 17th century, for its bawdy public life, sensuality and decadence, so much so that it became known as the Bay of All Saints...and of nearly all sins!

The first Black slaves were brought from Guinea in 1538, and in 1587 historian Gabriel Soares estimated that Salvador had 12,000 Whites, 8000 converted Indians and 4000 Black slaves. A Black man was worth six times as much as a Black woman in the slave market. The number of Blacks eventually increased to constitute half of the population and the traditions of Africa took root so successfully that today Salvador is called the African soul of Brazil.

In Salvador, Blacks preserved their African culture more than anywhere else in the New World. They maintained their religion and their spirituality, albeit wrapped in the outer layer of Catholicism. African food and music enriched the houses of Black and White. Capoeira, the dance of defiance, developed among the slaves. Quilombos, runaway slave communities, terrified the landed aristocracy; and uprisings of Blacks threatened the city several times.

In 1798, the city was the stage for the Conjuração dos Alfaiates (Conspiracy of the Tailors), which intended to proclaim a Bahian republic. Although this conspiracy was quickly quelled, the battles between those who longed for independence and those loyal to Portugal continued in the streets of Salvador for many years. It was only on 2 July 1823, with the defeat in Cabrito and Pirajá of the Portuguese troops commanded by Madeira de Melo, that the city found peace. At that time, Salvador numbered 45,000 inhabitants and was the commercial centre of a vast territory.

For most of the 19th and 20th centuries the city stagnated as the agricultural economy, based on archaic arrangements for land distribution, organisation of labour and production, went into uninterrupted decline.

Only recently has Salvador begun to move forward economically. New industries such as petroleum, chemicals and tourism are producing changes in the urban landscape, but the rapidly increasing population is faced with major social problems.

Orientation

Salvador sits at the southern tip of a V-shaped peninsula at the mouth of Baía de Todos os Santos. The left branch of the 'V' is on Baía de Todos os Santos; the right branch faces the Atlantic; and the junction of the 'V' is the Barra district, south of downtown.

Finding your way around Salvador can be a bitch. Besides the upper city and lower city, there are too many one-way, no-left-turn streets that wind through Salvador's valleys and lack any coherent pattern or relationship to the rest of the existing paved world. Traffic laws are left to the discretion of drivers. Gridlock is common at rush hour.

Perhaps most difficult for the visitor is the fact that street names are not regularly used by the locals; and when they are, there are often so many different names for each street that the one you have in mind probably doesn't mean anything to the person you're asking to assist you – the road along the Atlantic coast, sometimes known as Avenida Presidente Vargas, has at least four aliases.

Street name variations include:

Praça 15 de Novembro is popularly known as Terreiro de Jesus.
Rua Dr J J Seabra is popularly known as Bairro do Sapateiro (Shoemaker's Neighbourhood). In

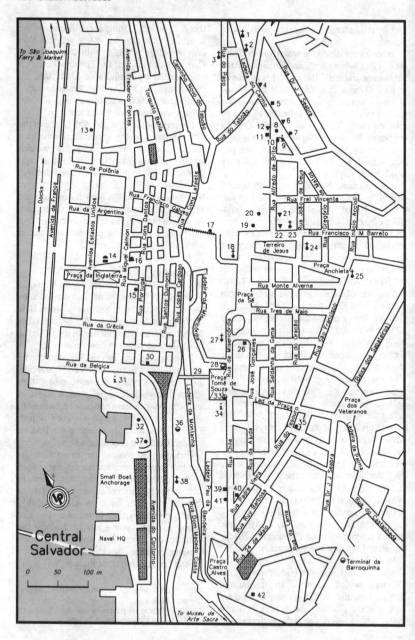

Central Salvador

To São Joaquim Ferry & Market

Docks

Small Boat Anchorage

Naval HQ

Praça Castro Alves

To Museu de Arte Sacra

Terminal da Barroquinha

Praça dos Veteranos

Terreiro de Jesus

Praça da Sé

Praça Tomé de Souza

Praça Anchieta

Praça da Inglaterra

0   50   100 m

■ PLACES TO STAY

5   Hotel Solara
11 Hotel Pelourinho
26 Hotel Themis
39 Hotel Chile
40 Palace Hotel
42 Hotel Maridina

▼ PLACES TO EAT

4   Casa do Benin Restaurant
6   Senac Restaurant
12 Banzo Restaurant
21 Meson Espanhol Restaurant
23 Cantina da Lua

OTHER

1   Igreja e Convento de NS do
    Carmo/Museu do Carmo
2   Igreja da Ordem Terceira do Carmo
3   Igreja do Santíssimo Sacramento da
    Rua do Paço
7   Olodum
8   Largo do Pelourinho
9   Emtursa Tourist Office
10 Museu da Cidade/Casa da Cultura
    Jorge Amado
13 Banco do Brasil
14 Central Post Office

15 Varig/Cruzeiro
16 VASP
17 Plano Inclinado Gonçalves (Funicular
    Railway)
18 Catedral Basílica
19 Museu Afro-Brasileiro/Museu de
    Arqueologia e Etnologia
20 Antiga Faculdade de Medicina (Old
    Medical Faculty)
22 Igreja São Pedro dos Clérigos
24 Igreja da Ordem Terceira de São
    Domingos
25 Igreja São Francisco
27 Igreja da Misericórdia
28 Police Post/Bus to Airport &
    Rodoviária
29 Lacerda Elevator
30 Casa dos Azulejos
31 Mercado Modelo & Bahiatursa Tourist
    Office
32 Boat to Itaparica
33 Buses to Barra & Rodoviária
34 Palácio Rio Branco & Bahiatursa
    Tourist Office
35 Casa de Ruy Barbosa
36 Buses to Mercado São Joaquim, São
    Joaquim Ferry & Igreja NS do
    Bonfim
37 Bunda Statue
38 Igreja NS da Conceição
41 VASP

early colonial days, this street was the site of a moat, the first line of defence against the Indians.

Rua Francisco Muniz Barreto is also called Rua das Laranjeiras (Street of Orange Trees).

Rua Inácio Accioli is also known as Boca do Lixo (Garbage Mouth)!

Rua Leovigildo de Caravalho is known as Beco do Mota.

Rua Padre Nobrega is commonly referred to as Brega. The street was originally named after a priest. It developed into the main drag of the red-light district and with time Nobrega was shortened to Brega, which in Brazilian usage is now synonymous with brothel!

A steep bluff divides central Salvador into two parts: Cidade Alta (Upper City) and Cidade Baixa (Lower City). These are linked by the Plano Inclinado Gonçalves (funicular railway), the Lacerda Elevator and some very steep roads (ladeiras).

Cidade Alta This is the historic section of Salvador. Built on hilly, uneven ground, the site of the original settlement was chosen to protect the new capital from Indian attacks. The most important buildings – churches, convents, government offices and houses of merchants and landowners – were constructed on the hilltops. Rational planning was not a high priority.

Today, the colonial neighbourhoods of Pelourinho, Terreiro de Jesus and Anchieta are filled with 17th-century churches and houses. Although these aren't the safest parts of town – several streets are centres of prostitution – they are certainly the most interesting.

Just around the corner from Praça da Sé and the Lacerda Elevator, you'll see a large, cream-coloured colonial building which houses Bahiatursa, the state tourism agency.

A few blocks further is Praça Castro Alves, a major hub for Carnival festivities.

From here, Avenida 7 de Setembro runs southwards and parallels the bay until it reaches the Atlantic Ocean and the Barra district, which has many of the city's upper and middle-end hotels and bars.

Heading east from Barra district, the main road along the Atlantic coast, sometimes called Avenida Presidente Vargas (at least on the maps), snakes along the shore all the way to Itapoã. Along the way it passes the middle-class Atlantic suburbs and a chain of tropical beaches.

Cidade Baixa This is Bahia's commercial and financial centre, and port. Busy during working days, and filled with lunch places, the lower city is deserted and unsafe at night. Heading north, away from the ocean and along the bay, you pass the port, the ferry terminal for Ilha de Itaparica (Itaparica island), and continue to the bay beaches of Boa Viagem and Ribeira (very lively on weekends). These are poor suburbs along the bay and the further you go from the centre, the greater the poverty. Watch for the incredible architecture of the *algados*, which are similar to favelas, but built on the bay.

CIA, the Centro Industrial de Aratu, is three times the size of Salvador and sprawls around the bay of Aratu, which empties into Baía de Todos os Santos. It's the first rationally planned industrial park of Brazil and over 100 firms operate there.

Information
Tourist Offices When we visited Salvador, there appeared to be a feud between Emtursa, the official tourist authority for the city of Salvador, and Bahiatursa, the state tourist authority for Bahia. This curious state of affairs meant that neither authority was interested in informing travellers about information or publications available from its counterpart.

Emtursa's main office (☎ 243-6150) is at Largo do Pelourinho, 12. For tourist information and maps, visit the nearby Emtursa information post (next to the Casa da Cultura Jorge Amado) – open from 8 am to noon and from 2 to 5 pm (Monday to Saturday).

The main tourist office of Bahiatursa (☎ 241-4333) is in Palácio Rio Branco, Rua Chile, 2 – open from 8 am to 6 pm (Monday to Friday). Although Bahiatursa's budget appears to have been cut to a shoestring, and very few publications are available, the few remaining staff try hard to provide advice about lodging, events, and where and when to see capoeira and Candomblé. During our visit, the staff were valiantly battling nausea caused by a rat which had expired under the office floor and started to decompose. Consult the message board inside the office to find friends, rent houses and boats, buy guidebooks and even overseas airline tickets, etc.

There are also Bahiatursa offices at: Mercado Modelo (☎ 241-0242), open from 8 am to noon and from 2 to 6 pm (Monday to Saturday); the rodoviária (☎ 231-2831), open from 9 am to 6 pm (Monday to Saturday; and the airport (☎ 204-1244), open from 8 am to 10 pm (Monday to Friday).

Bahiatursa operates an alternative lodging service to locate rooms in private houses and the like during Carnival and summer holidays. This can be an excellent way to find cheap rooms. Information on travel throughout the state of Bahia is also available, but don't expect much detail.

For general tourist information or help, you can try dialling 131 for a service called Disque Turismo (Dial Tourism).

For information about gay rights and AIDS, contact Centro Cultura (Triângulo Rosa; ☎ 242-3782)), Rua do Sodré, 45 which is close to the Museu de Arte Sacra.

Most newsagents and some of the tourist offices have maps on sale – the map entitled *Planta de Salvador* is useable. Emtursa publishes a glossy, detailed guide, *Guia Turístico Salvador*, which has useful listings. Most tourist offices and hotels have copies of *Itinerário*, a free monthly listing of cultural events in Salvador. The weekly magazine *Veja* also publishes a regular supplement containing excellent articles and listings for the latest cultural events in Bahia.

Dangers & Annoyances Salvador has a justifiable reputation for theft and muggings, and tourists clearly offer easy targets. Paranoia is not necessary, but you should be aware of the dangers and understand what you can do to minimise problems – for more detail, refer to the security section under Dangers & Annoyances in the Facts for the Visitor chapter. The following are some general points to remember when visiting Salvador.

Dress down; carry only a photocopy of your passport; and don't wear a watch or carry a camera. Look at a map for basic orientation before you set out to see the sights.

Stick to the main streets when walking during the day, and don't hesitate to use taxis at any time, but especially after dusk. Avoid side streets, and do not enter the area northeast of Pelourinho, which is a prostitution zone full of heavy dudes and ladies. The Lacerda Elevator is renowned for muggings, especially at night, and you should totally ignore any street touts offering to change money or sell drugs. Pickpocketing is very common on buses and in crowded places. Stay alert at all times and only take as much money with you as is necessary for your outing. Tourist police maintain a highly visible presence in the centre of Salvador, particularly Pelourinho, but this does not apply after dark.

On the beaches keep a close eye on juvenile thieves, often referred to as Capitões d'Areia (Captains of the Sand), who are quick to make off with unguarded possessions.

During Carnival, tourist authorities highly recommend that tourists form small groups, carry photocopies of passports, and avoid deserted places, especially narrow alleyways.

Emergency Useful numbers include: Disque Turismo (Dial Tourism) 131; Pronto Socorro (First Aid) 192; and Polícia Civil (Police) 197. There are several police posts in the city centre – for example, at the bus stop in Praça da Sé; and during the daytime in the same area there are often 'tourist' police (identified by an armband) on patrol.

Money The main branch of Banco do Brasil is at Avenida Estados Unidos, 561 in Cidade Baixa. Other useful branches of this bank are at Avenida 7 de Setembro, 733, and at the airport.

Whatever you do, don't change money on the street, particularly near the Lacerda Elevator or the Cantina da Lua. Out of every 100 foreigners who go near the Lacerda Elevator, 98 are approached by men posing as money changers and offering exchange rates that are too good to be true. Many of them will lead you to some side alley or empty lobby to conduct the transaction and rip you off.

American Express There's an American Express/Kontik-Franstur SA office (☎ 242-0433) in the Cidade Baixa at Praça da Inglaterra, 2 which holds mail for travellers. It's open Monday to Friday 8 am to 6 pm, but the mail office often closes for lunch.

Post Office The central post office is in Cidade Baixa. There are also post offices at: Avenida 7 de Setembro; Rua Ruy Barbosa, 19, in Cidade Alta; the airport; and the rodoviária. Watch out for price hikes and make sure items are franked.

Telephone Many hotels have international phone service, which is easier than running off to a phone station. If you are not so lucky, some of the convenient Telebahia posts are:

Telebahia Shopping Barra
    Avenida Centenário, 2992, Barra; open daily from 9 am to 10 pm; closes at 7 pm on Sunday.
Telebahia Rodoviária
    open daily, 6.30 am to midnight
Telebahia Aeroporto
    Aeroporto Internacional Dois de Julho; open daily 7 am to 10 pm

There are also phone stations in Iguatemi Shopping Centre, Campo da Pólvora and Centro de Convenções da Bahia.

Foreign Consulates The following countries maintain consulates in Salvador:

France
>Travessa Francisco Gonçalves 1, Comércio (☎ 241-0168). Open from 2.30 to 5 pm on Monday, Tuesday and Thursday.

Germany
>Rua Lucaia, 281, salas 204-6, Rio Vermelho (☎ 247-7106). Open from 9 am to noon, Monday to Friday.

UK
>Avenida Estados Unidos 4, salas 1109/1113, Comércio, (☎ 243-9222). Open from 8 to 11.30 am and 1.30 to 5 pm, Monday to Friday.

USA
>Avenida Antônio Carlos Magalhães, Edifício Cidadela Center I, sala 410, Pituba (☎ 358-9166). Open from 8.30 to 11.30 am, Monday to Friday.

Travel Agents Tatu Tours (☎ 237-3161), Rua Afonso Celso 447, sala 105, Barra, Salvador, CEP 40160, BA, deserves a mention for its informative and informal tours. The company specialises in natural and cultural history tours around Bahia, including specialist topics such as Afro-Brazilian culture and Carnival, and is happy to deal with groups or independent travellers. Tatu Tours is represented in the UK by Traveller's Tree (☎ (071) 935-2291), 116 Crawford St, London W1H 1AG.

The following travel agents sell bus tickets in addition to all the normal services. They can save you a trip out to the rodoviária, but check first as some agents do not sell tickets to all destinations:

Amaralina Viagens
>Barra (☎ 235-1263)

Itaparica Turismo
>Salvador Praia Hotel, Ondina (☎ 245-1455)

Itapemirim
>Avenida 7 de Septembro, 1420 (☎ 247-6633)

Itapoan Turismo
>Campo da Pólvora, 21, Centro (☎ 243-4648)

Rumo Turismo
>Avenida Antônio Carlos Magalhães, 1034, Loja 31, Pituba (☎ 258-1684)

Turbahia
>Cidade Baixa (☎ 242-3474)

Time In Salvador, shopkeepers close for lunch from noon to 3 pm (instead of 2 pm), and then go home at 3.45 pm instead of 5 pm. Café da manhã becomes *café da tarde*. Work has a different flavour: slow, relaxed and seemingly nonchalant.

The slow pace often frustrates and irritates visitors, but if you can reset your internal clock and not get uptight or unsettled, you are likely to be rewarded with many kindnesses and surprises. For example, whilst travelling in a taxi and unable to find an obscure restaurant, the taxi driver stopped, turned off his meter, and started to read our map. After 10 minutes we drove on and he turned the meter back on.

Walking Tour

Historic Salvador is easy to see on foot and you should plan on spending a couple of days wandering among the splendid 16th and 17th-century churches, homes and museums. One good approach is to ramble through the old city in the morning, head out to the beaches in the afternoon, and devote the evening to music, dance or Candomblé.

The most important sections of Salvador's colonial quarter extend from Praça Castro Alves along Ruas Chile and da Misericórdia to Praça da Sé and Terreiro de Jesus; and then continue down through Largo do Pelourinho and up the hill to Largo do Carmo.

There's no sense being too precise here; it's easy to wander through the colonial district if you keep yourself oriented with the map in this book.

Catedral Basílica Starting at the Praça da Sé, walk a block to the Terreiro de Jesus (Praça 15 de Novembro on many maps). The biggest church on the plaza is the Cathedral of Bahia, which served as a Jesuit centre until the Jesuits were expelled from Brazil in 1759. The cathedral was built between 1657 and 1672, and its walls are covered with Lioz marble which served as ballast for returning merchant ships. Many consider this the city's most beautiful church. The interior has many segmented areas and the emphasis is on verticality – raise your eyes to admire the superb

Top: Jaburú stork, Pantanal (SP)
Left: Cattle, Pantanal (SP)
Right: Stilt house, Pantanal (KB)

Top: Favela dwellers in Salvador, Bahia (JM)
Left: Resident of Salvador, Bahia (JM)
Right: A typical 'Baiana' in native dress, Salvador, Bahia (JM)

ceiling. The cathedral is open from 8 to 11 am and from 3 to 6 pm, Monday to Saturday; and from 5 to 6.30 pm on Sunday.

Museu Afro-Brasileiro Next door is the Antiga Faculdade de Medicina (Old Medical Faculty), which now houses our favourite museum in Bahia, the Afro-Brazilian Museum, with its small collection of displays focussing primarily on orixás from both Africa and Bahia. There is a surprising amount of African art from pottery to woodwork, and superb ceremonial Candomblé apparel. Other highlights include wooden panels representing Oxum (an orixá revered as the goddess of beauty) which were carved by Carybé, a famous Argentine artist who has lived in Salvador for many years. The museum (☎ 321-0383) is open Tuesday to Saturday, from 9 am to 5 pm.

In the basement of the same building is the **Museu de Arqueologia e Etnologia** (Archaeology & Ethnology Museum), which is open Monday to Friday, from 9 am to noon and 2 to 5.30 pm.

In the middle of the plaza you'll meet drug dealers, honest hammock vendors and rip-off money changers. Be careful: don't change money.

Igreja São Francisco As you exit the museum, turn left, walk to the far end of the plaza, and continue one block to Igreja São Francisco. Defying the teachings and vows of poverty of its namesake, this baroque church is crammed with displays of wealth and splendour. Gold leaf is used like wallpaper. There's an 80-kg silver chandelier and imported azulejos (Portuguese ceramic tiles).

Forced to build their masters' church and yet prohibited from practising their own religion (Candomblé terreiros were hidden and kept far from town), the African slave-artisans responded through their work: the faces of the cherubs are distorted, some angels are endowed with huge sex organs, some appear pregnant. Most of these creative acts were chastely covered by 20th-century sacristans. Traditionally Blacks were seated in far

corners of the church without a view of the altar.

Notice the polychrome of São Pedro da Alcântara by Manoel Inácio da Costa. The artist, like his subject, was suffering from tuberculosis. He made one side of the figure's face more ashen than the other so that São Pedro appears more ill as you walk past him. José Joaquim da Rocha painted the hallway ceiling using perspective technique, which was considered a novelty at the time.

The poor come to Igreja São Francisco on Tuesdays to venerate Santo Antônio and receive bread. The Candomblistas respect this church's saints and come to pray both here and in Igreja NS do Bonfim.

Depending on restoration work, opening hours are from 7.30 to 11.30 am and 2 to 6 pm, Monday to Saturday, and on Sunday from 7 am to noon.

Igreja da Ordem Terceira de São Francisco Next door to the Igreja São Francisco is the 17th-century Church of the Third Order of São Francisco. Notice the frontispiece, in the Spanish baroque or plateresco style, which remained hidden until it was accidentally discovered in the 1930s when a workman hammered off some plaster to install wiring. Opening hours are from 8 to 11.30 am and 2 to 5.30 pm, Monday to Friday.

Igreja São Pedro dos Clérigos The Igreja São Pedro dos Clérigos is back on Terreiro de Jesus and close to Cantina da Lua – a congenial restaurant. This rococo church, like many others built in the 18th century, was left with one of its towers missing in order to avoid a tax on finished churches. It opens only during mass, and if you visit during this time (usually from 8 to 9.30 am on Sunday), do not disturb the service.

Pelourinho To see the city's oldest architecture, turn down Rua Alfredo de Brito, the small street which descends into the Pelourinho district. If you're hungry while in the Pelourinho area, refer to the Places to Eat section for restaurant suggestions.

Pelourinho means whipping post, and this is where the slaves were tortured and sold (whipping of slaves was legal in Brazil until 1835). The old slave auction site on Largo do Pelourinho (also known as Praça José de Alencar) has recently been renovated and converted into the **Casa da Cultura Jorge Amado** (Jorge Amado Museum). According to a brass plaque across the street, Amado lived in the Hotel Pelourinho when it was a student house. The exhibition is disappointing but you can watch a free video of *Dona Flor* or one of the other films based on Amado's books. The museum is open Monday to Friday, from 8 am to noon and from 2 to 6 pm.

Next door is the **Museu da Cidade**. Among bits of whimsy (fleas in a matchbox dressed up to get married) there are costumes of the orixás of Candomblé and the personal effects of the Romantic poet Castro Alves, author of *Navio Negreiro* and one of the first public figures to protest against slavery. The museum is open Monday to Friday, from 8 am to noon and 2 to 5.30 pm.

Igreja NS do Rosário dos Pretos, across the Largo do Pelourinho, was built by and for the slaves. The 18th-century church has some lovely azulejos. Open from 8 am to 5.30 pm, Monday to Friday; and from 8 am to 2 pm on Saturday and Sunday.

Igreja do Santíssimo Sacramento da Rua do Paço From Pelourinho go down the hill and then continue uphill before climbing a set of steps to the left leading up to this church – an approach which is reminiscent of the Spanish steps of Rome. The first Brazilian film to win an award at the Cannes film festival, *O Pagador de Promessa*, was filmed here.

Igreja da Ordem Terceira do Carmo At the top of the hill, this church, founded in 1636, contains a baroque altar and an organ dating from 1889.

Igreja e Convento de NS do Carmo/ Museu do Carmo Next door, this religious complex is moderately interesting. Among the sacred and religious articles in the museum is a famous sculpture of Christ created by Francisco Chagas (also known as O Cabra). There's also a treaty declaring the expulsion of the Dutch from Salvador on 30 April 1625. The document was signed at the convent, which served as the general's quarters at the time. It's open Monday to Saturday, from 8 to 11.30 am and from 2 to 5 pm.

For a glimpse of unspoilt, old Salvador continue a few blocks past very old, dilapidated buildings which teem with life. Also notice an odd-looking public oratory, **Oratório da Cruz do Pascoal**, plunked in the middle of the street (Rua Joaquim Távora).

To continue on a walking tour of the city, it's best to retrace your steps to Praça da Sé.

Praça Tomé de Souza Starting at Praça da Sé again, walk over to the Praça Tomé de Souza. While not officially recognised or protected by the Brazilian historical architecture society SPHAN, this plaza has several beautiful and important sites. The **Palácio Rio Branco** was built in 1549 to house the offices of Tomé de Souza, the first governor general of Brazil; the palace has been rebuilt and refurbished over the years. The large, cream-coloured, birthday-cake building is now headquarters for Bahiatursa.

Elevador Lacerda The Lacerda Elevator, inaugurated in 1868, was an iron structure with clanking steam elevators until these were replaced with a new system in 1928. Today electric elevators truck up and down a set of 85-metre, vertical cement shafts in less than 15 seconds, and carry over 50,000 passengers daily.

Things weren't always so easy. At first, the Portuguese used slaves and mules to transport goods from the port in Cidade Baixa to Cidade Alta. By 1610, the Jesuits had installed the first elevator to negotiate the drop. A clever system of ropes and pulleys was manually operated to carry freight and a few brave souls.

You should be alert for petty crime and

mugging in and around the elevator, particularly after dusk – see the Dangers & Annoyances section.

Cidade Baixa Descending into the lower city you'll be confronted by the **Mercado Modelo**. Filled with souvenir stalls and restaurants, it's Salvador's worst concession to the tourism business. If you've missed capoeira, there are often impromptu displays for tourists outside the building – anyone contemplating taking photos is well advised to negotiate a sensible price beforehand or risk being suckered for an absurd fee. The horrendous modernist sculpture across the street is referred to as *bunda* (arse) by the locals. There are many cheap lanchonetes in Cidade Baixa and it's worth exploring.

Mercado São Joaquim

To see a typical market, take either the 'Ribeira' or the 'Bonfim' bus from the bus stop beside the elevator (base station). Ride for about three km and get off after the Pirelli Pneus store on your left. Mercado São Joaquim is a small city of waterfront barracas, open all day every day except Sunday. Watch out for the meat neighbourhood – it can turn the unprepared into devout vegetarians. You are bound to come across some spontaneous singing and dancing at the barracas serving cachaça.

Igreja NS do Bonfim

Further along the Itapagipe peninsula, past Mercado São Joaquim, is the **Igreja NS do Bonfim**. Built in 1745, the shrine is famous for its miraculous power to effect cures. In the Sala dos Milagres (ex-voto room) you'll see offerings: replicas of feet, arms, heads, hearts – the parts of the body devotees claim were cured by this power.

For Candomblistas, Bonfim is the church of Oxalá and thus their most important church. In January, the Lavagem do Bonfim, one of Bahia's most important festivals, takes place here and Candomblé priestesses (mães de santo) lead the festivities together with Catholic priests. See the Festivals section later in this chapter for more detail.

When you approach the church you'll undoubtedly be offered a *fita* (ribbon) to tie around your wrist. With the fita you can make three wishes that will come true by the time it falls off. This usually takes over two months and you must allow it to fall off from natural wear and tear. Cutting it off is said to bring bad luck.

The church is open from 6 am to noon and 2.30 to 6 pm, Tuesday to Sunday.

The Bay

From the church there's a very interesting half-hour walk to the bay, where you'll find the old Monte Serrat lighthouse and church (good crab at the barracas). Nearby is Praia da Boa Viagem where one of Bahia's most popular and magnificent festivals, Procissão do Senhor Bom Jesus dos Navegantes, takes place on New Year's Eve. See the Festivals section later in this chapter for more details.

The beach is lined with barracas and is very animated on weekends. It's a poorer part of town and quite interesting. From Boa Viagem there are frequent buses back to the bus stop beside the Lacerda Elevator (base station).

Museu de Arte Sacra da Bahia

The square belongs to the people as the sky belongs to the condor.

Castro Alves (Bahian poet)

From Praça Castro Alves, jammed with tens of thousands of people at Carnival time, it's a short walk to the Museu de Arte Sacra da Bahia at Rua do Sodré, 276. It's housed in a 17th-century convent which has been beautifully restored. The sacred art on display includes excellent and varied sculptures and images in wood, clay and soapstone – many were shipped to Salvador from Portugal. Opening hours are from 9.30 to 11.30 am and from 2 to 5.30 pm, Monday to Friday.

Museu de Arte Moderna

On the bay, further down from the centre toward Campo Grande, is the Solar do Unhão, an old sugar estate that now houses the small Museu de Arte Moderna, a restaurant (see Places to Eat) and a ceramic work-shop. It's a lovely spot; the art exhibits are often good and the restaurant is recommended for its tranquillity and view. The museum (☎ 243-6174) was closed for restoration in 1991, but scheduled to reopen within a year. Since this area has a reputation for crime (especially mugging of tourists), take a taxi to and from the Solar do Unhão – walking is not advisable. Opening hours are from 1 to 5 pm, Tuesday to Sunday.

Candomblé

Before doing anything in Salvador, find out about the schedule for Candomblé ceremonies so you don't miss a night in a terreiro. Bahiatursa has many Candomblistas on its staff who can provide a complete list of terreiros and advise you on the schedule for the month. Activities usually start around 8 or 9 pm and can be held any day of the week. For details about Candomblé refer to the religion section in the Facts about the Country chapter. For a description of an evening of Candomblé, see the introduction to the Bahia chapter.

Capoeira School

To visit a capoeira school it's best to get the up-to-date schedule from Bahiatursa, which has a complete listing of schools and class schedules. The Associação de Capoeira Mestre Bimba is an excellent school. It's at Rua Francisco Muniz Barreto 1, 1st floor, Terreiro de Jesus, and operates Monday to Saturday, 9 to 11 am and 4 to 7 pm. Speak to Manuel or Ari.

Beaches

Pituba, Armação, Piatãa, Placaford, and Itapoã beaches may not be as famous as Ipanema and Copacabana, but they are more beautiful. Although these beaches are all within 45 minutes by bus from the centre, Pituba, Armação and Piatã are becoming increasingly polluted and are not recommended for swimming. If you want to swim, it's advisable to head for Placaford, Itapoã or further north – for information on beaches

north of Itapoã see the North of Salvador section.

If you just want to wander through the city beach scene, Barra is the first Atlantic beach and the liveliest, but swimming is not advisable due to heavy pollution. There are plenty of restaurants, barracas and bars. You can see Bahia's oldest fort, the polygonal Santo Antônio da Barra, which was built in 1598 and fell to the Dutch in 1624. The view of Itaparica is splendid.

See the Getting Around section for details about transport to these beaches.

Festivals

Carnival in Salvador is justly world famous. For four nights and three days, beginning on a Thursday night, the masses go to the streets and stay until they fall. There's nothing to buy, so all you have to do is follow your heart – or the nearest trio elétrico – and play.

Carnival receives greatest emphasis, but it is by no means the only festival worth attending. There are many others, particularly in January and February, which attract huge crowds from the city. Since the 17th century, religious processions have remained an integral part of the city's cultural life. Combining elements of the sacred and profane, Candomblé and Catholicism, many of these festivals are as wild as Carnival and possibly more colourful.

Carnival Carnival, usually held in February or March, starts on a Thursday night and continues until the following Monday. Everything, but everything, goes during these four days. In recent years Carnival has revolved around the trios elétricos. The trios play distinctly upbeat music from the tops of trucks that slowly wind their way through the main Carnival areas (Praça Castro Alves, Campo Grande and Barra). Surrounding the trios is a sea of dancing, drinking revellers.

Carnival brings so many tourists and so much money to Salvador that there's been an inevitable tendency towards commercialisation, although this trend is still light years behind Rio. Fortunately, residents of the city have been very critical of recent Carnivals and in 1986, for example, control of Carnival arrangements was taken away from the bureaucrats and handed over to Waly Salomão, a local poet and friend of Gilberto Gil.

Waly promoted Carnival's most authentic manifestations: events were decentralised, and freer and more impromptu expression was encouraged. Let's hope the spontaneity continues.

Take a look at the newspaper or go to Emtursa or Bahiatursa for a list of events. Don't miss the afoxés (Afro blocos), such as Badauê, Ayê, Olodum, Ilê, Muzenza and the most famous, Filhos de Gandhi (Sons of Gandhi). The best place to see them is in Liberdade, Salvador's largest Black district.

Also, explore Carnaval Caramuru in Rio Vermelho and the smaller happenings in Itapoã, the old fishing and whaling village which has a fascinating ocean procession on the last day of Carnival, when a whale is delivered to the sea.

The traditional gay parade is held on Sunday at Praça Castro Alves. Many of Brazil's best musicians return to Salvador for Carnival, and the frequent rumours that so and so will be playing on the street are often true (for example, Gilberto Gil and Baby Consuelo have both taken part).

Many clubs have balls just before and during Carnival. If you're in the city before the festivities start you can also see the blocos practising. Just ask Emtursa or Bahiatursa.

Hotels do book up during Carnival, so reservations are a good idea. Stay near the centre or in Barra. Violence can be a problem during Carnival and some women travellers have reported violent approaches from locals. A common danger you may encounter at Carnival is when you are sucked into the pack right behind a trio elétrico and have to dodge all the dancers with their flying elbows! See the Dangers & Annoyances section for more details on avoiding crime.

Procissão do Senhor Bom Jesus dos Navegantes This festival, which originated in Portugal in 1750, is one of Bahia's most popular celebrations. On New Year's Eve, the image of Senhor dos Navegantes is taken to Igreja NS da Conceição, close to Mercado Modelo in Cidade Baixa. On the morning of New Year's Day, a maritime procession, consisting of dozens of boats, transports the image along the bay and returns it to the beach at Boa Viagem, which is packed with onlookers eager to celebrate with music, food and drink.

Festas de Reis Also of Portuguese origin, this festival is held in Igreja da Lapinha on 5 and 6 January.

Lavagem do Bonfim This festival, which takes place on the second Thursday in January and is attended by huge crowds, culminates with the ritual *lavagem* (washing) of the church by mães and filhas de santo. Abundant flowers and lights provide impressive decoration, and the party atmosphere continues with the Filhos de Gandhi and trios elétricos providing musical accompaniment for dancers.

Festa de São Lázaro This is a festival dedicated to the Candomblé orixá, Omulu, and culminates on the last Sunday in January with a mass, procession, festival and ritual cleansing of the church.

Festa de Iemanjá A grand maritime procession takes flowers and presents to Iemanjá, the Mãe e Rainha das Águas (Mother and Queen of the Waters). One of Candomblé's most important festivals, it's celebrated on 2 February in Rio Vermelho and accompanied by trios elétricos, afoxés and plenty of food and drink.

Lavagem da Igreja de Itapoã Celebrated in Itapoã, 15 days before Carnival, this warm-up for Carnival is all music and dance with blocos and afoxés.

Procissão do Encontro Sometime in mid-March, this large religious procession represents the meeting of NS das Dores with Sr dos Passos.

Festa São João This festival is celebrated on 23 and 24 June with pyrotechnics and many parties on the street where *genipapo*, a local liqueur, is consumed in liberal quantities.

Santa Bárbara The festival of Santa Bárbara is the Candomblé festa of the markets. Probably the best spot to see the festivities from 4 to 6 December is in Rio Vermelho at the Mercado do Peixe.

Festa de NS da Conceição This festival takes place on 8 December and features a procession in Cidade Baixa followed by Candomblé ceremonies in honour of Iemanjá.

Passagem do Ano Novo New Year's Eve is celebrated with all the zest of Carnival – especially on the beaches.

Places to Stay

Salvador has many hotels but they can all fill up during the Carnival season – reservations are a good idea. Bahiatursa can help you find lodging – just provide the staff with a general idea of your preferred price range and type of lodging. Bahiatursa also has lists of houses that take in tourists and these can be a source of excellent, cheap lodgings when hotels are full, especially during summer holidays and Carnival. But beware, the tourist office makes selective referrals and it helps if you don't look too burnt-out or broke.

Travellers who choose to stay in the historic centre should bear in mind the advice about crime included under Dangers & Annoyances in the Facts for the Visitor chapter. Several readers have commented that they felt safer staying south of the city centre or near the beaches.

Places to Stay – bottom end

Hostels – centre Most of Salvador's youth hostels, a relatively recent addition to the range of accommodation options, have been established away from the city centre and close to the beaches. One exception is *Albergue de Juventude Dois de Julho* (☎ 243-9513), Rua Areal de Cima, 44 which is just south of the city centre – very close to Praça Duque de Caxias.

Hostels – beaches The following beach hostels are listed in sequence, from Barra district along the Atlantic coast towards Itapoã. In Barra district, just a couple of blocks west of Shopping Barra, is *Albergue de Juventude Senzala* (☎ 247-5678), Rua Florianópolis, 134, Jardim Brasil, Barra. Close to Ondina beach is *Albergue de Juventude Solar* (☎ 235-2235) at Rua Macapá, 461. Moving further down the coast, Amaralina beach is a couple of minutes on foot from *Albergue de Juventude Lagash* (☎ 248-7399) at Rua Visconde de Itaboraí, 514. Next to Pituba beach there's *Albergue de Juventude Casa Grande* (☎ 248-0527) at Rua Minas Gerais, 122. Continuing along the coast, there's a hostel in Boca do Rio, *Albergue de Juventude Boca do Rio* (☎ 230-8371), at Avenida Dom Eugênio Sales, 72, Lote 11; and another hostel in Patamares, the *Albergue de Juventude CNEC* (☎ 249-4802), at Rua Bicuíba, s/n (no number), Loteamento Patamares.

Hotels The cheap hotels in the old part of town are around Praça da Sé, Terreiro de Jesus, Praça Anchieta, and Pelourinho.

Hotel Pelourinho (☎ 321-9022) at Rua Alfredo de Brito 20 is right in the heart of the historic Pelourinho area – a great central location during the day. It's an older, converted mansion with character (reputedly the setting for Jorge Amado's novel *Suor*), and the management appears to be security conscious. The lift seldom functions, so you earn the superb view from the top after puffing up five flights of stairs. Apartamentos are good value at US$10/21 for a single/double with view. Prices drop a little if you take a room without the view. Breakfast is included in the price and is served in a room that looks across the rooftops of Pelourinho. In the hotel courtyard there are handicraft shops and, right at the end, a restaurant-bar with a great view.

About 20 metres downhill from Largo do Pelourinho is *Hotel Solara* (☎ 321-0202) which has apartamentos starting at US$10/13/17 for a single/double/triple. Breakfast is included in the price.

Although it's a little more expensive, *Hotel Themis* (☎ 243-1668) at Praça da Sé 57, Edifício Themis (7th floor), offers perhaps the best value you'll find in the centre of town. A popular hangout with French travellers, it has a great view, a bar and a restaurant. Apartamentos with a view cost US$13/20/26 for a single/double/triple. Apartamentos without a view cost about US$1 less per person. All prices include breakfast.

Just a short walk from Bahiatursa is *Hotel Chile* (☎ 321-0246), at Rua Chile, 7 (1st floor). It's a bit grubby, but a good deal. Quartos start at US$7/10 for a single/double. Apartamentos cost US$17 for a double with air-con; and US$11/12 for singles/doubles without air-con. Close by is *Hotel Maridina* (☎ 242-7176) at Avenida 7 de Setembro, Ladeira de São Bento, 6 (1st floor). This is a friendly hotel which offers good value for money. Quartos cost US$8/13 for a single/double. Apartamentos start at US$10/16 for a single/double without TV – add US$3 to these prices if you want the box. All prices include breakfast.

Hotel Anglo-Americano (☎ 247-7681) at Avenida 7 de Setembro, 1838, is in a quieter location further away from the centre. Quartos cost US$7.50/10 for a single/double. Apartamentos start at US$11 for a double. Ask at the hotel desk about guides for visits to Candomblé ceremonies. Attached to the hotel is an Italian restaurant which gives a discount to hotel guests. In the same area, very close to Museu de Arte da Bahia, is *Hotel Caramuru* (☎ 247-9951) at Avenida 7 de Setembro, 2125 which has been highly recommended by readers. The hotel is a large colonial mansion with a leafy courtyard. Prices for single/double apartamentos start around US$9/12. Quartos are slightly cheaper.

In Barra district, readers have recommended *Hotel Bella Barra* (☎ 237-8401, 235-2313) at Rua Afonso Celso 439, which is run by a friendly family who came here from Hong Kong over 20 years ago. It's a much quieter place to stay than the hotels on the seafront, which suffer from constant traffic noise. Clean, bright apartamentos cost US$20/28 for singles/doubles.

If you plan to pass most of your days at the beach and just go into the city on occasion, consider staying in Itapoã, the nicest Atlantic beach suburb. From Itapoã, it's a good 45-minute ride to the city centre, but the beaches are topnotch, there are several hotels, and the town itself is an old fishing village with a good feel and few tourists. It's also close to the airport, which can make it convenient if you're flying out the next day.

Along the beach, in the heart of Itapoã, *Hotel Europa* (☎ 249-9344) is a personal favourite. It has very clean apartamento doubles around US$12. Across the street you have the beach, barracas for food and drink, and buses to the centre of Salvador.

Camping On the outskirts of Itapoã, there are several campgrounds, such as *Cabana da Praia* (☎ 248-8477), Alamedas da Praia, s/n (no number) which is open from December to March; and *Camping Clube do Brasil* (☎ 249-2101) also at Alamedas da Praia, s/n (no number).

Places to Stay – middle
The *Palace Hotel* (☎ 243-1155) at Rua Chile 20 is good value and right in the centre of the city. Apartamentos without air-con or TV cost US$28/33 for a single/double; with these amenities, singles/doubles are US$34/40.

If you'd rather stay opposite the beach in the Barra district, and within easy reach of the city centre, *Hotel Porto da Barra* (☎ 247-4939) at Avenida 7 de Setembro, 3783 has single/double apartamentos for US$27/30 (without air-con); and double apartamentos with air-con for US$33.

Places to Stay – top end

Sofitel Quatro Rodas (☎ 249-9611), Salvador's luxury palace (complete with helipad), is way out past Itapoã, near the lighthouse and just a stroll from the beach. Singles/doubles here are US$85/95. Facing the beach at Rio Vermelho is the *Meridien Bahia* (☎ 248-8011) which has singles/doubles for US$75/80. At Ondina beach, closer to the city, are two top-class hotels: *Bahia Othon Palace* (☎ 247-1044) which has singles/doubles around US$70/75; and *Salvador Praia* (☎ 245-5033) which has a private stretch of beach and charges US$80/90 for singles/doubles.

Places to Eat

Bahian cuisine is an intriguing blend of African and Brazilian recipes based on characteristic ingredients such as coconut cream, ginger, hot peppers, coriander, shrimp, and dendê oil. Dendê, an African palm oil with a terrific flavour, is used in many regional dishes (you'll also smell it everywhere). Since dendê has a reputation for stirring up trouble in travellers' bellies, you are advised to consume it in small quantities until you've become acclimatised. For names and short descriptions of typical Bahian dishes, refer to the food section in the Facts for the Visitor chapter.

With a large working population, Cidade Baixa has lots of cheap, lunch-only restaurants. Vegetarians will want to try *Restaurante Naturel* on Rua Conselheiro Lafayette – three doors to your right as you leave the elevator (base station). The restaurant is on the 2nd floor and offers an excellent self-service lunch – closed in the evenings. There are also several cafés across from Mercado Modelo serving standard fare.

Inexpensive food is also easy to find in Cidade Alta. A popular hangout with cheap victuals is *Cantina da Lua* on Terreiro de Jesus, at the edge of the Pelourinho district.

At Rua Alfredo de Brito 11, there's an excellent restaurant called *Meson Espanhol* (☎ 321-3523). It's on the 1st floor with a bird's-eye view of street life and the overgrown garden of the Antiga Faculdade de Medicina. Main dishes average US$6 – the *moqueca de peixe* (fish stew) and *doce de cajú* (supersweet cashew dessert) are excellent. Opening hours are from noon to 10 pm daily; closed on Sunday. To promote security for evening diners, this restaurant offers a free transport service (there and back) – just phone ahead for a reservation.

In Largo do Pelourinho, there's a restaurant in the courtyard of the *Hotel Pelourinho*. The main attraction is the great view of the bay. The dishes are adequate but overpriced, and the service can be surly.

Quite the opposite can be said for *Banzo*, the restaurant next door to the hotel, which is bright, animated and good value. There's a great selection of Bahian and European dishes plus all sorts of exotic drinks – expect to pay around US$5 for a main dish plus a drink. The décor features works of art by local artists, and there's often live music in the evening. Opening hours are erratic. When Grupo Olodum is giving one of its frequent, free Sunday evening concerts in Largo do Pelourinho, the Banzo balcony provides a good vantage point to view the gyrating crowds.

Across the street is *Senac* (☎ 321-5502), a cooking school which offers a huge spread of 30 regional dishes in the form of a self-service buffet. It's not the best Bahian cooking, but for US$8 you can discover which Bahian dishes you like...and eat till you explode! Senac is open from 6.30 to 9.30 pm every day except Sunday. Folklore shows are presented from 8 to 9 pm, from Thursday to Saturday – tickets cost US$2 per person. Check out the toilet décor: giant, lurid green taps and fluorescent pink soap dispensers!

At the crossroads downhill from Largo do Pelourinho is *Casa do Benin* (☎ 243-7629), a superb restaurant serving excellent African food in a small courtyard complete with palm trees, pond, and thatched hut. Main dishes start around US$6 – the *moqueca de peixe* and *frango ao gengibre* (ginger chicken) are close to culinary heaven! The restaurant is open daily from 11 am to 5 pm; closed on Sunday.

Solar do Unhão (☎ 321-5551), which houses the Museu de Arte Moderna described previously, also has a restaurant on the lower level in the old senzala (slave quarters). Legend has it that the place is haunted with the ghosts of tortured slaves. One look at the ancient pelourinho (whipping post) and torture devices on display makes the idea credible. Ironically, the view from the restaurant is one of the best in the city, and as good a reason as any for a visit. The Bahian cooking is unexceptional and you can expect to pay about US$4 for lunch and US$5 for dinner (reservations recommended). The restaurant is open daily (from noon to midnight), except Sunday. Dinner is usually accompanied by live music and a folklore show at 10 pm – expect to pay an extra US$3 cover charge. As mentioned previously for the Museu de Arte Moderna, crime is a problem in this area and you are advised not to walk to or from the Solar do Unhão – take a taxi.

Close to the rodoviária and adjacent to Hipermercado Paes Mendonça is *Baby Beef* (☎ 244-0811), a restaurant serving very fine steaks and ribs for about US$5. Open daily from 11.30 am to 3 pm and from 6 pm to midnight. For Japanese food, try *Restaurante Gan* (☎ 245-2206) at Praça Alexandre Fernandes 29, Fazenda Garcia – it's just east of Campo Grande, in the Garcia district. Open daily from 7 pm to midnight, but closed on the second and third Sundays of each month.

In Rio Vermelho, *O Marisco* (☎ 237-3910) at Rua Euricles de Matos 123 has great seafood, such as *mariscada tropical*, a sort of Bahian fish stew which can feed three for US$8; *polvo* (octopus) and *ensopado de camarão* (shrimp stew in a clay pot). Open daily from 11 am to 3.30 pm and from 6 to 11 pm – closed on Monday evening.

Excellent Bahian dishes at moderate prices are served at *Restaurante Iemanjá* (☎ 231-5570), Avenida Otávio Mangabeira, s/n (no number) on Armação beach. Open daily from noon to 5 pm and from 7 pm to midnight.

Last, best and hardest to find is *Bargaço* (☎ 231-5141) at Rua P, Quadra 43, Jardim Armação – it's on a small residential street near the Centro de Convenções (Convention Centre). National and international gourmets rate the seafood here as world class. The ensopada de camarão is divine, but you'll have to be prepared to splurge about US$12 – fame has set an upward trend for the prices. Open daily from noon to midnight.

Entertainment

Salvador is justly renowned for its music. The blending of African and Brazilian traditions produces popular styles, such as trio elétrico (which dominates Carnival), tropicalismo, afoxé, caribé, reggae, lambada, jazz and Gilberto Gil.

Bars and clubs tend to come and go quickly in Salvador, so ask around and check the newspaper to confirm the following suggestions. The weekly magazine *Veja* contains a supplement with tips on the hottest nightspots. In general, Barra has the most nightlife in Salvador, many of the city's best non-tourist places are in Rio Vermelho and many of the better hotels, such as the Salvador Praia, have fancy nightclubs. The security advice provided under Dangers & Annoyances is especially relevant after dark.

If you want to plug into the arts, the Fundação Cultural do Estado da Bahia (☎ 243-4555), Rua General Labatut 27, Barris, organises a listing of museums, libraries, theatres and cultural events (fine arts), including performances at the Teatro Castro Alves (☎ 235-7616), Praça Dois de Julho (Campo Grande). Call or stop by at either address for a monthly program. Teatro Castro Alves is the biggest music theatre in Salvador. The big acts play here and they're often Brazil's best.

The Pelourinho area often has blocos (musical street groups), such as Olodum, practising on Sunday nights and drawing crowds of dancers into the streets – definitely a musical highlight. Banzo, described under Places to Eat, is a great bar and restaurant in Pelourinho with live reggae music. African culture is kept alive in Liberdade, which is a good place to see afoxé. Go with someone who knows the area.

Barra is full of bars, discos and music. Some places are quite good, but it's more touristy and Westernised than other neighbourhoods. Habeas Copos (☎ 235-7274) at Avenida Marquês de Leão 172 is an old favourite with the bohemian crowd. Zimbabwe, Rua Afonso Celso 473, has good music and specialises in *afrodisíacos* (aphrodisiac drinks)!

Rio Vermelho district has some of Salvador's best music clubs. A pleasant bar with outside tables is Intermezzo at Largo da Mariquita s/n (no number). It's next to Cine-Teatro Maria Bethânia, a film theatre which may appeal to film buffs with its regular screenings of a wide range of national and international films. In the same district is the student hangout 68, at Avenida Cardeal da Silva s/n (no number). The number 68 refers to the worst year of repression during the 20-year military dictatorship. Although there is no live music the joint jumps. It's unpretentious and drinks are cheap. Outdoor seating provides refuge from the cigarettes.

Pituba beach has several bars with music, such as Tocaia Grande, Rua Minas Gerais 784, which specialises in Arabian appetisers.

Those in search of *danceterias* (dance halls) could try Souk Santana (☎ 247-7140), Rua João Gomes 88, in Rio Vermelho; or head towards Amaralina to visit New Fred's (☎ 247-4399), Rua Visconde de Itaboraí 125, which is a huge lambada mecca with room for 600 dancers.

Folklore shows, usually consisting of mini-displays of Candomblé, capoeira, samba, lambada, etc, are presented in the evening at: Senac (Pelourinho) – see Places to Eat; Solar do Unhão (south of city centre) – see Places to Eat; and Moenda (☎ 231-7915; Jardim Armação), next to the Centro de Convenções.

Things to Buy

For handicrafts, you can browse in Mercado Modelo, Praça da Sé, and Terreiro de Jesus – all places where articles and prices are geared to tourists. For a large, local market catering less to tourists, try Mercado São Joaquim (also known as Feira São Joaquim), which is just north of the city centre. Dedicated shoppers should head for Shopping Iguatemi (Salvador's largest shopping centre) and Shopping Barra, both of which are gigantic complexes with dozens of shops.

Getting There & Away

Air The big three domestic airlines all fly to Salvador, as does Nordeste, which goes to smaller cities in the region like Ilhéus and Porto Seguro. You can fly to most cities in Brazil from Salvador, but make sure you find out how many stops the plane makes: many flights in the Northeast operate as 'milk runs', stopping at every city along the Atlantic seaboard, which makes for a long ride. There are regular international flights between Salvador and: Miami; Frankfurt; Paris; Rome; and Buenos Aires. Following is a list of Brazilian and foreign airlines represented in Salvador:

Aerolineas Argentinas
    Rua da Bélgica 10, Loja D (☎ 242-1007)
Air France
    Rua Portugal, Edifício Regente Feijó, sala 606
    (☎ 242-4955)
Lanchile
    Rua Miguel Calmon 555, sala 609, Comércio
    (☎ 242-8144)
Lufthansa
    Rua Miguel Calmon 555, sala 401, Comércio
    (☎ 241-5100)
Nordeste
    Avenida D João VI, 259, Brotas (☎ 244-7755,
    249-2630)
TAP (Air Portugal)
    Avenida Estados Unidos 137, sala 401 (☎ 243-3673)
Transbrasil
    Rua Carlos Gomes 616, Centro (☎ 242-3344)
    airport (249-2467)
Varig/Cruzeiro
    Rua Carlos Gomes 6, Centro (☎ 243-1344)
    airport (☎ 204-1030)
VASP
    Rua Pinto Martins, Comércio (☎ 243-7044)
    Rua Chile 27, Centro (☎ 243-7044)
    airport (☎ 249-2495)

Bus There are numerous departures daily to Rio (28 hours; US$40) – US$80 for leito.

Buses to São Paulo leave four times daily (33 hours; US$48) – leito for US$95. There are four daily departures to Brasília (around 22 hours; US$40 – US$80 for leito) and Belo Horizonte (around 22 hours; US$33 – US$65 for leito).

There are six departures daily to Aracajú. The six-hour trip costs US$8.50, or take the leito (US$15). Five buses depart daily for Recife – the 12 to 14-hour trip costs US$20 (leito US$38). There are two daily departures to Fortaleza (20 hours; US$32), and a thrice-weekly leito (US$60). There's one daily departure to Belém (36 hours; US$50).

There are three daily departures to Lençóis (seven hours; US$9) – since the badly potholed road is currently under repair, the trip time may improve. There are frequent departures daily to Valença (five hours; US$7). Two buses depart daily for Ilhéus (seven hours; US$10). There are two evening departures to Porto Seguro (12 hours; US$15) – leito for US$32. There are frequent departures, between 5.30 am and 7 pm, to Cachoeira (two hours; US$3) – take the bus marked 'São Felix'.

Boat Boats to points on Baía de Todos os Santos leave from the Terminal Turístico Marítimo (☎ 242-9411) on Avenida da França, one block towards the water from the Mercado Modelo. There are tours of the bay featuring Itaparica and Frade islands, and boats to Maragojipe. (See Baía de Todos os Santos and recôncavo sections for schedules.) The other docks in front of the Mercado Modelo have motorboats to Mar Grande and Itaparica.

Getting Around

Venice has its canals and gondolas, Salvador has its bluff, elevators, hills, valleys and one-way streets. Bus strikes are very common. Our visit coincided with a mega advertising campaign for a huge tourism convention. Just a day or so before the convention was to begin, the bus drivers went on strike and paralysed the city for the duration of the event!

The Lacerda Elevator runs daily from 5 am to midnight linking the low and high cities. The Plano Inclinado Gonçalves, behind the cathedral near the Praça da Sé, makes the same link and is more fun, but only operates from Monday to Friday 6 am to 8 pm and Saturdays 6 am to 1 pm.

To/From the Airport Aeroporto Dois de Julho (☎ 204-1010) is over 30 km from the city centre, inland from Itapoã. At the airport there's a bilheteria (ticket office) for taxi transport. Check the price against the table displayed in the office window. A taxi ride to Praça da Sé costs US$20. The best way to go is to take the Executivo bus marked 'Praça da Sé/Aeroporto' (US$1). It starts at Praça da Sé (the stop is signposted), goes down Avenida 7 de Setembro to Barra, and continues all the way along the coast before heading inland to the airport. You can flag it down along the way. In light traffic, the ride to the airport takes 45 minutes; with traffic 1½ hours.

A municipal bus (fare 45c) marked 'Aeroporto' follows the same route but it gets very crowded and isn't recommended if you're carrying a bag.

Bus There are three municipal bus stops downtown worth knowing about: Praça da Sé, Avenida da França, and Barroquinha (described in the following Rodoviária section).

Buses from Praça da Sé go to Campo Grande, Vitória and Itapoã via Barra. Air-conditioned executive buses marked 'Praça da Sé/Aeroporto' also leave from here and go along the beaches from Barra to Itapoã (US$1). This is one way to go to the Atlantic coast beaches. Another way is to take the 'Jardineira' service which operates from 7.30 am to 7.30 pm daily between Campo Grande (bus stop outside Hotel da Bahia) and Itapoã. The trip on an open-deck bus following a scenic route along the coast takes 40 minutes and costs US$1.75.

The Avenida da França stop is in Cidade Baixa beside the Lacerda Elevator (base station). From here take either the 'Ribeira' or the 'Bonfim' bus to the Itaparica ferry (get

Baía de Todos os Santos & Recôncavo

off after a couple of km when you see the Pirelli Pneus store on your left); the Mercado São Joaquim market (get off at the stop after Pirelli Pneus); or continue to Igreja NS do Bonfim.

To/From the Rodoviária The rodoviária (☎ 231-5711) is five km from downtown, but it's a bit messy taking a bus there – many buses marked 'Rodoviária' drive all over the city – and can take up to an hour during rush hour. For a quicker trip it's advisable to take a taxi, which costs US$4 from Praça da Sé. At the rodoviária, there's a bilheteria which sells fixed price taxi tickets.

Buses to the rodoviária leave from Terminal da Barroquinha, just south of the city centre. Take the bus marked 'Rodoviária R3', get off at Iguatemi and use the pedestrian crossing which describes a huge arc above the highway. Alternatively, you can use the bus service between the rodoviária

and Campo Grande and change there to a bus for the city centre.

The rodoviária is a self-contained complex which contains a Bahiatursa office, Telebahia office, supermarket, left luggage service, and a couple of inexpensive eateries. For more complex needs, you can pop across the pedestrian crossing and visit Salvador's largest shopping centre – Shopping Iguatemi.

Around Salvador

ITAPARICA
Many Bahians love Itaparica, the largest island in Baía de Todos os Santos, but it's really not a must-see destination. Weekends are crowded, transportation is slow without a car, it's fairly expensive and the beaches aren't as pretty as the more accessible beaches north of the city.

Itaparica is popular with many Brazilians, who prefer a swim in the calm waters of the bay to the rough and tumble of the ocean. The island is built up with many weekend homes, but has few budget hotels. Many of the beaches are dirty and the best part of the island is owned by Club Med. Yet there still are a few clean beaches where you can just kick back on the sand, lie beneath wind-swept palms and gaze across the bay at the city (try Barra Grande for example).

Orientation

Itaparica City At the northern tip of the island is the city of Itaparica and its São Lourenço Fort. Built by the Dutch invaders in the 17th century, the fortress figured prominently in Bahia's battle for independence in 1823. The Solar Tenente Botas (Mansion of Lieutenant Botas) on the square of the same name, the Igreja Matriz do Santíssimo Sacramento on Rua Luis Gama and the Fonte da Bica (mineral water fountain) round out the city sights.

Along the Coast South along the coast, between Cidade de Itaparica and Bom Despacho, is Ponte da Areia, a thin strip of sand with barracas. The water is clear and shallow, the sandy floor slopes gently into the bay.

South of Mar Grande (perhaps the most likeable town on the island), the beaches of Barra do Gil, Barra do Pote and Coroa all have excellent views of Salvador, while on the other side of Club Med is Barra Grande, Itaparica's finest open-to-the-public beach. The beaches further to the south up to and including Cacha Pregos are dirtier and generally less beautiful, although many Bahians consider Cacha Pregos the best beach on the island.

Places to Stay & Eat

For an inexpensive place to stay, there's the pleasant youth hostel at Aratuba: *Albergue de Juventude Enseada de Aratuba* (☎ 321-8604), Quadra H, Lotes 12/13. There are campgrounds at Praia de Berlinque, Mar Grande, Praia de Barra Grande, and Praia de Cacha Pregos.

The best eating on the island is the seafood at the beach barracas. The *Timoneiro Restaurant*, 10 km from Cacha Pregos and three km from the Bom Despacho/Cacha Pregos junction, serves expensive but tasty shrimp dishes.

Getting There & Away

There are two boats from Salvador to Itaparica. The first is a small boat that leaves from the Mercado Modelo docks and goes directly to Mar Grande, Itaparica, where there are a few bars and restaurants. The trip costs 80c and takes around 50 minutes. Boats operate Monday to Saturday, from 6.30 am to 4 pm – departures every half hour or hour; and Sunday, 7 to 10 am and 2 to 5.45 pm – hourly departures. The last boat returns from Mar Grande at 4.30 pm Monday to Saturday. This schedule often changes.

The second boat is the giant car and passenger ferry from São Joaquim to Bom Despacho, Itaparica. The ferry leaves every half hour from near the São Joaquim market, a busy colourful place overflowing with produce, spices and hardware (open daily). Take either the 'Ribeira' or 'Bonfim' bus from the França bus stop beside the Lacerda Elevator (base station) for a couple of km and get off when you see a Pirelli Pneus store on your left.

The fare is 50c and the ride takes 45 minutes. Ferries operate Monday to Thursday, 6 am to 10 pm; and Friday to Sunday and holidays, from 6 am to midnight. If you're travelling by car, expect a long wait to get on the ferry returning to Salvador on Sunday nights.

Getting Around

Bom Despacho is the island's transportation hub. Buses, VW Kombi-vans and taxis meet the big boats and will take you to your desired beach. Bicycle rental is widely available, and a useful option if you want to explore under your own steam. A warning: although the São Joaquim-Bom Despacho ferry operates until midnight, island transport becomes scarce after 8 pm.

OTHER BAÍA DE TODOS OS SANTOS ISLANDS

The easiest way to cruise the lesser islands and the bay itself is to get one of the tourist boats that leave from the Terminal Turístico Marítimo (☎ 242-9411) close to Mercado Modelo in Salvador. There are various tours; most take half a day, stopping at Ilha dos Frades, Ilha da Maré and Itaparica. The cost is about US$12.

An alternative tour of the bay is possible by hiring a cheap, small boat from the small port near the Mercado Modelo. Bahiatursa's bulletin board often has ads for boat trips. The most popular islands include: Ilha Bom Jesus dos Passos which has traditional fishing boats and artisans; Ilha dos Frades, named after two monks who were eaten there by local Indians, which has attractive waterfalls and palm trees; and Ilha da Maré, which has the Igreja de NS das Neves and the beaches of Itamoabo and Bacia das Neves.

The Recôncavo Region

The recôncavo is the region of fertile lands spread around the Baía de Todos os Santos. Some of the earliest Brazilian encounters between Portuguese, Indian and African peoples occurred here and the lands proved to be among Brazil's best for growing sugar and tobacco.

Along with the excellent growing conditions, the region prospered due to its relative proximity to Portuguese sugar markets, the favourable winds to Europe and the excellent harbours afforded by the Baía de Todos os Santos. By 1570 there were already 18 mills and by 1584 there were 40. The sugar plantation system was firmly entrenched by the end of the 16th century and continued to grow from the sweat of African slaves for another 250 years.

Tobacco came a bit later to the recôncavo.

Traded to African slave-hunters and kings, it was the key commodity in the triangular slave trade. Tobacco was a more sensitive crop to grow than sugar and the estates were much smaller. Big fortunes were made growing sugar, not tobacco. On the other hand, fewer slaves were needed – about four per tobacco farm – so many poorer Portuguese settlers went into tobacco and a less rigid social hierarchy developed. Many even did some of the work!

A second subsidiary industry in the recôncavo was cattle ranching, which provided food for the plantation hands, and transport for the wood that fuelled the sugar *engenhos* (mills) and for delivery of the processed cane to market. Cattle breeding started in the recôncavo and spread inland, radiating west into the sertão and Minas Gerais, then north-west into Piauí.

If you have time for only one side trip from Salvador, visit Cachoeira and perhaps squeeze in Santo Amaro or Maragojipe on the way. A suggested itinerary is to take the weekday afternoon boat to Maragojipe and then the bus along the banks of the Rio Paraguaçu to Cachoeira. If you rent a car, drive up through Santo Amaro. If your timing is good, on Friday or Saturday nights, you may be invited to attend a terreiro de Candomblé at Cachoeira. From Cachoeira, there are frequent buses back to Salvador.

CACHOEIRA

Cachoeira, 121 km from Salvador and 40 km from Santo Amaro, stands below a series of hills beside the Rio Paraguaçu which is spanned by a bridge, built by the British in 1885 as a link with its twin town São Felix. Affectionately known as the jewel of the recôncavo, Cachoeira has a population of 28,000 and lies in the centre of Brazil's best tobacco growing region. Apart from tobacco, the main crops in the area are cashews and oranges.

The town is full of beautiful colonial architecture, uncompromised by the presence of modern structures. As a result, it was pronounced a national monument in 1971 and the state of Bahia started paying for

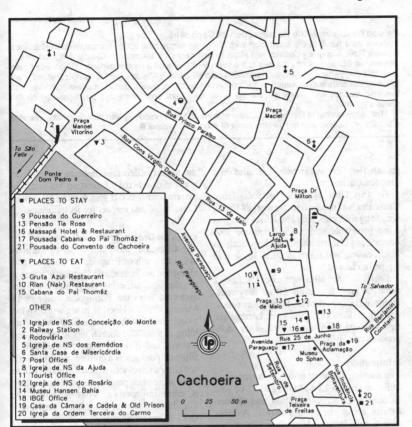

PLACES TO STAY

9 Pousada do Guerreiro
13 Pensão Tia Rosa
16 Massapé Hotel & Restaurant
17 Pousada Cabana do Pai Thomáz
21 Pousada do Convento de Cachoeira

▼ PLACES TO EAT

3 Gruta Azul Restaurant
10 Rian (Nair) Restaurant
15 Cabana do Pai Thomáz

OTHER

1 Igreja de NS do Conceição do Monte
2 Railway Station
4 Rodoviária
5 Igreja de NS dos Remédios
6 Santa Casa de Misericórdia
7 Post Office
8 Igreja de NS da Ajuda
11 Tourist Office
12 Igreja de NS do Rosário
14 Museu Hansen Bahia
18 IBGE Office
19 Casa da Câmara e Cadeia & Old Prison
20 Igreja da Ordem Terceira do Carmo

Cachoeira

0   25   50 m

restoration and preservation of historic buildings. However, these funds appear to have dried up and the municipal authorities in Cachoeira are continuing the work on their own dwindling budget.

Cachoeira is also a renowned centre of Candomblé orthodoxy and the home of many traditional artists and artisans. If you get an early start, Cachoeira can be visited in a day from Salvador, but it's less hectic if you plan to stay overnight.

Cachoeira and São Felix are best seen on foot. There's nothing you really *have* to see, so it's best to just take it easy and explore.

History

Diego Álvares, the father of Cachoeira's founders, was the sole survivor of a ship bound for the West Indies that was wrecked in 1510 on a reef near Salvador. The Portuguese Robinson Crusoe was saved by the Tupinambá Indians of Rio Vermelho, who dubbed the strange white sea creature Caramuru or Fish-Man. Diego Álvares lived 20 years with the Indians and married Catarina do Paraguaçu, the daughter of the most powerful Tupinambá chief. Their sons João Gaspar Aderno Álvares and Rodrigues Martins Alvares killed off the local Indians,

---

Nelson Napoleon & the Resurrection of Cachoeira

Perhaps as a result of the inspiration from his given names, the IBGE director, Nelson Napoleon Ferreira Reis, has many dreams and plans to resurrect past splendours. Clearly delighted by our interest, he whisked us off on a tour of the town, which proved a bizarre experience because it was clear that everywhere he indicated renovated colonial edifices – 'quase feito' or 'almost finished' – we followed the enthusiastic sweep of his arm and saw the opposite: gutted, roofless buildings with teetering facades and impromptu natural adornment from cacti or papaya trees perched on the remaining walls.

That is the appeal of Cachoeira, a town of surreal, faded grandeur, with friendly inhabitants who maintain enthusiasm and hope in the midst of economic decline. ∎

---

set up the first sugar-cane fazendas and founded Cachoeira.

By the 18th century, tobacco from Cachoeira was considered the world's finest, sought by rulers in China and Africa, and was more profitable than sugar. Tobacco also became popular in Brazil. The holy herb, as it was called, was taken as snuff, smoked in a pipe or chewed.

Early in the 19th century, Cachoeira achieved fame as a centre for military operations in Bahia to oust the Portuguese rulers, and on 25 June 1822, the town became the first to recognise Dom Pedro I as the independent ruler of Brazil.

Information

The municipal tourist office, in a renovated building on Rua 13 de Maio, should be able to help with accommodation and general details about the town's sights. Another source is the Instituto Histórico e Geográfico Brasileiro (IBGE) office on Praça da Aclamação. Some of the sights, especially churches, have experienced problems with theft and you may have to phone to arrange a visit. Bahiatursa no longer operates a tourist information office.

Candomblé

It at all possible, try to see Candomblé in Cachoeira. This is one of the strongest and perhaps purest spiritual and religious centres for Candomblé. Long and mysterious Candomblé ceremonies are held in small homes and shacks up in the hills, usually on Friday and Saturday nights at 8 pm. Visitors are not as common here as in Salvador and the tourist office is sometimes reluctant to give out this sort of information, but you may inspire confidence if you show an interest in Candomblé and respect for its traditions.

Igreja da Ordem Terceira do Carmo

The Church of the Third Order of Carmelites, just south of Praça da Aclamação, and alongside the Pousada do Convento, features a gallery of suffering polychrome Christs imported from the Portuguese colonies in Macau. Christ's blood is made with bovine blood mixed with Chinese herbs and sparkling rubies. The church has recently been restored and is now being promoted by the adjacent pousada as a convention centre. It's certainly a novel idea to seat delegates where there were once pews – the panelled ceiling is most impressive. Visiting hours are Tuesday to Saturday from 2 to 5 pm; and 9 to 11.30 am on Sunday.

Casa da Câmara e Cadeia

Nearby on the same square is the Casa da Camara e Cadeia, the old prefecture and prison. Organised criminals ran the show upstairs and disorganised criminals were kept behind bars downstairs. The structure in yellow with white trim dates back to 1698 and served as the seat of the Bahian government in 1822. The old marble pillory in the square was destroyed after abolition.

Museu do SPHAN

Across the square, a colonial mansion houses the humble SPHAN museum with squeaky bats flapping over colonial furnishings.

Open daily (except Monday) from 9 am to noon and 2 to 5 pm.

Museu Hansen Bahia

The Hansen Bahia Museum was set up in the home and birthplace of Brazilian heroine Ana Neri, who organised the nursing corps during the Paraguay War. Now the work of German (naturalised Brazilian) artist Hansen Bahia is displayed here. Among his powerful lithographs of human suffering is a series of illustrations of Castro Alves' poem *Návio Negreiro* (Slave Ship). The museum is open from 10 am to noon and from 2 to 5 pm and is closed Tuesday and Sunday afternoons. Prints are also on sale here.

Igreja de NS do Rosário do Porto do Cachoeira

The blue church with yellow trim, up from the Hansen Bahia Museum at the corner of Rua Ana Neri and Rua Lions Club, is the NS do Rosário do Porto do Cachoeira. The church has beautiful Portuguese tiles and a ceiling painted by Teófilo de Jesus. Opening hours are erratic, so it's best to phone 724-1294 and arrange for admission from the custodian who may also take you round the Museu das Alfaias on the 1st floor. This museum contains remnants from the abandoned 17th-century Convento de São Francisco do Paraguaçu.

Igreja de NS da Ajuda

On Largo da Ajuda is Cachoeira's oldest church, the tiny NS da Ajuda, built in 1595 when Cachoeira was known as Arraial d'Ajuda. Phone 724-1396 to arrange a visit to the church and the Museu da Boa Morte – an interesting museum with displays of photos and ceremonial apparel of the exclusively female Boa Morte cult.

Santa Casa de Misericórdia

This is the municipality's oldest hospital. The complex contains a pretty chapel (founded in 1734) with a painted ceiling, gardens and an ossuary. It's open weekdays from 2 to 5 pm.

Other Attractions in Cachoeira

At the far end of town near the bridge and train station is the Igreja de NS do Conceição do Monte. The climb to this 18th-century church is rewarded by a good view of Cachoeira and São Felix.

Across from the ruined grand facade of the train station, the wide, empty and cobblestoned Praça Manoel Vitorino feels like an Italian movie set. Try your Italian on the ice-cream seller or the pigeons, then move on to São Felix.

São Felix

When crossing the old Ponte Dom Pedro II, a narrow and dilapidated bridge where trains and cars must wait their turn, watch your step: loose planks have claimed the life of at least one person in recent years. Apart from the view towards Cachoeira, São Felix has two other attractions: the Casa da Cultura Américo Simas on Rua Celestino João Severino da Luz Neto (open from 8 am to 5 pm, Tuesday to Sunday); and the Centro Cultural Dannemann at Avenida Salvador Pinto, 29 (open from 8 am to 5 pm, Tuesday to Sunday).

The Centro Cultural Dannemann will delight cigar enthusiasts with its displays of old machinery and the techniques used for making *charutos* (cigars). The handmade cigars sold here make good souvenirs or presents.

Festivals

Festa da NS de Boa Morte falls on the Friday closest to 15 August and lasts three days. This is one of the most fascinating Candomblé festivals going – it's worth a special trip to see it. Organised by the Irmandade da Boa Morte (Sisterhood of the Good Death) – a secret, Black, religious society – the festival is celebrated by the descendants of slaves, who praise their liberation with dance and prayer and a mix of themes from Candomblé and Catholicism.

The Festa de São João, celebrated from 22 to 24 June, is the big popular festival of Bahia's interior. It's a great celebration of folklore with music and dancing, plenty of food and drink. Don't miss it if you're in Bahia at the time.

Other festivals include: NS do Rosário (second half of October) with games, music and food; NS da Ajuda (first half of November) which features ritual cleansing of the church and a street festival; and Santa Barbara or Iansã (4 December), a Candomblé ceremony held in São Felix at Fonte de Santa Bárbara (Fountain of Santa Bárbara).

Places to Stay – bottom end

Pensão Tia Rosa (☎ 725-1792) opposite Museu Hansen Bahia has pleasant quartos which cost US$9/10 for a single/double – superb breakfast included in the price. *Massapé* (☎ 725-1392) charges US$8 per person for adequate quartos and the price includes breakfast. *Pousada do Guerreiro* (☎ 725-1203) at Rua 13 de Maio, 14 has ragged but cheap quartos priced at US$10/13 for a single/double.

In São Felix, *Pousada do Paraguaçu* (☎ 725-1550), Avenida Salvador Pinto 1, has apartamentos priced around US$18/20 for a single/double.

Places to Stay – middle

Pousada do Convento de Cachoeira (☎ 725-1716) is a lovely hotel with a courtyard and swimming pool. The dark wood rooms of the old convent now have air-con, frigo bar and hot showers and cost US$24/29 for a single/double – including a major spread for breakfast. An extra bed costs US$7 or you can splurge on the suite for US$32. *Pousada Cabana do Pai Thomáz* (☎ 725-1288), Rua 25 de Junho, 12, has comfortable apartamentos which cost US$25/29 for a single/double. See the carved wooden panels in the restaurant downstairs.

Places to Eat

The *Gruta Azul* (☎ 725-1295), Praça Manoel Vitorino 2, is Cachoeira's best restaurant. The place has character: special recipes for seafood and batidas; a delightful shaded courtyard; and lots of forest birds in an aviary. Try the shrimp dishes for US$4 or

maniçoba, the spicy local dish composed of manioc and various meats. If you're adventurous ask for the *boa morte* (good death) drink. Opening hours are from 11 am to 3 pm and 7 to 9 pm, every day except Sunday when the restaurant is closed in the evening.

Next to the tourist office is the *Rian* restaurant, named after the owner, but locals delight in turning things around and calling it Nair. The menu includes excellent moqueca dishes and local specialities. On Rua 25 de Junho, there's more good food at *Cabana do Pai Thomáz* (the restaurant is part of the pousada) – open daily from 11 am to midnight; and *Massapé* (open daily from 11 am to midnight). In São Felix, you can try the restaurant in the *Pousada do Paraguaçu*, which is open from 11 am to 11 pm.

Entertainment

Check out the beer drinking and forró dancing at the riverside bars. On Wednesday and Saturday, there's an open market on Praça Maciel – a good place to pick up handicrafts and observe local life.

Things to Buy

Cachoeira has a wealth of wood sculptors, some of whom do very fine work and you will see plenty of studios as you walk through town. This is some of the best traditional art still available in Brazil. Two of the best sculptors are Doidão and Loucou, who carve beautiful, heavy pieces.

Getting There & Away

Bus There are frequent departures, between 5.30 am and 7 pm, to Salvador (two hours; US$3). The rodoviária (☎ 725-1214) in Cachoeira also has regular bus services to Maragojipe and Valença.

Train Salvador and Cachoeira are also connected by rail, but service is poor.

Boat After Rio Paraguaçu was blocked by Pedra do Cavalo Barragem (dam), Cachoeira no longer had the waterfalls for which it was named. The river has since silted up, making boat passage up from Maragojipe and Salvador difficult and irregular. Whilst researching this edition we were told in Cachoeira that long-distance boat travel has stopped completely, but you may want to check the latest information with the Vapor do Cachoeira boat service at the Companhia de Navegação Bahiano (Mercado Modelo docks, Salvador). Apparently, during the festival of São João there is an attempt at operating a regular boat service to Salvador.

Getting Around

Cachoeira is just the right size to cover on foot. If you want to cross the river to São Felix by canoe, rather than crossing the bridge on foot, you can hire one at the waterfront.

Around Cachoeira

If you have the use of a car or like long walks, you can visit the Pimantel Cigar Factory, 10 km out of town. Suerdieck is another cigar factory closer to the town.

There are also two old sugar mills near town: Engenho da Cabonha, eight km along the road to Santo Amaro; and Engenho da Guaiba, 12 km along the same road.

IGREJA E CONVENTO DE SANTO ANTÔNIO DO PARAGUAÇU

Construction of this magnificent Franciscan church and convent was started in 1658 and completed in 1686. The convent functioned as a hospital and training centre for novices until 1855, when an imperial decree forbidding the admission of novices put a stop to its activities and the buildings were gradually abandoned. In 1915, the contents of the convent and its walled grounds were sold. Today all that remains of this convent, with its superb position beside the Rio Paraguaçu, is a decaying shell. Although the place is in ruins (some efforts have been made at restoration), a visit is recommended if you enjoy powerful atmosphere and remote, faded glory.

A bus departs daily at noon from Cachoeira for the 44-km trip to the tiny village of São Francisco do Paraguaçu where the convent ruins face the Rio Paraguaçu.

The same bus returns to Cachoeira at 5.30 am the next day. The only lodgings in São Francisco are two pensões – ask for either Ednaide or José. José Gringa, who lives next to the telephone office, has the key to the convent, which is kept locked to prevent theft.

For information about plans to restore the convent, contact Movimento pró Recuperação e Preservação do Convento de Santo Antônio do Paraguaçu (☎ 321-1877), Rua General Labatut 462, apartamento 502, Barris, Salvador.

CANDEIAS

The Museu do Recôncavo (Vanderlei do Pinho) can be visited at the Engenho de Freguesia (sugar mill and plantation). In the restored colonial mansion and senzala (slave quarters) there are displays which graphically depict life on the plantations during the past centuries. The museum is open from 9 am to 3 pm, Tuesday to Sunday. Candeias is about 45 km from Salvador, and the museum is a further seven km outside the town – access is easiest if you have your own transport or take a taxi from Candeias.

SANTO AMARO

Santo Amaro is an old, run-down sugar town that knows no tourism. It's a town with unpretentious charm: if you're going to Cachoeira think about stopping for a few hours, especially if it's a market Saturday, when the town comes to life. If you decide to stay the night, there's often very good local music. The town's two pousadas are on the Praça da Purificação.

In colonial days, Santo Amaro made its fortune from sugar. Today the major industry is paper production at the paper mill along the road to Cachoeira. The mill has spoiled the Rio Subaé and bamboo has replaced sugar cane on the hillsides. Today's reminders of Santo Amaro's sugar legacy are the decrepit pastel mansions of the sugar barons and the many churches. The plantation owners lived on Rua General Câmara, the old commercial street.

Many of the churches have been closed

since a gang of thieves stole most of the holy images and exported them to France. The largest church, Santo Amaro da Purificação, is still open.

The Festa de Santo Amaro (6 to 15 January) is celebrated by the ritual lavagem of the church steps. Santo Amaro is the birthplace of two of Brazil's most popular singers: Caetano Veloso and his sister Maria Betânia. During Carnival, they've been known to put in an appearance between trios elétricos.

Step out to the square across from the church for an evening's promenade. Despite active flirting, the sexes circle separately.

Getting There & Away

There are frequent bus services between Salvador and Santo Amaro (US$2; 70 minutes); and many of these continue the 32 km to Cachoeira/São Felix.

MARAGOJIPE

Circled by Baía de Todos os Santos and rich green fields patched with crops, Maragojipe is a pleasantly decaying tobacco-exporting port – 32 km from Nazaré and 24 km from Cachoeira.

Would-be cowboys tie up their horses and hang out in dockside bars where posters of Jesus and automotive pin-ups vie for wall space. The crumbling plaster facades of the bars look out onto rows of *saveiros* (homemade fishing boats), dugout canoes and mangrove swamps.

Things to See

The Suerdieck & Company Cigar Factory (established 1920) is open for tours from 7 am to 6 pm Monday to Friday, and Saturday mornings. On weekend nights head down to the dockside bars for local music. Swimming off the cement pier is popular.

Strolling through town look out for the wrought-iron grill and sculpted facade of the pale-blue building on Rua D Macedo Costa.

Places to Stay & Eat

The *Oxumaré Hotel* (☎ 726-1104), Rua Heretiano Jorge de Souza 3, has cramped quartos which cost US$4/6 for singles/doubles.

To quench your thirst, visit the suco bar on Largo da Matriz. For a meal, try jumbo shrimp, the local delicacy served in the town's restaurants.

Getting There & Away

Bus Buses from Salvador to Maragojipe go via Santo Amaro and Cachoeira. There are six buses daily, the first at 7.10 am, the last at 6.20 pm. The trip takes three hours and costs US$3. There are no buses via Itaparica. We recommend going by boat.

Boat The boat from Maragojipe to Salvador leaves at 5 am, Monday to Friday. Get there an hour early to purchase your ticket (80c). Boats leave from Salvador to Maragojipe (Monday to Friday at 1 pm) from the Terminal Turístico Marítimo (☎ 242-9411) which is close to Mercado Modelo. Stops are made at São Roque, Barra do Paraguaçu and Enseada and the trip takes three hours.

There are no boats to Cachoeira since the Rio Paraguaçu has silted up but there are frequent buses.

NAZARÉ

Nazaré is an 18th-century city with some colonial buildings and churches and a good market known for its caxixis – small ceramic figures. For a place to stay, try the *Rio Jaguaripe* (☎ 736-1138) which is reasonably priced.

The big festivals are the folkloric NS de Nazaré (24 January to 2 February); and Feira dos Caxixis (Holy Week), which features a large market on Thursday and Good Friday of Holy Week, followed by the holiday of Micareta. For transport between Nazaré and Salvador you can either take the bus or the ferry boat.

North of Salvador

The coastal road north from Salvador is called the Rodovia do Côco (Coconut Highway). The excellent, paved road runs a few km from the ocean as far as the entrance to Praia do Forte, 80 km north of Salvador. There are several access roads along the way that get you down to the coconut beaches, fishing villages and, sadly, new housing developments. After Praia do Forte, a poor dirt road winds its way near the coast for about another 40 km.

Municipal buses go along the coast as far as Itapoã and then turn inland towards the airport. Buses to points further north along the coast – Arembepe, Praia do Forte and beyond – leave from the main rodoviária in Salvador or from Itapoã.

Note that the map entitled Beaches of North Bahia, Sergipe & Alagoas (Sergipe & Alagoas chapter) should be consulted in conjunction with the North of Salvador text.

AREMBEPE
Arembepe was one of Brazil's first hip beaches in the '60s. Mick Jagger and Janis Joplin got the joint rolling and many local and foreign hippies followed. It is no longer a particularly attractive or popular retreat. Exclusive private homes and pollution from the giant Tibras chemical plant have tainted the rocky coast.

We don't recommend Arembepe. If you want to head to the sea for a day from Salvador, there are prettier beaches, and if you're getting out of Salvador there are less spoiled fishing villages along the Bahian littoral.

Places to Stay
If you do end up in Arembepe, you can head for the campground or try *Pousada da Fazenda* (☎ 824-1030) which looks like one of the few holdovers from the hippie days. It has small cabanas and healthy cooking. Lodging costs US$22 a double. *Praias de Arembepe Hotel* (☎ 824-1115), across from

the praça, has more expensive apartamentos which cost around US$25/30 for a single/double.

NORTH TO PRAIA DO FORTE
Guarajuba
A few km south of Praia do Forte, Guarajuba is a beautiful beach accompanied by some tract housing which is clearly the beginning of major development. For places to stay you have a choice between the expensive *Guarajuba Praia* (☎ 874-1055) and the exorbitant *Pousada Canto do Mar* (☎ 874-1272).

Barra do Jacuípe
A more remote spot, Barra do Jacuípe sits at the mouth of a river only one km from the ocean. The beach is quite beautiful and, apart from a campground, there are no tourist facilities.

PRAIA DO FORTE
Praia do Forte has fine beaches, a beautiful castle fortress, a sea-turtle reserve and unfortunately only expensive hotels. Until recently a fishing village, Praia do Forte is being developed as an ecologically minded, upscale beach resort (European tourists, we are told, are now coming directly from Salvador's airport to Praia do Forte). While it's way too early to know how this attempt will fare – scepticism is the only sane attitude – the main result thus far is the absence of cheap accommodation.

Praia do Forte is the seat of one of the original 12 captaincies established by the Portuguese. The huge estate extended inland all the way to the present-day state of Piauí. Desperate to colonise and thereby hold his new land, the King of Portugal set about granting lands to merchants, soldiers and aristocrats. For no apparent reason Garcia d'Ávila, a poor, 12-cow farmer, was granted this huge tract of land.

Garcia chose a prime piece of real estate to build Castelo do Garcia d'Ávila as his home and castle: an aquamarine ocean-view plot studded with palm trees four km up the road from town on Morro Tatuapaçu. Today, the castle is in ruins, completely overgrown with weeds and grasses, but it still made a fine tropical setting for director Márcio Meyrelle's production of *Macbeth* a few years back. The castle is worth a visit.

TAMAR Turtle Reserve

The TAMAR turtle reserve is on the beach right next to the lighthouse and the over-priced Pousada Praia Forte. TAMAR (Tartaruga Marinha) is a jointly funded IBAMA and navy project started in 1982 to protect several species of marine turtles that are, or were, threatened: *tartaruga xibirro, tartaruga de pente, tartaruga mestica do cabeada* and *tartaruga de couro.*

What you see is actually quite modest: several small feeding pools with anywhere from two to several dozen turtles depending on the season. The TAMAR project gathers 30,000 turtle eggs a year along the coast. The eggs – moist, leathery, ping-pong-size balls – are buried in the sand to incubate. When the turtles hatch, they're placed in the feeding pools until big enough to tackle the Atlantic.

TAMAR also has stations at Comboios, Espírito Santo (north of Vitória near Lineares), to protect the leatherback and log-gerhead turtles and on Fernando de Noronha to preserve the green turtle.

Nowadays commerce in endangered turtle species is illegal, but shells are still sold in Salvador's Mercado Modelo, and in Sergipe, turtle eggs are still popular hors d'oeuvres. Of the 60 km of beach under the jurisdiction of the TAMAR project in Bahia, 13 km of coastline are patrolled by the scientists alone; the remainder is protected by a cooperative effort in which fishers – the very same who used to collect the eggs for food – are con-tracted to collect eggs for the scientists.

Places to Stay & Eat

The only cheap place to stay is at the camp-ground, which is just 10 minutes on foot from the beach, has cold-water showers, shady, sandy sites, and washbasins for clothes. One of the cheaper hotels is *João Sol* (☎ 876-1054) on Rua da Corvina. Prices for

most hotels are spiralling upwards. If you have an urge to splurge, the recently revamped *Pousada Praia do Forte* (☎ 835-1410) has bungalows on the beach for US$70 for two. This price also includes three meals. Speaking of appetites: everyone in town seems to be money hungry!

Getting There & Away

The São Luís bus company runs a bus service from Iguatemi Shopping Centre (opposite the rodoviária in Salvador) to Praia do Forte. The trip takes two hours and the service operates daily between 7.30 am and 6 pm. The last bus from Praia do Forte to Salvador leaves at 5 pm. More bus services are planned.

NORTH OF PRAIA DO FORTE

Access to the beaches north of Praia do Forte is still limited, but developers are eyeing the prospect of a continuous coastal road which would open up the beautiful beaches and fishing villages which have, as yet, been left undisturbed. All through this region there are fenced off tracts of land and small real-estate offices selling beachfront property. If the government goes ahead as planned and paves the Rodovia do Côco from Salvador all the way to Maceió, tremendous changes would be set in motion. With good roads, all these beaches would be close enough to major urban areas to become weekend beach resorts.

Subaúma, Porto Suipé & Palame

From Entre Rios there is a 75-km dirt road, curvy and precarious, to the beach town of Subaúma. There is no sign for the turnoff, so you should ask locals for directions. Hitch-ing is possible. From Subaúma, there is access to the tiny beach towns of Porto Suipé and Palame. These are very good, empty beaches but there are no hotels and the surf can be rough and dangerous.

Conde

On the Rio Itapicuru, Conde is about 12 km from the sea. It's the little big-town of the area and the jumping-off point for several beaches, the closest being Sítio. If you want beach there's little reason to stay in Conde – unless you are there on Saturday, when fisherfolk and artisans come to the market to peddle their goods.

Getting There & Away The town has regular bus services to Alagoinhas, Feira de Santana, and Salvador; and local shuttle services to nearby beaches. There's plenty of river traffic on market days which makes it easy to get a ride down the river to the ocean. From there you can hike or possibly hitch a ride on a tractor.

Sítio

From Conde it's a six-km drive to Sítio, which has a decent beach, although it's often windy with choppy surf. From Sítio you can reach more remote beaches by walking along the shore or finding a fishing boat travelling towards Rio Itapicuru.

Places to Stay The cheapest options are the campgrounds. Hotel construction is a booming business in this growing beach resort. One of the less expensive hotels is *Pousada Praia dos Coqueiros* (☎ 429-1152), which has apartamentos starting around US$25 for a double.

Getting There & Away The bus schedule is geared to getting the kids to school: Conde to Sítio 6.50 am, Sítio to Conde 2 pm, Sítio to Barra 9 am, Barra to Sítio 1.30 pm.

Barra de Itariri

Barra is a 14-km drive along a dirt road south from Sítio. There is little traffic, so be prepared for a walk/hitch combination or you can walk the entire route along the stunning beach. The road is never more than a few hundred metres from the sea, which is hidden behind a running dune spotted with coconut trees. The small village of Barra is a magic place. The beach is deserted except on weekends and the seas are choppy.

Places to Stay & Eat Barra has one lone restaurant overlooking the river. There are no pousadas, but some of the locals rent rooms (ask for Duda or Dona Nequinha) and there are some houses for rent on a long-term basis.

Getting There & Away The bus leaves Barra for Alagoinhas at 1.20 pm and returns from Alagoinhas at 6 pm, passing through Conde and Sítio.

Mangue Seco

Mangue Seco is a remote and tiny town on the northern border of Bahia, at the tip of a peninsula formed by the Rio Real. The town's main attraction is its expansive beach, but the surf is often rough.

Places to Stay & Eat If you want to camp, try *Camping Praias de Mangue Seco*. Other facilities in Mangue Seco include a couple of pousadas, a bar and a restaurant.

Getting There & Away Mangue Seco and Praia da Costa Azul can be reached via Jandaira (close to BR-101) along a very poor road, sometimes impassable after heavy rain, which weaves for 65 km until it reaches Mangue Seco. There is no bus service on this road.

You can also reach Mangue Seco by sea from Saco, a small town at the southern end of the coast of Sergipe state. To reach Saco, travel to Estância on the BR-101 in Sergipe. For more information, see the Sergipe & Alagoas chapter. From Estância there is a decent 28-km road to the coast and Praia do Abaís. Saco is another 23 km further south on a rough dirt road.

There are buses from Estância to Saco on Sundays and Mondays, but the timetable is rather flexible and you should check this information before making travel plans. From Saco you can catch a small boat to Mangue Seco. Reportedly, you can also reach Mangue Seco by boat from the towns of Pontal and Crasto in Sergipe.

Saco

Saco, actually across the border in the state of Sergipe, gets weekenders from Estância, but is quiet during the week. It's a fine beach with good swimming. There is no accommodation, but bars and restaurant open on weekends.

Abaís

This is another weekend spot, but with a pousada. The beach, however, is not as good as the others in the area.

South of Salvador

VALENÇA

For most travellers, Valença is simply a stepping stone to the beaches of Morro de São Paulo, but it's also a small, friendly city worth a visit en route.

After routing the local Tupininquin Indians, the Portuguese settled here along the Rio Una in the 1560s, but were in turn expelled by the Aimores tribes. In 1799 the Portuguese returned to resettle and found Vila de Nova Valença do Santíssimo Coração de Jesus.

Today everything centres around the busy port and large market beside the Rio Una, where there are buses and boats, historic buildings, food and lodging. The town's population includes an interesting assortment of shipbuilders, vaqueiros (cowboys), textile manufacturers, peasants, artisans and fisherfolk. It's a lively scene, well worth exploring.

Information

To obtain maps and information, visit the tourist office (☎ 741-1311) on Travessa General Labatut. It's open from 8 am to noon and 2 to 5 pm, Monday to Friday; and from 8 am to noon on Saturday. If you want to change money, Banco do Brasil and Banco Econômico are both on Rua Governador Gonçalves. There's a Vatur office on Rua Comendador Madureira.

Around Town

In the centre of town wander around the port, the central plaza and the market. At the far end of the port, the timbered ribbing of boat hulls resembles dinosaur skeletons. Some of the saveiros (wooden sail boats) are built for export to Uruguay and Paraguay. The remaining ones are used by the local fisherfolk, who pull out of port early in the morning and return by mid-afternoon with the catch of the day.

The smell of sap and sawdust, old fish and sea salt mingles with the wonderful smell of nutmeg. Picked from nearby groves of nutmeg trees, the cloves are set on a cloth and left to dry in the sun.

The cattle ranching a bit further upstream and downwind has its own peculiar aroma. Vaqueiros sporting leather caps with braided chin straps straddle their horses and guide the doomed cattle to market. Once in a while a loose bull goes charging through town.

For a good trek follow the left bank of the Rio Una upstream towards the Igreja NS de Amparo – the church up on the hill. At the base of the hill there's a trail straight up to the church which commands a beautiful view.

Cotton Factory

Back down the hill there's a large, white fortress-like building that houses a textile factory. Personal tours of the factory show the entire hot, noisy, smelly transformation of raw cotton into finished fabrics. This factory is typical of the old Brazilian economy – still prevalent in the Northeast – with its use of antiquated US machinery and cheap Brazilian labour. It's a good tour for those interested in economic development.

The factory is open for visits on Saturdays from 9 am to 5 pm and you may be able to arrange a tour on other days. Authorisation is provided at the colonial building which stands to the left of the factory front.

Festivals

In addition to the traditional festivals of Bahia, Valença also celebrates holidays peculiar to the area. Sagrado Coração de Jesus is a mass held for the patron of the city sometime in June or July. The festival in honour of the patron saint of workers, NS do Amparo, is celebrated on 8 November.

Boi Estrela is a folklore festival where men and women dressed as cowhands accompany Catarina the Baiana while they play tambourines and chant. Zabiapunga, another folklore fest, features musical groups playing weird instruments and running through the city streets on New Year's Eve.

There's a good Carnival, with trios elétricos and the Carnival-like Micareta festival held 15 days after Lent. Other festivals include Festa de Reis (6 January), São João (23 June), NS do Rosário (24 September to 3 October), São Benedito on Cairu Island (26 December to 6 January) and Iemanjá (31 December and 1 January).

Places to Stay & Eat

Hotel Valença (☎ 741-1807) at Rua Dr Heitor Guedes Melo, 15 has apartamentos for US$12/13 for singles/doubles. *Hotel Guaibim* (☎ 741-1110), Praça da Independência, 74 is one block in from the port. Apartamentos cost US$17/19 for singles/doubles – cheaper rooms are available without air-con or fridge.

Hotel Rio Una (☎ 711-1614) on Rua Maestro Barrinhão on the riverside has more comforts and is accordingly more expensive – apartamentos start around US$35/37 for singles/doubles.

There are plenty of typical lanchonetes in Valença. The *Recanto do Luís* in Cajaíba is recommended for seafood. *Restaurant Akuárius* is in the same building as the Hotel Guaibim, and the Hotel Rio Una has its own restaurant, the *Panorama*.

Getting There & Away

Air There is a small airport just outside town which is serviced by Nordeste.

Bus The rodoviária (☎ 741-1280) is on Rua Maçônica, next to the port. There's a frequent bus service operating daily to Salvador (five hours; US$7). Some buses go via Itaparica Island (190 km) and drop you off at Bom Despacho for the 45-minute ferry ride to Salvador; others go all the way around Baía de Todos os Santos (290 km) into Salvador.

Boat There are daily boat trips to Morro de São Paulo and Gamboa on Ilha de Tinharé, the large island facing Valença. Although Salvador is only 110 km away by sea, the boat service is irregular.

Around Valença

The best mainland beach in the vicinity is 16 km north of town at Guaibim, which is rapidly developing into a popular resort. There are local buses and the beach gets packed at weekends. *Pousada São Paulo* and *Santa Maria Praia*, both on Avenida Beira-Mar, have apartamentos around US$12/14 for singles/doubles.

The islands of Boipeba and Cairu have colonial buildings and churches, but their beaches don't compare with Morro de São Paulo.

VALENÇA TO ILHÉUS
Morro de São Paulo

What Porto Seguro must have been 15 years ago, Morro de São Paulo is today: a tranquil, isolated fishing village with incredible beaches, recently discovered by hip Brazilians and international travellers. Unfortunately, the secret is out. Morro is on everyone's lips and has even made it onto the best beach lists of several Brazilian magazines.

At the northern tip of Ilha de Tinharé, Morro de São Paulo has grass streets where only mules, beach bums and horses tread – no cars and few facilities for tourists. The waters around the island are very clear, ideal for scuba diving and the underwater hunt for lobster, squid and fish. The settlement is comprised of three hills – Morro de Mangaba, Morro de Galeão and Morro de Farol. Climb up from the harbour through the 17th-century fortress gate and up to the lighthouse (1835). From the top you can see over the island and its beaches. The west side of the island – the river or Gamboa side – is bordered by mangroves; the eastern side is sandy.

There are three beaches in Morro de São Paulo: the rather dirty village beach, the barraca and camping beach, and the fazenda beach. These three are merely preludes to the long lovely stretch of sand graced by tall swaying palms which borders the eastern half of the island.

Beware: there are many bichos de pé, little critters that burrow into human feet – so keep something on your feet when walking through town.

Places to Stay & Eat The food and lodging scene is changing quickly and accommodation can be scarce during the summer. Apart from a couple of campgrounds on the beaches, there are nearly 40 pousadas, or you could ask about renting a house from one of the local fishers. *Pousada da Praia* on Rua da Graça has inexpensive apartamentos.

The *Restaurante-Pousada Gaucho* charges US$5 per room which can sleep three people. They also rent two-room houses for US$12 per day. *Pousada da Praia* has quartos starting at around US$12/15 for a single/double; and *Ilha da Saúde Pousada-Restaurant* (☎ 741-1702 in Valença for reservations) has attractive single/double apartamentos for US$30/34. The restaurant serves a tasty shrimp prato feito excruciatingly slowly. *Naturalmente* serves a prato feito for US$3.

Getting There & Away Take the 'Brisa Biônica' (Bionic Breeze) or 'Brisa Triônica' between Morro de São Paulo and Valença for a relaxed 1½-hour boat ride (US$1.50). You'll pass mangroves, yachts, double-masted square-rigged Brazilian 'junks', and coconut palm-lined beaches that rival the Caribbean and South Pacific in beauty.

During the summer the schedule is as follows: Monday to Saturday, two boats per day go from Valença at 8 am and noon to Morro de São Paulo and return at 6 am and 12.20 pm. On Sundays they leave Valença at 6 am and 12.20 pm and leave Morro de São Paulo at 8 am and noon. Still, we recommend you check the times carefully; the increasing popularity of Morro de São Paulo will undoubtedly cause frequent schedule changes.

The rest of the year there is only one boat per day in either direction. It leaves Monday to Saturday at 6 am from Morro de São Paulo to Valença and returns at 12.30 pm. On Sundays there is a 6 am boat from Valença to Morro de São Paulo which returns at 12.30 pm. If you're coming from Salvador you can confirm these times at Bahiatursa.

Try a combination of *bolo* and *mingau* for breakfast when the boat stops at the Gamboa pier. Bolo is cake and mingau is a warm, white, sweet, gummy manioc-brew spiced with nutmeg cloves.

Camamu

On the mainland, further down the coast towards Ilhéus, Camamu sits on a hill behind a labyrinth of mangrove-filled islets and narrow channels (no beaches). The town is the port of call for the many tiny fishing villages in the region. There's a lively dockside morning market with fish, fruit and drying nutmeg.

Saveiro fishing boats are built and repaired right outside the port. The Açaraí waterfalls are five km away by bus or taxi and are worth a visit.

Places to Stay *Rio Açaraí* (☎ 255-2312) has simple apartamentos at US$12/14 for a single/double.

Getting There & Away Buses depart for Valença and Ubaitaba every hour or so.

Ponta do Mutá

If you want to get off the beaten path, this is the place. The peninsula that goes out to Ponta do Mutá has one long dirt road, no hotels, infrequent buses and a handful of very small fishing villages (you won't find any of them on a map). It's a completely unspoilt area but the beaches are hard to get to without a car.

Beer is sold in the villages, but little else, so you might have to work at finding food and lodging. At Barra Grande, on the tip of the peninsula, is *Ponta da Mutá*, a small hotel with quartos starting at around US$10/12 for singles/doubles and more expensive apartamentos. Several of the villages have small, early morning boats that take the locals to market across the bay to Camamu. This is a delicious two-hour voyage and it eliminates a heap of time backtracking on the peninsula.

Itacaré

Itacaré is a quiet colonial town at the mouth of the Rio de Contas. If movie moghuls could find the town they'd probably snap it up as a set to film *A Hundred Years of Solitude*. Distance and bad roads have shielded Itacaré from tourism (it's a two-hotel town). Ribeira beach is recommended for a swim. Be warned that there is no road along the coast, so you must return the way you came – unless you hike or hitch a ride on a fishing boat.

There is one blemish on this tropical hideaway, courtesy of Petrobras (the government oil company), which deposits little coin-sized spots of oil on many parts of the beach. To get to the beaches north of Itacaré, cross the river by long dugout canoe. This odd yet tranquil scene – mangrove trees lining the riverbanks and Petrobras choppers thrashing overhead – looks like the opening of *Apocalypse Now*, just before the jungle goes up in napalm flames.

In Itacaré you can also rent a canoe to visit O Pontal, a beautiful promontory just south of the bay. It's best to leave your camera behind as the canoes are unstable. The *Hotel-Restaurant Iemanjá* has quartos at US$7/8 for a single/double – with breakfast; or try the *Pousada Litoral*, close to the bus stop, which has more expensive apartamentos.

Getting There & Away There is no coastal road southwards from Itacaré, so you must return to the main highway inland, unless you sail or walk along the coast. Buses depart for Ilhéus at 6 am and 4 pm; for Ubaitaba at 9 am (for connections north); and for Itabuna at 5.30 am and 2 pm (via Ubaitaba).

On the map it appears possible to walk along the shore to the next town north, thereby eliminating a lot of backtracking. After getting several opinions, all conflicting, on the feasibility of this idea we decided to try it.

It is a long walk, around 20 km, and you have to cut inland at one point to reach the next road. It's only recommended if you want to camp out and explore some fantastic super-isolated stretches of beach.

Itacaré to Ilhéus

It's a four-hour trip by bus from Itacaré to Ilhéus. The journey is slow but stunning, one of our favourites in Brazil. The bus passes the occasional cacao plantation, stopping every few km to pick up another couple of locals whose features are an intriguing blend of Black, Indian and White.

For the first two hours the bus travels at a snail's pace from Itacaré to Uruçuca along a bad dirt road. Uruçuca is a tiny, secluded village surrounded by lush valleys of cacao trees – worth exploring if you have the time. Check what time the next bus is due, otherwise you could find yourself stuck here with nowhere to stay.

From here the road heads down through groves of cacao, coconut and enormous bamboo, to reach the coast shortly before Ilhéus.

ILHÉUS

Ilhéus, the town that Jorge Amado (Brazil's best known novelist) lived in and described with his novel *Gabriela, Cravo e Canela (Gabriela, Clove and Cinnamon)*, retains some of the charm and lunacy that Amado fans know well. There's a half-hearted attempt to portray the city as an up-and-coming tourist mecca, but nobody believes it will happen, and Ilhéus remains largely unaffected by tourism. The colonial centre is small and distinctive with its strange layout and odd buildings; the people are affable; the city beaches are broad and beautiful; and a short walk beyond these there are even better beaches.

The best thing to do in Ilhéus is just

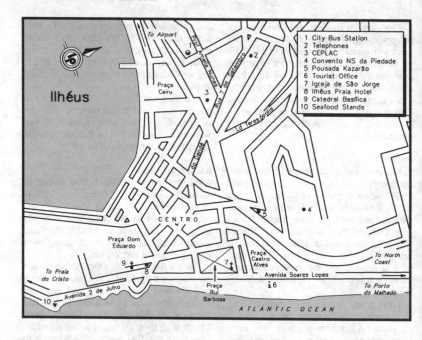

Ilhéus

1	City Bus Station
2	Telephones
3	CEPLAC
4	Convento NS da Piedade
5	Pousada Kazarão
6	Tourist Office
7	Igreja de São Jorge
8	Ilhéus Praia Hotel
9	Catedral Basílica
10	Seafood Stands

wander. The centre is lively, with several old, gargoyled buildings such as the Prefeitura. If you walk up the hill to the Convento NS da Piedade there's a good view of the city and littoral. Wherever you end up, it won't be more than a stone's throw from the beach. The Praia da Avenida (beach), close to the city centre, is always active, but has reportedly been polluted by the port.

History

Ilhéus was a sleepy town until cacao was introduced into the region from Belém in 1881. At the time, Brazil's many uncompetitive sugar estates, which had not followed the lead of other countries and introduced new production techniques to increase sugar output, were reeling from a drop in world sugar prices. Simultaneously, the slave system was finally coming to an end, with many slaves escaping and others being freed. With the sugar plantations in the doldrums,

impoverished agricultural workers from the Northeast – Black and White – flocked to the hills surrounding Ilhéus to farm the new boom crop: cacao, the *ouro branco* (white gold) of Brazil.

Sudden, lawless and violent, the scramble for the white cacao fruit displayed all the characteristics of a gold rush. When the dust settled, the land and power belonged to a few ruthless *coroneis* (rural landowners) and their hired guns. The landless were left to work, and usually live, on the fazendas, where they were subjected to a harsh and paternalistic labour system. This history is graphically told by Amado, who grew up on a cacao plantation, in his book *Terras do Sem Fim* (published in English as *The Violent Land*).

Cacao still rules in Ilhéus. The lush tropical hills are covered with the large, pod-shaped fruit that dangles from skinny trees, and if you take a drive you will still see the cacao fazendas and rural workers who

Autosuggestion
The basílica, the city's most important building, is an enormous edifice with a striking facade and a grand entrance. After climbing its many steps and passing through the massive doors, I entered the church's spacious interior where I was suddenly confronted by the bizarre sight of a sporty, bright-red, Ford Escort parked before the pews. The temporary use of the city's most famous House of the Lord to shelter an automobile was, it turned out, prompted by a raffle to fund a badly needed church restoration! ∎

look like they came right out of Amado's book. You can also visit the small Regional Museu do Cacao, the port, and, with a bit of effort and luck, a fazenda.

Information & Orientation
The city is sandwiched between hills, beach and a small harbour at the mouth of the Rio Cachoeira. The airport and the road to the Olivença beaches are in the southern part of town, beyond the circular harbour.

Tourist Office Tourist information and basic maps are provided by Ilhéustur (☎ 231-1861) on Praça Castro Alves.

Money Banco do Brasil is at Marques de Paranágua 112.

Travel Agency A reader recommended Grou Viagem (☎ 231-8741, 231-7883) for its reasonable prices and flexible attitude to planning. Trips to Rio Almada and Rio Santana are worthwhile – see descriptions in the Around Ilhéus section. However, don't bother with the trips to fazendas which are offered during the São João festival in June.

Churches
The Igreja de São Jorge (1534) is the city's oldest church and houses a small sacred art museum. It's on Praça Rui Barbosa, open Tuesday through Sunday 8 to 11 am and 2 to 5.30 pm. The Catedral de São Sebastião (Basílica) is on Praça Dom Eduardo.

Museu Regional do Cacao
The Museu Regional do Cacao displays cacao artefacts and modern painting by local artists. It's at Rua A L Lemos 126 and is open

Tuesday to Friday from 2 to 6 pm, Saturday and Sunday from 3 to 6 pm. During the holiday season, from December to March, it's also open from 9 am to noon.

Festivals
As any knowledgeable Jorge Amado fan would guess, Ilhéus has highly spirited festivals. The best are: the Gincana da Pesca in early January; Festa de São Sebastião (much samba and capoeira) from 11 to 20 January; Festa de São Jorge (featuring Candomblé) on 23 April; Festa das Águas (Candomblé) in December; and, of course, Carnival with its full complement of trios elétricos.

Places to Stay – bottom end
For campgrounds, see Places to Stay in Olivença. There is an undersupply of accommodation in Ilhéus; consequently hotels are generally overpriced and filled with guests. Most are within a 15-minute walk from the central bus station.

Pousada Kazarão (☎ 231-5031) at Praça Coronel Pessoa 38 has the nicest quartos in town for US$9/12 for a single/double – without breakfast. *Lukas* (☎ 231-3772), Rua 7 de Setembro, 177, offers adequate apartamentos for around US$15/16 for singles/doubles; as does *Britânia* (☎ 231-1722), Rua 28 Junho, 16, which is in a similar price range. *Pousada do Sol* (☎ 231-7000), just south of the airport, is very pleasant and reasonably priced.

Places to Stay – top end
The rather dingy *Ilhéus Praia Hotel* (☎ 231-2533) has apartamentos starting at around US$35/38 for singles/doubles. It's right across from the Catedral Basílica and the

Praia Ilhéus

beach on the Praça Dom Eduardo. Close to the airport, *Hotel Jardim Atlântico* (☎ 231-4541) is excellent but very expensive.

For a total splurge, there's *Transamérica Ilha de Comandatuba* (☎ 212-1122) which is on its own island (Ilha de Comandatuba) opposite the town of Una, 70 km south of Ilhéus. For US$155 per person (including meals) per day, you have the run of immense grounds, private beach, and every imaginable recreational facility.

Places to Eat

Behind the Catedral Basílica, along the beach, there are several reasonably priced seafood stands with outdoor tables. The centre is filled with cheap restaurants offering prato feito for a couple of dollars. The tiny, but mighty *Asa Branca*, with a wide array of natural juices and cheap sandwiches, is at Rua Pedro II, 110.

For good seafood, averaging US$4 for a main dish, try *Os Velhos Marinheiros* (open daily from 11 am to midnight) at Avenida 2 de Julho; and *O Céu é o Límite* (open daily from 11 am to 11 pm) four km west of town,

on Avenida Itabuna. *Bar Vezúvio* on Praça Dom Eduardo has been described in Amado's works and is consequently a popular hangout for tourists. For Swiss and Bahian food, try *Ô-lá-lá* at Avenida 2 de Julho, 785; for Japanese food you should head for *Tokyo* on the same street at No 1039.

Getting There & Away

Air There is a small airport which is serviced by Nordeste, VASP, Varig/Cruzeiro and air-taxis. You can fly to several major cities including Rio, Salvador, Recife and Belém. If you're returning to Rio, the flight stops at Salvador but is still cheaper than flying directly from Salvador.

Bus Ilhéus is about 460 km south of Salvador and 315 km north of Porto Seguro. From highway BR-101 at Itabuna, it's a beautiful 30-km descent passing through cacao plantations to Ilhéus and the sea. For most major destinations, buses leave more frequently from Itabuna than Ilhéus, so it's usually quicker to go to Itabuna first, then shuttle down to Ilhéus.

The rodoviária (☎ 231-4221) in Ilhéus is a 15-minute bus ride from the centre. Buses to Salvador use two different approach routes. The regular route follows the long sweep around the recôncavo and is recommended if you want to stop at Cachoeira on the way to Salvador. The other route runs via Nazaré and Itaparica Island, where you change to the ferry for a stunning 45-minute ferry ride into Salvador.

Ilhéus has several buses daily to Salvador, including one at 5.55 pm via the ferry (seven hours, US$10), two a day to Valença (four hours, US$4), three daily to Porto Seguro (4½ hours, US$6) and buses to Itacaré at 7 am and 4 pm (four hours, US$4).

Getting Around
To/From the Airport The airport (☎ 231-4900) is at Praia do Pontal, four km from the centre.

Bus The city bus station is on Praça Cairu on the edge of the centre. From here there are bus services to Olivença, the rodoviária and the airport.

AROUND ILHÉUS
Centro de Pesquisa do Cacao (CEPLAC)
You don't have to be a chocaholic to enjoy CEPLAC's model cacao plantation and research station at Itabuna. CEPLAC (☎ 214-3014), the government cacao agency, gives tours of the facility demonstrating the cultivation and processing of the fruit. Opening hours are from 8.30 to 11.30 am and 2.30 to 3.30 pm, Monday to Friday.

If you're in Ilhéus you can confirm these times in advance at CEPLAC's office, which is in the large building near the city bus station. Buses for Itabuna leave every 30 minutes from the rodoviária in Ilhéus. Ask the bus driver to let you off at CEPLAC, eight km before Itabuna.

Olivença
There are good clean beaches, many with barracas, all the way to Olivença, a small spa town 20 km south of Ilhéus. You can also continue south of Olivença to yet more remote beaches, but after a few km the coastal road turns inland. Beaches are busy on weekends and there's supposed to be some good surfing.

Places to Stay For campgrounds en route to Olivença, you can try *Camping Colónia da Stac* (☎ 231-7015) 13 km from Ilhéus; or *Camping Estância da Fonte* (☎ 212-2105) 18 km from Ilhéus. In Olivença proper there's *Pousada Olivença* (☎ 269-1107) at Praça Claudio Magalhães which offers apartamentos starting at around US$25/28 for singles/doubles; and the more expensive *Pousada Vila do Mar* (☎ 269-1136) at Rua Lúcio Soub, 5.

Getting There & Away To get there take the bus marked 'Olivença' from the central bus station in Ilhéus. The service is frequent and costs a few cents. The bus travels close to the beaches so you can pick one to your liking and quickly hop off.

Rio Almada & Rio Santana
A reader writes the following:

Rio Almada & Lagoa Encantada A drive along dirt tracks linking up the isolated communities north of Ilhéus took us to the settlement of Sambaituba where the emerald blue of the tidal reaches of the Rio Almada changes to a dark black, caused by the mangrove swamps on its fringes.

From here a boat took us upstream past isolated riverine hamlets, whose inhabitants engage in subsistence farming and fishing. Our guide informed us that life is impoverished and often violent. One settlement had been entirely wiped out by Federal Police following the discovery of a small marijuana plantation. Transport is entirely water-borne and consists largely of dugout canoes and rafts to ferry cattle.

Some 90 minutes from Sambaituba we emerged in Lagoa Itaipe, a large lagoon. A narrow channel took us to a pool at the foot of two waterfalls – a spot which tour operators have christened 'Lagoa Encantada'. One fall runs over a bed of curious porous rock which is indented with deep holes. Swimming is very refreshing, and it is possible to surface in a natural cave inside the waterfall. This trip is also a must for any bird enthusiast. However, the main attraction is to step back two centuries and leave the modern world behind. We saw the scar of a road leading to a fazenda on the banks of Lagoa Itaipe, but the one village on its shores has the water as its sole line of communication.

Rio Santana & Engenho This is a shorter trip into the past which can be made by local fishing boat from one of the jetties on the banks of Rio Cachoeira. The transition from the 20th century was accentuated for us by the Varig airliner which passed feet above us on its approach to the airport. Round the next bend we were back in the mangrove fishing communities, with dugout canoes taking old ladies to shop in Ilhéus.

Engenho lies at the head of the navigable part of the river, at the foot of shallow falls. The Jesuits founded the village, building the small church which is the third oldest in Brazil. A huge cauldron in the square was used by them to brew cachaça. There are at least half a dozen bars in the small village. Pitu, a delicious freshwater shrimp, can be bought at the one small shop. Behind the wattle-and-daub buildings lies jungle, full of colourful birds.

During the river trip several bare hillsides were seen, where the jungle has been cleared for cattle. Our guides told us that the destruction of the forest upstream, resulting in reduced waterflow and increased detritus from leeching of the soil, has helped to build up the bar which has closed Rio Cachoeira to all but small craft.

Commander M K Barritt (Royal Navy, UK)

Reserva Biológica Mico Leão de Una

This small (50 sq km) biological reserve was designed to protect the *mico leão* (lion monkey) in its natural habitat of coastal forest and attempt to save the species from extinction – less than 100 remain in this reserve. It's not a park and it does not cater to visitors. A reader recently wrote to say that Dr Saturnino Neto Souza, the director of the reserve, has been facing tourist pressure and consequent hostility from farmers and bureaucrats who are hostile to his conservation aims. At present, visits are discouraged.

If you are keen to visit, we suggest you make contact in advance with Dr Saturnino, either by phoning him at home in Una (☎ 236-2166 from 7 to 8 am or after 5.30 pm) or by writing to him at the following address: Rebio de Una, U5690, Una, Bahia.

The monkeys (*Leontopithecus rosalia chrysomelas*) have the look and proud gaze of miniature lions: a blazing yellow, orange and brown striped coat, a Tina Turner mane and a long, scruffy tail. The mico leões are hard to spot in the wild, but behind the biologist's quarters there is one monkey in captivity and one monkey-boarder who comes in from the forest every evening for milk, cheese, bananas and some shut-eye. If you're lucky you will also see tatu (armadillo), paca (agouti), capybara and veado (deer) which are also native to the area.

Getting There & Away Getting to the beasts is a bit difficult without a car. Take the bus marked 'Canaveiras' from the rodoviária in Ilhéus and travel 35 km south of Olivença along the coastal highway until an IBAMA sign marks the turnoff to the reserve.

From here you have to hitch, which is difficult, or hike. Follow the turnoff for five km on a pitted dirt track over the Rio Mariu and past a fazenda. Turn right at the marker; the working station is three km further within the park.

PORTO SEGURO

Porto Seguro, once a settlement of pioneers, is now a refuge for swarms of Brazilian and international tourists who come to party and take in some mesmerising beaches: tourism is the number one industry in Porto Seguro. At last count this small city had nearly 100 hotels and pousadas. Other regional industries are lumber, fishing, beans, sugar cane, manioc and livestock.

History

After sighting land off Monte Pascoal in April 1500, Cabral and his men sailed three days up the coast to find a safe port. The Portuguese landed not at Porto Seguro (literally Safe Port), but 16 km further north at Coroa Vermelha. The sailors celebrated their first mass in the New Land, stocked up on wood and fresh water and set sail after only 10 days on shore. Three years later the Gonçalvo Coelho expedition arrived and planted a marker in what is now Porto Seguro's Cidade Alta. Jesuits on the same expedition built a church in Outeiro da Glória, to minister to the early colonists and convert the Tupiniquin Indians. The church is now in ruins. In 1526, a naval outpost was built in Cidade Alta (Upper Town) and once

Top: Shanty town on the outskirts of Salvador, Bahia (JM)
Left: Catburger sign, north-east of Ilhéus, Bahia (MS)
Right: Beach scene, Bahia (JM)

Top: A coastal village, Maceió, Alagoas (JM)
Left: Fishermen in Alagoas (JM)

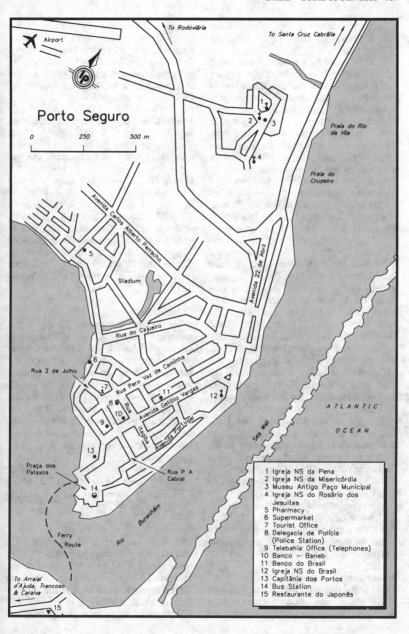

Porto Seguro

0   250   500 m

To Rodoviária
To Santa Cruz Cabrália

Airport

Praia do Rio da Vila

Praia do Cruzeiro

Avenida Carlos Alberto Parracho

Stadium

Avenida 22 de Abril

Rua do Cajueiro

Rua 2 de Julho

Rua Pero Vaz de Caminha

Avenida Getúlio Vargas

Rua Itagiba

Avenida Portugal

ATLANTIC

OCEAN

Sea Wall

Praça dos Pataxós

Rua P A Cabral

Ferry Route

Rio Buranhém

To Arraial d'Ajuda, Trancoso & Caraíva

1   Igreja NS da Pena
2   Igreja NS da Misericórdia
3   Museu Antigo Paço Municipal
4   Igreja NS do Rosário dos Jesuítas
5   Pharmacy
6   Supermarket
7   Tourist Office
8   Delegacia de Polícia (Police Station)
9   Telebahia Office (Telephones)
10 Banco – Baneb
11 Banco do Brasil
12 Igreja NS do Brasil
13 Capitânia dos Portos
14 Bus Station
15 Restaurante do Japonês

again the men from the Companhia de Jesus built a chapel and convent, the Igreja da Misericórdia.

In 1534, when the colonies were divided into hereditary captaincies, Porto Seguro was given to Pero de Campos Tourinhos. In the following year Tourinhos founded a village at the falls of the Rio Buranhém, Porto Seguro, and seven other villages each with a church. Despite the churches, Tourinhos was denounced to the Holy Inquisition as an atheist – apparently the captain didn't keep the holidays and, worse, he forced the colonists to work on Sundays, a blasphemy against God (and an abuse of cheap labour). Tourinhos was imprisoned, shipped off to Portugal and the Inquisition. His son Fernando inherited the captaincy.

Information recently unearthed at the Federal University of Bahia has revised some ideas about the history of the Indians during the colonial period. The Tupininquin, not the Pataxó, were the indigenous tribe when the Portuguese landed. They were rapidly conquered and enslaved by the colonists but the Aimoré, Pataxó, Cataxó and other inland tribes resisted Portuguese colonisation and constantly threatened Porto Seguro. Military outposts along the coast in Belmonte, Vila Viçosa, Prado and Alcobaça were built to defend the Portuguese from European attacks by sea and Indian attacks by land.

The Indians still managed to take Porto Seguro on two occasions, and according to documents sent by colonial judges to the Portuguese crown, attacks reduced Porto Seguro to rubble in 1612 (thus undermining Porto Seguro's claims to 16th-century buildings).

It is now believed that the Jesuit College in Cidade Alta was rebuilt after 1620. In 1759, the captaincy of Porto Seguro passed on to the crown and was incorporated into the province of Bahia.

Information & Orientation

Porto Seguro is connected by an asphalt road to BR-101 at Eunápolis, a little over 660 km south-west of Salvador. The town itself has no beaches, but it's the largest town in the area with the most facilities for tourists – there are plenty of perfect beaches nearby. Porto Seguro's coastline is protected by reefs; the ocean is clear, shallow, and as calm as a meeting of the Native Daughters of California. Swimming is safe.

Tourist Office Bahiatursa (☎ 288-2126) has an office in the Casa da Lenha on Praça Visconde de Porto. It's open from Monday to Saturday from 8 am to noon and 2 to 6 pm.

Money Banco do Brasil is on Avenida Getúlio Vargas.

Travel Agencies To arrange city tours or schooner trips to Trancoso, Coroa Alta or Monte Pascoal, contact BPS Agência de Viagem (☎ 288-2335) in BPS Shopping Centre; or Descobrimento Turísticos (☎ 288-2004), at Avenida Getúlio Vargas 330.

Cidade Alta

If not the first, then among the first settlements in Brazil, Cidade Alta is marked with a stone placed in 1503 by Gonçalvo Coelho. Walk north along the beach road about one km. Once you've arrived at the loop, don't follow the sign that points left to the historic city unless you're driving, but take the dirt road up the hill. The attractions of this part of the city include superb views of the beaches and the opportunity to see very old buildings such as Igreja NS da Misericórdia (perhaps the oldest church in Brazil), Museu Antigo Paço Municipal (1772, small museum), Igreja NS da Pena (1535, rebuilt 1773), Igreja NS do Rosário dos Jesuitas (1549) and the old fort (1503).

Reserva Biológica do Pau Brasil

This 10-sq-km reserve, 15 km from town, was set aside principally to preserve the pau brasil (brazil wood tree), which was almost completely wiped out along the littoral during the early years of colonisation. For details about visiting this reserve ask Bahiatursa or one of the travel agencies.

Festivals

Porto Seguro's Carnival is acquiring a reputation throughout Brazil as a hell of a party, though it is not at all traditional. Locals fondly remember the Carnival in 1984 when the theme was the Adam and Eve story. Costumes were pretty skimpy at first, then everyone stripped off as if on cue. The police were called in the following year.

Many of Brazil's favourite musicians have beach homes nearby and they often perform during Carnival. The Sunday before Carnival a beauty pageant is held at the Praia Hotel.

Municipal holidays celebrated include:

3 January until February
> Bumba meu boi is celebrated in the streets of the city with a musical parade (for details about this special event, see the section on São Luís in the Maranhão chapter).

5 to 6 January
> Terno de Reis is celebrated in the streets and at the churches. Women and children carrying lanterns and pandeiros (tambourines) sing *O Reis* and worship the Reis Magos (Three Wise Men).

20 January
> Puxada de Mastro festival features a group of men who parade a *mastro* (symbolic figure) to the door of Igreja NS da Penha. Decorated with flowers, the mastro is hung in front of the church with the flag and image of São Sebastião and women then sing to the saint.

19 to 22 April
> The 'discovery' of Brazil is commemorated with an outdoor mass and Indian celebrations. This seems a rather baffling celebration since the Indians were here first, and later fared badly at the hands of their 'discoverers'.

15 August
> Festa de NS d'Ajuda is the culmination of a pilgrimage starting on 9 April. A mass procession, organised in homage to the miraculous saint, is followed by food, drink and live music.

8 September
> Festa de NS da Pena is the same as Festa de NS d'Ajuda except for the additional enlivenment of fireworks.

25 to 27 December
> Festa de São Benedito is held on 27 December at the door of the church of NS do Rosário. Boys and girls from Cidade Alta blacken their faces and perform African dances, such as *congo da alma*, *ole* or *lalá*, to the music of drums, *cuíca atabaque* and *xeque-xeque*.

31 December
> On New Year's Eve everyone rushes around shouting 'Feliz ano novo Baiana!', strangers kiss and serious partying ensues.

Places to Stay

Accommodation in Porto Seguro is fancier and there is more of it than further south at Arraial d'Ajuda. During the low season there must be at least 20 vacant rooms per tourist, so bargain. On the other hand, in the high season (December to February) accommodation can be very tight. But fortunately, Porto Seguro has over a dozen hotels and more than 60 pousadas.

For campgrounds, you can try *Mundaí Praia* (☎ 288-2287) or *Camping da Gringa* (☎ 288-2076), both outside town on the road north to Santa Cruz da Cabrália; or take the road south towards Arraial d'Ajuda where there are more spots to camp.

Many of the middle-range pousadas are charming, homey hotels which reflect the character of their owners. The following prices are pitched for the high season – it should be possible to negotiate at least a 25% reduction during low season.

Pousada Aquarius (☎ 288-2738) at Rua P A Cabral 174 has apartamentos around US$25/27 for singles/doubles. *Pousada do Cais* (☎ 288-2111) at Avenida Portugal 382 has apartamentos around US$24/27 for singles/doubles. All the rooms are different and tastefully decorated. *Pousada dos Navegantes* (☎ 288-2390) at Avenida 22 de Abril 212 is a little bit out of the way. Apartamentos cost US$30/32 for singles/doubles with air-con. *Pousada Caravelas* (☎ 288-2210) at Avenida 22 de Abril s/n (no number), is near the sea and has pleasant apartamentos at US$23/24 for singles/doubles

The poshest hotel in the area, *Porto Seguro Praia* (☎ 288-2321), about four km north of town, is set back from the coastal road on Praia de Curuípe. *Hotel Phoenícia* (☎ 288-2411), at Avenida 22 de Abril 400, is closer to town and on the beach. Both are big, expensive and impersonal.

Places to Eat

The *Bar-Restaurant Tres Vintens*, Avenida Portugal 246, serves a delicious *bobo de camarão* (shrimp dish) for US$4. With a side dish this is a meal for two. For good sushi, sashimi and hot shrimp dishes (US$3 to US$6), take the ferry across to Arraial d'Ajuda and pop into the *Restaurante do Japonês* in the orange building. For dessert have a mango popsicle (*picole*) which you can buy nearby on the street.

La Tarrafa, at Avenida Portugal 360, is a rustic oyster bar. A plate of buttery clams or oysters costs a few dollars and goes best with a cold brew. *Restaurant Primadonna*, Praça dos Pataxos 247, is run by honest-to-God Italians from Turin who understand what *al dente* means. Pastas start at US$3, seafood is US$4.50 and up. It's open daily from noon until midnight – closed on Monday.

Casa da Esquina on Rua Assis Chateaubriand has been recommended for seafood. It's open from 7 pm to 1 am. *Nativo* on Avenida Getúlio Vargas is the place to go for pastries and juices. Try cacao juice – it's not at all like chocolate, but it is very good. *Tia Seissa* at Avenida Portugal 170 makes homemade liqueurs from tropical fruits and cachaça. Try *pitanga* (like cherry) and *jenipapo* at 75c a pop.

Entertainment

Porto Seguro is a hotspot for lambada enthusiasts. The lambada, recently elevated to international status, is an erotic and entertaining local dance which involves some agitated leg tangling and exaggerated hip wiggling whilst pressing belly buttons. The origins of the international hit, 'The Lambada', are disputed between Bolivians and Brazilians.

For live music and booze go to Porto Seguro's Passarela de Álcool (the equivalent of a 'booze alley'). It's a very popular street lined with bars and restaurants, most of which offer live music. Posto 38, a lambada dance hall, starts hopping after 10 pm. In Cidade Alta, try Pousada Estrela for drinks and lambada dancing at night.

Boat Trips

Excursions can be arranged with Companhia do Mar Passeios de Escunas (☎ 288-2981) on Praça dos Pataxos, which runs five-day schooner trips south along the coast and then out to Parque Nacional Marinho dos Abrolhos (described later in this chapter), an island archipelago 80 km offshore from Caravelas. Most of the travel agents can organise excursions to Recife de Fora (Coral Reef), Coroa Alta, Coroa Vermelha, and Trancoso.

For US$6 per hour you can windsurf in front of the Hotel Phoenícia, where the reef offers protection from choppy surf.

Things to Buy

Pataxó Indians imported from the interior of Brazil are nominally under the care of FUNAI. A few Pataxó are hanging on south of Caraiva and are trying to maintain some semblance of their traditional way of life. Those north of Porto Seguro sell trinkets (overpriced coloured feathers, pieces of coral, fibre wrist bands with beads) to tourists at Coroa Vermelha. This make-believe village is simply a sad little collection of thatched-roof huts and dugout canoes by the beach. Porto Seguro also has souvenir shops that sell Pataxó jewellery, basketware and earthenware ceramics.

Please *don't* buy items made of turtle shell or consume turtles or their eggs! Most of the species of tartaruga (turtle) found in Brazil are threatened with extinction. For more information about turtle conservation projects in Bahia, see the section on Praia do Forte and the TAMAR turtle reserve in this chapter.

Getting There & Away

Air Nordeste (☎ 288-2108) has a daily milk run to Porto Seguro, originating in São Paulo with stops in Rio (Santos Dumont airport), Brasília and Ipatinga (Minas Gerais). There are also daily services to Rio and Salvador, and flights on Saturday and Sunday to Belo Horizonte. Rio Sul (☎ 288-2321) operates Sunday flights to Vitória da Conquista and Rio. TAM flies to São Paulo on Saturdays.

Bus The new rodoviária (☎ 288-2239) is two km outside town on the road to Eunápolis. São Geraldo transport company runs a daily bus to São Paulo at 10.45 am (US$36; 25 hours) and Rio at 5.45 pm (US$28; 17 hours). During the high season, bus frequency is increased. Viação São Jorge bus company runs two daily buses to Salvador (12 hours; US$15) – leito for US$32. There are two daily departures for Vitória da Conquista (US$13; 11 hours) and there are three daily buses to Ilhéus (US$6; 4½ hours) and Itabuna.

Between 5.20 am and 8 pm, buses depart almost hourly to Eunápolis (US$2; 90 minutes), which is a large transport hub with more frequent bus departures than Porto Seguro. Buses to Santa Cruz Cabrália (30 minutes) run six times daily from 6.20 am to 7 pm.

Getting Around
For bike rentals enquire at the Bahiatursa office. The ferry across the Rio Buranhém provides access to the road towards Arraial d'Ajuda, Trancoso and Caraiva. The pedestrian ferry charges a few cents and seems to operate from dawn until late in the evening, but the car ferry charges US$2.50 per car and operates every half hour between 7 am and 9 pm. The *Nova Lusitânia* and *Iracema*, both tired barges converted for use as ferries, make the 10-minute crossing past the rotting and listing old hulks of beached fishing boats.

NORTH OF PORTO SEGURO
North of Porto Seguro, right by the paved coastal road, lie several attractive beaches such as Mundaí and Coroa Vermelha, and finally, at Km 25, is the town of Santa Cruz Cabrália. These beaches are easily accessible by bus and, consequently, not as primitive and pristine as those to the south.

About five km north of town is the nicest of the northern beaches, Mundaí, with barracas at the mouth of the Rio Mundaí. North of Rio dos Mangues at Ponta Grande, the highway cuts inland a bit. The beach is good – uncrowded, tranquil waters – and

hard to reach. Six km before Cabrália is Coroa Vermelha with Pataxos craft stands, a monument to the discovery of Brazil and some fair beaches.

SANTA CRUZ CABRÁLIA
There's not much to Cabrália, but its terracotta roofs and palm trees are pleasant enough. Climb up to the bluff for the view overlooking the town and to visit Igreja NS da Imaculada Conçeição, the lonely, white church which was built by the Jesuits in 1630. The elderly caretaker will tell you the history of the region as well as the inside scoop on Cabral's expedition. Fried shrimp and a batida de côco at the barracas by the church enhance the view of the offshore reef, the boats and the palm trees in and about the bay of Cabrália.

Places to Stay & Eat
Pousada Xica da Silva (☎ 282-1104), on Rua Frei Henrique de Coimbra (by the bus stop), has apartamentos at US$9/16 for singles/doubles. The pousada also has a restaurant, bar and swimming pool. Across the street at *Restaurante Vanda* lobster is sold for a hefty US$8.

Getting There & Away
For access from Porto Seguro, see the Getting There & Away section for Porto Seguro. The last bus back to Porto Seguro leaves at 4.30 pm, sometimes as late as 5.10 pm.

SOUTH OF PORTO SEGURO
After taking the ferry across the Rio Buranhém, you rejoin the road which continues along a long stretch of dreamlike beaches, with a bluff backdrop. Up on the bluff, a short walk from the beach, are the rapidly expanding villages of (Arraial d'Ajuda (also known as NS da Ajuda), Trancoso and Caraiva, which are 4½ km, 12 km and 37 km from the ferry crossing, respectively. The rush to develop the region south of Porto Seguro is in full swing in Arraial d'Ajuda and Trancoso, which are being developed to match the facilities in

Porto Seguro: paved roads, electricity, modern hotels as well as pousadas, chopp and, of course, bottled beer. South of Trancoso, a poor, unpaved road continues to Caraiva.

ARRAIAL D'AJUDA

Ten years ago, before the arrival of electricity or the road from Porto Seguro, Arraial was a poor fishing village removed from the world. Since then, the international tourist set has discovered Arraial and its desolate beaches, and a time-honoured way of life is dying. The village has gone too hip too fast: by day all is beach blanket Babylon, by night Arraial d'Ajuda is something out of a Fellini film – marijuana smoke clouds the main street, white horses gallop wildly through the town, wasted minstrels sing songs, and ancient village women wear Nina Hagen T-shirts.

Yet, for some, Arraial d'Ajuda is the place to be. Younger, hipper and wilder than Porto Seguro, small and rustic Arraial d'Ajuda is a wonderful place to tan and slough off excess brain cells. Newcomers soon fall into the delicious routine: going crazy every evening, recovering (hopefully) the following morning, only to stare blankly at strange, new bed-mates (read the Health section in the Facts for the Visitor chapter carefully!) and crawl weakly back onto the beach for more surf, sun and samba.

Information & Orientation

Arraial d'Ajuda is built on a little hilltop by the sea. The main street running from the church to the cemetery is called Broadway. The restaurants and bars plus a cheap pousada are here, and this is where the bus and taxis stop. Most of Arraial d'Ajuda's pousadas are located on the ocean-side of this hilltop in a maze of nameless dirt streets. Mucugê is the name of the beach below the maze.

From the ferry landing, the smooth 4½-km road to Arraial d'Ajuda runs about 100 metres inland of Praia do Arraial and passes several pousadas. Heading south from Arraial d'Ajuda towards Trancoso, the road

passes a series of beaches – Pitinga, Taipe, and Rio da Barra – before reaching Trancoso.

A Warning At less than one-third the cost in the USA, many people are tempted by cocaine, but be very cautious. Police in Porto Seguro are aware of Arraial d'Ajuda's drug traffic and there have been a couple of drug-related murders.

Beaches

Praia Mucugê is good until 3 or 4 pm when the sun hides behind the hill. Many of the beach barracas are home to do-it-yourself samba and guitar music. The barraca facing the ocean on the far right has great music and a fantastic *batida de abacaxi* (vodka and pineapple). The barraca to the far left, Tia Cleuza, has indescribably good fried shrimp for a couple of dollars.

Praia Pitinga, the river beach closest to Arraial d'Ajuda, has red and green striped sandstone cliffs, sparkling water and large grained sand.

Notes on nude sun-bathing: it's OK for women to go topless anywhere. Nude sun-bathing is OK for both men and women on Pitinga beach and points further south.

Places to Stay

Pousadas are popping up every day. Old pousadas change their names, management comes and goes, and owners trade property deeds like baseball cards. Information on accommodation changes very rapidly here. Out of season you should be able to negotiate heavy discounts on the prices quoted here. Pousadas in Arraial d'Ajuda tend to be rustic and often have fierce mosquitoes, so make sure your room has either a well-fitting mosquito net over the bed or preferably a fan.

Camping is permitted on the beaches around Arraial d'Ajuda. For organised campgrounds, try *Camping do Gordo* which has very basic facilities and is close to the ferry landing point; or *Camping Arraial d'Ajuda* which is closer to town on the beach at Praia de Mucugê and has better facilities.

For cheap deals check out the pousadas by the ferry crossing. *Pousada Iemanjá*, a dumpy little place on Broadway, has aparta-mentos with mosquito nets for about US$7 per person.

Pousada Coqueiros (follow the signs) is a very pretty, very hip and very noisy hangout for wandering musicians, the chic, the young and the wanna-be-young crowd. Aparta-mentos start around US$22/24 for singles/doubles. *Pousada e Restaurante Erva Doce* (☎ 875-1113) in the maze is quiet, with attractive split-level units. Aparta-mentos cost US$30/32 for singles/doubles. *Hotel Pousada Tororão* (☎ 875-1260) has single/double/triple apartamentos and chalets which start at around US$24/26/30. Cosy, very clean rooms, friendly staff, a res-taurant and bar make this a good deal. Across the street is *Pousada Cajueiros* (☎ 875-1233) which provides apartamentos around US$20/24 for singles/doubles – including good breakfasts, mosquito nets, and ham-mocks.

Places to Eat

Restaurants on Broadway serve the unavoid-able prato feito. Also on Broadway, *Restaurante Mama Mia* features people watching, drugs and respectable pizza. Other recommended restaurants include: *Erva Doce* (attached to the pousada); *Mão na Massa*, which specialises in Italian food; and *Varanda Grill*, which serves a wide variety of grilled meats and seafood. The barracas down at the beach have excellent fried shrimp and other seafood.

Entertainment

Arraial d'Ajuda is pretty lively in the eve-nings. Cruise Broadway for drinking and lambada or forró dancing. Arraial d'Ajuda's pousadas host open festas with musicians every evening. Pousada Coqueiros is a favourite party spot. Once a month people gather on Praia de Mucugê beach to sing, dance and howl at the moon.

Getting There & Away

For ferry details, see the Getting Around section for Porto Seguro. From the ferry landing there are four approaches to Arraial

d'Ajuda: a lovely four-km hike along the beach, a taxi to town, a VW Kombi-van to Mucugê beach or a bus to town.

TRANCOSO

Trancoso lies on a grassy bluff overlooking the ocean and fantastic beaches. Pousadas and restaurants are being revamped and going upmarket, but campgrounds are okay. Your best bet if you are planning a long stay is to rent a house on the beach. Trancoso has electricity, overpriced bottled beer, and a Telebahia office (☎ 867-1115) where you can leave a telephone message when making reservations for accommodation.

Places to Stay & Eat

Count on paying US$20/25 for single/double apartamentos – (negotiate sizeable reductions during low season) – at pousadas such as *Le Refuge*, *Canto Verde*, and *Hibis-cus*.

Caipim Santo, close to the central square, is recommended for its health food. It's open daily from 2.30 to 9.30 pm; closed on Sunday.

Getting There & Away

Trancoso is 22 km from Arraial d'Ajuda on a poor and winding road versus 13 km by foot along the beach. The bus from Arraial d'Ajuda to Trancoso leaves three times a day at 7 and 10 am, and 2 pm. It originates from the ferry landing opposite Porto Seguro and stops on Broadway in Arraial d'Ajuda. There are more buses during the high season. Pas-sengers must leave the bus while it crosses the rickety bridge spanning the Rio Taipe (to lighten the load and allow the *cobrador* (con-ductor) to fix the planks) and pray fervently while the bus attempts the 35° incline killer-hill just before town.

The walk from Trancoso back to Arraial d'Ajuda along the beach is beautiful. Hikers must ford two rivers ankle or arm-pit deep according to the tides and season. The road from Trancoso down to the beach is hidden near the right side of the square facing the ocean. One beach holds the coveted position between ocean surf and a freshwater lagoon.

CARAIVA

Without running water, electricity or throngs of tourists, the hamlet of Caraiva is primitive and beautiful. The beaches are lined with coconut palms and cashew trees and dashed by a churning white surf. Boats to Caraiva (40 km south of Trancoso) leave daily from Trancoso's pier during high season as soon as the boat fills (US$5 per person); and irregularly during the rest of the year. During high season there are also boat services operating to Caraiva from Porto Seguro.

PARQUE NACIONAL DE MONTE PASCOAL

On 22 April 1500 the Portuguese, sailing under the command of Pedro Álvares Cabral, sighted the broad, 536-metre hump of Monte Pascoal, their first glimpse of the new world. Pero Vaz de Caminha, who was with Cabral, wrote about the event nearly 500 years ago:

And thus we continue our course on this sea, at length, until Tuesday of the Oitavas of Easter, which made twenty-one days of April, being from that island a work of 660 or 670 leagues according to what the pilots said, we encountered some signs of land which were long grasses which the sailors call *botelho* just like others which are given the name asses' tail. And Wednesday the following morning we saw the birds they call *furabuchos*.

On this day, at vespers, we sighted land! First a great hill, very high and round, and other lower peaks to the south of it, and on the land great groves of tea: to the tall hill the captain gave the name of Monte Pascoal (Mount Easter) and the land, Terra de Vera Cruz (Land of the True Cross).

The park, 690 km from Salvador and 479 km from Vitória, contains a variety of ecosystems: Atlantic rainforest, secondary forests, swamplands and shallows, mangroves, beaches and reefs. The variety of the landscape is matched by the diversity in flora and fauna. There are several monkey species including the endangered spider monkey (brachyteles arachnoides), two types of sloths, anteaters, rare porcupines, capybaras (the world's largest rodent), deer, jaguar, cougar and numerous species of birds.

There are plans for a visitor's centre,

marked trails, picnic tables, etc. Visitors can climb Monte Pascoal and roam through the forests at the western/BR-101 end of the park. The coastal side is accessible by boat or on foot but the north-eastern corner of the park below Caraiva is home to a small number of Pataxó Indians and is closed to tourism.

According to recent reports, the Pataxó have succumbed to the lucrative offers of logging companies and allowed the park to be stripped of its valuable timber. The park currently covers only 12,000 hectares, a figure which represents half of its original size, and the shrinkage threatens to continue unchecked.

PRADO & ALCOBAÇA

South of Monte Pascoal is Prado (Meadow) which has fine beaches with very clean water and several hotels. Continuing south from Prado you reach the beach town of Alcobaça where you can arrange boat excursions with Agencia de Turismo Abrolhos (☎ 293-2295). Alcobaça is 27 km north of Caravelas (described in the next section), another beach town offering access to the Parque Nacional Marinho dos Abrolhos.

On a dirt track 12 km north of Prado are the semideserted beaches of Paixão and Tororão. The dirt road continues 22 km to the lovely and lonely Praia Areia Preta beach and the village of Cumuruxatiba. North of Cumuruxatiba past the ocean border of Parque Nacional de Monte Pascoal, the village of Caraiva and all the way to Trancoso is a 50-km stretch of undeveloped coastline. Judging by the interest currently being shown by developers, it is unlikely to stay that way. At present, there are just a few projects for upmarket beach tourism and a handful of low to middle-range tourist facilities. The road peters out beyond Caraiva and there is only a miserable unpaved road from Trancoso to Porto Seguro.

Places to Stay & Eat

Prado Just outside Prado on Praia Barra do Farol, try *Camping Clube do Brasil* which provides shady campsites near the beach.

Prado has one inexpensive pousada, *Costa Sul* (☎ 298-1069) on Avenida José Fontes Almeida. More expensive options include: *Hannah Pousada* (☎ 298-1385) at Avenida 2 de Julho, 180; *Pousada Caraívas* (☎ 298-1408) on Rua Calrício Cardoso dos Santos; and the very expensive *Praia do Prado* (☎ 298-1214) on Praia do Farol. *Tororão* restaurant (open only during the afternoon) on Praia Areia Preta does excellent shrimp dishes.

Cumuruxatiba At present, this beach community lacks telephone service. To make reservations for accommodation, you should phone the Telebahia office (☎ (073) 298-1509) and leave a message. For camping, try *Camping Aldeia da Lua* on Praia de Cumuruxatiba. On Praia Areia Preta, there's the inexpensive *Pousada Flamboyant* and the more expensive *Pousada Verde Verão*. The seafood at *Samburá* restaurant on Praia de Cumuruxatiba is recommended.

Alcobaça *Camping Clube do Brasil* has pleasant camping sites on Praia do Farol. For moderately priced lodging, try *Sul Americano* (☎ 293-2171) at Avenida Atlântica, 1111, or *Alcobaça* (☎ 293-2174) at Rua Joaquim Muniz, 223. For excellent grilled seafood, try *Grão d'Areia* (open until midnight) at Avenida Atlântica, 358.

CARAVELAS

Caravelas, 54 km from Teixeira de Freitas on BR-101, is not only a gateway to Parque Nacional Marinho dos Abrolhos (see the next section for access details); it's also a respectable beach town. In addition to Praia Grauçá (10 km north of town on a dirt track) and Pontal do Sul across the river, Caravelas has the island beaches of Coroa da Barra (30 minutes by boat) and Coroa Vermelha (1½ hours by boat).

Places to Stay & Eat

There's an attractive campground, *Camping Coqueiral*, on Praia Grauçá. On the same beach, there are a couple of inexpensive places to stay: *Pousada das Sereias*, which also rents out scuba gear, and *Pousada do Juquita*. For a low-priced place in town, try *Pousada Mirante*. Seafood enthusiasts should head for *Museu da Baleia* and *Chalé Barra*, both on Praia Grauçá.

PARQUE NACIONAL MARINHO DOS ABROLHOS

Abrolhos, Brazil's first marine park, covers part of an archipelago 80 km offshore from Caravelas. In 1832, Charles Darwin visited here whilst voyaging with HMS *Beagle*. The archipelago consists of five islands, but the only inhabited one is Santa Bárbara, which has a lighthouse, built in 1861, and a handful of buildings. Abrolhos is being preserved because of its coral reefs and crystal-clear waters. Underwater fishing within the park is prohibited. The only approach is by boat, and staying on the islands is prohibited. The Brazilian navy considers the area strategic, therefore only underwater photography is permitted.

Unfortunately, the archipelago's coral reefs, home to at least eight different species of coral, have been badly affected by toxic chemicals routinely dumped by industry, especially a pulp and paper company in southern Bahia. Dynamite fishing has depleted the fish stocks and thereby caused rapid growth of seaweed (normally kept in check by herbivorous fish), which is destroying the coral reefs. Experts now maintain that the erosion caused by deforestation along the coastline is responsible for heavy levels of sediment in the ocean which in turn block the penetration of sufficient light for underwater organisms like the coral.

Getting There & Away

Caravelas You can reach Abrolhos from Caravelas, the most popular gateway to the park, by fishing boats which leave early each morning (four-hour ride each way, US$75 per boatload). For more information call Antônio Carlos, Secretaria de Turismo de Caravelas (☎ (073) 297-1149). Another option in Caravelas is to contact Abrolhostur (☎ 297-1149), which organises boat trips to the park.

Porto Seguro From Porto Seguro, the Companhia do Mar Passeios de Escunas (☎ (073) 288-2381) on Praça dos Pataxós organises five-day schooner trips which cruise south along the Bahian coast, then on to Abrolhos. The fare of US$150 per person includes food, lodging (bunks on the boat), transport and visitor's licence from the Capitânia of Porto Seguro. A minimum of 10 passengers is needed.

West of Salvador

FEIRA DE SANTANA

At the crossroads of BR-101, BR-116 and BR-124, Feira de Santana is the main city of Bahia's interior, and a great cattle centre. There's not much to see here except the Feira de Gado, the big Monday cattle market (lots of tough leather), which is great fun but don't expect to buy much, and the Mercado de Arte Popular (open daily except Sundays). The Casa do Sertão (the folklore museum) and Museu Regional (Regional Museum) might also be worth a look.

Festivals

Two months after Carnival, Feira de Santana is the scene of the Micareta – a 60-year-old local version of Carnival which brings together the best trios elétricos of Salvador, with local blocos, samba schools and folklore groups.

The main action of the Micareta takes place on Avenida Getúlio Vargas, the city's main street, where 20 trios bop along for five days. The festivities begin on Thursday with a boisterous dance and opening ceremony. The Tennis and Cajueiro clubs sponsor large dances like the traditional Uma Noite no Havaí (A Night in Hawaii). For those who missed out on Carnival in Salvador, the Micareta could be the next best thing.

Places to Stay

There are many cheap hotels near the rodoviária, such as Hotel Samburá (☎ 221-8511) at Praça Dr Jackson do Amauri 132;

or Caroá (☎ 221-0158) at Avenida Getúlio Vargas 83.

In the top price range, there's the Feira Palace (☎ 221-5011) at Avenida Maria Quitéria 1572, a four-star affair with apartamentos starting at US$40/45 for singles/doubles.

Getting There & Away

Frequent buses make the two-hour journey from Salvador for US$2. The rodoviária features an eye-catching mural painted by Lénio Braga in 1967.

SALVADOR TO LENÇÓIS

The seven-hour bus odyssey from Salvador to Lençóis first goes through Feira de Santana and then continues through typical sertão countryside: patches of low scrub and cactus where scrawny cattle graze and hawks circle above. In 1991, hundreds of immense potholes were definitely winning the battle for supremacy of the road surface, but the local grapevine was buzzing with the wondrous news that road resurfacing teams were indeed advancing beyond Feira de Santana towards Lençóis.

The bus stops for lunch at Itaberaba where the rodoviária restaurant serves two typical sertão dishes: carne de sol com pirão de leite (dried salted beef with manioc and milk sauce to take the edge off the salt) and sopa de feijão (bean soup with floating UPO – Unidentified Pigs' Organs).

LENÇÓIS

Lençóis lies in a gorgeous, wooded, mountain region – the Chapada Diamantina – an oasis of green in the dusty sertão, where you'll find solitude, small towns steeped in the history and superstition of the garimpeiros (prospectors), and great hiking to peaks, waterfalls and rivers. If you want to see something completely different, and have time for only one excursion into the Northeastern interior, this is the one.

The natural beauty of the region and the tranquillity of the small, colonial towns has attracted a steady trickle of travellers for several years; some have never left. These

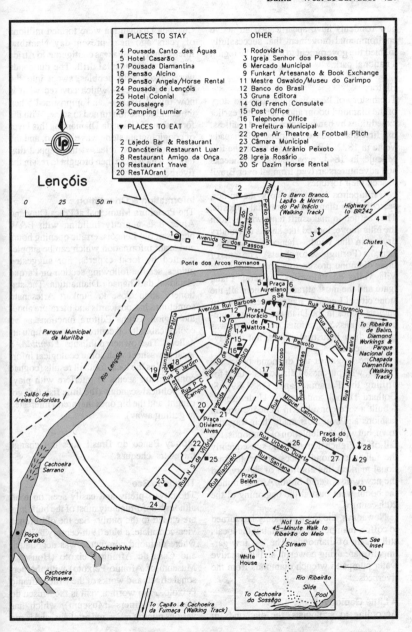

■ PLACES TO STAY

4 Pousada Canto das Águas
5 Hotel Casarão
17 Pousada Diamantina
18 Pensão Alcino
19 Pensão Angela/Horse Rental
24 Pousada de Lençóis
25 Hotel Colonial
26 Pousalegre
29 Camping Lumiar

▼ PLACES TO EAT

2 Lajedo Bar & Restaurant
7 Dancêteria Restaurant Luar
8 Restaurant Amigo da Onça
10 Restaurant Ynave
20 ResTAOrant

OTHER

1 Rodoviária
3 Igreja Senhor dos Passos
6 Mercado Municipal
9 Funkart Artesanato & Book Exchange
11 Mestre Oswaldo/Museu do Garimpo
12 Banco do Brasil
13 Gruna Editora
14 Old French Consulate
15 Post Office
16 Telephone Office
21 Prefeitura Municipal
22 Open Air Theatre & Football Pitch
23 Câmara Municipal
27 Casa de Afrânio Peixoto
28 Igreja Rosário
30 Sr Dazim Horse Rental

Lençóis

0   25   50 m

new residents have spearheaded an active environmental movement that successfully lobbied the government to declare the region a national park.

History

The history of Lençóis epitomises the story of the diamond boom and bust. After earlier expeditions by bandeirantes proved fruitless, the first diamonds were found in Chapada Velha in 1822. After large strikes in the Rio Mucujê in 1844, prospectors, roughnecks and adventurers arrived from all over Brazil to seek their fortunes.

Garimpeiros began to work the mines, searching for diamonds in alluvial deposits. They settled in makeshift tents which, from the hills above, looked like sheets of laundry drying in the wind – hence the name of Lençóis (Portuguese for sheets). The tents of these diamond prospectors grew into cities: Vila Velha de Palmeiras, Andaraí, Piatã, Igatú and the most attractive of them all, the stone city of Lençóis. Exaggerated stories of endless riches in the Diamantina mines precipitated mass migrations, but the area was rich in dirty industrial stones, not display-quality gems.

At the height of the diamond boom the French, who purchased diamonds – used for drilling the Panama Canal (1881-89), St Gothard Tunnel, and London Underground – built a vice-consulate in Lençóis. French fashions and *bon mots* made their way into town, but with the depletion of diamonds, the fall-off in French demand (and subsequently the fall in diamond prices on the international market), the abolition of slavery, and the newly discovered South African mines, the boom went bust at the beginning of the 20th century.

Nowadays, the town economy has turned to coffee, manioc and tourism, but the locals still dream of diamonds. The last few garimpeiros are using powerful and destructive water pumps to wrench diamonds from the riverbeds.

A Little Geology

According to geologists, the diamonds in Chapada Diamantina were formed millions of years ago near present-day Namibia. Interestingly, Bahia was contiguous to Africa before the continental drift. The diamonds were mixed with pebbles, swept into the depths of the sea – which covered what is now inland Brazil – and imprisoned when the conglomeration turned to stone. With the formation of Chapada Diamantina this layer of conglomerate stone was elevated, and the forces of erosion released the trapped diamonds which were then brought to rest in the riverbeds.

Information & Orientation

The Prefeitura Municipal at Praça Otaviano Alves 8 is a pretty building with B&W photos of old Lençóis, erratic opening hours and scant information which can be supplemented by local experts. For suggested guides, see the following section on Parque Nacional da Chapada Diamantina. The stationery shop close to Funkart Artesanato sometimes has postcards and literature about the region. Gruna Editora functions as an ecological/cultural centre and impromptu art gallery. The owner publishes *Lampião*, a local newssheet with some ecological information plus the local football results (cognac consumption seems to interfere with play) and political scandals (the little fish that got caught, and the big ones that aren't interested in getting away).

Money Banco do Brasil does not change travellers' cheques.

Things to See

The city is pretty and easily seen on foot, although unfortunately most of the buildings are closed to the public. See the old French vice-consulate, a blue 19th-century building where diamond commerce was negotiated; and Casa de Afrânio Peixoto (House & Museum of Afrânio Peixoto) with the personal effects and works of the writer Afrânio Peixoto. Also worth a visit is the Museu do Garimpô (Miners' Museum), which has various mining relics and artefacts, and is run by Mestre Oswaldo, a very knowledgeable local historian.

For details about hikes close to Lençóis and longer trips further afield in the park, see the following section on Parque Nacional da Chapada Diamantina.

Festivals
The principal holidays take place in January and September. Festa de Senhor dos Passos starts on 24 January and culminates on 2 February with the Noite dos Garimpeiros (Prospectors' Night). Semana de Afrânio Peixoto, a week dedicated to the author, is held from 11 to 18 December and coincides with the municipality's emancipation from slavery. Lamentação das Almas is a mystic festival held during Lent. Lençóis is also noted for Jarê, the regional variation of Candomblé.

Places to Stay
Lençóis has plenty of places to stay, but you should still try to reserve at weekends – and definitely book in advance during the high season: January and February.

Places to Stay – bottom end
Camping Lumiar on Praça do Rosário has shady sites, passable bathrooms, a bar and a restaurant – but watch out for Pablito and his marauding chickens. The cost is US$1 per person. *Hotel Casarão* (no phone) provides quartos for US$4.50 per person in a large, gently fading colonial building.

Pousalegre (☎ 334-1124) is a favourite with travellers. The rooms are certainly basic (lack of windows and furniture) but the friendly staff, amazing breakfast (and other meals) and reasonable price more than compensate. Quartos cost US$5/10 for a single/double.

Pensão Alcino (☎ 334-1171) is a bright, clean place which charges US$6 per person for quartos. The price includes a highly recommended breakfast. *Pensão Angela* (☎ 334-1167) provides similar quality at similar prices. Angela has horses available for rental for treks in the immediate area around Lençóis.

Pousada Diamantina (no phone) charges US$9/11 for a single/double quarto, and US$12/14 for a single/double apartamento.

Places to Stay – middle
Pousada Canto das Águas (☎ 334-1154) has a superb position in a landscaped garden beside the river. Facilities include a restaurant, bar, and swimming pool. The apartamentos overlook the cascades which provide the pousada's background music – hence the name Canto das Águas (Song of the Waters). Prices are around US$22/26 for singles/ doubles, including an enormous breakfast. At night, a dinner-plate size toad squats guard at the gate!

Hotel Colonial (☎ 334-1114) has pleasant apartamentos at US$13/18 for singles/ doubles.

Places to Stay – top end
At the top end of town, and the top end of the price range, is the attractive *Pousada de Lençóis* (☎ 334-1102) with gardens, swimming pool, restaurant and bar. Standard apartamentos with air-con cost US$30/33/41 for singles/doubles/triples. Deluxe versions of these rooms have frigobar and TV, and cost around US$8 more than the equivalent standard room. Books about the region are sold at the reception desk.

Places to Eat
If you like breakfast, you'll never want to leave Lençóis, where it's included in the room price of numerous lodgings which seem to be competing for the coveted 'BBB' (Best Breakfast in Brazil) title. A local breakfast staple is *baje* (a warm, buttered manioc pancake with the consistency of a very chewy styrofoam polymer). After breakfast, you've only got a few hours until you're faced with equally magnificent culinary options for the other meals of the day!

Pousalegre serves excellent, inexpensive meals with several natural foods on the menu, and a large community of cats attending the table. The *moqueca de peixe, salada do mato* (forest salad), and Chinese dishes are highly recommended. *ResTAOrant* is a type of New Age eatery run by a Berliner who paints and sells postcards of beach scenes in Bahia. Nets have been strung beneath a huge jackfruit tree to protect diners from plummeting fruit missiles. The food is not cheap, but there's a good selection of natural foods. Other restaurants in town worth visiting include *Ynave*, and those attached to Pousada de Lençóis and Pousada Canto das Águas.

The *Lajedo Bar & Restaurant* (across the bridge on the other side of town), *Amigo da Onça* (bar), and *Dançataria Restaurant Luar* are evening hangouts.

Things to Buy
Funkart Artesanato and other artisan/trinket shops sell crochet, lacework, and bottles of coloured sand collected at nearby Salão de Areias Coloridas.

Getting There & Away
Air Plans have been announced for an airfield at Palmeiras, 56 km from Lençóis.

Bus The rodoviária is on the edge of town, beside the river. Buses to Salvador leave daily at 9 am and 11 pm; on Sunday there's an additional departure at 9 pm. Buses from Salvador leave at 9.15 am and 8.15 pm. The trip currently takes seven hours – maybe less if the pesky potholes get filled – and the fare is US$9. Buses to Palmeiras and Seabra leave at 3 am and 4 pm.

Hitching Lençóis is on a sideroad 12 km off BR-242 (Salvador-Seabra highway). If you're hitching, you'll increase your chances of a lift if you stick your thumb out at the junction of the sideroad with the highway.

Car If you are using a car in Lençóis, there is a fuel station some 22 km east of town on BR-242, in Tanquinho. The nearest station to the west is around 30 km away. It's not a good idea to rely on the improvised fuel station in Lençóis which may or may not be open, have fuel or want to sell it.

Getting Around
The town is easily covered on foot. For transport further afield, see the following section on Parque Nacional da Chapada Diamantina.

PARQUE NACIONAL DA CHAPADA DIAMANTINA
Many of the foreigners and Brazilians who came only to visit have settled permanently in Lençóis. They have been the backbone of a strong ecological movement which is in direct opposition to the extractive mentality of the garimpeiros and many of the locals. Riverbeds have been dug up, waters poisoned and game hunted for food and sport. Much of the land has been ravaged by forest fires. The hunting and depletion of habitat has thinned the animal population severely.

After six years of bureaucratic battles, Roy Funch helped convince the government to create the Parque Nacional da Chapada Diamantina to protect the natural beauty of the area. Signed into law in 1985, the park roughly spans the quadrangle formed by the cities of Lençóis and Mucujê, Palmeiras and Andaraí. The park, 1520 sq km of the Sincora range of the Diamantina plateau, has several species of monkeys, beautiful views, clean waterfalls, rivers and streams, and an endless network of trails. Although bromelias, velosiaceas, philodendrons and strawflowers are protected by law, these plants have been uprooted nearly to extinction for the ornamental plant market.

The park is particularly interesting for rock hounds, who will appreciate the curious geomorphology of the region.

For information regarding minimising the impact of camping on fragile ecosystems, see the Minimum Impact Camping section under Accommodation in the Facts for the Visitor chapter.

Information
The park has little, if any, infrastructure for visitors. The map of the park included in this book should give you a good idea of the great hiking opportunities.

Knowledgeable guides, such as Roy Funch and Luís Krug, can greatly enhance

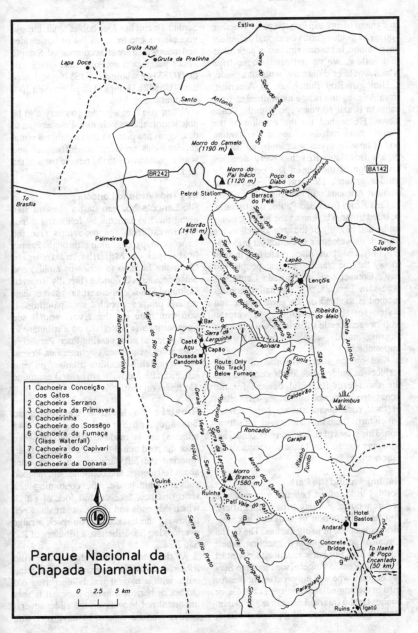

1 Cachoeira Conceição dos Gatos
2 Cachoeira Serrano
3 Cachoeira da Primavera
4 Cachoeirinha
5 Cachoeira do Sossêgo
6 Cachoeira da Fumaça (Glass Waterfall)
7 Cachoeira do Capivari
8 Cachoeirão
9 Cachoeira da Donana

Parque Nacional da Chapada Diamantina

0   2.5   5 km

enjoyment of any trip into the park. Whether you take a guide or not, you should definitely not go alone. In the descriptions of park hikes that follow, we've indicated those trips which would be dangerous without a guide.

Biologist Roy Funch, an ex-American from Arizona and now a naturalised citizen, came to Brazil 10 years ago with the Peace Corps. He pushed for the creation of the Parque Nacional da Chapada Diamantina and is now involved with lobbying for the park's interests. Roy has very detailed knowledge of the region and occasionally guides groups. He can be contacted at Funkart Artesanato in Lençóis.

Luís Krug, from São Paulo, is a friendly, bearded guide who knows the history, geography and biology of the area as well as the trails. Luís welcomes enquiries for information only, and shuns rates, preferring instead to say that he 'rarely charges; people just pay'. Contact Luís at Pousada Canto das Águas in Lençóis. An alternative contact method is to stand on the main square and watch for the 'Luísmobile', a veteran Volkswagen Beetle suffering from a chronic steering malady which renders left turns impossible!

Kids on the street will also offer their services as guides, but locals consider that the short-term financial benefit for the youngsters is negated by the long-term effect of their consequent truancy from school, which turns them into adults without education. This is less of an issue on weekends, but whatever you do, don't submit to requests for astronomical fees.

Getting Around the Park

For day trips around Lençóis, you can walk or hire a horse. For day trips further afield, you have the option of walking, hitching, hiring transport, or using the bus. The Grand Circuit, described later in this section, is best done on foot. For horse rental, either contact Angela at Pensão Angela (see Places to Stay in Lençóis), who will only rent out horses for trips in the immediate vicinity of Lençóis, or Senhor Dazim (marked on map as 'Sr Dazim Horse Rental'), who will go further afield.

Senhor Dazim has four horses available and you can choose from his list of horse rides and treks which are all accompanied. Sample prices per person are: one hour (50c); half day (US$14); whole day (US$20); and three days (US$42). Groups of three receive a 30% discount.

When you hire a guide, you may also be able to organise vehicle hire. Pousada Canto das Águas has plans to start a minibus rental service. Bus services are infrequent and scarce, particularly to the remote parts of the park.

Day Trips Around Lençóis

Rio Lençóis You can start a pleasant hike along the Rio Lençóis by following a trail south-west from the rodoviária (see the Lençóis map) continuing through Parque Municipal da Muritiba, upstream to Cachoeira Serrano (a series of rapids) and Salão de Areias Coloridas (literally Room of Coloured Sands), where artisans gather their matéria prima for bottled sand paintings. If you continue up the river, you'll see Cachoeirinha (a waterfall) on a tributary to your left, and after passing Poço Paraíso (a waterhole), you'll see Cachoeira da Primavera waterfall on another tributary on your left. From the rodoviária to here takes around 1½ hours on foot.

Ribeirão do Meio & Cachoeira do Sossêgo Another relaxing hike (45 minutes) can be made to Ribeirão do Meio. Take the road uphill from Camping Lumiar, ignoring the left turning you'll see after about 100 metres, and continue until the road ends at a white house. After continuing for a short distance, take the left fork of a trail which descends and crosses a stream. Keep following the track until you reach a ridge overlooking Rio Ribeirão, a tributary of Rio São José.

At the foot of the ridge you'll find Ribeirão do Meio, a series of swimming holes with a natural waterslide (bring old clothes or borrow a burlap sack). It is *very* important not to walk up the slide: several bathers who have done so have met with nasty accidents. Instead, swim across to the far side of the pool and climb the dry rocks at the side of the slide before launching off.

Upstream from Ribeirão do Meio, a trail leads to Cachoeira do Sossêgo waterfall. The hike involves a great deal of stone-hopping along the riverbed. On *no* account should you attempt this trail during high water or rain: the river stones are covered with lichen which becomes impossibly slippery.

Gruta do Lapão This is probably the largest sandstone cave in South America. Access is tricky and it's necessary to take a competent guide.

Day Trips Further Afield
Lapa Doce, Gruta da Pratinha & Gruta Azul These three sights are best visited by car. Lapa Doce (70 km from Lençóis, then a 25-minute hike to the entrance) is a huge cave formed by a subterranean river which dried up. Access to the cave is via an immense sinkhole; inside there's an impressive assortment of cave decorations which prompt erotic comparisons. You will need a guide – Luís is an expert on the place – and you should bring a torch. Admission costs 25c.

About 12 km from this cave are Gruta da Pratinha and Gruta Azul, two more caves of lesser interest which have been spoilt by pollution and vandalism. Admission to each of these costs 25c.

Rio Mucugêzinho This river, 30 km from Lençóis, is a super day trip. Take the 8 am 'Palmeiras/Seabra' bus, and ask the driver to let you off at Barraca do Pelé – the bus passes this place again around 4 pm on its return trip to Lençóis. From Barraca do Pelé, pick your way about two km downstream to Poço do Diabo (Devil's Well), a swimming hole with a 30-metre waterfall. Further upstream, you'll find Rita and Marco, who have set up housekeeping in a cave, and run a snack bar outside.

Morro do Pai Inácio & Barro Branco
Morro do Pai Inácio (1120 metres) is the most prominent peak in the immediate area. It's 27 km from Lençóis and easily accessible from the highway. An easy but steep trail takes you to the summit (200 metres above the highway) for a beautiful view.

Hikers may want to take the trail along Barro Branco between Lençóis and Morro do Pai Inácio – allow four or five hours one way for the hike.

Palmeiras, Capão & Cachoeira da Fumaça Palmeiras, 56 km from Lençóis, is a drowsy little town with a slow, slow pace and a scenic riverside position for its streets lined with colourful houses. There are several cheap pensões, including *Barreta* and *Cachoeira da Fumaça*.

The hamlet of Capão is 20 km from Palmeiras by road (see the Grand Circuit for a description of the hiking trail connecting Capão with Lençóis). From here, there's a six-km trail (two hours on foot) to the top of Cachoeira da Fumaça, also known as the Glass waterfall, after missionary George Glass, which plummets 420 metres – the longest waterfall in Brazil. Although marked on the map, the route to the bottom of the waterfall is very difficult and not recommended.

The Grand Circuit
The grand circuit of the park covers around 100 km and is best done on foot in a clockwise direction. It takes about five days, but you should allow eight days if you include highly recommended sidetrips, such as Igatú and Cachoeira da Fumaça.

Lençóis to Andaraí For this section you should allow two days. On the first night, camp at a site near Rio Roncador. On the way, you pass Marimbus, a microregion with characteristics similar to the Pantanal. In Andaraí, either camp or stay at the basic pensão called *Bastos*.

Sidetrips to Poço Encantado & Igatú these are two highly recommended sidetrips. Poço Encantado, 56 km from Andaraí, is an underground lake – clear blue and stunningly beautiful. You'll need a car to get there; hitching is difficult because there is very little traffic.

Igatú, 12 km from Andaraí, is a small community with an intriguing set of ruins (highly recommended). Either walk or drive to Igatú.

Andaraí to Vale do Patí & Ruinha This section takes a day, but you should allow an extra day to potter around the valley: for example, doing a sidetrip to Cachoeirão (a delightful waterfall) or enjoying the atmosphere in the tiny ghost settlement of Ruinha.

Vale do Patí to Capão This section, which crosses the beautiful plains region of Gerais do Vieira, is best covered in two comfortable days, although it's possible to do it in one very long day.

The tiny settlement of Capão serves as a base for the highly recommended hike to Cachoeira da Fumaça (see description in the Day Trips Further Afield section). In Capão, you can either camp or stay at *Pousada Candombá* for US$2.50 per person; breakfast costs US$1.50.

Capão to Lençóis You'll need a full day to hike this section. From Capão, follow the road through Caeté Açu and when you reach the 'bar', take the track to the right. Follow the main track east, crossing the river several times, before veering off to reach Lençóis. There are a couple of campsites along the track on the section between the 'bar' and Lençóis.

RIO SÃO FRANCISCO

For the Brazilian, particularly the Nordestino, it's impossible to speak about the Rio São Francisco without a dose of pride and emotion. The third most important river in Brazil, after the Amazon and Paraguay, there is no river that is anthropomorphised like the São Francisco. Everyone who knows the São Francisco, especially those who live along its banks, speak of it as a friend – hence the affectionate nickname *velho chico* or *chicão* (chico is short for Francisco).

The geographical situation of the São Francisco gave it a prominence in the colonial history of Brazil that surpassed the Amazon. Born in the Serra da Canastra, 1500 metres high in Minas Gerais, the Rio São Francisco descends from south to north, crossing the greater part of the Northeast sertão, and completing its 3160-km journey in the Atlantic Ocean after slicing through the states of Minas Gerais and Bahia, and delineating the borders of the states of Bahia, Pernambuco, Sergipe and Alagoas.

For three centuries the São Francisco, also called the 'river of national unity', represented the only connection between the small towns at the extremes of the sertão and the coast. 'Discovered' in the 17th century, the river was the best of the few routes available to penetrate the semi-arid Northeastern interior. Thus the frontier grew along the margins of the river. The economy of these settlements was based on cattle, to provide desperately needed food for the gold miners in Minas Gerais in the 18th century and, later, to feed workers in the cacao plantations in southern Bahia.

Although the inhabitants of the region were often separated by enormous distances, cattle ranching proved a common bond and produced a culture which can be seen today in the region's folklore, music and art.

The history of this area is legendary in Brazil: the tough vaqueiros who drove the cattle; the commerce in salt (to fatten the cows); the cultivation of rice; the rise in banditry; the battles between the big land owners; and the religious fanaticism of Canudos – see the History section in Facts about the Country.

The slow waters of the São Francisco have been so vital to Brazil because in a region with devastating periodic droughts, the river provides one of the only guaranteed sources of water. The people who live there know this and thus, over the centuries, they have created hundreds of stories, fairy tales and myths about the river.

One example is the *bicho da água* (beast of the water), part animal and part man who walks along the bottom of the river and snores. The crew on the riverboats must throw tobacco to the bicho da água for protection.

The river's width varies from two handspans at its source in the Serra da Canastre, an empty, uninhabitable region where nothing grows, to 40 km at the Lagoa do Sobradinho, the biggest artificial lake in the world. As a result, Nordestinos believe that São Francisco is a gift of God to the people of the sertão to recompense all their suffering in the drought-plagued land.

River Travel

People have always travelled by the São Francisco. In the beginning there were sailboats and rowboats, then came the motorboats, which became famous because of the personalities of the *barqueiros* who drove the boats and put *carrancas* on the front of them. Carrancas are wooden sculptures that represent an animal-like face – part dog, part wolf – with big teeth and open mouth. These sculptures are now popular as folk art, and are sold in Salvador and at fairs along the river.

Today, with the river cities linked by roads, river traffic has decreased drastically, but it's still possible to travel between the river towns of Pirapora and São Francisco, both in Minas Gerais. The trip is operated as an organised tour using the vintage American steamer, *Benjamin Guimarães,* which dates from the turn of this century and takes just under a week for the cruise. The boat leaves on Sunday from Pirapora and returns from São Francisco five days later. This schedule is subject to change. For more details about this trip, see the São Paulo River Trip section under Belo Horizonte in the Minas Gerais chapter.

Saturday (major market day) is the easiest day to find a boat up or down the São Francisco, for example, to Brejo Grande, but it shouldn't prove too hard to find boats for short local trips on the other days of the week.

These boat trips provide an impression of the harsh land and its riverside towns, some of which are very poor, but quite unusual. Bom Jesus da Lapa, on the São Francisco in the interior of Bahia, is the site of one of the most important religious festivals and processions in the sertão. The festival is held on 6 August.

A reader wrote to us recently with the following assessment of travel on the Rio São Francisco:

The river appears dead as a means of commercial travel, and only a small amount of transport by local narrow boat continues between the villages. The river has become sluggish as a result of construction of a hydroelectric plant on the seaward side of Lagoa do Sobradinho, and silting is so severe in some places that the shallow-draught local boats touch bottom.

Most of the commercial ventures have closed. The paddleboat which used to ply up and down the river is set in concrete as a restaurant on the esplanade. FRANAVE (☎ 811-2128/692) at Juazeiro is the only remaining commercial operator. Hiring local boats is possible, but expensive. An overnight one-way trip 200 km downstream to Xique-Xique costs US$60 per person. You must take your own hammock and food.

Xique-Xique, at the southern end of Lagoa do Sobradinho, appears to have a mainly school-age population, most of whom are learning English and are keen to use it. A couple of islands close to the town have been declared a reserve for the protection of anteaters, which are said to be the only ones in the area. Bookings to visit can be made at the kiosk just beyond the rodoviária on the opposite side of the road.

Commander M K Barritt (Royal Navy, UK)

Sergipe & Alagoas

Sergipe

Sergipe is Brazil's smallest state. It has all three zones typical of the Northeast: litoral, zona da mata and sertão. The coastal zone is wide and sectioned with valleys, with many towns dotted along the rivers.

What is there to see? There are a couple of interesting historical towns – Laranjeiras and São Cristóvão – and the towns along the Rio São Francisco have a unique, captivating culture – principally Propriá and Neópolis. The beaches, on the other hand, are not up to snuff, and the capital, Aracaju, is as memorable as last Monday's newspaper.

ESTÂNCIA

Estância, 68 km south of Aracaju, is one of the oldest towns in the state. The city has a certain amount of character and a few historic buildings in the centre, but there's little reason to stop in Estância unless you want to head to the nearby beaches (see the Mangue Seco section in Bahia chapter) or want to avoid spending the night in Aracaju – not a bad idea.

Information

Estância has most basic services, including a branch of Banco do Brasil. The São João festivals in June are the big event.

Places to Stay

The town has a couple of simple hotels facing the central plaza. The *Turismo Estanciano* (☎ 522-1404) has pleasant apartamentos around US$18/20 for singles/

Sergipe & Alagoas

doubles; and a couple of cheaper quartos which cost US$9/10 for singles/doubles. The *Hotel Bosco* has quartos for US$5 per person and apartamentos for US$7 per person.

Getting There & Away

The town is actually a bit off highway 101, but most long-distance buses still stop in Estância. There are buses directly from Salvador and São Cristóvão, Aracaju, Propriá and Maceió to the north.

SÃO CRISTÓVÃO

Founded in 1590, São Cristóvão is reputedly Brazil's fourth oldest town and was the capital of Sergipe until 1855. With the decline of the sugar industry, the town has long been in the economic doldrums and is trying to become a tourist attraction to bring in some cash.

Things to See

The old part of town, up a steep hill, has a surprising number of 17th and 18th-century colonial buildings along its narrow stone roads. Of particular distinction are: the Igreja e Convento de São Francisco, which has a good sacred art museum (at Praça São Francisco); the Igreja de Senhor dos Passos (Praça Senhor dos Passos); the Antiga Assembléia Legislativa; and the Antigo Palácio do Governo.

Festivals

Every year the town comes alive for a weekend with the Festival de Arte de São Cristóvão. The festival has both fine and popular arts, with lots of music and dance. The festival is held during the last 15 days of October.

Places to Stay & Eat

There is no real accommodation in town, but the old part of town has a better than expected Japanese restaurant. If you like sweets, São Cristóvão is renowned for its sweetmakers, who produce a wide variety of *doces caseiros* (tempting homemade sweets and cakes).

Getting There & Away

São Cristóvão is 25 km south of Aracaju on a good paved road, and seven km off the BR-101. The rodoviária is down the hill below the historic district on Praça Dr Lauro de Freitas. There are frequent buses from here to Aracaju and Estância. The 45-minute trip (fare 75c) from Aracaju by bus is particularly pleasant as the road traverses a plateau with a pretty view of the valleys. Catch the bus from Aracaju at the rodoviária velha (old bus terminal).

LARANJEIRAS

Nestled between three lush, green, church-topped hills, Laranjeiras is the colonial gem of Sergipe. Filled with ruins of old sugar mills, terracotta roofs, colourful colonial facades, and stone roads, the town is relatively unblemished by modern development. There are several churches and museums worth visiting and the surrounding hills offer picturesque walks with good views. It's a charming little town, easy to get to and well worth a few hours sightseeing or a day or two exploring the town, the nearby sugar mill and the countryside. The town centre has recently been renovated.

History

Laranjeiras was first settled in 1605. During the 18th and 19th centuries, it became the commercial centre for the rich sugar and cotton region along the zona mata west of Aracaju. At one point there were over 60 sugar mills in and around Laranjeiras. The processed sugar was sent down the Rio Cotinguiba about 20 km downstream to Aracaju and on to the ports of Europe. The large number of churches is a reminder of the past prosperity of the town.

Information

There is a city tourism office inside the Trapiche building in the Centro de Tradições on Praça Samuel de Oliveira where you can obtain brochures and information about guides for hire.

Engenho

This old, semi-restored sugar mill a few km from town is in a lovely setting. It's now owned by Paulistas, so you must go to the tourism office and have them call for permission to visit. You can walk, or hire a guide and a car to take you there.

Igreja de Camandaroba

Out at the Engenho Boa Sorte, two km from town along the river, is the baroque Igreja de Camandaroba, the second building that the Jesuits constructed back in 1731.

Igreja do Bonfim

This church is at the top of the hill called Alto do Bonfim. If the door is closed, go around to the back and ask to be let in. The short walk is rewarded with a fine view, but keep an eye out for snakes.

Trapiche

The Trapiche houses the tourism office. It's a large, impressive structure that was built in the 19th century to house the cargo waiting to be shipped downriver.

Gruta da Pedra Furada

This is a one-km tunnel built by the Jesuits to escape their persecutors. Check at the tourism office to make sure it's open. The gruta is three km out of town on the road leading to the small village of Machado.

Museums

The small Museu Afro-Brasileiro is on Rua José do Prado Franco s/n (no number). It's open Tuesday to Sunday, from 8 am to noon and from 2 to 5.30 pm. Also recommended is the Museu de Arte Sacra (Sacred Art Museum) in Igreja NS da Conceição, Rua Dr Francisco Bragança s/n.

Places to Stay

The only pousada in town is *Pousada Vale dos Outeiros* (☎ 281-1019) at Rua José do Prado Franco 124. It's a friendly place with cheap quartos for around US$5 per person, and apartamentos for around US$10/12 for a single/double.

Getting There & Away

Laranjeiras is 15 km from Aracaju and four km off the BR-101. Buses leave from and return to the rodoviária velha in Aracaju every hour. It's a 35-minute ride (50c) – the first bus leaves for Laranjeiras at 5 am and the last one returns at 9 pm. Any bus travelling the BR-101 can let you off at the turnoff for Laranjeiras. You can then walk, hitch or flag down a bus for the four km to town.

ARACAJU

Aracaju just may be the Cleveland of the Northeast. The city has little to offer the visitor – there is no colonial inheritance – and it is visually quite unattractive. Even the beaches are below the prevailing high standard in the Brazilian Northeast.

Aracaju, 367 km north of Salvador and 307 km south of Maceió, was Brazil's first planned city. The modest requirements of the original plan called for a grid-pattern intersected by two perpendicular roads less than two km long. The city outgrew the plan in no time, and the Brazilian norm of sprawl and chaotic development returned to the fore.

History

Some of its lack of appeal stems from the fact that Aracaju was not the most important city in the state during the colonial era. In fact, when it was chosen as the new capital in 1855, Santo Antônio de Aracaju was a small settlement with nothing but a good deep harbour – badly needed at the time to handle the ships transporting sugar to Europe.

With residents of the old capital of São Cristóvão on the verge of armed revolt, the new capital was placed on a hill five km from the mouth of the Rio Sergipe. Within a year an epidemic broke out that decimated the city. All the residents of São Cristóvão naturally saw this as an omen that Aracaju was destined to be a poor capital.

Information

Tourist Offices The state tourism office, Emsetur (☎ 231-9166), is in Centro de Interesse Comunitário (Ministério José Hugo Castelo Branco), Avenida Tancredo Neves,

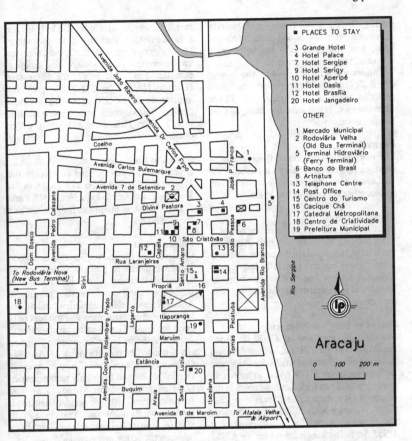

PLACES TO STAY

3 Grande Hotel
4 Hotel Palace
7 Hotel Sergipe
9 Hotel Serigy
10 Hotel Aperipé
11 Hotel Oasis
12 Hotel Brasília
20 Hotel Jangadeiro

OTHER

1 Mercado Municipal
2 Rodoviária Velha
   (Old Bus Terminal)
5 Terminal Hidroviário
   (Ferry Terminal)
6 Banco do Brasil
8 Artnatus
13 Telephone Centre
14 Post Office
15 Centro do Turismo
16 Cacique Chá
17 Catedral Metropolitana
18 Centro de Criatividade
19 Prefeitura Municipal

Aracaju

0   100   200 m

Distríto Industrial de Aracaju (DIA). The office is open from 7 am to 1 pm, Monday to Friday, but there's hardly any point in going there because it's very inconveniently positioned – absolutely miles out of town. Perhaps this keeps the workload to a minimum.

The Centro do Turismo in the centre of town is part of an artesanato market, and has little to offer in the way of information. There are also small tourist information booths (limited information; erratic opening hours) at the rodoviária nova (new bus terminal) and the airport.

Money There is a branch of Banco do Brasil at Praça General Valadão, 341 in the centre.

Post Office The central post office is at Rua Laranjeiras 229.

Beaches

On the sandy barrier island of Barra dos Coqueiros, at the mouth of the Rio Sergipe, is Praia Atalaia Nova (*atalaia* is Portuguese for watchtower), which is a popular weekend beach.

Praia das Artistas and Atalaia Velha are the closest beaches to the city. They are crowded (traffic jams on weekends) and heavily developed with hotels and motels, restaurants, bars and barracas – the latter are a source of inexpensive seafood.

Further south on the road to Mosqueiro, Praia Refúgio is the prettiest and most secluded beach close to Aracaju. It's 15 km from the city. There are a few bars, and the beach has calm water.

Festivals

The maritime procession of Bom Jesus dos Navegantes held on January 1 is probably the best event. Festa de Iemanjá is celebrated on 8 December at Praia Atalaia Velha.

Places to Stay

Most of the hotels are in the centre or out at Praia Atalaia Velha on Avenida Atlântica. For a short stay, hotels in the centre are much more convenient and generally less expensive. Ask for low-season discounts between March and June, and during August and September.

Places to Stay – bottom end

For camping, try *Camping Clube do Brasil* (☎ 243-1413) on Atalaia Velha. Also on Atalaia Velha, *Pousada das Redes (Albergue de Juventude)* (☎ 231-9165) is an agreeable youth hostel. For a rock-bottom choice in the centre of town, there's *Hotel Sergipe* (☎ 222-7898). Quartos cost US$2.50 per person; apartamentos without air-con cost US$5.50/8 for singles/doubles or US$2 more for equivalent rooms with air-con. You should also be aware that this hotel is favoured by local clientele as a 'short time' joint. For much better value, try *Hotel Oasis* (☎ 224-1181) which charges US$14/16 for single/double apartamentos. *Hotel Brasília* (☎ 222-5112) has apartamentos at US$14/21 for singles/doubles.

Places to Stay – middle

A popular mid-range hotel is the *Jangadeiro* (☎ 222-5115) in the city centre. It provides clean apartamentos at US$24/26 for singles/doubles. The *Serigy* (☎ 222-1210), at Rua Santo Amaro 269, has upgraded its aparta-

mentos, which now cost US$31/36 for singles/doubles. Just round the corner is *Hotel Aperipé* (☎ 211-1880) which offers apartamentos at US$20/26 for singles/doubles. For a bit more, the three-star *Grande Hotel* (☎ 211-1383) provides apartamentos at US$33/36 for singles/doubles. For similarly priced apartamentos, there's *Hotel Palace* (☎ 224-5000), which doesn't merit its four-star rating.

Places to Stay – top end

If you want a five-star hotel in Aracaju, the *Parque dos Coqueiros* (☎ 223-1511), out at Rua Francisco Rabelo Leite Neto 1075, Praia Atalaia Velha, is the place. Singles/doubles are US$80/88.

Places to Eat

Cacique Chá (closed on Sunday) is a good garden restaurant on Praça Olímpio Campos, a central location which has made it a popular meeting place for the 'in' crowd. *Artnatus* serves plain vegetarian food downtown at Rua Santo Amaro 282 but it is only open for lunch. Good seafood restaurants at Atalaia Velha include: *Taberna do Tropeiro* (live music in the evening) at Avenida Oceânica 6; *Chapéu do Couro* at Avenida Oceânica 128; and the highly recommended *O Miguel* (closed on Monday) at Rua Antônio Alves 340. For good Italian food, try *Villa Vietri* at Avenida Francisco Porto 896 in Bairro Salgado Filho – midway between the centre and Atalaia Velha.

Getting There & Away

Air The major airlines fly to Rio, São Paulo, Salvador, Recife, Maceió, Brasília, Goiânia and Curitiba.

You'll find a Varig/Cruzeiro office (☎ 222-7800) at Rua João Pessoa 86; VASP (☎ 222-3232) at Rua São Cristóvão 26; and Transbrasil (☎ 222-3037) at Rua São Cristóvão 14.

Bus Long-distance buses leave from the rodoviária nova (new bus terminal), which is about four km from the centre. There are six buses a day to Salvador (six hours; US$8.50

or US$15 for leito); and three daily departures for the five-hour trip (US$6.50) to Maceió – some sections of the road are heavily potholed, so it can be slow going. Two daily departures to Recife take nearly nine hours and cost US$13. There's one daily direct bus to Penedo (three hours; US$3.50).

For transport details on São Cristóvão and Laranjeiras, see their respective Getting There & Away sections. Note that bus services for these two towns operate from the rodoviária velha (old bus terminal) – not from the rodoviária nova.

Getting Around
To/From the Airport The airport (☎ 243-2721) is 11 km south of town, just past Atalaia Velha. From the rodoviária velha, take the bus marked 'Aeroporto'.

Bus The rodoviária nova (new bus terminal, four km from the town centre) is connected with the rodoviária velha (old bus terminal) in the centre by a frequent shuttle service (25 minutes; 30c). The requisite bus stop is a separate entity – look for a large shelter with a series of triangular roofs about 100 metres to your right as you exit the rodoviária nova. A taxi from the rodoviária nova to the centre costs around US$3.50.

The rodoviária velha is in the centre of town on Avenida Divina Pastora. This is the bus terminal to use for local trips, including visits to São Cristóvão and Laranjeiras. To reach Atalaia Velha, take any bus marked 'Atalaia' from the bus stop just south of the ferry terminal on Avenida Rio Branco.

Boat From the Terminal Hidroviário (Ferry Terminal), there are frequent ferries (20 minutes; 40c) to Atalaia Nova beach on Barra dos Coqueiros.

PROPRIÁ
Propriá is 81 km north of Aracaju where BR-101 crosses the mighty Rio São Francisco. While the town is less interesting than the downriver cities of Penedo and Neópolis, it has the same combination of colonial charm and a strong river culture. Thursday and Friday are the weekly market days in Propriá, when goods are traded from communities up and down the São Francisco.

Boat Trips
In recent years there has been a steady decline in long-distance boat travel on the Rio São Francisco. You should still be able to find boats going upriver as far as Pão de Açúcar, about a nine-hour ride by motorboat, with stops at all the towns along the way. One scheduled boat departure is the *Iolanda*, which leaves Propriá at 6.30 am Saturdays and Tuesdays and returns from Pão de Açúcar on Mondays and Wednesdays at 10 am.

There are also boats which leave irregularly – for example, downstream to Penedo and Neópolis. You can bargain a ride on any of them, including the beautiful *avelas* with their long, curved masts and striking yellow or red sails. The trip downriver to Penedo takes about four or five hours by avela or rowboat and should cost around 50c.

Festivals
Bom Jesus dos Navegantes, on the last Sunday in January, is a colourful affair with a maritime procession and *reisado* – a dramatic dance that celebrates the epiphany. It is highly recommended.

Places to Stay & Eat
The town's two hotels are near each other, facing the church. The *Hotel Imperial* (☎ 322-1294) charges by the room not the number of people, with quartos starting around US$7, and nice apartamentos (with fan) costing US$15. It's a very clean place with a pool table. A more expensive option is *Hotel do Velho Chico* (☎ 322-1941) with a fine riverside position and apartamentos starting at around US$30/32 for singles/doubles.

For a pleasant place to eat with a view of the river, we recommend *O Mangaba* on Avenida Nelson Melo.

Getting There & Away
Propriá is about 500 metres off BR-101.

There are bus connections with Neópolis, Penedo, Aracaju, and Maceió. Some buses don't go into town but drop off passengers at the closest junction with BR-101, which is a short walk from the town.

Alagoas

The small state of Alagoas is one of the pleasant surprises of the Northeast. The capital, Maceió, is a relaxed, modern city, and its beaches are enchanting, with calm, emerald waters. Penedo is the colonial masterpiece of the state, with a fascinating river culture on the Rio São Francisco.

Along the coast, there are many fishing villages (as yet undisturbed) with fabulous beaches shaded by rows of coconut trees. Buses trundle slowly along the coastal road (mostly unpaved) connecting the villages which are being 'discovered' by tourists and property developers.

History

The mighty republic of runaway slaves – Palmares – was in present-day Alagoas. During the invasion by the Dutch in 1630, many slaves escaped to the forest in the mountains between Garanhuns and Palmares. Today, where the towns of Viçosa, Capela, Atalaia, Porto Calvo and União dos Palmares stand, there were once virgin forests with thick growth and plenty of animals. Alagoas today has the highest population density in the Northeast.

MACEIÓ

Maceió, the capital of Alagoas, is 292 km north of Aracaju and 259 km south of Recife. A manageable place for the visitor, the city has a modern but relaxed feeling with endless sun and sea.

Orientation

The rodoviária is about four km north of the city centre, which has inexpensive hotels and is the bustle of commerce. On the east side of the city are Praia de Pajuçara and Praia dos

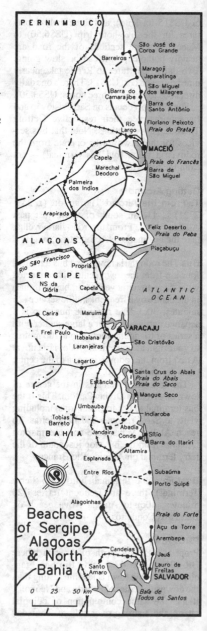

A Little Power Goes a Long Way

Alagoas has attracted much attention as the home state of President Fernando Collor and his wife, Rosane Malta Collor. Fernando Collor reached his present position in a linear progression: from mayor of Maceió to governor of Alagoas state and thence to the presidency of Brazil. Collor recently suffered acute embarrassment when it was revealed that the Malta family, to which his wife belongs, had received lavish funds, dozens of cushy jobs and titles, and amazing deals for contracts. Rosane was identified as a key figure in massive corruption perpetrated during her presidency of the nation's largest charity organisation. Some Brazilians joke that there is a '*dinheiroduto*' ('money duct') running directly from Brasília to Alagoas!

Certainly, the Hidrelétrica de Xingó (Xingó Hydroelectric Scheme) at Piranhas, on the banks of Rio São Francisco, is consuming money like water, and the construction funds are being ducted into the hands of the ruling elite...who just happen to live in the area. Impartial estimates have revealed that the US$3 billion price tag for the construction project (scheduled for completion in 1994) is at least US$600 million in excess of the cost of an equivalent project anywhere else in the world. ∎

Sete Coqueiros, which are three km and four km respectively from the centre, and recommended for beach enthusiasts.

Information

Tourist Office Ematur (☎ 221-9393), the state tourist agency, is on Avenida Siqueira Campos (Estádio Rei Pelé). There are information booths at the airport and at the rodoviária. The latter has erratic opening hours, but if you're lucky the staff will be in attendance and will provide a list of hotels with prices and will ring around to make a reservation for you.

Post & Telecommunications There is a post office at Rua João Pessoa 5, in the city centre. Telasa, the state phone company, has offices in the centre at Rua Cons Lourenço de Albuquerque 369 and Rua Joaquim Távora 320; and an office in Pajuçara at Avenida Zeferino Rodrigues 207.

Money There's a branch of Banco do Brasil on Rua Senador Mendonça.

Beaches

Just a short walk from the centre, the beaches of Praia do Sobral and Avenida are polluted. Your best bet is to head north for some of the best beaches in the Northeast. Protected by a coral reef, the ocean is calm and a deep emerald colour. On shore there are loads of barracas, *jangadas* (local sailboats) and plenty of beach enthusiasts.

The beaches to the north are Pajuçara (three km from the centre), Sete Coqueiros (four km), Ponta Verde (five km), Jatiúca (six km), Jacarecica (nine km), Guaxuma (12 km), Garça Torta (14 km), Riacho Doce (16 km) and Pratagi (17 km).

You won't go wrong with any of these tropical paradises, but they do get busy on weekends and throughout the summer when there are many local buses cruising the beaches. On Pajuçara, you'll find jangadas which will take you out about one km to the reef where you can swim in the *piscina natural* (natural swimming pool), and observe marine fauna and flora – the latter is best done at low tide.

Museums

In the centre, Museu do Instituto Histórico (open Monday to Friday, 8 am to noon and 2 to 5 pm) has exhibits about regional history. You might also like to browse through the Indian artefacts in Museu Theo Brandão (open Monday to Thursday from 8 am to 6 pm; and from 8 am to noon on Friday), which is in an attractive colonial building on the seafront.

Boat Trip

The schooner *Lady Elvira* departs daily from Restaurante do Alípio in Pontal da Barra for a five-hour cruise to islands and beaches.

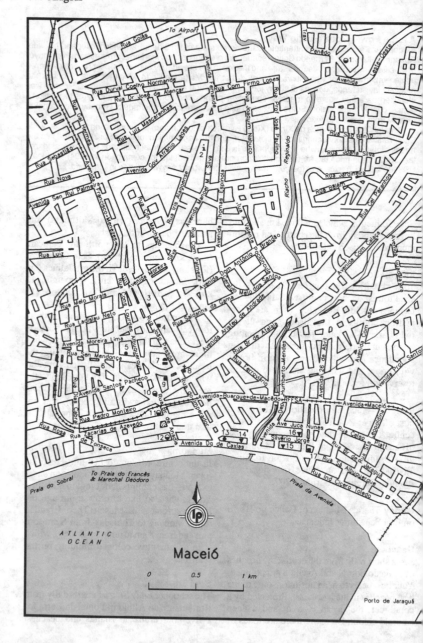

Maceió

0   0.5   1 km

PLACES TO STAY

4 Hotel Beiriz
6 Hotel Florida
9 Hotel Parque
17 Hotel Ney
18 Pousada da Praia
20 Anço Marzio Restaurant
   & Pousada
21 Pousada Saveiro
22 Hotel Praia Bonita
24 Praia Hotel Sete Coqueiros

PLACES TO EAT

14 Restaurant Lagostão
15 Restaurant Como Antigamente
16 Restaivant Nativa
19 Restaurant Gogo da Ema

OTHER

1 Rodoviária
2 Ematur Tourist Office
3 Instituto Histórico
5 Banco do Brasil
7 Post Office
8 Cathedral
10 Buses to Pajuçara
   & Ponte Verde (Beaches)
11 Buses to Marechal Deodoro
12 Minibuses to Marechal
   Deodoro & Praia do Francês
13 Museu Theo Brandão
23 Jangadas to Reef & Piscina Natural

The price per person is US$26 with lunch, or US$16 without lunch. For information and reservations, contact Restaurante do Alípio (☎ 225-2565) at Avenida Alípio Barbosa 321, Pontal da Barra.

Festivals
Maceió is reported to have a lively Carnival which is still considerably calmer and safer than Rio's, and features active samba clubs. Festa do Mar takes place in December.

Places to Stay – bottom end
Centre *Hotel Florida* (☎ 221-4485) has adequate apartamentos which cost US$9/16 for singles/doubles with fan; or US$13/20 with air-con. The recently renovated *Hotel Ney* (☎ 221-6500) is midway between the city centre and Praia de Pajuçara. Attractive apartamentos cost US$15/18 for singles/doubles. It's a clean, safe hotel.

Although conveniently central, *Hotel Parque* (☎ 221-9099) is rather institutional and drab, and doesn't merit its two stars. The staff insist that visitors should complete stacks of police forms and appear to be worried that hotel guests will abscond without paying for the contents of the frigobar in their room – in our case, the frigobar didn't even function! Apartamentos cost US$20/24 for singles/doubles.

Beaches For camping try *Camping Pajuçara* (☎ 235-7561) on Praia de Pajuçara or *Camping Jatiúca* (☎ 231-4183) on Praia Cruz das Almas, around six km from the centre.

There are three youth hostels close to Maceió: *Albergue de Juventude Pajuçara* (☎ 231-0631) at Rua Quintino Bocaiuva 63, Praia de Pajuçara; *Albergue de Juventude Nossa Casa* (☎ 231-2246) at Rua Prefeito Abdon Arroxelas 177, on Praia de Ponta Verde; and *Albergue de Juventude Stella Maris* (☎ 231-5217), Avenida Engenheiro Paulo Brandão Nogueira 336, on Praia Jatiúca.

Pousada da Praia (☎ 232-2697) has friendly management and is a good low-budget option with quartos at US$7/10 for

singles/doubles. Breakfast is included and monthly rates are good value at US$100/130 for singles/doubles. We recommend a room in the front, preferably upstairs; the rooms in the courtyard at the back include a bathroom, but are musty and gloomy.

Pousada Anço Marzio (☎ 231-0034) has bright rooms and an affable Italian manager. Quartos with fan cost US$7/11 for singles/doubles, and US$10/13 for singles/doubles with air-con. A suite with bath and balcony is available for US$21. *Pousada Saveiro* (☎ 231-9831) is friendly and offers apartamentos (with fan) at US$12/15 for singles/doubles. For an extra US$2, you can take an apartamento with air-con.

Places to Stay – middle
Centre If you want a good hotel in the centre, try the *Hotel Beiriz* (☎ 221-1080) at Rua João Pessoa 290. It's a large, three-star hotel with a swimming pool and restaurant. Room prices start around US$28/45 for singles/doubles.

The *Hotel California* (☎ 221-1200) at Rua Barão de Penedo 33, in the centre, has apartamentos around US$24/29 for singles/doubles, although you might find it to be one of those places where you can check out but never leave!

Beaches *Praia Hotel Sete Coqueiros* (☎ 231-8583) on Praia Pajuçara is a spiffy three-star hotel with swimming pool and coffee shop. Prices officially start around US$48/53 for singles/doubles, but payment in cash may earn a 30% discount.

Places to Eat
Centre *Nativa* is a good natural food eatery, close to the Hotel Ney. There's a set menu for US$3; vegetable salad for US$2; and excellent sandwiches and fruit juices. It's open for lunch and dinner, Monday to Friday, and until 3 pm on Saturday. If you want good seafood and feel like a splurge, visit *Lagostão* (☎ 221-6211) at Avenida Duque de Caxias 1384. A cheaper option, just one block to the east on the same road, is *Como Antigamente*, which does prato feito for

US$2.50 and has seating in a courtyard at the back of the restaurant away from the street noise.

Beaches Most of the beaches offer a wide choice of food in barracas and snack bars along the beachfront. Pestering from vendors and assorted sandpeople can become wearisome if you sit outside.

On Praia de Pajuçara, two pleasant restaurants are *Anço Marzio*, a recently renovated Italian restaurant with great homemade pasta – see Places to Stay for details about accommodation here; and *Gogo da Ema* (seafood dishes around US$5) with tables on an open patio.

Other good places for seafood are *Bem* (☎ 231-3316) at Rua João Canuto da Silva 21, Praia de Cruz das Almas; and *Restaurante do Alípio* (☎ 221-5186) at Avenida Alípio Barbosa 321, which is south-west of the centre in Pontal da Barra. All three of these restaurants are medium priced and open for lunch and dinner.

Entertainment
For reviews and listings of the latest bars, dance spots, and cultural events in Maceió, pick up a copy of *Veja*, which includes an

Women washing clothes, Maceió

assortment of these places in its weekly supplement entitled *28 Graus*.

Getting There & Away
Air Maceió is connected by air with Rio, São Paulo, Brasília, and all the major centres of the Northeast.

The major airline offices are in the centre. Varig/Cruzeiro (☎ 223-7334) is at Rua Dr Luiz Pontes de Miranda 42; VASP (☎ 221-2855) is at Rua do Comércio 56; and Transbrasil (☎ 221-8344) is at Rua Barão de Penedo 213.

Bus There are frequent daily departures to Recife (four hours; US$6); and Aracaju (five hours; US$6.50). Services operate five times daily to Salvador (10 hours; US$17).

Buses leave for Penedo at 5.20 and 9 am, noon, 6.20 pm (express) and 11.50 pm (express). The trip takes about three hours and costs US$5.50. The bus to Paulo Afonso leaves daily at 11 pm, takes around five hours, and costs US$10. And if you want to make a 2256-km bus trip to Rio (36 hours; US$58), there's a daily departure at 7 pm.

Walking For details of walking from Recife to Maceió, see the Getting There & Away section for Recife (Pernambuco chapter).

Getting Around
To/From the Airport Aeroporto Dos Palmares is 20 km from the centre. There is a circular bus route that stops at the rodoviária, the airport and downtown near the Hotel Beiriz at Rua João Pessoa 290 (ask about the schedule in the hotel). A taxi to the airport costs around US$12.

To/From the Rodoviária The rodoviária (☎ 223-4105) is about four km from the centre. To reach the centre, take the bus marked 'Ouro Preto'. A taxi to the centre costs around US$2.50, and a dollar more to Pajuçara.

To/From the Beaches Buses marked 'Santuário' or 'Ponta Verde' run from the centre to Pajuçara. The bus marked 'Fátima'

Around Maceió

will also get you to the beaches close to town. If you want to travel further away from the centre, the bus marked 'Jardineira' runs along the beaches north of town as far as Riacho Doce (recommended).

SOUTH OF MACEIÓ
Praia do Francês

Only 22 km from Maceió, this is a very pretty, popular weekend beach which is being rapidly developed. The beach is lined with barracas and the ocean is lined with reefs. The water is calm and better for wading than swimming. It's a very social beach on weekends, with plenty of drinking, seafood scoffing, football and music.

Places to Stay & Eat There are several expensive pousadas and restaurants at the beach, but the *Hotel do Mar* (☎ 231-6820) is cheaper than most. Apartamentos cost US$15/17 for a single/double. *Pousada Bougainville* (☎ 231-1079) is also close to the beach, and recommended for a splurge. The French owner has virtually submerged the pousada in bougainvillaea. Apartamentos cost US$30/35 for singles/doubles. The adjacent restaurant, *Chez Patrick*, is run by

the same Frenchman and specialises in seafood. Main dishes are expensive, but you can also drop in for an appetiser and drink served in the restaurant's shady courtyard. Numerous barracas along the beach are a good source of cheap seafood.

Getting There & Away From Maceió, either take the bus from the stop opposite the ferroviária (hourly departure), or use the more frequent minibus service which departs about 50 metres down the street. The same minibuses run between Praia do Francês and Marechal Deodoro.

Marechal Deodoro

Beside Lagoa Manguaba, a lagoon 21 km south-west of Maceió, is Marechal Deodoro, which was the capital of Alagoas between 1823 and 1839. Small and quiet, the town is worth a visit, perhaps combined with Praia do Francês as a day trip from Maceió.

Things to See

Marechal Deodoro has several churches, the most famous of which are the Igreja e Convento São Francisco, which was begun in the 17th century, and the Igreja de NS da Conceição.

Inside Igreja e Convento São Francisco is the Museu de Arte Sacra (Museum of Sacred Art). It's open daily from 9 am to 1 pm – except on Sunday, when it's closed.

Brazilian history buffs may want to see the old governor's palace and the house where Marechal Deodoro was born. The latter has been turned into the Museu Deodoro which is open daily from 9 am to 5 pm, except on Sunday, when it's closed. The exhibits give a 'deodorised' view of Manuel Deodoro da Fonseca, emphasising his role as a military hero and the first president of Brazil, but omitting to mention that he achieved this position with a military putsch in 1889 and later proved a poor politician. The artesanato shop next door sells the lace and homemade sweets for which the town is renowned. The Sunday market, held along the waterfront, is reported to be a lively, colourful event.

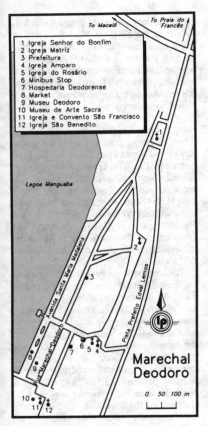

1 Igreja Senhor do Bonfim
2 Igreja Matriz
3 Prefeitura
4 Igreja Amparo
5 Igreja do Rosário
6 Minibus Stop
7 Hospedaria Deodorense
8 Market
9 Museu Deodoro
10 Museu de Arte Sacra
11 Igreja e Convento São Francisco
12 Igreja São Benedito

To Maceió

To Praia do Francês

Lagoa Manguaba

Avenida Santa Maria Madalena

Praça Prefeito Edval Lemos

Rua Marechal Deodoro

Marechal Deodoro

0   50   100 m

Place to Stay & Eat *Hospedaria Deodorense* is a clean, basic place to stay – usually booked solid on weekends. Quartos cost US$3/4 for singles/doubles. Breakfast costs US$1.50. If you order in advance, the landlady will serve lunch or dinner for US$2.50.

Getting There & Away Buses to Marechal Deodoro depart hourly from the bus stop outside the old ferroviária in Maceió. It's quicker to use the minibus service (30 minutes; fare 75c), just down the street, which departs when the minibus is full. Yes,

the minibus is definitely quicker: demon drivers keep their accelerator foot down to the board, and your heart pressed to the roof of your mouth!

An alternative route from Maceió is to take the boat from Trapiche across Lagoa Manguaba.

Barra de São Miguel

Barra is 35 km south of Maceió at the mouth of the Rio São Miguel. The fine beach is protected by a huge reef and there are kayaks for rent. Barra is not too crowded midweek, but it is being built up with summer homes for Maceió's wealthy.

A large sailboat will take you up the river for three hours for US$6. Boats leave from Bar do Tio at the dock on the river. During the trip, drinks and fruit are provided on board.

Places to Stay & Eat There are a couple of very expensive hotels in town. The *Pousada Mar e Sol* (☎ 272-1159) near the river has apartamentos at US$24/30 for singles/doubles. It's overpriced but in an attractive position.

Bar do Tio has good shrimp and fish dishes for US$3 to US$5. Try the super mussels.

Getting There & Away Barra is reached by paved road with a regular but infrequent bus service from Maceió. The last bus leaves Barra for the return trip at 5.30 pm.

Penedo

Penedo is best known as the *capital do baixo São Francisco* (capital of the lower São Francisco). The city has also been called *cidade dos sobrados* (city of two-storey homes) by the famous Brazilian sociologist Gilberto Freyre.

Amongst the attractions of the city, 42 km off the BR-101 and virtually untouched by tourism, are its many baroque churches and colonial buildings, and the opportunity to travel on the Rio São Francisco. Penedo bustles with people from the smaller villages up and down the river who come to sell and buy goods.

History

Penedo was founded in either 1535 or 1560 (opinions differ) by Duarte Coelho Pereira, who descended the Rio São Francisco in pursuit of Caete Indians responsible for the killing of bishop Pedro Fernandes Sardinhaeven. Penedo is claimed to be the river's first colonial settlement.

Information

There's a tourist information desk (open daily from 9 am to noon) and small city museum in the Casa da Aposentadoria, just up from the fort at Praça Barão de Penedo.

Market

The street market is held daily in Penedo, but Saturday is the big day when the city is transformed into a busy port-of-call for farmers, fisherfolk and artisans. The waterfront becomes a pageant as families disembark: old people with finely carved features topped by strange hats, many grasping chickens by the neck in one hand and boisterous children by the neck in the other. On shore, traditional musicians play the accordion. The market is filled with ceramics, baskets and shrimp traps made of reeds.

Churches

Penedo has a rich collection of 17th and 18th-century colonial buildings, including many churches. The Convento de São Francisco e Igreja NS dos Anjos on Praça Rui Barbosa is considered the finest church in the state. Even Dom Pedro II paid a visit to this church. Construction was begun in 1660 and completed in 1759. The rococo altar is made of gold. The church is open Tuesday to Sunday from 2 to 5 pm.

Igreja da Senhora das Correntes was completed in 1764. It has some fine work done with azulejos (glazed blue tiles) and a rococo altar. The church is open daily from 8 am to noon and 2 to 6 pm. You'll find it at Praça 12 de Abril.

The Igreja NS do Rosário dos Pretos, also

known as the Catedral do Penedo, was built by slaves. It's on Praça Marechal Deodoro and is open from Tuesday to Sunday, from 8 am to 6 pm. Igreja de São Gonçalo Garcia was built at the end of the 18th century and has some of the city's finest sacred art pieces. It's on Avenida Floriano Peixoto, but is closed for restoration.

Boat Trips

Saturday (major market day) is the easiest day to find a boat up or down the São Francisco, but it shouldn't prove too hard to find boats for short local trips on other days of the week. If you're going upriver, it's usually easy to find boats going as far as Propriá, but more difficult to continue beyond there to Pão de Açúcar in Alagoas. Beautiful sailboats travel to Propriá in four to five hours, depending on the wind, and charge around 50c for the trip.

The ferry between Penedo and Passagem, on the opposite side of the river, crosses every 30 minutes, but is only of interest if you're driving. From Passagem there's a road to Neópolis, which is linked by another road to BR-101. A better excursion is one of the motorboat crossings direct to Neópolis, a few km downriver. The 15-minute trip costs a few cents and boats depart every 30 minutes between 5.30 am and 11.30 pm. Neópolis is an old colonial town, on a hill overlooking the river, with some interesting buildings and good crafts for sale.

For another boat excursion only four km upriver, take one of the frequent boats (operating between 6 am and 6 pm) to Carrapicho, a small town noted for its ceramics. You can also hire a boat and just cruise the river a bit, possibly stopping at a sandbar for a swim.

Festivals

The Festa do Senhor Bom Jesus dos Navegantes, held on the second Sunday of January, features an elaborate procession of boats. Penedo also hosts a large annual Brazilian film festival.

Places to Stay

Penedo has some terrific hotels that are surprisingly cheap. Most are down by the waterfront, on or near Avenida Floriano Peixoto.

The *Hotel Imperial* (☎ 551-2198) on Avenida Floriano Peixoto is old but clean, with single/double quartos at US$4/6.

Perhaps the best deal in town is *São Francisco* (☎ 551-2273), on Avenida Floriano Peixoto, which is clean, quiet and has spacious apartamentos around US$15/20 for singles/doubles. Make sure you ask for a room with a view of the river and try to wake up early to enjoy the view at sunrise.

The *Pousada Colonial* (☎ 551-2677) at Praça 12 de Abril is more romantic than the São Francisco. It's a beautiful, converted colonial home on the waterfront with apartamentos at US$12/16 for singles/doubles.

Places to Eat

There are plenty of bars and lanchonetes where the locals eat. We recommend *Forte da Rocheira*, which is open for lunch and dinner (until 11 pm) and serves abundant portions of seafood and meat for US$2 to US$5. The restaurant is in an old fort overlooking the river. Just follow the signs to get there.

Getting There & Away

Bus The rodoviária is on Avenida Duque de Caxias. There are bus services to Maceió – the trip takes around three hours (three buses daily; US$5.50); and to Aracaju – the trip also takes three hours (one daily departure; US$3.50).

Car If you are driving to Penedo, there is a 41-km paved road from BR-101 in Sergipe to Neópolis, on the Sergipe side of the river, and then a short drive from Neópolis to Passagem, where a ferry boat makes the 10-minute river crossing to Penedo every 30 minutes (75c for a car).

There is also a dirt road (not marked on maps) that goes from BR-101 to Penedo along the north bank of the river. The turnoff from BR-101 is the first dirt road north of the bridge at Propriá. The only difficulty is staying on the right dirt road, but if you choose the fork that's closest to the river and stop and ask every once in a while you should be OK. There are good views of the river and some extremely poor hamlets along the way.

Around Penedo

The road is paved from Penedo down to the coast at Pontal do Peba. Along the way, there is a cheap hotel at the town of Piaçabuçu and a couple of restaurants. Praia do Peba, a couple of km from town, is a disappointing beach, well below the quality of those to the north.

The road north along the coast is unpaved, so the going is slow. The beaches are deserted until near Coruripe, a small fishing village with a hotel and a restaurant. Another 15 km of dirt road and you'll reach the coconut tree-lined beach at Poxim, which is even more beautiful than Coruripe; and the town is even smaller. There is no regular bus service along this stretch of coast.

NORTH OF MACEIÓ

If I had to choose one stretch of the Brazilian coast to spend several days exploring, this would be it. The Alagoas coast north of Maceió is ideal for independent travellers. The beaches are undisturbed and tropically perfect, and the sea is calm and warm. There are several fishing villages with no tourism apart from a simple hotel or two. The coastal road, which is unpaved and slow going along the most secluded stretch, runs within a few hundred metres of the ocean, a rare occurrence along the Brazilian littoral.

If you want to follow it, head down to Barra de Santo Antônio. This road is often in disarray and you have to cross some small rivers on local ferries, so check road conditions before departing.

Alternatively, from Maceió, AL-101 heads north and then divides outside Barra de Santo Antônio. The main road and most through traffic heads inland here on AL-465. It's a stunning drive through sugar-cane country (try to stop at Porto Calvo). AL-465 passes a large sugar-cane plant that processes the sugar-cane alcohol that fuels Brazil's cars. The Empresa de Santo Antônio employs about 800 workers in the factory and 4000 in the fields. Tours are possible and worthwhile, but hard to arrange.

A few buses from Maceió go all the way along the coast, but they are less frequent than those that follow the AL-465. Ask for a bus that goes to Porto de Pedras or São Miguel dos Milagres.

Barra de Santo Antônio & Ilha da Croa

Barra is along the mouth of the Rio Jirituba, below a small bluff. Only 40 km from Maceió, this fishing village is beginning to see a bit of tourism and beach-home construction. There is a boat that runs back and forth across the river.

The best beaches are out on the Ilha da Croa (narrow peninsula), 15 minutes by motorboat (US$1) from Barra de Santo Antônio.

Places to Stay & Eat The *Costa Verde Clube Hotel* (☎ 221-5581, 221-5308) is a fancy place, with a pool and horses, on the outskirts of town. Chalets cost US$35 for two people. There are also several cheap pensões which charge around US$4 per person for basic quartos.

Peixada da Rita along the river serves sensational seafood.

Getting There & Away Direct buses to Maceió operate from 4.30 am to 10.30 pm. You can also walk for 20 minutes or hire a local cab to the main road, where you can flag down those buses which bypass the town.

Barra do Camarajibe

This idyllic fishing village, 12 km further up the coast, offers fish, beer and beach. Ask around for a place to stay and for a ride in a fishing boat.

São Miguel dos Milagres

A bit bigger than its neighbours, São Miguel's soft beaches are protected by offshore reefs and the sea is warm and shallow. There's a petrol station in town.

Porto de Pedras

You've got to catch the local ferry to cross the river here. Porto de Pedras is a lively little fishing village with a road that connects to AL-465 at Porto Calvo. In the village there are bars, restaurants and the cheap and dingy *Hotel São Geraldo*.

Japaratinga

Japaratinga's shallow waters are protected by coral reefs and backed by coconut trees and fishing huts. Under the moonlight you can walk a couple of km into the sea. The town has a petrol station and a telephone.

Places to Stay & Eat The *Hotel Sol Mar*, on the south side of town, has a campground and simple quartos at US$5/6 for singles/doubles. *Rei dos Peixes* is a small pousada with similar prices. There's a large churrascaria by the road and several seafood eateries in town.

Getting There & Away There are regular buses from Japaratinga to Maceió and Recife (137 km).

Maragoji

Slightly more developed, Maragoji has some weekend homes for Pernambucanos and a couple of cheap hotels. The sea is protected by reefs and it's ideal for swimming.

Pernambuco

RECIFE

Recife is the country's fourth biggest city and the capital of Pernambuco. The Venice of Brazil (a rather hopeful Brazilian comparison), Recife is a city of water and bridges with *arrecifes* (stone reefs) offshore. Its sister city Olinda was once the capital of Brazil and today is a beautiful enclave of colonial buildings filled with artists, students and bohemians.

Amidst all the recent development Recife retains a rich traditional side, with some of Brazil's best folk art, including painting and sculpture, dance, music and festivals. It takes time to discover this side of the city, but it's well worth the effort.

Recife is the port of entry for many flights from Europe and has recently been trying to broaden its tourist appeal. The main beneficiary of these developments has been Boa Viagem, the Copacabana of Pernambuco. Site of the well-to-do nightclubs, restaurants and most of the mid to expensive hotels, Boa Viagem has good beaches which are essential for escaping Recife's muggy heat. However, unless you want be right on the beach, Olinda is a cheaper and more interesting place to stay.

History

Recife developed in the 17th century as the port for the rich sugar plantations around Olinda, which was the seat of the captaincy. With several rivers and offshore reefs, Recife proved to be an excellent port and began to outgrow Olinda. By the 17th century, Recife and Olinda combined were the most prosperous cities in Brazil, with the possible exception of Salvador (Bahia). The neighbouring Indians had been subdued after brutal warfare, and the colonial aristocracy living in Olinda was raking in profits with its many sugar engenhos (mills). Naturally all the work was done by slaves.

No European country had managed to grab a part of Brazil from the Portuguese until 1621, when the Dutch, who were active in the sugar trade and knew the lands of Brazil well, set up the Dutch West India Company to get their teeth into the Brazilian cake. A large fleet sailed in 1624 and captured Bahia, but a huge Spanish-Portuguese militia of 12,000 men recaptured the city the following year. Five years later the Dutch decided to try again, this time in Pernambuco. Recife was abandoned, the Dutch took the city and by 1640 they had control of a great chunk of the Northeast, from Maranhão to the Rio São Francisco.

The Dutch had hoped the sugar planters wouldn't resist their rule, but to their dismay many Brazilian planters took up arms against the non-Catholics. In 1654, after a series of battles around Recife, the Dutch finally surrendered. This was the last European challenge to Portuguese Brazil.

Recife prospered after the Dutch were expelled, but in spite of the city's growing economic power, which had eclipsed that of Olinda, political power remained with the sugar planters in Olinda and they refused to share it. In 1710 fighting began between the *filhos da terra* (the sugar planters of Olinda) and the *mascates* (the Portuguese merchants of Recife), the more recent immigrants. The Guerra dos Mascates (War of the Mascates), as it came to be known, was a bloody regional feud between different sections of the ruling classes and native Brazilians and immigrants. In the end, with the help of the Portuguese crown and their superior economic resources, the mascates of Recife gained considerable political clout at the expense of Olinda, which began its long, slow decline.

More dependent on the sugar economy than Rio or São Paulo, Recife was eclipsed by these two centres as the sugar economy floundered throughout the 19th century.

Orientation

Recife is large, modern and more difficult to

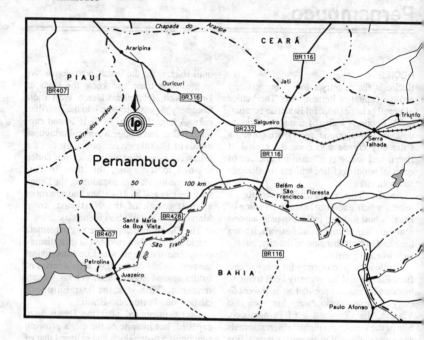

negotiate than most cities in the Northeast. The city centre is a confusing mixture of high-rise offices, colonial churches and popular markets. During the day, traffic and tourists get lost in the maze of winding, one-way streets.

The heart of Recife, containing the old section of town, ranges along the waterfront in Boa Vista district, across the Rio Capibaribe to Santo Antônio district and then across to Ilha do Recife (Island of Recife). All are connected by bridges.

Olinda is six km to the north over swamps and rivers while Boa Viagem is six km to the south.

Information
Tourist Office The headquarters of Empetur (☎ 231-7941), the state tourism bureau, is at Avenida Conde da Boa Vista 700. The tourist office, on the 2nd floor of the building, has plenty of brochures and maps. Smaller information booths are in the Casa da Cultura de Recife; Pátio de São Pedro, Loja 17 (municipal tourism organisation); and the rodoviária (good, but no literature). The information desk at the airport has been closed for lack of funds, organisation or both.

Useful publications available from tourist offices include *Walking Tour Schedule* (an illustrated map with a suggested walking route for daytime only); *Itinerário* (a monthly mini-guide for Recife) and *Shopping Map: Recife* (accurate and detailed). *Diário de Pernambuco*, one of the local newspapers, has cultural listings (museums, art galleries, cinemas, etc) in its daily Diversões (amusements) section.

Money There are convenient branches of Banco do Brasil at the airport, in the centre at Avenida Dantas Barreto, 541 (Santo Antônio), and in Boa Viagem at Avenida Conselheiro Aguiar, 3786.

Post & Telecommunications The main

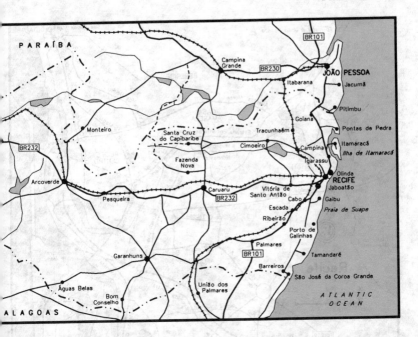

post office is at Avenida Guararapes 250. There are also convenient post offices at the airport and TIP (Terminal Integrado de Passageiros – rodoviária).

TELPE (the state phone company) has 24-hour phone stations with international service at TIP, the airport, and in the centre at Rua Diário de Pernambuco 38.

Foreign Consulates The following countries have consulates in Recife:

France
  Avenida Dantas Barreto, 1200, 9th floor, São José (☎ 224-6722)
Germany
  Avenida Dantas Barreto, 191, 4th floor, São José (☎ 224-3488)
UK
  Avenida Engenheiro Domingos Ferreira, 222, Boa Viagem (☎ 326-3733)
USA
  Rua Gonçalves Maia 163, Boa Vista (☎ 221-1429)

Visa Renewal If you need to renew a visa go to the Polícia Federal building on Cais do Apolo (Ilha do Recife). Since it's best to phone first, ask the tourist office for the appropriate information.

Travel Agencies Andratur (☎ 326-4388) at Avenida Conselheiro Aguiar, 3150, Loja 6 (Boa Viagem) provides national and international tickets at discounted prices (for example, US$960 for return flight from Recife to Miami with Transbrasil). This company also sells packaged trips for Fernando de Noronha.

Mubatur (☎ 341-4519) at Rua Barão de Souza Leão, 221, sala 23 (Boa Viagem) offers similar deals.

Bookshops There are several bookstalls along Rua do Infante Dom Henrique. The airport bookshop is a good bet if you are looking for English language books.

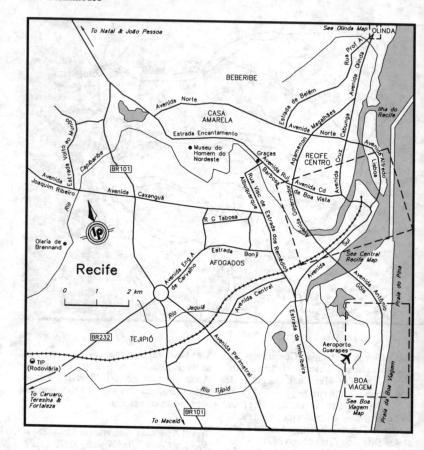

Museums & Galleries

With such a long and important history it's not surprising that Recife is loaded with churches and museums, but few are must-sees.

The best museum, Museu do Homem do Nordeste (Museum of the Northeast), is east of the city centre along Avenida 17 de Agosto. Catch the 'Dois Irmãos' bus from Parque 13 de Maio (in the centre) and ask the driver to let you off at the right spot. The museum is divided into three sections: an anthropology section about the people of the Northeast; a popular art section with some superb typical ceramic figurines; and a pharmacy exhibit about the region's rich herbal/indigenous medicine. Opening hours are from 11 am to 5 pm on Tuesday, Wednesday, and Friday; from 8 am to 5 pm on Thursday; and from 1 to 5 pm on Saturday, Sunday and public holidays.

The Horto Zoobotânico, with a zoo and botanical garden (both renovated in 1990), is in the same neighbourhood. Opening hours are from 7 am to 5 pm, from Tuesday to Sunday.

Train buffs may like to visit the Museu do Trem (Train Museum), which is adjacent to

Recife Metro Station – formerly known as Estação Central (Central Train Station). The museum is open from 9 am to noon and from 2 to 5 pm, Monday to Friday; from 9 am to noon on Saturday; and from 2 to 5 pm on Sunday.

For a look at paintings by renowned artists of Pernambuco, visit Galeria de Arte Metropolitana at Rua da Aurora 265. It's open from noon to 7 pm from Tuesday to Friday; and from 2 to 7 pm on Saturday and Sunday.

Archaeology enthusiasts will want to browse in the Museu Archeológico at Rua do Hospício, 130. It's open from 10 am to noon and from 2 to 4 pm, from Monday to Friday.

Old City

To see the old city start over at Praça da República where you'll see the **Teatro Santa Isabel** (1850) and the **Palácio do Governo** (1841). Take a look at *Igreja de Santo Antônio* (1753) in Praça da Independência and then visit **Catedral de São Pedro dos Clérigos** on Pátio de São Pedro, an artists' hangout. There are many intimate restaurants, shops and bars here, all with interesting local characters. On weekends there's often good music.

Walk down Rua Vidal de Negreiros to the **Forte das 5 Pontas**, which was built by the Dutch in 1630, then rebuilt in 1677. Inside there's the **Museu da Cidade**, which displays maps and photos of the city. Opening hours are 1 to 6 pm from Tuesday to Friday; and from 2 to 6 pm on Saturday and Sunday.

Nearby, at Praça Dom Vital, is the daily **Mercado do São José** (market) and **Basílica de NS da Penha**. The market used to be a major centre for food and crafts from throughout Pernambuco, but a fire in 1989 has curtailed the volume of business.

Casa da Cultura de Recife

The Casa da Cultura de Recife, across the street from Recife Metro Station, once served as a huge, colonial-style prison, but was decommissioned, renovated and redecorated in 1975. It's now home to many arts, crafts and trinket shops, but it's certainly not everyone's cup of tea because of its very touristy atmosphere. Good traditional music and dance shows are often performed outside the building, and the complex contains tourist information and phone offices. It's open from Monday to Saturday from 9 am to 8 pm, and on Sundays from 3 to 8 pm.

Olaria de Brennand

The Olaria, a ceramics factory and exhibition hall, is set in thickly forested surroundings, a rare landscape for suburban Recife and an even rarer chance for travellers in the Northeast to see what the Mata Atlântica looked like several centuries ago. The buildings and exhibits in Olaria de Brennand are perhaps the most bizarre highlight of the Northeast – highly recommended.

History The Irish forbears of the present owner, Francisco Brennand, arrived in Brazil in 1823 to work as peasant farmers. The unmarried daughter of a sugar magnate took a liking to Brennand's father, who was employed by her father. She later inherited her father's property, and, when she died, willed her entire estate and immense wealth to Brennand Senior.

The house in which Francisco Brennand was born in 1927 was imported from England in prefabricated form. Brennand's father founded a brickworks in 1917 and continued this business until 1945. Francisco left for France, where he studied art and was influenced by Picasso, Miró, Léger and Gaudi. The property in Recife remained abandoned from 1945 until 1971, when Brennand returned from France and set about restoring the dilapidated buildings.

The Gallery/Museum This contains a permanent exhibition of around 2000 pieces which are *not* for sale (see the end of this section for address of the sales outlet in Boa Viagem).

Wander around sculpted collages of cubes, spheres and rectangles absorbed into animal shapes: worms with balaclava hats; blunt-headed lizards bursting out of parapets; cuboid geckos straddling paths; geese

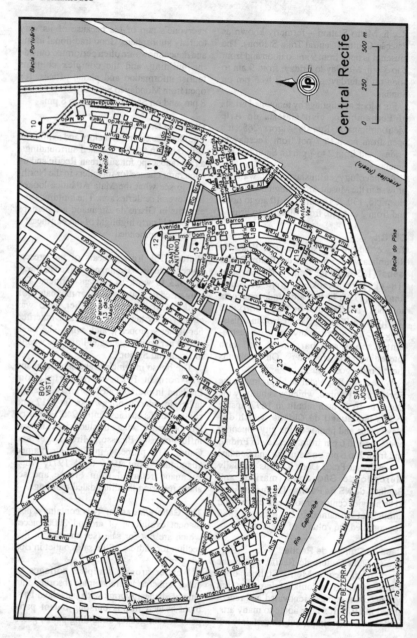

Central Recife

■ PLACES TO STAY

1 Hotel das Fronteiras
2 Hotel Central
4 Hotel Suiça
8 Hotel do Parque
9 Hotel América
16 Hotel 7 de Setembro
21 Hotel 4 de Outubro

OTHER

3 Empetur Tourist Office
5 Livro 7 Bookshop & China Brasil Restaurant
6 Galeria de Arte Metropolitana
7 Museu Archeológico
10 Fortaleza de São João Batista do Brum
11 Policia Federal
12 Palácio do Governo & Teatro Santa Isabel
13 Capela Dourada da Ordem Terceira de São Francisco
14 Post Office
15 Matriz de Santo Antônio
17 Praça da Independência
18 Praça 17
19 Mercado do São José
20 Pátio de São Pedro
22 Casa da Cultura de Recife
23 Recife Metro Station & Museu do Trem
24 Forte das 5 Pontas (Museu da Cidade)
25 Joana Bezerra Metro Station

with flying helmets; birds of prey hatching from half-shells lodged in the walls; pigs formed from giant nails; and vistas of busts, buttocks, breasts, and phalluses...meanwhile black swans glide through shoals of goldfish in ponds dotted with vulvas shaped like tortoises. Great fun: surely imagination cannot run more amok than this!

The gallery/museum is open from 8 am to 5 pm, Monday to Thursday; and from 8 am to 4 pm on Friday. For information, contact Oficina Ceramica Francisco Brennand (☎ 271-2466), s/a, Propriedade Santos Cosme e Damião, s/n (no number), Varzea, CEP 50741 Recife – PE.

Olaria Brennand produces superb ceramics which are sold in its shop (☎ 325-0025) at Avenida Conselheiro Aguiar 2966, Loja 4, Galeria Vila Real, in Boa Viagem.

Getting There & Away From the centre of Recife, take the bus marked 'Caxangá' for the long ride (around 11 km) to Caxangá bus terminal. Continue walking about 100 metres away from the city, and over the bridge; then take the first road on the left – easily recognised by the roadside statue of Padre Cicero. Walk about two km, past a couple of stray hotels, until you reach a gaudy housing development. At the T-junction, take the road to the left and continue for about 3 km through dense forest to the office. The walk takes about 75 minutes.

If you want to save time, you can take a taxi from the bus terminal or the bridge to the Olaria – and walk back after your visit. Tour companies and taxi companies will also do the trip from the centre of Recife or Olinda, but it's expensive unless you can form a small group to share the costs. For a recommended taxi company, see the Getting Around section for Olinda.

Festivals
The Recife-Olinda combination may be the best Carnival in Brazil but even if you decide to carnival in Rio or Salvador, Recife starts celebrating so early that you can enjoy festivities there and then go somewhere else for Carnival proper. Two months before the start of Carnival there are *bailes* (dances) in the clubs and Carnival blocos practising on the streets with frevo dancing everywhere. Galo da Madrugada, Recife's largest bloco, has been known to bring 20,000 people in costume onto the beaches at Boa Viagem to dance.

There are supposedly 500 different Carnival blocos in the Recife area and they come in all 'shakes' and colours. There are the traditional and well organised, the modern and anarchical. There are samba schools, there are afoxés, Indian tribes and *maracatus* (African processions accompanied by percussion musicians), but the main dance of Carnival in Pernambuco is the frenetic frevo.

The Fundação da Cultura do Recife, which runs Carnival, has on occasion organised public frevo lessons for the uninitiated at the Pátio de São Pedro.

Along Boa Viagem beach, Carnival groups practise on weekends and as Carnival approaches they add trios elétricos to the tomfoolery. The week before Carnival Sunday, unofficial Carnival really starts. Several groups march through the city centre each day and at least one baile kicks off each evening – time to practise that frevo.

Big-time Carnival takes place from Saturday to Tuesday, nonstop. The big Carnival groups parade in wonderful costumes, singing and dancing. For the parade route and schedule, check the local papers or the tourism office. Along Avenida Guararapes there's a popular frevo dance that starts on Friday night and goes on and on.

Places to Stay – bottom end

Although we've included details here for accommodation in Recife, most budget travellers prefer staying in Olinda: it's cheap and beautiful, there's lots happening and you can walk everywhere. If you want the beach, head to Boa Viagem, where the cheapest options are youth hostels.

Centre If you want to stay in central Recife there are a couple of good bets near Parque 13 de Maio. The Suiça (☎ 222-3534), Rua do Hospício 687, has quartos at US$5 per person. Apartamentos with fan cost US$6/8 for singles/doubles. Down the road is the busy and friendly Hotel do Parque (326-4666) at Rua do Hospício 51. Quartos with fan cost US$7/9. Apartamentos with air-con cost US$11 (same price for single/double). A block away the Hotel América (☎ 221-1300), Praça Maciel Pinheiro 48, has apartamentos at US$19/21 for singles/doubles. It doesn't merit two stars; some rooms are cramped without windows – see the room first.

Hotel das Fronteiras (☎ 221-0015) at Rua Henrique Dias 255 has friendly staff and clean apartamentos with fan at US$14/16 for singles/doubles. Equivalent apartamentos with air-con cost US$2 extra. Hotel 7 de Setembro, Rua Matias de Albuquerque 318 (near the Rio Capibaribe), has apartamentos at US$6/7 singles/doubles.

Boa Viagem For youth hostels, try Albergue de Juventude Maracatus do Recife (☎ 326-1221) at Rua Dona Maria Carolina 185; and Albergue de Juventude Maresias (☎ 326-6284) at Rua Mamanguape 678.

Places to Stay – middle

Centre The Central (☎ 221-1472) at Rua Manoel Borba 209 is a colonial mansion with a pleasant rambling design. Apartamentos cost US$26/29 for singles/doubles. You may be able to negotiate a 20% discount on these prices for cash.

Hotel 4 de Outubro (☎ 424-4477) is a modern, functional hotel opposite Recife Metro Station. Apartamentos start around US$30/32 for singles/doubles.

Boa Viagem The moderately priced hotels here are often full during the summer season. As a general rule, prices drop the further you go back from the seafront.

Hotel Pousada Aconchego (☎ 326-2989) at Rua Felix de Brito Melo 382 has apartamentos at US$21/23. Hotel Alameda Jasmins (☎ 325-1591) at Rua Felix de Brito 370 provides a friendly reception and a garden with swimming pool. Apartamentos start at around US$20/21 for singles/doubles. Seasonal discounts are available. Hotel Portal do Sol (☎ 326-9740) at Avenida Conselheiro Aguiar 3217 has similar prices but no swimming pool.

Hotel 54 (☎ 325-0695) at Rua Professor José Brandão 54 has rooms at US$34/38.

Places to Stay – top end

Almost all the better hotels are in Boa Viagem; there's no reason to stay in the centre of town. Remember it gets very humid in Recife. Hotel Tivoli (☎ 326-5669), at Rua Tenente João Cicero 47, charges US$45/50 for singles/doubles.

If you want the best, or at least the most expensive deals, try the four-star Othon

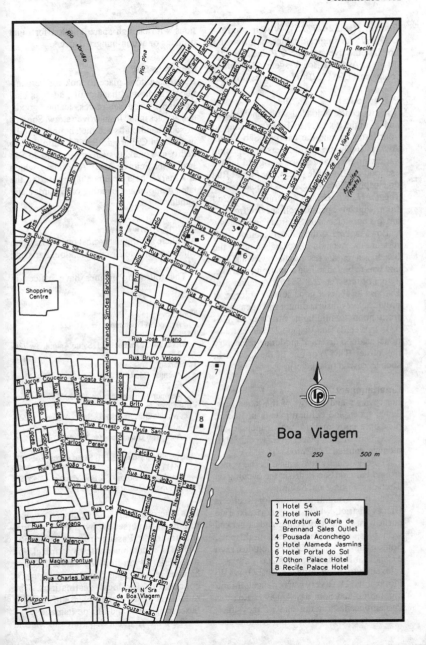

Boa Viagem

0   250   500 m

1 Hotel 54
2 Hotel Tivoli
3 Andratur & Olaria de
   Brennand Sales Outlet
4 Pousada Aconchego
5 Hotel Alameda Jasmins
6 Hotel Portal do Sol
7 Othon Palace Hotel
8 Recife Palace Hotel

Palace (☎ 326-7225), which charges US$69/75 for singles/doubles, or move up a notch to the five-star *Recife Palace* (☎ 325-4044) at Avenida Boa Viagem 4070 where rooms cost US$125/140 for singles/doubles.

Places to Eat

The city centre is loaded with lunch places and at night it's easy to find something to your liking around the Pátio de São Pedro. Always lively, the pátio offers a surprising variety of prices and styles. For good Japanese food at affordable prices, try *Fuji* at Rua do Hospício 354. Vegetarians should visit *O Vegetal II* at Avenida Guararapes 210, 2nd floor, which is open for self-service from 11 am to 3 pm – closed on Saturday and Sunday.

Boa Viagem has the bulk of Recife's good restaurants. Avenida Boa Viagem, along the beach, is a regular restaurant row. Walk here and you're bound to find something you like. The *Lobster* (☎ 268-5516), Avenida Rui Barbosa 1649, is a good lobster splurge. It provides live music at dinner and opens daily from noon to midnight. *Maxime* (☎ 326-5314), Avenida Boa Viagem 21, serves traditional seafood dishes at moderate prices; try the lobster (US$7) or one of the local fish, such as *cavala* (mackerel).

Entertainment

For reviews and listings of the latest bars, dance spots, and cultural events in Recife, pick up a copy of *Veja*, which includes an assortment of such places in its weekly supplement entitled *28 Graus*.

There is usually live music in the centre around Pátio de São Pedro in the evening on Thursday, Friday, and Saturday.

The major nightlife centre for Recife is Graças district, which is a short taxi ride north-west of the city centre and is packed with bars, clubs, and general nightspots. Some of the options in Graças include Cravo e Canela at Rua das Creoulas 260 – a suave, relaxed bar; New Hits at Rua Gervásio Fioravante 111 – a very active danceteria and night club; and Som das Aguas at Rua das Pernambucanas (at the end of the street, beside the river) – divided into separate sec-

tions with enough space allotted for quiet drinkers or action-hungry dancers.

Things to Buy

Recife is a good place to look for Pernambuco's traditional handicrafts, such as clay figurines, wood sculptures, leather goods, and articles made from woven straw. Sources of such handicrafts are the shops and stalls in Casa da Cultura de Recife, Pátio de São Pedro, and markets such as Mercado do São José or the Feira de Arte e Artesanato, which is a market held in Boa Viagem during the late afternoon and evening on Saturday and Sunday.

Getting There & Away

Air There are flights to most major Brazilian cities, and also to Lisbon, London, Paris and Miami.

The following airlines have offices in Recife:

Nordeste
    Aeroporto Guararapes (☎ 341-4222)
TAP
    Avenida Guararapes 111, Santo Antônio (☎ 224-2700)
Transbrasil
    Avenida Conde da Boa Vista 1546 (Boa Vista) (☎ 231-0522)
    Aeroporto Guararapes (☎ 326-2081)
Varig-Cruzeiro
    Avenida Guararapes 120, Santo Antônio (☎ 224-9066)
    Aeroporto Guararapes (☎ 341-4411)
VASP
    Avenida Guararapes 111, Santo Antônio (☎ 222-3611)
    Rua Manoel Borba 488, Boa Vista (☎ 421-3088)
    Aeroporto Guararapes (☎ 326-1699)

Bus The old rodoviária (rodoviária velha) has been superseded by TIP (Terminal Integrado de Passageiros; ☎ 251-4666), which is a combined Metro terminal and rodoviária, 14 km from the centre. TIP now handles all interstate departures and many connections for local destinations. The rodoviária velha is, however, still used for buses to Igarassu and Ilha de Itamaracá.

There are frequent departures to Maceió

(four hours; US$6); at least five daily departures to Salvador (12 to 14 hours; US$20; leito US$38); and daily departures to Rio (about 40 hours; US$50; leito US$100).

Heading north, it's two hours to João Pessoa (US$4.50); five hours to Natal (US$8.50); 12 hours to Fortaleza (US$22); 23 hours to São Luis (US$42); and 34 hours to Belém (US$50). There are frequent services to Caruaru (two hours; US$4.50); Garanhuns (2½ hours; US$7.50); and Triunfo (7½ hours; US$16).

Walking – from Recife to Maceió

Two Swedish travellers wrote to tell us about their walk from Recife to Maceió:

We started from Olinda, where we left most of our luggage at our pousada. From the centre of Recife we took the train (hourly departures) to Cabo, and then walked to the beach at Gaibu. The reason we started outside Recife was because we had been warned about walking around in the suburbs.

Sun protection is a must. If you walk from Maceió to Recife, the sun is in your face the whole time. We're happy we did it the other way round because the sun can really burn. You should carry a portable stove and always have at least one litre of water per person. Many villages can provide water and food. A big knife is useful as it's easy to pick coconuts along the way. A tent isn't strictly necessary, but it's good to have the option. You don't really need a mosquito net either.

After three hours of walking from Gaibu, we reached a little village and the first river. Don't try to cross it. We made this mistake and found ourselves in the Complexo Portuário e Industrial de Suape, a large oil refinery, where we had a terrible time finding a way out. It's far better to wait for a bus to NS do Ó, and walk from there to Porto de Galinhas; continue past the beautiful Praia de Galinhas until you come to a small river which you can wade across (waist level) at low tide.

At Barra de Sirinhaém, boats take you across the river for free. Unfortunately there is a lot of garbage along the beaches; people throw many things in the river, and you can even find needles and other things from hospitals.

At Rio Formoso, boats cross the river, but you may have to wait a while before one arrives. We got a lift for free right away. After about four more km we came to Tamandaré, a village with shops, bars, hotels, and boat rental.

At the next river, Rio Una, once again we got a ride across for free. Varza do Una is a very different village, and it can be difficult to find a place to stay, but ask around.

From here we had to hitchhike around a swamp area to São José da Coroa Grande. From here we continued into Alagoas state where the highway AL-101 runs not further than 100 metres from the beach. This makes it easy to walk up to the road to get around rivers.

Maragoji is a big beach with many bars, boat rentals, and other facilities. Japaratinga was the first place we slept at a pousada (Rei dos Peixes; quarto double for US$5). Our next stop was at the Rio Manguaba, where we were taken across by boat for US$1. It's also possible to walk to the highway and take a ferry. On the other side is a small town, Porto de Pedras, which is a nice, colourful place with good cheap restaurants and pousadas.

From here we started to follow the main road which was hot and boring until São Miguel dos Milagres (13 km from Porto de Pedras), where there is one pousada charging US$5/6 for a single/double quarto, breakfast included.

The following day we crossed the Rio Camarajibe by boat (fare 50c) and came to absolutely the nicest beach we found along this part of the coast. From there we walked three km to Barra de Santo Antônio.

Barra de Santo Antônio is nothing special. You can stay at Terezinha, a pensão which charges US$10 for a double quarto, including breakfast. Ilha da Croa is a peninsula. Take a boat across the river (50c), then walk along the beach to your right and cross to the other side of the peninsula. This only takes about 20 minutes.

This walk took us 11 days. We only walked in the morning and late afternoon. We often stopped for hours and sometimes for days. People invited us to stay with them. Fishing families are very generous and adore the company of foreigners. It's easily possible to do the walk in seven days, or even five days if you're in a hurry. We found enormous hospitality.

With blisters on our feet and red faces, we took a bus from here to Maceió – locals said the last 40 km to Maceió were nothing special. It was a great adventure and we loved every minute – almost!

Suzanne Gabrielsson & Lief Örnestrand

Getting Around

To/From the Airport Aeroporto Guararapes (☎ 341-1888) is 10 km south of the city centre. Taxis cost about US$12 to the centre; catch a regular taxi – not a special airport taxi, which is about twice as expensive.

From the airport there are regular buses and *micro* buses (more expensive) to NS do Carmo (Olinda) and Dantas Barreto (central Recife). Both routes stop at Boa Viagem. To get to the airport take a bus from NS do Carmo or Dantas Barreto.

Bus & Taxi Buses generally have signs which show the origin of the bus followed by its destination. For a telephone taxi dial 231-7533.

To/From Olinda From the city centre to Olinda, catch any bus marked 'Rio Doce'. The main bus stop in Olinda is Praça do Carmo. Taxis from the centre of Recife to Olinda cost about US$5 and take 20 minutes.

To/From Boa Viagem From the centre to Boa Viagem, take any bus marked 'Cidade Universitária/Boa Viagem'. To return to the centre, take any bus marked 'Dantas Barreto'. A taxi from the centre to Boa Viagem costs around US$5.

To/From TIP (Metro/Rodoviária) The shiny metro system is very useful for the 25-minute trip (50c) between TIP and the metro terminus at the Recife Metro Station) in the centre. Travellers who want to go straight to Boa Viagem from TIP should get off at metro stop 'Joana Bezerra' and catch a bus from there to Boa Viagem.

BEACHES SOUTH OF RECIFE

This is excellent beach territory: protected by coral reefs, the sea is calm, the waters are crystal clear, and the beaches are lined with coconut palms and white sand dunes. The coastal PE-060 road doesn't hug the ocean, like the road in northern Alagoas, so you have to drive a dozen or so km on an access road to see what each beach is like. There is a frequent direct bus service to all these beach towns from Recife. From Alagoas just take a coastal bus to Recife, and then catch another bus, hitch or walk the dirt access road to the beach. Many of these towns have one or two simple hotels and, away from Recife, all have excellent camping.

São José da Coroa Grande

The first beach town you reach after crossing into Pernambuco from Alagoas is São José da Coroa Grande, which has one of Pernambuco's finest beaches. It's 120 km from Recife on the PE-060 coastal road. The

fishing town is receiving attention from property developers, mostly for construction of weekend homes. There are a few restaurants and bars and two hotels, one moderately priced, the other a simple pensão.

Tamandaré

The next access road north of São José da Coroa Grande goes 10 km to the beach at Tamandaré. There's a small fishing village here with only a couple of bars and no hotel. The beach is idyllic and you can see the old 17th-century Forte Santo Inácio.

More Beaches

The dirt road going north along the coast from Tamadaré will take you past the beaches of Ponta dos Manguinhos, Guadalupe, Camela and then to Barra de Sirin-haém, where there is a 10-km access road back to the main road.

The only lodging in these towns is with the local fisherfolk. During the week the beaches are practically deserted. Off the coast is the Ilha de Santo Aleixo.

Porto de Galinhas

Seventy km south of Recife is Porto de Galinhas (Port of Chickens). The name came as a result of slave trade which secretly continued after abolition. Upon hearing that the chickens from Angola had arrived, the masters of Recife knew to expect another load of slaves.

Porto de Galinhas has one of Pernambuco's most famous beaches, which curves along a pretty bay lined with coconut palms, mangroves and cashew trees. Most of the beach, three km from town, is sheltered by a reef, but there are some waves for surfers. The water is warm and clear – you can see the colourful fish playing around your feet. There are plenty of jangadas for rent but they're not cheap (US$4 an hour).

Should you tire of Praia de Porto de Galinhas, head for Praia de Maracaípe, a beach three km away. From here you can sail on a jangada to Ilha de Santo Aleixo. The fishers charge US$10 per hour and take up to four passengers on their boats.

Places to Stay Most of the visitors here either own homes (the celebrities and politicos of Pernambuco), rent for the season or camp out (campground at Praia de Maracaípe). If you want to stay a few days, several houses are available to rent. *Pousada Armação de Porto* has a swimming pool and comfortable apartamentos at around US$25/28 for singles/doubles. *Solar Porto de Galinhas* is more expensive and plush, with a great position on the beach and a good restaurant. Apartamentos start at around US$32/36 for singles/doubles.

Places to Eat Famed for its seafood, Porto de Galinhas has several eateries, but the town's most renowned is *Peixada do Braz*. Don't miss the lobster, cooked in coconut or tomato sauce or just plain grilled. Other fine restaurants in town include *Peixada do Laercio*, *Restaurante Porto de Galinhas*, *Restaurante de Bras* and *Brisa Maritima*. All these restaurants serve lobster, squid, shrimp and local fish cooked with coconut milk, pepper and cumin sauces. The locally made genipapo liqueur is worth tasting, too.

Gaibu & Cabo de Santo Agostinho

Although Gaibu is the larger town further up the coast, beach bums should head only as far as Cabo de Santo Agostinho, one of the state's finest beaches. There are facilities for snorkelling and spear-fishing. Take a walk to the ruins of the Forte Castelo do Mar, which is next to the church.

On a hill between Gaibu and Calhetas (you have to ask around for directions) there's a small, freshwater stream that's used for nude bathing.

Suape & Ilha do Paiva

Suape has been developed as an industrial port. Heading north again, Ilha do Paiva, nicknamed the island of lovers, is popular for its nude beaches. Take a boat from Barra dos Jangandas – it's worth a visit.

The mainland beaches here – Candeias, Venda Grande, Piedade – are semi-urban beaches with many barracas, hotels and crowds on weekends. But they are still good beaches, with clean water and sometimes strong surf.

OLINDA

Beautiful Olinda, placed on a hill overlooking Recife and the Atlantic, is one of the largest and best preserved colonial cities in Brazil. Although many of the buildings in Olinda were originally constructed in the 16th century, the Dutch burnt virtually everything in 1631. Consequently, most of what you now see has been reconstructed at a later date. For an account of Olinda's history, refer to the History section in the introduction to Recife.

Whilst Recife plays the role of an administrative and economic centre, Olinda is recognised as its cultural counterpart: a living city with bohemian quarters, art galleries, museums, music in the streets, and always some kind of celebration in the works.

Orientation

Olinda is six km north of Recife. The historical district, which constitutes about 10% of the city, is concentrated around the upper streets of the hill and is easily visited on foot. The beaches immediately adjacent to the city, Milagres for example, suffer from pollution, and bathing is not recommended. Casa Caiada, the district at the foot of the hill, has several restaurants.

Throughout Olinda you'll no doubt hear the cry *guia* (guide). Olinda has more little kids throwing their services at you than anywhere in Brazil. If driving with an out-of-state licence plate, wearing a backpack or dawdling in front of a church, you'll be besieged. Offering services is fine, but the aggressive tactics employed by some of these characters should be ignored; and if you do take a guide, make sure the price is fixed *before* you start the tour.

Information

Tourist Office Whatever services you don't find in Olinda you can secure in Recife (eg airline offices, car-rental agencies). The main tourist office (☎ 429-0397), at Rua 13

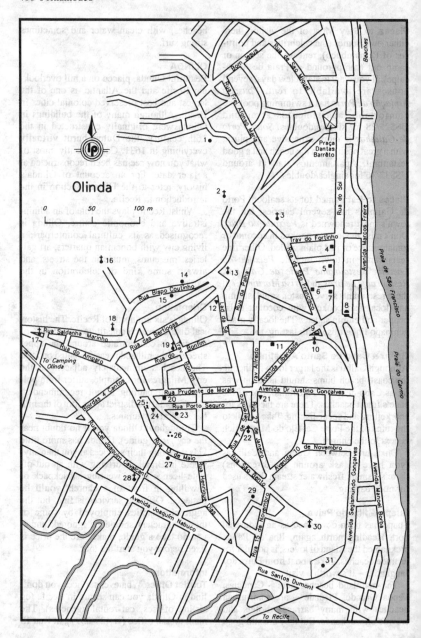

Olinda

0   50   100 m

Praça Dantas Barrêto

Bom Jesus

Rua de São Miguel

Rua Frei Afonso Maria

Rua do Sol

Rua Marcos Freire

Praia de São Francisco

Praia do Carmo

Beaches

1

2

3

Trav do Fortinho

4

5

6

7

8

9

10

11

Rua de São Francisco

Rua da Palma

14

13

15

Rua Bispo Coutinho

12

16

18

17

Rua Saldanha Marinho

Rua do Amparo

To Camping Olinda

Rua das Bertiogas

Ladeira de São Francisco

Rua do Bonfim

19

Rua do Bonfim

Trav Alfredo

Avenida Liberdade

Bordas & Cantos

Rua Prudente de Morais

20

Rua Porto Seguro

Avenida Dr Justino Gonçalves

21

25

24

23

22

26

Rua 13 de Maio

27

Rua Cel Joaquim Cavalcanti

Rua 7 de Setembro

Rua 7 de Janeiro

Avenida 10 de Novembro

28

Rua São Bento

Rua Henrique Dias

29

Avenida Joaquim Nabuco

30

Rua 15 de Novembro

Avenida Segismundo Gonçalves

Avenida Manoel Borba

31

Rua Santos Dumont

To Recife

■ PLACES TO STAY

4 Pousada do Fortim
5 Albergue de Olinda
6 Pousada Flor da Manhã
7 Hotel Pousada São Francisco
11 Albergue Pousada do Bonfim
20 Pousdada dos Quatro Cantos

▼ PLACES TO EAT

12 Restaurant Cantinho da Sé
21 Mourisco Restaurant
24 Atelier Restaurant

OTHER

1 Farol de Olinda (Lighthouse)
2 Seminário de Olinda/Igreja NS da
   Graça
3 Convernto São Francisco
8 Post Office
9 Praça do Carmo & Buses to Recife
10 Igreja NS do Carmo
13 Igreja da Sé
14 Museu de Arte Sacra de Pernambuco
15 Observatorio Astronômico
16 Recolhimento das Irmãs
   Dorotéias/Igreja NS da Conceição
17 Igreja NS do Amparo
18 Igreja da Misericódia
19 Igreja NS do Bonfim
22 Igreja São Pedro
23 Mercado da Ribeira
25 Tourist Office
26 Senado Ruins
27 Museu de Arte Contemporânea
28 Igreja da Boa Hora
29 Palaçio dos Governadores
30 Mosteiro de São Bento
31 Mercado Popular (Market)

---

de Maio 322, has good maps, walking tour brochures, information about art exhibitions, music performances, etc, and a small library of publications about Olinda. The office is open from 8 am to 1 pm, from Monday to Friday. There is also an information booth in Mercado Popular (market).

Post Office The main post office is on Praça do Carmo. It's open on Saturday mornings.

Walking Tour

Starting at Praça do Carmo, visit **Igreja NS do Carmo** (currently under restoration). Then follow Rua de São Francisco to **Convento São Francisco** (1585), which is a large structure containing three elements: the convent, the **Capela de São Roque** (chapel), and the **Igreja de NS das Neves** (church) – approximate daily opening hours for this group are from 8 to 11.30 am and 2 to 4.30 pm.

At the end of the street, turn left onto Rua Frei Afonso Maria and you'll see the **Seminário de Olinda** and **Igreja NS da Graça** (1549) on the hill above. Daily visiting hours are from 8 to 11.30 am and 2 to 5 pm.

Continue up the street, then turn left at Rua Bispo Coutinho and climb up to **Alto da Sé**, ('Cathedral Heights'), which is a good spot to enjoy superb views of Olinda and Recife. There are outdoor restaurants and a small craft market with some good woodcarvings, figurines and jewellery. It's a big hangout at night – good for meeting people, eating and drinking and, with a bit of luck, hearing some local music. The imposing **Igreja da Sé** (1537) is open from 7 am to 7 pm on Saturday and Sunday.

Continue a short distance along Rua Bispo Coutinho until you see the **Museu de Arte Sacra de Pernambuco** (MASPE) on your right. MASPE is housed in a beautiful building (1696) that once functioned as Olinda's Episcopal Palace & Camara (Government Council). The museum contains a good collection of sacred art and a photographic homage to the city. It's open Tuesday to Friday from 8 am to noon and 2 to 6 pm. On Saturdays and Sundays it's open from 2 to 5.30 pm.

About 75 metres further down the street, turn right into a patio to visit **Igreja NS da Conceição** (1585).

Retrace your steps and continue down the street, now named Ladeira da Misericórdia, to **Igreja da Misericórdia** (1540), which has fine azulejos and gilded carvings inside. It's open from 9 to 11 am, Monday to Friday, and from 2 to 5 pm on Saturday and Sunday.

From here, turn right onto Rua Saldanha Marinho to see **Igreja NS do Amparo** (1581) – currently under renovation.

Descend Rua do Amparo to join Rua 13 de Maio and walk about 100 metres until you see **Museu de Arte Contemporânea** (MAC) on your right. This museum of contemporary art is recommended for its permanent and temporary exhibits. The museum is housed in an 18th-century *ajube*, a jail used by the Catholic church during the Inquisition – with the new paint job you'd hardly guess its grim past. It's open Tuesday to Friday from 9 am to 5 pm, and Saturdays and Sundays from 2 to 5 pm.

Rua 13 de Maio continues in a tight curve to a junction with Rua Bernardo de Melo and Rua São Bento. If you walk up Rua Bernardo de Melo, you'll come to **Mercado da Ribeira**, an 18th-century structure that is now home to art and artisan galleries.

If you walk down Rua São Bento, you'll reach the huge **Mosteiro de São Bento** (1582) which has some exceptional woodcarving in the chapel. Do some exploring in here by going up the stone stairs on your left as you enter. There are all sorts of dark passageways and mysterious rooms. Brazil's first law school was housed here for 24 years (I'm not sure what lawyers did in colonial Brazil, but it had little to do with justice). The monastery is open daily from 8 to 11 am and 1 to 5 pm.

Beaches

The city beaches are polluted and not recommended for bathing. However, there are many excellent beaches north of Olinda which are described later in this chapter.

Festivals

Olinda's Carnival has been very popular with Brazilians and travellers for several years (see also the Carnival section in Recife). The old historic setting combined with the fact that so many residents know each other provides an intimacy and security that you don't get in big city Carnivals. It's a participatory Carnival: costumed blocos parade through the city dancing to frevo music and everyone else follows.

In recent years there have been complaints of creeping Carnival commercialisation in Olinda. On the other hand, Recife's Carnival has been getting better reviews lately. Since the two cities are so close, you could try out both of them at Carnival. Publications with full information on Carnival schedules and events are supplied by the tourist office in Olinda.

Carnival in Olinda lasts a full 11 days. There are organised Carnival events, including balls (of course), a night of samba, and a night of afoxé, but everything else happens in impromptu fashion on the streets. The official opening ceremonies – with the pomp and ceremony of the Olympic games – commence with a bloco of more than 400 'virgins' (men in drag) and awards for the most beautiful, the most risqué and for the biggest prude.

Everyone dresses for the Carnival, so you'll want some sort of costume. The Carnival groups of thousands dance the frevo through the narrow streets. It's very playful and very lewd. Five separate areas have orchestras playing nonstop from 8 pm to 6 am nightly.

Apart from Carnival, we also highly recommend the festival known as Folclore Nordestino, held at the end of August, which features dance, music, and folklore from many parts of the Northeast.

Places to Stay

The main choice in accommodation is whether you prefer to stay in the old city, which has fewer hotels, or north of town near the beaches at Bairro Novo or Farol. Reserve several months in advance and be prepared for massive price hikes if you want to stay in Olinda during Carnival.

For long stays (except during Carnival), the transport company Viagens Sob O Sol (☎ 429-3303) at Rua Prudente de Moraes 424 (opposite Pousada dos Quatro Cantos) lets a beach apartment (capacity up to 10 people) for US$150 per day, including rental of vehicle, or US$75 without vehicle.

Places to Stay – bottom end

At the low end there are several pousadas and a couple of albergues (hostels). There are several quasi-official pousadas that seem to come and go, which are good deals. Albergues have dorm-style sleeping, and sometimes a few quartos.

For camping within easy reach of the historical district, there's *Camping Olinda* (☎ 429-1365) at Rua do Bom Sucesso 262.

If you don't mind dorm-style sleeping, the *Albergue Pousada do Bonfim* (☎ 429-1674) at Rua do Bonfim 115-B is neat and clean and offers a bed in an eight-bed room for US$6. Keen dancers should ask here about frevo lessons. *Albergue de Olinda* (☎ 429-1592) at Rua do Sol 233 has collective quartos that sleep two to six people for US$6 a head. Apartamentos are also available at US$9/16 for singles/doubles. Similar hostel lodging is provided by *Albergue de Juventude Cheiro do Mar* (☎ 429-0101) at Avenida Marcos Freire 95; and *Hotel Albergue* (☎ 429-1409) at Avenida Marcos Freire 153.

Pousada Flor da Manhã (☎ 429-2266) at Rua de São Francisco 162 is an old villa, previously used as a radio station, now revamped as a hotel under German/Brazilian management. Individual apartamentos are assigned names of countries and decorated accordingly. 'India' is a spartan room with bunk beds which cost US$5 per person. 'Brazil' costs US$13/17 for single/double occupation. 'Chile', 'Peru' and 'Alemanha Romántica' (Romantic Germany – a homesick aberration?) cost US$18/22 for single/double occupation. Ask about discounts for stays longer than three days; during Carnival it may be possible to sling hammocks for a minimal fee.

Pousada do Fortim (☎ 439-1881) at Rua do Sol 311 has adequate apartamentos at US$12/13 for singles/doubles – for apartamentos with air-con you'll pay an additional US$3.

Places to Stay – middle

In the medium price range we'd recommend staying in *Pousada dos Quatro Cantos* (☎ 429-0220) at Rua Prudente de Morais 441. It's a fine colonial building with a leafy courtyard. Quartos cost around US$15/30. Apartamentos start at US$36/40; the splurge option is the suite (two rooms plus verandah) which costs US$48/53 for single/double occupation.

Hotel Pousada São Francisco (☎ 429-2109) at Rua do Sol 127, has recently been refurbished with upmarket facilities, including a swimming pool. Apartamentos cost US$40/45 for singles/doubles.

Places to Stay – top end

For luxury sleeping, *Hotel Quatro Rodas* (☎ 431-2955) is Olinda's five-star affair. It's north of town, on a so-so beach, with facilities for almost everything, including baby-sitting and a free bus to Recife. Room prices start at around US$75/85 for singles/doubles.

Places to Eat

Although *Cantinho da Sé* has a great view from Alto da Sé, it's overpriced. *Pousada Flor da Manhã* does good seafood meals and salads at reasonable prices. *Pousada dos Quatro Cantos* has a pricier menu, but the moqueca de peixe is superb. In a similar price range is *Mourisco*, one of Olinda's best fish restaurants. Try the *estrogonofe de camarão* (shrimp stroganoff). It's open daily from 11 am to 3 pm and from 7 to 11 pm – closed on Monday.

There are several good restaurants along the beach and within easy walking distance of the old city. For pizza try *Pizzaria Status* at Avenida José Augusto Moreira 379. *Sol na Brasa* at Avenida José Augusto Moreira 656 serves regional cuisine daily from 11 am to 3 pm and from 6 to 11 pm. Try the *linguiça do sertão* (sausage) for something new and different.

Out in Barra Novo, *Restaurant Taipei* at Avenida Marcos Freire 1161 has passable Chinese food. *Rei da Lagosta* (☎ 429-1565) at Avenida Marcos Freire 1255 gets mixed reviews but no one questions the fine view of the sea.

For fine dining the very expensive

Restaurante L'Atelier (☎ 429-3099) at Rua Bernardo Vieira de Melo 91 is considered the best. It has French cuisine and is open from 7 to 11.30 pm; closed on Tuesday. It's small, so you should reserve in advance.

Entertainment

Alto da Sé has several bars/restaurants open late with live music and a good mix of locals and travellers. Esperança is a good choice. In the old city there are several relaxed, hip bars that often have music. For dancing, try Olinda Caliente on Praça do Carmo.

For live music closer to the beach, there's Clã Destino at Rua do Sol 225 or Fruta Pão at Rua do Sol 349. A nearby nightspot for music and dancing is Las Vegas at Avenida Marcos Freire 1571.

On Friday and Saturday nights the beach restaurant/bars north of town come to life. The Ciranda de Dona Duda on Janga beach is famous for its participatory ciranda (round dance). The market at Milagres beach has a folk music show Tuesday nights.

Getting Around

Viagens Sob O Sol (☎ 429-3303), opposite Pousada dos Quatro Cantos, has a variety of vehicles for hire, with or without a driver/guide. This is an interesting option if you can form a group of three or more. Trips can be arranged, for example, to Porto de Galinhas, Itamaracá, Caruaru, Fazenda Nova (Nova Jerusalém), Olaria Brennand, and various art and handicraft showrooms. Sample prices for a minibus (maximum eight passengers) are US$150 for a trip to Nova Jerusalém, and US$20 for transfer between Olinda and the airport or TIP. The company is run by two affable 'ghostbuster' look-alikes, Mauro and Felipe, who are always keen to embark on 'night sorties', trips to remote beaches, or any other wild schemes!

To/From Recife The main bus stop in Olinda is on Praça do Carmo. Buses marked 'Rio Doce/Conde da Boa Vista' go to the centre of Recife. Taxis cost about US$5.

BEACHES NORTH OF OLINDA

You've got to get out of town a bit for a fine, clean beach. Head north to Janga beach (eight km) or at least Rio Doce (six km), and beyond to Praia do Ó (12 km); Praia do Pau Amarelo (14 km); Praia da Conceição (17 km); and Praia da Maria Farinha (23 km). The road goes along close to the beach, but don't be deterred by the ugly development beside the road: the beaches are generally undisturbed except for barracas and crowds on weekends. Enjoy the local *siri* (small crab) and *caranguejo* (big crab) at the barracas. There are local buses to these beaches from Praça do Carmo.

IGARASSU

One of the oldest cities in Brazil, Igarassu is 35 km north of Recife and 20 km shy of Ilha de Itamaracá. Igarassu is small, untouristed, and full of colonial buildings.

History

27 September 1535, the day of Saints Cosme and Damião, was a busy day for town hero Duarte Coelho and his men. They managed to fight off both the Potigar Indians at the mouth of the Rio Igarassu and the French pirates offshore. Later in the afternoon, after a big meal, Duarte Coelho founded the village, naming it São Cosme e Damião in honour of the saints. It later came to be known as Igarassu.

Information

Igarassu's tourist office (☎ 543-0435) at Praça da Bandeira 42, has brochures and beautiful free posters.

Historic Section

Walking up the hill to the historic section, you'll find Igreja Dos Santos Cosme e Damião, which dates back to the foundation of Igarassu and is the oldest standing church in Pernambuco state. Next door on Largo São Cosme e São Damião, the Museu Histórico de Igarassu (city museum) displays sacred art, weapons and furniture from noble families. It's open from 9 am to noon and

Jangada

from 2 to 5 pm, Tuesday to Saturday; and from 9 am to noon on Sunday.

The Convento de Santo Antônio (1588) on Avenida Hermes contains the Museu Pinacoteca (art museum) which has paintings depicting folk tales and popular legends. The convent and the museum are currently closed for restoration.

For typical food try the nearby *Restaurante Senzala* (closed on Sunday).

Engenho Mojope

The area surrounding the town also has a few treasures. The Engenho Mojope (1750), an old sugar estate with ruins of a mill, casa grande (plantation owner's mansion), chapel and slave quarters, is now a campground belonging to Camping Clube do Brasil. It's worth a stop if you're going by car: take BR-101 3½ km south from the Igarassu turnoff and turn right at the Camping Club

sign. The former plantation is one km further down the road.

Itapissuma

About 10 km from Igarassu is the small town of Itapissuma, which is worth visiting to see the Igreja São Gonçalvo do Amarante (1795) on Rua Manoel Lourenço.

Festivals

On 27 September Festa dos Santos Cosme e Damião celebrates the founding of Igarassu and honours its patron saints with bumba meu boi and the ciranda dance (which actually originated in Itamaracá). The Festa do Côco is held during the last week of November.

Getting There & Away

Buses leave every 15 minutes for the 45-minute trip to the rodoviária velha (old rodoviária) on Avenida Martins de Barros in Recife.

Itamaracá

Only 50 km from Recife, Itamaracá Island is a pleasant and popular weekend beach scene. During the week it's empty. There is a regular bus service to the island but getting to its many beaches takes some time if you don't have a car. There is a handful of hotels, few of which are cheap.

Beaches

Itamaracá has a long history and a lot of beach. The better beaches are north and south of Pilar, Itamaracá's town beach. Two km north of town is Jaguaribe, an emptier beach with barracas. For still more isolated beaches, hike five km further north along the coast to Praia Lance dos Cações and Fortinho. Immediately south of town is Praia Baixa Verde, and every three km south are more beaches: Praia Rio Ambo, Praia Forno de Cal, Praia de São Paulo and finally Praia de Vila Velha, which also is a historic old port near Forte Orange.

Forte Orange

This fort was built in 1630 by the Dutch and served as a base in a series of battles against the Portuguese colonies in Recife and Olinda. It's an impressive bastion, right on the water, but souvenir shops are rearing their ugly little heads.

Other Attractions

Engenho Amparo, an 18th-century sugar plantation, is just past Penitenciária Agricola, the island's agricultural penitentiary. Further from town is Vila Velha (1526), the first port in the Northeast, and its church, NS da Conceição (1526). Take a VW bus to get to these and other distant points from the town of Itamaracá.

Places to Stay

Inexpensive accommodation is not available. For apartamentos at around US$25/28 for singles/doubles, try *Hospedaria de Turismo Ilha do Sol* (☎ 554-1074) at Rua

Pereira Machado 281; or *Hotel do Marujo* (☎ 544-1157) at Praça Padre Machado 85.

Hotel Caravela (☎ 544-1130) on Praça João Felipe de Barros is a two-star Embratur resort hotel with a pool. Apartamentos cost US$35/40 for singles/doubles. Ocean view rooms with balconies cost more.

The *Hotel Pousada Itamaracá* (☎ 544-1152) at Rua Fernando Lopes 210 (near the centre of town) is a modern hotel with a swimming pool and comfortable apartamentos at US$40/48 for singles/doubles.

Things to Buy

At Engenho São João, about 10 km in the direction of Igarassu, inmates from the agricultural penitentiary sell their products such as lithographs and carrancas (carved figureheads).

Getting There & Away

There are 12 buses a day to the rodoviária velha (old rodoviária) on Avenida Martins de Barros in Recife.

PONTAS DE PEDRA

Pontas de Pedra, the last beach in Pernambuco if you're heading north, does its state proud. The reef two km offshore provides for calm, shallow water which is good for bathing and snorkelling.

Goiana, 22 km in from the coast at the junction of BR-101 and PE-49, has a few restaurants and bars, but no regular lodging.

CARUARU

If you like folk art and you wake up in Recife on a Wednesday or Saturday feeling like a day trip, you're in luck. Caruaru, South America's capital for ceramic figurine art, is only a couple of hours away.

Feira Livre

The Feira Livre (Grand Open Fair), held in the centre of Caruaru on Wednesdays and Saturdays, is a hot and noisy crush of Nordestinos: vendors, poets, singers, rural and town folk, tourists, musicians and artisans. *Zabumba* (drum) bands are accompanied by the music of *pífanos* (vertical flutes), veterans of the Paraguayan war fire rifles up in the hills of Bom Jesus, and *sulanqueiros*, Brazilian rag merchants, hawk their scraps of clothing.

The market has become a popular tourist attraction and many items on sale are produced for tourists. Alongside pots, leather bags and straw baskets are representations of strange beasts and mythical monsters crafted by artists as famous as Caruaru's master, Mestre Vitalino. To see the artists at work, visit Alto do Moura (described later in this section).

In addition to ceramic artwork you can hear singers and poets perform the *literatura de cordel* (literally 'string literature'): poetry by and for the people sold in little brochures which hang from the fair stands by string (hence the name). The poems tell of political events (the death of Tancredo Neves is likened to a mother giving birth to a nation and then expiring before she can suckle her infant), national figures (Getúlio Vargas, José Sarney, Fernando Collor), miracles and festivals, as well as traditional comedies and tragedies (for example, about a woman who lost her honour to Satan). Although its role in diffusing popular culture is threatened by TV, literatura de cordel is still written, sold and performed in public by Caruaru's street poets.

In a separate section of the main fair, there's the Feira do Troca-troca (Barter Market) where junk and treasure – depending on the perspective of the buyers and sellers – are traded.

Feira de Artesanato

This handicraft market on Parque 18 de Maio is open daily from 6 am to 5 pm.

Feira da Sulanca

This textile and clothing market, the largest in the Northeast, is set up on Parque 18 de Maio on Tuesday and Thursday.

Casa da Cultura José Condé

This cultural centre on Parque 18 de Maio contains a couple of museums. The most interesting is Museu do Forró, containing

exhibits about forró – records and musical instruments. It's open from 9 am to noon and from 2 to 5 pm, Monday to Friday; and from 9 am to 1 pm on Saturday.

Museu do Barro

This museum, containing displays of pottery produced by famous local artists, is inside the Espaça Cultural Tancredo Neves at Praça José Vasconcelos 100. It's open from 9 am to noon and from 2 to 5 pm, Monday to Friday; and from 9 am to 1 pm on Saturday.

Alto de Moura

Alto de Moura, six km from Caruaru, is a small community of potters which specialises in producing *figurinhas* (figurines). Many of the potters are descendants of Mestre Vitalino, the most famous artist, who brought fame to Alto de Moura. Other noted artists are Zé Caboclo, Manuel Eudocio, and Cunhado de Zé Caboclo. Museu Mestre Vitalino (Master Vitalino Museum), housed in the simple home of the master, contains his tools and personal effects. It's open from 9 am to noon and from 2 to 5 pm, Monday to Saturday.

You can wander the streets and browse through dozens of workshops and galleries where the figurines are on sale.

Places to Stay

Caruaru is an easy day trip from Recife, so there's no real need to stay here overnight. There are inexpensive hotels in town like *Hotel Central* (☎ 721-5880) at Rua Vigário Freire 71, and *Hotel Centenário* (☎ 721-9011) at Rua 7 de Setembro 24. Apartamentos start at around US$12/15 for singles/doubles.

Places to Eat

Fortunately there's plenty of cachaça and sugar-cane broth to quench your thirst, and local foods like *dobradinhas* (tripe stew), *chambaril* and *sarapatel* (a bloody goulash of pork guts) to appease your appetite. Spartan, inexpensive places for this type of food are *Bar do Biu* (open daily from 10 am to 7 pm; closed on Monday) at Rua Sanharó

8; and *Bar da Linguiça* (open daily from 10 am until early morning) at Rua Nunes Machado 278.

If the appeal of these local foods fades, try *Barrilândia* at Rua Silva Jardim 71. It's a good pizzeria with the feel of a Wild West saloon – you half expect a dramatic cowboy entrance through the swing doors. Open from 1 pm to the early morning; closed on Monday.

Getting There & Away
Caruaru is linked by shuttle buses to Recife every half hour. The trip takes two hours and costs US$4.50.

There is a daily bus service (one hour; US$1) to Fazenda Nova.

TRACUNHAÉM
If you've missed the fair at Caruaru, the next best thing, some say better, is to be in Tracunhaém for the Sunday fair. The village of Tracunhaém, 40 km from Recife in the direction of Carpina, is Pernambuco's number two craft centre. Look for the ceramic work of master artisans Zezinho de Tracunhaem, Severina Batista and Antônio Leão.

FAZENDA NOVA & NOVA JERUSALÉM
The small town of Fazenda Nova, 50 km from Caruaru, is famous for its theatre-city reconstruction of Jerusalem, known as Nova Jerusalém. Surrounded by a three-metre-high wall with seven gateways, 70 towers, and 12 granite stages, the reconstruction occupies an area equivalent to a third of the walled city of Jerusalem as it stood in the time of Jesus.

The time to visit is during Semana Santa (Holy Week, held in March or April – dates vary), when several hundred of the inhabitants of Fazenda Nova perform the Paixão de Cristo (Passion Play).

Places to Stay
There's a campground, *Camping Fazenda Nova*, at Nova Jerusalém. In the centre of Fazenda Nova, you can stay at the *Grande Hotel* (☎ 732-1137) at Avenida Poeta Carlos

Pena Filho, s/n (no number), which has apartamentos at US$18/20 for singles/doubles.

Getting There & Away
During Holy Week, there are frequent bus services direct from Recife and travel agencies sell package tours to see the spectacle. During the rest of the year, there are daily bus connections between Fazenda Nova and Caruaru.

GARANHUNS
Garanhuns, 100 km from Caruaru and 241 km from Recife, is popular as a holiday resort because of its relatively high altitude (900 metres) and healthy climate. Although it isn't quite the 'Suiça Pernambucana' (Switzerland of Pernambuco) touted in tourist brochures, it does possess pleasant parks, gardens, and cool air – all of which are a respite from the oppressive heat of the interior of the state.

Places to Stay & Eat
There's a campground, *Camping 13*, at Km 105 on BR-423. *Hotel Petrópolis* (☎ 761-0125) at Praça da Bandeira 129 has apartamentos around US$15/17 for singles/doubles. A more expensive option is *Hotel Village* (☎ 761-3624) at Avenida Santo Antônio 149.

For an inexpensive self-service buffet lunch, try *Jardim* at Praça Jardim 22. It's open daily (except Sunday) until 6 pm; closes at 3 pm on Saturday. Fondue enthusiasts prepared to pay a bit extra should visit *Chez Pascal* at Avenida Rui Barbosa 891. For regional dishes, there's *La Biritta* at Rua Dr José Mariano 152. It's open daily from 11 am to the very early hours of the morning. At the weekend there's live music after 11 pm.

Getting There & Away
There are several bus departures daily to Recife (2½ hours; US$7.50).

TRIUNFO
This small town, 448 km north-west of Recife, lies at an altitude of 1000 metres. The

cool climate and abundant vegetation have earned it the nickname 'cidade jardim' (garden city). For tourist information, contact the tourist office (☎ 846-1227) at Avenida José Veríssimo dos Santos 365.

Things to See & Do

The Museu do Cangaço (Bandit Museum) displays a collection of weaponry and assorted personal items used by cangaçeiros, or brigands, whose most famous and fearsome leader was Lampião (described in the history section in Facts about the Country). Opening hours are from 8 to 11 am and from 2 to 4 pm, Monday to Friday.

The town also has some fine examples of architecture – Cine Teatro Guarany (1922) on Praça Carolina Campos is a neo-classical stunner. It's open daily from 8 am to noon.

For excursions in the region around the town, you could visit: Pico do Papagaio, which is a peak (1230 metres) with a great view, seven km from town; Cachoeira do Grito (waterfall and swimming hole) – six km from town on the road to Flores, then one km on foot; or the pictoglyphs at Sítio Santo Antônio, three km from town. Ask the tourist office for more details about boat excursions, and other sights and access.

Places to Stay & Eat

Pousada Baixa Verde (☎ 846-1378) at Rua Manoel Paiva dos Santos 114 has apartamentos at US$9/11 for singles/doubles. *Lar Santa Elisabeth* (☎ 841-1236) at Rua Frei Fernanco, s/n (no number) has slightly more expensive apartamentos. It is also possible to order meals here; or try *Bar Guarany* at Rua Manoel Pereira Lima, s/n (no number).

Getting There & Away

There are daily bus departures for Recife (7½ hours; US$16).

Fernando de Noronha

Population: 1500
The archipelago of Fernando de Noronha lies 145 km from Atol das Rocas, 525 km from Recife and 350 km from Natal. The 21 islands of the archipelago cover a total area of only 26 sq km. In 1989, Fernando de Noronha was incorporated into the state of Pernambuco.

With its crystal-clear water (average water temperature 24°C) and rich marine life the archipelago is a heavenly retreat for underwater pleasures. The main island is sparsely populated and tourism has become the main source of income for locals. It's now easier for independent travellers to visit, but it is possible that organised tours will be made compulsory again if numbers of visitors prove detrimental to the environment of the archipelago. Although Fernando de Noronha is now protected as a national marine park, the effects of tourism on its fragile ecosystem need to be monitored carefully (see the following History section).

Before You Go

The rainy season is from February to July and the islands are one time-zone hour ahead of eastern Brazil. Bring everything you'll need for your stay (eg suntan lotion, insect repellent, magazines, snorkelling gear). There isn't much to buy on the island and, in any case, prices there are very high due to the cost of transporting goods from the mainland. Definitely take sufficient Brazilian money with you. Don't rely on changing money on Fernando de Noronha, where the exchange facilities are virtually nil and the rates are low.

History

Several hundred km off the coast from Natal, the archipelago of what is today known as Fernando de Noronha was discovered by the Spanish adventurer and cartographer Juan de la Costa. The islands first appeared on the maps by the name of Quaresma (which means Lent). A Portuguese expedition under the command of Fernando de Noronha sighted the islands once again in 1504. He was awarded the islands by his friend, King Dom Manoel. It was the first inherited captaincy of the Brazilian colonies.

The islands, with their strategic position between Europe and the New World, were coveted by the English, French and the Dutch who came to occupy the archipelago. But by 1557 the Portuguese managed to reclaim Fernando de Noronha and build a fortress. All that remains today of the European battles is the ruins of the fortress of NS dos Remédios and a few sunken shipwrecks.

Over the years, the islands were used as a military base by the USA during WW II, a prison, weather station, air base and most recently as a tourist resort.

There has already been some misguided tampering with the island ecology. The *teju*, a black and white lizard, was introduced to eat the island rats which had come ashore with the Europeans in colonial days. Unfortunately, the teju prefers small birds and crab to rat.

A struggle between developers and environmentalists over the future of the island was resolved in 1988 when most of the archipelago was declared a Parque Nacional Marinho (Marine National Park) to protect the island's natural treasures. These include: 24 different species of marine birds; two species of marine tortoise – one, *tartaruga-de-pente (Eretmochelys imbricata)*, in danger of extinction; sharks; stingrays; dolphins; whales; and a vast number of fish species.

Tourism has proved a blessing for the local economy and a bane for the ecosystem of the archipelago. Rapidly growing numbers of visitors have prompted locals to convert mangrove swamps into plots for cultivation of more food, thereby depriving marine life of important breeding grounds and food sources. It has also been noted that fish have become accustomed to being fed by tourists and have taken to biting them.

Orientation

On the largest and only inhabited island, the population is concentrated in Vila dos

Remédios. Although Pico hill, the highest point on the island, is only 321 metres above sea level, it is well over 4300 metres above the ocean floor, as the island is an extinct volcanic cone. The island-mountain is part of the mid-Atlantic ridge, an underwater mountain chain which is over 15,000 km long.

Information

Tourist Offices Information is available from Gerência do Meio Ambiente e Turismo (☎ 619-1244) in Centro de Convivência, Vila do Trinta. The prefectural tourism office (☎ 619-1414) is in the Palácio do Governo in Vila dos Remédios. The IBAMA (☎ 619-1210) office is on Alameda do Boldró.

Money The island's one and only bank is Banco Real in Vila dos Remédios.

Post & Telecommunications The post office is in Vila dos Remédios. The TELPE office is in the Hotel Esmeralda do Atlântico on Alameda do Boldró.

Emergency The Hospital São Lucas (☎ 619-1207) at Parque Flamboyant looks after medical emergencies. The Polícia Civil (☎ 619-1432) has its headquarters on Vila do Trinta.

Travel Agencies The island's two travel agencies are Dolphin Travel (☎ 619-4158) on Alameda do Boldró, and Mubatur (☎ 619-1154) also on Alameda do Boldró.

Island Rules Visitors are expected to obey the following rules: don't dump rubbish or food on the ground, in the sea or on the beach; don't take away or break off pieces of coral, shells, or marine creatures; don't use spearguns or traps; don't bring plants or animals to or from the archipelago; respect areas set aside for ecological protection; don't swim with the dolphins; and don't hunt under water. As mentioned in the introduction to this archipelago, tourism has already affected the ecosystem and it is hoped that observation of these rules will help redress such problems.

Beaches

Inside the boundaries of the park, IBAMA allows bathing at certain beaches, but restricts access to others to protect marine life.

The island beaches are deserted, clean and beautiful. The beaches of Caiera (no bathing, access only), Praia da Atalaia and Ponta das Caracas have rougher waters than Praia da Conceição. Cacimba do Padre beach is the only one with fresh water.

Baía dos Golfinhos (Dolphin Bay) is strictly off limits to swimmers, but access is permitted to Mirante dos Golfinhos, a viewpoint where you can watch hundreds of dolphins cavorting in the water every morning.

You can get to Baía do Sancho (no swimming; access only to Mirante do Sancho) either by boat or by following a rugged nature trail which leads through bramble and bush, past almond trees and over sharp rocks. Once at Baía do Sancho, you may be lucky to witness an odd meteorological phenomenon: without a cloud in sight, rain falls mysteriously on a spot of land 10 metres wide.

Diving

The Águas Claras company (☎ 619-1225) organises scuba diving excursions with instructors (variable quality) and will rent diving equipment. You can ask if diving is still permitted in Baía de Santo Antônio, where the *Paquistão* and *Ana Maria* wrecks lie seven metres under water. A Spanish corvette lies beneath 60 metres of water at Ponta da Sapata, the south-west tip of the island, but this area is now strictly out of bounds.

Places to Stay & Eat

The top hotel, *Esmeralda do Atlântico* (☎619-1355) on Alameda do Boldró, is very expensive and usually fully booked with package tours. There are over 20 pousadas and pensões, and many of the islanders let quartos in their private homes. Rates for apartamentos are around US$25/30 for singles/doubles, including breakfast, lunch and dinner. Quartos are about US$5 less per person.

Since accommodation prices usually include full board, restaurants are virtually nonexistent. There's a restaurant in Esmeralda do Atlântico hotel, or you could try *Restaurante e Bar Ilha Encantada* at Conjunto Vacária. Bars on the island include: *O Mirante* on Alameda do Boldró; *Bar do Meio* on Praia do Meio; *Bar da Angélica* in Vila do Trinta; and *Bar da Vila* in Vila dos Remédios.

Getting There & Away

Air Nordeste uses Bandeirante planes to fly twice daily between Recife and Fernando de Noronha. The flight takes 90 minutes and a return ticket costs around US$100.

Nordeste (☎ 619-1144) is on Alameda do Boldró. The airport (☎ 619-1188) is a couple of km from the centre of Vila dos Remédios.

Tours Organised tours sold by travel agencies in Recife usually include airfare to and from Fernando de Noronha, lodging (apartamento, including full board) and guided tours of the island by land and sea.

Prices per person for 4/5/8-day packages start at around US$550/600/800. Higher prices apply during high season and for apartamentos with air-con (not really necessary).

Assuming independent travellers are allowed to book flights only, they should have little difficulty negotiating lower prices for lodging and board on the island. This independent approach also allows travellers to pick and choose their accommodation. The accommodation included in most of the package tours is overpriced.

In Recife, Fernando de Noronha tours are packaged by Andratur and Mubatur – for phone numbers and address details, see the information section for Recife. In Rio, contact Quadratur (☎ 262-8011); in São Paulo, contact Vista (☎ 255-7330).

Getting Around

Buggies, cars and small motorbikes are available from Eduardo Galvào de Brito Lira (☎ 619-1355) at Esmeralda do Atlântico hotel on Alameda do Boldró.

Boats are available from Associação Noronhense de Pescadores Anpesca (☎ 619-1449) at Vila Porto de Santo Antônio.

Paraíba & Rio Grande do Norte

Paraíba

JOÃO PESSOA

Founded in 1585, the coastal city of João Pessoa is the capital of Paraíba. It lies 120 km north of Recife, 688 km south of Fortaleza and 185 km south of Natal.

The city derives its name from João Pessoa, the governor of Paraíba who formed an alliance with Getúlio Vargas to run for the presidency of Brazil in 1929. In response to advances from other political parties attempting to gain his support, João Pessoa uttered a pithy *nego* (I refuse) which is now given prominence in all Brazilian history books...and in bold letters on the state flag of Paraíba.

João Pessoa's aspirations to the vice-pres-

idency were shortlived: in July 1930 he was assassinated by João Dantas, an event which sparked a revolutionary backlash that eventually swept Getúlio Vargas to power (with ample help from the military) in October 1930.

Orientation

The rodoviária is on the western edge of the city. The main hotel and shopping district, known as Praça, is further east; and close by is Parque Solon de Lucena, a large lake circled by trees, which locals simply call 'Lagoa'. There are numerous bus stops here which are convenient for local transport (see Getting Around) – for example, to travel to the beach district of Tambaú or further up the coast to Cabo Branco.

A decidedly curious feature in the centre

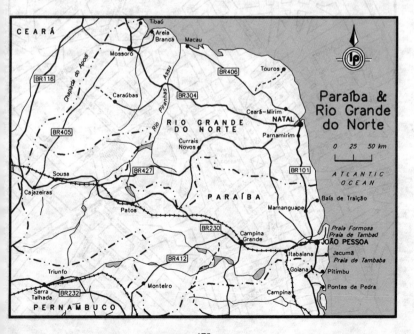

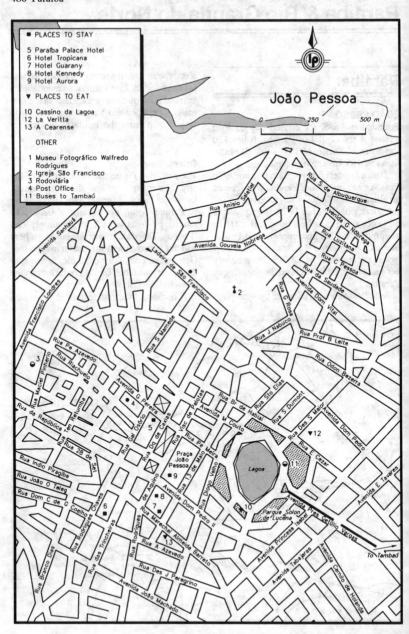

PLACES TO STAY

5 Paraíba Palace Hotel
6 Hotel Tropicana
7 Hotel Guarany
8 Hotel Kennedy
9 Hotel Aurora

PLACES TO EAT

10 Cassino da Lagoa
12 La Veritta
13 A Cearense

OTHER

1 Museu Fotográfico Walfredo Rodrigues
2 Igreja São Francisco
3 Rodoviária
4 Post Office
11 Buses to Tambaú

João Pessoa

0   250   500 m

Top: Woman selling corn on the street, Recife, Pernambuco (JM)
Left: The colonial village of Olinda, overlooking Recife, Pernambuco (JM)
Right: Family transportation, Brazil (JM)

Top: Two men near Natal, Rio Grande do Norte (JM)
Bottom: Genipabu, near Natal, Rio Grande do Norte (JM)

of the main square is a spiral moat which functions as a 'moatorway' for streams of noisy traffic.

Information

Tourist Offices PBTUR (☎ 226-7078) at Avenida Almirante Tamandaré 100 in Tambaú provides maps and leaflets. It's inside the shopping arcade, diagonally opposite Tambaú Hotel. There are also tourist information stands at the rodoviária (appears to be defunct) and the airport.

Money Banco do Brasil is on Praça João Pessoa – a couple of doors down from Hotel Aurora. The exchange counter on the 1st floor is open from 10 am to noon and from 1 to 3.30 pm, Monday to Friday.

Post & Telecommunications The main post office in the centre of town is on Avenida Guedes Pereira. The main office of TELPA, the state telephone company, is in the centre on Rua Visconde de Pelotas.

Dangers & Annoyances The municipality is clearly cutting costs when it comes to street maintenance: watch your step. Whilst looking for street names in the dark, one of the authors actually fell down a broken telephone access hole. And just at that moment a cuckoo character with a spaceship agenda arrived to chat, whilst the author, cussing loudly, tried to get out of the depths!

João Pessoa has many 'noisemobiles', vehicles converted to carry as many loudspeakers as possible, which cruise the streets deafening everyone with advertisements for underwear at amazing prices or airing political grievances at noise levels that make it impossible to understand the problem. Although the standard noisemobile is outfitted with a dozen or so loudspeakers, we saw a bus here which had been converted into a 'sound war monster' with no less than 96 speakers. Brazil may be the world's most musical country, but it's definitely at the top of the league for noise pollution.

Igreja São Francisco

The principal tourist attraction is the Igreja São Francisco, considered to be one of Brazil's finest churches. Construction was interrupted by successive battles with the Dutch and French, resulting in a beautiful but architecturally confused complex built over three centuries. The facade, church towers and monastery (of Santo Antônio) display a hodgepodge of styles. Portuguese tiled walls lead up to the church's carved jacaranda-wood doors. The church is currently undergoing renovation, but according to local optimists, should reopen soon. Provisional opening hours will be from 8 to 11 am and from 2 to 5 pm, Wednesday to Sunday.

Museu Fotográfico Walfredo Rodrigues

The Walfredo Rodrigues Photographic Museum in the old Casa da Pólvora (Powder House) on Ladeira de São Francisco has some interesting pictures of the old city. It's open daily from 7 am to noon and from 1 to 5.30 pm.

Beaches

Aside from the rusty remains of battles against the French and Dutch, the beaches are clean. Praia de Tambaú, seven km directly east of the centre, is rather built up, but nice. There are bars, restaurants, coconut palms and fig trees along Avenida João Maurício (north) and Avenida Almirante Tamandaré (south).

South of Tambaú is Praia Cabo Branco. From here it's a glorious 15-km walk along Praia da Penha – a beautiful stretch of sand, surf, palm groves and creeks – to Ponta de Seixas, the easternmost tip of South America. The combination of extremely clear water and coral make it a good spot for diving.

Immediately north of Tambaú, there are good urban beaches: Manaíra, Praia do Bessa I and II, Praia do Macaco (the surfers' beach) and Praia do Poço.

Twenty km north of Tambaú are Forte Santa Catarina, Costinha and Camboinha beaches.

July to November is whale-hunting season

in Costinha, so unless you particularly want to see whales being dismembered, those months are a good time to avoid the place.

Praia Cabedelo has restaurants, bars and boats to Ilha de Areia Vermelha, an island of red sand which emerges from the Atlantic at low tide. Camping is possible on many of these beaches.

Boat Trips

Navegar Turismo (☎ 226-5878) operates excursions on a motor schooner to Areia Vermelha and Praia de Santa Catarina, and various sunset/moonlight cruises. The trips last between three and four hours.

Places to Stay – bottom end

João Pessoa's main attraction is Tambaú beach and that's where many of the hotels are, although there are modest hotels in the centre as well. When enquiring about room prices, it's worth being persistent: many hotels will instantly claim that all the cheaper rooms are occupied and offer the most expensive rooms. A little encouragement to let you actually look at the list of room bookings may lower the price.

Centre For a central youth hostel, there's *Albergue de Juventude Cidade das Acácias* (☎ 222-2775) at Avenida das Trincheiras 554, Palácio dos Esportes. From the rodoviária, take the bus marked 'Cruz das Almas' and get off at the 'Palácio dos Esportes' (Sports Palace) stop, which is opposite the hostel.

Hotel Aurora (☎ 241-3238) at Praça João Pessoa 51 has adequate quartos at US$8/12 for singles/doubles. Apartamentos with air-con cost US$15/17 for singles/doubles, but you can shave a couple of dollars off the price if you take an equivalent room with fan only. Avoid the rooms overlooking the street, which can be noisy. The staff here, clearly worried about guests absconding with ashtrays, will supply saucers instead.

Hotel Guarany (☎ 241-2161) at Rua Marechal Almeida Barreto 181 is clean, but some rooms with fan have a gaping hole where air-con has been removed, and a

similar void in the wall above the door. Apartamentos with fan start at around US$17/19 for singles/doubles – air-con costs an additional US$5.

Hotel Kennedy (☎ 221-4924), at Rua Rodrigues de Aquino 17, has standard (with fan) apartamentos at US$12/15 for singles/doubles; and deluxe (with air-con) versions at US$20/23 for singles/doubles. These prices include a sumptuous breakfast.

Hotel Pousada Mar Azul (☎ 226-2660) at Avenida João Maurício 315 has apartamentos at US$8/12 for singles/doubles. Breakfast is not included.

Tambaú The local youth hostel, *Albergue de Juventude Tambaú* (☎ 226-5460), is at Rua Bezerra Reis 82. There's another youth hostel just south of Tambaú at Cabo Branco: *Albergue de Juventude Cabo Branco* (☎ 226-6504) at Avenida Padre José Trigueiro 104.

The best deal in Tambaú – if you can get a room – is the *Hotel Gameleira* (☎ 226-1576) at Avenida João Maurício 157, with quartos (no fan) at US$10/13 for singles/doubles, and standard (with fan) apartamentos at US$14/18 for singles/doubles. If you want to upgrade, luxury rooms and suites are also available.

Praia de Seixas If you fancy camping at the easternmost tip of Brazil, there's a campground, *Camping-PB-01*, run by Camping Clube do Brasil at Praia de Seixas, which is about 16 km from the centre of João Pessoa.

Places to Stay – middle

Centre *Paraíba Palace Hotel* (☎ 221-3107), at Praça Vidal de Negreiros, s/n (no number), is an impressive colonial palace which has recently been renovated and now includes a swimming pool and a restaurant. Although it is certainly a top-end hotel, its prices are currently a great bargain in the middle range. Standard apartamentos start at US$35/39 for singles/doubles; and luxury rooms cost US$45/50.

Hotel Tropicana (☎ 221-8445) at Rua Alice Azevedo 461 is a three-star hotel with swimming pool. Standard apartamentos cost US$35/39 for singles/doubles; and luxury versions cost US$45/50.

Tambaú *Hotel dos Navegantes* (☎ 226-4018) at Avenida NS dos Navegantes 602 has apartamentos at US$35/40 for singles/doubles. It's close to the beach and has a swimming pool.

Places to Stay – top end
Tambaú The five-star *Tropical Hotel Tambaú* (☎ 226-3660) at Avenida Almirante Tamandaré 229 on Praia de Tambaú is the city's entry into the world of modern architecture. From a distance this immense edifice (part of the Varig hotel group) bears a passing resemblance to a rocket launching pad. The hotel has standard singles/doubles for US$70/80; and luxury singles/doubles for US$100/120. Although the hotel has an immense swimming pool and rooms perched within a few feet of the waves, the scale is intimidating and impersonal.

Places to Eat
Centre *Cassino da Lagoa* has an open patio with a fine position beside the Lagoa. Seafood and chicken dishes are recommended. On Friday nights, there's live music here. *La Veritta* at Rua Desembargador Souto Maior 331 does good Italian food. *A Cearense* at Rua Almeida Barreto 270, is a good bet for regional dishes; diagonally opposite is *Sorveteria Tropical*, which is close to Hotel Guarany and serves ice cream in exotic flavours. Vegetarians can head for *O Natural* at Rua Rodrigues de Aquino 177, but it serves lunch only.

On the 3rd floor of the *Paraíba Palace Hotel* is an excellent restaurant with an international menu. Prices here are high, but you can also simply order a beer with an appetiser or snack and enjoy an aerial view of the weird traffic moat and city life from the terrace.

Tambaú *Adega do Alfredo* at Rua Coração de Jesus 22 specialises in Portuguese dishes. Live music on Fridays; closed on Mondays.

Wan Li at Rua Coração de Jesus 100 is an inexpensive option for Chinese food. For a splurge on French cuisine, there's *Casier* at Rua Coração de Jesus 144. It's closed on Monday. *Peixada do João* at Rua Coração de Jesus 147 does excellent seafood – the *ensopado de caranguejo* (crab stew) is superb.

Entertainment
Gulliver Pub at Avenida Olinda 500, Tambaú, is run by an Anglophile Brazilian who has duplicated the structure and atmosphere of a pub. Worth a visit to see what a pub feels like when it goes 'troppo'. It's closed on Monday.

For forró and lambada dancing in Tambaú, there's Palladium at Rua João Maurício 33, which bops after 11 pm on Friday, Saturday and Sunday. Admission costs US$6 and entitles the guest to two drinks. Beer House at Avenida Almirante Tamandaré 310 (opposite Tropical Hotel Tambaú) features live music with forró and lambada dancing on Friday and Saturday nights after 10 pm. Pizzas and seafood dishes are served, and there's a cover charge for live music nights.

Things to Buy
Avenida Rui Carneiro on Praia de Tambaú has ceramic, wicker, straw and leather goods for sale. On weekends, a food fair is held in front of Hotel Tropical Tambaú. In the city centre, Casa do Artesão Paraibano at Rua Maciel Pinheiro 670 also has craft work for sale.

Getting There & Away
Air Aeroporto Presidente Castro Pinto (☎ 229-3200) is 11 km from the city centre. Flights operate to Rio, São Paulo, and the major cities in the Northeast and the North.

Following are addresses for Brazilian airlines: Transbrasil (☎ 241-2822), Rua General Osório 177, sala 1; Varig/Cruzeiro (☎ 221-1133), Avenida Getúlio Vargas 183; and VASP (☎ 222-0715), Parque Solon de Lucena 530, Edifício Lago Center.

Bus The rodoviária (☎ 221-9611) is on

Avenida Francisco Londres. There are frequent buses to: Recife (two hours; US$4.50); Natal (2½ hours; US$5); and Fortaleza (10 hours; US$18). There are four departures daily direct to Sousa (seven hours; US$13).

Getting Around

Bus Local buses can be boarded at the rodoviária; at the bus stop next to the main post office; and at the bus stops next to the Lagoa. Bus No 510 runs frequently to Tambaú (25 minutes; 30c). Bus No 507 runs to Cabo Branco.

Taxi *Taxistas* on short hauls downtown may try to charge tariff 2 (generally applicable at night and on Sunday) instead of tariff 1, which applies during the daytime. Take a careful look at the price table and ignore absurd comments that the taxi requires 'more petrol'. One taxista took us for a spin round the rodoviária just to rack up extra income. Work out your position on the map and point out obvious 'detours'. It's also best to give exact money, otherwise there may be tiresome hassles over change.

A taxi to the airport costs around US$20; from the rodoviária to the centre costs around US$1.75. For a telephone taxi, call Teletaxi (☎ 222-3765).

SOUTH OF JOÃO PESSOA
Jacumã & Praia do Sol

Forty km south of João Pessoa, Praia Jacumã is a long thin strip of sand featuring coloured sand bars, natural pools, potable mineral water springs, a shady grove of palms and barracas (open for business on weekends). There are several campsites and a hotel with apartamentos at US$25/30 for singles/doubles (including full board).

Halfway between Jacumã and João Pessoa is Praia do Sol, which is similar to Jacumã and an equally good place to relax – swaying in a hammock, and sipping coconut milk in the shade. Welcome to the tropics.

The Buraquinho Forest Reserve, operated by IBAMA, is 10 km before João Pessoa on BR-230.

Tambaba

About nine km south of Jacumã is Praia de Tambaba, the only official nudist beach in the Northeast. This superb beach, rated by Brazilians as among the top 10 in Brazil, is divided into two parts: one section is reserved exclusively for nudists, and the other is open to clothed bathers. To prevent problems, the nude section has two public relations officers who explain the rules to bathers. When the beach is crowded, men are not allowed in the nude section unless accompanied by a woman.

The Associação dos Amigos da Praia de Tambaba (Association of Friends of Tambaba; (☎ 290-1037, evenings only) can provide more information. There's an organised campground with facilities, but fires are not allowed and you should bring a stove.

Pitimbu

Praia Pitimbu, 75 km south of João Pessoa, has a long, broad beach, a coconut grove, some thatched-roof houses and a couple of bars frequented by sugar-cane farmers, fishers and jangada sailmakers. There are no hotels, but if you look friendly and bring a hammock someone will put you up for a nominal fee.

Travelling north on BR-101 from Pernambuco state into Paraíba state, there's a turnoff (just after the border) which leads 35 km down a rough road to Praia Pitimbu.

BAÍA DA TRAIÇÃO

Despite the peaceful, reef-sheltered waters, coconut palms and gentle breezes, Baía da Traição has a bloody past. Here in 1501, the first Portuguese exploratory expedition was slaughtered by the Tabajara Indians. In 1625 the Portuguese had it out with the Dutch, claimed victory and left some rusty cannons and the ruins of a fortress in their wake.

This fishing village, 85 km north of João Pessoa, has no regular lodging, but the beach is better than the one at Barra do Cunhaú, which is further north along the coast in the state of Rio Grande do Norte.

Getting There & Away

There's a partially paved turnoff to the beach on BR-101 at Mamanguape. Rio Tinto bus company operates buses twice daily at 5.30 am and 3 pm from João Pessoa's rodoviária (two hours; US$4).

SOUSA

Sousa, 420 km west of João Pessoa, is known for an offbeat tourist attraction: dinosaur tracks. The tracks were discovered in 1920 by a geologist who was researching drought – a major preoccupation in the sertão. Later discoveries of tracks at over 13 sites along the Rio do Peixe showed that the whole region had once been a Vale dos Dinossauros (Valley of Dinosaurs). There are at least three sites in the proximity of Sousa. The best is four km from town at Passagem das Pedras da Fazenda Ilha, on the banks of the Rio do Peixe, where at least 50 prints have been left by dinosaurs which, judging by the depth and size of the imprints, weighed between three and four tonnes.

This site is subject to flooding during the rainy season and is best visited with a guide. Transport options are limited to either hiring a taxi at the rodoviária or asking the staff at the Hotel Gadelha Palace to arrange transport plus guide.

Travellers interested in handicrafts should make a sidetrip to the town of Aparecida, 14 km east of Sousa, which is famed as a centre for the production of superb hammocks, textiles, and goods made from leather and straw.

Places to Stay & Eat

Hotel Gadelha Palace (**☎** 521-1416) at Rua Presidente João Pessoa 2 has apartamentos around US$18/22 for singles/doubles. There's a restaurant in the hotel, or, if you hanker after pizza, try *Diagonal* at Rua Getúlio Vargas 2.

Getting There & Away

There are six bus departures daily which run via Patos and Campina Grande to João Pessoa (seven hours; US$13). Buses also depart four times daily to Juazeiro do Norte (described in the Ceará chapter).

Rio Grande do Norte

BAÍA FORMOSA

The fishing village of Baía Formosa has super beaches, a cheap pousada and practically no tourism.

Backed by dunes, Baía Formosa curves from the end of the village (on the southern part of the bay) to an isolated point to the north. Parts of the beach have dark volcanic rocks eroded into curious forms by the surf. The beaches further south of town are sweeping, empty and spectacular. Surfing is possible.

Places to Stay & Eat

Hotel Miramar (**☎** 236-2079) at the end of the road by the waterfront has dorm beds, quartos and apartamentos. It's clean enough for a cheapo small town hotel, but you'll probably find better value and comfort by

asking around for a room in a private home. There are two restaurants to choose from.

Getting There & Away

Seventeen km off BR-101 and 10 km from the Rio Grande do Norte and Paraíba border, Baía Formosa is serviced by one daily bus. The bus leaves town at 6.30 am and returns from the junction with BR-101 at 1.30 pm. Direct buses from Natal's rodoviária leave on weekdays at 7.30 am and 3.30 pm, Saturdays at 11.30 am and 3.30 pm, and Sundays at 7.15 am and 5.30 pm. The trip takes about two hours.

BARRA DO CUNHAÚ

Barra do Cunhaú, 10 km from Canguaretama on a dirt track, is a hybrid fishing village/resort town. You can camp in the coconut grove.

Getting There & Away

There are three buses a week on Monday, Thursday and Friday at 3.30 pm from Natal.

TIBAU DO SUL

The small and rocky beaches of Tibau do Sul – Praia da Madeira, Praia da Cancela and Praia da Pipa – are said to be among the finest in Rio Grande de Norte. From Goaininha, 75 km south of Natal on BR-101, there's a 20-km dirt road to the coast.

There's an expensive pousada with chalets on Praia da Madeira; and Praia da Pipa now has a campground, pousada, and restaurant.

SENADOR GEORGINO ALVINO TO BÚZIOS

This stretch of coast has some of the best beaches in Rio Grande do Norte, a state which has so many great beaches it's difficult to find one that's not worth praising.

Búzios is a lovely beach town 35 km south of Natal. A couple of hotels here cater to weekenders. *Varandas de Búzios* (☎ 239-2121) has inexpensive chalets.

Resist the temptation to get off the bus at Búzios. After Búzios the road is reduced to a rugged dirt track, then degenerates into two grooves. It crosses a stream and loses a

groove, leaving the bus bumping along a goat trail. Aside from the red coastal road, a stone road a few hundred metres inland, and the occasional surfer, there's nothing here but small waves crashing against the coast, white dunes, coconut palms, uncut jungle and pretty little farms. The place is idyllic. Get here before the road is finished and the developers move in.

Getting There & Away

From Natal there are two buses a day at 8.15 am and 4.30 pm that go directly to Senador Georgino Alvino, but it's more fun to take a bus along the barely negotiable coastal 'road'. From Natal take one of 10 Auto Viação Campos buses to Búzios (45 minutes).

PIRANGI DO SUL & PIRANGI DO NORTE

Fourteen km north of Búzios, the twin beach towns of Pirangi do Sul and Pirangi do Norte are split by a river which courses through palm-crested dunes on its way to the ocean. It's a quiet area where wealthy folk from Natal have put up their beach bungalows. There are a few hotels and restaurants too. Nearby is the world's largest cashew tree – its rambling sprawl of branches is over half a km in circumference and still growing!

BARREIRA DO INFERNO

Twenty km from Natal is Barreira do Inferno (Hell's Gate), the Brazilian air force (FAB) rocket base. The base is open to visitors on Wednesdays from 1 to 3 pm. The tour of the base includes a 30-minute talk with slides and films. Intending visitors must call 222-1638, extension 202, at least one day in advance to reserve a place on the tour.

PONTA NEGRA

Ponta Negra is 14 km south of Natal. The beach is nearly three km in length and full of hotels, pousadas, restaurants, barracas and sailboats – at weekends the place really jumps. The water is very calm and safe for weak swimmers. At the far end of the beach is a monstrous sand dune. Its face is inclined at 50° and drops straight into the sea. Bordered by jungle green, the slope is perfect for sand skiing. A good exercise for snow skiers is running down the hill. A good exercise for masochists is running up the hill.

Evening activities consist of beer drinking or snacking at the barracas, browsing at the restaurants, and gazing for shooting stars and straying rockets.

Places to Stay

For camping, try *Camping Vale das Cascatas* (☎ 236-3229). There are also two youth hostels: *Albergue de Juventude Lua Cheia* (☎ 236-2085) at Avenida Estrela do Mar 2215; and *Albergue de Juventude Verdes Mares* (☎ 236-2872) at Rua das Algas 2166.

There are dozens of pousadas and hotels. Some of the cheaper pousadas include: *Pousada do Flamboyant* (☎ 236-2622) at Avenida Engenheiro Roberto Freire 3110; *Pousada Bella Napoli Praia* (☎ 219-2666) at Avenida Beira-Mar 3188; *Pousada Maria Bonita II* (☎ 236-2941) at Rua Estrela do Mar 2143; and *Pousada Costa Sul* (☎ 236-3047) at Rua Pedro Fonseca Filho 1089.

NATAL

Natal, the capital of Rio Grande do Norte, is a clean, bright city which is being developed at top speed into the beach capital of the Northeast. There is very little to see of cultural or historical interest: the main attractions are beaches, buggy rides, and nightlife.

History

In 1535, a Portuguese armada left Recife for the falls of the Rio Ceará-Mirim (12 km north of present-day Natal) where it met strong opposition from the French and their Indian allies. For the next 60 years the territories remained abandoned until the French (recently expelled from Paraíba) began to use it as a base for attacks on the south. The Portuguese organised a huge flotilla from Paraíba and Pernambuco which met at the mouth of the Rio Potenji on Christmas Day 1597 to battle the French.

On 6 January, the day of Os Reis Magos (The Three Wise Kings), the Portuguese began to work on the fortress, which they used as their base in the war against the French. The Brazilian coastline was hotly contested, and in 1633 the fortress was taken by the Dutch, who rebuilt it in stone but retained the five-point star shape. First under Dutch and thereafter Portuguese occupation, Natal grew from the fortress, which was named the Forte dos Reis Magos.

With the construction of a railway and a port, Natal continued to develop as a small and relatively unimportant city until WW II. Recognising Natal's strategic location on the eastern bulge of Brazil, Getúlio Vargas and Franklin D Roosevelt decided to turn the sleepy city into the Allied military base for operations in North Africa.

Orientation

Natal is on a peninsula flanked to the north by the Rio Potenji and the south by Atlantic reefs and beaches. The peninsula tapers, ending at the Forte dos Reis Magos, the oldest part of the city. The city centre, Cidade Alta, was developed around the river port which was built in 1892.

Information

Tourist Offices Tourist information is currently not a strong point of the city, but changes are expected and warranted. The Centro de Turismo (☎ 221-3839) in the Casa de Detenção (old prison) on Rua Aderbal Figueiredo is quite useless. Locals reported that it was closed for lack of funds and alleged misappropriation of maps for personal gain. Although there's a fine view from the heights of this renovated prison, the artesanato shops command equally elevated prices.

Other sources of information are: EMPROTURN (☎ 221-1452), the state tourism authority, at Avenida Deodoro 249 – open from 7 am to 1 pm, Monday to Friday; and SEMITUR (☎ 221-5729), the municipal tourism authority, at Rua Trairi 563, Petrópolis (a district of Natal just east of the centre) – open from 8 am to noon and from

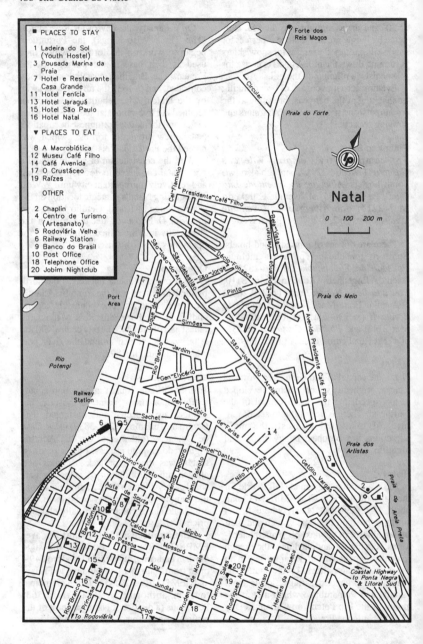

PLACES TO STAY
1 Ladeira do Sol
  (Youth Hostel)
3 Pousada Marina da
  Praia
7 Hotel e Restaurante
  Casa Grande
11 Hotel Fenícia
13 Hotel Jaraguá
15 Hotel São Paulo
16 Hotel Natal

PLACES TO EAT
8 A Macrobiótica
12 Museu Café Filho
14 Café Avenida
17 O Crustáceo
19 Raízes

OTHER
2 Chaplin
4 Centro de Turismo
  (Artesanato)
5 Rodoviária Velha
6 Railway Station
9 Banco do Brasil
10 Post Office
18 Telephone Office
20 Jobim Nightclub

Natal

0   100   200 m

Forte dos
Reis Magos

Praia do Forte

Praia do Meio

Praia dos
Artistas

Praia da
Areia Preta

Coastal Highway
to Ponta Negra
& Litoral Sud

Rio
Potengi

Port
Area

Railway
Station

To Rodoviária

2 to 6 pm, Monday to Friday. There's also an information booth at the rodoviária which appears to be open from Monday to Friday, from 4 to 10 pm.

Money Banco do Brasil is at Avenida Rio Branco 510.

Post & Telecommunications The main post office is at Avenida Rio Branco 538. The telephone office is at the intersection of Avenida Prudente de Morais and Jundiai.

Dangers & Annoyances The dramatic increase in visitors to the beaches has attracted petty thieves. There's no cause for paranoia, but you should take the usual precautions – refer to the Dangers & Annoyances section in the Facts for the Visitor chapter for general advice on beach security.

Things to See
The principal non-beach attractions of Natal are the pentagonal Forte dos Reis Magos (open from 7 am to 5 pm, Tuesday to Sunday) at the tip of the peninsula, and the Museu da Câmara Cascudo at Avenida Hermes da Fonseca 1400. This museum of folklore and anthropology features a collection of Amazon Indian artefacts. It's open from 8 to 11.30 am and from 2 to 5 pm, Tuesday to Friday; and from 8 to 11.30 am on Saturday.

The Museu Café Filho at Rua da Conceição 630 will probably only appeal to history buffs. This museum is housed in the mansion that once belonged to João Café Filho, and now displays his personal effects. It's open from 8 am to 6 pm, Tuesday to Friday; and from 8 am to 5 pm on Saturday and Sunday

In 1954, the military presented President Getúlio Vargas with an ultimatum to resign from the presidency, whereupon Vargas left a patriotic note and then shot himself through the heart. Café Filho, who had been vice-president, assumed the presidency and muddled through political crises until he suffered a major heart attack in 1955 and gave way to Carlos Luz. Although Café Filho

recovered quickly and tried hard to be reinstated, he'd missed his turn on the political carousel and had to be content with his brief moment of fame as the first person from the state of Rio Grande do Norte to become a president.

Beaches
Natal's city beaches – Praia do Meio, Praia dos Artistas, Praia da Areia Preta, Praia do Pinto and Praia Mãe Luiza –stretch well over nine km from the fort to the Farol de Mãe Luiza lighthouse. These are mostly city beaches, with bars, nightlife and big surf. The ones closest to the fort are rocky and closed in by an offshore reef.

Buggy Rides
Beach buggy excursions are offered by a host of *bugeiros* (buggy drivers), mostly in Brazilian-built vehicles with brand names such as Bird, Baby, Praya, or Malibuggy. An excursion lasting from 9 am to 6 pm costs around US$18 per person – assuming four passengers in the buggy (tight squeeze). The price includes transport and driver/guide, but excludes food and ferry fees (minimal). Take sunscreen, a tight-fitting hat, and swimwear; and keep all photo gear in a bag as protection from sand.

Bugeiros seem to be a crazy bunch of wannabe racing drivers intent on demonstrating a variety of buggy tricks and spins on the dunes. You may be treated to some or all of the following: Wall-of-Death; Devil's Cauldron; Vertical Descent; Roller-Coaster; and something best described as Racing the Incoming Tide – if you lose, the surf claims the buggy and the passengers scrabble for high ground. Bugeiros are well acquainted with the mechanical vagaries of their beasts: we were intrigued to watch large spanners being used to transfer charge from our buggy's battery to the dead battery of a stranded colleague.

There are pirate bugeiros and accredited bugeiros; the latter are represented by the Associação de Bugeiros (☎ 225-2077). You can usually arrange a deal through your hotel, and youth hostels may be able to negotiate a discount. Sergio-tur (☎ 211-2146) seemed a reliable outfit.

Although Brazilians and foreigners clearly have a fun time zooming around in buggies, the more remote beaches don't exactly benefit from the commotion and erosion. The coastline close to Natal has been claimed by bugeiros, but in years to come there may be a move to protect beaches further afield from their impact.

Places to Stay

Natal's hotel areas are in Cidade Alta and along the city beaches. Ponta Negra, 14 km south of the city, also has plenty of low-budget options – see the section on Places to Stay in Ponta Negra.

Cidade Alta One of the cheapest options is *Hotel Fenícia* (☎ 222-1366) at Avenida Rio Branco 586, which offers standard apartamentos at US$8/10 for singles/doubles; and luxury versions (with air-con) at US$12/17 for singles/doubles. Breakfast is not included in the price. *Hotel São Paulo* (☎ 222-4536), at Avenida Rio Branco 697, has apartamentos at US$12/15 for singles/doubles. One block down the street is *Hotel Natal* (☎ 222-2792), which has aparta mentos at similar prices. Both of these are good budget options.

Hotel e Restaurante Casa Grande (☎ 222-1513), Rua Princesa Isabel 529, is a quiet place directly opposite A Macrobiótica restaurant. Standard apartamentos (with fan) cost US$14/21 for singles/doubles; luxury versions (with air-con) cost US$21/29 – breakfast is not included in the price. The hotel also has a restaurant annexe.

The three-star *Hotel Jaraguá* (☎ 221-2355) at Rua Santo Antônio 665 has a sauna, swimming pool, and panoramic view from the 17th floor. Apartamentos cost US$36/50 for singles/doubles, but these prices can be discounted up to 30% if you pay in cash.

City Beaches There's a nifty youth hostel, *Albergue de Juventude Ladeira do Sol* (☎ 221-5361), at Rua Valentim de Almeida on Praia dos Artistas. *Pousada Marina da Praia* (☎ 222-0678) at Avenida Presidente Café Filho 860 has standard apartamentos (with fan) at US$13/15 for singles/doubles; and luxury versions (with air-con) at US$15/20.

For a splurge on a fancy beach hotel, try *Vila do Mar* (☎ 222-3755), five km south of town at Via Costeira 4223. Rooms cost around US$65/70 for singles/doubles.

Places to Eat

Natural food freaks will streak to *A Macrobiótica* on Rua Princesa Isabel. It's open from 11 am to 2 pm and from 6 to 8 pm, Monday to Friday; and from 11 am to 2 pm on Saturday.

Raízes, at Avenida Campos Sales 609, serves a rodízio dinner with a choice of 35 regional dishes: a real blowout meal of Northeastern specialities for US$6 per person. At lunch the restaurant opens a self-service section for inexpensive dishes and sandwiches. There's also a pleasant bar outside and live music in the evening. Raízes is closed on Sundays, except during the peak tourism months of January, February and July.

O Crustáceo at Rua Apodi 414 specialises in seafood – the ambience is enhanced by a large tree poking through the roof in the centre of the restaurant. Coffee enthusiasts should get their caffeine fix at *Café Avenida* on Avenida Deodoro.

Rio Grande do Norte boasts a few good brands of cachaça. Try a shot of Ohlo D'Água, Murim or Caranguejo with a bite of cashew fruit.

Entertainment

Chaplin is a pricey and popular bar on Praia dos Artistas. Jobim, at Rua Mossoró 561, is a combination nightclub/bar with live music and dancing – US$3 cover charge. For folk-loric shows and dancing, try Zás-Trás at Rua Apodi 500 in the Tirol district. Inexpensive food is served in the restaurant section and the shows start around 8 pm. After the show, the dancers will teach guests dances such as forró, *ciranda de roda* (round dancing), and something called *aeroreggae*. From 11 pm onwards, the dance floor gets crowded and the tempo rises.

Getting There & Away

Air There are flight connections to all major cities in the Northeast and the North, and to Rio and São Paulo.

Airline offices are in the Cidade Alta: VASP (☎ 222-2290) is at Avenida João Pessoa 220; Varig/Cruzeiro (☎ 221-1537) at Avenida João Pessoa 308; and Transbrasil (☎ 221-1805) at Avenida Deodoro 363. Nordeste (☎ 221-3139) is on the southern perimeter of the city in the district of Lagoa Nova at Avenida Senador Salgado Filho 1799.

Bus There are two daily departures to Salvador (21 hours; US$24); four daily buses to Recife (five hours; US$8); frequent departures to João Pessoa (2½ hours; US$5); and three regular buses (eight hours; US$19) and one leito (US$30) departing daily to Fortaleza. Buses depart twice a day for Rio (46 hours; US$63). There are eight daily departures to Mossoró (five hours; US$10); and two daily departures (at 8 am and 7 pm) for Juazeiro do Norte (10 hours; US$17).

Getting Around

To/From the Airport Natal's Augusto Severo airport (☎ 272-2811) is 15 km south of town on BR-101. There is a bus service from the rodoviária velha (old bus station) in the city centre to the airport. The taxi fare from the city centre is around US$14.

To/From the Rodoviária The rodoviária nova (☎ 231-1170) (new bus station – for long-distance buses) is about six km south of the city centre. There is a bus service connecting the rodoviária nova with the rodoviária velha (old bus terminal), which is on Praça Augusto Severo in the city centre. The taxi fare to the centre is around US$5.

To/From the Beaches The rodoviária velha is the hub for bus services to: the airport; the rodoviária nova; city beaches, such as Praia dos Artistas; beaches further south, such as

Ponta Negra and Pirangi; and beaches in the north, as far as Genipabu.

A taxi from the centre to Praia dos Artistas costs around US$2.50, while to Ponta Negra it's about US$9.

NORTH OF NATAL

The beaches immediately north of Natal, where sand dunes plunge into the surf, are beautiful, but not quite as spectacular as the southern beaches.

Praia Redinha

Twenty-five km by road north of Natal, Praia Redinha features 40-metre-high dunes, a good view of Natal, lots of bars and *capongas* (freshwater lagoons).

Genipabu

Five km further north is Genipabu, where golden sand dunes, palm trees and dune buggies converge on a beach lined with

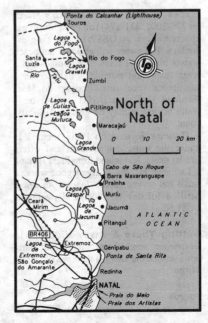

numerous barracas, pousadas, and restaurants. It's a popular, crowded place where you can swim, toboggan down the dunes, or take a 30-minute jangada trip (US$2.50 per person).

Places to Stay Amongst the cheapest pousadas are *Casa de Genipabu* (☎ 225-2141) and *Pousada Marazul* (☎ 225-2065).

Getting There & Away Buses to Genipabu and Redinha leave Natal regularly from the rodoviária velha.

Praia Jacumã to Praia Maxaranguape

A coastal road is being built which will head north from Genipabu towards praias Jacumã, Muriú, Prainha and Maxaranguape – little, palm-graced bay beaches separated from one another by rivers and hills. The beaches are readily accessible, but off the beaten track. Muriú and Prainha (still undeveloped) are especially nice.

Places to Stay & Eat *Marina's Muriú* (☎ 228-2001, 221-1741) on Praia Muriú has apartamentos at US$9/16 for singles/doubles. The owner will also rent out beach houses for longer stays. The pousada has a large restaurant outside which serves a sumptuous lunchtime 'Rodízio do Mar' (Seafood Buffet) at US$11 per person – youth hostellers may be given a 50% discount.

Marina's Jacumã on Praia Jacumã is under the same management and offers similar deals. Just inland from Praia Jacumã is Lagoa de Jacumã, a large lagoon where a small hut serves superb *lagosta na brasa* (grilled lobster tails on a skewer) for US$1.50.

Getting There & Away Viação Rio Grandense buses from Natal's rodoviária nova service the area via the town of Ceará-Mirim.

Touros

Sixty km north of Ceará-Mirim is Touros, a fishing village with several beaches, bars and a couple of cheap pousadas.

AREIA BRANCA

The town of Areia Branca, 50 km from Mossoró and BR-304, is a small fishing port. It's possible to visit the super-modern salt docks 25 km away, but only with advance notice.

Places to Stay

The hotel *Areia Branca Praia* (☎ 332-2344) is right on Upanema, the town beach. Apartamentos start at around US$12/18 for singles/doubles.

MOSSORÓ

To break the trip between Natal and Fortaleza, you might want to visit this town on the fringe of the sertão. About four km out of town there are hot springs at *Hotel Termas de Mossoró* – which is expensive, but you may be able to pay a small fee just to use the springs.

In town there's the Mercado Municipal, an interesting market where all kinds of artesanato (especially leatherwork and ceramics) and daily necessities for life in the sertão are sold. The Museu Histórico at Praça Antônio Gomes 514 has all sorts of personal effects, weapons, and documents connected with Lampião and his bandit colleagues, who attacked Mossoró in 1924. It's open from 8 am to 8 pm, Tuesday to Friday; from 8 am to 4 pm on Saturday; and from 8 to 11 am on Sunday. For more details about Lampião, see the History section in the Facts about the Country chapter.

Places to Stay

Lord (☎ 321-1137) at Rua Cel Gurgel 21 has inexpensive apartamentos; or try the more upmarket *Sol* (☎ 321-4342) at Rua Idalino de Oliveira s/n (no number).

Getting There & Away

The rodoviária is three km out of town on Rua Felipe Camarão. Mossoró has frequent bus services to Natal (four hours; US$4.50) and Fortaleza (four hours; US$4). There are also infrequent local bus services between Mossoró and Areia Branca.

TIBAÚ

Tibaú, 25 km from BR-304, is a bustling resort beach on the border between Ceará and Rio Grande do Norte. Truck caravans roll past the surf into Ceará, saving a few km and giving the place a frontier-town flavour. Locals sell bottles filled with sand in many different colours collected from the beach.

Four km west on the coast you come to a river and a friendly outdoor bar. The river's current is swift; nevertheless it's a popular bathing spot. Two men pull you and your vehicle across on a low-tech car ferry – a wooden platform and a piece of rope pegged to both banks – for US$1. Between ferry duty, the float serves as a diving platform for the bathers.

Follow the caravan of trucks. The coast from Tibaú (Rio Grande do Norte) to Ibicuitaba (Ceará) can be negotiated at low tide. From Ibicuitaba the road is paved again.

Ceará, Piauí & Maranhão

Ceará

Ceará's pride and glory is its coastline – nearly 600 km of glorious beaches. The beach in this part of the Northeast engenders a special way of life. In nearly all of the beach towns, the people of Ceará live out their folklore every day of the year. They make old-fashioned lacework and handicrafts, cook according to traditional recipes, sleep in hammocks, sail out on jangadas to catch fish, and live in thatched-roof homes.

Should you stray inland into the sertão, you will see a rugged, drought-plagued land, a bleak landscape of dust and caatinga, peopled by vaqueiros (cowboys) who rely on their cattle for almost everything. The dried meat serves as food, tools are fashioned from the bones, and the hides provide clothing: nothing is wasted. For a complete contrast, visit the Serra de Baturité, a small chain of hills south-west of Fortaleza, which features an agreeable climate and coffee and banana plantations.

For all its size and wealth of culture, Ceará is a poor and undeveloped state. Poverty and disease are rampant and dengue and yellow fever are endemic. Cars and buses are sprayed for mosquitoes at highway police stations, particularly at state borders.

FORTALEZA

Fortaleza is now a major fishing port and commercial centre in the Northeast. The tourist attractions of the city are limited to a small historical section, a large selection of regional handicrafts, a few good restaurants and some super beaches 20 km beyond the city limits in either direction.

History

According to revisionist Cearense historians, the Spanish navigator Vicente Yanez was supposed to have landed on Mucuripe beach on 2 February 1500, two months before Pedro Álvares Cabral sighted Monte Pascoal in Bahia. Despite this early claim to fame, it was only in 1612 that the first colonisers sailed from the Azores to settle on the banks of the Ceará river.

The settlement at present-day Fortaleza was hotly contested: it was taken over by the Dutch in 1635, then lost in turn to the Tabajara Indians. In 1639, the Dutch under the command of Matias Beck landed once again, fought off the Indians and constructed a fortress. In 1654 the Portuguese captured the fortress and reclaimed the site. A town grew around the fortress, which was given the name of Fortaleza de NS da Assunção (Fortress of Our Lady of Assumption). Ignored by most history books, fierce battles with the local Indians continued to delay colonisation for many years.

Orientation

The city is laid out in a convenient grid pattern. The centre lies above the old historical section and includes the Mercado Central (Central Market), the sé (cathedral), and major shopping streets and government buildings.

East of the centre are the beaches of Praia de Iracema and Praia do Ideal; then continuing eastwards, Avenida Presidente John Kennedy links Praia do Diário, and Praia do Meireles, which are lined with glitzy hotels and restaurants. Beyond here are Porto do Mucuripe (the port) and the Farol Velha (Old Lighthouse). Praia do Futuro begins at the lighthouse and extends five km southwards along Avenida Dioguinho to the Clube Caça e Pesca (Hunting & Fishing Club).

Information

Tourist Office EMCETUR, the state tourism organisation, has its Centro de Turismo (☎ 231-3566; main tourist office) at Rua Senador Pompeu 350 – inside a renovated prison. This was one of the best tourist infor-

Ceará, Piauí & Maranhão

mation centres we encountered in Brazil. Staff help with booking accommodation and organising tours to distant beaches, and can provide details on bus transport. Useful maps of the city are on sale for US$1.50 and there's even a computer information service. The Centro de Turismo is open from 7 am to 6 pm, Monday to Saturday; and from 7 am to noon on Sunday.

There are also EMCETUR kiosks at the airport (open daily from 6 am to 6 pm) and the rodoviária (open daily from 7 am to 11 pm).

A tourist information telephone service,

Disque Turismo (Dial Tourism), is also available – just dial 1516.

Money Banco do Brasil has a convenient branch in the city centre on Rua Floriano Peixoto.

Post & Telecommunications The main post office in the centre is on Rua Floriano Peixoto. Teleceará, the state phone company, has a convenient office in the city centre at the intersection of Rua Floriano Peixoto and Rua Dr João Moreira. Other useful phone

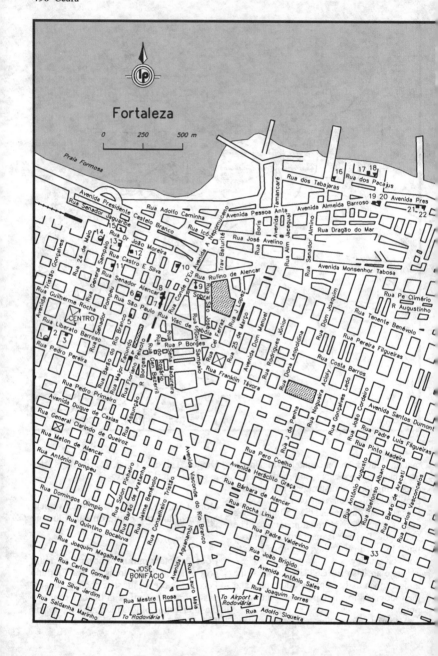

Fortaleza

0   250   500 m

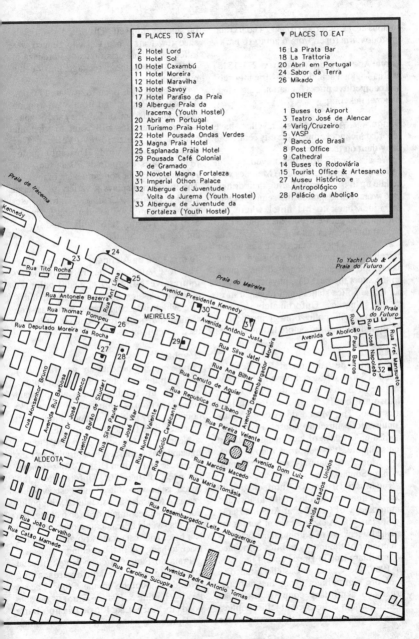

■ PLACES TO STAY

2 Hotel Lord
6 Hotel Sol
10 Hotel Caxambú
11 Hotel Moreira
12 Hotel Maravilha
13 Hotel Savoy
17 Hotel Paraíso da Praia
19 Albergue Praia da
   Iracema (Youth Hostel)
20 Abril em Portugal
21 Turismo Praia Hotel
22 Hotel Pousada Ondas Verdes
23 Magna Praia Hotel
25 Esplanada Praia Hotel
29 Pousada Café Colonial
   de Gramado
30 Novotel Magna Fortaleza
31 Imperial Othon Palace
32 Albergue de Juventude
   Volta da Jurema (Youth Hostel)
33 Albergue de Juventude da
   Fortaleza (Youth Hostel)

▼ PLACES TO EAT

16 La Pirata Bar
18 La Trattoria
20 Abril em Portugal
24 Sabor da Terra
26 Mikado

OTHER

1 Buses to Airport
3 Teatro José de Alencar
4 Varig/Cruzeiro
5 VASP
7 Banco do Brasil
8 Post Office
9 Cathedral
14 Buses to Rodoviária
15 Tourist Office & Artesanato
27 Museu Histórico e
   Antropológico
28 Palácio da Abolição

stations are at the airport (open 24 hours) and the rodoviária (open from 6 am to 10 pm).

Travel Agency Hoje Turismo (☎ 231-1515) at Rua Major Facundo 52 has friendly staff and competitive prices for national and international ticketing.

Dangers & Annoyances Travellers have reported pickpocketing in the city centre and petty theft on the beaches.

We also heard from one traveller about solicitous females on Praia do Meireles who cuddle up to travellers and drug their drinks. One woman transported the semiconscious foreigner back to his hotel where she attempted to gain entry to his room on the pretext that she was helping him because he was 'drunk'. Once in the room, she helped herself to his valuables and vanished. Fortunately, the traveller recognised the woman on the street the next day, physically towed her to the police station, and regained most of his valuables. Unfortunately, he was unable to stop the police from giving the thief an almighty thrashing before letting her go.

Museums
The Centro de Turismo at Rua Senador Pompeu 350 is a restored prison which now contains a folk museum, the main tourist information office and shops selling artesanato. The Museu de Arte e Cultura Popular (folk museum) houses a variety of interesting displays of local handicrafts, art and sculpture. It's open from 7 am to 6 pm, from Monday to Saturday; and from 7 am to noon on Sunday.

The Museu Histórico e Antropológico do Ceará, a museum devoted to the history and anthropology of Ceará, is at Avenida Barão de Studart 410. A bizarre exhibit here is the crushed wreckage of a light plane, which is a reminder of the murky politics associated with military rule in Brazil during the '60s. In 1964, the Cearense Castello Branco, a hardcore rightwinger from the military, organised a military coup to oust João Goulart, whom he accused of leftist politics, from the presidency and then assumed the presidency himself. Disgusted democrats shed few tears when Castello Branco was killed in a plane crash outside Fortaleza in 1967 – hence the wreckage outside the museum.

The museum is open from 7 am to 6 pm, Tuesday to Friday; and from 8 am to noon and from 2 to 6 pm, on Saturday and Sunday.

Car enthusiasts will want to visit the Museu do Automóvel (Veteran Car Museum) at Avenida Desembargador Manoel Sales de Andrade 70, in the Água Fria district on the southern edge of the city. The museum displays a variety of veteran Buicks, Pontiacs, Cadillacs, Citroens, etc. It's open from 8 am to noon and from 2 to 5.30 pm, Tuesday to Saturday; and from 9 am to 5 pm on Sunday.

Teatro José de Alencar
The José Alencar Theatre (1910) is an impressive building, a pastel-coloured hybrid of classical and art nouveau architecture which was constructed with cast-iron sections imported from Scotland. It is now used for cultural events.

Beaches
Fortaleza's city beaches are generally dirty and, with the exception of Praia do Futuro, are unfit for bathing. There are pleasant beaches within 45 minutes of town (1½ hours or so by public transport), but the best beaches all lie further from Fortaleza.

Near Ponte Metálica, the old port, Praia de Iracema was a source of inspiration to Luis Assunção and Milton Dias, Ceará's Bohemian poets of the '50s. Unfortunately this beach is now polluted and best avoided. Praia do Meireles is also tainted with pollution and not recommended for bathing, but it fronts Avenida Presidente Kennedy, which is a hotel and restaurant strip and a popular place to hang out in the evening.

Praia do Futuro, a clean length of sand stretching five km southwards along Avenida Dioguinho to the Clube Caça e Pesca (Hunting & Fishing Club), is the sole good city beach. Like Rio de Janeiro's Barra de Tijuca, it is being built up at an alarming rate. There are barracas here which serve fried fish and shrimp.

The beaches immediately north of Fortaleza, Cumbuco and Iparana, are both pleasantly tranquil. Harried travellers can relax from the tensions of tropical living, string up a hammock in the shade of some palm trees, sip coconut milk and rock themselves to sleep.

Parque Ecológico do Côco
This park, close to Shopping Center Iguatemi, was set up in 1991 after local ecological groups pressed for protection of the mangrove swamps from encroaching highways and the industrial zone. Entrances to the park, which is about seven km from the centre, are on Avenida Engenheiro Santana and Rua Vicente Leite. From the centre, take the bus marked 'Edison Quieroz' to Shopping Center Iguatemi, which is opposite the park.

Organised Tours
There are several tours available from Fortaleza, mostly to beach destinations such as Beach Park, Lagoinha, Jericoacoara, Canoa Quebrada, Morro Branco, Iguape, Prainha, etc. The tours can be a good idea if you're stuck in Fortaleza and don't have time to arrange your own transport or don't want to stay overnight at the beach towns. The buses will pick you up and drop you off at your hotel door. Details about tours to these destinations are given under their respective headings later in this chapter.

EMCETUR offers many such tours – ask at the Centro de Turismo. Other tour operators include: Protec Turismo (☎ 239-4788) at Avenida Washington Soares 260; Valtur (☎ 231-9157) at Avenida Monsenhor Tabosa 1078 (Praia de Iracema); Egoturismo (☎ 221-6461) at Rua Barão de Aracati 644; Petritur (☎ 252-3391) at Rua Padre Valdevino 197; and Hoje Turismo – for address and phone details see the previous Travel Agency section.

Festivals
The Regata de Jangadas, a jangada regatta between Praia do Meireles and Praia Mucuripe, is held in the second half of July.

The Iemanjá festival is held on 15 August at Praia do Futuro. The Semana do Folclore, the town's folklore week, takes place in the Centro do Turismo from 22 to 29 August.

Places to Stay
The main tourism office provides help finding accommodation.

Places to Stay – bottom end
Centre The *Albergue de Juventude da Fortaleza* (☎ 244-1850) at Rua Rocha Lima 1186 is good, but it's in Aldeota district, a long way from the centre and the beaches.

There are many dives on Rua Senador Pompeu: shop around for cleanliness not price. Readers have recommended the *Hotel Savoy* (☎ 252-2582) which has apartamentos (with fan) at US$8/13 for singles/doubles. Opposite is the *Hotel Maravilha*, with similar prices and an odd entrance that resembles an outdoor loo! One block south is *Hotel Moreira* (☎ 252-4665), with quartos at US$6/10 for singles/doubles.

The *Hotel Lord* (☎ 231-6188) at Rua 24 de Maio 642, right off Praça José Alencar, is in a convenient location, but several readers have commented that it's 'full of bugs', 'a rip-off', and 'really bad news'; and furthermore, the praça itself is renowned for theft at night. Food for thought. Apartamentos start at US$12/17 for singles/doubles.

City Beaches Praia de Iracema is generally less expensive for accommodation than Praia do Meireles. *Albergue de Juventude Praia de Iracema* (☎ 252-3267) at Avenida Almeida Barroso 998, on Praia de Iracema, is a convenient distance from the centre. *Albergue de Juventude Volta da Jurema* (☎ 244-1254) at Rua Frei Mansueto 370 is less comfortable, but close to the glitz of Praia do Meireles.

Abril em Portugal (☎ 231-9508) at Avenida Almeida Barroso 1006, on Praia de Iracema, has a friendly owner and new apartamentos at US$12/17 for singles/doubles. Downstairs is a good restaurant.

Hotel Pousada Ondas Verdes (☎ 226-0871) at Avenida Presidente Kennedy 934, Praia de Iracema, has bright double apartamentos at US$25 (with sea view); US$21 (with fan); and US$18 (without fan – wait for the breeze?). *Pousada Café Colonial de Gramado* (☎ 224-1499) at Rua Nunes Valente 275, close to Praia do Meireles, is recommended. Apartamentos cost US$14/16 for singles/doubles. Discounts are negotiable for cash payment. The pousada has a swimming pool and, if convenient for the owner, transport can be provided from the airport or rodoviária.

Rodoviária The *Hotel NS de Fátima* offers standard cheapo rodoviária digs for US$5 per person.

Places to Stay – middle

Centre *Hotel Caxambu* (☎ 231-0339) at Rua General Bezerril 22 has standard aparta mentos at US$19/24 for singles/ doubles; and luxury versions (with frigobar) at US$20/29 for singles/doubles. *Hotel Sol* (☎ 211-9166) at Rua Barão do Rio Branco charges similar prices for standard and luxury apartamentos. Travellers aspiring to higher rates will take the 'Suite Presidencial', which costs US$69/77 for single/double occupancy.

City Beaches *Hotel Paraíso da Praia* (☎ 231-3387) at Rua dos Pacajus 109, Praia de Iracema, has a swimming pool and spiffy standard apartamentos at US$33/40 for singles/doubles; and luxury versions (with sea view balcony) at US$40/44 for singles/ doubles. Discounts can be negotiated for cash payment. *Turismo Praia Hotel* (☎ 231-6133) at Avenida Presidente Kennedy 894/814, Praia de Iracema, provides good value with apartamentos at US$26/34 for singles/doubles. Discounts are negotiable for cash payment.

Rodoviária The *Hotel Amuarama* (☎ 272-2111) is a surprisingly good three-star hotel next to the rodoviária. Apartamentos start at

around US$21/27 for singles/doubles. The hotel has a café and a swimming pool.

Places to Stay – top end

Most of the top-end hotels are on Praia do Meireles, which has been heavily developed with competing hotels, many of which resemble multistorey carparks. There are two five-star hotels facing Meireles beach on Avenida Presidente Kennedy. The *Esplanada Praia Hotel* (☎ 244-8555), despite its star rating, has the outward appearance of a decaying tenement block. Room prices start around US$69/78 for singles/doubles. The *Imperial Othon Palace* (☎ 244-9177) at 2500 has single/double rooms for US$55/65.

Novotel Magna Fortaleza (☎ 244-1122) at Avenida Presidente Kennedy 2380 is a very slick four-star hotel with a swimming pool and the usual amenities (TV, air-con, phone, fridge). Room rates start at US$85/90 for singles/doubles.

Places to Eat

You can eat well in Fortaleza. There's delicious crab, lobster, shrimp and fish, and a fantastic variety of tropical fruits including cashews, coconut, mango, guava, sapoti, graviola, passionfruit, murici, cajá and others.

There are several local dishes worth tasting. *Peixe a delícia* is a highly recommended favourite. Try *paçoca*, a typical cearense dish made of sun-dried meat, ground with a mortar and pestle, mixed with manioc and then roasted. The tortured meat is usually accompanied by *baião de dois*, which is a mixture of of rice, cheese, beans and butter.

Centre The centre has lots of eateries which offer snacks and prato feito at lunch; in the evening, you have a much wider choice at the city beaches. Vegetarians can browse at *Restaurante Alivita* at Avenida Barão do Rio Branco 1486. Open for lunch only – closed on Sunday. In the courtyard inside the Centro de Turismo, there's *Xadrez*, a restaurant with tables outside in the shade – good for a cool beer and a snack.

City Beaches There are some excellent restaurants on Praia de Iracema. For Italian food, try *La Trattoria* where the owner proudly claims 'cutting spaghetti is a crime, ketchup is forbidden; and no-one will be served beans and rice'! It's open from 6 pm to midnight, Monday to Saturday; and from 11 am to 3 pm on Sunday. *Abril em Portugal* is run by an affable Portuguese from Alentejo. Main dishes start around US$3.50. The *galinha de cabidela* (chicken special) and *arroz de mariscos* (rice with shellfish) are delicious. It's closed on Monday.

Praia do Meireles is packed with restaurants. *Sabor da Terra* is a churrascaria on the beach, with a leafy setting and tables set out in the open to catch the breeze. The curiously named *Smell's* at Avenida Presidente Kennedy 4456 (towards the eastern end of the beach) is a sandwich bar serving pita bread sandwiches, juices, and sweets. The Japanese restaurant *Mikado* at Avenida Barão de Studart 600 (three blocks back from the beach) specialises in teppanyaki.

At the aptly named *Restaurante Água Na Boca* (literally Water in the Mouth), Rua República do Líbano 1084 (Varjota district), we highly recommend the *moqueca mixta*, a combination of seafood cooked in coconut cream and dendê oil. This restaurant is closed on Monday, and open for lunch only on Sunday. In Mucuripe, *Restaurante Osmar* at Rua São João 147 has been recommended for seafood. It's closed on Sunday.

Entertainment
Boite Apocalypse, at Avenida Duque de Caxias 309, is a major nightspot in the centre with videos, shows, beauty parades, striptease, live music and dancing. It's open from 6 pm to midnight, Tuesday to Thursday; from 11 pm to 4 am, Friday and Saturday. London London, at Avenida Dom Luis 131, prides itself on being the most animated pub in Fortaleza. There's live music in the bar area and a pizzeria restaurant in another section of the pub.

Pirata Bar at Rua dos Tabajaras 325, Praia de Iracema, is clearly the place to go, at least on Mondays when it claims 'a segunda feira mais louca do planeta' (the craziest Monday on the planet). The action includes live music for avid forró or lambada fans, who can dance until they drop. Admission costs US$2.50. Babilônia, at Avenida Santos Dumont 5779, is a gigantic dancehall with room for several thousand. If you like sweaty action, there's boxing and freestyle wrestling for men and women on Wednesdays. Admission costs US$4. Open from 11 pm to 3 am, Wednesday to Saturday.

Much of the action during holiday season is out on the hotel strip on Avenida Presidente Kennedy. There are outdoor bars, and merchants and artists hawking their goods. Oba Oba at Avenida Washington Soares 3199 (Água Fria district) has shows, dancing and live music.

Clube de Vaqueiro (☎ 229-2799) at Anel Contôrno, between BR-116/CE-04, is a huge forró club, a long way from the centre and best reached by taxi. On Fridays, there's a rodeo before 11 pm when the forró dancing kicks off.

Things to Buy
Fortaleza is one of the most important centres in the Northeast for crafts. Artisans work with carnaúba palm fronds, bamboo, vines, leather and lace. Much of the production is geared to the tourist, but there are also goods for urban and Sertanejo customers. The markets and fairs are the places to look for clothing, hammocks, wood carvings, saddles, bridles, harnesses and images of saints for pilgrims.

Markets are held about town (usually from 4 pm onwards) from Tuesdays to Sundays:

Tuesday
    Praça João Gentil in Gentilândia (on the southern edge of the city)
Wednesday
    Praça Luiza Távora in Aldeota district
Thursday
    Praça do Professor on Avenida Aguanambi in front of Jornal O Povo (newspaper office)

Friday
    Praça Portugal in Aldeota district
    Rua dos Tabajaras at Praia de Iracema
    Praça Farias Brito in Otávio Bonfim
    Praça da Igreja Redonda in Parquelândia district
    Praça José Bonifácio
Saturday
    Praça Pio IX on Avenida 13 de Maio
    Praça Presidente Roosevelt in Jardim América district
    Praça da Aerolândia – on BR-116 close to the Aeroclube de Fortaleza (Fortaleza Flying Club)
Sunday
    Praça da Imprensa in Aldeota district

You can purchase sand paintings on Calçadão da Avenida Presidente Kennedy, watch the artists work and have them customise your design. Best visited in the evening.

Lacework, embroidery, raw leather goods, ceramics and articles made of straw are also available from: the Central de Artesanato Luiza Távora (Handicrafts Centre) at Avenida Santos Dumont 1589 in Aldeota district; the Centro do Turismo at Rua Senador Pompeu 350; the Mercado Central on Rua General Bezerril; and tourist boutiques (clothing, jewellery, fashion) along Avenida Monsenhor Tabosa. Cashew nuts are also excellent value in Fortaleza.

Getting There & Away

Air Aeroporto Pinto Martins (☎ 272-1335) is six km south of the city centre. Flights operate to Rio, São Paulo, and major cities in the Northeast and the North.

Following are addresses for Brazilian and foreign airlines:

Air France
    Rua Pedro Borges 33, sala 409 (☎ 221-3533)
British Airways
    Rua Pedro Borges 135, sala 1501 (☎ 221-5370)
TAP (Air Portugal)
    Rua Pedro Borges 135, sala 302, Edifício Portugal (☎ 231-4345)
Transbrasil
    Rua Barão do Rio Branco (☎ 221-3922)
Varig/Cruzeiro
    Rua Barão do Rio Branco 1179 (☎ 211-9099)
VASP
    Rua Barão do Rio Branco 959 (☎ 244-2244)

Bus The rodoviária (☎ 272-1566) is about six km south of the centre.

Bus services run daily to Salvador (20 hours, US$32); thrice daily to Natal (eight hours; US$19) plus one leito service (US$30); at least twice daily to Teresina (nine hours; US$16 or US$33 for leito); thrice daily to São Luis (17 hours; US$28); once daily to Recife (12 hours; US$20); six times daily to Belém (25 hours; US$40); and twice daily to Rio de Janeiro (48 hours; US$75 or US$150 for leito).

Empresa Redenção bus company runs 10 buses a day to Quixada (3½ hours) and Quixeramobim (four hours), and 13 buses a day to Baturité (two hours). Ipu Brasileira bus company runs services to Ubajara seven times a day (six hours; US$9) and four times a day to Juazeiro do Norte (nine hours; US$14). The daily bus to Gijoca (for Jericoacoara) leaves at 8 am (eight hours). There are four buses a day to Aracati (two hours), the small town which provides access to Canoa Quebrada.

Train See the section on Serra de Baturité later in this chapter for details about a weekly rail excursion between Fortaleza and Baturité.

Getting Around

To/From the Airport Aeroporto Pinto Martins is six km south of the centre and just a couple of km from the rodoviária. From the airport, there are buses to Praça José Alencar in the centre. A taxi to the centre costs around US$7.

To/From the Rodoviária To reach the city centre, take any bus marked 'Alencar', 'Ferroviária', or 'Aguanambi'. A taxi to the centre costs around US$4.

To/From City Beaches From Rua Castro e Silva (close to the Centro de Turismo) take the bus marked 'Praia do Meireles' for Praia do Meireles, and the bus marked 'Praia de Iracema' for Praia de Iracema. A taxi from the centre to Praia de Iracema costs US$2.50.

From Praça Castro Carreiro (close to the

Centro de Turismo) take any of the following buses for Praia do Futuro: 'Praia do Futuro', 'Serviluz' or 'Caça e Pesca'.

To/From Beaches West of the City For beaches west of the city, such as Icaraí and Cumbuco, you should take the bus from Praça Capistrano Abreu on Avenida Tristão Gonçalves to Caucaia and then change to a bus to the beach. If you're short of time, take a taxi.

BEACHES SOUTH-EAST OF FORTALEZA

The coastal road from Fortaleza south to Aracati, CE-004, runs about 10 km inland. It's a flat, dry landscape of shrubs, stunted trees and some lakes. The towns are small with good beaches, jangadas, and dunescapes.

Prainha

Thirty-three km south of Fortaleza via BR-116 and seven km from Aquiraz, is the beach town of Prainha (the name means Little Beach'. Prainha is a great beach, and the local fishers will give you rides on their jangadas.

Places to Stay & Eat There are two mid-range hotels in Prainha: *Aquiraz Praia Hotel* (☎ 361-1177) and *Prainha Solar Hotel* (☎ 361-1000). Apartamentos start at US$25/30 for singles/doubles. Both hotels are set back from the beach. *O Leôncio* is a good seafood restaurant.

Getting There & Away São Benedito buses to Prainha leave every hour until 8 pm from Praça da Escola Normal in Fortaleza.

Iguape

Iguape, five km south of Prainha, is also a charming little beach with jangadas, a few lonely palm trees and sand dunes breaking the clean line of the horizon. Kids in town ski down the dunes on planks of wood.

In Iguape, women and children make wonderful lacework. Four or more wooden bobs are held in each hand and clicked rapidly and rhythmically. The bobs lay string around metal pins which are stuck in burlap cushions. Using this process, beautiful and intricate lace flowers are crafted.

Save your purchases for Centro das Rendeiras, six km inland, where the lacework is just as fine and cheaper. Also on sale are sweet cakes made from raw sugar cane broth which is boiled into a thick mass, pressed and reboiled in vats.

Places to Stay & Eat There are two hotels in town, but you can easily rent rooms or houses. Recommended restaurants are *Peixado do Iguape* and *Leão do Camarão*.

Getting There & Away São Benedito buses to Iguape leave every hour until 8 pm from Praça da Escola Normal in Fortaleza.

Tours Tour operators in Fortaleza offer day trips to Iguape for US$15 per person. The tour leaves at 8 am and returns at 5.30 pm. See the Fortaleza section for details about tour operators.

Praia do Morro Branco

This lovely beach, bounded on the coast by the rivers Rio Choro and Rio Piranji and inland by red cliffs, is four km south of the town of Beberibe. Spurn the annoying child-guides who swarm around beach gringos, and instead enjoy the following options: take a jangada ride to the caves, hike to the cliffs of coloured sands, drink from the natural springs of the Praia das Fontes, or simply savour the sun and surf.

The big festival here, dedicated to São Francisco, is held on 3 and 4 September and features a grand procession.

Places to Stay & Eat There are two hotels on the beach: *Hotel Recanto Praiano* (☎ 338-1144) and *Pousada do Morro Branco* (☎ 344-1144). They both have apartamentos around US$18/22 for singles/doubles, and both serve meals.

Getting There & Away Beberibe is 78 km south of Fortaleza on BR-116 and CE-004.

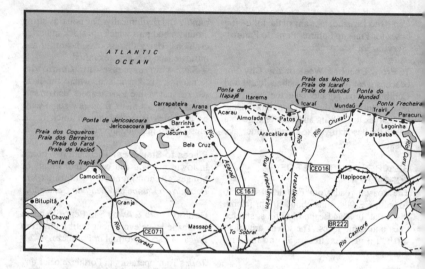

There are four daily São Benedito buses running via Beberibe to Morro Branco from Fortaleza's rodoviária, the first leaving at 6 am, the last at 5 pm (two hours). There are also two daily buses from Beberibe to Aracati.

Tours Tour operators in Fortaleza offer day trips to Morro Branco for US$15 per person. The tour leaves at 8 am and returns at 5.30 pm. See the Fortaleza section for details about tour operators.

Aracati

Aracati is a large town by the Rio Jaguaribe, a river that provided transport for sugar cane and thus wealth for Aracati in the 18th century.

Although the town is not in the best of shape architecturally, it's worth a few hours' to look at some of the historical buildings. The Igreja Matriz de NS do Rosário on Rua Dragão do Mar dates from the late 18th century and is a fine example of colonial architecture. The attractive Sobrado do Barão de Aracati houses the Museu Jaguaribano, which contains sacred art and local handicrafts. For a look at more colonial

houses, some of which have retained their azulejo facades, wander down Rua do Comércio (Rua Grande).

The town is also known for its handicrafts and the best time to see them is at the Feira do Artesão (Artisan Market) held on Saturdays.

The towns south of Aracati, poor little villages often without electricity or running water, are set on stunningly beautiful, wide beaches. Developers have moved in to construct regular accommodation, but it's still easy to camp out on barren beaches.

Places to Stay & Eat There are a couple of inexpensive hotels: *Hotel Casarão* (☎ 421-0079) at Rua Cel Alexandrino 841; and *Brisa Rio* (☎ 421-0081) at Rua Cel Alexandrino 1179. *Churrascaria Raimundo do Caranguejo* at Rua Hilton Gondim Bandeira 505 serves good crab dishes.

Getting There & Away From Fortaleza's rodoviária take one of four daily buses (7 and 11.50 am, and 2 and 5 pm) to Aracati. The 2½-hour trip costs about US$3.

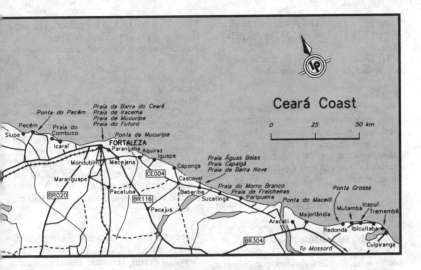

Ceará Coast

0   25   50 km

Canoa Quebrada

Once a tiny fishing village cut off from the world by its huge pink sand dunes, Canoa Quebrada, 13 km from Aracati, is still tiny and pretty, but it is no longer the Shangri-la of the past. There are lots of hip international types running about, but basically the village has peaked. Other than the beach, the main attractions are watching the sunset from the dunes, riding horses bareback and dancing forró or reggae by the light of gas lanterns. If you still have energy remaining after a night of dancing, hire a horse (four hours for US$7 after bargaining) and ride out early in the morning.

The electricity supply in town is erratic, so torches or candles are handy. Take care, bichos de pé are underfoot. Wear shoes all around town and wherever pigs, sheep, and dogs roam freely.

Despite the poor accommodation options, Canoa Quebrada is very crowded in the summer.

Places to Stay The cheapest option is *Albergue Lua Estrela* (☎ 421-1401) on Rua Principal, which is a youth hostel with 32 bunks, a restaurant and a bar.

Other options include *Pousada Maria Alice* (☎ 421-0401) on Rua Principal, and *Pousada Tenda do Cumbe* on Avenida da Praia.

Getting There & Away There are no direct buses to Canoa Quebrada. From Praça do Mercado Antigo in Aracati, there are infrequent buses and VW Kombis to Canoa Quebrada until 5.30 pm – after that the only option is a taxi.

Tours Tour operators in Fortaleza offer day trips (transport only) to Canoa Quebrada for US$18 per person. The tour leaves at 8 am and returns at 6.30 pm. See the Fortaleza section for details about tour operators.

Majorlândia

Majorlândia, 14 km south of Aracati, has a wide, clean beach with many barracas and jangadas.

Places to Stay & Eat Inexpensive places to stay include: *Hotel Sereia* (☎ 421-1748, ramal 130) on Rua Raimundo Rodrigues; *Pousada Gaúcho* (☎ 421-1748, ramal 195) on the beach; *Pousada Sol Nascente* on

Avenida da Praia; and *Apartamento Beira Mar* (☎ 421-1748, ramal 134) on Avenida da Praia.

Try *Restaurant Dengo da Bia* or the restaurant in Hotel Sereia for seafood.

Quixaba

Five km further south of Majorlândia on a sandy track are the distinctive, chalky white sandstone bluffs of Quixaba. From the bluffs, cut by gullies between cacti and palms, you can see the pink hills of Canoa Quebrada. You can rent a jangada and visit the neighbouring beaches.

Places to Stay *Fillo* has clean and quiet rooms to let with electricity.

SOUTH TO RIO GRANDE DO NORTE

The 50 km south-east from Quixaba to the border with Rio Grande do Norte is just a series of primitive little beaches and towns mostly off the maps and definitely out of the guidebooks: Lagoa do Mato, Fontainha, Retirinho and Retiro Grande Mutamba, Ponta Grossa, Redonda and Retiro (waterfall), Peroba, Picos, Barreiras and Barrinha, and, finally, Icapuí.

Three buses a day go from Fortaleza to the village of Icapuí; it's a 3½-hour ride. A road continues to Ibicuitaba and Barra do Ceará beach. It's possible to drive from there to Tibaú, in Rio Grande do Norte, at low tide.

BEACHES NORTH-WEST OF FORTALEZA

Beach Park

This full-blown beach resort, 22 km up the coast from Fortaleza, is one of the most modern in Brazil, with facilities such as ultralights, surfboards, and buggies. It also has an Aqua Park, which features a huge swimming pool complex with the highest water toboggan run (24 metres; and speeds up to 80 kp/h) in Brazil. It's quite expensive and would probably appeal more to travellers in search of structured fun.

Getting There & Away Tour operators in Fortaleza offer day trips (transport only) to Beach Park for US$10 per person. The tour leaves at 8 am and returns at 3 pm. See the Fortaleza section for details about tour operators.

Paracuru

About 100 km from Fortaleza on BR-222 and CE-135, Paracuru is a cearense version of Rio de Janeiro's Búzios. Coconut palms, natural freshwater springs and jangadas complete a tranquil beach picture. Although the beach attracts crowds from Fortaleza at weekends, it's quiet during the rest of the week. In recent years, Carnival in Paracuru has become a byword amongst Cearenses for hot beach action.

Places to Stay For budget accommodation, try *Pousada da Canoa* (☎ 344-1397) on Avenida Perilo Teixeira. Houses can be rented cheaply here, too.

Getting There & Away Frequent buses run from the rodoviária in Fortaleza to Paracuru (two hours; US$3).

Tour operators in Fortaleza offer day trips (transport only) to Paracuru for US$18 per person. The tour leaves at 8 am and returns at 4.30 pm. See the Fortaleza section for details about tour operators.

Praia da Lagoinha

Praia da Lagoinha, a short distance up the coast from Paracuru, has lots of coconut palms, good camping and a small but deep lagoon near the sand dunes.

Places to Stay & Eat If you're not camping, try the moderately priced *Pousada Sol e Mar* (☎ 344-1166, ramal 122). Have a beer and fish stew at *Bar Restaurante Seu Milton*.

Getting There & Away Tour operators in Fortaleza offer day trips (transport only) to Praia da Lagoinha for US$18 per person. The tour leaves at 8 am and returns at 4.30 pm. See the Fortaleza section for details about tour operators.

Mundaú, Guajira & Fleixeiras

The beaches of Mundaú, Guajira and Fleixeiras, 155 km from Fortaleza via BR-222, are traditional fishing areas with wide, unspoiled sweeps of sand.

Places to Stay On the beach at Fleixeiras, there's the mid-range *Solar das Fleixeiras* (☎ 344-1044, ramal 136). On Mundaú beach, there's *Mundaú Dunas Hotel* (☎ 344-1207, ramal 197). Both hotels have restaurants.

Getting There & Away Tour operators in Fortaleza offer day trips (transport only) to these beaches for US$18 per person. The tour leaves at 8 am and returns at 5 pm. See the Fortaleza section for details about tour operators.

Itapipoca

The city of Itapipoca, about 120 km west of Fortaleza, can be used as a staging point for exploring the beaches of Baleia, Pracianos, Inferno and Marinheiros.

Places to Stay *Hotel Municipal* (☎ 631-0197) is on Rua Anastácio Braga in Itapipoca. On Praia Baleia, there's *Pousada da Baleia*, which has a churrascaria.

Jericoacoara

This latest remote-and-primitive 'in' beach has become popular among backpackers and hipper Brazilians, thus replacing Canoa Quebrada in stature. Jericoacoara is a rough little fishing village where dozens of palms drowning in sand dunes face jangadas stuck on a broad grey beach. It's very hard to get there, so you might as well stay a while. Pigs, goats, sheep, horses, burros and dogs roam the sandy streets at will.

It's best to avoid bichos de pé and other parasites by not walking the streets barefoot. Stay clear of the mud-and-straw-walled homes, which may harbour Reduvid bugs, transmitters of Chagas' disease. If you do stay in a mud house, sleep with your body and head covered – for more details see the Health section in the Facts for the Visitor chapter.

You can boogie at the forró held every evening – just follow the music. You can also climb the sand dunes, hitch a ride on a jangada, or walk to Pedra Furada, a rock three km east along the beach. At low tide the beach route is safer than the hill route. You can also hire horses and gallop 18 km west along the beach from Jericoacoara to the still smaller town of Mangue Seco. Trucks go to Mangue Seco on Monday and Thursday.

Places to Stay Accommodation in Jericoacoara now includes more upmarket options – at a price. The cheap options aren't necessarily clean, and don't count on electricity or running water – just gas lanterns and running pigs. You can rent a local's house for about US$2.50 or hang your hammock for US$1. Words to the wise: bring a large cotton hammock or bed roll with sheet sleeping sack, as well as bottled water, which is sometimes scarce. A good inexpensive option is *Pousada Casa do Turismo* (☎ 261-2368 – Fortaleza number for reservations).

The upmarket lodgings include *Pousada Hippopotamus* (☎ 244-9191 – Fortaleza number for reservations); *Pousada Papagaio* (☎ 224-1515 – Fortaleza number for reservations); and *Pousada Matusa* (☎ 244-6500 – Fortaleza number for reservations). Package deals for these upmarket pousadas typically include return transport from Fortaleza, two nights accommodation, and one breakfast. For this type of package, expect to pay US$37/45 for standard/luxury apartamentos per person.

Places to Eat There are plenty of restaurants in town, such as *Acoara do Jérico*, *Pousada do Alemão*, *Freddyssimo* (Italian food), and *Da Isabel*. Most of the budget places to stay also serve food.

Getting There & Away There is a gruelling daily eight-hour bus ride leaving from Fortaleza's rodoviária at 8 am and arriving 24 km shy of Jericoacoara in Gijoca roughly by 4 pm. The road(s) to Gijoca are miserable and confusing. The route is best negotiated by a 4WD equipped with over-sized wheels, *figa* (good luck charm) hanging from the rear-view mirror and a plastic Jesus on the dashboard.

There is an informal and irregular jeep, pickup truck and sometimes burro service to Jericoacoara. When the bus from Fortaleza arrives, the vehicles fill up and leave en masse. Collective bargaining among the passengers should bring the fare to US$2.50 or less per person.

If you have come by car or even a VW Fusca, take your vehicle no further. Leave it parked in Gijoca, where some of the pousada owners can keep an eye on it. The ride over and around sweeping dunes, lagoons, bogs and flat scrub terrain is beautiful, but very hard on people and machines. Transport back to Gijoca usually leaves Jeri after 5 pm.

To get to Jericoacoara from Sobral take a Vale do Acaraú bus to Bela Cruz on an abysmally paved road and intercept the Fortaleza to Gijoca bus there.

For details about access from Camocim, see Getting There & Away in the Camocim section.

Tours Tour operators in Fortaleza and upmarket pousadas in Jericoacoara offer tour packages (see description and prices in section on Places to Stay) for Jericoacoara. The tours usually leave Fortaleza twice a week at 7 pm on Tuesday and Friday; and return from Jericoacoara on Thursday and Sunday at 3 pm. See the Fortaleza section for details about tour operators.

Camocim

Camocim is a fishing village and beach town at the mouth of the Rio Coreaú in northwestern Ceará near the Piauí border. The town's economy revolves around the salt works and lobster fishing. On Praia dos Barreiros and Praia do Farol, two and four km from town respectively, you can sip coconut water while tanning.

Places to Stay & Eat The three pousadas in town face the ocean. Riverbank restaurants serve local seafood and typical cearense dishes.

Getting There & Away Access to Jericoacoara along the beach in a 4WD is difficult but worthwhile. During high season there are boats sailing from Camocim to Jericoacoara – the trip takes four hours. Half the adventure is getting there.

SOBRAL

Sobral has two minor sights, faded glories from the past before all was changed by the construction of BR-222. The Museu Diocesano Dom José (a museum of sacred art) on Rua Dom José houses an eclectic collection of images of saints. It's open Monday to Saturday from 2 to 5 pm. The Teatro Municipal São João on Praça Antônio Ibiapina is an impressive neo-classical theatre (1880).

Places to Stay

The *Hotel Cysne* (☎ 611-0236) at Travessa do Xerez 215 has apartamentos at US$12/18 for singles/doubles.

Getting There & Away

There are seven buses a day to Camocim from Sobral. The earliest bus to make the 3½-hour trip leaves at 5.30 am, the last at 7.30 pm.

MARANGUAPE

Thirty-eight km from Fortaleza on the way to the Serra de Baturité is the town of Maranguape, famous for its Ypioca brand cachaça. The Ypioca aguardente factory is six km from town; the turnoff is near the Shell station. There is no regular transportation to the cachaça plant, but it's not a bad hike and most of the traffic is headed in your direction.

At the gate, ask for a tour of the 138-year-old plant. Before you step within the grounds, a pungent sour mash smell assaults the senses. Whirring, clanking, steam-spitting Industrial Revolution era machinery crushes the cane to pulp and mush. The raw sugar cane mash undergoes alcoholic fer-

Coffee picker

the evenings are cool and morning fog obscures Pico Alto (1115 metres), the highest point in the state.

Baturité

Founded in 1745, the town of Baturité (95 km west of Fortaleza) was once at the forefront of the fight against slavery, and is now the economic and commercial centre of the region. The town's attractions are grouped around the Praça Matriz and include the *pelourinho* (whipping post), the baroque church of Matriz NS de Palma (1764), the Palácio Entre-Rios, and the Museu Comendador Ananias Arruda, which contains exhibits from the town's past. There are a few *termas* (resorts with mineral pools) clustered around the town. Local handicrafts on sale in Baturité include embroidery, tapestry and straw goods.

Places to Stay Apart from the accommodation in the nearby villages of Guaramiranga and Pacoti (see next section), lodgings are also available at *Balneário Itamaracá Club* (☎ 347-0113) at Sítio Itamaracá.

Getting There & Away Although there's a weekly tourist train from Fortaleza to Baturité, it's probably not worth touring the area without a car. The tourist train leaves every Sunday at 7.30 am. Make reservations in advance at the station or contact Bec Turismo (☎ 244-9155) at Avenida Barão de Studart in Fortaleza. There are several daily bus services to Fortaleza (two hours) and Guaramiranga.

Guaramiranga & Pacoti

Two of of the prettiest villages on the heights of Serra de Baturité are Guaramiranga and Pacoti, 19 km and 26 km respectively from Baturité.

Places to Stay & Eat The *Hotel Escola de Guaramiranga* (☎ 226-7122; training centre for hotel staff) in Guaramiranga has spotless apartamentos, a bar, swimming pool, and ping-pong tables. Singles/doubles are US$12/14. It's unmarked and tricky to find

mentation, is distilled, then aged one to three years in huge wooden casks.

PACATUBA

Pacatuba is a cute little town in the shadow of the Serra de Baturité. The Balneário Bico das Andreas spring is smelly, dirty and not what it's cracked up to be.

Places to Stay

The *Pousada das Andreas* (☎ 345-1252) charges US$18 for a four-room bungalow that sleeps eight and comes with kitchenette and refrigerator.

SERRA DE BATURITÉ

Ceará's interior is not limited to the harsh landscapes of the sertão. There are also ranges of hills which break up the monotony of the sun-scorched land. The Serra de Baturité is the range of hills closest to Fortaleza. A natural watershed, it is an oasis of lush green where coffee and bananas are cultivated around the cliffs and jagged spines of the hills. The climate is tempered by rain,

(no sign), but it's a great deal. The *Remanso Hotel e Restaurante da Serra* (☎ 227-7395, ramal 195) is five km from Guaramiranga on the beautiful road to Pacoti. The hotel has pleasant apartamentos at US$20/25 for singles/doubles, a restaurant, and a swimming pool. Slightly more expensive, and closer to Pacoti, is the *Estância Vale das Flores* (☎ 381-1115 Ramal 188) at Sítio São Francisco. It's set in a park with a swimming pool, sports facilities, horse rental, and mini-zoo.

CANINDÉ

Canindé, only 110 km inland from Fortaleza on the BR-020, is the site of one of the Northeast's great religious pilgrimages, O Santuário de São Francisco das Chagas. Since 1775 pilgrims have been coming to Canindé to offer promises and favours to São Francisco de Assis. Nowadays around 250,000 fervent believers arrive each year, most from the sertão, almost all dirt poor. For Westerners the festival is both colourful and bizarre, and laced with superstition. You'll see many ex-voto offerings and miracle cures. It's a scene right out of a Glauber Rocha film.

The festival begins on 2 September at 4 am and continues until 4 October. On 30 September, the climax of the festival begins with the celebration for the *lavradores* (farm workers), which is followed in turn by celebrations for the vaqueiros (cowboys) on 1 October, and for the *violeiros* (guitarists and guitar makers) on 2 October.

The culmination of all the festivities begins at 3 am on 4 October, when the first of nine masses commences. These are followed by a 70,000-strong procession through the town.

PARQUE NACIONAL DE UBAJARA

The main attractions of the Parque Nacional de Ubajara, just a few km from the small town of Ubajara, are the cable-car ride down to the caves and the caves themselves.

Nine chambers with strange limestone formations extend over half a km into the side of a mountain. The main formations

seen inside the caves are: Pedra do Sino (Bell Stone), Salas da Rosa (Rose Rooms), Sala do Cavalo (Horse Room), and Sala dos Retratos (Portrait Room). The park and its beautiful vistas, forest, waterfalls and three-km trail to the caves are alone worth the visit.

In 1987 the lower station of the *teleférico* (cable car) was wiped out by boulders which fell after the winter rains. The station was jerked 18 metres off its foundation and pieces of the teleférico were flung 500 metres into the sertão. The cable-car system has been replaced and now operates from noon to 4 pm, Wednesday to Friday; and from 10 am to 4 pm on Saturday and Sunday. The ride costs US$2.50. Guides accompany you on the one-hour tour round the caves. Lighting has been reinstalled, but a torch is still useful.

Information

The IBAMA office (☎ 634-1388), five km from Ubajara proper, at the entrance to the park, provides guides for the tour, and a few brochures and maps. Phone to make a reservation for the tour – the first one is at 2 pm. If you fancy a strenuous hike, ask at the office if you can take the three-km 'trilha' (trail) down to the cave. Accompaniment by a guide is compulsory (and sensible). Allow at least half a day for the round trip, start in the cool of the early morning, wear sturdy footwear, and take enough to drink.

Places to Stay & Eat

Just 100 metres from the park entrance, the *Pousada da Neblina* (☎ 634-1270) on the Estrada do Teleférico has apartamentos at US$9/12 for singles/doubles, a campground, a swimming pool and a restaurant. It's a good place to stay and guests who decline breakfast receive a 30% discount.

The *Hotel Ubajara* (☎ 634-1261) at Rua Juvêncio Luís Pereira 370 in Ubajara has single/double apartamentos for US$9/12 and lower prices for quartos.

Getting There & Away

Empresa Ipu-Brasília has seven daily buses from Fortaleza to Ubajara (six hours; US$9).

The first bus leaves at 4 am, the last one at 9 pm. There are also bus connections to Teresina (six hours; US$8), the capital of Piauí state.

To reach the park entrance from the town of Ubajara, either walk or take a taxi – buses are very infrequent.

SERRA DA IBIAPABA

The Serra da Ibiapaba, a range of hills running along the undefined border with the state of Piauí, forms a rugged terrain of buttes, bluffs and cliffs, overlooking distant plains.

The town of Ipu lies 75 km south-east of Ubajara in the Serra da Ibiapaba. The main attraction of Ipu (the name means Waterfall in the Tabajara Indian language) is the Bico do Ipu, a powerful waterfall that jets 100 metres downwards and fans out into sheets of mist and spray. A few km out of town are strange stone stairs built by the Tabajara.

There is a sleazy restaurant under the falls, but no hotels in town. Ipu is worth a visit if it happens to be on your route, but it's not worth a special detour.

JUAZEIRO DO NORTE

Juazeiro do Norte, 528 km from Fortaleza, is a magnet for believers in Padre Cícero, who lived in this town and became a controversial figure of the sertão. Not only was he a curate with several miracles to his credit, he also exercised a strong political influence. His astonishing rise to fame was started when an elderly woman received the host from him at mass and claimed that it had miraculously turned to blood. Soon he was being credited with all kinds of miracles and later became drawn into a leading role in the social and political upheavals in the Northeast. Padre Cícero died in 1934, but despite attempts by the Catholic church to deny his sainthood, the claims and adoration of his followers seem to be as strong as ever.

The best time to see this magnetic attraction and devotion is during the festivals and pilgrimages in honour of Padre Cícero. On 24 March, the Aniversário do Padre Cícero celebrates Padre Cícero in legend and song.

The *romaria* (pilgrimage) to Juazeiro do Norte in honour of Padre Cícero takes place on 1 and 2 November and is known as the Dia do Romeiro e Festa do Padre Cícero.

The city of Padre Cícero is rich in wood and ceramic sculpture. Look for the work of Expedito Batista, Nino, Cizinho, José Celestino, Luis Quirino, Maria de Lourdes, Maria Cândida, Francisca, Daniel, José Ferreira and Maria das Dores.

Logradouro do Horto

On the hill above the town – accessible either by road or via a path laid out with the stations of the cross – is the colossal statue of Padre Cícero (25 metres) which was built in 1969 and now ranks fourth in the record books – its taller statue competitors include Cristo Rey (Cochabamba, Bolivia), Cristo Redentor on Corcovado (Rio) and the Statue of Liberty (New York). Nearby is a small chapel and a building filled with votive offerings which depict the afflictions and problems from which the worshippers have been freed: wooden or wax replicas of every conceivable body part, and graphic representations of survival from accidents.

Túmulo do Padre Cícero

Padre Cícero's tomb is beside the Capela NS do Perpétua Socorro on Praça do Socorro.

Gráfica de Literatura de Cordel

If you are interested in literatura de cordel (literally string literature), visit this workshop on Rua Santa Luzia where you can see the pamphlets being produced for sale on the premises. It's open from 7 to 11 am and from 1 to 5 pm, Monday to Friday; closed Saturday afternoon.

Places to Stay

Since this town is a pilgrimage centre, there is no lack of accommodation except during the main festivals. For inexpensive apartamentos, try *Juá Palace* (☎ 511-0844) at Avenida Castelo Branco 2558, or *Viana Palace* (☎ 511-2585) at Rua São Pedro 746.

Getting There & Away

There are four daily departures for Fortaleza (nine hours; US$14), and regular bus services to all the major cities in the Northeast.

Piauí

Piauí, one of the largest states in the Northeast, is one of the poorest states in Brazil, due to the oppressively hot and arid climate in its eastern and southern regions. The odd shape of the state – broad in the south, tapered at the coast – is due to a unique pattern of settlement which started from the sertão in the south and gradually moved towards the coast.

The climate on the Litoral Piauiense (Piauí Coast) is kept cool(er) by sea breezes. If you're heading into the interior of the state, the best time for festivals and cool breezes is during July and August. Absolutely the worst time, unless you want to be sunbaked to a frazzle, is between September and December.

Although Piauí is usually bypassed by travellers, it offers superb beaches along its short coast; interesting rock formations and hikes in the Parque Nacional de Sete Cidades; prehistoric sites and rock paintings in the Parque Nacional da Serra da Capivara, which ranks as one of the top prehistoric monuments in South America; and the chance for rock hounds to visit Pedro Segundo, the only place in South America where opals are mined.

TERESINA

Teresina, the capital of Piauí, is famed as the hottest city in Brazil. Promotional literature stresses heat and yet more heat, with blurb bites such as 'Even the Wind Here Isn't Cool' or 'Teresina – As Hot As Its People'.

It's an interesting, quirky place which seems addicted to giving a Middle Eastern slant to the names of its streets, hotels, and sights. Our taxi driver, who had been absorbing the landscapes of the Gulf War on TV, thought that Teresina would probably compare well with Iraq for its climate – but definitely nothing else! The city itself is a Mesopotamia of sorts, sandwiched between the Rio Poty and Rio Parnaíba, and there's even a hotel shaped like a pyramid. Teresina is untouristed and unpretentious and the inhabitants will stop you on the street to ask 'Where are *you* from?' Like the British, residents of Teresina instantly warm to discussion of the weather, and especially of their favourite topic: 'O Calor' (The Heat).

We recommend a visit if you yearn for attention or would like to feel famous for a day or so. And there's got to be something good going for a city that hosts an annual festival of humour!

Information

Tourist Offices PIEMTUR (☎ 223-0775), the state tourism organisation, at Rua Alvaro Mendes 1988, has helpful staff who appear delighted to see stray travellers and happily dole out literature and advice. It's open from 9 am to 6 pm, Monday to Friday.

The IBAMA office (☎ 232-1652) at Avenida Homero Castelo Branco 2240 (Jockey Club district) was one of the most active we encountered in Brazil. Leaflets about the national parks in Piauí are available here. It's open from 8 am to 5.45 pm, Monday to Friday.

Travel Agencies For tours to sights in Piauí, contact Servitur Turismo (☎ 223-2065) at Rua Eliseu Martins 1136, or Espaço Turismo (☎ 223-3777), inside the shopping gallery of the Hotel Luxor.

Museu Histórico do Piauí

This state museum is divided into a series of exhibition rooms devoted to the history of the state; religious art; popular art; archaeology; fauna, flora and minerals; and an eclectic assortment of antique radios, projectors and other ancient wonders. Hidden in the corner of one room is a pathetic cabinet containing flag, kerchief, and scribbled notes from 'Comunistas', a flexible term used here to describe a group of independent thinkers,

Top: Lacemaker, south of Fortaleza, Ceará (MS)
Left: The day's catch, Ceará (JM)
Right: Fishermen, Ceará (JM)

Top: Ruins of Igreja de São Matías, Alcântara, Maranhão (RS)
Left: A lazy afternoon in an amphitheatre, São Luís, Maranhão (DS)
Right: Projeto Reviver rooftops, São Luís, Maranhão (DS)

Teresina

0   250   500 m

JOCKEY CLUB

Rio Poty

Rio Parnaíba

CENTRO

TIMON, MARANHÃO

To Airport

To São Luís & Belém

To Rodoviária

PLACES TO STAY
- 1 Rio Poty Hotel
- 5 Hotel Sambaíba
- 6 Hotel Fortaleza
- 8 Royal Palace Hotel
- 9 Hotel Luxor Palace Hotel
- 14 Hotel Central
- 20 Teresina Palace Hotel
- 22 Hotel São José

OTHER
- 2 Railway Station
- 3 PIEMTUR Tourist Office
- 4 Museu de Arte Didática
- 7 Banco do Brasil
- 10 Praça da Bandeira (aka Praça Marechal Deodoro)
- 11 Museu Histórico do Piauí
- 12 Mercado Central
- 13 Mercado Troca-Troca
- 15 Teatro 4 de Setembro
- 16 Post & Telephone Office
- 17 Palácio de Karnak
- 18 Praça Pedro II
- 19 Centro Artesanal & Restaurante Típico do Piauí
- 21 Praça Saraiva

who were wiped out by the government in 1937.

Admission costs 40c and the museum is open from 8 am to 5 pm, Tuesday to Friday; and from 8 am to noon on Saturday and Sunday. A free guide is provided; in our case it was a delightful woman who not only gave us a guided tour of the museum, but also a very detailed account of her family life and the cruel grip that TV exerted on her daughter's cultural interests.

Museu de Arte Didática

For a complete cultural change – in line with Piauí's empathy for the Middle East – you can visit this museum's collection of artworks from the ancient civilisations of Assyria, Babylon, Egypt, and more. Opening hours are from 7 am to 11 pm and from 1 to 6 pm, Tuesday to Friday.

Palácio de Karnak

This Greco-Roman structure once functioned as the governor's residence and contained valuable works of art and antiques. In the late '80s, the outgoing governor made a quick exit together with all the contents, and the building has been left to deteriorate.

Centro Artesanal

This centre for artesanato from Piauí is a pleasant spot to browse among shops which sell: leather articles; furniture made from fibres; extremely intricate lacework; colourful hammocks; opals and soapstone (from Pedro Segundo); and liqueurs and sweets made from genipapo, cajú, maracujá, etc. The Cooperativa de Rede Pedro Segundo, a producer of high-quality hammocks, sells beautiful linen hammocks at prices ranging from US$55 to US$130. Cotton hammocks start at around US$26.

Mercado Troca-Troca

In an attempt to perpetuate the old traditions of 'troca troca' (barter), the government has made a permanent structure out of what was once an impromptu barter market. Unless you are curious to see the river, it's not worth a visit.

Potycabana

If you hanker after aquatic frolics and games as a respite from the searing heat, visit the Potycabana, an aquatic entertainment centre with water tobogganing and a surf pool close to the Rio Poty.

Festivals

The main festivals, with typical dancing, music, and cuisine of the Northeast, are held between June and August. The Salão Internacional de Humor do Piauí (Piauí Festival of Humour) is held during the first two weeks of September and features comedy shows, exhibitions of cartoons, comedy routines, and lots of live music.

Places to Stay – bottom end

Rua São Pedro is the street to look for rock-bottom options. For more comfort, try *Hotel Fortaleza* (☎ 222-2984) on Praça Saraiva with apartamentos (with fan) at US$8/14 for singles/doubles – equivalent apartamentos with air-con cost US$13/24; and *Hotel Central* (☎ 222-3222) on Rua 13 de Maio 85, which provides apartamentos (with fan) at US$12/15 for singles/doubles – equivalent apartamentos with air-con cost US$17/20.

Camping *PIEMTUR Camping* (☎ 222-6202) is 12 km out of the city on Estrada da Socopo, the road running east towards União.

Places to Stay – middle

The two-star *Hotel Sambaiba* (☎ 222-6711) at Rua Gabriel Ferreira 340 gives a good deal, with apartamentos at US$35/39 for singles/doubles. *Hotel São José* (☎ 223-2176) at Rua João Cabral 340 has a swimming pool and apartamentos (with air-con) at US$40/46 for singles/doubles. The two-star *Hotel Teresina Palace* (☎ 222-2770) at Rua Paissandu 1219, also with swimming pool, provides apartamentos (with air-con) at US$48/52. The *Royal Palace Hotel* (☎ 222-8707) at Rua 13 de Maio 233 offers apartamentos (with air-con) at US$46/54.

Places to Stay – top end

Shaped like a lazy pyramid, perhaps in deference to the prevailing Middle Eastern theme in Teresina, the five-star *Rio Poty Hotel* (☎ 223-1500), at Avenida Marechal Castelo Branco 555, is the poshest place in town. Rooms cost US$100/125 for singles/doubles. Travelling potentates will find the 'Suite Presidencial' a snip at US$293.

Another luxury pad is the *Luxor Palace Hotel* (☎ 222-4911) at Praça Marechal Deodoro 310, which has rooms at US$93/110 for singles/doubles.

Places to Eat

Restaurante Típico do Piauí inside the Centro Artesanal serves regional dishes such as *paçoca* (dried meat with manioc flour and onions) and *sarapatel* (ingredients include blood and intestines). For seafood, try *Camarão do Elias* at Avenida Pedro Almeida 457, or *O Pesqueirinho* which is at Avenida Jorge Velho 6889, several km outside town on the riverside, and serves crab and shrimp stew. For a splurge, visit the *Forno e Fogão* inside the Hotel Luxor which charges US$8 per person for a gigantic buffet lunch. *Chez Matrinchan* at Avenida NS de Fatima 671 (Jockey Club district) is divided into three elements: a restaurant serving French cuisine; a pizzeria; and a nightclub. There's live music here on Friday and Saturday nights – US$1.50 cover charge.

Getting There & Away

Air The airport is on Avenida Centenário, six km north of the centre. There are flights between Teresina and Rio, São Paulo, and the major cities in the Northeast and North.

Bus Teresina has regular bus connections with: Sobral (seven hours; US$10); Fortaleza (nine hours; US$16 or US$33 for leito); São Luis (seven hours; US$10 for frequent daily service or US$20 for midnight leito which runs twice a week); and Belém (four times a day; 16 hours; US$25).

To Parnaíba there are executivo (four hours; US$11) and standard (six hours: US$8) buses – both types run twice daily.

There are bus connections thrice daily to: Esperantina (about three hours; US$6); São Raimundo Nonato (10 hours; US$18); São João do Piauí (seven hours; US$15); and Oeiras (five hours; US$9). To Piracuruca (3½ hours; US$6), there are departures at 8.15 and 11.40 am, and 3.40 and 6.15 pm. Buses depart hourly between 7 am and 6 pm for Piripiri (three hours; US$8). Bus services direct to Pedro Segundo are infrequent, so it may be better to take the bus to Piripiri and continue from there.

Car If you're driving to São Luis, the *Pousada Buriti Corrente* (☎ 521-1668) (between Codó and Caxias) on BR-316 at Km 513 is a beautiful hotel with apartamentos at US$19/25 for singles/doubles and a small zoo. It's 14 km from an alcohol factory. For tours ask for Sérgio or Marcos.

Getting Around

To/From the Rodoviária The cheapest, slowest and hottest option is to take the bus from the stop outside the rodoviária.

Although the rodoviária has a bilheteria with a mandatory price table posted on the window, the ticket price for a taxi ride to the city centre is calculated at US$6.50 – exactly twice what you pay when hailing a taxi in the centre for the ride out to the rodoviária. Clearly a scam. Try flagging down a taxi outside the perimeter of the rodoviária.

LITORAL PIAUIENSE

Parnaíba

Parnaíba, once a major port at the mouth of the Rio Parnaíba, is being developed as a beach resort along with the town of Luís Correia which is 18 km away. Porto das Barcas, the old warehouse section currently under restoration, contains a PIEMTUR information office, a youth hostel, a maritime museum, an artesanato centre, and several bars and restaurants.

Beaches & Lagoons Praia Pedra do Sal, 15 km north-east of the centre on Ilha Grande Santa Isabel, is a good beach divided by rocks into a calm section suitable for swimming, and a rough section preferred by surfers. Lagoa do Portinho is a lagoon surrounded by dunes about 14 km east of Parnaíba on the road to Luís Correia. It's a popular spot for swimming, boating, sailing, and fishing.

The prime beaches closer to Luís Correia are Praia do Coqueiro and Praia de Atalaia. The latter is very popular at weekends and has plenty of barracas selling drinks and seafood. The nearby lagoon, Lagoa do Sobradinho, is renowned for its shifting sands which bury surrounding trees.

Boat Trips Day trips by boat to Tutóia on the coast of Maranhão state are operated on weekends from Porto das Barcas. For more details about the trips which leave at 8 am, contact Parnatur (☎ 322-3569) in Parnaíba.

Places to Stay There's a youth hostel in Porto das Barcas (Parnaíba) and a campground at Lagoa do Portinho, where the *Centro Recreativa Lagoa do Portinho* (☎ 322-2165) provides apartamentos and chalets. The *Hotel Cívico* (☎ 322-2470) at Avenida Governor Chagas Rodrigues 474, in the centre of town, has a swimming pool and apartamentos at US$15/19 for singles/doubles.

The two-star *Hotel das Araras* (☎ 322-3580) is an expensive resort hotel with swimming pool and sports facilities. It's 10 km from Parnaíba on the road to Luís Correia.

Getting There & Away For bus services between Parnaíba and Teresina see the Getting There & Away section for Teresina.

PARQUE NACIONAL DE SETE CIDADES

Sete Cidades is a small national park with interesting rock formations, estimated to be at least 190 million years old, which resemble *sete cidades* (seven cities). Various researchers have analysed nearby rock inscriptions and deduced that the formations are ruined cities from the past. The Austrian historian Ludwig Schwennhagen visited the area in 1928 and thought he'd found the ruins

of a Phoenician city. The French researcher Jacques de Mabieu considered Sete Cidades as proof that the Vikings had found a more agreeable climate in South America. And Eric van Daniken, the Danish ufologist, theorised that extraterrestrials were responsible for the cities which were ruined by a great fire some 15,000 years ago. There's clearly lots of scope here for imaginative theories. See what you think!

The road around the park's geological monuments starts one km further down from the Abrigo do IBAMA (IBAMA office and hostel). The loop is a leisurely couple of hours' stroll. It's best to start your hike early in the morning and bring water because it gets hot; watch out for the *cascavelas* – poisonous black and yellow rattlesnakes. The park is open from 6 am to 6 pm. Ask at the IBAMA office for information; guides may be available.

Sexta Cidade (Sixth City) and Pedra do Elefante, the first sites on the loop, are lumps of rock with strange scaly surfaces. The Pedra do Inscrição (Rock of Inscription) at Quinta Cidade (Fifth City) has red markings which some say are cryptic Indian runes. The highlight of Quarta Cidade (Fourth City) is the Mapa do Brasil (Map of Brazil), a negative image in a rock wall. The Biblioteca (Library), Arco de Triunfo (Triumphal Arch) and Cabeça do Cachorro (Dog's Head) are promontories with good views.

Places to Stay & Eat

Abrigo do IBAMA is an inexpensive hostel at the park entrance. Designated campsites are also available here.

Hotel Fazenda Sete Cidades (☎ 276-1664), a two-star resort hotel, has attractive apartamentos for US$14/18 for singles/doubles. It's a cool and shady spot, just six km from the park entrance, and the restaurant serves a delicious grilled chicken for US$2.50. Even if you don't stay overnight it's good for lunch and a quick dip in the pool. Guests may be able to arrange transport between the fazenda and Piripiri on arrival or departure.

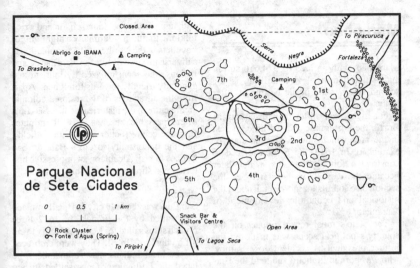

Parque Nacional de Sete Cidades

Getting There & Away
The park is 180 km from Teresina and 141 km from Ubajara (Ceará state) on a fine paved road. Buses depart hourly between 7 am and 6 pm for Piripiri (three hours; US$8). There are several daily bus departures to Fortaleza (nine hours; US$9).

Getting Around
IBAMA courtesy bus transport for the trip (26 km) to the park leaves from Piripiri at 7 am and returns from Abrigo do IBAMA at 4 pm. A taxi costs around US$13. Hitchhiking is also effective. In the park itself, you can drive on the roads or follow the trails on foot.

PEDRO SEGUNDO
The town of Pedro Segundo lies in the hills of the Serra dos Matões, around 50 km south of Piripiri. Close to the town are several mines which are the only source of opals in South America.

Place to Stay
The town's hotel is *Hotel Rimo Pedro Segundo* (☎ 271-1543) on Avenida Itamaraty.

Getting There & Away
For bus services between Pedro Segundo and Teresina see the Getting There & Away section for Teresina.

PARQUE NACIONAL SERRA DA CAPIVARA
The Parque Nacional Serra da Capivara, in the south-west of the state, was established in 1979 to protect the many pre-historic sites and examples of rock paintings in the region.

There are over 300 excavated sites which are opened to the public depending on the research schedule. If the staff have time, you may be lucky enough to receive a lift and be shown around. For details about access and archaeological sites, contact Doutora Niede Guidon at FUMDHAM (Fundação Museu do Homem Americano; (☎ 582-1612) at Rua Abdias Neves 551, São Raimundo Nonato. There are plans to open a museum and conduct guided tours of some of the sites.

Getting There & Away
For bus services between São Raimundo Nonato and Teresina see the Getting There & Away section for Teresina.

Maranhão

Maranhão, with an area of 324,616 sq km and a population of five million, is the second largest state in the Northeast, after Bahia.

For many years after their discovery of Brazil, the Portuguese showed little interest in the area which now forms the state of Maranhão. In 1612, the French arrived to construct a fort at São Luís, which later became the capital of the state. See the section on São Luís for more detail about the historical and economic development of Maranhão.

The state's most recent impact on the country's political scene was made by the former president-by-accident José Sarney, who was born in Pinheiro and held the Brazilian presidency from April 1985 until March 1990. Sarney is now a senator for the state of Amapá.

Although the southern and eastern areas of Maranhão are characterised by vast expanses of babaçu palms and typical sertão landscapes, the western and north-western regions merge into humid Amazon rainforests.

The rural economy of Maranhão is dependent on the babaçu palm, which serves an amazing multitude of purposes: the nuts can be eaten straight out of the fruit or crushed to produce vegetable oil (margarine) or industrial lubricating oils; the tips of the young palms can be eaten as 'palm hearts'; the older trunks are used for construction of huts, with roofing material supplied by the leaves – which can also be used for the production of cellulose and paper. The residue from the crushed nuts provides excellent fertiliser and cattle feed; and the hulls of the fruits are used in the production of acetates, tar, and methyl alcohol. Finally, the hulls are turned to charcoal for use in smelting. Things go better with babaçu!

SÃO LUÍS

São Luís, the capital of Maranhão, is a city with unpretentious colonial charm and a rich folkloric tradition – definitely a highlight for travellers in the Northeast. The population is a diverse mixture of Europeans, Blacks, and Indians who seem unfazed by tourism and generally friendly towards foreigners. Apart from the attractions of the restored colonial architecture in the historical centre, São Luís offers passable beaches only 30 minutes from the centre (better ones further afield), and the opportunity to cross Baía de São Marcos to visit Alcântara, an impressive historic town slipping regally into decay.

History

São Luís was the only city in Brazil founded and settled by the French. In 1612 three French ships sailed for Maranhão to try to cut off a chunk of Brazil. They were embraced by the local Indians, the Tupinambá, who hated the Portuguese. Once settled in São Luís, named after their King Louis XIII, the French enlisted the help of the Tupinambá to expand their precarious foothold by attacking tribes around the mouth of the Amazon.

But French support for the new colony was weak and in 1614 the Portuguese set sail for Maranhão. A year later the French fled. The Tupinambá, abandoned to fend for themselves, were 'pacified' by the Portuguese.

Except for a brief Dutch occupation between 1641 and 1644, São Luís developed slowly as a port for the export of sugar, and later trade switched to cotton exports. As elsewhere, the plantation system was established with slaves and Indian labour, despite the relatively poor lands. When demand for these crops slackened in the 19th century, São Luís went into a long and slow decline.

In recent years the economy of São Luís has been stimulated by several mega-projects. A modern port complex has been built to export the mineral riches of the Serra dos Carajás, a range of hills in the Amazon which has the world's largest deposits of iron ore. In 1984, Alcoa Aluminium built an enormous factory for aluminium processing – you'll see it along the highway south of the city. The US$1.5 billion price tag for this project was the largest private investment in Brazil's history. A missile station has been built near Alcântara, and oil has been found in the bay.

Orientation

Perched on a hill overlooking the Baía de São Marcos, São Luís is actually on an island of the same name. The historic core of São Luís, now known as Projeto Reviver (Project Renovation), lies below the hill. Going north from the old town, one crosses Ponte José Sarney bridge to São Francisco, the new and affluent area with many hotels, restaurants and nightspots.

It's easy to get around on foot – despite hills and confusing street layout – because everything is so close. In fact, as long as you're in the old part of town, a bus is rarely needed.

The most confusing thing about getting around São Luís is the existence of several names for the same streets. There are the new official names that are on street signs and the historical names or nicknames that the locals use. No two city maps seem to be the same.

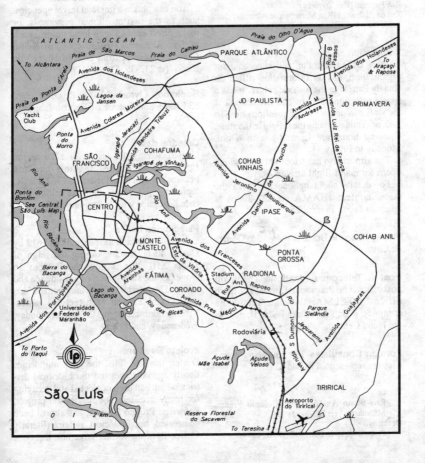

Alternative Street Names The following is a short list of streets with their common alternative names in brackets:

28 de Julho (Rua do Giz)
Rua da Estrêla (Rua Candido Mendes)
Rua Afonso Pena (Rua Formosa)
Rua do Sol (Rua Nina Rodrigues)
Rua do Egito (Rua Tarquinho Lopes)
Rua do Veado (Rua Celso Magalhães)
Rua dos Afogados (Rua José Bonifácio)
Rua de Nazaré (Rua de Nazaré e Odilo)
Rua das Barrocas (Beco dos Barqueiros; Rua Isaacs Martins)
Rua Jacinto Maia (Rua da Cascata)
Rua Portugal (Rua Trapiche)
Rua da Alfândega (Rua Marcelino de Almeida)
Praça Dom Pedro II (Avenida Dom Pedro II)

Information

Tourist Office Maratur, the state tourism organisation, has an information office on Rua da Estrêla in the historic centre. It has a sparse selection of maps and literature, but the staff can answer most questions on São Luís or destinations further afield in the state. Opening hours are from 8 am to 6 pm, Monday to Friday.

The airport also has a tourist booth which opens for major flight arrivals only.

For details about national parks in the state, contact IBAMA (☎ 222-3006) at Avenida Jaime Tavares 25.

Money Banco do Brasil is at Avenida Gomes de Castro 46.

Post & Telecommunications The main post office is on Praça João Lisboa. The main office of TELMA, the state telephone company, is on Praça Dom Pedro II, next to the Hotel Central.

Foreign Consulates The following countries are represented in São Luís:

France
    Rua Santo Antônio 259 (Colégio Franco Maranhense) (☎ 222-2732)
Germany
    Praça Gonçalves Dias, 310 (☎ 221-2294)

USA
    Avenida Daniel de La Touche, Jardim Buriti (☎ 226-4535)

Travel Agencies & Tour Guides In the shopping gallery at Rua do Sol 141, there are several travel agencies offering guides and organised tours to Alcântara and other destinations in the state. An efficient agency in the shopping gallery is Taguatur (☎ 222-0100) at Loja 14 which also sells bus tickets. Babaçu Viagens (☎ 222-7028) at Loja 3 in the same gallery is also reliable, and has another office in the Hotel Central.

You can obtain a guide at travel agencies, such as the two mentioned previously, or make direct contact with local guides, such as Simon Ramos (☎ 236-4069) or Nelito (leave message at front desk of Hotel Vila Rica – (☎ 232-3535).

Bookshop Livraria ABC at Rua de Nazaré 533 has a small stock of English-language books.

Catedral da Sé

Constructed by the Jesuits in 1726 as the Igreja NS da Boa Morte, this building became the official cathedral in 1762. Inside, there's a fine baroque altar and ceiling frescoes decorated with babaçu motifs.

Palácio dos Leões

Originally a French fortress built in 1612 by Daniel de la Touche, during the reign of Louis XIII, this is now the Palácio do Governo, the state governor's residence and office. The interior reflects the pomp of Versailles and French architectural tastes. Visiting hours are from 3 to 6 pm on Monday, Wednesday, and Friday.

Projeto Reviver

During the late '80s, the state authorities finally agreed to restore the historical district, which had been neglected and decaying for many decades. The restoration project, known as Projeto Reviver, has almost been completed, but Epitácio Cafeteira (literally Coffee-Pot), the former governor, has been replaced by Edison Lobão (literally Big Wolf), who has stalled further work.

Over 200 buildings have been restored and the district has been turned into one of the architectural highlights of Brazil. To appreciate the superb colonial mansions and the many designs and colours of their azulejo facades, just wander around the district. Azulejos were first produced in Portugal and later became a popular product in France, Belgium and Germany. Since azulejos provided a durable means to protect outside walls from the humidity and heat in São Luís, their use became standard practice during colonial times.

Museu de Artes Visuais This museum has a fine collection of old azulejos, engravings, prints, and paintings. It's open from 8 am to 1 pm and from 4 to 6 pm, Monday to Friday.

Opposite the museum is the old round market where you can shop with the locals for dried salted shrimp (eaten with shell and all), cachaça, dry goods, and basketwork, or visit the lunch counters for cheap local cooking.

Cafua das Mercês & Museu do Negro This museum is housed in the old slave market building where slaves were once kept after their arrival from Africa – notice the absence of windows – and then sold. A small and striking series of displays documents the history of slavery in Maranhão. The museum is open from 1.30 to 6 pm, Monday to Friday; and from 2.30 to 5.30 pm on Saturdays and public holidays.

The African slaves brought to Maranhão were Bantus from West Africa who were used primarily on the sugar plantations, and to a lesser extent for the cultivation of rice and cotton. They brought their own type of Candomblé, which is called Tambor de Mina in this part of Brazil. The museum director, Jorge Babalaou, is an expert on Candomblé and Bantu/Maranhense folklore. He may be able to indicate where you can visit a ceremony, but the major houses, the Casa das Minas, Casa de Nagô and Casa Fanti-Ashanti-Nagô, don't welcome visitors.

Museu do Centro de Cultura Popular This museum is at Rua 28 de Julho 221, just a few minutes on foot from the Cafua das Mercês. The displays include a good collection of handicrafts from the state of Maranhão, and Bumba meu boi costumes and masks. It's open from 8 am to 6 pm, Monday to Friday.

Igreja do Desterro

This church, notable for its facade, was built between 1618 and 1641 and is the only Byzantine church in Brazil. There's a small adjoining museum, the Museu de Paramentos Eclesiásticos, with a display of ecclesiastical apparel.

Fonte das Pedras

This fountain, built by the Dutch during their brief occupation of São Luís, marks the spot where, on 31 October 1615, Jerônimo de Albuquerque and his troops camped before expelling the French. It's closed at present, but you can ask for the key at the house next door.

Museu Histórico e Artístico do Estado de Maranhão

This museum, housed in a restored mansion originally built in 1836, provides an idea of daily life in the 18th century with an attractive display of artefacts from wealthy Maranhão families. There are furnishings, family photographs, religious articles, coins, sacred art – and President José Sarney's bassinet.

Opening hours are from 2 to 6 pm, Tuesday to Friday; and from 3 to 6 pm, on Saturdays, Sundays, and public holidays.

Fonte do Ribeirão

This is a delightful fountain, built in 1796, with spouting gargoyles. The three metal gates once provided access to subterranean tunnels which were reportedly linked to churches as a means to escape danger.

Beaches

The beaches are beyond São Francisco district and they are all busy on sunny weekends. You should beware of rough surf

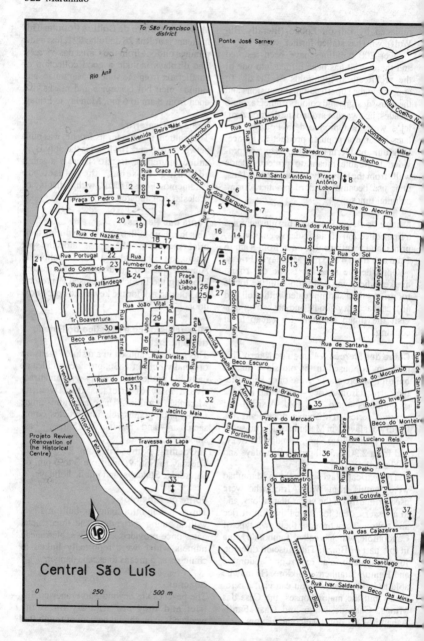

Central São Luís

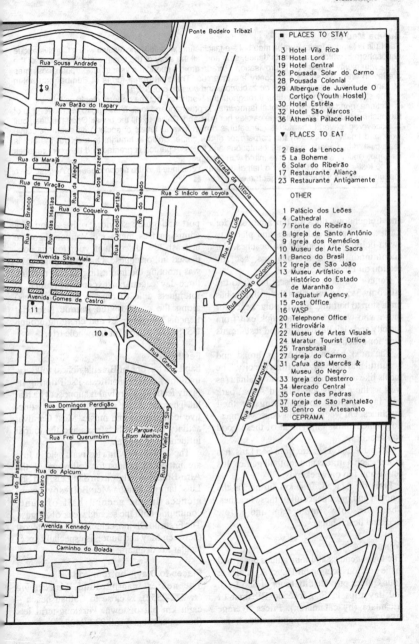

Ponte Bodeiro Tribazi

■ PLACES TO STAY

3 Hotel Vila Rica
18 Hotel Lord
19 Hotel Central
26 Pousada Solar do Carmo
28 Pousada Colonial
29 Albergue de Juventude O
   Cortiço (Youth Hostel)
30 Hotel Estrêla
32 Hotel São Marcos
36 Athenas Palace Hotel

▼ PLACES TO EAT

2 Base da Lenoca
5 La Boheme
6 Solar do Ribeirão
17 Restaurante Aliança
23 Restaurante Antigamente

OTHER

1 Palácio dos Leões
4 Cathedral
7 Fonte do Ribeirão
8 Igreja de Santo Antônio
9 Igreja dos Remédios
10 Museu de Arte Sacra
11 Banco do Brasil
12 Igreja de São João
13 Museu Artístico e
   Histórico do Estado
   de Maranhão
14 Taguatur Agency
15 Post Office
16 VASP
20 Telephone Office
21 Hidroviária
22 Museu de Artes Visuais
24 Maratur Tourist Office
25 Transbrasil
27 Igreja do Carmo
31 Cafua das Mercês &
   Museu do Negro
33 Igreja do Desterro
34 Mercado Central
35 Fonte das Pedras
37 Igreja de São Pantaleão
38 Centro de Artesanato
   CEPRAMA

Bumba Meu Boi

São Luís is famous for its Bumba meu boi – a fascinating, wild, folkloric festival with a Carnivalesque atmosphere in which participants dance, sing and tell the story of the death and resurrection of the bull – with plenty of room for improvisation. Parade groups spend the year in preparation, costumes are lavish and new songs and poetry are invented. There are three forms of Bumba meu boi in Maranhão: *bois de matraca*; *bois de zabumba*; and *bois de orquestra*.

The story and its portrayal differ throughout the Northeast, but the general plot is as follows:

Catirina, goddaughter of the local farmowner, is pregnant and feels a craving to eat the tongue of the best *boi* (bull) on the farm. She cajoles her husband, Chico, to kill the beast. Once the dead bull is discovered, several characters (caricatures drawn from all levels of society) do some detective work and finally track down the perpetrator of the crime. Chico is brought to trial, but the bull is resuscitated by various magical incantations and tunes. A pardon is granted and the story reaches its happy ending when Chico is reunited with Catirina.

The festivals start in the second half of June and continue into the second week in August. Give the tourism office a quick call to get the exact date. ■

and tremendous tides in the area: ask for local advice about safe times and places to swim before you head for the beaches. For accommodation at the beaches, see the section on Places to Stay.

Ponta d'Areia is the closest beach to the city, only 3½ km away, but the pollution has put a stop to bathing. It's a popular beach for those who want to make a quick exit from the city and visit the barracas and restaurants here for beach food.

The next beach, Calhau, is broad and beautiful and only 7½ km from the city. The locals like to drive their cars onto Calhau (as well as the next beach, Olho d'Agua) park and lay out their towels alongside their machines. On weekends this causes congestion which spoils enjoyment of these good city beaches.

Olho d'Agua, 11½ km from São Luís, has more beach barracas and football games. It's active and fun on weekends.

Praia do Araçaji, four km further, is the quietest and most peaceful of these beaches. There are only simple bars and a few weekend beach houses.

Tours

The tour agencies and tour guides described in the previous section on Travel Agencies & Tour Guides provide city tours of São Luís, and day trips to São José do Ribamar or Alcântara (by catamaran). Prices average US$33 per person per day and include trans-

port and guide services only – you pay admission fees, meals, etc. You can negotiate at least 30% discount if your tour is conducted in Portuguese. One guide told us he was mooting the interesting idea of running three-day catamaran excursions (suited to foreigners able to cope with rough seas) along the coast to the Parque Nacional Lençóis Maranhenses and charging around US$80 per person for the whole trip.

Festivals

São Luís has one of Brazil's richest folkloric traditions, which manifests itself during its many festivals. Carnival is supposedly a real hit. There are active samba clubs and distinctive local dances and music. Most Carnival activity is out on the streets and the tourist influence is minimal.

The Tambor de Mina festivals held in July are important events for followers of the Afro-Brazilian religions in São Luís, and São Luís' famous Bumba Meu Boi festival commences in the second half of June, continuing until the second week of August. The Festa do Divino, celebrated on Pentecost (between May and June), is especially spectacular in Alcântara.

Places to Stay – bottom end

The nearest campground, *Unicamping* (☎ 222-2552), is close to Calhau beach – eight km out of town. For long-term lets (houses or rooms) call 222-2425.

Centre The youth hostel, *Albergue de Juventude O Cortiço* (☎ 222-6258) at Rua 14 de Julho 93, is in a refurbished colonial mansion and provides excellent value. *Hotel Estrêla* (☎ 222-1083) at Rua da Estrêla 370 is a good cheapie in the heart of the historic district. Quartos (with fan) cost US$6 per person. Don't leave valuables in your room.

There are several very cheap places along Rua da Palma, which is a convenient location, right in the heart of town, but not too safe at night. *Hotel São Marcos* (☎ 221-4761) at Rua do Saúde 178 has started to disintegrate and is not recommended unless the management sees the potential of this hotel and cleans up its act. Apartamentos cost US$17/22 for singles/doubles. There are two swimming pools: one filled with murky water and rubbish; the other without water and also full of rubbish.

A much better deal is *Hotel Lord* (☎ 222-5544) at Rua de Nazaré 258. It's a large, timeworn hotel with clean, comfortable quartos at US$15/24 for singles/doubles; and apartamentos (including air-con) at US$24/29 for singles/doubles.

The *Athenas Palace Hotel* (☎ 221-4163) at Rua Antônio Rayol 431 – just east of the Mercado Central – also offers good value. Apartamentos cost US$15/21 for singles/doubles. The area is not too safe at night (if you have a car make sure the hotel staff let you use the locked parking lot behind the hotel).

Beaches The *Pousada Tia Maria* (☎ 227-4338) at QD 1 Lote 12, on Ponta d'Areia beach, has attractive apartamentos at US$18/25 for singles/doubles.

Places to Stay – middle
Centre The *Hotel Central* (☎ 232-3855) at Praça Dom Pedro II 258 has a couple of cheapie double apartamentos (with fan only) at US$21; and other overpriced apartamentos starting at US$34/42 for singles/doubles.

The *Pousada Colonial* (☎ 232-2834), at Rua Afonso Pena 112, is in a recently restored colonial mansion and offers excel-lent value. Clean and comfortable apartamentos cost US$37/45 for singles/doubles – discounts can be negotiated for cash payment. If you do negotiate a discount, make certain it is noted on your bill at the same time as you check in. Avoid confusion by getting the figures in writing before taking the room.

Pousada Solar do Carmo (☎ 222-2455) at Praça João Lisboa 400 has apartamentos at US$33/39.

Beaches At Araçagi beach there's one medium-priced hotel, the *Chalé da Lagoa* (☎ 226-4196), which is a relaxing place surrounded by gardens.

Places to Stay – top end
Centre The five-star *Vila Rica* (☎ 232-3535) is very central at Praça Dom Pedro II 299, with a view overlooking the bay. Singles/doubles cost US$95/110 – discounts for cash payment may also be available.

São Francisco There are several upmarket hotels in the São Francisco district – north of town, on the other side of the Rio Anil. These are not recommended unless you have a car or prefer to stay outside the city centre.

The *Hotel São Francisco* (☎ 227-1155) at Rua Luís Serson 77 has singles/doubles for US$45/55. The *Panorama Palace Hotel* (☎ 227-0067) at Rua dos Pinheiros Q-16, 15, has singles/doubles for US$37/44 or you could splurge US$77 for the presidential suite (600 sq metres!), which the management claims is the largest of its kind in Brazil.

Beaches The five-star *Sofitel Quatro Rodas* (☎ 227-1683) is at Calhau beach, a 15-minute drive from town. It has singles/doubles for US$70/76.

Places to Eat
The best maranhense food comes from the sea. In São Luís you'll find many of the familiar dishes of the Northeast and regional specialities such as *torta de sururu* (mussel pie), *casquinha de caranguejo* (stuffed crab), *caldeirada de camarão* (shrimp stew)

and the city's special rice dish – *arroz de cuxá* (rice with vinegar, local vegetables and shrimp).

Centre There are plenty of lanchonetes downtown serving typical, cheap food. Across from the Fonte do Ribeirão, you'll find a couple of good snack bars with sucos.

The *Base da Lenoca* on Praça Dom Pedro II is a popular restaurant with a great position overlooking the Rio Anil – order a beer and a snack and enjoy the breeze. Good regional seafood is served at *Solar do Ribeirão* (☎ 222-3068) at Rua das Barrocas 141. Just down the street at Rua das Barrocas 48 is *La Boheme*, an upmarket restaurant with international cuisine and live music on Friday and Saturday nights – closed on Sunday. *Restaurante Aliança* at Rua de Nazaré 300 serves pizzas, chicken dishes, and steaks. In the heart of the historic district on Rua da Estrêla there's the *Restaurante Antigamente*, which is a convenient spot to pause for refreshment. Live music is offered here in the evening on weekends.

São Francisco The main drag through São Francisco has many new restaurants, particularly pizzerias, and bars. The *Oriental* at Avenida Presidente Castelo Branco 47 has a nice view and serves Chinese food. For vegetarian food, try *O Naturista* at Rua 3, 738 – closed on Sunday.

Further from the Centre The seafood is highly recommended at *Base do Germano* (☎ 222-3276) at Avenida Wenceslau Brás, in Camboa district. Another recommended seafood restaurant is *Base do Edilson* (☎ 222-7210) at Rua Paulo Kruger de Oliveira 32 – in the Vila Bessa district. It's only a 10-minute drive from the city centre, but it's worth taking a taxi as it's difficult to find. The restaurant starts serving lunch at 11.30 am and dinner at 7 pm. The portions are not big for what you pay, but very tasty. We'd suggest *ensopado de camarão com molho pirão* and *peixada com pirão*, for US$5, but everything's good and it's well worth the trip.

Beaches At , *Tia Maria* has good seafood and it's also a fine place to watch the sunset over a cool drink. This is also the closest beach to the city with barracas serving food.

Entertainment

São Luís is currently the top reggae centre of the Northeast and many of the nightspots cater to *reggeiros* or 'reggae fans'. Ask the tourist office for the best places to catch live music. The Cooperativa de Reggae, just a few doors down from the tourist office, might be a good place to start.

For dancing, two of the current hotspots are Boate Génesis at Avenida dos Holandeses Qd-28, 4, at Calhau beach; and Boate Tucanos at Avenida Jerônimo Albuquerque, Curva do 90 – in the Vinhais district, north-east of the city centre.

If you have a radio, São Luís has two radio stations that play great Brazilian pop/jazz late at night.

Things to Buy

São Luís is the place to look for the traditional handicrafts of Maranhão, such as woodcarving, basketry, lacework, ceramics, leatherwork, and woven goods made from linen, local plant fibres, and straw. Also on sale are featherwork, and items made from woven straw or plant fibres (from baskets to bracelets) by the Urubus-Caapor Indians and the Guajajara Indians, both from the interior of Maranhão state.

CEPRAMA (Centro de Artesanato), at Rua de São Pantaleão 1232, is housed in a renovated factory and functions as an exhibition hall and sales outlet for handicrafts. It's open from 3 to 9 pm on Sundays and Mondays; and from 9 am to 9 pm, Tuesday to Saturday. Also worth visiting are the Centro Artesanal do Maranhão at Avenida Marechal Castelo Branco 605, and the Mercado Central. The Mercado Central is open from 7 am to 4 pm, Monday to Saturday; and the Centro Artesanal do Maranhão is open from 8 am to 8 pm, Monday to Friday; and from 8 am to 1 pm on Saturday.

Getting There & Away
Air Air services connect São Luís with Rio, São Paulo, and the major cities in the Northeast and the North.

Following are the addresses for Brazilian and foreign airlines:

Air France
    Praça Gonçalves Dias 301(☎ 222-0344)
Transbrasil
    Praça João Lisboa 432 (☎ 223-1414)
Varig/Cruzeiro
    Rua do Sol, 141, Loja 10 (☎ 222-5322)
VASP
    Rua do Sol 43 (☎ 222-4655)

Bus The rodoviária is about eight km southeast of the city centre. Bus tickets can be booked and purchased in the city centre at several travel agencies listed under Information earlier in this section.

There are regular bus services to Teresina (seven hours; US$10 for frequent daily service or US$20 for midnight leito which runs twice a week); Belém (twice daily; 12 hours; US$21); Carolina (once daily via Imperatriz; 12 hours; US$25); Fortaleza (18 hours; US$23); and Recife (24 hours; US$40).

Boat The *hidroviária* (boat terminal) is on the quayside, just beyond the western end of Rua Portugal. From here, it's possible to take passage on boats sailing along the coast. Sailing times are always approximate, and depend on the tides. The regular daily service to Alcântara is described in the Getting There & Away section for Alcântara. There are regular local services to Pinheiro, Porto de Itaúna and São Bento.

There are also regular departures at least once a week to Guimarães, a major centre for boat-building and fishing, and infrequent departures from there to destinations further along the western coast, such as Turiaçu, Luís Domingues, and Carutapera (on the Pará border).

Getting Around
To/From the Airport The Aeroporto do Tirirical (☎ 225-0044) is 15 km south-east of the city. The bus marked 'São Cristóvâo' runs from the bus stop beside Igreja de São João (on Rua da Paz) to the airport in 45 minutes. There's a bilheteria system for taxis – from the airport to the centre costs about US$10.

To/From the Rodoviária The rodoviária (☎ 223-0253) is about eight km south-east of the city on Avenida dos Franceses. From the bus stop at the junction of Avenida Magalhães de Almeida and Rua Regente Braulio, catch the bus marked 'Rodoviária'. There's a bilheteria system for taxis – from the rodoviária to the city centre centre costs around US$5.

Our taxi trip out to the rodoviária proved confusing when the taxista 'forgot' to turn on the meter and was unable to tell us the price. We stopped for a heated discussion, but were suddenly interrupted by a donkey braying right next to the car. We raised the tempo and volume of the altercation, but had to quit when another donkey (attached to a cart) came trotting down the road and commenced a braying duet – through the open car windows – with the donkey by the roadside. After the donkeys had passed, we unplugged our ears, settled the argument, and drove on.

To/From the Beaches For buses to Ponta d'Areia and Calhau, there's a convenient bus stop on Avenida Beira Mar – take buses marked 'Ponta d'Areia' or 'Calhau'. The bus stop in front of Igreja do Carmo (on Praça João Lisboa) is handy for buses to Olho d'Água and Araçagi. For buses to Raposa and São José do Ribamar, there's a bus stop beside the Mercado Central.

ILHA DE SÃO LUÍS
Praia da Raposa
Out at the tip of the Ilha de São Luís, 30 km from the city, is the interesting fishing centre of Raposa, also known for its lacework. It's a poor town, built on stilts above mangrove swamps – which gives it an unusual appearance. The bulk of the town's population is descended from Cearense immigrants. There are no tourist facilities but the ocean here is

The São José do Ribamar Miracle

The origins of the town date back to the early 18th century when a Portuguese sailing ship went astray and started to founder on the sandbanks of the Baía de São José. The desperate crew begged for mercy from São José das Botas and promised to procure the finest statue of the saint and construct a chapel for it if they were spared.

The ship and its crew were miraculously saved, and several years later the promise was kept when a fine statue of the saint was installed in a chapel at the tip of the cape where disaster had been narrowly avoided. The settlement on this site later received the name of São José do Ribamar: a fusion of the saint's name and the local Indian name for the rock formation at the cape.

According to local legend, the statue was moved away from its site beside the shore, but miraculously reappeared in its original position the next day – without any signs of human intervention. This miracle was repeated a couple more times until the locals decided the statue should be left in its preferred place. During its trek, the statue left deep footprints along the rocky coastline which are now venerated by the townsfolk, who host the annual Festa do Padroeiro (held in September) in honour of the saint. ■

---

pretty and very shallow. There are lots of small fishing boats and it's not too hard to negotiate a ride. Bathing at the beach is dangerous – due to extreme tidal variations, the water recedes up to one km at low tide.

Getting There & Away There are frequent buses from São Luís – a convenient bus stop is the one beside the Mercado Central. The trip takes 35 minutes.

São José do Ribamar

This fishing town is on the east coast of the island, 30 km from the city. There's a busy little waterfront with boats leaving for small towns along the coast – a good way to explore some of the untouristed villages on the island. On Sundays buses go from São José to nearby Ponta de Panaquatira, a popular weekend beach.

Places to Stay & Eat There are two hotels: *Hotel Mar e Sol* and *Hotel Tropical* – both offer simple quartos for about US$4 per person, and both have restaurants. Beach camping is permitted at Panaquatira beach. The seven-metre tide is very fast, so don't camp close to the water.

Getting There & Away Frequent buses leave from São Luís (convenient bus stop beside the Mercado Central) for the 40-minute trip to São José do Ribamar. The last bus back to São Luís leaves at 10.30 pm.

AROUND SÃO LUÍS

Alumar

One of the world's largest aluminium processing plants is on the outskirts of São Luís. Alumar is a cooperative venture between the Brazilian government and a Shell Oil/Alcoa consortium. Bauxite ore is extracted from mines in Pará and brought by rail to the Alumar plant for processing. Tours are conducted on Saturdays – call 216-1155 a few days in advance for reservations. A company bus leaves from Praça Teodoro in São Luís.

ALCÂNTARA

Across the Baía de São Marcos from São Luis is the old colonial town of Alcântara. Founded in the early 1600s with extensive slave labour, the town was the hub of the region's sugar and cotton economy. The beneficiaries of this wealth, Maranhão's rich landowners, preferred living in Alcântara to São Luís.

While the town has been in decline since the latter half of the 19th century, it is still considered an architectural treasure and some experts claim that it is the most homogeneous group of colonial buildings and ruins from the 17th and 18th centuries in Brazil.

Construction of the Centro do Lançamento de Alcântara (CLA), a nearby rocket-launching facility, has caused mutterings amongst residents, who disagreed with the forceful resettlement policy undertaken to

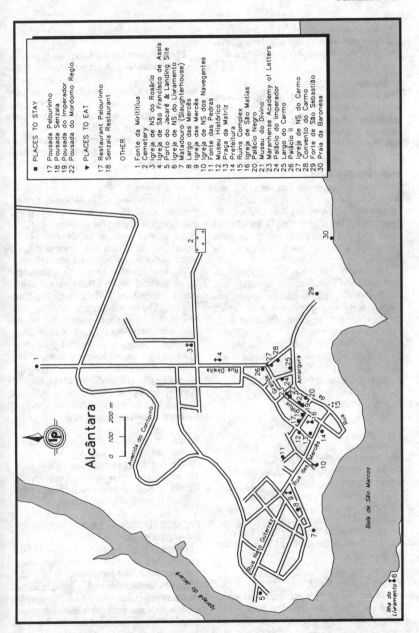

Alcântara

0   100   200 m

PLACES TO STAY
- 17 Pousada Pelourinho
- 18 Pousada Senzala
- 19 Pousada do Imperador
- 22 Pousada do Mordomo Regio

PLACES TO EAT
- 17 Restaurant Pelourinho
- 18 Senzala Restaurant

OTHER
- 1 Fonte da Mirititiua
- 2 Cemetery
- 3 Igreja de NS do Rosário
- 4 Igreja de São Francisco de Assis
- 5 Porto do Jacaré & Landing Site
- 6 Igreja de NS do Livramento
- 7 Matadouro (Slaughterhouse)
- 8 Largo das Mercês
- 9 Igreja das Mercês
- 10 Igreja de NS dos Navegantes
- 11 Fonte das Pedras
- 12 Museu Histórico
- 13 Praça da Matriz
- 14 Prefeitura
- 15 Ruins Complex
- 16 Igreja de São Matias
- 20 Palácio Negro
- 21 Museu do Divino
- 23 Maranhense Academy of Letters
- 24 Palácio do Imperador
- 25 Largo do Carmo
- 26 Palácio II
- 27 Igreja de NS do Carmo
- 28 Convento do Carmo
- 29 Forte de São Sebastião
- 30 Praia da Baronesa

Avenida do Contorno

Rua Direita

Amargura

Grande

Rua das Mercês

Rua Nelo Guterres

Baía de São Marcos

Ilha do Livramento

Igarapé do

clear the construction site. There couldn't be a greater contrast with this slumbering colonial town than a space-age launching pad!

Information

The tourist office in São Luís has brochures about Alcântara. Phone connections with Alcântara are effected through the TELMA office in Alcântara, where you can leave a message.

Things to See & Do

The town is very poor and decaying, but don't miss the following: the beautiful row of two-storey houses on Rua Grande; the Igreja de NS do Carmo (1665), Rua Amargura; and the best preserved pelourinho (whipping post) in Brazil, on Praça da Matriz.

The Museu Histórico on the Praça da Matriz displays a collection of sacred art, festival regalia, and colonial furniture. Each room has its own guardian – a source of employment for the locals. Opening hours for the museum are from 8 am to 2 pm, Tuesday to Saturday; and from 8 am to 1 pm on Sunday. Admission costs 50c and is not included in the price of tours from São Luís.

Once you've seen the main sights, you can walk to the beaches or take a boat trip out to nearby islands.

Festival

The Festa do Divino is held on the first Sunday after Ascension Day. Check the date for the festival (usually held in May) with the tourist office in São Luís.

This is considered one of the most colourful annual festivals in Maranhão, a fusion of African and Catholic elements with two children dressed as the 'Emperor' and 'Empress' paraded through the town and accompanied by musicians.

Places to Stay & Eat

Alcântara has simple campsites close to Praça da Matriz and near the farol (lighthouse). Kids at the quayside will offer very cheap lodgings – basically a place to sling a hammock.

There are also several inexpensive hotels, such as *Pousada do Mordomo Régio* (☎ 101) – recommended – and *Pousada do Imperador* on Rua Grande; and *Pousada Senzala* and *Pousada Pelourinho* beside Praça da Matriz. If you value relaxation, peace and quiet, stay a night or two.

Most of the hotels have restaurants and there are also a couple of eateries along Rua Neto Guterrez.

Getting There & Away

The boat from São Luís to Alcântara departs from the hidroviária (boat terminal) on the quayside, just beyond the western end of Rua Portugal. Buy your ticket the day before departure and check the departure time which varies according to the tide.

The boat leaves at around 8 am (depending on the tide) but it's often crowded so get there between 7 and 7.30 am for the 1½-hour journey. The two sailboats used for this service, the *Newton Belle* and *Mensageiro da Fé*, are real beauties – the stuff of pirate tales. Pandemonium reigns as the last passengers and cargo get stuffed below at sailing time. If you want to avoid the crush and sit outside (no sitting allowed on the top deck), head to the very front of the boat. The boat leaves Alcântara for the return trip around 2 pm, but has been known to go a bit earlier.

Tours For details about tours to Alcântara, see the sections on Travel Agencies & Tour Guides and Tours included under São Luís. The catamaran trip is highly recommended, but you should be prepared for rough seas. Protect cameras, etc, with plastic.

PARQUE NACIONAL DOS LENÇÓIS MARANHENSES

The natural attractions of this national park include 1550 sq km of beaches, mangroves, lagoons, dunes and local fauna (turtles and migratory birds). The park's name refers to the immense dunes which look like *lençóis* (bedsheets) strewn across the landscape. Since 1981 this parcel of land has been set aside as a protected ecological zone, staving off the ruinous effects of land speculation.

It's a real expedition to reach the park, but there are plans afoot to allow supervised access for tourists. The park has minimal infrastructure, but it's currently possible to arrange a visit from the town of Barreirinhas, which is two hours by boat from the dunes. The tiny fishing villages of Mandacaru and Ponta da Mangue, around 22 km north-east of Barreirinhas, are very hard to reach and have no tourist facilities (take your own hammock).

Information

For more information, contact Ana Maria (see Places to Stay & Eat in Barreirinhas), the tourist office in São Luís or IBAMA (☎ 222-3006) at Avenida Jaime Tavares 25, also in São Luís.

Place to Stay & Eat

Pousada da Ana Maria (☎ 238-1334 – contact number in São Luís) in Barreirinhas, belongs to – guess who? – Ana Maria. She also runs Cafua Turismo, a tour agency specialising in excursions into the park.

Getting There & Away

Bus There's a daily bus service to Barreirinhas from the rodoviária in São Luís. The bus departs at 7 am and the trip takes about eight hours (US$11). The return service from Barreirinhas departs daily at 7 am. From Barreirinhas, there's a dirt road to Tutóia, but transport is infrequent.

Boat See the section on Parnaíba (in the state of Piauí) for details about day trips by boat between Parnaíba and Tutóia.

Tours Tour guides and travel agencies in São Luís are considering organising trips to the park from São Luís – possibly as a road/sea combination. Check the latest ideas with the companies and individuals listed in the São Luís section under Travel Agencies & Tour Guides and Tours.

THE NORTH COAST

The town of Guimarães, about 420 km by road from São Luís, is a centre for boat-building and fishing. Further north is Cururupu, a small town which is the gateway to the Lençóis de Cururupu – a huge expanse of coastal dunes similar to, but not to be confused with, those in the Parque Nacional dos Lençóis Maran-henses.

About 80 km offshore is Atol de Manoel Luís, a coral reef named after the *Manoel Luís* – the first ship to be lost there! According to experts, this reef, extending over 288 sq km, is the largest in South America and there are plans to turn it into a marine park. There are also plans to exploit it as one of the world's top attractions for divers – especially divers with fat wallets tucked into their wetsuits.

RESERVA BIOLÓGICA DO GURUPI

This biological reserve in the Serra do Tiracambu on the western border of the state is not open to the public. This news does not seem to have reached the sawmill owners, loggers and assorted industrialists clustered on the fringe of the reserve, who are plundering it at top speed.

IMPERATRIZ

Imperatriz, 636 km from São Luís, is a rapidly expanding city on the border with Pará. The expansion is due to the rabid logging and mining of the surrounding region which is turning the forests into ecological nightmares and attracting plenty of low-life characters to make a quick killing. The only possible reason to visit would be to change buses – otherwise just keep going. The airports at Imperatriz and nearby Açailândia are frequently closed for days on end because of the huge clouds of smoke from forest fires.

CAROLINA

The town of Carolina, 242 km south of Imperatriz, lies beside the Rio Tocantins and provides a handy base for visiting nearby natural attractions.

Pedra Caída, 35 km from town on the road

towards Estreito, is a dramatic combination of rock canyons and waterfalls. Other spectacular waterfalls in the region are: Cachoeira do Itapecuruzinho, 27 km from town on the road towards Riachão; Cachoeira de São Simão, at Fazenda São Jorge about 10 km from town; and Cachoeira da Barra da Cabeceira. There are rock paintings and inscriptions at Morro das Figuras, close to Fazenda Recanto; and bat enthusiasts will want to visit the colony of bats in Passagem Funda, a large cave 70 km from Carolina.

Places to Stay

The town has several inexpensive hotels, including *Santa Rita* (☎ 731-1224), *Maia* (☎ 731-1284), *Sansão* (☎ 731-1297) and *Imperial* (☎ 731-1151).

Pousada Rio Lajes (☎ 731-1348), three km outside town on the road towards Riachão, has chalets. *Pousada Pedra Caída*, is a tourist complex with chalets and sports facilities at the Pedra Caída waterfalls.

Getting There & Away

There's a daily bus service from São Luís (12 hours; US$25); and four services daily from Imperatriz (four hours).

Getting Around

A frequent ferry service (15-minute ride) operates across the Rio Tocantins to the town of Filadélfia, which is in the state of Tocantins.

THE NORTH

The North

The North of Brazil is composed of seven states: Pará, Amapá, Tocantins, Amazonas, Roraima, Rondônia, and Acre.

History

In 1541, the Gonzalvo Pizarro expedition ran short of food supplies while searching for El Dorado, the mythical kingdom of gold. Captain Francisco de Orellana, who had joined the expedition earlier, offered to take a small group of soldiers and forage for supplies.

Orellana floated down the Rio Napo all the way to the Amazon, which received its name after the group reported attacks by female warriors, thereby prompting comparisons in the West with the Amazons of Greek myth. Although Orellana had disobeyed orders, his exploits found favour with the Spanish king, who sent him back on a second expedition, during which Orellana died from malaria.

Despite this foray into the region, the Spanish were not interested in claiming the territory which had been assigned to the Portuguese under the terms of the Treaty of Tordesillas signed in 1494.

For later developments in the history of the region, see the sections on Manaus (in the Amazonas & Roraima chapter) and Belém (in the Pará, Amapá & Tocantins chapter).

Geography

The Amazon Basin, six million sq km of river and jungle, is the world's largest in terms of volume and drainage area. Its flow is 12 times that of the Mississippi, with 12 billion litres of fresh water flowing down the river every minute – enough to supply New York City for 60 years! There are 80,000 km of navigable rivers in the Amazon system. Ocean-going vessels can sail deep into South America: from the mouth of the Amazon (300 km east of Belém) to the Solimões and Marañon rivers, and all the way to Iquitos, Peru.

Although the Amazon river dominates the record books, many of its tributaries are also enormous: the Rio Juruá is a 3280-km-long tributary of the Solimões; the Rio Madeira-Mamoré flows for 3240 km; the Rio Purus/Pauini is 3210 km in length (1667 km navigable); and the Rio Tocantins is a respectable 2640 km in length. The Rio Negro runs 1550 km (only the lower half is navigable and fully explored). For the people who live in the Amazon interior, the rivers are their only roads.

Flora & Fauna

For details about Amazon flora and fauna, refer to the Flora & Fauna section of the Facts about the Country chapter.

Ecology & Environment

For discussion of ecological and environmental issues concerning the Amazon, refer to the Ecology & the Environment section of the Facts about the Country chapter.

Things to Bring

Protect yourself from the sun with a baseball cap or visor, sunglasses and sunblock. Things can get very wet, so bring along a hooded poncho or windbreaker to keep your-

Health Care in the Amazon

In the field of health care, there is hope for the poor of the Amazon. Although to most denizens of the Amazon little or no health care is available, the situation is changing thanks to the efforts of Fundação Esperança (Hope Foundation), founded by the late Father Luke Tupper. The primary health care project is so successful that the United Nations is using it as a model for health projects in Africa.

The problems of providing health care in the Amazon are manifold. Homesteaders are scattered far apart on minor tributaries, and other than river travel, there is no transportation network to reach them. The economic resources of these people are scanty.

During its first 10 years, Fundação Esperança's health care programme was centred upon a riverboat fitted with fancy medical equipment and staffed by interns and surgeons. The mobile hospital did not prove very effective. True, 150,000 people were vaccinated, but there was no continuity in health care. After a while the boat would only show up in communities during election years.

In 1978 the World Health Organization defined the task of cost-effective use of medicinal resources emphasising the preventative medicine needs of women and children (formerly overlooked), stressing community participation and education. In the following year the Fundação Esperança began to mobilise rural communities in three areas – improving diet, sanitary practices and medical care. Physicians and nurses sent into the rural villages would not stay very long, despite the best intentions, as they were overqualified for the task and nearly universally preferred to live in bigger cities.

The third and current approach to health care involves the transfer of information, control and prestige from health care professionals to chosen villagers. These villagers are briefly trained as paramedics in Santarém. They lead their communities in digging wells and developing sanitation, teach fellow villagers a little hygiene and preventative medicine, treat some ailments and refer what they can't handle to urban medical centres.

Financial support for Fundação Esperança health projects comes from the Interamerican Bank of Development, the Companhia do Vale Doce hydroelectric plant and the Lion's Club. You can also help. If you wish to contact the organisation, the address is Fundação Esperança, Caixa Postal 222, CEP 68100 Santarém, Pará, Brazil. ∎

---

self dry. Use Ziplock plastic storage bags to compartmentalise tickets, travellers' cheques and other valuables (unless you prefer to entrust them to a hotel safe). You'll also need a hammock (fabric is preferable to net), sheet, blanket and some rope. To keep your possessions dry, the backpack should be waterproofed, wrapped in a groundcloth or a large plastic bag and suspended above the floor of the boat.

Long-sleeved cotton shirts and light cotton trousers with elastic drawstrings at the ankles keep some of the bugs from nipping. Cloth or rubber thongs and sneakers are also comfortable boat/jungle gear. Bring a day pack stashed with toilet paper/tissues, toiletries, focusing backpacker's torch, pocket knife, water bottle, a thick novel and plenty of insect repellent. Don't forget a camera, binoculars and a good birding guide. For suggested reading and reference material, see the Books & Maps section in the Facts for the Visitor chapter. Finally, antimalarials

and pure drinking water should take care of most medical problems.

Organised River Trips

To see the wildlife of the Amazon – jacarés, monkeys, hawks, anacondas, toucans and botos (freshwater dolphins) – you must leave the major rivers and head for the *igarapés*, narrow channels cutting through the jungle where the forest brushes up to your face. If you opt for river travel with an independent operator, part of your agreement should include a canoe tour of the igarapés, since noisy motorboats only scare the wildlife away.

Remind your guide to bring fishing gear, straps and cords (to suspend packs) and of course cachaça, sugar and lemons for caipirinhas at the end of the day. Shop for food with your guide and inflict your tastes on the guide, rather than vice versa. Don't scrimp on water – be conservative and have

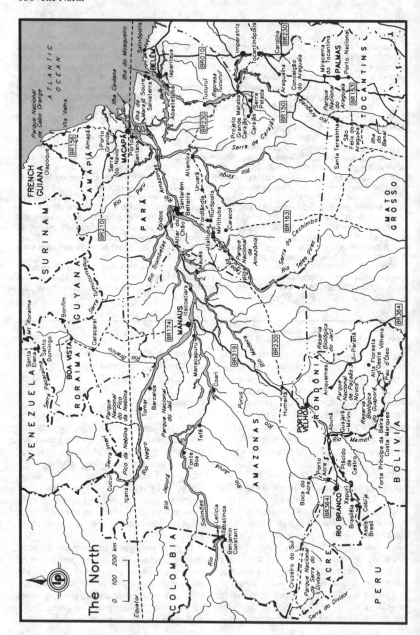

The North

at least two litres of bottled water per person per day. It's nice to have two styrofoam coolers on board, one to keep perishables from spoiling, and the second to keep valuables dry when the weather becomes wet and wild. Last, but definitely not least, insist on life jackets.

For information on long-distance river trips, refer to the discussions under Belém, Manaus, and Tabatinga/Benjamin Constant.

The Amazon by Road

Buses are a good way to cover lots of ground cheaply. Most of the river crossings throughout the back country are simple, motor-driven ferries that take one truck at a time. As it is a slow process, trucks are often lined up, especially at night when the ferry isn't operating. The ferries often break down and may take hours, or in the worst cases days, to repair.

Pará, Amapá & Tocantins

Brazil's territory in eastern Amazonia is composed of the states of Pará, Amapá and Tocantins.

The state of Pará covers over one million sq km and includes a major stretch of the Amazon, and huge tributaries, such as Rio Trombetas, Rio Tapajós and Rio Xingu. The attractions of the state include the cities of Belém and Santarém, and Ilha de Marajó, one of the largest fluvial islands in the world. The state of Amapá straddles the equator in the north-eastern corner of Brazil. Most visitors to the state arrive or leave via the challenging route to or from French Guiana. Tocantins, Brazil's newest state, was carved out of Goiás state in 1989. The main attraction in Tocantins is the Parque Nacional do Araguaia on Ilha do Bananal, the world's largest fluvial island.

Pará

The Tupi tribe who lived beside the Amazon estuary prior to colonisation used the term '*pa'ra*' (vast ocean) to describe its awesome size. In 1500, the Spanish navigator Vicente Yáñez Pinzón sailed past the estuary, noted the huge volume of freshwater issuing into the ocean, and turned back to investigate a short distance up the estuary. He concluded that navigation to the source of such a gigantic 'ocean river' was too risky and headed back to Spain to report his discovery. For more details about the history of Pará state, see the History section for Belém.

The economic development of the state is concentrated on giant mining projects, such as Projeto Grande Carajás, and grandiose hydroelectric schemes, such as the Tucuruí dam. Much of the southern part of the state has been deforested and there are serious ecological problems involved with uncontrolled mining, land disputes, and ranching.

Pará state is divided into two time zones.

The delineation of the time zone seems to depend on local assessment, but as a general rule, the section of the state east of the Rio Xingu is on Brazilian standard time; the section to the west of the river is one hour behind Brazilian standard time.

BELÉM

Belém is the economic centre of the north and the capital of the state of Pará. It's a city with a unique and fascinating culture derived from the peoples and ways of the forest, and animated by the exuberance of the port. Although Belém is clearly in a state of decay, the central area is pleasant, the sites of interest are close by and the people are friendly.

History

The Portuguese, sailing from Maranhão, landed at Belém in 1616 and promptly built the Forte do Castelo at an entrance to the 'Rio Mar' (River Sea) to prevent French, English, Spanish and Dutch boats from sailing up the Amazon and claiming territory. By 1626 the area encompassed by the present-day states of Pará and Maranhão was set up as a separate colony from the rest of Brazil. It had its own governor, who reported directly to the Portuguese king, and its own capital in São Luís do Maranhão. This colony remained officially separate from the rest of Brazil until 1775.

The king's decision to create a separate administration for the territory stretching from Belém to São Luís made sense. Due to prevailing winds and ocean currents along the coast of Brazil, it was extremely difficult for ships to leave Belém and reach Salvador, and the inland route was long and perilous. The trip from Belém to Lisbon lasted only six weeks, whereas the journey to Salvador took considerably longer.

Belém's economy relied on *drogas do sertão* (the spices of the backlands). The White settlers, most of whom were poor farmers who had emigrated from the islands of the Azores off the coast of Portugal, were entirely dependent on the labour of the *filhos do mato* (sons of the forest), native Indians who knew the ways of the Amazon and could find the cacao, vanilla, cassia and cinnamon for export to Europe. Belém became a relatively prosperous settlement due to these riches and the enslavement and destruction of the Indians. For hundreds of years the settlement survived by striking further and further into the Amazon, destroying tribes of Indians in one slaving expedition after another.

As elsewhere in Brazil, the Jesuits came to the Amazon to save the Indians and install them in *aldeias* (mission villages) throughout the region. Terrible epidemics killed many Indians and Catholicism killed their culture. Indians who chose to escape this fate fled further into the Amazon along its smaller tributaries.

By the end of the 18th century, as its Indian labour force became depleted, the economy of Belém began to decline. In the 1820s a split between the White ruling classes led to civil war. It quickly spread to the dominated Indians, mestizos, Blacks and mulattos, and after years of fighting, developed into a popular revolutionary movement that swept through all of Pará like a prairie fire. The Cabanagem rebellion was a guerrilla war of the wretched of the Amazon.

In 1835 the guerrilla fighters marched on Belém and after nine days of bloody fighting took the city. They installed a popular government which expropriated the wealth of the merchants, distributed food to all the people and declared its independence. But the revolutionary experiment was immediately strangled by a British naval blockade, Britain being the principal beneficiary of the Brazil trade in the 1800s.

A year later, a large Brazilian force took back Belém. The vast majority of the city's population fled to the interior to resist again. Over the next four years the military hunted down, fought and slaughtered two-thirds of the men in the state of Pará – they killed anyone they found who was black or brown – 40,000 out of a total population of some 100,000. The Cabanagem was one of the bloodiest and most savage of many Brazilian military campaigns against its own people.

Decades later the regional economy was revitalised by the rubber boom. A vast number of poor peasants fled the drought-plagued Northeast, particularly Ceará, to tap the Amazon's rubber trees. Most of the *seringuieros* (rubber gatherers) arrived and then died in debt.

By 1910 rubber exports constituted 39% of the nation's total exports. Belém grew from a city of 40,000 in 1875 to over 100,000 people in 1900. It had electricity, telephones, streetcars and a distinctly European feel, in the middle of the tropical heat. The rubber boom provided the money for the city to erect a few beautiful monuments, like the Teatro da Paz.

Climate

Belém is one of the rainiest cities in the world. There is no dry season – October has the least rain – but it rains more often and with greater abundance from December to June. This is not as bad as it sounds: the rain is often a brief welcome relief from the heat.

Orientation

As it approaches the Atlantic, the Amazon splinters into many branches and forms countless channels, fluvial islands, and, finally, two great estuaries. These estuaries separate the Ilha de Marajó, the 'island-continent', from the mainland. The southern estuary is joined by the mighty Rio Tocantins and is known as the Baía de Marajó before it enters the Atlantic.

Belém is 120 km from the Atlantic at the point where the Rio Guamá turns north and becomes the Baía do Guajará, which soon feeds into the massive Baía de Marajó. It's the biggest port on thé Amazon. From Belém you can set sail for any navigable port of the Amazon and its tributaries. Distances are great, river travel is slow and often dull, and you may have to change ships along the way, but it is possible and very cheap.

The heart of town is along Avenida Presidente Vargas from the bay to the Teatro da

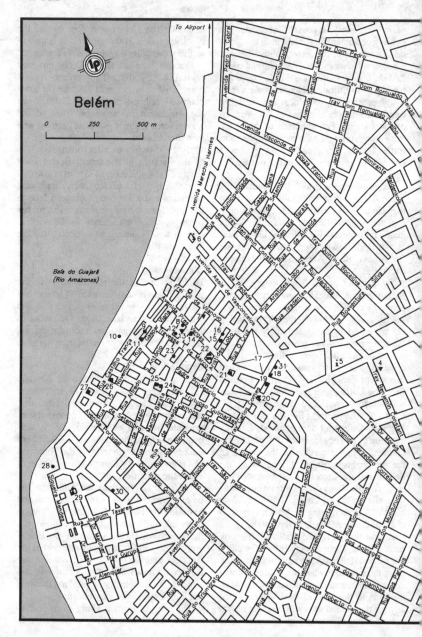

Belém

Baía do Guajará
(Rio Amazonas)

To Airport

■ PLACES TO STAY

9 Hotel Canto do Rio
11 Hotel Transamazônica
14 Hotel Central
15 Vidonho's Hotel
19 Hilton Hotel
21 Excelsior Grão Pará & Hotel Milano
24 Hotel Fortaleza
25 Hotel Vitória Regia
26 Hotel Ver-o-Peso

▼ PLACES TO EAT

4 Cantina Italiana
7 Restaurant Inter
13 Hakata Restaurant
18 Bar do Parque
20 Miako

OTHER

1 Rodoviária
2 Museu Emílio Goeldi
3 Basílica de NS de Nazaré
5 Municipal Tourist Office
6 Paratur Park and Tourist Office
8 Banco do Brasil
10 ENASA Ferry Landing (Boats to Soure)
12 Mercado do Natural (Natural Foods Store)
16 TABA Office
17 Praça da República
22 Post Office
23 Casa do Cruzeiro Câmbio
27 Mercado Ver-o-Peso
28 Forte do Castelo
29 Cathedral
30 Palácio Lauro Sodré
31 Teatro da Paz

Paz in the Praça da República. Here, you'll find most of the best hotels and restaurants. Praça da República is a large central park and a good place to relax and socialise in the early evening.

Just west of Avenida Presidente Vargas are several narrow shopping streets. Rua João Alfredo is good for cheap clothes and hammocks. Continue a few blocks and you reach the Cidade Velho (Old Town), with its colonial architecture, or turn right to see the Mercado Ver-o-Peso and waterfront.

Information

Tourist Offices Paratur (☎ 224-9633), the state tourism agency, has its main office at the Feira de Artesanato do Estado, Praça Kennedy. The staff are helpful and provide free maps. It's open from 9 am to 5 pm, Monday to Friday. Outside the office is a small garden with caged animals and birds. Watch out for the monkeys, who have honed to perfection their capacity to perform their natural duties through the bars with random timing and accurate aim. Revenge is sweet! There are other information offices at the airport and rodoviária (irregular hours).

There is also a good municipal tourism office (☎ 223-5802) which has maps and a small library of good regional literature that's worth a look if you read Portuguese. It's at Avenida Nazaré 231, about a 10-minute walk from Praça da República.

Money The main branch of Banco do Brasil is at Avenida Presidente Vargas, 248; and there's another branch at the airport. Another good place for currency and travellers' cheque exchange is Casa do Cruzeiro Câmbio (☎ 241-5558) at Rua 28 de Setembro, 62.

Post & Telecommunications The central post office is at Avenida Presidente Vargas, 498. The central office of Telepará, the state phone company, is nearby at Avenida Presidente Vargas, 620.

Foreign Consulates If you're travelling to other countries in South America, for example via the Amazon, Belém is one of the best cities in the region to stock up on visas. The following countries are represented in Belém:

Bolivia
    Avenida Governador Magalhães Barata, 661 (☎ 229-6829)
Colombia
    Avenida Governador José Malcher, 1332 (☎ 241-0311)
France
    Avenida Presidente Pernambuco, 269 (☎ 224-6818)
Germany
    Travessa Campos Sales, 63, 4 Andar (☎ 222-5634)
Peru
    Avenida Conselheiro Furtado, 767 (☎ 241-4108)
UK
    Rua Gaspar Viana 490 (☎ 224-4822)
USA
    Avenida Oswaldo Cruz 165 (☎ 223-0800)
Venezuela
    Avenida Governador José Malcher, 187 (☎ 222-6396)

Travel Agencies City tours, river tours, and excursions to Ilha de Marajó are offered by agencies such as: Vianney Turismo (☎ 241-5638) at Travessa Padre Eutíquio, 2296; Mendestur (☎ 235-0841) on Praça Kennedy; and Mundial Turismo (☎ 223-1981) at Avenida Presidente Vargas, 780.

Bookshop For a reasonable selection of English books go to Ponto e Virgula, at Avenida Conselheiro Furtado, 1142.

Emergency The local police force has set up POLITUR, a special division which is responsible for the security of tourists. The number to call is 224-9460.

Dangers & Annoyances Many readers have written to warn about the pickpockets operating in gangs or singly at Mercado Ver-O-Peso – don't take anything of value to this market. If you intend to travel by boat from Belém, watch your gear carefully – theft is becoming increasingly common. Theft at the rock-bottom hotels is also commonplace – see comments under Places to Stay.

For more advice, see the security section

under Dangers & Annoyances in the Facts for the Visitor chapter. The same section contains a salutary tale about a bogus official at the boat dock in Belém.

Mercado Ver-o-Peso

Spanning several blocks along the waterfront, this is one big market that goes all day, every day. The name of this market originated from the fact that it was established as a checkpoint where the Portuguese would '*ver o peso*' (watch the weight) in order to impose taxes.

Peixe-boi (manatee)

Many readers have commented unfavourably on the smell of putrefaction and the rampant crime in the market. There's not much for tourists to buy, but the display of fruits, vegetables, plants, animals and fish, not to mention the people, is fascinating. It's best to get there early when the boats are unloading their catches at the far end of the market. Watch for the *mura*, a human-size fish.

The most intriguing section is filled with medicinal herbs and roots, dead snakes, jacaré teeth, amulets with mysterious powers, and potions for every possible occasion. There are many restaurants for good, cheap meals.

Teatro da Paz

Constructed in neo-classical style in 1874, this theatre has hosted performances by numerous Brazilian stars and various international favourites, such as Anna Pavlova, the Vienna Boys Choir, and the Cossacks. The architecture has all the sumptuous trappings of the era: columns, busts, crystal mirrors, and an interior decorated according to Italian theatrical tastes. Opening hours are from 8 am to noon and from 2 to 6 pm, Monday to Friday. The theatre is in the centre on Praça da República.

Museu Emílio Goeldi

Recent renovation has greatly improved this museum, which we'd rate as the top attraction in Belém – the zoo is one of the best we've seen in South America – recommended for kids.

The museum consists of three parts: a park and zoo; an aquarium; and an ethnology museum. The zoo has *peixe-boi* (manatees) browsing on underwater foliage; huge and beautiful *pirarucu* fish (some specimens here weigh at least 100 kg!); jungle cats; *ariranha* (giant river otters); and many strange Amazonian birds. There's even a roving band of *pacas* (agoutis) scurrying free through the park.

The aquarium displays an extraordinary sample of the 1500 fish species identified in local waters (there are dozens of fish species still to be identified in the Amazon region), including hoover fish, window cleaner fish, butterfly fish, and leaf fish – the names are self-explanatory.

The museum, founded in 1866, has good displays of Marajó Indian ceramics, many stuffed birds and old photos. There's an exhibit of a modern Brazilian kitchen filled with indigenous Amazonian devices that have made their way into our modern lifestyle; and various bugs and spiders to give you happy nightmares – arachnaphobes will shiver at a spider the size of a human hand! This is also a research facility with a library that's worth exploring if you have a particular interest in the region.

The Museu Emílio Goeldi is open from 9 am to noon and from 2 to 5 pm, Tuesday to Thursday; from 9 am to noon on Friday; and from 9 am to 5 pm, on Saturday and Sunday. Admission to all three sections costs US$2, except on Wednesday from 9 am to noon, when it's free. Guided tours are given at 9.30 and 10.30 am, and 2.30 and 5.30 pm, from Tuesday to Thursday; at 9.30 am on Friday;

Our Lady of Nazaré

The origins of the image of Our Lady of Nazaré, the devotion to the Virgin and the story of how she came to Belém are shrouded in myth and misunderstanding, but many people accept the following account of the events as the true version.

According to the Portuguese, the holy image was sculpted in Nazareth in Galilee. The image of the Virgin made its way through many European monasteries before arriving at the monastery of Gauliana in Spain. In 714, the forces of King Roderick, the last Visigoth king, were routed by the Moors at the battle of Gaudelette. Retreating to the only remaining patch of Christian soil in Iberia at Asturias, the king took refuge at the monastery of Gauliana. Still pursued by the Moors, Roderick fled to Portugal with Abbot Romano, who had the presence of mind to bring the Virgin with him. Before his capture and slaughter, the abbot hid the Virgin from the iconoclastic Muslims while King Roderick escaped unharmed (no miracle, he wasn't lugging a statue around).

Four hundred years later, shepherds in the mountains of Siano (now São Bartolomeu) found the Virgin of Nazaré, and the statue became known as a source of protection. The first miracle occurred on 9 October 1182. Dom Fuas Roupinho was riding in pursuit of a stag when he was miraculously saved from falling off a cliff. According to local belief, his horse stopped so suddenly that bits of iron from the horseshoes were embedded into the stones underfoot. The miracle was attributed to the Virgin of Nazaré, upon whose help he had called in his moment of danger.

In the 17th century, Jesuits brought the cult and the image to Northeastern Brazil and somehow the Virgin made her way to Vigia in Pará, where she was worshipped. An attempt was made to bring the Virgin to Belém, but the image was lost in the jungle and forgotten. In October of 1700, Placido José de Souza, a humble rancher, led his cattle to drink from Murucutu Igarapé and rediscovered the Virgin. Placido placed the statue on a rough altar in his hut. News spread and many of the faithful gathered from miles around. Before long, Placido's hut became the sanctuary of NS de Nazaré. In 1721 Bishop Dom Bartolomeu do Pilar confirmed the image as the true Virgin of Nazaré. In 1793 Belém had its first Círio (see the section on Festivals later in this chapter), and the city has staged an annual celebration ever since. ■

and at 10 am and 3 pm on Saturday and Sunday. Inside the grounds, the museum shop sells an excellent selection of posters and publications about the museum; and booklets about Amazon fauna and flora, and Amazon culture. A gift shop sells a variety of T-shirts, minerals, etc.

The museum is at Avenida Governador Magalhães Barata 376. From the centre, take the bus marked 'Aeroclube 20'. If you feel like walking from the centre, it takes about 35 minutes and you can include a couple of sights en route. Starting from the Teatro da Paz, walk down Avenida Nazaré, which merges into Avenida Governador Magalhães Barata, and continue past Basílica de NS de Nazaré (see description in next section), which is close to the museum.

Basílica de NS de Nazaré

The basílica is visited annually by over one million worshippers during the Círio de Nazaré. Built in 1909, the church has a Roman architectural style inspired by the Basilica of St Paul in Rome. Inside there is fine marble and gold, and downstairs is a sacred art museum. The church is on Praça Justo Chermont – a short walk from the Museu Emílio Goeldi – and it's open daily from 6.30 to 11.30 am and from 3 to 9 pm.

Bosque Rodrigues Alves

This park at Avenida Almirante Barroso 1622 covers 16 hectares and contains a lake and a zoo with turtles and jacarés. Apart from the Museu Emílio Goeldi, this is the only large patch of greenery close to the city centre. It's a pleasant place to relax, but avoid it on Sundays when little brats torment the turtles and jacarés by throwing plastic bags filled with water at their heads – one reader felt like feeding the perpetrators to the victims!

Opening hours are from 7 am to noon and from 2 to 5 pm, Tuesday to Sunday. From the centre, take the bus marked 'Aeroclube 20'.

Cidade Velho

The old part of Belém is run-down but authentic. There are many colonial buildings notable for their fine azulejos (blue Portuguese tiles). It's a good area in which to walk, drink and explore. The large Palácio Antônio Lemos and Palácio Lauro Sodré are also in the neighbourhood. The latter now houses the state government. A particularly striking example of the colonial style is Loja Paris N'America on Rua Alfredo Santo Antônio.

River Tours & Beach Excursions

The travel agencies mentioned previously in this chapter under the Information section offer various river tours and excursions to nearby beaches. Prices range from US$22 per person for the standard river tour, to US$31 per person for an excursion to the beach at Ilha do Mosqueiro. For excursions to Ilha de Marajó, see the requisite section later in this chapter.

The 'canned tours' of the Rio Guamá are heavily promoted, but not particularly exciting. In three hours you cruise the river, go down a channel, get out on an island and walk down a path where many have travelled before to see the local flora (rubber, mahogany trees, açaí palms, sumauma, mangoes, and cacao trees) and have the rare opportunity to pass a souvenir stand every 100 metres. This voyage into the known is recommended only if you have no time to really see the jungle and rivers.

Festivals

Every year on the morning of the second Sunday of October the city of Belém explodes with the sound of hymns, bells and fireworks. Started in 1793 as a tribute to the Virgin of Nazaré, the Círio de Nazaré is Brazil's biggest religious festival. People from all over Pará and Brazil flock to Belém, and even camp in the streets to participate in the grand event. In 1985 over 700,000 people filled the streets to march from the Catedral Metropolitana (also known as the Igreja da Sé) to the Basílica de NS de Nazaré. The 1993 Círio is expected to attract even larger crowds to celebrate the 200th anniversary of the festival.

The image of the Virgin, centrepiece of the procession, is placed on a flower-bedecked carriage. While the faithful pray, sing hymns, give thanks or ask favours of the Virgin, the pious (often barefoot) bear heavy crosses and miniature wax houses, and thousands squirm and grope in their emotional frenzy to get hold of the 300-metre cord for an opportunity to pull the carriage of the Virgin. Five hours and only 2½ km later the Virgin reaches the basílica, where she remains for the duration of the festivities.

After the parade, there is the traditional feast of *pato no tucupi* (duck cooked in manioc juice): Círio de Nazaré without this dish is akin to Thanksgiving in the USA without turkey. From the basílica, the multitudes head to the fairgrounds for mayhem of the more secular kind: food, drink, music and dancing. The party continues unabated for a fortnight. On Monday, 15 days after the first procession, the crowd reassembles for the Recírio parade in which the Virgin is returned to her proper niche and the festivities are concluded.

Places to Stay

With an abundance of two-star hotels at one-star prices, Belém has some of the best hotel deals in Brazil. Several of the hotels with middle-range facilities charge very reasonable rates. Consequently, even travellers on a low budget may want to consider a minor splurge on the hotels described in the middle range. Most of these hotels are central – along or close to Avenida Presidente Vargas (an ideal location). There are also cheap dives and opulent, old hotels. If you're just passing through there are hotels in front of the rodoviária.

Places to Stay – bottom end

Hotels There are very cheap places scattered along the waterfront on Rua Castilho França. The prices are definitely rock bottom, but you may have to compromise on security and cleanliness. The *Hotel Canto do Rio* appears to be caving in and is not recommended.

There have been consistent reports from several readers that the *Palácio das Musas* is prone to robberies by someone using double keys – avoid it. Try hotels such as *Transamazônica, Grajaú, São Jorge* and *Miranda Nova*. Prices average US$5/6.50 for a single/double quarto.

However, for the same prices or just a little more, there are much better options with cleaner, safer and more comfortable rooms. *Hotel Fortaleza* (☎ 222-2984) at Travessa Frutuoso Guimarães, 276 provides good value quartos at US$5/6.50 for single/doubles.

The *Vitória Régia* (☎ 241-3475) at Travessa Frutuoso Guimarães 260 offers good deals, with standard apartamentos at US$10/12 for singles/doubles, and special apartamentos (with air-con) at US$14/16 for singles/doubles. *Hotel Central* (☎ 222-3011) at Avenida Presidente Vargas 290 is a large hotel, popular with foreign travellers. It charges US$9/12 for single/double apartamentos (with fan); single/double apartamentos (with air-con) cost US$13/17. Watch your valuables carefully – several travellers have reported robberies in this hotel.

Youth Hostel *Albergue de Juventude Ver-O-Verde* (☎ 229-2006) is at Travessa Francisco Caldera Castelo Branco 1128 (São Brás district) – in the vicinity of the rodoviária.

Places to Stay – middle
Vidonho's Hotel (☎ 225-1444), at Rua Ó de Almeida 476, is a modern, spic-and-span place with all the amenities of an expensive hotel (colour TV, refrigerator-bar). Apartamentos cost US$18/24 for singles/doubles.

The *Hotel Milano* (☎ 224-7045) faces the Praça da República at Avenida Presidente Vargas, 640. The staff are very friendly and the hotel provides a reliable safe deposit. Standard apartamentos (with fan) cost US$18/24. Apartamentos with air-con cost US$3 more; and luxury versions with a view cost US$27/30 for singles/doubles.

If you like the waterfront, the *Ver-o-Peso* (☎ 224-2267) – across from the market at

Rua Castilho França 208 – offers standard apartamentos at US$16/18 for singles/doubles, and plusher versions for US$28/30. All rooms have air-con. The rooftop restaurant is closed. One reader wrote that his sleep was constantly interrupted by prostitutes knocking at the door.

The *Cambará Hotel* (☎ 224-2422), in the Cidade Velho at Avenida 16 de Novembro 300, is in the same league as Vidonho's and charges slightly more for its apartamentos. Also in the Cidade Velho, the *Plaza* (☎ 224-2800) at Praça da Bandeira 130 is recommended.

The *Excelsior Grão Pará* (☎ 222-3255) at Avenida Presidente Vargas 718 is more upmarket, with apartamentos priced at US$36/40 – the rooms facing the square are the best. The *Regente* (☎ 224-0755) at Avenida Governador José Malcher 485 is also a good deal, with apartamentos at US$26/30 for singles/doubles.

Places to Stay – top end
The *Hilton Hotel* (☎ 223-6500), at Avenida Presidente Vargas 882, reminded us of the fancy, sterile hotels where the CIA always stays in movies about the Third World. Singles/doubles cost US$130/150.

The *Equatorial Palace* (☎ 241-2000), at Avenida Braz de Aguiar 612, has lost its intimate atmosphere and become a bit dismal. Rooms here cost US$75/80 for singles/doubles. The *Novotel* (☎ 229-8011) at Avenida Bernardo Sayão 4804 is about five km from the centre – an inconvenient location. Rooms cost US$50/56 for singles/doubles. Close to the airport is *Hotel Vila Rica* (☎ 233-4222) at Avenida Júlio César 1777. Rooms cost US$80/90 for singles/doubles.

Places to Eat
The food in Belém is tasty and varied, with a bewildering variety of fish and fruit and, unlike much of Brazil, a distinct regional cuisine that features several delicious dishes. *Pato no tucupi* is a lean duck cooked in fermented manioc extract; *unhas de caranguejo* and *casquinho de caranguejo* are

crab claws and stuffed crab, and *maniçoba* is a stew with dried meat.

Endangered species which are regularly served in restaurants in Belém include tartaruga (turtle) and peixe-boi (manatee). Since so many other dishes are available, we see no reason to contribute to the extinction of endangered species – choose something else.

Three of the best local fish are filhota, pescada amarela and dourada – great fish. And you are no doubt familiar with açai, uxi, murici, bacuri and sapoti, just a few of the luscious Amazonian fruits available.

For cheap victuals, there are loads of snack bars throughout the city offering sandwiches and regional juices. Mercado Ver-o-Peso has a thousand and one food stands serving big lunches for small prices. It's also a good place to try the local fish.

Vegetarians can try the *Restaurante Vegetariano Mercado do Natural* at Rua Alfredo Santo Antônio. For heavenly sucos made from one or more of the many Amazon fruits available in Pará, you should go to *Casa do Suco* at Avenida Presidente Vargas 794 (close to the Hilton Hotel). Close by is the *Bar do Parque*, an outside bar and popular meeting place where you can order a snack and a drink.

There is decent, cheap pasta at *Cantina Italiana*, Travessa Benjamin Constant 1401. It's closed on Mondays. For typical Brazilian fare try the *Inter Restaurant* at Rua 28 de Setembro 304, which has meat, fish, rice, etc for about US$3.

Belém has several excellent restaurants where you can do some fine dining for US$4 to US$7. *Lá Em Casa* and *O Outro* (☎ 225-0320) are two restaurants on the same site, at Avenida Governador José Malcher 237, which have all the best regional dishes. The *O Círculo Militar*, at the old Forte do Castelo on Praça Caetano Brandão, has a great bay view and good regional cooking.

The *Hakata* has decent Japanese food, but the *Miako*, behind the Hilton Hotel, is one of Brazil's best Japanese restaurants north of São Paulo. And if you don't like Japanese food, typical Brazilian dishes are also available. The Miako is closed on the second and last Sundays of each month.

Casa Portuguesa, at Rua Senador Manoel Barata 897, and *Avenida*, at Avenida Nazaré 1086, are also recommended.

Entertainment

There's lots of music in town. The best samba clubs at which to shake, rattle and roll on weekends are Rancho Não Posso me Amofiná (☎ 225-0918) at Travessa Honório José dos Santos 764, in the Jurunas district; and Arco-Íris (☎ 226-1926) on the corner of Travessa Castelo Branco and Silva Castro, in the Guamá district. The new kid on the block is Imperio de Samba 'Quem São Eles' (which translates as 'Who Are They') (☎ 225-1133) at Avenida Almirante Wandenkolk 680, in the Umarizal district. This is the closest samba club to the city centre. The clubs operate all year and admission usually costs US$1.

Belém has many night clubs, known in Brazilian as 'boites' or 'boates', which are popular night spots with music, shows and dance. Mistura Fina at Rod Augusto Montenegro 39, Km 3, is a teenybopper hangout; and Lapinha (☎ 229-3290) at Travessa Padre Eutíquio 3901 presents good shows. The Safari Bar (☎ 223-7553) at Avenida 16 de Novembro 528 has a good reputation. Sabor da Terra (☎ 223-6820), at Avenida Visconde de Souza Franco 685, is a combined restaurant and club which presents folkloric shows from Monday to Saturday at 9.30 pm.

The region has some great traditional music and dance which unfortunately is hard to find in Belém. One place to try is Samumbia. There are also performances occasionally arranged for tour groups, which may not be your cup of tea but it's worth doing anything to see and hear the old music and dance. Call the tourism office and tell them you want to see *carimbó* (the origin of which goes back to the Bantu slaves from northern Africa), *lundú* or *siriá*. If you have a cassette player, pick up a tape by the great local musician Pinduca, who is a carimbó maestro. Other popular local musicians and groups to look out for are Nelson Chaves, Marcos Monteiro, Grupo Oficina, and Vital Nima.

If you want to escape the Amazon for a couple of hours, the Cultural Center Tancredo Neves at Avenida Gentil Bittencourt 650, often shows English-language films.

Getting There & Away

Air Air services connect Belém with the major Brazilian cities. There are daily flights to Macapá (Amapá state), Santarém and Manaus. International destinations available from Belém include Cayenne, (French Guiana), Paramaribo (Surinam), and Miami. Frantur (☎ 241-1540) sometimes sells tickets for one-way or return flights to Cayenne. The price for a one-way/return ticket is about FFr 900/1400.

The following national and international airlines have offices in Belém:

Air France
    Rua Boaventura da Silva, 1457 (☎ 223-7547)
British Airways
    Avenida Presidente Vargas, 620, Sala 204, (☎ 241-2805)
Surinam Airways
    Rua Alfredo Santo Antônio, 432, Salas 1204/1206 (☎ 224-7144)
TABA
    Rua Ó de Almeida, 408 (☎ 223-6300)
TAP (Air Portugal)
    Rua Senador Manoel Barata, 704, Sala 1401 (☎ 223-4385)
Transbrasil
    Avenida Presidente Vargas, 580 (☎ 224-6977)
Varig/Cruzeiro
    Avenida Presidente Vargas, 768/363 (☎ 225-4222)
VASP
    Avenida Presidente Vargas, 620, Loja B (☎ 224-5588)

Air Taxi In Belém, air taxis fly from the separate Aeroporto Júlio César (☎ 233-3868) at Avenida Senador Lemos 4700. There are several carriers, such as Kovacs (☎ 233-1600), Bandeirantes (☎ 233-2868) and Dourado (☎ 226-2351).

Bus There are regular bus services to: São Luís (12 hours; US$21); Fortaleza (25 hours; US$40); Recife (34 hours; US$50); and Rio

(56 to 60 hours; US$85). There also direct buses from Belo Horizonte, São Paulo and Brasília.

There is one direct bus a week running from Belém to Santarém. The trip costs US$35 and frequent delays can turn it into a gruelling two-day marathon – only recommended if you are deathly afraid of boats.

Boat There are two ways to travel by boat on the Amazon: with the government-operated Empresa de Navegação da Amazônia (ENASA) which operates large, regularly scheduled passenger boats along several river routes; or with various and sundry small cargo boats that also have cabins and hammock space on deck for a couple of dozen passengers.

The cargo boats usually have a few very cramped cabins with four, six or eight bunk beds. The best option is to hang a hammock on deck where you can at least catch the occasional cooling breeze. These boats stay closer to shore so there's more to see. Food is usually included, and includes lots of rice, beans and some meat. Prices are standard and don't vary too much between boats. Downriver travel is considerably faster than up, but upriver traffic goes closer to the shore and the trip is consequently more scenic.

To find a boat go to the docks and climb aboard for information. Most boats take a day or two to load up before they depart. The best places to look are Porto 9 and 10 CDP which always seem to have a couple of boats preparing to leave. The entrance is at the guard station where Travessa Quintino Bocaiúva meets Avenida Marechal Hermes. Boats also depart from the Porto do Sal in Cidade Velho and at the Porto das Lanchas, Rua Castilho França, between Ver-o-Peso Market and the Forte do Castelo.

Beware of theft on boats – a very common complaint. Also, do not entrust baggage into the care of a boat official or allow it to be stored in a locker unless you are quite certain about the identity of the official. Bogus officials and related locker thefts have been reported by readers. For more advice, see the security section under Dangers & Annoyances in the Facts for the Visitor chapter.

To/From Santarém & Manaus ENASA has reduced the frequency of its Cruzeiro Pelo Rio Amazonas (Amazon Cruise) tourist service to Manaus and back. This service, currently operating only once a month, seems to be embroiled in controversy – it's not making money, and could be eliminated. It's also expensive and you pay for 'love boat' distractions such as a swimming pool. This is not a good way to see the Amazon because the boat usually stays too far out in the middle of the wide river for passengers to see the forested riverbanks. The cruise from Belém to Manaus takes five days and prices start at US$250 per person for cabin accommodation.

The ENASA office (☎ 223-3011) is at Avenida Presidente Vargas 41. For tickets go to the dock where the boats (new catamarans) depart – on Rua Castilho França, near Mercado Ver-o-Peso. Both places have the most up-to-date schedule; if you're having any difficulties there are English speakers at the ENASA office who are quite friendly. For more information on the ENASA services between Manaus and Belém, see the Getting There & Away section for Manaus.

Boats on the regular ENASA service leave Belém every Wednesday at 9 pm, and arrive at Santarém on Saturday and Manaus on Tuesday morning. The fare to Santarém/Manaus is US$36/73 *classe regional* with food included; it's best to sleep in hammocks. The boat holds 600 passengers and is usually crowded – arrive early on the day of departure. Several readers have written to say that these regular ENASA services are very crowded, serve poor food, and are prone to theft. Although the smaller operators may be slightly more expensive, the quality of their service is generally much better. The boat stops at several towns along the way. The return service departs Manaus on Thursday night at 8 pm, reaches Santarém on Saturday and Belém a couple of days later.

VINAVE (☎ 224-2339, 224-7656 for passenger reservations) at Avenida Bernardo Sayão 1242 operates a weekly service to Santarém, departing Belém at 6 pm on Fridays and returning on Tuesdays at 6 pm. The trip takes 48 hours and costs US$31/42 for hammock space/cabin accommodation.

The Porto Fé Em Deus company (☎ 229-4022) at Avenida Bernardo Sayão 3590 operates a weekly service to Santarém, departing at 6 pm on Fridays and returning on Fridays at noon. The trip takes 72 hours and costs US$39 for hammock space.

The Cidade de Terezina IV company (☎ 522-2371) at Armazem 15, Docas do Pará, operates services to Santarém and Manaus, departing on Tuesday, Wednesday, and Friday, and returning on Saturdays at 6 pm. The fare to Santarém is US$39/53 for hammock space/cabin accommodation, and to Manaus it's US$66/93 for hammock space/cabin accommodation.

To/From Soure (Ilha de Marajó) A regular ENASA ferry to Soure on Ilha de Marajó departs on Wednesday at 8 pm, Friday at 8 pm and Saturday at 2 pm. The return services leave from Soure on Thursday at 2 am and on Sunday at 3 pm. It's a five-hour trip for US$14/26 economy/1st class (the only difference is a separate cabin with more comfortable chairs).

To/From Macapá The Superintendência de Navegação do Amapá (SENAVA) service departs for Macapá (Amapá state) from Belém on Tuesdays at 10 am, and returns from Macapá on Fridays at 10 am. The journey takes 24 hours and costs US$13/53 for hammock space/cabin accommodation. One boat is currently being renovated so the usual schedule has been temporarily reduced. Check the current schedule with the SENAVA office (☎ 222-8710) in Belém at Rua Castilho França, 234.

ENAL (☎ 224-5210), at Avenida Bernardo Sayão 1740, operates services to Macapá via Breves, Curralinho, Santana, Jari, and Monte Dourado. The trip takes 28 hours and costs US$18. Boats depart Belém at 6 pm on Tuesday and Saturday, and return from Macapá at 6 pm on Tuesday and at 11 am on Sunday.

VINAVE (☎ 222-2339) at Avenida Bernardo Sayão 1242 provides a weekly service via Breves to Macapá, departing Tuesdays at 6 pm and returning on Sundays at 6 pm. The trip costs US$26 for hammock space. ENASA has stopped services to Macapá.

Getting Around

To/From the Airports Belém's main airport, Aeroporto Internacional Val de Cans (☎ 233-4122), is on Avenida Júlio César. Airport facilities include a Paratur tourist information office, a branch of Banco do Brasil, a newsagent, post office and restaurant.

Take the bus marked 'Perpétuo Socorro' from the centre – it's quick (30 minutes) and, of course, cheap. There's a bilheteria system for taxis – from the airport to the centre costs about US$10.

Remember, air taxis leave from a different airport, Aeroporto Júlio César (☎ 233-3868), which is at Avenida Senador Lemos 4700.

To/From the Rodoviária The rodoviária (☎ 228-0500) is at the corner of Avenida Almirante Barroso and Avenida Ceará – about a 15-minute bus ride from the city. To reach the city centre from the rodoviária, take any bus marked 'Aeroclube 20', 'Cidade Nova 6', or 'Universidade (Presidente Vargas)'. Buses marked 'Cidade Nova 5' or 'Souza' run via Mercado Ver-o-Peso.

Bus The bus marked 'Aeroclube 20' is especially convenient because it runs from the city centre via the main city attractions of Basílica de NS de Nazaré, Museu Emílio Goeldi, and Bosque Rodrigues Alves to the rodoviária.

Frequent buses run to the beaches at Ilha do Mosqueiro. For details, see the Getting There & Away section for Ilha do Mosqueiro.

ILHA DO MOSQUEIRO

Mosqueiro is the weekend beach for Belenenses (inhabitants of Belém), who attempt to beat the heat by flocking to the island's 19 freshwater beaches on the east side of the Baía de Marajó. It's close enough for plenty of weekend beach houses, and some well-to-do Belenenses even commute to the city. The island is particularly crowded during the holiday period between July and October. The beaches are not nearly as nice as those on Ilha de Marajó or on the Atlantic coast, but if you want to get out of Belém for just a day they're not bad.

Beaches

The best beaches are Praia do Farol, Praia Chapéu Virado and the more remote Baía do Sol.

Festivals

Mosqueiro has a traditional folklore festival in June with the dance and music of carimbó and *bois-bumbas*. In July, there is the Festival de Verão, when the island shows off some of its art and music. On the second Sunday of December is the Círio de NS do Ó, the principal religious event on the island. Like Belém's Círio, it's a very beautiful and joyous event, and well worth a special trip if you're in Belém at the time.

Places to Stay & Eat

There are campsites on the island and a handful of hotels. The *Ilha Bela* (☎ 771-1448) at Avenida 16 de Novembro 409/463 has air-con apartamentos around US$25/30 for singles/doubles, and a restaurant. *Hotel Farol* (☎ 771-1219) at Praça Princesa Isabel 3295, on Praia do Farol, offers quartos around US$14/17 for singles/doubles, and more expensive apartamentos.

Maresias at Praia Chapéu Virado is a recommended seafood restaurant. On Praia do Murubira, *Hotel Murubira* (☎ 771-1256) has apartamentos at US$32/37 for singles/doubles.

Getting There & Away

Ilha do Mosqueiro is a 90-minute bus ride (84 km) from Belém. The island is linked by good, paved roads and a bridge. Buses leave from the rodoviária in Belém every hour on weekdays and every half-hour on weekends.

PRAIA DO ALGODOAL & MARUDÁ

Algodoal attracts younger Belenenses and a handful of foreign travellers. It's a beautiful spot with dune-swept beaches and at times a turbulent sea. It's very remote, with a small fishing village and a couple of very basic hotels. But all this will change, hopefully not too radically, as it is in the process of being discovered.

Marudá is a poor fishing village with a couple of cheap hotels and a respectable beach, so it's no problem if you're stuck there overnight. Cars cannot make the journey to Algodoal and will have to be left in Marudá.

Places to Stay

Pousada da Aldeia (☎ 224-2096) and *Caldeirão* are both inexpensive places to stay on Praia do Algodoal.

Getting There & Away

Algodoal is north-east of Belém, on the tip of a cape jutting into the Atlantic. Getting there requires a three-hour bus ride from Belém to the town of Marudá, and then a boat across the bay. When you get off the boat you have to negotiate with a taxi driver to take you to the other side of the cape.

The road from Belém is not in good condition and buses can be delayed by bad weather. Buses leave the rodoviária in Belém daily at 7 and 10 am, 1.30, 3.30 and 5.30 pm; and, additionally, at 8 pm on Fridays. The last bus leaves Marudá for Belém at 5 pm. There are sometimes additional buses on weekends – check this by phoning the rodoviária.

SALINÓPOLIS

Salinópolis is Pará's major Atlantic coast resort with good beaches, such as Praia da Atalaia, and some mineral spas. There are plenty of summer homes here and during the July holiday month Salinópolis is very crowded. If you want beautiful, deserted Brazilian beaches, this is not really the best place to go.

Places to Stay

For camping, there's *Amapá Camping* (☎ 823-1422) on Avenida Dr Miguel Sta Brigida. Hotel accommodation is generally expensive in Salinópolis. *Hotel Salinas* (☎ 823-1173) at Passagem Guarani 190 offers apartamentos for around US$30/38 for singles/doubles.

Getting There & Away

There is a regular bus service from Belém (three hours; US$4).

ILHA DE MARAJÓ

Ilha de Marajó, one of the largest fluvial islands in the world, lies at the mouths of the Amazon and Tocantins rivers. The island's 250,000 inhabitants live in 13 municipalities and in the many fazendas spread across the island. Although it's fairly straightforward for independent travellers to visit the island, many travel agencies in Belém offer packaged tours to the main town of Soure and remote fazendas – see the section on Tours under Soure.

History

Researchers have discovered that the island was inhabited between 1000 BC and 1300 AD by successive Indian civilisations. The first of these, known as the Ananatuba civilisation, was followed by those of the Mangueiras, the Formiga Marajoara and, finally, the Aruã. The ceramics produced by these civilisations were ornamented with intricate designs in black, red and white. The best examples of these ceramics are displayed at the Museu Emílio Goeldi (museum) in Belém.

The resemblance of these designs to those found in Andean civilisations prompted the theory amongst some researchers that the inhabitants of Ilha de Marajó had originally floated down the Amazon from the Andes. In 1991, a team of international archaeologists reported the discovery of pottery fragments near Santarém which were estimated to be between 7000 and 8000 years old. As these fragments predate what was previously considered the oldest pottery in the Americas, it

Marajó Buffalo

Legend has it that a French ship was sailing to French Guiana with a load of buffalo picked up in India, but never made it. The boat sank off the shore of Ilha de Marajó and the buffalo swam to shore. The rest is history.

Today, Marajó is the only place in Brazil where the buffalo roam in great numbers, and there are thousands of them. These are not the furry American bison that Buffalo Bill and other rough-riders slaughtered on the American plains, but a tough-skinned hairless buffalo that looks like a macho Indian Brahma bull.

There are four different uses for buffalo on Marajó: meat, dairy products, traction, and breeding. Buffalo are better suited than cattle to Marajó's environment because of three qualities. During the wet season, when much of the land turns into swamps or lagoons, buffalo can walk on the soft ground with their wide hooves and can swim when the water gets deep. Their tough three-layered hide is able to withstand the bites of the island's many snakes and parasites; and they can eat almost anything, even diving underwater to obtain food. ∎

---

now seems quite possible that Amazonia may have been home to pottery-age cultures which were indigenous, and not introduced from other regions.

Geography

Ilha de Marajó, slightly larger in size than Switzerland, has close to 50,000 sq km of land which divides into two geographical regions of almost equal magnitude. The eastern half of the island is called the *região dos campos*, an area characterised by low-lying fields with savannah-type flora, and sectioned by strips of remaining forest. Various palm trees and dense mangrove forests line the coast. The island's western half, the *região da mata*, is primarily forest.

Climate

Marajó has two seasons: the very rainy, from January to June; and the dry (less rainy!), from July to December. During the rainy season much of the island turns into swamp and the região dos campos becomes completely submerged under a metre or more of water. The island's few roads are elevated by three metres, but they are often impassable during the rainy season nonetheless.

Fauna

The herds of buffalo which wander the fields provide Marajó's sustenance. They are well-adapted to the swampy terrain. There are many snakes, most notably large boas. The island is filled with birds, especially during the dry season, including the *guará*, a graceful flamingo with a long, curved beak. The sight of a flock of deep-pink guarás flying against Marajó's green backdrop is truly spectacular.

Soure

Soure (pronounced 'sorry'), the island's principal town, is on the Rio Paracauari, a few km from the Baía de Marajó. The tide along the city's shore oscillates a remarkable three metres. With regular boat services from Belém and easy access to several of the best beaches and fazendas, it's probably the best place to go on the island.

Like all the island's coastal towns, Soure is primarily a fishing village, but it's also the commercial centre for the island's buffalo business and buffaloes rule the place like kings. The townsfolk work around the buffaloes, or sometimes with or on them, but never obstruct their passage: right of way in town belongs indisputably to the buffaloes!

Warning There are bichos de pé (unpleasant bugs that burrow into human feet) in and around the towns, in addition to many other nasty parasites. Keep your head on your shoulders and shoes on your feet.

Beaches The bay beaches near Soure are excellent and look more like ocean beaches. Praia Araruna, the most beautiful beach, is also the closest, just a 10-minute taxi drive from town. Ask the driver to pick you up at a set hour...and pay then. You can also walk the five km to the beach; ask for directions in town. At the end of the road, follow two pedestrian bridges across the lagoons to the beach. The bay here, 30 km from the ocean, has both fresh and salt water: at low tide you can walk about five km in either direction. The beach is deserted during the week and could scarcely be called crowded on weekends. There's often a strong wind: one Belenense I met was planning a two-month windsurfing trip around the island. Another nearby beach is Praia Mata Fome, only two km from town.

Praia do Pesqueiro is 13 km from town (a 25-minute drive). Ask about buses at Pousada Marajoara. There are a couple of barracas with great caranguejo (crab) and casquinha de caranguejo (stuffed crab) but lousy shrimp. When you're facing the sea, the best beach section lies on your right. Do not swim in the shallow lagoon between the barracas and the sea: it harbours prickly plants.

O Curtume As you head upriver, about a 10-minute walk from town, there is an old, simple tannery which sells sandals, belts, etc, made from buffalo and boa. When I visited, the tanning of a jacaré skin was in progress – illegal but quite common. The stuff on sale isn't very good (don't buy products made from endangered species such as jacaré or tartaruga) but it's illuminating to see the way it's made.

Festivals On the second Sunday of November, Soure has its own Círio de Nazaré. There's a beautiful procession and the town bursts with communal spirit. Everyone in the region comes to town, so accommodation can be difficult to find. The festival of São Pedro on 29 June is a very colourful celebration, and includes a maritime procession. If you're into buffalo culture there's an Agro-Pecuária fair during the third week of September.

Places to Stay – Soure Although travel agencies in Belém are keen to promote their package tours to Ilha de Marajó with pre-booked accommodation in Soure, independent travel on the island is really no more difficult than anywhere else in the Amazon region. Providing you have a flexible schedule, it's easy to set out on your own.

Pousada Marajoara (☎ 741-1287 in Soure; 223-2128 for reservations in Belém) does most of its business through package excursions. A one-day trip by plane costs US$75. A three-day trip by boat is US$125/190 for a single/double apartamento – food and lodging included. The pousada buses you around to a fazenda with buffalo and the local beaches. If you're in a hurry or want someone else to take care of everything for you it's a good deal, but otherwise there is no reason to take the packaged option.

The pousada accommodation is fine, if a bit touristy, and it serves the best food in town. The local fish is the best dish but there's also buffalo meat – and for dessert, don't miss the fantastic flan made from buffalo milk. Independent travellers may be able to reserve rooms direct – apartamentos cost around US$35/40 for singles/doubles.

For about the same price on the other side of town is the *Hotel Marajó* (☎ 741-1376 in Soure; 229-6302 for reservations in Belém) which is less crowded on weekends. For cheaper lodging, try the *Soure Hotel* (☎ 741-1202) in the centre of town which has apartamentos at US$14/18 for singles/doubles. It's simple but a bit dowdy.

Places to Stay – remote fazendas The fazendas where the buffalo roam are enormous estates which occupy most of the island's eastern half. They are also beautiful, rustic refuges filled with birds and monkeys. Most of the fazendas have dormitories with an extra bunk or a place to hitch a hammock, but not all welcome outsiders. The fazendas listed here have primitive dorms for tourists and will show you around by jeep or on foot.

Fazenda Bom Jardim (☎ 231-3681 in Soure; 222-1380 for reservations in Belém) is reportedly the most beautiful. It's a three-hour boat ride or a slightly shorter taxi ride from Soure. Air taxis take 30 minutes from Belém. The fazendeiro, Eduardo Ribeira, often comes to Soure, so you can also try to track him down in town if you want to stay at Bom Jardim and maybe organise transport out there with him.

Fazenda Providencia is two hours by boat from Soure. It reportedly has beds available for a couple of guests. Travel agencies in Belém arrange day trips there on weekends and claim the fazenda is loaded with monkeys.

Fazenda Jilva (☎ 225-0432), 40 km from Soure, has accommodation for about 20 people and charges around US$70 per person per day. It's a 45-minute flight from Belém to the fazenda.

For information about other fazendas in Belém, try Paratur or the travel agencies described under Tours in the Getting There & Away section. Another strategy would be to talk to the air-taxi companies at the Aeroclube Júlio César in Belém (☎ 233-3868). Some of the old pilots know the island very well.

Around Ilha de Marajó

It's a short boat trip from Soure across the river to Salvaterra. Shuttle boats go every 15 minutes during the day and cost 20c. Salvaterra has restaurants and an expensive hotel, the *Pousada dos Guarás* (☎ 241-0891 – number for reservations in Belém). A 10-minute walk from town, Praia Grande de Salvaterra is a long, pretty beach on the Baía de Marajó. The beach is popular on weekends when the barracas open, but often windy. It's a good place to see the beautiful fence corrals which dot Marajó's coastline (the best view is from a small plane). The corrals are simple fences with netting that use the falling tide to capture fish.

From Salvaterra there is a dirt road that goes to Câmara (24 km) and then continues to Cachoeira do Arari (51 km), which is a very pretty, rustic town and reportedly has a pousada.

To the north, accessible only by plane, is the town of Santa Cruz do Arari, on the immense Lagoa Arari (lagoon). This town is completely submerged under water during the rainy season, and is famous for its fishing.

The eastern half of the island is less populated and less interesting for travellers. There are boat services to the city of Breves, which has a pousada. Afuá, on the northern shore, is built on water and also has a pousada. Both of these cities are linked to Belém by air taxi.

Ilha Caviana, an island lying off the north coast of Ilha de Marajó, is an excellent base from which to observe the *pororoca* (the thunderous collision between the Atlantic tide and the Amazon). The best time to see this phenomenon is between January and April at either full or new moon. Marcelo Morelio (☎ 241-1317, 225-3366) is a local pilot/guide who shuttles between Belém and Ilha de Marajó. He charges US$200 per person or US$1000 for a group (maximum six people) to fly to Ilha Caviana to see the pororoca.

Getting There & Away

Air Air taxis fly regularly between Belém and Soure, and to other towns on the island. It's a beautiful 25-minute flight over thick forest to Soure. The standard price per passenger is US$50, but it's cheaper if you form a small group. A five-seater from Belém to Soure, for example, costs US$175. Split five ways, that's only US$35 a person. For details about air-taxi companies, see the Getting There & Away section under Belém.

Boat For details about boat services between Belém and Ilha de Marajó, see the Getting There & Away section for Belém.

From Macapá (Amapá state) there are boats to Afuá on Ilha de Marajó. Local fishing boats sail the high seas and it's possible to use them to get all the way around the island and to some of the fazendas.

Tours Excursions to Ilha de Marajó are offered by agencies in Belém, such as: Gran-Pará Turismo (☎ 224-3233) at Avenida

Presidente Vargas 676; Vianney Turismo (☎ 241-5638) at Travessa Padre Eutíquio, 2296; and Mundial Turismo (☎ 223-1981) at Avenida Presidente Vargas, 780. Excursions include transport by either boat or plane and full board at a hotel in Soure or at one of the remote fazendas. As a rough rule of thumb, most of these package deals cost around US$75 per person per day if the trip is done by plane, or US$50 per person per day if the trip is done by boat.

PROJETO GRANDE CARAJÁS

If any project defies superlatives to describe its scale, it is the Projeto Grande Carajás, designed to whittle away Brazil's US$110 billion debt. The multifocal project centres around the world's largest deposit of iron ore, but only US$4.5 billion out of US$60 billion budgeted for the project will be directed towards the extraction of iron ore. The rest of the money will be invested in the extraction of the other metals of the area – manganese, copper, bauxite, nickel and gold, all found near the Serra Pelada – and the development of an industrial zone 400,000 sq km in area, thus rivalling California in size.

In the tradition of previous Amazonian-scaled enterprises, Henry Ford's Fordlândia and Daniel K Ludwig's Jari pulpwood project, the Carajás project began with American support. The venture began as a partnership between US Steel and the Companhía Vale do Rio Doce. Since iron has been depressed on the world market, US Steel bowed out of the collaboration. Some of the projects currently planned by the company include diversification into aluminium products and coffee production. Projects already completed include the 900-km railroad from Carajás to the Atlantic coast at São Luis, Maranhão, where a port for large ships and an ore-loading terminal are now in operation. Eight million kilowatts of power for the project are already being generated by the Tucuruí dam on the Rio Tocantins and seven more dams are planned for the Tocantins and its tributaries. The environmental effects of clearing this much jungle, burning this much wood, and flooding this much land will undoubtedly be stupendous.

SERRA PELADA

The Serra Pelada gold mines near the Carajás project west of Marabá are some of the world's largest mines. The mines are dug by hand and the enterprise rivals the pyramids in scale and epic sweep. Not whips but the promise of gold drives prospectors to work like slaves. The mine area, a huge pit with criss-crossing claims, is a human anthill where 150,000 miners and hangers-on scrape away at the earth. During the '80s, the Companhía Vale do Rio Doce (CVRD), which operates the nearby Projeto Grande Carajás, claimed the mineral rights to the area and attempted to wrest control of the mines from the prospectors. The enraged prospectors protested strongly, staged a march on Brasília, and threatened to raid Projeto Grande Carajás. In 1984, the government compromised by paying US$60 million to CVRD in compensation and then recognising the prospectors' claims.

SANTARÉM

Santarém is a pleasant city with a mild climate (22 to 36°C), Atlantic breezes, calm waters and forests. The region around Santarém was originally inhabited by the Tapuiçu Indians. In 1661, over three decades after Captain Pedro Teixeira's expedition first contacted the Tapuiçu, a Jesuit mission was established at the meeting of the Tapajós and Amazon rivers. In 1758 the village which grew around the mission was named Santarém after the city of the same name in Portugal.

In 1867, a group of 110 Confederates from the breakaway Southern states of the United States emigrated to Santarém, where they attempted to start new lives as farmers or artisans. Only a handful of these settlers managed to prosper; the rest drifted away from Santarém, were killed off by disease, or accepted the offer of a free return passage on an American boat to the USA.

Later developments in Santarém's history

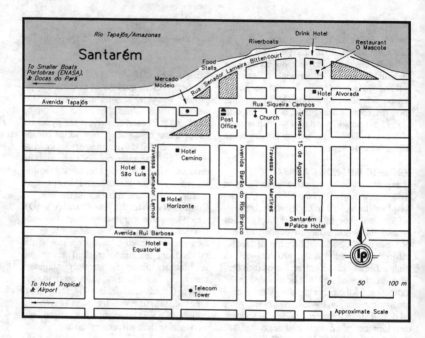

Santarém

included the boom-and-bust cycle of the rubber plantations (for the story of the 'bust', see the section called Henry Wickham – Executioner of Amazonas, in the History section of the Facts about the Country chapter) and a series of gold rushes which started in the 1950s and have continued to this day. The construction of the Trans-amazônica highway in 1970 and the Santarém-Cuiabá highway, completed six years later, has attracted hordes of immigrants from the Northeast, few of whom have been able to establish more than a brief foothold before abandoning the region for the favelas of Manaus or Belém.

The economy is based on rubber, hard woods, brazil nuts, black pepper, mangoes and fish. More recently, soybeans and jute have been added to the list and in the past 10 years there has been rapid development with the discovery of gold and bauxite and the construction of the Curuá-Una hydroelectric dam.

Orientation

Santarém lies 2½° south of the equator at the junction of the Tapajós and Amazon rivers, about halfway between Manaus and Belém (and only 30 metres above sea level). Although it's the third largest city on the Amazon, it's merely a sleepy backwater in comparison to Manaus and Belém.

The city layout is simple: the Cuiabá-Santarém highway runs directly to the Docas do Pará, dividing the city into old (eastern) and new (western) halves. East from the Docas do Pará, where the large boats dock, is Avenida Tapajós, which runs along the waterfront and leads to the market place and commercial district.

Information

Tourist Office There is no tourist office, but you may be able to get tourist information by phoning the municipal department of tourism on 522-1185. Two additional sources of information in Santarém are Bill

Legends of Santarém
Beware of walking the streets after the bells of Catedral NS da Conceicáo ring, for you may encounter a fire-breathing pig. Even if you avoid the pig, legend has it that at midnight a woman in white kneels at the crossroads to pray; if you set eyes on her you will die! ■

Dieter, an American bush pilot, who flies gold prospectors in and out of the Amazon; and Mr Alexander, an expatriate American English teacher who is the author of *Alexander's Guide to Santarém*. The guide is available from Amazon Tours (address given under Tour Agencies) and Mister: English Communications (☎ 522-2620) at Travessa Turano Meira 1084.

Money Banco do Brasil is at Avenida Rui Barbosa 794.

Tour Agency Amazon Tours (☎ 522-2620), at Travessa Turiano Meira 1084, organises jungle tours. Gil Serique (☎ 522-5174) at the Quick & Easy English School, Rua 24 de Outubro 1111, takes time off from teaching to guide visitors on trips around Santarém.

Waterfront
Walk along the waterfront of Avenida Tapajós from the Docas do Pará to Rua Adriano Pimentel. This is where drifters, loners and fishers congregate. Include a stop at the Mercado de Peixes (Fish Market) and the floating market.

Casa da Cultura
The Casa da Cultura at the corner of Avenida Borges Leal and Avenida Barão do Rio Branco features a small collection of pre-Columbian pottery.

River Beaches
Santarém's natural river beaches are magnificent. Like elsewhere in the Amazon, the seasonal rise and fall of the waters uncovers lovely white river beaches and sweeps them clean of debris at the end of the beach season.

Festivals
The Indian Festa do Sairé and the Christian ceremony of NS da Saude have been celebrated on 23 June at Alter do Chão since 1880. The Sairé is a standard which is held aloft to lead a flower-bedecked procession. This is perhaps a re-enactment of the historic meeting between the Tapuiçus and the Portuguese, or possibly a ritual which originated when the Jesuits introduced Christianity to the Indians. The patron saint of fisherfolk, São Pedro, is honoured with a river procession on 29 June when boats decorated with flags and flowers sail before the city.

Fishing enthusiasts should note that the Tucunaré fishing championship takes place during the second half of September and that October and November are the best months to fish for pirarucu in the Rio Itaqui and Lago Grande de Curuaí.

Places to Stay – bottom end
Hotel São Luís (☎ 522-1043), Travessa Senador Lemos 118, is cheap but dumpy. Quartos cost US$5/8 for singles/doubles – meals and laundry service are also available.

Restaurante e Hotel Ponte Certo on the corner of Avenida Cuiaba and Mendoza Fortado is a cleanish place but unfortunately a bit out of the way. Apartamentos here cost US$11/13 for singles/doubles.

Hotel Camino (☎ 522-2981), at Praça Rodrigues dos Santos 877, near the market, and *Hotel Central Plaza*, also by the market, have apartamentos at US$12/14 for singles/doubles with fan, and air-con versions for a couple of dollars more.

Places to Stay – middle & top end
The two middle-range hotels are inferior in quality but they're still adequate. The *Santarém Palace Hotel* (☎ 522-5285), at Avenida Rui Barbosa 726, and the *Hotel Nova Olinda* (☎ 522-1531), at Avenida Ad-

riano Pimentel 140, provide apartamentos for about US$20/25 for singles/doubles.

The *Hotel Tropical* (☎ 522-1533), at Avenida Mendoça Furtado 4120, is the only luxury hotel in Santarém. Despite the amenities, such as air-con, swimming pool, restaurant and bar, it's definitely a bit frayed around the architectural edges. Room rates start around US$30/35 for singles/doubles.

Places to Eat

Succulent species of local fish include curimatá, jaraqui, surubim, tucunaré and pirarucu. Local dishes use cassava: maniçoba is made from pork and cassava, while pato no tucupi is a duck and cassava root concoction.

Restaurante O Mascote on Praça do Pescador 10 (just off Rua Senador Lameira Bittencourt) is Santarém's best restaurant and music hangout. Fried crab costs US$2.50 and fish dinners are US$6 and up. Try the *peixe caldeirada* and *moqueca*, and listen to singer/guitarist Vianey Sirotheau. *Restaurant Tapaiu* in the lobby of the Hotel Tropical also has a pleasing menu.

Ice-cream fans will stampede to *Sorveteria Go-Go* at Rua Siquiera Campos 431, which offers old favourites and great new flavours such as graviola and milho verde (corn).

Things to Buy

Fabrica de Redes Aparecida (☎ 522-5958) at Avenida Borges Leal 2561 manufactures high-quality hammocks, a cheap and handy souvenir of the Amazon. Visitors may be given a tour of the 19th-century textile works. Artesanato Dica Frazão, a clothing/craft store, is at Rua Floriano Peixoto 281. The proprietor, Senhora Dica, creates women's clothing from natural fibres.

Getting There & Away

Air TABA serves the small towns of the Amazon interior while Varig/Cruzeiro and VASP provide connections to other major cities in Brazil via Manaus and Belém.

TABA (☎ 522-1939) is at Rua Floriano Peixoto 607, Varig/Cruzeiro (☎ 522-2084) is at Rua Siquiera Campos 277 and VASP (☎ 522-1680) is at Avenida Rui Barbosa 786.

Bus The rodoviária (☎ 522-1342) is five km from the Docas do Pará, on Avenida Cuiabá. During the dry season there are buses to: Cuiabá; Belém (1369 km) via Imperatriz; Itaituba (370 km); and Marabá (1087 km).

The Transamazônica highway (BR-230) and Santarém-Cuiabá highway (BR-163) intersect 190 km south of Santarém, at Rurópolis. Bus travel can be miserable/impossible during the rainy season because about 1800 km of BR-163 (between Itaituba and Sinop) is unpaved. Most travellers still rely on river transport.

Boat For details about boat services to Manaus, Santarém and Belém, see the respective Getting There & Away sections for Belém and Manaus. Boat schedules are erratic, but anticipate three days to Manaus, three days to Belém and 12 hours to Itaituba. The ENASA office (☎ 522-5855) is at Rua Senador Lameira Bittencourt 459.

The river trip between Santarém and Belém includes an interesting section downstream from Monte Alegre at the Narrows, where the boat passes closer to jungle. The boat trip is pleasant, and the food is plentiful. It's a breezy ride and the endless view of long, thin, green strips of forest and wider bands of river and sky is OK for the first day, but after a while you'll start talking to your hammock and chewing on the life belts.

There are also boat services twice a week (two days; US$18/21 for 2nd/1st class) between Santarém and Porto Santana, the major port 20 km down the coast from Macapá (Amapá state) – see also the Getting There & Away section under Macapá.

Getting Around

To/From the Airport The airport is 15 km from the centre and there's a bus service to the centre which operates from 6 am to 7 pm. Alternatively, you may be able to use the courtesy shuttle bus which runs between the Hotel Tropical and the airport. The taxi fare is US$12.

AROUND SANTARÉM
Encontro das Águas & Alter do Chão
The meeting of the waters (águas barrentas), where the clear Tapajós and the light brown Amazon merge, is worth a boat excursion or at least a glimpse from land at Praça Mirante near Restaurante O Mascote.

This trip can be combined with an excursion up the Rio Tapajós to the village of Alter do Chão, a weekend resort for the people of Santarém. Alter do Chão has good fishing and a beautiful turquoise lagoon, which was once a sacred spot for the Tapajós Indians. The village is three hours by boat or 50 km by bus on a dirt road through jungle.

Getting There & Away The Hotel Tropical organises a day tour (US$25 per person) to the meeting of the waters and Alter do Chão; or you can do it yourself by taking a scheduled boat from the town docks or a bus from the rodoviária. The bus leaves at 4 am and returns at 6 pm.

Fordlândia & Belterra
Fordlândia and Belterra, Henry Ford's huge rubber plantations, date from the 1920s. Ford successfully managed to transplant an American town, but his Yankee ingenuity failed to cultivate rubber efficiently in the Amazon. Abandoned by Ford, the rubber groves are now operated by the Ministry of Agriculture as a research station.

During the dry season, there is one bus a day to Belterra, which is 60 km south of Santarém. It departs at 11.30 am and returns at 2.30 pm. Amazon Tours (for address, see the Information section under Santarém) or the travel agent at the Hotel Tropical in Santarém can arrange trips to Belterra and Fordlândia (50 km further south).

Curuá-Una Hydroelectric Dam
The Curuá-Una Hydroelectric Dam at Cachoeira de Palhão, 72 km from Santarém, meets the growing energy needs of a rapidly developing region. It's open to visitors.

PARQUE NACIONAL DA AMAZÔNIA
This national park lies close to the town of Itaituba on the western boundary between the states of Pará and Amazonas. Most sources agree that at least 10% of the park's original one million hectares has been devastated as a result of depredação (predatory behaviour) by garimpeiros and prospective landgrabbers, who face an utterly absurd force of four IBAMA employees attempting to protect the park.

Information & Permission
To arrange a visit to the park, you should contact Senhor Raimundo Egido Castro Ferreiro (☎ 518-1530) at IBAMA, Posto do Fomento Estrada, 53 Bis – Km 02 –, Itaituba.

Providing you seek prior permission from this IBAMA office, which is 73 km from the park entrance, it is possible to visit the park. Once your visit has been approved, you may be given assistance with transport to the park station. The park administration operates on less than a shoestring, so don't expect too much.

The administrative station inside the park at Uruá has rudimentary facilities, such as a campsite, but no special infrastructure for tourists. From this station there are rough trails leading into the forest.

Getting There & Away
Air The easiest option is to take a TABA flight from Belém or Santarém to Itaituba. There's one daily flight leaving Belém at 9.30 am which costs US$120/246 one-way/return; and one daily flight leaving Santarém at 6.30 am which costs US$75/150 one way/return.

Bus There's a bus service between Santarém and Itaituba which takes about eight hours (assuming the road conditions are favourable) and costs around US$10. The bus service between Belém and Itaituba is unreliable and only recommended if you are prepared to spend up to three days slogging through delays.

Amapá

There's not much to the state of Amapá other than Macapá, where three-quarters of the state's inhabitants live. During the 18th century the Portuguese built a fort at Macapá to protect access to the Amazon. The discovery of gold in the region prompted several attempts by the French to invade from French Guiana and claim Amapá. At the turn of this century, after international arbitration had snubbed the French and definitively awarded Amapá to Brazil, it was promptly annexed by Pará. This annexation greatly displeased the Amapaenses, who relentlessly pursued autonomy until it was finally granted by the Brazilian government in 1943. Today the state's economy is based on lumber and the mining of manganese, gold, and tin ore.

MACAPÁ

Macapá, capital of the state of Amapá, lies close to the equator. It was officially founded in 1815 in a strategic position on the Amazon estuary.

Information

The DETUR provisional tourist information office (☎ 222-0733) is at Avenida FAB, Centro Cívico Administrativo.

Travellers planning to continue north into French Guiana will require a visa. There are French consulates in Belém, Manaus, Recife, Salvador, Rio de Janeiro, São Paulo and Brasília, but *not* in the state of Amapá.

Forte São José de Macapá

The fort was built in 1782 by the Portuguese to defend against French invasions from the Guianas. It is still in good condition and worth a visit.

Curiaú

This African village, eight km from Macapá, was founded by escaped slaves.

Marco Zero do Equador

If you absolutely *have* to have that picture of yourself astride the equator, you can catch a bus at Praça São José which goes to the equator via Porto Santana and Fazendinha and then returns to Macapá. At the equator, the bus driver pauses long enough for travellers to race to the roof of the tourist restaurant, snap their pics, and hop back onto the bus. Allow around three hours for the whole excursion.

Festivals

O Marabaixo is an Afro-Brazilian holiday celebrated 40 days after Semana Santa (Holy Week).

Places to Stay

The *Mara Hotel* (☎ 222-0859) on Rua São Jose has single/double quartos for US$7/9. The *Hotel Tropical* (☎ 231-3739), at Avenida Antônio Coelho de Carvalho 1399, offers good-value apartamentos at around US$7/9 for singles/doubles.

The *Amapaense Palace* (☎ 222-3366) on Avenida Tiradentes is a two-star hotel with standard apartamentos at US$25/35 for singles/doubles. Also known as the Amazonas, the *Novotel* (☎ 223-1144), at Avenida Engenheiro Azarias Neto 17, is a hotel on the waterfront which falls far short of its four-star rating. Singles/doubles here are US$36/42.

Places to Eat

Eat your meals either at the *Peixaria* (☎ 222-0913) at Avenida Mãe Luzia 84 or *Restaurante Boscão* (☎ 231-4097) at Rua Hamilton Silva, 997.

Getting There & Away

Air It's possible to fly with Air France from Paris to Cayenne, French Guiana, and then continue overland to Amapá; however, travellers who want to avoid overland hassles may prefer to take the more convenient flight which is operated by Air France between Belém and Cayenne.

The Varig/Cruzeiro office (☎ 223-1743) is at Rua Candido Mendes 1039; VASP

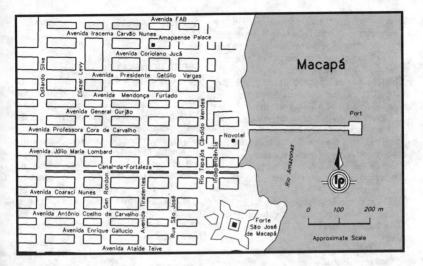

Macapá

(☎ 223-2411) is at Avenida Júlio Maria Lombard 115; and TABA (☎ 222-2083) is on Avenida Independência. Check the latest schedules and prices for flights to Oiapoque, Cayenne or Belém with these airlines.

At the time of writing, TABA was operating daily flights (except Sundays) between Macapá and Oiapoque, which departed Macapá at 11.50 am and returned from Oiapoque at 4.50 pm. The one-way fare for the 75-minute flight was US$65.

Bus Macapá is linked by BR-156 to Oiapoque, the Brazilian border town beside the Rio Oiapoque on the border with French Guiana. The 560-km road is paved as far as Calçoene and then degenerates into an 'unpaved track'. The road is frequently washed out and you should be prepared to hire vehicles or hitch on an impromptu basis. Transport between Macapá and Oiapoque is erratic and best attempted in two stages: by bus from Macapá to Calçoene (nine hours; US$15); and from there to Oiapoque (minimum seven hours; US$12) by occasional 'colectivo' (collective taxi or minibus). For details about crossing the border, see the relevant section in this chapter.

Boat For information about boat schedules and fares contact SENAVA (☎ 222-3648) at Avenida Engenheiro Azarias Neto 20; or Capitânia dos Portos (☎ 222-0415) at Avenida FAB, 427.

There is at least one boat a month to Oiapoque, but there appears to be no set pattern for departures, so you'll have to ask at the docks.

For details about boat services to Belém and Santarém, see their respective Getting There & Away sections. Note: boats to Santarém and Belém depart from Porto Santana, the main port 20 km down the coast from Macapá. If you need to stay overnight in this archetypal Amazon port (the exotic wares in the market are reportedly worth a look), a reader has recommended *Hotel Muller* (☎ 632-6881) at Rua Filinto Muller 373 which charges US$5 per person for an apartamento with fan. There is a regular bus service between Porto Santana and Macapá.

Crossing the Border The Brazilian border town of Oiapoque, 560 km north of Macapá, is the main crossing point for overland travellers between Brazil and French Guiana.

The transport options available from

Macapá to the border include a flight to Oiapoque; a privately arranged boat ride from the Macapá docks to Oiapoque; or a bus trip to Calçoene where you can change to a colectivo for a long and rugged trip to Oiapoque. For specific details, see the respective air, bus and boat descriptions in this Getting There & Away section.

Unless you have a great deal of time and patience or absolutely *have* to do the trip overland, you may prefer to avoid all the hassles and hop on a plane. For more advice, refer to the French Guiana section in the discussion of land routes in the Getting There & Away chapter.

There's a clean, state-owned hotel in Calçoene which is excellent value at US$5 for a double apartamento. The two hotels in Oiapoque charge US$5 for a double quarto and US$6 for a double apartamento.

Get your Brazilian exit stamp from the Polícia Federal in Oiapoque and your French Guianese entry stamp at the *gendarmerie* in St Georges (French Guiana), which is reached by a 20-minute motorboat ride (US$2.50) from Oiapoque. There are also plans to construct a bridge over the river. If you need to change money, there's a casa de câmbio at the harbour in Oiapoque.

Around Macapá

Bonito and the Igarapé do Lago, 72 km and 85 km from Macapá, are good places for swimming, fishing and jungle walks. There's a bus service to Praia da Fazendinha, the local beach 19 km from town.

Cachoeira de Santo Antônio is a pretty waterfall in the municipality of Mazagão, an 18th-century Portuguese town which is accessible by ferry from Porto Santana.

RIO ARAGUARI & THE POROROCA

At the mouth of the Rio Araguari, about 100 km north of Macapá, you can observe (and hear!) the pororoca (thunderous collision between Atlantic tide and the Amazon). The best time to see this phenomenon is between January and April at either the full or new moon. Excursions by boat (15 hours) to see the pororoca are organised by Martinica

Agência de Turismo (☎ 222-3569) in Macapá.

SERRA DO NAVIO

Serra do Navio, a mining town built in the 1950s to support the extraction of 40 million tonnes of manganese in the area, lies about 200 km north-west of Macapá. By 1990, the manganese reserves had been exhausted and the original mining consortium is currently negotiating to hand over the town to national and international organisations which are interested in using Serra do Navio as a base for research into ecology, meteorology, hydrology and anthropology in the Amazon region. The University of São Paulo has already set up a small research station in the town.

Getting There & Away

Serra do Navio is connected to Porto Santana by a railway (departures on Friday and Sunday), or you can drive there in about four hours, passing through beautiful forests, on BR-210. For more information, contact Indústria e Comércio de Minérios (ICOMI), the mining consortium, by phoning 632-6160.

NATIONAL PARKS, RESERVES & RESEARCH STATIONS IN AMAPÁ

The Piratuba Reserva Biológica do Lago Piratuba (biological reserve) and Estação Ecológica de Maracá-Jipioca (ecological research station) are managed by IBAMA as part of a project to study and protect turtles, manatees, toucans, and many other species in the mangrove swamps and tropical forests of Amapá.

The Parque Nacional de Cabo Orange, also managed by IBAMA, extends along the northern tip of Amapá and is of prime importance as a breeding ground for sea turtles. For more information about these protected areas, contact IBAMA (☎ 222-2099), Superintendência Estadual, Rua Hamilton Silva 1570, Bairro Santa Rita, in Macapá.

Tocantins

On 1 January 1989 a constitutional amendment creating the new state of Tocantins came into effect. The new state, which encompasses what was previously the northern half of the state of Goiás, was supposedly created to give the Indians of the region greater autonomy; however, they appear to have been conveniently shuffled aside to make way for grandiose Big Plans with lavish use of statistics and slogans, such as '20 Anos em 2 'or '20 Years (of progress) in 2 years'.

Siqueira Campos, the man who proposed the creation of the state some 25 years ago, took part in a bitter tussle with rival politicians before emerging victorious as the new governor of the state. The political debate produced some strange claims. José Freire, one of Campos' toughest rivals, tried to prove that Campos was in fact a murderer who had changed his name in the '60s. Freire offered a substantial reward to anyone who could prove this theory by producing the relevant birth certificate and other pertinent papers. One curious flaw in his argument was his inability to identify Campos' real name.

After ferocious politicking between three or four rival towns, the town of Palmas was officially declared the state capital. Campos immediately launched into dozens of development projects, and the grandiose Palácio Araguaia, seat of the state government, was one of the first buildings to be completed.

At this early stage in the life of the state, very little information is available. Tocantins currently has 1.2 million inhabitants in 124 municipalities assigned to 15 administrative regions. The largest cities are Araguaína, Gurupi, and Porto Nacional. In 1991, Palmas had 2000 inhabitants, mostly public officials and construction workers, but optimistic estimates envisage the town's population growing to 30,000 in 1992, 150,000 in 1995, and achieving a target of 500,000 by the turn of the century.

RIO ARAGUAIA

The Rio Araguaia begins in the Serra dos Caiapós and flows 2600 km northwards, forming the borders of Mato Grosso, Goiás, and Pará before joining the Rio Tocantins, where the states of Goiás, Maranhão and Pará come to a point near Marabá. About 500 km from its source the Araguaia bifurcates into the greater and lesser Araguaia rivers, which course west and east respectively and then rejoin, having formed the largest river island in the world, Ilha do Bananal.

The river is not easily accessible, so tours are a good idea. The best access from Mato Grosso is via Barra do Garças, about 500 km from Cuiabá. Barra do Garças has the Parque de Águas Quentes (hot springs). Camping facilities are open from May to October. It's a rapidly growing agricultural boom-town of 30,000 people. There are four simple hotels in town.

The stretch of the Rio Araguaia from the town of Aruanã up to the Ilha do Bananal is considered one of the best freshwater fishing areas in the world. The region is beginning to attract Brazilian vacationers during the dry season – June to September – when the receding waters uncover white beaches along the riverbank. Many Brazilians camp on the banks of the river. During the May through October fishing season, pintado, pirarucu, pacu, tucunaré, suribim and matrinchã are there for the taking.

If you're serious about fishing and have the money, there are tours, arranged in Brasília and Goiânia (Goiás state), where you meet a boat-hotel in Aruanã and sail around the island. If you want to explore the river without a tour, catch a boat in Aruanã or Barra do Garças; however, if you want to get as far north as Ilha do Bananal and don't have a lot of money, it's best to take a bus up to São Felix do Araguaia and hire a boat from there.

ILHA DO BANANAL

The Ilha do Bananal, formed by the splitting of the Rio Araguaia, is the world's largest river island, covering 20,000 sq km. Much of the island is covered with forest and a big chunk is an Indian reserve, the Parque Nacional do Araguaia, inhabited by Carajás and Javaés Indians. There is plenty of wildlife but only birds are visible in abundance.

At sunset or sunrise you can reel in all sorts of fish, including dogfish with teeth so large that the Indians use them to shave with. There are also tucunaré with colourful moustaches, ferocious tabarana, pirarucu (two-metre-long, 100-kg monsters) and several other slimy critters. The river also harbours boto (freshwater dolphin), jacaré, soia (a rare one-eyed fish) and poraquê (an electric fish).

Peter Fleming describes an excursion in this region in his excellent travelogue entitled *Brazilian Adventure* (see the Books & Maps section in the Facts for the Visitor chapter). Fleming's route took him down the Araguaia to São Felix do Araguaia where his group prepared for an expedition up the Rio Tapirapé in an attempt to establish what had happened to Colonel Fawcett, an English explorer who had disappeared there in 1925.

Permission to visit the park can be obtained from IBAMA (the national parks service) in Brasília, or from the park director (☎ 224-2457, 224-4809) who lives in Goiânia (Goiás state). Of course, if you just show up you may save a lot of time and hassle and get in just the same. The ranger responsible is Senhor Bonilho, who knows the park quite well. There is simple accommodation available on the island but no food other than what you bring. Senhor Bonilho can provide 4WDs and boats.

Places to Stay & Eat

São Felix do Araguaia São Felix is a town of around 3000 inhabitants on the Rio das Mortes. It has a few simple hotels. On the river's edge you'll find the very basic *Hotel Araguaia*. You may be tempted to take one of the rooms with air-con, but don't. The electricity turns off at 11 pm, and those tomb-like rooms turn into ovens. Get a room that has a ceiling vent through to the hallway.

In town, you can arrange boat rides from fisherfolk and locals who hang out on the water's edge. The pizzeria and fish restaurant overhanging the water is recommended. In July, the town may well be flooded with tourists from the area looking to 'catch some rays'.

Santa Teresinha Another gateway to Ilha do Bananal is the small town of Santa Teresinha (Mato Grosso state). A small hotel on the water's edge is popular with foreign naturalists who use it as a base for visits to the Parque Nacional do Araguaia. Costs in this region, as in all of the Amazon, are higher than what one would expect to pay in Rio or Salvador – so be prepared.

Getting There & Away

To/From Barra do Garças The long and dry road to Ilha do Bananal begins 400 km west of Goiânia at Barra do Garças in Mato Grosso. Buses leave early in Mato Grosso, not to beat the heat, but to suffer a bit less. The bus from Barra do Garças to São Felix do Araguaia leaves daily at 5 am.

If you don't want to take the bus, air taxis are available and cover the distance in one hour.

To/From Aruanã It's probably easier to reach the Araguaia from the state of Goiás (Goiânia in particular) than from Mato Grosso. For those without a 4WD at their disposal, the town of Aruanã, accessible by bus from both Goiânia (310 km) and Goiás Town, is the gateway to the Araguaia. There is a campground (open in July) at Aruanã. Hire a *voadeira* (a small aluminium motorboat) and guide for a river trip to Ilha do Bananal.

Amazonas & Roraima

Amazonas

Amazonas, covering an area of over 1.5 million sq km, is Brazil's largest state. Approximately 75% of its two million inhabitants live in the metropolis of Manaus or the much smaller cities of Manacapuru, Itacoatiara, Parintins, and Coari.

For further coverage of the Amazon region, including Amazonas state, see the Facts about the Country chapter (Flora & Fauna; Ecology & Environment; National Parks). For details about getting around the Amazon region see the North introductory chapter.

Amazonas state is one hour behind Brazilian standard time.

MANAUS

Manaus lies beside the Rio Negro – 10 km upstream from the confluence of the Rio Solimões and Rio Negro which join to form the Amazon. In 1669 the fortress of São José da Barra was built by Portuguese colonisers who named Manaus after a tribe of Indians who inhabited the region. The village which grew from the fort was little more than a minor trading outpost populated by traders, Black slaves, Indians and soldiers, until the rubber boom pumped up the town.

Although Manaus continues to be vaunted in countless glossy advertising brochures as an Amazon Wonderland, the city itself has few attractions. In addition, it is dirty, ugly and becoming increasingly crime-ridden, and the flora and fauna has been systematically despoiled for hundreds of km around the city. Many travellers now only use the city for the briefest of stopovers before making excursions far beyond Manaus, where it is still possible to experience the rainforest wonders that Manaus glibly promises but cannot deliver.

The current governor of Amazonas, Gilberto Mestrinho, is now in his fourth term at the post. Mestrinho, who captivates voters with promises of jobs and development, styles himself as 'the governor of men, not of animals and the forest' and maintains 'there are hardly any healthy trees in Amazônia and they should all be used before the woodworm gets to them'. In the long term, this is clearly neither a recipe for sustainable use of the region's resources nor a viable option to produce jobs and development. Critical observers encapsulate such a policy as 'smash, grab and run'.

History

In 1839 Charles Goodyear developed the vulcanisation process which made natural rubber durable, and in 1888 John Dunlop drew a patent for pneumatic rubber tires. Soon there was an unquenchable demand for rubber in the recently industrialised USA and Europe, and the price of rubber in the international markets soared.

In 1884, the same year that Manaus abolished slavery, a feudal production system was established that locked the seringueiros (rubber tappers) into a cruel serfdom. Driven from the sertão by drought, and lured into the Amazon with the false promise of prosperity, they signed away their freedom to the *seringalistas* (owners of rubber plantations).

The seringalista sold goods to the seringueiro on credit – fishing line, knives, manioc flour, hammocks – and purchased the seringueiro's balls of latex. The illiteracy of the seringueiros, the brutality of *pistoleiros* (gun-toting henchmen hired by seringalistas), deliberately rigged scales, and the monopoly of sales and purchases all contributed to the perpetuation of the seringueiro's debt and misery. The seringueiros also had to contend with loneliness, jungle fevers, hostile Indian attacks and all manner of deprivation. Seringueiros who attempted to escape their serfdom were hunted down and tortured by the pistoleiros.

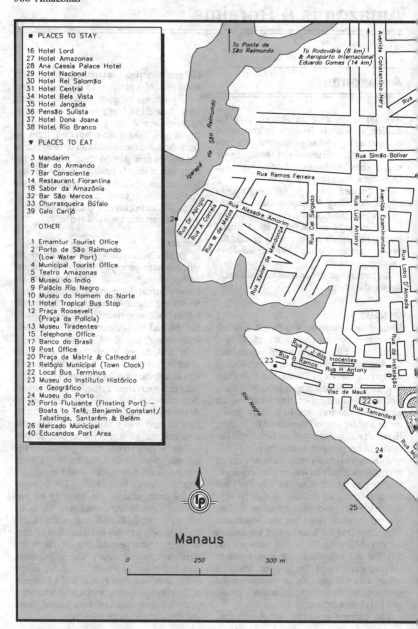

■ PLACES TO STAY
16 Hotel Lord
27 Hotel Amazonas
28 Ana Cassia Palace Hotel
29 Hotel Nacional
30 Hotel Rei Salomão
31 Hotel Central
34 Hotel Bela Vista
35 Hotel Jangada
36 Pensão Sulista
37 Hotel Dona Joana
38 Hotel Rio Branco

▼ PLACES TO EAT
3 Mandarim
6 Bar do Armando
7 Bar Consciente
14 Restaurant Fiorantina
18 Sabor da Amazônia
32 Bar São Marcos
33 Churrasqueira Búfalo
39 Galo Carijó

OTHER
1 Emamtur Tourist Office
2 Porto de São Raimundo
   (Low Water Port)
4 Municipal Tourist Office
5 Teatro Amazonas
8 Museu do Índio
9 Palácio Rio Negro
10 Museu do Homem do Norte
11 Hotel Tropical Bus Stop
12 Praça Roosevelt
   (Praça da Polícia)
13 Museu Tiradentes
15 Telephone Office
17 Banco do Brasil
19 Post Office
20 Praça da Matriz & Cathedral
21 Relógio Municipal (Town Clock)
22 Local Bus Terminus
23 Museu do Instituto Histórico
   e Geográfico
24 Museu do Porto
25 Porto Flutuante (Floating Port) –
   Boats to Tefé, Benjamin Constant/
   Tabatinga, Santarém & Belém
26 Mercado Municipal
40 Educandos Port Area

Manaus

0   250   500 m

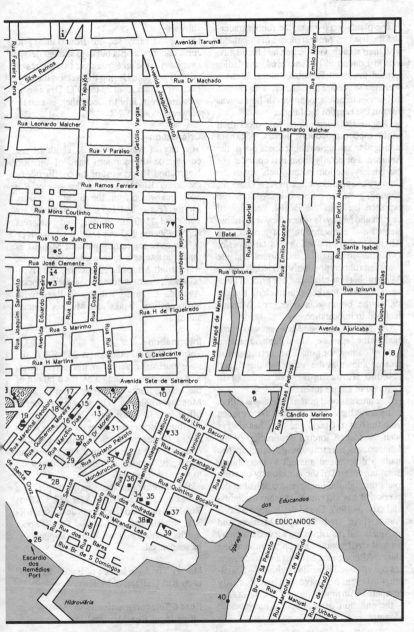

The plantation owners, the rubber traders and the bankers prospered and built palaces with their wealth. Gentlemen had their shirts sent to London to be laundered, and ladies sported the latest French fashions. Manaus became the second city after Rio de Janeiro to get electricity, and an opera house was built in the heart of the jungle.

Despite Brazilian efforts to protect their world rubber monopoly, Henry Wickham managed to smuggle rubber seeds out of the Amazon. For details about this episode, see the History section in the Facts about the Country chapter. Botanists in Kew Gardens, London, grew the rubber tree seedlings and exported them to the British colonies of Ceylon and Malaysia where they were transplanted and cultivated in neat groves. The efficient Asian production was far superior to haphazard Brazilian techniques and the Brazilian rubber monopoly eroded. As more Asian rubber was produced, the price of latex on the world market plummeted. By the 1920s the boom was over, and Manaus declined in importance.

During WW II when Malaysia was occupied by the Japanese, Allied demand created a new rubber boom. The seringueiros became known as the 'rubber soldiers', and 150,000 Nordestinos were once again recruited to gather rubber.

The international port of Manaus is still in many ways the capital of a land far removed from the rest of Brazil, and there has always been the fear of foreign domination of the Amazon. As a result, the government has made a determined attempt to consolidate Brazilian control of the Amazon by creating roads through the jungle and colonising the interior. It has also made Manaus an industrial city. In 1967, Brazil established a Zona Franca (Free Trade Zone) in Manaus, and multinational industries drawn to the area by tax and tariff benefits set up manufacturing plants. Although the Manaus free trade zone has not spawned Brazilian industry – Brazilian entrepeneurs have not successfully competed with multinationals in the Amazon – the infusion of money has invigorated Manaus.

Climate

During the rainy season, from January to June, count on a brief but hard shower nearly every day – the area gets over two metres of rainfall per year. During this season the temperature ranges from 23 to 30°C. Dry season weather, from July to December, is usually between 26 and 37°C.

Orientation

The city of Manaus lies 3° south of the equator on the northern bank of the Rio Negro, and 10 km west of the confluence of the lesser Rio Negro and the greater Rio Solimões which form the mighty Amazon. Iquitos (Peru) and Leticia (Colombia) are 1900 and 1500 km upriver, and Santarém and Belém are 700 and 1500 km downriver.

The most interesting parts of Manaus as far as the tourist is concerned are close to the waterfront: Mercado Municipal, the riverboat port, customs house and floating docks. Avenida Eduardo Ribeiro is lined with airline offices, banks and Manaus' fancier stores.

Information

Tourist Office Emamtur (☎ 243-5983), the state tourism organisation, has its headquarters at Avenida Tarumã 379. It's a bit out of the way and only open from 7 am to 1 pm, Monday to Friday. The municipal tourist office (☎ 232-1646) at the Canto da Cultura (Culture Corner), opposite the Teatro Amazonas (Manaus Opera Theatre) is more convenient. It's open from 9 am to noon and 2 to 6 pm, Monday to Friday; and from 9 am to noon on Saturday.

For information about national parks in Amazonas, contact IBAMA (☎ 237-3718) at Rua Ministro João Gonçalves de Souza, BR-319, Km 01, Distrito Industrial. Don't expect much – management of the parks appears to be suspended.

Money The main branch of Banco do Brasil is on Rua Guilherme Moreira.

Post & Telecommunications Manaus' post office is on Rua Marechal Deodoro and is

Escadaria dos Remédios Port

Most of the people you will observe at the Escadaria dos Remédios Port have Indian features, with straight, jet-black hair and tawny skin. The thin and stoop-shouldered stevedores lug barrels, casks and boxes between the trucks and riverboats, whose curved decks are filled with boxes and people, and draped with hundreds of hammocks. Fishers look on from the sidelines while they smoke cigarettes and drink beer.

Men toss banana stalks from their dugout canoes to shore and then onto the waiting trucks. A speaker blares out nonstop love songs from warped tapes until the boats pull out at 6 pm. The boats leave one by one: bells ring, horns blow and thin boys scurry about selling their last lengths of rope to tie up travellers' hammocks. ∎

open Monday to Saturday, 8 am to 6 pm; and Sunday 8 am to 2 pm. The Amazon postal system has a poor reputation, and foreign residents in Manaus don't entrust their correspondence to Brazilian correios, but wait for US or Europe-bound couriers and friends to take it. For this reason US stamps (as well as vanilla spice) are valuable commodities among expatriates residing in the Amazon.

There's a central office of TELE-AMAZON, the state telephone company, on Rua Guilherme Moreira. It's open daily from 8 am to 11 pm.

Foreign Consulates It's best to arrange visas to neighbouring countries well in advance through consulates in Manaus.

If you're going beyond Leticia to Colombia, tell the consul, who'll probably demand to see an onward ticket and proof of 'sufficient funds' before issuing a visa.

Bolivia
    Avenida Tefé, Bloco B4A, Apartamento 202, Parque Solimões (☎ 237-8686)
Colombia
    Rua Dona Libânia, 262 (☎ 234-6777) – see preceding comment on visas
Ecuador
    Rua 6 Casa 6 (Jardim Belo Horizonte) (☎ 236-3698)
France
    Rua Monsenhor Coutinho, 164 (☎ 233-6851)
Germany
    Rua Barroso 355, 1 Andar, sala A (☎ 232-5877)
Peru
    Conjunto Aristocrático, Rua A, Casa 19, Chapada (☎ 236-3666)
UK
    Edifício Manaus Shopping Center, sala 1212 (☎ 234-1018)
USA
    Rua Recife, 1010 (Pq 10) (☎ 234-4546)
Venezuela
    Rua Recife, 1620 (☎ 236-0406)

Dangers & Annoyances Theft at rock-bottom hotels is common – double keys are sometimes used to gain access to your room. When travelling by boat, watch your gear very carefully. Taxi drivers in Manaus have a poor reputation. Watch out for blatant rip-off attempts: spurious 'extra charges'; slack use of meters; and cosy 'deals' whereby hotel clerks are paid a fat commission by taxi drivers who are willing to pay for the privilege of being able to rip-off foreign tourists. In our case, this system backfired because we saw the deal between the clerk and the driver, and promptly called in the police at the airport when the driver tried to double the price. Perhaps there are some decent taxistas in Manaus, but we encountered so many crooked ones that taxi travel turned into a sick joke.

For more advice, see the security section under Dangers & Annoyances in the Facts for the Visitor chapter.

Hunting & Fishing Although hunting is widely practised, it is illegal. Hunting has already brought peixe-boi and many species of turtles close to extinction. Fishing, however, is acceptable anywhere, and is best from September to November. These are also the best months for swimming.

Serpent Support for the Theatre

According to the historian Daniel Fausto Bulcão, there was once a couple who lived in the interior far from the city. The woman became pregnant, and in the course of her pregnancy she had the misfortune to kill a cobra. When her nine months were up she gave birth to two cobras, male and female, which she raised as her own children.

The cobras began to grow and the mother was unable to control her unruly offspring, so she threw them into the river. The female cobra earned a reputation for being evil by tipping over riverboats, devouring children and drowning adults – killing simply for the pleasure of it. Her brother was of a milder temperament, and the two cobras fought continuously. One day brother snake killed his sister, but not without suffering the loss of one eye. He is still alive and well and has grown considerably over the years. Caboclos believe that he now lives beneath Manaus and that his enormous head supports the Teatro Amazonas while his body supports the many river beaches of the Amazon. ∎

Escadaria dos Remédios Port

The Escadaria dos Remédios port by the Mercado Municipal is quite a scene and is well worth a visit. For a description, see the aside in this section.

Mercado Municipal

Looming above the dock is the imposing cast-iron structure of the Mercado Municipal, designed in 1882 by Adolfo Lisboa after the Parisian Les Halles. Although the art nouveau ironwork was imported from Europe, the place has acquired Amazonian character. Inside and about the market you can purchase provisions for jungle trips: strange fruit, old vegetables, several varieties of biscuits, sacks of beans and rice, lanterns, rope, straw hats, perhaps some Umbanda figurines, powders and incense.

At the back end of the market there's a grimy cafeteria where you can have lunch and contemplate Manaus' complete ignorance regarding sanitation. The water which keeps enormous fish and fly-covered meats cool, drains from the stalls, mingles with meat, fish and urine, flows underfoot, runs off into the river and mixes with discarded meats and produce and all the sewage of Manaus. Urubu vultures swarm around the refuse and roost in the rusty ironwork of the cafeteria and the new scaffolding by the docks. Take the tables at either end for the best view.

Teatro Amazonas

Teatro Amazonas, the famous opera house of Manaus, was designed by Doménico de Angelis in Italian renaissance style at the height of the rubber boom in 1896. More than any other building associated with the administration of Mayor Eduardo Ribeiro, this opera house is symbolic of the opulence that was Manaus. Renovated in 1990, it's now open from 10 am to 5 pm, Tuesday to Sunday. Admission costs US$2.50 and includes a compulsory guided tour. Opera and ballet performances are held here throughout the year. Ask the guide about the schedule or check the entertainment section in the local newspaper.

Palácio Rio Negro

The Palácio Rio Negro, built as a home for eccentric German rubber baron, Waldemar Scholz, now serves as the seat of the state government. It's on Avenida Sete de Setembro beside the first bridge over the Igarapé do Manaus.

British Customs House

The British Customs House (Alfândega) dates back to 1906. The sandy-coloured building with its neat brown trim seems out of place in this dilapidated city. The building was imported from the UK in prefabricated blocks and now serves as the Inspetoria da Receita Federal do Porto do Manaus.

Porto Flutuante

The Porto Flutuante (floating docks), also installed in 1906, were considered a technical marvel because of their ability to rise and fall as the water level of the river changes with the seasons.

Amazon Research Institute

The central project of the Instituto Nacional de Pesquisa da Amazônia (INPA) (☎ 23-9400), the National Amazon Research Institute, is a joint study with the Smithsonian Institute to determine the 'minimal critical size of ecosystems' – the smallest chunk of land that can support a self-sustaining jungle forest and all its attendant creatures. The ambitious 20-year project, under the direction of Dr Thomas Lovejoy, has consumed a great deal of money and drawn some criticisms of its methods and effectiveness. Various sized parcels of jungle are studied first in their virgin state and later after the surrounding land has been cleared, creating islands of jungle. Changes in plant and animal populations are carefully scrutinised. Initial conclusions show that the complex interdependence of plants and animals and the heterogeneity of species poses a barrier to maintaining an isolated patch of jungle. INPA scientists are also studying aquatic mammals: fresh-water manatee, river otter and porpoises. These animals are on display for visitors.

The grounds are open Monday to Friday from 8 am to noon and 2 to 6 pm, and are located at Bola do Coroado, Estrada de Aleixo 1756, Km 4. Call ahead (☎ 236-9400) to find out about the topic (and language) of Tuesday's seminar series. To reach INPA, either take the bus marked 'São José' or use a taxi.

Museu do Homem do Norte

The Museu do Homem do Norte (Museum of Northern Man) (☎ 232-5373), at Avenida Sete de Setembro 1385, is an ethnology/anthropology museum dedicated to the way of life of the river-dwelling Caboclos. It's open Tuesday to Friday from 9 am to noon and 2 to 6 pm; and from 9 am to noon on Monday. To reach the museum from the city centre, take the bus marked 'Coroado'.

Museu do Indio

This Indian museum, at the intersection of Avenida Duque de Caxias and Avenida Sete de Setembro, displays ceramics, featherwork, weavings and ritual objects of the tribes of the upper Rio Negro. It's open Monday to Friday, from 8 am to noon and 2 to 5 pm; and from 8 am to noon on Saturday.

Parque Zoológico – CIGS

If you want to feel nauseated, visit this military zoo, which boasts more jaguars born in captivity than anywhere else in the world. The zoo is attached to the Centro de Instrução de Guerra na Selva (CIGS), a jungle warfare training centre. The animals on display – tapir, monkeys, armadillos, snakes and birds – were collected by Brazilian soldiers on jungle manoeuvres and survival training programmes. The conditions in the zoo are abysmal: the animals are badly kept, ill-fed, and there have been reliable reports that animals regularly perish during mock combat with soldiers. Given their miserable existence in this zoo, these animals probably welcome the release from their suffering. This is definitely not a tourist attraction, but rather a cause for outrage. One reader described the plight of the animals as 'heartbreaking'. We'd like to hear from readers if complaints to Amamtur have any effect.

To get to the zoo, on Estrada da Ponta Negra at Km 12, near the beach and Hotel Tropical, take a taxi or a municipal bus marked 'Compensa' or 'São Jorge'. Zoo hours are Tuesday to Sunday 8 to 11.30 am and 1 to 5 pm. Admission is US$1.

Praia da Ponta Negra & Waterfalls Around Manaus

Praia da Ponta Negra, the chic river beach of the Amazon, has a full range of amenities, such as restaurants and bars. The best time to go is from September to November (and sometimes as early as July) when the waters recede, but it's still a popular hangout even when the high waters flood the sand and cleanse the beach for the following season.

From the city centre, take the bus marked 'Praia da Ponta Negra'.

If you've missed the beach season, December to February is the best time to visit the waterfalls near Manaus: Cascatinha do Amor and Cachoeira do Tarumã. Further west from Manaus, near the opposite bank of the Rio Negro, is Cachoeira do Paricatuba.

Reserva do Tarumã

The Reserva do Tarumã is an animal rehabilitation centre, close to Ponta Negra, where you can observe and photograph local wildlife. The animals are cared for properly and allowed to roam free. A visit is recommended if you want a guided tour (languages available include English, French, German, Dutch and Portuguese) or would like to camp in the forest and hike the trails. The forest camps have been set up with spartan cabanas and basic equipment and cooking facilities – bring your own food. The cost per person per day is US$10.

All arrangements *have* to be made in advance by phoning Dr Marc & Betsy van Roosmalen (☎ 238-1394, 232-7171) who will then organise a boat for the 20-minute trip to the reserve. This procedure is strictly necessary to avoid poaching and commercialisation, both of which run contrary to the purpose of the reserve and lead to unnecessary disturbance of the wildlife.

São (Rabbi) Moyal

In Cemitério São João Batista, the general cemetery of Manaus (Praça Chile, Adrianópolis), is the tomb of Rabbi Moyal of Jerusalém. The rabbi came to the Amazon to minister to a small community of Jewish settlers, mostly merchants who had established a cacao, lumber and rubber trading network. He died in 1910, and over the years his tomb has become a shrine for an odd Roman Catholic cult. This cult, complete with rosary beads, candles, coins and devoted followers, probably arose with the Jewish custom of placing pebbles on tombs when visiting grave sites. The people of Manaus, unfamiliar with Jews and their ways (of Brazil's 120,000 Jews, less than 1000 inhabit Manaus) attribute the mysterious pebbles to the miraculous powers of the dead rabbi. Followers believe that the rabbi is a saint and insist that he performs miracles for faithful supplicants.

Encontro das Águas

The Encontro das Águas (Meeting of the Waters), when the inky black waters of the Rio Negro meet with the lemon-yellow waters of the Rio Solimões, is well worth seeing, but it's not absolutely necessary to take a tour to see this phenomenon. It can be seen just as well from the ferry which shuttles between Careiro and the Porto Velho highway (BR-319). If you do include the meeting of the waters in your tour, you may lose time spent exploring the more interesting sights further along the river.

Jungle Tours

The number one priority for most visitors to Manaus is to take a jungle tour to see the wildlife and experience the jungle close at hand. Here it's possible to arrange anything from standard day trips and overnights excursions, to months of travel in the hinterland. It is common for travellers to be greeted at the airport by groups of tour agency representatives keen to sign them up for trips. These representatives are a useful source of information, and may even offer transport into the centre to a budget hotel, but you should hold off booking a tour until you've had time to shop around for the best deals.

There are now dozens and dozens of agencies vying for your custom with trendy names ('Eco' and 'Green' have quickly become standard prefixes) and glossy brochures touting all sorts of encounters with wildlife and Indians just a few km from the city.

What you *can* expect on day trips or tours by boat lasting three or four days is a close-up experience of the jungle flora, with abundant birdlife and a few jacaré (more easily located at night by guides using powerful torches). It is also a chance to see what life is like for the caboclos in the vicinity of Manaus.

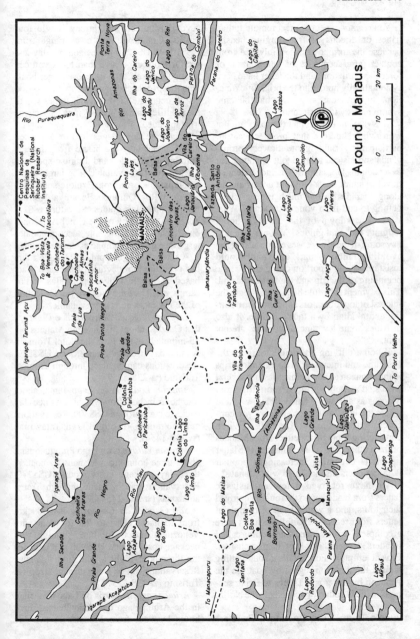

Around Manaus

0   10   20 km

Centro Nacional de
Pesquisas da
Seringueira (National
Rubber Research
Institute)

To Itacoatiara

To Boa Vista &
Venezuela

Rio Puraquequara

Ponta Terra Nova

Rio Amazonas

Ilha do Jenico

Lago do Rei

Paraná do Cambixi

Lago do Careiro

Lago do
Jenico

Lago do
Mandu

Lago do
Jabenico

Lago de
Arroz

Paraná do Careiro

Lago do
Capitari

Lago Jassua

Ponta das
Lajes

Balsa

Vila do
Careiro

Lago
Comprido

Ilha do
Xiborema

Lago Manguiri

Lago
Alvares

Lago Araçá

Encontro das
Águas

Lago
Janauari

Fazenda Santo
Antônio

Ilha do
Machantaria

Cachoeira
do Tarumã

Cachoeira
das Almas

MANAUS

Cascalho
do Amor

Balsa

Janauarylândia

Ilha do
Curari

Igarapé Tarumã Açu

Praia da Lua

Praia Ponta Negra

Praia de
Guedes

Vila do
Irandubo

Lago do
Irandubo

Ilha
Paciência

Rio Negro

Colônia
Paricatuba

Cachoeira
do Paricatuba

Colônia Lago
do Limão

Lago do
Limão

Rio Ariaú

Ilha da
(Amazonas)

Lago
Grande

Lago
Janaucá

Rio
Solimões

Jutaí

Igarapé Arara

Cachoeira
dos Araras

Ilha Sacada

Praia Grande

Lago
Acajatuba

Lago do
Bim

Lago do
Matias

Colônia
Boa Vista

Ilha do
Borroso

Manaquiri

Lago
Coapiranga

Igarapé Acajatuba

To Manacapuru

Lago
Santana

Rio Manaquiri
Paraná

Lago
Redondo

Lago
Miraúá

To Porto Velho

You *cannot* expect to meet remote Indian tribes or dozens of free-ranging beasts, because the former have sensibly fled from contact (after centuries of annihilation or forced assimilation) and the latter have been systematically hunted to the brink of extinction. In both cases, access has become synonymous with destruction.

This does not mean that the tours are not worthwhile, merely that prospective tour participants should ignore flowery propaganda and instead ask the tour operators for exact details. Does the tour include extended travel in small boats (without use of motor) along igarapés? How much time is spent getting to and from your destination? What is the breakdown of the costs for food, lodging, fuel, and guides? You may want to pay some of these expenses en route, thereby avoiding fanciful mark-ups, and should insist on paying a portion of the costs at the beginning of the trip and the rest at the end. This payment schedule helps to maintain the interest of tour operators and guides in defining and abiding by a tour schedule. It also provides some leverage if promises are not kept.

If you are trying out jungle tours for the first time and intending to do extended trips in the Amazon region perhaps lasting several weeks, it's useful to do a short trip from Manaus as a 'taster'. This will allow you to assess the idea in practice and give you confidence to 'iron out the bugs' when considering longer trips either from Manaus or from other parts of the Amazon. The latter option is becoming increasingly popular with travellers disenchanted with Manaus.

We have received a few enthusiastic letters from readers who thoroughly enjoyed their tours, and a whole heap of complaint letters from readers who felt the tours were a complete rip-off – see the section called Readers' Experiences later in this chapter. Caveat emptor! For details about getting around the Amazon region by boat see the Amazon by River and Things to Bring sections in the introductory chapter to the North.

Jungle Tours – Big Operators There are several reputable but pricey jungle tour outfits. Organised tour costs range from US$100 to US$200 per person per day and are far more expensive than tours you can arrange yourself. The tours use larger boats than those of the independent operators – too big to negotiate the narrow igarapés where the wildlife roams – but they may have canoe trips included.

There are advantages to the organised tours in that they are hassle free, there is nothing to arrange, and English-speaking guides are often available. The larger firms are reputable. Amazon Explorers (☎ 232-3052) at Rua Quintino Bocaiúva 189 has English speaking guides. Selvatur (☎ 622-2088), in the lobby of the Hotel Amazonas on Praça Adalberto Valle, accommodates large tour groups on huge catamaran boats.

A recent trend in upmarket jungle tours has been the introduction of package tours based at jungle lodges, pousadas, safari camps, etc. The following is a brief selection of the packages currently available.

Tropical Lago de Salvador is on Igarapé dos Guedes, about 30 km from Manaus – a 35-minute boat trip from the Hotel Tropical. A three-day package costs around US$280. Reservations can be made through Tropical Turismo (☎ 238-5757).

Amazon Lodge is on Lago Juma, about four hours by boat from Manaus. A three-day package costs around US$300. Reservations can be made through Transamazonas (☎ 232-1454).

Amazon Village is on Lago Puraquequara, about three hours from Manaus by boat. A three-day package costs around US$270. Reservations can be made through Transamazonas (☎ 232-1454).

São Gabriel da Cachoeira is 1000 km from Manaus, close to the frontiers with Venezuela and Colombia. An eight-day package costs around US$900 and includes the three-hour flight to and from Manaus. Reservations can be made through Tropical Turismo (☎ 238-5757).

Ariaú Jungle Tower is on Lago do Ariaú, in the Arquipélago das Anavilhanas, three hours by boat from Manaus. A two-day package costs around US$200. Reservations can be made through Rio Amazonas Turismo (☎ 234-7308).

Janauacá Jungle Lodge is on Lago do Janauacá, south-west of Manaus. A three-day package costs around US$260. Reservations can be made through Tropical Turismo (☎ 238-5757).

Acajatuba Jungle Lodge is on Lago Acajatuba, in the municipality of Iranduba (north-west of Manaus). A three-day package costs around US$250. Reservations can be made through Tropical Turismo (☎ 238-5757).

Adventure Camp is on Igarapé do Tarumã, 40 km from Manaus – two hours by boat. A four-day package costs around US$350, and includes accommodation in hammocks. Reservations can be made through Tarumã (☎ 642-2100).

Amazon Camp is on the Rio Urubu, about 200 km east of Manaus. A three-day package costs around US$230. Reservations can be made through Tropical Turismo (☎ 238-5757).

Pousada dos Guanavenas is on Ilha de Silves (an island), 300 km east of Manaus – about five hours by car. A three-day package costs around US$350. Reservations can be made through Guanavenas (☎ 236-5758).

Jungle Tours – Smaller Operators If you speak Portuguese and don't mind travelling a bit rough, there are plenty of smaller operators offering tours. It takes a while to hammer out a deal, change money, arrange supplies and buy provisions – you must allow at least a day for this. When serious haggling is called for, you should ask the tour operator to itemise expenses. Disproportionately inflated estimates can work in your favour. If the food budget seems unreasonable, buy provisions in and about the Mercado Municipal. If the fuel budget seems too high, offer to pay at the floating gas stations. Subtract the items from your original quote. As a rough rule of thumb, expect prices to start around US$90 for two people on a two-day (one night) trip including boat transport, guide, food and hammock

lodging. For more advice, see the comments at the beginning of this section, and the Readers' Experiences entry at the end of this section.

Moaçir Fortes (☎ 232-7492) speaks English and operates his own boat from the Porto Flutuante. He runs a small and first-class operation, charging US$80 to US$100 per person per day depending on the number of passengers on board (maximum 14; minimum four). Everyone sleeps in a clean cabin that has hot showers. His boat is fitted out with canoes and a small outboard, and has a well-stocked bar, a library full of wildlife guidebooks, binoculars, and there's even a telescope on board.

Sivilino Moeira do Santo is an amiable, honest and knowledgeable guide who works out of the Escadaria dos Remédios and goes by the nickname 'Capibara'. I've made two trips with him, an overnight to Lago Janauário, and six months later, a five-day tour up the Rio Negro. If I ever have the opportunity to go again I'll look him up once more.

Gerry Hardy is an English guide operating tours from Manacapuru together with a Brazilian guide, Elmo de Morais Lopes. Readers have generally liked the tours, but some have found the tone of the ecological explanations a bit patronising. Contact these guides through the Hotel Rio Branco (☎ 233-4019).

Suggested Excursions An overnight trip to Lago Janauário reserve (15 km from Manaus) – a standard excursion often including the meeting of the waters – or a three-day (two nights) trip to Lago Mamori, can both be recommended. The latter is especially good when the waters are high, as it has been in recent years, when boats could float past the treetops. A glimpse of life at the level of the jungle canopy is far richer than the view from the jungle floor.

A suggested longer tour is 100 km up the Rio Negro to the Arquipélago das Anavilhanas, near Nova Airão. This trip is best from July to December. Whichever tour you choose, make sure to take a canoe ride on the igarapés: it's a Disneyland top-price-ticket

The Amazon Circuit

It seems odd that in the millions of sq km that make up the Amazon, everyone seems to be congregating upon such a small spot, but during the pre-Carnival season, Lago Janauário draws hordes of visitors. One thing that cheapens the jungle experience is the feeling of being pumped through a tourist circuit: everyone bangs on the flying buttresses of the same sambaiaba tree, cuts the same rubber tree for latex-sap, then pulls over to an authentic jungle house where a monkey, a sloth, a snake and a jacaré are tied up to amuse visitors.

After a quick bite at a jungle restaurant, take the elevated walk to the Vitória Regia water lilies beyond the make-believe Indian craft stalls (10 stores operated by one athletic Indian who follows alongside the group and pushes feathered novelty-shop junk). At this point one disregards the water lilies and the Kodak boxes floating alongside and compares notes with one's neighbour about respective tour costs, boat sizes and whether or not a flush toilet has been provided.

The water lilies, metre-wide floating rimmed dishes adorned with flowers above and protected by sharp spikes below, are lovely despite it all. ∎

experience. On a Lago Janauário canoe trip I've seen bats on a rotting branch, twisted Tarzan vines and monkeys scattering and crashing over the treetops.

Readers' Experiences What you get out of your trip depends on several factors: expectations, previous experience, competence and breadth of knowledge of tour operators and guides; and the ability to accept life in the the Amazon at face value – one enterprising tour operator advertises 'Selva sem Sofrimento' (the Jungle Without Suffering!). Although the 'jungle' is often described in exaggerated terms as a 'Green Hell', it seems rather odd to want to turn it into a luxury outing with all mod cons, thereby distancing travellers from experiencing the 'wild' characteristics that are its hallmark.

The following selection of readers' experiences may help you with your choices. We welcome letters and comments for future editions.

'A good, medium-sized operation is Amazonas Indian Turismo, at Rua dos Andradas 335. I paid US$100 for three days.'

'Jungle tours are not that expensive. I had a three-day tour with Amazonas Indian Turismo and spent a wonderful time for US$100 (three days, everything included). During this trip I saw toucans, colibris, jacaré, Indians, mosquitoes and plenty more. A canoe trip at night in the swamps I'll never forget. Wow, how much I would like to go back there! The only problem

was that the Indian guide didn't speak more than two words of English and I didn't speak any Portuguese.'

'We took a three-day (two nights) trip with Cristóvão Amazonas Turismo (☎ 233-3231). We paid US$200 each and felt we were cheated. It was a canoe trip staying with Indian families and included all food. Instead, we recommend contacting the boatmen's union direct. All the canoe guides have formed an association. The tour companies only pay the guides US$400 for a three-day trip with four people – and the guides do everything (arranging lodging, meals, etc). We had a guide called Raimundo (59 years old) and he was excellent. Take some money with you for the trip as Indian handicrafts can be purchased at a much cheaper price (than in Manaus). There really weren't any animals to be seen. Although we saw a few cows, cranes, and jacaré, and caught piranha, there wasn't any wildlife in the jungle during the day. Due to too many people touring the jungle, the animals probably come out at night – if at all. Besides the jungle trip there is nothing else to do in Manaus.'

'You might warn travellers arriving in Manaus airport about the tourist-hunting girls who work freelance or for certain tour agencies. On my arrival, I felt insecure about finding a place to stay, so I was an easy victim. However, there was one good side to being caught: I got free transport to town and didn't have to worry about looking for a hotel – the girl put me into one that was good value. The bad side was the three-day boat trip she sold me. The experience of being on the Amazon is something I'll never forget – and I hope to get back there one day – but the trip as such was pure shit: a ridiculous 'guide' who had no interest in explaining anything; boring food (basically rice and noodles); 'mineral water' that tasted of gasoline; no visits to igarapés; and not even a trip to Lago Janauário. The agency was OCA Turismo at Rua 10 de Julho 695 and they demanded US$70 per day. Well, next time I'll take more time to compare, but how to know who's keeping promises and who's not?'

Top: Manaus Opera House, Amazonas (RS)
Bottom: Floating house, Rio Solimões, Amazonas (GC)

Top: Still backwaters of the Rio Negro, Amazonas (GC)
Bottom: Kids at a river town, Rio Amazonas, Pará (GC)

'We were told it's almost a must to go on a jungle tour if you go to Manaus. Unfortunately, we must say that it was very disappointing. We didn't see many animals on our two-day tour and it was also very expensive (US$85 per person), especially if you compare it, for example, to Ecuador where you can go on similar tours. We don't think the tours of the various tour agencies differ much. We went with Green Life Expeditions (☎ 234-3759) at Rua Miranda Leão 167. The one-day tour is not good: you spend 10 hours on the boat!'

'I took the three-day tour with Green Life Expeditions for US$120. This was very nicely done and had a really good local flavour. We spent the first night in a hut with a nice family about 60 km outside Manaus and were passed to two other sets of guides – locals who knew some English. I especially appreciated the home cooking and non-touristic approach and the fact that they asked for my comments and suggestions upon my return. Top marks!'

'We enjoyed a lot our trip with Enric Marsa (a Catalan guy from Spain) and Andreu Comas Casas from the travel agency Santo Agostinho (☎ 238-8009) at Rua Retiro Santa Luzia 399. The trip included various activities in the jungle (fishing, swimming, collecting fruits, etc) and was very worthwhile indeed.'

An Aussie couple we met told us about a tour they took with a local operator. All went well on the first day until the group took the advice of the guide and went for a swim. The cook waited until the group had returned to the boat and then took a quick dip even though he had admitted to being a poor swimmer. Suddenly, the Aussies heard the cook scream 'Ajuda-me' (help me) and before they could rush to his aid, he'd disappeared into the depths. All attempts to locate the cook proved fruitless and the locals advised waiting until morning before using hooks to drag the river.

The body (clearly mangled by various fish including piranhas) was duly fished out by this method and returned to Manaus draped across the boat. When the Aussies approached the operator (a red-headed lady) for a refund, having missed half their tour and endured such a gruesome incident, their demand was refused point blank and they had to call in the police before she gave in. Nobody could explain the sudden disappearance of the cook so close to the boat, but locals attributed it to some unidentified underwater beastie(s).

Festivals

A folklore festival held during the second half of June coincides with a number of saints' days and culminates in the Procissão Fluvial de São Pedro (São Pedro River Procession) when hundreds of regional boats parade on the river before Manaus to honour São Pedro, the patron saint of fisherfolk.

Places to Stay – bottom end

Camping Reserva do Tarumã (Tarumã Reserve), described under the sights for Manaus, has supervised campsites.

Youth Hostels There are two hostels in Manaus which have both been criticised by travellers for lack of cleanliness and security. Given the surfeit of cheap hotels in the centre of Manaus, you may want to give them a miss. The hostels are *Albergue de Juventude Explorador* (☎ 234-6796) at Rua Silva Ramos 685; and *Albergue de Juventude CETUR* (☎ 233-1703) at Km 13, Rodovia Tarumã, Ponta Negra.

Hotels There's plenty of cheap lodging, ranging from grungy to decent, off Avenida Joaquim Nabuco, with some establishments charging as little as US$6 for double quartos.

The *Hotel Rio Branco* (☎ 233-4019) on Rua dos Andradas is a popular budget place with apartamentos (with fan) at US$6/10 for singles/doubles; and apartamentos with air-con at US$8/13 for singles/doubles. The breakfast is very poor. *Pensão Sulista* (☎ 234-5814) at Avenida Joaquim Nabuco 347, near the junction with Rua Quintino Bocaiúva, has clean quartos at US$5/8 for singles/doubles. Make sure your room has a fan and try to get a room without a tin roof as it gets hot. Breakfast is served after 7 am and there are clotheslines and washing tubs for your laundry.

Hotel Jangada (☎ 232-2248) on Rua dos Andradas offers dorm beds for US$4 and quartos for US$5/7 for singles/doubles. Breakfast is included in the price. *Hotel Bela Vista* at the junction of Rua dos Andradas and Avenida Joaquim Nabuco is in the same price range. Readers have warned that the *Hotel Paraíso* is notorious for theft and the use of double keys.

Hotel Dona Joana (☎ 233-7553), at Rua dos Andradas 553, is one of the best budget hotels. Apartamentos (with air-con) start around US$17 for singles/doubles, and the suite costs US$24. The rooms at the top have good views across the river.

Places to Stay – middle

There is a significant drop in quality between the top and middle-range hotels, many of which appear to cater to Brazilians making a flying visit to Manaus to shop like crazy for duty-free goods. Check your rooms for working air-con and showers before paying. The middle-range hotels in the centre are clustered along Rua Dr Moreira.

Hotel Nacional (☎ 233-7533) at Rua Dr Moreira 59 has barely decent apartamentos for US$25/33. *Hotel Rei Salomão* (☎ 232-8479) at Rua Dr Moreira 119 is a spiffy three-star hotel with apartamentos at US$39/48 for singles/doubles. *Hotel Aquarius* (☎ 232-5526) at Rua Dr Moreira 116 is another three-star hotel with similar prices to Hotel Rei Salomào. *Hotel Central* (☎ 622-2600) at Rua Dr Moreira 202 offers apartamentos at US$45/55 for singles/doubles. The *Ana Cassia Palace Hotel* (☎ 622-3637) at Rua dos Andradas 14 provides rather cranky service, but the apartamentos are passable at US$35/44 for singles/doubles. Discounts are available for cash payment.

Places to Stay – top end

For details about jungle tours and package tours based on upmarket jungle lodges, pousadas and safari camps, refer to the previous section called Jungle Tours – Big Operators.

The *Tropical Hotel* (☎ 238-5757), Manaus' premier luxury hotel, is a self-contained resort 16 km out of Manaus at Ponta Negra. Rooms start around US$135/150 for singles/doubles, and suites are available for a mere US$333. The hotel belongs to Varig's chain of Tropical hotels and Varig passengers travelling as a couple are given a double room for the cost of a single room less 25%. A discount is also given if you arrive without a reservation and pay cash.

Even if you don't stay here, you may want to visit this huge complex, which has a well-arranged mini-zoo (watch out for the bats at dusk – one of the authors was hit smack on the forehead!); a superb giant pool with waves, sloping beach, palm trees, and even Vitória Regia lilies; coffee shop; and a staff of 1000 to keep guests happy. The bookshop sells an attractive mini-guide to the fauna and flora in the mini-zoo.

The hotel also provides a shuttle service (US$2.50) to and from the centre of Manaus. Buses leave every couple of hours between 8.30 am and 7 pm. Pick up a timetable at the reception desk. The requisite bus stop in the centre of Manaus is on Rua Dr Moreira.

Hotel Amazonas, (☎ 232-2957, 234-7979), a four-star hotel on Praça Adalberto Valle, has singles/doubles starting at US$70/90. Readers have complained about poor soundproofing. *Hotel Lord* (☎ 622-2844) offers standard apartamentos at US$45/53 for singles/doubles and luxury versions at US$79/85. The bar of this hotel used to be a popular watering hole where the wealthier adventurer types congregated to exchange old campaign stories.

Places to Eat

Before taking a long riverboat ride or foray into the jungle, splurge on a few good meals in Manaus. The local fish specialties are tucunaré, tambaqui and pirarucu served grilled (a la brasa), pickled (escabeche) or stewed (caldeirada).

There are two good seafood restaurants a bit out of the way in the Adrianópolis neighbourhood: *Chapéu de Palha* (☎ 234-2133) at Rua Fortaleza 619 enjoys the best reputation, but excellent fish dishes can also be found at *Restaurante Panorama* (☎ 232-3177), Rua Recife 900.

For surprisingly good pizza and pasta dishes, try *Restaurante Fiorentina* (☎ 232-1295) at Praça Roosevelt 44. Vegetarians should head for *Chapaty Restaurante Vegetariano*, near the Opera House, at Rua Costa Azevedo 105. It's open from 11 am to 2.30 pm, from Sunday to Friday. *Churrasqueira Búfalo* at Avenida Joaquim Nabuco 628 is a decidedly non-vegetarian place serving massive steaks. *Mandarim*, at Avenida Eduardo Ribeiro 650, serves inexpensive

Chinese food. *Sabor da Amazônia*, at the intersection of Rua Marechal Deodoro and Rua Quintino Bocaiúva, specialises in regional cuisine and exotic ice cream. *Galo Carijó*, opposite Hotel Dona Joana on Rua dos Andradas, is recommended for local fish and favoured by locals who drop in for 'uma cerveja estupidamente gelada' (an idiotically cold beer).

Adventurous palates will venture to the street stalls and sample *tacacá*, a gummy soup made from lethal-if-not-well-boiled manioc root, lip-numbing jambu leaves and relatively innocuous dried shrimp.

For dessert there's always strange fruit to taste, including pupunha, bacaba and buriti. *Pinguinzinho*, Avenida Eduardo Ribeiro 523, is a popular ice-cream parlour.

Finally, one disgruntled reader wrote: 'Manaus is a pit – the restaurant at Hotel Amazonas is a bigger pit. I'm still not sure if I got the fish I ordered or some genuine Brazilian latex!'

Entertainment

Praça do Congresso, at the inland end of Avenida Eduardo Ribeiro, is the centre of Manaus' nightlife. Bars and restaurants lie along Avenida Eduardo Ribeiro, Avenida Sete de Setembro and Avenida Getúlio Vargas. Papagaio at Ponta Negra has live music and folkloric shows for tourists. Bar Consciente on Avenida Joaquim Nabuco is a good place to listen to music in a quiet setting. Bar do Armando, opposite the Opera House, is a traditional rendezvous – open from noon to midnight. São Marcos on Rua Floriano Peixoto is another traditional bar, recommended for the best chopp and fishballs in town.

The dancing establishments are clustered in the Cachoeirinha district, north-east of the centre. Nostalgia (☎ 233-9460) at Avenida Ajuricaba 800 is a hotspot for forró.

Things to Buy

Indian crafts are sold at the Museu do Indio, where FUNAI has a shop selling articles produced by the Wai-wai and Tikuna tribes. The store is open Monday to Friday, 8 am to noon and 2 to 6 pm; and from 8 am to noon on Saturday. Casa do Beija-Flor, at Rua Quintino Bocaiúva 224, sells a variety of Amazon arts and handicrafts. Casa das Redes, a couple of blocks inland from the Mercado Municipal in front of the Hotel Amazonas, has a good selection of hammocks at reasonable prices.

Manaus is a free trade zone. This means that locally manufactured products with foreign labels – particularly electronic goods – are available for less than elsewhere in Brazil. This doesn't mean all that much in the way of savings to foreigners, but as a result, everyone entering or leaving the city must theoretically go through customs. People entering by bus from the south pass through customs at the Careiro ferry landing. Customs is no problem with smaller riverboats, which are far less likely to attract the attention of customs officials. Travellers arriving via Manaus airport are supposed to declare foreign goods (eg cameras) to avoid a tariff upon departure, but nobody seems to worry about this rule anymore.

Foreigners can purchase as much as US$1200 worth of tariff-free goods. However, it's worth pointing out that this exceeds the value of goods which may be imported tax free into the USA and elsewhere. The Zona Franca commercial district is bounded by Avenida Eduardo Ribeiro, Avenida Sete de Setembro and Avenida Floriano Peixoto.

Getting There & Away

Air The Aeroporto Internacional Eduardo Gomes (☎ 621-1431) is on Avenida Santos Dumont, 14 km from the city centre. A reader wrote that 'if you want to save some money the observation deck at the airport is a great place to lay out a sleeping bag and spend the night before an early morning flight'.

From Manaus, it's five hours to Miami on Lloyd Aereo Boliviano (LAB) or Varig/Cruzeiro and four hours to Rio de Janeiro. There are international flights to: Caracas, Venezuela; Iquitos, Peru; Bogotá, Colombia; and La Paz, Bolivia. US-bound flights from Manaus are in flux. In general it's cheaper to purchase the ticket abroad and have it sent to Brazil by registered mail.

VASP, Transbrasil, and Varig/Cruzeiro serve all major cities in Brazil, and air taxis and TABA fly to smaller Amazonian settlements.

Varig/Cruzeiro (☎ 234-1116) is at Rua Marcílio Dias, 284; Lloyd Aereo Boliviano (☎ 232-7428) is at Avenida Getúlio Vargas, 759; TABA (☎ 232-0224) is at Avenida Eduardo Ribeiro 664; VASP (☎ 234-1266) is at Rua Guilherme Moreira 179; and nearby is Transbrasil (☎ 233-2288) at Rua Guilherme Moreira 150.

Air France (☎ 234-0794) is at Rua Marechal Deodoro, 63-Altos; British Airways (☎ 234-6209) is at Rua Barroso, 307; Japan Airlines (JAL) (☎ 234-4077) is at Avenida Eduardo Ribeiro, 520, 4 Andar, sala 403; and Delta Airlines (☎ 234-5915) is at Avenida Joaquim Nabuco, 2338.

Bus The rodoviária (☎ 236-2732) is six km from the town centre, at the junction of Rua Recife and Avenida Constantino Nery. Phone for information on road conditions. All roads from Manaus involve ferry transport.

In the dry season (July to December south of the equator) it's sometimes possible to travel overland from Manaus southwards to Porto Velho on BR-319 (two daily Andorinho buses, 22 hours and 990 km). In the rainy season, river travel along the Rio Madeira takes up the slack. In 1991, the road had become impassable and all bus services had been suspended.

The 770-km road from Manaus north to Boa Vista (BR-174) has more unpaved sections, but is usually passable. It lies on either side of the equator which means that travellers must contend with two rainy seasons. In addition, 100 km of this unpaved road cuts through the tribal lands of the Waimiris. Despite the FUNAI posts there have been Indian attacks on this route.

The daily Andorinho bus to Boa Vista takes about 15 hours, but delays are common and the trip can take a lot longer. The ticket costs US$38.

There are also bus services to Manacapuru, 85 km south-west of Manaus, and Itacoatiara, 290 km east of Manaus.

Boat Three major ports in Manaus function according to high and low water levels. Bairro Educandos is the port for sailings to Porto Velho. For sailings on the Rio Negro as far as Caracaraí, the requisite high-water port is Ponte de São Raimundo or, during low water, Bairro de São Raimundo, about 2½ km away. The Porto Flutuante serves mainstream Amazon destinations – Belém, Santarém, Tefé and Benjamin Constant – and is the port used by ENASA.

For information, you should visit Voz Praiana, at Rua Barão de São Domingos 30, just behind the Mercado Municipal. This is a radio station which broadcasts complete details of sailings and you should ask to see its up-to-date lists. The ENASA ticket office (☎ 234-3478) is at Rua Marechal Deodoro 61. Another place to get information about sailing times, fares, distances and ports of call is the Superintendência Nacional de Marinha Mercante (SUNAMAM) (Merchant Marine Headquarters), on the 10th floor of the Edifício Manaus on Avenida Eduardo Ribeiro.

A more time-consuming method to locate a boat is to go to Escadaria dos Remédios, the docks by the Mercado Municipal, and poke around. Don't waste time with the Capitânia do Porto.

Ports of call are marked on the boats and fares are pretty much standardised according to distance. The boats usually pull out at 6 pm regardless of the destination. Remember the waters drop roughly 10 to 14 metres during the dry season and this restricts river traffic, particularly in the upper Amazon tributaries.

Although food and drink are included in the fare, it's a good idea to bring bottled water and snacks as a supplement. Unless you have cabin space, you will need a hammock, as well as rope to string it up. It can get windy and cool at night so a sleeping bag is also recommended. Spend a bit more money and hang your hammock in the cooler upper deck, preferably towards the bow.

Beware of theft on boats – a very common complaint. For more advice, see the security section under Dangers & Annoyances in the Facts for the Visitor chapter.

To/From Santarém & Belém Going downriver, the big boats go in the faster central currents several kms from shore. Upriver they stay more in the slow currents by the riverbanks, but not as close as the smaller boats which hug the shore. You won't miss much, as there's not much to be seen on the Amazon anyway. If seeing wildlife is a priority, this is not the way to go.

ENASA ferry-catamarans take two days to Santarém , and four days downstream to Belém. Cabin accommodation for the five-day tourist cruise from Manaus to Belém starts at US$250 per person. For details about regular ENASA services and other companies operating to Santarém and Belém, see the Getting There & Away sections for the respective cities.

To/From Benjamin Constant & Tabatinga
From Manaus it's a seven-day trip to Tabatinga on the *Almirante Monteiro*, if all goes well. On the *Avelino Leal* and *Cidade de Terezina* it's at least a week's journey to Tabatinga, with stops at Fonte Boa, Foz do Jutaí, Vila Nova, Santo Antônio do Içá, Amaturé, São Paulo de Olivença and Benjamin Constant. Average prices for passage are US$110/65 for cabin/hammock accommodation.

To/From Leticia (Colombia) & Iquitos (Peru) Travellers can cruise the river between Manaus and Iquitos, Peru. The return or outgoing leg can be flown with Varig/Cruzeiro (four flights a week) between Iquitos and Manaus via Tefé and Tabatinga. From Tabatinga it's three more days and 280 km to Iquitos via Leticia. *Oro Negro* is a recommended boat for this trip.

For details about travelling to or from Peru on this route, see the overland section in the Getting There & Away chapter. Travellers

coming downriver from Peru and Colombia should remember to get their passports stamped in Manaus at the customs house beside the Porto Flutuante.

To/From Porto Velho Another long river trip can be taken from Manaus up the Rio Madeira to Porto Velho. The trip takes about a week and tickets cost US$55/40 for cabin/hammock accommodation. For more details, see the Getting There & Away section under Porto Velho.

To/From Caracaraí The *Rio Uaquiry* leaves every Friday from Manaus and arrives on Monday in Caracaraí. It leaves Caracaraí on Tuesday and arrives back in Manaus on Thursday. Passage costs US$50/30 for cabin/hammock accommodation. Food is included in the price, but it's of marginal quality – bring water and some extra snacks. The high-water port in Manaus for this boat is Ponte de São Raimundo, which is changed to Bairro de São Raimundo during low water. There's a bus service between Boa Vista and Caracaraí – the trip takes about four hours.

Getting Around
To/From the Airport Aeroporto Internacional Eduardo Gomes (☎ 621-1431) is 14 km from the city centre on Avenida Santos Dumont. The bus marked 'Aeroporto Internacional' runs between the local bus terminus and the airport from 6 am to midnight. The trip takes 40 minutes and costs 50c. There's a bilheteria system for taxis – from the airport to the centre costs US$15. When taking a taxi from the centre to the airport, taxistas may try to extract more money – see Dangers & Annoyances in the introduction to Manaus.

Bus The local bus terminus is on Praça da Matriz – near the cathedral and a few blocks from the Hotel Amazonas. Beware of the child pickpockets here. From this terminus you can catch buses to Ponta Negra and the sights in town (details provided under the individual sights). A more expensive but quicker option to reach Ponta Negra is the

River town on the Amazon

Tropical Hotel shuttle bus (details provided in Places to Stay under Tropical Hotel).

To/From the Rodoviária The rodoviária (☎ 236-2732) is six km from the centre of town. Buses marked 'Ileia', 'Santos Dumont', or 'Aeroporto Internacional' run from the centre via the rodoviária. A taxi to the centre costs around US$7.

MANACAPURU

It's possible to get an idea of the poverty of life in the interior without resorting to days of river travel. Manacapuru, 85 km southwest of Manaus and the Rio Negro, is a river town on the Rio Solimões. The river port and its traffic, the market, the homes and the people of Manacapuru all make for an interesting day trip.

I went to Manacapuru to visit my friend, a 33-year old man who works in Manaus and on the rivers. Manacapuru's residential area is a collection of corrugated tin roof shacks. His home is a three room, eight by 24 foot building elevated less than two feet off the ground by stilts. 'It's ugly, but it's my house.' The house is tiny and spare, but tidy, and the floors are rough wood planks. Folded hammocks and tinted black and white prints of the matriarch, father and favourite daughter (now living in Porto Velho) adorn the walls.

My friend's extended family lives here: his wife (married since age 15), his mother, two of his six children, his brother, sister-in-law and their child (all three suffering with measles). The entire family is illiterate. There is no running water. Foot-wide canals are simply dug into the earth as an open sewerage system – not surprisingly, the water supply is contaminated. The poor sanitation is a direct cause of the high mortality rate from infectious diseases – of my friend's 14 brothers and sisters, only four have survived to adulthood.

Places to Stay

There are hotels in town in case you miss the boat or the last bus back to Cacau Pirera. The *Hotel Coqueiro* (☎ 261-1505) is at Avenida Eduardo Ribeiro 725.

Getting There & Away

It's possible to take the ferry from São Raimundo to Cacau Pirera (30 minutes) then the bus to Manacapuru (2½ hours). Although there are daily boats to Manaus from Manacapuru, six hours down the Rio Solimões, only the Thursday and Sunday boats run at reasonable hours.

Take the São Raimundo bus from the cathedral in Manaus to the ferry terminal of São Raimundo. There are nine ferries a day in each direction from 5 am to 11 pm; passage is free. Ferry schedules coincide with buses between Cacau Pirera and Manacapuru.

MAUÉS

In November, the Festa do Guaraná is celebrated in the town of Maués (about 220 km east of Manaus), the largest cultivator of *guaraná*.

The first people to cultivate guaraná were the Saterê-Maûé Indians of the Amazon. Originally the Saterê-Maûé lands encompassed the vast stretch of jungle between the Madeira and Tapajós rivers. Today the Maûé live in a small tribal reservation. They believe that their place of origin, Noçoquem, is on the left bank of the Tapajós where the rocks talk, and their creation myth links them to guaraná.

TEFÉ

The port of Tefé is about 600 km upstream from Manaus on the Rio Solimões (the Brazilian name for this stretch of the Amazon) and can be visited for jungle tours.

Joaquim de Jesus Lopes is a 63-year-old local who can tailor trips for the requirements of biologists, ornithologists, botanists, and curious travellers. Trips can last a minimum of three days, but Joaquim Lopes prefers to take full-week tours, and is prepared to do longer tours if advance notice is given. Only Portuguese is spoken and travellers either take along their own tent and hammock or use jungle shelters. Tour costs include fuel, food, boat hire, and guiding fee. Discuss the price of each tour component individually. Expect to pay at least US$35 per day for a group of three people. Contact Joaquim Lopes at his home at Rua Marechal Deodoro 801.

Places to Stay
Hotel Anilceis is preferable to *Hotel Cassandra* which is cheaper, but less secure.

Getting There & Away
Varig/Cruzeiro serves Tefé from Manaus and has an office in Tefé (☎ 743-2466) at Rua Duque de Caxias, 25. The daily boat from the Porto Flutuante in Manaus leaves at 6 pm and arrives in Tefé about 36 hours later.

TABATINGA & BENJAMIN CONSTANT

These two Brazilian ports are on the border between Brazil, Colombia and Peru, known as the Triple Frontier. Neither are particularly attractive and most travellers view them as transit points. If you have to wait a few days for a boat, the Colombian border town of Leticia is a much more salubrious place to hang out.

Getting There & Away
Air From Tabatinga there are four flights weekly to Manaus (US$90) and two flights weekly to Iquitos (US$75). Apart from these commercial passenger flights there are cargo planes operating irregularly from Tabatinga

The Origin of Guaraná

Long ago at Noçoquem, in the beginning of all things, lived two brothers and a sister, Ohiamuaçabe. Ohiamuaçabe, also known as Uniai, was so beautiful and wise that all the animals desired her. Of all the animals, the snake was the first to express his desire and act upon it. With a magic perfume the snake enchanted Uniai and made her pregnant.

Her brothers were none too pleased and kicked her out of Noçoquem. The child was born far from Noçoquem, but Uniai often told her son about Noçoquem and the brazil-nut tree which grew there. Although the brothers had a parakeet and a macaw on guard before the brazil-nut tree, the child insisted on tasting the delicious nuts, for as he grew stronger and more beautiful, his desire to taste the fruit also grew. Finally he convinced his mother to accompany him to the tree.

The birds had spotted the ashes of a fire in which mother and child roasted the delicious brazil nuts. After the birds reported the incident, the brothers replaced the inept guard-birds with a reliable monkey guard. Now that the boy knew the path to Noçoquem, he returned to the tree alone the following day. The monkey spied the boy, drew his bow and shot the child full of arrows.

GUARANÁ DO AMAZONAS

SANITAS

50 CÁPSULAS

CADA CAPSULA CONTEM 0,5g DE GUARANÁ EM PÓ.

Uniai found her dead child beneath the tree. She buried him and vowed: 'You will be great; the most powerful tree will grow from you; you will cure sickness, provide strength in war and in love.' From the boy's left eye grew the false guaraná *uaraná-hop*, then from his right eye grew the true guaraná *uaraná-cécé* This is why the berries of the guaraná look like eyes.

Days later a child was born from the guaraná tree and emerged from the earth. The child was Uniai's, and he was the first Maúé Indian.

To this day the Maúé call themselves sons of guaraná, and because of this plant, their favourite decorative colours are red and green. The ritual drink of the Sateré-Maúé Indians is çapo of guaraná which is prepared from the eye-like berries. The berries, collected before the fruit opens, are dried, washed in running water and cooked in earth ovens. Water is added and the guaraná is moulded into black sticks which are then dried in a smokehouse. The Maúé shave guaraná flakes from the black sticks, using either the raspy tongue of the pirarucu or a rough stone. The flakes are then mixed into water to make the çapo.

The Maúé drink çapo of guaraná on important occasions to affirm the life force, to cure all illness, to gird their strength in times of war and to gird their loins in times of peace.

Most Brazilians take their guaraná in the form of a tasty sweetened and carbonated soft drink. Coca-Cola bottles one of the most popular brands of guaraná soda, Taí Guarana. Like Coke, guaraná is a mild stimulant, although unlike Coke guaraná is said to have aphrodisiac powers. Brazilians take guaraná to keep themselves up for Carnival. Pharmacies and herbal medicine shops also sell guaraná in the form of syrups, capsules and powders. ∎

to Manaus, and military planes from Ramón Castilla (Peru) to Iquitos.

Boat Boats down the Amazon to Manaus leave from Benjamin Constant. There are regular boats departing (theoretically) on Wednesday and Saturday nights, taking four days and costing US$35 in your own hammock or US$40 in a cabin. Many other irregular cargo boats take passengers on deck, and some have cabins. Prices and journey times are similar. In the opposite direction, upstream from Manaus to Benjamin Constant, the trip takes between six and 10 days. Food is included but is of poor quality.

There are frequent colectivos between the Leticia and Tabatinga ports (40c), otherwise it's a 20-minute walk. In Tabatinga you must get an entry stamp in your passport from Brazilian officials who like prospective foreign visitors to dress neatly. There is a ferry service with two boats daily between Tabatinga and Benjamin Constant (US$2; 1½ hours).

Upstream to Iquitos (Peru) there are irregular boats which leave from Ramón Castilla (Peru), across the river from Tabatinga, and Islandia (Peru), on an island opposite Benjamin Constant. The journey takes about three days and costs about US$35, food included. Travelling in the opposite direction, downstream from Iquitos to Ramón Castilla, the trip takes around 36 hours. You can obtain your entry stamp from Peruvian officials in Puerto Alegría. For information on Islandia, see the requisite section later in this chapter.

LETICIA (COLOMBIA)

Leticia, on the Amazon River where the borders of Colombia, Brazil and Peru meet, is the most popular place in Colombian Amazonia. This is due principally to its developed tourist facilities and its good flight connections with the rest of the country. Leticia has become the leading tourist centre for Colombians thirsty to see primitive tribes and buy their handicrafts, and to get a taste of the real jungle. The influx has broken the natural balance and today the Indians work hard on their crafts to keep up with tourist demand. This has also caused prices to rise, so food, accommodation and especially the tours offered by local people and travel agents, are quite expensive.

For travellers, Leticia is interesting because it is linked via the Amazon to Manaus and Iquitos, and therefore offers reasonably easy travel between Brazil, Colombia and Peru. The best time to visit the region is in July or August which are the only relatively dry months.

Information
Tourist Office The Corporación Nacional de Turismo (CNT) office is at Calle 10 No 9-86.

Money The Banco de la República is at the corner of Calle 10 and Carrera 10. It changes only hard-currency cash and travellers' cheques for pesos. There are several casas de cambio near the corner of Calle 8 and Carrera 11 which convert to or from US dollars, pesos, cruzeiros and soles. If you want to change cash dollars for pesos, try the casas de cambio first as they pay slightly more than the bank. There are also several casas de cambio in Tabatinga, Brazil, with similar exchange rates.

Immigration The DAS (security police) office on Calle 9 is open daily from 8 am to 6 pm. This is where you get your passport stamped when leaving or entering Colombia.

Foreign Consulates The Brazilian Consulate is on Calle 9 next to the DAS office; the Peruvian Consulate is on Carrera 11 next to the Hotel Anaconda.

Things to See
Leticia has become a tourist town not for what the town itself offers, but for the surrounding region. However, as all transport is by river and there are no regular passenger boats, it's difficult to get around cheaply on your own. All trips are monopolised by tourist agents and locals with their own boats, and are dreadfully expensive.

The cheapest one-day tour offered by agents will cost you around US$40. It works out cheaper to contract a local, but you must bargain ferociously as the starting price is usually astronomical. Whatever you do, make sure you clearly delineate the conditions of the trip, the places to be visited and the price.

A reader has recommended Antonio Cruz Perez (☎ 9819-27121), at Calle 8, No 9-22A – near Hotel La Manigua. Antonio Perez is a guide who is knowledgeable about the Indian way of life but does not want commercialisation to destroy it.

Two major travel agencies are Turamazonas, in Parador Ticuna, and Amaturs, in Hotel Anaconda. Independent sharks are waiting on the riverfront.

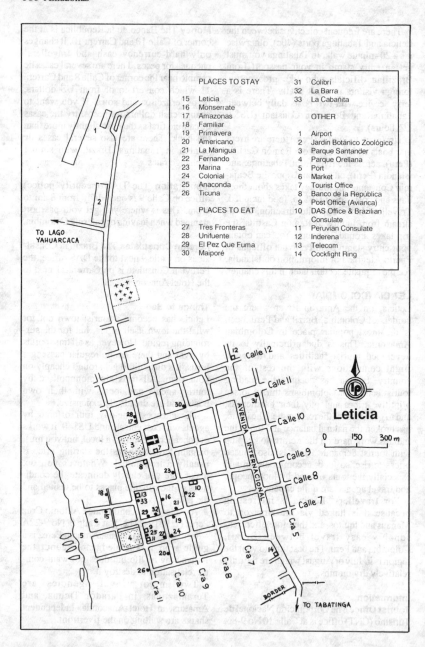

PLACES TO STAY

15 Leticia
16 Monserrate
17 Amazonas
18 Familiar
19 Primavera
20 Americano
21 La Manigua
22 Fernando
23 Marina
24 Colonial
25 Anaconda
26 Ticuna

PLACES TO EAT

27 Tres Fronteras
28 Unifuente
29 El Pez Que Fuma
30 Maiporé

31 Colibrí
32 La Barra
33 La Cabañita

OTHER

1 Airport
2 Jardín Botánico Zoológico
3 Parque Santander
4 Parque Orellana
5 Port
6 Market
7 Tourist Office
8 Banco de la República
9 Post Office (Avianca)
10 DAS Office & Brazilian Consulate
11 Peruvian Consulate
12 Inderena
13 Telecom
14 Cockfight Ring

TO LAGO YAHUARCACA

Leticia

0   150   300 m

Calle 12
Calle 11
Calle 10
Calle 9
Calle 8
Calle 7

AVENIDA INTERNACIONAL

Cra 5
Cra 7
Cra 8
Cra 9
Cra 10

BORDER

TO TABATINGA

Among the places to visit, Monkey Island, some 40 km up the Amazon from Leticia, is the number one spot for the tour business. There are over 10,000 small, yellow-footed monkeys living on the island. A footpath has been made through a part of the island where you can see the lush jungle vegetation.

The Parque Nacional Amacayacu is a nature reserve which takes in a large area of jungle to the north of Puerto Nariño. A spacious visitors' centre with food and accommodation facilities has been built beside the Amazon. From the centre you can explore the park, but most places are accessible by water only.

The main Indian tribes living in the region are the Ticunas and Yaguas. The major settlement of the Ticunas is Arara, but the village is on the route taken by almost every tour, and has become something of a theatre with Indians as the actors. The Yaguas are more primitive and ethnically different; they are noted for their *achiote*, a red paint used on the face.

Places to Stay

The best budget bet is the *Leticia*, a quiet, clean and friendly hotel in the market area. Singles/doubles with fan cost US$2.50/4. At the same price, but poorer value and without fans, is the *Monserrate* on Carrera 10 between Calles 8 and 9. It has its own cheap restaurant. Also worth consideration is the *Primavera* on Calle 8, half a block from the Monserrate. It is not bad, with singles/ doubles with fans and bath costing US$3.50/5, but its bar with music at full volume can be quite irritating. Just across the street, Hotel La Manigua has slightly better rooms and slightly higher prices.

For something flashier, check the *Fernando* or the *Marina*, both near the DAS office.

Places to Eat

The food is not bad in Leticia, though it is fairly expensive. Obviously, the local speciality is fish; don't miss the delicious *gamitana*. Also try *copoasú* juice, known to Brazilians as *cupuaçu*, which is a local fruit

somewhat similar in taste to *guanábana*. Fizzy drinks and beer are expensive.

Tres Fronteras, on the corner of Calle 7 and Carrera 10, is one of the best for cheap eats. It has good food and service and a long menu with dishes for less than US$2.50. *Maiporé*, on Calle 11, two blocks from the Parque Santander, serves good set meals. The gamitana is excellent and portions are huge. *La Barra*, on the corner of Calle 8 and Carrera 10, and *La Cabañita*, on the corner of Carrera 11 and Calle 9, are two good places for fruit juices.

Getting There & Away

Air Air Avianca has four flights weekly to Bogotá, US$70. Aerosucre runs several cargo flights a week to Bogotá and it sometimes takes passengers for about US$40. Enquire at the airport.

There are no international flights from Leticia, but from Tabatinga, just across the border in Brazil, you can fly to Manaus or Iquitos – see the Getting There & Away section for Tabatinga.

Boat Boats down the Amazon to Manaus leave from Benjamin Constant – see the Getting There & Away section for Benjamin Constant. For connections between Leticia, Benjamin Constant and Tabatinga, see the Getting There & Away section for Benjamin Constant and Tabatinga.

Irregular cargo boats to Puerto Asís (Colombia), on the upper reaches of the Rio Putumayo, can take up to 20 days, and the price varies substantially – from US$60 to US$120, food usually included. From Puerto Asís you can continue on by road to Pasto or head to Ecuador via San Miguel. It's much better to do this route in reverse, ie downstream, as it is faster and cheaper.

ISLANDIA (PERU)

Islandia is a grubby Peruvian river village on an island opposite Benjamin Constant. There's no accommodation available at Islandia, so boat passengers arriving from Iquitos must travel by motorised canoe ferry to Benjamin Constant, where they can find a hotel and/or arrange river transport to Manaus. The downstream trip from Iquitos to Islandia takes about 36 hours and costs around US$35 if you bargain. If you intend to exit Peru here, you'll either have to pick up a stamp at immigration in Iquitos or arrange with the boat captain to stop at Puerto Alegría, the riverside guard post in the border area. Entering Brazil, visit the Polícia Federal in either Benjamin Constant or Tabatinga.

In Iquitos, there's a Brazilian Consulate at Calle Morona 283 and a Colombian Consulate at Calle Malecón Tarapaca 260.

Roraima

The rugged, remote and beautiful mountain region straddling the Venezuelan border to the north of Roraima is perhaps the ultimate Amazon frontier. This rugged land is home to the Yanomami, who represent about one-third of the remaining tribal Indians of the Amazon. Because the Indian lands are sitting on huge deposits of iron, cassiterite and gold, the Yanomami are threatened by the building of roads and encroachment from garimpeiros and others seeking to expropriate these lands. Although the Brazilian government has declared the area a special Indian reserve, this declaration will be worthless unless the government is prepared to enforce it and eject trespassers on Yanomami lands.

For a description of the Yanomami, see the section on Indians under Population & People in the Facts about the Country chapter.

Roraima state is one hour behind Brazilian standard time.

BOA VISTA

Boa Vista, the capital of Roraima, is a planned city on the banks of the Rio Branco. Although the city is growing at a bounding pace there is much poverty. Most travellers consider this city 'the ultimate bore' or 'one of the armpits of the universe', bereft of any interest, and nothing more than a transit point between Brazil and Venezuela. However, there appear to be some intriguing sights in the vicinity of Boa Vista.

Orientation

The city is shaped like an archway with the base of the arch on the Rio Branco and the arch itself formed by Avenida Major Williams and Avenida Terencio Lima. Avenues radiate from the top dividing the outskirts into wedges. The city planners were clearly a race of giants: the scale of the place is totally unsuited to pedestrians who could quite easily spend a whole day trying to do a couple of errands on foot.

The government buildings are located dead centre at the intersection of Avenida Ville Roy and Avenida Capitan Ene Garcez, while the commercial district runs from the centre of town along Avenida Jaime Brasil to Avenida Floriano Peixoto, on the waterfront.

Information

Tourist Office There's an information booth at the rodoviária, with efficient staff who can supply you with a map and help with booking accommodation. The booth is open from 8 am to 5.30 pm, Monday to Friday. There's a similar booth at the airport which opens erratically, usually for major flight arrivals only.

The Secretaria Municipal de Obras, Coordenadoria de Turismo (☎ 224-9977), the municipal tourism administration, is on Rua Prof Angelo Bittencourt, in the Edifício Boa Vista (behind the Parque de Exposição de Agropecuária). It's a very long hike northeast of the centre.

Money Banco do Brasil is in the centre, close to Praça do Centro Cívico. A useful money changer, with longer opening hours than the bank, is Casa de Câmbio Pedro José (☎ 224-4277) on Rua Araújo Filho. It's open from 8 am to 6 pm, Monday to Friday.

Post The post office is on the north side of the Praça do Centro Cívico.

Venezuelan Consulate The Venezuelan

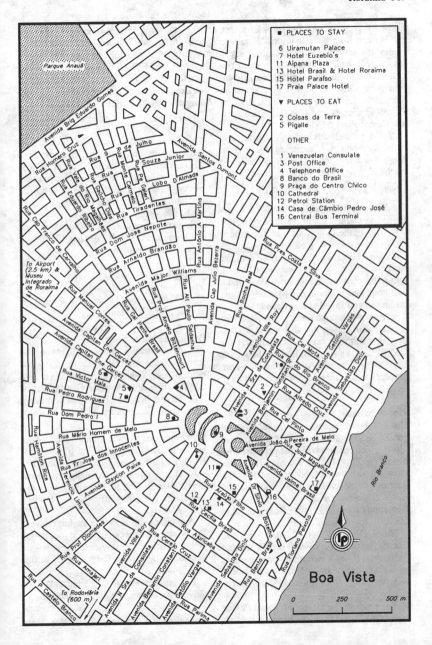

PLACES TO STAY
6 Uiramutan Palace
7 Hotel Euzebio's
11 Aipana Plaza
13 Hotel Brasil & Hotel Roraima
15 Hotel Paraíso
17 Praia Palace Hotel

PLACES TO EAT
2 Coisas da Terra
5 Pigalle

OTHER
1 Venezuelan Consulate
3 Post Office
4 Telephone Office
8 Banco do Brasil
9 Praça do Centro Cívico
10 Cathedral
12 Petrol Station
14 Casa de Câmbio Pedro José
16 Central Bus Terminal

Boa Vista

0   250   500 m

Consulate is on Avenida Benjamin Constant, and is open from 8 am to noon, Monday to Friday. If you arrive early in the morning you may be able to pick up your visa at noon. You will require one photo, a completed application form, and an outbound ticket from Venezuela. Current visa fees are US$10 for British applicants, and US$2 for US nationals. Cash dollars only!

You'd be well advised to get your visa beforehand and avoid the delay in Boa Vista. More visa details for Venezuela can be found in the section called Visas for Adjoining Countries, in the Facts for the Visitor chapter.

Travel Agency Acqua (☎ 224-6576) at Rua Floriano Peixoto 505, organises a variety of boat trips in the region, such as a four-hour excursion to Fazenda São Marcos (cattle ranch) and Forte São José (ruins of a colonial fort) for US$90; a four-hour Serra Grande tour to beaches and creeks for US$90; and a two-hour tour to Ponte dos Macuxí, Paraná do Surrão and Ilha da Praia Grande – inclusive of a walk through forest to an inland lake – for US$50. The agency also provides transport to campsites on the Rio Branco for US$30, and kayak rental (three hours for US$10 per person). All prices given here (except kayak rental) are for a group of up to five persons.

Places to Stay

Cheaper hotels include the *Hotel Paraíso* (☎ 224-9335) at Rua Araújo Filho 228, a real 'dive' which charges US$6 per person; *Hotel Brasil* (☎ 224-9421) at Avenida Benjamin Constant 331 – a rock-bottom cheapie with quartos at US$4/8 for singles/doubles; and *Hotel Roraima* (☎ 224-9843) at Avenida Benjamin Constant 351 which has quartos at US$6/10 for singles/doubles.

Hotel Euzebio's (☎ 224-0300) at Rua Cecília Brasil 1107, provides excellent value for money. It has a swimming pool, garden, and restaurant, and offers comfortable apartamentos for around US$16/25 for singles/doubles.

The upmarket hotels include *Praia Palace Hotel* (☎ 224-8111) at Rua Floriano Peixoto 352 with single/double rooms at US$37/51; the *Uiramutan Palace* (☎ 224-9912) at Avenida Capitan Ene Garcez 427 which charges US$49/55 for single/double rooms; and the *Aipana Plaza* (☎ 224-4500) at Praça do Centro Cívico, Joaquim Nabuco 53, with single/double rooms at US$51/68.

Places to Eat

There are lots of food stalls selling inexpensive food at the municipal bus terminal. *Coisas da Terra* on Avenida Benjamin Constant serves savoury snacks, quiche, pastries, cakes, and sucos. *Pigalle* on Avenida Capitan Ene Garcez does great pizza and hosts live music at weekends. Also worth trying are the various hotel restaurants such as those at Euzebio's, Aipana Plaza, and Uiramutan Palace.

Things to Buy

The Centro de Artesanato at Avenida Marechal Floriano, 158 and the shop at the airport both sell Indian crafts.

Getting There & Away

Air Varig/Cruzeiro operates flights to and from Manaus and Georgetown (Guyana) twice weekly. The Varig/Cruzeiro (☎ 224-2226) office is at Avenida Getúlio Vargas 242. Flights between Boa Vista and Santa Elena were discontinued in 1989.

Bus From Boa Vista to Manaus is a 15-hour bus ride (road conditions and trip time are erratic) with two ferry crossings along the way. There's one departure daily at 8 am and the ticket costs US$38. Hitching is very difficult as most of the traffic – gravel trucks – is only local.

Another option is to take the bus between Boa Vista and Caracaraí (US$5; four hours) where there's a boat service to Manaus – for details see the Getting There & Away section for Manaus.

For bus services to the Venezuelan and Guyanese borders, see the next section.

Crossing the Borders From Boa Vista,

there are overland routes to Venezuela and Guyana.

Venezuela If the weather cooperates, it's a beautiful six-hour ride between Boa Vista and Santa Elena (Venezuela). The bus departs daily at 8 am from the rodoviária in Boa Vista. Tickets (US$13) seem to sell out fast – buy yours the day before departure. For more details about the border crossing, see the Getting There & Away section under Santa Elena.

Guyana There's a bus from Boa Vista to Bonfim leaving Monday, Thursday and Friday at 4 pm. The 125-km trip takes four hours and costs US$8.50. Once in Bonfim, pick up your exit stamp from the Polícia Federal and slog the five km from there to the border at the Rio Tacutu. There, you can hire a canoe across to Lethem in Guyana. Although Lethem is linked to the rest of Guyana by air, there's no road access beyond the immediate vicinity. Beware that Guyanese officials worry about illegal immigration from Brazil and tend to scrutinise travellers fairly carefully here.

You may want to save yourself the trouble of a difficult overland passage by flying directly to Georgetown from Boa Vista.

Getting Around
Whoever planned Boa Vista on such a vast scale clearly didn't think about pedestrians – getting around on foot is a real slog.

The airport (☎ 224-3680) is four km from the city centre. Take a bus marked 'Aeroporto' from the municipal bus terminal. The taxi fare from the airport to the centre is about US$7.

The rodoviária (☎ 224-0606) is about three km from the centre – about 40 minutes on foot! Take a bus marked '13 de Setembro' from the municipal bus terminal and get off at the bus stop beside a supermarket which is opposite the rodoviária. A taxi from the centre to the rodoviária costs about US$5.

AROUND BOA VISTA
Mt Roraima (2875 metres) is one of Brazil's highest peaks and straddles the Brazilian/Venezuelan/Guyanese border. The easiest access for climbers is from the Venezuelan side – for more details see the section called Mt Roraima and the Gran Sábana, later in this chapter.

Lago Caracanã, a large lake 180 km from Boa Vista, is a popular weekend destination. A bus departs for the lake from the rodoviária in Boa Vista at 10 am on Saturday and returns at noon on Sunday. There's a campsite and a basic hotel at the lake.

The Estação Ecológica da Ilha de Maracá (an ecological reserve), 120 km from Boa Vista on the Rio Uraricoera, can only be visited with permission from IBAMA (☎ 224-4011) in Boa Vista.

SANTA ELENA (VENEZUELA)
Santa Elena is on the only land border crossing between Venezuela and Brazil.

Information
If you're heading for Brazil, pick up an exit stamp from the DIEX (immigration) office which is on a hill opposite the bus terminal at the northern edge of town. It's open Monday to Saturday from 9 am to 5 pm, and is closed on Sundays and holidays.

Money Money may be changed at the bus terminal, the supermarket/*tienda* (shop) opposite the Hotel Mac-King, and the Hotel Auyantepuy, but the rates are relatively poor. Travellers' cheques cannot be changed here.

Places to Stay
There is no shortage of places to stay and eat in Santa Elena. Expect to pay US$5 minimum for a standard room.

Getting There & Away
For details about crossing the border to Boa Vista in Brazil, see the next section.

Buses to San Francisco de Yuruaní depart at 9 am and 3 pm (US$1.50). See also Getting There & Away in the section on Mt Roraima & the Gran Sábana.

Crossing the Border A paved road runs through the Venezuelan towns of Ciudad Bolívar, Tumeremo and El Dorado to Santa Elena, then continues to Boa Vista, Brazil. Unfortunately, Santa Elena is no longer served by Aeropostal flights, so you'll have to rely on the buses which leave from the *terminal terrestre* in Ciudad Bolivar several times daily for around Venezuelan bolívares 550 (US$10). (Venezuelan currency in this section is abbreviated to B$.) Whether entering or leaving Venezuela at Santa Elena, you can count on numerous unpleasant encounters with police and border patrols. They have a well-deserved reputation for 'confiscating' travellers' belongings.

Most people arrive in Santa Elena in the evening, but if at all possible, try to arrive earlier if you hope to secure a hotel room. To avoid having to endure morning border mayhem, go for your exit stamp at DIEX the day before crossing.

When departing for Brazil, pick up your exit stamp from DIEX and board the bus for Boa Vista at the bus terminal opposite the immigration office. Be wary of fellow passengers and officials who board the bus. Theft is common, particularly during the periodic clumsy searches which punctuate the ride to the border.

Brazilians are strict about border control here, and carefully scrutinise travellers. If you've ever overstayed a Brazilian visa and found your way onto their records, you may want to try an alternative border crossing or simply fly in.

If the weather cooperates, it's a beautiful six-hour ride. The bus departs at 8 am from Santa Elena to Boa Vista, and the fare is B$750 (US$13) payable in bolívares or cruzeiros.

For details about the Venezuelan Consulate and obtaining Venezuelan visas in Boa Vista, refer to the Boa Vista section in this chapter.

MT RORAIMA & THE GRAN SÁBANA

From the Indian village of San Francisco de Yuruaní, 60 km north of Santa Elena, you can hire a guide to take you to the geographically spectacular and botanically unique area around Mt Roraima, which straddles the Brazilian/Venezuelan/Guyanese border.

From there, it's 22 km to Paray Tepui, a small Indian village and the entrance to the park. You may also hire a guide here. From Paray Tepui, the trail is easy to follow, although it quickly deteriorates after rain. There's the odd rattlesnake but no other large wildlife.

Although you must bring food from Santa Elena, good water may be found in streams every four or five km along the way. The trail passes one of the world's highest waterfalls. The top of Roraima is a moonscape; it would be very easy to get lost, so don't wander far. Consider spending an extra day on top of the mountain, but prepare for cool drizzle and fog.

The return trip from Santa Elena will take five days but some people allow up to two weeks in the area.

In San Francisco de Yuruaní, the starting point for climbs up Roraima, you can hire a guide for US$15-19 per day and for just a few dollars more, the guide will carry your gear. Guides are cheaper and easier to obtain in the Indian village of Paray Tepui. Hire a guide, because the dense cloud cover and strange landscape on top can get a person lost very quickly. Furthermore, guides know of two 'hotels' on the mountain, cliff overhangs under which you can camp and stay dry!

Jeeps to Paray Tepui charge a set rate of US$31 each way. If you choose not to hire a jeep, the hike between San Francisco and Paray Tepui is a full day. The best days for hitching between the two towns are on Sunday and Monday going to Paray Tepui, and on Friday returning to San Francisco, as the school teachers at Paray Tepui leave the town for the weekend. Mosquito repellent is absolutely essential.

Pack light but for wet weather. The trail runs under a waterfall when there is a lot of rain. If you want hot food on top, bring a stove, because there is absolutely no firewood there.

The trail from Paray Tepui runs over open savannah and crosses several small streams. You will cross one river which is about 10 metres wide and is called Quebrada de Piedras or Río de Atuc. The next large river is Cuquenan. It is 10 to 20 metres wide. Camp on the far side of Cuquenan. The next day, you can make it all the way to the 'hotel' on top of Roraima, or you can camp at the base just before the trail enters the jungle. On the return trip, try to make it as far as the Quebrada de Piedras on the first night. If it is raining on Cuquenan, the levels of the rivers can rise very rapidly. You should cross them as quickly as possible – you may even need a rope.

Greg & Kevin Merrell, USA

The Gran Sábana has been described as 'beautiful open rolling grassland with pockets of cool jungle, all eerily deserted and silent'. It's best to visit the area in the dry season from December to March, but even then you can still plan to be wet much of the time.

Getting There & Away

You can travel by bus from Santa Elena to San Francisco de Yuruaní (60 km) and hike for six to eight hours to Paray Tepui, or hire a jeep in Santa Elena (at least US$80). If you'd rather hitch, the best chances of finding a lift will be at the petrol station at the north end of Santa Elena.

Neotropic Cormorants

Rondônia & Acre

The states of Rondônia and Acre, previously undeveloped frontier regions, have undergone rapid development – mainly as a result of the construction of BR-364, which already runs from Cuiabá via Porto Velho to Rio Branco, and is projected to extend as far as Cruzeiro do Sul. The two states are of intense interest to environmentalists studying the effects of deforestation. Many travellers will only be passing through these states en route to or from Peru or Bolivia – probably all will be impressed by the massive deforestation which has left vast tracts of land looking like the aftermath of a holocaust.

Travellers should be aware that both these states, especially Rondônia, are major distribution centres for cocaine from neighbouring Peru and Bolivia. Travellers are generally left alone, providing they mind their own business.

Guajará-Mirim is an entry point for the 'Rota Formiguinha' (Ant Route) favoured by small-scale smugglers – hence the reference to ants – who arrive from Bolivia with the white stuff hidden in their baggage or concealed in false compartments in vehicles. Large-scale smugglers use *aviãozinhos* (light aircraft) to pick up the cocaine in Bolivia and then fly it to secret landing strips in Rondônia – for example, in the vicinity of Cacoal, Ji-Paraná, and Rolim Moura. From there, the goods are distributed to Rio, São Paulo and fazendas in Mato Grosso state.

Another of the so-called 'Transcoca' highways runs from San Joaquim in Bolivia to the Rio Guaporé, where the cocaine is ferried across to the Brazilian town of Costa Marques for distribution in Brazil.

Some of the cocaine is destined for domestic consumption, but most is exported to the USA and Europe. Recent reports indicate that drug kingpins in both Rondônia and Acre have moved into the processing business. Whilst the smugglers have literally hundreds of light aircraft at their disposal, a recent newspaper article claimed that Rondônia's 140 federal agents did not have the use of a single plane or radar tracking system, and that the agents had to use a payphone to call headquarters! It is an open secret that various politicians in Rondônia are involved in drug-running: in 1991, two brothers of a federal deputy from Rondônia were arrested in connection with a 554-kg cocaine bust in São Paulo.

Rondônia

In 1943, Getúlio Vargas created the Territory of Guaporé from chunks of Amazonas and Mato Grosso. In 1981, the Territory of Guaporé became the state of Rondônia, named in honour of Marechal Cândido Mariano da Silva Rondon, the soldier who tamed the region. A legendary figure, Rondon was honoured by the Indians he helped subdue. He linked Cuiabá, Porto Velho and Rio Branco by telegraph to the rest of Brazil.

In recent years, roads and a gold rush displaced the Nordestinos from the desert into the jungles and the few remaining Indians from the jungles into the cities. Rondônia's population consists of mostly poor but hopeful migrants from the Northeast.

Rondônia state is one hour behind Brazilian standard time.

National Parks & Biological Reserves
In Porto Velho, contact IBAMA (☎ 223-33607) at Avenida Jorge Teixeira 3477, Bairro C E Silva, for details about national parks and ecological reserves in Rondônia. This office is clearly overworked and restricted in its powers and facilities, but travellers with a genuine interest and the ability to travel rough may be helped with

introductions to park staff and details about access options. Only Portuguese is spoken.

Reserva Biológica do Guaporé The main attractions in this reserve are fauna and flora similar to those found in the Pantanal – hence the reserve's nickname 'Pantanal de Rondônia'. To reach the reserve, take a boat from Costa Marques to Pau d'Óleo (160 km; about six hours) where there is a government fazenda with accommodation (cabanas) and transport into the reserve. Prior to departure from Costa Marques, you should contact Senhor Amos (☎ 651-2239), who is in charge of the local IBAMA (Posto da Fiscalização) office, and ask for the latest information on access and facilities.

Reserva Biológica do Jaru At present there are two options to organise a trip to this reserve, which is in the north-east corner of Rondônia. The long-distance option is to contact Doutor Eurico (☎ 421-4164), the regional director of IBAMA in the town of Ji-Paraná, 376 km from Porto Velho. The closest access to the park is provided by a private guide, Ubalde Almeida (☎ 521-2827), who arranges tours from Cachoeira Nazaré, where he also offers accommodation (cabanas).

Parque Nacional de Pacáas Novas As yet, there is no tourist access or infrastructure available for this park. Those interested in a visit must contact the IBAMA (☎ 421-4164) office in Ji-Paraná and seek permission from either Doutor Eurico or Gilson Macedo. These officials may then be willing to arrange 4WD transport from Ouro Preto do Oeste along Linhea 81 into the park, where there is rough accommodation in camps.

Estação Biológica Cuniã Lago do Cuniã, a biological reserve 110 km north of Porto Velho on the Rio Madeira, contains the state's largest spawning area for fish and is renowned for its abundant birdlife. Access to this reserve is only possible by boat.

PORTO VELHO

Now capital of the young state of Rondônia, Porto Velho is rapidly losing its frontier ways. The streets are being paved, the Indians are nearly all dead and the forests are rapidly being felled. Nevertheless, 20th-century Porto Velho still has all the elements of the American Wild West – land-hungry cattle ranchers, fierce Indians, gold prospectors, deadly pistoleiros and desperadoes of all stripes.

The newspaper headlines tell the whole story: articles range from the gold strike to taxi cab lynch mobs and examples of rude frontier justice, border cocaine trafficking, Indian attacks against garimpeiros (prospectors), poaching, and conflicting land claims settled at gunpoint.

History

During the 17th and 18th centuries, Portuguese bandeirantes, hot in pursuit of gold and Indian slaves, crossed the lines drawn according to the Treaty of Tordesillas and entered what is now known as Rondônia to roam the Guaporé and Madeira river valleys. Since the Spanish were incapable of defending themselves from these incursions, the occupation was officially sanctioned in lofty Latin terms which meant that it was ignored. The Portuguese secured their new possessions by building the fortress of Principe da Beira (1783) at the confluence of the Mamoré and Guaporé rivers.

The Treaty of Tordesillas was kept more in the breach than the observance; the Portuguese continued to push west and occupy Bolivian lands. The Brazil-Bolivia Treaty of Friendship (1867) and the Treaty of Petrópolis (1901) addressed Bolivian grievances. The Bolivians ceded the region – known today as the state of Acre – in return for UK£2,000,000 and the construction of a railway along the upper reaches of the Rio Madeira to give landlocked Bolivia access to world rubber markets via the Amazon.

The Public Works Construction Company of London had started work on a railway in 1872, but abandoned the project after two

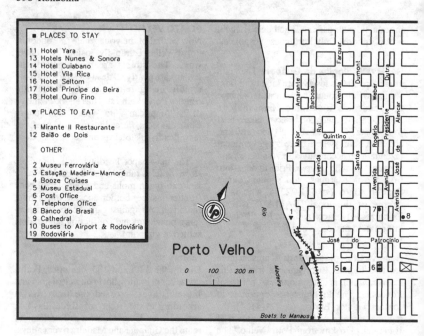

PLACES TO STAY

11 Hotel Yara
13 Hotels Nunes & Sonora
14 Hotel Cuiabano
15 Hotel Vila Rica
16 Hotel Seltom
17 Hotel Principe da Beira
18 Hotel Ouro Fino

▼ PLACES TO EAT

1 Mirante II Restaurante
12 Baião de Dois

OTHER

2 Museu Ferroviária
3 Estação Madeira—Mamoré
4 Booze Cruises
5 Museu Estadual
6 Post Office
7 Telephone Office
8 Banco do Brasil
9 Cathedral
10 Buses to Airport & Rodoviária
19 Rodoviária

Porto Velho

0   100   200 m

Boats to Manaus

years due to rampant disease and Indian attacks. These swampy jungle lands earned the unenviable reputation of being the most hostile in the world.

In 1907, the North American company Jeckyll & Randolph began work on the 364-km railway from the vicinity of Vila do Santo Antônio do Rio Madeira to the Bolivian border town of Riberalta on the Rio Mamoré. German, Jamaican and Cuban workers, and old Panama Canal hands, were brought in as labourers to do the job. The track was completed in 1912; however, this achievement claimed the lives of thousands of workers, who perished from malaria, yellow fever and gunfights.

Since the railway did not go as far as intended (above the rapids of Rio Mamoré at Riberalta) and the price of rubber had plummeted on the world market, it was effectively useless. However, the towns of Guajará-Mirim and Porto Velho were founded at either end of the completed railway, which

functioned sporadically until it was officially closed in 1972.

Today the road between Porto Velho and Guajará-Mirim uses the railway bridges, but the line itself is used only occasionally as a tourist novelty from the Porto Velho end. Marcio Souza chronicles the whole brutal story in his book *Mad Maria* (available in an English paperback edition by Avalon), which is mandatory reading for anyone interested in how a small parcel of the Green Hell was briefly conquered.

During WW II, when the Japanese occupation of Malaysia cut Allied rubber supplies, rubber production in the Amazon picked up briefly once again. In 1958, cassiterite (tin ore) was discovered. The mining of cassiterite and timber extraction now constitutes Rondônia's principal source of wealth, but other minerals – gold, iron, manganese and precious stones – are also found in the region.

In fact, Porto Velho is riding out the tail

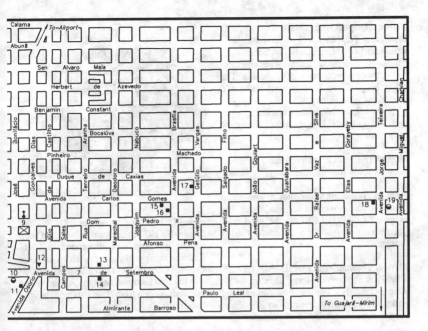

end of a gold rush: in the space of three blocks along Avenida 7 de Setembro you can find over 30 gold shops, all empty save for the old-fashioned powder scales in glass cases. The prospectors haven't seen much gold, but they're still working the old claims and dumping mercury in the river. The economy is completely extractive, and most food is 'imported' from São Paulo, half a continent away.

Orientation

Porto Velho sits on the right bank of the Rio Madeira, almost contiguous with the state of Amazonas. The Madeira, a 3240-km long tributary of the Amazon, is formed by the Mamoré and Abunã rivers.

Porto Velho's main street is Avenida 7 de Setembro, stretching almost two km from the riverfront docks and Madeira Mamoré train station to Avenida Jorge Teixeira.

If you take a walk along this main drag, you'll pass gun and munitions stores, gold

shops, mining supply houses and cheap hotels. The new capital is a little raw: electric wires slump and dangle over muddy dirt roads; scrawny dogs pick their way through garbage, roaming for scraps; and street vendors fry up potatoes and plantains for passers-by. *Compra-se ouro* signs indicate the gold shops where prospectors bring their gold powder to be weighed and sold. The powder is melted into bullion and smuggled out to avoid government taxes.

You won't fail to notice the appalling volume of distorted street 'music' which is brought to a crescendo by a cruising 'Noisemobile', complete with a battery of eight giant loudspeakers mounted on the roof. We'd willingly have foregone the advertised 30% discount at a local clothing shop if the infernal machine had only stopped broadcasting immediately!

Information

Tourist Offices There is a DETUR tourist

office (Departamento de Turismo de Rondônia; (☎ 223-2276) at Avenida Padre Chiquinho 670, Esplanada das Secretarias. The staff can help with details about access to the more remote parts of Rondônia. The office is open from 8 am to noon and 2 to 6 pm, Monday to Friday.

The tourist office in the Prefeitura, opposite the cathedral, is a poor source of information.

Money The main branch of Banco do Brasil is on Avenida José de Alencar.

Post & Telecommunications The main post office is on Avenida Rogério Weber. The main office of TELERON, the state telephone company, is on Avenida Carlos Gomes.

IBAMA The state office of IBAMA (☎ 223-33607) is at Avenida Jorge Teixeira 3477, Bairro C E Silva. For details about national parks and ecological reserves in Rondônia, see the separate section in this chapter.

Bookshop A reasonable selection of books is available at Livraria da Rose at Avenida Rogério Weber 1967. For a survey in Portuguese of the history of Rondônia, pick up a copy of *Kayan* by Emanuel Pinto.

Tour Agencies Baretur (☎ 221-6642), a tour agency at the train station docks, runs daily booze cruises between 2 and 11 pm (one hour; US$2.50, excluding drinks), and excursions to the Santo Antônio rapids.

Estação Madeira-Mamoré & Museu Ferroviário

The original terminal of the Madeira-Mamoré railway is Porto Velho's main tourist attraction. For details about the history of this railway, see the History section for Porto Velho. The terminal is currently drifting into extreme dilapidation.

A museum housed in a huge train shed displays train relics, memorabilia and photographs of the construction of the railway and history of the Madeira-Mamoré line. Com-

Old Steam Locomotive, Museu Ferroviário

pleted in 1912, the railway quickly fell into disuse. By 1931 the private railway had been nationalised and was abandoned in 1966. Railway buffs will also get a kick out of the Colonel Church. Built in 1872, this dinosaur was the first locomotive in the Amazon. The museum is open from 8 am to 6 pm, Tuesday to Sunday.

Train Trips In 1981, in tribute to its historical origins, the new state government reinstated 28 km of the famous Madeira to Mamoré railway. Depending on funds and government permission – both were being withheld in 1991 – sporadic train trips are arranged using the Maria Fumaça steam locomotive to chug to and from Santo Antônio (seven km from Porto Velho). A return ticket for this excursion costs US$1.50.

It may be possible to arrange for a special trip to be laid on, providing you have assembled a group of at least 15 passengers and can give at least one day's advance notice. For more information, contact the staff at the railway terminal. The railway is closed during the rainy season for maintenance and repairs.

Museu Estadual

The State Museum, at the intersection of Avenida 7 de Setembro and Avenida Farquar, houses modest displays of the state's archaeology, mineralogy, ethnology and natural history collection. The museum is open Monday to Friday, from 8 am to 6 pm.

River Beaches

There are several river beaches near town: ask the tourist office for directions to Areia Branca (three km), and Candeias (20 km off BR-364; take the Linha Novo Brasil bus). The fishing village of Belmont, 20 km from Porto Velho, is a calm place to swim or fish.

Rubber Trees

If you are interested in seeing rubber trees, but aren't inclined to launch an expedition into the wilderness to do so, visit the Parque Circuito on Avenida Lauro Sodré, four km from town on the way to the airport.

Jungle Lodge Tours

Tapiri Selva Hotel (☎ 221-4785 for reservations) is a jungle lodge complex with wooden huts in the midst of forest, close to Lago de Cujubim, which is 70 km from Porto Velho. Access to the lodge is provided by boat from the docks. On Friday, Saturday and Sunday, boats depart from Porto Velho at 8 am and return at 5 pm. A day trip costs US$22 per person. If you want to stay one or more nights, the price is around US$44 per person per night (transport included).

Festivals

Indian legends and traditions were corrupted by Jesuit missionaries to the extent that Indians circulated stories of the Virgin Mary visiting the Amazon. However, theatrical interpretations of authentic Amerindian legends, ritual dances and ceremonies are becoming popular in Porto Velho among students. *A Jara*, *O Mapinguari* and *O Boto* are recent productions of the amateur theatre groups. Call the Teatro Municipal Secretaria do Cultura (☎ 223-3836, extension 136) for information.

Along with the Northeastern settlers, folklore was also transplanted from the sertão to the jungle. In the month of June the saints' days of Santo Antônio, São João and São Pedro are celebrated.

Places to Stay – bottom end

Readers have recommended avoiding the rock-bottom *Villas Hotel* which is a sleaze pit catering to a short-time clientele.

The best of the budget hotels is *Hotel Nunes* (☎ 221-1389), which has quartos at US$6/7 for singles/doubles and apartamentos at US$7/8 for singles/doubles. Just a few metres away are the slightly cheaper *Hotel Sonora* and *Hotel Cuiabano* (☎ 221-4084). The *Hotel Ouro Fino* (☎ 223-1101) at Avenida Carlos Gomes 2844, near the rodoviária, has clean, but musty quartos (with fan) at US$5/7 for singles/doubles.

Places to Stay – middle

Hotel Yara on Avenida Osorio has comfortable apartamentos at US$11/14 for singles/doubles. *Hotel Principe da Beira* (☎ 221-0086) is on the edge of the centre, at Avenida Getúlio Vargas 2287. It's a friendly place with an in-house travel agency, Princetur. Apartamentos cost US$21/29 for singles/doubles.

Places to Stay – top end

The three-star *Hotel Seltom* (☎ 221-7535) at Rua Brasília 2323 charges US$34/50 for singles/doubles and is part of the same chain as the adjacent five-star *Hotel Vila Rica* (☎ 221-2286) which is Porto Velho's finest hotel. Singles/doubles here cost US$66/80.

Places to Eat

Porto Velho is not known for its haute cuisine, but it does have good fish. The best place for fish is *Remanso do Tucunaré* at Avenida Brasília 1506. Try the caldeirada of *tucunaré* and *tambaqui*.

Baião de Dois is open daily from 7 am to midnight. It has a wide range of snacks and main dishes on its menu, including bauru, pizza, seafood, and pasta, and special pasta or seafood buffets on Saturday and Sunday nights. A highlight here is the amazing variety of Amazon juices. For a multi-fruity resurrection of the spirit, try 'Ressurreição' (US$1), or take it to the limit with 'Guaraná até que em Fim' (Guaraná to the Very End).

Restaurante Mirante II serves fish dishes

and has an outdoor patio with a great view of the river. Unfortunately, this is often shrouded in smoke: enjoy your meal as the forest on the opposite bank of the river burns before your eyes and a light sprinkling of vegetal ash descends on the diners. Insects in the trees above the tables wreak revenge by generating a deafening noise similar to the honking of impatient commuters caught in a traffic jam.

The popular floating restaurant that was once moored at the docks was recently cast off by the authorities after a disagreement with the management and has now disappeared down the river.

Getting There & Away
Air There are flights from Porto Velho to all major Brazilian cities. The airline offices are: VASP (☎ 223-3755) at Rua Tenreiro Arenha 2326; Varig/Cruzeiro (☎ 221-8555) at Rua Campos Sales 2666; and TABA (☎ 221-5172) at Rua Prudente de Moraes 39.

TABA and air taxis serve smaller destinations within the state, such as Guajará-Mirim and Costa Marques.

Bus Porto Velho has bus connections to: Manaus, Rio Branco, Guajará-Mirim, Cuiabá, Humaitá, and Costa Marques. Road conditions are generally poor (often impassable during the wet season) and you should view schedules and trip times as optimistic approximations.

To/From Manaus There are two departures daily to Manaus (22 hours; US$50) during the dry season. Watch your belongings. However, the road is generally in poor shape and all services were suspended in 1991 – see also Getting There & Away for Manaus in the Amazonas & Roraima chapter.

To/From Rio Branco There are four or five daily departures from Porto Velho to Rio Branco. The trip takes at least 15 hours (many delays for ferry crossings) and costs around US$26.

To/From Guajará-Mirim There are four daily departures from Porto Velho to Guajará-Mirim (eight to 12 hours; US$20).

Boat There are boat services between Porto Velho and Manaus. The fare of US$40/55 for hammock/cabin accommodation on the four or five-day trip does include three meals a day, but you need to take bottled water. The boats are small and the ride is long, so check out fellow passengers for unsavoury characters before committing yourself.

Some boats go directly to Manaus, others require transfer halfway down the Madeira at Manicoré. The trip takes anywhere from three days to a week, depending on the level of the water, the number of breakdowns and availability of onward connections. One reader recommended taking a bus to Humaitá (203 km from Porto Velho), and then catching a boat to Manaus – this shaved about 24 hours off the normal trip time.

Getting Around
To/From the Airport Aeroporto Belmont (☎ 221-3935) is seven km out of town. You can catch a bus to the centre from the main road outside the airport. In the centre, a convenient bus stop for the bus to the airport is on Avenida 7 de Setembro, close to Hotel Yara. The set price for a taxi from the airport to the centre is US$7, but it's considerably cheaper (US$4) if you walk out to the main road and flag down a taxi there.

To/From the Rodoviária The rodoviária (☎ 221-2141) is about two km from the centre on Avenida Jorge Teixeira. In the centre, a convenient bus stop for the bus to the rodoviária is on Avenida 7 de Setembro, close to Hotel Yara.

Around Porto Velho
Santo Antônio, a small riverside settlement seven km from Porto Velho, is popular with the residents of Porto Velho who come here to fish and swim. You can get here by boat (see information on Tour Agencies under Porto Velho). The fishing village of Teotônio (Km 23 off BR-364, 38 km from Porto Velho), situated by the longest waterfall on

the upper Madeira, is the site of an annual fishing championship held in August and September.

Salto do Jirau is an impressive waterfall on the Rio Madeira, 132 km south-west of Porto Velho on BR-364. About 215 km down BR-364, south-west of Porto Velho and near the town of Abunã, is the Cachoeira Três Esses – a spectacular waterfall on the Rio Abunã with Indian rock inscriptions nearby.

VILHENA

Vilhena, at the border between Rondônia and Mato Grosso, is a good access point for a look at Brazilian frontier life. From Vilhena, take a bus east into Mato Grosso state to Juina or further on to Fontanilhas. These are towns straight from the Wild West, complete with Indian wars, gold miners, rustlers and homesteaders. The real treat in the area is the route north from Juina direct to Aripuanã, on a dirt road. There is an alternate route via Juruena, but it is not nearly as spectacular as the direct route, which passes through the mountains.

Just outside Aripuanã are the spectacular Dannelles Falls. A local guide may be able to take you on some longer hikes through the area, which is rapidly being deforested. Note that trees marked with painted bands indicate disputed Indian territory, and you are well advised to stay out of these areas.

FORTE PRÍNCIPE DA BEIRA & COSTA MARQUES

Remote and little visited Forte Príncipe da Beira, 170 river km south of Guajará-Mirim, was constructed between 1776 and 1783 on the eastern bank of the Guaporé. The fort has 10-metre-high walls with four towers, each holding 14 cannons which took five years to carry from Pará. The fortress walls, nearly one km in perimeter, are surrounded by a moat and enclose a chapel, armoury, officers' quarters, and prison cells where bored convicts scrawled poetic graffiti. Underground passageways lead from the fortress directly to the river. Nearby, there's a mini 'Meeting of the Waters' where the clear, dark Baures flows into the murky brown Guaporé.

The region around Costa Marques has many Indian archaeological sites, inscriptions, and cemeteries. Notable sites here are Pedras Negras and Ilha das Flores. For details about the Reserva Biológica do Guaporé, see the section on National Parks & Biological Reserves earlier in this chapter.

Getting There & Away

Air There are regular flights operated by TABA and air taxis between Costa Marques and Porto Velho and Guajará-Mirim. The TABA office (☎ 651-2323) in Costa Marques is at Avenida Guaporé 512.

Bus It's at least a 22-hour trip to the fort from Guajará-Mirim: eight to 12 hours to Porto Velho, then 278 km on BR-364 to Presidente Medici and 363 km along the unpaved BR-429 to Costa Marques. This is as far as you can go by bus, and from there it's still 20 km to Forte Príncipe da Beira. West of Presidente Medici is a wild stretch of road and the environmental destruction is heartbreaking. Because the land has been cleared and settled only recently, there's a significant risk of malaria and other tropical diseases.

Boat A preferable alternative to the bus is to travel by boat up the Mamoré and Guaporé rivers. ENARO government boats ply this stretch of the river and reach the military post at Forte Príncipe da Beira from Guajará-Mirim in two to three days. They then continue to Costa Marques where food and accommodation are available. Enquire about schedules at the Capitânia dos Portos in Guajará-Mirim, but don't expect much help.

GUAJARÁ-MIRIM

The contrast between Guajará-Mirim on the Brazilian/Bolivian border and its Bolivian counterpart Guayaramerín is striking. While the Brazilian town is a bustling metropolitan area with restaurants, shops, parks and traffic, the Bolivian town is still a small, dusty, frontier settlement. For a discussion of the history of Guajará-Mirim, see the History section for Porto Velho.

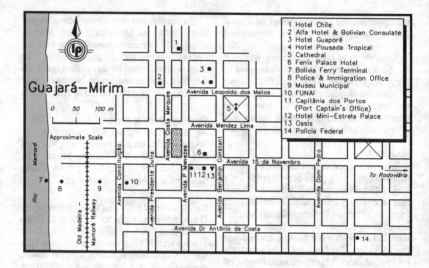

Guajará—Mirim

0   50   100 m

Approximate Scale

Rio Mamoré

Old Madeira – Mamoré Railway

Avenida Constituição

Avenida Presidente Dutra

Avenida Costa Marques

Avenida P. Menezes

Avenida Benjamin Constant

Avenida Dom Pedro

Avenida Leopoldo dos Matos

Avenida Mendez Lima

Avenida 15 de Novembro

Avenida Dr Antônio de Costa

To Rodoviária

1 Hotel Chile
2 Alfa Hotel & Bolivian Consulate
3 Hotel Guaporé
4 Hotel Pousada Tropical
5 Cathedral
6 Fenix Palace Hotel
7 Bolivia Ferry Terminal
8 Police & Immigration Office
9 Museu Municipal
10 FUNAI
11 Capitânia dos Portos
   (Port Captain's Office)
12 Hotel Mini-Estrela Palace
13 Oasis
14 Policia Federal

Information

Bolivian Consulate If you're entering Bolivia and require a visa, there is a Bolivian Consulate (☎ 541-2862) in Guajará-Mirim, open only on weekday mornings. It's a small, unassuming cubbyhole upstairs in the Alfa Hotel building at Avenida Leopoldo dos Matos, 239; there's no sign. Have two photographs ready.

Museu Municipal

With a couple of old steam locomotives parked outside, the marginally interesting museum housed in the old railway station on Avenida 15 de Novembro focuses on the history of the region and contains the remains of some of Rondônia's fiercely threatened wildlife. Particularly interesting are the huge anaconda which stretches the length of the main salon and a pathetically hideous turtle which inhabits the aquarium area. The museum's collection of photographs has an especially intriguing portrayal of an Indian attack – or defence, depending upon your reference – taken in the 1960s.

The museum is open weekdays from 7.30 am to noon and 2.30 to 5.30 pm. On weekends and holidays, it opens at 8 am.

Places to Stay

A favourite for travellers is *Hotel Guaporé* on Avenida Benjamin Constant. It costs US$11/18 a single/double quarto including breakfast. Cheaper still is the *Fenix Palace Hotel* (☎ 541-2326), Avenida 15 de Novembre 459, which costs US$8.50/14 a single/double quarto and US$14/19 for a single/double apartamento, including electric fan. The popular *Hotel Mini-Estrela Palace* (☎ 541-2399) across the road charges US$11/18 for single/double apartamentos with fan or US$14/19.50 with air-conditioning. The *Hotel Pousada Tropical* (☎ 541-3308) is quite comfortable, with single/double air-conditioned apartamentos for US$11/14 or US$8.50/11 with just a fan. The hotel charges US$3 for each additional occupant.

Moving slightly up the scale, the *Alfa Hotel* (☎ 541-3121) costs US$19.50/30.50 for single/double apartamentos. Additional beds cost US$7 and breakfast will cost an extra US$3 per person.

Places to Eat

Universally recommended as Guajará-

Mirim's best restaurant, the *Oasis* is next door to the Hotel Mini-Estrela Palace.

Getting There & Away

Air TABA (☎ 541-2609) flies three times weekly to and from Porto Velho, and operates a similar schedule to Costa Marques.

Bus During the dry season – May to September – there are bus connections twice daily to Porto Velho along a stretch of road commonly known – for what should be obvious reasons – as one of the 'Transcoca Highways'. The trip takes between eight and 12 hours and costs US$20.

Boat It's possible to travel by boat up the Mamoré and Guaporé rivers to Costa Marques via Forte Príncipe da Beira. Enquire about schedules at the not-terribly-helpful Capitânia dos Portos (☎ 541-2208). For more details see Getting There & Away for Forte Príncipe da Beira & Costa Marques.

Crossing the Border Even if you're not planning to travel further into Bolivia, you can pop across the Rio Mamoré and visit Guayaramerín, a dusty frontier settlement with more charm and cheaper accommodation than Guajará-Mirim. Between early morning and 6.30 pm, small motorised canoes and larger motor ferries cross the river from Guajará-Mirim every few minutes for US$1. After hours, there are only express motorboats which cost US$4 to 5.50 per boat. You may travel back and forth across the river at will, but those travelling beyond the frontier area will have to complete border formalities.

Leaving Brazil, you may need to have your passport stamped at the Bolivian Consulate in Guajará-Mirim before getting a Brazilian exit stamp from the Polícia Federal (☎ 541-2437) at Avenida Dr Antônio da Costa 842, five blocks from the port in Guajará-Mirim. Once across the Rio Mamoré, pick up an entrance stamp at Migración (Bolivian Immigration) at the ferry terminal.

If you're leaving Bolivia from Guayaramerín, you must have your passport stamped at Migración and again at the Polícia Federal in Guajará-Mirim, where you'll get a Brazilian entry stamp. Although officials don't always check, technically everyone needs a yellow fever vaccination certificate to enter Brazil here. If you don't have one, there is a convenient and relatively sanitary clinic at the port on the Brazilian side. The medical staff use an air gun rather than a hypodermic needle.

GUAYARAMERÍN (BOLIVIA)

Guayaramerín, on the Rio Mamoré opposite the Brazilian town of Guajará-Mirim, is a rail town where the railway never arrived. The line that would have connected the Rio Beni town of Riberalta and the Brazilian city of Porto Velho was completed only as far as Guajará-Mirim just over the border – it never reached Bolivian territory! See the History section for Porto Velho for more details about the railway.

Guayaramerín retains a strong frontier atmosphere and is a typically friendly Amazon town with a population of just 14,000. The town serves as a river port and an entry point to or from Brazil; it is also the terminus of the brand new road linking it and Riberalta, 90 km away, with Santa Ana, Rurrenabaque and La Paz. This road is impassable after rain.

Information

Brazilian Consulate There is a Brazilian Consulate in Guayaramerín, one block south of the main plaza. It's open from 9 am to 1 pm Monday to Friday and the friendly and efficient consul will issue visas on the same day. They are free for US citizens but other applicants must pay US$10.

Money Cash US dollars may be exchanged at Hotel San Carlos for a good rate. Alternatively, exchange US dollars, bolivianos (abbreviated in this section to 'B') or Brazilian cruzeiros with the aggressive cambistas who hang around the port area. In 1992, the going rate was B3.6 for US$1.

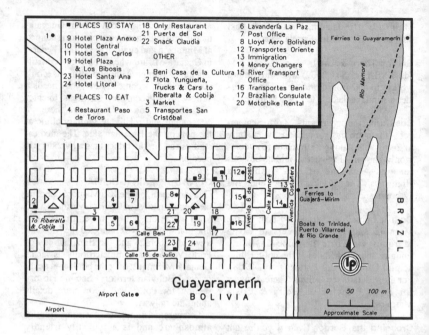

PLACES TO STAY	18 Only Restaurant	6 Lavandería La Paz
9 Hotel Plaza Anexo	21 Puerta del Sol	7 Post Office
10 Hotel Central	22 Snack Claudia	8 Lloyd Aero Boliviano
11 Hotel San Carlos		12 Transportes Oriente
19 Hotel Plaza	OTHER	13 Immigration
& Los Bibosis		14 Money Changers
23 Hotel Santa Ana	1 Beni Casa de la Cultura	15 River Transport
24 Hotel Litoral	2 Flota Yungueña,	Office
	Trucks & Cars to	16 Transportes Beni
▼ PLACES TO EAT	Riberalta & Cobija	17 Brazilian Consulate
	3 Market	20 Motorbike Rental
4 Restaurant Paso	5 Transportes San	
de Toros	Cristóbal	

Ferries to Guayaramerín

Rio Mamoré

Ferries to Guajará–Mirim

Calle Mamoré

Avenida 6 de Agosto

Avenida Costañera

Boats to Trinidad, Puerto Villarroel & Rio Grande

B R A Z I L

To Riberalta & Cobija

Calle Beni

Calle 16 de Julio

Guayaramerín

BOLIVIA

Airport Gate ●

Airport

0   50   100 m

Approximate Scale

Places to Stay

The mellowest budget place to stay in Guayaramerín is undoubtedly the *Hotel Litoral* near the airport. Private baths, refreshingly tepid showers and clean rooms are offered here for only B15 per person. In the courtyard there's a snack bar where you may meet the Litoral's inedibly scrawny and independently minded pet chicken called Pinky; not just a dumb cluck, she spurns feathered company and fraternises instead with hotel staff and clientele, insistently making her demands known.

Across the street, the quiet and shady *Hotel Santa Ana* (☎ 2206) offers similar amenities for B15/12 per person with/without private bath.

The *Hotel Central* (☎ 2042) costs B10 per person. It's a low-budget option with no double beds and only shared baths. *Hotel Plaza* (☎ 2085) charges B20/15 per person with/without private bath. It's a bit run-down and not particularly good value, but it's worth having a look at the high-security telephone box which looks more like a drying-out cage for drunks!

Nicer is the *Hotel Plaza Anexo* (☎ 2086), with clean rooms, electric hot showers and a pleasant ambience, for B20 per person.

The *Hotel San Carlos* (☎ 21152) at Calle 6 de Agosto is the upmarket place to stay in town, with TV, sauna, air-conditioning, a billiards room and hot water at all times. Rooms cost B56/90 for singles/doubles, and a gimmicky room called the Suite costs B120. All rooms have private baths.

Places to Eat

Guayaramerín's best restaurant is appropriately called the *Only Restaurant* (☎ 2397)! With an extensive international menu and a pleasant outdoor garden area, it's very popular with Brazilians. Out of town but also very good is *Sujal*; motorbike taxis will get you there for B1 each way. On the corner of the plaza, *Pollo Pio Pio* isn't bad for cold drinks and snacks, but check your bill for spontaneous additions. The *Puerto del Sol* is frequently recommended by locals but we reckon it's grossly overrated: the food is only average and serious overcharging of foreigners is in effect.

Getting There & Away

Air Guayaramerín's airport, right at the edge of town, takes air safety seriously; just prior to our most recent visit, a bull had been mown down on the runway and the airport was closed down for two weeks!

The LAB office in Guayaramerín isn't yet on the computer line, so book flights out of Guayaramerín from elsewhere or risk not getting a seat. LAB has flights from Trinidad daily except Tuesday; from Cochabamba and Santa Cruz on Wednesday and Sunday; and from La Paz on Friday. From Guayaramerín, TAM has flights from La Paz on Monday and Wednesday, and to La Paz on Tuesday and Thursday. You can fly to Cobija with TAM on Tuesday and LAB on Friday for B165.

Bus Bus services to and from Guayaramerín operate only during the dry season – roughly from May to October. The two-hour journey to Riberalta on Flota Trans-Oriente costs B10 – departures at 8 am and 3 pm daily. Transportes Beni operates buses to La Paz via Santa Rosa, Reyes, San Borja and Rurrenabaque according to no particular schedule; sporadic service to Cachuela Esperanza and Cobija is planned as soon as the road opens. Flota Yungueña departs for Riberalta, Rurrenabaque and La Paz on Tuesday and Sunday at 3 pm from the car and *camión* (truck) stop at the western end of town (see the discussion of Hitching which follows later in this section). The 36-hour trip to La Paz costs B140. Scheduled service to Cobija is planned for the near future.

Beware of bus companies cancelling trips. If tickets aren't sold out, the run may be cancelled and irate would-be passengers are given a lame excuse.

Boat From the port, ships leave frequently for Trinidad, five to seven days up the Mamoré. For information regarding departures, the port captain's office has a notice board which lists any activity into or out of town.

Hitching Camiones (trucks) to Riberalta leave from the main street 2½ blocks west of the market near the Flota Yungueña office. They charge the same as buses but make the trip in less time. If you'd like to travel a bit more comfortably, cars charge US$7.50 and you're spared exposure to the choking red dust that seems to get into everything. To Cobija, YPFB petrol trucks and a white Volvo freight carrier depart occasionally from the same place.

Crossing the Border For information about onward travel into Brazil, see Getting There & Away in the section on Guajará-Mirim.

Getting Around

You'll quickly discover that there are no automobile taxis in Guayaramerín, but then the town is so small you can walk just about anywhere you'd like to go. Motorbike taxis cost B1 anywhere around town. Those who want to do some exploring of the surrounding area can hire a motorbike from the main plaza for about B75 per 24-hour day. Don't be tempted to take a swig of the stuff sold in Coke bottles on the street: it's motorbike petrol!

Acre

The state of Acre has become a favoured destination for developers and settlers, who have followed BR-364 and started claiming lands, clearing forest, and setting up ranches. This has caused a major conflict over land ownership and sustainable use of the forest with the indigenous tribes and rural workers, mostly rubber tappers, who are descended from settlers who arrived many decades ago. This conflict received massive national and

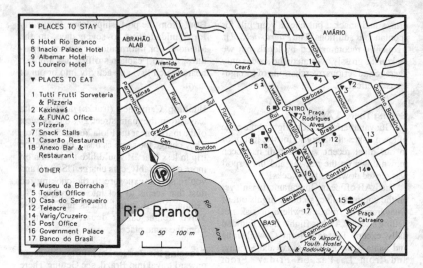

PLACES TO STAY

6 Hotel Rio Branco
8 Inacio Palace Hotel
9 Albemar Hotel
13 Loureiro Hotel

PLACES TO EAT

1 Tutti Frutti Sorveteria
   & Pizzeria
2 Kaxinawá
   & FUNAC Office
3 Pizzeria
7 Snack Stalls
11 Casarão Restaurant
18 Anexo Bar &
   Restaurant

OTHER

4 Museu da Borracha
5 Tourist Office
10 Casa do Seringueiro
12 Teleacre
14 Varig/Cruzeiro
15 Post Office
16 Government Palace
17 Banco do Brasil

Rio Branco

0   50   100 m

international attention when Chico Mendes, a rubber tapper and opponent of rainforest destruction, was assassinated in 1988. For a discussion of Chico Mendes, see the section on Xapuri. For details about the history of Acre, see the History section for Porto Velho.

Time: most of the state is two hours behind Brazilian standard time.

RIO BRANCO

Rio Branco, capital of Acre state, was founded in 1882 on the banks of the Rio Acre, which is navigable via the Rio Purus to the Amazon. There's a relaxed feel to this city, which has a few attractions close to the centre, and other points of interest, including intriguing religious communities, further afield.

Information

Tourist Office The Departamento de Turismo (☎ 224-3997) at Avenida Getúlio Vargas 659 is helpful. It's open from 8 am to 1 pm, Monday to Friday.

Money The main branch of Banco do Brasil is at Rua Acre, 85.

Post & Telecommunications The central post office is on Avenida Epaminondas Jácome. The main office of TELEACRE, the state phone company, is on Avenida Brasil.

Travel Agency Acretur (☎ 224-2404), inside the lobby of the Hotel Rio Branco at Rua Rui Barbosa 193, offers good deals for domestic flights and also organises tours to local sights.

Casa do Seringueiro

This museum has a collection of photos, paintings, replicas of housing and utensils which portray the life of a typical seringueiro (rubber tapper). Also on display are videos and pictures of Chico Mendes.

The museum is open from 8 to 11 am and from 3 to 8 pm, Tuesday to Friday; and from 4 to 8 pm on Saturday and Sunday.

Museu da Borracha

The collection in this museum is divided into sections relating to the archaeology, palaeontology, ethnology and recent history of Acre. It's well worth a visit. The museum is open from 9 am to 6 pm, Tuesday to Friday; and from 4 to 8 pm on Saturday and Sunday.

Colônia Cinco Mil

The Colônia Cinco Mil (literally Colony of the 5000) is a religious community which follows the doctrine of Santo Daime introduced in 1930 by Raimundo Irineu Serra, also known as Mestre Irineu. For more details about this cult based on the sacred hallucinogenic drink called ayahuasca, see the section on Religion in the Facts about the Country chapter. Mestre Irineu founded the first centre at Alto Santo, seven km from Rio Branco. Various schisms amongst his followers led to the establishment of other centres, such as Casa de Jesus Fonte de Luz in the Vila Ivonete district, three km from Rio Branco; Centro Fonte Luz Universal (CEFLURIS) in the agricultural community of Côlonia Cinco Mil, 12 km from Rio Branco; and Ceú da Mapiá, a similar community which is based at Mapiá, accessible by boat (two days) from Boca do Acre (Amazonas state).

Visits can be arranged to Colônia Cinco Mil either through a travel agency – Acretur for example – or by contacting the Daimistas at Kaxinawá, the Daimista restaurant in Rio Branco. The best day to visit is Wednesday, when the main weekly festival is celebrated. If you stay overnight, no fee will be charged but you will be expected to share costs of transport and food.

In the grounds of the restaurant is a shop sponsored by the Fundação de Tecnologia do Estado do Acre (FUNTAC), a state organisation promoting sustainable use of forest products, which are sold here.

Horto Florestal

This municipal forest park in the Vila Ivonete district, three km from the centre, contains a selection of Amazon flora, a lake, and various paths which make a pleasant change from the traffic in the centre. A taxi from the centre costs about US$2.50. The park is open daily from 8 am to 4 pm.

Lago do Amapá

Lago do Amapá is a large, U-shaped lake, eight km south-east of Rio Branco, which is a popular spot for swimming and boat excursions. A taxi from the centre costs around US$6.

Parque Ecológico Plácido de Castro

In 1991, an ecological park was opened at Plácido de Castro, 94 km east of Rio Branco, on the Brazilian/Bolivian border. This park offers good swimming at river beaches, and it is possible to take walks through the forests along the paths originally used by rubber tappers.

There are two bus departures daily from Rio Branco to Plácido de Castro, where there's a hotel, *Hotel Carioca* (☎ 237-1064) on Rua Juvenal Antunes, and various inexpensive pensões, restaurants and even a danceteria. Acretur runs Sunday excursions to the park which leave Rio Branco at 8.30 am and return from Plácido de Castro at 6 pm. The cost of the excursion is US$7 per person.

Places to Stay

Youth Hostel *Albergue de Juventude Fronteira Verde* (☎ 225-7128) on Travessa Natanael de Albuquerque is a cheap, friendly place to stay, just a short walk from the city centre. From the airport, take the bus marked 'Norte/Sul' and get off at the 'Cine Recreio'. From the rodoviária, take the same bus and get off at the same bus stop. From the city centre, the hostel is a short walk across the bridge at the southern end of Avenida Getúlio Vargas.

Hotels *Albemar Hotel* (☎ 224-1938), at Rua Franco Ribeiro 99, has comfortable apartamentos at US$12/15/25 for singles/doubles/triples, and a friendly bar and restaurant in the same building. *Loureiro Hotel* (☎ 224-3560), at Rua Marechal Deodoro 196, has apartamentos (without TV) at US$8/12 for singles/doubles – rooms with TV are more expensive.

For good value, try *Hotel Rio Branco* (☎ 224-1785) at Rua Rui Barbosa 193. This place has efficient service, bright decor, and neat apartamentos. Cost is US$19 per person, and an excellent breakfast is included.

Inácio Palace Hotel (☎ 224-6397) at Rua Rui Barbosa 72 provides rather dismal apartamentos at US$14/28 for singles/doubles. *Pinheiro Palace* (☎ 224-7191), across the street and under the same management, is a three-star luxury establishment which charges US$45/66 for single/double rooms.

Places to Eat

Anexo Bar & Restaurant does a good buffet lunch for US$3 per person. *Pizzeria*, at the junction of Rua Rui Barbosa and Rua Marechal Deodoro, and *Tutti Frutti Sorveteria & Pizzeria*, at Avenida Ceará 1132, both serve tasty Italian dishes. *Casarão Restaurant* at Avenida Brasil 310 serves regional dishes and is popular with locals who come for the live music in the evening. On Praça Rodrigues Alves, you might want to stop at the snack stalls which sell ice creams with exotic flavours. Vegetarians can browse in the health food shop next to the Hotel Rio Branco. *Kaxinawá* has been described previously in the section on Colônia Cinco Mil.

Entertainment

For some strange reason, the big day in Rio Branco is Tuesday, when it seems as if the entire town stops work in the afternoon to go to a football match and then boogies through the night to live music at Kaxinawá. Sunday and Monday are the complete opposite: dead days when virtually all commercial activity in the centre ceases.

Getting There & Away

Between October and June, when the rivers are at their highest, roads are usually impassable and the only viable options are plane or boat. From July to September, when the rivers are at their lowest, the roads are passable, but river traffic is restricted.

Air There are flights between Rio Branco and Cruzeiro do Sul, Manaus, Porto Velho, Cuiabá, Rio and São Paulo. VASP (☎ 224-6585) is at Avenida Epaminondas Jácome 611, and Varig/Cruzeiro (☎ 224-2226) is at Rua Marechal Deodoro 115. There are also various air taxi companies at the airport, such as TACEZUL (☎ 224-3242), TAFETAL (☎ 224-2465), and TAVAJ (☎ 224-5981).

Bus There are bus services between Rio Branco and Porto Velho (four departures daily; 15 hours minimum; US$26), Brasiléia (four departures daily; six hours; US$11), Plácido de Castro, and Boca do Acre.

Boat To enquire about boats, either visit the tourist office or go direct to the port, which is at the eastern end of Avenida Epaminondas Jácome. It should be possible to find a ride at least as far as Boca do Acre (Amazonas state), where there is river traffic along the Rio Purus as far as the Amazon, and even Manaus.

Getting Around

The airport, Aeroporto Internacional Presidente Medici (☎ 224-6833), is about two km out of town at AC-40, Km 1. The rodoviária (☎ 224-1182) is also a couple of km out of town at AC-40, 1018 (Cidade Nova district).

From the airport, the bus marked 'Norte/Sul' runs via the rodoviária to the centre. A taxi from the centre to the airport costs US$3, and it's about the same price to the rodoviária.

XAPURI

Xapuri, 188 km south-west of Rio Branco, was founded in the late 19th century on territory formerly inhabited by the indigenous Xapuri, Latiana, and Maneteri tribes. In 1902, it achieved historical fame as the site where Plácido de Castro proclaimed Acrean independence from Bolivia. In 1988, the town hit international and national headlines with the assassination of Chico Mendes, a rubber tapper and opponent of rainforest destruction.

Places to Stay & Eat

There are two inexpensive hotels on Rua Major Salinas – *Hotel Veneza* (☎ 542-2397) and *Santo Antônio Hotel* (☎ 542-2408). For places to eat in the centre of town, try *Restaurante Eldorado* on Rua Coronel

Top: Sunset on the Rio Negro, Amazonas (KB)
Left: View over the Amazon (VS)
Right: Deforestation in the Amazon (JM)

Top: Old man, Santarém, Pará (MS)
Left: On the Rio Negro, Amazonas (KB)
Right: On the Rio Negro, Amazonas (KB)

Chico Mendes

Chico Mendes was born in 1944 at Seringal Cachoeira in Acre into a family descended from generations of rubber tappers. At an early age he became interested in asserting the rights of rubber tappers to their lands. In the '70s, the Plano de Integração Nacional (PIN), an ambitious government plan to tame the Amazon, attracted developers, ranchers, logging companies, and settlers into Acre. In 1975, Chico Mendes organised a rural workers' union to defy the tactics of violent intimidation and dispossession practised by the newcomers, who were destroying the forest and thus robbing the rural workers of their livelihood.

Mendes organised large groups of rural workers to form non-violent human blockades around forest areas threatened with clearance, and soon attracted the wrath of developers, who were used to getting their way either through corrupt officials or by hiring pistoleiros to clear human impediment. These empates or 'confrontational stand-offs' proved effective in saving thousands of hectares of forest, which were set aside as *reservas extrativistas* (extractive reserves) where rural workers could continue to tap rubber and gather fruits, nuts and fibres.

International interest focussed on Mendes as a defender of the forests, but his role as a leader also made him a natural target for frustrated and infuriated opponents. Early in December 1988, he moved to establish his birthplace, Seringal Cachoeira, as an extractive reserve and defied the local landowner and rancher, Darly Alves da Silva, who disputed ownership of the land. On 22 December, Chico Mendes, who had received numerous death threats, momentarily left his bodyguards inside his house and stepped out onto the back porch. He was hit at close range by shots fired from the bushes and died shortly afterwards.

For almost two years there was much speculation about the murderers who, although well known, were considered out of legal reach because of their connections with the influential landowners and corrupt officials of the region – a common arrangement in the frontierlands of Brazil. Intense national and international pressures finally brought the case to trial. In December 1990, Darly Alves da Silva received a 19-year prison term for ordering the assassination; his son, Darci, was given an identical term of imprisonment for pulling the trigger.

The verdict pleased the rural workers, world opinion, and the Brazilian government, which badly needed to demonstrate – to Brazilians and foreigners – a modicum of control in the Amazon region. The media spotlight moved on to new sensations, and the murders continued.

However, documentation shows that this exhibition of justice was a rare flash in the media pan. Between 1980 and 1989, there were hundreds of murders of union leaders and land rights campaigners: the only murder that was thoroughly investigated and prosecuted was that of Chico Mendes.

Ilzamar Mendes, Chico's wife, was courted by Hollywood to sell the film rights to her husband's story for one million dollars, international organisations made posthumous awards, and several city parks in Brazil were named after Chico Mendes. In Xapuri, his house has been made into a commemorative museum. Having lost their most charismatic leader, the rubber tappers and rural workers of the region are keen to keep up the pressure, not only to establish more extractive reserves throughout the Amazon region, but most importantly, to force the Brazilian government to enforce the laws governing the establishment of such reserves and to punish all who violate them.

On February 29 1992, the state appeals court in Rio Branco annulled the conviction of Darly Alves da Silva. Osmarino Rodrigues, the man who replaced Chico Mendes as head of the rubber tappers' union, declared that this outrageous decision was effectively the second killing of Chico. For those who had hoped to see a glimmer of justice in Brazil, it was just another nail in the country's coffin.■

Brandão or *Pensão O Escadão* on Rua 17 de Novembro.

Getting There & Away

There are several bus services daily between Rio Branco and Xapuri.

BRASILÉIA

The small town of Brasiléia lies on the Bra-

zilian border with Bolivia and is separated from Cobija, its Bolivian counterpart, by the Rio Abunã and the Rio Acre. Brasiléia has absolutely nothing of interest to travellers, save an immigration stamp into or out of Brazil. The Polícia Federal is two km from the centre; dress nicely – no shorts allowed – or officials may refuse to stamp your passport. For information on crossing the

Around Brasiléia

0   250   500 m

Approximate Scale

Brazilian/Bolivian border see the section on Getting There & Away.

Information

Bolivian Consulate There is a Bolivian Consulate in Brasiléia at Rua Major Salinas 114.

Places to Stay & Eat

If you're stuck in Brasiléia, try the *Carioca Charmé Hotel* (☎ 546-3045) near the church in the centre. Apartamentos cost US$8/10 for singles/doubles. The *Restaurant Carioca* beside the hotel serves drinks, chicken and beef dishes and standard prato feito (a veritable feast of Brazilian carbohydrates). Alternatively, there's the *Hotel Kador* (☎ 546-3283) at Avenida Santos Dumont 25, on the road between the international bridge and the Polícia Federal – near the turnoff to the centre of Brasiléia.

Getting There & Away

From the rodoviária, there are four buses daily to Rio Branco (six hours; US$11).

Crossing the Border If you're going to or coming from Bolivia, you'll have to get entry/exit stamps from Migración (Immigration) in Cobija and the Polícia Federal just outside Brasiléia. A yellow fever vaccination certificate is required to enter Brazil from Cobija, but there is no vaccination clinic in Brasiléia – you'll have to track down a private physician if your health records aren't in order.

Since it's a rather long up-and-down slog from Cobija across the bridge to Brasiléia, you may want to take a taxi, but negotiate the routing and the fare in advance. For about US$3.50, the driver will take you from Cobija to the Polícia Federal in Brasiléia, wait while you complete immigration formalities and then take you to the centre or to the rodoviária.

Alternatively, take the rowboat ferry (30c per person) across the Rio Acre to the landing in the centre of Brasiléia. From here it's one km to the rodoviária and two km in the opposite direction to the Polícia Federal.

COBIJA (BOLIVIA)

The Bolivian border town of Cobija is linked to its Brazilian counterpart, Brasiléia, by the International Bridge. Founded in 1906 under the name of Bahia, Cobija experienced a boom as a rubber-producing centre during the 1940s; when the rubber industry declined, so did Cobija's fortunes, and the town was reduced to a forgotten hamlet of 5000 people. Today, Cobija's population has almost doubled and it has at least one claim to fame: with 1770 mm of precipitation falling annually, it is the rainiest spot in Bolivia.

At present, Cobija has no surface link with the rest of Bolivia, but a highway to Riberalta and La Paz should be open by the time this book is published. Cobija is also the site of a brand-new international airport which will accommodate Boeing 727s flying the popular La Paz/Santa Cruz/Panama City/ Miami flights. Hmmm?

Information

Tourist Office There has been a Pando tourist office in Cobija on and off, but it wasn't operating at the time of writing. If you read Spanish, the best source of background information on this remote area will be the book *Pando es Bolivia* by Alberto Lavadenz Ribera, published in 1991. It's available at the LAB office in Cobija and outlines the history, development and official story of the entire Pando department of which Cobija is the capital.

Brazilian Consulate For US citizens and others who need a visa to enter Brazil, there is a Brazilian Consulate (☎ 2188) on the corner of Calle Beni and Fernandez Molina. It's open from 8.30 am to 12.30 pm, Monday to Friday.

Immigration Bolivian immigration is located in the Prefectural building on the main plaza. The office opens at 9 am on weekdays but the immigration officer is often taken with wanderlust, so you may have to hunt him up to get your entry or exit stamp.

Money Casa Horacio changes cruzeiros, bolivianos (abbreviated in this section to 'B') and US dollars for official rates. Travellers' cheques changed to US dollars or cruzeiros are charged 10% commission because they must be sent to La Paz. In 1992, the going rate was B3.6 for US$1. If you're exchanging money over the border in Brasiléia, be sure to check official tourist and parallel rates before handing money over to a shopkeeper.

Things to See

There are a few interesting things to see in the area, including rubber and Brazil nut plantations, a number of lakes and places to observe rainforest wildlife, but transportation is difficult and Cobija's hinterlands are not easily accessible.

A relatively new destination and a favourite with residents is Lago Bay, a freshwater lake and picnicking and fishing site near the Rio Manuripi, about 150 km south of Cobija along the Chivé road. There are basic cabañas to rent if you want to stay there. A return taxi from Cobija to Lago Bay will cost around B50.

If you're really bored, take a look at the monument in front of the old hospital. It commemorates an apocryphal local youth who, during the Brazilian takeover of the Acre, shot a flaming arrow and set the fire that sent invading Brazilians packing back across the river.

Places to Stay

The very friendly Spanish-run *Hotel Prefectural* (☎ 2230), also known as Hotel Pando, is under new management and has recently been upgraded considerably. Nice breezy rooms with fans and private baths cost B25 per person or B45 for a room with a double bed. Breakfast is included in the price. While you're there, say hello to their chatty parrot and take a look at the immense anaconda skin stretched across the reception area.

The *Residencial Frontera* is clean and relatively inexpensive at a negotiable B20 per person or B30 with a double bed. It's pleasant if you can get a room with a window onto the patio.

A third option is the *Residencial Cocodrilo* which charges B12 per person – also negotiable – for a pleasant but far from opulent room in a nice, tropical-style wooden building.

Rock-bottom accommodation is found for B6 per person at *Alojamiento 24 de Septiembre*; it's used mostly by locals.

Places to Eat

In the early morning, the market sells chicken *empanadas*, but that's about all in the way of prepared food. Nothing stays fresh very long in this stifling and sticky climate so most people wouldn't want to touch the meat available in the market. There are, however, fresh fruits and vegetables and lots of tinned Brazilian products, so with a stove, one can whip up something different.

During the day, try *Confitería La Favorita*, which has snacks, drinks and sandwiches, or *Restaurant Nina*, which has basic, inexpensive meals.

The *Churrasquería La Estancia* is Cobija's nicest restaurant, with outdoor tables beneath big sheltering trees. Try their excellent *parrillada* (barbecue) served with salad and yuca for B10. Local dogs seem to be impressed, anyway, and they patiently wait around for something to drop from tables. *Discoteca Restaurant Pachahuara* just opposite is Cobija's swinging night spot, serving snacks, standard meals and parrillada.

Getting There & Away

Air On Friday, TAM (☎ 2267), the Bolivian military airline, flies from La Paz to Cobija and back; it's a popular run, so book at least a week in advance. Every second week, TAM flies a circle route from La Paz on Monday, stopping at Cobija, Riberalta, Guayaramerín, and Cochabamba, returning by the reverse route the following day. LAB (☎ 2170), the Bolivian national airline, flies to and from La Paz with intermediate stops in Riberalta, Guayaramerín and Trinidad. If you're on the LAB Fokker which flies this run, look for the golden plaque that hangs over the seat occupied by the Pope on his most recent visit to Bolivia.

On arrival at the airport, you may claim baggage immediately or pick it up at the LAB office in town, a good idea if you're walking the two km to the centre in Cobija's sticky heat. Most taxis into town are motorbikes and it's not easy to find one that will accommodate much luggage. Between November and March, Cobija runs are often cancelled; sometimes several weeks pass without a flight.

Bus At the time of writing, there was no surface transportation from Cobija to the rest of Bolivia without travelling literally thousands of km on a loop through Brazil; however, that's due to change soon with the opening of the newly completed road to Riberalta. Freight and YPFB petrol trucks are already doing the trip and Flota Yungueña is on line to begin bus service at the earliest possible moment. Flota Cobija buses connect Cobija with the village of Porvenir, 30 km away. They depart at 11.30 am daily from Confitería La Favorita and leave Porvenir for the return trip at 3 pm. The trip takes one hour each way and costs B3.

Details about bus connections from Brasiléia (Brasil) are given in the Getting There & Away section for Brasiléia.

Crossing the Border For details about crossing the border between Brasiléia (Brazil) and Cobija, see Crossing the Border in the Getting There & Away section for Brasiléia.

ASSIS BRASIL & IÑAPARI (PERU)

Although we haven't tried the route described here, locals reckon that access from Assis Brasil to Iñapari (Peru) is possible for the adventurous traveller. Unfortunately, Peru's Madre de Dios department has recently been a stage of operations for the Sendero Luminoso (Shining Path) guerrillas, drug-running, lawless gold digging and other renegade activities. We don't recommend trying, but if you do manage to get through, please write and let us know how it went!

Places to Stay & Eat

There's one hotel in Assis Brasil, the *Assis Brasil Palace Hotel* on Rua Eneide Batista. For places to eat in the town centre, try *Restaurante Seridó* at Rua Valério Magalhães 62, or *Bar & Restaurante Petisco* on Rua Raimundo Chaar.

Getting There & Away

Crossing the Border The route involves taking a bus from Brasiléia to Assis Brasil, 110 km west of Brasiléia. It may be simpler to complete Brazilian immigration procedures in Brasiléia.

Across the Rio Acre from Assis Brasil is the muddy little Peruvian settlement of

Iñapari, where you must check into Peru with the police. There is a road of sorts from there to Puerto Maldonado, which is accessible to Cuzco on the Peruvian road system but for practical purposes is impassable to all but pedestrian or motorbike traffic. You may be able to fly from Iñapari – there is an airport seven km from the village – to Puerto Maldonado on a Grupo Ocho cargo flight; just don't count on it.

CRUZEIRO DO SUL

Another option to reach Peru – and a decidedly bad idea due to heavily entrenched drug-running and Sendero Luminoso activity in the area – is to either fly or hitch on a truck (654 km along BR-364) from Rio Branco to Cruzeiro do Sul in western Acre, and then fly from there to the Peruvian Amazon city of Pucallpa.

Places to Stay & Eat

In Cruzeiro do Sul, there are a couple of hotels – *Plínio Hotel* (☎ 322-3445) at Blvd Thaumaturgo 155, and *Sandra's Hotel* (☎ 322-2481) at Avenida Coronel Mâncio Lima 241. For places to eat in the town centre, try *Restaurante Popular* on Rua Joaquim Távora or *Zanzibar Bar & Restaurante* at Avenida Getúlio Vargas 19.

Glossary

ABCD Cities – refers to Brazil's industrial heartland; the cities of São André, São Bernardo, São Caetano and Diadema, which flank the city of São Paulo.

Abandonados – abandoned children.

Abertura – opening; refers to the process of returning to a civilian, democratic government which was begun in the early 1980s.

Afoxé – music of Bahia with strong African rhythms and close ties to the Candomblé religion.

Aguardente – firewater, rotgut; any strong drink, but usually cachaça.

Albergue – lodging house or hostel.

Álcool – car fuel made from sugar cane; about half the cars in Brazil and all new cars run on álcool.

Aldeia – originally a mission village built by Jesuits to 'save' the Indians, but now any small village of peasants or fisherfolk.

Andar – the verb 'to walk', but also used to denote the floor number in a multistorey building.

Apartamento – hotel room with a bathroom.

Arara – macaw.

Autódromo – racing track. The race track near Barra in Rio is the site of the Brazilian Grand Prix.

Automotriz – tourist train.

Avelã – hazelnut.

Azulejos – Portuguese ceramic tiles which have a distinctive blue glaze. You will often see them in churches.

Bandeirantes – bands of Paulistas (people from São Paulo) who explored the vast Brazilian interior while searching for gold and Indians to enslave. The bandeirantes were typically born of an Indian mother and a Portuguese father.

Banzo – a slave's profound longing for the African homeland which often resulted in a 'slow withering away' and death.

Barraca – any stall or hut, including those omnipresent food and drink stands at the beach, park, etc.

Bateria – any rhythm section, including the enormous ones in samba parades.

Beija-flor – humming bird; also the name of Rio's most famous samba school.

Berimbau – fishing rod-like musical instrument used in the martial art/dance of capoeira

Bicho de Pé – parasite that burrows into the bottom of the foot and then grows, until it is cut out. It's found near the beach and in some jungle areas.

Bloco – large groups, usually in the hundreds, of singing Carnival revellers in costume. Most blocos are organised around a neighbourhood or theme.

Boate, Boîte – nightclub; refers to both the expensive joint and the strip joint.

Bogó – leather water pouch typical of the sertão.

Bonde – cable car; tram/trolley.

Bossa Nova – music that mixes North American jazz with Brazilian influences.

Boto – freshwater dolphin of the Amazon. Indians believe the boto has magical powers, most notably the ability to impregnate unmarried women.

Brazilian Empire – the period from 1822 to 1889 when Brazil was independent of Portugal but was governed by monarchy.

Bumba Meu Boi – the most important festival in Maranhão; a rich folkloric event that revolves around a carnivalesque dance/procession.

Bunda – an African word for buttocks.

Caatinga – scrub vegetation of the Northeast sertão.

Cabanagem – the popular revolt that swept through Pará state in the 1830s until a large government force defeated the uprising and then massacred 40,000 of the state's 100,000 people.

Caboclo – literally copper-coloured; a person of White and Indian ancestry.

Cachaça – Brazil's national drink: a sugarcane rum, also called pinga and aguardente.

Hundreds of small distilleries produce cachaça throughout the country.

Cachoeira – waterfall.

Café – means café da manha (breakfast) or just coffee.

Caipirinha – made from cachaça and crushed citrus fruit such as lemon, orange or maracujá.

Câmara – town council during colonial days.

Camisa-de-Vênus, Camisinha – literally cover or shirt of Venus, but is used to refer to a condom.

Candomblé – Afro-Brazilian religion of Bahia.

Canga – wrap-around fabric worn going to and from the beach and for sitting on at the beach.

Cangaceiro – legendary bandits of the sertão.

Capanga – hired gunman, usually employed by the rich landowners in the Northeast.

Capitania Hereditária – hereditary province or estate. To settle Brazil at minimum cost to the crown, the king of Portugal divided Brazil into 12 capitanias hereditárias in 1531.

Capivara (Capybara) – the world's largest rodent; it looks like a large guinea pig and lives in the waters of the Pantanal.

Capoeira – martial art/dance performed to the rhythms of an instrument called the berimbau; developed by the slaves of Bahia.

Capongas – a freshwater lagoon.

Carioca – a native of Rio de Janeiro.

Casa Grande – plantation owner's mansion.

Casa de Câmbio – money exchange house.

Casal – married couple; also, double bed.

Castanha – brazil nut.

Catamarãs – typical boats of the Amazon.

Chapadões – tablelands or plateaux running between river basins.

Churrascaria – restaurant featuring meat, which should be churrasco (barbecued).

Círio de Nazaré – in Belém, this is Brazil's largest religious pilgrimage.

Cobra – any snake.

Collectivá – bed in a shared room or dorm-style accommodation.

Comunidade de Base – neighbourhood organisations of the poor led by the progressive Catholic Church and inspired by liberation theology. They are involved in many struggles for social justice.

Congelamento – freeze, as in a price freeze.

Coronel – rural landowner who typically controlled the local political, judicial and police systems; any powerful person.

Cruzeiro – national currency.

Delegacia – police station.

Dendê – palm-tree oil; the leading ingredient in the cuisine of Bahia.

Drogas do Sertão – plants of the sertão such as cacao and cinnamon.

Economic Miracle – period of double-digit economic growth while the military was in power during the late 1960s and early 1970s. Now mentioned sarcastically to point to the failures of the military regime.

Embolada – kind of Brazilian rapping, where singers trade-off performing verbal jests, teasing and joking with the audience. It is most common in Northeastern fairs.

EMBRATUR – federal government tourism agency.

Empire – the Brazilian Empire. Era from 1822 to 1889 when Brazil had declared its independence from Portugal but continued under the rule of a monarchy.

ENASA – government-run passenger ships of the Amazon.

Engenho – sugar mill or sugar plantation.

Escolas de Samba – these aren't schools, but large samba clubs. In Rio the escolas have thousands of members and compete in the annual Carnival parade. The escolas begin weekend rehearsals around November and continue until Carnival; rehearsals are open to the public.

Estado Novo – literally New State. Dictator Getúlio Vargas' quasi-fascist state that lasted from 1937 to the end of WW II.

Estância Hidromineral – spa, hot springs.

Exús – spirits that serve as messengers between the gods and humans in Afro-Brazilian religions.

Facão – large knife or machete.

Fantasia – Carnivalesque costume.

Farinha – flour made from the root of the manioc plant. Farinha was the staple food of Brazil's Indians before colonisation and remains the staple for many Brazilians today, especially in the Northeast and the Amazon.

Favela – slum, shantytown.

Fazenda – ranch or farm, usually a large landholding; also cloth, fabric.

Ferroviária – railway station.

Ficha – token. Due to inflation, machines (eg telephones) take tokens not coins.

Fidalgos – gentry.

Figa – good luck charm formed by a clenched fist with the thumb between index and middle finger. The figa originated with Afro-Brazilian cults but is popular with all Brazilians.

Filhos de Gandhi – Bahia's most famous Carnival bloco.

Fio Dental – literally dental floss. This is what Brazilians call their famous skimpy bikinis.

Flamengo – Rio's most popular football team. Also, one of Rio's most populated areas.

Fluminense – native of Rio state. Also the Rio football team that is the Flamengo's main rival.

Forró – the music of the Northeast, which combines the influences of Mexico and the Brazilian frontier. The characteristic instruments used are the accordion, harmonica and drums.

Frevo – fast-paced, popular music that originated in Pernambuco.

FUNAI – government Indian agency.

Fusca – a Volkswagen beetle, long Brazil's most popular car; they stopped making them in 1986.

Garimpeiro – a prospector or miner; originally an illegal diamond prospector.

Gaúcho – pronounced gaoooshoo, a cowboy of southern Brazil.

Gíria – slang.

Gringo – you don't have to be from the USA – any foreigner or person with light hair and complexion, including Brazilians, qualifies. It's not necessarily a derogatory term.

Guaraná – an Amazonian shrub whose berry is believed to have magical and medicinal powers; also a popular soft drink.

Iemanjá – the god of the sea in Afro-Brazilian religions.

Igapó – flooded Amazon forest.

Igarapés – pools formed by the changing paths of the rivers of the Amazon.

INPA – national agency for research on the Amazon.

Jaburú – giant white stork of the Pantanal with black head and red band on neck.

Jagunço – the tough man of the sertão.

Jangada – beautiful sailboat of the Northeast, usually made by the fisherfolk themselves with building techniques passed from generation to generation.

Jangadeiros – fishers who use jangadas.

Jeito (Dar um Jeito or Jeitinho) – possibly the most Brazilian expression, jeito means finding a way to get something done, no matter how seemingly impossible. It may not be an orthodox, normal or legal way but is nonetheless effective in the Brazilian context. Jeito is both a feeling and a form of action.

Jogo de bicho – a popular lottery, technically illegal but played on every street corner by all Brazilians, with each number represented by an animal. The banqueiros de bicho, who control the game, have become almost a kind of mafia and have traditionally helped fund the escolas de samba. Many consider the jogo de bicho the most honest and trustworthy institution in the country.

Jogo dos Búzios – type of fortune-telling performed by a pai or maê de Santo throwing shells.

Karaoke – bar or nightclub where anyone can get up and perform.

Labour Code – labour legislation, modelled on Mussolini's system, which is designed to keep government control over labour unions.

Ladrão – thief.

Lanchonete – stand-up snack bar. They are found all over Brazil.

Lavrador – peasant, small farmer or landless farm worker.

Leito – super-comfortable overnight express bus.

Liberation Theology – movement in the Catholic Church that believes the struggle for social justice is part of Christ's teachings.

Literatura de Cordel – literally Literature of String. Popular literature of the Northeast, where pamphlets are typically hung on strings. It is sold at markets where authors read their stories and poems.

Maconha – type of marijuana.

Maê de Santo – female spiritual leader of Afro-Brazilian religions.

Maharajás – pejorative term for government employees getting rich from the public coffers; it usually refers to army and police officers.

Malandro do Morro – vagabond; scoundrel from the hills. A popular figure in Rio's mythology.

Mameluco – offspring of a White father and an Indian mother.

Manatee, Peixe-boi – literally cow fish. An aquatic mammal of the Amazon rivers that grows to five feet in length; now rare.

Manchete – number two national TV station and popular photo magazine.

Maracanã – football stadium in Rio; supposedly the world's largest. The stadium allegedly holds 200,000, but it looks full with 100,000.

Maté – popular tea of southern Brazil.

Mestiço – a person of mixed Indian and European parentage.

Mineiro – miner; also, person from the state of Minas Gerais.

Mocambo – community of runaway slaves; small version of a quilombo.

Moço – waiter or other service industry worker.

Morro – hill, but used to indicate person or culture of the favelas.

Motel – sex hotel with rooms to rent by the hour.

Mulatto – person of mixed Black and European parentage.

Novela – soap opera. Novelas are the most popular TV shows in Brazil. They are much funnier and have more insights than their American counterparts. From directors to actors to composers, many of Brazil's most talented and famous artists work on novelas.

NS – Nosso Senhor (Our Father), or Nossa Senhora (Our Lady).

O Globo – Brazil's number one media empire. O Globo owns the prime national TV station and several newspapers and magazines.

Old Republic – period from the end of the Brazilian Empire in 1889 to the coup that put Getúlio Vargas in power in 1930. There were regular elections but only a tiny percentage of the population was eligible to vote.

Orixás – the gods of the Afro-Brazilian religions.

Pagode – todays's most popular samba music.

Pai de Santo – male spiritual leader in Afro-Brasilian religions.

Pajé – shaman, witchdoctor.

Palafitas – houses built on sticks above water, as in Manaus.

Paralelo – the parallel, semi-official exchange rate that reflects the currency's market value, not the government's regulated official value.

Paruara – Amazon resident who came from Ceará.

Pau Brasil – brazil wood tree. It produces a red dye that was the colony's first commodity. The trees are scarce today.

Paulista – native of São Paulo.

PCB – Communist Party of Brazil.

Pelourinho – stone pillar used as a whipping post for punishing slaves.

Petrobras – the government-owned oil company. Brazil's largest corporation is so powerful that it's referred to as a 'government within a government'.

Pinga – another name for cachaça, the sugar cane brandy.

Pistoleiro – gun-toting henchman

Planalto – enormous plateau that covers a part of almost every state in Brazil

PMDB – the governing party a loose coalition that encompasses a wide variety of ideologies and interests from far right to centre.

Posseiro – squatter.

Pousada – hotel.

Prato Feito, Prato do Dia – literally, made plate, plate of the day. They are typically enormous meals and incredibly cheap.

PT – Worker's Party. Brazil's newest and most radical political party. It came out of the massive strike waves of the early 1980s and is led by Lula. The PT's support is largely in São Paulo, and among industrial workers and the Catholic base communities.

PTD – Democratic Workers' Party. A social democratic party dominated by the charismatic populist Leonel Brizola.

Puxar – means pull, not push.

Quarto – hotel room without a bathroom.

Quilombo – community of runaway slaves. They posed a serious threat to the slave system as hundreds of quilombos dotted the coastal mountains. The Republic of Palmares was the most famous – it survived for most of the 17th century and had as many as 20,000 people.

Rede – hammock.

Revolution of '64 – the military takeover in 1964.

Rodízio – a smorgasbord with lots of meat (similar to a churrascaria).

Rodoferroviária – bus and train station.

Rodoviária – bus station.

Sambódromo – the road and bleachers where the samba parade takes place on Rio's north side.

Senzala – slave quarters.

Sertão – drought-stricken region of the Northeast, known as the backlands. It has a dry, temperate climate, and the land is covered by thorny shrubs.

Shiita – term derived from the Shiite Muslims of Iran, used to describe any zealot or radical, no matter their cause.

Suco – juice bar or juice.

Terra de Vera Cruz – Land of the True Cross. This was the original but short-lived Portuguese name for the country. Generations of Portuguese believed Brazil was the work of the devil (who, according to common wisdom, was very active in the sinful colony).

Terreiro – house of worship for Afro-Brazilian religions.

Travesti – tranvestite. A popular figure throughout Brazil and considered by some to be the national symbol.

Treaty of Tordesillas – agreement between Spain and Portugal dividing Latin America.

Trio Eléctrico – literally a three-pronged electric outlet. Also, a musical style that is a sort of electrified frevo played on top of trucks, especially during Carnival in Bahia.

Tropicalismo – important cultural movement centred in Bahia in the late 1960s.

Tupi – the Indian people and language that predominated along the Brazilian coast at the time of the European invasion. Most animals and places in Brazil have Tupi names.

Umbanda – Rio's version of the principal Afro-Brazilian religion.

Vaqueiro – cowboy of the Northeast.

Várzea – Amazonian floodplain

Velho Chico – literally old Chico, the fond nickname for the great Rio São Francisco.

Violeiros – guitarists and guitar makers.

Zona da Mata – bushland just inside the littoral in the Northeastern states.

Index

ABBREVIATIONS

A	-	Argentina	G	-	Guyana	RGN	-	Rio Grande do Norte
B	-	Brazil	GOI	-	Goias	RGS	-	Rio Grande do Sul
ACRE	-	Acre	MAR	-	Maranhão	RJ	-	Rio de Janeiro State
ALA	-	Alagoas	MG	-	Mato Grosso	RON	-	Rondônia
AMA	-	Amapá	MGS	-	Mato Grosso do Sul	ROR	-	Roraima
AMAZ	-	Amazonas	MINAS	-	Minas Gerais	SC	-	Santa Caterina
BAH	-	Bahia	P	-	Paraguay	SER	-	Sergipe
BOL	-	Bolivia	PAR	-	Paraná	SP	-	São Paulo
C	-	Colombia	PARÁ	-	Pará	TOC	-	Tocantins
CEA	-	Ceará	PARAI	-	Paraíba	U	-	Uruguay
DF	-	Distrito Federal	PER	-	Pernambuco	V	-	Venezuela
ES	-	Espirito Santo	PERU	-	Peru			
FG	-	French Guiana	PIA	-	Piauí			

MAPS

Air Routes 130
Alcântara (MAR) 529
Aracaju (SER) 439
Arraial do Cabo, Cabo Frio & Búzios (RJ) 204
Baía de Todos os Santos & Recôncavo (BAH) 396
Bahia 374
Beaches of Sergipe, Alagoas & North Bahia 442
Belém (PARÁ) 540-541
Belo Horizonte (MINAS) 221
Blumenau (SC) 305
Boa Viagem (PER) 461
Boa Vista (ROR) 589
Brasiléia, Around (ACRE) 610
Brasília (DF) 332-333
Brasília, Central (DF) 334
Brazil 12-13
Cachoeira (BAH) 399
Campo Grande (MGS) 365
Canela (RGS) 322
Caxambu (MINAS) 247
Ceará Coast 504-505
Ceará, Piauí & Maranhão 495
Central West 330
Copacabana, Ipanema & Leblon (RJ) 166-167
Corumbá (MGS) 359
Cuiabá (MG) 344
Cuiabá, Central (MG) 346
Curitiba (PAR) 281
Diamantina (MINAS) 243
Espírito Santo 210
Fernando de Noronha (PER) 476

Florianópolis (SC) 307
Fortaleza (CEA) 496-497
Foz do Iguaçu (PAR) 292
Glória, Catete & Flamengo (RJ) 165
Goiânia (GOI) 337
Goiás Velho (GOI) 340
Gramado (RGS) 321
Guajará-Mirim (RON) 602
Guayaramerín (BOL) 604
Iguaçu Falls (PAR) 294
Ilha de Santa Catarina (SC) 310
Ilha do Mel (PAR) 290
Ilhéus (BAH) 412
Itatiaia Region (RJ) 201
João Pessoa (PARAI) 480
Joinville (SC) 301
Lençóis (BAH) 427
Leticia (C) 586
Macapá (AMA) 561
Maceió (ALA) 444-445
Maceió, Around (ALA) 448
Manaus (AMAZ) 566-567
Manaus, Around (AMAZ) 573
Marechal Deodoro (ALA) 449
Minas Gerais 219
Natal (RGN) 488
Natal, North of (RGN) 491
Natal, South of (RGN) 485
National Parks, Biological Reserves & Ecological Stations 40
North, The 536
Nova Friburgo (RJ) 196
Olinda (PER) 466

Ouro Prêto (MINAS) 227
Pantanal 352
Paraíba & Rio Grande do Norte 479
Paraná 279
Paranaguá (PAR) 287
Parati Islands & Beaches (RJ) 187
Parque Nacional da Chapada Diamantina (BAH) 431
Parque Nacional de Sete Cidades (PIA) 517
Pernambuco 454-455
Petrópolis (RJ) 191
Poconé (MG) 351
Ponta Porã (MGS) 369
Porto Alegre (RGS) 316
Porto Seguro (BAH) 417
Porto Velho (RON) 596-597
Rainfall 44
Recife (PER) 456
Recife, Central (PER) 458
Rio Branco (ACRE) 606
Rio de Janeiro City (RJ) 140-141
Rio de Janeiro City, Central (RJ) 148-149
Rio de Janeiro State 182
Rio Grande do Sul 314
São João del Rei (MINAS) 236
São Lourenço (MINAS) 249
São Luís (MAR) 519
São Luís, Central (MAR) 520-521
São Paulo City (SP) 256

619

São Paulo City, Central (SP) 258-259
São Paulo State 254
Salvador (BAH) 378
Salvador, Central (BAH) 380
Santa Catarina 299

Santarém (PAR) 556
Sergipe & Alagoas 436
States of Brazil 27
Teresina (PIA) 513
Teresópolis (RJ) 194
Time Zones 77

Tiradentes (MINAS) 240
Triple Frontier 583
Vitória (ES) 211
Vitória, Central (ES) 212

TEXT

Map references are in **bold** type

Abaís (BAH) 408
Abraão (RJ)183-184
Acre 605-613
Alagoas 442-452, **436, 442**
Alcântara (MAR) 528-530, **529**
Alcobaça (BAH) 424, 425
Alter do Chão (PAR) 559
Alto do Moura (PER) 473
Alumar (MAR) 528
Amapá 560-562
Amazon 31-32, 34-37
    Jungle Tours 572-577
Amazonas 565-588
Anastácio (MGS) 364
Anchieta (ES) 214-215
Andaraí (BAH) 433
Angra dos Reis (RJ)184-185
Antonina (PAR) 286
Aquidauana (MGS) 364
Aracaju (SER) 438-441, **439**
Aracati (CEA) 504
Areia Branca (RGN) 492
Arembepe (BAH) 405
Arraial d'Ajuda (BAH) 421, 422-423
Arraial do Cabo (RJ) 204-205, **204**
Aruanã (GOI) 564
Assis Brasil (ACRE) 126, 612
Asunción (P) 127, 363

Bahia 92, 374-435, **374, 442**
Baía da Traição (PARAI) 484
Baía de Guanabara (RJ) 160, 181
Baía de Paranaguá (PAR) 286-292
Baía de Todos os Santos (BAH) 396-398, **396**
Baía do Sancho (PER) 477
Baía do Sol (PARÁ) 550
Baía dos Golfinhos (PER) 477
Baía Formosa (RGN) 485-486
Balneário Camboriú (SC) 304
Barão de Melgaço (MG) 350
Barra da Itabapoana (RJ) 209
Barra da Tijuca (RJ) 103, 144

Barra de Itariri (BAH) 407
Barra de Santo Antônio (ALA) 452, 463
Barra de São João (RJ) 208
Barra do Camarajibe (ALA) 452
Barra do Cunhaú (RGN) 486
Barra dos Coqueiros (SER) 439
Barra Velha (SC) 303
Barreira do Inferno (RGN) 486
Barreiras (CEA) 506
Barrinha (CEA) 506
Barro Branco (BAH) 433
Baturité (CEA) 509
Beaches
    Armação (BAH) 388
    Arpoador (RJ) 151
    Atalaia Velha (SER) 439
    Barra (BAH) 388
    Barra da Lagoa (SC) 309
    Barra da Tijuca (RJ) 144
    Barra de Itariri (BAH) 407
    Barra de Santo Antônio (ALA) 451, 452
    Barra de São João (RJ) 208
    Barra de São Miguel (ALA) 449
    Barra do Gil (BAH) 397
    Barra do Pote (BAH) 397
    Barra do Sirinhaém (PER) 463
    Barra Grande (BAH) 397
    Boiçucanga (SP) 272-273
    Botafogo (RJ) 151, 170, 173-174
    Búzios (RJ) 206-208, **204**
    Cabo de Santo Agostinho (PER) 465
    Cacha Pregos (BAH) 397
    Caiera (PER) 477
    Calhau (MAR) 524
    Canasvieiras (SC) 311
    Copacabana (RJ) 143-144, 151, 164, 168, 171, 174, **166-167**
    Coroa Vermelha (BAH) 421
    Cumbuco (CEA) 499
    Domingas Dias (SP) 269
    Enseada (SP) 269
    Flamengo (RJ) 151, 164, 167-168, 170
    Flamengo (SP) 269

Fleixeiras (CEA) 507
Garça Torta (ALA) 443
Grumari (RJ) 152
Guajira (CEA) 507
Guarujá (SP) 273
Guaxuma (ALA) 443
Iguape (CEA) 503
Ipanema (RJ) 144, 152, 168, 171-172, 174, **166-167**
Iparana (CEA) 499
Itajuba (SC) 303
Itamambuca (SP) 269
Itapoã (BAH) 388
Jacarecica (ALA) 443
Janga (PER) 470
Japaratinga (ALA) 452
Jatiúca (ALA) 443
Jericoacoara (CEA) 507
Jurerê (SC) 311
Lazaro (SP) 269
Leblon (RJ) 144, 152, 168, 172, 174, **166-167**
Leme (RJ) 151, 168
Majorlândia (CEA 505
Mar Grosso (SC) 312
Maragoji (ALA) 452
Marambaia (RJ) 152
Mundaí (BAH) 421
Mundaú (CEA) 507
Olho d'Agua (MAR) 524
Pajuçara (ALA) 443
Pepino (RJ) 152
Piatãa (BAH) 388
Piçarras (SC) 303
Pirangi do Norte (RGN) 486
Pirangi do Sul (RGN) 486
Pituba (BAH) 388
Placaford (BAH) 388
Ponta d'Areia (MAR) 524, 526
Ponta das Caracas (PER) 477
Ponta Negra (RGN) 486-487
Ponta Verde (ALA) 443
Pontal do Sul (PAR) 289
Pontas de Pedra (PER) 472
Ponte da Areia (BAH) 397
Praia Atalaia Nova (SER) 439
Praia Barra da Tijuca (RJ) 152
Praia Barra Grande (RJ) 190
Praia Bombas (SC) 304

Praia Bombinhas (RJ) 304
Praia Cabo Branco (PARAI) 481
Praia Chapéu Virado (PARÁ) 550
Praia da Areia Preta (RGN) 489
Praia da Armação (SC) 311
Praia da Atalaia (PER) 477
Praia da Conceição (PER) 470, 477
Praia da Figueira (SP) 271
Praia da Joaquina (SC) 309
Praia da Lagoinha (CEA) 506
Praia da Maria Farinha (PER) 470
Praia da Penha (PARAI) 481
Praia da Trindade (RJ) 190
Praia das Artistas (SER) 439
Praia de Camburí (ES) 211
Praia de Enseada (SC) 303
Praia de Iracema (CEA) 498
Praia de Leste (PAR) 289
Praia de Parati-Mirim (RJ) 190
Praia de Seixas (PARAI) 482
Praia de Tambaba (PARAI) 484
Praia de Tambaú (PARAI) 481, 482
Praia de Ubatuba (SC) 303
Praia do Algodoal (PARÁ) 551
Praia do Araçaji (MAR) 524
Praia do Campeche (SC) 311
Praia do Farol (PARÁ) 550
Praia do Forte (RJ) 188
Praia do Forte (SC) 311
Praia do Francês (ALA) 448
Praia do Futuro (CEA) 498
Praia do Gato (SP) 271
Praia do Gi (SC) 312
Praia do Grant (SC) 303
Praia do Jabaquara (RJ) 188
Praia do Meio (RGN) 489
Praia do Meireles (CEA) 498
Praia do Moçambique (Praia Grande) (SC) 309
Praia do Morro Branco (CEA) 503-504
Praia do Ó (PER) 470
Praia do Pau Amarelo (PER) 470
Praia do Pesqueiro (PARÁ) 553
Praia do Pinho (SC) 304
Praia do Pinto (RGN) 489
Praia do Pontal (RJ) 188
Praia do Santinho (SC) 309
Praia do Sol (PARAI) 484
Praia do Sono (RJ) 190
Praia do Tabuleiro (SC) 303
Praia dos Artistas (RGN) 489
Praia dos Castelhanos (SP) 271

Praia dos Ingleses (SC) 309
Praia Grande (PAR) 290, 303
Praia Jabaquara (SP) 271
Praia Jacumã (PARAI) 484
Praia Jacumã (RGN) 492
Praia Mãe Luiza (RGN) 489
Praia Maxaranguape (RGN) 492
Praia Pedra do Sino (SP) 271
Praia Pitimbu (PARAI) 484
Praia Redinha (RGN) 491
Prainha (CEA) 503
Prainha (RJ) 152
Prainha (SC) 303
Pratagi (ALA) 443
Riacho Doce (ALA) 443
São Conrado (RJ) 152
São José da Coroa Grande (PER) 464
Sete Coqueiros (ALA) 443
Tamandare (PER) 464
Tibaú (RGN) 493
Toninhas (SP) 269
Torta (ALA) 443
Ubatumirim (SP) 269
Vermelha (SP) 269
Vidigal (RJ) 152
Bela Vista (SP) 265
Belém (PARÁ) 103, 538-550, 581, 540-541
Belo Horizonte (MINAS) 220-224, 221
Belterra (PARÁ) 559
Benjamin Constant (AMAZ) 125, 581, 583-585, 583
Biological Reserves
    Reserva Biológica do Gurupi (MAR) 531
    Reserva Biológica do Jaru (RON) 595
    Reserva Biológica do Lago (AMA) 562
    Reserva Biológica do Pau Brasil (BAH) 418
    Reserva Biológica do Poço das Antas (RJ) 208
    Reserva Biológica Mico Leão de Una (BAH) 416
Bixiga (SP) 265
Blumenau (SC) 304-305, 305
Boa Viagem (PER) 460, 461
Boa Vista (ROR) 126, 588-591, 589
Boiçucanga (SP) 272-273
Bom Despacho (BAH) 397
Bom Jardim da Serra (SÇ) 313
Bonfim (ROR) 126, 591
Bonito (MGS) 367-368
Botafogo (RJ) 143, 170, 173-174

Brasiléia (ACRE) 125, 609-610, 610
Brasília (DF) 329-336, 332-333, 334
Búzios (RGN) 486
Búzios (RJ) 104, 206-208, 204

Cabo de Santa Marta (SC) 312
Cabo Frio (RJ) 205-206, 204
Cáceres (MG) 125, 350
Cachoeira (BAH) 117, 398-403, 399
Cachoeira da Farofa (MINAS) 40
Cachoeira da Fumaça (BAH) 433
Cachoeira das Tocas (SP) 272
Cachoeira do Sossêgo (BAH) 432
Cachoeira Saia Velha (DF) 336
Cachoeira Topázio (DF) 336
Caldas Novas (GOI) 342
Camamu (BAH) 410
Camocim (CEA) 508
Campo Grande (MGS) 364-367, 365
Campos (RJ) 208
Campos do Jordão (SP) 133, 274-276
Cananéia (SP) 274
Candeias (BAH) 403
Candomblé 60-61
    Cachoeira (BAH) 399, 400
    Salvador (BAH) 388
Canela (RGS) 323, 322
Canindé (CEA) 510
Canoa Quebrada (CEA) 505
Canyon das Bandeirinhas (MINAS) 40
Capão (BAH) 433, 434
Capão da Canoa (RGS) 318
Capoeira
    Bahia 375
    Salvador (BAH) 388
Caracaraí (AMAZ) 581
Caraguatatuba (SP) 270
Caraiva (BAH) 421, 424
Caravelas (BAH) 425
Carnival
    Ilha do Mel (PAR) 291
    Ilhéus (BAH) 413
    Maceió (ALA) 446
    Olinda (PER) 468
    Paracuru (CEA) 506
    Porto Seguro (BAH) 419
    Recife (PER) 459
    Rio de Janeiro City (RJ) 161-163
    Salvador (BAH) 388, 389
    São João (MINAS) 238

São Luís (MAR) 524
Valença (BAH) 409
Carolina (MAR) 531-532
Caruaru (PER) 117, 472-474
Cascatinha (PAR) 285
Cassino (RGS) 321
Catete (RJ) 143, 164, 167-168, 170, **165**
Caxambu (MINAS) 245-248, **247**
Ceará 494-512, **495, 504-505**
Central West 328-370, **330**
Cerqueira César (SP) 265
Chapada dos Guimarães (MG) 349-350
Chuí (RGS) 126, 319
Chuy (U) 126, 319
Cidade Alta (BAH) 418
Cinelândia (RJ) 143, 166, 170
Ciudad Bolívar (V) 592
Ciudad del Este (P) 126, 295
Cobija (BOL) 610-612
Conceição da Barra (ES) 217
Conde (BAH) 406-407
Congonhas (MINAS) 226-227
Copacabana (RJ) 117, 118, 143-144, 164-165, 168, 171, 174, **166-167**
Corcovado (RJ) 153-154, 160
Corumbá (MGS) 125, 127, 133, 359-364, **359**
Coruripe (ALA) 451
Costa Verde (RJ) 181
Coxim (MGS) 367
Criciúma (SC) 313
Cruzeiro do Sul (ACRE) 613
Cuiabá (MG) 344-349, **344, 346**
Cumuruxatiba (BAH) 425
Curitiba (PAR) 133, 279-285, **281**
Curuá-Una Hydroelectric Dam (PARÁ) 559
Cururupu (MAR) 531

Diamantina (MINAS) 242-245, **243**
Distrito Federal 329-336
Domingos Martins (ES) 216

El Dorado (V) 592
Ecological Stations
 Parque Ecológico do Côco (CEA) 499
 Parque Ecológico Plácido de Castro (ACRE) 607
Encontro das Águas (PARÁ) 559, 572
Engenho (BAH) 416

Environmental Movements 37-39
Espírito Santo 210-217, **210**
Estação Biológica Cuniã (RON) 595
Estância (SER) 436-437
Estância de Agua de Itiquira (GOI) 336

Fazenda Babilônia (GOI) 341
Fazenda Bananal-Engenho de Murycana (RJ) 190
Fazenda Nova (PER) 474
Feira de Santana (BAH) 426
Fernando de Noronha (PER) 42, 475-478, **476**
Ferradura (RGS) 323
Flamengo (RJ) 164, 167-168, 170, **165**
Florianópolis (SC) 303, 306-308, **307**
Fontainha (CEA) 506
Fordlândia (PARÁ) 559
Fortaleza (CEA) 494-503, **496-497**
Forte Príncipe da Beira (RON) 601
Foz do Iguaçu (PAR) 125, 126, 293-298, **292**

Gaibu (PER) 463, 465
Garanhuns (PER) 474
Garopaba (SC) 312
Gávea (RJ) 172
Genipabu (RGN) 491
Georgetown (G) 591
Glória (RJ) 164, **165**
Goiânia (GOI) 336-339, **337**
Goiás 336-343
Goiás Velho (GOI) 339-341, **340**
Gramado (RGS) 321-322, **321**
Gran Sábana (V) 592-593
Gruta Azul (BAH) 433
Gruta da Pratinha (BAH) 433
Gruta do Lapão (BAH) 433
Grutas das Encantadas (PAR) 290
Guaibim (BAH) 409
Guajará-Mirim (RON) 125, 601-603, **602**
Guaramiranga (CEA) 509
Guarapari (ES) 214
Guarujá (SP) 273
Guayaramerín (BOL) 603-605, **604**
Guimarães (MAR) 531

Icapuí (CEA) 506
Igarassu (PER) 470-472

Igatú (BAH) 433
Iguaçu Falls (PAR) 293-295, **294**
Iguape (CEA) 503
Iguape (SP) 273-274
Ilhabela (SP) 103, 271-272
Ilha Bom Jesus dos Jesus (BAH) 398
Ilha da Croa (ALA) 452
Ilha da Maré (BAH) 398
Ilha da Paquetá (RJ) 157
Ilha da Paz (SC) 303
Ilha das Peças (PAR) 291
Ilha de Itamaracá (PER) 472
Ilha de Marajó (PARÁ) 551-554
Ilha de Santa Catarina (SC) 304, 309-312, **310**
Ilha de São Francisco (SC) 303
Ilha de São Luís (MAR) 527-528
Ilha do Bananal (TOC) 43, 563-564
Ilha do Mel (PAR) 289-291, **290**
Ilha do Mosqueiro (PARÁ) 550
Ilha do Paiva (PER) 465
Ilha do Superagui (PAR) 292, 293
Ilha dos Currais (PAR) 291
Ilha dos Frades (BAH) 398
Ilha dos Lobos (SC) 312
Ilha Grande (RJ) 181, 183-184
Ilha Itaparica (BAH) 396-398
Ilhéus (BAH) 409, 411-415, **412**
Imperatriz (MAR) 531
Iñapari (PERU) 126, 612
Ipanema (RJ) 117, 144, 168, 171-172, 174, **166-167**
Ipu (CEA) 511
Iquitos (PERU) 126, 581
Islandia (PERU) 126, 587-588
Itacaré (BAH) 411
Itaipu Dam (PAR) 295
Itajaí (SC) 304
Itaparica City (BAH) 397
Itapipoca (CEA) 507
Itapissuma (PER) 471
Itatiaia (RJ) 198, **201**

Japaratinga (ALA) 452
Jericoacoa (CEA) 507-508
Jesuit Missions 324-326
 Candelaria (A) 325
 Jesus (P) 325
 San Ignacio Miní (A) 325
 Santa Maria la Mayor (A) 325
 Santa Rosa (P) 325
 Santiago (P) 325
 São João Batista (RGS) 325
 São Lourenço das Missoes (RGS) 325

São Miguel das Missoes (RGS) 325

Trinidad (P) 325

João Pessoa (PARAI) 479-484, **480**

Joinville (SC) 133, 300-303, **301**

Juazeiro do Norte (CEA) 511-512

Lago Caracanã (ROR) 591

Lago do Amapá (ACRE) 607

Lagoa da Conceição (SC) 311

Lagoa do Mato (CEA) 506

Lagoa Encantada (BAH) 415

Laguna (SC) 312

Lapa (RJ) 143, 170, 173

Lapa Doce (BAH) 433

Laranjeiras (SER) 437-438

Largo do Machado (RJ) 170

Leblon (RJ) 144, 168, 172, 174, **166-167**

Leme (RJ) 168, 170

Lençóis (BAH) 426-430, **427**

Lethem (G) 591

Leticia (C) 125, 581, 585-587, **583, 586**

Liberdade (SP) 263, 265

Litoral Gaúcho (SC) 317-319

Litoral Piauiense (PIA) 515-516

Macaé (RJ) 208

Macapá (AMA) 560-562, **561**

Maceió (ALA) 442-448, 463, **444-445, 448**

Manacapuru (AMAZ) 582-583

Manaus (AMAZ) 565-582, **566-567, 573**

Mangue Seco (BAH) 407

Mar Grande (BAH) 397

Maragoji (ALA) 452, 463

Maragojipe (BAH) 404

Maranguape (CEA) 508

Maranhão 518-532, **495**

Marataízes (ES) 215-216

Marechal Deodoro (ALA) 448-449, **449**

Mariana (MINAS) 235

Marudá (PARÁ) 551

Marumbi State Park (PAR) 285

Mata Atlântica 32, 33-34, 372

Mata da Araucaria 32-33

Mato Grosso 343-351

Mato Gross do Sul 359-370

Maués (AMAZ) 583

Miguel dos Milagres (PER) 463

Minas Gerais 117, 218-252, **219**

Morretes (PAR) 285-286

Morro de São Paulo (BAH) 409-410

Morro do Pai Inácio (BAH) 433

Mossoró (RGN) 492-493

Mt Roraima 43, 591, 592-593

Natal (RGN) 487-491, **488, 485 491**

National Parks 39-43, **40**
Parque Nacional da Amazônia (PARÁ) 43, 559

Parque Nacional da Chapada Diamantina (BAH) 42, 430-434, **431**

Parque Nacional da Chapada dos Guimarães (MG) 42

Parque Nacional da Chapada dos Veadeiros (GOI) 42, 342-343

Parque Nacional da Lagoa do Peixe (RGS) 42

Parque Nacional da Serra da Bocaina (RJ) 39, 190-191

Parque Nacional da Serra da Canastra (MINAS) 39, 252

Parque Nacional da Serra da Capivara (PIA) 42

Parque Nacional da Serra Divisor (ACRE) 43

Parque Nacional da Serra do Cipó (MINAS) 40, 251-252

Parque Nacional da Serra dos Órgãos (RJ) 181

Parque Nacional da Tijuca (RJ) 39, 142, 154-155, 159, 172

Parque Nacional das Emas (GOI) 42, 343

Parque Nacional de Aparados da Serra (SC) 41, 323-324

Parque Nacional de Brasília (DF) 42, 331

Parque Nacional de Cabo Orange (AMA) 43, 562

Parque Nacional de Caparaó (MINAS) 39, 251

Parque Nacional de Monte Pascoal (BAH) 42, 424

Parque Nacional de Monte Roraima (ROR) 43

Parque Nacional de Pacaás Novas (RON) 43, 595

Parque Nacional de São Joaquim (SC) 41, 313

Parque Nacional de Sete Cidades (PIA) 42, 516-517, **517**

Parque Nacional de Ubajara (CEA) 42, 510-511

Parque Nacional do Araguaia (TOC) 43

Parque Nacional do Itatiaia (RJ) 39, 200-202

Parque Nacional do Jaú (AMAZ) 43

Parque Nacional do Pantanal Matogrossense (MG, MGS) 42

Parque Nacional do Pico da Neblina (AMAZ) 43

Parque Nacional do Superagui (PAR) 40, 289, 292, 293

Parque Nacional dos Lençóis Maranhenses (MAR) 43, 530-531

Parque Nacional Grande Sertão Veredas (MINAS) 40

Parque Nacional Marinho de Fernando de Noronha (PER) 42, 475-478, **476**

Parque Nacional Marinho dos Abrolhos (BAH) 42, 425-426

Parque Nacional Serra da Capivara (PIA) 517

Parque Nacional Serra dos Órgãos (RJ) 195

Nazaré (BAH) 404

Niterói (RJ) 104, 160

Nova Friburgo (RJ) 196-197, **196**

Nova Jerusalém (PER) 474

NS da Ajuda (see Arraial d'Ajuda

Oiapoque (AMA) 126, 561

Olinda (PER) 465-470, **466**

Olivença (BAH) 415

O Pico do Bandeira (MINAS) 39

Ouro Prêto (MINAS) 218, 227-235, **227**

Pacatuba (CEA) 509

Pacoti (CEA) 509

Palame (BAH) 406

Palmas (TOC) 563

Palmeiras (BAH) 433

Pantanal 29-31, 34, 104, 351-358, **352**
Mato Grosso 356
Mato Gross do Sul 356-357
Tours 360-361

Pão de Açúcar (RJ) 153, 159-160

Pará 538-559

Paracuru (CEA) 506

Paraíba 479-485, **479**

Paraná 279-298, **279**

Paranaguá (PAR) 133, 282, 286, 288, **287**

Parati (RJ)185-190, **187**

Paray Tepui (V) 592

Parnaíba (PIA) 515-516

Parque Estadual do Caracol (SC) 323
Parque Recreativo de Brasília Rogerio Pithon Farias (DF) 334
Pedro Juan Caballero (P) 126, 368
Pedro Segundo (PIA) 517
Pelotas (SC) 319
Penedo (ALA) 449, 451,
Penedo (RJ) 449, 198-199
Penha (SC) 303
Pernambuco 117, 453-478, **454-455**
Peroba (CEA) 506
Petrópolis (RJ) 181, 191-192, **191**
Piauí 512-517, **495**
Piçarras (SC) 303
Pico 31 de Março (AMAZ) 43
Pico da Neblina (AMAZ) 43
Picos (CEA) 506
Pirangi do Norte (RGN) 486
Pirangi do Sul (RGN) 486
Pirenópolis (GOI) 341-342
Piúma (ES) 215
Poço Encantado (BAH) 433
Poconé (MG) 351, **351**
Ponta do Lobo (SC) 304
Ponta do Mutá (BAH) 410, 411
Ponta Grossa (CEA) 506
Ponta Negra (RGN) 486-487
Ponta Porã (MGS) 126, 368, **369**
Pontal do Sul (PAR) 289
Pororoca (AMA) 562
Porto Alegre (SC) 314-317, **316**
Porto Belo (SC) 304
Porto de Galinhas (PER) 464-465
Porto de Pedras (PER) 452, 463
Porto Seguro (BAH) 103, 416-421, 426, **417**
Porto Suipé (BAH) 406
Porto Velho (RON) 581, 595-601, **596-597**
Prado (BAH) 424
Prados (MINAS) 242
Praia de Leste (PAR) 289
Praia do Forte (BAH) 405-406
Praia Ponta Negra (AMAZ) 571
Prainha (CEA) 503
Projeto Grande Carajás (PARÁ) 555
Propriá (SER) 441-442
Puerto Iguazú (A) 295

Quijarro (BOL) 362, 363
Quixaba (CEA) 506

Ramón Castilla (PERU) 126
Recife (PER) 453-464, **456, 458**
  Entertainment 462
  Places to Eat 462
  Places to Stay 460-462
Recôncavo Region (BAH) 398-404, **396**
Redonda (CEA) 506
Resende (RJ) 198
Restinga de Marambaia (RJ)181
Retirinho (CEA) 506
Retiro (CEA) 506
Retiro Grande Mutamba (CEA) 506
Ribeirão da Ilha (SC) 311
Ribeirão do Meio (BAH) 432
Rio Almada (BAH) 415
Rio Aquidauana 104
Rio Araguaia 104
  Mato Grosso 343
  Tocantins 563
Rio Araguari 562
Rio Branco (ACRE) 588, 606-608, **606**
Rio Camarajibe 463
Rio das Mortes 564
Rio das Ostras (RJ) 208
Rio de Janeiro City 139-180, **140-141, 148-149, 165**
  Beaches 151-152, **166-167**
  Entertainment 173-176
  Places to Eat 169-173
  Places to Stay 163-169
  Samba Schools 175
  Walking Tour 147-151
Rio de Janeiro State 103-209, **182**
Rio Grande (SC) 320
Rio Grande do Norte 485-493, **479**
Rio Grande do Sul 314-326, **314**
Rio Iguaçu 293
Rio Mamoré 603
Rio Manguaba 463
Rio Mucugêzinho 433
Rio Nhundiaquara 285
Rio Paraguay 104, 127
Rio Santana 416
Rio São Francisco 39
  Bahia 434-435
  Minas Gerais 222-223
  Sergipe 441
Rio Sergipe 439
Rio Tacutu 591
Rio Una 463
Rondônia 594-605
Roraima 588-593
Ruinha (BAH) 434

Sabará (MINAS) 224-226
Saco (BAH) 407
Salinópolis (PARÁ) 551
Salvador (BAH) 117, 377-396, **378, 380**
  Entertainment 393
  Places to Eat 392-393
  Places to Stay 390-392
  Walking Tour 384-387
Salvador da Bahia (see Salvador)
Salvaterra (PARÁ) 554
Sambaqui (SC) 311
San Francisco de Yuruaní (V) 592
Santa Catarina 299-313, **299**
Santa Cruz (BOL) 362, 363
Santa Cruz Cabrália (BAH) 421
Santa Elena (V) 126, 591-592
Santa Teresa (RJ) 143, 154, 166, 170
Santa Teresa (ES) 216-217
Santa Teresinha (MG) 564
Santarém (PARÁ) 555-558, 581, **556**
Santo Amaro (BAH) 403
Santo Antônio de Leverger (MG) 347
Santo Antônio do Pinhal (SP) 133
Santos (SP) 133, 273
São Borja (SC) 325
São Cristóvão (SER) 437
São Felix (BAH) 401
São Felix do Araguaia 564
São Francisco do Sul (SC) 303
São João del Rei (MINAS) 133, 235-240, **236**
São Joaquim (SC) 313
São José da Coroa Grande (PER) 463, 464
São José do Norte (SC) 320
São Lourenço (MINAS) 248-250, **249**
São Luís (MAR) 518-527, **519, 520-521**
São Miguel dos Milagres (ALA) 452
São Paulo City (SP) 116, 133, 253-269, **256, 258-259**
  Entertainment 266
  Places to Eat 264-266
  Places to Stay 262-264
São Paulo State 253-276, **254**
São Sebastião (SP) 270-271
São Tomé das Letras (MINAS) 250
Saquarema (RJ) 202
Senador Georgino Alvino (RGN) 486

Sergipe 436-442, **436, 442**
Serra da Ibiapaba 511
Serra de Baturité 509-510
Serra de São Jose 241
Serra do Mar 41, 293
Serra do Navio 562
Serra do Rio do Rastro 313
Serra dos Caiapós 563
Serra dos Órgãos 181
Serra Gaúcha 321
Serra Pelada 555
Serro (MINAS) 245
Sítio (BAH) 407
Sobral (CEA) 508
Soccer
  Maracanã Stadium, Rio de
  Janeiro City 152-153
Soure (PARÁ) 552
Sousa (PARAI) 485
St Georges (FG) 126
Suape (PER) 465

Subaúma (BAH) 406
Sugar Loaf (see Pão de Açúcar)

Tabatinga (AMAZ) 125, 581,
  583-585, **583**
Tamandaré (PER) 464
Tefé (AMAZ) 583
Teresina (PIA) 512, **513**
Teresópolis (RJ) 181, 193-195,
  194
Tibau do Sul (RGN) 486
Tiradentes (MINAS) 133, 240-
  242, **240**
Tocantins 563-564
Torres (SC) 318
Touros (RGN) 492
Tracunhaém (PER) 474
Tramandaí (SC) 318-319
Trancoso (BAH) 421, 423
Transpantaneira 355-356, 357-
  358

Triunfo (PER) 474-475
Tubarão (SC) 313
Tumeremo (V) 592

Ubatuba (SP) 269-270
Uruguaiana (SC) 326

Vale do Patí (BAH) 434
Valença (BAH) 408-409
Vassouras (RJ) 192-193
Véu de Noiva (MG) 349
Vila Velha (ES) 211
Vila Velha (PAR) 285
Vilhena (RON) 601
Visconde de Mauá (RJ) 198,
  199-200
Vitória (ES) 210-214, **211, 212**

Xapuri (ACRE) 608-609

THANKS

Thanks to all the following travellers and others (apologies if we've misspelt your name) who took time to write to us about their experiences in Brazil. If you can't see your name immortalised below, don't fear! You have probably been credited in Lonely Planet's *South America on a shoestring*.

Payson Adams (USA), Bharat Aggarwal, Comm M K Barritt (UK), Lori Borg (USA), Terezinha Brandao Vieira, David Bruton (USA), Stanley Campbell (USA), Els Clement (NL), Briggitte Coppecters (Bra), Steve Cuff (Aus), Mrs J de Massano (CH), Maria Desseaux, Oriane Eisenbarth (D), Paulo & Luciane Farber (Bra), Claudia Marcia Ferreira (Bra), Tom Field (USA), Vicki Findel, Marineu Florencio (Bra), Jerry Foster (USA), Georie & Ronda (USA), David M Gerstein (USA), Creed Greer (USA), Joel Gueguen , Andre Guit (NL), Ben Herman (USA), Dieter Herzberg, Elizabeth Hillman (UK), Michael Hohl (D), Russell Hosking (NZ), Barbara Jans (NL), Anthony John (UK), C A Johnson Jr (USA), Anja Kessler, Joan Klein (C), Mr D G Knighton (UK), Jose Leonadidas, Eric Long (USA), Mabel MacDonald (USA), Axel Mahler (A), Paugl Marijnissen (NL), Mark & Kate (UK), Geoffrey Martyn (USA), R N McLean (NZ), Chris Meshens (B), Paulo Nurmberger (Bra), Thomas L Pinkerton (USA), Joan Rankin (USA), Rosa Abadia Resende, Prof Kenneth Ribet (USA), Henrik Rosenc (D), Claude Samuel, Palle Schrwelins (CH), Alain Segers (B), Marisol Olva Segura (Sp), Reinhard Senkowski, Gil Serique, Martin Sichel, Ted Stroll (USA), Jerry Swallow (USA), Paolo Vacchina (USA), Marc G M van Roosmalen, Alex Verstraeten (NL), Jonathan Weiland (USA), Rinette Werkman, Oliver Williams (UK), Paul Wooldridge (Aus), Xcentrek Xcursions (Bra), Graham Youdale (Aus) and Joseph & Lucia Yserbyt

A – Austria, Aus – Australia, B – Belgium, Bra – Brazil, C – Canada, CH – Switzerland, D – Germany, NL – Netherlands, NZ – New Zealand, Sp – Spain, UK – United Kingdom, USA – United States of America

Keep in touch!

We love hearing from you and think you'd like to hear from us.

The Lonely Planet Newsletter covers the when, where, how and what of travel. (AND it's free!)

When...is the right time to see reindeer in Finland?
Where...can you hear the best palm-wine music in Ghana?
How...do you get from Asunción to Areguá by steam train?
What...should you leave behind to avoid hassles with customs in Iran?

To join our mailing list just contact us at any of our offices. (details below)

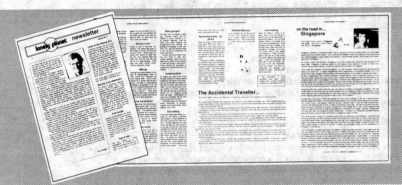

Every issue includes:

- *a letter from Lonely Planet founders Tony and Maureen Wheeler*
- *travel diary from a Lonely Planet author - find out what it's really like out on the road*
- *feature article on an important and topical travel issue*
- *a selection of recent letters from our readers*
- *the latest travel news from all over the world*
- *details on Lonely Planet's new and forthcoming releases*

Also available Lonely Planet T-shirts. 100% heavy weight cotton (S, M, L, XL)

LONELY PLANET PUBLICATIONS
Australia: PO Box 617, Hawthorn, 3122, Victoria (tel: 03-819 1877)
USA: Embarcadero West, 155 Filbert Street, Suite 251, Oakland, CA 94607 (tel: 510-893 8555)
UK: Devonshire House, 12 Barley Mow Passage, Chiswick, London W4 4PH (tel: 081-742 3161)

Guides to the Americas

Alaska – a travel survival kit
Jim DuFresne has travelled extensively through Alaska by foot, road, rail, barge and kayak. This guide has all the information you'll need to make the most of one of the world's great wilderness areas.

Argentina, Uruguay & Paraguay – a travel survival kit
This guide gives independent travellers all the essential information on three of South America's lesser known countries. Discover some of South America's most spectacular natural attractions in Argentina; friendly people and beautiful handicrafts in Paraguay; and Uruguay's wonderful beaches.

Baja California – a travel survival kit
For centuries, Mexico's Baja peninsula – with its beautiful coastline, raucous border towns and crumbling Spanish missions – has been a land of escapes and escapades. This book describes how and where to escape in Baja.

Bolivia – a travel survival kit
From lonely villages in the Andes to ancient ruined cities and the spectacular city of La Paz, Bolivia is a magnificent blend of everything that inspires travellers. Discover safe and intriguing travel options in this comprehensive guide.

Canada – a travel survival kit
This comprehensive guidebook has all the facts on the USA's huge neighbour – the Rocky Mountains, Niagara Falls, ultramodern Toronto, remote villages in Nova Scotia, and much more.

Central America on a shoestring
Practical information on travel in Belize, Guatemala, Costa Rica, Honduras, El Salvador, Nicaragua and Panama. A team of experienced Lonely Planet authors reveals the secrets of this culturally rich, geographically diverse and breathtakingly beautiful region.

Chile & Easter Island – a travel survival kit
Travel in Chile is easy and safe, with possibilities as varied as the countryside. This guide also gives detailed coverage of Chile's Pacific outpost, mysterious Easter Island.

Colombia – a travel survival kit
Colombia is a land of myths – from the ancient legends of El Dorado to the modern tales of Gabriel Garcia Marquez. The reality is beauty and violence, wealth and poverty, tradition and change. This guide shows how to travel independently and safely in this exotic country.

Costa Rica – a travel survival kit
This practical guide gives the low down on exceptional opportunities for fishing and water sports, and the best ways to experience Costa Rica's vivid natural beauty.

Ecuador & the Galápagos Islands – a travel survival kit
Ecuador offers a wide variety of travel experiences, from the high cordilleras to the Amazon plains – and 600 miles west, the fascinating Galápagos Islands. Everything you need to know about travelling around this enchanting country.

Hawaii – a travel survival kit
Share in the delights of this island paradise – and avoid its high prices – both on and off the beaten track. Full details on Hawaii's best-known attractions, plus plenty of uncrowded sights and activities.

La Ruta Maya: Yucatán, Guatemala & Belize – a travel survival kit
Invaluable background information on the cultural and environmental riches of La Ruta Maya (The Mayan Route), plus practical advice on how best to minimise the impact of travellers on this sensitive region.

Mexico – a travel survival kit
A unique blend of Indian and Spanish culture, fascinating history, and hospitable people, make Mexico a travellers' paradise.

Peru – a travel survival kit
The lost city of Machu Picchu, the Andean altiplano and the magnificent Amazon rainforests are just some of Peru's many attractions. All the travel facts you'll need can be found in this comprehensive guide.

South America on a shoestring
This practical guide provides concise information for budget travellers and covers South America from the Darien Gap to Tierra del Fuego. The *New York Times* dubbed the author 'the patron saint of travellers in the third world'.

Trekking in the Patagonian Andes
The first detailed guide to this region gives complete information on 28 walks, and lists a number of other possibilities extending from the Araucanía and Lake District regions of Argentina and Chile to the remote icy of South America in Tierra del Fuego.

Also available:
Brazilian phrasebook, **Latin American Spanish** phrasebook and **Quechua** phrasebook.

Lonely Planet Guidebooks

Lonely Planet guidebooks cover every accessible part of Asia as well as Australia, the Pacific, South America, Africa, the Middle East, Europe and parts of North America. There are five series: *travel survival kits*, covering a country for a range of budgets; *shoestring guides* with compact information for low-budget travel in a major region; *walking guides*; *city guides* and *phrasebooks*.

Australia & the Pacific
Australia
Bushwalking in Australia
Islands of Australia's Great Barrier Reef
Fiji
Melbourne city guide
Micronesia
New Caledonia
New Zealand
Tramping in New Zealand
Papua New Guinea
Bushwalking in Papua New Guinea
Papua New Guinea phrasebook
Rarotonga & the Cook Islands
Samoa
Solomon Islands
Sydney city guide
Tahiti & French Polynesia
Tonga
Vanuatu
Victoria

South-East Asia
Bali & Lombok
Bangkok city guide
Myanmar (Burma)
Burmese phrasebook
Cambodia
Indonesia
Indonesia phrasebook
Malaysia, Singapore & Brunei
Philippines
Pilipino phrasebook
Singapore city guide
South-East Asia on a shoestring
Thailand
Thai phrasebook
Vietnam, Laos & Cambodia
Vietnamese phrasebook

North-East Asia
China
Mandarin Chinese phrasebook
Hong Kong, Macau & Canton
Japan
Japanese phrasebook
Korea
Korean phrasebook
Mongolia
North-East Asia on a shoestring
Seoul city guide
Taiwan
Tibet
Tibet phrasebook
Tokyo city guide

West Asia
Trekking in Turkey
Turkey
Turkish phrasebook
West Asia on a shoestring

Middle East
Arab Gulf States
Egypt & the Sudan
Egyptian Arabic phrasebook
Iran
Israel
Jordan & Syria
Yemen

Indian Ocean
Madagascar & Comoros
Maldives & Islands of the East Indian Ocean
Mauritius, Réunion & Seychelles

Mail Order

Lonely Planet guidebooks are distributed worldwide. They are also available by mail order from Lonely Planet, so if you have difficulty finding a title please write to us. US and Canadian residents should write to Embarcadero West, 155 Filbert St, Suite 251, Oakland CA 94607, USA; European residents should write to Devonshire House, 12 Barley Mow Passage, Chiswick, London W4 4PH; and residents of other countries to PO Box 617, Hawthorn, Victoria 3122, Australia.

Indian Subcontinent

Bangladesh
India
Hindi/Urdu phrasebook
Trekking in the Indian Himalaya
Karakoram Highway
Kashmir, Ladakh & Zanskar
Nepal
Trekking in the Nepal Himalaya
Nepal phrasebook
Pakistan
Sri Lanka
Sri Lanka phrasebook

Africa

Africa on a shoestring
Central Africa
East Africa
Trekking in East Africa
Kenya
Swahili phrasebook
Morocco, Algeria & Tunisia
Moroccan Arabic phrasebook
South Africa, Lesotho & Swaziland
Zimbabwe, Botswana & Namibia
West Africa

Central America

Baja California
Central America on a shoestring
Costa Rica
La Ruta Maya
Mexico

North America

Alaska
Canada
Hawaii

Europe

Dublin city guide
Eastern Europe on a shoestring
Eastern Europe phrasebook
Finland
Iceland, Greenland & the Faroe Islands
Mediterranean Europe on a shoestring
Mediterranean Europe phrasebook
Poland
Scandinavian & Baltic Europe on a shoestring
Scandinavian Europe phrasebook
Trekking in Spain
Trekking in Greece
USSR
Russian phrasebook
Western Europe on a shoestring
Western Europe phrasebook

South America

Argentina, Uruguay & Paraguay
Bolivia
Brazil
Brazilian phrasebook
Chile & Easter Island
Colombia
Ecuador & the Galápagos Islands
Latin American Spanish phrasebook
Peru
Quechua phrasebook
South America on a shoestring
Trekking in the Patagonian Andes

The Lonely Planet Story

Lonely Planet published its first book in 1973 in response to the numerous 'How did you do it?' questions Maureen and Tony Wheeler were asked after driving, bussing, hitching, sailing and railing their way from England to Australia.

Written at a kitchen table and hand collated, trimmed and stapled, *Across Asia on the Cheap* became an instant local bestseller, inspiring thoughts of another book.

Eighteen months in South-East Asia resulted in their second guide, *South-East Asia on a shoestring*, which they put together in a backstreet Chinese hotel in Singapore in 1975. The 'yellow bible' as it quickly became known to backpackers around the world, soon became *the* guide to the region. It has sold well over half a million copies and is now in its 7th edition, still retaining its familiar yellow cover.

Today there are over 120 Lonely Planet titles in print – books that have that same adventurous approach to travel as those early guides; books that 'assume you know how to get your luggage off the carousel' as one reviewer put it.

Although Lonely Planet initially specialised in guides to Asia, they now cover most regions of the world, including the Pacific, South America, Africa, the Middle East and Europe. The list of *walking guides* and *phrasebooks* (for 'unusual' languages such as Quechua, Swahili, Nepalese and Egyptian Arabic) is also growing rapidly.

The emphasis continues to be on travel for independent travellers. Tony and Maureen still travel for several months of each year and play an active part in the writing, updating and quality control of Lonely Planet's guides.

They have been joined by over 50 authors, 54 staff – mainly editors, cartographers, & designers – at our office in Melbourne, Australia, 10 at our US office in Oakland, California and another three at our office in London to handle sales for Britain, Europe and Africa. In 1992 Lonely Planet opened an editorial office in Paris. Travellers themselves also make a valuable contribution to the guides through the feedback we receive in thousands of letters each year.

The people at Lonely Planet strongly believe that travellers can make a positive contribution to the countries they visit, both through their appreciation of the countries' culture, wildlife and natural features, and through the money they spend. In addition, the company makes a direct contribution to the countries and regions it covers. Since 1986 a percentage of the income from each book has been donated to ventures such as famine relief in Africa; aid projects in India; agricultural projects in Central America; Greenpeace's efforts to halt French nuclear testing in the Pacific and Amnesty International. In 1993 $100,000 was donated to such causes.

Lonely Planet's basic travel philosophy is summed up in Tony Wheeler's comment, 'Don't worry about whether your trip will work out. Just go!'